DICTIONARY OF
American History

Third Edition

EDITORIAL BOARD

DICTIONARY OF
American History

Third Edition

Stanley I. Kutler, *Editor in Chief*

Volume 10
Contributors, Learning Guide, and Index

CHARLES SCRIBNER'S SONS

New York • Detroit • San Diego • San Francisco • Cleveland • New Haven, Conn. • Waterville, Maine • London • Munich

THOMSON
★
GALE

Dictionary of American History, Third Edition

Stanley I. Kutler, *Editor*

For permission to use material from this product, submit your request via Web at http://www.gale-edit.com/permissions, or you may download our Permissions Request form and submit your request by fax or mail to:

Permissions Department
The Gale Group, Inc.
27500 Drake Rd.
Farmington Hills, MI 48331-3535
Permissions Hotline:
248-699-8006 or 800-877-4253, ext. 8006
Fax: 248-699-8074 or 800-762-4058

LIBRARY OF CONGRESS CATALOGING-IN-PUBLICATION DATA

Dictionary of American history / Stanley I. Kutler—3rd ed.
   p. cm.
     Includes bibliographical references and index.
     ISBN 0-684-80533-2 (set : alk. paper)
     1. United States—History—Dictionaries. I. Kutler, Stanley I.

E174 .D52 2003
973'.03—dc21

Printed in United States of America
10 9 8 7 6 5 4 3 2 1

EDITORIAL AND PRODUCTION STAFF

(continued on next page)

Captions
Richard Slovak

Primary Source Document Selection
Mark D. Baumann   Cynthia R. Poe   Honor Sachs   Christopher Wells

Cartography
Donald S. Frazier
Robert F. Pace

Tina Bertrand   Robert Wettemann

McMurry University
Abilene, Texas

Line Art
Argosy Publishing

Index
Coughlin Indexing Services, Inc.

Page Design
Pamela Galbreath

Cover Design
Jennifer Wahi

Imaging
Robert Duncan   Leitha Etheridge-Sims   Mary Grimes   Lezlie Light
Dan Newell   David G. Oblender   Chris O'Bryan   Kelly A. Quin
Luke Rademacher   Robyn Young

Permissions
Margaret Chamberlain

Compositor
Impressions Book and Journal Services, Inc.

Manufacturing
Wendy Blurton

Publisher
Frank Menchaca

CONTENTS

Directory of Contributors . . . *1*

Guide to Research and Learning . . . *61*

Index . . . *91*

DICTIONARY OF
American History
Third Edition

DIRECTORY OF CONTRIBUTORS

†signifies contributors to previous editions.

Carl Abbott
Portland State University
Capitals
City Planning
Denver
Portland
Urbanization

Charles C. Abbott†
War Finance Corporation

Wilbur C. Abbott†
Delaware, Washington Cross-
ing the
"Yankee Doodle"

Sandra Schwartz Abraham
Educational Testing Service
Educational Testing Service

Shirley S. Abrahamson
Wisconsin Supreme Court
Bill of Rights in State Constitu-
tions

William J. Aceves
California Western School of Law
Cole Bombing
Embassy Bombings
World Trade Center Bombing,
1993

Sam H. Acheson†
Texan Emigration and Land
Company

Rolf Achilles
School of the Art Institute of Chicago
Art: Decorative Arts
Art: Glass
Art: Pottery and Ceramics
Collecting
Furniture
Metalwork
Miniature
Porcelain

Earl W. Adams†
Federal Reserve System

Henry H. Adams†
Atlantic, Battle of the

Randolph G. Adams†
Arnold's March to Quebec
Arnold's Raid in Virginia
Arnold's Treason
Morse, Jedidiah, Geographies of

Michael R. Adamson
Sonoma State University
Balance of Trade
British Debts
Council of Economic Advisors
Depletion Allowances

James F. Adomanis
*Maryland Center for the Study of His-
tory*
National Association for the
Advancement of Colored
People
Organized Crime Control Act
Primary, Direct
Reparation Commission

Robert G. Albion†
Merchant Marine
Naval Stores
Shipping, Ocean

John Albright†
Booby Traps

Michele L. Aldrich†
Geological Surveys, State

Edward P. Alexander†
Rogers' Rangers
Ticonderoga, Capture of

Richard D. Alford†
Naming

F. Hardee Allen†
Cod Fisheries
Fishing Bounties
Mackerel Fisheries

James B. Allen
Brigham Young University
Tabernacle, Mormon

Patrick N. Allitt
Emory University
American Dilemma, An
Christianity
Church and State, Separation of
*How to Win Friends and Influence
People*
National Review
Political Correctness
Power of Positive Thinking, The
Religious Liberty
Silent Spring
Walden

Donna Alvah
Saint Lawrence University
Causa, La
Civil Disobedience
Civil Rights Movement
Integration
Loyalty Oaths
March on Washington

S. M. Amadae
University of California, Berkeley
Political Science

Patrick Amato
New York, New York
Amtrak

Charles H. Ambler†
Conestoga Wagon
Henry, Fort

Nancy T. Ammerman
Hartford Institute for Religious Research, Hartford Seminary
Women in Churches

Kristen Amundsen[†]
Women in Public Life, Business, and Professions

Gary Clayton Anderson
University of Oklahoma
Indian Political Life

George L. Anderson[†]
Colorado Coal Strikes
Crime of 1873
Cripple Creek Strikes

Margo Anderson
University of Wisconsin–Milwaukee
Statistics

Russell H. Anderson[†]
Fencing and Fencing Laws

Carol Andreas[†]
National Woman's Party
Women's Rights Movement:
The Nineteenth Century

Susan Andrew[†]
Biosphere 2
Physician Assistants

Matthew Page Andrews[†]
Singleton Peace Plan
Virginia Declaration of Rights

Wayne Andrews[†]
America First Committee

Paul M. Angle[†]
Freeport Doctrine
Illinois and Michigan Canal
Illinois Fur Brigade
Mormon War
Rail Splitter

Thomas Archdeacon
University of Wisconsin–Madison
Assimilation

Ethel Armes[†]
Alexandria

David Armstrong[†]
Machine Guns

Joseph L. Arnold
University of Maryland at Baltimore
Greenbelt Communities

Donna E. Arzt
Syracuse University
Pan Am Flight 103

George Frederick Ashworth[†]
Baltimore Riot
Fredericksburg, Battle of

Lori Askeland
Wittenberg University
"Forty Acres and a Mule"

Lewis E. Atherton[†]
Stores, General

Philip G. Auchampaugh[†]
Elections, Presidential: 1856
Hunkers

Francis R. Aumann[†]
Conciliation Courts, Domestic
Litchfield Law School

Richard L. Aynes
University of Akron
Munn v. Illinois
Slaughterhouse Cases
Springer v. United States
Stafford v. Wallace

Willoughby M. Babcock[†]
Northfield Bank Robbery

Andrew J. Bacevich[†]
Volunteer Army
War Powers Act

Charles H. Backstrom[†]
Gerrymander
Ripper Legislation

Douglas Bacon
Mayo Clinic
Anesthesia, Discovery of

Paul Bacon
New York, New York
Accidents

Lawrence Badash
University of California, Santa Barbara
Cyclotron

Physics: Overview
Physics: High-Energy Physics
Physics: Nuclear Physics

Judith A. Baer[†]
Frontiero v. Richardson
General Electric Company v. Gilbert
Griswold v. Connecticut
Harris v. McRae
Planned Parenthood of Southeastern Pennsylvania v. Casey
Roberts et al. v. United States Jaycees
Rotary International v. Rotary Club of Duarte
Taylor v. Louisiana

John Bakeless[†]
Molly Maguires

Gladys L. Baker[†]
Rural Free Delivery

John H. Baker[†]
Local Government

Nadine Cohen Baker
University of Georgia
California Higher Educational System

Gordon Morris Bakken
California State University at Fullerton
Land Acts
Proposition 13
Proposition 187
Proposition 209
Ruby Ridge
Simpson Murder Trials
Unabomber

Leland D. Baldwin[†]
Allegheny River
Bargemen
Flatboatmen
Galley Boats
Keelboat
River Navigation
Whiskey Rebellion

Sidney Baldwin[†]
Job Corps

Rebecca Bales
Diablo Valley College
Klamath-Modoc
Modoc War

Shelby Balik
University of Wisconsin–Madison
American Bible Society
Burghers
Cabot Voyages
Civil Religion
Colonial Assemblies
Duke of York's Laws
Education, Experimental
Hundred
Jehovah's Witnesses
Jenkins's Ear, War of
King George's War
King Philip's War
King William's War
Latitudinarians
Navigation Acts
Toleration Acts
Townshend Acts

Milner S. Ball
University of Georgia School of Law
Cherokee Nation Cases

Randall Balmer
Barnard College
Protestantism

William M. Banks
University of California, Berkeley
Black Nationalism
Magazines and Newspapers,
    African American
Nation of Islam

Charles Pete Banner-Haley
Colgate University
Black Power
Organization of Afro-American
    Unity
White Supremacy

Lance Banning
University of Kentucky
Jeffersonian Democracy
Republicans, Jeffersonian

Robert C. Bannister Jr.
Swarthmore College
Swarthmore College

William J. Barber[†]
Rhodes Scholarships

Thomas S. Barclay[†]
McNary-Haugen Bill
Minor v. Happersett
Normalcy

Packers and Stockyards Act
Pujo Committee

Elliott R. Barkan
*California State University at San
Bernadino*
Multiculturalism

Gilbert Hobbs Barnes[†]
Oberlin-Wellington Rescue
    Case

James A. Barnes[†]
Trade, Foreign

Viola F. Barnes[†]
Chartered Companies
Council for New England
Duke of York's Proprietary
Farmer's Letters
Plymouth, Virginia Company of
Providence Island Company
Randolph Commission
Sow Case

Gene Barnett
*University of Wisconsin–Madison
Alabama*

William C. Barnett
Madison, Wisconson
Hurricanes
Mexico, Gulf of

Georgia Brady Barnhill
American Antiquarian Society
Catlin's Indian Paintings
Wood Engraving

Daniel P. Barr
Kent State University
Army on the Frontier
Explorations and Expeditions:
    British
Explorations and Expeditions:
    Dutch
Frontier
Frontier Thesis, Turner's
La Salle Explorations
Laramie, Fort
Lewis and Clark Expedition
Westward Migration

Mark V. Barrow Jr.
*Virginia Polytechnic Institute and State
University*
Ornithology

Paul C. Bartholomew[†]
Boundary Disputes Between
    States
Expatriation
McCulloch v. Maryland

Bob Batchelor
San Rafael, California
Armory Show
Ashcan School
AT&T
AT&T Divestiture
Bank of America
Bootlegging
Cartoons
Chambers of Commerce
Cyborgs
Fair-Trade Laws
Fiber Optics
Gray Panthers
Hell's Angels
Insider Trading
Kent State Protest
Mass Production
Pittsburgh
Quiz Show Scandals
Radio
Robber Barons
San Francisco
Scandals

Robert L. Bateman
United States Military Academy
Mims, Fort, Massacre at

Scott C. Bates
WestEd, San Francisco, California
Substance Abuse

Edwin A. Battison[†]
Typewriter

James L. Baughman
University of Wisconsin–Madison
Television: Programming and
    Influence

Timothy Bawden
University of Wisconsin–Eau Claire
Camp Fire Girls
Forty-Eighters
Fox-Wisconsin Waterway
National Geographic Society
Vacation and Leisure

Heather Becker
Chicago Conservation Center
Murals

Thomas Becker[†]
  Society for the Prevention of
    Cruelty to Children

Robert L. Bee
University of Connecticut
  Mohave

Kirk H. Beetz
Davis, California
  ACTION
  Assembly Line
  Auto Emission Testing and
    Standards
  Automobile Industry
  Buckboards
  Central Europe, Relations with
  Cereal Grains
  Cereals, Manufacture of
  Citizenship
  Connecticut
  Executive Orders
  French Decrees
  Fuels, Alternative
  Kansas
  Massachusetts Circular Letter
  Michigan, Upper Peninsula of
  Nebraska
  New Hampshire
  Nicaraguan Canal Project
  Pennsylvania
  Polar Exploration
  Portsmouth, Treaty of
  Rhode Island
  Savannah
  Tennessee
  Treaties, Commercial

Michal R. Belknap
*California Western School of Law and
University of California, San Diego*
  Alexander v. Holmes County
    Board of Education
  In Re Gault
  Schenck v. United States
  War and the Constitution

John L. Bell
Western Carolina University
  North Carolina

Whitfield J. Bell Jr.[†]
  American Philosophical Society

Phil Bellfy
*White Earth Anishnaabe and Michigan
State University*

  Indians in the Civil War
  Native Americans
  Ojibwe
  Ottawa

James H. Belote[†]
  Bataan-Corregidor Campaign
  Okinawa

William M. Belote[†]
  Bataan-Corregidor Campaign
  Okinawa

Samuel Flagg Bemis[†]
  German-American Debt Agree-
    ment
  Lausanne Agreement
  Plan of 1776
  Taft-Katsura Memorandum
  Webster-Ashburton Treaty

Byron W. Bender[†]
  Linguistics

Margaret Bendroth
Calvin College
  United Church of Christ

Michael L. Benedict
Ohio State University
  Baker v. Carr
  Civil Rights Act of 1866
  Civil Rights Act of 1875
  Committee on the Conduct of
    the War
  Impeachment Trial of Andrew
    Johnson
  Joint Committee on Recon-
    struction

Richard R. Benert[†]
  Nader's Raiders

Stefanie Beninato
Santa Fe, New Mexico
  Colonial Administration, Spanish

William Ira Bennett[†]
  Post-Traumatic Stress Syndrome

George C. S. Benson[†]
  Interstate Compacts

Keith R. Benson
National Science Foundation
  Marine Biology
  Oceanography

Elbert J. Benton[†]
  Liberal Republican Party
  Western Reserve

Glenn H. Benton[†]
  Ballinger-Pinchot Controversy

Megan L. Benton
Pacific Lutheran University
  Prizes and Awards: MacArthur
    Foundation "Genius"
    Awards
  Prizes and Awards: Pulitzer
    Prizes

Clarence A. Berdahl[†]
  Berlin, Treaty of
  Boston Police Strike
  Caucus
  Confirmation by the Senate
  Equal Rights Party
  Yap Mandate

Julie Berebitsky
University of the South
  Adoption

Robert L. Berg[†]
  Territories of the United States

Carl Berger[†]
  World War II, Air War against
    Japan

Mark T. Berger
University of New South Wales
  Foreign Aid
  Good Neighbor Policy
  Gunboat Diplomacy
  India and Pakistan, Relations with
  Latin American Wars of Inde-
    pendence
  League of Nations
  Organization of American
    States
  Pan-American Union
  Southeast Asia Treaty Organiza-
    tion
  United Nations

Laura A. Bergheim
Columbus, Ohio
  Anarchists
  Barbados
  Distilling
  Hispanic Americans
  Manumission

Maternal and Child Health
    Care
National Endowment for the Arts
Press Associations
Voice of America

Barbara R. Bergman
American University
    Glass Ceiling

Don H. Berkebile[†]
    Trucking Industry
    Wagon Manufacture

Edward D. Berkowitz
George Washington University
    Health and Human Services,
        Department of
    War on Poverty

Leslie Berlowitz
American Academy of Arts and Sciences
    American Academy of Arts and
        Sciences

John S. Berman
New York University
    Sex Education

Larry Berman
University of California, Davis
    Vietnam, Relations with

Lila Corwin Berman
Yale University
    Institute for Advanced Study
    Rafts and Rafting

William C. Berman
University of Toronto
    Bitburg Controversy
    Clinton Scandals
    Clinton v. Jones
    Domino Theory
    Eagleton Affair
    Kosovo Bombing
    Tonkin Gulf Resolution

Daniel Bernardi
University of Arizona
    Citizen Kane
    Star Wars

Celeste-Marie Bernier
University of Nottingham
    Creole Slave Case
    Slave Rescue Cases

Slave Trade

Jennifer L. Bertolet
George Washington University
    Cambridge Agreement
    Empresario System
    Great Migration
    Homestead Movement
    Mussel Slough Incident
    Oñate Explorations and Settle-
        ments

Gary Dean Best
University of Hawaii (emeritus)
    Hawaii

Loren P. Beth[†]
    Implied Powers

Charles F. Bethel
San Diego, California
    Indemnities
    National Lawyers Guild

John K. Bettersworth[†]
    Cotton Money

Herman Beukema[†]
    West Point

Fred W. Beuttler
University of Illinois at Chicago
    Carnegie Corporation of New
        York
    Carnegie Foundation for the
        Advancement of Teaching
    Encyclopedias
    Foundations, Endowed
    MacArthur Foundation
    Mayo Foundation
    Pew Memorial Trust
    Philanthropy
    Revolution, Right of
    Rockefeller Foundation

Gary Bevington
Northeastern Illinois University
    Cherokee Language
    Custer Died for Your Sins
    Indian Languages
    Lakota Language
    Navajo Language

Rae Sikula Bielakowski
Loyola University of Chicago
    Dime Novels
    Jungle, The

Objectivism

Joseph C. Bigott
Purdue University, Calumet
    Bathtubs and Bathing

Monroe Billington[†]
    Primary, White
    States' Rights

Ray Allen Billington[†]
    Maria Monk Controversy
    Nativism
    Philadelphia Riots
    United Americans, Order of
    Ursuline Convent, Burning of

Robert W. Bingham[†]
    Great Lakes Naval Campaigns
        of 1812
    Niagara, Carrying Place of
    Niagara Campaigns
    Niagara Falls
    Stoney Creek, Battle of

Arthur C. Bining[†]
    Industries, Colonial
    Iron Act of 1750

Mary Jo Binker
George Mason University
    Ames Espionage Case
    Hanssen Espionage Case

Robert H. Birkby[†]
    Delegation of Powers

Martina B. Bishopp
Washington University in St. Louis
    Music: Classical
    Opera

Erin Black
University of Toronto
    Battle Fleet Cruise Around the
        World
    World Bank

Liza Black
University of Michigan
    Remington and Indian and
        Western Images

Ned Blackhawk
University of Wisconsin–Madison
    Ex Parte Crow Dog
    Fox War

Indians and Slavery
Lone Wolf v. Hitchcock
Lyng v. Northwest Indian Ceme-
tery Association
Navajo War
Paiute
Pontiac's War
Seminole Tribe v. Florida
Seminole Wars
Sioux Uprising in Minnesota
Sioux Wars
Tecumseh's Crusade
Tribes: Great Basin
United States v. Sioux Nation
Wounded Knee (1973)
Yakima Indian Wars

Martha Royce Blaine
Oklahoma State Historical Center
Pawnee

John B. Blake[†]
Malaria

Ellen Sue Blakey
Wyoming Folk Center
Honolulu

G. Robert Blakey
University of Notre Dame Law School
RICO

Edwin H. Blanchard[†]
Peninsular Campaign

Thomas E. Blantz, C.S.C.[†]
Holy Cross, Priests of

T. C. Blegen[†]
Northwest Angle
Snelling, Fort

Arthur R. Blessing[†]
Bonhomme Richard-Serapis
Encounter

Daniel K. Blewett
The College of DuPage Library
Aix-la-Chapelle, Treaty of

Jack Blicksilver[†]
Cotton

David W. Blight
Amherst College
Souls of Black Folk, The

Jack S. Blocker Jr.
Huron University College, University
of Western Ontario
Alcohol, Regulation of
Alcoholics Anonymous
Prohibition

Irene Bloemraad
Harvard University
Naturalization

Lansing B. Bloom[†]
California Trail

Francis X. Blouin
University of Michigan, Ann Arbor
Michigan
University of Michigan

Albert A. Blum[†]
Yellow-Dog Contract

Martin Blumenson[†]
Anzio
Cherbourg
Gothic Line
Gustav Line
Kasserine Pass, Battle of
Monte Cassino
North African Campaign
Saint-Lô
Salerno
Sicilian Campaign

Edith L. Blumhofer[†]
Wheaton College
Adventist Churches
Millennialism

Lance R. Blyth
Northern Arizona University
Encomienda System

Robert C. Boardman[†]
Audubon Society

Mody C. Boatright[†]
Tall Stories

Louis H. Bolander[†]
Constitution
"Don't Give Up the Ship"
Dreadnought
Golden Hind
Jersey Prison Ship
Mortars, Civil War Naval
Nautilus

Prisoners of War: Prison Ships
Ships of the Line
Twenty-One Gun Salute

Bruce A. Bolt[†]
Earthquakes

Charles K. Bolton[†]
"Don't Fire Till You See the
White of Their Eyes"

Ethel Stanwood Bolton[†]
Wax Portraits

Theodore Bolton[†]
Silhouettes

Beverley W. Bond Jr.[†]
Miami Purchase

Martyn Bone
University of Copenhagen
City on a Hill
"Dixie"
Jazz Age
Soccer

Milledge L. Bonham Jr.[†]
Bull Run, First Battle of
Caroline Affair

Jeremy Bonner
Washington, D.C.
African Methodist Episcopal
Church
Assemblies of God
Church of God in Christ
Disciples of Christ
Episcopalianism
Frazier-Lemke Farm Bankrupt-
cy Act
Idaho
Latter-day Saints, Church of
Jesus Christ of
Lutheranism
Moravian Brethren
Pentecostal Churches
Progressive Party, 1924
Reorganized Church of Jesus
Christ of Latter-day Saints
Scandinavian Americans
Utah

Timothy G. Borden
Toledo, Ohio

American Federation of State,
County, and Municipal
Employees
Americorps
Black Panthers
Indiana
International Union of Mine,
Mill, and Smelter Workers
Wayne, Fort

Georg Borgstrom[†]
Meatpacking

Douglas E. Bowers
*Economic Research Service, U.S.
Department of Agriculture*
Agriculture, Department of

Ray L. Bowers[†]
Air Force Academy

Julian P. Boyd[†]
Baynton, Wharton, and Morgan
Paxton Boys

Anne M. Boylan
University of Delaware
Sunday Schools

Eric William Boyle
University of California, Santa Barbara
Childbirth and Reproduction
Endangered Species
Wildlife Preservation

Frederick A. Bradford[†]
Banking: Banking Acts of 1933
and 1935
Banking: Banking Crisis of 1933
Bills of Credit
Glass-Steagall Act
Gold Exchange
Gold Purchase Plan
Inflation in the Confederacy
Liberty Loans
McFadden Banking Act
National Bank Notes
National Monetary Commission

Phillips Bradley[†]
Hylton v. United States

Richard Bradley
Central Methodist College
Anti-Semitism

E. Douglas Branch[†]
Buffalo Trails
Pack Trains

Robert M. Bratton
*Salmon P. Chase College of Law,
Northern Kentucky University*
U.S. Steel

Susan Roth Breitzer
University of Iowa
Amalgamated Clothing Workers of America
Child Labor
Discrimination: Race

Marion V. Brewington[†]
France, Quasi-War with

Howard Brick
Washington University in St. Louis
Sociology

William W. Brickman[†]
Education, Higher: Colleges
and Universities
Education, United States Office
of
Exchange Students
Schools, Private

Ron Briley
Sandia Preparatory School
Audio Technology Industry
Thrift Stamps

Tom A. Brindley[†]
Corn Borer, European

Jerry Brisco
Arizona State University
Dime Stores
Macy's
Retailing Industry
Sears Roebuck Catalog

James E. Brittain[†]
Electric Power and Light Industry
Lighting
Microwave Technology
Niagara Falls

David Brody[†]
American Labor Party
Socialist Party of America

Carolyn Bronstein[†]
Achille Lauro
Jonestown Massacre
Mount St. Helens

Philip Coolidge Brooks[†]
Convention of 1818 with England
Era of Good Feeling

R. P. Brooks[†]
Bankhead Cotton Act

Robert C. Brooks[†]
Canvass

Alfred L. Brophy
University of Alabama School of Law
Common Law
Property
Tulsa Race Riot

Cornelius James Brosnan[†]
Coeur d'Alene Riots

Dorothea Browder
University of Wisconsin–Madison
Coeur d'Alene Riots
Gasoline Taxes
Medicine, Occupational

Dee Brown[†]
Galvanized Yankees

Harry James Brown[†]
Wool Growing and Manufacture

James A. Brown
Northwestern University
Adena
Hopewell
Natchez
Spiro

L. Carl Brown
Princeton University
Arab Nations, Relations with

Lloyd A. Brown[†]
Cabot Voyages

Phillip M. Brown[†]
Deerfield Massacre

R. Blake Brown
Dalhousie University
    Eminent Domain
    Grosjean v. American Press Company
    Jury Trial
    Staggers Rail Act

Richard Maxwell Brown
University of Oregon
    Violence

William Lincoln Brown[†]
    Schooner

W. Elliot Brownlee
University of California, Santa Barbara
    Hamilton's Economic Policies
    Taxation

Kathleen Bruce[†]
    White House of the Confederacy

Mia Sara Bruch
Stanford University
    Ethical Culture, Society for

John Brudvig
University of Mary
    North Dakota
    Union, Fort

Lester H. Brune
Bradley University
    Jay-Gardoqui Negotiations
    Joint Occupation

Erik Bruun[†]
    Animal Rights Movement
    Junk Bonds
    Small Business Administration
    Stagflation

G. S. Bryan[†]
    Campaign Songs

David R. Buck
West Virginia University
    Extraterritoriality, Right of
    Monongahela, Battle of the
    Open Door Policy

Solon J. Buck[†]
    Braddock's Expedition
    Duquesne, Fort
    Great Meadows

    Ohio Company of Virginia
    Proclamation of 1763

Jay H. Buckley
Brigham Young University
    Fur Companies
    Fur Trade and Trapping

Peter Buckley
Cooper Union for the Advancement of Science and Art
    Cooper Union for the Advancement of Science and Art

Raymond A. Bucko, S.J.
Creighton University
    Sioux

John Budd
University of Minnesota
    Arbitration
    Comprehensive Employment and Training Act

Arthur F. Buehler
Louisiana State University
    Asian Religions and Sects
    Islam

John D. Buenker
University of Wisconsin–Parkside
    Progressive Party, Wisconsin
    Referendum
    University of Wisconsin

Paul Buhle
Brown University
    Socialist Labor Party

David Buisseret
University of Texas, Arlington
    Creoles and Creolization

John J. Bukowczyk
Wayne State University
    Polish Americans

Vern L. Bullough[†]
    Prostitution

Craig Bunch
Coldspring-Oakhurst High School, Texas
    Museum of Modern Art

Flannery Burke
University of Wisconsin–Madison

    Audubon Society
    Bay of Pigs Invasion
    Boxer Rebellion

George R. Burkes Jr.
Library of Congress
    Encounter Groups
    Family Values

Roger Burlingame[†]
    International Harvester Company
    Rum Trade

David Burner
State University of New York at Stony Brook
    Hudson River School
    Polling
    Trusts
    Water Supply and Conservation

Christina Duffy Burnett
Princeton University
    Territorial Governments

Edmund C. Burnett[†]
    Independence Day

John C. Burnham[†]
    Gasoline Taxes

Chester R. Burns[†]
    Hygiene

Jennifer Burns
University of California, Berkeley
    Leatherstocking Tales
    Leaves of Grass
    Modernists, Protestant
    Mysticism

Lawrence J. Burpee[†]
    Abraham, Plains of
    Montreal, Capture of (1760)
    Saint Lawrence River
    United Empire Loyalists

Harold L. Burstyn[†]
    International Geophysical Year

Stephen Burwood
State University of New York at Geneseo
    Marketing

Alfred Bush
Princeton University Library

Association on American Indian
Affairs

Richard Lyman Bushman
Columbia University
Nauvoo, Mormons at

Pierce Butler[†]
Mafia Incident

Stephen R. Byers
University of Wisconsin–Milwaukee
Newspapers

John J. Byrne[†]
Health Food Industry
Home Shopping Networks
New Age Movement

Mark E. Byrnes
Middle Tennessee State University
Chappaquiddick Incident
Checkers Speech
National Aeronautics and Space
Administration

Mark S. Byrnes
Wofford College
Spain, Relations with
Yugoslavia, Relations with

Anthony Christopher Cain
*College of Aerospace Doctrine Research
and Education*
Air Force, United States
Armored Vehicles
Helicopters
Korean War, Air Combat in

Philip D. Caine[†]
Cambodia, Bombing of

J. M. Callahan[†]
Mexican-American War

George H. Callcott
University of Maryland
Maryland

Colin G. Calloway
Dartmouth College
Abenaki

Krista Camenzind
University of California, San Diego
Tea Trade, Prerevolutionary

Charles S. Campbell[†]
Atlantic Charter
Bretton Woods Conference
Cairo Conferences
Four Freedoms
McCarran-Walter Act
Rio de Janeiro Conference
Smith Act
United Nations Declaration
Yalta Conference

Gregg M. Campbell[†]
Sacramento

Gregory Campbell
University of Montana, Missoula
Indian Reservations

Ian Campbell[†]
Petrography

Martin Campbell-Kelly
University of Warwick
Software Industry

Jack Campisi
*Mashantucket Pequot Museum and
Research Center*
Mahican
Mashpee
Mohegan
Pequots

Dominic Candeloro
Governors' State University
Italian Americans

Carl L. Cannon[†]
Albatross
Army Posts
Bonanza Kings
Doubloon
Drogher Trade
Forty-Mile Desert
Freeman's Expedition
Great Valley
Kelly's Industrial Army
Mangeurs de Lard
Marcy, R. B., Exploration of
Passes, Mountain
Sovereigns of Industry
Train Robberies

David Canon
University of Wisconsin–Madison
Voting Rights Act of 1965

Gregg Cantrell
University of North Texas
Texas

Gerald M. Capers Jr.[†]
Mississippi Plan
Natchez Trace

Antoine Capet
University of Rouen, France
Versailles, Treaty of

James H. Capshew
Indiana University
Psychology

Michael Carew
New York University
Albuquerque
Brooklyn Bridge
Buffalo
Empire State Building
Massachusetts Institute of Tech-
nology
Prizes and Awards: Academy
Awards
Wall Street Journal

Jim Carl
Cleveland State University
School Vouchers

Douglas W. Carlson
Northwestern College
Temperance Movement

Laurie Winn Carlson
Washington State University
Cattle
Overland Companies
Pioneers
Polk Doctrine
Puget Sound
Textbooks, Early
Washington, State of

Victor Carlson
*Los Angeles County Museum of Art
(emeritus)*
Art: Painting
Cubism
Genre Painting
Printmaking

W. N. C. S. Carlton[†]
Cumberland, Army of the

Neil Carothers[†]
Dollar Sign
Silver Legislation
Trade Dollar

William S. Carpenter[†]
Holmes v. Walton
Midnight Judges
Rights of Englishmen

Bret E. Carroll
California State University at Stanislaus
Church of Christ, Scientist
Spiritualism

James T. Carroll
Iona College
Indian Boarding Schools
Pike, Zebulon, Expeditions of

Clayborne Carson
Stanford University
King, Martin Luther, Assassination

Mina Carson
Oregon State University
Algonquin Round Table
Nightclubs
Personal Ads
Ragtime
Sexual Harassment
Track and Field
Vaudeville
Women's Studies

Carolle Carter
San Jose State University and Menlo College
San José

Dan T. Carter[†]
Scottsboro Case

Harvey L. Carter[†]
Four Hundred
Oratory

Lynn M. Case[†]
Algeciras Conference

David W. Cash[†]
Species, Introduced

W. T. Cash[†]
New Smyrna Colony
Ocala Platform

John Cashman
Boston College
Brotherhood of Sleeping Car Porters
Homestead Strike
International Brotherhood of Teamsters
Lawrence Strike
Paterson Silk Strike

Alfred L. Castle[†]
Post-structuralism

Norman Caulfield
Fort Hays State University
Electrical Workers
International Longshoremen's and Warehousemen's Union

Dominic Cerri
University of Wisconsin–Madison
Belize, Relations with
El Salvador, Relations with
Guatemala, Relations with

Martha L. Chaatsmith
Ohio State University
Indian Child Welfare Act

Thomas Chaffin
Emory University
Filibustering
Force Acts

Ranes C. Chakravorty
Virginia Polytechnic Institute and State University
Transplants and Organ Donation

John Whiteclay Chambers[†]
Desertion

Howard M. Chapin[†]
Gaspée, Burning of the
Mount Hope
Newport, French Army at

William C. Chapman[†]
Aircraft Carriers and Naval Aircraft

Thomas Chappelear
University of Chicago
Pure and Simple Unionism

Alan Chartock[†]
Political Action Committees

Eric L. Chase[†]
Erie Railroad Company v. Tompkins
Extra Sessions
Poll Tax
State Laws, Uniform
Trade with the Enemy Acts

Harold W. Chase[†]
Erie Railroad Company v. Tompkins
Expenditures, Federal
Extra Sessions
Poll Tax
State Laws, Uniform
Trade with the Enemy Acts

L. A. Chase[†]
Menominee Iron Range

Gabriel J. Chin
University of Cincinnati College of Law
Chinese Exclusion Act
Insular Cases

Leslie Choquette
Assumption College
Huguenots

Lawrence O. Christensen
University of Missouri at Rolla
Missouri

Howard P. Chudacoff
Brown University
Adolescence

Christopher Clark
University of Warwick
Manufacturing, Household

Dan E. Clark[†]
Big Horn Mountains
"Hell on Wheels"
Homestead Movement
Jumping-Off Places
Public Lands, Fencing of
Railroad Surveys, Government
South Pass

Ellery H. Clark Jr.[†]
Spanish-American War, Navy in

John B. Clark[†]
Elkins Act

Keith Clark[†]
Covered Wagon

R. C. Clark[†]
Walla Walla Settlements

T. D. Clark[†]
"Dark and Bloody Ground"
Feuds, Appalachian Mountain
Kentucky Conventions

Victor S. Clark[†]
Carriage Making
Friends of Domestic Industry
Hemp
Linen Industry
Sawmills
Soda Fountains
Tar

Jeffrey J. Clarke[†]
Ordnance

Sally Clarke
University of Texas, Austin
Agricultural Price Support

Dane S. Claussen[†]
Lever Act

Martin P. Claussen[†]
Arrest, Arbitrary, during the
Civil War
Conspiracies Acts of 1861 and
1862
Plumb Plan
Prize Cases, Civil War
Railroad Administration, U.S.
Smuggling of Slaves

Lyn Clayton
Brigham Young University
Fur Companies
Fur Trade and Trapping

J. Garry Clifford[†]
Conscription and Recruitment
Gulf of Sidra Shootdown
Persian Gulf War
Vietnam War Memorial

Scott Cline
Seattle Municipal Archives
Seattle

Kenneth Cmiel
University of Iowa
Atlantic, The
Dictionaries

Robert W. Coakley[†]
Military Academy

Daniel M. Cobb
University of Oklahoma
Indian Self-Determination and
Education Assistance Act

Justin Cober
InteLex Corporation
Great Train Robbery, The

Thomas C. Cochran[†]
Brewing
Debt and Investment, Foreign

John Colbert Cochrane[†]
Fourierism
Jones Act
Tallmadge Amendment

Rexmond C. Cochrane[†]
National Academy of Sciences

Robert P. Tristram Coffin[†]
Little Red Schoolhouse

Seddie Cogswell[†]
Bonuses, Military
Memorial Day
Midway Islands

Charles L. Cohen
University of Wisconsin–Madison
Great Awakening

Ronald D. Cohen
Indiana University Northwest
National Education Association

Barbara Cohen-Stratyner
Performing Arts Museum, New York
Public Library for the Performing Arts
Ballet

Jan Cohn
Trinity College, Hartford
Saturday Evening Post

Elbridge Colby[†]
Billeting

Bounties, Military
Cold Harbor, Battle of
Quebec, Capture of
Shiloh, Battle of
World War II

Arthur C. Cole[†]
Compromise of 1850
Irrepressible Conflict
Omnibus Bill

Fred Cole[†]
Guano

Kenneth Colegrove[†]
Boxer Rebellion
China Clipper

Arica Coleman[†]
Peace Movement of 1864

Charles H. Coleman[†]
Canada, Confederate Activities
in
Copperheads
Elections, Presidential: 1868
and 1872
General Order No. 38
National Union (Arm-in-Arm)
Convention
Northwest Conspiracy
Saint Albans Raid
Vallandigham Incident

David G. Coleman
Miller Center of Public Affairs, University of Virginia
Antiwar Movements
Berlin Airlift
Berlin Wall
Cuban Missile Crisis
Hijacking, Airplane
Hostage Crises
Peace Corps

R. V. Coleman[†]
Ludlow's Code

Francis J. Colligan[†]
Fulbright Act and Grants

Henry B. Collins[†]
Ethnology, Bureau of American

James L. Collins Jr.[†]
Germany, American Occupation
of

Richard B. Collins
University of Colorado School of Law
Native American Rights Fund

Robert M. Collins
University of Missouri at Columbia
Employment Act of 1946
Keynesianism
National Association of Manufacturers

Jerald A. Combs[†]
Strategic Arms Limitation Talks

Mary Commager[†]
North American Free Trade Agreement

Carl W. Condit[†]
Building Materials
Tunnels

Stetson Conn[†]
Reserve Officers' Training Corps

C. Ellen Connally
University of Akron
Davis, Imprisonment and Trial of

Margaret Connell-Szasz
University of New Mexico
Education, Indian

Marie D. Connolly[†]
International Monetary Fund

Timothy C. Coogan
Rutgers University–Newark
New Jersey

Jacob E. Cooke[†]
American Independent Party
Compromise of 1790
Doves and Hawks
White Citizens Councils

Dane Coolidge[†]
Death Valley

B. Franklin Cooling[†]
Civil Defense
Energy Research and Development Administration

Terry A. Cooney
University of Puget Sound
New York Intellectuals

Evelyn S. Cooper
Arizona Historical Foundation, Arizona State University
Arizona
Photographic Industry

Gail A. Cooper
Lehigh University
Air Conditioning

Grace R. Cooper[†]
Cotton Gin
Sewing Machine

Susan J. Cooper[†]
Conservation Biology
Environmental Business
Wetlands

Elmer E. Cornwell Jr.[†]
Elections, Presidential: Overview

Graham A. Cosmas
Joint History Office, Joint Chiefs of Staff
Vietnam War

Sarah Costello
University of Wisconsin–Madison
[Various revisions]

Jeffrey T. Coster
University of Maryland, College Park
Bail
Direct Mail
Home Rule
Initiative
McDonalds
Procter and Gamble
Soft Drink Industry

George B. Cotkin
California Polytechnic State University
Existentialism
Historiography, American

Carl H. Cotterill[†]
Lead Industry
Zinc Industry

R. S. Cotterill[†]
Black Belt
Hermitage

Robert C. Cottrell
California State University at Chico
American Civil Liberties Union
Espionage Act

E. Merton Coulter[†]
Bowles's Filibustering Expeditions
Chisholm v. Georgia
Georgia Platform
Jenkins's Ear, War of
Savannah, Siege of (1779)
Southwest Territory

Edward Countryman
Southern Methodist University
Committees of Correspondence
Committees of Safety
Intolerable Acts
Loyalists
Revolution, American: Political History
Sons of Liberty (American Revolution)
Stamp Act
Stamp Act Congress
Stamp Act Riot

Robert D. Couttie
Balangiga Research Group
Philippine Insurrection

Akiba J. Covitz
University of Richmond
Extradition
Fletcher v. Peck
Gelpcké v. Dubuque
Loving v. Virginia
Miscegenation
Presidents and Subpoenas
Privacy
Search and Seizure, Unreasonable
Statutes of Limitations
Supreme Court Packing Bills
United States v. Virginia

David L. Cowen
Rutgers, The State University of New Jersey
Pharmacy
Resorts and Spas

Thomas W. Cowger
East Central University
National Congress of American Indians

Isaac J. Cox[†]
Elections, Presidential: 1800
and 1804

Thomas H. Cox
State University of New York at Buffalo
Shreveport Rate Case

Jerry Craddock
University of California, Berkeley
Spanish Language

Wesley Frank Craven[†]
Two Penny Act

Martin Crawford
Keele University
Confederate States of America
Nashville Convention
Southern Unionists

Donald T. Critchlow
Saint Louis University
Brookings Institution
Think Tanks

Ann Jerome Croce
DeLand, Florida
Homeopathy

James B. Crooks[†]
Jacksonville

Philip A. Crowl[†]
Caroline Islands
Gilbert Islands
Saipan
Tinian

Robert D. Cuff
York University
National War Labor Board,
World War I
National War Labor Board,
World War II
World War I, Economic Mobi-
lization for

Katherine Culkin
Pace University
Women's Rights Movement:
The Nineteenth Century

David O'Donald Cullen
Collin County Community College
Cow Towns
Music: Gospel

United Brotherhood of Carpenters and Joiners
United Textile Workers

Kathleen B. Culver[†]
Los Angeles Riots
Pyramid Schemes
Robberies

Charles Cummings
*Newark Public Library/Newark City
Historian*
Newark

Noble E. Cunningham Jr.[†]
Quids

Lynne Curry
Eastern Illinois University
Child Abuse
Domestic Violence

Cathy Curtis
Los Angeles, California
Dentistry
Disasters
Emigration
Poverty
Urban Redevelopment

Christopher M. Curtis
Emory University
Debt, Imprisonment for

Jane E. Dabel
*California State University at Long
Beach*
Draft Riots
Quilting

Edward Everett Dale[†]
Abilene
Abilene Trail
Boomer Movement
Cherokee Trail
Chisholm Trail
Indian Brigade
Prairie Schooner
Rustler War
Singing Schools
Sooners
Southwest

Matthew L. Daley
Bowling Green State University
Baltimore
City Directories
Detroit

Detroit Riots
Galveston
Great Lakes Steamships
Green Bay
Independence, Mo.
Kansas City
Tulsa

R. W. Daly[†]
Archangel Campaign
Gunboats
Meuse-Argonne Offensive
Monitor and *Merrimack*, Battle
of
Murmansk
Naval Academy
Naval Operations, Chief of
Navy, Department of
Pensions, Military and Naval
Somme Offensive
Warships

Robert Daly
State University of New York at Buffalo
Scarlet Letter, The

Brian Isaac Daniels
San Francisco State University
Archaeology and Prehistory of
North America

Maygene F. Daniels
National Gallery of Art
National Gallery

Roger Daniels
University of Cincinnati
Grand Army of the Republic
Immigration
Immigration Act of 1965
Immigration Restriction
Internment, Wartime
Japanese American Incarcera-
tion

Allison Danzig[†]
Tennis

W. M. Darden[†]
Bougainville

Arthur B. Darling[†]
Elections, Presidential: 1816
and 1820

R. J. Davey[†]
Hogs

13

Lee Davis
San Francisco State University
Tribes: California

Matthew R. Davis
University of Puget Sound
Jazz Singer, The

Ronald W. Davis[†]
Liberia, Relations with

Jared N. Day
Carnegie Mellon University
New York City

Jane Sherron De Hart
University of California, Santa Barbara
Discrimination: Sex
Equal Rights Amendment
Reed v. Reed
Roe v. Wade

Guillaume de Syon
Albright College
Balloons
Space Program
X-1 Plane

William Tucker Dean[†]
Licenses to Trade

Ada E. Deer
University of Wisconsin–Madison
Menominee

Christian Mark DeJohn
Wyncote, Pennsylvania
Air Defense
Bombing

Denys Delage
Laval University
Huron/Wyandot

Andrew Delbanco
Columbia University
Moby-Dick

Vincent H. Demma
United States Army Center for Military History
Atrocities in War
Liberty Incident
My Lai Incident
Navajo Code Talkers
Prisoners of War: Exchange of Prisoners

Special Forces
Vietnamization

Michael Aaron Dennis
Cornell University
Laboratories

David Dent
Towson University
Mexico, Relations with

Jeremy Derfner
Columbia University
Amusement Parks
Assistant
Bowling
Central Park
College Athletics
Golf
Government Ownership
Government Publications
Governors
Graffiti
Grants-in-Aid
Harlem
Inspection, Governmental
Ironclad Oath
Lecompton Constitution
Lindbergh's Atlantic Flight
Niagara Movement
Political Subdivisions
Radical Republicans
Reconstruction Finance Corporation
Resettlement Administration
Shays's Rebellion
Sons of Liberty (Civil War)
Tillmanism
Union Party
War Democrats
War Powers

Andy DeRoche
Front Range Community College
South Africa, Relations with

Chester M. Destler[†]
Ohio Idea
Pendleton Act
Ten-Forties
Union Labor Party

Tracey Deutsch
University of Minnesota
Boycotting
Chain Stores

Michael J. Devine
Harry S. Truman Library
Illinois

H. A. DeWeerd[†]
Embalmed Beef
War Industries Board

Lynda DeWitt
Bethesda, Maryland
Discrimination: Religion
Electricity and Electronics
Federal Register
Petrochemical Industry
Public Utilities

Herbert Maynard Diamond[†]
Walsh-Healey Act

Everett Dick[†]
Adobe
Arbor Day
Long Drive
Sorghum

W. M. Dick[†]
Labor Parties

Edwin Dickens
Drew University
Building and Loan Associations
Check Currency
Credit Unions
Investment Companies
Open-Market Operations
Redlining

O. M. Dickerson[†]
Colonial Councils
Enumerated Commodities
Indentured Servants
Navigation Acts
Parson's Cause
Sugar Acts
Sumptuary Laws and Taxes, Colonial
Tea, Duty on
Townshend Acts
Trading Companies
Writs of Assistance

Irving Dilliard[†]
"Tippecanoe and Tyler Too!"
United We Stand, Divided We Fall
"We Have Met the Enemy, and They Are Ours"

14

Robert W. Dimand
Brock University
    Laffer Curve Theory

Eli Moses Diner
New York, New York
    American Association of University Professors
    American Association of University Women
    Big Sisters
    Dugout
    Mexican American Women's National Association
    National Conference of Puerto Rican Women
    National Federation of Business and Professional Women's Clubs
    9 to 5, National Association of Working Women
    Phi Beta Kappa Society
    Scrabble

Hasia R. Diner
New York University
    Lower East Side

Shira M. Diner
Brookline, Massachusetts
    Apalachin Conference
    Bronson v. Rodes
    Ex Parte Merryman
    Freedom of Information Act
    Iraq-gate
    Israeli-Palestinian Peace Accord
    Motor Carrier Act
    Platt Amendment
    Reynolds v. United States
    Society for Women's Health Research
    Speed Limits
    Toxic Substance Control Act
    United States–Canada Free Trade Agreement

Bruce J. Dinges
Arizona Historical Society
    Tombstone

P. Allan Dionisopoulos†
    Federal Government
    Powell Case

Robert B. Dishman†
    State Constitutions

Charles M. Dobbs
Iowa State University
    Canadian-American Waterways
    China, Relations with
    Guadalupe Hidalgo, Treaty of
    House-Grey Memorandum
    Jay's Treaty
    Kellogg-Briand Pact
    London Naval Treaties
    Marshall Plan
    Monroe Doctrine
    Most-Favored-Nation Principle
    North Atlantic Treaty Organization
    Paris, Treaty of (1783)
    Perry's Expedition to Japan

J. Frank Dobie†
    Bowie Knife
    Cattle Brands
    Cattle Drives
    Herpetology
    Horse Stealing
    Medicine Show
    Mesa
    Mesquite
    Mule Skinner
    Stampedes
    Trail Drivers
    Windmills

John M. Dobson†
    General Agreement on Tariffs and Trade
    Trade Agreements

Gordon B. Dodds
Portland State University
    Oregon
    Portland

Rick Dodgson
Ohio University
    Beat Generation
    Hippies
    Surfing
    Woodstock

Justus D. Doenecke
University of South Florida
    Bricker Amendment
    Casablanca Conference
    Dollar Diplomacy
    Dumbarton Oaks Conference
    Hague Peace Conferences
    Intervention
    Operation Dixie

    Potsdam Conference
    Roosevelt Corollary
    Teheran Conference
    United Nations Conference
    Washington Naval Conference

Jameson W. Doig
Princeton University
    George Washington Bridge

Jay P. Dolan
University of Notre Dame
    Catholicism

Paul Dolan†
    Myers v. United States
    Statutory Law

Marc Dollinger
San Francisco State University
    Jewish Defense League
    Zionism

Melanie M. Domenech-Rodriguez
Utah State University
    Filipino Americans
    Substance Abuse

Susan Dominguez
Michigan State University
    Society of American Indians

Greg Donaghy
Department of Foreign Affairs and International Trade
    Canadian-American Reciprocity

Gregory Michael Dorr
University of Alabama
    Breast Implants
    Dalkon Shield
    DNA

Jonathan T. Dorris†
    Cumberland Gap
    Cumberland River

Lyle W. Dorsett†
    Pendergast Machine

Joseph A. Dowling†
    Blacklisting
    Enemy Aliens in the World Wars
    Sedition Acts
    Test Laws

15

Donald A. Downs
University of Wisconsin–Madison
    Book Banning
    Contempt of Congress
    First Amendment
    Supreme Court

Robert C. Doyle
Franciscan University of Steubenville
    Prisoners of War: Overview

Edmund Lee Drago
College of Charleston
    Red Shirts

Dennis Dresang
University of Wisconsin–Madison
    Legislatures, State

Henry N. Drewry[†]
    Berea College v. Kentucky
    Black Codes
    Education, African American
    Equal Employment Opportuni-
        ty Commission
    Nat Turner's Rebellion
    Slave Insurrections

Robert S. Driscoll
    Joint Chiefs of Staff
    War Casualties

Stella M. Drumm[†]
    Missouri River
    Missouri River Fur Trade

John Duffy[†]
    Cholera
    Influenza
    Sanitation, Environmental

Jonathan R. Dull
The Papers of Benjamin Franklin
    Revolution, American: Diplo-
        matic Aspects

Foster Rhea Dulles[†]
    Cushing's Treaty
    Kearny's Mission to China
    Sino-Japanese War

Lynn Dumenil[†]
    Fraternities and Sororities

Wayland F. Dunaway[†]
    Free Society of Traders

Louise B. Dunbar[†]
    Meetinghouse
    Mourt's Relation

Robert G. Dunbar[†]
    Reclamation
    Sheep
    Wheat

James T. Dunham[†]
    Copper Industry

E. Melanie DuPuis
University of California, Santa Cruz
    Packaging

Dawn Duquès
Nova Southeastern
    Education, Cooperative
    Homework
    Self-Help Movement

Donald F. Durnbaugh
Juniata College
    Amish
    Brethren
    Mennonites
    Pietism

George Matthew Dutcher[†]
    Pequot War

Meaghan M. Dwyer
Boston College
    Great Books Programs
    Irish Americans

Linda Dynan
Cincinnati, Ohio
    Hospitals
    Seniority Rights
    Strikes
    Trade Unions

Mary Ann Dzuback
Washington University
    University of Chicago

Vicki L. Eaklor[†]
    Gay and Lesbian Movement

Polly Anne Earl[†]
    Clothing Industry

Gerald Early
Washington University in St. Louis

    Literature: African American
        Literature

Robert A. East[†]
    Dutch Bankers' Loans

Clare Virginia Eby
University of Connecticut
    Naturalism

H. J. Eckenrode[†]
    Monroe, Fortress

R. David Edmunds
University of Texas, Dallas
    Mesquakie
    Miami (Indians)
    Potawatomi
    Shawnee
    Wars with Indian Nations:
        Early Nineteenth Century
        (1783-1840)

Rebecca Edwards
Vassar College
    Farmers' Alliance

Thomas L. Edwards[†]
    Free Trade

Martha Avaleen Egan
Emory & Henry College
    Anthracite Strike
    Prisoners of War: Prison
        Camps, World War II

Michael Egan
Washington State University
    Colorado River Explorations
    Dust Bowl

Michael J. Eig
Michael J. Eig and Associates
    Disabled, Education of the

John F. Eisenberg
University of Florida
    Mammalogy

Charles Winslow Elliott[†]
    Chapultepec, Battle of
    Mexico City, Capture of
    Newburgh Addresses

Angela Ellis
University of Wisconsin–Madison
    Arlington National Cemetery

Army of Northern Virginia
Army of Virginia
Backlash
Jersey Prison Ship
Korea War of 1871
Nonferrous Metals
Prize Courts
Soldiers' Home
Southern Commercial Conventions
Volunteer Army
War and Ordnance, Board of

Elmer Ellis[†]
Elections, Presidential: 1896
Elections, Presidential: 1900
Elections, Presidential: 1912
Elections, Presidential: 1916
Greenbacks
Silver Democrats
Silver Republican Party

L. Ethan Ellis[†]
Dartmouth College Case

J. W. Ellison
"Fifty-Four Forty or Fight"
"Go West, Young Man, Go West"
Legal Tender Act

Lucius F. Ellsworth[†]
Boot and Shoe Manufacturing

Fred A. Emery[†]
Japanese Cherry Trees

Eugene M. Emme[†]
Missiles, Military

Judith E. Endelman
Henry Ford Museum and Greenfield Village
Henry Ford Museum and Greenfield Village

Francene M. Engel
University of Michigan
Executive Privilege

Jeffrey A. Engel
Yale University
Great Britain, Relations with

Hugh English
Queens College of the City University of New York
Celebrity Culture

Lisa A. Ennis
Georgia College and State University
Assisted Suicide
Cardiovascular Disease
Chiropractic
Cosmetic Surgery
General Motors
G.I. Joe
Livestock Industry
Osteopathy
Paper and Pulp Industry
Post-Traumatic Stress Disorder
Tariff
Video Games
Vietnam Syndrome
West Virginia

Jonathan L. Entin
Case Western Reserve University
Miranda v. Arizona

David J. Erickson
Berkeley, California
Budget, Federal

Erik McKinley Eriksson[†]
Blue Eagle Emblem
Brain Trust
Corrupt Bargain
Elections, Presidential: 1836
Elections, Presidential: 1932 and 1936
Frazier-Lemke Farm Bankruptcy Act
Gold Reserve Act
Interests
"Kitchen Cabinet"
Majority Rule
National Labor Relations Board v. Jones and Laughlin Steel Corporation
Pump-Priming
Resumption Act
Specie Circular
War Trade Board

Grover Antonio Espinoza
Columbia University
Cabeza de Vaca Expeditions

Emmett M. Essin III[†]
Cavalry, Horse

Elizabeth W. Etheridge[†]
Centers for Disease Control and Prevention
Legionnaires' Disease

Alona E. Evans[†]
Women, Citizenship of Married

C. Wyatt Evans
Drew University
Anti-Saloon League
Bourbons
Bull Moose Party
Cleveland Democrats
Muckrakers
Mugwumps
New Freedom
Recall
Square Deal

David S. Evans
University of California, Davis
Deaf in America
Gallaudet University

Stephen H. Evans[†]
Coast Guard, U.S.

Bruce J. Evenson[†]
Beirut Bombing
Black Monday Stock Market Crash
Challenger Disaster
Korean Airlines Flight 007
Waco Siege

Robert Eyestone[†]
Blocs
Unit Rule

Regina M. Faden
University of Missouri at St. Louis
Chanukah
Volunteerism

William B. Faherty
Saint Louis University
Louisiana Purchase Exposition

Robert B. Fairbanks[†]
Austin

Charles Fairman[†]
Bank of Augusta v. Earle
Cohens v. Virginia
Cooley v. Board of Wardens of Port of Philadelphia
Ex Parte Bollman

Leslie A. Falk[†]
Leyte Gulf, Battle of
Medicine, Occupational

17

Stanley L. Falk[†]
  Bismarck Sea, Battle of
  Coral Sea, Battle of the
  Guadalcanal Campaign
  Lingayen Gulf
  Peleliu
  Rabaul Campaign
  Tarawa

Alving F. Farlow[†]
  Beaver Hats

Hallie Farmer[†]
  Bloody Shirt
  Emancipation, Compensated
  Freedman's Savings Bank
  "King Cotton"
  Montgomery Convention
  Wormley Conference

Karenbeth Farmer
University of Kansas
  Housing and Urban Develop-
    ment, Department Of
  Norsemen in America
  Sovereignty, Doctrine Of
  State Constitutions

Brenda Farnell
*University of Illinois at Urbana-Cham-
paign*
  Dance, Indian
  Sign Language, Indian

V. J. Farrar[†]
  Klondike Rush

H. U. Faulkner[†]
  China Trade
  In Re Debs

Jefferson Faye Sina
Michigan State University
  Aleut

Loren Butler Feffer
Aberdeen, New Jersey
  Ague
  Creationism
  Evolutionism
  LSD
  Primal Therapy
  Prozac
  Semiconductors
  Vegetarianism
  Videocassette Recorder

Roger Feinstein
University of Massachusetts at Boston
  Massachusetts

Werner Feld[†]
  Prize Courts

Andrew Feldman[†]
  Air Traffic Controllers Strike

Daniel Feller
University of New Mexico
  Albany Regency
  Antibank Movement
  Expunging Resolution
  Jacksonian Democracy
  Removal of Deposits
  Spoils System

David Fellman[†]
  Suffrage: Exclusion from the
    Suffrage

Ann Harper Fender
Gettysburg College
  Blast Furnaces, Early
  Coffee
  Health Maintenance Organiza-
    tions
  Monopoly

John H. Fenton[†]
  Property Qualifications

Ellen Fernandez-Sacco
University of California, Berkeley
  Museums

Sarah Ferrell[†]
  Lost Generation

Lenore Fine[†]
  Engineers, Corps of
  River and Harbor Improve-
    ments
  Roads, Military

Charles J. Finger[†]
  Shanty Towns

Gary M. Fink[†]
  Labor, Department of

Leslie Fink[†]
  Human Genome Project

Roger Finke
Pennsylvania State University
  Religion and Religious Affilia-
    tion

Paul Finkelman
University of Tulsa College of Law
  Ableman v. Booth
  Calder v. Bull
  Civil Rights Act of 1991
  Dred Scott Case
  Fugitive Slave Acts
  Palimony
  Personal Liberty Laws
  *Prigg v. Commonwealth of Penn-
    sylvania*
  Zenger Trial

Bernard S. Finn[†]
  Cables, Atlantic and Pacific

Martin H. Fishbein[†]
  Patents and U.S. Patent Office

Lillian Estelle Fisher[†]
  Presidio

Robert Fishman[†]
  Atlantic City

Michael Fitzgerald
Saint Olaf College
  South, the: The New South

Lena G. FitzHugh[†]
  Candles

John Fitzpatrick
Charles Scribner's Sons
  Appalachian Trail
  City University of New York
  Music: Theater and Film

John C. Fitzpatrick[†]
  Conway Cabal
  Elections, Presidential: 1789
    and 1792
  Seal of the Confederate States
    of America
  Seal of the United States

Donald L. Fixico
University of Kansas
  American Indian Movement
  Native American Studies

Martin S. Flaherty
Fordham Law School
    Antifederalists

Douglas Flamming
Georgia Institute of Technology
    Georgia

Maureen A. Flanagan
Michigan State University
    Consumers Leagues
    General Federation of Women's
        Clubs
    National Organization for
        Women
    Sanitary Commission, United
        States
    Women, President's Commis-
        sion on the Status of
    Women's Bureau
    Women's Clubs

Richard M. Flanagan
College of Staten Island of the City Uni-
versity of New York
    Black Caucus, Congressional
    Bonus Army
    Bosses and Bossism, Political
    Contract with America
    Democracy
    Drug Trafficking, Illegal
    Great Society
    Kerner Commission
    Narcotics Trade and Legislation
    Port Authority of New York
        And New Jersey
    Violence Commission
    Watergate

Michael A. Flannery
University of Alabama at Birmingham
    Diets and Dieting
    Nutrition and Vitamins
    Obesity

James Rodger Fleming
Colby College
    Climate
    Meteorology

K. E. Fleming
New York University
    Greece, Relations with

A. C. Flick[†]
    Albany Plan
    Bennington, Battle of

    Burghers
    Duke of York's Laws
    Dutch West India Company
    Fulton's Folly
    Half Moon
    King William's War
    Leisler Rebellion
    New York City, Capture of
    Oriskany, Battle of
    Patroons
    Petition and Remonstrance of
        New Netherland
    Saratoga Springs
    White Plains, Battle of
    Workingmen's Party

James J. Flink[†]
    American Automobile Association
    Automobile

Percy Scott Flippin[†]
    Hundred

Matthew J. Flynn
San Diego State University
    Flapper
    Oregon Trail
    Washington's Farewell Address

S. J. Folmsbee[†]
    Franklin, State of
    Tennessee River

William E. Forbath
University of Texas School of Law
    Antitrust Laws
    Clayton Act, Labor Provisions
    Danbury Hatters' Case
    Hague v. Committee on Industrial
        Organization
    Injunctions, Labor
    International Labor Organization
    Right-to-Work Laws
    Taft-Hartley Act

Bonnie L. Ford
Sacramento City College
    Association of Southern
        Women for the Prevention
        of Lynching
    Birth Control Movement
    Coalition of Labor Union
        Women
    Colonial Dames of America
    Convention on the Elimination
        of All Forms of Discrimina-
        tion Against Women

    Daughters of the American
        Revolution
    DES Action USA
    Explorations and Expeditions:
        Spanish
    Girl Scouts of the United States
        of America
    Junior Leagues International,
        Association of
    League of Women Voters
    Menéndez de Avilés, Pedro,
        Colonization Efforts of

Guy Stanton Ford[†]
    Committee on Public Informa-
        tion

Michael James Foret
University of Wisconsin–Stevens Point
    Houma

Cornelius P. Forster, O.P.[†]
    Dominicans

Harold S. Forsythe
Fairfield University
    Underground Railroad

Robert Fortenbaugh[†]
    Dissenters
    Great Law of Pennsylvania
    Harrisburg Convention

Philip L. Fosburg[†]
    Elevators

Gaines M. Foster
Louisiana State University
    United Daughters of the Con-
        federacy

Kristen Foster[†]
    Literature: Native American
        Literature

Joseph H. Foth[†]
    Safety First Movement

Steve M. Fountain
University of California, Davis
    Great Salt Lake

Arlen L. Fowler[†]
    Black Cavalry in the West
    Black Infantry in the West

Daniel M. Fox[†]
Acquired Immune Deficiency
Syndrome

Stephen Fox
California State University
Relocation, Italian-American

John Francis Jr.[†]
Sequoia
Whiskey Ring

Perry Frank
American Dream & Associates, Inc.
Battle Hymn of the Republic
Circus and Carnival
Motels
Social Register

Norma Frankel[†]
Savings Bonds

W. Neil Franklin[†]
Virginia Indian Company

Eric M. Freedman
Hofstra University School of Law
Habeas Corpus, Writ of

Douglas Southall Freeman[†]
Appomattox
Bull Run, Second Battle of
Pickett's Charge

Frank Freidel[†]
Civil War General Order No.
100
Mexican-American War Claims

Allen French[†]
Bunker Hill, Battle of
Lexington and Concord, Battles
of
Minutemen
Revere's Ride

Tony Freyer[†]
Griggs v. Duke Power Company
*International Brotherhood of
Teamsters v. United States*
*Meritor Savings Bank v. Mechelle
Vinson*
*Personnel Administrator of Massa-
chusetts v. Feeney*
Richmond v. J. A. Croson Company
Rust v. Sullivan
Santa Clara Pueblo v. Martinez

Russell W. Fridley[†]
Farmer-Labor Party of Minnesota

Amy Fried[†]
Rape Crisis Centers

Max Paul Friedman
Florida State University
Agency for International Devel-
opment
Armistice of November 1918
Bermuda Conferences
Carter Doctrine
Eisenhower Doctrine
Geneva Conferences
Genocide
Hay-Bunau-Varilla Treaty
Hay-Pauncefote Treaties
Lend-Lease
Olney Corollary
Panama Revolution
Propaganda
Pugwash Conferences
Reciprocal Trade Agreements
Reykjavik Summit
Summit Conferences, U.S. and
Russian
Unconditional Surrender
X Article

Monroe Friedman
Eastern Michigan University
Hidden Persuaders, The
Product Tampering

Herman R. Friis[†]
Cartography

Derek W. Frisby
University of Alabama
Censorship, Military
Enlistment
Thresher Disaster

Morton J. Frisch[†]
Republic

Henry E. Fritz
Saint Olaf College
Billings
Board of Indian Commissioners
Meriam Report

Percy S. Fritz[†]
Prospectors
Smelters

Joseph Fronczak
University of Wisconsin–Madison
Rock and Roll

Clifford Frondel[†]
Mineralogy

Polly Fry
University of Minnesota
Blizzards
Hennepin, Louis, Narratives of
Midwest
Mississippi Valley
Prairie
Trans-Appalachian West

Ralph T. Fulton[†]
Fruit Growing

Tom Fulton[†]
Horse

Robert Frank Futrell[†]
Korean War, Air Combat in

John Lewis Gaddis[†]
Geneva Conferences
Paris Conferences

David W. Galenson[†]
Tennis

Gilbert J. Gall[†]
*Automobile Workers v. Johnson
Controls, Inc.*
*Ward's Cove Packing Co., Inc., v.
Atonio*

Ruth A. Gallaher[†]
Iowa Band

Robert E. Gallman[†]
National Bureau of Economic
Research
Standards of Living

Perrin C. Galpin[†]
World War I, U.S. Relief in

W. Freeman Galpin[†]
Entail of Estate
Magna Carta
Primogeniture

Oscar H. Gandy Jr.
University of Pennsylvania
Communications Industry

Paul Neff Garber†
Gadsden Purchase

Robert Garland
Colgate University
Emigrant Aid Movement
Marathons
Passports

Raymond L. Garthoff†
Strategic Arms Limitation Talks

Ellen Gruber Garvey
New Jersey City University
Magazines
Magazines, Men's
Reader's Digest

Carol Gaskin†
Aerobics

K. Healan Gaston
University of California, Berkeley
Bay Psalm Book
National Council of Churches

Paul W. Gates†
Alien Landholding
Bounties, Commercial
Claim Associations
Cornell University
Deposit Act of 1836
Glebes
Indian Trade and Intercourse
Act
Land Bounties
Land Grants: Land Grants for
Education
Land Grants: Land Grants for
Railways
Land Office, U.S. General and
Bureau Plans Management
Land Scrip
Land Speculation
Mesabi Iron Range
Morrill Act
Public Domain
Public Land Commissions
School Lands
Subsidies
Timber Culture Act
Western Lands

Robert Moulton Gatke†
Discovery
Pacific Fur Company

Anthony Gaughan
Harvard University Law School
Belknap Scandal
Executive Agreements
Presidents, Interment of
Sherman Silver Purchase Act
Tweed Ring

Gary Gault
Maryland Air National Guard
National Guard

Daniel Geary
University of California, Berkeley
Book-of-the-Month Club
Environmental Movement
Frankfurt School
Time
Welfare System

Noah Gelfand
New York University
Mount Rushmore

Karen E. Geraghty
Chicago, Illinois
American Medical Association
Medical Societies

Scott D. Gerber
*Pettit College of Law, Ohio Northern
University*
Commerce Clause

Louis S. Gerteis
University of Missouri at St. Louis
Gag Rule, Antislavery
Liberty Party
Locofoco Party
Minstrel Shows
Webster-Hayne Debate

Irwin N. Gertzog†
Caucuses, Congressional
Comparable Worth
Tailhook Incident
Violence Against Women Act
Women's Educational Equity
Act

Pierre Gervais
University of Paris
Industrial Revolution

Marvin E. Gettleman
Brooklyn Polytechnic University
Abraham Lincoln Brigade

Norman Gevitz
*Ohio University, College of Osteopathic
Medicine*
Medicine, Alternative

David Ghere
*General College, University of Min-
nesota*
Passamaquoddy/Penobscot

Guy Gibbon†
Cahokia Mounds
Poverty Point

Arrell M. Gibson†
Midcontinent Oil Region

Paul H. Giddens†
Pipelines, Early

James B. Gilbert
University of Maryland
Scopes Trial

Carolyn Gilman
Missouri Historical Society
Mandan, Hidatsa, and Arikara

Nils Gilman
University of California, Berkeley
Catch-22
Unsafe at Any Speed

Rhoda R. Gilman
Minnesota Historical Society
Minnesota

Lawrence Henry Gipson†
Colonial Assemblies

Philippe R. Girard
McNeese State University
America's Cup
Class Conflict
Earth Day
Monopoly
Olympic Games, American Par-
ticipation in
Pork Barrel
Running
TWA Flight 800

Betsy Glade
Saint Cloud State University
Wedding Traditions

Joseph T. Glatthaar
University of Houston
Civil War

Frederic W. Gleach
Cornell University
Powhatan Confederacy

George W. Goble[†]
West Coast Hotel Company v. Parrish

Dorothy Burne Goebel[†]
Elections, Presidential: 1840

Jennifer Gold
University of California, Berkeley
Ripley's Believe It or Not

Joseph P. Goldberg[†]
Labor, Department of

Joseph Goldenberg
Virginia State University
Shipbuilding

Phyllis Goldfarb
Newton, Massachusetts
Rape

David Goldfield
University of North Carolina at Charlotte
Atlanta
Charlotte

Ellen Goldring
Vanderbilt University
Magnet Schools

Pedro M. Pruna Goodgall
Smithsonian Institution Archives
Zoology

Judith R. Goodstein
California Institute of Technology
California Institute of Technology

Colin B. Goodykoontz[†]
Jefferson Territory
Missionary Societies, Home
Union Colony

Nancy M. Gordon[†]
Earthquakes

Ozone Depletion
Volcanoes
Wildfires

Stephanie Gordon
University of Georgia
House Made of Dawn

Dayo F. Gore
New York University
Stanford University

Daniel Gorman
McMaster University
British Empire, Concept of
Victorianism

Hugh Gorman[†]
Acid Rain

Ken Gormley
Duquesne University School of Law
Special Prosecutors

T. P. Govan[†]
Commission Merchants And
Factors

William Graebner
State University of New York at Fredonia
Common Sense Book of Baby and Child Care

Hugh Davis Graham[†]
Busing

Otis L. Graham Jr.[†]
Youth Administration, National

Pete Granger
University of Washington
Salmon Fisheries

W. Brooke Graves[†]
Enabling Acts
Guinn and Beal v. United States
Lochner v. New York
Minnesota Moratorium Case
Mugler v. Kansas
Original Package Doctrine
Rule of Reason
Transportation Act of 1920
Victory Loan of 1919
Wisconsin Railroad Commission v. Chicago, Burlington and Quincy

A. A. Gray[†]
Camels in the West

Ellen Gray[†]
Rockefeller Commission Report

Ralph D. Gray[†]
Waterways, Inland

Fletcher M. Green[†]
Address of the Southern Delegates
Peculiar Institution
Star of the West

John C. Green[†]
Elections, Presidential: 1976
Elections, Presidential: 1980
Elections, Presidential: 1984
Elections, Presidential: 1988
Elections, Presidential: 1992

Michael S. Green
Community College of Southern Nevada
Las Vegas

David Greenberg
American Academy of Arts and Sciences
Impeachment Trial of Bill Clinton
9/11 Attack
Nixon, Resignation of
Nixon Tapes

Mary Greenberg[†]
Brown University

Kent Greenfield
Boston College School of Law
Administrative Discretion, Delegation of
Administrative Justice
Airline Deregulation Act
Business, Big
Business, Minority
Code, U.S.
Employment Retirement Income Security Act
Equal Protection of the Law
Group Libel Laws
Hate Crimes
Leveraged Buyouts
Meat Inspection Laws
Mergers and Acquisitions
Romer v. Evans
Smith v. Oregon Employment
Telecommunications Act

Washington v. Glucksberg
Williamson v. Lee Optical

Linda Greenhouse
New York Times
  Bush v. Gore

Richard A. Greenwald
United States Merchant Marine Academy
  Sweatshop
  Women's Trade Union League

Ross Gregory[†]
  Korea-gate

Thomas G. Gress[†]
  Bakke v. Regents of the University
    of California
  Deregulation

James M. Grimwood[†]
  Moon Landing

R. Dale Grinder
United States Department of Trans-
portation
  Interstate Commerce Commis-
    sion
  Transportation, Department of

Erwin N. Griswold[†]
  Panhandle

Dean Grodzins
Meadville/Lombard Theological School
  Transcendentalism

Bethany Groff
Bradford, Massachusetts
  Salem

Theodore G. Gronert[†]
  Yellow Journalism

Norman Gross
American Bar Association Museum of
Law
  American Bar Association

Wayne Grover[†]
  Council of National Defense

Farley Grubb
University of Delaware
  Convict Labor Systems

J. Justin Gustainis
Plattsburgh State University of New
York
  Counterculture
  Credibility Gap
  Pornography Commission
  Solid South

Robert M. Guth[†]
  Nuclear Power
  Serial Killings
  Vigilantes

K. R. Constantine Gutzman
Western Connecticut State University
  Enumerated Powers
  Hartford Convention
  Maysville Veto
  Mazzei Letter

William Haber[†]
  Employment Service, U.S.

Kurt Hackemer
University of South Dakota
  Armored Ships

Sally E. Hadden
Florida State University
  Common Sense
  Continental Congress
  General Court, Colonial

LeRoy R. Hafen[†]
  Cripple Creek Mining Boom
  Mail, Overland, and Stage-
    coaches
  Mail, Southern Overland
  Mountain Men
  Pikes Peak Gold Rush

Steve Hageman
University of Illinois at Urbana-Cham-
paign
  Compromise of 1890

Edward Hagerman
York University
  Chemical and Biological Warfare

Travis Haglock
Boston College
  Work

Peter L. Hahn
Ohio State University
  Diplomatic Missions

Executive Agent
Nonimportation Agreements
Papal States, Diplomatic Service
  to

E. Irvine Haines[†]
  Cowboys and Skinners

Gerald Haines[†]
  Intelligence, Military and
    Strategic

Michael R. Haines
Colgate University
  Demography and Demographic
    Trends

J. Evetts Haley[†]
  Cattle Rustlers

Elizabeth Armstrong Hall
Manassas, Virginia
  Apartment Houses
  Saint Louis

Joseph Hall
Bates College
  [Various revisions]

Timothy D. Hall[†]
  Fundamentalism

Mark Haller
Temple University
  Crime, Organized

George H. Hallett Jr.[†]
  Preferential Voting

Holman Hamilton[†]
  Elections, Presidential: 1848

Michael S. Hamilton
Seattle Pacific University
  Evangelicalism and Revivalism

Milton W. Hamilton[†]
  Pamphleteering
  Printer's Devil

W. J. Hamilton[†]
  Craig v. State of Missouri

C. H. Hamlin[†]
  Doughfaces
  Gastonia Strike

Peter Hammond
University of Nottingham
Folklore

Samuel B. Hand
University of Vermont
Vermont

Jack Handler[†]
Civil Rights Restoration Act of 1987
Patients' Rights
Quality Circles
Sudden Infant Death Syndrome

Richard Carlton Haney
University of Wisconsin–Whitewater
Wisconsin

A. J. Hanna[†]
Florida, Straits of

Jonathan M. Hansen
Boston University
Beyond the Melting Pot
Pluralism

Mary Anne Hansen
Montana State University
Archives
Children's Bureau
Family of Man Exhibition
Gulf Stream
Interior, Department of the
Knights of the Golden Circle
Mineral Springs
Northwest Passage
Penobscot Region
Pinckney Plan
Sequoyah, Proposed State of
Tornadoes

Carl E. Hanson[†]
Noise Pollution

Elizabeth Hanson
Rockefeller University
Rockefeller University

Joseph Mills Hanson[†]
Belleau Wood, Battle of
Château-Thierry Bridge, Americans at
Far West
"Lafayette, We Are Here"
Leavenworth Expedition
Petersburg, Siege of

Saint-Mihiel, Campaigns at
Seven Days' Battles
Somme Offensive
Spotsylvania Courthouse, Battle of

Russell L. Hanson
Indiana State University
Equality, Concept of
Liberty, Concept of

Fraser Harbutt
Emory University
Anti-Imperialists
Foreign Policy
Wise Men

D. B. Hardeman[†]
Rules of the House
Whip, Party

Mary W. M. Hargreaves[†]
Deserts

Alvin F. Harlow[†]
Airmail
Backcountry and Backwoods
Black Laws
Boomtowns
Broadway
Cincinnati Riots
Civil Aeronautics Act
Dollar-a-Year Man
Eads Bridge
Economic Royalists
Ferris Wheel
"Forgotten Man"
Gallatin's Report on Roads, Canals, Harbors, and Rivers
Harlem, Battle of
Inland Lock Navigation
Lifesaving Service
Lincoln Highway
Maple Sugar
May Day
Military Order of the Loyal Legion of the U.S.A.
Mint, Federal
Mints, Private
Monterrey, Battles of
Mooney Case
Moonshine
Narrows
National Union for Social Justice
New Lights
Niblo's Garden

Old North Church
Onions
Oxen
Paving
Post Roads
Potatoes
Richmond Junto
Scab
Sheridan's Ride
Snake River
Southern Campaigns
Tar and Feathers
Telephone Cases
Veracruz Incident
Volstead Act
Wall Street Explosion
Wells, Fargo and Company
Western Federation of Miners
Whiskey
Wickersham Commission

George D. Harmon[†]
Bonus Bill of 1816
Mexico, Confederate Migration to

Gillis J. Harp
Grove City College
Positivism

Lawrence A. Harper[†]
Hat Manufacture, Colonial Restriction on
Molasses Trade

John W. Harpster[†]
Wagoners of the Alleghenies

Katy J. Harriger[†]
Set-Asides
Son-of-Sam Law
Tower Commission

Ben Harris
University of New Hampshire
Behaviorism

Ruth Roy Harris[†]
Bionics
Clinical Research
Heart Implants
Lyme Disease

Thomas L. Harris[†]
"In God We Trust"
Liberty-Cap Cent
Pine Tree Shilling

Cynthia Harrison[†]
Equal Pay Act
Women in Public Life, Business, and Professions

Jennifer Harrison
College of William and Mary
American Ballet Theatre
American Protective Association
Barbie Doll
Burr-Hamilton Duel
Cambridge
Dance
Feminine Mystique, The
Martha Graham Dance Company
Melting Pot
New York City Ballet
Resolutions, Congressional
Williamsburg, Colonial
XYZ Affair

Howard L. Harrod
Vanderbilt University
Sun Dance

D. G. Hart
Westminster Theological Seminary in California
Denominationalism
Presbyterianism
Reformed Churches
Religious Thought and Writings

Hendrik Hartog
Princeton University
Divorce and Marital Separation
Marriage

Gordon E. Harvey
University of Louisiana at Monroe
"Chicken in Every Pot"
Irrepressible Conflict

Susan Haskell
University of California, Berkeley
Hinduism
Quakers

Adele Hast
Newberry Library
Newberry Library

Dorothea E. Hast
Eastern Connecticut State University
Music: Early American
Music: Folk Revival

W. B. Hatcher[†]
Dark Horse

Guy B. Hathorn[†]
Commerce, Department of
Comptroller General of the United States

Laurence M. Hauptman
State University of New York at New Paltz
Onondaga

Raymond E. Hauser
Waubonsee Community College
Illinois (Indians)
Sauk

Bernice L. Hausman
Virginia Polytechnic Institute and State University
Gender and Gender Roles

Miriam Hauss
American Historical Association
American Historical Association

Richard A. Hawkins
University of Wolverhampton
Duties, Ad Valorem and Specific
Wal-Mart

Ellis Hawley
University of Iowa
New Era

Paul L. Haworth[†]
Elections, Presidential: 1876

Thomas Robson Hay[†]
Army of Northern Virginia
Army of the James
Army of Virginia
Brannan Plan
Brown v. Maryland
Burlington Strike
Chattanooga Campaign
Columbia River Treaty
Davis-Johnston Controversy
Donelson, Fort, Capture of
Elections, Presidential: 1824
Fallen Timbers, Battle of
Harpers Ferry, Capture of
Hood's Tennessee Campaign
Kenesaw Mountain, Battle of
Levy
McHenry, Fort

Maryland, Invasion of
New York City, Plot to Burn
Organization for Economic Cooperation and Development
Pennsylvania, Invasion of
Pennsylvania Troops, Mutinies of
Perryville, Battle of
Powhatan Incident
"Public Be Damned"
Railroads in the Civil War
Red River Campaign
Savannah, Siege of (1864)
Shenandoah Campaign
Stuart's Ride
Tidelands
Tydings-McDuffie Act
Vicksburg in the Civil War
Wilderness, Battles of the

Stephen Haycox
University of Alaska at Anchorage
Alaska
Alaska Native Claims Settlement Act
Alaskan Pipeline
Tribes: Alaskan

John D. Hayes[†]
World War I, Navy in
World War II, Navy in

John Earl Haynes
Library of Congress
Anticommunism
Communist Party, United States of America

Sarah E. Heath
Texas A&M University, Corpus Christi
Young Women's Christian Association

Charles W. Heathcote[†]
Brandywine Creek, Battle of

Darlene L. Brooks Hedstrom
Wittenberg University
Egypt, Relations with

Paul Hehn
Who2.com
Elections, Contested
Iranian Americans
Nevada
Police

Prizefighting
Television: Technology

Carol Heim
University of Massachusetts at Amherst
Capitalism

Ronald L. Heinemann
Hampden-Sydney College
Pentagon

Robert Debs Heinl Jr.[†]
Iwo Jima
Wake, Defense of

John Heitmann
University of Dayton
Automobile Safety

Leonard C. Helderman[†]
Financial Panics
Hurtado v. California
United States v. Lee

Douglas Helms
United States Department of Agriculture
Insecticides and Herbicides

Michael B. Henderson
Louisiana State University
Smoke-Filled Room

Kimberly A. Hendrickson
Rhodes College
Blue Laws
Mann Act
National Traffic and Motor
Vehicle Safety Act
Pierce v. Society of Sisters
Restraint of Trade
Sherman Antitrust Act

David Henry[†]
Iran-Contra Affair

Gary R. Hess[†]
Prisoners of War: POW/MIA
Controversy, Vietnam War

W. B. Hesseltine[†]
Belknap Scandal
Elmira Prison
Prisoners of War: Prison
Camps, Confederate

Norriss Hetherington
University of California, Berkeley
Astronomy

James E. Hewes Jr.[†]
War Department

Richard G. Hewlett[†]
Hydrogen Bomb
Nuclear Power

DuBose Heyward[†]
Sumter, Fort

John D. Hicks[†]
Citizens' Alliances
Elections, Presidential: 1904
Granger Movement
Middle-of-the-Road Populists
Patrons of Husbandry

Dennis R. Hidalgo
Adelphi University
Manifest Destiny

Kenneth B. Higbie[†]
Aluminum

Don Higginbotham
University of North Carolina at Chapel Hill
French in the American Revolution
Revolution, American: Military History

Carol L. Higham
Davidson College
Indian Missions

John Higham
Johns Hopkins University
Statue of Liberty

Jim Dan Hill[†]
Horse Marines
Press Gang
Rough Riders
San Juan Hill and El Caney, Battles of
Texas Navy

Roscoe R. Hill[†]
Journal of Congress

Willam G. Hines
United States Navy

Office of Price Administration
Office of Price Stabilization

Curtis M. Hinsley Jr.
Northern Arizona University
National Museum of the American Indian

Leo P. Hirrel
United States Army Center for Military History
Awakening, Second
Bismarck Archipelago Campaign
Edwardsean Theology

Adam Hodges
University of Houston, Clear Lake
Machine, Political
Oregon System
World War I

Graham Russell Hodges
University of Kansas
Art: Photography
Family and Medical Leave Act
Film
Flags
Music: Theater and Film
Nationalism
New York Slave Conspiracy of 1741
Pregnancy Discrimination Act
Republicanism
Women's Equity Action League

M. H. Hoeflich
University of Kansas
Housing and Urban Development, Department of
Norsemen in America
Sovereignty, Doctrine of
State Constitutions

J. David Hoeveler
University of Wisconsin–Milwaukee
Postmodernism

Abraham Hoffman
Los Angeles Valley College
Salton Sea

Christine E. Hoffman
Colgate University
Art: Sculpture
Automobile Racing
Education, Department of

Hymns and Hymnody
Lake Okeechobee
Marching Bands
Mines, U.S. Bureau of
National Bureau of Standards
National Women's Political
    Caucus
New Albion Colony
New Castle
Nonpartisan League, National
Pacific Northwest
Sagadahoc, Colony at

J. H. Hoffman[†]
Coal

Raymond H. Hoffman[†]
Big Brother Movement

L. Lynn Hogue
*Georgia State University College of
Law*
    Military Law

E. Brooks Holifield
Emory University
    Baptist Churches

Cecelia Holland
Fortuna, California
    Alcaldes
    Bear Flag Revolt
    California
    Donner Party
    Florida
    Forty-Niners
    Kearny's March to California
    Mountain Meadows Massacre
    Saint Augustine

Max Holland
Miller Center of Public Affairs, University of Virginia
    Warren Commission

Stanley C. Hollander
Michigan State University
    Hardware Trade
    Traveling Salesmen

David A. Hollinger
University of California, Berkeley
    Great Gatsby, The
    Patterns of Culture

Peter C. Holloran
Worcester State College

Cape Cod
Nantucket
New England
Plymouth Rock
Yankee

Tom Holm
University of Arizona
    Indians in the Military

John Dewey Holmes
University of California, Berkeley
    International Ladies Garment
        Workers Union

Ryan F. Holznagel
Belmont, Massachusetts
    Boy Scouts of America
    Mother's Day and Father's Day
    Nickelodeon
    Weather Service, National

Herbert T. Hoover
University of South Dakota
    South Dakota

T. N. Hoover[†]
    Marietta

Vincent C. Hopkins[†]
    Fair Deal

Brian C. Hosmer
*Newberry Library and University of
Illinois at Chicago*
    Arapaho
    Indian Policy, U.S.: 1830–1900

Neil Howe[†]
    Generational Conflict

Joel D. Howell[†]
    Chronic Fatigue Syndrome

William G. Howell
Harvard University
    Removal, Executive Power of

Frederick E. Hoxie
University of Illinois at Urbana-Champaign
    From the Deep Woods to Civilization
    Sand Creek Massacre
    Wounded Knee Massacre
    Wyoming Massacre

David C. Hsiung
Juniata College
    Coyote

Donald W. Hunt[†]
    Rio Grande

John J. Hunt[†]
    Iceland, U.S. Forces in

Richard A. Hunt[†]
    Geneva Conventions
    Photography, Military

Richard T. Hunt
Idaho National Engineering and Environmental Laboratory
    Hydroelectric Power

Leslie Gene Hunter[†]
    Prisoners of War: Prison
        Camps, Union

Louis C. Hunter[†]
    Waterpower

R. Douglas Hurt
Iowa State University
    Agricultural Machinery
    Agriculture, American Indian

James A. Huston[†]
    Logistics
    Munitions

John Hutchinson[†]
    Espionage, Industrial

Bradley Hyman[†]
    Alzheimer's Disease

Jeffrey Hyson
Saint Joseph's University
    Zoological Parks

Dennis Ippolito[†]
    Literacy Test

Benjamin H. Irvin
Brandeis University
    "E Pluribus Unum"

Chippy Irvine
Patterson, New York
    Glassmaking
    Kitchens

27

Ray W. Irwin[†]
Ogden v. Saunders
Washington Burned

Bliss Isely[†]
Homesteaders and the Cattle
Industry
Johnny Appleseed
Santa Fe Trail
Yellowstone River Expeditions

Andrew C. Isenberg
Princeton University
Buffalo (Bison)
Dodge City

Peter Iverson
Arizona State University
Defiance, Fort
Indians and the Horse
Navajo

Brenda Jackson
Washington State University
Ghost Towns
Sutter's Fort
Trading Posts, Frontier

Kenneth T. Jackson
New York Historical Society
Columbia University

Philip E. Jacob[†]
Pacifism

David Jacobs
Temple University
Unidentified Flying Objects

Ruth Harriet Jacobs
*Wellesley College Center for Research on
Women*
Old Age

John A. Jakle
University of Illinois at Urbana-Champaign
Food, Fast

Alfred P. James[†]
Allegheny Mountains, Routes
Across
Chancellorsville, Battle of
Commander in Chief of British
Forces
Lookout Mountain, Battle on
Mason-Dixon Line

Monongahela River
Mosby's Rangers
Nashville, Battle of
Tidewater

Marquis James[†]
Alamo, Siege of the
San Jacinto, Battle of

Duncan R. Jamieson
Ashland University
Bicycling

Reese V. Jenkins[†]
Photographic Industry

Robert Jenkins
Mississippi State University
Mississippi

Matthew Holt Jennings
University of Illinois at Urbana-Champaign
Panton, Leslie and Company
Stockbridge Indian Settlement
Timucua

John E. Jessup Jr.[†]
Cemeteries, National
Decorations, Military
Guerrilla Warfare
Office of Strategic Services
Rangers

Philip C. Jessup[†]
Root Arbitration Treaties
Root Mission
Root-Takahira Agreement

Andrew Jewett
American Academy of Arts and Sciences
Bartlett's Familiar Quotations
National Science Foundation
New Republic, The
Office of Scientific Research
and Development

Robert W. Johannsen
University of Illinois at Urbana-Champaign
Lincoln-Douglas Debates

Benjamin H. Johnson
Southern Methodist University
Forestry
Gold Rush, California
Irrigation

Lumber Industry
United Farm Workers of America
ica
Water Pollution

Daniel J. Johnson
*California State University at Long
Branch*
Hollywood
Long Beach
Los Angeles
McNamara Case
Oakland
San Diego
Symbionese Liberation Army

Hugh Buckner Johnston[†]
United Confederate Veterans

Leon W. Johnson[†]
Ploesti Oil Fields, Air Raids on

Robert W. Johnson[†]
Installment Buying, Selling, and
Financing

Samuel A. Johnson[†]
Jayhawkers
Kansas Committee, National
Lawrence, Sack of
Quantrill's Raid
Wyandotte Constitution

Sharon L. Johnson
Denver, Colorado
Western Union Telegraph
Company

Troy Johnson
California State University at Long Beach
Red Power

Arnita A. Jones
American Historical Association
National Trust for Historic
Preservation

Chester Lloyd Jones[†]
Elections, Presidential: 1908

Dorothy V. Jones
Newberry Library
Indian Treaties, Colonial

Edgar A. Jones Jr.[†]
Picketing

Fred M. Jones[†]
Commodity Exchanges
Markets, Public

Gwyn Jones[†]
Vinland

J. Wayne Jones
University of Georgia
Utopian Communities

James E. Jones Jr.
University of Wisconson Law School
Philadelphia Plan

Karen Jones
University of Essex
Everglades National Park
National Park System
Yellowstone National Park
Yosemite National Park

Katherine M. Jones
University of Virginia
Blue Sky Laws
Fair Labor Standards Act
General Welfare Clause
Gold Clause Cases
Minimum-Wage Legislation
Norris-LaGuardia Act
Robinson-Patman Act
Social Legislation

R. Steven Jones
Southwestern Adventist University
Buenos Aires Peace Conference
Colonization Movement
Colored National Labor Union
Consumerism
Department Stores
Indian Treaties
Nullification
Ostend Manifesto
Palsgraff v. Long Island
Savannah
Suburbanization
Toys and Games
Transcontinental Railroad,
Building of

Veda Boyd Jones
Institute of Children's Literature
American Indian Gaming Regu-
latory Act
Architecture, American Indian
Art, Indian
Ethnohistory

Indian Territory
Little Bighorn National Monu-
ment
Mission Indians of California
Pueblo Revolt
Stevens, Isaac, Mission
Winnebago/Ho-Chunk

Shibu Jose
University of Florida
Forest Service

D. George Joseph
Yale University School of Medicine
Epidemics and Public Health
Hantavirus
Leprosy
Sexually Transmitted Diseases
Tuberculosis

Louis Joughin[†]
Sacco-Vanzetti Case

Robert J. T. Joy[†]
Medicine, Military

Fred B. Joyner[†]
Blue and Gray
Ducking Stool

Suzanne White Junod[†]
*United States Food and Drug Adminis-
tration*
Food and Drug Administration
Toxic Shock Syndrome

David Kahn
Great Neck, New York
Cryptology

Ronald Kahn
Oberlin College
Federal-Aid Highway Program

Yale Kamisar[†]
Gideon v. Wainright

Harmke Kamminga
University of Cambridge
Biochemistry

I. Howell Kane[†]
Gideon Bibles

Daniel Kanstroom
Boston College School of Law
Aliens, Rights of

Deportation
Green Card
Political Exiles to the United
States
Refugee Act of 1980
Refugees

Shawn Kantor
University of Arizona
Southern Tenant Farmers'
Union

Jeffrey Kaplan
Sullivan and Cromwell
West Indies, British and French

Lawrence S. Kaplan[†]
Convention of 1800

Ruth Kaplan
New York, New York
Hoover Dam
New Yorker, The
Verrazano-Narrows Bridge
Whitney Museum

Stefan J. Kapsch[†]
Office of Management and
Budget

Carol F. Karlsen
University of Michigan
Witchcraft

James Kates[†]
Citizens Band (CB) Radio
Cultural Literacy
National Public Radio

Kenneth D. Katkin
Northern Kentucky University
Scientific Fraud

Bruce Kaufman
Georgia State University
Industrial Relations

Thomas Kavanagh
Bloomington, Indiana
Comanche

Margaret Keady
Astoria, New York
Contract Labor, Foreign
Labor's Non-Partisan League
Mercantilism
Privatization

Linda Nelson Keane
School of the Art Institute of Chicago
    Art: Interior Decoration
    Art: Interior Design

Mark Keane
University of Wisconsin–Milwaukee
    Art: Interior Decoration
    Art: Interior Design

Louise Phelps Kellogg†
    Connolly's Plot
    Dunmore's War
    Howard, Fort
    Jesuit *Relations*
    Jolliet-Marquette Explorations
    Prairie du Chien, Indian Treaty
        at
    Wisconsin Idea

Alfred H. Kelly†
    Constitution of the United
        States

John Haskell Kemble†
    Coasting Trade
    Coastwise Steamship Lines
    Navigation Act of 1817

Donald L. Kemmerer†
    Banking: Overview
    Banking: Bank Failures
    Banking: State Banks
    Brokers
    Federal Reserve System
    Financial Panics
    Gold Standard
    Hard Money
    Independent Treasury System
    International Monetary Fund
    Repudiation of Public Debt

Emory L. Kemp
Institute for the History of Technology and Industrial Archaeology, West Virginia University
    James River and Kanawha
        Company

John S. Kendall†
    New Orleans Riots
    White League

John W. Kendrick†
    Productivity, Concept of

Lawrence W. Kennedy
University of Scranton
    Boston
    Faneuil Hall

William V. Kennedy†
    Conscription and Recruitment

Linda K. Kerber†
    Alien and Sedition Laws

Kevin F. Kern
University of Akron
    Racial Science

K. Austin Kerr†
    Railroad Mediation Acts

Louise B. Ketz
Louise B. Ketz Agency
    Chess

Daniel J. Kevles†
    Allison Commission
    Carnegie Institution of Wash-
        ington
    Physics: Overview

Clara Sue Kidwell
University of Oklahoma
    Choctaw
    Indian Technology

John A. Kidwell
University of Wisconsin Law School
    Copyright
    Intellectual Property
    Mineral Patent Law
    Patents and U.S. Patent Office
    Trademarks

Vincent Kiernan†
    Artificial Intelligence
    Cold Nuclear Fusion
    Cybernetics
    Weather Satellites

John D. Kilbourne†
    Cincinnati, Society of the

Sukkoo Kim
Washington University in St. Louis and National Bureau of Economic Research
    Distribution of Goods and Ser-
        vices

Christine K. Kimbrough
New York University
    Railroads

John M. Kinder
University of Minnesota
    Abstract Expressionism
    Bungee Jumping
    Pop Art
    Rollerblading
    Skateboarding
    Tennis

William E. King
Western State College of Colorado
    English Language
    Recycling
    Slang
    Telecommunications

Connie Ann Kirk
Mansfield University
    America the Beautiful
    Barn Raising
    Bloomers
    Ellis Island
    Flag of the United States
    Liberty Bell
    Literature: Children's Literature
    "My Country, 'Tis of Thee"
    New York State
    Provincetown Players
    "Star-Spangled Banner"

Dan Kirklin
Liberty Fund
    Printing Industry

Tristan Hope Kirvin
New York University
    World Trade Center

Joel D. Kitchens
Texas A&M University
    Barnstorming

Ruth A. Kittner
Carnegie Mellon University
    Comics

Margaret Klapthor†
    Inauguration, Presidential

Harvey Klehr
Emory University
    Rosenberg Case
    Subversion, Communist

Frank M. Kleiler[†]
National Labor Relations Act

Milton M. Klein[†]
Suffrage: Colonial Suffrage

Herbert M. Kliebard[†]
Curriculum

Frank J. Klingberg[†]
Coercive Acts

James T. Kloppenberg
Harvard University
Democracy in America
Liberalism
Locke's Political Philosophy

James C. Klotter
Georgetown College, Kentucky
Kentucky

Daniel Knapp[†]
Community Action Program

Joseph G. Knapp[†]
Cooperatives, Tobacco

Edgar W. Knight[†]
Charity Schools
Dame School
Latin Schools
Peabody Fund

Dudley W. Knox[†]
"Damn the Torpedoes"
Five-Power Naval Treaty
Ironclad Warships
Naval Operations, Chief of
Navy, Department of the
Parity in Naval Defense
"White Squadron"

Anne Meis Knupfer
Purdue University
National Association of Colored
Women
National Council of Negro
Women

Louis W. Koenig[†]
Watergate

Sheilah R. Koeppen[†]
Freedom Riders

Martha Kohl
Montana Historical Society
Montana

Sally Gregory Kohlstedt
University of Minnesota,
Minneapolis/St.Paul
American Association for the
Advancement of Science

Paul A. C. Koistinen
California State University at North-
ridge
Military-Industrial Complex

Charles C. Kolb
National Endowment for the Humani-
ties
Great Lakes
Johnstown Flood
Ohio River
Ohio Valley

Maureen Konkle
University of Missouri at Columbia
Son of the Forest, A

David B. Kopel
Independence Institute
Gun Control

Ronald J. Kopicki[†]
Electrification, Household

Charles P. Korr
University of Missouri at St. Louis
Baseball Union

Jeremy L. Korr
University of Maryland, College Park
Railways, Urban, and Rapid
Transit
Toll Bridges and Roads

J. Morgan Kousser
California Institute of Technology
Disfranchisement
Election Laws
Grandfather Clause
Jim Crow Laws
Plessy v. Ferguson
Reitman v. Mulkey
Voter Registration
Voter Residency Requirements
Voting

Bill Kovarik[†]
Energy, Renewable

Stewart Koyiyumptewa
Hopi Tribe, Hopi Cultural Preservation
Office
Hopi

Nathan Ross Kozuskanich
Ohio State University
Civilized Tribes, Five

Benjamin R. Kracht
Northeastern State University, Okla-
homa
Kiowa
Powwow

Ellen Percy Kraly[†]
Russian and Soviet Americans

Barbara Krauthamer
New York University
Treaty Councils (Indian Treaty-
making)

Michael L. Krenn
Appalachian State University
Chile, Relations with
Dominican Republic
Haiti, Relations with
Hay-Herrán Treaty

Sheldon Krimsky[†]
Biological Containment

Carol Herselle Krinsky
New York University
Frick Collection

Samuel Krislov[†]
Chicago Seven

Charles A. Kromkowski
University of Virginia
Articles of Confederation
Census, U.S. Bureau of the
Suffrage: Overview
Suffrage: African American Suf-
frage
Suffrage: Woman's Suffrage

Barbara Krueger
Stained Glass Association of America
Art: Stained Glass Windows

Warren L. Kuehl[†]
Hague Peace Conferences

Bruce Kuklick
University of Pennsylvania
Philosophy
Pragmatism

Gary Kulik
Winterthur Museum, Garden, and Library
Winterthur

Eric Kupferberg
Harvard University
Microbiology

Stanley I. Kutler
University of Wisconsin–Madison
Charles River Bridge Case

Robert B. Kvavik[†]
Proportional Representation

Modupe G. Labode
Colorado Historical Society
Colorado

Mark Ladov
New York University
Tenements

Marcel C. LaFollette
Washington, D.C.
Science Journalism and Television

Lionel H. Laing[†]
Antelope Case

Lewis E. Lawes[†]
Hanging

Eric E. Lampard[†]
Dairy Industry

Rosalyn LaPier
Piegan Institute
Blackfeet

Edward J. Larson
University of Georgia
Science and Religion, Relations of

Henrietta M. Larson[†]
Cooke, Jay, and Company

Christopher Lasch[†]
Elections, Presidential: 1940
Elections, Presidential: 1944
Elections, Presidential: 1948
Elections, Presidential: 1952
Elections, Presidential: 1956
Elections, Presidential: 1960
GI Bill of Rights
War Crimes Trials

Carol Lasser
Oberlin College
Oberlin College

Robert N. Lauriault
University of Florida
Citrus Industry
Tampa–St. Petersburg

Mark A. Lause
University of Cincinnati
Industrial Workers of the World
Knights of Labor
National Trades' Union
Railroad Strike of 1877
Railroad Strike of 1886

Michael K. Law
University of Kansas
Christiana Fugitive Affair
Cotton Kingdom
Vesey Rebellion

Alan Lawson
Boston College
Civilian Conservation Corps
Farm Security Administration
Home Owners' Loan Corporation
National Recovery Administration
New Deal
Works Progress Administration

R. A. Lawson
Vanderbilt University
Harlem Renaissance

Edwin T. Layton Jr.[†]
Engineering Societies

Eugene E. Leach
Trinity College, Hartford
American Railway Union

Railroad Brotherhoods

Calvin B. T. Lee[†]
Apportionment

Mark H. Leff
University of Illinois at Urbana-Champaign
Medicare and Medicaid

Hugh T. Lefler[†]
Bundling
Charleston Harbor, Defense of
Cowpens, Battle of
Gilbert's Patent
Great Smoky Mountains
Society for the Propagation of the Gospel in Foreign Parts
Tobacco as Money
Wilmington Riot

Richard M. Leighton[†]
Defense, National
War Costs

Keith A. Leitich
Seattle, Washington
School Prayer

Thomas C. Leonard
University of California, Berkeley
New York Times

Henry Lesesne
University of South Carolina
South Carolina

W. Bruce Leslie
State University of New York at Brockport
State University of New York

Harvey Levenstein
McMaster University
Food and Cuisines

Jane Freundel Levey
D.C. Heritage Tourism Coalition
White House

Zach Levey
University of Haifa, Israel
Israel, Relations with

Werner Levi[†]
Nuclear Test Ban Treaty

Robert M. Levine
University of Miami
Alliance For Progress
Confederate Expatriates in
Brazil
González, Elián, Case
Mariel Boatlift

David Levinson[†]
Kinship

Alan Levy
Slippery Rock University
Symphony Orchestras

David W. Levy
University of Oklahoma
Bork Confirmation Hearings
Brandeis Confirmation Hear-
ings
Thomas Confirmation Hearings

Anne Lewandowski
Minneapolis, Minnesota
Soil

Anna Lewis[†]
Arkansas River
Cimarron, Proposed Territory
of

Charles Lee Lewis[†]
Chesapeake-Leopard Incident
Decatur's Cruise to Algiers
Intrepid
Island Number Ten, Operations
at
Mobile Bay, Battle of

David K. Lewis[†]
Laser Technology

David Rich Lewis
Utah State University
Ute

Emanuel Raymond Lewis[†]
Fortifications

James G. Lewis
Falls Church, Virginia
Fire Fighting
Geological Survey, U.S.

Yolanda Chávez Leyva
University of Texas, El Paso
El Paso

O. G. Libby[†]
Dakota Expeditions of Sibley
and Sully
Dakota Territory
Little Bighorn, Battle of
Red River Cart Traffic

Willard F. Libby[†]
Radiocarbon Dating

Nelson Lichtenstein
*University of California, Santa Bar-
bara*
American Federation of Labor-
Congress of Industrial
Organizations
Collective Bargaining
Sit-down Strikes
Socialist Movement
United Automobile Workers of
America

Nhi T. Lieu
University of Michigan
Southeast Asian Americans

Blanche M. G. Linden
Fort Lauderdale, Florida
Cemeteries
Erector Sets
Lincoln Logs

Leslie J. Lindenauer
*Hartford College for Women of the
University of Hartford*
Carolina, Fundamental Consti-
tutions of
Charter of Liberties
Colonial Agent
Farmer's Letters
Holy Experiment
Hutchinson Letters
Instructions
Ipswich Protest
Kinsey Report
Massachusetts Bay Colony
Narragansett Bay
Narragansett Planters
New England Colonies
New England Company
Plans of Union, Colonial
Port Royal
Royal Colonies
Royal Disallowance
Salem Witch Trials
Smuggling, Colonial

Christina Lindholm
Virginia Commonwealth University
Clothing and Fashion
Textiles

Edward T. Linenthal
University of Wisconsin–Oshkosh
Holocaust Museum

**Christina Linsenmeyer-van
Schalkwyk**
Washington University in St. Louis
Blues
Jazz

Seymour Martin Lipset[†]
Radical Right

Julia E. Liss
Scripps College
Anthropology and Ethnology

Kimberly Little
Ohio University
Barbecue

T. L. Livermore
Triple T Double L Research
Bank of the United States
Explosives
Merchant Adventurers
Oil Fields
Pet Banks
Petroleum Industry
Petroleum Prospecting and
Technology
Surveying
Wildcat Oil Drilling

Terri Livermore
Triple T Double L Research
Oil Fields
Pet Banks
Petroleum Industry
Petroleum Prospecting and
Technology
Surveying
Wildcat Oil Drilling

H. Matthew Loayza
University of Wisconsin–La Crosse
Geneva Accords of 1954
Nicaragua, Relations with

Hartman H. Lomawaima
Arizona State Museum
Hopi

John A. Lomax[†]
Cowboy Songs

Kyle Longley
Arizona State University
Contra Aid
Cuba, Relations with
Latin America, Relations with
Panama Canal

Paul K. Longmore[†]
Disability Rights Movement

Ella Lonn[†]
Blockade Runners, Confederate
Confederate Agents

Brad D. Lookingbill
Columbia College of Missouri
Conquistadores
Coronado Expeditions

James J. Lorence
Gainesville College
Trade Union Educational
League
Trade Union Unity League

Justin T. Lorts
Rutgers, The State University of New Jersey
SAT

Arnold S. Lott[†]
Minesweeping

Leland P. Lovette[†]
Flag Day

John Low
Pokagon Band Potawatomie and Indiana University Northwest
Indian Civil Rights Act
Indian Country

Bradford Luckingham
Arizona State University
Phoenix

Kenneth M. Ludmerer
Washington University in St. Louis
Health Care
Medical Education

Elizabeth A. Lunbeck
Princeton University
Psychiatry

Philip K. Lundeberg[†]
Convoys
Dry Docks

Mary Lou Lustig
West Virginia University
Catskill Mountains
Colonial Settlements
Colonial Society
Dongan Charters
Hudson River

Denis Tilden Lynch[†]
Tweed Ring

William O. Lynch[†]
National Republican Party

Willem Maas
Yale University
Public Opinion

Laurie McCann
AARP Foundation Litigation
Discrimination: Age

John McCarthy
Marquette University
Nashville
Officers' Reserve Corps

Carl S. McCarthy[†]
Soldiers' Home

James P. McCartin
University of Notre Dame
Anti-Catholicism
Liberation Theology
Vatican II

Wilfred M. McClay
University of Tennessee, Chattanooga
Individualism
Lonely Crowd, The
Political Theory

Timothy P. McCleary
Little Big Horn College
Crow

William M. McClenahan Jr.
University of Maryland at College Park
Banking: Export-Import Banks

Dennis McClendon
Chicago CartoGraphics
Dallas
Sears Tower

Robert McColley
University of Illinois at Urbana—Champaign
War Hawks

Kent A. McConnell
Dartmouth College
Assassinations and Political Violence, Other
Education, Higher: Denominational Colleges
Gettysburg Address
Ireland, Relations with
Yale University

Stephanie Wilson McConnell
Bowling Green State University
Camp David Peace Accords
Iran Hostage Crisis

Donald R. McCoy[†]
Libraries, Presidential

Mary McCune
State University of New York at Oswego
National Council of Jewish Women

David P. McDaniel[†]
Chess

Allan Macdonald[†]
Malmédy Massacre
Normandy Invasion
Oneida Colony

Charles B. MacDonald[†]
Bastogne
Bulge, Battle of the
Elbe River
Guantánamo Bay
Java Sea, Battle of
Lafayette Escadrille
Lebanon, U.S. Landing in
Marshall Islands
Siegfried Line

Dedra S. McDonald
Hillsdale College
New Mexico

Girard L. McEntee[†]
Champagne-Marne Operation

Lisa MacFarlane
University of New Hampshire
Uncle Tom's Cabin

Eliza McFeely
College of New Jersey
Zuni

William S. McFeely[†]
Freedmen's Bureau

Richard McGowan, S.J.
Boston College
Lotteries

Reginald C. McGrane[†]
Financial Panics
Repudiation of State Debts

John T. McGreevy
University of Notre Dame
Jesuits

Rebecca C. McIntyre
University of Alabama
Tourism

David MacIsaac[†]
Bombing
World War II, Air War against
Germany

Effie Mona Mack[†]
Comstock Lode
Deseret
Great Basin

Guian McKee
Miller Center of Public Affairs, University of Virginia
Albany

John P. Mackenzie[†]
Baker Case

C. H. McLaughlin[†]
Executive Agreements

Judson MacLaury
United States Department of Labor
Federal Mediation and Conciliation Service

Don E. McLeod[†]
Demobilization
Mobilization
Psychological Warfare

Jonathan W. McLeod
San Diego Mesa College

American Federation of Teachers
Checkoff
Lockout

Donald L. McMurry[†]
Coxey's Army
Pensions, Military and Naval

Neil MacNeil[†]
Hoover Commissions

Rebecca McNulty
University of Illinois at Urbana-Champaign
American Indian Defense Association
Indian Rights Association

John A. McQuillen Jr.[†]
Gliders

Michael R. McVaugh[†]
Parapsychology

Jeffrey D. Madura
Duquesne University
Chemistry

James D. Magee[†]
Adamson Act
Gallatin's Report on Manufactures
Gold Act
Hoosac Tunnel
Horizontal Tariff Bill
National Trades' and Workers' Association
Public Credit Act
Soft Money
Subtreasuries
Wildcat Money

C. Peter Magrath[†]
Yazoo Fraud

Jennifer Lane Maier
Worthington, Ohio
Maritime Commission, Federal
Migration, Internal
Oceanographic Survey
Pithole

Pauline Maier
Massachusetts Institute of Technology
Declaration of Independence

Susan L. Malbin
District of Columbia Public Library
Folger Shakespeare Library

Edward S. Malecki[†]
Lobbies

James C. Malin[†]
Dry Farming
Pottawatomie Massacre

W. C. Mallalieu[†]
Lyceum Movement

Mark G. Malvasi
Randolph Macon College
Consumer Purchasing Power
Hockey
Judaism
Stock Market

Meg Greene Malvasi
Midlothian, Virginia
Arab Americans
Assay Offices
Baby Bells
Bank for International Settlements
Business Forecasting
Cost of Living
Cost of Living Adjustment
Debt, Public
Economic Indicators
Exchange, Bills of
Financial Services Industry
Individual Retirement Account
Interest Laws
Iraqi Americans
Lebanese Americans
Money
Moody's
Options Exchanges
Peter Principle
Price and Wage Controls
Revenue Sharing

Peter Mancall
University of Southern California
Indians and Alcohol

Herbert Manchester[†]
Blacksmithing

Daniel R. Mandell
Truman State University
Narragansett
Praying Towns

Joan D. Mandle[†]
   Women's Rights Movement:
      The Twentieth Century

Patrick Maney
University of South Carolina
   La Follette Civil Liberties
      Committee Hearings
   Legislative Reorganization Act

A. M. Mannion
University of Reading
   Aleutian Islands

Daniel Mannix[†]
   Slave Ships

W. W. Manross[†]
   Church of England in the
      Colonies

Deanna B. Marcum
*Council on Library and Information
Resources*
   Libraries

Sarah S. Marcus
Chicago Historical Society
   Lincoln Tunnel

Robert A. Margo
*Vanderbilt University and National
Bureau of Economic Research*
   Inflation
   Prices

Norman Markowitz
*Rutgers, The State University of New
Jersey*
   American Liberty League
   Progressive Party, 1948
   Radicals and Radicalism

Scott P. Marler
Rice University
   Country Store
   Mail-Order Houses
   Malls, Shopping
   Peddlers

Edward J. Marolda
Naval Historical Center
   Navy, United States

Alice Goldfarb Marquis
University of California, San Diego
   Middlebrow Culture

Timothy Marr
*University of North Carolina at Chapel
Hill*
   Pledge of Allegiance
   Thanksgiving Day

Kevin R. Marsh
Boise State University
   Sauk Prairie

John F. Marszalek
Mississippi State University
   Eaton Affair
   Sherman's March to the Sea

James Marten
Marquette University
   Childhood

Albro Martin[†]
   Railroad Rate Law

Asa E. Martin[†]
   Stalwarts

Joel W. Martin
University of California, Riverside
   Indian Religious Life

Judith A. Martin
University of Minnesota
   Minneapolis-St. Paul

Russell Martin
Southern Methodist University
   Almanacs

Joseph Mason
LeBow College of Business, Drexel University
   Banking: Savings Banks

Mary Ann Mason
University of California, Berkeley
   Children's Rights

James I. Matray
California State University at Chico
   Burlingame Treaty
   Dawes Plan
   Japan, Relations with
   Japanese Americans
   Korean Airlines Flight 007

Yoshihisa T. Matsusaka
Wellesley College
   Manchuria and Manchukuo

Albert Matthews[†]
   Uncle Sam

Jeffrey G. Matthews
University of Puget Sound
   Young Plan

Robert Matthews
Federal Aviation Administration
   Airports, Siting and Financing of
   Civil Aeronautics Board
   Federal Aviation Administration
   Interstate Highway System

Aaron Mauck
University of California, San Diego
   Medical Profession

Thomas Maulucci
State University of New York at Fredonia
   European Union
   Germany, Relations with

Seymour H. Mauskopf[†]
   Parapsychology

Dean L. May
University of Utah
   Salt Lake City

Robert E. May
Purdue University
   Contraband, Slaves as
   Crittenden Compromise
   Missouri Compromise

Martin Mayer
Brookings Institution
   Savings and Loan Associations

Dennis Mazzocco
Hofstra University
   Communications Workers of
      America

Karen Rae Mehaffey
Sacred Heart Major Seminary, Detroit
   Automated Teller Machines
   Death and Dying
   Dueling
   Funerary Traditions
   Lafayette's Visit to America
   Peonage
   Prizes and Awards: Guggen-
      heim Awards

Perry Mehrling[†]
    Banking: Overview

August Meier[†]
    Congress of Racial Equality
    Student Nonviolent Coordinat-
    ing Committee

Marcia L. Meldrum[†]
    Aquired Immune Deficiency
    Syndrome

Caroline Waldron Merithew
University of Dayton
    Birds of Passage
    Hanging
    Lynching
    Mining Towns
    United Mine Workers of Amer-
    ica

R. L. Meriwether[†]
    Charleston Indian Trade
    Eutaw Springs, Battle of

James H. Merrell
Vassar College
    Catawba

Myrna W. Merron[†]
    Academic Freedom
    Coeducation
    Education, Experimental
    Head Start
    Schools, For-Profit
    Teacher Training

Thomas J. Mertz
University of Wisconsin–Madison
    Aldrich-Vreeland Act
    California Alien Land Law
    Enabling Acts

Donna Merwick
Centre for Cross-Cultural Research,
Australian National University
University, Canberra, Australia
    New Netherland

Timothy Messer-Kruse
University of Toledo
    Memorial Day Massacre
    Pure Food and Drug Movement

Jeffrey F. Meyer
University of North Carolina at Char-
lotte
    Washington Monument

Susan Gluck Mezey[†]
    Equal Employment Opportuni-
    ty Commission

Debra Michals
New York, New York
    Ms. Magazine

Sonya Michel
University of Maryland
    Child Care

Christopher Miller
Marquette University
    Milwaukee
    Railways, Interurban

Christopher L. Miller
University of Texas, Pan American
    Tribes: Northwestern

Glenn H. Miller Jr.[†]
    Mortgage Relief Legislation

Glenn T. Miller[†]
    Civil Religion
    Congregationalism
    Jehovah's Witnesses
    Nazarene, Church of the
    Orthodox Chuches
    Salvation Army

Jason Philip Miller
Nashville, Tennessee
    Pinkerton Agency

Jay Miller
Cultrix Research
    Delaware Indians
    Indian Oral Literature
    Nativist Movements (American
        Indian Revival Movements)
    Ozette
    Yakama

John C. Miller[†]
    Mutiny Act
    Quartering Act

Karl Hagstrom Miller
University of Texas, Austin
    Music Industry

Perry Miller[†]
    Antinomian Controversy
    Brownists
    Cambridge Platform

    Covenant, Church
    Divine Providences
    Fast Days
    Indian Bible, Eliot's
    Puritans and Puritanism
    Saybrook Platform
    Separatists, Puritan
    Theocracy in New England

Toby Miller
New York University
    Mass Media

Allan R. Millett
Ohio State University
    Defense Policy

John D. Milligan[†]
    Pillow, Fort, Massacre at

Patricia Hagler Minter
Western Kentucky University
    Antimonopoly Parties
    State Sovereignty

Steven Mintz
University of Houston
    Family

Cecilia S. Miranda
University of California, San Diego
    Nursing

Charlene Mires
Villanova University
    Centennial Exhibition

Broadus Mitchell[†]
    Federal Aid
    Interstate Trade Barriers
    Sinking Fund, National

Kris Mitchener
Santa Clara University
    Intermediate Credit Banks

Raymond A. Mohl
University of Alabama at Birmingham
    Miami

Frank Monaghan[†]
    Crystal Palace Exhibition
    Elections, Presidential: 1796
    Pan-American Exposition

Paul Monroe[†]
    School, District

Chalmers A. Monteith[†]
Debts, State
Sales Taxes

Royal E. Montgomery[†]
Coppage v. Kansas

Richard W. Moodey[†]
Veterans Affairs, Department of

Robert E. Moody[†]
Penobscot Expedition
Webster-Parkman Murder Case

Gregory Moore
Notre Dame College of Ohio
French and Indian War
Mixed Commissions
Nez Perce War
Oregon Treaty of 1846
Overland Trail
Pension Plans
Philippines
Retirement
Retirement Plans
Wars with Indian Nations:
Later Nineteenth Century
(1840–1900)
Wilmot Proviso

John H. Moore
University of Florida
Cheyenne

Leonard J. Moore
McGill University
Ku Klux Klan

John Morelli[†]
Superfund
Times Beach

John A. Morello
DeVry University
Agent Orange
Love Canal

Michelle M. Mormul
California State University at Fullerton
Amistad Case
Assemblies, Colonial
Board of Trade and Plantations
Charter of Privileges
Chesapeake Colonies
Colonial Charters
House of Burgesses
Middle Colonies

Molasses Act
New Amsterdam
New York Colony
Privy Council
Proprietary Colonies
Providence Plantations, Rhode
Island and
Raleigh Colonies
Virginia Company of London

Richard B. Morris[†]
Appeals from Colonial Courts
Borough
Capitation Taxes
Justice of the Peace
Philadelphia Cordwainers' Case
Rights of the British Colonies
Asserted and Proved

Alan B. Morrison
Stanford Law School
Public Interest Law
Veto, Line-Item

Jarvis M. Morse[†]
Providence Plantations, Rhode
Island and

Eric J. Morser
University of Wisconsin–Madison
Army, Confederate
Army, Union
Army of Occupation
Army of the Potomac
Arrest, Arbitrary, during the
Civil War
Billeting
Contraband of War
Germany, American Occupation
of
In Re Debs
Preparedness

David Morton
IEEE History Center, Rutgers University
Answering Machines
Automation
Business Machines
Electronic Mail
Fax Machine
Office Technology

Louis Morton[†]
Dartmouth College

Rebekah Presson Mosby
Hamilton, New York
Alvin Ailey American Dance
Theater
Arts and Crafts Movement
Ballads
Disco
Music: African American
Music: Popular
Theater

Vincent Mosco
Carleton University
Electronic Commerce

John E. Moser
Ashland University
Panay Incident
Peace Conferences
Peacekeeping Missions

Wilson J. Moses
Pennsylvania State University
Pan-Africanism

Kenneth B. Moss[†]
Military Base Closings
Oil Crises
Silicon Valley

Douglas M. Muir
The World Bank
Samoa, American
Trust Territory of the Pacific

John Muldowny
University of Tennessee, Knoxville
Titanic, Sinking of the

Charles F. Mullett[†]
East India Company, English

Robert P. Multhauf[†]
Borax
Heating
Potash
Refrigeration
Salt

Dana G. Munro[†]
ABC Conference
Bryan-Chamorro Treaty

M. Susan Murnane
Case Western Reserve University
Conspiracy

Joseph M. Murphy
Georgetown University
Santeria

Robert E. Mutch
Washington, D.C.
Campaign Financing and
Resources

Margaret G. Myers[†]
Clearing House, New York
Clearinghouses

William Starr Myers[†]
Elections, Presidential: 1860
Elections, Presidential: 1864
Elections, Presidential: 1928
Sovereignty, Doctrine of

Joanne Nagel
University of Kansas
Trail of Broken Treaties

June Namias
University of Alaska at Anchorage
Captivity Narratives

David Nasaw
*Graduate Center, City University of
New York*
San Simeon

Gerald D. Nash[†]
Natural Gas Industry

Jan Olive Nash
Tallgrass Historians, L.C.
Wolves

National Archives
National Archives

Michael S. Neiberg
United States Air Force Academy
Aachen
Conscientious Objectors
Courts-Martial
Martial Law
Uniform Code of Military Jus-
tice

Daniel Nelson
University of Akron
Business Unionism
Labor
Scientific Management

E. Clifford Nelson[†]
Norwegian Churches

Patricia Nemetz
Eastern Washington University
Industrial Management

Bruno Nettl
*University of Illinois at Urbana-Cham-
paign*
Music: Indian

C. T. Neu[†]
"Remember the Alamo!"

Caryn E. Neumann
Ohio State University
Mount Holyoke College
Seven Sisters Colleges
Young Men's and Young
Women's Hebrew Associa-
tion

Nancy P. Neumann
Albing International Marketing
Marketing Research

Mark Neuzil
University of Saint Thomas
Steamboats

Allan Nevins[†]
Alabama Claims
Black Friday
Elections, Presidential: 1884
Elections, Presidential: 1888
Elections, Presidential: 1892
Financial Panics
Kerosine Oil
Olney-Pauncefote Treaty
Standard Oil Company
Washington, Treaty of

Jason Newman
Cosumnes River College
Vietnam, Relations with

Kent Newmyer[†]
Contract Clause

L. W. Newton[†]
Buena Vista, Battle of
Dodge City Trail
Grand Prairie
Survey Act

J. Harley Nichols[†]
Mulligan Letters
Rights of Man

Jeannette P. Nichols[†]
Aldrich-Vreeland Act
Bland-Allison Act
Coin's Financial School
Free Silver
Gold Democrats
Kansas-Nebraska Act
University of Pennsylvania
World Economic Conference

Roger L. Nichols
University of Arizona
Tucson

Roy F. Nichols[†]
Elections, Presidential: 1852

Freda H. Nicholson[†]
Science Museums

Edgar B. Nixon[†]
Natchez Campaign of 1813
Orleans, Territory of

Ransom E. Noble Jr.[†]
Ex Parte Merryman
*Humphrey's Executor v. United
States*
Nebbia v. New York
Strauder v. West Virginia
United States v. Cruikshank
United States v. Harris
*United States v. Trans-Missouri
Freight Association*

James D. Norris[†]
Nonferrous Metals
North Sea Mine Barrage

Walter B. Norris[†]
Alexandria Conference
Barbary Wars
Essex, Actions of the
Lake Erie, Battle of
Lexington
Maine, Sinking of the
Perry-Elliott Controversy
Princeton, Explosion on the
"Yankee"

Walter Nugent
University of Notre Dame (emeritus)
West, American

Grace Lee Nute[†]
Grand Portage
Hudson's Bay Company
North West Company
Voyageurs

James P. O'Brien[†]
Students for a Democratic Society
Youth Movements

Kenneth P. O'Brien
State University of New York at Brockport
State University of New York

Kym O'Connell-Todd
Gunnison, Colorado
Rivers
San Juan Islands
Telegraph
Tennessee Valley Authority
Whaling

Alice O'Connor
University of California, Santa Barbara
Welfare Capitalism

William F. O'Connor
Asia University
Barnum's American Museum

Catherine O'Dea[†]
Tammany Hall

Michael O'Malley
George Mason University
Daylight Saving Time

E.H. O'Neill[†]
Godey's Lady's Book
Poor Richard's Almanac

Kenneth O'Reilly
University of Alaska at Anchorage
Abscam Scandal
Amerasia Case
COINTELPRO
Freedom of Information Act
Federal Bureau of Investigation
Hiss Case
House Committee on Un-American Activities
Investigating Committees
ITT Affair
John Birch Society
Palmer Raids

James Oakes
Graduate Center, City University of New York
Impending Crisis of the South
Overseer and Driver
Plantation System of the South
Slavery

D. W. Oberlin[†]
Saint Lawrence Seaway

James Oberly
University of Wisconsin–Eau Claire
Land Claims
Land Companies
Land Grants: Overview
Land Patents
Land Policy

Kerry A. Odell
Scripps College
Banking: Investment Banks

Paul H. Oehser[†]
Smithsonian Institution

Adele Ogden[†]
Sea Otter Trade

Christine A. Ogren[†]
Education, Higher: Colleges and Universities
Teacher Corps

Morris S. Ogul[†]
Filibuster, Congerssional

Gary Y. Okihiro[†]
Asian Americans
Asian Indian Americans

Bill Olbrich
Washington University in St. Louis
American Legion
Associations
Clubs, Exclusionary
Fraternal and Service Organizations
National Rifle Association
Political Cartoons
Secret Societies
Veterans' Organizations
War Memorials

John W. Oliver[†]
Pension Act, Arrears of

Martha L. Olney
University of California, Berkeley
Advertising
Credit
Credit Cards

David J. Olson[†]
Backlash

Peter S. Onuf
University of Virginia
Ordinances of 1784, 1785, and 1787

Ernest S. Osgood[†]
McCormick Reaper
Packers' Agreement
Stockyards

Molly Oshatz
University of California, Berkeley
Social Gospel
Swedenborgian Churches

Brian Overland
Bellevuw, Washington
Computers and Computer Industry
Microsoft

Christopher Owen
Northeastern State University, Oklahoma
South, the: The Antebellum South
Southern Rights Movement

Robert M. Owens
University of Illinois at Urbana-Champaign
Cahokia Mounds
Greenville Treaty
Indian Agents
Indian Land Cessions
Indian Oratory
Indians in the Revolution
Kickapoo
Ohio Wars
Osage
Scalping
Tomahawk

Linda E. Oxendine
University of North Carolina at Pembroke
Lumbee

Keith Pacholl
California State University at Fullerton
Embargo Act
Nonintercourse Act

Dominique Padurano
Rutgers, The State University of New Jersey
Camp David

Mary Borgias Palm, S.N.D.[†]
Company of One Hundred Associates

Aaron J. Palmer
Georgetown University
Dominion of New England
Dorchester Company
"Give Me Liberty or Give Me Death!"
Mayflower Compact
New England Confederation
"Our Federal Union! It Must Be Preserved!"
Plymouth Colony
Suffolk Resolves
"Taxation without Representation"

Diane Nagel Palmer
Center for Civic Education
Communication Satellites
Gentrification
Manners and Etiquette
Plastics
Polygamy

Nancy B. Palmer[†]
Pro-Choice Movement
Pro-Life Movement

Alex Soojung-Kim Pang
Stanford University
Geodesic Dome

Wayne Parent
Louisiana State University
"Benign Neglect"

David Park
Madison, Wisconsin
Centralia Mine Disaster
Commonwealth v. Hunt
Employers' Liability Laws
Ex Parte Milligan
Korea, Relations with
Korean Americans

Labor Day
Labor Legislation and Administration
Triangle Shirtwaist Fire

Alison M. Parker[†]
Pornography

Frank Parker[†]
Sherman Silver Purchase Act
Depression of 1920
Export Debenture Plan
Safety Fund System

Jerry L. Parker
Truckee Meadows Community College
American Fur Company
Fisk Expeditions
Free Society of Traders
Starving Time

Robert J. Parker[†]
Stockton-Kearny Quarrel

E. T. Parks[†]
Galápagos Islands

George B. Parks[†]
Hakluyt's *Voyages*

Donald L. Parman
Purdue University
Bureau of Indian Affairs
Indian Policy, U.S.: 1900–2000

Julius H. Parmelee[†]
Latrobe's Folly

Jon Parmenter
Saint Lawrence University
Warfare, Indian
Wars with Indian Nations: Colonial Era to 1783

Jay Parrent
Madisonville Community College
Talk Shows, Radio and Television

Jeffrey Pasley
University of Missouri at Columbia
Aurora

Thomas G. Paterson
University of Connecticut
Iron Curtain

Donald M. Pattillo
Atlanta, Georgia
Air Transportation and Travel
Aircraft Industry

Timothy R. Pauketat
University of Illinois at Urbana-Champaign
Indian Mounds

Arnold M. Paul[†]
Income Tax Cases

Philip J. Pauly
Rutgers, The State University of New Jersey
Eugenics

Brian Payne
University of Maine, Orono
Maine

Robert L. Peabody[†]
Caucus

Haywood J. Pearce Jr.[†]
Lower South
Navy, Confederate

C. C. Pearson[†]
Readjuster Movement
Virginia v. West Virginia

Louis Pelzer[†]
Food Preservation
Cattle Associations
Star Route Frauds

Mark Pendergrast
Colchester, Vermont
Coca-Cola

Pamela E. Pennock
University of Michigan, Dearborn
Spirits Industry
Wine Industry

Joshua Perelman
New York University
Guggenheim Museum
Huntington Library and Museum
Jews

J. R. Perkins[†]
Central Pacific-Union Pacific Race

Linda M. Perkins
Hunter College and Graduate Center,
City University of New York
    Education, Higher: African
        American Colleges

Hobart S. Perry[†]
    Hepburn Act
    Seamen's Act

Lewis Perry
Saint Louis University
    Shakers

John J. Pershing[†]
    American Expeditionary Forces

Allan Peskin
Cleveland State University
    Assassinations, Presidential

Lawrence A. Peskin
Morgan State University
    Manufacturing

Shannon C. Petersen
Law Firm of Latham & Watkins
    Clean Air Act
    Clean Water Act
    Environmental Protection
        Agency
    Highway Beautification Act
    Occupational Safety and Health
        Act
    Sierra Club

William J. Petersen[†]
    Galena-Dubuque Mining Dis-
        trict
    Inland Waterways Commission
    National Waterways Commis-
        sion
    New Orleans
    Towboats and Barges

Paul C. Phillips[†]
    Helena Mining Camp

Robert Phillips[†]
    Mesa Verde, Prehistoric Ruins
        of

William Philpott
Illinois State University
    Leadville Mining District

Donald K. Pickens
University of North Texas
    Agrarianism
    Brownsville Affair
    Buccaneers
    Capital Punishment
    Corruption, Political
    Crédit Mobilier of America
    Flogging
    Gone with the Wind
    Political Scandals
    Red River Indian War
    Rifle
    Tennessee, Army of
    Texas Rangers
    Tribute

Gordon K. Pickler[†]
    Flying Tigers

Ezra H. Pieper[†]
    Fenian Movement

Frank C. Pierson[†]
    Wages and Hours of Labor,
        Regulation of

Stanley R. Pillsbury[†]
    Astor Place Riot
    Dearborn Wagon
    Fraunces Tavern
    Jingoism
    Pine Tree Flag
    Proclamation Money
    Speakeasy
    Tin Pan Alley

Harvey Pinney[†]
    Briscoe v. Bank of the Common-
        wealth of Kentucky
    Capper-Volstead Act
    Field v. Clark
    Near v. Minnesota
    Sturges v. Crowninshield
    United States v. Butler

Mark Pitcavage
Anti-Defamation League
    Militia Movement
    Militias

John D. R. Platt[†]
    Independence Hall

Cynthia R. Poe
University of Wisconsin–Madison
    Antiquities Act

    Busing
    Comparable Worth
    Congress of Racial Equality
    Daughters of Bilitis
    "Don't Ask, Don't Tell"
    Doves and Hawks
    Fuel Administration
    "Lost Cause"
    Molly Maguires
    River Navigation
    Water Law
    White Caps

Frank Pommersheim
University of South Dakota School of
Law
    Indian Tribal Courts

Gerald M. Pomper[†]
    Elections, Presidential: 1964
    Elections, Presidential: 1968
    Elections, Presidential: 1972

Nancy A. Pope
National Postal Museum
    Pony Express

Samuel H. Popper[†]
    Teachers' Loyalty Oath

David L. Porter
William Penn University
    Hatch Act

Kenneth Wiggins Porter[†]
    East Indies Trade

Theodore M. Porter
University of California, Los Angeles
    Statistics

Amanda Porterfield
University of Wyoming
    Televangelism

W. B. Posey[†]
    Camp Meetings

Brian D. Posler
Millikin University
    Cloture
    District, Congressional
    Filibuster, Congressional
    Speaker of the House of Repre-
        sentatives
    Ways and Means, Committee on

Charles Postel
University of California, Berkeley
Populism

Kenneth Potter[†]
Tripartite Agreement

A. L. Powell[†]
Lamp, Incandescent

Norman John Powell[†]
Profiteering

William S. Powell[†]
Albemarle Settlements

Julius W. Pratt[†]
Paris, Treaty of (1898)
Teller Amendment

Charles Prebish
Pennsylvania State University
Buddhism

Christopher A. Preble
Woodbury, Minnesota
Missile Gap

Heather Munro Prescott[†]
Eating Disorders

Stephen B. Presser
Northwestern University School of Law
Barron v. Baltimore
Erie Railroad Company v. Tompkins
Gibbons v. Ogden
Hayburn's Case
Higher Law
Impeachment
Impeachment Trial of Samuel
Chase
Inherent Powers
Judicial Review
Judiciary
Judiciary Act of 1789
Judiciary Act of 1801
Natural Rights
Separation of Powers
Swift v. Tyson
Ware v. Hylton

B. Byron Price
University of Oklahoma
Cowboys

Walter Prichard[†]
Code Napoléon

Code Noir
Elections, Presidential: 1844
Lake Pontchartrain
Mississippi Bubble
New Orleans, Battle of
New Orleans, Capture of
Pieces of Eight
Vieux Carré

Carl E. Prince
New York University
Boston Common
Checks and Balances
Colonial Commerce
Committee of Inspection
Confederation
Customs Service, U.S.
Debts, Revolutionary War
Declaration of Rights
Declaratory Act
East Jersey
Insurrections, Domestic
Logrolling
Manhattan
Massachusetts Government Act
New Haven Colony
New Sweden Colony
Postal Service, U.S.
Proclamations
Provincial Congresses
Riots, Urban
Riots, Urban, of 1967
Rotation in Office
Selectmen
Treasury, Department of the
Vancouver Explorations
Vice President, U.S.
Wilkes Expedition
Wyoming Valley, Settlement of

C. Herman Pritchett[†]
Privileges and Immunities of
Citizens

John R. Probert[†]
Washington Naval Conference

Robert N. Proctor
Pennsylvania State University
Cancer
Smoking

Raymond H. Pulley[†]
Virginia

Carol Pursell[†]
Steam Power and Engines

John C. Putman
San Diego State University
Ludlow Massacre

Steve Pyne[†]
Geophysical Explorations

M. M. Quaife[†]
Chicago Fire
Clark's Northwest Campaign
Dearborn, Fort
French Frontier Forts
Griffon
Mackinac, Straits of, and Mack-
inac Island
Portages and Water Routes
Thames, Battle of the
Tippecanoe, Battle of

Ellen G. Rafshoon
Atlanta, Georgia
Ambassadors
Annexation of Territory
Embassies
Isolationism
State, Department of
Treaties, Negotiation and Rati-
fication of
Truman Doctrine

Allen E. Ragan[†]
Addyston Pipe Company Case
*Wolff Packing Company v. Court
of Industrial Relations*

Jack Rakove
Stanford University
Annapolis Convention
Bill of Rights in U.S. Constitu-
tion
Federalist Papers
Independence

Charles W. Ramsdell[†]
Army, Confederate

Stephen J. Randall[†]
Offshore Oil

Armin Rappaport[†]
Retaliation in International Law

Ronald S. Rasmus
Tacoma, Washington
Censorship, Press and Artistic
Physiology

Nicolas Rasmussen
University of New South Wales
    Molecular Biology

Wayne D. Rasmussen[†]
    Cattle Industry
    Corn
    Food Preservation
    Sugar Industry

W. P. Ratchford[†]
    Texas Public Lands

Donald J. Ratcliffe
University of Durham
    South Carolina Exposition and
        Protest
    Whig Party

Sidney Ratner[†]
    Excess Profits Tax
    Trade Agreements

Eric Rauchway
University of California, Davis
    Progressive Movement

P. Orman Ray[†]
    California Alien Land Law
    Claims, Federal Court of
    Cummings v. Missouri
    Golden Gate Bridge
    In Re Neagle
    Kearneyites
    Lame-Duck Amendment
    Morgan-Belmont Agreement
    Old Hickory
    Pairing
    *Panama Refining Company v.
        Ryan*
    Vanhorne's Lessee v. Dorrance
    Weeks Act

Allen Walker Read[†]
    America, Naming of

T. T. Read[†]
    Anaconda Copper
    Naval Oil Reserves

Donna W. Reamy
Virginia Commonwealth University
    Carpet Manufacture
    Honky-Tonk Girls
    Trade, Domestic

David Reddall
University of Alberta
    Literature: Overview

Robert Nelson Reddick
*Rutgers, The State University of New
Jersey*
    Rutgers University

Amanda Rees
University of Missouri at Kansas City
    Great Plains

Jonathan Rees
University of Southern Colorado
    Iron and Steel Industry
    National Labor Union
    Steel Strikes
    United Steelworkers of America

Linda Reese
University of Oklahoma
    Oklahoma
    Oklahoma City

Rosalie Jackson Regni
Virginia Commonwealth University
    Silk Culture and Manufacture
    Trade, Domestic

Michael Regoli
Organization of American Historians
    Compact Discs
    Internet

Andrew Rehfeld
Washington University
    Representation
    Representative Government

Joseph D. Reid
George Mason University
    Patronage, Political

Roddey Reid
University of California, San Diego
    Tobacco Industry

Janice L. Reiff
University of California, Los Angeles
    Pullman Strike

Conrad L. Rein
Our Lady of Holy Cross College
    Houston

Nathan Reingold[†]
    Lighthouse Board

Thomas Reins
California State University at Fullerton
    Amnesty
    Defoliation

Jesse A. Remington[†]
    Roads, Military

Barbara O. Reyes
University of New Mexico
    Santa Fe

Clark G. Reynolds[†]
    Philippine Sea, Battle of the
    Task Force 58

Judith Reynolds
LaCrosse, Kansas
    Capitol at Washington
    France, Relations with
    Housing
    Real Estate Industry

David Rezelman
Temple University
    Arms Race and Disarmament
    Hydrogen Bomb
    Manhattan Project
    Nuclear Weapons
    Strategic Defense Initiative

Samuel Rezneck[†]
    Financial Panics

Leo R. Ribuffo
George Washington University
    Conservatism
    Fascism, American
    Neoconservatism

Rupert N. Richardson[†]
    Bridger, Fort
    Virginia City

Jeffrey Richelson
National Security Archive
    Central Intelligence Agency
    National Security Agency
    National Security Council

Monica Rico
Lawrence University
    Frémont Explorations

Long, Stephen H., Explorations of

S. F. Riepma[†]
"Young America"

Andrew C. Rieser
State University of New York at Geneseo
Camp Meetings
Chautauqua Movement
Chesapeake-Leopard Incident
Chickamauga, Battle of
Cummings v. Missouri
Income Tax Cases
Knox, Fort
Lochner v. New York
McCarran-Walter Act
Mugler v. Kansas
National Labor Relations Board v. Jones and Laughlin Steel Corporation
Standard Oil Company of New Jersey v. United States

Steven A. Riess
Northeastern Illinois University
Madison Square Garden
National Collegiate Athletic Association
Sports

Elizabeth Ring[†]
Aroostook War

Natalie J. Ring
Tulane University
Chain Gangs
Sharecroppers

R. Volney Riser
University of Alabama
American Tobacco Case
Balanced Budget Amendment
Collector v. Day
Craig v. Boren
Ex Parte Garland
Granger Cases
Missouri v. Holland
Saenz v. Roe
United States v. Butler

C. C. Rister[†]
Red River Indian War
Sheep Wars

Donald A. Ritchie
United States Senate Historical Office

Appropriations by Congress
Congress, United States

Christine M. Roane
Springfield, Massachusetts
Floor Leader
Gardening
Nitrates
Soybeans
Telephone

Dana L. Robert
Boston University
Missions, Foreign

Frédéric Robert
University Jean Moulin Lyon III, France
Marijuana
U-2 Incident

Margaret Roberts
Venice, California
Oklahoma City Bombing

Philip J. Roberts
University of Wyoming
Wyoming

Timothy M. Roberts
Bilkent University, Turkey
America as Interpreted by Foreign Observers
Autobiography of Malcolm X
Freemasons
Harpers Ferry Raid
Immediatism
Kennebec River Settlements
"Kilroy Was Here"
Know-Nothing Party
New England Antislavery Society
New England Emigrant Aid Company
Oberlin Movement
Port Authorities

Andrew W. Robertson
Herbert H. Lehman College and the Graduate Center, City University of New York
Democratic Party
Elections
Federalist Party
Jacobin Clubs
Political Parties
Republican Party

William Spence Robertson[†]
Foraker Act
Hay-Pauncefote Treaties
Latin America, Commerce with
Mexico, French in

Doane Robinson[†]
Badlands
Black Hills

Edgar Eugene Robinson[†]
Elections, Presidential: 1828 and 1832
Elections, Presidential: 1920
Elections, Presidential: 1924
Taft-Roosevelt Split

George C. Robinson[†]
Congressional Record
Grain Futures Act

Michael Robinson
University of Southern California
Literature: Popular Literature

Victor Robinson[†]
Scurvy
Yellow Fever

W. A. Robinson[†]
Bayard-Chamberlain Treaty
Commerce, Court of
Freeholder
Gristmills
Moratorium, Hoover
Railroad Retirement Acts
Railroad Retirement Board v. Alton Railroad Company
Tolls Exemption Act
Trevett v. Weeden
United States v. Wong Kim Ark
Veazie Bank v. Fenno

William A. Robinson[†]
Reed Rules

William M. Robinson Jr.[†]
Privateers and Privateering
Rams, Confederate

Nathan C. Rockwood[†]
Cement

John Rodrigue
Louisiana State University
Louisiana

Junius P. Rodriguez
Eureka College
Kwanzaa

George H. Roeder Jr.
School of the Art Institute of Chicago
Art Institute of Chicago
Metropolitan Museum of Art

Naomi Rogers
Yale University
Women's Health

Ron Roizen
Wallace, Idaho
Alcoholism

Jon Roland
Constitution Society
American Party
Appointing Power
Boston Committee of Correspondence
Charlotte Town Resolves
Colonial Policy, British
Constitutional Union Party
Council of Revision, New York
Parliament, British
States' Rights in the Confederacy
Subsistence Homesteads
Titles of Nobility
Treason
Virginia Resolves

David C. Roller[†]
Distilling

Philip Ashton Rollins[†]
Saddles

Charles F. Romanus[†]
Burma Road and Ledo Road
Merrill's Marauders

Katharine Metcalf Roof[†]
Samplers

Winfred T. Root[†]
Proprietary Agent
Toleration Acts

F. Arturo Rosales
University of Arizona
Mexican Americans

Frances Rose-Troup[†]
Dorchester Company

Eugene H. Roseboom[†]
Black Swamp
Geographer's Line
Morgan's Raids
Osborn v. Bank of the United States
Tammany Societies

Norman Rosenberg
Macalester College
Kidnapping
Libel
Lindbergh Kidnapping Case

Denise Rosenblatt
National Library of Education
Pacific Islanders

Ross Rosenfeld
State University of New York at Stony Brook
Polling
Trusts
Water Supply and Conservation

Paul C. Rosier
Villanova University
Indian Claims Commission

Frank Edward Ross[†]
Ginseng, American
Hide and Tallow Trade

M. W. Rossiter[†]
Lawrence Scientific School

David Rossman
Boston University School of Law
Plea Bargain

Michael S. Roth
California College of Arts and Crafts
Getty Museum

Morton Rothstein[†]
Elevators, Grain

Kristen L. Rouse
Florida State University
ACT UP
AIDS Quilt
Birth of a Nation, The
Mardi Gras
Military Service and Minorities: Homosexuals
Westerns

Peter L. Rousseau
Vanderbilt University
Financial Panics

James M. Rubenstein
Miami University of Ohio
Roads
Transportation and Travel

Ted Rubin[†]
Juvenile Courts

David Rudenstine
Benjamin N. Cardozo School of Law, Yeshiva University
New York Times v. Sullivan
Pentagon Papers

John Rury
DePaul University
Education

Jerrold G. Rusk[†]
Ballot

Jonathan S. Russ
University of Delaware
Delaware

R. R. Russel[†]
Railroad Conventions

Carl P. Russell[†]
Astoria
Bullboats

Don Russell[†]
Ensign
Muster Day

Nelson Vance Russell[†]
Camden, Battle of
Guilford Courthouse, Battle of

Paul B. Ryan[†]
Contraband of War
Merchantmen, Armed
Pueblo Incident
Warships

Robert W. Rydell II
Montana State University
World's Fairs

Frank Rzeczkowski
Northwestern University
Burke Act

46

Century of Dishonor
Dawes Commission
Dawes General Allotment Act
Ghost Dance
Indian Citizenship
Indian Reorganization Act
Laramie, Fort, Treaty of (1851)
Laramie, Fort, Treaty of (1868)
Termination Policy
Tribes: Great Plains

Paul Sabin
Yale University
Global Warming

George Sabo III
University of Arkansas
Caddo

Honor Sachs
University of Wisconsin–Madison
Alamo, Siege of the
Black Cavalry in the West
Black Hills
Claims, Federal Court of
Flying Tigers
France, Quasi-War with
Impressment of Seamen
Lawrence, Sack of
London, Declaration of
Navy, Confederate
Piracy
Unknown Soldier, Tomb of

J. Fred Saddler
Temple University
Charleston
Virginia Beach

Cameron L. Saffell
New Mexico Farm and Ranch Heritage Museum
Boll Weevil
Rural Life

Ernesto Sagas
Rutgers, The State University of New Jersey
Caribbean Policy

Kelly Boyer Sagert
Lorain, Ohio
Downsizing
Profit Sharing
Thirty-Hour Week

John Saillant
Western Michigan University
Hartford Wits

Frank Salamone
Iona College
Italy, Relations with

Kirkpatrick Sale[†]
Bioregionalism

Matt T. Salo
Cheverly, Maryland
Gypsies

Shelia Salo
Cheverly, Maryland
Gypsies

Stephen Salsbury[†]
Soap and Detergent Industry

Bradford W. Sample
Indiana University–Purdue University, Indianapolis
Indianapolis

Terry Samway
United States Secret Service
Secret Service

Kathleen Waters Sander
University of Maryland University College
Johns Hopkins University
Woman's Exchange Movement

Peggy Sanders
Oral, South Dakota
Cooperatives, Consumers'
Cooperatives, Farmers'
County and State Fairs
Gambling
Mule
Taverns and Saloons

Andrew K. Sandoval-Strausz
University of New Mexico
Hotels and Hotel Industry

Margaret D. Sankey
Auburn University
American Republican Party
Anti-Rent War
Boston Tea Party
Brook Farm
Culpeper's Rebellion
Green Mountain Boys

Greenback Movement
Olive Branch Petition
Revolutionary Committees
Saratoga Campaign

Vilma Santiago-Irizarry
Cornell University
Puerto Rico

Jack Santino
Bowling Green State University
Holidays and Festivals

Leo Sartori[†]
Submarines

Richard A. Sattler
University of Montana
Seminole

Claudio Saunt
University of Georgia
Creek
Indian Policy, U.S.: 1775-1830
Tribes: Southeastern

Max Savelle[†]
Indiana Company
Paris, Treaty of (1763)
Ryswick, Peace of

Ken W. Sayers[†]
Submarines

T. Laine Scales
Baylor University
Charity Organization Movement
Social Work

Jennifer Scanlon
Bowdoin College
Magazines, Women's

Margaret Schabas
University of British Columbia
Economics

Ludwig F. Schaefer[†]
German-American Bund

Elizabeth D. Schafer
Loachapaha, Alabama
Digital Technology
DVD
Horse
Mustangs
Robotics

Sealing
Space Shuttle

Joseph Schafer[†]
Farmers Institutes
Russian Claims

Harry N. Scheiber
University of California, Berkeley
Canals

Paul J. Scheips[†]
Signal Corps, U.S. Army

John T. Schlebecker[†]
Grasshoppers

Kurt C. Schlichting
Fairfield University
Grand Central Terminal

Janet Schmelzer
Tarleton State University
Fort Worth

John R. Schmidhauser[†]
Stare Decisis

Leigh E. Schmidt
Princeton University
Secularization

Steffen W. Schmidt
Iowa State University
Bermuda Islands
Coast and Geodetic Survey
Long Island
Sailing and Yacht Racing

Bernadotte E. Schmitt[†]
Four-Power Treaty
Fourteen Points
Lusitania, Sinking of the
Sussex Case

Dorothee Schneider
University of Illinois at Urbana-Champaign
German Americans

James C. Schneider
University of Texas at San Antonio
San Antonio

Brent Schondelmeyer[†]
Clothing Industry

Hubble Space Telescope
Insurance
Rust Belt
Supply-Side Economics
Trade, Foreign

Zachary M. Schrag
Baruch College of the City University of New York
Washington, D.C.

Sarah Schrank
California State University at Long Beach
Artists' Colonies

Ellen Schrecker
Yeshiva University
McCarthyism

Stephen A. Schuker[†]
World War I War Debts

Susan Schulten
University of Denver
Geography

Kevin Schultz
University of California, Berkeley
Social Darwinism

Scott T. Schutte[†]
American Association of Retired Persons

Philip Schwadel
Pennsylvania State University
Religion and Religious Affiliation

Carlos A. Schwantes
University of Missouri at St. Louis
Stagecoach Travel

Anna J. Schwartz[†]
Devaluation

Ira M. Schwartz
Temple University
Foster Care

Larry Schweikart
University of Dayton
Banking: Private Banks
Bimetallism
Free Banking System
Trickle-Down Economics

Dorothy Schwieder
Iowa State University
Iowa

James T. Scott
Gahanna, Ohio
African American Religions and Sects
Border Slave State Convention
Conglomerates
Corporations
International Labor Defense
Justice, Department of
Race Relations
Taft Commission
Viagra

Louis Martin Sears[†]
Elections, Presidential: 1808 and 1812
Joint Commissions
Slidell's Mission to Mexico

Bruce Seely
Michigan Technological University
Engineering Education

Jeff Seiken
Ohio State University
Colonial Wars

Amanda I. Seligman
University of Wisconsin–Milwaukee
Museum of Science and Industry

J. Paul Selsam[†]
Germantown

Ted Semegran
Chemical Industry Consultant
Chemical Industry

Alfred E. Senn[†]
Afghanistan, Soviet Invasion of

R. Stephen Sennott
Illinois Institute of Technology, College of Architecture
Monticello

Jennifer Sepez
University of Washington
Makah

Gilbert T. Sewall[†]
Educational Technology
Textbooks

Stacy Kinlock Sewell
Saint Thomas Aquinas College
    Affirmative Action

Esa Lianne Sferra
University of Richmond
    Extradition
    Fletcher v. Peck
    Gelpcké v. Dubuque
    Loving v. Virginia
    Miscegenation
    Presidents and Subpoenas
    Privacy
    Search and Seizure, Unreasonable
    Statutes of Limitations
    Supreme Court Packing Bills
    United States v. Virginia

William G. Shade[†]
    American Colonization Society
    Antislavery
    Scalawag

Benjamin F. Shambaugh[†]
    Pit

Bertha M. H. Shambaugh[†]
    Amana Community

Henry T. Shanks[†]
    Impressment, Confederate
    Sons of the South

Kathryn W. Shanley
University of Montana
    Surrounded, The

Fred A. Shannon[†]
    Army, Union
    Army of the Potomac
    Bounties, Military
    Bounty Jumper
    Substitutes, Civil War

Shelby Shapiro
University of Maryland at College Park
    Log Cabin
    Sheffield Scientific School

Robert P. Sharkey[†]
    Specie Payments, Suspension
        and Resumption of

G. Terry Sharrer
Smithsonian Institution
    Flour Milling
    Smallpox

Augustus H. Shearer[†]
    Barnburners
    Broadsides
    Walloons

Deirdre Sheets
Chicago, Illinois
    Barbed Wire
    Beauty Contests
    Bees
    Benefit Concerts
    Bible Commonwealth
    Burlesque
    Fertilizers
    Feudalism
    Grand Ole Opry
    Ice Skating
    Kensington Stone
    Miss America Pageant
    Mountain Climbing
    Oats
    Peace Commission (1867)
    Piecework
    Rocky Mountains
    Rodeos
    Showboats
    Trailer Parks

H. H. Shenk[†]
    Fries' Rebellion

Massey H. Shepherd Jr.[†]
    Oxford Movement

Samuel C. Shepherd
Centenary College of Louisiana
    New Orleans
    Richmond

Steve Sheppard
University of Arkansas School of Law
    Bioterrorism
    Civil Rights Act of 1957
    Due Process of Law
    Enron Scandal
    Ex Parte McCardle
    Legal Profession
    Marbury v. Madison
    Martin v. Mott
    Neutral Rights
    Neutrality
    Petition, Right of
    Police Power
    Regulators
    *United States v. E. C. Knight
        Company*
    War, Laws of

Michael Sherfy
University of Illinois at Urbana-Champaign
    Glaize, The
    Indian Removal
    Osage Orange
    Trail of Tears

Thomas E. Sheridan
University of Arizona
    Akimel O'odham and Tohono
        O'odham

Carol Sheriff
College of William and Mary
    Erie Canal

Caroline R. Sherman
Princeton University
    Botanical Gardens
    Botany
    Weeds

Daniel John Sherman
Cornell University
    County Government
    Energy, Department of
    Federal Agencies

H. Shimanuki[†]
    Beekeeping

Clifford K. Shipton[†]
    Pillory
    Stocks

Frank R. Shirer
*United States Army Center of Military
History*
    D Day
    Pearl Harbor

Frank C. Shockey
University of Minnesota
    Inuit

Fred Shore
University of Manitoba
    Cree

Jack Shulimson[†]
    Marine Corps, United States

Wilbur H. Siebert[†]
    Burns Fugitive Slave Case

Robert H. Silliman
Emory University
    Geology

John R. Sillito
Weber State University
    Farmer-Labor Party of 1920

David J. Silverman
Wayne State University
    Wampanoag

Faren R. Siminoff
Nassau Community College
    Bowery
    Brooklyn
    Ghent, Treaty of
    Greenwich Village
    Indian Policy, Colonial
    Nicolls' Commission
    Times Square

Francis B. Simkins[†]
    Hamburg Riot
    Indigo Culture
    Tithes, Southern Agricultural

Edwin H. Simmons[†]
    China, U.S. Armed Forces in
    Spanish-American War

Harvey G. Simmons
York University
    Terrorism

Stephanie R. Sims
Rutgers, The State University of New Jersey
    Princeton University

Bruce Sinclair[†]
    Franklin Institute
    Mechanics' Institutes

Daniel J. Singal
Hobart and William Smith Colleges
    Fugitive-Agrarians

Joseph M. Siracusa
Griffith University
    Australia and New Zealand, Relations with
    Pacific Rim
    Recognition, Policy of

J. Carlyle Sitterson[†]
    Sugar Industry

Alfred Lindsay Skerpan[†]
    Schools, Private

William Z. Slany
University of Wisconsin–Milwaukee
    Foreign Service

Susan Sleeper-Smith
Michigan State University
    Indian Social Life

Michael A. Sletcher
Yale University
    Scotch-Irish

Charles W. Smith
Queens College and Graduate Center of the City University of New York
    Auctions

Dale C. Smith
Uniformed Services University
    Medical Research
    Medicine and Surgery

Dale O. Smith[†]
    Air Power, Strategic

E. C. Smith[†]
    Union Sentiment in Border States

Hilda L. Smith
University of Cincinnati
    Declaration of Sentiments

J. F. Smith[†]
    Mormon Handcart Companies

Janet S. Smith
Slippery Rock University
    Appalachia
    Maps and Mapmaking
    Mississippi River
    Mohawk Valley
    Vinland
    Yukon Region

Jason Scott Smith
Harvard University
    Virtual Reality

John Howard Smith
Texas A&M University, Commerce
    Eagle, American

Richard K. Smith[†]
    Dirigibles

Stephen A. Smith
University of Arkansas
    Liberty Poles

Theodore Clark Smith[†]
    Chickamauga, Battle of
    Elections, Presidential: 1880

Victoria A. O. Smith
University of Nebraska
    Apache
    Apache Wars
    Tribes: Southwestern

Willard H. Smith[†]
    Tenure of Office Act
    Wade-Davis Bill

William Paul Smith[†]
    Holding Company

J. F. Smithcors[†]
    Veterinary Medicine

John Smolenski
University of California, Davis
    Philadelphia

Charles W. Smythe[†]
    Mexico, Punitive Expedition into

David L. Snead
Texas Tech University
    Cold War

Itai Sneh
Columbia University
    Christian Coalition
    Cross of Gold Speech
    Emily's List
    Ferguson Impeachment
    Gabriel's Insurrection
    Iran, Relations with
    Moral Majority
    Panama Canal Treaty
    Suez Crisis
    Tiananmen Square Protest

Dean Snow
Pennsylvania State University
    Iroquois
    Tribes: Northeastern

Michael M. Sokal
Worcester Polytechnic Institute
    Phrenology

Winton U. Solberg
University of Illinois at Urbana-Champaign
    Universities, State

Rayman L. Solomon Jr.
Rutgers School of Law–Camden
    Circuits, Judicial
    Law Schools

Frank J. Sorauf[†]
    Two-Party System

Mary Deane Sorcinelli[†]
    Free Universities
    Schools, Community

Frank A. Southard Jr.[†]
    Emergency Fleet Corporation
    Export Taxes
    Shipping Board, U.S.

James Spady
College of William and Mary
    Apprenticeship
    Class

Oliver Lyman Spaulding[†]
    Aisne-Marne Operation
    Antietam, Battle of
    Boston, Siege of
    Doughboy
    Trenches in American Warfare

Ronald Spector[†]
    Blockade
    Warships
    Torpedo Warfare

Mark David Spence
Knox College
    Columbia River Exploration
        and Settlement
    Explorations and Expeditions:
        U.S.
    Mandan, Fort
    Northwest Territory
    Western Exploration

Robert F. Spencer[†]
    Indians and Tobacco
    Sachem
    Wampum

Jonathan P. Spiro
University of California, Berkeley
    American Museum of Natural
        History
    Conservation

Michael H. Spiro[†]
    Gramm-Rudman-Hollings Act

Harold H. Sprout[†]
    Ludlow Resolution

James Duane Squires[†]
    EPIC
    Ipswich Protest

C. P. Stacey[†]
    Montreal, Capture of (1775)
    Preparedness

Martin H. Stack
Saint Mary College
    Boeing Company
    Canning Industry
    Ford Motor Company

Amy Stambach
University of Wisconsin–Madison
    Charter Schools

Henry E. Stamm IV
Lucius Burch Center for Western Tradition at the Wind River Historical Center
    Shoshone

Edith Kirkendall Stanley[†]
    Woman's Christian Temperance
        Union

Warner Stark[†]
    Aircraft, Bomber
    Aircraft, Fighter
    Aircraft Armament
    Artillery
    Flying the Hump
    Paratroops
    Revolution, American: Profiteering
    Rifle, Recoilless

Warren Stark[†]
    Decorations, Military

Raymond P. Stearns[†]
    Debts, Colonial and Continental
    Halfway Covenant

    King George's War
    King Philip's War
    London, Treaty of
    Lords of Trade and Plantation
    Louisburg Expedition
    Lovejoy Riots
    Massachusetts Body of Liberties
    New England Way

Francis Borgia Steck[†]
    Apalachee Massacre
    Santa Maria

Michael Stein
College of William and Mary
    Americans with Disabilities Act
    Discrimination: Disabled

Wayne J. Stein
Montana State University
    Tribal Colleges

Wendell H. Stephenson[†]
    Alabama Platform
    Border Ruffians
    Border War
    Fire-Eaters
    "Full Dinner Pail"
    Topeka Constitution

Keir B. Sterling
United States Army Combined Arms Support Command
    Exploration of America, Early

Kyes Stevens
Waverly, Alabama
    Alabama

Mitchell Stevens
Hamilton College
    Home Schooling

Wayne E. Stevens[†]
    Vandalia Colony

John W. Stewart
Princeton Theological Seminary
    Higher Criticism

Kenneth M. Stewart[†]
    Black Hawk War
    Black Hills War
    Canoe
    Cherokee Wars
    Cibola
    Creek War

National Indian Youth Council
Soto, Hernando de, Explorations of

Meredith L. Stewart
University of Richmond
Extradition
Fletcher v. Peck
Gelpcké v. Dubuque
Loving v. Virginia
Miscegenation
Presidents and Subpoenas
Privacy
Search and Seizure, Unreasonable
Statutes of Limitations
Supreme Court Packing Bills
United States v. Virginia

Phia Steyn
University of the Free State, South Africa
Cook, James, Explorations of
Exxon Valdez

Robert Stockman
DePaul University
Bahá'í

Marvel M. Stockwell[†]
Single Tax

James J. Stokesberry[†]
Underwater Demolition Teams

Michael E. Stoller
New York University
Library of Congress

Lisa Stone
Roger Brown Study Collection of the School of the Art Institute of Chicago
Art: Self-Taught Artists

Samuel M. Stone[†]
Colt Six-Shooter

Ronald Story
University of Massachusetts
Harvard University

William Stott
University of Texas, Austin
Let Us Now Praise Famous Men

Mulford Stough[†]
Carlisle Indian Industrial School

David Stradling
University of Cincinnati
Currier and Ives
Landscape Architecture
Municipal Government
Municipal Ownership
Municipal Reform
Preservation Movement

Roxanne Struthers
University of Minnesota
Medicine, Indian

William W. Stueck Jr.
University of Georgia
Korean War

Paul E. Sultan[†]
Closed Shop

Justin Suran
University of California, Berkeley
Death of a Salesman, The
Health Insurance

Jeremi Suri
University of Wisconsin–Madison
Diplomacy, Secret
Helsinki Accords
Imperialism
Monroe-Pinkney Treaty
Nuclear Non-Proliferation Treaty
Nuclear Test Ban Treaty
Treaties with Foreign Nations

Marc J. Susser
Department of State
Human Rights

Charles Süsskind[†]
Radar

William R. Swagerty
University of the Pacific
Beaver
Indian Trade and Traders
Nez Perce
Taos

Charles B. Swaney[†]
Colonial Ships
Plank Roads

John P. Swann[†]
Pharmaceutical Industry

Mack Swearingen[†]
Vicksburg Riots
White Caps
Williams v. Mississippi

Martin J. Sweet
University of Wisconsin–Madison
Book Banning
Contempt of Congress
First Amendment
Supreme Court

William W. Sweet[†]
Calvinism
Circuit Riders
Evangelical Alliance
Finney Revivals
Latitudinarians
Theosophy

Robert P. Swierenga[†]
Corn Belt

Peter Swirski
University of Alberta
Literature: Overview

Carl Brent Swisher[†]
Jury Trial
Legal Tender Cases

Richard Sylla
New York University
Comptroller of the Currency

Marcia G. Synnott
University of South Carolina
Ivy League

John Syrett
Trent University
Baseball
Basketball
Black Sox Scandal
Confiscation Acts
Little League

Aissatou Sy-Wonyu
University of Rouen, France
Clayton-Bulwer Treaty
Virgin Islands

Rick Szostak
University of Alberta
Business Cycles
Great Depression

Tad Szulc[†]
Bay of Pigs Invasion

Joel A. Tarr[†]
Hazardous Waste
Waste Disposal

Paul S. Taylor[†]
Farmhand

Jon C. Teaford
Purdue University
Charters, Municipal
Chicago
Cincinnati
City Councils
City Manager Plan
Cleveland
Columbus, Ohio
Commission Government
Enterprise Zones
Levittown
Local Government
Memphis
Metropolitan Government
Sectionalism
Town Government
Zoning Ordinances

David J. Teece
University of California, Berkeley
Industrial Research

James Tejani
Columbia University
Columbia
Federal Trade Commission
Food Stamp Program
Galloway's Plan of Union
McClellan Committee Hearings

Lisa Tetrault
University of Wisconsin–Madison
Rock and Roll
Women, Citizenship of Married
Yellow Journalism

Charles Marion Thomas[†]
Pribilof Islands

David Y. Thomas[†]
Ex Parte Garland

Hugh Thomas[†]
Pocket Veto

Robert S. Thomas[†]
American Expeditionary Forces
In Italy
Army of Occupation
Benning, Fort
Independence Rock
Long Island, Battle of
Lost Battalion
Marion, Battle at
Moultrie, Fort, Battle of
World War I Training Camps

W. Scott Thomason
Cornelia Strong College, University of North Carolina at Greensboro
Andersonville Prison
Atlanta Campaign
Gettysburg, Battle of
Richmond Campaigns

Elizabeth Lee Thompson
Palo Alto, California
Commodities Exchange Act
Confiscation of Property
Webster v. Reproductive Health Services

Mark Thompson
University of North Carolina at Pembroke
Yorktown Campaign

Robert Thompson
Syracuse University
All in the Family
I Love Lucy
Infomercials
March of Time
Music Television
Saturday Night Live
Sesame Street
60 Minutes
Soap Operas
Today
Tonight

Elizabeth H. Thomson[†]
Sheffield Scientific School

Ross D. Thomson
University of Vermont
Leather and Leather Products
Industry

Russell Thornton
University of California, Los Angeles
Indian Intermarriage

Native American Graves Protection and Repatriation Act

Peter J. Thuesen
Tufts University
Bible

Antonine S. Tibesar[†]
Franciscans

John A. Tilley
East Carolina University
Packets, Sailing

Richard H. Timberlake Jr.[†]
Counterfeiting

C. A. Titus[†]
Elizabethtown Associates
Monmouth, Battle of
Princeton, Battle of
Trenton, Battle of

Kathleen A. Tobin
Purdue University, Calumet
Abortion
Birth Control

Frederick P. Todd[†]
Unknown Soldier, Tomb of the

Mark Todd
Western State College of Colorado
Bell Telephone Laboratories
Electronic Surveillance
Energy Industry
Middle Passage
Observatories, Astronomical
Strontium 90

Rebecca Tolley-Stokes
East Tennessee State University
Genealogy
March of Dimes

Anthony R. Tomazinis
Transportation Studies Laboratory, University of Pennsylvania
Infrastructure

Maria Emilia Torres-Guzman
Columbia University
Education, Bilingual

John Townes[†]
Courier Services
Hydroponics
Sun Belt

James Tracy
Boston University Academy
Christmas

Roger R. Trask[†]
Defense, Department of
General Accounting Office

Hans L. Trefousse
Brooklyn College of the City University of New York
Emancipation Proclamation
Reconstruction

Anton Treuer
Bemidji State University
Ojibwe Language

Stanley W. Trimble
University of California, Los Angeles
Bluegrass Country
Piedmont Region
Potomac River
Shenandoah Valley

Ronald L. Trosper
Northern Arizona University
Indian Economic Life

Gil Troy
McGill University
Conventions, Party Nominating
First Ladies
New Frontier
New Nationalism
Platform, Party
Third Parties

Samuel Truett
University of New Mexico
Spanish Borderlands

Patricia Trutty-Coohill
Siena College
Yaddo

Andie Tucher
Columbia University
Nation, The

Thaddeus V. Tuleja[†]
Midway, Battle of

Richard W. Tupper[†]
Selden Patent

Diana B. Turk
Turk University
Education, Higher: Women's
Colleges
Schools, Single-Sex

Richard W. Turk[†]
Grenada Invasion
Panama Invasion

James Turner
University of Notre Dame
Agnosticism

William B. Turner
Saint Cloud State University
Defense of Marriage Act
Sexual Orientation
Sexuality

Mark V. Tushnet
Georgetown University Law Center
Brown v. Board of Education of
Topeka
Civil Rights Act of 1964
Civil Rights and Liberties
Desegregation
Segregation

James H. Tuten
Juniata College
Rice Culture and Trade

Robert Twombly
City College of New York
Architecture
Skyscrapers

Robert W. Twyman[†]
Bayou
Fall Line
Poor Whites

Carl Ubbelohde[†]
Gold Mines and Mining
Silver Prospecting and Mining

Peter Uhlenberg
University of North Carolina at Chapel Hill
Life Expectancy

B. A. Uhlendorf[†]
German Mercenaries

Gregory Fritz Umbach
John Jay College of the City University of New York
Police Brutality

Betty Miller Unterberger
Texas A&M University
Siberian Expedition

Bernard Unti
American University
Animal Protective Societies
Society for the Prevention of
Cruelty to Animals

Paul Uselding[†]
Clock and Watch Industry

R. W. G. Vail[†]
Chapbooks
King's Province
Massachusetts Ballot
Mayflower

Michael Valdez
Triple T Double L Research
Explosives
Merchant Adventurers

Richard W. Van Alstyne[†]
Impressment of Seamen
London, Declaration of

John Vickrey Van Cleve
Gallaudet University
Sign Language, American

Ruth G. Van Cleve[†]
Guam

John G. Van Deusen[†]
Detroit, Surrender of

Jon M. Van Dyke
William S. Richardson School of Law, University of Hawaii at Manoa
Admiralty Law and Courts

Ruth M. Van Dyke
Colorado College
Ancestral Pueblo (Anasazi)
Hohokam
Pueblo

David Van Leer
University of California, Davis
Romanticism

A. Bowdoin Van Riper
Southern Polytechnic State University
Bermuda Triangle
Rockets
Supersonic Transport

Paul P. Van Riper[†]
Civil Service
Interstate Commerce Laws

Rupert B. Vance[†]
Peonage

Philip R. VanderMeer
Arizona State University
Gold Bugs

Charles Garrett Vannest[†]
Clipper Ships
Hornbook

James Varn
Johnson C. Smith University
Huckleberry Finn

Christopher Vecsey
Colgate University
American Indian Religious
Freedom Act
Native American Church

David W. Veenstra
University of Illinois at Chicago
Bicentennial

Charles Vevier[†]
"Yellow Peril"

John R. Vile
Middle Tennessee State University
Electoral College

Gilberto Villahermosa
United States Army
Military Service and Minorities:
African Americans
Military Service and Minorities:
Hispanics
Women in Military Service

Erik B. Villard
United States Army Center of Military History
Army, United States
Cambodia Incursion
Chosin Reservoir
Mayaguez Incident

Tet Offensive
Thirty-eighth Parallel

Alan Villiers[†]
Cape Horn

Tom Vincent
North Carolina State University
Raleigh

Margaret Vining
National Museum of American History, Smithsonian Institution
Uniforms, Military

Dale Vinyard[†]
Cabinet
Steering Committees

Paul S. Voakes[†]
Alcatraz

Vernon L. Volpe
University of Nebraska at Kearney
Kansas Free-State Party

John Vosburgh[†]
Yellowstone National Park
Yosemite National Park

Clement E. Vose[†]
Statutes at Large, United States

Barbara Schwarz Wachal
Saint Louis University
American Studies
Arminianism
Autobiography of Benjamin Franklin
Carpetbaggers
Deism
Gateway Arch
Invisible Man
Louisiana Purchase
Methodism
Pilgrims
Poet Laureate
Roots

Israel Waismel-Manor
Cornell University
Federal Communications Commission

Michael Wala
University of Erlangen–Nürnberg
Belgian Relief

Brady Photographs
Essex Junto
Fee Patenting
Freedom of the Seas
Georgiana
Horse Racing and Showing
Intelligence, Military and Strategic
Legislatures, Bicameral and Unicameral
Macon's Bill No. 2
Martha's Vineyard
Moral Societies
Muscle Shoals Speculation
Nominating System
Nonintervention Policy
Pinckney's Treaty
Point Four
Randolph Commission
Russia, Relations with
Spies
States' Rights
Trent Affair
Two-Thirds Rule
War of 1812

Harvey Walker[†]
Legal Tender
Pools, Railroad
Riders, Legislative

J. Samuel Walker
United States Nuclear Regulatory Commission
Nuclear Regulatory Commission

Charles C. Wall[†]
Mount Vernon

Wendy Wall
Colgate University
Elections, Presidential: 1996
Elections, Presidential: 2000
Prohibition Party
Recreation
Skid Row
Skiing
Southern Christian Leadership Conference
Swimming

Anthony F. C. Wallace
University of Pennsylvania
Removal Act of 1830

D. D. Wallace[†]
Columbia, Burning of

Peter Wallenstein[†]
Virginia

James Elliott Walmsley[†]
Beecher's Bibles
Dismal Swamp
Draper's Meadows
Hampton Roads Conference
Huguenots
Virginia Dynasty

Jessica Wang
University of California, Los Angeles
Science Education

M. L. Wardell[†]
Cherokee Strip

Harry R. Warfel[†]
McGuffey's Readers
New England Primer
Spelling Bee
Webster's Blue-Backed Speller

Colston E. Warne[†]
Consumer Protection

Elizabeth Warren[†]
Revolution, American: Financial
Aspects

Harris Gaylord Warren[†]
Technocracy Movement

Stephen Warren
Augustana College
Tribes: Prairie

Manfred Waserman[†]
National Institutes of Health

Wilcomb E. Washburn[†]
Bacon's Rebellion

Janet Wasko
University of Oregon
Disney Corporation

Mary Lawrence Wathen
Southern Methodist University
Dow Jones
Standard & Poor's

Gordon S. Watkins[†]
Conciliation and Mediation,
Labor

Haywood-Moyer-Pettibone
Case
Laissez-Faire
Syndicalism
Truax v. Corrigan
Walking Delegate

Myron W. Watkins[†]
Codes of Fair Competition
*Northern Securities Company v.
United States*
Trust-Busting

Annette Watson
University of Minnesota
Greely's Arctic Expedition

R. L. Watson[†]
Africa, Relations with
Somalia, Relations with

John Sayle Watterson
James Madison University
Football

Jill Watts[†]
Cults
Rainbow Coalition

John W. Wayland[†]
Baltimore Bell Teams

Spencer Weart
Center for the History of Physics, American Institute of Physics
Physics: Solid-State Physics

John B. Weaver
Sinclair Community College
Ohio
Toledo

Warren E. Weber
Federal Reserve Bank
Suffolk Banking System

Charles A. Weeks[†]
Music: Bluegrass
Music: Country and Western
Music Festivals

Ross Weeks Jr.[†]
William and Mary, College of

Murray L. Weidenbaum[†]
Revenue, Public

Marc D. Weidenmier
Claremont McKenna College and National Bureau of Economic Research
Exchanges

Russell F. Weigley[†]
Air Cavalry

Steven Weiland[†]
Prizes and Awards: Nobel Prizes

James Weinstein
In These Times, Chicago, Illinois (retired)
National Civic Federation
Wages and Salaries

Carol Weisbrod
University of Connecticut School of Law
Displaced Homemakers Self-
Sufficiency Assistance Act
Family Education Rights and
Privacy Act
Married Women's Property Act,
New York State
Megan's Law
Right to Die Cases
Sheppard-Towner Maternity
and Infancy Protection Act

Francis Phelps Weisenburger[†]
Cumberland Road

Anne C. Weiss[†]
Children, Missing

Jane Weiss
State University of New York at Old Westbury
Love Medicine
Pennsylvania Germans

Nancy J. Weiss[†]
National Urban League

Ralph Foster Weld[†]
Burgoyne's Invasion

Paul I. Wellman[†]
Dull Knife Campaign
Hays, Fort
Scouting on the Plains
Shelby's Mexican Expedition

Christopher Wells
University of Wisconsin–Madison
Automobile

Bowles's Filibustering Expeditions
Cambodia, Bombing of
Expatriation
Galvanized Yankees
McFadden Banking Act
Merrill's Marauders
Prisoners of War: Prison Camps, Union
Profiteering
Railroads in the Civil War
Scouting on the Plains
Serial Killings
Trucking Industry
Tydings-McDuffie Act
Waco Siege

Wyatt Wells
Auburn University, Montgomery
Reaganomics

Peter C. Welsh[†]
Flour Milling

Raymond C. Werner[†]
Coutume de Paris

Edgar B. Wesley[†]
Frontier Defense
Indian Trading Houses

Marilyn F. Wessel[†]
4-H Clubs

Elizabeth Howard West[†]
Chickasaw-Creek War

Allan Westcott[†]
Manila Bay, Battle of
Marque and Reprisal, Letters of
Merrimac, Sinking of
Sampson-Schley Controversy

R. E. Westmeyer[†]
Beef Trust Cases

Carmen Teresa Whalen
Williams College
Cuban Americans
Puerto Ricans in the United States

Robert Whaples
Wake Forest University
Education, Parental Choice in
Inheritance Tax Laws
Negative Income Tax

Social Security
Unemployment
Workers' Compensation

Jeannie Whayne
University of Arkansas
Arkansas

Steven C. Wheatley
American Council of Learned Societies
Learned Societies

Arthur P. Whitaker[†]
Blount Conspiracy
Spanish Conspiracy

Matthew Whitaker
Arizona State University
African Americans
Migration, African American

Devin Alan White
University of Colorado, Boulder
Archaeology
Archaeology and Prehistory of North America

Ronald C. White Jr.
San Francisco Theological Seminary
Lincoln's Second Inaugural Address

J. G. Whitesides
University of California, Santa Barbara
Bioethics
Euthanasia
Genetic Engineering
Genetics
Persian Gulf Syndrome

Stephen J. Whitfield
Brandeis University
Frank, Leo, Lynching of
Leopold-Loeb Case
Till, Emmett, Lynching of

Theodore M. Whitfield[†]
Connecticut Compromise
Entangling Alliances
House Divided

Marcus Whitman[†]
Lakes-to-Gulf Deep Waterway

Donald R. Whitnah[†]
Weather Service, National

James P. Whittenburg
College of William and Mary
Triangular Trade

Christine Whittington
Greensboro College
Columbus Quincentenary
Wild West Show

A. W. Whittlesey[†]
Bank of North America

William M. Wiecek
Syracuse University College of Law
Adkins v. Children's Hospital
Alden v. Maine
Attainder
Boerne v. Flores
Carter v. Carter Coal Company
Chicago, Milwaukee, and Saint Paul Railway Company v. Minnesota
Child Labor Tax Case
Dorr's Rebellion
Georgia v. Stanton
Jones v. Van Zandt
License Cases
Luther v. Borden
McCray v. United States
Martin v. Hunter's Lessee
Mississippi v. Johnson
Missouri ex rel Gaines v. Canada
Muller v. Oregon
Schechter Poultry Corporation v. United States
United States v. Lopez
United States v. Reese

Thomas Wien
Université de Montréal
Acadia
Champlain, Samuel de, Explorations of
Explorations and Expeditions: French
Grand Banks
Lake Champlain
New France
Nicolet, Explorations of

Henry Mark Wild
California State University at Los Angeles
American System

Harry Emerson Wildes[†]
Franklin Stove

Korea War of 1871
Valley Forge

Mira Wilkins
Florida International University
Foreign Investment in the United States

Brien R. Williams
American Red Cross
Locomotives
Red Cross, American

C. Fred Williams
University of Arkansas, Little Rock
Little Rock

Charles E. Williams
Clarion University of Pennsylvania
Floods and Flood Control

Daniel T. Williams[†]
Tuskegee University

Dennis Williams[†]
Air Pollution
Marine Sanctuaries
Organic Farming

Ernest W. Williams Jr.[†]
Ferries

Mary Wilhelmine Williams[†]
Clayton Compromise

Samuel C. Williams[†]
Cumberland Settlements
Indian Trails

Stanley T. Williams[†]
Sleepy Hollow

Vernon J. Williams Jr.
Purdue University
African American Studies

Brady C. Williamson Jr.
University of Wisconsin Law School
Bankruptcy Laws

Hugh E. Willis[†]
Juilliard v. Greenman

C. A. Willoughby[†]
Mormon Expedition
Villa Raid at Columbus

John Wills
University of Essex
Agriculture
San Francisco Earthquakes
Three Mile Island

Angela Cavender Wilson
Arizona State University
Spirit Lake Massacre

Bobby M. Wilson[†]
Birmingham

Daniel J. Wilson
Muhlenberg College
Poliomyelitis

G. Lloyd Wilson[†]
Railroad Rate Wars

Graham K. Wilson
University of Wisconsin–Madison
Bureaucracy
Interest Groups
President, U.S.
Veto Power of the President

Paul J. Wilson
Nicholls State University
Chicago Riots of 1919
Crown Heights Riots
Watts Riots

Samuel M. Wilson[†]
Wilderness Road

William E. Wingfield
Christian Brothers University
Mental Illness

Robin W. Winks[†]
Canada, Relations with

James E. Winston[†]
Butler's Order No. 28

Robert W. Winston[†]
Bayard v. Singleton

Thomas Winter
Bilkent University, Turkey
Gilded Age
Young Men's Christian Association

Oscar Osburn Winther[†]
Promontory Point

David A. Wirth
Boston College School of Law
International Court of Justice
International Law
Territorial Sea

Harvey Wish[†]
De Lima v. Bidwell
Haymarket Riot
Pollock v. Farmers' Loan and Trust Company
Progress and Poverty
Pullmans
Railway Shopmen's Strike
Smith-Hughes Act
Smith-Lever Act
Social Democratic Party
Texas v. White

Clark Wissler[†]
Wigwam

John Witte
University of Wisconsin–Madison
Surplus, Federal

Martin Wolfe[†]
Currency and Coinage

Julienne L. Wood
Noel Memorial Library, Louisiana State University, Shreveport
Anti-Masonic Movements
Conscience Whigs
Copperheads
Free Soil Party
Popular Sovereignty

William Woodruff[†]
Rubber

C. Vann Woodward[†]
Share-the-Wealth Movements
Townsend Plan

Richard D. Worthington[†]
Herpetology

William E. Worthington Jr.
National Museum of American History, Smithsonian Institution
Bridges
Plumbing

A. J. Wright
University of Alabama at Birmingham
Tuskegee University

Ivan Wright[†]
Joint-Stock Land Banks

James D. Wright[†]
Brady Bill

Jon Wright
Hartlepool, United Kingdom
Atheism
Emerson's Essays

Peter H. Wright[†]
Chemotherapy
Magnetic Resonance Imaging

Malcolm G. Wyer[†]
Pikes Peak

George Wycherley[†]
Piracy

John Cook Wyllie[†]
University of Virginia

Rufus Kay Wyllys[†]
Grand Canyon
Wagon Trains

Kerry Wynn
University of Illinois at Urbana-Champaign
Cherokee

John Wyzalek
Weehawken, New Jersey
Discrimination: Sexual Orientation
Federal Government
Government Regulation of Business
Hairstyles
Office of Economic Opportunity

Publishing Industry
Scientific Information Retrieval

Larry Yackle
Boston University School of Law
Arrest
Attica
Crime
Prisons and Prison Reform
Punishment
Reformatories
San Quentin
Sing Sing

Gaynor Yancey
Baylor University
Settlement House Movement

Richard E. Yates[†]
Union Sentiment in the South
Zimmermann Telegram

C. K. Yearley[†]
Coal Mining and Organized Labor
Guffey Coal Acts

Eric S. Yellin
Princeton University
Columbine School Massacre
Delaney Amendment
Operation Rescue
Riots
Sabotage
Sacco-Vanzetti Case
Teapot Dome Oil Scandal

Diana H. Yoon
New York University
Chinese Exclusion Act
Insular Cases

L. E. Young[†]
Mormon Battalion
Mormon Trail

Nigel J. Young
Colgate University
Peace Movements
Women and the Peace Movement

Rosemarie Zagarri
George Mason University
Seneca Falls Convention

Jamil Zainaldin
Georgia Humanities Council
National Endowment for the Humanities

Edmund Zalinski[†]
Insurance

Albert Louis Zambone
Saint Cross College, Oxford University
Secession

Christine Clark Zemla
Rutgers, The State University of New Jersey
Intelligence Tests

Xiaojian Zhao
University of California, Santa Barbara
Chinese Americans

Larry J. Zimmerman
University of Iowa
Tipi

Harold Zink[†]
Black Horse Cavalry
Rings, Political

Andrei A. Znamenski
Alabama State University
Explorations and Expeditions: Russian

Hiller B. Zobel[†]
Boston Massacre

GUIDE TO RESEARCH AND LEARNING

We have designed this section to help students and educators use the large number of articles, maps, and primary source documents gathered in the *Dictionary of American History,* 3rd edition, for classroom study and research.

Part One of this guide correlates the *Dictionary'*s contents to three widely used American history textbooks from Wadsworth publishers:

- *American Passages: A History of the American People* (Edward L. Ayers, Lewis L. Gould, David M. Oshinsky, Jean R. Soderlund, 2000).

- *The American Past: A Survey of American History,* 6th ed. (Joseph R. Conlin, 2001).

- *Liberty, Equality, Power: A History of the American People,* 3rd ed. (John M. Murrin, Paul E. Johnson, James M. McPherson, Gary Gerstle, Emily S. Rosenberg, Norman L. Rosenberg, 2002).

Part Two consists of a research guide that provides essential information on gathering data for, and writing, a research paper in history.

The Editors of Charles Scribner's Sons

PART ONE: USING THE *DICTIONARY OF AMERICAN HISTORY* WITH CLASSROOM TEXTBOOKS

The *Dictionary of American History,* 3rd edition, is, like its predecessors, a reference book, which necessarily locates it not only in the library, but as part of the noncirculating collection. Nevertheless, the *Dictionary* contains much information that directly supports classroom work and textbook use in particular. Its articles, maps, and primary materials add depth and detail to topics that textbooks only touch upon or omit. In so doing, they provide a point of departure for a variety of assignments and papers.

History textbooks present chronological narratives. American historians tend to tell the story of the U.S. in periods bracketed by the beginning or end of significant events: the Civil War, World War II, and so on. To make *Dictionary of American History* content accessible to textbook readers, we have organized it into eight chronological segments:

To 1760
1761–1788
1789–1860
1861–1877
1878–1920
1921–1945
1946–1974
1975–2002

This scheme follows no particular textbook's arrangement. Rather, it adopts a common-sense approach intended to be capacious and flexible enough to suit many U.S. history texts.

In the pages that follow, we correlate chapters from the above-cited textbooks to content in the eight periods. A student or educator can, of course, substitute others. The central point is that periodizing the *Dictionary*'s entries allows the reader to relate them to specific topics that are found in textbooks and provides a basis for class discussions and written investigations. In the 1761–1788 period, for example, a student or educator can pursue a paper topic or group examination spurred by a textbook allusion to Shays's rebellion. Using this guide she can quickly identify not only the *Dictionary*'s entry on this event, but also a primary account. Combine these with information contained in the archival maps on the revolutionary period and the result is an array of resources that usefully amplifies textbook information.

Apart from its link to specific textbook topics, each chronological grouping of *Dictionary* content provides a cluster of information for spurring new research on a period, in the process creating an opportunity for new knowledge. An original class unit or major paper about the Civil War, for example, can be built from the entries, maps, and primary sources covering the 1861–1877 period. Evidentiary (maps, primary sources) and secondary (articles) materials coalesce in a way that supports fresh connections by the student or educator. Thus, the *Dictionary of American History* can be used beyond the confines of the reference collection and outside the walls of the library.

TO 1760:

PERTINENT TEXTBOOK CHAPTERS

American Passages
1. Contact, Conflict, and Exchange in the Atlantic World to 1590
2. Colonization of North America, 1590–1675
3. Crisis and Change, 1675–1720
4. The Expansion of Colonial British America, 1720–1763

The American Past
1. When Worlds Collide: America and Europe before 10,000 B.C.–A.D. 1550
2. England in America: The Struggle to Plant a Colony 1550–1624
3. Puritans and Proprietors: Colonial America 1620–1732
4. Colonial Society: English Legacies, American Facts of Life
5. Other Americans: The Indians, French, and Africans of Colonial North America
6. British America: The Colonies at the Equinox

Liberty, Equality, Power
1. When Old Worlds Collide: Contact, Conquest, Catastrophe
2. The Challenge to Spain and the Settlement of North America
3. England Discovers Its Colonies: Empire, Liberty, and Expansion
4. Provincial America and the Struggle for a Continent

DICTIONARY OF AMERICAN HISTORY ENTRIES

Articles
Albany Plan
Albemarle Settlements

America, Naming of
Ancestral Pueblo (Anasazi)
Antinomian Controversy
Apalachee Massacre
Appeals from Colonial Courts
Archaeology and Prehistory of North America
Arminianism
Assemblies, Colonial
Assistant
Attainder
Autobiography of Benjamin Franklin
Bacon's Rebellion
Bible Commonwealth
Board of Trade and Plantations
Braddock's Expedition
Brownists
Buccaneers
Buffalo Trails
Burghers
Cabeza de Vaca Expeditions
Cabot Voyages
Cahokia Mounds
Cambridge Agreement
Cambridge Platform
Carolina, Fundamental Constitutions of
Champlain, Samuel de, Explorations of
Charity Schools
Charleston Indian Trade
Charter of Liberties
Charter of Privileges
Chartered Companies
Church of England in the Colonies
Cibola
Code Noir
Colonial Agent
Colonial Assemblies
Colonial Charters

Colonial Commerce
Colonial Councils
Colonial Policy, British
Colonial Settlements
Colonial Ships
Colonial Society
Colonial Wars
Company of One Hundred Associates
Conquistadores
Coronado Expeditions
Council for New England
Covenant, Church
Culpeper's Rebellion
Dame School
"Dark and Bloody Ground"
Deerfield Massacre
Divine Providences
Dominion of New England
Dongan Charters
Dorchester Company
Draper's Meadows
Ducking Stool
Duke of York's Laws
Duke of York's Proprietary
Dutch West India Company
East Jersey
Edwardsean Theology
Elizabethtown Associates
Encomienda System
Exploration of America, Early
Fast Days
Feudalism
Franklin Stove
Free Society of Traders
French Frontier Forts
General Court, Colonial
Germantown
Gilbert's Patent
Golden Hind
Governors
Great Law of Pennsylvania
Great Migration
Griffon
Hakluyt's Voyages
Half Moon
Halfway Covenant
Hat Manufacture, Colonial Restriction on
Hennepin, Louis, Narratives of
Hohokam
Holy Experiment
Homework
Hornbook
House of Burgesses
Huguenots
Hundred
Indentured Servants
Indian Bible, Eliot's

Indian Mounds
Instructions
Ipswich Protest
Iron Act of 1750
Jenkins' Ear, War of
Jolliet-Marquette Explorations
Kennebec River Settlements
King George's War
King Philip's War
King William's War
King's Province
La Salle Explorations
Latin Schools
Latitudinarians
Leisler Rebellion
Liberty Bell
Locke's Political Philosophy
London, Treaty of
Lords of Trade and Plantation
Louisburg Expedition
Ludlow's Code
Magna Carta
Markets, Public
Massachusetts Ballot
Massachusetts Bay Colony
Massachusetts Body of Liberties
Mayflower
Mayflower Compact
Meetinghouse
Mercantilism
Merchant Adventurers
Mesa Verde, Prehistoric Ruins of
Molasses Act
Monongahela, Battle of the
Mount Hope
Mourt's Relation
Narragansett Planters
Navigation Acts
New York Slave Conspiracy of 1741
New Albion Colony
New Castle
New England Company
New England Confederation
New England Primer
New England Way
New France
New Haven Colony
New Lights
New Netherland
New Sweden Colony
New York City, Capture of
New York Colony
Nicolet, Explorations of
Nicolls' Commission
Norsemen in America
Oñate Explorations and Settlements
Orleans, Territory of

63

Parliament, British
Parson's Cause
Patroons
Pennsylvania Germans
Penobscot Region
Pequot War
Petition and Remonstrance of New Netherland
Pieces of Eight
Pilgrims
Pillory
Pine Tree Flag
Pine Tree Shilling
Plans of Union, Colonial
Plymouth Colony
Plymouth Rock
Plymouth, Virginia Company of
Port Royal
Poverty Point
Powhatan Confederacy
Privy Council
Proprietary Agent
Proprietary Colonies
Providence Island Company
Providence Plantations, Rhode Island and
Pueblo Revolt
Puritans and Puritanism
Quebec, Capture of
Raleigh Colonies
Randolph Commission
Royal Colonies
Royal Disallowance
Ryswick, Peace of
Sagadahoc, Colony at
Santa Maria
Saybrook Platform
Soto, Hernando de, Explorations of
Sow Case
Starving Time
Suffrage, Colonial
Sumptuary Laws and Taxes, Colonial
Tea Trade, Prerevolutionary
Theocracy in New England
Titles of Nobility
Tobacco as Money
Toleration Acts
Tomahawk
Trading Companies
Two Penny Act
Vinland
Virginia Company of London
Virginia Indian Company
Walloons

Maps: Early Maps of the New World
Die Nüw Welt (1540)
Mondo Nuovo (1576)
Norumbega et Virginia (1597)

Provinciae Borealis Americae non itapridem dete ctae aut magis ab europaeis excuitae (1703)

Maps: The Colonies
A Map of Virginia and Maryland, Sold by Thomas Basset in Fleet Street and Richard Chiswell in St. Pauls Church Yard (1676)
A Map of New England, Being the first that was ever here cut (1677)
A Mapp of New England by John Seller Hydrographer to the King (1675)
A New Map of the Most Considerable Plantations of the English in America, Dedicated to His Highness William Duke of Glocester (1722)
An accurate map of the English colonies in North America bordering on the River Ohio (1754)
New England, New York, New Jersey and Pensilvania (1736)
Virginiae partis australis et Floridae partis orientalis (1671)

Maps: Explorations of the American Continent
A Map of Louisiana and of the River Mississippi, by John Senex (1721)
A New Map of the River Mississippi from the Sea to Bayagoulas (1761)
Carte de la Louisiane et du Cours du Mississippi (1730)
Louisiana, as formerly claimed by France, and now containing part of British America to the East & Spanish America to the West of the Mississippi (1765)
Unidentified French manuscript map of the Mississippi River (1683)

Maps: Colonial Wars
Map of that part of America which was the Principal Seat of War in 1756
Plan of the City & Fortifications of Louisburg, from a Survey made by Richard Gridley (1745)
A Plan of the River St. Lawrence, from the Falls of Montmorenci to Sillery; with the Operations of the Siege of Quebec (1759)

Maps: New York: The Development of a City
Plan de Manathes ou Nouvelle Yorc (1675)
A Plan of the City of New York from an actual Survey, Made by James Lyne (1728)

Primary Source Documents
A Dialogue Between Piumbukhou and His Unconverted Relatives
An Act Concerning Religion
Captivity Narrative of a Colonial Woman
Charter to Sir Walter Raleigh
Earliest American Protest Against Slavery
Evidence Used Against Witches
Excerpt from The History and Present State of Virginia
Excerpt from Voyages of the Slaver St. John
Letter Describing Plantation Life in South Carolina

Massachusetts School Law
Maxims from Poor Richard's Almanack
Powhatan's Speech to John Smith
Spanish Colonial Official's Account of the Triangular
    Trade with England
Starving in Virginia
The Mayflower Compact
The Origin of the League of Five Nations
Trial of Anne Hutchinson at Newton
Untitled Poem

1761–1788:

PERTINENT TEXTBOOK CHAPTERS

American Passages
4. The Expansion of Colonial British America, 1720–1763
5. Wars for Independence, 1764–1783
6. Toward a More Perfect Union, 1783–1788

The American Past
7. Years of Tumult: The Quarrel with Great Britain 1763–1770
8. Riot to Rebellion: The Road to Independence 1770–1776
9. War for Independence: Winning the Revolution 1776–1781
10. Inventing a Country: American Constitutions 1781–1789

Liberty, Equality, Power
5. Reform, Resistance, Revolution
6. The Revolutionary Republic

DICTIONARY OF AMERICAN HISTORY ENTRIES

Articles
Alexandria Conference
Annapolis Convention
Antifederalists
Arnold's March to Quebec
Arnold's Raid in Virginia
Arnold's Treason
Articles of Confederation
Associations
Bank of North America
Bayard v. Singleton
Baynton, Wharton, and Morgan
Bennington, Battle of
Billeting
Bonhomme Richard–Serapis Encounter
Boston Committee of Correspondence
Boston Massacre
Boston, Siege of
Boston Tea Party
Brandywine Creek, Battle of
British Empire, Concept of
Bunker Hill, Battle of

Burgoyne's Invasion
Camden, Battle of
Charleston Harbor, Defense of
Cherokee Wars
Clark's Northwest Campaign
Coercive Acts
Commander in Chief of British Forces
Committees of Correspondence
Committees of Safety
Common Sense
Confederation
Connecticut Compromise
Connolly's Plot
Continental Congress
Conway Cabal
Cook, James, Explorations of
Council of Revision, New York
Cowboys and Skinners
Cowpens, Battle of
Cumberland Settlements
Declaration of Independence
Declaration of Rights
Declaratory Act, 1766
Delaware, Washington Crossing the
"Don't Fire Till You See the White of Their Eyes"
"Don't Give Up the Ship"
Dunmore's War
Duquesne, Fort
Dutch Bankers' Loans
Essex Junto
Eutaw Springs, Battle of
Farmer's Letters
Federalist Papers
Franklin, State of
French in the American Revolution
Galloway's Plan of Union
Gaspée, Burning of the
Geographer's Line
Georgiana
German Mercenaries
"Give Me Liberty or Give Me Death!"
Great Meadows
Greenville Treaty
Guilford Courthouse, Battle of
Harlem, Battle of
Henry, Fort
Holmes v. Walton
Hutchinson Letters
Independence
Indiana Company
Indians in the Revolution
Committees of Inspection
Intolerable Acts
Jay-Gardoqui Negotiations
Jeffersonian Democracy
Jersey Prison Ship
Kentucky Conventions

Lexington and Concord, Battles of
Liberty Poles
Long Island, Battle of
Loyalists
Marietta
Massachusetts Circular Letter
Massachusetts Government Act
Minutemen
Mississippi Bubble
Monmouth, Battle of
Montreal, Capture of (1760)
Montreal, Capture of (1775)
Morse, Jedediah, Geographies of
Moultrie, Fort, Battle of
Mutiny Act
New Smyrna Colony
Newburgh Addresses
Newport, French Army at
Nonimportation Agreements
Olive Branch Petition
Ordinances of 1784, 1785, and 1787
Oriskany, Battle of
Paris, Treaty of (1763)
Paris, Treaty of (1783)
Paxton Boys
Pennsylvania Troops, Mutinies of
Penobscot Expedition
Pinckney Plan
Plan of 1776
Pontiac's War
Princeton, Battle of
Prisoners of War: Prison Ships
Proclamation of 1763
Provincial Congresses
Quartering Acts
Revere's Ride
Revolution, American: Military History
Revolution, American: Political History
Revolution, Diplomacy of the
Revolution, Financing of the
Revolution, Profiteering in the
Revolutionary Committees
Rights of the British Colonies Asserted and Proved
Rogers' Rangers
Saratoga Campaign
Savannah, Siege of (1779)
Shays's Rebellion
Sons of Liberty (American Revolution)
Southern Campaigns
Stamp Act
Stamp Act Congress
Stamp Act Riot
Suffolk Resolves
"Taxation Without Representation"
Ticonderoga, Capture of
Townshend Acts
Trenton, Battle of

Trevett v. Weeden
United Empire Loyalists
United We Stand, Divided We Fall
Valley Forge
Vandalia Colony
Virginia Declaration of Rights
Virginia Resolves
War and Ordnance, Board of
White Plains, Battle of
Wyoming Massacre
Yorktown Campaign
Zenger Trial

Maps: Explorations of the American Continent

Carte de la Californie et des Pays Nord-Ouest separés de l'Asie par le détroit d'Anian (1772)

Maps: The Revolutionary War

A Map of the Country which was the scene of operations of the Northern Army; including the Wilderness through which General Arnold marched to attack Quebec (1806)
A Map of Part of Rhode Island, Showing the Positions of the American and British Armies at the Siege of Newport (1778)
A Map of the United States of America, As settled by the Peace of 1783 (1785)
Plan of the Town and Harbour of Boston, and the Country adjacent with the Road from Boston to Concord, shewing the Place of the late Engagement between the King's Troops & the Provincials (1775)
Plan of the Battle of Bunkers Hill (1775)

Maps: The Early Republic

A Chorographical Map of the Northern Department of North America (1780)
A Plan of the Boundary Lines between the Province of Maryland and the Three Lower Counties of Delaware with Part of The Parallel of Latitude which is the Boundary between the Provinces of Maryland and Pennsylvania (1768)

Primary Source Documents

A Soldier's Love Letter
Address of the Continental Congress to Inhabitants of Canada
Battle of Lexington, American and British Accounts
Constitution of the United States
Correspondence Leading to Surrender
Declaration and Resolves of the First Continental Congress
Declaration of Independence
Excerpt from Life and Adventures of Colonel Daniel Boon
Excerpt from "Common Sense"
Eyewitness Account of the Boston Massacre
From Annapolis to Philadelphia

Indentured "White Slaves" in the Colonies
Letter Describing Catholic Missions in California
Letters of Abigail and John Adams
Letters of Eliza Wilkinson
Life at Valley Forge, 1777–1778
Logan's Speech
Massachusetts Circular Letter
Patrick Henry's Resolves
Paul Revere's Account of His Ride
Shays's Rebellion
Slave Andrew's Testimony in the Boston Massacre Trial
Stamp Act
The Call for Amendments
The Continental Association
The Pennsylvania Farmer's Remedy
Townshend Revenue Act
Treaty with the Six Nations, 1784
Virginia Declaration of Rights
Writ of Assistance

1789–1860:

PERTINENT TEXTBOOK CHAPTERS

American Passages
7. The Federalist Republic
8. The New Republic Faces a New Century, 1800–1814
9. Exploded Boundaries
10. The Years of Andrew Jackson, 1827–1836
11. Panic and Boom: 1837–1845
12. Expansion and Reaction: 1846–1854
13. Broken Bonds: 1855–1861

The American Past
11. We the People: Putting the Constitution to Work 1789–1800
12. The Age of Jefferson: Expansion and Frustration 1800–1815
13. Beyond the Appalachian Ridge: The West in the Early Nineteenth Century
14. Nation Awakening: Political, Diplomatic, and Economic Developments 1815–1824
15. Hero of the People: The Age of Andrew Jackson 1824–1830
16. In the Shadow of Old Hickory: Personalities and Politics 1830–1842
17. Sects, Utopias, Visionaries, Reformers: Popular Culture in Antebellum America
18. A Different Country: The South
19. The Peculiar Institution: Slavery as It Was Perceived and as It Was
20. From Sea to Shining Sea: American Expansion 1820–1848
21. Apples of Discord: The Poisoned Fruits of Victory 1844–1854
22. The Collapse of the Old Union: The Road to Secession 1854–1861

Liberty, Equality, Power
7. The Democratic Republic, 1790–1820
8. Completing the Revolution, 1789–1815
9. The Market Revolution, 1815–1860
10. Toward an American Culture
11. Society, Culture, and Politics, 1820s–1840s
12. Jacksonian Democracy
13. Manifest Destiny: An Empire for Liberty—or Slavery?
14. The Gathering Tempest, 1853–1860

DICTIONARY OF AMERICAN HISTORY ENTRIES

Articles
Ableman v. Booth
Address of the Southern Delegates
Alabama Platform
Alamo, Siege of the
Albany Regency
Albatross
Alcaldes
Alien and Sedition Laws
American Fur Company
American Party
American Republican Party
American System
Amistad Case
Anesthesia, Discovery of
Antelope Case
Antibank Movement
Anti-Rent War
Aroostook War
Astoria
Aurora
Baltimore Bell Teams
Bank of Augusta v. Earle
Barbary Wars
Bargemen
Barnburners
Barron v. Baltimore
Bathtubs and Bathing
Bear Flag Revolt
Beecher's Bibles
Black Hawk War
Black Laws
Bloomers
Blount Conspiracy
Bonus Bill of 1816
Border Ruffians
Border War
Bridger, Fort
Briscoe v. Bank of the Commonwealth of Kentucky
British Debts
Brown v. Maryland
Buena Vista, Battle of
Bullboats
Burns Fugitive Slave Case
Burr-Hamilton Duel

Calder v. Bull
Capitals
Chapultepec, Battle of
Charles River Bridge Case
Charlotte Town Resolves
Chesapeake-Leopard Incident
Chickasaw-Creek War
Chisholm v. Georgia
Christiana Fugitive Affair
Claim Associations
Clayton Compromise
Clayton-Bulwer Treaty
Cohens v. Virginia
Commonwealth v. Hunt
Compromise of 1790
Compromise of 1850
Conscience Whigs
Constitutional Union Party
Convention of 1800
Convention of 1818 With England
Cooley v. Board of Wardens of Port of Philadelphia
Corrupt Bargain
Cotton Gin
Cotton Kingdom
Craig v. State of Missouri
Creek War
Crystal Palace Exhibition
Cushing's Treaty
Dartmouth College Case
Dearborn Wagon
Debts, Revolutionary War
Decatur's Cruise to Algiers
Defiance, Fort
Democracy in America
Deposit Act of 1836
Detroit, Surrender of
Donner Party
Dorr's Rebellion
Doughfaces
Dred Scott Case
Drogher Trade
Eaton Affair
Embargo Act
Emerson's Essays
Emigrant Aid Movement
Entangling Alliances
Era of Good Feeling
Essex, Actions of the
Ex Parte Bollman
Fallen Timbers, Battle of
"Fifty-Four Forty or Fight"
Finney Revivals
Fire-Eaters
Fletcher v. Peck
Forty-Niners
France, Quasi-War with
Free Soil Party

Freeman's Expedition
Freeport Doctrine
Frémont Explorations
French Decrees
Friends of Domestic Industry
Fries' Rebellion
Fulton's Folly
Gabriel's Insurrection
Gadsden Purchase
Gag Rule, Antislavery
Gallatin's Report on Manufactures
Gallatin's Report on Roads
Georgia Platform
Ghent, Treaty of
Gibbons v. Ogden
Godey's Lady's Book
Gold Rush, California
Great Lakes Naval Campaigns of 1812
Guadalupe Hidalgo, Treaty of
Guano
Hamilton's Economic Policies
Harpers Ferry Raid
Harrisburg Convention
Hartford Convention
Hartford Wits
Hayburn's Case
Higher-Law Doctrine
Howard, Fort
Hudson River School
Hunkers
Hylton v. United States
Illinois Fur Brigade
Immediatism
Impeachment Trial of Samuel Chase
Impending Crisis of the South
Impressment of Seamen
Independent Treasury System
Indian Trade and Intercourse Act
Indian Trading Houses
Inland Lock Navigation
Intrepid
Irrepressible Conflict
Jacksonian Democracy
Jacobin Clubs
Jayhawkers
Jay's Treaty
Jefferson Territory
Johnny Appleseed
Joint Occupation
Jones v. Van Zandt
Judiciary Act of 1789
Judiciary Act of 1801
Kansas Committee, National
Kansas Free-State Party
Kansas-Nebraska Act
Kearny's March to California
Kearny's Mission to China

King Cotton
"Kitchen Cabinet"
Lafayette's Visit to America
Lake Erie, Battle of
Laramie, Fort
Laramie, Fort, Treaty of (1851)
Latin American Wars of Independence
Latrobe's Folly
Lawrence, Sack of
Leatherstocking Tales
Leavenworth Expedition
Lecompton Constitution
Levy
Lewis and Clark Expedition
Liberty Party
Liberty-Cap Cent
License Cases
Lincoln-Douglas Debates
Locofoco Party
Long, Stephen H., Explorations of
Louisiana Purchase
Lovejoy Riots
Luther v. Borden
McCulloch v. Maryland
McHenry, Fort
Macon's Bill No. 2
Mail, Southern Overland
Mandan, Fort
Marbury v. Madison
Marcy, R. B., Exploration of
Maria Monk Controversy
Married Women's Property Act, New York State
Martin v. Hunter's Lessee
Martin v. Mott
Maysville Veto
Mazzei Letter
Mechanics' Institutes
Mexican-American War
Mexico City, Capture of
Midnight Judges
Mims, Fort, Massacre at
Missouri Compromise
Moby-Dick
Monroe-Pinkney Treaty
Monterrey, Battles of
Mormon Battalion
Mormon Expedition
Mormon Handcart Companies
Mormon Trail
Mormon War
Morrill Act
Mountain Meadows Massacre
Muscle Shoals Speculation
Muster Day
My Country, Tis of Thee
Nashville Convention
Nat Turner's Rebellion

Natchez Campaign of 1813
National Republican Party
Nautilus
Nauvoo, Mormons at
Navigation Act of 1817
Navy, Confederate
New England Antislavery Society
New England Emigrant Aid Company
New Orleans
New Orleans, Battle of
Niagara Campaigns
Nonintercourse Act
Oberlin Movement
Oberlin-Wellington Rescue Case
Ogden v. Saunders
Old Hickory
Omnibus Bill
Oregon Treaty of 1846
Osborn v. Bank of the United States
Ostend Manifesto
"Our Federal Union! It Must Be Preserved!"
Overland Companies
Overseer and Driver
Oxford Movement
Pacific Fur Company
Peculiar Institution
Perry-Elliott Controversy
Perry's Expedition to Japan
Pet Banks
Philadelphia Cordwainers' Case
Philadelphia Riots
Pike, Zebulon, Expeditions of
Pikes Peak Gold Rush
Pinckney's Treaty
Plank Roads
Polk Doctrine
Pony Express
Popular Sovereignty
Pottawatomie Massacre
Prairie du Chien, Indian Treaty at
Prigg v. Commonwealth of Pennsylvania
Princeton, Explosion on the
Public Credit Act
Quids
Rail Splitter
Railroad Conventions
Red River Cart Traffic
"Remember the Alamo"
Removal Act of 1830
Removal of Deposits
Republicans, Jeffersonian
Richmond Junto
Rights of Man
Romanticism
Russian Claims
Safety Fund System
San Jacinto, Battle of

Savannah
Scarlet Letter, The
Seminole Wars
Seneca Falls Convention
Silhouettes
Slaughterhouse Cases
Slidell's Mission to Mexico
Smuggling of Slaves
Sons of the South
South Carolina Exposition and Protest
South Pass
Southern Rights Movement
Southwest Territory
Specie Circular
Spirit Lake Massacre
Star-Spangled Banner
Stockton-Kearny Quarrel
Stoney Creek, Battle of
Sturges v. Crowninshield
Suffolk Banking System
Survey Act of 1824
Sutter's Fort
Swift v. Tyson
Tallmadge Amendment
Tammany Societies
Tecumseh's Crusade
Texan Emigration and Land Company
Texas Navy
Texas Public Lands
Thames, Battle of the
"Tippecanoe and Tyler Too!"
Tippecanoe, Battle of
Tolls Exemption Act
Topeka Constitution
Trail of Tears
Transcendentalism
Tribute
Uncle Tom's Cabin
Underground Railroad
United Americans, Order of
Upper Peninsula of Michigan
Ursuline Convent, Burning of
Vancouver, George, Explorations of
Vanhorne's Lessee v. Dorrance
Vesey Rebellion
Virginia Dynasty
Wagoners of the Alleghenies
War Democrats
War Hawks
War of 1812
Ware v. Hylton
Washington Burned
Washington's Farewell Address
Wayne, Fort
"We Have Met the Enemy, and They Are Ours"
Webster-Ashburton Treaty
Webster-Hayne Debate

Webster-Parkman Murder Case
Whig Party
Whiskey Rebellion
Wildcat Money
Wilkes, Charles, Expedition of
Wilmot Proviso
Workingmen's Party
Wyandotte Constitution
XYZ Affair
Yakima Indian Wars
Yankee
Yazoo Fraud
Yellowstone River Expeditions
"Young America"

Maps: The Early Republic
An Exact Map of North America from the best Authorities (c. 1780)

Maps: The War of 1812
Attack on Fort Bowyer (1814)
Attack on New Orleans (1815)

Maps: The United States Expands
A Map of the eclipse of Feb.y 12th. in its passage across the United States (1831)
Map of the Northern parts of Ohio, Indiana and Illinois with Michigan, and that part of the Ouisconsin Territory Lying East of the Mississippi River (1836)
Map of the Western Territory &c. (1834)
North America (1812)
North America (1851)
Sketch of the Lower portion of the White Fish River (1857)

Maps: Texas and the Mexican War
Map of Texas and the Country Adjacent (1844)
Ornamental Map of the United States and Mexico (1848)
Untitled [map of U.S. and Mexico] (1849)

Maps: Transportation
A Complete Map of the Feather and Yuba Rivers, With Towns, Ranches, diggings, Roads, distances […] (1851)
Map of the Country between the Atlantic & Pacific Oceans […] shewing the proposed route of a Rail Road from the Mississippi Valley to the ports of St. Diego, Monterey, & St. Francisco […] (1848)
Map of the United States, Shewing the principal Steamboat routes and projected Railroads connecting with St. Louis. Compiled for the Missouri Republican, Jan 8[?], 1854

Maps: Gold Rush in California
Run for Gold, from all Nations, Geographically Explained (1849)

Map of the Gold Regions of California, Compiled from the best Surveys (1849)

Plan of Benicia, California; Founded by Thomas O. Larkin and R. Simple Esq'rs (1847)

California (1855)

Maps: New York: The Development of a City

Plan of the City of New York for the Use of Strangers (undated)

Primary Source Documents

A House Divided

A Pioneer Woman's Letter Home

American Party Platform

Americans in Their Moral, Social and Political Relations

Civil Disobedience

Constitution of the Committee of Vigilantes of San Francisco

Excerpt from Across the Plains to California in 1852

Excerpt from An Expedition to the Valley of the Great Salt Lake of Utah

Excerpt from Glimpse of New Mexico

Excerpt from Memories of the North American Invasion

Excerpt from Notes Illustrative of the Wrong of Slavery

Excerpt from On the Equality of the Sexes

Excerpt from Running a Thousand Miles for Freedom

Excerpt from Sociology for the South

Excerpt from The Impending Crisis of the South: How to Meet It

Excerpt from The Oregon Trail

Excerpt from The Vigilantes of Montana

Fort Laramie Treaty

Human Rights Not Founded on Sex, October 2, 1837

John Brown's Last Speech

Letter Replying to Manuel de la Peña y Peña

Life of Ma-ka-tai-me-she-kai-kiak, or Black Hawk

Madison's War Message

Message on the Lewis and Clark Expedition

Mill Worker's Letter on Hardships in the Textile Mills

National Songs, Ballads, and Other Patriotic Poetry, Chiefly Relating to the War of 1846

On the Underground Railroad

Polk's Message on the War with Mexico

Sleep Not Longer, O Choctaws and Chickasaws

South Carolina Declaration of Causes of Secession

Text of the Pro-Slavery Argument

The Journals of the Lewis and Clark Expedition

The Monroe Doctrine and the Roosevelt Corollary

The Nat Turner Insurrection

The Seneca Falls Declaration

The Story of Enrique Esparza

What If I Am a Woman?

When Woman Gets Her Rights Man Will Be Right

1861–1877:

PERTINENT TEXTBOOK CHAPTERS

American Passages

13. Broken Bonds: 1855–1861
14. Descent into War, 1861–1862
15. Blood and Freedom, 1863–1867
16. Reconstruction Abandoned, 1867–1877

The American Past

23. Tidy Plans, Ugly Realities: The Civil War 1861–1862
24. Driving Old Dixie Down: General Grant's War of Attrition 1863–1865
25. Reconstruction: Rebuilding the Shattered Union: 1863–1877
26. Parties, Patronage, and Pork: Politics in the Late Nineteenth Century
27. Big Industry, Big Business: Economic Development in the Late Nineteenth Century
28. Living with Leviathan: Americans React to Big Business and Great Wealth
29. We Who Made America: Factories and Immigrant Ships
30. Bright Lights and Squalid Slums: The Growth of Big Cities
31. The Last Frontier: Winning the Rest of the West 1865–1900
32. Stressful Times down Home: The Crisis of American Agriculture 1865–1896

Liberty, Equality, Power

15. Secession and Civil War, 1860–1862
16. A New Birth of Freedom, 1862–1865
17. Reconstruction, 1863–1877
18. Frontiers of Change: Politics of Stalemate, 1865–1890

DICTIONARY OF AMERICAN HISTORY ENTRIES

Articles

Abilene Trail

Alabama

Alabama Claims

Andersonville Prison

Antietam, Battle of

Antimonopoly Parties

Appomattox

Army of the Potomac

Army, Confederate

Army, Union

Army of the James

Army of Virginia

Army of Northern Virginia

Arrest, Arbitrary, during the Civil War

Atlanta Campaign

Baltimore Riot

Battle Hymn of the Republic

Belknap Scandal
Black Codes
Black Friday
Black Hills War
Bland-Allison Act
Blockade Runners, Confederate
Bloody Shirt
Blue and Gray
Border Slave State Convention
Bounty Jumper
Brady Photographs
Bronson v. Rodes
Bull Run, First Battle of
Bull Run, Second Battle of
Burlingame Treaty
Butler's Order No. 28
Canada, Confederate Activities in
Caroline Affair
Carpetbaggers
Catlin's Indian Paintings
Centennial Exhibition
Central Pacific-Union Pacific Race
Chancellorsville, Battle of
Chattanooga Campaign
Chickamauga, Battle of
Civil Rights Act of 1866
Civil Rights Act of 1875
Civil War
Civil War General Order No. 100
Cold Harbor, Battle of
Collector v. Day
Colorado River Explorations
Columbia, Burning of
Committee on the Conduct of the War
Comstock Lode
Confederate Agents
Confederate Expatriates in Brazil
Confederate States of America
Confiscation Acts
Conspiracies Acts of 1861 and 1862
Contraband, Slaves as
Cooke, Jay, and Company
Cotton Money
Crédit Mobilier of America
Crime of 1873
Crittenden Compromise
Cumberland, Army of the
Cummings v. Missouri
Dakota Expeditions of Sibley and Sully
Dakota Territory
"Damn the Torpedoes"
Davis, Imprisonment and Trial of
Davis-Johnston Controversy
Donelson, Fort, Capture of
Draft Riots
Elmira Prison
Emancipation Proclamation

Embalmed Beef
Ex Parte Garland
Ex Parte McCardle
Ex Parte Merryman
Ex Parte Milligan
Far West
Fisk Expeditions
"Forty Acres and a Mule"
Fredericksburg, Battle of
Freedmen's Bureau
Galvanized Yankees
Gelpcké v. Dubuque
General Order No. 38
Georgia v. Stanton
Gettysburg Address
Gettysburg, Battle of
Gilded Age
Gold Act
Gold Exchange
Granger Cases
Granger Movement
Greenbacks
Hamburg Riot
Hampton Roads Conference
Harpers Ferry, Capture of
Hays, Fort
"Hell on Wheels"
Hood's Tennessee Campaign
Horizontal Tariff Bill
House Divided
Impeachment Trial of Andrew Johnson
Impressment, Confederate
Indian Brigade
Indians in the Civil War
Inflation in the Confederacy
Ironclad Oath
Island Number Ten, Operations at
Joint Committee on Reconstruction
Kasserine Pass, Battle of
Kenesaw Mountain, Battle of
Korea War of 1871
Laramie, Fort, Treaty of (1868)
Legal Tender Act
Little Bighorn, Battle of
Lookout Mountain, Battle on
"Lost Cause"
Marion, Battle at
Maryland, Invasion of
Mexican-American War Claims
Mexico, Confederate Migration to
Mexico, French in
Mineral Patent Law
Minor v. Happersett
Mississippi v. Johnson
Mobile Bay, Battle of
Modoc War
Molly Maguires

Monitor and *Merrimack*, Battle of
Montgomery Convention
Morgan's Raids
Mortars, Civil War Naval
Mosby's Rangers
Mulligan Letters
Munn v. Illinois
Nashville, Battle of
National Union (Arm-in-Arm) Convention
Navajo War
New Orleans, Capture of
New Orleans Riots
New York City, Plot to Burn
Northfield Bank Robbery
Northwest Conspiracy
Ohio Idea
Peace Movement of 1864
Peninsular Campaign
Pennsylvania, Invasion of
Perryville, Battle of
Petersburg, Siege of
Pickett's Charge
Pillow, Fort, Massacre at
Pipelines, Early
Pithole
Powhatan Incident
Prisoners of War: Prison Camps, Confederate
Prisoners of War: Prison Camps, Union
Prize Cases, Civil War
Progress and Poverty
Quantrill's Raid
Railroad Strike of 1877
Railroads In the Civil War
Rams, Confederate
Readjuster Movement
Reconstruction
Red River Campaign
Red River Indian War
Red Shirts
Regulators
Resumption Act
Richmond Campaigns
Saint Albans Raid
Sand Creek Massacre
Sanitary Commission, United States
Savannah, Siege of (1864)
Scalawag
Seal of the Confederate States of America
Secession
Seven Days' Battles
Shelby's Mexican Expedition
Shenandoah Campaign
Sheridan's Ride
Sherman's March to the Sea
Shiloh, Battle of
Singleton Peace Plan
Sioux Uprising in Minnesota

Society for the Prevention of Cruelty to Children
Sons of Liberty (Civil war)
Southern Commercial Conventions
Southern Unionists
Sovereigns of Industry
Spotsylvania Courthouse, Battle of
Star of the West
Stuart's Ride
Substitutes, Civil War
Sumter, Fort
Ten-Forties
Tennessee, Army of
Tenure of Office Act
Texas v. White
Timber Culture Act
Tithes, Southern Agricultural
Trent Affair
Tweed Ring
Twenty-One Gun Salute
Union Party
Union Sentiment in Border States
Union Sentiment in the South
United States v. Cruikshank
United States v. Reese
Vallandigham Incident
Veazie Bank v. Fenno
Vicksburg in the Civil War
Vicksburg Riots
Wade-Davis Bill
Washington, Treaty of
Whiskey Ring
White League
Wilderness, Battles of the
Wormley Conference

Maps: The Civil War
Sketch of the country occupied by Federal and Confederate Armies (1861)
Map of the United States, Showing the Territory in Possession of the Federal Union (1864)
Plan of Cantonment Sprague near Washington, D.C. (1861)
White House to Harrison's Landing (1862)

Primary Source Documents
A Confederate Blockade-Runner
Address to President Lincoln by the Working-Men of Manchester, England
Benjamin Butler's Report on Contrabands of War
Black Code of Mississippi, November, 1865
Congress Debates the Fourteenth Amendment
Emancipation Proclamation
Excerpt from Half a Century
Excerpt from My Army Life
Excerpt from Roughing It
Excerpt from The Crime Against Kansas
Gettysburg Address

Head of Choctow Nation Reaffirms His Tribe's Position
Lee's Farewell to His Army
Letter to President Lincoln from Harrison's Landing
Letters from Widows to Lincoln Asking for Help
Lincoln's Second Inaugural Address
Police Regulations of Saint Landry Parish, Louisiana
President Andrew Johnson's Civil Rights Bill Veto
Prisoner at Andersonville
Speech of Little Crow on the Eve of the Great Sioux
      Uprising
Women in the Farmers' Alliance

1878–1920:

PERTINENT TEXTBOOK CHAPTERS

American Passages
17. The Economic Transformation of America, 1877–1887
18. Urban Growth and Farm Protest
19. Domestic Turmoil and Overseas Expansion, 1893–1901
20. Theodore Roosevelt and Progressive Reform
21. Progressivism at its Height
22. Over There and Over Here: The Impact of World War I

The American Past
26. Parties, Patronage, and Pork: Politics in the Late Nineteenth Century
27. Big Industry, Big Business: Economic Development in the Late Nineteenth Century
28. Living with Leviathan: Americans React to Big Business and Great Wealth
29. We Who Made America: Factories and Immigrant Ships
30. Bright Lights and Squalid Slums: The Growth of Big Cities
31. The Last Frontier: Winning the Rest of the West 1865–1900
32. Stressful Times down Home: The Crisis of American Agriculture 1865–1896
33. In the Days of McKinley: The United States Becomes a World Power 1896–1903
34. Theodore Roosevelt and the Good Old Days: American Society in Transition 1890–1917
35. Age of Reform: The Progressives after 1900
36. Victors at Armageddon: The Progressives in Power 1901–1916
37. Over There: The United States and the First World War 1914–1918
38. Over Here: World War I at Home 1917–1920

Liberty, Equality, Power
18. Frontiers of Change: Politics of Stalemate, 1865–1890
19. Economic Change and the Crisis of the 1890s

20. An Industrial Society, 1890–1920
21. Progressivism
22. Becoming a World Power, 1898–1917
23. War and Society, 1914–1920

DICTIONARY OF AMERICAN HISTORY ENTRIES
Articles
ABC Conference
Adamson Act
Addyston Pipe Company Case
Aisne-Marne Operation
Aldrich-Vreeland Act
Algeciras Conference
Allison Commission
Amalgamated Clothing Workers of America
American Expeditionary Forces
American Expeditionary Forces In Italy
American Federation of State, County, and Municipal Employees
American Federation of Teachers
American Museum of Natural History
American Protective Association
American Railway Union
American Tobacco Case
Anaconda Copper
Anthracite Strike
Anti-Imperialists
Archangel Campaign
Armistice of November 1918
Army of Occupation
Ballinger-Pinchot Controversy
Battle Fleet Cruise Around the World
Bayard-Chamberlain Treaty
Beef Trust Cases
Belgian Relief
Belleau Wood, Battle of
Berea College v. Kentucky
Birth of a Nation, The
Black Horse Cavalry
Boomer Movement
Boston Police Strike
Bourbons
Boxer Rebellion
Brotherhood of Sleeping Car Porters
Brownsville Affair
Bryan-Chamorro Treaty
Bull Moose Party
Burke Act
Burlington Strike
Carlisle Indian Industrial School
Century of Dishonor
Champagne-Marne Operation
Château-Thierry Bridge, Americans at
Chautauqua Movement
Chicago, Milwaukee, and Saint Paul Railway Company v. Minnesota
Chinese Exclusion Act

Cimarron, Proposed Territory of
Cincinnati Riots
Citizens' Alliances
Civil Aeronautics Act
Clayton Act, Labor Provisions
Cleveland Democrats
Coeur d'Alene Riots
Coin's Financial School
Colorado Coal Strikes
Commerce, Court of
Committee on Public Information
Communication Workers of America
Compromise of 1890
Consumerism
Coppage v. Kansas
Council of National Defense
Coxey's Army
Cripple Creek Mining Boom
Cripple Creek Strikes
Cross of Gold Speech
Danbury Hatters' Case
Dawes Commission
Dawes General Allotment Act
De Lima v. Bidwell
Depletion Allowances
Dreadnought
Dull Knife Campaign
Electrical Workers
Elkins Act
Emergency Fleet Corporation
Equal Rights Party
Espionage Act
Farmer-Labor Party of 1920
Farmers' Alliance
Field v. Clark
Foraker Act
"Forgotten Man"
Four Hundred
Fourteen Points
Fuel Administration
"Full Dinner Pail"
Gold Bugs
Gold Democrats
Great Train Robbery, The
Greely Arctic Expedition
Guinn and Beal v. United States
Hague Peace Conferences
Hay-Bunau-Varilla Treaty
Hay-Herrán Treaty
Hay-Pauncefote Treaties
Haymarket Riot
Haywood-Moyer-Pettibone Case
Hepburn Act
Homestead Strike
House-Grey Memorandum
Huckleberry Finn
Hurtado v. California

In Re Debs
In Re Neagle
Income Tax Cases
Industrial Workers of the World
Inland Waterways Commission
Insular Cases
Interests
International Harvester Company
International Ladies Garment Workers Union
International Longshoremen's and Warehousemen's
    Union
Japanese Cherry Trees
Johnstown Flood
Jones Act
Juilliard v. Greenman
Jungle, The
Kearneyites
Kelly's Industrial Army
Klondike Rush
Lafayette Escadrille
"Lafayette, We Are Here"
Lawrence Strike
League of Nations
Legal Tender Cases
Lever Act
Liberal Republican Party
Liberty Loans
Lochner v. New York
London, Declaration of
Lost Battalion
Louisiana Purchase Exposition
Lusitania, Sinking of the
McCray v. United States
McNamara Case
Mafia Incident
Maine, Sinking of the
Manila Bay, Battle of
Mann Act
Meat Inspection Laws
Merrimac, Sinking of
Metropolitan Museum of Art
Meuse-Argonne Offensive
Mexico, Punitive Expedition into
Middle-of-the-Road Populists
Missouri v. Holland
Morgan-Belmont Agreement
Muckrakers
Mugler v. Kansas
Mugwumps
Mussel Slough Incident
National Monetary Commission
National Trades' and Workers' Association
National War Labor Board, World War I
National Woman's Party
New Freedom
New Nationalism
Niagara Movement

Nickelodeon
Normalcy
North Sea Mine Barrage
Northern Securities Company v. United States
Ocala Platform
Occupational Health and Safety Act
Oil Fields
Olney Corollary
Oregon System
Packers' Agreement
Palmer Raids
Pan-American Exposition
Panama Revolution
Paris, Treaty of (1898)
Pendleton Act
Pension Act, Arrears of
Philippine Insurrection
Platt Amendment
Plessy v. Ferguson
Plumb Plan
Pollock v. Farmers' Loan and Trust Company
Populism
Portsmouth, Treaty of
Preparedness
Progressive Movement
Promontory Point
"Public Be Damned"
Pujo Committee
Pullman Strike
Railroad Administration, U.S.
Railroad Rate Law
Railroad Strikes of 1886
Reed Rules
Roosevelt Corollary
Root Arbitration Treaties
Root Mission
Root-Takahira Agreement
Rough Riders
Rustler War
Saint-Mihiel, Campaigns at
Sampson-Schley Controversy
San Juan Hill and El Caney, Battles of
Schenck v. United States
Seamen's Act of 1915
Selden Patent
Sequoyah, Proposed State of
Sherman Antitrust Act
Sherman Silver Purchase Act
Shreveport Rate Case
Siberian Expedition
Silver Democrats
Silver Republican Party
Single Tax
Sino-Japanese War
Smith-Hughes Act
Smith-Lever Act
Social Democratic Party

Somme Offensive
Sooners
Souls of Black Folk, The
Southern Tenant Farmers' Union
Spanish-American War
Spanish-American War, Navy in
Springer v. United States
Square Deal
Stalwarts
Standard Oil Company of New Jersey v. United States
Star Route Frauds
Statue of Liberty
Strauder v. West Virginia
Sussex Case
Syndicalism
Taft Commission
Taft-Katsura Memorandum
Taft-Roosevelt Split
Telephone Cases
Teller Amendment
Tillmanism
Titanic, Sinking of the
Transportation Act of 1920
Triangle Shirtwaist Fire
Trust-Busting
Union Labor Party
United States v. E. C. Knight Company
United States v. Harris
United States v. Lee
United States v. Trans-Missouri Freight Association
United States v. Wong Kim Ark
Veracruz Incident
Versailles, Treaty of
Victory Loan of 1919
Villa Raid at Columbus
Virginia v. West Virginia
Volstead Act
Wall Street Explosion
War Industries Board
War Trade Board
Washington Monument
Weeks Act
Western Federation of Miners
White Caps
"White Squadron"
Williams v. Mississippi
Wilmington Riot
Wisconsin Idea
World War I
World War I Training Camps
World War I War Debts
World War I, Economic Mobilization for
World War I, Navy in
World War I, U.S. Relief in
Wounded Knee Massacre
"Yellow Peril"

Maps: New York: The Development of a City
A map of Manhattan issued as a publicity brochure by
   the Navarre Hotel (1913)

Primary Source Documents
A Letter from Wovoka
A Soldier's Account of the Spanish-American War, 1898
America's War Aims: The Fourteen Points
Conditions in Meatpacking Plants
Excerpt from A Century of Dishonor
Excerpt from Path Breaking
Excerpt from Peace and Bread in Time of War
Excerpt from The Principles of Scientific Management
Excerpt from The Theory of the Leisure Class
Excerpt from The War in Its Effect upon Women
Gentlemen's Agreement
In the Slums
Letters from the Front, World War I, 1918
Lyrics of "Over There"
Platform of the Anti-imperialist League, 1899
The Pullman Strike and Boycott
Women in Industry (Brandeis Brief)
Women in the Farmers' Alliance

1921–1945:

PERTINENT TEXTBOOK CHAPTERS

American Passages
23. The Age of Jazz and Mass Culture
24. The Great Depression
25. The New Deal, 1933–1939
26. The Second World War, 1940–1945

The American Past
39. In the Days of Harding: Time of Uncertainty
   1919–1923
40. Calvin Coolidge and the New Era: When America
   Was a Business 1923–1929
41. National Trauma: The Great Depression 1930–1933
42. Rearranging America: Franklin D. Roosevelt and
   the New Deal 1933–1938
43. Headed for War Again: Foreign Relations
   1933–1942
44. America's Great War: The United States at the Pin-
   nacle of Power 1942–1945

Liberty, Equality, Power
24. The 1920s
25. The Great Depression and the New Deal, 1929–1939
26. America during the Second World War

DICTIONARY OF AMERICAN HISTORY ENTRIES
Articles
Aachen
Abraham Lincoln Brigade

Adkins v. Children's Hospital
Airmail
America First Committee
American Dilemma, An
American Indian Defense Association
American Liberty League
Anzio
Ashcan School
Atlantic Charter
Atlantic, Battle of the
Bankhead Cotton Act
Banking: Banking Acts of 1933 and 1935
Banking: Banking Crisis of 1933
Bastogne
Bataan-Corregidor Campaign
Berlin, Treaty of
Bismarck Sea, Battle of
Blue Eagle Emblem
Bonus Army
Bougainville
Brain Trust
Bretton Woods Conference
Buenos Aires Peace Conference
Bulge, Battle of the
Burma Road and Ledo Road
Cairo Conferences
California Alien Land Law
Capper-Volstead Act
Caroline Islands
Carter v. Carter Coal Company
Casablanca Conference
Centralia Mine Disaster
Cherbourg
China Clipper
Citizen Kane
Civilian Conservation Corps
Codes of Fair Competition
Commodities Exchange Act
Coral Sea, Battle of the
Council of Economic Advisors
Dawes Plan
D Day
Depression of 1920
Dumbarton Oaks Conference
Economic Royalists
Elbe River
Empire State Building
Employment Act of 1946
EPIC
Erie Railroad Company v. Tompkins
Export Debenture Plan
Fair Labor Standards Act
Farm Security Administration
Farmer-Labor Party of Minnesota
Federal Mediation and Conciliation Service
Five-Power Naval Treaty
Flying the Hump

Flying Tigers
Four Freedoms
Four-Power Treaty
Frazier-Lemke Farm Bankruptcy Act
Gastonia Strike
German-American Bund
German-American Debt Agreement
Gilbert Islands
Glass-Steagall Act
Gold Clause Cases
Gold Purchase Plan
Gold Reserve Act
Golden Gate Bridge
Good Neighbor Policy
Gothic Line
Grain Futures Act
Great Gatsby, The
Grosjean v. American Press Company
Guadalcanal Campaign
Guffey Coal Acts
Gustav Line
Hague v. Committee on Industrial Organization
Harlem Renaissance
Hatch Act
Hiss Case
Home Owners' Loan Corporation
Hoover Dam
How to Win Friends and Influence People
Humphrey's Executor v. United States
Iceland, U.S. Forces in
Indian Reorganization Act
Iwo Jima
Japanese American Incarceration
Java Sea, Battle of
Jazz Singer, The
Kellogg-Briand Pact
Keynesianism
"Kilroy Was Here"
La Follette Civil Liberties Committee Hearings
Lame-Duck Amendment
Lausanne Agreement
Lend-Lease
Let Us Now Praise Famous Men
Leyte Gulf, Battle of
Lindbergh Kidnapping Case
Lindbergh's Atlantic Flight
Lingayen Gulf
London Naval Treaties
Lost Generation
Ludlow Resolution
McFadden Banking Act
McNary-Haugen Bill
Malmédy Massacre
Manhattan Project
Marshall Islands
Meriam Report
Merrill's Marauders

Midway, Battle of
Minnesota Moratorium Case
Missouri ex rel Gaines v. Canada
Monte Cassino
Mooney Case
Moratorium, Hoover
Myers v. United States
National Congress of American Indians
National Labor Relations Act
National Labor Relations Board v. Jones and Laughlin Steel Corporation
National Recovery Administration
National Union for Social Justice
National War Labor Board, WWII
Near v. Minnesota
Nebbia v. New York
New Deal
New Era
Normandy Invasion
Norris-La Guardia Act
North African Campaign
Office of Strategic Services
Okinawa
Packers and Stockyards Act
Panama Refining Company v. Ryan
Panay Incident
Pearl Harbor
Peleliu
Philippine Sea, Battle of the
Pierce v. Society of Sisters
Ploesti Oil Fields, Air Raids on
Potsdam Conference
Progressive Party, 1924
Rabaul Campaign
Railroad Retirement Acts
Railroad Retirement Board v. Alton Railroad Company
Railway Shopmen's Strike
Reconstruction Finance Corporation
Reparation Commission
Resettlement Administration
Robinson-Patman Act
Sacco-Vanzetti Case
Saint-Lô
Saipan
Salerno
Schechter Poultry Corporation v. United States
Scottsboro Case
Share-the-Wealth Movements
Sheppard-Towner Maternity and Infancy Protection Act
Sicilian Campaign
Siegfried Line
Sit-down Strikes
Smith Act
Stafford v. Wallace
Tarawa
Task Force 58
Teapot Dome Oil Scandal

Technocracy Movement
Teheran Conference
Tinian
Townsend Plan
Tripartite Agreement
Truax v. Corrigan
Tydings-McDuffie Act
Unconditional Surrender
United Nations Declaration
United States v. Butler
Unknown Soldier, Tomb of the
Wake, Defense of
Walsh-Healy Act
Washington Naval Conference
West Coast Hotel Company v. Parrish
Wickersham Commission
Wisconsin Railroad Commission v. Chicago, Burlington and Quincy Railroad
Wolff Packing Company v. Court of Industrial Relations
Works Progress Administration
World Economic Conference
World War II
World War II, Air War against Japan
World War II, Air War against Germany
World War II, Navy in
Yalta Conference
Yap Mandate
Young Plan
Youth Administration, National

Primary Source Documents
Advice to the Unemployed in the Great Depression
"America First" Speech
Dedicating the Tomb of the Unknown Soldier
Excerpt from Land of the Spotted Eagle
Excerpt from Who Shall be Educated?
Fireside Chat on the Bank Crisis
Ford Men Beat And Rout Lewis
Franklin D. Roosevelt's Message on War Against Japan
Hobby's Army
Letter to Franklin Roosevelt on Job Discrimination
Living in the Dust Bowl
Pachucos in the Making
Power
Proclamation on Immigration Quotas
Total Victory
Vanzetti's Last Statement
War and The Family
Women Working in World War II

1946–1974:

PERTINENT TEXTBOOK CHAPTERS

American Passages
27. Post-War America, 1946–1952

28. The White House Years, 1953–1960
29. Turbulent Years, 1961–1968
30. Crisis of Confidence, 1969–1980

The American Past
45. Anxiety Time: The United States in the Early Nuclear Age 1946–1952
46. Eisenhower Country: American Life in the 1950s
47. Consensus and Camelot: The Eisenhower and Kennedy Administrations 1953–1963
48. Years of Turbulence: Conflict at Home and Abroad 1961–1968
49. Presidency in Crisis: Policies of the Nixon, Ford, and Carter Administrations 1968–1980

Liberty, Equality, Power
27. The Age of Containment, 1946–1954
28. Affluence and Its Discontents, 1954–1963
29. America during Its Longest War, 1963–1974

***DICTIONARY OF AMERICAN HISTORY* ENTRIES**

Articles
ACTION
Air Cavalry
Air Force Academy
Alaska Native Claims Settlement Act
All in the Family
Alliance For Progress
American Independent Party
American Indian Movement
Anticommunism
Association on American Indian Affairs
AT&T Divestiture
Attica
Autobiography of Malcolm X
Automation
Backlash
Baker Case
Baker v. Carr
Bay of Pigs Invasion
Beat Generation
Berlin Airlift
Berlin Wall
Bermuda Conferences
Beyond the Melting Pot
Black Panthers
Black Power
Brannan Plan
Bricker Amendment
Brown v. Board of Education of Topeka
Busing
Cambodia Incursion
Cambodia, Bombing of
Chicago Seven
Civil Rights Act of 1957
Civil Rights Act of 1964
Civil Rights Movement

Cold War
Columbia River Treaty
Communication Satellites
Community Action Program
Cuban Missile Crisis
Doves and Hawks
Downsizing
Eagleton Affair
Eisenhower Doctrine
Equal Employment Opportunity Commission
Existentialism
Fair Deal
Family Education Rights and Privacy Act
Family of Man Exhibition
Feminine Mystique, The
Freedom Riders
Geneva Accords of 1954
Great Society
Hidden Persuaders, The
Hoover Commissions
House Committee on Un-American Activities
Hydrogen Bomb
Indian Civil Rights Act
Indian Claims Commission
International Geophysical Year
Interstate Highway System
Invisible Man
Iron Curtain
ITT Affair
Kent State Protest
Kerner Commission
Kinsey Report
Korean War
Korean War, Air Combat in
Lebanon, U.S. Landing in
Legislative Reorganization Act, 1946
Liberty Incident
Lonely Crowd, The
McCarran-Walter Act
McClellan Committee Hearings
Marshall Plan
Miranda v. Arizona
Moon Landing
Nader's Raiders
National Council of Churches
New Frontier
New Left
Nixon, Resignation of
Nuclear Test Ban Treaty
Organization of Afro-American Unity
Paris Conferences
Pentagon Papers
Point Four
Powell Case
Power of Positive Thinking, The
Pueblo Incident
Quiz Show Scandals

Red Power
Revenue Sharing
Rio de Janeiro Conference
Roe v. Wade
Rosenberg Case
Saint Lawrence Seaway
Silent Spring
Software Industry
Southeast Asia Treaty Organizations
Strategic Arms Limitation Talks
Student Nonviolent Coordinating Committee
Students for a Democratic Society
Suez Crisis
Taft-Hartley Act
Termination Policy
Tet Offensive
Thresher Disaster
Tonkin Gulf Resolution
Truman Doctrine
Unit Rule
United Nations Conference
Vatican II
Vietnam War
Vietnamization
Voting Rights Act of 1965
War Crimes Trials
War on Poverty
Warren Commission
Watergate
White Citizens Councils
Wise Men
Women's Educational Equity Act
X-1 Plane
Youth Movements

Primary Source Documents

A Personal Narrative of the Korean War
An Interview with Fannie Lou Hamer
Black Power Speech
Constitutional Faith
Eisenhower's Farewell Address
Excerpt from American Diplomacy
Excerpt from Chicano Nationalism: The Key to Unity
    for La Raza
Excerpt from The Blue Book of the John Birch Society
Excerpt from the Pentagon Papers
Excerpts from Dear America: Letters Home from Viet-
    nam
General Douglas MacArthur's Speech to Congress
Letter to Nguyen Van Thieu
Lyndon B. Johnson's Speech Declining to Seek Re-elec-
    tion
NOW Statement of Purpose
President Gerald R. Ford's Proclamation 4311, Granting
    a Pardon to Richard Nixon
Statement by Committee Seeking Peace with Freedom
    in Vietnam

Student Nonviolent Coordinating Committee Founding Statement
The Arrest of Rosa Parks
The Christmas Bombing of Hanoi was Justified
Vietnamization and Silent Majority
Voice from Moon: The Eagle Has Landed
War Story
Watergate Investigation Address

1975–2002:

PERTINENT TEXTBOOK CHAPTERS

American Passages
30. Crisis of Confidence, 1969–1980
31. The Reagan-Bush Years
32. Toward the Twenty-First Century: The Clinton Presidency

The American Past
49. Presidency in Crisis: Policies of the Nixon, Ford, and Carter Administrations 1968–1980
50. Morning in America: The Reagan Era 1980–1993
51. Millennium: Frustration, Anger, Division, Values

Liberty, Equality, Power
30. Economic and Social Change in the Late 20th Century
31. Power and Politics since 1974

DICTIONARY OF AMERICAN HISTORY ENTRIES

Articles
Abscam Scandal
Achille Lauro
Acquired Immune Deficiency Syndrome
ACT UP
Aerobics
Affirmative Action
Afghanistan, Soviet Invasion of
Africa, Relations with
Agent Orange
Agriculture, Department of
AIDS Quilt
Air Pollution
Air Traffic Controllers Strike
Aircraft Industry
Airline Deregulation Act
Alaskan Pipeline
Albuquerque
Alzheimer's Disease
America's Cup
American Association of Retired Persons
American Indian Religious Freedom Act
Americans with Disabilities Act
Americorps
Ames Espionage Case

Archives
Arms Race and Disarmament
Artificial Intelligence
Assimilation
Astronomy
Atlantic City
Automobile Industry
Automobile Workers v. Johnson Controls, Inc.
Bakke v. Regents of the University of California
Baltimore
Baseball
Basketball
Beirut Bombing
Bicentennial
Biochemistry
Biological Containment
Bionics
Bioregionalism
Biosphere 2
Bitburg Controversy
Black Monday Stock Market Crash
Bork Confirmation Hearings
Boston
Botany
Brady Bill
Budget, Federal
Cardiovascular Disease
Carter Doctrine
Caucuses, Congressional
Celebrity Culture
Centers for Disease Control & Prevention
Challenger Disaster
Child Care
Children, Missing
China, Relations with
Chronic Fatigue Syndrome
Cincinnati
Citizens Band (CB) Radio
Civil Rights Act of 1991
Civil Rights Restoration Act of 1987
Clean Air Act
Clean Water Act
Clubs, Exclusionary
Cold Nuclear Fusion
College Athletics
Columbus Quincentenary
Communications Industry
Compact Discs
Comparable Worth
Computers and Computer Industry
Congress, United States
Conservation Biology
Contra Aid
Contract with America
Cost of Living Adjustment
Courier Services
Craig v. Boren

Credit Cards
Crown Heights Riots
Cuba, Relations with
Cuban Americans
Cultural Literacy
Cybernetics
Cyborgs
Dalkon Shield
Death and Dying
Defense, Department of
Dentistry
Denver
Deregulation
Desegregation
Detroit
Direct Mail
Discos
Domestic Violence
"Don't Ask, Don't Tell"
Earthquakes
Economic Indicators
Education, Cooperative
Education, Department of
Education, Experimental
Education, Higher: African American Colleges
Education, Parental Choice in
Educational Technology
El Paso
Employment Retirement Income Security Act
Endangered Species
Energy Industry
Energy Research and Development Administration
Energy, Department of
Energy, Renewable
Enterprise Zones
Environmental Business
Environmental Movement
Environmental Protection Agency
Equal Pay Act
European Union
Euthanasia
Exxon Valdez
Family and Medical Leave Act
Federal Bureau of Investigation
Fertilizers
Fiber Optics
Filipino Americans
Financial Services Industry
Food and Drug Administration
Food, Fast
Football
Foreign Investment in the United States
Fort Worth
Foster Care
Free Universities
Freedom of Information Act
Frontiero v. Richardson

Gambling
Gay and Lesbian Movement
General Accounting Office
General Agreement on Tariffs and Trade
General Electric Company v. Gilbert
Genetic Engineering
Gentrification
Geology
Global Warming
Golf
Graffiti
Gramm-Rudman-Hollings Act
Grenada Invasion
Griggs v. Duke Power Company
Griswold v. Connecticut
Gulf of Sidra Shootdown
Gun Control
Hairstyles
Haiti, Relations with
Harris v. McRae
Head Start
Health and Human Services, Department of
Health Care
Health Food Industry
Health Maintenance Organizations
Heart Implants
Helsinki Accords
Hispanic Americans
Home Shopping Networks
Hostage Crises
Housing
Hubble Space Telescope
Human Genome Project
Hydroponics
Indian Rights Association
Indianapolis
International Brotherhood of Teamsters v. United States
Internet
Iran-Contra Affair
Iranian Americans
Iraq-gate
Iraqi Americans
Israeli-Palestinian Peace Accord
Japan, Relations with
Jewish Defense League
Jews
Jonestown Massacre
Junk Bonds
Justice, Department of
Korea-gate
Korean Airlines Flight 007
Laffer Curve Theory
Laser Technology
Latin America, Relations with
Legionnaires' Disease
Leveraged Buyouts
Libraries

Life Expectancy
Los Angeles Riots
Love Canal
Loving v. Virginia
LSD
Lyme Disease
Manners and Etiquette
Mariel Boatlift
Marine Biology
Marriage
Medicare and Medicaid
Mental Illness
Meritor Savings Bank v. Mechelle Vinson
Microbiology
Military Base Closings
Millennialism
Milwaukee
Minneapolis-St. Paul
Moral Majority
Mount St. Helens
Multiculturalism
Music Television
National Association for the Advancement of Colored
    People
Native American Graves Protection and Repatriation
    Act
Native American Rights Fund
Neoconservatism
New York City
9/11 Attack
North American Free Trade Agreement
North Atlantic Treaty Organization
Nuclear Non-Proliferation Treaty
Nuclear Regulatory Commission
Office Technology
Offshore Oil
Oklahoma City Bombing
Olympic Games, American Participation in
Options Exchanges
Paleontology
Palimony
Pan Am Flight 103
Panama Canal Treaty
Panama Invasion
Peace Movements
Pentecostal Churches
Persian Gulf War
Personnel Administrator of Massachusetts v. Feeney
Planned Parenthood of Southeastern Pennsylvania v. Casey
Political Correctness
Pregnancy Discrimination Act
Printing Industry
Prizefighting
Prizes and Awards: MacArthur Foundation "Genius"
    Awards
Prizes and Awards: Nobel Prizes
Pro-Choice Movement

Pro-Life Movement
Product Tampering
Publishing Industry
Pure Food and Drug Movement
Pyramid Schemes
Rainbow Coalition
Reaganomics
Real Estate Industry
Recycling
Redlining
Reed v. Reed
Refugee Act of 1980
Reorganized Church of Jesus Christ of Latter-day Saints
Retailing Industry
Richmond v. J. A. Croson Company
Robberies
Roberts et al. v. United States Jaycees
Rockefeller Commission Report
Roots
Rotary International v. Rotary Club of Duarte
Ruby Ridge
Rust v. Sullivan
Rust Belt
Saint Louis
San Diego
Santa Clara Pueblo v. Martinez
Scandals
Schools, For-Profit
Scientific Fraud
Semiconductors
Set-Asides
Sexual Harassment
Sexually Transmitted Diseases
Skiing
Soccer
Son-of-Sam Law
Sports
Star Wars
State, Department of
Strategic Defense Initiative
Superconducting Super Collider
Superfund
Supply-Side Economics
Surrogate Motherhood
Tailhook Incident
Taylor v. Louisiana
Telecommunications
Televangelism
Tennis
Terrorism
Textbooks
Thomas Confirmation Hearings
Three Mile Island
Tiananmen Square Protest
Times Beach
Tourism
Tower Commission

Toxic Shock Syndrome
Toxic Substance Control Act
United States–Canada Free Trade Agreement
Unsafe at Any Speed
Veterans Affairs, Department of
Vice President, U.S.
Video Games
Vietnam War Memorial
Violence Against Women Act
Virtual Reality
Voice of America
Volcanoes
Volunteer Army
Waco Siege
Ward's Cove Packing Co., Inc., v. Atonio
Webster v. Reproductive Health Services
Wine Industry
Women in Military Service
Women's Health

Megan's Law
Telecommunications Act
TWA Flight 800

Maps: New York: The Development of a City
Bird's Eye View of Manhattan
The Day After

Primary Source Documents
Address on Energy Crisis
Deming's 14 Points for Management
Excerpt from Maya in Exile: Guatemalans in Florida
Excerpt from The New American Poverty
Excerpt from The New Right: We're Ready to Lead
Interrogation of an Iran Hostage
Pardon for Vietnam Draft Evaders
Report on the Iran-Contra Affair
The Fall of Saigon

PART TWO: A GUIDE TO HISTORICAL RESEARCH

In addition to being a scholarly enterprise, research is a social activity intended to create new knowledge. Historical research leads to an informed response to the questions that arise while examining the record of human experience: What was life like under Jim Crow? How did New York City develop? Why were women tried as witches in Salem, Massachusetts, in the late seventeenth century?

This guide defines the terminology and describes the processes involved in investigating and writing about history, in asking and answering questions about the past. It includes the following topics:

I. Understanding Historical Resources

II. Analyzing Sources

III. Developing a Research Assignment

IV. Beginning and Organizing a Research Paper

V. Drafting and Revising a Research Paper

VI. Works Cited in This Guide

VII. Works to Consult

I. Understanding Historical Resources

Every historical period leaves traces—records of what occurred and who lived during a time. These traces reside in newspaper articles, books, studies, photographs, advertisements, corporate files, and more. Historians call this disparate array of materials *sources*.

Historians classify sources in two major categories: primary and secondary. Secondary sources are created by someone who was either not present when the event the source refers to occurred, or removed from it in time. Historians use secondary sources for overviews, and to help familiarize themselves with a topic and com-

pare that topic with other events in history. Secondary sources are a good starting point in the research process. History books, encyclopedias, historical dictionaries, and academic articles are secondary sources. All of the entries in the *Dictionary of American History*, volumes 1 through 8, are secondary sources.

Primary sources are created by individuals who participated in, or witnessed, an event and recorded that event while, or immediately after, it occurred. Volume 9 of the *Dictionary of American History* is a rich repository of primary sources. It includes maps, speeches, memoirs, articles, and much more.

Both primary and secondary sources vary in the kind of information they contain and how they present that information. A primary source like Mathew Brady's photographs of Civil War battlefields, for example, provides important visual evidence of how the war was fought: the landscape, how soldiers looked, what they wore, etc. Yet Brady and his photographers did not simply point their cameras and capture a set of facts. They made conscious decisions about the composition of their pictures, sometimes arranging the positions of soldiers. They both *recorded* and *interpreted* the scenes they shot.

This is also the case with secondary sources. Each has a design, a slant of some kind on the information it conveys. An economic historian's study of the Great Depression emphasizes certain facts that a political historian's account downplays or omits. Their differing purposes require asking different questions; they examine different evidence and arrive at different conclusions.

Some sources are also more credible than others. The economist's study, for example, could be more thoroughly researched than the political historian's, supplying more balanced information. Discerning the slant and quality of primary or secondary sources requires careful analysis.

II. Analyzing Sources

The historian determines the "five W's" for every piece of information he examines. Who authored the source? What is it about? When was it produced, written, or published? Where did it originate? Why was it created? Subjecting a source to these and similar questions, a historian determines its context, its motive, and, often, its credibility.

Analysis does not necessarily lead a historian to the truth; this presumes there is, in the end, only one true account or interpretation of an event. Rather, good historical research requires examining many, often conflicting, sources to arrive at a subtle and meaningful understanding, the "new knowledge" that is the object of investigation. This is why the *Dictionary of American History* includes a variety of primary source documents, maps, photos, and entries.

III. Developing a Research Assignment

With this analytical framework in mind, a student or researcher can develop an assignment or activity for research. Choosing a topic is the first step. Textbooks frequently suggest topics at the ends of chapters. Skimming reference works, critical essays, and periodical articles can also help you choose a topic. Another method consists of reviewing tables of contents of secondary sources, identifying a concept or concepts of interest, and reading the opening paragraph of each, while looking at illustrations and checking captions.

Having a topic in mind does not mean you can begin writing. What if the idea is too large for the assignment at hand—covering the entire Civil War in a five-page paper—or misguided? Rather, your idea must

be refined and tested. Historians (and other researchers) refer to a topic at this stage as a *hypothesis*, a proposition made without necessarily being factually correct.

A good researcher avoids committing to any one hypothesis early in the research process. Rather, she uses it as a general direction for careful reading of primary and secondary sources. All the while, the researcher takes notes and the hypothesis changes and matures. Initial sources lead to new ones. New information prompts rereading of old. This is the trajectory of investigation: more spiraling or iterative than strictly linear.

Along the way, you can refine a working hypothesis by asking:

- Is it *broad* enough to promise a variety of sources?
- Is it *limited* enough to be investigated thoroughly and suit the assignment at hand?
- Is it *original* enough to interest you and your readers? Has it been overdone?
- Is it *worthwhile* enough to offer information and insights of substance? Is it trivial?
- Can it be *verified?* Is it supported by facts and sources?

From a refined hypothesis the main idea of a research assignment, or *thesis*, can be crafted. The thesis is a declarative sentence that

- focuses on a well-defined idea or set of ideas
- makes an arguable assertion that facts can support
- prepares your readers for the body of your paper and foreshadows the conclusion

An example of a thesis statement for a research paper on World War II is: "Air warfare had an important influence on the outcome of World War II."

Like the hypothesis, the thesis is not carved in stone and, if necessary, can be revised during the research process. As you research, it is important to continue to evaluate the thesis for breadth, practicality, originality, and verifiability—the same criteria used to refine your hypothesis.

With a well-formed thesis, a researcher returns to the primary and secondary literature, this time to support, illuminate, and document the idea. How many primary and secondary sources you should use depends on your topic, the length of your writing assignment, and specific guidelines given by a teacher or professor. There is no general rule, but emphasis on the use of primary materials is increasing at all levels of the curriculum. They are the essential tools of the historian. For the research paper on World War II mentioned above, a student might consult the following sources:

- articles from *Military History Quarterly* on World War II air warfare
- articles under Battles, Air, from an encyclopedia on World War II

- firsthand reports of air battles in Britain from the *Times* of London

- memoirs of air war by former German and Japanese pilots

The bibliographies of these sources would, of course, lead to other sources.

Where and how do you find historical materials? Today the availability of primary and secondary literature is not restricted to a school, public, or academic library. The Internet also provides a vast array of primary and secondary texts for research. As with all sources, you should ask the questions associated with the "five W's" mentioned above. The sheer amount and widely varying quality of Internet information requires extra rigor. Many students and researchers end up combining library research with Internet investigation, with the guidance of the librarian often informing the latter.

In "Introduction to the Library," the *Modern Language Association Handbook for Writers of Research Papers* suggests that you become familiar with the library you use by:

- taking a tour or enrolling for a brief introductory lecture

- referring to the library's publications describing its resources

- introducing yourself and your project to the reference librarian

The *Handbook* also lists guides to the use of libraries (Gibaldi, 5–6). Among them are Jean Key Gates, *Guide to the Use of Libraries and Information* (7th ed., New York: McGraw-Hill, 1994) and Thomas Mann, *A Guide to Library Research Methods* (New York: Oxford University Press, 1987).

Today most libraries have their holdings listed on a computer. The online catalog may offer access to Internet sites, Web pages, and commercial databases that relate to a university or community's needs. It may also include academic journals and online reference books. Below are three search techniques for accessing references to primary and secondary literature in an online library catalog:

1. Index Search. Although online catalogs may differ slightly from one library to another, listings are usually accessible by:

   - Subject Search: Enter the subject terms related to your topic. If, for example, your paper topic focuses on the significance of the Saint Lawrence River, you can enter "River, Saint Lawrence." To determine whether you need to follow a particular sequence of terms, as this example does, check with a reference librarian.

   - Author Search: Enter an author's name to find out the library's holdings of works written by the author.

   - Title Search: Enter a title to obtain a list of all the books the library carries with that title.

2. Keyword Search/Full-text Search. A one-word search, e.g., "Kennedy," will produce an overwhelming number of sources, as it will call up any entry that includes the name "Kennedy." To narrow the focus, add one or more keywords, e.g., "John Kennedy, Peace Corps." Be sure to use precise keywords.

3. Boolean Search. Boolean searches use words such as "and," "or," and "not," which clarify the relationship between keywords, narrowing the search. "John Dean and senate hearings," for example, will retrieve materials related to Nixon administration counsel John Dean's testimony during the Ervin committee's Watergate hearings.

There may be far more books and articles listed than you have time to read, so be selective when choosing a reference for further investigation. Take information from works that clearly relate to your thesis, remembering that you may not use them all.

As you identify sources for review, it is important to keep them organized and to take good notes. Keeping a complete and accurate bibliography during the research process is a time- (and sanity-) saving practice. If you have ever needed a book or pages within a book only to discover that an earlier researcher has failed to return it or torn pages from your source, you will understand the need for good documenting and note taking. Every researcher has a favorite method for taking notes. Here are some suggestions to customize for your own use.

- Note cards. In an age when students and researchers routinely bring laptops into the library, this low-tech method may seem out of date, but it does have its advantages. Keeping a 3 in. × 5 in. note card with bibliographic information on one side and notes on another is a convenient and time-tested practice.

- Digital files. Another method for recording a working bibliography, of course, is to enter sources and notes into a computer file. Adding, removing, and alphabetizing titles is a simple process. Be sure to save often and to create a backup file.

Most researchers use hard copy notes and computer files in tandem. Regardless of your method, your bibliographic entry should include some basic information. Most of the information required for a book entry (Gibaldi, 112) includes:

Author's name
Title of a part of the book [preface, chapter title, etc.]
Title of the book
Name of the editor, translator, or compiler
Edition used
Number(s) of the volume(s) used
Name of the series
Place of publication, name of the publisher, and date of publication

Page numbers

Supplementary bibliographic information and annotations

Most of the information required for an article in a periodical (Gibaldi, 141) includes:

Author's name

Title of the article

Name of the periodical

Series number or name (if relevant)

Volume number (for a scholarly journal)

Issue number (if needed)

Date of publication

Page numbers

Supplementary information

Citations for electronic versions of books and articles are generally the same as for print sources. For information on how to cite other sources, refer to the *Chicago Manual of Style*, MLA *Handbook*, the American Historical Association's and/or the Organization of American Historians' web site.

Effective note taking ensures your research is productive. Focus on points in sources that support and enhance your thesis as well as those that conflict with it or call it into question. A good researcher sharpens her thesis when confronted with new and challenging information. Be concise. Do not weave in the author's phrases. Read the information first and then capture the main points in your own words. If necessary, simplify the language of the source and list the ideas in the same order. A good paraphrase can be as long as the original phrase. Paraphrasing is also helpful when you struggle to understand a particularly difficult passage. It also helps you analyze the text you are reading and evaluate its strengths and weaknesses (Barnet and Bedau, 13). If you quote, copy patiently word for word. Quote from the original source, if possible. A secondary source may have misquoted the original.

Whether you paraphrase or quote directly from another work, you *must* acknowledge the original source. Remember, taking the words and ideas of others without crediting them is plagiarism. From the Latin *plagium*, meaning kidnapping, plagiarism, whether intentional or not, is stealing someone else's ideas and expressions. It is unethical and illegal.

Just as you would not misappropriate others' ideas, do not neglect your own. Ralph Waldo Emerson warns you to "look sharply after your thoughts. They come unlooked for, like a new bird seen on your trees, and, if you turn to your usual task, disappear." To differentiate these insights from those of the source you are reading, initial them as your own in your notes.

IV. Beginning and Organizing a Research Paper

When you have amassed substantial research on your thesis, you are ready to write your paper. Where to begin? If you feel overwhelmed staring at a blank page,

you are not alone. Many students—and many published writers—find beginning to write the most daunting part of the entire research process. "The best antidote to writer's block is—to write" (Klauser, 15).

To an extent, if you have been following the methods for research and annotation mentioned earlier, you have already begun writing your paper. The next step is to structure and amplify the ideas captured in your notes. Organize your notes according to key topic headings. This involves grouping like ideas and assigning a general label to them. These headings will eventually serve as your paper's main points.

Taking time to assess key topic headings will lead you to build up, or omit, certain topics, thus sharpening your argument. Does one topic have few primary or secondary sources supporting it, compared with another? If so, you may need to perform more research, or you may delete it. Each key topic should have approximately the same amount of information associated with it. Have you resolved or at least accounted for a topic's conflicting information? If not, further research and thought are required.

Once you have assembled key topics, you can consider two different methods for organizing them: deduction or chronological order.

Deduction. From the Latin *deducere*, meaning to lead away from, deduction is a process of reasoning, and writing, in which one point leads into another. Usually, the first point is a general one and the second is a more specific point related to it. In a paper, the thesis statement is the generalization that leads to specific points. These specific points are the key topics assembled from research and supported by primary and secondary sources. The thesis is stated early in the paper. The body of the paper then provides the facts, examples, and analogies that flow logically from that thesis. The thesis contains keywords that are reflected and enhanced in the subordinate points drawn from research. These keywords become a unifying element throughout the paper, as they reappear in the detailed paragraphs that support and develop the thesis. The conclusion of the paper circles back to the thesis, which is now far more meaningful because of the deductive development that supports it. An old saying sums it up this way: "Tell 'em what you're going to tell 'em, tell 'em, and then tell 'em what you told 'em."

In the example given earlier on air warfare in World War II, the structure of the research paper could be:

Thesis: "Air warfare had an important influence on the outcome of World War II."

Key Topic 1: Overall effects of air battles on the outcome of the war.

Notes from Military History Quarterly

—the Allied air campaign against Germany destroyed many weapons factories, compromising German offense and defense.

Key Topic 2: Air warfare was crucial to England's successful self-defense against a German invasion, an important factor in the outcome of the war.

Notes from German former pilot's memoir

—the strategy the Germans pursued is recalled as follows....

Note that topics support and detail the thesis in increasing levels of specificity and always refer to sources.

Chronological Order. A chronological organizing principle presents key topics gathered in research as events in a story. If you are analyzing a specific historical event, such as the Triangle Shirtwaist fire, or exploring cause and effect, a chronological organization is useful.

Whether you develop your paper's argument using a deductive or chronological method, you will need to cite the sources behind your key topics. A works cited page at the paper's end is not sufficient documentation to acknowledge the ideas, facts, and opinions you have included within your text. The MLA *Handbook for Writers of Research Papers* describes an efficient parenthetical style of documentation—this guide uses it—to be used within the body of your paper. The author's last name and the page number referred to appear in the text in parentheses. A full bibliographic description of the source follows on the works cited page. There are numerous styles for parenthetical and full bibliographic citations. Your instructor may direct you to use a specific one. Refer also to the American Historical Association's Web site.

There are a variety of titles for the page that lists primary and secondary sources (Gibaldi, 106–107). A Works Cited, also called a Bibliography, page lists those works you have cited within the body of your paper. The reader need only refer to it for the information required for further independent research. An Annotated Bibliography or Annotated Works Cited page offers brief descriptions of the works listed. A Works Consulted page lists those works you have used but not cited.

Regardless of the style you adopt, a citation should accompany the following pieces of information:

- direct quotations
- paraphrases and summaries
- information that is not common knowledge and can be traced to a specific source
- borrowed material that could be mistaken for your own in the absence of a citation

V. Drafting and Revising a Research Paper

"There are days when the result is so bad that no fewer than five revisions are required. In contrast, when I'm greatly inspired, only four revisions are needed."—John Kenneth Galbraith

You have assembled the research paper's key topics. You have determined an organizing principle. You have settled on a method of citing sources. Now you need to put your ideas into prose for a first draft. Some writing teachers suggest "freewriting" your first draft. Freewriting is a process during which the writer freely moves from idea to idea, not necessarily imposing a strict order or sequence at first. In *Writing without Teachers*, Peter Elbow asserts that "[a]lmost everybody interposes a massive and complicated series of editings between the time words start to be born into consciousness and when they finally come off the end of the pencil or typewriter [or word processor] onto the page" (Elbow, 5). Regardless of the method you use, your primary intention in drafting your paper should be to write your ideas so that you can begin the process of revising and refining your work.

Subsequent drafts focus on writing a paper that is grammatically correct, flows smoothly, supports your thesis fully, and speaks clearly and interestingly. This involves reviewing the language and structure of your paper. Although a thorough discussion of grammar and style is beyond the scope of this guide, here is a checklist of major points that will help you in reviewing your first draft and revising it to produce a more refined piece of writing.

Grammar. In reviewing your paper for grammatical correctness, you should bear the following factors in mind:

1. *Sentence completeness.* Be sure sentences are complete. Eliminate fragments.

   Example: Because Roosevelt believed in the cause [fragment], he hewed to his New Deal program [completion].

2. *Subject and verb agreement. Do subjects and verbs agree in number?*

   Example: The trouble with truth **is** [not are] its many varieties.

3. *Pronoun and noun agreement.* Review pronouns for agreement in number (this, these, that, those) and gender (his, hers) with the nouns to which they refer. Remember that a pronoun refers back to the noun preceding it.

4. *Punctuation.* Are you using correct punctuation throughout your paper?

What follows are some basic punctuation guidelines:

- A period completes a sentence, which is a complete thought.
- A semicolon separates two complete, related thoughts within the same sentence.
- Use of a colon implies introduction of an example.
- A comma introduces a pause after a phrase or in a sequence within a sentence.

   Examples: Speed, skill, and agility constituted success factors. Or: Her journey ended, she began to edit her travel journal.

- Avoid the use of exclamations in formal prose.

- Use the apostrophe in "it's" to signify a contraction of "it is." Use "its" for the possessive of "it."

Style. Consider the following points:

1. *Voice.* Do you speak in the first person in your paper? Avoid using phrases such as "I think…" in formal expository prose.
2. *Passive constructions.* Are you frequently using passive verb constructions? Passive sentences hide cause and effect relationships and obscure responsibility. You can revise passive sentences to restore agency:

   It was decided to remain in the building.

   The firefighters decided to remain in the building.

   The consequences of his actions were shown to him.

   The scientists showed him the consequences of his actions.

3. *Verbs.* Favor vivid verbs over verb and adverb combinations. The first sentence shows a weak, wordy expression. The second shows a forceful, efficient expression. Emphasize vivid verbs over forms of "to be."

   She too hastily arrived at a conclusion.

   She rushed to a conclusion.

4. *Repetition.* As you review your first draft, eliminate repeated thoughts and phrases. As stated elsewhere, however, judicious repetition of your thesis statement's keywords throughout your argument can signal the introduction of an important idea.
5. *Transition.* Transition between thoughts is essential if you want your reader to follow you from introduction to conclusion. Transitional words and phrases, such as "however," "then," "next," "therefore," "first," "moreover," and "on the other hand," signal changes in your argument. You should not overuse them, however.
6. *Organization.* Throughout revision, check and recheck your paper's organization for logical sequencing of ideas. Continue the practice of labeling key topics in your prose. Write the main idea of each paragraph in the margin and review the progression of your paper in shorthand form as you revise. This technique produces a "living outline" of your paper.
7. *Sound.* As you revise sentences and paragraphs, read them aloud. Hearing your own words puts them in a new light. Listen to the use of language and flow of ideas. Does the writing sound awkward or wordy? Reading your work aloud will likely lead you to shorten sentences, generally a positive editorial decision.
8. *Peer review.* Find a peer reader to read your paper with you present. Or, visit your college or university's writing lab. Guide your reader's responses by asking specific questions. Can he follow your argu-

ment? Is your reasoning convincing? Does your conclusion relate to your thesis?

9. *Spelling.* Do not rely only on spell-checking programs. The program will not pick up correctly spelled words that are misused, such as "affect," "effect," "it's," and "its." When you edit for spelling errors, read sentences backward. This procedure will help you look closely at individual words.

These points constitute major areas of concern. There are dozens of others. Following this guide's suggestions for research and writing will not ensure an unqualified success in historiography. Rather, we hope we have provided a useful point of departure for utilizing the *Dictionary of American History.*

Two lists follow. The first identifies sources cited in this guide; the second lists other works to consult. Both contain further suggestions for historical research and for writing papers.

VI. Works Cited in This Guide

Barnet, Sylvan, and Hugo Bedau. *Critical Thinking, Reading, and Writing: A Brief Guide to Argument.* Boston: Bedford/St. Martin's, 1998.

Elbow, Peter. *Writing without Teachers.* New York: Oxford University Press, 1973.

Gibaldi, Joseph. *MLA Handbook for Writers of Research Papers.* 4th ed. New York: Modern Language Association of America, 1995.

Klauser, Henriette Anne. *Writing on Both Sides of the Brain: Breakthrough Techniques for People Who Write.* San Francisco: HarperSanFrancisco, 1987.

VII. Works to Consult

Barzun, Jacques, and Henry F. Graff. *The Modern Researcher.* 6th ed. Stamford, Conn.: International Thomson, 2002.

Brent, Doug. *Reading as Rhetorical Invention: Knowledge, Persuasion, and the Teaching of Research-Based Writing.* Urbana, Ill.: National Council of Teachers of English, 1992.

Davidson, James West, and Mark H. Lytle. *After the Fact: The Art of Historical Detection.* 2nd ed. New York: Knopf, 1986.

Furay, Conal, and Michael J. Salevouris. *The Methods and Skills of History: A Practical Guide.* 2nd ed. Wheeling, Ill.: Harlan Davidson, 2000.

Rico, Gabriele Lusser. *Writing the Natural Way: Using Right Brain Techniques to Release Your Expressive Powers.* Los Angeles: J. P. Tarcher, 1983.

Sorenson, Sharon. *How to Write Research Papers.* New York: Arco, 2002.

Steffens, Henry J., Mary Jane Dickerson, Toby Fulwiler, and Arthur W. Biddle. *Writer's Guide: History.* Boston: D.C. Heath, 1987.

Strunk, William, Jr., and E. B. White. *The Elements of Style.* 4th ed. Boston: Allyn and Bacon, 2000.

Turabian, Kate L. *A Manual for Writers of Term Papers, Theses, and Dissertations.* Chicago: University of Chicago Press, 1996.

INDEX

Index preparation by Jennifer Burton, Nedalina (Dina) Dineva, and Marianna Wackerman at Coughlin Indexing Services, Inc., with the assistance of Maria Coughlin and Scott Smiley.

Volume numbers are in **boldface** and precede page numbers. Page numbers in **boldface** refer to the main entry on the subject. Pages with illustrations, tables, or figures are cited in *italics*.

A

AA. *See* Alcoholics Anonymous
AAA. *See* Agricultural Adjustment Act; Agricultural Adjustment Administration; American Automobile Association
AAAS. *See* American Association for the Advancement of Science
Aachen (Germany), **1:**1
AAFL. *See* All America Football League
AAIA. *See* Association on American Indian Affairs
AALS. *See* Association of American Law Schools
Aandahl, Fred G., **6:**132
Aaron, Henry (Hank), **1:**421
AARP. *See* American Association of Retired Persons
AAS. *See* American Anti-Slavery Society
AAU. *See* Amateur Athletic Union
AAUP. *See* American Association of University Professors
ABA. *See* American Bar Association
Abbe, Cleveland, **2:**235
Abbey, Edward, **5:**552
Abbott, Berenice, **1:**301
Abbott, Gilbert, **1:**185
Abbott, Jacob, **5:**127
Abbott, Lyman, **8:**263
Abbott, Robert, **6:**98
ABC bill (Act for Better Child Care Services) (1990), **2:**139
ABC Conference (1914), **1:**1

ABC television network, **8:**72, 73, 138
cartoons on, **2:**64
Abduction. *See* Kidnapping
Abdul-Jabbar, Kareem, **1:**425
Abel, Rudolph Ivanovich, **8:**247
Abenaki, **1:1–2; 8:**219
in 20th century, **1:**2
in colonial era, **1:**1; **5:**21; **6:**56; **8:**311
France's alliance with, **1:**1; **2:**293; **8:**311
Iroquois and, **5:**21; **8:**311
member tribes of, **1:**1
in New Hampshire, **6:**56
in Vermont, **1:**2; **5:**21; **8:**311
Abercromby, James, **5:**21; **7:**193
Abilene (Kansas), **1:**2; **2:**442
cattle market at, **2:**75, 158
railroads and development of, **7:**34
Abilene Trail, **1:**2
Ableman, Stephen V., **1:2–3**
Ableman v. Booth, **1:2–3; 3:**482
ABM. *See* Anti-ballistic missile
Abolitionism
and boycotts, **1:**528
censorship of, **2:**84
and colonization movement, **2:**297
goals of, **1:**208
Liberty Party and, **5:96–97**
and Lovejoy riots, **5:**165
in New York, **6:**88
organized, **5:**96
in Pennsylvania, **6:**278
Quakers and, **7:**2
Second Great Awakening and, **2:**163

Uncle Tom's Cabin (Stowe) and, **8:248–249**
women and, **8:505–506, 512**
See also Antislavery movement
Abortion, **1:3–7**
in 19th century, **1:**4, 5
in 20th century, **1:4–7**
adolescent girls and, **2:**149
black-market, **1:5–6**
in colonial era, **1:**3
Comstock law and, **1:**467
contraception and, **1:4–5**
criminal regulation of, **2:**459
in electoral politics, **3:**168
gender roles and, **1:**4
legislative restrictions on, **1:4–7**
under Medicaid, **1:**7; **4:**100
methods of, **1:3–4, 7**
partial-birth, **1:**7
perceptions of fetus and, **1:3–4, 5**
pro-choice movement and, **6:**489
pro-life movement against, **1:**4, 6; **2:**165; **6:**489
Moral Majority in, **5:**456
Operation Rescue in, **5:**549; **6:199–200**
rates of, **1:**3, 4, 5
religious protests against, **2:**165
right to privacy and, **4:**497; **6:**479
Supreme Court on
discussion of, **7:**216
legalization of *(Roe v. Wade)*, **1:6–7; 7:192–193; 8:**517
as litmus test for Court nominees, **1:**7
under Medicaid, **4:**100

Abortion, (*continued*)
reactions to, **1:**6–7
restrictions on, **1:**7, 45–46;
6:361–362; **8:**433–434
right to privacy and, **4:**497
women's rights movement and,
8:511, *518*
Abourezk, James, **5:**72
Abraham, Plains of, **1:**7
Abraham, Spencer, **5:**72
Abraham Lincoln Brigade, **1:**7–8
Abrams, Creighton W., **8:**335
Abrams, Elliott, **6:**32
Abscam scandal, **1:**8; **3:**338
Abstract art
cubism, **2:**475–476
expressionism, **1:**8–10, 298
ABT. *See* American Ballet Theatre
Abuse
child (*See* Child abuse)
domestic (*See* Domestic violence)
sexual, Catholic Church scandal
involving, **2:**71
Abzug, Bella, **8:***517*
AC. *See* Alternating current
ACA. *See* Automobile Club of Amer-
ica
Academia
growth of, **5:**67
middlebrow culture and, **5:**366
Academic freedom, **1:**10–11
American Association of University
Professors and, **1:**10, **142–143**
American Federation of Teachers
and, **1:**155
Academy Awards, **6:485–486**
Acadia, **1:***11,* 11–12; **6:**52
ACC. *See* Air Combat Command
Accelerators, **6:**339, 342–343
Accidents, **1:12–13**
airplane (*See* Airplane crashes)
automobile, **1:**12, 376–377
environmental, **3:**228
Exxon Valdez oil spill, **3:**39, 233,
305, **305–306**
industrial, Safety First Movement
and, **7:**222
Accommodations, equal
Civil Rights Act of 1875 on, **2:**194
Civil Rights Act of 1964 on,
2:195–196
Accounting scandals, **4:**27–28
Acculturation, **1:**336
Acharya, Pandit, **1:**326

Acheson, Dean G.
Cuban missile crisis and, **2:**471
in Korean War, **4:**545
Acheson, Lila Bell, **7:**51, *51*
Achille Lauro hijacking, **1:**13
Acid rain, **1:13–14,** *14,* 80; **3:**480
Canadian complaints about, **2:**27
fossil fuels and, **3:**214
Ackerman, James, **1:***70*
ACLS. *See* American Council of
Learned Societies
ACLU. *See* American Civil Liberties
Union
ACLU, Reno v., **2:**85
*ACLU Greater Pittsburgh Chapter,
County of Allegheny v.,* **2:**166
ACLU v. Reno, **3:**340
Acquired immune deficiency syndrome (AIDS), **1:14–18; 2:**512;
3:37, 241
activists on, **1:**16, *16,* 18–19; **7:**327
in Africa, **1:**18, 40, 41
and gays and lesbians, **3:**514; **7:**327
incidence of, **7:**332–333
by state, **1:***17*
people with, **1:**15, 16, 17
prostitution and, **6:**514
public attitudes toward, **1:**16–17
quilt dedicated to victims of,
1:72–73, *73;* **7:**6
recognition of, **2:**88
research on, **1:**15–16
sex education and, **1:**17, 18
treatment for, **1:**15–16, 17–18
tuberculosis in, **8:**237
Acquisitions. *See* Mergers and acquisitions
Across the Plains to California in 1852
(Frizzell), excerpt from,
9:229–233
Acrylic, **6:**366
ACS. *See* American Colonization
Society
Act for Better Child Care Services
(ABC bill) (1990), **2:**139
Act for International Development
(1950), **6:**381
Act for the Government and Protec-
tion of Indians (1850), **8:**214
Act for the Impartial Administration
of Justice. *See* Coercive Acts;
Intolerable Acts
Act for the Punishment of Certain
Crimes (1798), **1:**123–124

Act of Chapultepec (1945), **8:**272
ACT UP (AIDS Coalition to
Unleash Power), **1:**16, **18–19**
ACTION, **1:19**
Action figures (toys), **8:**153
Action for Progress, **1:**128
Active life expectancy, **5:**106
Actors' Equity, **8:**114
Actors' Society of America, **8:**114
Actors Studio, **8:**115
Acuff, Roy, **5:***491*
ACWA. *See* Amalgamated Clothing
Workers of America
Ad valorem duties, **3:**97
vs. specific duties, **8:**50
ADA. *See* Americans with Disabili-
ties Act
Adair v. United States, **2:**408; **8:**578
Adam, Robert, **1:**291
Adam of Bremen, **8:**337
Adams, Abigail, **3:**375; **7:**7; **8:**512
letters of, excerpts from, **9:**144–145
Adams, Alice, **1:**309
Adams, Ansel, **1:**301; **4:***200*
Adams, Arthur, **3:**521, 522
Adams, Bud, **3:**411
Adams, C. F., **1:**106
Adams, Charles Francis, **4:**31; **5:**90;
8:290
and Free Soil Party, **2:**361
Adams, Douglas, *The Hitchhiker's
Guide to the Galaxy,* **2:**338
Adams, Franklin P., **1:**123
Adams, George Burton, **1:**159
Adams, Henry, **1:**55; **3:**280; **4:**138
Adams, Herbert Baxter, **1:**158
Adams, John
and Alien and Sedition Acts, **6:**145
American Academy of Arts and
Sciences and, **1:**139; **5:**66
birthplace of, **1:**508
Blount conspiracy and, **1:**489
Boston Massacre and, **1:**513
and Declaration of Independence,
2:521–522
and Declaration of Rights, **2:**524
diplomacy of, **2:**394; **7:**146, 147
and Dutch bankers' loans, **3:**96
and Essex Junto (term), **3:**255
estimate of number of Loyalists,
5:167
foreign policy of, **2:**398; **7:**117
and France, relations with, **3:**450
and independence, goal of, **2:**520

legal training of, **5**:56, 73
letters of, excerpts from, **9**:144–145
Locke's political philosophy and, **5**:141
midnight judges appointed by, **5**:367
and Navy, Department of, **6**:23
and Plan of 1776, **6**:361
presidency of, **3**:351
in presidential campaign of 1789, **3**:150, 171
in presidential campaign of 1792, **3**:150
in presidential campaign of 1796, **3**:150, 171; **8**:322
in presidential campaign of 1800, **3**:150, 351–352
and presidential open house, **8**:471
on republican order, **2**:315
and Seal of the United States, **3**:99
on state representation, **2**:86
subpoena to, **6**:456
Thoughts on Government, **7**:136
and Treaty of Paris, **1**:541; **6**:248
and Virginia dynasty, **8**:348
and XYZ affair, **8**:570
Adams, John Quincy
Adams-Onís Treaty and, **1**:188; **8**:204
in *Amistad* case, **1**:176
on astronomy, **1**:343
birthplace of, **1**:508
caucus supporting, **6**:113
and civil service, **2**:206
against gag rule, **3**:502
on metric system, **5**:529
and Monroe Doctrine, **5**:46
and National Republican Party, **5**:555
on natural dominion, **1**:187
in presidential campaign of 1824, **2**:420; **3**:152, 171; **5**:555; **8**:322–323
in presidential campaign of 1828, **3**:152
Vancouver explorations and, **8**:307
and westward expansion, **1**:187–188; **8**:307
Adams, Lewis, **8**:241
Adams, Robert, **5**:129
Adams, Samuel, **1**:509; **7**:135
and Boston Committee of Correspondence, **1**:512; **2**:314
and Boston Tea Party, **1**:514

British attempt to arrest, **2**:287
and Federalists, **2**:381
at First Continental Congress, **2**:524
Massachusetts Circular Letter by, **5**:272; **8**:349
text of, **9**:122–123
Adams, Samuel Hopkins, **6**:554
Adamson Act (1916), **1**:19; **6**:54; **7**:24, 25; **8**:360
Adams-Onís Treaty, **1**:188; **3**:386, 425; **5**:159; **8**:204
Arkansas River in, **1**:264
Adarand Constructors v. Pena, **1**:581; **7**:316
ADC. *See* Aid to Dependent Children; American Arab Anti-Discrimination Committee
Addams, Jane, **2**:132, 349; **5**:91; **6**:267, 317, 440; **8**:114, 499, 521
Peace and Bread in Time of War, excerpt from, **9**:365–367
in settlement house movement, **1**:146; **7**:317–318
social gospel and, **7**:414
Addes, George, **8**:261
Address of the Southern Delegates, **1**:19–20
Addyston Pipe Company case, **1**:20
ADEA. *See* Age Discrimination in Employment Act
Adena, **1**:20
Aderholt, O. F., **3**:512
ADHD. *See* Attention-deficit/hyperactivity disorder
Adirondack Mountains, **6**:86
Adirondack Park Agency Act (1971), **5**:38
Adkins v. Children's Hospital, **1**:20–21; **3**:308; **5**:394–395; **8**:445
Adler, Felix, **1**:55; **3**:256
Adler, Mortimer, **3**:124; **4**:40
and *Encyclopaedia Britannica*, **3**:204
Administration of Justice Act (1774), **4**:408
Administration Reorganization Act (1939), **6**:44
Administrative agencies, federal. *See* Federal agencies
Administrative discretion, delegation of, **1**:21–22
Administrative justice (adjudication), **1**:22–23

Administrative law, **3**:333
Administrative Procedure Act (APA) (1946), **1**:22
Admiralty law and courts, **1**:23–24
Adobe, **1**:24
Adolescence, **1**:24–27
social recognition of, **2**:137; **3**:73
violent crime in, **2**:460
See also under Juvenile
Adoptees' Liberty Movement Association, **1**:29
Adoption, **1**:27–30
international, **1**:29
legislation on, **1**:27–29; **2**:137; **3**:443
of Native Americans, **4**:263–264
open, **1**:29
transracial, **1**:29
Adoption and Safe Families Act (ASFA) (1997), **2**:137; **3**:443
Adoptions Assistance and Child Welfare Act (1980), **3**:443
Adorno, Theodor, **1**:196, 207; **3**:454
ADR. *See* Alternative dispute resolution; Applied Data Research
Adult education, **3**:115
Chautauqua movement and, **2**:113
Adultery, Uniform Code of Military Justice on, **8**:256
Advanced Research Projects Agency (ARPA), **4**:398; **8**:66
Advanced Research Projects Agency Network (ARPANET), **2**:337; **3**:184–185; **4**:398–399; **8**:65, 66, 70
Advanced Technology Program, **5**:529
Adventist churches, **1**:30–31
origins of, **8**:501
Adventurers, merchant, **5**:316–317
Adventures of Augie March, The (Bellow), **8**:294
Adverse possession, **6**:506–507
Advertising, **1**:31–35
in 19th century, **1**:32–33
in 20th century, **1**:33–34
in almanacs, **1**:129
for borax, **1**:505
on cable television, **8**:76
celebrities and, **2**:79, 98
for Coca-Cola, **2**:260, *260*
in colonial era, **1**:31
and consumerism, **2**:388, 389–390
cowboy imagery in, **2**:444

Advertising, (*continued*)
  department stores and, **3:**7
  flag used in, **3:**380
  The Hidden Persuaders (Packard)
    on, **4:**130
  on Internet, **1:**34
  in magazines, **1:**32; **5:**193, 198;
    7:252
  in mail-order catalogs, **5:**206
  mass marketing, **5:**245–246
  men as targets of, **2:**391
  motivation research in, **4:**130
  in newspapers, **6:**96, 97
  online, **2:**323
  outdoor, **1:**34
  and packaging, **6:**229
  in print, **1:**31–32
  with product placement, **1:**34
  on radio, **1:**34
  roadside, **2:**389
  slogans in, **1:**33
  for smoking, **1:**34; **7:**404, 405;
    8:136
  for soap, **7:**408
  for spirits, **7:**504, 505
  on television, **1:**34; **8:**72, 73, 75–76
    infomercials, **4:354–355**
  volume of, **1:**34*t*, 34–35
  women as targets of, **2:**390–391
Advertising agencies, **1:**32–33
Advocate, The (magazine), **5:**198
AEC. *See* Atomic Energy Commission
AEI. *See* American Enterprise Institute
Aerial Phenomenon Research Organization (APRO), **8:**255
Aerobics, **1:35**
Aerospace industry, **1:**96
Aesthetic preservationism,
  2:368–369
AFC. *See* America First Committee;
  American Fur Company
AFDC. *See* Aid to Families with
  Dependent Children
Affirmative action, **1:35–37; 3:**49
  arguments against, **1:**386; **2:**205;
    3:249, 250
  in employment, **1:**35–37; **4:**66;
    7:315–316
  in higher education, **1:**37
  neoconservatives on, **6:**32
  Philadelphia Plan and, **6:**314
  Proposition 209 and, **6:**509–510
  set-asides as, **7:**315–316

  Supreme Court on, **1:**36–37, 386;
    4:66; **7:**157
  for women, **1:**36–37
Affluent Society, The (Galbraith),
  6:438
Afghanistan
  CIA operations in, **2:**92
  Soviet invasion of, **1:37–38,** *38;*
    2:269, 270
    chemical weapons used in, **2:**119
    U.S. response to, **2:**60
    and U.S. relations with Pakistan
      and India, **4:**260
  U.S. bombing campaign in, **1:**496;
    6:109
  armed forces used in, **1:**277–278;
    2:365
AFL. *See* American Federation of
  Labor; American Football
  League
AFL-CIO. *See* American Federation
  of Labor–Congress of Industrial
  Organizations
Africa
  African American alliances with,
    1:138
  African American colonization of,
    1:147–148, 208–209, 477;
    2:296–297; **3:**197; **6:**47
  AIDS in, **1:**40, 41
  Cuban troops in, **2:**471
  economic and political crises in,
    1:38
  foreign aid to, **3:**416, 418
  foreign observers from, **1:**138
  immigration from, **4:**221
  Pan-Africanism and, **6:**234–236
  religion in, **1:**41
  and slave culture, **7:**396
  slavery within, **7:**386–387, 389–390
  U.S. aid to, **1:**40–41
  U.S. relations with, **1:38–41**
  World War II in, **6:123–124;**
    8:549
See also specific countries
African Abroad or His Evolution in
  Western Civilization, Tracing His
  Development Under Caucasian
  Milieu, The (Ferris), **6:**236
African American(s), **1:47–53**
  in 18th century, **1:**48
  in 19th century, **1:**48–50
  in 20th century, **1:**51–52
  activist organizations of, **5:**371

  adoption of, **1:**28, 29
  affirmative action for, **1:35–37**
  African alliances with, **1:**138
  in Alabama, **1:**103
    civil rights movement and,
      1:104–105
  in Alvin Ailey Dance Theater,
    1:131
  in American Bar Association, **1:**145
  in American Revolution, **1:**48;
    7:116, 146, 152
  anti-Semitism among, **1:**207; **6:**32
  in Arkansas, **1:**261, 263
  bank for, **3:**462
  black arts movement among,
    5:194; **8:**115
  and black nationalism, **1:477–478,**
    479
  boycotting by, **1:**529
  in California
    Los Angeles, **5:**153
    Oakland, **6:**151
  on chain gangs, **2:**99, *99*
  Christianity and, **7:**8, 87–88
  churches of, **2:**477; **7:**89 (*See also*
    specific churches)
    membership in, **7:***91*
  citizenship for, **2:**180, 193, 219
  civil rights for (*See* Civil rights
    movement)
  in Civil War, **1:**510; **2:**212, 215,
    395–396
    Confederate States of America,
      2:343
    Fort Pillow Massacre and, **6:**356
    New York City Draft Riots and,
      3:84; **7:**164
  after Civil War, **7:**10
    political participation of, **7:***61*
  in Civilian Conservation Corps,
    2:220
  in colonial era, **1:**47–48 (*See also*
    Slave[s])
  colonization movement and,
    1:147–148, 208–209; **2:**296,
    296–297; 6:47
  in Communist Party, **2:**327
  compensation for, **3:**440
  in Congressional Black Caucus,
    1:471
  in Connecticut, **2:**358
  cowboys, **2:***443*
  cultural pluralism and, **6:**375, 376
  culture of, in 18th century, **1:**48

dance among, **2:**497
and Democratic Party, **2:**195, 201, 552; **6:**398
discrimination against (*See* Racial discrimination)
disfranchisement of, **3:**57
  and Dorr's Rebellion, **3:**80
  legal challenge to, **8:**483
  Mississippi Plan for, **5:414–415**
  through voter registration laws, **8:**354
education for, **3:**115, 117, 118, **120–121**
  African American Studies and, **1:**46–47; **3:**119
  colleges, **3:**121, **125–127; 8:**263
  at Oberlin College, **6:**152
  universities, **8:**263
emigration to Africa, **1:**477; **2:**296–297; **3:**197
family life of, **3:**313
farmers' alliance created by, **3:**323; **6:**417
as farmhands, **3:**325
FBI operations targeting, **2:**266
in Florida, **3:**386, 388
folklore of, **3:**394–395
foreign observers on, **1:**138
in foster care, **1:**29
free
  in 18th century, **1:**48
  in 19th century, **1:**48–49; **7:**465
  kidnapping, **6:**294, 462
  in Louisiana, **5:**160
  in Lower East Side, **5:**166
  in South, **7:**465
Freedom Riders, **3:464**
as freemasons, **3:**466
gender roles of, **3:**519, 520
genealogical community of, **3:**522–523
in Georgia, **3:**555–558
  Atlanta, **1:**348–349
in Great Depression, **1:**51; **5:**563
and gun control, **4:**74, 75
gun violence among, **2:**460
hairstyles of, **4:**84
Harlem Renaissance and, **4:**94, **95–97**
heritage of, **7:**197
holiday celebrations by, **4:**148, 149, 553
in Illinois, **4:**217
  Chicago, **2:**133, 134, 201

in Indiana, **4:**317, 319
International Labor Defense and, **4:**389
in Iowa, **4:**417
Jim Crow laws and, **4:479–480**
as jurors, **4:**503; **7:**555
in Kentucky, **4:**521
Kwanzaa among, **4:**148, **553**
as law students, **5:**58
literature by, **2:**205; **4:**95–96; **7:**197; **8:**248
in Louisiana, New Orleans, **6:**74
lynching of, **5:**179, *179;* **8:**337
  and NAACP, **5:**526
  of Till (Emmett), **8:126,** *126*
  during World War I, **8:**537
magazines of, **5:**193, 194, **199–200**
marriage among, interracial (miscegenation), **4:**479; **5:**405–406
in Maryland, Baltimore, **1:**393
in Massachusetts, Cambridge, **2:**18
in Michigan, Detroit, **3:**20
migration by, **5:369–371,** *370*
  in 20th century, **1:**51; **8:**537
  from Georgia, **3:**557
  to Liberia, **1:**148
military service by, **2:**201; **5:380–382,** *381*
  black cavalry, **1:471–472**
  black infantry, **1:**475, *476*
  Brownsville affair, **1:549–550**
  women, **8:**505
minstrel shows and, **5:402,** 489–490, 496
in Mississippi, **5:**412–413
in Missouri, Saint Louis, **7:**227
music of, **4:**96; **5:489–490,** 492
  blues, **1:491–492**
  gospel, **5:497–498**
  jazz, **4:**467–468
  ragtime, **7:22**
  rock and roll, **7:**185
names of, **5:**509
National Urban League and, **5:**563
Native Americans and, **4:**324; **7:**8–9; **8:**249
in Nebraska, **6:**31
in New Hampshire, **6:**58
in New Jersey, **6:**63
in New York City, **4:**94
newspapers of, **5:**193, 194, **199–200; 6:**88, 96–97, 98
  censorship of, **6:**99
in North Carolina, Raleigh, **7:**46

in Ohio, **6:**174
in Oklahoma, **6:**185, 186
in old age, **6:**189
in Oregon, **6:**206, 207
in Organization of Afro-American Unity, **6:**211
in Pennsylvania, **6:**278, 312
picketing, **6:**350
pioneers, **6:***358*
in political office
  in 19th century, **1:**50; **8:**8
  in 20th century, **8:**9
  and African policies, **1:**38, 39
  in Virginia, **8:**345
  Voting Rights Act and, **8:**357
political participation of, after Civil War, **7:***61*
poverty among, **6:**437, 440
in prison, **6:**477, 478
rape laws and, **7:**49, 50
in Reconstruction era, **1:**49–50; **3:**462–463; **4:**374; **8:**23
relations with whites, **7:**9–10
religions of, **1:41–46** (*See also specific denominations*)
in Republican Party, **8:**356
in Rhode Island, **7:**152
rights of
  Force Acts and, **3:**413–414
  and liberalism, **5:**92
rioting by
  in 1960s, **7:**165
  Rodney King riots, **7:**12, 165
  Watts riots, **2:**12; **8:430–431,** *431*
separatists, **4:**375
sexuality of, **7:**329
sharecroppers, **7:**335
in South, New, **7:**468
in South Carolina, **7:**456–457
  Charleston, **2:**107
in sports, **7:**511
  baseball, **1:**420, 421, 422, 547
  basketball, **1:**424–425
  football, **3:**412
  prizefighting, **6:**483, 484, 485; **7:**510
  track and field, **8:**154–156
in State Department, **7:**530
steelworkers, compensation of, **8:**278
stereotypes regarding, **2:**223
as strikebreakers, **3:**49
suburbanization and, **7:**575
suffrage for, **1:***542;* **3:**145; **7:**106; **8:6–9,** 7, 355, 356

African American(s), (*continued*)
  in 20th century, **8:**9
  after Civil War, **7:**58, 59, *59*, 62
  Federal Elections Bill (1890) and,
    2:332
  Mississippi Plan and, **5:414–415**
  in Reconstruction, **8:**7–9
  resistance to, **3:**146, 147; **7:**58;
    8:8–9, 273, 275
  in Tennessee, **8:**85–86
  in Texas, **8:**101
  in textile industry, **8:**111
  in theater, **8:**113
  in trade unions, **2:**301–302;
    3:49–50; **8:**172, 263
  Uncle Tom's Cabin (Stowe) and,
    8:248
  unemployed, during Great Depression, **4:**47; **5:**563
  urban experience of, **8:**285, 291
  urban renewal program and, **8:**286
  in Utah, **8:**298
  in vaudeville, **8:**309
  in Vietnam War, **8:***333*
  violence against, **8:**337–338
    lynching of Till (Emmett), **8:**126
    and NAACP and, **5:**526
    political, **1:**332–333
    during World War I, **8:**537
  in Virginia, **8:**344, 345, 346, 347
    Richmond, **7:**156
  volunteerism among, **8:**353
  voter registration by, **8:***354*, 357
    SNCC and, **7:**561
  voting by, **8:***356*
    constraints on, **8:**356
      grandfather clause, **4:**35, 73;
        5:526
      property qualifications and,
        6:508
      white primaries and, **6:**463
    in Georgia, **3:**555–556, 557–558
    NAACP and, **5:**526–527
    Voting Rights Act and, **8:**357
  in Washington (D.C.), **8:**410
  white flight from
    in Philadelphia, **6:**313
    in Virginia, **8:**347
  women
    activists, **8:**510, 512
    clubs for, **8:**514
    double jeopardy for, **8:**521
    on mainstream women's right
      movement, **3:**519, 520

  in military, **8:**505
  National Association of Colored
    Women and, **5:**527
  National Council of Negro
    Women and, **5:**534
  as nurses, **6:**146–147
  suffrage organizations of, **8:**514
  in track and field, **8:**155
  in workforce, **8:**507
  in World War I, **8:**537, *537*
  in World War II, **1:***49*, 51; **8:***545*
  and World's Columbian Exposition, protesting against, **8:**558
  in Wyoming, **8:**566
  in Young Men's Christian Association, **8:**584
  See also Civil rights movement
African American colleges, **3:**121,
  125–127; 8:263
  in Reconstruction era, **1:**50
  Tuskegee University, **8:241**
African American Studies, **1:46–47;**
  3:119
African Civilization Society, **6:**235
African Methodist Episcopal Church
  (AMEC), **1:53–54; 8:**501
  origins of, **1:**43–44, *44*, 53
  and Vesey Rebellion, **8:**317
African Methodist Episcopal Zion
  (AMEZ) Church, **1:**44, 53–54
African Union Church, **1:**43
Afrikaners, **7:**451, 452
Afrocentrism, **1:**47
AFS. *See* American Folklore Society
AFSA. *See* Armed Forces Security
  Agency
AFSCME. *See* American Federation
  of State, County, and Municipal
  Employees
AFT. *See* American Federation of
  Teachers
After the New Criticism (Lentricchia),
  6:429
Agassiz, Alexander, **6:**160, 161
Agassiz, Louis, **1:**140, 141, 192, 520;
  2:446; **3:**541; **5:**59, 240; **7:**13
Agbebe, Mojola, **6:**236
Age
  discrimination based on, **3:46–47;**
    7:129
  shares of population by, **2:***557*
  voting, **7:**106
Age Discrimination Act (1975), **5:**15

Age Discrimination in Employment
  Act (ADEA) (1967), **3:**46–47;
  5:15
Age of Reason (Paine), **2:**539
Agee, James, *Let Us Now Praise
  Famous Men: Three Tenant Families* (with Walker Evans),
  5:83–84
Agencies, federal. *See* Federal agencies
Agency for International Development (USAID), **1:**54
  in Africa, **1:**40
  criticism of, **1:**54
  functions of, **1:**54
  in South Vietnam, **3:**417
Agency for Nuclear Stewardship,
  3:210
Agency shop, **2:**243
Agent Orange, **1:54–55; 2:**119, 537
  illnesses attributed to, **2:**538
Aging, **2:**560
  See also Old age
Agnew, Spiro T., **3:**166
  resignation of, **8:**323
  on Skinner (B. F.), **1:**438
Agnosticism, **1:**55
Agrarianism, **1:55–58,** *56*
  Granger movement, **4:**36–37
  Jefferson on, **1:**55, 56–57, 62
  Nonpartisan League and, **6:**118
  Southern, **3:**481
  Tillmanism, **8:**126
Agribusiness, **1:**67
Agricultural Adjustment Act (AAA)
  (1933), **1:**66, 71, 396; **6:**43;
  8:273
  Thomas Amendment to, **1:**459;
    4:15
Agricultural Adjustment Administration (AAA), **1:**60; **3:**318–319
  in Arkansas, **1:**262
Agricultural education, land-grant
  colleges for, **5:**28, 29–30
Agricultural machinery, **1:58–60**
  grain elevators, **3:187–188**
  by International Harvester Company, **4:389**
  McCormick reaper, **5:183–184**
  wagons, **8:362**
Agricultural policy, *United States v.
  Butler* and, **8:**273
Agricultural science, Morrill Act
  and, **2:**415

Agricultural workers
  American, **5**:4
  immigrant, **5**:4
    illegal, **4**:229
  migrant, **5**:374
  occupational health issues for,
      5:297, 298–299
  trade union of, **8:266–267**
  See also Farmers
Agriculture, **1:61–68**
  in 19th century, **1**:63–65; **7**:207
  in 20th century, **1**:65–67, *66*
  in Alabama, **1**:102, 103, 104, 105
  in American Revolution, **1**:62
  apprenticeship in, **1**:228
  in Arkansas, **1**:260, 261, 262
  botanical gardens and, **1**:516
  Brannan Plan for, **1:533**
  capitalist, **2**:42
  child labor in, **2**:140
  in Civil War, **1**:63
  in colonial era, **1**:61–62, *62*;
      2:96–97; **3**:108; **4**:125–126,
      349; **6**:151; **8**:12–13
  commercialization of, **1**:67; **2**:387
  dry farming, **3:87–88**
  electrification and, **1**:67
  fertilizers in (*See* Fertilizers)
  in Florida, **3**:478, 479
  gardening, **3:509–511**
  in Georgia, **3**:555, 556
  grants-in-aid for, **7**:401–402
  grasshoppers and, **4**:37
  Great Depression and, **8**:162
  in Great Lakes basin, **4**:51–52
  in Great Plains, **4**:57
  health issues in, occupational,
      5:297, 298–299
  hydroponic, **4:204**
  in Idaho, **4**:212, 213
  in Illinois, **4**:216, 217
  in Indiana, **4**:318, 320
  insecticides and herbicides in, **1**:67;
      4:361–362
  in Iowa, **4**:414–417
  irrigation in (*See* Irrigation)
  in Kansas, **4**:508, 509, 510
  in Kentucky, **4**:519
  legislation on, **1**:63; **4**:30
    New Deal, **1**:66–67, 71; **7**:474
  loans for, by intermediate credit
      banks, **4**:384–385
  in Maine, **5**:208–209
  in Minnesota, **5**:399

  in Mississippi, **5**:413
  in Montana, **5**:450
  Native American, **1**:61, **68–71;**
      2:96, 413
    Akimel O'odham, **1**:100
    economics of, **4**:267–269
    fruit growing, **3**:478
    gardening, **3**:509
    in Great Plains, **8**:218
    Hopi, **4**:165
    in New England, **8**:220
    potatoes, **6**:432
    on prairie, **8**:224
    of Pueblo, **6**:540; **8**:227
    technology in, **4**:307–308
  in Nebraska, **6**:30, 31
  New Deal legislation on, **1**:66–67,
      71; **7**:474
  in New Hampshire, **6**:58–59
  in New Jersey, **6**:61
  in North Dakota, **6**:133
  no-till, **7**:445
  in Oregon, **6**:205–206
  organic farming, **4**:118; **6:210**
  origins of, **2**:95–96
  in Plymouth Colony, **6**:378
  population on farms, **1**:66
  on prairie, **6**:447; **8**:224
  price supports in, **1:60–61,** 66
    export debenture plan, **3:302**
    McNary-Haugen Bill, **5:189**
  productivity of, **1**:67, 72
  radio broadcasting on, **7**:274–275
  railroads and, **8**:165
  research on, **1**:63, 71, 72; **5**:17–18
  sharecropping in, **1**:63; **7:335–336**
  slavery and, **7**:383–384, 385
  in South
    in 19th century, **1**:63
    antebellum, **7**:463–464
    in Civil War, **1**:63
    in colonial era, **1**:62
    plantation system, **6:363–365**
  in South Carolina, **7**:454
  in South Dakota, **7**:460
  statistics used in, **7**:539
  subsidies for, **7**:565
  surpluses in, **1**:71–72
  tariffs and, **3**:460
  teaching, **3**:325
  in Texas, **8**:101–102
  in tidewater region, **8**:125
  transportation and, **1**:63; **3**:390
  unsustainable, and Dust Bowl, **3**:96

  in Utah, **8**:297
  in Utopian communities, **8**:301
  in Vermont, **8**:313, 314
  in Virginia, **1**:62; **8**:341–342, 343,
      346
  in Washington, **8**:413
  weed control in, **8**:436
  in West, **1**:64–65; **3**:18
  World War II and, **8**:162
  in Wyoming, **8**:565
  See also Livestock industry; *specific
      crops*
Agriculture, Department of
    (USDA), **1:71–72;** **3**:331
  agrarianism and, **1**:57
  animal disease and, **8**:319
  establishment of, **1**:57, 63, 71;
      8:319
  Food Safety and Inspection Service
      in, **5**:278
  food stamp program of, **3**:408–409;
      6:150
  Forest Service in (*See* Forest Ser-
      vice)
  and 4-H Clubs, **3**:445
  functions of, **1**:71–72
  and genetically modified plant
      species, **1**:463
  head of, **2**:2
  microbiology research by, **5**:358
  and organic farming, **6**:210
  soil mapping by, **7**:444
Ague, **1:72**
Aguinaldo, Emilio, **6**:319–320, 322
AHA. *See* American Historical Asso-
      ciation; American Hospital
      Association
Ahlquist, Jon, **6**:215
Ahrens-Fox Manufacturing Compa-
      ny, **3**:372
Ahtnas, **8**:213
AIAA. *See* American Institute of
      Aeronautics and Astronautics
AIC. *See* Art Institute of Chicago
AICF. *See* American Indian College
      Fund
Aid. *See* Federal aid; Foreign aid
Aid to Dependent Children (ADC),
      2:146; **7**:416; **8**:440
Aid to Families with Dependent
      Children (AFDC), **6**:438; **8**:440
  abolition of, **8**:442
  expansion of, **8**:441–442

AIDA. *See* American Indian Defense Association

AIDS. *See* Acquired immune deficiency syndrome

AIDS Coalition to Unleash Power. *See* ACT UP

AIDS Quilt, **1:**72–73, *73;* **7:**6

Aiello, Geduldig v., **3:***525*

AIHEC. *See* American Indian Higher Education Consortium

Aiken, Conrad, **5:**120

Aiken, Howard, **2:***334*

Ailey, Alvin, **1:**131; **2:***498,* 499

AIM. *See* American Indian Movement

AIP. *See* Airport Improvement Program

Air Cavalry, **1:**73–74

Air Combat Command (ACC), **1:**82

Air Commerce Act (1926), **1:**82, 98; **3:**336; **6:**427

Air Commerce Act (1938), **1:**84

Air conditioning, **1:**74–75

Air defense, **1:**75–76

Air Force, U.S., **1:**76–78
  and aerial bombing, **1:**495
  in Cold War, **1:**76–77
  creation of, **1:**76
  in Korean War, **1:**76–77; **4:**550
  medicine in, **5:**296
  in Persian Gulf War, **1:**77; **6:**293
  Special Forces of, **7:**494
  SR-71 fleet of, **2:**93
  and UFO research, **8:**255
  in Vietnam War, **1:**77
  in World War II, **8:**545

Air Force Academy, **1:**78

Air Force Cross, **2:**526

Air Guard, **5:**542

Air Medal, **2:**527

Air pollution, **1:**78–81
  in 19th century, **1:**78–79
  and acid rain, **1:**13–14, *14;* **3:**480
  automobiles and, **8:**190
  in cities, **1:***80*
  crisis of 1950s, **2:**371
  emissions trading and, **1:**80
  energy use and projections for, **3:**213
  fossil fuels and, **3:**214
  gasoline taxes and, **3:**511
  indoor, **1:**80–81
  legislation on, **1:**79, 362 (*See also* Air Quality Act; Clean Air Act)
  and auto industry, **1:**362

effectiveness of, **1:**13–14
  resistance to, **1:**79
  in Los Angeles, **5:**154
  in New Jersey, **6:**64
  and search for alternative fuels, **3:**480
  sources of, **1:**79

Air power, strategic, **1:**81–82
  helicopters in, **4:**123–124
  in Korean War, **4:**550

Air Quality Act (1967), **1:**79
  limitations of, **1:**362

Air Traffic Control (ATC), **3:**336

Air traffic controllers strike (1981), **1:**82; **2:**275; **5:**11; **7:**559; **8:**172

Air Transport Association (ATA), **1:**84

Air transportation and travel, **1:**82–86; **8:***189,* 190–191
  accidents in, **1:**13; **3:**35–36
    Korean Airlines flight 007, **4:**543
    Pan Am flight 103, **6:**233–234
    TWA flight 800, **8:***241,* 241–242
  air traffic controllers strike (1981) and, **1:**82; **8:**172
  airplane hijackings in, **4:**132–133
  airports
    hub system of, **1:**97
    siting and financing of, **1:**98–99
    in Alaska, **1:**110
    Civil Aeronautics Board and, **2:**190–191
  commercial airlines in, **1:**83, 84
  deregulation of, **1:**96–97
  Federal Aviation Administration and, **3:**336–337
  infrastructure of, **1:**84
  jets in, **1:**84–85
  after 9/11 attack, **1:**86; **6:**108, 109; **8:**192
  regulation of, **1:**84
  subsidies for, **7:**565
  and vacation activities, **8:**305
  after World War I, **1:**82–84
  after World War II, **1:**84

Air war. *See* Bombing

Airborne units. *See* Paratroops

Aircraft
  armament on, **1:**88–89
  bombers, **1:**86–87; **5:**480
    on aircraft carriers, **1:**89
    B-1, **1:**87
    B-2, **1:**87
    B-17, **1:**86, 494

B-24, **1:**86, *86*
B-25, **1:**86, *87, 90*
B-26, **1:**86
B-29, **1:**86, 494
  in air war against Japan, **8:**554–555
B-36, **1:**76, 86
B-45, **1:**86
B-47, **1:**86
B-52, **1:**87, 496
B-70, **2:**528
FB-111A, **1:**87
  manufacture of, **1:**335–336
China Clipper, **2:**153
commercial, **1:**83, 84
dirigibles, **3:**30–32, *31*
executive, **1:**95
fighters, **1:**87–88
  on aircraft carriers, **1:**89
insurance for, **4:**368–369
Liberty engine, **5:**481–482
naval, **1:**89–92
private ownership of, **1:**93, 94, 95
supersonic transport (Concorde), **8:**21
X-1 plane, **8:***569,* 569–570
See also Airplane; Helicopters

Aircraft carriers, **1:**89–92
  development of, **1:**89; **8:**406
  first battle of, **2:**412
  radar room on, **7:***14*
  in World War II, **1:**89–91; **8:**557
    Pearl Harbor attack and, **8:**556
    Task Force 58, **8:**53

Aircraft industry, **1:**92–96
  aluminum in, **1:**130
  automation in, **1:**364
  Boeing Company, **1:***493,* 493–494
  in California, **2:**11
    Long Beach, **5:**149
    Southern, **5:**152–153
  Federal Aviation Administration and, **3:**337
  in Great Depression, **1:**93
  holding companies in, **1:**93
  on Long Island, **5:**149
  mergers in, **1:**95
  regulation of, **1:**93
  in Vietnam War, **1:**96
  in World War I, **1:**92
  in World War II, **1:**93–94

AIRFA. *See* American Indian Religious Freedom Act

Airline Deregulation Act (1978),
  1:96–97; 8:191
Airline industry
  deregulation of, **3:**13
  See also Air transportation and trav-
    el; Aircraft industry
Airmail, **1:**82, 83, **97–98; 6:**427;
  8:190–191
Airmail Act (1925), **1:**82; **8:**190
Airmail Act (1930), **1:**83
Airplane crashes, **1:**13; **3:35–36**
  Korean Airlines flight 007, **4:**543
  Pan Am flight 103, **6:233–234**
  TWA flight 800, **8:***241*, **241–242**
Airplane hijacking, **4:132–133**
Airport Improvement Program
  (AIP), **1:**98, 99
Airports
  hub system of, **1:**97
  regulation of, **1:**98
  siting and financing of, **1:98–99**
Airy, George B., **3:**552
Aisne-Marne Operation, **1:99**
Aitken, Robert, **1:**447, 552
Aityes, Victor, **5:**72
Aix-la-Chapelle, Treaty of (1748),
  1:99–100; 4:313
  and Louisburg expedition, **5:**157
Akimel O'odham, **1:***100*, **100–101;**
  8:227
  agriculture among, **1:**100
  language of, **1:**100
  water rights for, **1:**100, 101
Akron Rule (1872), **5:**176
Al Qaeda, **6:**108–109
  and *Cole* bombing, **2:270–271**
  and embassy bombings, **3:**194
  See also Bin Laden, Osama
Alabama, **1:101–105**
  African Americans in
    civil rights movement and,
      1:104–105
    during Reconstruction, **1:**103
  agriculture in, **1:**102, 103, 104, 105
  Alabama Platform in, **1:106**
  Black Belt in, **1:471**
  civil rights movement in,
    1:104–105
  in Civil War, **1:**102–103
    Battle of Mobile Bay, **5:428–429**
  in colonial era, **1:**102
  constitution of, **1:**102, 103; **7:**525
  Creek War in, **1:**102

Democratic Party in, **1:**102, 103,
  104
emblems, nicknames, mottos, and
  songs of, **7:***532*
governors of, **1:**102, 104
Great Depression in, **1:**104
industry in, **1:**103, 105
Ku Klux Klan in, **1:**103, 104
Montgomery Convention in
  (1861), **5:452**
Muscle Shoals speculation in,
  5:483–484
Native Americans in, **1:**101–102
in New Deal era, **1:**104
population of, **1:**102, 105
Populist Party in, **1:**103
Reconstruction in, **1:**103
school desegregation in, **1:**104
Scottsboro case in, **1:**104; **7:286**
segregation in, **1:**104; **3:**464
slavery in, **1:**102
statehood for, **1:**102
strike in textile industry in, **8:**111
tidelands in, ownership of, **8:**125
Union sentiment in, **8:**260
voter requirements in, **1:**103
women in, **1:**103–104
in World War I, **1:**103
in World War II, **1:**104
Alabama (ship), **1:105–106**
Alabama, Powell v., **3:**575
Alabama, Thornhill v., **6:**350
Alabama claims, **1:106; 6:**35
  Treaty of Washington on, **1:**106;
    8:416
Alabama Claims Arbitration (1871),
  6:35
Alabama Platform, **1:106**
ALAM. *See* Association of Licensed
  Automobile Manufacturers
Alamo, Siege of, **1:106–107,** *107*,
  354; **8:**100
  eyewitness account of, **9:**212–214
Alar, **6:**210
Alarcón, Hernando de, **1:**256; **2:**301,
  416; **3:**296
Alarcón, Martín de, **8:**99
Alaska, **1:107–112**
  annexation of, **1:**108–109, 189;
    3:425; **8:**94
  boundary question regarding, **2:**26;
    7:215
  coal mining in, **1:**110
  constitution of, **1:**110

earthquakes in, **3:**101, *101*, 102
economy of, **1:**110
emblems, nicknames, mottos, and
  songs of, **7:***532*
Exxon Valdez oil spill in, **1:**13, 111,
  113; **3:**233, *305*, **305–306;**
  6:304
fisheries in, **1:**109–110
  salmon, **7:**231
fur trapping in, **1:**108, 121
gold in, **1:**109–110; **4:**11
legislature of, **1:**109, 111
Libertarian Party in, **8:**120
maps of, **1:***109, 110*
national parks in, **5:552–553**
Native Americans in, **1:**108, 109,
  110, 111, 112
  Aleut, **1:120–121**
  Inuit, **4:**408–409
natural resources in, **1:**108,
  109–110
oil in, **1:**111, 112, 113; **6:**171, 179,
  180
oil pipeline in, **1:**111, 112, **113;**
  6:180
population of, **1:**109, 110
public lands in, distribution of,
  5:30
purchase of, **8:**201, 204
Russian exploration and expansion
  in, **1:**108, 120–121; **3:***293,*
  293–294; 4:409
statehood for, **1:**110–111, 112
U.S. purchase of, **7:**210
volcanoes in, **8:**351
wilderness of, **1:**108, 109, 111
winter in, **1:***486*
in World War II, **1:**110, 121–122
Alaska Highway, **2:**27; **7:**180
Alaska National Interest Lands Conservation Act (ANILCA) (1980),
  1:111; **5:**553
Alaska Native Claims Settlement Act
  (ANCSA) (1971), **1:**111, **112;**
  8:212
  impact on Aleut, **1:**121
Alaska Permanent Fund, **1:**111
Alaska Pipeline Authorization Act
  (1973), **1:**111
Alaska Purchase Treaty (1867), **8:**204
Alaska Syndicate, **1:**110
Alaskan Indians. *See* Tribes, Alaskan
Alaskan Petroleum Reserve, **3:**547
Albanel, Charles, **3:**291

Albany (New York), **1:113**
  Dongan charter and, **3:**79
  Dutch post at, **3:**290
Albany Convention, **5:**81
  See also Leisler Rebellion
Albany Plan, **1:113–114; 6:**363
Albany Regency, **1:**114
Albatross (ship), **1:**114
Albee, Edward, **8:**309
  Who's Afraid of Virginia Woolf?,
    5:122
Albemarle settlements, **1:**114
Albers, Josef, **1:**298
Albertson, Ralph, **8:**302
Albizu Campos, Pedro, **6:**545, 546
Albright, Horace, **3:**268; **5:**549,
    550–551; **8:**580
Albright, Madeleine
  and Cuba relations, **2:**472
  and Kosovo bombing, **4:**551
Albright, Miller v., **1:**125
Albuquerque (New Mexico),
    1:114–115, *115;* **6:**69
Alcaldes, **1:**115
Alcaraz, Lalo, **6:**395
Alcatraz, **1:115–116,** *116;* **6:**477
  AIM occupation of, **1:**115–116,
    161; **7:70,** *70;* **8:**215
Alcindor, Lew, **1:**425
Alcoa. *See* Aluminum Company of
    America
Alcohol
  abuse of, **7:**567–568 (*See also* Alco-
    holism)
  consumption rates for, **1:**116, 117
    in colonial era, **2:**292
  distilling of, **2:**97; **3:59–61,** *60*
  and driving, **1:**118
  legal age for use of, **1:**118
  moonshine, **5:455**
  and Native Americans, **1:**116;
    4:321–323
  recreation and, **7:**64
  regulation of, **1:116–118** (*See also*
    Prohibition; Temperance
    movements)
    in 19th century, **1:**116–117
    in 20th century, **1:**117–118
    in colonial era, **1:**116
    federal, **1:**117
    after Prohibition, **1:**117–118
    state, **1:**117–118
  research on, **1:**118, 119
  at speakeasies, **7:492–493**

spirits industry, **7:504–505**
Alcoholics Anonymous (AA), **1:118,**
    119; **7:**570
  and self-help movement,
    7:304–305
Alcoholism, **1:118–120**
  as disease, **1:**118, 119
  among Native Americans, **4:**323
  origin of term, **1:**118–119
  treatment of, **1:**118; **7:**569–570
Alcott, Abigail, **8:**301
Alcott, Bronson, **7:**194; **8:**179, 180,
    301
Alcott, Louisa May, *Little Women*,
    5:127
Alcott, William, **8:**310
Alden v. Maine, **1:**120
Alderman, Edward A., **8:**283
Aldrich, Nelson W., **7:**343
Aldrich-Vreeland Act (1908), **1:120,**
    397
  and National Monetary Commis-
    sion, **5:**547
  for panic of 1907, **3:**344, 366
Aldrin, Edwin E. (Buzz), Jr., **5:**454,
    524; **7:**480
Alemany, José Sadoc, **3:**77
Alembert, Jean d', *Encyclopédie*, **3:**204
Aleut, **1:120–121; 8:**211–212
  housing of, **4:***180*
  Russians and, **1:**120–121
Aleutian Islands, **1:***121,* **121–122**
Alexander, Sir Harold
  in Anzio, **1:**217
  in Sicilian Campaign, **7:**354
Alexander, James, **2:**292; **6:**61, 95;
    8:590
Alexander, Jane, **5:**536
Alexander v. Choate, **2:**196
*Alexander v. Holmes County Board of
    Education*, **1:**122
Alexander v. Sandoval, **2:**196
Alexander VI, Pope, **3:**284
Alexandria (Virginia), **1:**122
Alexandria Conference (1785),
    1:122
Alexie, Sherman
  *The Lone Ranger and Tonto Fistfight
    in Heaven*, **5:**129
  Smoke Signals, **5:**129
Algeciras Conference (1904), **1:123**
Alger, Commonwealth v., **6:**387
Alger, Horatio, **2:**227; **8:**325
Algeria, in World War II, **1:**233

Algiers
  Decatur's cruise to, **2:520**
  U.S. relations with, **1:**232
  war with, **1:**415
Algonquin Indians
  and Champlain explorations, **2:**103
  French alliance with, **2:**293
  languages of, **8:**219, 223
  in Pontiac's War, **8:**392
  in Rhode Island, **7:**151
  teachers among, **3:**133
Algonquin Round Table, **1:**123
Ali, Muhammad, **5:**520; **6:**484–485
  as conscientious objector, **2:**362
Alianza movement, **7:**12
Alien(s)
  deportation of, **1:**125
  detention of, **1:**125
  enemy, in world wars, **3:207–208,**
    254
  green card for, **4:60–61**
  landholding by, **1:124–125,** 126;
    4:464
  naturalization of, **6:**13–14
  rights of, **1:125–126**
    Proposition 187 and, **6:**509
  wartime internment of, **4:**399–400
Alien and Sedition Acts, **1:123–124;**
    2:84; **7:**301
  of 1798, **5:**97
  and asylum principle, **6:**396
  Aurora and, **1:**360
  convictions under, **1:**124; **3:**374
  and deportation, **3:**11
  and Jeffersonian Republicans, **6:**96
  and newspapers, **3:**351
  opposition to, **1:**124; **6:**145, 297;
    8:349
  provisions of, **1:123–124; 7:**301
  Supreme Court on, **7:**301
  Virginia Resolves on, **1:**124; **8:**349
Alien Enemies Act (1798), **1:**123
Alien Friends Act (1798), **1:**123
Alien Registration Act. *See* Smith Act
Alien registration receipt card. *See*
    Green card
Alkalimat, Abdul, **1:**47
All America Football League
    (AAFL), **3:**412
All in the Family (TV show), **1:***126,*
    126–127
All the King's Men (Warren), **5:**121
All Things Considered (radio pro-
    gram), **5:**554; **8:**44

Allegheny Mountains, **6:**86
  Monongahela River in, **5:444**
  and pack trains, **6:**228
  routes across, **1:127**
  wagoners of, **8:**365
Allegheny River, **1:127**
Allegheny Transportation Company,
  6:359
Allen, Arthur, **1:**248
Allen, Ethan, **8:**311
  achievements in American Revolu-
    tion, **7:**142
  in capture of Ticonderoga, **8:**124
  Green Mountain Boys formed by,
    4:61
Allen, Forrest (Phog), **1:**423, 424
Allen, Frederick Lewis, **1:**33–34
Allen, Gracie, **8:**309
Allen, Henry T., Army of Occupa-
  tion under, **1:**278
Allen, Horatio, **7:**30
Allen, Ira, **4:**61
Allen, Ivan, Jr., **3:**557
Allen, Lewis F., **2:**489
Allen, Macon Bolling, **5:**74
Allen, Mueller v., **2:**169
Allen, Paul, **2:**336; **3:**184; **5:**359–360
Allen, Richard, **1:**43–44, *44*, 53, *53;*
  8:501
Allen, Steve, **8:**142
Allen, William, **1:**494; **3:**358
Allen, Woody, **3:**364; **5:**123
Allen v. Board of Election, **8:**357
Allende, Salvador, **2:**150; **5:**49
Allgeyer v. Louisiana, **1:**21
Alliance, Treaty of (1778),
  8:199–200
Alliance for Progress, **1:127–128;**
  3:143, 417–418; **5:**48
  in Guatemala, **4:**70
Allin, Darcy v., **6:**255
Allison, W. B., **1:**484
Allison, William B., **1:**128
Allison Commission, **1:128**
Allport, Gordon, **6:**376
Allred, James V., **8:**103
Allston, Washington, **1:**295
All-Volunteer Force (AVF), **3:**223
Allwright, Smith v., **3:**147; **5:**526;
  6:463
Almanacs, **1:129–130**
  Poor Richard's Almanac, **1:**129;
    6:413
  excerpt from, **9:**113–114

Almond, Edward, **2:**160
Almond, J. Linsey, Jr., **8:**344
Almshouses, **6:**476
  as hospitals, **4:**172
ALP. *See* American Labor Party
Altair (personal computer), **2:**336
Alternating current (AC), **3:**178, 211
Alternative dispute resolution
  (ADR), **1:**236; **3:**343
Alternative Dispute Resolution Act
  (1990), **3:**343
Alternative medicine, **5:290–292,**
  301
  chiropractic, **5:**291–292
  homeopathy, **5:**291, 301
  medicine shows, **5:305–306,** *306*
  New Age, **5:**292
Altgeld, John Peter, **6:**550
Altman, Robert, **3:**364
  Short Cuts, **5:**123
*Alton Railroad Company, Railroad
  Retirement Board v.*, **7:28–29**
Altria Group, Inc., **8:**137
Aluminum, **1:130–131**
  applications for, **1:**130–131
  as building material, **1:**564–565
  demand for, **6:**116
  electrolytic process for, **6:**115
  metalwork, **5:**330
  production of, **1:**130; **6:**114,
    115–116
  recycling of, **6:**116; **7:**67
Aluminum Company of America
  (Alcoa), **1:**130; **6:**114, 115–116
Alvarado, Hernando de, **3:**296
Alvarez, Luis W., **6:**343
Álvarez de Pineda, Alonso, **8:**98–99
Alvin (submersible research vessel),
  6:161, 162
Alvin Ailey Dance Theater, **1:**131,
  131
Alzheimer, Alois, **1:**131
Alzheimer's disease, **1:131–132**
Am Olam movement, **8:**302
AMA. *See* American Medical Associ-
  ation
Amador, Manuel, **6:**243
Amalgamated Association of Iron,
  Steel and Tin Workers, **7:**545
Amalgamated Clothing Workers of
  America (ACWA), **1:132–133;**
  2:249, 250; **8:**278
Amana Community, **1:133**
Amaraks, **1:**413–414

Amateur Athletic Union (AAU),
  5:530
Amateur Sports Act (1978), **5:**530
Amazon.com, **2:**324; **3:**183
Ambach v. Norwick, **1:**126
Ambassadors, **1:133–134; 3:**28;
  7:528
Ambler Realty Company, Euclid v.,
  6:505; **8:**593
AMEC. *See* African Methodist Epis-
  copal Church
Amelung, John Frederick, **4:**3
Amendments, Constitutional,
  1:456–457
  See also Bill of Rights; *specific
    amendments*
Amerasia case, **1:134–135**
America
  definition of, in American Studies,
    1:170
  exploration of (*See* Exploration[s])
  flora of, **1:**518
  as interpreted by foreign observers,
    1:135–139, 148–149
  naming of, **1:**135; **3:**284
  as New Israel, **1:**447
America 2000 Excellence in Educa-
  tion Act, **3:**124
America First Committee (AFC),
  1:139; 4:440
"America First" speech, Lindbergh's,
  text of, **9:**393–395
America Online (AOL), **2:**323, 337;
  8:127
"America the Beautiful" (song),
  1:139
American Academy of Arts and Sci-
  ences, **1:139–140; 5:**66
  astronomy in, **1:**343
American Academy of Dramatic
  Arts, **8:**114
American Airlines, **1:**83
  crash of flight 191 (1979), **1:**13
American and Foreign Christian
  Union, **6:**4
American Anti-Slavery Society
  (AAS), **1:**209, 210; **3:**502; **5:**96
American Anti-Vivisection Society,
  1:186
American Arab Anti-Discrimination
  Committee (ADC), **5:**72
American Art Union, **3:**537
American Association for Public
  Opinion Research, **6:**534

American Association for the Advancement of Science (AAAS), **1:**140–142; **3:**548, 550; **5:**66–67

American Association of Advertising Agencies, **1:**33

American Association of Retired Persons (AARP), **1:**142; **6:**189

American Association of University Professors (AAUP), **1:**10, **142–143**

American Association of University Women, **1:**143
  on coeducation, **2:**263

American Atlas (Carey), **2:**60

American Automobile Association (AAA), **1:143–144**

American Ballet Theatre (ABT), **1:**144, 390; **2:**498–499

American Banking Group, **6:**197

American Bar Association (ABA), **1:144–145; 5:**74
  on Federal Trade Association, **3:**349
  and legal education, **5:**56–57
  and National Lawyers Guild, **5:**546

American Bible Society, **1:145–146**, 447

American Board of Psychiatry and Neurology, **6:**521

American Broadcasting Company. *See* ABC television network

American Civil Liberties Union (ACLU), **1:146–147; 2:**84
  and church-state separation, **2:**169
  on electronic surveillance, **3:**186
  establishment of, **1:**146
  legal cases involving (*See under* ACLU)
  on Palmer Raids, **6:**232
  on physician-assisted suicide, **3:**262
  and prisons, **6:**477
  on prostitution, **6:**513
  public interest law carried out by, **6:**530
  in Sacco-Vanzetti case, **1:**146
  in Scopes Trial, **1:**146
  in Scottsboro case, **1:**146

American Civil Liberties Union, Reno v., **3:**374; **8:**68

American Civil War, The: Explorations and Reconsiderations (Grant), **5:**568

American Class Reader (Wilson), **5:**127

American Colonization Society (ACS), **1:147–148**, 208–209, 477; **3:**197; **6:**47
  on manumission, **5:**230

American Commonwealth (Bryce), **1:**137; **6:**455

American Communist Party. *See* Communist Party, USA

American Company (theater), **8:**113

American Council of Learned Societies (ACLS), **5:**67, 537

American Crisis, The (Paine), **5:**118

American Dilemma, An (Myrdal), **1:**138, **148–149**

"American Diplomacy" (Kennan), excerpt from, **9:**411–413

American Economic Association, **3:**108; **5:**67

American Enterprise Institute (AEI), **1:**545; **8:**117–118

American Expeditionary Forces (AEF), **1:**149; **8:**535
  and American Legion, **8:**318
  Americanism of, **8:**318
  buildup of, **5:**338
  in France, **1:**149
  in Italy, **1:**149
  transport of, **8:**540

American Express, **1:**580; **2:**451; **8:**443

American Federation of Labor (AFL), **1:**150–151, 589; **5:**7, 10, 16, 17
  Amalgamated Clothing Workers of America in, **1:**132
  on child labor, **2:**140
  discrimination in, **1:**150
    racial, **3:**49
  establishment of, **1:**150
  ideology of, **1:**150
  immigrants in, **1:**150
  and Labor Day, **5:**13
  merger with CIO, **1:**151; **8:**172
  and National Civic Federation, **5:**530
  New Deal and, **1:**150–151
  and Progressive Party, **6:**498
  and Railroad Brotherhoods, **7:**24
  Railway Employees Department of, **7:**40
  size of, **1:**150, 151

thirty-hour week proposed by, **8:**120
  and Trade Union Educational League, **8:**170
  and Trade Union Unity League, **8:**170
  on unemployment insurance, **2:**227
  and United Brotherhood of Carpenters and Joiners, **8:**262–263
  and United Electrical, Radio, and Machine Workers of America, **3:**176
  and United Mine Workers of America, **8:**267
  and United Textile Workers, **8:**278
  and Women's Trade Union League, **8:**522
  in World War I, **1:**150; **8:**536
  in World War II, **1:**151
  See also American Federation of Labor–Congress of Industrial Organizations

American Federation of Labor–Congress of Industrial Organizations (AFL-CIO), **1:149–154**
  anticommunism of, **1:**151, 152, 197
  civil rights movement and, **1:**152; **8:**172
  in Democratic Party, **1:**151, 152–153
  discrimination in, **1:**152
  in domestic affairs, **1:**151–152
  on ergonomic workplace standards, **5:**12
  in foreign affairs, **1:**152
  functions of, **1:**149
  International Brotherhood of Teamsters in, **1:**151; **4:**386
  as monopoly, **1:**151
  No-Strike Pledge of, **8:**171
  size of, **1:**151, 153
  Supreme Court on, **4:**82–83
  and United Automobile Workers, **8:**262
  and United Mine Workers of America, **8:**268
  and youth movements, **8:**587

American Federation of State, County, and Municipal Employees (AFSCME), **1:154**

American Federation of Teachers (AFT), **1:154–157**
  on academic freedom, **1:**155

in Great Depression, **1:**155–156
National Education Association
    and, **1:**155, 156, 157; **5:**534
origins of, **1:**155
on racial discrimination, **1:**155
rightward shift of, **1:**156–157
on school desegregation, **1:**155,
    156
in World War I, **1:**155
in World War II, **1:**156
American Fiber Manufacturers
    Association, **8:**108
American First Army, **1:**149
American Folklore Society (AFS),
    3:394
American Football League (AFL),
    3:411
American foulbrood disease, **1:**436
American Fur Company (AFC),
    1:157–158; 3:298, 487, 494;
    8:175
    Illinois Fur Brigade by, **4:219**
    and Red River cart traffic, **7:**71
American Genealogist, The (TAG)
    (magazine), **3:**522
American Geographical Society,
    3:540, 541, 543
American Gothic (Wood), **3:**538
American Grocer (journal), **6:**554
American Health Convention, **8:**310
American Historical Association
    (AHA), **1:158–159; 5:**67
    and archives, **1:**255
*American History and Its Geographic
    Conditions* (Semple), **3:**542–543
American Hospital Association
    (AHA), **6:**257
American Independent Party, **1:**159;
    3:165; **7:**16; **8:**119
American Indian College Fund
    (AICF), **8:**211
American Indian Dance Theater,
    2:501
American Indian Day, **8:**215
American Indian Defense Associa-
    tion (AIDA), **1:159–160**
    Meriam Report compared to, **5:**323
American Indian Gaming Regulato-
    ry Act (1988), **1:**160; **8:**489
American Indian Higher Education
    Consortium (AIHEC), **8:**211
American Indian Movement (AIM),
    1:160–161; 7:165
    activities of, **1:**160–161

establishment of, **1:**160
magazine publication and, **5:**192
prosecution of, **7:**71
protests by, **1:**161
    Alcatraz occupation, **1:**115–116,
        161; **7:**70; **8:**215
    Wounded Knee occupation, **1:**161;
        7:70, 71; **8:560–561,** *561*
    "Trail of Broken Treaties" orga-
        nized by, **8:**177
American Indian Religious Freedom
    Act (AIRFA) (1978), **1:161–162;**
    5:180
American Institute of Aeronautics
    and Astronautics (AIAA), **8:**255
American Institute of Public Opin-
    ion, **6:**409
American Journal of Nursing, **6:**147
American Journal of Physiology, **6:**349
American Journal of Psychology, **6:**524
American Kinship (Schneider), **5:**251
American Labor Party (ALP), **1:**162;
    5:16, 17
American Land Company, **5:**36
American Law Institute, on prostitu-
    tion, **6:**513
American Legion, **1:162–163**
    Americanism of, **1:**163; **8:**318
    creation of, **1:**162–163; **8:**318
American Liberty League,
    1:163–164
American Library Association, **5:**98
American Lutheran Church, **5:**177;
    6:137
American Mathematical Society. *See*
    Learned Societies
American Medical Association
    (AMA), **1:164–165**
    on abortion, **1:**4
    birth control and, **1:**5, 466, 468
    and chiropractic, opposition to,
        2:157
    on contraception, **1:**5
    education standards of, **1:**164
    establishment of, **1:**164;
        5:284–285, 288
    on health insurance, **4:**119
    lobbying by, **1:**164–165
    on medical ethics, **1:**164
    organizational structure of, **1:**164
    on physician assistants, **6:**334
    radio broadcasting by, **7:**275
American Medical Political Action
    Committee (AMPAC), **6:**393

American Medico-Psychological
    Association, **6:**521
American Museum (of P. T. Bar-
    num), **5:**487
American Museum of Natural His-
    tory, **1:**165
American Nazi Party, **3:**328
American Notes (Dickens), **1:**136;
    6:537
American Nurses Association
    (ANA), **6:**147
American Party, **1:165–166**
    platform of (1856), **9:**242–243
    See also Know-Nothing Party
American Peace Society (APS),
    1:216
American Pharmaceutical Associa-
    tion, **6:**309
American Philosophical Society,
    1:166–167; 5:66
    astronomy in, **1:**342
American Physical Society, **6:**335,
    337, 346, 347, 348
American Physiological Society
    (APS), **6:**349
American Political Science Associa-
    tion (APSA), **6:**402–403
American Political Science Review
    (journal), **6:**402, 404
American Press Company, Grosjean v.,
    4:67
American Printing House for the
    Blind, **3:**123
American Professional Football
    Association, **3:**410
American Protection Association,
    6:4
American Protective Association
    (APA), **1:**167, 196
    and little red schoolhouse, **5:**134
American Protective League, **6:**232
American Protestant Society, **6:**4
American Psychiatric Association
    (APA), **6:**521, 522
    on homosexuality, **3:**514; **7:**327
American Psychological Association
    (APA), **6:**524
American Railway Union (ARU),
    1:167–168; 7:24
    and Pullman Strike, **6:**549
American Relief Administration
    (ARA), **8:**541
American Renaissance (Matthiessen),
    1:169, 170

American Republican Party, **1:**168; **6:**4

American Samoa, **7:**235–236

"American Scholar, The" (Emerson), **5:**119; **8:**180

American Ship Building Co. v. NLRB, **5:**141

American Sign Language (ASL), **2:**508, 509; **7:355–357**
opposition to, **3:**32

American Soccer League (ASL), **7:**410

American Social Hygiene Association, **6:**513

American Social Science Association (ASSA), **5:**66–67; **7:**432

American Society for Colonizing the Free People of Color, **6:**235

American Society for Psychical Research, **6:**246

American Society for the Promotion of Temperance, **8:**78

American Society of Composers, Authors, and Publishers (ASCAP), **5:**502

American Society of Genealogists (ASG), **3:**521

American Society of Hospital Pharmacists, **6:**311

American Society of Mammalogists, **5:**217

American Society of Newspaper Editors, **6:**99

American Sociological Association (ASA), **7:**432, 434, 435

American Spelling Book, The (Webster), **8:**106

American Standard Code for Information Interchange (ASCII), **3:**24

American Stock Exchange (AMEX), **3:**275; **7:**548–549

American Studies, **1:168–171**

American System (economic policy), **1:171**

American System (of manufacturing), development of, **5:**262

American Teachers Association (ATA), **5:**534

American Telephone and Telegraph. *See* AT&T

American Temperance Society (ATS), **1:**116; **8:**78, 80

American Temperance Union, **8:**78

American Textbook of Physiology (Howell), **6:**349

American Tobacco case, **1:**172

American Tobacco Company, **8:**135
antitrust measures against, **1:172;** **2:**418

American Tobacco Company, United States v., **1:**172

American Tragedy, An (Dreiser), **5:**120; **6:**12

American Trial Lawyers Association, **5:**75

American Veterans Committee, **8:**318

American Veterinary Association, **8:**319

American Veterinary College, **8:**319

American Veterinary Journal, **8:**319

American Veterinary Medical Association, **8:**319

American Veterinary Review, **8:**319

American Volunteer Group (AVG), **3:**392

American Woman's Suffrage Association (AWSA), **8:**11

Americana ballets, **1:**390

American-Arab Anti-Discrimination Committee, Reno v., **1:**125

Americanism, **1:**163; **8:**318

American-Medico-Psychological Association (AMPA), **5:**314

Americans (Sherman), **6:**494

Americans and Chinese (Hsu), **1:**138

Americans in Their Moral, Social and Political Relations (Grund), excerpt from, **9:**215–218

Americans with Disabilities Act (ADA) (1990), **1:172;** **3:**47–48; **5:**15

America's Coming of Age (Brooks), **5:**120

America's Cup, **1:***172,* **172–173;** **7:**223–224

AmeriCorps, **1:**173; **8:***353*

Ameryk, Richard, **1:**135

Ames, Aldrich, **2:**92
espionage case of, **1:173–174**

Ames, Elizabeth, **8:**570

Ames, Fisher, **3:**225, 255

Ames, James Barr, **5:**58

Ames, Jessie Daniel, **1:**339

Ames, John, **6:**245

Ames, Mary Clemmer, **3:**375

Ames, Nathaniel, **1:**129

Ames, Oakes, **2:**453

Ames, Rosario, **1:**174

Ames, Sarah Fisher Clampitt, **1:**308

AMEX. *See* American Stock Exchange

AMEZ. *See* African Methodist Episcopal Zion

Amherst, Jeffrey, **2:**286; **3:**470; **6:**411; **7:**193

Amin, Hafizullah, **1:**37

Amish, **1:174–176,** *176;* **6:**279, 280
barn raising by, **1:**417
and education of children, **2:**170
Hutterites compared with, **8:**301

Amistad case, **1:176–177**

Amistead, Lewis, in Battle of Gettysburg, **3:**569

Amity and Commerce, Treaty of (1778), **8:**198

Amlie, Tom, **6:**500

Ammann, Jakob, **1:**174

Ammann, Othmar H., **1:**539; **8:**315
George Washington Bridge designed by, **3:**553

Amnesty, **1:177–178**
Proclamation of, by Johnson (Andrew), **6:**491

Amnesty International, benefit concerts by, **1:**441

Among the White Moon Faces (Lim), **5:**123

Amoskeag Manufacturing Company, **6:**58

AMPA. *See* American-Medico-Psychological Association

AMPAC. *See* American Medical Political Action Committee

Ampère, André Marie, **3:**172

Amphetamines, **7:**568

Amphibious assault operations, **8:**557

Amsden, Alice, **2:**43, 44

AMSII. *See* Association of Medical Superintendents of American Institutions for the Insane

Amskapi Pikuni, **1:**481

Amtrak, **1:***178,* **178–179;** **7:**39; **8:**191

Amundsen, Roald, **3:**286; **6:**136, 383–384

Amusement parks, **1:179–180**
Coney Island, **1:***546,* 547; **2:**178
family vacationing at, **8:**305

Amvets, **8:**318

ANA. *See* American Nurses Association

Anabaptists, **1:**411, 533
and Amish, **1:**174
Mennonites, **5:308–309**
See also Baptist churches

Anaconda Copper Company, **1:180;**
2:409; **5:**449

Analytic philosophy, **6:**327

Anarchists, **1:180–182**
in 19th century, **1:**180–181
assassinations by, **1:**181
bombings by, **1:**182, 198; **8:**95
at Haymarket riot, **4:**109
nonviolent, **1:**181–182
Palmer Raids and, **6:**232
in Seattle protests (1999), **7:**165
and Utopian communities, **8:**303
violent, **1:**180–181

Anasazi. *See* Ancestral Pueblo

Anaya, Pedro María, **9:**218–219

Ancestral Pueblo (Anasazi),
1:182–183, *183,* 243–244; **6:**540
in Colorado, **2:**297
in Mesa Verde, prehistoric ruins of,
5:*325,* **325–326**
in Nevada, **6:**37
in New Mexico, **6:**65
in Utah, **8:**296
and Zuni, **8:**598

ANCSA. *See* Alaska Native Claims
Settlement Act

Andersen, Arthur, LLP, **2:**419; **3:**223

Anderson, Alexander, **8:**522

Anderson, Carl, **6:**336, 341, 344

Anderson, George M., in Philippine
Insurrection, **6:**319

Anderson, John, **8:**119–120
in presidential campaign of 1980,
2:548; **3:**167

Anderson, Kenneth, in North
African Campaign, **6:**124

Anderson, Laurie, **1:**307; **8:**115

Anderson, Marian, **2:**504; **5:**526

Anderson, Mary, **8:**508

Anderson, Maxwell, **5:**121

Anderson, Philip W., **1:**440

Anderson, Richard, in Battle of
Spotsylvania Courthouse, **7:**512

Anderson, Robert, **7:**523; **8:**17

Anderson, Sherwood, **6:**13, *13*
Winesburg, Ohio, **5:**120

Anderson, Thomas J., **1:**166

Anderson, William, **6:**403

Anderson v. Dunn, **2:**393

Andersonville Prison, **1:184**
firsthand account of, **9:**304–307

"Andes Initiative," **5:**512–513

Andover Seminary, **7:**96, 97

Andre, Carl, **1:**307

André, John, **1:**282; **7:**145, 502

Andreessen, Marc, **2:**337

Andreotti, Giulio, **4:***448*

Andrews, Elisha Benjamin, **1:**548

Andrews, John, **5:**297

Andrews, William, on railroad liability, **6:**232

Andros, Sir Edmund, **3:**77; **4:**417;
5:271; **6:**83, 363
control of Connecticut, **2:**281
control of Rhode Island, **7:**151
Duke of York's proprietary and, **3:**93
retirement to England, **2:**280

Androscoggin River, **6:**56

Andrus, Ethel Percy, **1:**142

Anesthesia
in dentistry, **1:**184; **3:**3
discovery of, **1:184–185**

ANFO (ammonium nitrate-fuel oil
mixtures), **3:**302

Angell, George, **1:**186

Angell, Thorndike, **6:**553

Angelou, Maya, **5:**123
I Know Why the Caged Bird Sings,
1:500; **5:**126

Angier, Joel, **6:**301–302

Anglican Church. *See* Church of
England

Anglin, Jay P., **3:**522

Anglo-African Magazine, **5:**199

Anglo-American relations. *See* Great
Britain, U.S. relations with

Anglo-conformity, **1:**337

Angola, U.S. relations with, **1:**38–39

ANILCA. *See* Alaska National Interest Lands Conservation Act

Animal(s)
abuse of, legislation on, **4:**168–169
in circuses, **2:***176,* 176–177
disease in, **2:**73; **8:**318–320
domestic, Native Americans and,
8:318
industrialization of, **1:**185
medical research on, **1:**185, 186
Native Americans and, **8:**318, 496
physiology of, **6:**349
protective societies for, **1:185–186**
SPCAs, **1:**185, 186; **7:429–430**

rights of, **1:**186–187
study of, **8:596–598**
veterinary medicine for,
8:318–320
See also Wildlife

Animal Liberation Front, **1:**186

Animal rights movement,
1:186–187

Animal Welfare Act (1966), **1:**186

Animation. *See* Cartoons

Anishinabe culture, **8:**496

Anka, Paul, **5:**72

Annan, Kofi, **8:**272

Annapolis (Maryland)
city plan for, **2:**185
Naval Academy in, **2:**530
South River Club in, **2:**251

Annapolis Convention (1786), **1:187**
text of proceedings of, **9:**156–159

Annapolis Royal, **6:**421

Annexation of territory, **1:187–189**
See also specific territories

Annie Allen (Brooks), **5:**125

Anorexia nervosa, **3:**104

Another Country (Baldwin), **5:**126

ANP. *See* Associated Negro Press

Anslinger, Harry, **5:**511

Anson, Cap, **1:**420

Answering machines, **1:189–190**

Antarctic Treaty (1961), **6:**384

Antarctica. *See* South Polar explorations

Antebellum period
agriculture in, **1:**62–63
and gender roles, **3:**519
in South, **7:462–467**
vacationing in, **8:**305

Antelope case, **1:190**

Anthem, national
"America the Beautiful" proposed
as, **1:**139
Confederate, **3:**66
first, **2:**302
Ripley (Robert LeRoy) on, **7:**168
"Star-Spangled Banner," **7:**524

Anthology of American Folk Music
(Smith), **3:**396

Anthony, Susan B., **1:**489; **3:**248;
6:88, 97; **7:***311;* **8:**11
at Centennial Exhibition, **2:**87
as Quaker, **7:**3
and voting rights for women,
7:106; **8:**513

Anthony, William A., **3:**173

Anthracite coal, **2:**251–252, 253; **8:**567

Anthracite Coal Strike Commission, **1:**190; **7:**557

Anthracite strike (1902), **1:190–191; 6:**279; **7:**557

Anthrax, **1:**465; **3:**241
  experimentation with, **2:**118
  mail contaminated with, **6:**109

Anthropology, **1:191–195**
  archaeology in, **1:**239–240
  natural history museums and, **5:**488
  Patterns of Culture (Benedict), **6:**259–260
  racial science and, **7:**13
  radiocarbon dating and, **7:**21

Anti-abortion movement. *See* Pro-life movement

Anti-ballistic missile (ABM) systems, **1:**75; **6:**144–145

Anti-Ballistic Missile Treaty (1972), **2:**269; **6:**145; **8:**202, 206
  See also Strategic Arms Limitation Talks

Antibank movement, **1:195**

Anti-Bigamy Act (1862), **5:**54

Antibiotics, **3:**241; **6:**307

Anti-Catholicism, **1:195–197; 2:**69, 163, 164
  of American Protective Association, **1:167**, 196
  in colonial era, **7:**93, 94
  and Irish Americans, **4:**223, 424
  of Ku Klux Klan, **1:**196; **2:**167
  in nativism, **6:**4
  Order of United Americans and, **8:260**
  Philadelphia riots and, **6:315**
  rightist backlash and, **7:**16
  Ursuline Covenant burning and, **8:295**

"Anti-Chain Store Act." *See* Robinson-Patman Act

Anticommunism, **1:197–199; 2:**327–328; **7:**17
  in AFL-CIO, **1:**151, 152, 197
  and African policies, **1:**38, 39
  and China, relations with, **2:**151
  Congress of Industrial Organizations as target of, **2:**225; **8:**278
  conservative, **1:**197
  in Democratic Party, **1:**197
  and FBI activities, **3:**338
  in government, **1:**198–199

and homosexuality, **3:**513
  HUAC and, **4:**178
  impact on student movements, **8:**587
  in John Birch Society, **4:**481
    excerpt from manifesto of, **9:**429–433
  and loyalty oaths, **5:**168
  in Marshall Plan, **5:**252
  of McCarthyism, **5:181–183**
  and Mexico, bargained negligence policy with, **5:**348–349
  Monroe Doctrine as justification for, **5:**447
  National Union for Social Justice and, **5:**563
  in nativism, **6:**5
  and Palmer Raids, **6:**232
  political, **1:**197–198
  religious, **1:**197
  in Republican Party, **1:**197
  and Russia, interference in, **7:**211
  sedition legislation and, **7:**401
  in Socialist Party, **1:**197–198
  and Vietnam War, **8:**330, 332
    backlash against, **2:**328

Anticult movement, **2:**477–478

Antidepressants, **6:**521, 522

Anti-Drug Abuse Act (1988), **5:**511

Antietam, Battle of, **1:***199*, **199–200; 2:**212; **3:**191; **5:**259

Anti-Evolution League, **3:**484

Antifederalists, **1:200–202; 2:**381; **8:**243
  on bill of rights, **1:**454, 455
  failure of, **1:**201
  ideology of, **1:**200, 201
  impact of, **1:**201–202
  on implied powers, **4:**247
  leaders of, **1:**200–201
  origin of term, **1:**200
  writings of, **1:**200–201

Antigen, **8:**182

Anti-immigrant sentiment
  epidemics and, **3:**236
  eugenicists and, **2:**371
  evolutionism and, **3:**269–270
  Order of United Americans and, **8:260**
  See also Nativism

Anti-imperialism, **1:202–203**
  and Philippines, **6:**320, 321

Anti-Imperialist League, **1:**202
  text of platform of, **9:**263–264

Anti-Masonic movements, **1:203–204; 3:**466
  in Vermont, **8:**313

Anti-Masonic Party, **2:**399; **7:**16; **8:**467
  in presidential campaigns, **3:**152, 153

Anti-Missourian Brotherhood, **6:**137

Antimonopoly parties, **1:***204*, **204–205**
  in presidential campaign of 1884, **3:**157

Antinomian controversy, **1:205; 3:**329; **5:**271

Antinomians, in Rhode Island, **7:**151

Antiquarks, **6:**338

Antiques, collecting, **2:**271

Antiquities Act (1906), **1:205–206; 6:**529
  preservationists and, **2:**369
  and president establishing national monuments, **5:**550

Anti-Rent War, **1:206**

Anti-Saloon League, **1:206; 6:**501; **8:**81

Anti-Semitism, **1:206–208**
  in 20th century, **1:**206–207
  among African Americans, **6:**32
  anti-Catholicism compared to, **1:**195
  in colonial era, **1:**206
  conservatism and, **2:**375
  and Crown Heights riots, **2:**466
  decline after 1945, **7:**94
  Great Depression and, **3:**327–328
  and lynching of Frank (Leo), **3:**453
  racial-religious communities and, **8:**303
  Rosenberg Case and, **7:**197

Antislavery movement, **1:208–212**
  African colonization in, **1:**147–148, 208–209
  arguments for, in original documents, **9:**269–271, 280–284, 288–292
  Brown (John) in, **4:**97–100
    last speech of, **9:**286–287
  Burns Fugitive Slave Case and, **1:577**
  forms of, **1:**208
  Free Soil Party and, **3:**459–460
  Fugitive Slave Acts and, **3:**482; **6:**146
  gag rule and, **3:502**
  gradualism in, **1:**208

immediatism in, **1:**209–210; **4:219**
leaders of, **1:**209
manumission in, **5:230–231**
Massachusetts leadership in, **5:**266
Mennonites on, **9:**97–98
among Methodists, **5:**333
New England Antislavery Society,
    6:47
of Oberlin Movement, **6:152–153**
pacifism and, **6:**227
Pan-Africanism and, **6:**234–235
in Pennsylvania, **6:**277, 278
political, **1:**210–211
in popular press, **5:**199
among Quakers, **6:**277
Sewall's tract against, **5:**118
slave insurrections and, **7:**387–388
slave rescue cases and, **7:**381
in South, **1:**208
state sovereignty in, **7:**534
Tallmadge Amendment and, **8:**45
Uncle Tom's Cabin and, **8:**248
Underground Railroad and,
    8:249–251, *250*
in Vermont, **8:**313
violence in, **1:**211
Antistrike decrees, **6:**121
Anti-Terrorism and Effective Death
    Penalty Act (1996), **4:**81–82
Antitrust legislation, **1:212–215;**
    4:26–27; **5:**21
in 19th century, **1:**213–214; **4:**26
Beef Trust cases, **1:435–436**
under Clinton, **1:**215
international enforcement of, **1:**215
litigation under
    against AT&T, **1:**347; **8:**235
    against IBM, **8:**235
    against railroad industry, **8:**275
    against Standard Oil, **7:**521
    against sugar industry, **8:**274
    against tobacco industry, **1:**172;
        8:135
on mergers and acquisitions, **5:**323
Packers and Stockyards Act (1921),
    6:229
and railroads, **6:**135; **8:**275
under Reagan, **1:**215
Robinson-Patman Act, **1:**215;
    3:348; **7:183; 8:**235
under Roosevelt (Franklin
    Delano), **3:**348
under Roosevelt (Theodore),
    4:26–27; **8:**233, 234

by states, **1:**213; **7:**343
under Wilson, **1:**214–215; **3:**348;
    6:54, 63; **8:**235
See also Clayton Antitrust Act;
    Monopoly(ies); Sherman
    Antitrust Act
Antivice campaigns, **7:**64
Antiwar movements, **1:215–217**
Cambodia bombing and, **2:**16, 17
Catholics and, **2:**70
Chicago Seven and, **1:**479; **2:135**
in Civil War, **1:**284
and environmentalism, **3:**227
and McNamara's resignation, **2:**528
in Socialist Party, **7:**426–427
student participation in, **3:**119;
    8:587
in Vietnam War, **1:**216–217, *217;*
    6:268
    Kent State protest, **4:517–518**
    Students for a Democratic Soci-
        ety, **7:**561–562
See also Pacifism; Peace move-
    ment(s)
Antonius, George, **1:**232–233
ANWR. *See* Arctic National
    Wildlife Refuge
Anza, Juan Bautista de, **6:**67; **8:**451
Anzio (Italy), **1:217–218**
ANZUS Treaty (1952), **1:**361–362
AOL. *See* America Online
AP. *See* Associated Press
APA. *See* Administrative Procedure
    Act; American Protective Asso-
    ciation; American Psychiatric
    Association; American Psycho-
    logical Association
Apache, **1:218–220; 8:**218, 228
bands of, **1:**218–220
defeat of, **7:**9
language of, **6:**18
in Nebraska, **6:**29
in New Mexico, **6:**65, 67, 69
Pueblo and, **1:**219, 220
raids in Arizona, **1:**257
on reservations, **1:**221; **6:**263
seminomadic lifestyle of, **8:**227
in Texas, **8:**98
Apache Wars, **1:220–221**
Apalachee, **8:**225
Apalachee Massacre (1704), **1:221–222**
Apalachin Conference (1957), **1:222**
Apartheid, in South Africa, **1:**38, 39;
    7:452–453

Apartment houses, **1:222–224;**
    4:182; **8:**292
public housing debacle of 1950s
    and, **8:**287
APEC. *See* Asia-Pacific Economic
    Cooperation
Apess, William, *A Son of the Forest,*
    5:128; **7:448**
Apgar, Virginia, alma mater of, **2:**304
Aphorisms, **8:**528
Apollo Hall, **8:**54
Apollo program, **5:**523–524, *524;*
    7:480, *481*
Apollo 1, **3:**41
Apollo 11, **5:**454–455
    excerpt from transcript of,
        9:435–444
See also Moon landing
Appadurai, Arjun, **1:**194
Appalachia, **1:**224, *224*
Cumberland Gap, **1:**562; **2:479;**
    8:461
feuds in, **3:**356–357
Great Smoky Mountains, **4:**57
migration across, **8:**460–461
moonshine in, **5:**455
mountain passes in, **6:**253–254
religious revivals in, **3:**44
in Tennessee, **8:**83
Trans-Appalachian West, **8:179**
Appalachian Trail, **1:224–225**
*Appeal, in Four Articles, Together with
    a Preamble, to the Colored Citizens
    of the World* (Walker), **6:**235
Appeals, from colonial courts, **1:**225
Privy Council, **6:482**
Appert, Nicolas, **2:**35–36; **3:**406
Appiah, Anthony, **1:**47
Apple Computer, **2:**336, 337
Appleby, John, **1:**59
Apples, **3:**478
Applewhite, Marshall Herff, **2:**478
Appliances, electrical, **3:179–183,**
    182; **4:**535, 536
Applied Data Research (ADR), **7:**441
Appointment(s), political, **1:**573
criteria for, **1:**225
of midnight judges, **5:367**
power of, **1:**225–226
removal of, Supreme Court on,
    5:506
Appomattox, **2:**215, 343
Lee's surrender at, **1:226–227;**
    8:344

Apportionment, **1:227; 2:**351; **7:**106–107
  Constitutional amendment on, **1:**457
  gerrymandering and, **3:**564
  in House of Representatives, **1:**227
  in state legislatures, **1:**227
    of Tennessee, **1:**385
    of Vermont, **8:**314
    of Virginia, **8:**344
  Supreme Court on, **1:**227; **8:**357
Apportionment Act (1842), **1:**227
Apprenticeship, **1:228–229; 2:**223
  in legal education, **5:**55–56
  printer's devil, **6:465–466**
Appropriations, by Congress, **1:229–230**
Appropriations Committees, **1:**229
APRO. *See* Aerial Phenomenon Research Organization
APS. *See* American Peace Society; American Physiological Society
APSA. *See* American Political Science Association
Aptucxet Trading Post, **8:**160
Aquariums, **8:**594
Aquash, Anna Mae, **1:**161
Aquino, Benigno, **6:**323
Aquino, Corazon, **6:**323
ARA. *See* American Relief Administration
Arab Americans, **1:230–232**
  culture of, **1:**231
  nativist movements against, **6:**5
  notable, **1:**231–232
  number of, **1:**230
  professional activities of, **1:**230–231
  religions of, **1:**231
Arab nations
  in Arab-Israeli wars, **1:**233, 234; **4:**440–441
  Carter Doctrine on, **1:**233
  Eisenhower Doctrine on, **1:**233
  foreign investment from, **3:**422
  at Geneva Conference (1973), **3:**535
  immigration from, **1:**230–231
  Islam in, **4:**436
    fundamentalist, **1:**234
  military coups in, **1:**233–234
  U.S. relations with, **1:232–234**
  in World War II, **1:**233
  See also specific countries
Arabella (ship), **5:**270

Arab-Israeli wars, **1:**233, 234; **4:**440–441
Arafat, Yasir
  and *Achille Lauro* hijacking, **1:**13
  Israeli negotiations with, **4:***442, 443
Arapaho, **1:234–235**
  in Colorado, **2:**298
  Fort Laramie Treaty with, text of, **9:**227–229
  and Ghost Dance, **3:**573
  land of, **1:**235
  in Nebraska, **6:**29
  on reservations, **1:**235; **6:**263
Arbella (ship), **4:**55, 56
Arbenz, Jacobo, **2:**54; **5:**48
Arbitration, **1:235–238**
  commercial, **1:**236, 237–238
  vs. conciliation, **2:**339
  international, **6:**263
    development of, **4:**394
    international law in, **4:**394
    by joint commissions, **4:**484–485
  labor, **1:**236–237
  mixed commissions, **5:**428
  process of, **1:**236
Arbor Day, **1:238**
Arboretums, **1:**515, 516, 517
Arbus, Diane, **1:**301
Arc light, **5:**108
Arcadia conference, **8:**545
Archaeoastronomy, **4:**308
Archaeology, **1:238–241**
  anthropological, **1:**239–240
  dating in, **1:**240
  of prehistoric North America, **1:***241, **241–247**, *243, 245;* **6:**441
  public and, **1:**240
  radiocarbon dating and, **7:**21
Archaic Indians, **8:**83
Archaic period
  in Maine, **5:**207
  in Southwest, **1:**243
Archambault, A. L., **1:**59
Archangel Campaign, **1:247–248**
Archbald, Robert W., **2:**310
Archer, Dennis W., **1:**145; **3:**20
Architecture, **1:248–254**
  after American Revolution, **1:**249–250
  of apartments, **1:**222–223
  Arts and Crafts, **1:**320
  building materials, **1:563–565**

  of Chicago, **2:**132–133; **8:**290
  colonial, **1:**248–249
  of Denver, **3:**6, *6*
  eclecticism in, **1:**249–250, 253
  geodesic dome, **3:***539, **539–540**
  Gothic Revival, **1:**250
  Greek Revival, **1:**249–250
  modernist, **1:**251–252, 288
  of Monticello, **5:452–453,** *453*
  of Mount Vernon, **5:465–466,** *467*
  murals and, **5:**483
  of museums, **5:**485, 487
  Native American, **1:254–255**
    Ancestral Pueblo (Anasazi), **1:**182–183, *183;* **5:***325, 325–326*
    Iroquois, **1:***238*
  neoclassical, **1:**251
  in New Orleans, **6:**73
  of New York City, **6:**80
  of Pentagon, **6:**285–286
  postmodern, **6:**430; **7:**376
  preservation of, **6:**452–453
  of skyscrapers, **1:**252; **7:**375–377
  statehouse, **2:**48
  of University of Virginia, **8:**283
  Victorian, **8:**326
  of White House, **8:**470–471, *471*
  of World Trade Center, **8:**532
  See also Landscape architecture
Archival maps. *See* Maps and mapmaking, archival
Archives, **1:255–256**
  National Archives and Records Administration, **5:524–526**
Arctic. *See* North Polar explorations
Arctic National Wildlife Refuge (ANWR), **6:**304
  oil drilling in, **1:**111; **6:**171, 179
Area 51, **6:**39
Area studies, and political science, **6:**404–405
Arendt, Hannah, **5:**121; **6:***404*
Arent, Arthur, *Power,* excerpt from, **9:**388–390
Argall, Samuel, **2:**540–541; **8:**347
Argand, Aimé, **5:**107
Argentina
  at ABC Conference, **1:**1
  commerce with, **5:**44–45
  independence of, **5:**50
  trade agreements with, **6:**125
  U.S. relations with, **5:**49
Argosy (magazine), **5:**196

Arias, Oscar, **6:**105
Arikara Indians, **1:**383; **5:**219–220, *220*
  Fort Laramie Treaty with, text of, **9:**227–229
Aristide, Jean-Bertrand, **2:**55; **4:**85; **5:**49
Aristophanes, **1:**575
Aristotle, **6:**407; **8:**527
Arizin, Paul, **1:**424
Arizona, **1:256–260**
  astronomical observatories in, **6:**155, 156–157
  in colonial era, **1:**256–257
  copper mining in, **2:**409
  Democratic Party in, **1:**259
  education in, **1:**259
  emblems, nicknames, mottos, and songs of, **7:***532*
  governors of, **1:**259
  in Great Depression, **1:**258
  industry in, **1:**257–258, 259
  mining in, **1:**257; **8:**141
  Native Americans in, **1:**100–101, 256–257; **6:**230, 540
  New Deal and, **1:**258
  population of, **1:**259
  purchase of, **3:**425
  reclamation projects in, **7:**55
  Republican Party in, **1:**259
  Spanish exploration in, **3:**296
  statehood for, **1:**258
  Territory of, **1:**257–258
  water rights in, **1:**100–101
  women in, **1:**258–259
Arizona (battleship), **6:**273
Ark (ship), **2:**290
Arkansas, **1:260–263**
  African Americans in, **1:**261, 263
  agriculture in, **1:**260, 261, 262
  in Civil War, **1:**261
  constitution of, **1:**260–261
  Democratic Party in, **1:**261, 263
  economy of, **1:**263
  emblems, nicknames, mottos, and songs of, **7:***532*
  flood of 1927 in, **1:**262
  freedmen in, **1:**261
  governors of, **1:**261, 263
  industry in, **1:**261–263
  legislature of, **1:**261
  Native Americans in, **1:**260
  Progressivism in, **1:**262
  race riots in, **1:**262

  Reconstruction in, **1:**261
  Republican Party in, **1:**263
  school desegregation in, **1:**263
  slavery in, **1:**260, 261
  statehood for, **1:**260–261
  Whig Party in, **1:**260
Arkansas, Epperson v., **1:**500
Arkansas River, **1:264**
  Long's explorations of, **5:**150
  Pike expedition to, **6:**354
Arks. *See* Flatboat(s)
Arkwright, Richard, **8:**108
Arlandes, François d', **1:**391
Arledge, Roone, **3:**411
Arlington National Cemetery, **1:264; 2:**82
  Tomb of the Unknown Soldier at, **8:***284*, **284–285**
  United States v. Lee and, **8:**274
Armajani, Siah, **1:**307
Armaments. *See* Weapons
Armas, Carlos Castillo, **5:**48
Armed forces. *See* Military; *specific branches*
Armed Forces Security Agency (AFSA), **5:**558
Armijo, Manuel, **6:**68
Arm-in-Arm (National Union) Convention, **3:**155
Arminianism, **1:264–265**
Arminius, Jacobus, **1:***264*, 264–265
Armistice of November 1918, **1:265; 8:**539
Armored ships, **1:265–266**
Armored vehicles, **1:266–268; 5:**480
Armory Show (1913), **1:268–269**, 297, 321–322
Armour, Philip and Simeon, **5:**135
Arms race and disarmament, **1:269–273; 6:**144–145
  Anti-Ballistic Missile Treaty (1972) and, **6:**145; **8:**202, 206
  antiwar movements on, **1:**216
  beginning of U.S.-Soviet negotiations on, **7:**212
  in Cold War, **1:**271–272; **2:**269, 528, 532
  in Eisenhower's farewell address, **9:**434–435
  imperialism and, **1:**270
  military-industrial complex in, **5:376–378**
  missile gap in (U.S. and USSR), **5:406–407**

  missiles in, **5:407–408**
  nuclear, **1:**271–272
  Nuclear Non-Proliferation Treaty (1968) and, **6:138**, 139–140
  Nuclear Test Ban Treaty (1963) and, **3:**427; **6:142–143**
  origins of, **1:**269–271
  and peace movement, **6:**268–269
  Reykjavik Summit and, **7:149–150**
  Strategic Arms Limitation Talks (SALT I) and, **8:**202, 206
  Strategic Arms Limitation Talks II (SALT II) and, **8:**202, 206
  Strategic Arms Reduction Talks (START) and, **8:**203
  Strategic Defense Initiative in, **1:**75; **7:554–555**
  Washington Naval Conference and, **6:**264; **8:**555
  in World War II, **1:**270–271
  See also Nuclear weapons; Strategic Arms Limitation Talks
Armstrong, C. Michael, **1:**346
Armstrong, E. Howard, **7:**20
Armstrong, John, Jr., **6:**94
Armstrong, Lance, **1:**452
Armstrong, Louis, **4:**468
Armstrong, Neil A., **2:**102; **5:**454, *454*, 524; **7:**480
Armstrong, Samuel, **6:**317
Army, Confederate, **1:273; 2:**210, 215
  activities in Canada, **2:24–25**; **6:**136
  Army of Northern Virginia in, **1:278**
  at Battle of Antietam, **1:**200
  cavalry in, **2:**78
  impressment in, **4:**248
  organization of, **1:**274
  uniforms of, **1:**490; **8:***256*, 257
  veterans of, **8:264–265**, 318
  in Vicksburg, **8:**324
Army, Continental, **1:**509, 511; **7:**141
  cavalry in, **2:**77
  Congress and, **2:**394
  disbanding officers of, society of, **2:**174
  organization of, **1:**275
  recruiting poster for, **2:***363*
  training by Steuben, **7:**144
  at Valley Forge, **8:306**
  Washington as commander in chief of, **2:**394
  Yorktown campaign and, **8:**580

Army, Union, **1:273–274; 2:**210, 215
  Army of Tennessee in, **8:**87
  Army of the Cumberland in, **2:**479
  Army of the James in, **1:**279
  Army of the Potomac in, **1:**279
  Army of Virginia in, **1:**279
  cavalry in, **2:**78
  desertion from, **1:**524
  Military Order of the Loyal Legion
      of the U.S.A., **5:**380
  organization of, **1:**274, 276
  transportation of, **7:**40
  uniforms of, **1:**490; **8:**257–258
  veterans of
    bonuses for, **1:**499
    pensions for, **7:**127
  in Vicksburg, **8:**324
  women nurses in, **8:**502
Army, U.S., **1:274–278**
  armored vehicles in, **1:**267–268
  artillery regiments in, **1:318–319**
  black infantry in the West, **1:**475,
      476
  cavalry in, **2:77–78**
  in Cold War, **1:**277
  communist infiltration in, **4:**411
  Corps of Engineers in, **3:218–220**
  doughboy in, **3:**82
  early history of, **2:**530
  forts of, **1:**280–281
  on frontier, **1:279–280**
    firsthand account of, **9:**244–248
  intelligence testing in, **4:**378–379
  in Korean War, **1:**277; **4:***547*
  liquor ration for, **3:**59
  Medical Department of,
      5:286–287, 293
  medicine in, **5:**293–296
  missions of, **1:**274–275
  and National Rifle Association,
      5:556–557
  Native Americans in, **4:**328–329
  ordnance of, **6:**201–202
  organization of, **1:**275–278
  in Persian Gulf War, **1:**277
  Signal Corps of, **7:358**
  in Spanish-American War, **1:**276;
      7:486
  Special Forces of, **7:**494
  uniforms in, **8:**257, 258
  in Vietnam War, **1:**277
  volunteer, **8:352**
  in War of 1812, **1:**275–276
  before World War II, **2:**531

in World War II, **1:**277
Army Corps of Engineers. *See* Engi-
    neers, U.S. Army Corps of
Army of Northern Virginia, **1:**278
  at Battle of Antietam, **1:**200
Army of Occupation, **1:**278
Army of Tennessee, **8:**87
Army of the James, **1:**279
Army of the Potomac, **1:**279; **9:**67
Army of Virginia, **1:**279
Army on the Frontier, **1:**279–280
Army posts (forts), **1:**280–281
  in archival maps, **9:***55, 56*
  life at, firsthand account of,
      9:244–248
  See also specific forts
Army School of Nursing, **6:**147
Arnall, Ellis, **3:**557
Arnaz, Desi, **4:**209, *209*
Arneson, Robert, **1:**305
Arnim, D. Juergen von, in Battle of
    Kasserine Pass, **4:**514
Arnold, Benedict, **1:**574; **8:**311
  achievements in American Revolu-
      tion, **7:**142, 143
  in Battle of Valcour Island, **4:**77
  in capture of Ticonderoga, **8:**124
  court-martial of, **2:**440
  march to Quebec by, **1:**281–282;
      5:208; **9:***34*, 36
  raid in Virginia, **1:**282
  in Saratoga Campaign, **7:**251, *251*
  treason by, **1:**282; **7:**144–145, 502;
      8:447
Arnold, Henry H., **8:**554
Arnold, James, **1:**517
Arnold, Thurman W., **6:**44; **8:**263
Aroostook War, **1:282–283**
ARPA. *See* Advanced Research Pro-
    jects Agency
ARPANET (Advanced Research
    Projects Agency Network),
    2:337; **3:**184–185; **4:**398–399;
    8:65, 66, 70
ARPC. *See* Associate Reformed
    Presbyterian Church
Arpino, Gerald, **1:**390
Arrears Act (1879), **4:**31
Arrest(s), **1:283–284**
  arbitrary, during Civil War, **1:**284;
      2:210, 377, 411; **3:**272
  as search and seizure, **1:**283; **7:**290
  Supreme Court on, **1:**283, 284;
      7:290

Arrhenius, Svante, **4:**6
Arrow, Kenneth, **3:**107, 110
Arrowsmith (Lewis), **5:**18
Arroyo, Gloria, **6:**323
Arsenals, establishment of, **6:**201–202
Art(s), **1:285–314**
  artists' colonies, **1:**319–320
  ceramics, **1:**286, **303–305**
    porcelain, **6:**418
  collecting, **2:**272, 272–273
  cubism in, **2:**475–476
  decorative, **1:285–288**
    Art Deco style, **1:**287–288
    ceramics, **1:**286
    chairs, **1:**286
    early colonial style, **1:**285
    industrialization and, **1:**287
    modernist, **1:**288
    Oriental style, **1:**287
    pottery, **1:**285–286
    silver, **1:**286–287
    in Victorian era, **8:**326
    Winterthur Museum for, **8:489**
  exhibitions
    Armory Show, **1:**268–269
    photography, **3:**316, *316*
  existentialism in, **3:**280
  glass, **1:**288–290; **4:**4
  graffiti, **4:**30
  of Harlem Renaissance, **4:**96–97
  interior decoration, **1:**290–292
  interior design, **1:**292–294
  by Kentuckians, **4:**520–521
  National Endowment for the Arts
      and, **5:**535–536
  Native American, **1:**314–316
    Iroquois, **4:***431*
  painting, **1:**294–299
    abstract expressionism, **1:**8–10,
        298
    genre painting, **3:***537*, **537–538**
    Hudson River School of,
        4:188–190
    miniatures, **5:**393–394, *394*
    murals, **5:**483
    postmodernist, **6:**430
    theft of, **7:**182
  photography, **1:**299–302; **6:**330
    in Civil War, **1:***199*, 200, 299, *530*
    Family of Man Exhibition, **3:**316,
        316
  pop, **6:**414–415
  postmodernism, **6:**430
  pottery, **1:**303–305**, 321

printmaking, **6:470–472**
sculpture, **1:305–309**
   Mount Rushmore, **5:464–465**, *465*
   by self-taught artists (folk art), **1:309–313**
   stained glass windows, **1:313–314**, *320*
   in Victorian era, **8:**326
   wax portraits, **8:431**
   See also Museum(s)
Art Deco, **1:287–288**
Art Institute of Chicago (AIC), **1:316–317**
Art of Beautifying Suburban Home Grounds of Small Extent, The (Scott), **3:**510
Arthur, Chester Alan, **2:**400; **3:**157
   immigration restriction under, **4:**232
   presidency of, **2:**485; **8:**322
   and tariffs, **8:**51
Arthur, Gabriel, **8:**85
Arthur, Timothy Shay, **8:**80
Articles of Confederation, **1:317**; **2:**344, 394; **7:**136
   Annapolis Convention on, **1:187**; **9:156–159**
   Congress under, **2:**350
   deficiency of, **2:**378
   on enumerated powers, **3:**225
   on privileges and immunities of citizens, **6:**481–482
   ratification of, **7:**140
   states' claims to western lands and, **8:**455
   system of representation under, **3:**170; **7:**109
Articles of War (1775), **8:**256
   as military law, **5:**379
Artificial insemination technology, **2:**73
Artificial intelligence, **1:318**; **2:**486
Artificial perception, **1:**318
Artificial Transmutation of the Gene (Muller), **3:**532
Artillery, **1:318–319**, *319*
   See also Munitions; Nuclear weapons; Weapons
Artists' colonies, **1:319–320**
   Yaddo, **8:570–571**
Arts and Crafts movement, **1:320–321**
   in furniture, **3:**498

handcrafted silver in, **5:**328
   and Native American art, **1:**315
   in pottery and ceramics, **1:**304
ARU. *See* American Railway Union
As I Lay Dying (Faulkner), **5:**121
ASA. *See* American Sociological Association
Asad, Talal, **1:**194
Asante, Molefi Kete, **1:46–47**
Asawa, Ruth, **1:**309
Asbury, Francis, **1:**44; **2:**162, 175; **5:**333; **7:**87
   and religious liberty, **7:**93
ASCAP. *See* American Society of Composers, Authors, and Publishers
ASCII (American Standard Code for Information Interchange), **3:**24
ASFA. *See* Adoption and Safe Families Act
ASG. *See* American Society of Genealogists
Ashcan School, **1:321–322**
   Armory Show by, **1:268–269**, 297, 321–322
   members of, **1:**297, 321
   printmaking by, **6:**471
Ashcroft, John, as NRA life member, **5:**557
Ashe, Arthur, **1:**17
Ashford, Bailey K., **5:**294
Ashiwi. *See* Zuni
Ashley, James M., **8:**564
Ashley, William Henry, **2:**301; **5:**70
   and fur trade, **1:**158; **3:**487, 493; **8:**563
Ashmun Institute, **3:**121, 125
Asia
   dollar diplomacy in, **3:**71
   foreign observers from, **1:**138
   immigration from, **1:**322, 324; **2:**10; **7:**10, 470–471; **8:**291
   and religious affiliation, **7:**91
   Japanese power in, **4:**457–458
   religions and sects of, **1:325–327**
   State Department experts on, **7:**530
   U.S. imperialism in, **4:**242–243, 245
   See also specific countries
Asian Americans, **1:322–325**
   challenges faced by, **1:**323–324
   definition of, **1:**322–323
   discrimination against, **2:**10, 13, 157; **8:**577–578

Supreme Court on, **1:**324
   gender roles of, **3:**520
   geographic distribution of, **1:**324
   hate crimes against, **1:**323–324
   as law students, **5:**58
   as "model minority," **1:**323
   nativist laws and, **6:**5
   in New Jersey, **6:**63
   number of, **1:**322
   in old age, **6:**189
   science education for, **7:**273
   from Southeast Asia, **7:470–472**
   in Virginia, **8:**346
Asian Indian Americans, **1:325**
   in California, **1:**324, 325
   in New Jersey, **6:**63
   number of, **1:**325
   religious practices of, **4:**133
Asian religions and sects, **1:325–327**
   See also specific types
Asia-Pacific Economic Cooperation (APEC), **6:**226
Asimov, Isaac, **5:**130
ASL. *See* American Sign Language; American Soccer League
Asphalt, **6:**260–261, 301; **7:**181
Aspin, Les, **2:**529; **8:**504
Aspinwald, Nathan, **7:**361
ASSA. *See* American Social Science Association
Assassination(s), **1:327–333**; **8:**339
   of ambassadors, **1:**134
   by anarchists, **1:**181
   attempted
      of Field (Stephen J.), **4:**250
      of Ford, **1:**330–331
      of Jackson (Andrew), **1:**327–328
      of Johnson (Andrew), **1:**328
      of Nixon, **1:**330
      of Reagan, **1:**330, 331; **2:**79; **8:**339
      of Roosevelt (Franklin Delano), **1:**329
      of Roosevelt (Theodore), **1:**329, 566
      of Truman, **1:**329; **4:**135
      of Wallace (George C.), **3:**166
   of Evers (Medgar), **2:**203; **5:**527
   of Garfield, **1:328**, 572; **2:**23; **8:**339
   of Kennedy (John F.), **1:**330; **3:**165; **8:**339
      conspiracy theories on, **1:**330; **2:**378

Assassination(s), (*continued*)
  and gun control, **4:**75; **5:**557
  Malcolm X on, **5:**520
  media coverage of, **8:**339
  and Vietnam War, **8:**331
  Warren Commission on,
    8:394–395
  of Kennedy (Robert F.), **3:**165
  and gun control, **4:**75; **5:**557
  and Violence Commission, **8:**340
  of King, **2:**204; **4:528–530; 8:**339
  conspiracy theories on, **4:**530
  and gun control, **4:**75; **5:**557
  prosecution of Ray after,
    4:529–530
  riots after, **4:**528; **7:***164;* **8:**338
  trade union support and, **1:**154
  and Violence Commission, **8:**340
  of Lincoln, **1:**328; **2:**218; **8:**339
  of Malcolm X, **5:**520
  of Mboya, **1:**138
  of McKinley, **1:328–329; 2:**84,
    227; **6:**236; **8:**323, 339
  anarchism and, **1:**181
  of presidents, **1:327–331; 8:**339
Assay Offices, **1:**333
Assemblies, colonial. *See* Colonial
  assemblies
Assemblies of God, **1:**334; **6:**288
  membership in, **7:***91*
Assembly, right of. *See* First Amendment
Assembly lines, **1:334–336**
  in automobile industry, **1:***335,*
    335–336, 372; **4:**334; **5:**262,
    263
  at Ford Motor Company, **2:**389;
    3:414; **8:**189
  See also Mass production
Assimilation, **1:336–338**
  of Native Americans, **1:**492; **3:**115
  stages of, **1:**336–337
Assiniboin Indians, **5:**23
  Fort Laramie Treaty with, text of,
    9:227–229
  gambling by, **3:**506–507
Assistant, **1:338–339**
Assisted suicide, **1:**339; **3:**261–263
  court cases on, **3:**262; **7:**160–161;
    8:418
  definition of, **1:**339
Associate Reformed Presbyterian
  Church (ARPC), **6:**451
Associate trading companies, **8:**174

Associated Negro Press (ANP),
  5:200
Associated Press (AP), **6:**458
  first commercial facsimile service
    introduced by, **3:**329
Associated Press of Illinois, **6:**458
Associates of New Jersey Company,
  6:62
Association(s), **1:340–341**
  definition of, **1:**340
  *See also specific associations; specific
    types*
Association Against the Prohibition
  Amendment, **6:**501
Association football. *See* Soccer
Association of American Geogra-
  phers, **3:**541
Association of American Geologists
  and Naturalists, **1:**140; **3:**550
Association of American Law
  Schools (AALS), and legal edu-
    cation, **5:**56–57
Association of Forest Service
  Employees for Environmental
    Ethics, **3:**437
Association of Intercollegiate Athlet-
  ics for Women, **5:**531
Association of Junior Leagues Inter-
  national, **4:501**
Association of Licensed Automobile
  Manufacturers (ALAM), **1:**367
Association of Medical Superinten-
  dents of American Institutions
    for the Insane (AMSAII), **5:**313,
    314
Association of Morning Newspa-
  pers, **6:**458
Association of Negro Life and His-
  tory, **5:**200
Association of Southern Women for
  the Prevention of Lynching
    (ASWPL), **1:339–340; 5:**180
Association of Women Geoscien-
  tists, **3:**550
Association on American Indian
  Affairs (AAIA), **1:**159, **340**
Assumption, Fort, **8:**85
Aston, F. W., **6:**341
Astor, Caroline Webster Schermer-
  horn, **3:**445
Astor, John Jacob, **1:**404; **3:**298; **8:**490
  American Fur Company of,
    1:157–158; 3:487, 491; **8:**175
  Astoria founded by, **1:**342

  and land speculation, **5:**36, 37
  Lewis and Clark Expedition and,
    8:307
  Pacific Fur Company of, **3:**492;
    6:225
Astor Place riot, **1:***341,* **341–342**
Astoria (Oregon), **1:**342
  founding of, **1:**342
  fur trading in, **1:**342; **8:**307
  Albatross and, **1:**114
  by American Fur Company,
    1:157
  by Pacific Fur Company, **6:**225
Astronomical observatories, **1:**343,
  344, 345; **6:154–157**
Astronomy, **1:342–346; 3:**552
  among Native Americans, **4:**308
  See also Telescopes
ASWPL. *See* Association of South-
  ern Women for the Prevention
    of Lynching
Asylum. *See* Political exiles
Asylums. *See* Mental illness
ATA. *See* Air Transport Association;
  American Teachers Association
Atanasoff, John V., **3:**25
Atari, **8:**327
ATC. *See* Air Traffic Control
Atchison, David R., **1:**505;
  4:512–513; **5:**59, 420
Atchison, Topeka & Santa Fe Rail-
  road, **7:**34
ATF. *See* Bureau of Alcohol, Tobac-
  co, and Firearms
Atget, Eugene, **1:**301
Athapascans, **1:**219
  in Alaska, **8:**211, 213
  in New Mexico, **6:**65
Atheism, **1:347–348**
  definition of, **1:**347
"Athens of the South." *See* Nashville
Athey, Ron, **5:**536
Athletic shoes, **1:**503
Athletics. *See* Sports
Atkinson, Henry, **8:**580
Atlanta (Georgia), **1:***348,* **348–350**
  in Civil War, **1:**350–351; **7:**346
  damages to, **2:***217*
  after Civil War, **1:**348
  Empowerment Zone program in,
    8:287
  higher education in, **1:**349
  origins of, **7:**32
  race relations in, **1:**348–349

Atlanta Campaign, **1:**350, **350–351**
 Army of the Cumberland in, **2:**479
 Battle of Kenesaw Mountain in,
  4:516
"Atlanta Compromise" (Washington), **3:**556
Atlanta Olympic bombing case,
 3:339
Atlantic, Battle of, **1:**352, **352–353**
Atlantic Charter (1941), **1:**353;
 8:273, 543
 as executive agreement, **3:**277
 imperialism of, **4:**244–245
Atlantic City (New Jersey), **1:**353
Atlantic Community, **8:**166
Atlantic Intracoastal waterway, **8:**430
Atlantic Monthly (magazine), **1:**351,
 351–352; 8:233
Atlantic Ocean, cables across, **2:**3–4
Atmospheric sciences. *See* Meteorology
ATMs. *See* Automated teller
 machines
Atomic bomb, **6:**144, 342
 development of
  media coverage of, **7:**275
  in Soviet Union, **1:**271
  in U.S., **4:**203–204; **6:**143, 336,
   342; **8:**414–415 (*See also*
   Manhattan Project)
  U.S. use against Japan, **6:**143, 342;
   8:551–552, 555
 See also Nuclear weapons
Atomic Café, The (Loader, Rafferty,
 Rafferty), **5:**121
Atomic Energy Act (1946), **6:**141
Atomic Energy Act (1954), **3:**213;
 6:140, 141
Atomic Energy Commission (AEC),
 3:213
 accelerator construction by, **6:**339
 designing nuclear power plants,
  6:138–139
Atomic physics, **6:**340
Atoms, **6:**339, 340
Atoms for Peace program, **3:**208;
 6:140
*Atonio, Ward's Cove Packing Co., Inc.,
 v.*, **2:**196, 197; **8:389–390**
Atrocities in war, **1:353–355**
 in American Revolution, on Jersey
  Prison Ship, **4:**473
 Americans as victims of, **1:**354
 in Indian wars, **1:**353–354; **8:**337

international agreements on, **1:**354
in Mexican-American War, **1:**354
prosecutions for (*See* War crimes
 trials)
in Vietnam War, **1:**354; **8:**333
ATS. *See* American Temperance
 Society
AT&T (American Telephone and
 Telegraph), **1:346,** 440
 antitrust suit against, **8:**235
 breakup of, **1:**381; **3:**13
 and cable advances, **2:**3
 and code making, **2:**468
 divestiture of, **1:346–347**
 foundation of, **8:**65, 70
 industrial research at, **4:**339, 342
 innovations resisted by, **6:**169
 lawsuits by, **8:**70
 as monopoly, **8:**65, 70
 research laboratory of, **5:**18
 service provided by, **8:**65, 66
 and trade unions, **2:**324–325
 and Western Union, **8:**456, 457
AT&T, United States v., **1:**347
Attainder, **1:355**
Attakullakulla (Cherokee chief), **8:**85
Attaway, William, *Blood on the Forge*,
 5:125
Attention-deficit/hyperactivity disorder (ADHD), **7:**568–569
Attenuated vaccine, **6:**389
Attica State Prison, **1:355–356,** 356;
 7:165
Attorney(s)
 African American, first, **5:**74
 and counselors at law, Supreme
  Court's distinction between,
  5:73
 female
  first admitted to practice before
   Supreme Court, **5:**74
  first black, **5:**75
  first in U.S., **5:**74
 See also Legal profession
Attorneys general, **4:**503
Attucks, Crispus, **1:**48, 509; **7:**7, 164
Atwater, W. O., **3:**325; **6:**148
Atwood, Leland, **3:**498
Atzerodt, George, **1:**328
Aubuisson, Roberto d', **3:**144
Auchmuty, Robert, **1:**513
Auctions, **1:356–357**
Auden, W. H., **1:**389; **3:**280; **5:**194
Audiencias, **2:**278–279

Audiffron, Marcel, **3:**182
Audio technology industry,
 1:357–359
 film industry and, **1:**358;
  3:362–363; **4:**470
Audubon, John James, **1:**359, 360;
 3:268; **8:**259, 597
 Birds of America, **6:**214, 214
 exploration of American West and,
  3:299
Audubon Society, **1:359–360; 6:**215
Auenbrugger, Leopold, **2:**53
Auerbach, Red, **1:**424
Augsburg Confession, **5:**176, 177
Auguilar, Martin de, **7:**173
Auguste Comte and Positivism (Mill),
 6:424
Augustine, Saint, **3:**261
Aum Shinrikyo (Japanese cult),
 1:465
Aurora (newspaper), **1:360–361;**
 2:393
Auster, Paul, *New York Trilogy*, **5:**122
Austin (Texas), **1:361**
Austin, Hudson, **4:**65
Austin, Mary, **1:**320
Austin, Moses, **5:**61
Austin, Stephen F., **1:**361; **3:**202;
 8:104
Australia
 in ANZUS Treaty, **1:**361–362
 convict transportation to, **2:**402
 U.S. relations with, **1:361–362**
 in World War II, **1:**361
Australian ballot, **1:**392; **3:**146–147
Austria
 U.S. relations with, **2:**88
 after World War I, **2:**89
Austrian State Treaty (1955), **8:**205
Authoritarian Personality, The
 (Adorno), **3:**454
Autobiography of an Ex-Colored Man
 (Johnson), **5:**124
Autobiography of Benjamin Franklin,
 1:363; **5:**118
Autobiography of Malcolm X, The,
 1:363; **5:**126
*Autobiography of Miss Jane Pittman,
 The* (Gaines), **5:**126
Autoflow, **7:**441
Autologous transplantation, **8:**182
Automated teller machines (ATMs),
 1:363–364
 and theft, **7:**182

Automation, **1:364–366**
  applications for, **1:**364–366
  definitions of, **1:**364
  robotics, **7:183–185**, *184*
  Technocracy Movement on, **8:**63
Automobile(s), **1:366–371;**
    8:189–190
  accidents in, **1:**12, 376–377
  alcohol use and, **1:**118
  alternative fuels for, **3:**480–481
  catalytic converters for, **1:**362
  culture of, **2:**389
  early development of, **1:***366,*
    366–367; **8:**189
  effects of, **1:**368; **8:**190
  emissions from
    and air pollution, **1:**79
    regulation of, **1:**79, 362
    testing and standards for, **1:362**
  and historic preservation, **6:**452
  and hotel industry, **4:**176
  hybrid, **1:**79
  installment financing of,
    4:364–365
  insurance for, **4:**370
  internal combustion engine in,
    patent on, **7:304**
  mass production of, **5:**262–263,
    263
  problems with, **1:**369–370
  racing, **1:**366–367, **374–376**, *376;*
    2:436
  and recreation, **7:**65–66
  reliance on, **1:**369–370
  and road construction, **7:**177–178
  safety of, **1:**144, **376–377; 5:**105
  speed limits for, **7:500–501**
  in suburbanization, **7:**573–574
  technological improvements in,
    1:368–369
  and tourism, **8:**146
  and urbanization, **8:**290
  and vacation activities, **8:**305
  See also Automobile industry
Automobile associations, **1:**143–144
Automobile Club of America (ACA),
    1:143–144
Automobile industry, **1:371–374**
  air pollution regulations and, **1:**79,
    362
  aluminum used in, **6:**116
  assembly lines in, **1:***335,* 335–336;
    2:389; **3:**414; **4:**334; **5:**262,
    263

  automation in, **1:**364
  competition in, **1:**368–369
  computers and, **2:**392
  in Detroit, **3:**20
  disregard for consumer safety,
    exposé of, **8:**285
  early, **1:**366–368
  energy crisis and, **1:**370
  foreign trade and, **8:**167
  industrialization and, **5:**228–229
  and installment credit, **2:**449
  of Japan, **1:**336, 373–374; **3:**422
  legislation on, **1:**369
  manufacturing process in,
    1:367–368
  mass production in, **1:**367,
    371–373
  in Michigan, **5:**355
  National Traffic and Motor Vehi-
    cle Safety Act and, **5:**561
  origins of, **1:**371
  in Rust Belt, **7:**215
  safety and design changes in,
    1:376–377; **2:**384
  strikes in
    newspaper account of, **9:**385–387
    sit-down, **7:**372
  trade unions in, **1:**373; **5:**355; **8:
    260–262**
  vulcanized rubber in, **7:**202
  in Wisconsin, **8:**492
  after World War II, **1:**369–370;
    3:527
Automobile racing, **1:374–376**, *376*
  in early auto industry, **1:**366–367,
    374–375, *375*
  at fairs, **2:**436
Automobile safety, **1:376–377;**
    5:105
  American Automobile Association
    and, **1:**144
  consumer movement and, **2:**384
  disregard for, exposé of, **8:**285
  governmental inspection for, **4:**364
*Automobile Workers v. Johnson Con-
    trols, Inc.,* **1:377**
Autonomous workers, **5:**6
Avant-garde art, **1:**298
Avedon, Richard, **1:**301
Avery, Byllye, **8:**511
Avery, Oswald, **3:**67, 533; **7:**188
AVF. *See* All-Volunteer Force
AVG. *See* American Volunteer
    Group

Aviation. *See* Air transportation and
    travel; Aircraft
Aviation and Transportation Securi-
    ty Act (2001), **8:**185
Aviation insurance, **4:**368–369
Avilés, Pedro Menéndez de, **3:**296
Awakening. *See* Great Awakening
*Awful Disclosures of the Hotel Dieu
    Nunnery of Montreal* (Monk),
    5:238
AWSA. *See* American Woman's Suf-
    frage Association
Aycock, Alice, **1:**307
Ayer, J. C., and Co., **1:**129
Ayer, N. W., & Son, **1:**32
Ayer's American Almanac, **1:**129
Ayllón, Lucas Vázquez de, **3:**295
Ayres, Clarence E., **3:**109
Ayub Khan, Mohammad, **4:**259
Azidothymidine (AZT), **1:**16
Aztec Club, **8:**318
Azziz, Tariq, **6:**292

B

Babbage, Charles, **2:**334
Babbitt, Irving, **2:**375
Babbitt (Lewis), **5:**120; **8:**290, 292
Babcock, Stephen M., **2:**490
Bábí movement, **1:**384
Baby Bells, **1:381**
Baby boom generation
  in adolescence, **1:**25–26
  and crime, **2:**460
  and education, **3:**117
  and fashion, rejection of, **2:**247
  and unemployment rate, **8:**252
Bache, Alexander Dallas, **1:**141;
    2:257; **6:**160, 335
Bache, Benjamin Franklin, **1:**360
Bacher, Robert, **2:**15
Bachstrom, Friedrich, **6:**148
Bacillus-Calmette-Guérin (BCG)
    vaccine, **8:**237
Backcountry and backwoods,
    1:381–382
Backlash, **1:382**
Backlist titles, **6:**538
Bacon, Francis, **3:**204, 262; **6:**335
  on common law, **2:**316
  on leisure, **8:**526
Bacon, Nathaniel, Jr., **1:**62, 382–383,
    383; **8:**342

Bacon, Roger, **3**:301
Bacon's Rebellion, **1**:62, **382–383**; **2**:280; **8**:125, 342
Bacteriology. *See* Microbiology
Bad Axe, Battle of, **8**:401
"Bad tendency test," **3**:374
Baden-Powell, Robert, **1**:527
Badlands, **1:383–384**, *384*
Baehr v. Levin, **2**:532
Baekeland, Leo, **6**:366
Baer, Ralph, **8**:327
Baez, Joan, **8**:499
Baffin, William, **3**:286; **6**:136
Baffin Bay, **6**:136
Bagley, Sarah, **8**:505
Bahá'í, **1:384**
BAI. *See* Bureau of Animal Industry
Bail, **1:385**
Bailey, DeFord, **3**:395
Bailey, Gamaliel, **5**:96
Bailey, George, **2**:177
Bailey, Hachaliah,**2**:177
Bailey, James A., **2**:177
Bailey, Liberty Hyde, **1**:57
Bailey, Theodorus, **5**:87
Bailey v. Drexel Furniture Company, **2**:140, **142**
Bailyn, Bernard, **7**:148
Bain, Alexander, **3**:329
Bainbridge, William, **1**:415; **2**:378
Bainter, Fay, **6**:*485*
Baird, Eisenstadt v., **5**:251
Baird, John Logie, **3**:357; **8**:76
Baird, Robert, **3**:2
Baird, Spencer Fullerton, **8**:597
Bakelite, **6**:366
Baker, Edward M., **8**:404
Baker, Eugene, **3**:300
Baker, Gardiner, **5**:486
Baker, James Addison, III
   influence of, **2**:2
   and Persian Gulf War, **6**:292, 293
Baker, James Jay, **5**:557
Baker, Josephine, **2**:497
Baker, Newton (Cleveland mayor), **2**:233
Baker, Newton D. (secretary of war), **8**:378–379, 540
Baker, Ray Stannard, **2**:*73*
Baker, Robert G. (Bobby), **1**:385; **2**:421
Baker Case, **1:385**
Baker Island, **1**:189

Baker v. Carr, **1**:227, **385–386**; **5**:79; **7**:108; **8**:357
Baker v. Selden, **2**:412
Bakke, Allan, **1**:386
Bakke v. Regents of the University of California, **1**:37, **386**; **3**:119
Bakker, Jim, **8**:*71*
Bakker, Tammy Faye, **8**:*71*
Bakunin, Michael, **1**:180–181
Balaguer, Joaquin, **3**:76
Balance of trade, **1:386–387**; **2**:517
   with Japan, **4**:459
Balanced Budget Act (1997), **1**:388; **2**:515
Balanced Budget Amendment, **1:388**
Balanced Budget and Emergency Deficit Control Act. *See* Gramm-Rudman-Hollings Act
Balanchine, George, **2**:498, 499; **6**:81, *82*
Balboa, Vasco Nuñez de, **3**:284
Balch, Emily Green, **8**:499
Baldrige National Quality Program, **5**:529
Baldwin, Abraham, at Constitutional Convention, **2**:379
Baldwin, Billy, **1**:292
Baldwin, James, **3**:197; **8**:248
   Another Country, **5**:126
   Blues for Mister Charlie, **5**:126
   The Fire Next Time, **5**:126
   Go Tell It on the Mountain, **5**:121, 125
   Tell Me How Long the Train's Been Gone, **5**:126
Baldwin, Marcus W., *American Eagle*, **3**:*100*
Baldwin, Matthias W., **5**:142
Baldwin, Roger, **1**:146, 147
Baldwin, Ruth Standish, **5**:563
Baldwin, Samuel, **6**:61
Baldwin, Simeon Eben, **1**:144
Baldwin, Thomas Scott, **3**:30
Balfour Declaration, **8**:592
Balkans. *See specific countries*
Ball, Caroline Peddle, **1**:308
Ball, Lucille, **4**:209, *209*
Ball, Thomas, **1**:306
Balladares, Ernesto Pérez, **6**:241
Ballads, **1:388–389**
   on Mexican-American War, **9**:221–222
Ballard, Guy W., **2**:477
Ballard, Robert, **8**:132

Ballet, **1:389–391**; **2**:497, 498–499
   American Ballet Theatre, **1:144**, 390; **2**:498–499
   New York City Ballet, **1**:390; **2**:498; **6:81–82**, *82*
Ballet Society, **6**:81
Ballinger, R. A., and naval oil reserves, **6**:19
Ballinger-Pinchot controversy, **1:391**
Ballistic Missile Defense System, **1**:75
Ballistic missiles, inter-continental (ICBMs), **1**:75
Balloon-frame construction, **5**:173
Balloons, **1:391–392**
Ballot, **1:392**
   Australian, **1**:392; **3**:146–147
   canvassing of, **2**:38
   Massachusetts, **5:269**
   vs. voice voting, **3**:146
Ballou, Hosea, **2**:350
Baltimore (Maryland), **1:392–393**
   Empowerment Zone program in, **8**:287
   fire of 1904 in, **3**:38
   flour milling in, **3**:389, 391
   Fort McHenry in, **5:185**, *186*
Baltimore, Barron v., **1:419**, 457; **2**:198
Baltimore, Cecilius Calvert, 2nd Baron, **2**:67, 280, 287
Baltimore, Charles Calvert, Lord, **1**:392
Baltimore, David, **3**:68, 533; **7**:279
Baltimore, George Calvert, Lord, **1**:196, 333; **2**:171, 287; **5**:255; **6**:433
Baltimore Afro-American (newspaper), **6**:98, 99
Baltimore and Ohio Railroad, State of Maryland v., **2**:438
Baltimore Bell Teams, **1:393**
Baltimore Riot, **1:393**
Bambara, Toni Cade, **5**:124
Bamberger, Louis, **4**:366
Bamberger, Simon, **8**:297
Bananas, **3**:479; **4**:69–70
Banca Nazionale del Lavoro (BNL), **4**:422
Bancroft, George, **2**:485; **4**:137–138; **6**:19
Bands, marching, **5:237–238**
Bangladesh
   Concert for, **1**:441
   creation of, **4**:260

Bank(s)
building and loan associations and, **1:**563
in capitalist economy, **2:**41
central, **4:**258
and check currency, **2:114–115**
commercial, **1:**396, 405
credit provided by, **2:**447–448
decline of, **3:**367–368
export-import, **1:402–404**
failures (*See* Bank failures)
Gold Exchange Bank, **4:**10
intermediate credit, **4:384–385**
investment, **1:404–406**
Jay Cooke and Company, **2:404–405**
regulation of, **1:**405–406
Japanese, **3:**422
joint-stock land, **4:**486
national, **2:**333
regulation of, **5:**185
private, **1:406**
redlining by, **7:72–73**
robberies of, **7:**182
savings, **1:406–408; 2:**447
state, **1:**406, **408–409**
notes issued by, **8:**310
regulation of, **5:**185
wildcat, **8:**477
See also Banking; *specific banks*
Bank failures, **1:400–401**
contractionary impact of, **1:**585
deregulation in 1980s and, **4:**27
Freedman's Savings Bank, **3:**462
during Great Depression, **4:**45
Safety Fund System and, **7:222**
Bank for International Settlements (BIS), **1:393–394**
creation of, **8:**585
Bank Holiday Proclamation, **6:**491
Bank notes, **5:**528
vs. check currency, **2:**114
counterfeit, **2:433–434**
Bank of America, **1:394–395**
Bank of Augusta v. Earle, **1:**395
Bank of North America, **1:**395, 396; **2:**447; **3:**344
Bank of the Commonwealth of Kentucky, Briscoe v., **1:540**
Bank of the United States (BUS), **1:395–396,** 396–397
as central bank, **3:**344
and foreign investment, **2:**516; **3:**420

foundation of, **3:**365
Hamilton's proposal for, **4:**89–90; **8:**195
implied powers of Congress and, **4:**247
Jackson's campaign against, **1:**395, 397; **3:**152; **7:**103
and antibank movement, **1:**195; **3:**365
and pet banks, **6:**295
and panic of 1792, **3:**365
and panic of 1819, **3:**365
and panic of 1837, **3:**365
Second, removal of deposits from, **7:103**
state taxation of, Supreme Court on, **4:**247; **5:184; 6:**218
Bank of the United States, Osborn v., **6:218–219**
BankAmerica, **3:**368
Bankers Trust, **3:**370
Bankhead Cotton Act (1934), **1:396**
Bankhead-Jones Farm Tenancy Act (1937), **2:**371
Banking, **1:396–400**
antibank movement in, **1:195**
ATMs in, **1:363–364**
in Charlotte (North Carolina), **2:**109
and clearinghouses, **2:231–232**
crisis of 1933 in, **1:402**
and gold standard, **4:**15–16
Roosevelt's fireside chat on, text of, **9:**377–379
Roosevelt's response to, **7:**62–63
free, **3:**458
interest rates in, **4:**382
under Jackson, **1:**195
Jacksonian assaults on, opposition to, **8:**467
Lebanese Americans in, **5:**71
monetary system, **5:**440–441
Morgan-Belmont Agreement, **5:457–458**
offshore, **8:**447
open-market operations in, **6:**198
and organized crime, **2:**463
under Polk, **1:**195
regulation of, **1:**405–406
Comptroller of the Currency and, **2:**333
savings and loan associations and, **7:256–258**
in South Dakota, **7:**460–461

subtreasuries in, **7:571**
Suffolk Banking System, **8:3**
under Van Buren, **1:**195
Banking Act (1933). *See* Glass-Steagall Act
Banking Act (1935), **1:402; 3:**345
Banking Modernization Bill (Gramm-Leach-Bliley Act of 1999), **1:**402
Bankruptcy laws, **1:409–411**
Frazier-Lemke Farm Bankruptcy Act, **3:457**
state, Supreme Court on, **6:**171; **7:**562
Banks, Dennis, **1:**160, *160*, 161; **8:**561
Banks, Nathaniel P.
in Army of Virginia, **1:**279
in Red River Campaign, **7:**71
Banneker, Benjamin, **1:**48
Banning, Margaret Culkin, "War and the Family" speech by, **9:**403–404
Bannister, Robert, **6:**424
Bantam Books, **6:**539
Banting, William, **6:**153
Baptist churches, **1:411–413,** *413*
African Americans in, **1:**42, 43, *43*, 44–45
and camp meetings, **7:**86, 87
membership in, **7:**87, *90*, 91
and religious liberty, **7:**93
spread of, **7:**86
and Underground Railroad, **8:**250
Bar associations, **5:**74
See also American Bar Association
Barak, Ehud, **4:**442–443
Baraka, Imamu Amiri, **1:**478; **5:**123, 126; **8:**115
Blues People, **5:**126
The Dead Lecturer, **5:**126
Dutchman, **5:**126
Home: Social Essays, **5:**126
Preface to a Twenty-Volume Suicide Note, **5:**126
Baran, Paul, **4:**398; **8:**66
Baranov, Aleksandr, **1:**108; **3:**294
Barbadians, **7:**453, 454
Barbados, **1:413–415,** *414*
Barbara, Joseph, **1:**222
Barbary states, U.S. relations with, **1:**232
Barbary Wars, **1:415**
Constitution (frigate) in, **2:378**

Decatur's cruise to Algiers, **2:520**
gunboats in, **4:**77
Intrepid in, **4:**408
sailing warships in, **8:**405
Barbecue, **1:415–416**
Barbed wire, **1:416**, *416*
and cattle ranching, **2:**443
and farmer-rancher relations, **8:**463
fencing with, **3:**353
and livestock industry, **2:**73, 76
and windmills, **8:**486
Barber, Red, **1:**421
Barbera, Joe, **2:**64
Barbie doll, **1:**417; **8:**153
Barbiturates, **7:**568
Barboncito (Navajo leader), **6:**16
Barbour, John S., **7:**52
Barclay, Robert H., **5:**21
Bardeen, John, **1:**346, 440; **6:**337, 346
Barents, Willem, **6:**381–382
Barents Sea, **6:**382
Murmansk in, **5:**483
Bargained negligence policy, **5:**348–349
Bargaining for a Horse (Mount), **3:**537
Bargemen, **1:417**
Barges, **8:***147*, 147–148
Barker, Bernard L., **8:**426
Barker, Mary, **1:**155
Barkley, Alben W., **3:**164
Barkley, Charles, **6:**547
Barlow, Joel, **4:**101
Barn raising, **1:417**, 436
Barnard, Christiaan, **4:**121
Barnard, Edward Emerson, **1:**344
Barnard, Henry, **3:**114, 138
Barnard College, **3:**131; **7:**319–320
Barnburners, **1:417–418**; **2:**400; **4:**195
Barnes, Albert C., **2:**273
Barnes, Hazel E., **3:**280
Barnes and Noble, **3:**183; **6:**538, 539
Barnett, Claude, **5:**200
Barnett, Samuel, **7:**317
Barnette, West Virginia State Board of Education v., **3:**374; **6:**370
Barnstorming, **1:418**
Barnum, P. T., **1:**32, 418, *418*
American Museum of, **1:418–419**; **5:**487; **8:**593
burlesques sponsored by, **1:**575

and circus, development of, **2:**177
and Crystal Palace Exhibition, **8:**558
Davis (Jefferson) trial and, **2:***505*
Barnum & Bailey, **2:**177
Baroody, William, **8:**118
Baroody, William, Jr., **8:**118
Baroque furniture, **3:**496
Barr, Alfred H., Jr., **5:**484
Barr, Elizabeth, **7:**264
Barras, Comte de, **3:**473
Barreiro, Antonio, **9:**201–203
Barrett, David D., **6:**199
Barrie, Dennis, **5:**535
Barron, Clarence, **3:**83; **8:**367
Barron, James, **2:**129
Barron, Samuel, **1:**415
Barron, William Wallace, **8:**450
Barron v. Baltimore, **1:**419, 457; **2:**198
Barrows and Company, **6:**359
Barry, John, **5:**87
Barry, Marion, **8:**411
Barry, Rick, **1:**425
Barry, William T., **6:**426
Barth, Carl G., **7:**281
Barth, John
Coming Soon!!!, **5:**122
Lost in the Funhouse, **5:**122
Barth, Karl, **7:**414
Barthold, Richard, at Hague Peace Conference, **4:**82
Bartholdi, Frédéric Auguste, **7:**540
Bartlam, John, **1:**304
Bartlett, Frederic Clay, **1:**316
Bartlett, James H., **6:**343
Bartlett, John, **1:**419
Bartlett, John Russell, **1:**192
Bartlett's Familiar Quotations, **1:419**
Barton, Andrew, **6:**199
Barton, Clara, **6:**317
and American Red Cross, **7:**68; **8:**502
Bartram, John, **1:**166, 516, 519; **2:**292
Bartram, William, **2:**181; **6:**214
Baruch, Bernard M., **2:**189; **8:**380
Barus, Carl, **3:**552
Baryshnikov, Mikhail, **1:**144
Bascom, Florence, **6:**300
Baseball, **1:419–422**
in 19th century, **7:**508
in 20th century, **7:**509

African Americans in, **1:**420, 421, 422, 547
Black Sox scandal, **1:479–480**
college, **2:**276
women in, **2:**277
First World Series, **1:***420*
salaries in, **8:**361
and social stratification, **7:**65
trade union for, **1:422–423**; **7:**511
Bases, military. *See* Military base closings
Basketball, **1:423–426**
in college athletics, **2:**276
invention of, **8:**584
Bass, Edward, **1:**464
Bass, Robert, **6:**58
Bassett, Rex, **3:**182
Bastogne, **1:426–427**
BAT. *See* British-American Tobacco Company
Bataan-Corregidor Campaign, **1:427**; **8:**547
Bates, Katharine Lee, **1:**139
Bathroom fixtures, **6:**372
Bathtubs and bathing, **1:427–428**
Batista, Fulgencio, **2:**54, 470; **5:**47–48
Battery, electric, **3:**172–173
Battle Fleet Cruise Around the World, **1:428–429**, *429*
"Battle Hymn of the Republic," **1:429**; **2:**192–193; **4:**100
Battle of Lake Erie (Cooper), **6:**290–291
Battles of the American Revolution, 1775–1781 (Harrington), **5:**145
Battleships, **8:**407
Batts, Nathaniel, **1:**114
Batts, Thomas, **8:**447
Baum, Frederick, **1:**442
Baum, L. Frank, *The Wonderful Wizard of Oz*, **5:**127
Baumann, Eugene, **6:**149
Baxter, William, **1:**347
Bay of Pigs invasion, **1:430–431**; **2:**55, 470–471; **4:**22
Bay Psalm Book, **1:431**; **6:**468, 536
Bayard, James, **2:**542
Bayard, Thomas F., **3:**156
Bayard v. Singleton, **1:431**
Bayard-Chamberlain Treaty, **1:431**
Bayh, Evan, **4:**320
Baylor, Elgin, **1:**424

Baynton, Wharton, and Morgan, **1:431–432**

Bayou, **1:432**, *432*

Baziotes, William, **1:**10

BBC. *See* British Broadcasting Corporation

BBN. *See* Bolt, Beranek, and Newman

BBS. *See* Bulletin board systems

BCG. *See* Bacillus-Calmette-Guérin vaccine; Board for Certification of Genealogists

BEA. *See* Budget Enforcement Act; Bureau of Economic Analysis

Beach, Alfred Ely, **8:**240

Beach, Frederick C., **3:**204

Beadle, Erastus, **5:**129; **6:**537

Beadle, George Wells, **3:**532–533

Beadle, William Henry Harrison, **7:**459, 460

Beads. *See* Wampum

Beal, Fred E., **3:**512

Beale, Francis, **8:**521

"Bean bag" chair, **3:**499

Beans, Native American cultivation of, **1:**68

Bear Dance, **8:**299

Bear Flag Revolt, **1:432–433**; **3:**468

Bear Island, **6:**382

Beard, Charles A., **1:**139; **2:**382; **4:**139; **6:**403

Beard, Daniel, **2:**21

Beard, Dita, **4:**449

Bearden, Romare, **1:**298

Beards, **4:**84

Beasley, Daniel, **5:**389

Beat generation, **1:433**; **2:**433; **5:**121

Beatles, The, **2:**79; **7:**185

Beattie, Anne, **5:**122

Beatty, Willard W., **3:**136

Beauharnais v. Illinois, **4:**67; **6:**91

Beaujeu, Daniel, **1:**530

Beaumont, Andrew, **2:**411

Beaumont, William, **5:**286, 295; **6:**148, 348

Beauregard, Pierre G. T., **1:**567; **2:**211

Beauty contests, **1:433–434**, *434*
  Miss America pageant, **5:**406

Beauvoir, Simone de, **3:**279, 280
  The Second Sex, **3:**281

Beaver, **1:434–435**
  in Colorado, **2:**298
  hats, **1:**434, **435**

Native Americans and, **5:**207

Beaver, Tony, **8:**45

Bebop, **4:**469

Beccaria, Cesare, **2:**40; **6:**476

Beck, Dave, **4:**385, 386; **5:**183

Beck, Julian, **8:**115

Beck, Thomas, **8:**481

Becker, Gary, **3:**108

Becker, George F., **3:**552; **6:**300

Becker, H., **6:**340

Beckley, John James, **5:**100

Beckmann, Max, **1:**298

Becknell, William, **6:**68; **7:**248; **8:**363

Beckwith, E. G., **7:**30

Bedford, Gunning, at Constitutional Convention, **2:**379

Beech, Walter H., **1:**418

Beecher, Catharine, **3:**114, 131, 180; **7:**195; **8:**106
  Congregationalism and, **2:**349

Beecher, Henry Ward, **1:**435, 448; **6:**333; **7:**195; **8:**263
  on John Brown, **2:**163

Beecher, Lyman, **1:**377, 378, 379; **7:**195; **8:**78

Beecher's Bibles, **1:435**

Beef Trust Cases, **1:435–436**

Beekeeping, **1:436**

Beer, **7:**504, 505, 567
  brewing of, **1:***536*, **536–537**

Bees (social gatherings), **1:436–437**

Beetlecreek (Demby), **5:**125

Begin, Menachem, **3:**141

Behavior, codes of. *See* Manners and etiquette

Behavioral Science Unit of FBI, **3:**338

Behaviorism, **1:437–438**
  and political science, **6:**403–404
  and psychology, **6:**524–525

Behrman, Martin, **6:**74

Beiber, Owen, **8:**262

Beidler, John, **8:**336

Beirne, Joseph, **2:**325

Beirut bombing, **1:438–439**

Beissel, Conrad, **1:**534

Békésey, Georg von, **1:**463

Belasco, David, **8:**114

Belcher, Jonathan, **3:**466

Belgian Relief, **1:439**

Belgium
  in European Common Market, **8:**157

during World War I, **1:**439

during World War II, **1:**426

Belin, Edouard, **3:**329

Belize, **1:439**

Belknap, Tomlinson, **1:**440

Belknap, William W., **1:**440

Belknap scandal, **1:440**

Bell, Alexander Graham, **1:**440; **2:**388; **8:***70*
  on American Sign Language, **7:**356
  Bell Company founded by, **1:**346; **8:**70
  at Centennial Exhibition, **2:**87
  and deaf education, **3:**32, 34
  and fiber optics, **3:**357
  and gramophone, **1:**357
  on "grand system," **8:**65
  and National Geographic Society, **5:**541
  and telephone, **3:**577; **8:**65, 69, 456

Bell, Buck v., **3:**258

Bell, Daniel, **6:**32; **7:**428

Bell, E. N., **6:**288

Bell, Eudorus N., **1:**334

Bell, Fiallo v., **1:**125

Bell, Griffin, **3:**206

Bell, Grove City College v., **2:**206

Bell, James Ford, **2:**98

Bell, James Franklin, **6:**320

Bell, John, **1:**164; **4:**205
  in presidential campaign of 1860, **2:**383; **3:**154

Bell, Larry, **1:**299, 307

Bell, Terrel H., **3:**123

Bell Curve, The (Herrnstein and Murray), **1:**194; **7:**13

Bell System
  microwave communications, **5:**361
  and trade unions, **2:**324–325

Bell Telephone Company. *See* AT&T

Bell Telephone Laboratories, **1:**346, **440–441**; **4:**339, 342
  transistor invented at, **2:**335

Bell X-1 plane, **8:***569*, **569–570**

Bellah, Robert, **2:**192

Bellamy, Edward, **4:**333; **6:**417; **7:**424, *426*; **8:**304
  Looking Backward, **8:**303

Bellamy, Francis M., **5:**168; **6:**370; **8:**558

Bellamy, Joseph, **7:**96

Bellamy, Mr., in XYZ affair, **8:**570

Bellamy, Samuel, **2:**38

Belle of Orleans (steamboat), **3:***508*
Belleau Wood, Battle of, **1:441**
Bellecourt, Clyde, **1:**160
Bellecourt, Vernon, **1:**161
Bellei, Rogers v., **2:**181
Bellenger, Étienne, **3:**291
Bellmon, Henry, **6:**186
Belloc, Hilary, **1:**57–58
Bellow, Saul, **5:**121
   The Adventures of Augie March,
    8:294
Bellows, George, **1:**268, 297, 320,
   321, *321*; **3:**538; **6:**471
Bellows, Henry Whitney, **7:**244
Belluschi, Pietro, **6:**207
Belmont Report, The , **1:**462
Beloved (Morrison), **5:**123, 126
Belter, John Henry, **3:**497
Bemen, Solon S., **1:**252
Bemis, Samuel Flagg, **4:**467
Ben Franklin Stores, **3:**26
Ben Hur, burlesque parody of, **1:**575
Benchley, Robert, **1:**123
Benedict, David, **1:**412
Benedict, Ruth, **1:**193; **6:**259; **8:**599
Benefit concerts, **1:***441*, 441–442
Benham, Philip (Flip), **6:**199
Benicia (California), archival map of,
   9:62, *62*
Benign neglect, **1:442**
Benjamin, Judah P., **2:**341
Bennett, Gordon, **1:**374
Bennett, Hugh Hammond, **2:**371
Bennett, James Gordon, **2:**3; **6:**96;
   8:577
Bennett, Louis (Deerfoot), **8:**154
Bennett, William
   as director of Office of National
    Drug Control Policy, **5:**511
   on National Endowment of the
    Humanities, **5:**537; **6:**33
Bennett College, **3:**132
Benning, Fort, **1:442**
Benning, Henry L., **1:**442
Bennington, Battle of, **1:442–443**;
   4:61
Benny, Jack, **8:**309
Benson, Crowell v., **1:**22
Benson, Elmer A., **3:**322
Benson, O. H., **3:**445
Bent, Charles, **1:**220; **6:**68; **8:**48
Bent, William, **8:**364
Benteen, Frederick, and Battle of
   Little Bighorn, **5:**131–132

Bentham, Jeremy, **6:**476, 534
Bentley, Arthur F., **6:**376–377, 402
Bentley, Elizabeth, **8:**1, 2
Bentley, William, **2:**271
Benton, Thomas Hart (artist),
   1:297–298; **6:**471
Benton, Thomas Hart (senator),
   2:351; **4:**512, 513; **5:**420;
   8:434–435
Benton, William, **3:**204
Benton-Banai, Eddie, **1:**161
Bentsen, Lloyd, **3:**168
Benz, Karl, **1:**366
Benzodiazepines, **7:**568
Berea College v. Kentucky, **1:443**
Berenson, Bernard, **2:**272
Berenson, Senda, **2:**277
Berg, Paul, **3:**529
Berger, Victor, **6:**98; **7:**426
Bergh, Henry, **1:**186
Bergstresser, Charles M., **3:**83
Bergstrom, G. Edwin, **6:**286
Bering, Vitus, **1:**108, 121; **2:**8; **3:**286,
   293, 491; **8:**453
Berkeley, Frances Culpeper
   Stephens, **2:**476
Berkeley, John, Lord, **2:**289; **3:**112;
   6:60, 511
Berkeley, Sir William, **1:**62, 114,
   382–383, *383*; **2:**280; **8:**447
Berkman, Alexander, **1:**181
Berkman v. Parker, **3:**199
Berkowitz, David, **7:**448
Berle, Adolf, in Brain Trust, **6:**42
Berle, Milton, **8:**72, 309
Berlin, Edward A., **7:**22
Berlin, Irving, **3:**396
Berlin, Treaty of (1921), **1:443**
Berlin Airlift, **1:***443*, 443–444; **2:**269
Berlin Wall, **1:***444*, *444*; **2:**269
Berliner, Emile, **1:**358
Berlitz, Charles, **1:**446
Bermuda Company, **2:**111
Bermuda Conferences, **1:444–445**
Bermuda Islands, **1:445–446**
Bermuda Triangle, **1:***445*, **446**
Bermúdez, Juan de, **1:**445
Bernard, Claude, **6:**348
Bernard, John, **2:**326
Berners-Lee, Tim, **7:**280
Bernhardt, Sarah, **8:**309
Bernstein, Leonard, **3:**280
Bernston, Jackie, **7:**185
Berry, Chuck, **7:**185

Berry, Clifford E., **3:**25
Berry, Don, **6:**207
Berry, George L., **5:**17
Berryman, John, **5:**122
Bertoia, Harry, **3:**499
Bessemer, Henry, **4:**427
Best Friend of Charleston (locomo-
   tive), **7:**30
Betamax, **8:**327
Bethe, Hans A., **6:**344
Bethune, Mary McLeod, **1:**51
   education of, **3:**126
   and National Council of Negro
    Women, **5:**534
Betio Island, **3:**576
Better Business Bureau, **2:**383–384
Betts v. Brady, **3:**575
Beverages. *See* Brewing; Soft drink
   industry; Spirits industry;
   Whiskey; Wine industry
Beverly, Robert, *The History and Pre-
   sent State of Virginia*, **1:**191;
   9:109–111
Bey, Dawoud, **1:**302
Beyond the Melting Pot (Glazer and
   Moynihan), **1:446–447**
Bezos, Jeff, **3:**183
   See also Amazon.com
Bhaktivedanta, A. C., **2:**477
BIA. *See* Bureau of Indian Affairs
Biasone, Danny, **1:**424
Bibb, William Wyatt, **1:**102
Bible, **1:447–449**
   distributed by Gideon Society, **3:**575
   Eliot's Indian, **4:262**
   geology and, **3:**549
   Gutenberg, **6:**468
   science and, **7:**269–271
Bible box, **3:**495
Bible Commonwealth, **1:449–450**;
   8:116
Bible Presbyterian Synod (BPS),
   6:451
Bible societies, **1:**145–146; **3:**575
Biblical studies, **1:**448
   higher criticism in, **4:130–131**
Bicameralism, **5:78**
   See also Legislature
Bicentennial, **1:450**
Bickford, William, **3:**301
Bicycle messenger services, **2:**439
Bicycling, **1:450–451**, *451*
   and road construction, **1:**451;
    7:178

Bidault, Georges, **1:**445

Biddle, Charles, **6:**237

Biddle, Nicholas, **1:**396, 397, 404
   removal of deposits and, **7:**103

Biden, Joseph, **8:**339
   on Persian Gulf War, **6:**292

Biderman, Jacques Antoine, **8:**489

Bidwell, De Lima v., **2:**545; **4:**367

Bidwell, John, **6:**502

Bien, Julius, **2:**61

Bienville, Jean-Baptiste Le Moyne,
   Sieur de, **2:**262; **5:**158; **6:**73

Bierstadt, Albert, **1:**295; **4:**189;
   8:583

Big Bang, **6:**339, 347

Big Bear (Cree leader), **2:**455

"Big Bend State." *See* Tennessee

Big Brother movement, **1:**452

Big business. *See* Business, big

Big Dig. *See* Central Artery/Tunnel
   Project

Big Foot (Miniconjou leader), **8:**562

Big Horn Mountains, **1:***452*,
   452–453

Big Money (Dos Passos), **5:**121

Big Science, **6:**337–338

Big Sisters, **1:**453

Big Sleep, The (Chandler), **5:**121

Bigamy, **6:**410

Big-band swing era, **4:**468–469

Bigelow, Erastus B., **2:**58

Bigelow, Jacob, **1:**519; **5:**301

Bigelow, Julian, **2:**486

Biggs, Hermann, **3:**239

Bilingual education, **3:**121–122, 136

Bilingual Education Act (1968),
   3:118

Bilingualism. *See* Education, bilingual

Bill of Rights
   in state constitutions, **1:453–454;**
      3:89; **7:**525
   in U.S. constitution, **1:**453,
      454–457; 2:198; **3:**341; **6:**10
      (*See also specific amendments*)
   Antifederalists and, **1:**201–202
   children under, **4:**250
   and Congressional powers, **2:**350
   debate over adoption of,
      9:159–169
   and First Amendment freedoms,
      3:374
   privacy in, **6:**479
   and right to petition, **6:**297

Second, **5:**92
   Supreme Court on, **8:**24–25

Billboards, **1:**34
   regulation of, **4:**132

Billeting, **1:457–458,** 512
   Muntiny Act, **5:505**

Billings (Montana), **1:**458

Billings, Frederick K., **1:**458

Billings, John Shaw, **4:**482;
   5:295–296

Billings, Warren K., **1:**146; **5:**455

Billings, William, **5:**494

Billington, James H., **5:**102

Bills of credit, **1:**458
   Supreme Court on, **2:**446

Bills of exchange, **3:**273–274

Bimetallism, **1:458–460,** 484; **4:**14
   failure of, **7:**363
   reasons for, **7:**363

Bin Laden, Osama, **6:**108–109
   and *Cole* bombing, **2:270–271**
   and embassy bombings, **3:**194
   and 9/11 attack, **3:**41

Binckes, Jacob, **6:**82

Binders, grain, **1:**58

Binet, Alfred, **3:**116; **4:**378, 379;
   6:524

Binford, Lewis, **1:**240

Bing, Siegfried, **1:**287

Bingham, Eula, **5:**11

Bingham, George Caleb, **3:**537

Bingham, Hiram, **5:**542

Bingham, John A., **4:**485

Bini, Lucio, **6:**522

Bini (prophet), **6:**7

Biochemical genetics, **3:**532

Biochemistry, **1:460–461**

Biodiesel, **3:**480

Bioengineering, and transplants, **8:**183

Bioethics, **1:461–462**

Biograph, **3:**361

Biological containment, **1:462–463**

Biological Survey, Bureau of, on
   mammalogy, **5:**217

Biological warfare. *See* Chemical and
   biological warfare

Biological Warfare Convention,
   2:119

Biologics Control Act (1902), **6:**554

Biology
   conservation, **2:**372–374
   culture and, **1:**194
   marine, **5:**240–241
   molecular, **5:**359, **437–438**

taxonomy, **5:**217–218
   See also Zoology

Biomass, as alternative energy
   source, **3:**212, 214, 215

Bionics, **1:**463

Biophysics, **5:**437

Bioregionalism, **1:**464

Bioremediation, **3:**531

Biosphere 2, **1:**464

Biotechnology
   future directions for, **5:**19
   venture capital in, **4:**341

Bioterrorism, **1:464–465**
   CDC activities aimed to prevent,
      2:88
   See also Chemical and biological
      warfare

BIPAC. *See* Business-Industry Political Action Committee

Birch, John M., **4:**481

Bird, Larry, **1:**425

Birds
   protection of, **6:**215
   See also Ornithology

Birds of America (Audubon), **6:**214, *214*

Birds of passage, **1:**465

Birdseye, Clarence, **3:**407; **7:**78

Birge, Raymond T., **6:**341

Birge, Robert, **1:**463

Birmingham (Alabama), **1:**466
   church bombing in, **1:**332; **2:**203
   civil rights movement in, **1:**104

Birmingham (cruiser), **1:**89

Birney, James G., **3:**153; **8:**119
   Liberty Party and, **5:**96–97

Birth. *See* Childbirth

Birth cohort, **5:**103

Birth control, **1:**466
   abortion and, **1:**4–5
   AMA on, **1:**5
   Dalkon Shield, **1:**469; **2:493–494**
   and gender roles, **3:**519
   legalization of, **5:**274
   pill, **1:**466
      development of, **1:**468
   restrictions on, **5:**274
   in sex education, **7:**321, 322
   and sexuality, **7:**330
   Supreme Court on, **1:**6; **4:**66–67;
      6:479

Birth control movement, **1:466–469**
   abortion and, **1:**4–5

Birth defects, March of Dimes and,
   5:236

Birth of a Nation, The (film), **1:***469,* **469–470; 3:**362; **4:**552; **5:**569
BIS. *See* Bank for International Settlements
Biscoe, John, **6:**383
Bishop, Maurice, **4:**65; **8:**447
Bishop of Durham clause, **6:**511
Bismarck Archipelago Campaign, **1:**470
Bismarck Sea, Battle of, **1:**470
Bison. *See* Buffalo
Bissell, George H., **6:**302
Bissell, Wilson S., **7:**205
Bitburg Controversy, **1:**471
Bitter, Karl, **1:**306
Bitumen, **6:**301
Bituminous coal, **2:**251
Bitzer, Fitzpatrick v., **1:**120
Bitzer, G. W. (Billy), **1:**469
Black, Calvin, **1:**312
Black, G. V., **3:**4
Black, Hugo C.
  appointment to Supreme Court, **1:**104
  on religious freedom, **2:**168
  on right to privacy for birth control, **4:**67
  Thirty-Hour Work Week Bill of, **8:**120
Black, James, **6:**502
Black, Jesse, **3:**73
Black, Ruby, **1:**312
Black Americans. *See* African American(s)
Black arts movement, **8:**115
  periodicals in, **5:**194
Black Ball Line, **6:**230
Black Belt, **1:**471
Black Boy: A Recollection of Childhood and Youth (Wright), **5:**125
Black Caucus, Congressional, **1:**471
Black cavalry in the West, **1:471–472**
Black codes, **1:**50, **472; 7:**15
  Code Noir, **2:262–263**
  of Mississippi, text of, **9:**319–322
  in Texas, **8:**101
Black Elk (prophet), **6:**6, 8
Black Friday, **1:472–473**
Black Hawk (Colorado), **3:**574
Black Hawk (Sauk chief)
  excerpt of autobiography of, **9:**210–212
  resistance to removal by, **8:**401

Black Hawk War, **1:473–474; 8:**300, 490
Black Hills, **1:**474; **8:**275
  Custer's expedition to, **1:**474; **3:**300
  gold rush in, **1:**474; **2:**493
  Mount Rushmore in, **5:464–465,** *465*
Black Hills War, **1:474–475; 5:**41
Black horse cavalry, **1:**475
Black infantry in the West, **1:**475, *476*
Black Kettle (Cheyenne chief), **2:**298; **7:**243
Black laws, **1:475–476**
Black Militia, Free, **5:***381*
Black Monday stock market crash (1987), **1:476–477,** 563, 585
Black Muslims. *See* Nation of Islam
Black nationalism, **1:477–478,** 479; **5:**124
  of Malcolm X, **6:**211
  Nation of Islam and, **5:**519–521
  Pan-Africanism and, **6:**234–236
Black No More (Schuyler), **5:**125
Black Panthers, **1:478–479; 7:***18,* 167
"Black powder," **3:**301
Black Power, **1:479,** *480;* **2:**204; **6:**376; **7:**167
  Carmichael's speech on, text of, **9:**452–454
  Congress of Racial Equality (CORE) and, **2:**355
  at Olympics of 1968, **6:**193, *193*
  in SNCC, **7:**561
Black (covert) propaganda, **6:**503
Black Regiment, in American Revolution, **7:**152
Black Scholar, The (journal), **5:**200
Black Sox scandal, **1:479–480**
Black Star Line steamship company, **3:**197
Black Swamp, **1:**480
Black Thunder (Bontemps), **5:**125
Blackbeard (Edward Teach), **1:**550, *550*
Blackett, P. M. S., **6:**343
Blackface minstrelsy. *See* Minstrel shows
Blackfeet, **1:481–483; 8:**218
  camp of, **1:***482*
  chief of, **1:***483*
  and fur trade, **3:**490
  in Montana, **5:**449

Blackfoot Confederacy, and fur trade, **3:**491
Blacklisting, **1:**483
  in film industry, **4:**178; **5:**183
Blackmun, Harry, **2:**197; **7:**198
  on abortion, **1:**6; **7:**192
Blacks. *See* African American(s)
Blacksburg (Virginia), settlement of, **3:**84
Blacksmithing, **1:483–484,** *484*
Blackstone, William, **5:**90; **6:**387, 505; **7:**134, 151
  on common law, **2:**316
Blackton, James Stuart, **2:**63
Blackwell, Antoinette Brown, **8:**506
Blackwell, Elizabeth, **7:**244; **8:**506, 509
Blagdon, Emery, **1:**311
Blaine, James G., **5:**46, 210, 473; **8:**156
  Crédit Mobilier of America and, **2:**453
  and Harrison (Benjamin), **3:**158
  and "Mulligan Letters," **2:**453
  in presidential campaigns, **3:**156, 157
Blair, Francis P., **3:**146
Blair, Frank, **3:**155
Blair, Montgomery, **2:**551
Blair, Vilray, **2:**422
Blaisdell et al., Home Building and Loan Association v., **5:401**
Blake, Eubie, **8:**309
Blake, Eugene Carson, **5:***533*
Blake, Luther Lee, **7:**520
Blake, Lyman, **1:**503; **5:**69
Blake, or the Huts of America (Delany), **6:**235
Blake, Peter, **1:**173
Blanchard, Jean-Pierre, **1:**391
Blanchard, Jonathan, **1:**203
Blanchard, Thomas, **5:**262
Blanchet, Francis, **6:**205
Bland, R. P., **1:**484
Bland-Allison Act (1878), **1:**459, **484; 3:**458
Blanshard, Paul, **1:**337
Blanton, Smiley, **6:**442
Blasdel, Gregg N., **1:**312
Blashfield, Edwin H., *The Evolution of Civilization,* **5:***101*
Blast furnaces, **1:**485
Blatch, Harriot Stanton, **8:**514
Blatchford, Samuel, **2:**134

Blathwayt, William, **5**:151

Blatty, William Peter, *The Exorcist*, **5**:130

Blavatsky, Helena Petrovna, **5**:507; **7**:*505*; **8**:116–117

Blazejowski, Carol, **1**:425

BLE. *See* Brotherhood of Locomotive Engineers

Bleeding Kansas, **1**:505, 506; **3**:196

Blimps (dirigibles), **3**:30–32, *31*, 35

Blind, education of, **3**:34

Bliss v. Commonwealth, **4**:74

Blithedale Romance, The (Hawthorne), **7**:194; **8**:292

Bliven, Bruce, **6**:76

Blizzards, **1**:485–487, *486, 487*; **3**:42

BLM. *See* Bureau of Land Management

Bloch, Felix, **6**:*336*

Block, Adrian, **2**:357

Block, Herbert (Herblock), **6**:395

Block, Sherman, **6**:509

Blockade(s), **1**:487

in American Revolution, **8**:466

in Civil War, **1**:487–488; **2**:214, 217, 396

firsthand account of, **9**:296–297

of Cuba, **2**:471

and trade with enemy, **8**:173

in War of 1812, **8**:384

in World War I, **2**:396

Blockade runners, Confederate, **1**:487–488; **8**:446

firsthand account by, **9**:296–297

Blockaders (moonshiners), **5**:455

Blocs, political, **1**:488

Blondie (comic strip), **2**:308

Blood, Henry, **8**:298

Blood on the Forge (Attaway), **5**:125

Blood transfusion, **8**:183

AIDS transmitted through, **1**:15

Bloodless Revolution, in Rhode Island, **7**:153

Bloody Monday, **1**:332

Bloody shirt, **1**:488

Bloom, Allan, **6**:395

Bloom, Sol, **8**:272

Bloomer, Amelia, **1**:489; **6**:88, 96; **8**:513

Bloomers, **1**:488–489, *489*

Bloomfield, Leonard, **5**:115

Bloomingdale, Alfred, **2**:450, 451

Blount, William, **1**:489; **2**:135

in Southwest Territory, **7**:476

Blount conspiracy, **1**:489–490

Blow molding, **6**:366

Blowers, Sampson Salter, **1**:513

BLS. *See* Bureau of Labor Statistics

Blue and Gray, **1**:490

Blue Book of the John Birch Society, The, excerpt from, **9**:429–433

Blue Cross–Blue Shield, **4**:119, 120, 121, 173

Blue Eagle emblem, **1**:490

Blue Helmets, **6**:270

Blue Jacket (Shawnee chief), **6**:178

Blue Lake, **6**:69; **8**:48

Blue Laws, **1**:490–491

Blue Ridge Gap, **6**:254

Blue sky laws, **1**:491

Bluegrass country, **1**:491, *491*

Bluegrass music, **5**:490–491, *491*

Blues, **1**:491–492; **5**:490

African American folklore and, **3**:395

in Memphis, **5**:308

Blues for Mister Charlie (Baldwin), **5**:126

Blues People (Baraka), **5**:126

Bluford, Guion, **7**:481

Blum, Virgil, **3**:137

Blume, Judy, *Forever*, **1**:500

Blumenschein, Ernest, **8**:48

Blumstein, Dunn v., **8**:355

Bluntschli, Johann, **8**:371

Blyden, Edward Wilmot, **1**:477; **6**:*234*, 235, 236

BMI. *See* Broadcast Music, Inc.

B'nai B'rith, **5**:166

BNL. *See* Banca Nazionale del Lavoro

Board for Certification of Genealogists (BCG), **3**:521–522

Board of Education, Everson v., **2**:168

Board of Education, McCollum v., **2**:168

Board of Education of Oklahoma City v. Dowell, **1**:590

Board of Education of Topeka, Brown v. See Brown v. Board of Education of Topeka

Board of Education v. Lindsay Earls, **2**:149

Board of Education v. Mergens, **2**:169

Board of Election, Allen v., **8**:357

Board of Indian Commissioners, **1**:492

reorganization of, **5**:323

Board of Public Instruction of Orange County, Florida, Cramp v., **8**:62

Board of Regents of University of State of New York, Knight v., **8**:62

Board of Trade and Plantations, **1**:493; **5**:151

instructions from, **4**:366

Board of Wardens of Port of Philadelphia, Cooley v., **2**:310, **405**

Boarding schools, for Native Americans, **2**:55, 145; **3**:135–136

Boas, Franz, **1**:192–193, 239; **3**:396; **5**:115; **7**:13

Boat(s)

bullboats, **1**:568–569

canoes, **2**:37, *37–38*

See also Ship(s)

Boat people, **7**:471

Boatbuilding. *See* Shipbuilding

Bodie (California), **3**:574

Bodmer, Karl, **1**:295; **8**:259

Body, human, men's magazines and, **5**:196

Boehn, Max von, **1**:441

Boeing, William E., **1**:493; **8**:414

Boeing Company, **1**:83, 84, *493*, **493–494**

supersonic transport by, **8**:21

in Washington (state) economy, **8**:414, 415

during World War II, **1**:*94*

Boerne v. Flores, **1**:494; **2**:318

Boff, Leonardo, **5**:93

Boggs, Hale, **8**:340

in Warren Commission, **8**:394

Boggs Act (1951), **5**:511

Bogus laws, **6**:435

Bohlen, Charles, ambassadorship of, **1**:134

Bohr, Niels, **1**:271; **6**:338, 340, 343, 345

Boise (Idaho), **4**:212

Bok, Edward, **4**:158; **5**:193

Boland Amendments. *See* Iran-Contra Affair

Boldt, George, **8**:415

Bolívar, Simón, **5**:51–52

Bolivia

commerce with, **5**:45

relations with, drug trafficking and, **5**:512–513

Boll weevil, **1**:495

in Black Belt, **1**:471

Bolles, Eugene, **2**:272

Bolling v. Sharpe, **3:**245
Bollinger, Grutter v., **1:**386
Bollman, Justus Erlich, **3:**270
Bolm, Adolf, **1:**390
Bolshakov, Georgi, **2:**475
Bolshevik Revolution (1917), and anticommunism, **1:**197, 198
Bolt, Beranek, and Newman (BBN), **4:**398
Bolton, John, **1:**313
Bolton, William, **1:**313
Boltwood, Bertram B., **6:**344
Bomb(s)
  atomic (*See* Atomic bomb)
  hydrogen, **4:**203–204
  in arms race, **1:**271
Bombers. *See* Aircraft, bombers
Bombing(s), **1:**495–497, *496*
  of Afghanistan, **1:**496
  of American embassies, **6:**109
  by anarchists, **1:**182, 198; **8:**95
  of Beirut, **1:**438–439
  of Birmingham church, **1:**332; **2:**203
  of Cambodia, **2:**16, *16*
  of *Cole* (destroyer), **2:**270–271; **6:**109
  in Fraunces Tavern, **8:**96
  of Kosovo, by NATO, **4:**551
  at La Guardia Airport, **8:**96
  letter, **8:***247*, **247–248**
  of Los Angeles Times Building, **2:**10
  in Mooney case (1916), **5:**455
  in Oklahoma City, **3:**41, 328; **5:**385; **6:**186, *187*, **187–188**; **8:**95, 339
    and FBI, **3:**339
  of Vietnam, **2:**532
  Wall Street Explosion (1920), **8:366**
  of World Trade Center (1993), **3:**41; **6:**109; **8:**96, 532, **533–534**
  in World War I, **1:**495
  in World War II (*See* World War II, air war)
Bonanza Kings, **1:**497
Bonaparte, Charles, **3:**337; **4:**503
Bond(s)
  junk, **4:501–502**
  Moody's ratings, **5:454**
  savings, **7:258–259**
Bond, Alan, **1:**172

Bond, Christopher (Kit), **5:**422
Bond, Julian, **3:**558
Bond, William Cranch, **1:**343
Bonds, Barry, **1:**421, 422
Bondwoman's Narrative (Crafts), **5:**124
Bone marrow transplantation, **8:**183
Bonesetter's Daughter, The (Tan), **5:**123
Bonfanti, Maria, **1:**389
Bonham, M. L., **1:**567
Bonhoeffer, Dietrich, **2:**165
Bonhomme Richard (warship), **6:**24
Bonhomme Richard-Serapis encounter, **1:***497*, **497–498**
Bonifacius: Essays to Do Good (Mather), **6:**316
Bonneville, Benjamin L. E., **8:**363
Bonneville Dam, **4:**201; **8:**414
Bonney and Bush, **8:**192
Bonnin, Gousse, **1:**304
Bonny, Anne, **1:**550
Bono, **1:**41
Bonpland, Aimé, **3:**551
Bonsack, James, **8:**135
Bontemps, Arna
  Black Thunder, **5:**125
  God Sends Sunday, **5:**125
Bonus Army, **1:498**, *499*; **7:**166
Bonus Bill of 1816, **1:**498
Bonuses, military, **1:498–499**
  GI Bill of Rights and, **3:**574
Bonvouloir, Julien-Alexandre Archard de, **7:**147
Booby traps, **1:499–500**
Book banning, **1:500**
Book of Mormon, The (Smith), **1:**447; **2:**163; **5:**53
Book publishing, **2:**322–323
  See also Publishing industry
Book-of-the-Month Club, **1:500–501**; **6:**538
  first black writer selected by, **5:**125
Booksellers, **6:**538
  online, **6:**539
  superstores, **6:**538–539
Boomer movement, **1:501**
Boomtowns, **1:501–502**, *502*
Boone, Daniel, **3:**297
  captivity narrative involving, **2:**51
  excerpt from biography of, **9:**104–107
  and Wilderness Road, **2:**479; **8:**478
Boone, Jamima, **2:**51

Boone and Crockett Club, **2:**366, 367; **8:**480
Boorstin, Daniel J., **4:**139; **5:**102; **6:**407
Booster (Rauschenberg), **6:**471
Boot and shoe manufacturing, **1:502–503**
Booth, Ableman v., **1:2–3**; **3:**482
Booth, Catherine Mumford, **7:**234
Booth, Charles, **6:**533
Booth, Edmund, **2:**509
Booth, John Wilkes, **1:**328; **2:**218
Booth, Sherman, **1:**2–3
Booth, William, **7:**234, *235*
Bootlegging, **1:503–504**
  moonshine, **5:**455
  and organized crime, **2:**463
BOR. *See* Reclamation, Bureau of
Borax, **1:504–505**; **2:**513
Borbridge, John, **1:**112
Borchgrevink, Carsten, **6:**383
Borden, Gail, **2:**490
Borden, Luther v., **5:**175
Border disputes. *See* Boundary disputes
Border ruffians, **1:505**, 506
Border Slave State Convention, **1:505–506**
Border War, **1:506**
  Quantrill's Raid, **7:**4
Borderlands. *See* Spanish Borderlands
Borders Bookstore, **6:**539
Boreman, Arthur, **8:**449
Boren, Craig v., **2:445–446**; **3:**246
Borglum, Gutzon, **5:**464–465
Boring, Edwin G., **6:**525–526
Bork, Robert Heron, **1:***506*, 506–507; **5:**137
  confirmation hearings for, **1:506–507**; **2:**346; **4:**497
  CORE support for, **2:**355
  National Rifle Association and, **5:**557
  under Nixon, **7:**495
  Watergate scandal and, **8:**427
Borough, **1:507**
Borrowing. *See* Debt
Bosch, Juan, **3:**76
Boskin, Michael, **2:**423
Boskin Committee, **2:**423–424
Bosnia
  atrocities committed in, **8:**588
  NATO bombing campaign in, **1:**496

Bosnia-Herzegovina. *See* Yugoslavia
Bosons, **6:**339
Bosses and bossism, political,
  1:507–508; 2:388
 in California, **2:**10
 municipal government and, **5:**475
 municipal reform and, **5:**478
 political machines, **5:186–187**
Boston (Massachusetts), **1:508–511,**
  509
 American Academy of Arts and
  Sciences, **5:**66
 in American Revolution, archival
  maps of, **9:**29, *29–33, 32, 33*
 architecture of, **1:**510, *510;* **5:**266
 arts in, **5:**268
 Central Artery/Tunnel Project (Big
  Dig) in, **8:**240
 in colonial era, **1:508–509; 8:**289
 economy of, **1:**509, 510
 embargo on British imports in,
  6:116
 Federal period in, **5:**265–266
 fire fighting in, **3:**371
 furniture manufacturing in, **3:**496,
  497
 gentrification of, **3:**539
 geography of, **5:**266
 glassmaking in, **4:**3–4
 Massachusetts Bay Colony at, **5:**265
 Mount Auburn Cemetery in, **2:**80,
  81
 newspapers published in, **6:**95
 Old North Church in, **6:**190, *190*
 police strike of 1919, **1:513–514;**
  7:164–165
 riots in, Burns Fugitive Slave Case
  and, **1:**577
 siege of, **1:***511,* **511–512; 5:**88–89;
  7:142
  capture of Ticonderoga and,
   8:124
 symphony orchestra in, **8:**38
 transportation projects in, **5:**267–268
 water system of, **8:**292
Boston and Illinois Land Company,
  5:26
Boston and Sandwich Glass Company, **4:**3
Boston Athletic Association, **8:**154
Boston Classicists, **5:**492
Boston Committee of Correspondence, **1:**512; **2:**314
Boston Common, **1:**512, *513*

Boston Crown Glass Company, **4:**4
Boston Gazette (newspaper), **6:**95
Boston Latin School, **1:**509; **3:**111,
  112
Boston Massacre, **1:**458, 509,
  512–513, *514;* **2:**286; **7:**164
 eyewitness account of, **9:**128–130
 first victim of, **7:**7–8
 newspapers on, **6:**95
 trial of soldiers after, transcript of
  slave testimony in, **9:**130–131
Boston Massacre, The (Revere), **6:**470
Boston News-Letter (newspaper), **6:**95
Boston Pilot (newspaper), **6:**294
Boston Port Act (1774), **4:**408
Boston Public Library, **5:**98
Boston Quarterly Review (magazine),
  8:179
Boston Social Club, **7:**557
Boston Symphony, **8:**38
Boston Tea Party, **1:**509, **514–515,**
  515; **2:**286–287; **3:**103; **8:**60, 150
 British policies following, **7:**134
 and Intolerable Acts, **4:**408
 Massachusetts Government Act
  and, **5:**272
 and North Carolina, **6:**127
Boston Veterinary Institute, **8:**319
Bosworth, F. F., **8:**302
Botanical gardens, **1:515–518**
Botany, **1:518–520**
Bothe, Walther, **6:**340
Böttger, Johann Friedrich, **6:**418
Boudinot, Elias, **1:**145, 501, *501;*
  3:99
Bougainville, **1:520–521,** *521*
Bouguer, Pierre, **3:**551
Boulder Dam. *See* Hoover Dam
Boulding, Kenneth, **3:**109
Bound East for Cardiff (O'Neill), **6:**519
Boundary disputes
 over Indian Country, **4:**266
 Kansas in, **4:**466
 Maine in, **1:**282–283
 in maps, archival, **9:**37
 Mason-Dixon line and,
  5:259–260, *260*
 Massachusetts in, **8:**311
 Missouri in, **4:**466
 New Hampshire in, **8:**311
 New York in, **8:**311
 Rhode Island in, **4:**528
 between states, **1:521–523,** *522;*
  2:355–356

 U.S.-Canada, **8:**434
 Vermont in, **8:**311
Bounties
 commercial, **1:523–524**
  on British goods, **6:**21–22
 fishing bounties, **3:**376–377
 military, **1:524**
  in Civil War, **2:**211, 363
Bounty jumper, **1:524**
Bouquet, Henry, **6:**277
Bourbons, **1:524**
 in Alabama, **1:**103
 in Mississippi, **5:**413
Bourgeois, Leon, *La Société des*
  Nations, **5:**63
Bourgmont, Étienne Véniard de,
  3:292; **6:**29; **8:**451
Bourne, Randolph, **1:**337; **6:**375
Boussingault, Jean-Baptiste, **6:**148
Boutros-Ghali, Boutros, **8:**271, 272
Boutwell, George S., **1:**473
 anti-imperialism of, **1:**202
Bovine growth hormone, **3:**531
Bovine spongiform encephalopathy,
  2:73
Bowditch, Henry P., **6:**349
Bowditch, Nathaniel, **1:**343
Bowdler, Thomas, **8:**325
Bowen, Anthony, **8:**584
Bowen, Daniel, **5:**486
Bowen, Norman L., **6:**301
Bowers, Birdie, **6:**383
Bowers v. Hardwick, **6:**480
Bowery, **1:525**
Bowie, James, **1:**106–107
Bowie knife, **1:525**
Bowlegs, Billy, **8:**402
Bowler, Jack, **7:**379
Bowles, Samuel, **3:**505
Bowles, William Augustus, filibus-
  tering expeditions of, **1:**525
Bowling, **1:525–526,** *526;* **7:***508*
Bowman, Isaiah, **3:**543
Bowyer, Fort, **9:**42, *43*
Boxer, Marilyn, **8:**520
Boxer Rebellion, **1:***526,* **526–527**
Boxing. *See* Prizefighting
Boy Scouts of America, **1:527; 2:**21;
  7:65
Boyce, William, **1:**527
Boycotting, **1:***528,* **528–530; 6:**227
 by associations, **1:**340
 of British imports, **2:**284, 286
 Pullman cars, **6:**549

Boyd, Belle, **7**:502

Boyd, R., **1**:44

Boyer, Ernest, **2**:56–57; **7**:536

Boyle, Stack v., **1**:385

Boyle, Tony, **8**:268

Boylston, Zabdiel, **3**:235

Boys from Brazil (Levin), **5**:122

Bozeman Pass, **6**:254

Bozeman Trail, Treaty of Fort
    Laramie and, **5**:40

BPD. *See* Bureau of the Public Debt

BPS. *See* Bible Presbyterian Synod

Brace, Charles Loring, **1**:27; **8**:291
    Children's Aid Society founded by,
        2:136

Brackenridge, Hugh Henry, **5**:118

Bradbury, Ray, **5**:130

Braddock, Edward
    in Battle of the Monongahela,
        5:443–444
    expedition of, **1**:122, **530**; **3**:95
    in Allegheny Mountains, **1**:127
    in French and Indian War, **3**:469

Braddock's Road, **6**:254; **8**:461

Bradford, Andrew, *The American
    Magazine*, **5**:118

Bradford, William, **1**:129; **4**:137;
    5:117; **6**:95, 363, 378, 536; **9**:71

Bradley, Bill, **3**:169

Bradley, David, *The Chaneysville Inci-
    dent*, **5**:126

Bradley, Joseph P., **2**:134; **3**:156

Bradley, Milliken v., **1**:590; **2**:199;
    3:118

Bradley, Omar N., **1**:565
    in liberation of France, **8**:550
    in Normandy Invasion, **6**:119
    in Saint-Lô, **7**:227

Bradstreet, Anne Dudley, **9**:91–92
    Several Poems, **5**:118

Bradwell, Myra, **5**:74

Brady, Betts v., **3**:575

Brady, Dorothy, **3**:110

Brady, James, **1**:331, 530

Brady, Mathew B., **1**:*199*, 299,
    530–531
    photographs by, **1**:*530*, 530–532

Brady Bill (Handgun Violence Pre-
    vention Act) (1993), **1**:530;
    4:76; **5**:557; **6**:213

Brady Campaign, **4**:76

Bragg, Braxton
    and Army of Tennessee, **8**:87
    in Battle of Chickamauga, **2**:135

in Battle of Perryville, **6**:291

in Chattanooga Campaign, **2**:113

at Cumberland Gap, **2**:479

in Kentucky Campaign, **7**:35, 157

at Pensacola, **3**:386

Brain Trust, **1**:532; **6**:42

Branch Davidians, **2**:478
    See also Waco Siege

Brancusi, Constantin, **1**:297, 310

Brandeis, Louis D., **5**:91
    on big business, **1**:214
    on censorship, **2**:84
    "clear and present danger test"
        established by, **3**:374
    confirmation hearings for, **1**:532
    on diversity-of-citizenship cases,
        3:254
    on Espionage and Sedition Acts,
        3:254
    on industrial democracy, **2**:273
    and New Freedom, **6**:54, 70, 495
    on regulatory takings, **6**:505
    on right to privacy, **6**:479
    Women in Industry (Brandeis Brief),
        excerpt of, **9**:357–360
    and Zionist movement, **8**:592

Branden, Nathaniel, **6**:154

Brandenburg v. Ohio, **3**:374

Branding, cattle, **2**:74, 76

Brando, Marlon, **8**:115

Brandon, Barbara, **6**:395

Brandt, Bill, **1**:301

Brandt, Edward, **1**:15

Brandt, Willy, **8**:271

Brandywine Creek, Battle of, **1**:532;
    7:143

Brannan, Charles, **1**:533

Brannan, Sam, **2**:9

Brannan Plan, **1**:533

Bransfield, Edward, **6**:382–383

Braque, Georges, **2**:475

Brass, **6**:115
    metalwork, **5**:329

Brattain, Walter H., **1**:346, 440;
    6:337, 346

Braun, Braunfeld v., **2**:169

Braun, Carol Moseley, **5**:549; **8**:507

Braun, Wernher von, **7**:479

Braunfeld v. Braun, **2**:169

Brave New World (Huxley), **8**:599

Bray, John Randolph, **2**:63

Brazil
    at ABC Conference, **1**:1
    capitalist development in, **2**:44

commerce with, **5**:43–45

Confederate expatriates in, **2**:340

independence of, **5**:52

Rio de Janeiro Conference (1947)
    in, **7**:163

rubber in, **7**:202

slave trade in, **7**:387

trade agreements with, **6**:125

Breast implants, **1**:533

Breathed, Berkley, **2**:309

Breckinridge, John C., **3**:154, 155;
    5:244
    and Democratic Party, **2**:551
    and land speculation, **5**:36
    in presidential campaign of 1860,
        2:400

Breech-loading rifles, **5**:479

Breen, T. H., **1**:528

Breit, Gregory, **6**:343

Brennan, William J., Jr.
    on new federalism, **1**:454
    on sex discrimination, **2**:445;
        3:478, 525
    on voting rights, **1**:385

Brenner, Sidney, **3**:533

Brent, Charles, **3**:243

Brent, Margaret, **8**:9–10

Brereton, Lewis H., **6**:371

Breslin, Jimmy, **5**:122

Brest-Litovsk, Treaty of (1918),
    1:247; **7**:211; **8**:315

Brethren (Dunkers), **1**:533–535
    pacifism of, **6**:227
    and Underground Railroad, **8**:250

Brett, George Sidney, **6**:525

Bretton Woods Conference (1944),
    1:536; **8**:531
    International Monetary Fund at,
        4:396

Brewer, David J., **6**:410

Brewer, Lucy, **5**:243

Brewing, **1**:*536*, 536–537
    in Milwaukee, **5**:389

Brewster, William, **4**:474; **6**:215

Breyer, Stephen G.
    on line-item vetoes, **8**:320, 321
    on presidential election of 2000,
        1:579

Breyman, Heinrich von, **1**:442

Brezhnev, Leonid, **2**:269, 270; **3**:427;
    7:212
    in SALT agreement, **1**:272
    at summit conferences, **8**:16

Briand, Aristide, **4**:515

Bribery, **2**:420
See also Corruption, political
Brice, Calvin S., **3**:158
Bricker, John W., **3**:163; **8**:204
Bricker Amendment, **1**:537; **8**:204
Brickwedde, Ferdinand G., **6**:341
Bridge at San Luis Rey, The (Wilder),
 5:120
Bridger, Fort, **1**:537
Bridger, James, **1**:537; **4**:57
Bridger, Jim, **2**:301; **3**:299; **7**:190
Bridger's Pass, **6**:254
Bridges, **1**:537–540
 Brooklyn Bridge, **1**:547, *547*
 building materials for, **1**:564
 covered, **1**:538, *538*
 disasters involving, **3**:41
 Eads Bridge, **3**:99, *99*
 George Washington Bridge,
  3:553, *553*
 Golden Gate Bridge, **4**:18, *18*
 suspension, **1**:539, *547*
 toll, **8**:*139*, **139**–140
 Verrazano-Narrows, **1**:539; **8**:315
Bridges, Calvin Blackman, **3**:532
Bridges, Harry, **1**:151; **2**:11; **4**:395
Briggs, Charles Augustus, **1**:448;
 4:131
Bright, William, **8**:564
Brightman, Lehman, **1**:161
Brinster, Ralph, **3**:530
Brinton, Daniel Garrison, **1**:192
Brisbane, Albert, **3**:446
Brisbane, Arthur, **8**:301
*Briscoe v. Bank of the Commonwealth
 of Kentucky*, **1**:540
Bristow, Benjamin H., **1**:144; **3**:156;
 8:470
Britain. *See* Great Britain
Britannia metal, **5**:328
British Broadcasting Corporation
 (BBC), **8**:65
British debts, **1**:540–541
British Empire, concept of, **1**:541–543
 See also Great Britain
British-American Tobacco Company
 (BAT), **8**:135
Broadcast journalism. *See* News pro-
 gramming
Broadcast Music, Inc. (BMI), **5**:502
Broadsides, **1**:543
Broadway, **1**:*543*, **543**–544; **8**:115,
 128, 129
 burlesque on, **1**:575

musicals on, **5**:500
Brock, Isaac, **3**:21
Brock, William E., **5**:12
Brockenbrough, John, **7**:157
Brockway, Zebulon, **7**:75
Broder, Samuel, **1**:15–16
Broderick, David, **2**:9
Brodie, Bernard, **6**:144
Brodie, Maurice, **6**:388
Brodovitch, Alexy, **1**:301
Brokers, **1**:544–545
Bronk, Detlev, **1**:141
Bronson, Ruth Muskrat, **3**:136
Bronson v. Rodes, **1**:545
Bronze Star Medal, **2**:527
Brook Farm, **1**:545; **3**:446; **7**:424,
 425; **8**:179, 181, 301
Brooke, Fort, **8**:47
Brookings, Robert S., **1**:545
Brookings Institution, **1**:545–546
 foundation of, **8**:117
 on gentrification, **3**:538
 Keynesianism at, **8**:117
 on New Deal, **8**:117
 presidents of, **8**:117
Brooklyn, **1**:*546*, **546**–547; **6**:80
 Coney Island in, **1**:179, *179*
 Greenwood Cemetery in, **2**:*80*
Brooklyn Botanic Garden, **1**:517
Brooklyn Bridge, **1**:539, 546, **547**,
 547, 564
Brooklyn Dodgers, **1**:421, 547
Brooks, Byron A., **8**:245
Brooks, Gwendolyn, *Annie Allen*,
 5:125
Brooks, James, **2**:453
Brooks, Preston, Sumner caned by,
 1:332
Brooks, Rodney A., **7**:183–184
Brooks, Van Wyck, *America's Coming
 of Age*, **5**:120
Brooks, William Keith, **5**:240
Brooks v. United States, **2**:311
Brooks-Coffey, Lillian, **2**:172
Broom, Wood v., **1**:227
Broonzy, Big Bill, **1**:492
Brotherhood of Carpenters and
 Joiners of New York, **5**:12
Brotherhood of Locomotive Engi-
 neers (BLE), **7**:24, 25
 Burlington strike, **1**:576, *576*
Brotherhood of Railway and Airline
 Clerks, **1**:548

Brotherhood of Sleeping Car
 Porters (BSCP), **1**:*547*,
 547–548; **5**:*9*, 237; **8**:172
 African Americans in, **3**:50
"Brothers and Sisters" (Gray), **3**:323
Brough, Charles, **1**:262
Broughton, William, **2**:303; **6**:204
Broun, Heywood, **1**:123
Broward, Napoleon Bonaparte,
 3:387
Browder, Earl, **1**:198; **2**:326, 327
Brower, Abraham, **7**:42, 43
Brower, David, **3**:230
Brown, Antoinette, **8**:501
Brown, B. Gratz, **5**:90
Brown, Charles Brockden, **5**:118
Brown, Charles L., **1**:347
Brown, Claude, *Manchild in the
 Promised Land*, **5**:126
Brown, Edmund, Sr., **2**:11, 12
Brown, Edmund G., Jr. (Jerry),
 1:479; **2**:12; **8**:266
Brown, Elaine, **1**:479
Brown, H. Rapp, **7**:167
Brown, Harold, **2**:529
Brown, Henry (Box) (slave), **7**:*381*
Brown, Henry Billings (Supreme
 Court justice), on racial segre-
 gation, **6**:370–371
Brown, Henry Kirke, **1**:306
Brown, Hugh, **5**:55; **8**:298
Brown, Jacob, **8**:384
Brown, James, **5**:490
Brown, John, **4**:98; **5**:59; **7**:17
 as biblical avenger, **2**:163
 Gaspée, burning of, **3**:512
 Harpers Ferry raid by, **1**:332;
  2:192; **4**:97–100, *98*; **8**:448
 historical assessment of, **9**:287–288
 last speech by, text of, **9**:286–287
 Pottawatomie Massacre by, **1**:505,
  506; **4**:98, 509; **6**:435
Brown, John Carter, and land specu-
 lation, **5**:36
Brown, Joseph E., **2**:341
Brown, Lee, **5**:511
Brown, Lewis, **8**:118
Brown, Louise, **1**:462
Brown, Margaret Wise, *Goodnight
 Moon*, **5**:128
Brown, Moses, **7**:152
 and land speculation, **5**:36
Brown, Nicholas, **1**:548
Brown, NLRB v., **5**:141

Brown, Oliver, **1:**549

Brown, Robert McAfee, **5:**93

Brown, Roger, **1:**298, 311

Brown, Ron, as Commerce secretary, **2:**310

Brown, Sonia Gordon, **1:**308

Brown, Tina, **6:**92

Brown, William Hill, *The Power of Sympathy*, **5:**118

Brown, William Wells, **7:**381
    Clotel; Or, The President's Daughter: A Narrative of Slave Life in the United States, **5:**124
    Experience; Or, How to Give a Northern Man Backbone, **5:**124
    Narrative of William Wells Brown, a Fugitive slave, **5:**124
    Three Years in Europe; Or, Places I Have Seen and People I Have Met, **5:**124

Brown Girl, Brownstones (Marshall), **5:**126

"Brown scare," **3:**328

Brown University, **1:**548
    establishment of, **3:**111, 127; **7:**152

Brown v. Board of Education of Topeka, **1:**548–549; **3:**118, 121, 246; **5:**161
    and distinction between desegregation and integration, blurring of, **3:**14–15
    judicial review in, **4:**493
    NAACP and, **5:**527
    and role of federal government, **3:**341
    ruling in *Plessy v. Ferguson* reversed by, **3:**342
    and school desegregation, **1:**589; **2:**199, 202
    Southern governors defying, **4:**29
    and special education, **3:**34
    and state sovereignty, **7:**534
    and white resistance in Georgia, **3:**557

Brown v. Maryland, **1:**549; **6:**387
    original package doctrine in, **6:**213

Browne, Carl, **2:**444

Browne, Robert, **1:**549; **7:**313

Brownell, Herbert, **2:**194

Brownfields, **6:**64

Browning, John M., **5:**186

Brownists, **1:**549; **7:**313

Brownmiller, Susan, **8:**511

Browns Ferry fire, **6:**141

Brownson, Orestes, **8:**179, 180–181

Brownsville affair, **1:**549–550

Bruce, Ailsa Mellon, **5:**539–540

Bruce, Blanche K., **1:**50

Bruce, David K. E., ambassadorship of, **1:**134

Bruce, John Edward, **6:**236

Bruce, Patrick Henry, **2:**476

Bruch, Hilde, *The Golden Cage*, **3:**104

Brûlé, Étienne, **5:**353

Brunel, Marc Isambard, **8:**240

Brunot, James, **7:**287

Brush, Charles F., **2:**232; **3:**173; **5:**108

Brutality, police, **6:**385, *386*, **386–387**

Bryan, Charles W., **3:**162

Bryan, Kirk, **2:**237

Bryan, William Jennings, **2:***465*; **6:**30
    anti-imperialism of, **1:**202
    arbitration agreements negotiated by, **6:**263
    and Bryan-Chamorro Treaty, **1:**550
    "cooling off" treaties, **5:**428
    and creationism, **2:**446
    Cross of Gold speech by, **1:**459; **2:**400, **465**, 551; **3:**458
    and Democratic Party, **2:**551
    Farmers' Alliances and, **2:**227
    free-silver arguments of, **2:**265
    and fundamental Protestantism, **2:**164
    and Japanese expansionism, **4:**457
    populists and, **5:**366
    in presidential campaign of 1896, **2:**46; **3:**158–159; **6:**418; **8:**234
    in presidential campaign of 1900, **3:**159; **6:**320
    in presidential campaign of 1908, **3:**160, *160*
    in Scopes trial, **7:**283, 284; **8:**86
    on silver coinage, **7:**362
    against teaching evolution, **3:**484

Bryan-Chamorro Treaty (1914), **1:550–551**

Bryant, Roy, **8:**126

Bryant, William Cullen, **5:**118

Bryce, James, **1:**137; **6:**455

Bryce Canyon National Park, **5:***551*

Bryn Mawr College, **3:**131, 133; **7:**319–320

Brzezinski, Zbigniew, **6:**392

BSCP. *See* Brotherhood of Sleeping Car Porters

Buade, Louis de, Comte de Frontenac et Pallau, **5:**1

Buccaneers, **1:**551, *551*

Buchanan, Franklin, **5:**442–443

Buchanan, James (economist), **3:**110

Buchanan, James (president), **5:**110; **6:**278
    and Lecompton Constitution, **5:**73
    as log cabin president, **5:**145
    in Mormon expedition, **5:**458
    vs. Mormon state, **8:**296
    and Mormons in Utah, **5:**53–54
    Ostend Manifesto and, **1:**189; **6:**219
    in presidential campaign of 1852, **3:**154
    in presidential campaign of 1856, **3:**154; **7:**111

Buchanan, Patrick (Pat)
    and GATT, **3:**524
    in presidential campaign of 1992, **2:**376; **3:**169
    right-wing forces and, **7:**16

Buchanan v. Warley, **5:**526

Buck v. Bell, **3:**258

Buckboards, **1:551–552**, *552*

Buckingham, Thomas, **8:**572

Buckland, William, **1:**249

Buckley, James, **5:**556

Buckley, William F., Jr., **5:**556
    and conservative movement, **2:**375

Buckley Amendment. *See* Family Education Rights and Privacy Act

Bucklin, Joseph, **3:**512

Buckman Act (1905), **3:**387

Buckner, Simon Bolivar, **6:**182–183

Buddhism, **1:552–554**; **7:**91, 94
    forms of, **1:**325–326
    growth of, **1:**325
    prevalence of, **1:**325

Budge, Don, **8:**90, *90*

Budget, federal, **1:554–560**
    balanced, **8:**197–198
    Balanced Budget Amendment, **1:388**
    Congressional appropriations in, **1:**229
    goals of, **1:**556
    Gramm-Rudman-Hollings Act and, **4:**31
    history of, **1:**558–560
    and military base closings, **5:374–375**

Budget, federal, (*continued*)
  OMB in, **1:**229; **6:**164
  surplus in, **8:***28*, 28–29
Budget and Accounting Act (1921),
  3:523
Budget Enforcement Act (BEA)
  (1990), **2:**515; **4:**31
Buell, Don Carlos, **7:**157
  Army of the Cumberland under,
    2:479
  in Battle of Perryville, **6:**291
  in Battle of Shiloh, **7:**346
Buena Vista, Battle of, **1:560**
Buenos Aires Peace Conference,
  1:560–561
Buffalo (New York), **1:561**
  flour milling in, **3:**390
  foundation of, **4:**52
Buffalo (bison), **1:***561*, 561–562
  and Blackfeet culture, **1:**481
  in hide and tallow trade, **4:**130
  hunting of, **5:***426*
  near extinction of, **8:**480
  and Ute culture, **8:**299
Buffalo Tamer (chief), **5:***518*
Buffalo trails, **1:**562; **4:**2
Buffon, Georges-Louis Leclerc de,
  2:234
Buffum, Arnold, **6:**47
Buford, Abraham, **2:**128
Buford, Jefferson, **3:**196
Buford, John, **3:**567
Bugs Bunny, **2:**64
Building and Loan Associations,
  1:562–563
Building materials, **1:563–565**
  adobe, **1:**24
  cement, **2:**79
  plastics, **6:**366
Bulfinch, Charles, **1:**249; **2:**49; **3:**318
Bulganin, Nikolai, at summit confer-
  ences, **8:**15
Bulge, Battle of the, **1:**426, *565*,
  565–566; **8:**550–551, *551*
  Malmédy Massacre in, **5:**217
Bulimia, **3:**104
Bull, Calder v., **6:**10
Bull, Clarence Sinclair, **1:**300
Bull Moose Party, **1:566**, *566*; **3:**160;
  8:43
  See also Progressive Party
Bull Run (Manassas), **2:**211
  First Battle of, **1:567**; **2:**211
    archival map of, **9:***65*, 65–66

Second Battle of, **1:568**; **2:**212
Bullboats, **1:568–569**
Bulletin board systems (BBS), **8:**304
Bulletin of the Atomic Scientists, **6:**337
Bullfinch, Charles, **5:**266
Bullitt, William, **7:**211
  ambassadorship of, **1:**134
Bulloch, James D., **1:**105
  securing ships for Confederacy,
    6:23
Bullwhackers, **5:**472
Bultmann, Rudolf, **5:**93
Bulwer, Sir Henry Lytton, **2:**229;
  6:237
Bumpers, Dale Leon, **1:**263
Bumppo, Natty, **5:**70
Bunau-Varilla, Philippe, **4:**108;
  6:237, 238
Bunche, Ralph, **8:**270
Bundling, **1:569**
Bundy, McGeorge
  as head of Ford Foundation, **6:**318
  and National Security Council,
    5:560
  on nuclear warfare, **1:**271
Bundy, Omar, **1:**441
Bungee jumping, **1:569**, *569*
Bunker, Ellsworth, **6:**240
Bunker Hill, Battle of, **1:**509, 511,
  569–570, *570*; **7:**142
  archival maps of, **9:***33*, 33–35
  "Don't fire till you see the white of
    their eyes," **3:**78
  trenches in, **8:**207
Buntline, Ned, **8:**476
Bunyan, John, *Pilgrim's Progress*,
  5:127
Bunyan, Paul, **8:**45, 288
Burchard, Samuel D., **3:**157
Burden, Chris, **1:**307
Burden, Scott, **1:**307
Burdick, Eugene, with Harvey
  Wheeler, *Fail-Safe*, **5:**121
Burdick, Quentin N., **6:**132
Bureau of Agricultural Economics,
  1:71
Bureau of Air Commerce, **1:**82, 93
Bureau of Alcohol, Tobacco, and
  Firearms (ATF), **3:**331
Bureau of Animal Industry (BAI),
  1:63; **8:**319–320
Bureau of Chemistry, **3:**403–404
Bureau of Economic Analysis (BEA),
  3:105

Bureau of Immigration and Naturalization, of Department of
  Labor, **5:**11
Bureau of Indian Affairs
  occupation of, **8:**177
  tribal councils organized by, **8:**215
Bureau of Indian Affairs (BIA),
  1:570–572; **3:**115
  under Collier, **4:**288
  establishment of, **4:**272, 384
  functions of, **4:**384
  and reclamation projects, **7:**56
  reservations under, **4:**272
  schools operated by, **3:**136
  termination policy in, **4:**288
Bureau of Investigation, **3:**337
Bureau of Labor, **5:**10; **6:**492
Bureau of Labor Statistics (BLS),
  5:10–11
  faulty procedures used by, **2:**423
  Monthly Labor Review, **3:**106
  and unemployment rate, **8:**251
Bureau of Labor-Management Relations and Cooperative Programs, **5:**12
Bureau of Land Management (BLM)
  archive of land patents, **5:**32
  functions of, **4:**383; **5:**31
Bureau of Lighthouses, **5:**106
Bureau of Public Roads, **3:**335
Bureau of Refugees, Freedmen, and
  Abandoned Lands. *See* Freed-
  men's Bureau
Bureau of the Public Debt (BPD),
  2:515–516
Bureaucracy, **1:572–573**; **3:**329–333
  civil service, **2:206–208**
Burford, Anne, **3:**229
Burgdorfer, Willy, **5:**178
Burger, Warren Earl
  Court under, **4:**497; **8:**25
  on doctrine of free speech, **3:**374
  on executive privilege of presi-
    dents, **3:**279
  on separation of church and state,
    3:374
  on subpoenas to presidents, **6:**457
Burgess, Anthony, **1:**438
Burgess, John W., **6:**401
Burghers, **1:573**
Burgoyne, John, **1:**442, *574*; **2:**29;
  7:143
  in Battle of Oriskany, **6:**213

and Fort Ticonderoga, **8**:124, 312; **9**:35

invasion by, **1:573–574**

in Saratoga Campaign, **7**:250–251; **9**:35–36

Burial
methods of, **3**:486
of presidents, **6**:457–458

Burke, Charles, **1**:492

Burke, Edmund
and conservatism, **2**:374
Reflections on the Revolution in France, **7**:149, 162
on representative government, **7**:109

Burke, John, **6**:132

Burke Act (1906), **1:574**
effects of, **4**:299

Burleigh, Charles, **8**:240

Burleigh, Walter, **7**:459

Burleson, Albert S., **3**:208

Burlesque, **1:575**

Burlingame Treaty (1868), **1:575–576**; **2**:154, 157

Burlington strike, **1:576**, *576*

Burma Road, **1:576–577**; **7**:181
Merrill's Marauders (GALAHAD), **5:324**

Burnap, Daniel, **2**:241

Burnham, Daniel, **2**:132–133, *187*; **3**:498; **8**:410
design for World's Columbian Exhibition, **2**:187

Burning Bush, Society of, **8**:302

Burns, Allan F., *Maya in Exile: Guatemalans in Florida*, excerpt from, **9**:509–515

Burns, Anthony, **1**:577

Burns, Arthur F., **2**:431; **3**:346

Burns, George, **8**:309

Burns, John A., **4**:108

Burns, Lucy, **8**:514

Burns, Tommy, **6**:484

Burns Fugitive Slave Case, **1:577**

Burnside, Ambrose E., **2**:212, 213
in Battle of Antietam, **1**:200
at Battle of Fredericksburg, **3**:457
in Battle of Spotsylvania Courthouse, **7**:512
General Order No. 38 issued by, **3**:527
side-whiskers of, **4**:84
and Vallandigham incident, **3**:527; **8**:306

Burr, Aaron, **1**:577; **3**:359; **5**:37, 86
charged with treason, **8**:193, 194
and Democratic Party, **2**:549
duel with Hamilton, **1:577–578**; **3**:*92*
in presidential campaign of 1796, **3**:150
in presidential campaign of 1800, **3**:148, 150, 171; **8**:322
in Spanish Conspiracy, **3**:270; **7**:490
treason trial of, **2**:377; **7**:156

Burr, Theodore, **1**:538

Burr, United States v., **3**:279; **6**:456; **8**:194

Burrill, Thomas J., **5**:357

Burritt, Elihu, **6**:267

Burroughs, Edgar Rice, **5**:129

Burroughs, George, **8**:494

Burroughs, William (inventor), **2**:334

Burroughs, William S. (writer), **1**:433; **2**:433; **5**:121

Burroughs-Wellcome, **1**:16

Burrows, Larry, **1**:301

Bursum Bill, opposition to, **1**:340

Burt, William A., **8**:244

Burton, Dan, **2**:472

Burton, Ernest DeWitt, **8**:281

Burton, Isaac, **4**:169

Burton, Phillip, **1**:15

Burton, William, **2**:542

BUS. *See* Bank of the United States

Bus system, desegregation of, **1**:529, 548; **2**:202; **3**:15

Busemann, Adolf, **8**:569

Bush, Barbara, **3**:376

Bush, George H. W.
and abortion, **6**:361
on ACLU, **1**:147
AIDS research under, **1**:16
arms race under, **7**:553–554
birthplace of, **1**:508
censorship measures of, **2**:85
child care policies of, **2**:139
and civil rights legislation, **2**:196, 197
Cuba policy of, **2**:472
defense policy of, **2**:529
and Department of Transportation, **8**:185
drug law enforcement under, **5**:511, 513
education policies of, **3**:119, 123

energy policies of, **3**:210; **6**:304
environmental policies of, **2**:230
and European Community, policies toward, **3**:260
Family and Medical Leave Act vetoed by, **3**:315
and family-planning programs, **7**:216
and Federal Mediation and Conciliation Service, **3**:343
and flag protection, **3**:381
foreign policies of, **3**:427; **7**:114; **8**:588
and German unification, **3**:563
Gorbachev and, **2**:270
HUD under, **4**:184
intelligence activities under, **4**:377
Iraq-gate and, **4**:422
Israel and, **4**:442
Latin American policies of, **2**:55; **5**:49
and NAFTA, **3**:309–310; **6**:124; **8**:199
and National Endowment for the Arts, **5**:535
and nonprofit organizations, **6**:319
and Panama Canal, **6**:241, 242–243
and peacekeeping missions, **6**:271
Persian Gulf address by, text of, **9**:515–517
and Persian Gulf War, **6**:292–293
in presidential campaign of 1980, **3**:167
in presidential campaign of 1984, **3**:168
in presidential campaign of 1988, **3**:168, 229
in presidential campaign of 1992, **3**:168, 169
presidential library of, **5**:100
and regulatory relief, **5**:11–12
and Strategic Arms Reduction Talks, **8**:203
at summit conferences, **8**:16
tax increases under, **2**:515
and taxation, **8**:59
and Tiananmen Square Protest, **8**:123
vetoes cast by, **8**:321
Vietnam syndrome and, **8**:328
in World War II, **8**:557

Bush, George W.
on ABM Treaty, **7**:553
AIDS policy under, **1**:18, 41

Bush, George W., (*continued*)
AmeriCorps under, **1:**173
on "Axis of Evil," **1:**40; **8:**96
biological weapons policies of, **2:**119
conservatism advocated by, **2:**376
defense policy of, **2:**529
education policies of, **3:**124
energy policy of, **6:**179, 304
environmental policies of, **3:**230,
231; **8:**424
and Federal Mediation and Conciliation Service, **3:**343
foreign policies of, **3:**428; **8:**588
on genetic engineering, **3:**532
on global warming, **3:**511
Head Start under, **4:**113
HUD under, **4:**184
immigration regulation under,
4:229
on international trade, **3:**309–310
Job Corps under, **4:**481
judicial nominations of, **7:**313
and Kyoto Protocol, **4:**8
labor policies of, **5:**12
on Libya, **1:**40
and National Endowment for the
Humanities, **5:**537
on 9/11 attack, **6:**108; **8:**96
and Office of Faith-Based Community Initiatives, **3:**330
and Office of Homeland Security,
3:330; **6:**109
in presidential campaign of 2000,
1:578; **3:**119, 148, 149, **170,**
171, 221
response to Court decision,
9:525–526
at summit conferences, **8:**16
Superfund under, **4:**112
tax policies of, **3:**273; **8:**59
as Texas governor, **8:**103
Thanksgiving Day Proclamation
by, **6:**490
War on Terrorism address by, text
of, **9:**526–530
Bush, George Washington, **8:**412–413
Bush, Vannevar, **5:**18–19;
6:166–167; **7:**279–280
Science–The Endless Frontier, **5:**19,
557
Bush v. Gore, **1:**578–579; **3:**170, 171,
246
Bush's response to, **9:**525–526
Florida constitution in, **7:**527

Gore's response to, **9:**523–525
judicial review in, **4:**494
Bushnell, Horace, **2:**349; **5:**431;
6:324; **7:**97
Bushnell, Nolan, **8:**327
Bushrod, Richard, **3:**80
Bushwackers, **1:**505
Business
bankruptcy provisions for,
1:409–410
big, **1:579–581**
and antitrust laws, **1:**213
critics of, **1:**214
industrialization and, **5:**228
mergers and acquisitions in,
5:322–323
monopolies in, **5:444–445**
rise of, **1:**213, 214
Supreme Court on, **1:**214
conglomerates, **2:347–348**
environmental, **3:225–226**
military-industrial complex,
5:376–378
minority, **1:581–582**
set-asides for, **7:315–316,** 398
Small Business Administration
and, **7:**398
regulation of (*See* Government
regulation of business)
and Republican Party, **2:**23
Small Business Administration and,
7:398
See also Corporations
Business cycles, **1:582–586,** *583*
National Bureau of Economic
Research on, **5:**528
Business forecasting, **1:586–588**
marketing research and,
5:247–248
Business indicators. *See* Economic
indicators
Business machines, **1:588–589**
typewriter, **8:***244,* **244–245,** *245*
Business unionism, **1:589; 7:**25
National Association of Manufac-
turers, **5:**527–528
Business-Industry Political Action
Committee (BIPAC), **6:**393
Busing, **1:589–590; 3:**119
in Charlotte (North Carolina),
2:108–109
Butane, **6:**301
Butler, Benjamin F., **3:**157
Army of the James under, **1:**279

and black enlistment in Civil War,
2:212
New Orleans occupied by,
6:73–74, 75
Order No. 28, **1:590**
on slaves as contraband of war,
2:395
text of report on, **9:**294–296
Butler, Ed, **5:**421
Butler, John, **8:**567
Butler, Josephine Elizabeth, **6:**513
Butler, Judith, **3:**516–517, 518
Butler, Nicholas Murray, **3:**274
Butler, Thomas, **4:**84
Butler, United States v., **1:**396; **3:**527;
8:273
Butler, Zebulon, **8:**566
Butterfield, Alexander, **6:**112
Butterfield, John, **6:**411
Butterfield Overland Mail, **5:**204;
6:411, 412; **7:**514
Butternuts (Peace Democrats),
2:218, 411
Button, Thomas, **3:**286
Buttrick, John, **5:**88
Butts, Alfred Mosher, **7:**287
Byck, Samuel, **1:**330
Byers, Walter, **5:**531
Byllynge, Edward, **6:**60, 511
Bylot, Robert, **3:**286
Byrd, Harry Flood, **1:**507; **8:**344
Byrd, James, **5:**179
Byrd, Raines v., **8:**320–321
Byrd, Richard Evelyn, **6:**382, 384
Byrd, Robert C., **2:**230; **8:**450
Byrd, Robert E., **5:**542
Byrd, William, I, **3:**57; **7:**155–156
Byrd, William, II, **1:**248; **5:**118;
7:156; **8:**343, 447
Byrne, Ethel, **1:**468
Byrne, Leslie L., **8:**345
Byrne, William M., **6:**287
Byrnes, James F., **3:**163
Byrnes, Thomas, **1:**299
Byron, John, **6:**473

C

CAA. *See* Civil Aeronautics Admin-
istration; Civil Aeronautics
Authority; Clean Air Act
CAB. *See* Civil Aeronautics Board

Cabazon Band of Mission Indians, California v., **3:**509; **8:**223

Cabell v. Chavez-Salido, **1:**126

Cabeza de Vaca, Álvar Núñez
expeditions of, **1:**256; **2:**1–2, *2*, 360; **3:**284, 295, 296
in New Mexico, **6:**65
in Texas, **8:**99
La Relacion, **2:**1, *1*
in Soto expedition, **1:**102

Cabinet, **2:**2–3; **3:**331–332
nominations for, Senate confirmation of, **2:**353
See also specific departments

Cabinet-Maker and Upholsterer's Drawing Book (Sheraton), **3:**496

Cabinet-Maker and Upholsterer's Guide (Hepplewhite), **3:**496

Cabinets (collections), **5:**485
See also Museum(s)

Cable Act (1922), **5:**65
See also Married Women's Property Act (1922)

Cable News Network (CNN), **8:**74

Cable Services Bureau, **3:**340

Cable television, **1:**381; **2:**322; **8:**74
advertising on, **8:**76

Cable Television Consumer Protection and Competition Act (1992), **3:**340

Cables, Atlantic and Pacific, **2:**3–4
lithograph celebrating, **2:***4*

Cabot, George, **3:**255, 256; **8:**108

Cabot, John, **4:**32
on cod fisheries, **2:**261
voyages of, **2:**4–5, *5*; **3:**285, 287

Cabot, Sebastian, **2:**4–5, *5*

Cabral, Pedro Alvarez de, **3:**283

Cabrillo, Juan Rodríguez, **3:**285, 296, 491; **8:**451

CAD. *See* Computer-aided design

Caddo, **2:**5–6; **8:**223
in Texas, **8:**98

Cadmus, Paul, **1:**298

Cadwalader, John, **2:**543

Caffe Cino, **8:**115

"Cagers," **1:**423

Cagle, Daryl, **6:**395

Cahill, Holger, **1:**310

Cahn, Julius, **8:**114

Cahokia Mounds, **1:***247;* **2:**6, *6–7;* **4:**278; **8:**225

Cahuenga, Treaty of. *See* Mexican-American War

Cain, James M., **5:**120
Double Indemnity, **5:**121
The Postman Always Rings Twice, **5:**121

Caine Mutiny (Wouk), **5:**121

Cairo Conferences, **2:**7

Cajon Pass, **6:**254

Cakewalk, **2:**497

Calculators, **6:**169
basis for, **2:**392
invention of, **1:**588

Caldecott, Helen, **6:**268; **8:**499

Calder, Alexander, **1:**306; **8:**475

Calder, Alexander Mine, **1:**306

Calder, Alexander Stirling, **1:**306

Calder v. Bull, **2:**7; **6:**10

Caldwell, Charles, **6:**333

Caldwell, Philip, **3:**415

Caledonia (ship), **5:**21

Caledonian Clubs, **8:**154

Calhoun, John C.
Address of the Southern Delegates by, **1:**20
antislavery movement and, **1:**210
Bonus Bill of 1816 and, **1:**498
doctrine of "concurrent majority," **2:**374
Eaton affair and, **3:**105
and Long's explorations, **5:**150
and military forces, plan for, **2:**530
and Nashville Convention, **5:**516
Native American removal under, **4:**295
and navigation projects, **7:**168–169
on nullification, **7:**293, 457
in presidential campaign of 1824, **3:**152; **8:**322–323
in presidential campaign of 1828, **3:**152; **8:**323
resignation of, **6:**400
on secession, **7:**293
in Senate, **8:**323
on slavery, **8:**485
South Carolina Exposition and Protest, **7:**457
on southern rights, **7:**473–474
on state sovereignty, **7:**534
and states' rights, **2:**550; **8:**435
and tariffs, **3:**460; **6:**145
vice presidency of, **8:**322–323
and War Department, **8:**378
and Yellowstone River expeditions, **8:**580

Calhoun doctrine, **2:**331

Califano, Joseph A., **4:**114

California, **2:**7–13
admission to Union, **2:**331
application for, **8:**462
affirmative action in, **1:**37
Proposition 209 and, **6:**509–510
African Americans in, **6:**151
alcaldes in, **1:**115
alien landholding in, **1:**124
architecture in, **1:**248–249
Asian Indian Americans in, **1:**324, 325
Bear Flag Revolt in, **1:432–433**
blizzards in, **1:**486
Catholic missions in, firsthand account of, **9:**107–109
cession by Mexico of, **2:**550
charter schools in, **2:**110
Chinese immigrants in, **2:**154
citrus industry in, **2:**182
Death Valley, **1:**505; **2:**513, *513*
development of, Bank of America and, **1:**394
earthquakes in, **3:**37, 101–102
electric industry in, deregulation of, **3:**175–176; **4:**27
emblems, nicknames, mottos, and songs of, **7:***532*
floods in, **3:***42*
fruit growing in, **3:**478, 479
gold rushes in (*See* Gold rush[es], in California)
gun control in, **4:**75
hide and tallow trade in, **4:**130
higher educational system of, **2:13–14; 6:**509–510 (*See also* University of California)
affirmative action in, **1:**386
Hispanic Americans in, **4:**134
Hopkins Marine Station in, **5:**240, 241
Iranian Americans in, **4:**421
Japanese Americans in, **4:**457, 462–463, 464
Kearneyites in, **4:**514
Kearny's march to, **4:514–515**
and land claims, **5:**26
Long Beach, **5:148–149**
maps of, **2:***8*
archival, **9:**10, *57, 58–64, 60, 61, 63*
Mexican-American War in, **5:**341
military base closings in, **5:**376
mission Indians of, **5:408–409**

California, (*continued*)
modern, **2:**11–12
Mussel Slough incident in,
 5:503–504
Native Americans in, **2:**7, 8, 9, 10,
 12; **8:***214*, **214–216**
oil in, **6:**179, 298
prehistoric, **1:**242
Progressivism in, **2:**10
Proposition 8, **6:**509
Proposition 13, **2:**12; **6:508–509**
Proposition 14, **7:**82
Proposition 187, **4:**229
Proposition 187 of, **6:509**
Proposition 209, **6:509–510**
Proposition 227, **6:**510
Salton Sea in, **7:234**
Scripps Institution of Oceanogra-
 phy in, **5:**241
scurvy in, **7:**287
Silicon Valley in, **7:**306, **360–361**
smoking in public places, ban on,
 8:136
southern, rise of, **2:**10–11
Spanish, **2:**8
Sutter's Fort in, **8:33**
toll roads in, **8:**140
trade unions in
 for teachers, **1:**157
 United Farm Workers, **8:**266
U.S. takeover of, **2:**8–9
Utopian communities in, **8:**303
welfare in, **7:**222
wine industry in, **8:**487
Yosemite National Park,
 8:582–583
California (battleship), **6:**273
California, Hurtado v., **4:198**
California, Miller v., **6:**419
California, United States v., **8:**124
California Alien Land Law (1913),
 2:13
*California Federal Savings and Loan
 Association v. Guerra,* **6:**449
California Federation of Teachers
 (CFT), **1:**157
California Indian Basketweavers
 Association, **8:**215
California Indian Education Associ-
 ation, **8:**215
California Indian Legal Services,
 8:215
California Indian Rancheria Act
 (1958), **8:**215

California Indian Storytellers Asso-
 ciation, **8:**215
California Institute of Technology
 (Caltech), **2:14–15; 3:**217
 rocket research at, **7:**189
California Land Act (1851), **5:**25
California Native American Her-
 itage Commission, **8:**215
California State University, **2:13–14**
California Trail, **2:15; 6:208–209**
*California v. Cabazon Band of Mission
 Indians,* **3:**509; **8:223**
Caliguiri, Richard, **6:**361
Calkins, Robert, **8:**117
Call, Richard, **8:**402
Call girls. *See* Prostitution
Call It Sleep (Roth), **6:**13
Call of the Wild, The (London), **5:**119
Call Off Your Old Tired Ethics
 (COYOTE), **6:**514
Callender, Guy S., **4:**6
Callender, James T.
 in Chase impeachment trial, **4:**241
 conviction under sedition act,
 1:124
Callery, Mary, **1:**309
Calley, William L., Jr., court-martial
 of, **2:**440; **5:**505
Calorie, **6:**148
Caltech. *See* California Institute of
 Technology
Calvert, Cecil, **6:**511
Calvert, Cecilius. *See* Baltimore,
 Cecilius Calvert, 2nd Baron
Calvert, George. *See* Baltimore,
 George Calvert, Lord
Calvert, Leonard, **5:**255
Calvin, John, **7:**75
 on right of revolution, **7:**148
 and work ethic, **8:**526, 527
Calvinism, **2:15–16**
 vs. Arminianism, **1:**264–265
 Cambridge Platform and, **2:**19
 Edwardsean theology, **3:**140
 and Puritanism, **6:**556
 and Reformed Churches, **7:**75
 Second Awakening in, **1:**378
 and United Church of Christ,
 8:263
CAM. *See* Computer-aided manu-
 facture
Cambodia
 bombing of, **2:**16, *16*
 immigration from, **7:**470–471

incursion in, **2:16–17,** *17*
independence for, **8:**330
Mayaguez incident in, **5:275**
in Vietnam War, **8:**332, 334, 335
neutrality of, **6:**36
Cambodian Americans, **7:**471
Cambridge (Massachusetts),
 2:17–18
 Charles River Bridge at, **1:**537
Cambridge Agreement (1629),
 2:18–19; 4:56
Cambridge Platform, **2:19,** 349
Camcorders, **6:**331
Camden (New Jersey), **6:**62, 63, 64
Camden, Battle of, **2:19; 3:**261
Camels, in American West, **2:**19
Camels (cigarettes), **8:**135
Cameras, **6:**329
 digital, **6:**330, 331
 electronic, **6:**330
Cameron, James, **8:**132
Cameron, Simon, **2:**420
Cameron, William E., **7:**52
Caminetti, Anthony, **6:**232
Cammerer, Arno B., **5:**551
Camouflage uniforms, **8:**258, *258*
Camp, Carter, **1:**161
Camp, Walter, **2:**276; **3:**410
Camp David, **2:19–20,** *20*
Camp David Peace Accords, **2:20,**
 21; **3:**141, 427
Camp Fire Girls, **2:21**
Camp meetings, **2:21–22; 7:***86*
 Chautauqua movement and, **2:**113
Campaign(s), political
 almanacs in, **1:**129
 barbecue as site of, **1:**415–416
 songs in, **2:**24; **3:**153
 television advertising in, **8:**75
 See also Election(s)
Campaign financing and resources,
 2:22–24
 civil servants and, restrictions on,
 4:103–104
 Emily's List and, **3:**198
 reform attempts, **2:**548; **3:**147
 regulation of, **3:**144
 soft money in, **7:**439
Campaign to End Discrimination
 Against Pregnant Women,
 6:449
Campanius, John, **2:**234
Campbell, Alexander, **3:**44, *44*
Campbell, George W., **8:**241

Campbell, H. W., **3**:88
Campbell, Joan, **8**:*501*
Campbell, John (printer), **6**:95
Campbell, John A. (governor), **8**:564
Campbell, John W., **5**:130
Campbell, Joseph, **2**:36
Campbell, Sir Malcolm, **1**:375
Campbell, Robert, **8**:176
Campbell, Thomas (minister), **3**:44
Campbell, Thomas E. (Arizona governor), **7**:55
Campbell, W. Glenn, **8**:118
Campbell Soup Can (Warhol), **6**:414
Camping, **8**:305
Campoli, Cosmo, **1**:311
Camus, Albert, **3**:279, 280
Canada
    acid rain in, **1**:13
    air defense systems in, **1**:75
    Alabama claims and, **1**:106
    in American Revolution, **7**:142
        Arnold's march to Quebec,
            1:281–282
        Continental Congress address to,
            9:134–135
    in American Studies, **1**:170
    in Aroostook War, **1**:282–283
    borders of
        in archival maps, **9**:52
        Oregon Treaty on, **6**:209–210
    British acquisition of, **2**:295
    in Civil War
        Confederate activities in,
            2:24–25; **6**:136
        Saint Albans Raid, **7**:224; **8**:313
    explorations of, **3**:285–286
        by Ogden, **6**:37
    foreign investment from,
        3:421–422
    French colonial settlements in,
        2:329; **6**:51–53
    French legal system in, **2**:440
    hockey in, **4**:143–144, 209–210
    immigration to
        after American Revolution,
            7:137; **8**:266
        after Vietnam War, **3**:197
    Inuit in, **4**:410
    in King William's War, **4**:527
    Klondike Rush in, **4**:538–539
    Mennonites in, **5**:310
    North American Free Trade
        Agreement with, **3**:309;
        6:124–125; **8**:199

Paris, Treaty of (1763) and, **6**:248
Saint Lawrence Seaway in, **7**:225
trade with, **2**:27–28; **8**:276–277
U.S. relations with, **2**:25–28
    Bayard-Chamberlain Treaty,
        1:431
    Caroline affair and, **2**:58
    Columbia River Treaty,
        2:303–304
    Fenian movement and, **3**:354
    Northwest Angle and, **6**:135–136
    Vermont and, Haldimand Negotiations between, **8**:312
    in War of 1812, **8**:383–384
    in World War II, Normandy Invasion, **6**:119–120
    Yukon region of, **8**:589, *589*
Canada, Missouri ex. rel. Gaines v.,
    3:14; **5**:526
Canadian Football League (CFL),
    3:411
Canadian River, Long's explorations
    of, **5**:150
Canadian-American reciprocity,
    2:28–29
Canadian-American waterways, **2**:29
    and Great Lakes steamships,
        4:53–55
    Niagara Falls, **6**:103
    Saint Lawrence Seaway,
        7:225–226
Canal(s), **2**:29–34, *30*; **8**:187
    advantages and disadvantages of,
        2:30–31
    Chesapeake and Ohio Canal, **2**:32,
        32
    Chicago Sanitary and Ship, **5**:22
    construction of, **8**:429
        federal support for, **7**:169
    Erie (*See* Erie Canal)
    Gallatin's report on, **3**:503
    Illinois and Michigan Canal, **2**:132;
        4:219; **5**:22
    inland lock navigation in, **4**:361
    Lakes-to-Gulf Deep Waterway
        and, **5**:22–23
    and market shipping, **2**:387
    Nicaraguan Canal Project, **6**:105
    in Ohio, **6**:172
    Panama (*See* Panama Canal)
    Schuylkill Canal, **8**:239
    subsidies for, **7**:564
    toll, **8**:140
    tunnels built for, **8**:239

Union Canal, **8**:239
Whitewater Canal, **8**:239
Canarsies, **6**:79
Canary Currents, **4**:73
Canby, Edward R. S., **5**:433; **8**:404
Canceaux (British man-of-war),
    5:208
Cancer, **2**:34–35
    protection from, federal government's role in, **2**:540
    smoking and, **7**:404, 405
Candler, Asa G., **2**:260; **7**:438
Candles, **2**:35
    as lighting, **5**:107
    in soap industry, **7**:408
Cane (Toomer), **5**:125
Canine distemper, **8**:319
Cannibalism
    during blizzards, **1**:486
    Donner party and, **3**:79
Canning, George, **5**:52
Canning (food), **3**:405–406
Canning industry, **2**:35–37
    fruits, **3**:479
Cannon, James, **2**:326
Cannon, Marion, **6**:417
Cannon, Sylvester, **8**:298
Cannon, Walter B., **6**:349
Canoes, **2**:37, **37**–38
Canticle for Leibowitz (Miller), **5**:121
Cantonment Sprague, archival map
    of, **9**:66, *66*–67
Cantwell v. Connecticut, **2**:167–168
Canvass, **2**:38
Capa, Robert, **1**:301
Cape Ann, settlement on, **3**:80
Cape Canaveral (Florida), **1**:502
Cape Cod (Massachusetts), **2**:*38*,
    38–39
    origins of name, **2**:261
Cape Horn, **2**:39, *39*
Caperton, William Gaston, III, **8**:450
Capital(s)
    nation's (*See also* Washington
        [D.C.])
        Philadelphia as, **6**:277, 278, 312
    state, **2**:47–48
Capital punishment, **2**:39–41
    doubts about, **6**:478
    evasion of, in Leopold-Loeb case,
        5:82
    by hanging, **4**:91–92
    opposition to, **4**:92
    Supreme Court on, **6**:552

Capitalism, **2:41–47**
  class formation within, **2:**222
  collective bargaining and, **2:**273
  Declaration of Independence as
    reaffirmation of, **2:**284
  Marx on, **7:**424
  socialism on, **7:**424–425
  uneven development of, **2:**45–46
  welfare, **2:**43; **8:437–438**
Capitalism and Freedom (Friedman),
  6:31
Capitation taxes, **2:48**
  See also Poll taxes
Capitol(s)
  state, **2:**47, 48, *48*
    first, **8:**483
  U.S., **2:48–50**, *49*, 352
    burning of, **8:**417
    heating systems in, **4:**122
Capone, Al, **1:**504; **2:**133; **3:**60
Caponigro, Paul, **6:**330
Capote, Truman, *In Cold Blood,*
  5:122
Capper-Volstead Act (1922), **1:**71;
  2:50, 407
Captivity narratives, **2:50–52**, *51,*
  52; **3:**84; **4:**524–525
  by Rowlandson (Mary), **9:**101–103
Car(s). *See* Automobile
Car culture, **2:**389
Carbon dioxide
  in atmosphere, **4:**5–6, 7, 8
  concentrations of, Keeling curve
    of, **2:**237, *237*
  emissions of, energy use and pro-
    jections for, **3:**213
*Carbon Dioxide and Climate: A Scien-
  tific Assessment* (Charney), **4:**6
Carbon paper, **6:**168
Cárdenas, García López de, **2:**301,
  416; **3:**296
Carder, Frederick, **1:**288, 290
Cardiovascular disease, **2:52–54**
  heart implants for, **4:121–122**
Cardona, José Miró, **1:**431
Cardozo, Benjamin N., **2:**317; **6:**232
Cardozo, Jacob, **3:**108
Carey, Henry C., **3:**108
Carey, Hugh, **1:**355
Carey, James, **3:**176
Carey, Matthew, **1:**447
  American Atlas, **2:**60
Carey, Ronald R., **4:**386
"Cargo cults," **6:**6

Caribbean
  British and French territories in,
    8:445–447, *446*
  buccaneers in, **1:551**, *551*
  slave trade in, **7:**387, *387*
  U.S. interventions in, **4:**406–407
  U.S. policies in, **2:54–55**
    dollar diplomacy and, **3:**71
    Good Neighbor Policy and,
      3:426; **4:22–23**, 77
    Grenada Invasion and, **4:**65
    gunboat diplomacy and, **4:**76–77
    manifest destiny and, **3:**75
    Providence Island Company and,
      6:518–519
  See also specific countries
Caribbean Basin Initiative, **5:**49
Caribs, **1:**414
Carillon, Fort, **5:**21
Carleton, Sir Guy, **1:**281; **4:**467;
  7:143
Carleton, James H., **6:**16, 19; **8:**404
Carlile, John S., **8:**449
Carlisle Indian Industrial School,
  2:55, 145
Carlos, John, **6:**193, *193*
Carlos III. *See* Charles III
Carlson, A. J., **6:**349
Carlson, Chester F., **1:**325, *588;*
  6:169
Carlson, Henry (Doc), **1:**423
Carlton, George, **1:**221
Carlucci, Frank C., **2:**529
Carmack, George, **1:**109; **4:**538
Carmichael, Stokely, **1:**479, *480;*
  2:204; **6:**376; **7:**561, *561*
  "Black Power" speech by, text of,
    9:452–454
  sexism of, **8:**516
Carnahan, Jean, **5:**422
Carnahan, Mel, **5:**422
Carnap, Rudolf, **3:**204; **6:**425
Carnegie, Andrew, **1:**580; **8:**233,
  295, 295
  anti-imperialism of, **1:**202; **6:**320,
    321
  and astronomy, **1:**344
  Homestead strike and, **2:**224
  philanthropy of, **2:**55–57, 227;
    3:443; **6:**317
  and public libraries, **2:**56; **5:**98;
    7:65
  public perception of, **7:**181
  rags-to-riches story of, **8:**529

  and rail transportation, **2:**388
  in steel industry, **4:**427–428
    Homestead strike and, **4:**157;
      7:556
  on trade unions, **7:**556
Carnegie, Dale, *How to Win Friends
  and Influence People,* **4:186**
Carnegie Corporation of New York,
  2:55–56; **3:**444
Carnegie Foundation for the
  Advancement of Teaching
  (CFAT), **2:56–57**
Carnegie Institution of Washington
  (CIW), **2:57**; **5:**18
  Geophysical Laboratory of, **3:**552
Carnegie Steel Company, **4:**157
Carnes, Peter, **1:**391
Carnivals, **2:177–178**, 436
"Carnivore" (software), **3:**186
Carnivore Diagnostic Tool, **3:**339
Carolene Products Co., United States v.,
  3:246
Carolina(s)
  colonial assembly of, **1:**333
  Fundamental Constitutions of,
    2:57–58
  westward migration in, **8:**459
  See also North Carolina; South
    Carolina
Caroline affair, **2:58**
Caroline Islands, **2:58**
  in Trust Territory of the Pacific,
    8:95, 232
Carothers, Wallace H., **2:**123; **8:**110
Carpal tunnel syndrome, **5:**298
Carpathia (ship), **8:**131
Carpenter, Charles C., **1:**501
Carpenter, James, **1:**290
Carpenter, Liz, **8:**517
Carpet manufacture, **2:58–59**, *59*
  nylon and, **2:**121
Carpetbaggers, **2:**59; **3:**386
Carr, Baker v., **1:**227, **385–386; 5:**79;
  7:108; **8:**357
Carr, Benjamin, **5:**495
Carr, Dabney, **1:**512
Carr, Sir Robert, **6:**41
Carranza, Venustiano, **1:**1; **5:**346
Carré, Ferdinand, **7:**77
Carriage, horse-drawn, **7:**42–43
Carriage making, **1:**551–552;
  2:59–60
Carrier, Willis, **1:**74
Carrier Indians, **8:**221

Carrington, Frances C., **9**:244–248

Carroll, Charles, **2**:67–68; **8**:187
  revolutionary committees and, **7**:149

Carroll, John, **2**:67, 68; **3**:129; **4**:474
  and religious learning, **7**:97

Carson, Christopher (Kit), **1**:221, 257; **2**:537; **3**:299; **8**:404
  and Apaches, **6**:69
  in folklore, **3**:394
  and Navajos, **6**:19, 69
  in Taos, **8**:47

Carson, Johnny, **8**:142, *142*

Carson, Rachel, *Silent Spring*, **1**:67; **3**:205, 227, 232; **4**:362; **6**:210; **7**:359; **8**:285, 423

Carson City (Nevada), **6**:37

Carswell, Harold, **5**:548

Carte Blanche, **2**:451

Carter, Harlan, **5**:557

Carter, Henry W., **7**:124

Carter, James Earl (Jimmy)
  African policies under, **1**:39
  airline deregulation under, **1**:96
  arms race under, **1**:272
  and bureaucracy, **1**:573
  and Camp David Peace Accords, **2**:20
  Carter Doctrine of, **1**:233; **2**:60; **3**:142
  Collazo pardoned by, **1**:329
  Community Services Administration under, **6**:164
  conservative opposition to, **2**:376
  and Contra aid, **2**:395
  Cuba policy of, **2**:471–472; **5**:239
  defense policy of, **2**:529
  and Department of Education, **3**:332
  and Department of Energy, **3**:332
  and draft registration, **2**:365
  energy crisis address by, text of, **9**:492–494
  energy policies of, **3**:209, 215; **6**:304
  and European Community, policies toward, **3**:260
  and Federal Mediation and Conciliation Service, **3**:343
  fiscal policies of, **2**:423
  foreign policy of, **3**:427
  as Georgia governor, **3**:558
  and Guatemala, **4**:70
  Haiti and, **4**:85
  Health and Human Services Department under, **4**:114
  and Holocaust Museum, **4**:150
  HUD under, **4**:183
  human rights policy of, **5**:49
  Indian relations under, **4**:260
  inflation under, **7**:516
  Iran hostage crisis and, **4**:174, 418, *418*, 420–421
  Israel and, **4**:441
  labor policies of, **3**:245; **5**:11
  Latin American policies of, **3**:143; **5**:49
  and neoconservatives, **6**:32
  and Nicaragua, **6**:105
  and 1980 Olympics, **6**:193–194
  Pakistani relations under, **4**:260
  and Panama Canal, **6**:239–240, 242
  and Peace Corps, **6**:266
  and Philippines, **6**:323
  in presidential campaign of 1976, **3**:166–167; **6**:517–518
  in presidential campaign of 1980, **3**:167
  presidential library of, **5**:100
  refusing price controls, **6**:460
  religious beliefs of, **2**:165
  South African policy of, **7**:452
  Soviet invasion of Afghanistan and, **1**:37; **4**:260
  and Strategic Arms Limitations Talks II, **8**:202
  at summit conferences, **8**:16
  Three Mile Island accident investigated by, **8**:122
  vetoes cast by, **8**:321
  Vietnam draft evaders pardoned by, **1**:177
    text of, **9**:479–480
  and Wise Men, **8**:493
  in World War II, **8**:557

Carter, Rosalynn, **8**:*517*
  and White House furnishings, **8**:471

Carter, William, **8**:318

Carter Coal Company, Carter v., **4**:71

Carter Doctrine, **1**:233; **2**:60; **3**:142

Carter Fund, **3**:443

Carter v. Carter Coal Company, **2**:60, 311; **4**:71

Carteret, Sir George, **2**:289; **3**:103; **6**:60, 511

Carteret, Philip, **3**:188

Cartier, Jacques, **3**:285, 291
  exploring St. Lawrence River, **3**:488; **4**:50

Cartier-Bresson, Henri, **1**:301

Cartography, **2**:60–63, *61*
  See also Maps and mapmaking

Cartoons, **2**:63–65
  by Disney Corporation, **3**:58
  political, **6**:393–395, *394*
  and toys, **8**:153

Cartwright, Alexander, **1**:419

Cartwright, Peter, **2**:175

Carver, George Washington, **7**:478

Carver, John, **5**:276, 317

Carver, Raymond, **5**:123

Casablanca (film), **3**:363

Casablanca Conference, **2**:65; **8**:549, 552

Cascade Tunnel, **8**:240

Casco (ship), **1**:*266*

Casely Hayford, Joseph Ephraim, **6**:235–236

Casey, Planned Parenthood of Southeastern Pennsylvania v., **1**:7; **4**:497–498; **6**:361–362; **8**:434

Casey, William, **4**:377

Casimir, Fort, **6**:41

Casinos
  in Las Vegas, **5**:42
  Native American tribes operating, **2**:359
  organized crime and, **2**:463
  theming of, **5**:42
  See also Gambling

Caskets, **3**:486

Caslon, William, **6**:468

Cass, Lewis, **1**:158; **4**:295; **6**:415, 447
  and Compromise of 1850, **2**:331
  and popular sovereignty, **8**:485
  in presidential campaign of 1848, **1**:418; **3**:154
  in presidential campaign of 1852, **3**:154

Cassady, Neal, **1**:433

Cassatt, Mary, **1**:296, 316; **2**:272; **3**:197; **6**:470

Cast iron, **5**:330

Castañeda, Jorge G., **5**:349–350

Castañeda, Pedro de, **4**:33

Castillo, Alonso del, **2**:360

Castillo, Ann, **5**:123

Castillo, Domingo del, **9**:10

Castro, Fidel, **2**:54–55, 470; **5**:48, 49
  and Cuban missile crisis, **2**:474
  FBI arrest and interrogation of, **2**:470
  and Mariel boatlift, **2**:472

Casualties. *See* War casualties

CASVA. *See* Center for Advanced Study in the Visual Arts

CAT. *See* Convention Against Torture

Catalogs, mail-order, **1**:32; **5**:204–207, *205*
  Sears Roebuck, **7**:290–291

Catalytic converters, **1**:362

Catawba Indians, **2**:65, *66*; **8**:225

Catch-22 (Heller), **2**:66–67; **5**:121

Catesby, Mark, **6**:213

Catherine II (empress of Russia), **1**:108; **7**:210

Catholic Worker (newspaper), **6**:99

Catholic Worker Movement, **8**:303

Catholicism, **2**:67–71
  on abortion, **1**:5
  and adoption, **1**:28
  anticommunism in, **1**:197; **5**:563
  in colonial era, **1**:195–196
  Council of Trent and, **8**:309
  denominational colleges, **3**:129, 130
  diplomatic service to papal states, **6**:244–245
  Dominican Order, **3**:77
  ecumenicalism in, **8**:308
  evangelicalism and, **3**:267
  growth of, **7**:88–89
  among immigrants, **1**:196
  individual responsibility in, **8**:309
  individualism and, **1**:196
  among Irish Americans, **4**:223, 423, 424–425
  Irish immigrants and, **2**:163
  among Italian Americans, **4**:445
  Latin American immigrants and, **7**:91–92
  lay leadership in, **8**:309
  liberal vs. conservative wings of, **8**:309
  and liberation theology, **5**:93
  Luther and, **6**:515
  in Maryland, **1**:196; **2**:287
  mass in, **8**:309
  membership in, **7**:*87, 90*
  missions of, **4**:276
    in California, firsthand account of, **9**:107–109
  mysticism in, **5**:507
  and *National Review*, **5**:556
  in New Mexico, **6**:67
  papacy in, **1**:195–196

Polish Americans and, **6**:391

Priests of Holy Cross in, **4**:151

and Protestantism, conflict of, **1**:447

Puritans on, **1**:195–196

on religious freedom, **4**:475; **8**:308

and religious learning, **7**:97

revival campaign of, **7**:89

and revivalism, **3**:264–265

schools of, **3**:129, 130; **4**:474–475; **7**:268

sexual abuse scandal involving, **2**:71

sexuality in, **1**:196

temperance and, **1**:117

Vatican II and, **8**:308–309

women's role in, **8**:500

See also Anti-Catholicism; Jesuits

Catlin, G. E. G. (political scientist), **6**:403

Catlin, George (artist), **1**:295; **8**:259
  exploration of American West and, **3**:299
  on Indian games, **3**:507
  Indian paintings of, **2**:71–72, *72*
  and national park movement, **5**:549
  on preservation of environment, **2**:366

Cato, Gavin, **2**:466

Cato's Revolt, **7**:379

Cats, disease in, **8**:319

Cat's Cradle (Vonnegut), **5**:121

Catskill Mountains, **2**:72; **6**:86

Catt, Carrie Chapman, **5**:65; **8**:514

Cattell, James McKeen, **1**:141; **4**:378

Cattle, **2**:72–74, 489
  disease in, **8**:319, 320
  protection of, legislation for, **1**:185
  in Texas, **8**:101

Cattle Associations, **2**:74

Cattle brands, **2**:74, 76

Cattle drives, **2**:74–75, 442, 443
  on Abilene Trail, **1**:2
  on Chisholm Trail, **2**:158
  Dodge City Trail and, **3**:69
  and fencing of public lands, **6**:532
  homesteaders and, **4**:157
  railroads and, **2**:387; **7**:34
  stampedes in, **7**:519–520
  trail drivers and, **8**:176
  transcontinental railroad and, **5**:149

Cattle frontier, **8**:463

Cattle industry
  barbed wire and, **2**:443

in Colorado, **2**:299

Great Britain in, **4**:157

homesteaders and, **4**:157–158

in Montana, **5**:449

rise of, **1**:64; **4**:157–158

sheep wars in, **7**:339–340

stockyards in, **7**:551–552

Cattle rustlers, **2**:75–76, 443

Cattle towns. *See* Cow towns

Caucus(es), **2**:76–77; **6**:113
  Congressional, **2**:76, 77
    Black, **1**:471

Causa, La, **2**:77

Cavalier Hotel, **8**:346

Cavalry
  Air, **1**:73–74
  horse, **2**:77–78

Cavendish, Lord, **8**:347, 348

Cavill, Frederick, **8**:36

Cayetano, Ben, **3**:361

Cayuga, **6**:86

Cayuse, **8**:221

Cazneau, Jane McManus Storms, **3**:75

Cazneau, William, **3**:75

CB radio, **2**:179

CBC. *See* Black Caucus, Congressional

CBDs (Central Business Districts). *See* Cities

CBN. *See* Christian Broadcasting Network

CBO. *See* Congressional Budget Office

CBOE. *See* Chicago Board of Options Exchanges

CBS television network, **8**:72, 73, 138
  cartoons on, **2**:64

CCC. *See* Civilian Conservation Corps; Commodity Credit Corporation

CDA. *See* Communications Decency Act

CDC. *See* Centers for Disease Control and Prevention

CD-ROM, **2**:329
  dictionaries on, **3**:23
  encyclopedias on, **3**:205
  use in education, **3**:139

CDs, **2**:328–329, 392

CEA. *See* Council of Economic Advisors

Cecil, Robert, **5**:63

Cédras, Raoul, **5:**49
Celanese Corporation, **6:**366
Celebration community, **8:**304
Celebrity culture, **2:78–79**
  and advertising, **2:**79, 98
Celera Genomics, **4:**192
Celler-Kefauver Antimerger Act
    (1950), **1:**215; **3:**348
Cellular telephones, **8:**67
  commercial use of, **6:**169
Celluloid, and plastics, **6:**366
Celluloid Manufacturing Company,
    6:366
Cellulose, **8:**110
Celmins, Vija, **1:**309
Cement, **2:**79
Cemeteries, **2:**80, 80–82, 81, 511
  national, **2:**81–82, 82, **82–83**
    Arlington National Cemetery,
        1:264
    National Cemetery System,
        8:317
Censorship
  during Civil War, **6:**97
  economic, **2:**84, 85
  military, **2:83,** 84
  press and artistic, **2:83–86**
    ACLU on, **1:**146
    of African American press, **6:**99
    of beat literature, **1:**433
    book banning, **1:500**
    of movies, **6:**419
    and National Endowment for the
        Arts, **5:**535
    Near v. Minnesota and, **6:**27
    pornography and, **6:**419
    by Postal Service, U.S.,
        6:426–427
    and publishing industry, **6:**537
    Supreme Court on, **3:**374; **6:**419
Censure, presidential, **3:**303
Census, U.S., **2:**554–555
  statistical mapping in, **5:**233
Census, U.S. Bureau of, **2:86–87**
  and emigration data, **3:**197
  maps and atlases published by, **2:**62
Centennial Exhibition (1876),
    2:87–88, 88
Center for Advanced Study in the
    Visual Arts (CASVA), **5:**540
Centers for Disease Control and
    Prevention (CDC), **2:**88
  and AIDS, **1:**15
  on obesity, **6:**153–154

on toxic shock syndrome, **8:**150
Central Artery/Tunnel Project (Big
    Dig), **8:**240
Central banks, **3:**344; **8:**160
Central Business Districts (CBDs).
    See Cities
Central Europe, **2:88–91**
  foreign aid to, **3:**418
  propaganda to, **6:**503
  See also Eastern Europe; *specific*
    countries
Central Intelligence Agency (CIA),
    2:91–93
  and African policies, **1:**38
  Ames espionage case in,
      1:173–174
  establishment of, **7:**503
  failures of, **4:**377
  functions of, **7:**503
  propaganda by, **6:**503
  and U-2 incident, **8:247**
Central Labor Union (New York
    City), and Labor Day, **5:**12
Central nervous system stimulants,
    7:568–569
Central Overland California and
    Pikes Peak Express Company
    (COC&PP), **5:**204; **6:**411–413
Central Pacific Railroad, **2:**9; **8:**181,
    188
  and transcontinental roadway, **7:**34
    Golden Spike Ceremony, **7:**34
    race with Union Pacific Railroad,
        2:94; **6:**502; **8:**181, 188
Central Park (New York City), **2:**94,
    94–95; **6:**453
  Menagerie in, **8:**594
Centralia Mine disaster, **2:**95
Century 21 Exposition, **8:**560
Century of Dishonor, A (Jackson), **2:**95
  excerpt from, **9:**257–259
Century of Progress Exposition
    (1933), **8:**559
  furniture at, **3:**498
CEQ. *See* Council on Environmen-
    tal Quality
Ceramics, **1:**286, **303–305**
  collecting, **2:**271
CERCLA. *See* Comprehensive
    Environmental Response, Com-
    pensation, and Liability Act
Cereal grains, **2:**95–98, 96
  corn, **2:**413, **413–414,** 414
  milling of, **3:**388–392

oats, **6:151–152**
  storage of, **3:**187
  wheat, **2:**96, 97; **8:466–467**
  winter, **3:**88
Cereals, manufacture of, **2:98–99**
Ceremony (Silko), **5:**129
Cerletti, Ugo, **6:**522
Cermak, Anton, **1:**329; **2:**133
CERN. *See* European Organization
    for Nuclear Research
Cerography (wax engraving), in
    mapmaking, **5:**233
Cervera, Pascual, **7:**486, 488
CES. *See* Committee on Economic
    Security
CETA. *See* Comprehensive Employ-
    ment and Training Act
Cézanne, Paul, **2:**475
  exhibitions of, **1:**268, 297
CFA. *See* College Football Associa-
    tion
CFAT. *See* Carnegie Foundation for
    the Advancement of Teaching
CFCs. *See* Chlorofluorocarbons
CFL. *See* Canadian Football League
CFT. *See* California Federation of
    Teachers
CFTC. *See* Commodities Futures
    Trading Commission
C&GS. *See* Coast and Geodetic Sur-
    vey
Chaco Canyon, **1:**244, *244*
  irrigation in, **4:**307–308
Chadwick, Donald, **3:**499
Chadwick, Edwin, **3:**238
Chadwick, Henry, **1:**419
Chadwick, James, **6:**340–341
Chafee, Zechariah, **2:**84
Chaffee, Adna R., **1:**267; **6:**320
Chain booksellers, **6:**538–539
Chain gangs, **2:**99, 99–100
"Chain migration," **3:**313
Chain stores, **2:100–101,** *101;* **3:**9,
    10, 26; **7:**125
  Robinson-Patman Act and, **7:183**
  Wal-Mart, **1:**263; **8:**368
Chakrabarty, Ananda, **3:**530
Chakrabarty, Diamond v., **3:**530;
    6:256
Challenge of Nationhood, The
    (Mboya), **1:**138
Challenger disaster, **2:101–102,** *102;*
    3:41; **5:**524; **7:**481, 483
Chalmers, Lionel, **2:**235

Chamberlain, Daniel H., **4**:87

Chamberlain, Edward, **3**:109

Chamberlain, John W., **3**:182

Chamberlain, Joshua L., in Battle of Gettysburg, **3**:568; **5**:209

Chamberlain, Wilt, **1**:424, 425

Chamberlin, Clarence, **1**:83

Chamberlin, Thomas C., **2**:235; **3**:552; **4**:6

Chambers, Ephraim, **3**:204

Chambers, John Graham, **6**:483

Chambers, Whittaker, **3**:280
HUAC testimony by, **4**:136; **8**:1, 2

Chambers of commerce, **2**:102–103

Chamorro, Emiliano, **1**:550

Chamorro, Violeta Barrios de, **2**:395

Chamoun, Camille, **5**:72

Champagne-Marne Operation, **2**:103
French vs. American strategy, **5**:338

Champagny, Jean-Baptiste Nompère de, duc de Cadore, **8**:382

Champlain, Samuel de, **3**:285–286, 291
explorations of, **2**:103–104, *104*; **5**:21
in Cape Cod, **2**:38
and fur trade, **3**:488
Lake Ontario and Huron, **4**:50
mapmaking, **5**:231–232
and trading posts, **8**:175
in Vermont, **8**:311

Chancellorsville, Battle of, **2**:104, 213; **6**:280
trenches in, **8**:207

Chancy, Israel, **8**:572

Chandler, Alfred, **2**:42

Chandler, Charles F., **2**:122

Chandler, John, **7**:552

Chandler, Raymond, **5**:120, 129
The Big Sleep, **5**:121

Chandler, Zechariah, **2**:313

Chandra X-ray Observatory, **6**:157

Chaney, James, **1**:332; **2**:203

Chaneysville Incident, The (Bradley), **5**:126

Chang, Min-Chueh, **1**:468

Channing, J. Parke, **3**:218

Channing, William Ellery, **2**:350; **7**:97; **8**:179

Chanukah, **2**:104–105

Chapbooks, **2**:105

Chaplet, Ernest, **1**:304

Chaplin, Charles (public health official), **3**:240

Chaplin, Charlie (actor), **3**:362

Chapman, John (Johnny Appleseed), **3**:478; **4**:481

Chapman, John Gadsby (wood engraver), **8**:522

Chapman, Mark David, **2**:79

Chapman, William S., and land speculation, **5**:36

Chapman showboat, **7**:350–351

Chapmen. *See* Peddlers

Chappaquiddick incident, **2**:105

Chappell, Walter, **6**:330

Chapter 7 bankruptcy, **1**:409, 410

Chapter 11 bankruptcy, **1**:409–410

Chapter 13 bankruptcy, **1**:410

Chapultepec, Battle of, **2**:105

Charbonneau, Toussaint, **5**:86

Chargaff, Erwin, **3**:67

Charismatic Christianity, **8**:303

Charity
vs. philanthropy, **6**:315
"scientific," **6**:436
in Victorian era, **8**:325–326

Charity organization movement, **2**:105–106
Woman's Exchange, **8**:497

Charity Organization Society, **6**:436; **8**:82

Charity schools, **2**:106

Charles I (king of Great Britain)
charters issued by, **2**:287
and colonial policy, **2**:285
and Great Migration, **4**:55

Charles II (king of Great Britain), **1**:383
and colonial charters, **2**:281; **8**:455
and colonial policy, **2**:285, 287, 289; **3**:77
death of, **2**:109
and Duke of York's proprietary, **3**:93
on fur hats, **1**:434
land grants by, **5**:149; **6**:126, 276, 511, *511*, 512; **8**:311
and Lords of Trade and Plantation, **5**:151
and Nicolls' Commission, **6**:106–107
Sunday law of, **1**:490

Charles III (king of Spain), **1**:257; **7**:489

Charles V (Holy Roman emperor), **3**:274, 295

Charles, Ray, **1**:389

Charles River Bridge, construction of, **1**:537

Charles River Bridge case, **2**:106–107; **4**:495

Charles Town, siege of, **7**:145
See also Charleston (South Carolina)

Charleston (South Carolina), **2**:107–108
Civil War damages in, **2**:107, *107*
in colonial era, **8**:289
trade with Native Americans, **2**:108
earthquake near, **3**:101
Fort Sumter in, **8**:17–18
siege of, in American Revolution, **7**:145
Vesey Rebellion in, **8**:316–317

Charleston (dance), **2**:497

Charleston Harbor, defense of, **2**:108; **8**:17

Charleston Library Association, **5**:485

Charlotte (North Carolina), **2**:108–109; **6**:130

Charlotte Temple (Rowson), **5**:118

Charlotte Town Resolves, **2**:109

Charlotte-Mecklenburg Board of Education, Swan v., **1**:589; **2**:108–109, 199; **3**:118

Charlotte's Web (White), **5**:127

Charney, Jule G., **4**:6

Charter of Liberties, **2**:109–110; **3**:93

Charter of Privileges, **2**:110
commemoration of, **5**:95

Charter schools, **2**:110–111; **3**:119
states with, **2**:*110*

Chartered companies, **2**:111

Charters
colonial (*See* Colonial charters)
municipal, **2**:111–112
forms of government and, **5**:474
home rule and, **4**:152–153

Chase, Chevy, **7**:253

Chase, Lucia, **1**:144; **2**:498

Chase, Martha, **3**:533

Chase, Martin, **7**:126

Chase, Salmon P., **3**:155; **4**:487; **5**:76
and antislavery politics, **5**:96–97
and banking system, **1**:397, 404

and Davis (Jefferson), trial of,
  2:505
and Emancipation Proclamation,
  3:191
and financing of Civil War, 2:215
in Free Soil Party, 3:459
in Johnson's impeachment trial,
  4:237
Liberty Party and, 5:96–97
on powers of habeas corpus, 3:271
in presidential campaign of 1864,
  2:218
as Radical Republican, 7:15
as secretary of Treasury, 8:196
Chase, Samuel
  at Alexandria Conference, 1:122
  impeachment trial of, 4:234, 241
  on judicial review, 2:7
  on state vs. federal laws, 8:390
  and subpoena to Adams (John),
    6:456
Chase, Stuart, 2:390; 6:42
Chase, Thornton, 1:384
Chase, William Merritt, 1:296,
  319–320; 3:537
Château-Thierry Bridge, Americans
  at, 1:441; 2:112
Chattanooga campaign, 2:112–113,
  213; 5:151
Chauncey, Charles, 6:65
Chauncey, Isaac, 4:53
Chautauqua movement, 2:22,
  113–114; 3:115; 5:178; 7:65
Chávez, César Estrada, 2:77; 5:3;
  8:172, 266, 267
Chavez, Denise, 5:123
Chavez-Salido, Cabell v., 1:126
Chavez-Thompson, Linda, 3:49
Chebeir, Camille, 5:72
Check currency, 2:114–115
  clearing of, 2:232
Checkers, 8:153
Checkers speech, 2:115
Checkoff, 2:115–116
Check-row planter, 1:58
Checks and balances, 2:116–117
  Senate confirmation and, 2:346
Cheesemaking, 2:490
Cheever, Ezekial, 3:112
Cheever, John, 5:121
Chemehuevi, 8:228
Chemical Analyses of Igneous Rocks
  (U.S. Geological Survey), 6:301

Chemical and biological warfare,
  2:117–119
  Agent Orange, 1:54–55
  international agreements banning,
    1:270
  smallpox in, 7:399, 400
  in Vietnam War, 2:537–538
Chemical industry, 2:119–121
  automation in, 1:364–365
  Du Pont Company and, 2:542
  petroleum industry and, 2:121;
    3:211
  and plastics, 6:366
  research in, 2:123
Chemical Science and Technology
  Laboratory, 5:529
Chemical societies, 2:121–122
Chemical spills, 3:39
Chemical Weapons Convention,
  2:119
Chemistry, 2:121–123
  mineral, 5:391
  Nobel Prizes in, 6:487
Chemotherapy, 2:124
Cheney, Benjamin, 2:241
Cheney, Lynne, 5:537
Cheney, Richard (Dick), 6:243
  in presidential campaign of 2000,
    3:170
  as secretary of defense, 2:529
Chennault, Claire L., 2:152; 3:392
Cherbourg, 2:124
Cherokee, 2:124–126; 8:225
  adaptation of, 8:226
  in American Revolution,
    4:329–330; 6:128; 8:85
  Baptist mission to, 2:163
  in Civil War, 4:326–327
  constitution of, 2:125
  in Georgia, 3:554
  language of, 2:124–125, 126–127,
    127; 4:275
  removal of, 2:125, 127; 3:278;
    4:272, 285–286, 296, 314;
    6:183–184
    Trail of Tears, 2:125, 127, 128;
      6:183; 8:177
  schools of, 3:134–135
  in Tennessee, 8:84–85, 87
  in Texas, 8:100
  treaty with, 8:206
  written language of, 4:275
Cherokee Nation cases, 2:127–128

Cherokee Nation v. Georgia,
  2:127–128
Cherokee Strip, 2:128
Cherokee Trail, 2:128
Cherokee Wars, 2:128–129
Cherry Hill, 6:476
Chesapeake (American frigate),
  3:78–79
Chesapeake and Ohio Canal, 2:32,
  32
Chesapeake Bay, cleanup of, 3:233
Chesapeake Bay Bridge and Tunnel,
  8:240
Chesapeake colonies, 2:129, 287
  city planning in, 2:184
  families in, 3:311–312
  slave society of, 7:391–392
Chesapeake plantation system,
  6:363, 364
Chesapeake-Leopard incident,
  2:129–130; 3:192
Chesnutt, Charles Waddell, 5:124
  The Marrow of Tradition, 5:124
Chess, 2:130, 130–131; 8:153
  computer programs, 2:130, 338
Chester (U.S.S.), 5:94
Chesterfield (cigarettes), 8:135
Chester's Gap, 6:254
Chesterton, Gilbert Keith, 1:57–58
Chevreul, Eugène Michel, 6:148
Chevron v. NRDC, 3:333
Chewing tobacco, 8:134, 135
Cheyenne, 2:131, 131; 8:218
  at Battle of Little Bighorn, eyewit-
    ness account of, 9:253–255
  in Colorado, 2:298
  Dull Knife Campaign of, 3:94
  Fort Laramie Treaty with, text of,
    9:227–229
  and Ghost Dance, 3:573
  Jackson's A Century of Dishonor on,
    9:257–259
  in Nebraska, 6:29
  on reservations, 6:263
  Sand Creek Massacre of, 4:326;
    7:243–244, 244
  in Wyoming, 8:564, 566
Cheyney State College, 3:125
Chiang Kai-Shek, 7:530
  at Cairo Conference, 2:7
Chiari, Roberto, 6:239
Chicago (Illinois), 2:131–133, 132
  African Americans in, 2:133, 134,
    201

Chicago (Illinois), (*continued*)
  architecture of, **1**:252; **2**:132–133;
    8:290
  Art Institute of Chicago in,
    1:316–317
  Democratic National Convention
    in (1968), **2**:400; **7**:165
  Empowerment Zone program in,
    8:287
  fire of 1871 in, **1**:12; **2**:132,
    133–134; 3:37
  founding of, **4**:52
  furniture manufacturing in, **3**:497
  gang warfare during Prohibition,
    1:504
  growth of, **8**:290
  Haymarket Riot in (1886), **2**:132;
    8:259
  land speculation in, **5**:37
  mayor of, first, **7**:53
  meatpacking in, **2**:73, *73*, 132;
    5:277, 279; **8**:463
    The Jungle on, **4**:500–501
    stockyards of, **5**:*136;* **7**:551
  Memorial Day Massacre in, **5:307**
  Museum of Science and Industry
    in, **5:484–485**
  Native Americans in, **2**:509
  Newberry Library in, **6:93–94**
  paved streets in, **6**:260
  Polish Americans in, **6**:391
  political machine in, **5**:187
  politics in, **4**:216
  population of, **4**:217
  Puerto Ricans in, **6**:543
  Pullman Strike in (1894), **2**:132;
    8:303
  riots of 1919, **2**:133, **134**
  self-taught art in, **1**:311–312
  settlement houses in, **7**:317–318
  skyscrapers in, **7**:375–376
    Sears Tower, **7**:*291,* 291–292
  steel strikes in, **7**:*545,* 546
  World's Columbian Exposition in,
    3:174; **8**:290, 297, 558–559
    furniture at, **3**:498
*Chicago, Burlington and Quincy Rail-
    road, Wisconsin Railroad Commis-
    sion v.,* **2**:311; **8:493**
*Chicago, Burlington and Quincy Rail-
    road v. Chicago,* **3**:198
Chicago, Judy, **1**:309

*Chicago, Milwaukee, and Saint Paul
    Railway Company v. Minnesota,*
    2:134
Chicago Board of Options
    Exchanges (CBOE), **6**:200
Chicago Commons, **7**:317
Chicago Defender (newspaper), **2**:134;
    5:199, 200; **6**:98, 99
Chicago Federation of Labor, **3**:320
Chicago Seven, **1**:479; **2:135**
Chicago Tribune (newspaper), **6**:97
Chicano movement, **5**:344–345;
    9:484–486
"Chicano Nationalism: The Key to
    Unity for La Raza" (Gonzáles),
    excerpt from, **9**:484–486
Chicanos
  Alianza movement of, **7**:12
  See also Mexican Americans
Chickamauga, Battle of, **2:135**, 213
Chickasaw, **8**:225
  adaptation of, **8**:226
  Tecumseh's speech to, **9**:199–200
  in Tennessee, **8**:84–85
  trade with, **6**:244
  treaty with (1832), and land ces-
    sion, **5**:34
Chickasaw Bluffs, in Civil War,
    8:324
Chickasaw-Creek War, **2:135–136**
"Chicken in Every Pot," **2:136;**
    7:113
Chihuly, Dale, **1**:290; **4**:4
Chilcotin, **8**:221
Child, Francis James, **1**:388; **3**:394
Child, Lydia Maria, **2**:40; **6**:47; **8**:512
Child abuse, **2:136–138; 3**:73
  in 19th century, **3**:313
  court cases on, **3**:74
  and foster care, **3**:442
  protective agencies for, **7**:430
  repressed memory of, primal thera-
    py and, **6**:462
Child care, **2:138–140**
  *Common Sense Book of Baby and
    Child Care* (Spock and Spock),
    2:318–319
  shifts in prescriptions for, **2**:144
Child Citizenship Act (2000), **6**:14
Child labor, **2:140–141,** *141,* 146, 148
  health issues with, **5**:274
  in industrial revolution, **4**:*344*
  minimum-wage legislation and,
    5:394–395

  regulation of, **4**:27; **5**:5; **8**:111
  in New Hampshire, **6**:58
  in textile industry, **8**:111
Child Labor Act (1916), **3**:308
Child labor tax case, **2**:142; **5**:184
Child Support Recovery Act (1992),
    3:317
Childbirth, **2:142–144**
  in 19th century, **3**:312–313
  in 20th century, **3**:314
  in colonial era, **2**:291; **3**:311
  maternal and child health care,
    5:273–275
Childhood, **2:144–147**
Childhood leukemia, **2**:35
Children
  in 20th century, **3**:313–315
  adoption of, **1:27–30**
  breakfast cereals for, **2**:99
  in civil rights movement, **2**:203
  clothing for, **2**:246
  in colonial families, **3**:311
  death rate for, **2**:510
  encyclopedias for, **3**:204
  exposed to violence on TV, **3**:340
  factory work by, **7**:64
  in foster care, **3:442–443**
  health of
    legislation on, **7**:342
    SIDS and, **8**:2
  in juvenile court system, **4**:250,
    504–506
  kidnapping of, **4**:525
  marketing to, **5**:246
  missing, **2**:147
    Megan's Law and, **5**:306
  National Commission on, **7**:186
  Native American, removal of,
    4:262–264
  obesity among, **6**:154
  poverty among, **6**:437; **7**:186
  in prostitution, **6**:514
  protective agencies for, **7**:430
  recreation for, **7**:65
  in Republican families, **3**:312–313
  rights of, **2:148–150**
    Family Education Rights and Pri-
      vacy Act and, **3**:315–316
    Supreme Court on, **4**:250
  substance abuse by, **7**:568–569
  volunteerism among, **8**:353
  welfare programs for, **8**:439–440
  See also Adolescence

Children of God (Family of Love), **2**:477
Children's Aid Societies, **2**:136, 146
Children's Bureau, **2**:137, 146, **147–148; 5**:11; **8**:439
Children's Code of Minnesota (1917), **1**:28
Children's Hospital, Adkins v., **1:20–21; 3**:308; **5:394–395; 8**:445
Children's Television Act (1990), **2**:65
Childs, Richard, **2**:183
Chile
  at ABC Conference, **1**:1
  astronomical observatories in, **6**:157
  commerce with, **5**:43–45
  independence of, **5**:50
  nonferrous metal production in, **6**:115
  U.S. relations with, **2**:150; **5**:46–47, 49
Chin, Frank, *Donald Duk,* **5**:123
Chin, Vincent, **1**:323–324; **7**:12
China
  air route to, **3**:392
  Boxer Rebellion in, **1**:*526,* **526–527**
  dollar diplomacy in, **3**:71
  at Dumbarton Oaks Conference, **3**:94
  immigration from, **2**:150–151, 154–156; **7**:10 (*See also* Chinese Americans)
  and Christian churches, **7**:91
  restrictions on, **1**:324; **4**:224, 227, 232
  and Japan
    biological warfare employed by, **2**:118
    war of 1894-1895, **2**:151
    Japanese invasion of, **4**:457–458
  Kearny's mission to, **4:515**
  Manchuria and Manchukuo, **5:218–219**
  "most favored nation" status to, **8**:198
  Nuclear Test Ban Treaty and, refusal to sign, **6**:143
  "one child" policy of, **7**:81
  Operation Dixie in, **6**:199
  printing in, **6**:466
  religions of, **1**:326
  in Sino-Japanese War, **7**:367
  smallpox in, **7**:399
  Tiananmen Square Protest in, **8**:*123,* **123–124**
  tobacco factories in, **8**:135
  trade with, **2**:150, **153; 6**:226
    Cushing's Treaty on, **4**:515
    embargo against, **8**:173
    in ginseng, **3**:578
    Hawaii in, **4**:105–106
    Nixon opening door to, **8**:173
    trade dollar and, **8**:158
    Wangxia Treaty on, **5**:462
  U.S. armed forces in, **2:152–153**
    Burma Road and Ledo Road build by, **1:576–577**
    Flying Tigers, **3**:392–393
    Merrill's Marauders, **5:324**
    and *Panay* incident, **6:243–244**
  U.S. relations with, **2:150–152**
    Burlingame Treaty and, **1:575–576; 2**:154, 157
    Cairo Conference and, **2**:7
    Clinton and, **2**:240
    Cushing's Treaty and, **2:484**
    Korean War and, **8**:270
    loss of nuclear-weapons secrets, **3**:210
    Open Door policy in, **2**:151; **4**:243, 457; **5**:218–219; **6**:196–197
    right of extraterritoriality, **3**:304
China Clipper, **2:153**
Chinese Americans, **1**:*323, 324;* **2:153–157,** *154*
  boycott of Japanese goods by, **1**:529
  and Buddhism, **1**:552–553
  community organization and activities of, **2**:155
  gender roles of, **3**:520
  immigration restrictions on, **6**:5, 14, 396
  labor of, **2**:10, *156;* **8**:578
  nativist laws and, **6**:5
  racial exclusion of, **5**:250
  racism against, **2**:154 (*See also* Chinese Exclusion Act)
  as railroad workers, **8**:181
Chinese Exclusion Act (1882), **1**:125; **2:154–155, 157; 3**:207; **6**:14; **8**:276, 578
  passage of, **4**:232
  repeal of, **4**:227
Chinese immigrants
  deportation of, **3**:11
  prostitution among, **2**:154; **8**:436
  See also Chinese Americans
Ching, Cyrus, **3**:343
Chinook, **8**:221
Chipley, William Stout, **3**:104
Chippendale, **1**:*285*
Chippendale furniture, **3**:496
Chippewa
  Indian Treaty at Prairie du Chien and, **6:447–448**
  See also Ojibwe
Chirac, Jacques, **3**:452
  and AIDS research, **1**:15
Chiricahuas, **1**:219, 220, 221; **8**:228
Chirikov, Aleksey, **1**:121; **3**:286, 293; **8**:453
Chiropractic, **2:157–158; 5**:291–292
Chisholm, Shirley, **1**:52, 546
Chisholm Trail, **2:158**
Chisholm v. Georgia, **1**:120; **2:158**
Chittenden, Hiram M., **7**:55
Chittenden, Thomas, **8**:312
Chivington, John, **2**:298; **4**:326; **7**:243
Chiwere Sioux, **8**:224
Chlorofluorocarbons (CFCs), **6**:223
Chlorpromazine, **6**:522
Choate, Alexander v., **2**:196
Choate, Joseph H., at Hague Peace Conference, **4**:82
Choctaw, **2:158–159,** *159;* **8**:225
  adaptation of, **8**:226
  in Civil War, Pitchlynn on, **9**:302–303
  encoding messages during World War I, **6**:17
  gambling by, **3**:507
  Tecumseh's speech to, **9**:199–200
  trade with, **6**:244
  treaty with (1830), and land cession, **5**:34
Choctaw Academy, **3**:135
Chokonens, **1**:221
Cholera, **2:159–160,** *160;* **3**:236–237; **8**:576
  1866 outbreak of, **4**:363
  navy research on, **5**:296
  sanitary reform and, **7**:245
Chomsky, Noam, **1**:182; **5**:115, 122
  on behaviorism, **1**:438
  on censorship, **2**:86
Chong, Albert, **1**:302
Chorographical maps, **9**:37, *39*
Chosin Reservoir, **2:160–161,** *161*

Chouteau, Auguste, **1:**157; **5:**419
Chouteau, Pierre, **1:**158; **8:**175
Chovet, Abraham, **5:**485
Christanna, Fort, **8:**349
Christenberry, Grove Press v., **1:**500
Christensen, Lew, **1:**390
Christensen, Parley P., **3:**320–321
Christensen, William, **1:**390
Christian Broadcasting Network
   (CBN), **8:**71
Christian Church. *See* Disciples of
   Christ
Christian Coalition, **2:**161; **3:**485;
   8:71
Christian Commonwealth Colony,
   8:302
Christian Life Commission (CLC),
   1:413
Christian Methodist Episcopal
   (CME) Church, **1:**44
Christian Reformed Church (CRC),
   7:76, 89
Christian Science, **2:**170–171; **8:**501
   See also Church of Christ, Scientist
Christian socialists, **3:**107; **8:**302
Christiana fugitive affair, **2:**161–162
Christianity, **2:**162–166
   and abolitionism, **2:**163
   among African Americans,
      1:41–46; **7:**8, 87–88
   charismatic, **8:**303
   evolutionism and, **3:**270
   growth of adherence to, **7:**299
   individualism in, **1:**196; **4:**331, 332
   laws of war in, **8:**370
   liberal, **5:**431
   and National Council of Churches,
      5:532–533
   among Native Americans, **1:**447,
      482; **2:**125; **4:**293
   Orthodox churches in, **6:**215–217
   and politics, **2:**164–165
   in school curriculum, **7:**299
   Second Awakening in, **1:**377–379
   on slavery, **1:**41–42
   among slaves, **1:**42; **7:**396
   social gospel movement in,
      7:412–414
   See also Mission(s); *specific denomi-
      nations*
Christina, Fort, **6:**77
Christmas, **2:**166
   evolution of celebration of, **4:**149
   Kwanzaa and, **4:**148

Christmas Conference (1784), **5:**333
Christy, Edwin P., **5:***402*
Christy's Minstrels, **5:**496
Chromosomes, **3:**532
Chronic fatigue syndrome,
   2:166–167
Chrysler Building, **6:**80; **7:***376*
Chrysler Motor Corporation, **1:**373
   and United Automobile Workers,
      8:261, 262
Chryssa, **1:**307
Chu, Steven, **1:**440
Chubb, John, **3:**137
Chumash, **2:**7
Chunnel, **8:**240
Church(es)
   diversity of, **3:**2
   parochial, in North Carolina,
      6:129
   Weber on, **3:**1
   women in, **8:***500*, **500–502**, *501*
      Christian Science, **2:**171
      Church of God in Christ, **2:**172
      ordination of, in Methodism,
         1:44, 53
Church, Frederic Edwin, **1:**295;
   4:189
Church, William, **5:**556
Church and state, separation of,
   2:167–170**, *168*; **7:**82, 93
   Democratic Party on, **4:**453
   Jefferson on, **6:**374
   Massachusetts Bay Colony and,
      5:270–271
   Pinckney Plan and, **6:**356
   school prayer and, **7:**265–266
   Supreme Court on, **3:**374
Church Covenant, **2:**440–441**
Church of Christ, **3:**44, 45
Church of Christ, Scientist,
   2:170–171**
Church of England, **3:**242
   in colonies, **2:**171–172**; **7:**93
      and freedom of religion, **8:**139
      and glebes, **4:**5
      Methodism and, **5:**332–333
      missionaries from, **7:**430
      New England Way and, **6:**50
   dissenters from, **3:**59
   Oxford Movement in, **6:**222
   vs. Puritanism, **2:**162
   upstart sects and threat to, **7:**86
   Westminster Assembly on, **3:**1
Church of God, **6:**287, 288

Church of God in Christ (COGIC),
   2:172–173**; **6:**287
   growth of, **7:**90
   membership in, **7:***91*
   origins of, **1:**45
Church of Jesus Christ of Latter-day
   Saints, **8:**296
   division within, **7:**103
   growth of, **7:**90
   membership in, **7:***91*
   See also Mormon(s)
Church of the Disciples, **8:**179
*Church of the Lukumi Babalu Aye, Inc.
   v. Hialeah,* **3:**374
Church Universal and Triumphant,
   2:478
Churchill, Winston S.
   on aerial bombing, **1:**495
   at Arcadia conference, **8:**545
   arms race under, **1:**270–271
   at Bermuda Conference, **1:**445
   at Cairo Conferences, **2:**7
   at Camp David, **2:**20
   at Casablanca Conference, **2:**65;
      8:549
   on Iron Curtain, **4:**429; **8:**574
   on Lend-Lease, **5:**81–82
   at Potsdam Conference, **6:**434
   and Roosevelt, **8:**543
   at Teheran Conference, **8:**64
   United Nations Declaration and,
      8:273
   on U.S. entry in World War II,
      8:546
   in World War I, armored vehicles
      and, **1:**266
   in World War II, **4:**43; **8:**249
      Anzio Campaign, **1:**217
      Atlantic Charter, **1:**353
      strategic air power under, **1:**81
      at summit conferences, **8:**15
      at Yalta Conference, **8:**573, 574,
         574
Chymosin, **3:**531
CIA. *See* Central Intelligence
   Agency
Cíbola, **2:**173**, 360, 416; **3:**296;
   8:451
Cicero, **4:**131
Cicotte, Ed, **1:**480
Cigarettes
   filtered-type, **8:**136
   low-nicotine, **8:**137
   low-tar, **8:**137

mass production of, **8:**133, 135
mentholated, **8:**136
See also Smoking
Cigars, **8:**134
Cimarron, proposed territory of,
 2:173
Cincinnati (Ohio), **2:173–174**
 fire-fighting force in, **3:**372
 furniture manufacturing in, **3:**497
 Pike's Opera House in, **2:***174*
 pork supplies in, **3:**398
 riots of 1883 in, **2:175**
 soap industry in, **7:**407
 Spring Grove Cemetery in, **2:**81,
 81
 Western Museum, **5:**487
Cincinnati, Society of the, **2:**173,
 174; **8:**318
Cinco de Mayo, **4:**148
Cinema. *See* Film
Cino, Joe, **8:**115
Cinque, Joseph, **1:***177*
CIO. *See* Congress of Industrial
 Organizations
Circuit riders, **2:175**
 Methodism and, **5:**333
Circuits, judicial, **2:175–176**
Circular Letter, Massachusetts,
 5:272; **8:**349
 text of, **9:**122–123
Circuses, **2:***176*, **176–177**, *177*
 dances in, **2:**497
Cisneros, Henry, **4:**184
Citibank, **3:**370; **7:**460, 461
Cities
 air pollution in, **1:***80*
 as air power target, **1:**81
 annexation of, **5:**334
 apartments in, **1:**222–223
 automobiles in, **1:**368
 botanical gardens in, **1:**517
 capital, **2:47–48**
 crime in, **2:***459*
 crowding in, **7:**572
 decline in, **5:**475
 economic redevelopment in,
 5:477–478
 gentrification of, **3:**538–539
 housing in, **1:**222–223; **4:**180–181
 infrastructure of, **4:**355–358
 inner, **7:**576; **8:**285–286
 Irish Americans in, **4:**223
 Main Street, death of, **5:**215

malls in, and urban revitalization,
 5:216
metropolises, industrialization and,
 5:228
metropolitan government in,
 5:334–335
migration to, **5:**373
municipal government in,
 5:474–476
municipal ownership of,
 5:476–478
municipal reform in, **5:478**
Native Americans in, AIM and,
 1:160–161
parks and open space in, **5:**475,
 476, 477
political machines and, **5:186–187**
population decline in, **7:**575–576
poverty in, **6:**437, 439, 440
prostitution in, **6:**513
public markets in, **5:**248
public transportation in, **4:**356–357
revitalization of, **7:**576
riots in, **8:**337–338
 of 1967, Kerner Commission on,
 4:522
skid rows in, **7:373–374**
tenements in, **8:**81–82
utility services in, **5:**476
See also Urbanization
Citigroup, **3:**368
Citizen Kane (film), **2:***178*, **178–179**;
 3:363
Citizens' Alliances, **2:179**
Citizens band (CB) radio, **2:179**
Citizens for Humane Abortion
 Laws, **1:**6
Citizenship, **2:179–181**
 acquired through naturalization,
 6:13–14
 for African Americans, **2:**193, 219
 alien rights and, **1:**125
 for Chinese immigrants, denial of,
 2:155; **8:**276 (*See also* Chinese
 Exclusion Act)
 Civil Rights Act of 1866 on, **2:**193
 Fourteenth Amendment on, **2:**198
 marriage and, **5:**250; **6:**14;
 8:497–498
 in Massachusetts Bay Colony,
 5:270
 for Native Americans, **1:**574;
 4:264, 287, 299; **8:**215
 passport as proof of, **6:**254–255

and privileges and immunities of
 citizens, **6:481–482**
for Puerto Ricans, **4:**135; **6:**542,
 544–545
suffrage and, Supreme Court on,
 5:401–402
for women, **2:**180, 181
 married, **6:**14; **8:497–498**
Citizenship Act (1924), **8:**215
Citrus industry, **2:181–182**; **3:**479
City Beautiful Movement, **2:**187;
 5:39
City councils, **2:182–183**
 vs. managers, **2:**184
City directories, **2:**183
City manager plan, **2:183–184**
*City of Cleburne v. Cleburne Living
 Center*, **3:**247
City of New York, Clinton v., **8:**321
City of St. Paul, R.A.V. v., **4:**67, 105
"City on a Hill," **1:**169; **2:184**
 manifest destiny and, **5:**223
City planning, **2:184–189**, *186*
 in Chicago, **2:**132–133
 in Detroit, **3:**19
 and gentrification, **3:**538–539
 legislation on, **4:**355
 and paving streets, **6:**260–261
 in Washington (D.C.), **2:**49, 185,
 187; **7:**52; **8:**409, 410
 zoning ordinances and, **2:**187;
 8:593
City University of New York
 (CUNY), **2:189–190**
Ciudad Juárez (Mexico), **3:**142
Civil Aeronautics Act (1938), **2:190**
Civil Aeronautics Administration
 (CAA), **1:**84; **2:**190
Civil Aeronautics Authority (CAA),
 1:84, 94
Civil Aeronautics Board (CAB),
 1:84, 96, 97; **2:190–191**; **8:**191
Civil defense, **2:191**
Civil disobedience, **2:191–192**
 pacifism and, **6:**227
"Civil Disobedience" (Thoreau),
 5:119; **7:**194; **8:**180; **9:**339–340
Civil disorder. *See* Riots
Civil liberties. *See* Civil rights
Civil religion, **2:192–193**
Civil rights, **2:198–200**
 during Civil War, **1:**284
 Democratic Party and, **2:**553
 FBI activities and, **3:**338

Civil rights, (*continued*)
  Johnson (Lyndon B.) and, **2**:194,
      195, 199, 203, 553
  and liberalism, **5**:91
  martial law to enforce, **5**:254
  for Native Americans, legislation
      on, **4**:264–265; **7**:247
  privileges and immunities of citi-
      zens, **6:481–482**
  Supreme Court on, **8**:24–25
  during war, **8**:374–375
  See also Civil rights movement
Civil Rights Act (1866), **2:193**, 197
  Force Act strengthening, **3**:413
  Johnson's veto of, text of,
      9:317–318
Civil Rights Act (1875), **2:194**, 199
Civil Rights Act (1957), **2:194–195**
  NAACP and, **5**:527
Civil Rights Act (1964), **1**:549;
      2:195–197; **3**:15–16, 51–52;
      5:66, 116; **8**:517
  affirmative action as violation of,
      1:386
  backlash against, **1**:382
  civil rights movement and, **2**:204
  and education funding, **3**:123
  equal employment section of,
      1:36–37
  and Georgia politics, **3**:557
  provisions of, **1**:51–52
  and role of federal government,
      3:341
  and school desegregation, **1**:589
  sexual harassment under, **5**:324;
      7:322
  Title II of, **2**:195–196, 199
  Title VI of, **2**:196, 200
  Title VII of, **2**:196, 200; **3**:52, 243;
      5:15
    exclusion of age from, **3**:46
    key amendments to, **3**:52
    sex discrimination provisions in,
        3:54
  on women, **1**:36–37
Civil Rights Act (1991), **2:197–198**;
      5:15
  settlements under, **1**:37
Civil rights movement, **1**:51–52;
      2:199–200, **200–206**; **8**:587
  AFL-CIO and, **1**:152
  African American press and, **5**:200
  in Alabama, **1**:104–105
    Birmingham, **1**:466

and American Studies, **1**:170
backlash against, **1**:382
and bilingual education, **3**:121
boycotts and, **1**:529
and children, **2**:146, 149
Christian teachings and, **2**:164–165
Congress of Racial Equality
    (CORE) and, **2**:354–355
and country clubs, **4**:19–20
desegregation in, **4**:374–375
on domestic violence, **3**:74
and environmentalism, **3**:227
firsthand accounts of, **9**:445–446,
    447–452
folk music and, **5**:497
Freedom Riders and, **3:464**, 465
in Georgia, **3**:557–558
Griggs v. Duke Power Company and,
    4:66
impact of, **1**:52
legacies of, **2**:205
legislation in, **1**:51
and lynching, **5**:179–180
Malcolm X on, **5**:520
March on Washington (1963),
    5:237, 237
in Maryland, **5**:258
among Mexican Americans, **5**:344
in Mississippi, **5**:413–414
NAACP and, **5**:526–527
National Review on, **5**:556
National Urban League and, **5**:563
The New Republic on, **6**:77
Niagara movement and,
    6:103–104
original documents on, **9**:445–454
origins of, **1**:51
principles of, **3**:249
and prisons, **6**:477
and Protestantism, **6**:517
radicalization of, **7**:167
right-wing resistance to, **7**:16
Scottsboro Boys incident in, **1**:104
sexism of, **8**:515–516
in South Carolina, **7**:456–457
Southern Christian Leadership
    Conference in, **7**:472–473
Student Nonviolent Coordinating
    Committee in, **4**:375; **7**:561
student participation in, **3**:119
Students for a Democratic Society
    in, **7:561–562**
in Tennessee, **8**:86
and theater, **8**:115

trade unions and, **8**:262
United Church of Christ and,
    2:349
Civil Rights Restoration Act (1987),
    2:206
Civil service, **2:206–208**
  aliens in, **1**:126
  number of people in, **3**:330, 342
  patronage workers, **6**:258
  Pendleton Act (1883) and, **6**:275
  and pension plans, **6**:283
  political activities in, regulation of,
      4:103–104
  spoils system in, **7:506–507**
  women in, sex discrimination
      against, **6**:295
  See also Government employment
Civil Union Act (Vermont, 2000),
    8:314
Civil War, **2:208–220**
  African Americans in, **1**:510; **2**:212,
      215, 395–396
    Fort Pillow Massacre and, **6**:356
  and African colonization, **1**:148
  agriculture during, **1**:63
  Alabama in, **1**:102–103; **5**:428–429
  Alabama claims in, **1:106**; **5**:428
    Treaty of Washington on, **1**:106;
        8:416–417
  alcohol regulation in, **1**:117
  Andersonville Prison in, **1:184**
    firsthand account of, **9**:304–307
  antiwar protests in, **1**:284
  arbitrary arrest during, **1:284**
  Arkansas in, **1**:261
  Atlanta Campaign in, **1:350–351**
    Battle of Kenesaw Mountain in,
        4:516
  ballad inspired by, **1**:*388*
  ballooning used in, **1**:391
  Baltimore Riot during, **1**:393
  bank notes issued during, **5**:528
  Battle at Marion in, **5**:244
  Battle of Antietam in, **1:199–200**;
      2:212; **3**:191; **5**:259
  Battle of Bull Run in
    First, **1:567**; **2**:211; **9**:*65*, 65–66
    Second, **1:568**; **2**:212
  Battle of Chancellorsville in,
      2:104, 213; **6**:280
  Battle of Chickamauga in, **2:135**,
      213
  Battle of Cold Harbor in, **2**:214,
      266

Battle of Fair Oaks in, **6:**275

Battle of Fredericksburg in, **2:**213;
3:457–458

Battle of Gettysburg in, **2:**214;
3:566–569, *568–570;* **6:**278
New Yorkers in, **6:**88
Pickett's charge in, **6:**351, *351*

Battle of Hampton Roads in, **6:**25

Battle of Kenesaw Mountain in,
4:516

Battle of Mobile Bay in,
5:428–429

Battle of Nashville in, **2:**214; **5:516**

Battle of Perryville in, **6:**291

Battle of Shiloh in, **2:**213;
7:346–347

Battle of Spotsylvania Courthouse
in, **7:512**

Battle of the *Monitor* and the *Merrimack* in, **5:442–443**

Battle on Lookout Mountain in,
5:151

Battles of the Wilderness in, **2:**214;
8:477–478

blockade in, **1:**487–488; **2:**214, 217

bounties in, **1:**524

Canada during, **2:**26
Confederate activities in,
2:24–25; 6:136

and canning industry, **2:**36

casualties in, **2:**213, 214, 219,
510–511

causes of, **2:**208

censorship during, **2:**83, 84; **6:**97

Chattanooga Campaign in,
2:112–113, 213; **5:**151

Christian beliefs in, **2:**163–164,
192–193

Committee on the Conduct of the
War, **2:313–314**

Confiscation Acts in, **2:346**

confiscation of property during,
2:347

Connecticut during, **2:**358

conscientious objectors during,
2:361

consequences of, **2:**219

and conservative politics,
2:374–375

constitutional predicate for, **3:**225

contraband of war in, slaves as,
Butler's report on, **9:**294–296

contraband policy in, **2:**395–396

Copperheads during, **2:**218, **411**

cost of, **2:**219; **3:**282; **8:**377

Cumberland Gap in, **2:**479

and defense policy, **2:**534

Delaware during, **2:**542

demobilization after, **2:**546

and Democratic Party, **2:**551

desertion in, **1:**524; **3:**17

and domestic trade, **8:**159, 160

draft in, **1:**274; **2:**210–211,
363–364
Confederate, **2:**340–341
riots over, **2:**211; **3:**84; **7:**164,
166; **8:**338
substitutes for, **7:571**

early, **2:***210,* 211–212

economy during, **2:**215–217

efforts to prevent, **1:**505–506

elections in era of, **3:**146

Emancipation Proclamation,
2:212, 217; **3:190–192,** *191*

enlistment and conscription in,
2:210–211

Excess Profits Tax in, **3:**273

financing of, **2:**215–216, 342–343

and flag, **3:**380

Florida in, **3:**386

and foreign investment in U.S.,
3:420–421

foreign labor during, **2:**397

and foreign policy, **3:**425

and foreign service, **3:**428

and foreign trade, **8:**165

Fort Donelson capture in, **3:**79;
8:249

Fort Henry in, **4:**126

Fort Pillow Massacre, **6:356**

Fort Sumter in, **8:**17

fortifications during, **3:**439

Fortress Monroe in, **5:**446

Galvanized Yankees in, **3:**505

General Order No. 100, **2:220**

and "generation touched with fire,"
3:528

Georgia in, **3:**555

Great Britain in, **1:**105, 106; **3:**425;
4:41–42

greenbacks issued during, **4:**9, 14,
62

guerrilla warfare in, **4:**70

and gun control, **4:**74

gunboats in, **4:**77

Hampton Roads Conference in,
4:91

Harpers Ferry in, Capture of, **4:97**

Hood's Tennessee Campaign in,
4:160

Indiana in, **4:**318

inflation in, **4:**353

Iowa in, **4:**415

Irish Americans in, **4:**424

ironclad warships in, **4:**430–431

Island Number Ten in, **4:438**

Kansas in, **4:**509

Kentucky in, **4:**519

laws of war in, **8:**371

logistics in, **5:**146

and "Lost Cause," **5:**155

Maine in, **5:**209–210

maps of
1861-1862, **2:***210*
1863, **2:***213*
1864-1865, **2:***216*
archival, **9:65–67**

Marine Corps in, **5:**242

Maryland in, **5:**257
invasion of, **5:**259

Mason-Dixon line in, **5:**260

McClellan's letter to Lincoln on,
9:298–299

medical knowledge and, **5:**302

medicine and surgery in, lessons
from, **5:**302

military forces in, **2:**530

military uniform in, **8:***256,*
257–258

militias and, **5:**387

minorities serving in
African Americans, **5:**380
Hispanic Americans, **5:**383

Mississippi River in, **5:**417

Missouri in, **5:**420–421

mobilization for, **5:**429
funds for, **5:**76

Morgan's raids in, **5:458**

Mosby's Rangers in, **5:462**

munitions in, **5:**479–480, 481

and nationalism, **5:**568

Native Americans in, **1:**501; **2:**126,
158, 492–493; **4:326–327,** 328
Choctaw leader on, **9:**302–303
in Indian Brigade, **4:263**
from Indian Territory, **6:**184

and nativism, **6:**4

naval mortars in, **5:460**

and Navy, **6:**25

and Navy, Department of, **6:**23

Nebraska in, **6:**30

Nevada in, **6:**37–38

Civil War, (*continued*)
  New Hampshire in, **6:**58
  New Mexico in, **6:**69
  New Orleans during, **6:**73–74,
    75–76
  New York City in, **6:**80, 82
  New York (state) in, **6:**88
  and newspapers, **6:**97
  North Carolina in, **6:**129
  nursing in, **6:**146
  Ohio in, **6:**173
  Oklahoma in, **6:**184–185
  onset of, **2:**209
  and paper and pulp industry, **6:**245
  and Peace Movement of 1864,
    6:266
  Peninsular Campaign in, **6:275**
  Pennsylvania in, **6:**278
  and philanthropy, **6:**317
  photography in, **1:***199,* 200, 299,
    530, 530–532; **6:**329, 331–332
  and plantation systems, **6:**365
  and pluralism, **6:**374
  politics during, **2:**218
  Powhatan incident, **6:443**
  and prices, **6:**461
  and Princeton University, **6:**465
  prisoners of war in, **6:**472
    exchange of prisoners, **6:**473
    prison camps, **6:**473–474
  Prize cases, **6:482–483**
  and Protestantism, **6:**516
  railroads during, **7:**35, *36,* 40, *41*
  Red River Campaign in, **7:71**
  Rhode Island in, **7:**153
  Richmond (Kentucky) Campaigns
    in, **7:156–157**
  role of rivers in, **7:**175
  Saint Albans Raid in, **7:**224; **8:**313
  sectionalism in, **7:**296
  Seven Days' Battles in, **2:**212;
    6:275; **7:319**; **9:**67, *68*
  Shenandoah Campaign in, **7:341**
  Sherman's March to the Sea in,
    7:345–346
  Siege of Petersburg in, **6:295–296,**
    296
  Siege of Savannah in, **7:255–256**
  Singleton Peace Plan in, **7:366**
  and smoking, **8:**134
  Sons of Liberty in, **7:449**
  South Carolina in, **7:**455
  southern Unionists in, **7:474–475**
  spies in, **7:**502

  spread of disease during, **3:**238
  state sovereignty in, **7:**534
  Stuart's Ride in, **4:**99; **7:560**
  submarines in, **7:**562
  substance abuse during, **5:**510
  surrender at Appomattox,
    1:226–227
  and tariffs, **8:**51, 156
  taxation during, **2:**215, 216; **7:**132;
    8:56–57
    Confederacy and, **2:**342–343
  telegraph used in, **8:**69
  ten-forties issued during, **8:**81
  Tennessee in, **8:**85
  Texas in, **8:**101
  and textile industry, **8:**109
  trading with enemy in, **8:**173
  Trans-Mississippi Theater, **2:***215*
  and Treasury, **8:**196
  trenches in, **8:**207
  Trent affair in, **8:**207–208
  Uncle Tom's Cabin and, **8:**248
  Union sentiment during
    in border states, **8:260**
    in South, **8:260**
  Union victory in, road to,
    2:213–215
  Vallandigham incident in, **3:**527;
    8:305–306
  Vermont in, **7:**224; **8:**313
  veterans' organizations, **8:**264–265,
    318
  Vicksburg in, **8:324,** *324*
  Virginia in, **8:**344
  war crimes trial after, **1:**184
  War Democrats in, **8:**378
  warships in, **8:**405
    ironclad, **4:**430–431
  Washington (D.C.) in, **8:**410
  West Virginia in, **8:**448–449
  Western theater, **2:**212–213
  widows of, letters to Lincoln by,
    9:303–304
  women in, **2:**215; **8:**502, 509
  See also Confederate States of
    America; Union
Civil Works Administration (CWA),
  8:440
Civiletti, Benjamin R., **1:**8
Civilian Conservation Corps (CCC),
  2:*220,* 220–221, 371; **3:**432,
  436; **6:**43; **8:**440, 441
  and natural resource preservation,
    8:423

Civilized Tribes, Five, **1:**501; **2:**221
  in Civil War, **4:**327
  removal of, **4:**285–286, 309, 314
  Sequoyah (proposed state) for,
    7:314
CIW. *See* Carnegie Institution of
  Washington
*CLA Journal. See College Language
  Association Journal*
Claesen, Dirck, **1:**285, 303
Clagett, William H., **8:**579
Claiborne, F. L., **5:**518
Claiborne, William C. C., **5:**159;
  6:213
Claim associations, **2:**221
Claims, Federal Court of,
  2:221–222
Clancy, Tom, **5:**130
Clans, **6:**86
Clanton, Billy, **8:**141
Clanton, Ike, **8:**141
Clap, Thomas, **8:**573
Clark, Beauchamp (Champ), in pres-
  idential campaign of 1912,
  3:160
Clark, Field v., **3:358**
Clark, George Rogers, **1:**382; **4:**214;
  6:177
  Northwest Campaign of, **2:222**
Clark, Jim, **2:**337
Clark, John Bates, **3:**108, 109
Clark, Larry, **1:**301
Clark, Mark, in Anzio Campaign,
  1:217–218
Clark, Mary Higgins, **5:**130
Clark, Tom, on Japanese American
  incarceration, **4:**460
Clark, William, **3:**297; **5:**41, 86–87,
  449, 487; **6:**447
  on Columbia River, **2:**303
  and fur trade, **3:**298–299
Clark Sisters, the, **1:**441
Clark University, **8:**280
Clarke, Arthur C., **2:**319
Clarke, Charles, **2:**404
Clarke, Edward, **3:**131
Clarke, Frank W., **2:**122
Clarke, Hans T., **1:**460
Clarke, James Freeman, **8:**179
Clarke, John, **1:**411
Clarke, William E., **1:**184
Clarke, William Newton, **1:**413
Clarke-McNary Act (1924), **3:**432
Clarkson, Matthew, **3:**236

Clash of Civilizations (Huntington), **6:**405

Class(es), **2:222–226**
  and abortion, **1:**4, 5
  capitalism and shifts in, **2:**45
  in Democratic Party, **4:**453–454
  and food and cuisines, **3:**399, 402
  and life expectancy, **5:**105–106
  middlebrow culture, **5:365–366**
  in South, **7:**464
  in Spanish colonial settlements, **7:**207
  and sports, **7:**509
  and vacationing, **8:**305
  Veblen's *Theory of the Leisure Class* on, excerpt from, **9:**347–351
  See also Middle classes; Working class
Class conflict, **2:226–228**
Classical conditioning, **6:**524
Classical music, **5:491–492**
  by symphony orchestras, **8:38–39**
Clausewitz, Carl von, **8:**370
Clay, Cassius. *See* Ali, Muhammad
Clay, Cassius M., **2:**84; **7:**210
Clay, Clement C., **1:**102
  and Peace Movement of 1864, **6:**266
Clay, Edward William, **6:**394
Clay, Henry, **5:**116
  and African colonization, **1:**148
  American System of, **1:**171
  caucus supporting, **6:**113
  and colonization movement, **2:**296
  and Compromise of 1850, **2:**9, 331
  and Compromise Tariff (1833), **8:**50–51
  duel with Randolph, **3:**93
  economic policies sponsored by, **7:**111
  vs. Jackson (Andrew), **7:**103
  as Kentucky native, **4:**519
  and Latin America, **5:**46
  and navigation projects, **7:**168
  party nomination of, **2:**399
  and presidential campaign of 1812, **3:**151
  in presidential campaign of 1824, **3:**152, 171; **5:**555
  in presidential campaign of 1832, **3:**152
  in presidential campaign of 1844, **3:**153
  as war hawk, **8:**379, 382

Clay, Lucius D., **1:**443
Claypoole, James, **3:**459
Clayton, John, **6:**237
Clayton, John Middleton, **2:**229
Clayton Antitrust Act (1914), **2:**418; **5:**21
  amendments to, **1:**215
  and FTC, **3:**348; **4:**27
  labor provisions of, **2:228–229**, 496; **6:**121
  provisions of, **1:**215
  Sherman Antitrust Act and, **2:**311
  Supreme Court on, **6:**121
  on trade union activity, **8:**171
  Wilson and, **6:**497; **8:**235
Clayton Compromise, **2:**229
Clayton-Bulwer Treaty (1850), **1:**439; **2:229–230**; **4:**41; **6:**104, 237
  Hay-Pauncefote Treaties and, **4:**110
CLC. *See* Christian Life Commission
Clean Air Act (1963), **8:**190
  provisions of, **1:**79
Clean Air Act (1970)
  1973 amendments to, **1:**362
  1977 amendments to, **1:**14, 362
  1979 amendments to, **1:**79–80
  1990 amendments to (*See* Clean Air Act [1990])
  and acid rain, **1:**13–14
  effects of, **1:**13–14
  and EPA, creation of, **1:**362
  provisions of, **1:**79
Clean Air Act (1990), **1:**14, 362; **2:**230; **3:**100, 227, 228, 232; **6:**9; **8:**423
  and coal mining, **2:**253
  on emissions, **1:**80
  and ethanol-powered vehicles, **3:**480
Clean Water Act (CWA) (1972), **2:230–231**; **3:**100, 227, 232; **8:**422, 423
  enforcement of, **3:**219
  on sewage, **4:**356
Cleanliness, and food production, **3:**400
"Clear and present danger test," **3:**374
Clear Channel Radio, **7:**21
Clearcutting, **3:**431
Clearing House, New York, **2:**231
Clearinghouses, **2:231–232**
Cleary, Fran, **2:***493*

Cleaveland, Parker, **5:**390
Cleaver, Eldridge, **1:**478–479
Cleburne Living Center, City of Cleburne v., **3:**247
Clemenceau, Georges, at Paris peace conference, **8:**315
Clemens, Samuel Langhorne. *See* Twain, Mark
Clement, Frank, **8:**86
Clement XIV, Pope, **4:**474
Clements, William P., Jr., **8:**103
Clerc, Laurent, **7:**355–356
Clermont (Fulton's Folly) (steamboat), **3:483–484**; **7:***171*, 172; **8:**187
Cleveland (Ohio), **2:232–233**
  Cuyahoga River fire in, **3:**228, 232
  Czech population in, **2:**89
  Empowerment Zone program, **8:**287
  foundation of, **4:**52
  race riots in, **7:**166
  Rock and Roll Hall of Fame and Museum, **2:**232; **7:**186
  school choice program in, **3:**138
Cleveland, Frances Folsom, **3:**375
Cleveland, Grover
  anti-imperialism of, **1:**202
  conservation policies of, **2:**367
  and Dawes Commission, **2:**506
  and Democratic Party, **2:**551
  embassies established by, **3:**193
  on fencing of public lands, **6:**532
  fiscal policies of, **1:**459
  and foreign service, **3:**428
  and forest conservation, **3:**433
  Hawaiian annexation under, **4:**107
  illegitimate children of, **6:**400
  Labor Day established by, **5:**13
  Latin American policies of, **1:**550
  on military pensions, **6:**285
  Monroe Doctrine and, **5:**446
  and panic of 1893, **3:**366
  in presidential campaign of 1884, **2:**453; **3:**157
  in presidential campaign of 1888, **3:**157, 158, 171; **8:**233
  in presidential campaign of 1892, **3:**158
  in Pullman strike, **4:**249
  on silver coinage, **7:**362
  on silver purchase, **3:**458
  Sino-Japanese War and, **7:**367
  and tariffs, **8:**51
  veto power exercised by, **2:**375

Cleveland, Moses, **2**:232; **8**:456
Cleveland Democrats, **2**:233
Cleveland Foundation, **6**:317
Cliff dwellings, of Mesa Verde, pre-
 historic ruins of, **5**:*325*,
 325–326
Clifford, Clark M., **2**:528
Clifford, James, **1**:194
Clifford, William, **1**:55
Clifton, Lucille, **5**:126
Climate(s), **2:233–238**
 annual rainfall, **2**:*236*
 average regional temperature,
 2:*234*
 global warming and, **4**:5–9, *7*
 Gulf Stream and, **4**:73
 meteorology, **5**:330–332
 regional, **2**:235–236
Climate change
 in 19th century, **2**:235
 in 20th century, **2**:237–238
Clinch, Duncan, **8**:401
Cline, Martin, **3**:531
Cline, Patsy, **5**:*493*
Clinical research, **2:238–239**
 ethics in, **1**:461–462
Clinton, DeWitt, **3**:151, 352; **6**:79
 and Erie Canal, **3**:252; **8**:187
Clinton, George, **5**:37
 antifederalism of, **1**:201
 and Democratic Party, **2**:549
 idea of Erie Canal by, **6**:87
 on King George's War, **6**:83
 in presidential campaign of 1792,
 3:150
 in presidential campaign of 1808,
 3:151
Clinton, Sir Henry, **1**:574; **2**:108;
 7:143, 144; **8**:581
 at Charles Town, **7**:145
 in Saratoga Campaign, **7**:251
 in southern campaigns, **7**:472
 victories of, **8**:447
 in Virginia, **1**:282
Clinton, Hillary Rodham, **3**:376;
 6:89
 in Senate campaign of 2000, **3**:198
 in Whitewater scandal, **2**:239;
 7:496
Clinton, William Jefferson (Bill)
 on abortion, partial-birth, **1**:7
 affirmative action under, **1**:37
 AFL-CIO and, **1**:153
 AIDS policy under, **1**:18
 and air traffic controllers, **1**:82
 and Al Qaeda, **6**:109
 AmeriCorps under, **1**:173
 antitrust legislation under, **1**:215
 as Arkansas governor, **1**:263
 and Balanced Budget Act (1997),
 1:388
 and bioethics, **1**:462
 censorship measures of, **2**:85
 child care policies of, **2**:139
 and civil servants' political activities, **4**:104
 Congressional appropriations
 vetoed by, **1**:229
 conservative opposition to, **2**:376
 Cuba policy of, **2**:472
 and Defense of Marriage Act,
 2:532
 defense policy of, **2**:529
 defense policy of, **2**:553
 and Democratic Party, **2**:553
 and Domestic Policy Council,
 3:330
 "don't ask, don't tell" policy of,
 3:78
 drug law enforcement under,
 5:511–512, 513
 economic policies of, **3**:224
 energy policies of, **3**:210, 212;
 6:304
 environmental policies of, **3**:207,
 230, 233; **8**:298
 executive orders of, **3**:278
 and federal aid, **3**:334
 and Federal Mediation and Conciliation Service, **3**:343
 foreign policy of, **3**:428
 and forest conservation, **3**:431
 and Forest Summit of 1993, **3**:207
 and Freedom of Information Act,
 3:463
 and gasoline tax, **3**:511
 and GATT, **3**:524
 and global warming, **4**:8
 and Grand Staircase-Escalante
 National Monument, **8**:298
 and gun control, **4**:76
 health care plan of, **1**:153; **4**:114,
 120, 372
 HHS under, **4**:114
 HUD under, **4**:184
 immigration regulation under,
 4:229
 impeachment trial of, **2**:240, 353;
 3:169; **4**:235–236, **238–241**,
 240; **7**:114
 and Indian education, **3**:137
 on Iraq-gate, **4**:422
 Israeli relations under, **4**:442–443
 Japanese relations under, **4**:459
 Job Corps under, **4**:481
 Kosovo bombing under, **4**:551
 labor policies of, **3**:244
 Latin American policies of, **2**:55;
 5:49
 and line-item veto, **8**:320
 and national debt, **2**:515, 517
 and National Economic Council,
 3:330
 and National Endowment for the
 Arts, **5**:536
 and National Endowment for the
 Humanities, **5**:537
 national monuments created by,
 1:206
 National Performance Review of,
 3:332–333
 and National Security Council,
 3:330
 and National Trust for Historic
 Preservation, **5**:550
 Native American policies of, **1**:162;
 4:301
 and North American Free Trade
 Agreement, **3**:309, 524
 and Office of National AIDS Policy, **3**:330
 pardons by, **2**:240
 on partial-birth abortion, **1**:7
 and peacekeeping missions, **6**:271
 in presidential campaign of 1992,
 2:24; **3**:169
 in presidential campaign of 1996,
 3:169
 presidential library of, **5**:100
 on Proposition 209, **6**:510
 public debt under, **7**:367
 Republican Party during presidency of, **7**:114
 scandals involving, **2:239–240**;
 6:400, 401
 extramarital affairs, **2**:79, 239,
 240, **240–241**; **3**:169;
 4:238–240; **7**:496
 media coverage of, **7**:261
 Rose Garden statement on,
 9:522–523

Whitewater, **4:**238; **7:**496
and sexual orientation, ban on discrimination based on, **3:**56, 78
South African policy of, **7:**453
subpoena to, **6:**457
at summit conferences, **8:**16
Superfund under, **4:**112
and taxation, **8:**59
on Tienanmen Square Protest, **8:**124
and Transportation, Department of, **8:**185
and Treasury, **8:**197
vetoes cast by, **1:**7, 229; **8:**321
Vietnam visited by, **8:**328
welfare policies of, **2:**228; **3:**485; **6:**439; **8:**442
Clinton v. City of New York, **8:**321
Clinton v. Jones, **2:**240–241
Clipper ships, **2:**241
marine insurance on, **4:**368
Clock and watch industry, **2:**241–242
peddlers and, **6:**273–274
Clockwork Orange, A (Burgess), **1:**438
Cloisters, The (New York), **5:**336
Cloning, **3:**532
and cattle industry, **2:**73
study of DNA and, **3:**67
Closed primary, **6:**463
Closed shop, **2:**242–244
Taft-Hartley Act outlawing, **2:**243; **7:**161
Closing of the American Mind, The (Bloom), **6:**395
Clotel; Or, The President's Daughter: A Narrative of Slave Life in the United States (Brown), **5:**124
Clothing and fashion, **2:**244–248
beaver hats, **1:**434, **435**
cowboy, **2:**443
Godey's Lady's Book and, **4:**9
in hairstyles, **4:**83–84
in men's magazines, **5:**196–197
women's
bicycling and, **1:**451
bloomers, **1:**488–489, *489*
women's rights movement and, **8:**513
Clothing industry, **2:**245, 248–250, *249*
Lebanese Americans in, **5:**71
sewing machines in, **7:**321, *321*

strikes in, **1:**132; **2:**247; **3:**512; **4:**390, 391; **8:**521–522
sweatshops in, **2:**247, 248–249; **8:**34–35, *35*
trade unions in, **1:**132; **2:**247, 249–250
International Ladies Garment Workers Union, **4:**390–393, 478
Cloture, **2:**250; **3:**358–359
Cloud, Henry Roe, **3:**136
Clovis points, **1:**242, *242*
Cloward, Richard A., **6:**440
Clubs
exclusionary, **2:**251
sex discrimination in, ban on, **7:**183, 198
women's, **8:**508–510, 514
CLUW. *See* Coalition of Labor Union Women
CME. *See* Christian Methodist Episcopal
CNLU. *See* Colored National Labor Union
CNN. *See* Cable News Network
CNO. *See* Naval operations, chief of
Coachman, Alice, **8:**155
Coal, **2:**251–253; **3:**210, 212
and iron production, **1:**485
in smelters, **7:**400
Coal Mine Inspection Act (1941), **5:**391
Coal mining, **2:***251, 252,* 252–253
in Alaska, **1:**110
Centralia Mine disaster, **2:**95
health hazards of, **5:**297, 298
and Ludlow Massacre, **5:**169–170
Molly Maguires and, **5:**438
in Montana, **5:**450–451
in North Dakota, **6:**133
trade unions in, **2:**253–256, *254, 255;* **5:**6, *6* (*See also* United Mine Workers of America)
anthracite strike by (1902), **1:**190–191; **5:**6; **7:**557
establishment of, **1:**190; **5:**6
U.S. Bureau of Mines and, **5:**391–393
in West Virginia, **8:**449–450
in Wyoming, **8:**564, 565
in Wyoming Valley, **8:**567
Coalition for a Democratic Majority, **6:**32

Coalition for Essential Schools, **3:**124
Coalition for Women's Appointments (CWA), **5:**566
Coalition of Labor Union Women (CLUW), **2:**256
Coalition to Stop Gun Violence, **4:**76
Coard, Bernard, **4:**65
Coase, Ronald, **3:**109
Coast and Geodetic Survey (C&GS), **2:**62, **256–257;** **6:**160–161
Coast Guard, U.S., **2:**257–259; **5:**106
ensigns in, **3:**223
and lighthouses, **5:**107
recruiting poster for, **2:***258*
Coast Survey, U.S., **6:**159, 160, 161
Coastal Lowlands, **6:**55
Coasting trade, **2:**259
drogher, **3:**86
Navigation Acts and, **6:**21–22
Coastwise steamship lines, **2:**260
Coates, Robert, **1:**9
Cobb, Howell, **2:**485
Cobblestones, **6:**260
Coca-Cola, **2:**260–261, 388; **7:**438–439
advertisement for, **2:***260*
cocaine in, **7:**569
and wine industry, **8:**487
Cocaine, **5:**512, 513; **7:**569, 570
Cochise (Chokonen headman), **1:**221
Cochrane, Alexander, **8:**417
Cochrane, Elizabeth, **6:**98
Cockburn, George, **8:**417
Cockcroft, John D., **6:**342–343
"Coconut" chair, **3:**499
Cocopah, **8:**228
COC&PP. *See* Central Overland California and Pikes Peak Express Company
Cod fisheries, **2:**261–262
fishing bounties and, **3:**376–377
on Grand Banks, **4:**32
Coddingston, John Insley, **3:**521, *522*
Coddington, William, **7:**151
Code, U.S., **2:**262
Code breaking, **2:**467–468
in World War II, **2:**334, 467
Code Napoléon, **2:**262

Code Noir, **2:262–263**

Codes of fair competition, **1:**490; **2:**263

Codman, Ogden, Jr., **1:**292

Cody, William F. (Buffalo Bill), **8:**476, *476*

  Wild West Show of, **7:**191; **8:**457, *475*, **475–477**

Coeducation, **2:263–264**

Coercive Acts (Intolerable Acts), **1:**509, 515, 542; **2:**264, 287; **4:408; 7:**134

  and colonial trade, **2:**284

  Massachusetts Government Act, **5:272**

  opposition to, **8:**3

  protests against, Committee of Inspection and, **2:**313

  Quartering Act, **7:**4

  response of Continental Congress to, **2:**393

Coeur d'Alene riots, **2:**264; **8:**454

Coffee, **2:264–265**

  from Latin America, **5:**44–45

  in Nicaragua, **6:**104

Coffee, Linda, **7:**192

Coffelt, Leslie, **1:**329

Coffin, Levi, **7:**2

COGIC. *See* Progressive National Baptist Convention

Cognitive psychology, **6:**525

Cognitive Psychology (Neisser), **6:**525

Cohan, George M., "Over There" lyrics by, **9:**364–365

Cohen, George, **1:**311

Cohen, Katherine M., **1:**308

Cohen, Morris, **6:**445

Cohen, Stanley, **3:**529

Cohen, Wilbur, **2:**431

Cohen, William S., **2:**529

Cohens v. Virginia, **2:**265, 381

Cohl, Emil, **2:**63

Cohn, Carol, **8:**499

Cohn, Edward, **1:**461

Cohn, Fannia, **3:**53

Coinage. *See* Currency and Coinage; Currency and coinage

Coin's Financial School (Harvey), **2:265**

COINTELPRO (Counterintelligence Program), **2:265–266; 3:**338

Coit, Henry L., **2:**490

Coke, Edward, **4:**491

Coke, Richard, **8:**101

COLA. *See* Cost-of-Living Adjustment

Cold Harbor, Battle of, **2:**214, 266

Cold nuclear fusion, **2:**266

Cold War, **2:266–270**, *268*

  and Africa policies, **1:**38, 39

  air defense during, **1:**75

  Air Force (U.S.) in, **1:**76–77

  air power after, **1:**82

  Amerasia case in, **1:134–135**

  anthropology in, **1:**193–194

  anticommunism during, **2:**327–328

  antiwar movements in, **1:**216

  armored warfare in, **1:**267–268

  arms race and disarmament in, **1:**271–272; **2:**269, 528, 532; **6:**144–145

  Army (U.S.) in, **1:**277

  and ARPANET, **8:**66

  Bay of Pigs invasion in, **1:430–431**

  Berlin Airlift in, **1:***443*, 443–444

  Berlin Wall in, **1:444**, *444*

  biological agents created in, **1:**465; **2:**118

  blacklisting during, **1:**483

  Central European states during, **2:**89–90

  Central Intelligence Agency during, **2:**92, 93

  conservatives during, **2:**375, 376

  containment policy in, **2:**268; **7:**212

    Kennan on, **9:**411–413

  Cuban missile crisis, **1:**430; **2:**55, 269, 471, **474–475**, *475*

  defense policy during, **2:**535–536

  détente in, **2:**269; **7:**212

  diplomacy during, **3:**28–29

  domino theory in, **2:**151; **3:**78

  end of, **2:**266

  and European integration, **3:**259

  FBI activities during, **3:**338

  foreign aid after, **3:**418

  foreign aid during, **3:**416–418; **6:**381

  and foreign policy, **3:**426–427

  and foreign service, **3:**429

  and foreign trade, **8:**166–168

  fruit growing during, **3:**479

  GATT during, **3:**523

  and Georgia, **3:**557

  and Germany, U.S. relations with, **3:**562–563

  and Great Britain, U.S. relations with, **4:**43–44

  gunboat diplomacy during, **4:**77

  Helsinki Accords in, **4:125**

  imperialism in, **4:**245

  industrial espionage during, **3:**255

  and Internet development, **4:**397

  Iron Curtain in, **4:429–430**

  Israel in, **4:**440

  and journalism, **6:**99

  laws of war in, **8:**372

  McCarthyism, **5:**182

  and Middle East policies, **3:**141, 142

  military and strategic intelligence in, **4:**377

  military-industrial complex in, **5:376–378**

  missile gap in, **5:406–407**

  missiles in, **5:407–408**

  mobilization plans in, **5:**430

  multilateral treaties in, **8:**202–203

  and NASA, **5:**523

  and NATO, **6:**125–126

  Navy (U.S.) in, **6:**26–27

  and neoconservatism, **6:**31–33

  and New Mexico, **6:**69

  New York Times on, **6:**90

  newspapers on, **6:**90

  and Nuclear Test Ban Treaty, **6:**143

  Olympics during, **7:**512

  original documents from, **9:**411–444

  and political exiles, **6:**397

  and political science, **6:**403

  propaganda in, **6:**503–504

  Reagan's policies in, **2:**269–270; **7:**212–213

  research during, **5:**19

  roots of, **2:**267

  science education in, **7:**272–273

  segregation in, **4:**375

  South Africa in, **7:**452

  spies in, **7:**503

  State Department in, **7:**529–530

  submarines in, **7:**563

  tariffs during, **3:**461

  Time on, **8:**127

  and trade unions, **5:**545

  treason trials in, **8:**195

  Truman's policies in, **1:**197; **8:**231–232

  U-2 incident in, **7:**212; **8:247**

  United Nations during, **8:**269–270

peacekeeping missions of, **6:**270
U.S. intervention in, **4:**407
in post–World War II years,
  2:267–269
"X" article and, **8:569**
Yalta Conference and, **8:**574
Colden, Cadwallader, **1:**518, 519;
  7:245
Colden, Jane, **1:**518
Cole, Bruce, **5:**537
Cole, David, **3:**343
Cole, Eunice, **8:**494
Cole, Mildred Wiese, **6:**376
Cole, Stewart G., **6:**376
Cole, Thomas, **1:**295, *296;* **4:**189;
  6:507
Cole bombing, **2:**270–271; **6:**109
Colegrove v. Green, **1:**385
Coleman, Bessie, **1:**418
Coleman, James, **3:**118
Colfax, Schuyler, **2:**453; **3:**155
  resignation of, **8:**323
Colfax Massacre (1873), **5:**160
Colgate-Palmolive-Peet, **7:**408
Coligny, Gaspard de, **3:**285
Colijn, Michiel, **9:**10
Colket, Meredith, **3:**522
Collazo, Oscar, **1:**329
Collecting, **2:271–273**
  at Huntington Library and Muse-
    um, **4:195–196**
See also Museum(s)
*Collection of Hymns and Spiritual
  Songs* (Occom), **5:**128
Collective bargaining, **2:273–275**;
  5:14–15, 141
  by federal employees, **1:**154, 156;
    7:558
  industrial relations and, **4:**336, 337
  institutionalization of, **5:**7
  La Follette Civil Liberties Com-
    mittee hearings on, **5:**1
  miners' unions and, **5:**6
  National Labor Relations Act
    establishing right to,
    5:544–545; **8:**42
  New Deal and, **5:**5
  by railroad workers, **5:**7
  by teachers, **1:**156, 157
Collector v. Day, **2:275–276**
College(s), **3:127–129**
  in 19th century, **3:**115
  African American, **3:**121,
    125–127; 8:263

Tuskegee University, **8:241**
community, **3:**117, 127
denominational, **2:**70; **3:129–131**
military training in, **7:**119–120
Native American, **3:**129
private, **8:**279, 280
  black, **3:**125–126
social activism in, **8:**586–587
women's, **3:131–133**
  Seven Sisters Colleges,
    7:319–320
See also Education, higher; *specific
  colleges*
College athletics, **2:276–278; 7:**511
basketball, **1:423–426**
football, **3:**409–410, 411–412;
  4:449; **5:**530–531
National Collegiate Athletic Association and, **5:**530–531
track and field, **8:**154, 155
women in, **2:**276–277, *277*
College Board, **2:**56; **3:**140
College Football Association (CFA),
  3:412
*College Language Association Journal
  (CLA Journal),* **5:**200
College of New Jersey, **6:**465
College of William and Mary. *See*
  William and Mary, College of
College Retirement Equities Fund
  (CREF), **2:**56
Collegiate dictionary, **3:**23
Collier, John, **1:**492; **3:**136
  in American Indian Defense Asso-
    ciation, **1:**159, 340
  attacks on Bureau of Indian Affairs,
    1:571
  and Indian boarding schools, **4:**263
  and Navajos, **6:**16
  reform under, **4:**263, 288, 297
Collins, Al, **8:**142
Collins, Anthony, **2:**539
Collins, J. Lawton, **2:**124
Collins, John F., **1:**510
Collins, Michael, **5:**454
Collins, Thomas v., **6:**297
Colman, Norman Jay, **1:**71
Colombia
  commerce with, **5:**43–45
  and Panama Canal, **6:**237–238
  U.S. relations with, **2:**54; **5:**47
    drug trafficking and, **5:**512
  Panama and, **4:**108–109
Colombo Plan, **3:**416

Colonial administration
  Hundred in, **4:195**
  Lords of Trade and Plantation and,
    5:151
  Privy Council and, **5:**151
  Spanish, **2:**278–279
Colonial agents, **2:279–280**
  proprietary agents, **6:**510
Colonial assemblies, **1:333–334**;
  2:280–281
  Massachusetts Bay Colony General
    Court, **5:**270, 271–272
  Mayflower Compact, **5:**276
  in New York Colony, **6:**83
  Privy Council, **6:**482
  See also General Court, colonial
Colonial charters, **2:281–282**
  Charter of Liberties, **2:109–110**
  Dongan, **3:**79
  municipal, **2:111–112**
  New Albion, **6:**39–40
  to New Haven Colony, **6:**60
  for North Carolina, **6:**126
  to Plymouth Colony, **6:**379–380
  and proprietary colonies,
    6:510–512
  Rights of Englishmen in,
    7:161–162
  and trading companies, **8:**174
  to Virginia Company of London,
    8:347–348
  to Sir Walter Raleigh, text of,
    9:82–84
Colonial commerce, **1:**431–432;
  2:282–284, *283;* **8:**159–160
  Alexandria Conference on, **1:122**
  balance of trade in, **1:**386–387
  coasting, **2:**259
  domestic, **8:**159–160
  foreign, **4:**25; **6:**20, 21–22;
    8:163–164
  fur, **4:**349–350
  with Native Americans, **4:**267–268,
    310, 322–323
  naval stores, **6:**20
  Navigation Acts and, **6:**21–22
  New France and, **6:**51–53
  New Netherland and, **6:**71, 72
  New York Colony and, **6:**83
  peddlers in, **6:**273
  public markets, **5:**248
  tariffs and, **8:**49–50
  tea, **8:**60, 61, 150
  textiles, **8:**108

Colonial commerce, (*continued*)
  tobacco, **8**:134
  Townshend Acts and (*See* Townshend Acts)
  Trade with Enemy Acts and, **8**:173
  See also Piracy; Smuggling
Colonial councils, **2:284–285**
Colonial courts, appeals from, **1**:225
Colonial Dames of America, **2**:285
Colonial era
  adoption in, **1**:27
  advertising in, **1**:31
  African Americans in, **1**:47–48 (*See also* Slave[s])
  agriculture in, **1**:61–62; **2**:96–97; **3**:509; **4**:349
    hemp, **4**:125–126
    oats, **6**:151
    sugar, **8**:12–13
    tobacco, **1**:62
  alcohol in
    and Native Americans, **4**:322–323
    regulation of, **1**:116
  anti-Semitism in, **1**:206
  apprenticeship in, **1**:228
  architecture in, **1**:248–249
  art in
    decorative, **1**:285–286
    glass, **1**:289
    interior decoration, **1**:290–291
    painting, **1**:294–295
    pottery, **1**:285–286, 303–304
    sculpture, **1**:305
  associations in, **1**:340
  astronomy in, **1**:342
  Bible's influence in, **1**:447
  billeting in, **1:457–458**
  Boston in, **1:508–509**; **8**:289
  bounties in, **1**:523
  British colonial offices in, **1**:493
  business regulation in, **4**:25
  Catholicism in, **1:195–196**
    anti-Catholicism and, **1**:195–196; **4**:474
    Jesuits, **4**:473–474
  censorship in, **2**:83
  child care in, **2**:138
  children in, **2**:146, 148
  Christianity in, **2**:162
  Church of England in, **2:171–172**; **7**:93
  cities in, **8**:289, 292
  city planning in, **2**:184–185
  clothing and fashion in, **2**:244

coinage in, **2**:480–481
collecting objects of, **2**:271
committees of correspondence in, **1**:512
crime in, **2**:458
death and dying in, **2**:510
debts in, **2:518**
defense system in, **2**:534
disease in, **2**:291
  ague, **1:72**
  influenza, **4**:353–354
divorce in, **2**:291; **3**:63
economics in, **3**:108
education in, **2**:263, 291; **3**:111–112
  and college athletics, **2**:276
  district schools in, **7**:264
  hornbook in, **4**:*166*, **166–167**
  Massachusetts school law on, **9**:92–93
  for Native Americans, **3**:133
elections in, **3**:145
entailing of estates in, **3**:224
enumerated commodities in, **3**:224
environmental sanitation in, **7**:245
families in, **3**:311–312
feudalism in, **3**:356
financial schemes in, Mississippi bubble, **5:414**
fishing in, **4**:349
flour milling in, **3**:388–389
food and cuisines of, **3**:398
foreign investment in, **3**:419
foreign policy in, **3**:425
forest industries in, **4**:350
fortifications in, **3**:438–439
Franciscans in, **3**:453
fruit growing in, **3**:478
funerary traditions in, **3**:486
fur companies in, **3**:486–487
furniture in, **3**:495–496
gender in, **3**:518
general court in, **3**:525
glassmaking in, **4**:3
government and politics in, **2**:22
governors in, **4**:28
  instructions for, **4:366–367**
gun control in, **4**:74
hairstyles in, **4**:83
hat manufacture in, **4:103**
historiography of, **4**:137
holidays in, **4**:148–149
horse racing in, **4**:169
hotels in, **4**:175

housing in, **4**:179–180
hymns in, **4**:206
immigration in, **4**:220–222
indentured servants in, **4**:252–254
industries in, **4**:*349*, 349–350
  blacksmithing, **1:483–484**, *484*
  naval stores and, **6**:20
insurance in, **4**:367, 369, 370
iron industry in, **4**:350, 426
isolationism in, **4**:438
Italian Americans in, **4**:444
Judaism in, **4**:476
judiciary in, **4**:494
justices of the peace in, **4**:504
kidnapping in, **4**:525
  firsthand account of, **9**:101–103
kitchens in, **4**:534
Mackinac Island and Straits in, **5**:188
manifest destiny in, **5**:223
manufacturing in, **5**:227
mapmaking in, **5**:232
maps of, archival, **9**:2, **12–18**
marriage in, **2**:291; **3**:63
medicine and surgery in, **5**:299–300
meetinghouses in, **5:306**
merchant marine in, **5**:318
meteorology in, **5**:330–331
military uniforms in, **8**:257
militias in, **3**:222; **5**:386
mineralogy in, **5**:390
Mourt's Relation in, **5:468–469**
Native Americans in
  alcohol and, **4**:322–323
  policies on, **4:281–283**
  trade with, **4**:267–268, 310, 322–323
  treaties with, **4**:312–313, **315–316**
  wars with, **8**:395–399, *397*
newspapers in, **6**:94–95
original documents from, **9**:81–126
paper and pulp industry in, **6**:245
patents in, **6**:255
petitions in, **6**:297
philanthropy in, **6**:315–316
plans of union in, **6:362–363**
ports in, **2**:*284*
poverty in, remedies for, **8**:439
press in, freedom of, **6**:95
prices during, **6**:461
primogeniture in, **6**:464
printing in, **6**:468

Protestantism in, **7:**95–96
publishing in, **1:**129
punishment in, **6:**551
  flogging, **3:383**; **6:**551
  pillory, **6:356**
  prisons, **6:**476, 551–552
  tar and feathers, **8:49,** *49*
race relations in, **7:**7–8
religion in, **2:**291–292; **7:**83–85, *88*
  Antinomian controversy in,
    1:205
  freedom of, **7:**93; **8:**139
  science and, **7:**269
roads in, **7:***175,* 175–176; **8:**186
rural life in, **7:**206
science in, religion and, **7:**269
sexuality in, **7:**328–329
shipbuilding in, **4:**349; **7:**347
smuggling in (*See* Smuggling)
soap in, **7:**407
society in, **2:290–293**
sports in, **7:**507–508
suffrage in, **8:**4, **6,** 355
sugar industry in, **8:**12–13, *13*
sumptuary laws and taxes in, **8:**17
tariffs in, **8:**49–50
taxation in, **8:**55
  under Stamp Act, **8:**55
  under Townshend Acts, **8:**49–50,
    55, 150
textiles in, **4:**350; **8:**108
theater in, **8:**112–113
tobacco as money in, **8:**133
tobacco production in, **1:**62
tobacco use in, **7:**404
toys and games in, **8:**152
trade in (*See* Colonial commerce)
trading companies in, **8:**174
transportation in, **8:**186
vacationing in, **8:**305
veterinary medicine in, **8:**318–319
wars in, **2:293–296,** *295*
  archival maps of, **9:***25,* **25–28,** *27,*
    28
water transportation in, **8:**429
westward migration during,
  8:459–460
whaling in, **4:**349
witchcraft in, **7:**83; **8:**494–495
Colonial policy, British
  Hutchinson letters and, **4:199**
  on manufacturing, American,
    5:227
  mercantilism, **5:**271, **315–316**

taxation, **5:**271; **8:**49–50, 55, 150
  See also specific laws
Colonial settlements, **2:287–290,**
  288; **3:**288
  See also specific colonies
Colonial ships, **2:290**
  Arabella, **5:**270
  Fortune, **5:**317
  Little James, **5:**317
  Mayflower, **5:**265, **275**
  Speedwell, **5:**275
Colonization
  arguments for, **3:**287
  charter companies and, **2:**111
  vs. nation building, **3:**297
Colonization movement, **1:**208–209,
  477; **2:***296,* **296–297; 6:**47
  American Colonization Society in,
    1:147–148, 208–209
  rise of, **1:**208–209
Color Additives Amendment (1960),
  3:404
Color television, **8:**77
Colorado, **2:297–300**
  Amendment 2 in, **7:**196
  anti-discrimination laws in, **3:**56
  capital of, **2:**47–48
  emblems, nicknames, mottos, and
    songs of, **7:***532*
  exploration of, **3:**300
  gold in, **2:**298; **4:**11, 314
    Pikes Peak Gold Rush, **6:355**
  Jefferson Territory in, **4:470–471**
  Leadville Mining District, **5:**63
  Ludlow Massacre in, **5:**169–170
  Mesa Verde, prehistoric ruins of,
    5:*325,* **325–326**
  Native Americans in, **2:**297,
    298–299; **4:**314–315; **8:**299,
    300
    Sand Creek Massacre of,
      7:243–244
  reclamation projects in, **7:**55, *56*
  silver in, **7:**364
  ski resorts in, **7:**122
  smelters in, **7:**400
  Spanish language in, **7:**491
  Union Colony in, **8:**259
Colorado coal strikes, **2:300–301**
Colorado River
  explorations of, **2:301; 4:**33
  Hoover Dam on, **4:161–162,** *162,*
    200
  Mohave tribe and, **5:**433–434

Colorado River Compact, **8:**297
Colorado River Indian Tribes reser-
  vation, **8:**228
Colorado River Reservation, **5:**434,
  435
Colored Farmers' National Alliance,
  3:323
Colored Methodist Episcopal
  Church, **1:**44
Colored National Labor Union
  (CNLU), **2:301–302**
Color-field painters, **1:**9–10, 298
Colson, Charles W., **8:**425
Colt, Samuel, **2:**302; **8:**558
Colt revolvers, **2:**302; **5:**479
Colter, John, **8:**579
Colton, Frank, **1:**468
Columbia (Maryland), **2:**188
Columbia (South Carolina), burning
  of, **2:302–303**
Columbia (space shuttle), **2:**101
"Columbia" (term), **2:302**
Columbia Broadcasting System. *See*
  CBS television network
Columbia Institute for the Instruc-
  tion of the Deaf, Dumb, and
  Blind, **3:**504
Columbia River, **7:**173
  Bonneville Dam on, **4:**201; **8:**414
  development of, **8:**430
  exploration and settlement of,
    2:303; 6:204; **8:**412
  fur trade on, **3:**298
  Grand Coulee Dam on, **4:**200–201;
    8:414
Columbia River Treaty, **2:303–304**
Columbia University, **2:304–305**
  and beat generation, **1:433**
  biochemistry department at, **1:**460
  establishment of, **3:**112, 127
  Frankfurt School at, **3:**454
  pragmatism at, **6:**445
  sociology at, **7:**433
Columbine school massacre, **2:305,**
  305
Columbus (Ohio), **2:**47, *48,*
  305–306
  streetcar strike in, **2:**306
Columbus, Christopher, **3:**283, 287
  Santa Maria of, **7:**249
Columbus (New Mexico), Villa raid
  at, **5:**346; **8:336–337**
Columbus Quincentenary (1992),
  2:306–307

Comanche, 2:*307*, **307–308**; 8:216, 218
  captives of, 2:50
  emigrants attacked by, 2:*441*
  and Ghost Dance, 3:573
  in KCA Indian coalition, 4:532
  in New Mexico, 6:67, 69
  on reservations, 6:263
  in Texas, 8:100
  treaty with, Congressional violation of, 5:147–148
"Comanche peace," 6:67
Combat neurosis, 6:431
Combe, George, 6:333
Combines, 1:59
Combs, Roberta, 2:161
Comic almanacs, 1:129
Comics, **2:308–309**, 390
  The Yellow Kid, 2:308; 8:577
Coming Soon!!! (Barth), 5:122
COMINT. *See* Communications intelligence
Comintern. *See* Communist International
Comiskey, Charles, 1:421, 479
Commander in Chief of British Forces, **2:309**
Commentaries on the Laws of England (Blackstone), 6:387
Commentary (magazine), 6:32, 85
Commerce
  chambers of, 2:102–103
  See also Interstate commerce; Trade
Commerce, Court of, **2:309–310**
Commerce, Department of, 2:310; 3:331
  Bureau of Economic Analysis in, 3:105
  head of, 2:2
  Import Administration in, 3:309
  U.S. Bureau of Mines in, **5:391–393**
  Weather Bureau in, 5:332
Commerce clause, 1:549; **2:310–312**; 8:274
  Supreme Court on, 2:310, **405**; 3:575; 4:26
Commercial arbitration, 1:236, 237–238
Commercial banks, 1:396
  and investment banks, separation of, 1:405, 406

Commercial Bureau of the American Republics, 5:46
Commission, 8:193
Commission government, **2:312**
Commission merchants, **2:312–313**
Commission on Industrial Relations, 3:444
Commissions, mixed. *See* Mixed Commissions
Committee for Industrial Organization. *See* Congress of Industrial Organizations
Committee for Public Education v. Nyquist, 3:138
Committee for the Free World, 6:32
Committee of Forty-Eight, 3:320
Committee of Inspection, **2:313**
Committee of Secret Correspondence, 3:472
Committee on Economic Security (CES), 7:418
Committee on Equal Employment Opportunity, 1:36
Committee on Industrial Organization, Hague v., **4:82–83**; 5:546
Committee on Political Education (COPE), 6:393
Committee on Public Information (CPI), 2:313; 3:254; 6:503; 8:535
Committee on the Conduct of the War, **2:313–314**
Committee Seeking Peace with Freedom in Vietnam, statement by, 9:459–462
Committees of correspondence, **2:314–315**; 7:135, 149
  Boston, **1:512**
  New York (Committee of Inspection), **2:313**
Committees of safety, 1:512; **2:315**; 7:136, 149
Commodities Exchange Act (1936), **2:315–316**
Commodities Futures Trading Commission (CFTC), 3:276
Commodity Credit Corporation (CCC), 1:60–61, 66; 2:408
Commodity Exchange Act (1936), 4:30
Commodity exchanges, **2:316**
  Pit, **6:360**

Commodore (train engine), derailment of, 1:*568*
Common Carrier Bureau, 3:340
Common law, **2:316–318**
  attainder in, **1:355**
  in colonies, 2:291
  constitutional law and, 4:496
  on family relations, 3:72
  riparian doctrine in, 8:420
  in Sherman Antitrust Act, 1:213–214
  treatment of child abuse in, 2:136
Common Law, The (Holmes), 2:317
Common Market, 7:54
  U.S. abandoning gold standard and, 4:17
  See also European Community; European Economic Community
Common school reform, 3:114, 116, 131
"Common Sense" (Paine), 1:515; **2:318**, 520; 3:378; 5:118; **6:232**, 396; 7:109, 136
  excerpt from, 9:137–138
Common Sense Book of Baby and Child Care (Spock and Spock), **2:318–319**
Commons, John R., 3:109; 6:42; 8:254
  and University of Wisconsin, 8:284
Commonwealth, Bliss v., 4:74
Commonwealth of Pennsylvania, Prigg v., 3:482; 6:278, 294, **452–453**
Commonwealth v. Alger, 6:387
Commonwealth v. Hunt, **2:319**
Commonwealth v. Pullis, 5:13
Communes. *See* Utopian communities
Communication
  electronics and, 3:179
  See also Telecommunications
Communication satellites, **2:319–320**, *320*
Communications Act (1934), 3:185, 339, 340
Communications Assistance for Law Enforcement Act (1994), 3:185
Communications Decency Act (CDA) (1996), 2:85
Communications industry, **2:320–324**
  fiber optics and, 3:357–358
  mass media, **5:260–261**

in military intelligence, **4**:376
regulation of, **3**:340–341
Western Union in, **8**:456
Communications intelligence (COMINT), **5**:558
Communications Satellite Act (1962), **3**:339
Communications Security (COMSEC), **5**:559
Communications Workers of America (CWA), **2**:324–325
Communism
  censorship of, **2**:85
  and class politics, **2**:225
  containment of, **2**:268
  in Eastern/Central Europe, **2**:89
    overthrow of, **2**:270
  exclusion policy for individuals supporting, **3**:207
  in film industry
    Disney's testimony on, **9**:413–417
    HUAC on, **4**:178, 411
  during Great Depression, **2**:227
  homosexuality and, **7**:326
  perceived threat of, **2**:531
  and Spanish Civil War, **1**:7–8
  in State Department, **4**:136; **7**:530
  subversion in, **8**:1–2
  in trade unions, **3**:176
    International Union of Mine, Mill, and Smelter Workers, **4**:397
  See also Anticommunism
Communist International (Comintern), **2**:325, 326; **7**:57
Communist Labor Party, Palmer Raids and, **6**:232
Communist Party, USA (CPUSA), **2**:325–328; **7**:17
  blacklisting of members, **1**:483
  counterintelligence program against, **2**:265
  decline of, **1**:198–199; **7**:427
  headquarters of, **2**:327
  internal divisions in, **7**:427
  International Labor Defense under, **4**:389
  labor agitation by, **2**:326, 326
  McCarthyism, **5**:182
  Palmer Raids and, **6**:232
  and peace movements, **6**:267
  Roosevelt (Franklin Delano) and, **1**:198
  subversion by, **8**:1

and Trade Union Educational League, **8**:170
and Trade Union Unity League, **8**:170
Communitarianism, **7**:424
  vs. individualism, **4**:333
Community Action Program, **2**:328; **8**:386
Community colleges, **3**:117, 127
  in Virginia, **8**:345
Community of Christ, **7**:104
Community Reinvestment Act, **8**:287
Community schools, **7**:266–267
Community Services Administration (CSA), **6**:164; **8**:387
Commuter railroads, **5**:373–374
Compact discs (CDs), **2**:328–329, 392
Company of Laconia, **6**:56
Company of One Hundred Associates, **2**:329
Company towns, **2**:387; **8**:437–438
Company unions, **8**:277
Comparable worth, **2**:329–330
Comparative advantage, **3**:460
Compensation, eminent domain and, **6**:505–506
Competition, fair, codes of, **1**:490; **2**:263
Competition Advocacy Program, **3**:349
Comprehensive AIDS Resource Emergency Act (1990), **1**:17
Comprehensive Employment and Training Act (CETA) (1972), **2**:330; **3**:201; **5**:11
Comprehensive Environmental Response, Compensation, and Liability Act (CERCLA) (1980), **3**:228, 232; **4**:111
  See also Superfund
Compromise of 1790, **2**:330
Compromise of 1850, **2**:9, **331–332**; **5**:110
  Georgia accepting, **3**:558
  nullification of, **6**:146
  and presidential campaign of 1852, **3**:154
Compromise of 1890, **2**:332
Compromise Tariff (1833), **8**:50–51
Compton, Arthur H., **6**:336
Compton, Frank E., **3**:204

Comptroller General of the United States, **2**:332–333
Comptroller of the Currency, **2**:333
Computer(s), **1**:589; **2**:333–338
  in air defense, **1**:75
  artificial intelligence in, **1**:318
  in automation, **1**:364
  and chess programs, **2**:130, 338
  commercial use of, **6**:169–170
  and consumerism, **2**:392
  development of, **6**:169–170
  digital, **3**:25
  and DVD technology, **3**:98
  early, **2**:334, 334–335, 335
  in education, **3**:139
  environmental dangers associated with, **8**:420
  graphics in movies, **3**:365
  hackers, **7**:219
  impact of, **3**:179
  and industrial espionage, **3**:255
  MITS Altair (first home computer), **5**:359
  occupational health hazards, **5**:298
  and online information industry, **2**:323
  and patents, **6**:256
  personal, software for, **7**:442–443
  privacy concerns about, **6**:480
  in publishing industry, **6**:99
  and railroad operations, **5**:144
  scientific information retrieval by, **7**:279–280
  security issues involving, **2**:338
  video games for, **8**:327
  virtual reality on, **8**:350
  See also Internet
Computer Associates, **7**:441
Computer industry
  foreign investment in, **3**:423
  graphical interface user (GUI), **5**:360
  operating systems and, **5**:360
  venture capital in, **4**:341
  See also Software industry
Computer Usage Corporation (CUC), **7**:440
Computer-aided design (CAD), **8**:110
Computer-aided manufacture (CAM), **8**:110
COMSEC. *See* Communications Security

Comstock, Anthony, **1:**4, 466, 467; **2:**84
  and publishing industry, **6:**537
Comstock, William A., **1:**402
Comstock Act (1873), **1:**4, 5, 500; **2:**84; **3:**313, 317; **5:**274; **6:**419
Comstock Lode, **1:**497; **2:**9, **338;** **3:**300; **4:**11; **6:**37
Comte, Auguste, **6:**423; **7:**431–432
Con Edison, **4:**188
Conant, Roger, **3:**80
Concanen, Richard L., **3:**77
Concentration camps, **6:**474
Conceptual pragmatism, **6:**445
Concerned United Birthparents, **1:**29
Concert of Europe, **5:**64
Conciliation and mediation, labor, **2:338–339**
  Federal Mediation and Conciliation Service and, **3:**343
Conciliation commissions, **5:**428
Conciliation courts, domestic, **2:339**
Conciliation Service, of Department of Labor, **5:**11
Concord coach, **7:**515–516
Concorde, **8:21**
Concrete, as building material, **1:**564–565
Condensed-matter physics, **6:**347
Condit, Gary, **6:**400
Conditioning, classical, **6:**524
Condon, Edward U., **4:**178; **6:**342
Cone, Claribel, **2:**273
Cone, Etta, **2:**273
Cone, James H., **5:**93
Conestoga wagon, **2:**339, 441; **7:**177; **8:***462*
Coney Island, **1:**179, *179*
  amusement park in, **1:***546,* 547; **2:**178
  streetcars and, **7:**66
Confederate States of America, **2:**208–209, **340–344**
  agents of, **2:339**
  anthem of, **3:**66
  blockade of, **1:**487–488; **2:**214, 396; **8:**446
    firsthand account of, **9:**296–297
  comparative advantages of, **2:**209
  conscription by, **2:**210–211, 340–341
  Constitution of, **2:**340, *341*
  cotton money used by, **2:429–430**

currency in, **2:**434
defeat of, **2:**343–344
disaffected citizens in, **8:**260
economy of, **2:**216–217, 342–343
expatriates, in Brazil, **2:340**
flag of, **3:**381
foreign policy of, **3:**425
foreign relations of, **2:**342
founding of, **2:**340
Georgia and, **3:**555
government and politics of, **2:**341
heritage of, preservation of, **8:**265
inflation in, **4:353**
and "Lost Cause," **5:**155
in maps, archival, **9:**67, *69*
and Mexico, postwar migration to, **5:345**
military strategy and administration of, **2:**217
Mississippi in, **5:**412
Missouri and, **5:**421
Montgomery Convention and, **5:452**
Native Americans in, **4:**326–327
organization and mobilization of, **2:**340–341
politics in, **2:**218
prison camps of, **6:473–474**
Seal of, **7:288**
society of, **2:**343
states' rights in, **7:**537
taxation by, **2:**342–343
and tithes, **8:**132
United Confederate Veterans, **8:264–265**
United Daughters of the Confederacy, **8:265–266**
White House of, **8:472,** *472*
See also Army, Confederate; Civil War; Navy, Confederate
Confederation, **2:344–346; 7:**140
  cession of western lands and, **8:**455, 456
  Muscle Shoals speculation and, **5:**483–484
  See also Articles of Confederation
Confederation Congress, **2:**344, 378
  debts incurred by, **2:**518
  ordinances of, **6:**200–201
  See also Continental Congress, Second
Conference for Progressive Political Action (CPPA), **3:**162; **6:**498
  La Follette and, **5:**16

Conference on Science and World Affairs (1957), **6:**547
Confidence man (con man), **2:**458
Confirmation, by Senate, **2:**346, 353
  of Brandeis (Louis D.), **1:**532
  of cabinet members, **2:**2
  of Thomas (Clarence), **8:**121
Confiscation Acts, **2:**346, 377
Confiscation of property, **2:**346–347
  eminent domain power and, **3:**198–199
Conflict of interest, and political corruption, **2:**420
Conglomerates, **2:**347–348, 419
  Clayton Act and, **4:**27
  in food industry, **3:**400, 403
Congo, United Nations operation in, **8:**270–271
Congregationalism, **2:348–350;** **3:**242; **8:**263
  membership in, **7:***87,* 90
  in New England, **7:**84, 93
  New England Way and, **6:**50
  religious intolerance of, **7:**151
  revivalism and, **3:**264
  Second Awakening in, **1:**378
  separation from state, **2:**167
  upstart sects and threat to, **7:**86
  women's role in, **8:**501
Congress, Confederate, **2:**341
Congress, Confederation, **2:**344, 378
  debts incurred by, **2:**518
  ordinances of, **6:**200–201
  See also Continental Congress, Second
Congress, Continental. *See* Continental Congress
Congress, U.S., **2:350–354; 3:**341
  Abscam scandal and, **1:**8
  administrative discretion delegation by, **1:21–22**
  African Americans in, during Reconstruction, **1:**50
  appropriations by, **1:229–230**
  authority of, over monetary policy, **4:**10
  Balanced Budget Amendment and, **1:**388
  Bank of the United States and, **5:**184
  bicameral structure of, **5:**78
  Black Caucus in, **1:**471
  boundary disputes settled by, **1:**522

caucuses in, **2:**76, **77**

censuring/expulsion of members of, **2:**352

Committee on the Conduct of the War (Civil War), **2:313–314**

committee system of, **5:**77

Constitutional interpretation by, **3:**342

Contempt of, **2:392–393**

controlling federal agencies, **3:**333

currency regulation by, **8:**310

and delegation of powers, **2:**545

district representation in, **3:**62; **7:**107–108

extra sessions of, **3:303**

and federal budget, **1:**557, 559

floor leaders in, **3:**384–385

grants-in-aid to states from, **4:**37

implied powers of, **4:246–248**

investigating committees of, **4:410–411**

investigations by, **2:**352

Joint Committee on Reconstruction, **4:485–486**

Journal of Congress, **4:488**

in Korea-gate, **4:**542–543

leadership of, **2:**352

legal standing of, **8:**320–321

Legislative Reorganization Act and, **5:77–78**

line-item veto and, **8:**320

and national parks, **5:**549, 550

pairing in, **6:230**

party whip in, **8:468**

policy-making power of, **1:**21

presidential elections decided by, **3:**148, 152, 156, 171

printing needs of, **4:**24

and Reconstruction, **4:**236–237; **7:**59–61

resolutions of, **7:120–121**

and riders, legislative, **7:159**

role in foreign affairs, **3:**277–278

separation of powers and, **7:**312

spending power of, **3:**527–528

states sued by, **1:**120

Statutes at Large, **7:540–541**

statutory law by, **7:541**

steering committees in, **7:546–547**

Supreme Court and, relationship between, **8:**22

taxation power of, Supreme Court on, **5:**184

transportation regulation by, **4:**26

vetoes overridden by, **8:**321

war powers of, **8:**373–374, 387–388

women in, **5:**566; **8:**507, 517

See also House of Representatives; Senate

Congress of Industrial Organizations (CIO), **1:**151; **2:**227; **5:**8, 17

Amalgamated Clothing Workers of America in, **1:**132

anticommunist campaign against, **2:**225; **8:**278

communist activists and, **2:**326–327; **7:**17

establishment of, **1:**151; **8:**171, 268

ideology of, **1:**151

International Union of Mine, Mill, and Smelter Workers in, **4:**397

Memorial Day Massacre (1937), **5:307**

merger with AFL, **1:**151; **8:**172

political action committee created by, **6:**393

and racial discrimination, **3:**49

sit-down strikes by, **7:**371

Taft-Hartley Act and, **8:**42–43

and United Brotherhood of Carpenters and Joiners, **8:**262–263

and United Electrical, Radio, and Machine Workers of America, **3:**176

and United Steelworkers of America, **8:**277

and United Textile Workers, **8:**278

in World War II, **1:**151

See also American Federation of Labor–Congress of Industrial Organizations

Congress of Racial Equality (CORE), **2:**201, *354*, **354–355**

and Freedom Rides, **2:**354; **3:**15

political violence against, **1:**332

radicalism and, **7:**18

Congressional Budget and Impoundment Act (1974), **1:**229

Congressional Budget Office (CBO), **1:**555; **6:**165

Congressional districts. *See* Districts, congressional

Congressional Record, **2:**351, **355**; **4:**488

Congreve, Richard, **6:**423

Conkling, Mabel Viola Harris, **1:**308

Conkling, Roscoe, **3:**156, 157; **7:**517

Conley, Jim, **3:**453

Connally, Tom, **8:**272

Connally "Hot Oil" Act, **6:**303

Connecticut, **2:***355*, **355–359**

claims to western lands, **8:**455, 456

colonial assembly of, **1:**333; **2:**280

colonial charter of, **2:**281

in colonial era, **2:**357

emblems, nicknames, mottos, and songs of, **7:***532*

founding of, **2:**289; **5:**271

geography of, **2:**355–356

legal system of, Ludlow's Code and, **5:**170

in modern era, **2:**358–359

Native Americans in, **2:**356–357

Mohegan, **5:435**

and New York, boundary dispute between, **1:**521; **2:**355–356

prehistory of, **2:**356–357

statehood of, **2:**357–358

sumptuary laws in, **8:**17

temperance movements in, **8:**78

toll canals in, **8:**140

town government in, **8:**148

and Western Reserve, **8:**456

Connecticut, Cantwell v., **2:**167–168

Connecticut, Griswold v., **1:**6, 466, 468; **4:66–67**; **6:**479; **7:**192

Connecticut Compromise (Great Compromise), **2:**350, **359**, 380; **3:**170

Connecticut River, **7:**174

Connelie, Foley v., **1:**126

Connell, Bob, **3:**516

Conner, Dennis, **1:**172–173

Connerly, Ward, **6:**509

Connick, Charles, **1:**314

Connolly, James B., **6:**192

Connolly, John, **2:**360; **3:**77

Connolly, Richard (Slippery Dick), **7:**162

Connolly's Plot, **2:360**

Connor, Dennis, **7:**223

Connor, Eugene (Bull), **1:**104

Conquest of Canaan, The (Dwight), **5:**118

Conquistadores, **2:**360; **7:**206

Conrail, **6:**481; **8:**191

Conscience Whigs, **2:**360–361

Conscientious objectors, **2:**361–362; **6:**227, 269

"Consciousness revolution," **3:**528

Conscription Act (1863), **7**:571
Conscription and recruitment, **2**:362–365; **3**:222–223
  bounties for, **1**:524; **2**:211, 363
  in Civil War, **1**:274; **2**:210–211, 363–364, 530
    Confederate, **2**:340–341
    substitutes for, **7**:571
  dental standards in, **3**:4
  through militias, **5**:386
  mobilization, **5**:429–430
  muster day, **5**:504–505
  press gangs and, **6**:459
  in Vietnam War, **1**:278; **2**:532; **8**:352
  in World War II, **8**:543
Consensus history, **4**:139
Conservation, **2**:366–372
  vs. alternative energy, **3**:215
  under Antiquities Act, **1**:205–206
  in Bermuda, **1**:445
  botanical gardens and, **1**:517–518
  and environmental movement, **3**:226, 227
  eugenics and, **2**:370–371
  of forests, **3**:433–438
  of mammals, **5**:218
  in marine sanctuaries, **5**:244
  national park movement and, **5**:549–553
  and petroleum industry, **6**:304
  vs. preservation, **7**:355; **8**:479
  public land commissions and, **6**:531
  and public ownership, **6**:528
  Roosevelt (Theodore) and, **2**:366, 367, 368, 369; **3**:226; **8**:422–423, 480
  of sequoias, **7**:314
  by Tennessee Valley Authority, **8**:89
  terrorism and, **8**:424
  and tourism, **8**:146
  Weeks Act and, **8**:423, **437**
  Wisconsin progressivism and, **8**:492
  in Yellowstone National Park, **8**:579
  zoological parks and, **8**:594
  See also Environmental movement
Conservation biology, **2**:372–374
Conservatism, **2**:374–376
  American Enterprise Institute and, **8**:117–118
    anticommunism in, **1**:197
    and consumer movement, attacks on, **2**:384
    and criticism of welfare programs, **2**:228; **8**:442
    Heritage Foundation and, **8**:118
    laissez-faire, **2**:375
    National Review and, **5**:556
    New Right in, Viguerie on, **9**:495–499
    and Protestantism, **6**:516, 518
    Reader's Digest and, **7**:51
    See also Neoconservatism
Conspiracies Acts (1861 and 1862), **2**:376–377
Conspiracy, **2**:377–378
Constitution(s)
  Cherokee, **2**:*125*
  Confederate, **2**:340, *341*
  state (See also under specific states)
    after American Revolution, **7**:138
    bills of rights in, **1**:453–454; **3**:89
Constitution, U.S., **2**:345, **378–383**
  on admiralty law, **1**:23
  alien rights under, **1**:125, 126
  amendments to, **1**:456–457 (See also specific amendments)
  on amnesty power, **1**:177
  Annapolis Convention and, **1**:187; **9**:156–159
  Antifederalists on, **1**:200
  on appointing power, **1**:225
  on apportionment, **1**:227
  Article II, Section 3 of, **3**:278
  Articles of Confederation and, **1**:317
  Bill of Rights in, **1**:453, **454–457**
  on branches of federal government, **3**:341
  on capitation taxes, **2**:48
  checks and balances of, **2**:116–117
  on citizenship, **2**:180
  civil rights and liberties guaranteed by, **2**:198
  commerce clause in, **1**:549; **2**:310–312; **8**:274
  on Congress, **6**:453
    appropriations by, **1**:229–230
    implied powers of, **4**:246–247
    investigating committees of, **4**:410
    policy-making power of, **1**:21
    spending power of, **3**:527–528
    on Congressional mandate, **2**:350, 351
  contract clause in, **2**:107, **397**
  Declaration of Independence principles added to, **2**:523
  drafting of, **2**:378–381
  due process of law provisions in, **3**:88
  on enumerated powers, **3**:225
  on executive agreements, **3**:277
  Federalist Papers on, **3**:350
  on impeachment, **4**:234
  on inauguration, **4**:250
  inherent powers in, **4**:358
  on international law, **4**:393
  interpreting, **3**:342
  on interstate commerce, **4**:401
  on interstate compacts, **4**:403
  on judicial power, and administrative adjudication, **1**:22
  judicial review and, **4**:491–494; **5**:235
  on judiciary, **4**:498–499
  on jury trial, **4**:502
  on line-item veto power, **8**:320
  majority rule, **5**:212
  on membership denied by House of Representatives, **6**:441
  on military law, **5**:378
  military provisions in, **7**:146
  on national defense, **8**:373
  Native Americans under, **4**:264–265; **7**:247
  natural rights and, **6**:10
  opening phrase of, **2**:179–180
  on police power, **6**:387
  on president, **6**:453–454
  on privileges and immunities of citizens, **6**:481–482
  ratification of, **2**:381–382
    debate over, **9**:159–169
  Rhode Island's refusal to accept, **7**:152
  on Senate, **8**:243–244
  on separation of powers, **7**:312
  speech and debate provision of, **2**:352
  vs. state constitutions, **7**:525
  on subsidies, **7**:564
  on suffrage, **8**:4–5
  supremacy clause in, **2**:380
  on Supreme Court, **8**:22
  on taxation, **8**:55
  territories under, **4**:367

text of, **9:**169–178
on treason, **8:**193
on treaties, **8:**199, 203
on veto power, **8:**321
line-item, **8:**320
on vice presidency, **8:**322
on war powers, **8:**373–375, 387
Constitution (frigate), **1:**415, 508;
    2:378; **6:**24
Constitutional Convention (1787),
    2:345, 378–381; **7:**138
    Connecticut Compromise at,
        2:359
    electoral college created by, **3:**170
    Shays's Rebellion and, **5:**266; **7:**338
    on state representation, **2:**86, 350
Constitutional facts, **5:**473
Constitutional Procession (1788),
    5:566–567
Constitutional Union Party, **2:**383;
    3:154
Consular Service, **3:**428
Consulates, **3:**28
Consumer bankruptcy, **1:**410
Consumer cooperatives, **2:**406
Consumer credit, **2:**448–449
Consumer Federation of America,
    2:384
Consumer Information Bureau of
    Federal Communications Com-
    mission, **3:**340
Consumer price index (CPI), **2:**385,
    422; **3:**106; **6:**460
    distorting effects of, **2:**423–424
    and inflation, **4:**350
Consumer protection, **2:**383–385,
    388–389, 391–392
    Food and Drug Administration
        and, **3:**403–405
    governmental inspection for, **4:**363
    Nader and, **2:**384; **5:**509; **7:**18;
        8:285
    National Traffic and Motor Vehi-
        cle Safety Act (1966) and,
        5:561
    product tampering and, **6:**491–492
    and public interest law, **6:**530
    Pure Food and Drug Movement
        and, **6:**553–555
Consumer purchasing power,
    2:385–386; **6:**460
Consumerism, **2:**386–392
    advertising and, **1:**34; **2:**388,
        389–390

automobiles and, **5:**229
financial panic of 1893 and, **7:**128
installment sales and, **4:**364–365
liberated, **2:**391–392
marketing and, **5:**246–247
shopping malls and, **5:**215, 216
technology and, **2:**388, 392
transportation and, **2:**387
women's magazines and, **5:**198
Consumers Leagues, **2:**392
Consumption, business cycles and,
    1:582
Containerization, in shipping, **5:**320
Containment policy, **2:**268; **3:**426;
    7:212
    Kennan on, **9:**411–413
    "X" article and, **8:**569
Contempt of Congress, **2:**392–393
Conti, Pietro, **8:**244
Continental Army. *See* Army, Conti-
    nental
Continental Association, **1:**340
    text of, **9:**123–126
Continental Congress, **2:**344, 378,
    393–395
    Articles of Confederation by,
        1:317; **2:**344; **7:**140
    Conway Cabal at, **2:**403
    debts incurred by, **2:**516, 518
    Delaware delegates at, **2:**541
    First (1774), **2:**393; **7:**135, 139
        Coercive Acts and, **2:**284, 287
        "Continental Association" by,
            1:340
            text of, **9:**123–126
        "Declaration and Resolves" by,
            text of, **9:**132–134
        and Declaration of Rights, **2:**523
        and foreign relations, **2:**394–395
        French assistance to, **7:**147
        and Galloway's plan of union,
            3:504–505
        in Philadelphia, **6:**277, 312
        and provincial congresses, **6:**520
        record of proceedings, **4:**488
        and Seal of the United States, **3:**99
    Second (1775), **2:**393–394; **7:**139
        address to Canadians by, text of,
            9:134–135
        and Articles of Confederation,
            2:344; **7:**140
        and Declaration of Indepen-
            dence, **2:**520–523

Olive Branch Petition by,
    6:190–191
states' claims to western lands and,
    8:455
Continuous-roll press, *6:*468, 469
Contra aid, **2:**395
    in Iran-Contra Affair, **4:**419–420
Contraband of war, **2:**396
    Plan of 1776 and, **6:**361
    slaves as, **2:**395–396
        Butler's report on, **9:**294–296
Contraception. *See* Birth control
Contract(s)
    arbitration in, **1:**237
    liberty of, **5:**394–395, 472–473
    Supreme Court on, **3:**382
Contract clause, **2:**397
    Minnesota moratorium case and,
        5:401
Contract labor, foreign, **2:**397–398
Contract with America (Republican
    Party), **2:**384, **398**; **3:**485;
    7:114; **8:**442
Contractors, government
    discrimination by, **1:**35–36
    set-asides for, **7:**315–316
    standards for work by, **8:**368
Contrast, The (Tyler), **8:**113
Convention Against Torture (CAT),
    7:81
Convention of 1800, **1:**124; **2:**398
Convention of 1818, **2:**398
    and fishing privileges, **2:**261
Convention of 1818 with England,
    and Northwest Angle, **6:**136
Convention of Miramar, **5:**345
Convention on the Elimination of
    All Forms of Discrimination
    Against Women, **2:**398–399
Conventions, party nominating,
    2:399–401; **3:**148, 152;
    6:113–114
    vs. caucus, **2:**76
    and unit rule, **6:**113; **8:**260
*Conversations with Children on the
    Gospels* (Alcott), **8:**180
Convict labor systems, **2:**401–402,
    402
    chain gangs, *2:*99, **99–100**
Convoys, **2:**402–403, *403*
Conway, Thomas, **2:**403
Conway Cabal, **2:**403
Coode, John, **6:**512
Cook, Flora, **3:**116

Cook, Frederick Albert, **6:**382

Cook, George Cram, **6:**519

Cook, James, **2:***404*
  companion ship to, **3:**46
  explorations of, **2:**403–404; **8:**453
    in Aleutian Islands, **1:**121
    in Hawaii, **4:**105
    Polar, **6:**382

Cook books, **3:**398, 399

Cooke, Jay, **1:**404
  and financing of Civil War, **2:**215
  investment bank firm of,
    2:404–405

Cooke, Morris L., **7:**281

Cooke, Morris Llewellyn, **3:**211

Cooke, Philip St. George, **8:**363

Cooke, Terence Cardinal, **8:**340

Cookery. *See* Food and cuisines

Cooley, Denton, **1:**463

Cooley v. Board of Wardens of Port of Philadelphia, **2:**310, **405**

Coolidge, Calvin
  advertising and, **1:**33
  agrarianism of, **1:***57*
  and bonus payments to veterans,
    1:499
  Boston police strike and, **1:**513
  and Garvey (Marcus), pardon of,
    1:478
  Geneva Conference (1927) called
    by, **3:**534
  in presidential campaign of 1920,
    3:161
  in presidential campaign of 1924,
    3:161; **8:**323
  and Republican Party, **7:**113
  special prosecutors under, **7:**495
  and Treasury, **8:**197

Coolidge, Grace, **3:**376

Coolidge, William D., **3:**175; **5:**24, 108

"Cooling-off" treaties, **5:**428

Coontz, Stephanie, **3:**317

Co-op programs, educational,
  3:122–123

Cooper, Charles, **2:**485

Cooper, James Fenimore, **2:**375;
  3:197, 434; **5:**118–119, 129;
  8:288
  Battle of Lake Erie by, **6:**290–291
  The Deerslayer, **5:**70
  *History of the Navy of the United
    States of America* by, **6:**290
  The Last of the Mohicans, **5:**70, 119

Leatherstocking Tales, **5:**70, 119;
  8:457, 479
  The Pathfinder, **5:**70, 119
  The Pioneers, **5:**70, 119
  The Prairie, **5:**70, 119

Cooper, John A., **1:**263

Cooper, John Sherman, **8:**394

Cooper, Kenneth H., **1:**35

Cooper, Leon, **6:**337, 346

Cooper, Peter, **2:**405; **5:**142; **6:**317;
  7:30

Cooper, Thomas, **1:**124; **6:**456

Cooper, United States v., **6:**456

Cooper Union for the Advancement
  of Science and Art, **2:***405*,
  405–406

Cooperative Forest Management
  Act (1950), **3:**432

Cooperative Forestry Assistance Act
  (1978), **3:**432

Cooperatives
  consumers', **2:**406
  farmers', **2:406–408**
    Capper-Volstead Act and, **2:**50
  tobacco, **2:**408

Coosuc, **6:**56

Coote, Richard, **6:**359

Coover, Robert, **5:**122

COPE. *See* Committee on Political
  Education

Cope, Edward D., **1:**167; **7:**270

Copeland, E. J., **3:**182; **7:**78

Copland, Aaron, **5:**492

Coplay (Pennsylvania), **2:**79

Copley, John Singleton, **1:**294–295;
  3:197

Coppage v. Kansas, **2:**408; **8:**578

Copper imports, from Latin America, **5:**45

Copper industry, **2:408–410,** *409;*
  6:114, 115
  Anaconda Copper in, **1:180**
  in Arizona, **1:**257
  metalwork, **5:**329
  in Michigan, **5:**355
  in Montana, **5:**449–450; **6:**115
  in Utah, **6:**115; **8:**297

Copperheads, **2:**218, **411;** **4:**540;
  6:136

Coppinger, William, **1:**148

Coppola, Francis Ford, **3:**364

Copway, George
  *The Life, History, and Travels of
    Kah-ge-ga-gah-bowh*, **5:**128

The Ojibway Conquest, **5:**128

Copyright, **2:411–412; 6:**256, 507
  functions of, **4:**375
  magazines and, **5:**191
  of music, **5:**502–503
  protection of
    domestic, **6:**537
    international, **6:**537
    and publishing industry, **6:**536,
     537
  registration of, **5:**100–101
  See also Trademarks

Coral Sea, Battle of, **1:**90;
  2:412–413

Corbett, Gail Sherman, **1:**308

Corbin, Abel Rathbone, **1:**472

Corbusier, Charles-Édouard Jean-
  neret Le, **8:**286

CORE. *See* Congress of Racial
  Equality

Corfield v. Coryell, **6:**482

Cori, Carl F., **1:**461

Cori, Gerty Radnitz, **1:**461

Corliss, George, **8:**108

Corn, **2:***413,* **413–414,** *414*
  Indian cultivation of, **1:**68–69;
    4:307
  storage of, **3:**187

Corn Belt, **2:**413, **414–415**

Corn borer, European, **2:**415

Corneal transplantation, **8:**183

Cornell, Ezra, **2:**415; **5:**28; **8:**456

Cornell University, **2:415–416**
  African American Studies at, **1:**46
  engineering program at, **3:**216, 217
  establishment of, **3:**115
  as land-grant college, **5:**28

Corning, Erastus, **1:**113

Corning Glass Works, **3:**357; **4:**4

Cornish, Samuel, **5:**199; **6:**96

Cornwallis, Charles, Lord
  in Battle of Camden, **2:**19
  in Battle of Cowpens, **2:**444
  in Battle of Guilford Courthouse,
    4:72; **6:**128
  in Battle of Princeton, **6:**464
  and College of William and Mary,
    occupation of, **8:**483
  correspondence with Washington,
    9:152
  invading North Carolina, **6:**128
  in southern campaigns, **7:**472
  surrender of, **7:**145; **8:**582, *582*
  vs. Washington, **2:**543

in Yorktown Campaign, **8**:581–582
defeat of, **3**:473; **6**:94
Coronado, Francisco Vázquez de, **2**:1, 360; **3**:285, 296
expeditions of, **1**:256; **2**:*416, 416–417*
to Cibola, **2**:173; **8**:451
Great Plains, **4**:56
in Kansas, **4**:508
in New Mexico, **6**:66
in Rocky Mountains, **7**:190
in Texas, **8**:99
Coronary heart disease, **5**:105
Corporate crime, **2**:461–462
Corporation for Public Broadcasting (CPB), and National Public Radio, **5**:554
Corporations, **1**:580; **2**:417–420
accounting practices of, scandals surrounding, **2**:419
and business forecasting, **1**:586–588
vs. cooperatives, **2**:407
debt of, **2**:42
downsizing by, **3**:83
as interest groups, **4**:380
mergers and acquisitions in, **5**:322–323
municipal, constitutions of, **2**:111–112
vs. trade unions, **2**:275
Corregidora (Jones), **5**:126
Corrigan, Truax v., **8**:230
Corrupt bargain, **2**:420
in presidential campaign of 1824, **5**:555
Corruption, political, **2**:420–421
Baker case, **1**:385
Black Horse cavalry and, **1**:475
bosses and bossism, **1**:507–508
in California, **2**:10
in city councils, **2**:182
Crédit Mobilier of America and, **2**:452–453
Ferguson (James), **3**:354; **8**:103
in Korea-gate, **4**:542–543
Mulligan letters and, **5**:473
municipal government and, **5**:475, 477
municipal reform and, **5**:478
Pendergast machine and, **6**:274–275
political machines, **5**:186–187
in post–Civil War era, **2**:206
in Prohibition era, **1**:504
rings and, **7**:162

Tammany Hall and, **8**:46
Teamsters Union, **8**:172
Teapot Dome oil scandal, **8**:63
Tweed Ring, **1**:*508*; **7**:162; **8**:46, **242**
Whiskey Ring, **8**:470
Corso, Gregory, **1**:433
Cortelyou, George B., **3**:366
Corte-Real, Gaspar, **3**:283
Cortés, Hernán (Hernando), **2**:360; **3**:203, 284, 294
and colonial administration, **2**:278
Corwin, Edward S., **6**:403
Coryell, Corfield v., **6**:482
Cosa, Juan de la, **5**:232
Cosby, William, **2**:292; **6**:83, 95; **8**:589, 590
Cosmetic surgery, **2**:421–422
breast implants, **1**:533
Cosmographia (Munster), **9**:*6*, 6–7
Cosmopolitan (magazine), **5**:198
Cost of living, **2**:422–424
Cost of living index. *See* Consumer price index
Costa Rica
Bryan-Chamorro Treaty and, **1**:550
Nicaraguan contras in, **2**:395
Costello, Frank, **2**:463
Cost-of-Living Adjustment (COLA), **2**:424
Cott, Nancy, **8**:520
Cotton, **2**:424–428
confiscated, **2**:*425*
in foreign trade, **8**:164
in Georgia, **3**:555, 556
in industrial revolution, **4**:343–344, 345
as "king," **4**:526
in Louisiana, **6**:364
manufacturing, **2**:426–427, *427*
mechanical pickers for, **1**:59
Native American cultivation of, **1**:68
plantations, **6**:363, 364–365
production, **2**:424–426, *426*
in Black Belt, **1**:471
boll weevil invasion and, **1**:495
Confederate States of America and, **2**:342
limits on, **1**:396
rise of, **1**:63; **7**:393, 463
and sharecroppers, **6**:365
and slavery, **1**:48; **6**:364; **7**:393

in Texas, **8**:101
Cotton, John, **1**:205, 431, 449; **7**:95; **8**:116
Spiritual Milk for Boston Babes, **5**:127
Cotton Futures Act (1914), **1**:71
Cotton gin, **2**:427, **428–429**; **3**:555; **6**:364; **8**:109
invention of, **2**:387, 425
and cotton production, **1**:63
and slavery, **1**:48; **7**:393
Cotton Kingdom, **2**:429
Cotton money, **2**:429–430
Cotton Oil Trust, **4**:26
Cotton Whigs, **2**:361
Couch, W. L., **1**:501
Coughlin, Charles E., **2**:375; **3**:208; **7**:16
anti-Semitism of, **1**:207; **3**:327, 328
National Union for Social Justice organized by, **5**:563
Coughlin, Paula A., **8**:44
Coulter, Ernest K., **1**:452
Coulthard, Alfred, **3**:176
Council for New England, **2**:111, **430**
Council for Tobacco Research, **8**:136
Council of Economic Advisors (CEA), **2**:430–432; **3**:110, 307, 330
Council of National Defense, **2**:432
War Industries Board and, **8**:380
Council of Revision, New York, **2**:433
Council of Trent, **8**:309
Council on Environmental Quality (CEQ), **3**:330
Global Energy Futures and the Carbon Dioxide Problem by, **4**:6–8
Counsel, right to, **3**:575–576
Counterculture, **2**:433, *433*
hippies in, **4**:134
Counterfeiting, **2**:433–434
Counterintelligence Program (COINTELPRO), **2**:265–266; **3**:338
Country clubs, **2**:251; **4**:19–20
Country music, **5**:493–494
African American folklore and, **3**:395
bluegrass, **5**:490–491
honky-tonk girls and, **4**:159
See also Cowboy songs; Nashville

Country Party, **6:**83
Country store, **2:434–436,** *435, 436*
Country-dancing, **5:**495
County, **6:**406
County and state fairs, **2:436,** *437*
County government, **2:436–439**
  home rule by, **4:**153
County of Allegheny v. ACLU Greater
    Pittsburgh Chapter, **2:**166
Courier services, **2:439–440**
  See also Postal Service, U.S.
Cournand, André, **2:**53
Cournot, August, **5:**444–445
Court(s)
  juvenile, **2:**137, 146, 149, 461
  small claims, **2:**339
Court of Commerce, **2:309–310**
Court of Industrial Relations, Wolff
    Packing Company v., **8:495**
Court of Private Land Claims, **5:**26
Court packing. *See under* Supreme
    Court
Court Party, **6:**83
Courtship
  bundling, **1:569**
  among Native Americans, **8:**435
  among slaves, **8:**436
Courts-martial, **2:440**
  in military law, **5:**379–380
Coutume de Paris, **2:440**
Couturier, Henri, **1:**294
Covenant, Church, **2:440–441**
  New England Way and, **6:**50
  New Haven Colony and, **6:**60
Covenanters, **6:**450–451
Covered wagon, **2:441,** *441;* **8:**463
Covert, Reid v., **3:**272
Covert (black) propaganda, **6:**503
Coverture, women under, **5:**249, 252
  See also Marriage
Covey, James, **1:**176
Cow towns, **2:442**
  Abilene (Kansas), **1:**2; **2:**75, 158,
    442
  Dodge City (Kansas), **2:**158; **3:**69
Cowboy(s), **2:***443,* **443–444,** *495*
  and cattle drives, **2:**74–75
  honky-tonk girls and, **4:**159
  Remington's images of, **7:***100*
  and rodeos, **2:**444; **7:***191,* **191–192**
  trail drivers, **8:**176
  work of, **4:**157
Cowboy songs, **2:442–443**
Cowboys and Skinners, **2:444**

Cowens, Dave, **1:**425
Cowles, Henry Chandler, **1:**520
Cowley, Malcolm, **6:**76
  The Literary Situation, **5:**121
  on Lost Generation, **5:**157
Cowpens, Battle of, **2:444**
Cox, Archibald, **1:**507; **7:**495
  in Watergate investigation, **8:**427
Cox, Harvey, **5:**432
  The Secular City, **5:**93
Cox, James M., **3:**161; **6:**174
Cox Committee, **6:**318
Coxey, Jacob, **2:**444; **6:**417
Coxey's Army, **2:444–445**
  Kelly's Industrial Army and, **4:**516
Coyle v. Smith, **3:**202
Coyote (animal), **2:445**
COYOTE (Call Off Your Old Tired
    Ethics), **6:**514
CPB. *See* Corporation for Public
    Broadcasting
CPC. *See* Cumberland Presbyterian
    Church
CPCA. *See* Cumberland Presbyter-
    ian Church of America
CPI. *See* Committee on Public
    Information; Consumer price
    index
CPPA. *See* Conference for Progres-
    sive Political Action
CPUSA. *See* Communist Party, USA
Crackers, **3:**386
"Cradle of Liberty, The." *See*
    Faneuil Hall
Craft, Ellen, **9:**272–274
Craft, William, *Running a Thousand*
    Miles for Freedom, excerpt from,
    9:272–274
Craft apprenticeship, **1:**228
Crafts, Hannah, *Bondwoman's Narra-*
    tive, **5:**124
Craftsman (Mission) style furniture,
    3:497
Craig, Charles F., **5:**294
Craig, Hiram, **2:**446
Craig v. Boren, **2:445–446; 3:**246
Craig v. State of Missouri, **1:**540;
    2:446
Cram, Ralph Adams, **1:**313–314
Cramer, Stuart, **1:**74
Cramer v. United States, **8:**194
Cramp v. Board of Public Instruction of
    Orange County, Florida, **8:**62
Crandall, Luciean S., **8:**245

Crandall v. Nevada, **6:**297
Crane, Frederick, **1:**468
Crane, H. R., **6:**342
Crane, Hart, **5:**157
Crane, Stephen, **3:**280
  The Red Badge of Courage, **5:**119
Crawford, Adair, **6:**148
Crawford, Thomas, **1:**305
Crawford, William H.
  caucus supporting, **6:**113
  in presidential campaign of 1816,
    3:151
  in presidential campaign of 1824,
    3:152, 171
Cray, Seymour, **2:**338
Crazy Horse (Sioux leader), **1:**475;
    7:370, 371
  in Battle of Little Bighorn, **8:**404
Crazy Snake (Creek leader), **2:**506
Crazy Tennesseans (Smoky Moun-
    tain Boys), **5:***491*
CRC. *See* Christian Reformed
    Church
Creationism, **2:446–447**
  vs. evolutionism, **3:**270
  geology and, **3:**549
  in school curriculum, **7:**284
  science and, **7:**271
Credibility gap, **2:447**
Credit, **2:447–451,** *448*
  automobile industry and use of,
    2:389
  bills of, **1:458**
    Supreme Court on, **2:**446
  bills of exchange, **3:273–274**
  consumer, **2:**448–449
  democratization of, savings banks
    and, **1:**407
  installment, **2:**449–450; **4:**364–365
  intermediate credit banks,
    4:384–385
  producer, **2:**447–448
Credit card(s), **2:**450, **451–452;**
    3:368; **4:**365
  automobile industry and introduc-
    tion of, **2:**389
  debt, rise in, **1:**410; **2:**452
  and direct mail, **3:**29
Crédit Mobilier of America,
    2:452–453
Credit Union National Association
    (CUNA), **2:**453, 454
Credit unions, **2:453–454**
Cree, **2:***454,* **454–455;** **8:**218

Creek Confederation, in Alabama, **1**:101–102
Creek Indians, **2**:*455*, **455–456**; **8**:225
  adaptation of, **8**:226
  in American Revolution, **4**:330
  Bowles's filibustering expeditions and, **1**:525
  in Everglades, **3**:268
  in Georgia, **3**:554
  in Oklahoma, **8**:239
  in Tennessee, **8**:84–85
  trade with, **6**:244
  war with Chickasaw Indians, **2**:135–136
Creek War, **2**:456; **7**:8
  backwoodsmen and, **1**:382
  end of, **1**:102
  Massacre at Fort Mims, **5**:389
  Natchez Campaign of 1813, **5**:518
Creel, George, **2**:313; **6**:98, 503; **8**:535
CREF. *See* College Retirement Equities Fund
Cremation, **2**:81, 511–512; **3**:486
Creole slave case, **2**:457
Creoles and creolization, **2**:*457*, **457–458**; **5**:158, 159, 160
  in Spanish America, **5**:50
Cresson, Margaret French, **1**:308
Crèvecoeur, Fort, **5**:2
Crèvecoeur, J. Hector St. John de, **1**:62, 136, 337; **6**:373
Crew, in college athletics, **2**:276
Cribb, Tom, **6**:483
Crick, Francis, **3**:67–68, 529, 533
Crim, William H., **2**:272
Crime, **2**:458–462
  bootlegging and, **1**:504
  in Central Park, **2**:94
  of conspiracy, **2**:377–378
  counterfeiting as, **2**:434
  in Detroit, **3**:20
  hate (*See* Hate crimes)
  juvenile, **1**:26; **4**:504–506
  organized, **2**:462–464
    Apalachin Conference (1957), **1**:222
    FBI against, **3**:338
    federal measures against, **2**:377
    legislation on, **6**:212–213
    Mafia incident, **5**:191
    Prohibition and, **3**:60
    prostitution and, **6**:513

  publications on, Son-of-Sam Law and, **7**:448–449
  rates in 20th century, **2**:459–460
  robberies, **7**:182–183
  statutes of limitations on, **7**:541
  tools for fighting, **3**:185
  white-collar, **2**:461–462
  See also Punishment
"Crime Against Kansas" speech, Sumner's, excerpt from, **9**:288–292
Crime Control and Law Enforcement Act (1994), Megan's Law (1996), **5**:306
Crime of 1873, **2**:464; **3**:458
Criminal law policy, changes in, **2**:460–462
Criner, Greg, **7**:*18*
Crippen, Robert L., **7**:482
Cripple Creek mining boom, **2**:464; **4**:11
Cripple Creek strikes, **2**:464–465; **8**:454
Crisis, The (magazine), **5**:200; **6**:104
Critical theory, **3**:454
Crittenden, John J., **2**:383, 465
Crittenden, William, **2**:469
Crittenden Compromise, **1**:505; **2**:465
Croatan Island, **7**:47
Croatia. *See* Yugoslavia
Croce, Jim, **1**:388
Crocker, Chester, **7**:452
Crocker, Richard, **6**:79
Crockett, David (Davy), **1**:107; **2**:74
  in folklore, **3**:394; **8**:45
  on logrolling, **5**:146
  as national hero, **5**:567
Croghan, George, **4**:313
  and land companies, **5**:35
Croker, Richard, **8**:46
Croll, James, **3**:552
Croly, David G., **6**:424
Croly, Herbert, **6**:70, 76, 424, 495
Croly, Jane Cunningham, **3**:526; **8**:510
Cromartie, Easley v., **3**:62
Cromwell, Oliver, and colonial policy, **2**:285
Cromwell, William, **6**:237
Croner, Ted, **1**:301
Cronin, Thomas, **1**:533
Cronkite, Walter, **7**:20; **8**:44
Crook, George, **1**:221, 475

Crook, United States ex rel. Standing Bear v., **8**:224
Crooks, Ramsay, **1**:158
Crosland, Alan, **4**:470
Cross, Christopher, **7**:361
Cross of Gold speech, **1**:459; **2**:400, **465**, 551; **3**:458
Crossley, Archibald, **6**:409, 533–534
Croton Aqueduct, **8**:240
Crow dance, **6**:444
Crow Dog, **3**:271
Crow Dog, Mary, **8**:177
Crow Indians, **2**:466, *466*; **8**:218
  Fort Laramie Treaty with, text of, **9**:227–229
Crowell, Benedict, **8**:379
Crowell v. Benson, **1**:22
Crowley, Leo T., **5**:82
Crown Heights riots, **2**:466–467
Crowninshield, Sturges v., **7**:562
Crozat, Antoine, **2**:262; **5**:158
Crozier, William B., **6**:202
Crude oil
  fractions of, **6**:301
  Native Americans using, **6**:298, 305
Cruikshank, George, **1**:129; **2**:308
Cruikshank, United States v., **6**:297; **8**:273
Cruisers, **8**:407–408
Crum, Denny, **1**:425
Crumbling Idols (Garland), **6**:12
Crummell, Alexander, **1**:477; **6**:235, 236
Crump, Edward, **1**:507
Cruzan, Nancy, **7**:160
Cruzan v. Director, Missouri Department of Health, **3**:263
Cryonics, **3**:486
Cryptology, **2**:467–468
Crystal Hall, **8**:*310*
Crystal Palace Exhibition, **2**:468, *469*; **8**:558
  elevator demonstration at, **3**:186
Crystallography, **5**:391
Crystals, **6**:345
CSA. *See* Community Services Administration
C-SPAN, **2**:353
Cuba, **2**:468–473
  attempted annexation of, **1**:188–189; **7**:484
  Bay of Pigs invasion of, **1**:430–431; **2**:55, 470–471

Cuba, (*continued*)
  under Castro, **2:**470
  CIA operations in, **2:**92
  confiscation of American-owned
    property in, **2:**347
  embargo against, **8:**173
  filibuster armies targeting, **3:**359
  Elián González case and, **2:**472;
    4:21
  immigration from, to Florida,
    5:351
  Maine sinking in, **5:**211
  Mariel boatlift from, **5:**238–239
  migratory accords with, **2:**55
  Operation Mongoose in, **2:**471
  in Organization of American
    States, **6:**211
  Ostend Manifesto on, **1:**189; **6:**219
  Platt Amendment and, **2:**470; **4:**69;
    6:369
  as protectorate, **1:**189
  refugees from, **2:***471*, 472, 473
  revolution in, **2:**54–55
  Santería in, **7:**249–250
  Spanish rule in, **2:**469–470
  in Spanish-American War, **7:**484,
    485–486
  struggle for independence,
    2:469–470
  Treaty of Paris (1763) and, **6:**248
  Treaty of Paris (1898) and, **3:**360;
    6:250; **8:**201
  U.S. acquisition efforts, **2:**469
  U.S. blockade of (1962), **1:**487
  U.S. imperialism in, **4:**243
  U.S. military occupation of (1898-
    1902), **2:**54
  U.S. relations with, **5:**47, 48, 50
    in Cuban missile crisis, **1:**271,
      430; **2:**55, 269, 471,
      474–475, *475*
    Elián González case and, **4:**21
    Good Neighbor policy and, **4:**22
    Guantánamo Bay and, **4:**69
    Teller Amendment, **8:**78
  Voice of America in, **8:**351
  yellow journalism and, **8:**577
Cuban Americans, **2:***473,* **473–474**
  and Elián González case, **4:**21
  in Florida, **3:**388
    Miami, **2:**473; **5:**351–352; **8:**291
  in New Jersey, **6:**64
  number of, **4:**134
  as political exiles, **6:**397

Cuban missile crisis, **1:**430; **2:**55,
    269, 471, **474–475,** *475*
  and arms control, **1:**271
Cubism, **2:**475–476; **6:**471
CUC. *See* Computer Usage Corpo-
    ration
Cudahy Packers, **5:**135
Cuffe, Paul, **1:**48, 147; **2:**296; **6:**234
Cugnot, Nicolas J., **8:**230
Cugoano, Ottobah, **6:**234
Cullen, Countee, **4:***97;* **5:**125
Cullen, Michael, **7:**125
Culpeper, John, **2:**476
Culpeper's Rebellion, **2:**476
Cult of domesticity, **8:**326
Cults, **2:**476–478; **7:**94; **8:**303
  Jonestown Massacre, **4:**488, *488;*
    8:339
  Waco Siege, **8:**359
Cultural homogenization, **1:**446
Cultural imperialism, mass media
    and, **5:**261
Cultural literacy, **2:**478–479
Cultural pluralism, **1:**337, 338;
    6:375–376
Cultural rebellion of 1960s, **1:**433
Cultural regionalism, **7:**297–298
Cultural relativism, **1:**192–193
Culture
  American Studies on, **1:**168–171
  American vs. European, **5:**365
  anthropology and ethnology on,
    1:191–195
  biology and, **1:**194
  middlebrow, **5:**365–366
  multiculturalism, **5:**473–474
  See also Folklore; Popular culture
*Culture and Democracy in the United
    States* (Kallen), **6:**375
"Culture industry," **3:**454
Culture of Narcissism, The (Lasch),
    6:429
Cumberland, Army of the, **2:**479
Cumberland Gap, **1:**562; **2:**479;
    6:254; **8:**478
  and westward migration, **8:**461
Cumberland Plateau, **8:**83
Cumberland Presbyterian Church
    (CPC), **6:**451
Cumberland Presbyterian Church of
    America (CPCA), **6:**451
Cumberland River, **2:**479
Cumberland Road, **2:**479–480;
    6:433; **7:**177, 181; **8:**186–187

Cumberland settlements, **2:**480
Cuming, Alexander, **8:**85
*Cumming v. School Board of Education
    of Richmond County, Georgia,*
    3:115
cummings, e. e., **5:**120, 157
Cummings v. Missouri, **2:**480; **8:**96
Cummins, Albert B., **8:**185
CUNA. *See* Credit Union National
    Association
Cunningham, Imogen, **1:**301
Cunningham, Merce, **2:***497,* 499
Cunningham, Sumner A., **8:**264, 318
Cunningham, Winfield Scott, **8:**365
CUNY. *See* City University of New
    York
Curie, Irène, **6:**340, 341
Curlett, Murray v., **1:**347
Curley, James Michael, **1:**510
Curran, James, **1:**15
Currency Act (1764), **4:**25
Currency and coinage, **2:**480–482;
    5:75–76
  American eagle on, **3:**100
  during American Revolution,
    7:148
  bimetallism, **1:**458–460; **4:**14
  check, **2:**114–115
  during Civil War, **7:**118
  in Confederate States of America,
    2:434
  in Confederation period, **2:**345
  cotton money, **2:**429–430
  devaluation of, **3:**21–22
  dollar sign, **3:**71–72
  doubloon, **3:**82
  euro, **3:**261
  free silver, **3:**458–459; **4:**10
  gold standard (*See* Gold standard)
  greenbacks (*See* Greenbacks)
  Hamilton on, **4:**90
  hard money policies, **2:**550; **4:**93
  "In God We Trust" on, **4:**249
  liberty-cap cent, **5:**97
  money, **5:**438–442
  pieces of eight, **6:**351
  pine tree shilling, **6:**357
  proclamation money, **6:**490
  regulation of, litigation on, **8:**310
  silver
    Democratic Party on, **7:**344–345,
      362–363
    legislation on, **7:**344–345,
      363–364

specie circular, **7:497**
specie payments, **7:497–499**
trade dollar, **8:158**
Current History (periodical), **6:**90
Curriculum, **2:482–483**
  McGuffey's Readers, **5:**185
  multiculturalism and, **5:473–474**
Currie, Lauchlin, **3:**110
Currie, William, **2:**235
Currier, Charles, **2:**484
Currier, Nathaniel, **2:**484; **6:**470
Currier and Ives, **2:483–484**
  The Mississippi in Time of Peace,
    2:483
*Currie's Administrators v. Mutual
  Assurance Society,* **6:**10
Curry, John Steuart, **1:**298; **7:**297
Curtice, Cooper, **8:**320
Curtis, Benjamin R., on commerce
  clause, **2:**310, 405
Curtis, Charles, **3:**162
Curtis, Cyrus H. K., **1:**32; **7:**252
Curtis, Edward S., **1:***68, 100,* 299,
  314
Curtis, Edwin U., **7:**557
Curtis, G. G., **3:**174
Curtis, James L., **1:**166
Curtiss, Glenn, **1:**92
*Curtiss-Wright Export Corporation,
  United States v.,* **8:**198, 388
Curzon Line, **8:**573
Cushing, Caleb, and land specula-
  tion, **5:**36
Cushing, Frank Hamilton, "My
  Adventures in Zuni," **8:**599
Cushing, Harvey W., **6:**349
Cushing's Treaty (1842), **2:**484;
  4:515; **5:**462
Cushman, Robert, **5:**317
Custer, George Armstrong, **5:***131*
  in Battle of Little Bighorn, **1:**354,
    453, 475; **5:**131–132;
    7:370–371
  expedition to Black Hills, **1:**474;
    3:300
  uniform of, **8:**257
Custer Died for Your Sins (Deloria),
  2:484–485
Custis, George Washington Parke,
  8:274
Custis, Peter, **3:**297, 298; **8:**453
Customs Service, U.S., **2:485–486**
  drug enforcement by, **5:**512
Cutting, Bronson, **2:**84

Cuyahoga River, **3:**228, 232
CWA. *See* Civil Works Administra-
  tion; Clean Water Act; Coali-
  tion for Women's Appoint-
  ments; Communications Work-
  ers of America
Cyanide process of gold separation,
  4:11
Cybernetics, **2:486**
Cyberspace, **8:**350
Cyborgs, **2:486**
Cyclical unemployment, **8:**252
"Cyclone" dust collector, **3:**390
Cyclones, **3:**42; **4:**197
Cyclotron, **2:486–487**, *487;* **6:**338
Czech Republic, creation of, **2:**91
Czechoslovakia
  after Cold War, **2:**91
  Prague Spring in, **2:**90
  in Siberian expedition, **7:**353
  Soviet intervention in, **2:**269
  in World War II, **2:**89
Czechs, immigration to U.S., **2:**89
Czolgosz, Leon, **1:**181, 328–329;
  2:84, 227

D

D Day, **2:507–508**, *508;* **6:**118–120,
  119; **8:**549
  casualties on, **6:**120
  Navy in, **6:**26
  use of gliders on, **4:**5
Daboll, Nathan, **1:**129
Dabrowski, Joseph, **6:**391
Dadd, George H., **8:**319
Daddy's Roommate (Willhoite), **1:**500
Dade, Francis, **8:**401
Dagenhart, Hammer v., **2:**140, 142,
  149, 311; **3:**308
Daguerre, Louis-Jacques-Mandé,
  1:299; **6:**328
Daguerreotype, **1:**299; **6:**328–329
  See also Photography
Dagyr, John Adam, **1:**502
Dahl, Robert A., **6:**376
Dahlgren, John A., **1:**319
Daimler, Gottlieb, **1:**366
Dairy industry, **2:**72, 73, **489–492**
  in Vermont, **8:**314
  in Wisconsin, **2:**489, 490; **8:**491
Dairy products, per capita consump-
  tion of, **2:***492*

Dakota. *See* Sioux
Dakota expeditions, of Sibley and
  Sully, **2:492–493**
Dakota Territory, **2:**493; **6:**132;
  8:564
  establishment of, **7:**459
Dale, Chester, **5:**539
Dale, James, **1:**527
Daley, Richard J., **1:**507; **2:**133, 135;
  5:187, *187;* **7:**165
Daley, Richard M., **2:**133
Dali, Salvador, **1:**310
Dalkon Shield, **1:**469; **2:493–494**
  protests against, **2:**493, 494
Dallas (Texas), **2:**494, **494–495**, *495;*
  8:103
Dallas, Alexander
  and tariffs, **8:**50
  and taxation, **8:**56
Dallas, George M., **3:**153
Dallas (TV show), **7:**409
Dalton (Georgia), **2:**58
Dalton, John C., Jr., **6:**348–349
Daly, Marcus, **1:**180; **5:**449
Daly, Mary, **5:**93
Dam(s)
  beaver-engineered, **1:**434
  Bonneville Dam, **4:**201; **8:**414
  building of, **4:**200–201, 435
  collapses of, **3:**36
  environmental problems with,
    4:201–202, 436
  Grand Coulee Dam, **4:**200–201;
    8:414
  Hoover Dam, **4:161–162**, *162*
  hydroelectric power from,
    4:199–203
  for irrigation, **4:**435
  on Mississippi River, **5:**417
  on Missouri River, **5:**426
  in reclamation of arid lands, **7:**56
  in Yosemite National Park, contro-
    versy over, **2:**368–369
  See also Hydroelectric power
Dame schools, **2:**138, **495–496**;
  3:112
Damien, Father (Joseph De
  Veuster), **5:**83
"Damn the Torpedoes," **2:496**
Dana, Charles A., **1:**137; **3:**204
  on Godkin (E. L.), **5:**521
Dana, Francis, **3:**255; **7:**210
Dana, James Dwight, **5:**390

Dana, Richard Henry, *Two Years Before the Mast*, **3**:86, 383
Danbury Hatters' Case, **2**:228, **496**
Dance, **2**:496–499, *497, 498, 499*
 African American, **2**:497
 Alvin Ailey Dance Theater, **1**:131
 ballet, **1**:389–391; **2**:497, 498–499
  American Ballet Theatre, **1**:144, 390; **2**:498–499
  New York City Ballet, **1**:390; **2**:498; **6**:81–82, *82*
 burlesque, **1**:575
 country-dancing, **5**:495
 in gold mining towns, **9**:240–242
 Martha Graham Dance Company, **5**:252–253, *253*
 modern, **2**:497–498, 499
 Native American, **2**:*500*, **500–501**, *501*
  Ghost Dance, **3**:573; **4**:294; **6**:7, 231; **8**:562
  Wovoka's letter on, **9**:259–260
  powwows, **5**:498; **6**:444
  sun dance, **4**:292–293; **8**:18–19, 223
 quadrille, **5**:495
Dandridge, Dorothy, **5**:*41*
Dane, Nathan, **3**:255, 256
Danforth, John C., **2**:197; **5**:422
 on Wago Siege, **8**:359
Danforth, William H., **2**:98
Daniel, John W., **7**:52
Daniels, Charles, **8**:36
Daniels, Josephus, **6**:23
Danish Americans, **7**:262
Danish West India Company, **3**:286
DAR. *See* Daughters of the American Revolution
Darby, Michael, **8**:252
Darby Lumber Company, United States v., **3**:308
Darcy v. Allin, **6**:255
Darger, Henry, **1**:311, 312
"Dark and Bloody Ground," **2**:501–502
Dark horse(s), **2**:399, **502**
 Garfield (James A.) as, **2**:400
 Pierce (Franklin) as, **2**:502; **3**:154
 Polk (James K.) as, **2**:399, 502; **3**:153
Darkness in Saint Louis BearHeart (Vizenor), **5**:129
Darley, Felix Octavius Carr, **8**:522
Darling, Jay Norwood (Ding), **8**:481

Darnall, Carl Rogers, **5**:294
Darnall, Henry, **6**:510
Darrow, Charles B., **5**:445
Darrow, Clarence, **1**:146; **2**:446
 in Leopold-Loeb case, **5**:82
 and Scopes trial, **3**:484; **8**:86
 and Sweet trial, **4**:75
Darsee, John R., **7**:278
Dart, Joseph, **3**:187, 390
Dartmouth College, **2**:502–503; **3**:*128*
 athletic program at, **2**:276
 establishment of, **3**:111
 Native Americans at, **3**:112, 134
 skiing at, **7**:374
Dartmouth College case, **2**:111, 397, 418, 502, **503**; **3**:127; **6**:316
 due process of law in, **3**:89
Darwin, Charles
 Origin of Species
  American Academy of Arts and Sciences on, **1**:140
  and anthropology/ethnology, **1**:192
  and philosophy, **6**:324
  and pragmatism, **6**:444
  theory of evolution, **1**:520; **3**:268–269
  responses to, **2**:446
  social applications for, **1**:192–193; **7**:411–412
 See also Evolutionism
Darwin, George H., **3**:552
Dasch, George, **3**:338
Date rape, **7**:50
Daugherty, Harry M., Railway Shopmen's strike and, **7**:40
Daugherty, McGrain v., **2**:352
Daughters of Bilitis (DOB), **2**:503–504; **3**:513; **7**:326
Daughters of the American Revolution (DAR), **2**:504
 barring Marian Anderson from performing, **5**:526
 and Flag Protection Movement, **3**:380
Davenport, Charles B., **3**:258
Davenport, John, **2**:289; **6**:59–60
Davenport, Thomas, **3**:172
Davidson, Bruce, **1**:301
Davidson, Donald, **3**:481; **7**:297
Davies, Arthur B., **1**:268, 297, 321
Davies, Donald, **4**:398
Dávila, Carlos G., **1**:137–138

Davis, Alexander Jackson, **1**:250; **5**:39
Davis, Andrew Jackson, **7**:505
Davis, Angela, **2**:*204*
Davis, Cummings E., **2**:271
Davis, David, **3**:156
 on military trials of civilians, **3**:272
Davis, Deane, **8**:314
Davis, Dwight F., **8**:90
Davis, Edmund J., **8**:101
Davis, Harry, **6**:105
Davis, Helvering v., **3**:528
Davis, Henry Gassaway, **3**:159
Davis, Henry W., **8**:359
Davis, Hugh, **2**:493, 494
Davis, Jack, **8**:179
Davis, Jefferson
 and Army of Tennessee, **8**:87
 and Atlanta Campaign, **1**:351
 bread riots and, **2**:343
 charged with treason, **8**:194
 during Chattanooga campaign, **2**:113
 and Confederate agents, **2**:339
 economic troubles and, **2**:216
 election as Confederate president, **2**:208, 340, 341
 at First Battle of Bull Run, **2**:211
 imprisonment and trial of, **2**:*504*, **504–505**, *505*
 inauguration of, **1**:103
 and Johnston (Joseph E.), controversy between, **1**:567; **2**:505–506
 as leader, **2**:219
 military strategy and administration of, **2**:217
 opposition to, **2**:210, 218, 341, 506
 and railroad surveys, **7**:30
Davis, John (explorer), **6**:383
Davis, John (mariner), **3**:285
Davis, John H., **1**:67
Davis, John W., as presidential candidate, **2**:400; **3**:161, 162
Davis, Marguerite, **6**:149
Davis, Miles, **4**:469
Davis, Nathan S., **1**:164
Davis, Norman, **8**:316
Davis, Parker v., **5**:76
Davis, Phineas, **5**:142
Davis, Sammy, Jr., **8**:309
 Yes I Can, **5**:126
Davis, Stuart, **1**:297; **2**:476
Davis, Varina, **8**:472

Davis, Washington v., **3**:247
Davis, William (inventor), **3**:407
Davis, William Morris (geologist),
	3:541
Davis Cup, **8**:90
Davis et al., Zadvydas v., **1**:125
Davis-Bacon Act (1931), **3**:308; **5**:11
Davis-Johnston controversy, **1**:567;
	2:505–506
Davison, Henry P., **7**:68
Davisson, Clinton J., **1**:440; **6**:336
Dawes, Charles G., **3**:161;
	7:104–105
Dawes, Henry L., **2**:506
Dawes, William, **5**:88; **7**:133
Dawes Act (1883), agrarianism and,
	1:57
Dawes Commission, **2**:506
Dawes General Allotment Act
	(1887), **1**:69, 574; **2**:506–507;
	3:352; **5**:128, 148; **7**:208; **8**:206
	effects of, **4**:273, 286–287
	and Great Basin Indians, **8**:217
	and Great Plains Indians, **8**:219
	in Montana, **5**:449
	and Northwestern Indians, **8**:222
	provisions of, **4**:264, 273, 286, 287
	and Southeastern Indians, **8**:226
Dawes Plan (1924), **2**:507, 516;
	3:426, 562; **7**:105
Dawes Severalty Act (1887), **8**:215
Dawn Valcour Community, **8**:303
Dawson, Charles, **7**:278
Dawson, William, **1**:311
Day, Arthur L., **6**:300
Day, Benjamin, **6**:96
Day, Collector v., **2**:275–276
Day, Dorothy, **1**:57; **2**:70; **6**:99
	and peace movement, **8**:499
Day, William R., **6**:250
Day care. *See* Child care
Day of Doom, The (Wigglesworth),
	5:117
Day of the Dead, **4**:148
Day of the Locust, The (West), **5**:121
Daye, Matthew, **6**:468
Daye, Stephen, **1**:129; **6**:468, 536
Daylight saving time, **2**:507
DBS (satellite direct broadcasting
	services), **2**:322
DDT, **3**:227
	and agricultural productivity, **1**:67
	ban on, **1**:67; **3**:232, 233
	development of, **4**:361

ecological side effects of, **1**:67;
	4:362; **7**:359
	Silent Spring on, **7**:359
De Andrea, John, **1**:307
De Beauvoir, Simone. *See* Beauvoir,
	Simone de
De Costa, J., **9**:29
De Forest, Lee, **7**:19
De Gaulle, Charles. *See* Gaulle,
	Charles de
De Grasse, **8**:581
De Klerk, F. W., **7**:453
De Kooning, Elaine, **1**:10
De Kooning, Willem, **1**:10, 298;
	6:471
De la Beckwith, Byron, **1**:332
De Lacy, Hugh, **2**:326
De Lancey, James, **5**:166; **6**:83;
	8:590
De Lavallade, Carmen, **1**:131
De Leon, Daniel
	in Industrial Workers of the
		World, **4**:346; **7**:424
	in Socialist Labor Party, **7**:424
De Lima v. Bidwell, **2**:545; **4**:367
De L'Isle, Guillaume, **9**:*20*, 20–21,
	21
De Maria, Walter, **1**:307
De Mille, Agnes, **1**:144; **8**:115
De Montebello, Philippe, **5**:337
De Smet, Pierre Jean, **2**:493; **8**:259
De Soto. *See* Soto, Hernando de
De Veuster, Joseph, **5**:83
De Witt, Simeon, **2**:62
De Wolfe, Elsie, **1**:291, 293
DEA. *See* Drug Enforcement
	Administration; Drug Enforce-
	ment Agency
Dead Lecturer, The (Baraka), **5**:126
Deadbeat Parents Punishment Act
	(1998), **3**:317
Deadwood (South Dakota),
	1:501–502
Deaf community, **2**:508–509
	bionics and assistance to, **1**:463
	disability rights movement and,
		3:33
	education for, **3**:34; **7**:355–357
	at Gallaudet University, **2**:509;
		3:33, 123, **504**, 504
	"oralist" movement and, **3**:32
	sign language of, **7**:355–357
Dean, John W., III, **8**:425, 426, 427,
	427

Deane, Silas, **3**:449–450
	diplomacy of, **3**:27; **7**:147
*Dear America: Letters Home from
	Vietnam* (Edelman), excerpt
	from, **9**:473–474
Dearborn, Fort, **2**:132, **509–510**
Dearborn, Henry, **2**:509, 510; **8**:383
Dearborn wagon, **2**:510
Death and dying, **2**:510–512
	accidental, **1**:12
	assisted suicide, **1**:339
Death of a Salesman, The (Miller),
	2:512–513
Death penalty. *See* Capital punish-
	ment
Death Valley (California), **2**:513,
	513
	borax production in, **1**:505
DeBardeleben, Henry, **1**:103
Debbane, Raymond, **5**:72
Debit cards, **2**:450
Debreu, Gérard, **3**:109, 110
Debs, Eugene V., **4**:*249*; **7**:17
	in American Railway Union, **1**:167,
		168; **7**:24, 556–557
	on colonization, **7**:412
	conviction of, **4**:249
	indictment of, **3**:254
	in Industrial Workers of the
		World, **4**:346
	and peace movements, **6**:267
	as People's Party candidate, **6**:417
	presidential bids of, **2**:227; **3**:160,
		161; **8**:119
	and Pullman Strike, **6**:549
	Social Democratic Party and,
		7:412
	as Socialist Party candidate, **8**:119
	in Socialist Party of America, **7**:425
Debs, Richard, **5**:72
Debt(s)
	colonial and continental, **2**:518;
		3:96
	consumer, rise in, **1**:410; **2**:385
	corporate, **2**:42
	credit card, **1**:410; **2**:452
	domestic, under Hamilton, **4**:87–88
	foreign, **2**:516–518
		under Hamilton, **4**:87
	to Great Britain, **1**:540–541
	Hoover Moratorium (1931), **5**:456
	imprisonment for, **2**:513–514
	mortgage relief legislation,
		5:460–462

Debt(s), (*continued*)
  public (national/federal), **1:**560;
      2:514–516
    under Clinton, **7:**367
    foreign trade and, **8:**168
    and gold reserves, **4:**17
    Gramm-Rudman-Hollings Act
        and, **4:**31
    national sinking fund for, **7:366–367**
    as percentage of GDP, **1:***558*
    under Reagan, **2:**517; **7:**132, 367
    repudiation of, **7:118–119**
    Revolutionary War, **2:518–519**
    Hamilton on, **4:**87–89
  state, **2:519–520**
    under Hamilton, **4:**88–89
    readjuster movement for, **7:**52
    repudiation of, **7:119**
Debt servitude, **6:**289
Decatur, Stephen, **1:**232, 415; **8:**229
  cruise to Algiers, **2:520**
Declaration of Independence, **2:**287,
    520–523; 7:136
  adoption by Continental Congress,
      2:394
  announcement of, **2:**522–523
  bicentennial of, **1:**450
  celebration of, **2:**523
  Constitution compared with, **2:**382
  drafting of, **2:**521–522
  equality principle in, **3:**245, 248
  hundredth anniversary of, celebra-
      tion of, **2:87–88**
  philosophical tradition informing,
      3:89
  printing, **6:**468
  and race relations, **7:**8
  as reaffirmation of capitalism, **2:**284
  text of, **9:**139–141
Declaration of Principles, **6:**103
Declaration of Rights, **2:523–524**
Declaration of Rights and Griev-
    ances, **2:**393
Declaration of Rights and Senti-
    ments (Seneca Falls), **2:**87,
    524–525; 6:88; **8:**506, 513
  text of, **9:**332–334
Declaration of Rights of Woman
    and Citizen, **2:**524
Declaratory Act (1766), **2:**286, **525;**
    7:134
Decolonization
  civil rights movement compared
      with, **2:**201–202

and United Nations, **8:**270–271
DeConcini, Dennis, **6:**242
DeConde, Alexander, **4:**467
Deconstructionism, **6:**431
Decoration Day. *See* Memorial Day
Decorations, military, **2:525–527,**
    526
  awarded to African Americans,
      5:381–382
  awarded to Hispanic Americans,
      5:383–384
Decter, Midge, **6:**32
Deep ecology, **3:**226
Deep Thought computer program,
    2:338
Deere, John, **1:**58, 63
Deerfield Massacre, **2:**527
Deering, Duplex Printing Press Co. v.,
    2:229; **6:**121
Deerslayer, The (Cooper), **5:**70
Defenders of Christian Faith, **3:**327
Defense
  civil, **2:**191
  national, **2:529–532**
    air defense, **1:75–76**
    Council of, **2:**432
    expenditures for, **1:**560; **2:**517;
        3:282
Defense, Department of (DOD),
    2:528–529
  Armed Forces Security Agency of,
      5:558
  "Don't ask, don't tell" policy of,
      3:56
  head of, **2:**2
  research budget of, **5:**19
  See also Pentagon
Defense industry, in California, **2:**11
Defense of Marriage Act (1996),
    2:532–533; 3:317, 514
  defiance of, **2:***533*
Defense policy, **2:533–537**
Defense Satellite Communications
    System (DSCS), **5:**559
Defiance, Fort, **2:537; 3:**311
Deficit, federal. *See* Debt(s), public
Deficit Reduction Act (1985), **6:**481
Deflation, **4:**350
  gold standard and, **4:**15
Defoe, Daniel, **2:**222
Defoliation, **2:537–538**
Deforestation, energy consumption
    and, **3:**214
Deganawidah (prophet), **6:**87

Degeneration, **6:**12
Deism, **2:538–540**
DeJoseph, Roni, **8:***335*
DeKoven, James, **3:**242
Delaherche, Auguste, **1:**304
Delaney Amendment, **2:**540
Delany, Martin, **1:**477; **6:**235
  and colonization movement, **2:**297
Delaunay, Robert, **2:**476
Delaware, **2:540–543,** *541*
  in colonial era, **5:**362
    New Castle, **6:**41
    as proprietary colony, **6:***510,* 512
    provincial congresses in, **6:**520
    as royal colony, **6:**511
  economy of, **2:**541–542
  emblems, nicknames, mottos, and
      songs of, **7:***532*
  Federalist Party in, **3:**351
  maps of, archival, **9:**37, *38*
  social structure of, **2:**543
  Winterthur Museum, **8:**489
Delaware Indians, **2:544–545**
  in American Revolution, **4:**329
  land cession treaties with, **4:**271
  Quakers and, **7:**2
  treaty with, **8:**206
Delaware River
  discovery of, **2:**540
  Washington's crossing of,
      2:543–544, *544;* **8:**208
DeLay, Tom, **8:**468
Delegation of powers, **2:545**
  by Congress, **1:**21–22
DeLillo, Don, *Underworld,* **5:**122
Delineator (magazine), **1:**28
Dellinger, Dave, **6:**269
Delmonico Building (Sheeler), **6:**471
DeLoatch, Gary, **1:**131
Deloria, Vine, Jr., *Custer Died for
    Your Sins,* **2:484–485**
Delta Airlines, **1:**83
Delta Force, **7:**494
Demby, William, *Beetlecreek,* **5:**125
Dementyev, Pyotr, **8:**47
Demers, Modeste, **6:**205
D'Emilio, John, **3:**514
Demilitarized zone (DMZ), in Viet-
    nam, creation of, **8:**329
Deming, Barbara, **8:**499
Deming, W. Edwards, **1:**373
  14 Points for Management, text of,
      9:499–500
Demobilization, **2:545–546**

Democracy, **2:**546–548
  cities and, **8:**291
  conservation and, **2:**367
  direct, **7:**109
    measures aimed at, **2:**548; **7:**53
  election systems in, **3:**145
  industrial, **2:**273
  majority rule, **5:**211–213
  party system and, **2:**547
  representative, **2:**546–547;
    7:109–110
  state universities and, **8:**280
  transition from federalism to,
    3:152
  trust in, **2:**548
Democracy and Social Ethics (Addams),
    6:440
Democracy in America (Tocqueville),
    1:137; **2:**548–549; **3:**249, 450;
    7:82
  on individualism, **4:**331
Democratic Party, **2:**549–554
  AFL-CIO and, **1:**151, 152–153
  African Americans in, **2:**195, 201,
    552; **6:**398
  in Alabama, **1:**102, 104
  in antebellum era, **2:**550
  anticommunism in, **1:**197
  in Arizona, **1:**259
  in Arkansas, **1:**261, 263
  on banks, **4:**258
    antibanking movement in, **1:**195;
    5:142
  Barnburners within, **1:**417–418
  and civil rights, **2:**553
  and civil service assessments, **2:**23
  Civil War and, **2:**411, 551
  class in, **4:**453–454
  and conservationism, **2:**371
  and Eagleton Affair, **3:**100
  economic policies of, **4:**453
  electoral base of, **3:**149
    19th-century, **3:**146
  and EPIC movement, **3:**233–234
  and federal agencies, **3:**332
  and federal aid, **3:**334
  and Free Soil Party, **3:**459
  in Georgia, **3:**555–556
  Gold Democrats in, **4:**10; **7:**362
  and homesteading, **5:**33
  in Idaho, **4:**213–214
  in Illinois, **4:**216
  immigrants and, **5:**187
  in Indiana, **4:**320

  in Iowa, **4:**416
  Jackson (Andrew) and, **2:**550
  Jacksonian, **4:**453–455
  Jefferson (Thomas) and, **2:**549–550
  Jeffersonian Republicans and,
    7:117
  labor and, **2:**23
  labor policies of, **5:**12, 15, 16, 17
  and Locofoco Party, **5:**142
  in Louisiana, **5:**159–160, 161
  in Massachusetts, **5:**268
  in Michigan, **5:**356
  middle-of-the-road populists and,
    5:366
  in Mississippi, during Reconstruc-
    tion, **5:**412–413
  national conventions of, **2:**399;
    6:113–114
    of 1848, **1:**106
    of 1860, **1:**106
    of 1968, **2:**400; **7:**165
  in New York, Hunkers in, **4:**195
  New York Times and, **6:**89, 90
  nominations by, **6:**113–114
  Nonpartisan League and, **6:**118
  in North Dakota, **6:**132–133
  in Ohio, **6:**172
  in Oklahoma, **6:**185–186
  organization of, **4:**453
  platform of, **6:**368
  political action committees and,
    6:393
  political machines, **5:**186, 187
  post-Watergate, **2:**553
  on Prohibition, **6:**501
  and Rainbow Coalition, **7:**46
  on separation of church and state,
    4:453
  on separation of powers, **7:**313
  Silver Democrats in, **7:**344–345,
    362–363
  and slavery, **6:**416
  in Solid South, **7:**446
  in state legislatures, **5:**80
  steering committees in, **7:**546–547
  on subsidies, **7:**564
  Tammany Hall and, **8:**45–46
  and tariffs, **8:**51, 57, 156
  and taxation, **8:**57, 58
  in Tennessee, **8:**86
  in Texas, **8:**101, 102, 103
  and trade unions, **8:**172, 262, 278
  in two-party system, **6:**398; **8:**243
  and unit rule, **8:**260

  in Utah, **8:**297, 298
  in Vermont, **8:**314
  in Virginia, **8:**344–345
  War Democrats in, **8:**378
  in West Virginia, **8:**449
  and Working Men's movement,
    5:142
Democratic-Farmer-Labor party,
    3:322
Democratic-Republican Party, **5:**555
  nominations by, **6:**113
Demographic transition, **2:**557–560,
    558
Demography and demographic
    trends, **2:**554–562
  in 19th century, **3:**312–313
  in 20th century, **3:**314
  in colonial era, **3:**311
  immigration and, **2:**556–557
  of pharmacists, **6:**311
  population density in 1790, **2:***554*
  population density in 1850, **2:***556*
  population density in 1900, **2:***559*
  population density in 1940, **2:***560*
  population density in 2000, **2:***561*
  population distribution, **2:**556
  westward expansion and, **5:**223
Dempsey, Jack, **6:**484; **7:**65
Dempsey, Moore v., **4:**81
Demuth, Charles, **1:**310; **3:**538
DeMuth, Christopher, **8:**118
Denby, Edwin, and naval oil
    reserves, **6:**19–20
Denmark, Virgin Islands under,
    8:340
Dennett, Mary Ware, **1:**468
Denney, Reuel, **5:**148
Dennis, Eugene, **2:**327
Dennis, Martin, **5:**69
Dennis, United States v., **2:**377
Dennison, Aaron, **2:**242
Denny, Reginald, **5:**155
Denominationalism, **3:**1–3; **5:**532
Densmore, James, **8:**244
Dentistry, **3:**3–5
  anesthesia in, **1:**184
  insurance for, **4:**372
Denver (Colorado), **1:**501; **2:**47–48;
    3:5–6
  founding of, **2:**298
  modern, **3:**6
  Welcome Arch, **3:***5*
Denver Trail, **6:**30

Deoxyribonucleic acid (DNA),
    3:67–69, *68*; **7:**188
Department stores, **3:**6–11;
    7:124–125
  Macy's, **5:**189–190, *190*
  in shopping malls, **5:**215–216
Depletion allowances, **3:**11
Depo-Provera, **1:**469
Deportation, **3:**11–12
  alien rights and, **1:**125
  Palmer Raids, **6:**232, 396
  Supreme Court on, **1:**125
Deposit Act (1836), **3:**12, 365
Depository Institutions Deregula-
    tion and Monetary Control Act
    (1980), **3:**347
Depression. *See* Great Depression
Depression (disorder), treatment of,
    6:521, 522
Depression of 1920, **3:**12–13
DePriest, Oscar, **2:**220
Deregulation, **3:**13
  of airlines, **1:**96–97
  of California power industry, **4:**27
  of public utilities, **6:**536
  of railroads, **7:**39–40, 517
  of savings and loan industry, **4:**27
  of trucking industry, **5:**463
Dern, George, **8:**297, 298
Derrida, Jacques, **6:**430–431
DES Action USA, **3:**13–14
*Des Moines Independent Community
    School District, Tinker v.,* **1:**26;
    2:149; **3:**119
Desai, Morarji, **4:**260
Desegregation, **3:**14–16, *15,* 118
  in civil rights movement,
    4:374–375
  in Delaware, **2:**543
  and electoral politics, **3:**166
  enforcement of, **2:**196
  Freedom Riders and, **3:**464
  NAACP and, **5:**526–527
  National Urban League and, **5:**563
  political violence and, **1:**332–333
  of schools, **3:**14–15, 16, 118
    in Alabama, **1:**104
    American Federation of Teachers
      on, **1:**155, 156
    in Arkansas, **1:**263; **5:**134, *134*
    busing and, **1:**589–590
    Civil Rights Act of 1964 and,
      2:196, 200
    in Louisiana, **5:**161

  magnet schools, **5:**201
  in Mississippi, **1:**122
  of public schools, **5:**425
  and state sovereignty, **7:**534
  Supreme Court on, **1:**122, 589;
    2:199; **3:**341; **4:**374; **5:**425,
    527
  in Tennessee, **8:**86
  in Virginia, **8:**344
  of sports, **7:**511
  of transportation, Montgomery bus
    boycott and, **1:**529, 548;
    2:202; **3:**15
  white resistance to, **3:***14,* 15
Deseret, **3:**16; **5:**53
Desert Land Act (1877), **1:**65; **5:**25;
    6:528
Desert Solitaire (Abbey), **5:**552
Desert Storm, Operation. *See* Per-
    sian Gulf War
Desertion, **1:**524; **3:**16–17
Deserts, **3:***17,* 17–19, *18*
  Forty-Mile Desert, **3:**441
Desha, Mary, **2:**504
*DeShaney v. Winnebago County
    Department of Social Services,*
    2:137; **3:**74
DeSilva, Ashanti, **3:**531
Desktop publishing, **6:**470
Destroyers, **8:**408
Détente, **2:**269; **7:**212
  summit conferences on, **8:**16
Detergent industry, **7:**408
Detroit (Michigan), **3:**19–21, *20*
  Empowerment Zone program,
    8:287
  founding of, **4:**52
  riots in, **3:**21, *22;* **7:**166, *167*
  in War of 1812, **3:**21
Detroit, surrender of, **3:**21
Detroit (ship), **5:**21
Detroit River Tunnel, **8:**240
Deukmejian, George, **2:**12
Deuterium, **6:**341
Deuteron, **6:**341
Devaluation, **3:**21–22
  in 1970s, **8:**168
Developing countries, lending to
    World Bank and, **8:**532
  See also Foreign aid
Development, real estate. *See* Real
    estate development
*Development of American Political Sci-
    ence: From Burgess to Behavioral-*

    ism, The (Somit and Tanenhaus),
    6:401
Developmentalism, pre-Darwinian,
    1:192
Devereux, James P. S., **8:**365
Deviancy, social, mental illness and,
    5:313
Devine, Edward T., **2:**106
"Devolution," **6:**12
Dew, Thomas, *Pro-Slavery Argu-
    ment,* text of, **9:**267–269
Dew, Thomas Roderick, **6:**507
Dewey, George, **1:**189; **5:**225; **6:**321
  in Spanish-American War, **7:**486,
    487–488
Dewey, John, **3:**116, 195; **5:**91, 122;
    6:*327*
  academic freedom and, **1:**143
  on Catholicism, **1:**196
  on individualism, **4:**333
  and instrumentalism, **6:**326, 445
  School and Society by, **8:**106
Dewey, Thomas E.
  and American Labor Party, **1:**162
  in presidential campaign of 1944,
    3:163
  in presidential campaign of 1948,
    6:409
  and State University of New York,
    7:535
Dewing, Thomas W., **1:**297
DeWitt, John L., **4:**460, 463; **7:**99
Dhegiha Sioux, **8:**223
DI. *See* Diffusion index
Diaghilev, Serge, **1:**390; **2:**498
*Diagnostic and Statistical Manual of
    Mental Disorders* (DSM-III)
    (American Psychiatric Associa-
    tion), **6:**522
Dial, The (magazine), **7:**194; **8:**179
Dialect, vs. slang, **7:**377
Dialectic of Enlightenment
    (Horkheimer and Adorno),
    3:454
Dialects, **3:**220
Diallo, Amadou, **6:**385
Diamond v. Chakrabarty, **3:**530;
    6:256
Diana (Princess of Wales), **2:**79
Dianetics, **7:**283
Díaz, Adolfo, **3:**71
Diaz, Mathews v., **1:**126
Díaz, Melchior, **2:**301
Díaz, Porfirio, **5:**348

Dick Act (1903), **5:**387, 542

Dicke, Robert, **1:**344

Dickens, Charles, **1:**136; **2:**166; **6:**537

Dickey, James, **5:**123

Dickhoff, Robert Ernest, **1:**326

Dickinson, Charles, duel with Jackson, **3:**93

Dickinson, Emily, **5:**119

Dickinson, John
  at Annapolis Convention, **1:**187
  on Britain, affinity with, **2:**520
  at Constitutional Convention, **2:**379
  Farmer's Letters by, **3:**320
  "Liberty Song," **8:**278
  and Olive Branch Petition, **6:**190
  and Plan of 1776, **6:**361
  "The Pennsylvania Farmer's Remedy," **9:**127–128
  writings by, **7:**136

Dickinson, Jonathan, **6:**465

Dickman, Joseph T., **2:**112

Dickstein, Samuel, **4:**178

Dictaphone Corporation, **6:**168

Dictionaries, **3:**22–23, 203, 220–221
  slang in, **7:**377–378

Dictionary of the English Language (Johnson), **6:**387

Diderot, Denis, *Encyclopédie*, **3:**204

Didion, Joan, **5:**122

Didrikson, Mildred (Babe), **4:**19, **8:**155

Diebenkorn, Richard, **1:**299

Diebold, John, **1:**364

Diem, Ngo Dinh, **3:**417; **8:**330–331
  canceling 1956 elections, **3:**534
  death of, **8:**331
  Eisenhower and, **8:**330
  U.S. aid to, **8:**330
  Viet Minh and, **8:**330

Dies, Martin, in HUAC, **1:**198; **4:**178, 411

Diesel fuel, **6:**301

Diethylene glycol, **3:**404

Diethylstilbestrol (DES), **3:**13–14

Diets and dieting, **3:**24
  body image and, **3:**401
  cereal grains in, **2:**97
  class distinction and, **3:**399, 402
  colonial, **3:**398
  and eating disorders, **3:**104
  during Great Depression, **3:**401; **6:**150

immigrants and, **3:**399–400, 401, 402
  nutrition and, **6:**148–150
  vegetarianism, **8:**310
  See also Nutrition

Diffie, Whitfield, **2:**468

Diffusion index (DI), **3:**106

Digestion, studies on, **6:**148

Digital cameras, **6:**330, 331

"Digital divide," **8:**67

Digital technology, **3:**24–25
  compact discs (CDs), **2:**328–329

Digital versatile discs (DVDs), **2:**329, 392; **3:**97–98; **8:**77

Dilling, Elizabeth, **3:**327

Dillon, John F., **2:**112

Dillon, Read and Company, **4:**412

DiMaggio, Joe, **1:**421

Dime museums, **5:**487

Dime novels, **3:**25–26; **6:**537; **8:**457

Dime Song Book, A, **6:**537

Dime stores, **2:**100, *101*; **3:**9–10, *10*, 26–27; **7:**125

Dimethyl ether, **3:**480

Diné. *See* Navajo

Diné College (Navajo Community College), **8:**210

Diners Club, **2:**450, 451

Dingell, John, **3:**206

Dingley Act (1897), **8:**51

Dinkins, David, **2:**466–467

Dinosaur National Monument, **2:**372

Dinosaurs. *See* Paleontology

Dinsmoor, S. P., **1:**312

Dinwiddie, Robert, **3:**95, 469

Dioxins, **3:**39
  in Agent Orange, **1:**54
  in Times Beach, **8:**127

Diphtheria
  disease control efforts against, **3:**239–240
  epidemic of 1931, **3:**37

Diplomacy
  by ambassadors, **1:**133–134
  during American Revolution, **7:**146–147
  Confederate, **2:**342, 344
  dollar, **3:**70–71
  executive agents in, **3:**277
  Lincoln's, in Civil War, **2:**217
  secret, **3:**27
  See also Foreign policy; Foreign Service

Diplomatic immunity, **1:**134

Diplomatic missions, **3:**27–29
  in 1990s, **3:**429–430
  during Civil War, **3:**428
  during Cold War, **3:**429
  during World War I, **3:**428
  during World War II, **3:**429

Dirac, P. A. M., **6:**341, 345

Direct Initiative, **5:**79, 80

Direct investment
  foreign, **3:**420, 423
  vs. portfolio investment, **3:**419

Direct mail, **3:**29–30

Direct primary. *See* Primary, direct

Directly Observed Treatment Short Course (DOTS), **8:**237

Directories, city, **2:**183

Dirigibles, **3:**30–32, *31*
  disasters involving, **3:**35

Dirksen, Everett, **2:**195

Disability rights movement, **3:**32–33

Disabled persons
  accommodations for, **1:**172
  Americans with Disabilities Act and, **1:**172
  discrimination against, **1:**172; **3:**47–48
  education for, **3:**33–35
  federal government and, **3:**123

DiSalle, Michael, **6:**166

Disasters, **3:**35–44
  blizzards, **1:**485–487, *486, 487*
  Cherry mine (1909), **5:**14
  Monongah mine (1907), **5:**14
  Mount St. Helens eruption, **5:**465, *466*
  Titanic, sinking of, **8:**131–132, *132*
  tornadoes, **8:**143–144, *144*
  See also Airplane crashes; Fire(s); Floods

Disch, Thomas M., **5:**123

Disciples of Christ (Christian Church), **3:**44–45; **8:**263–264
  formation of, **7:**87

Disciplinary maturity, **6:**403

Disco, **3:**45–46

Discount stores, **7:**126

Discourse on the Transient and Permanent in Christianity (Parker), **8:**180

Discovery, doctrine of, and land policy, **5:**32

Discovery (ship), **3:**46

Discovery (space shuttle), **2:**102; **3:46**
Discovery of the Titanic, The (Ballard),
   8:132
Discrimination, **3:46–57**
 in AFL-CIO, **1:**150, 152
 age, **3:46–47; 7:**129
 against aliens, **1:**125–126
 against Catholics, **1:195–197**
 against disabled persons, **1:**172;
   3:47–48
 employment, **1:**35–37
  AFL-CIO and, **1:**152
  age, **3:46–47**
  against aliens, **1:**125
  Civil Rights Act of 1964 on, **2:**196
  disability-based, **1:**172
  efforts to eliminate, **3:**243–245
  gender-based
   pregnancy and, **3:**525; **6:**449
   Supreme Court on, **1:**377
  letter to Roosevelt on, **9:**376–377
  of minority groups, **3:**48
  and Philadelphia Plan,
   6:314–315
  sex, **3:53–55**
  sexual harassment as, **7:**322–323
  sexual-orientation-based, **7:**327
  standards for evaluating, Supreme
   Court on, **8:**389–390
 housing, prohibition of, **2:**200
 intelligence testing and, **4:**379
 against Jews (*See* Anti-Semitism)
 against Mexican Americans, **5:**344
  in Los Angeles, **9:**407–409
 race, **3:48–51** (*See also* Racism)
  benign neglect, **1:442**
  combating, **3:**48–49
  redlining, **7:72–73**
  reverse, claims regarding, **1:**386
 religious, **3:51–53**
 sex, **3:53–55**, 249 (*See also* Sexual
   harassment)
  Civil Rights Restoration Act on,
   2:206
  vs. comparable worth principles,
   2:329–330
  constitutional test for, **2:**445–446
  Convention on the Elimination
   of All Forms of Discrimination Against Women,
   2:398–399
  glass ceiling and, **4:**2–3
  in higher education, law outlawing, **2:**277

9 to 5, National Association of
   Working Women fighting,
   6:109–110
 in private associations, **7:**183, 198
 sexual harassment as, **7:**322–323
 Supreme Court on, **1:**377; **3:**478,
   525; **6:**295; **7:**73, 183, 198;
   8:275–276
 sexual orientation, **3:56–57; 7:**196,
   325–326
 as social disorder, recognition of,
   1:207
 in trade unions, **4:**387
Disease(s)
 Agent Orange and, **2:**538
 alcoholism as, **1:**118, 119
 Alzheimer's, **1:131–132**
 in animals, **2:**73; **8:**318–320
 Army medicine and, **5:**294–295
 cancer, **2:34–35**
 cardiovascular, **2:52–54**
 in Chesapeake colonies, **2:**129
 cholera, **2:159–160**, *160;*
   3:236–237; **8:**576
  1866 outbreak of, **4:**363
  navy research on, **5:**296
  sanitary reform and, **7:**245
 in Civil War, **2:**211
 in colonial era, **1:**72; **2:**290, 291,
   360; **3:**291; **5:**300
 diagnosis and treatment of, study
   of DNA and, **3:**67
 environmental sources of, **3:**234
 germ theory of, **3:**239–240
  and bioterrorism, **1:**465
 herbicide use and, **2:**538
 Human Genome Project and,
   4:191–192
 Huntington's, **4:**191
 influenza, **4:353–354**, *354*
 "intermittent fever," **5:**300
 mammalian studies and, **5:**218
 parasitology, **5:**294
 polio, **5:**236; **6:388–389**, *389*
 sanitation systems and, **7:**245
 scurvy, **7:287**
 self-limited, theory of, **5:**301
 sexually transmitted, **7:332–333**
 on slave ships, **5:**364
 smallpox, **5:**219–220, 300;
   7:398–400
 typhoid, **5:**294–295
 war casualties from, **8:**375, *375*
 in War of 1812, **2:**235

 water pollution and, **8:**421
 yellow fever, **5:**294
Disfranchisement, **3:57**
 and Dorr's Rebellion, **3:**80
 legal challenge to, **8:**483
 Mississippi Plan for, **5:414–415**
 through voter registration laws,
   8:354
Disintermediation, **3:**368
Dismal Swamp, **3:57–58**
Disney, Roy, **3:**58
Disney, Walter E., **2:**63; **3:**58, *58*
 HUAC testimony by, text of,
   9:413–417
Disney Corporation, **3:58–59**
 boycotts of, **1:**529
 cartoons produced by, **2:**63–64
 Celebration community of, **8:**304
 and consumerism, **2:**391
 and toys, **8:**153
Disney World, **1:**180
Disneyland, **1:**179–180; **2:**178
 freeways and, **7:**66
Displaced Homemakers Self-Suffi-
   ciency Assistance Act (1990),
   3:59
Displaced Persons Act (1948), **6:**397
"Disquisition on Government." *See*
   *South Carolina Exposition and
   Protest*
Dissent (magazine), **6:**85
Dissenters, **3:59**
Dissociation, **6:**431
Disston, Hamilton, **5:**22
Distiller and Cattle Feeders Trust,
   4:26
Distilling, **2:**97; **3:59–61**, *60;* **8:**468
Distinguished Flying Cross, **2:**527
Distinguished Service Cross, **2:**526
Distinguished Service Medal, **2:**526
Distribution Act (1841), **5:**33
Distribution of goods and services,
   3:61–62
Distribution-Preemption Act (1841),
   6:527
District of Columbia. *See* Washing-
   ton (D.C.)
District schools, **7:264–265**
Districts, congressional, **3:62;**
   7:107–108
 in 19th century, **8:**356
 gerrymandering and, **3:**564
 See also Apportionment
Ditmars, Raymond Lee, **4:**129

Divine providences, **3:**63
Divorce and marital separation, **3:63–66**
  in 19th century, **3:**312, 313
  in 20th century, **3:**313–314
  collusive, **3:**64–65
  in colonial era, **2:**291; **3:**63, 311
  "no fault," **3:**65
  and property rights, **6:**506
  public opinion on, **3:**317
  rates of, **5:**249, 251
    growth in, **3:**65
Dix, Dorothea, **1:**509; **5:**313; **6:***146*
  in Civil War, **8:**502
  nurses' uniform prescribed by, **8:***257, 258*
Dix-Hill Cartel, **6:**472, 473
Dixie. *See* South, the
"Dixie" (song), **3:66–67**
Dixiecrats, **8:**119
Dixon, Jeremiah, **5:**260; **9:**37
Dixon, Joseph, **5:**552
Dixon, Thomas, Jr., **1:**470
Djerassi, Carl, **1:**468
DMZ. *See* Demilitarized zone
DNA (deoxyribonucleic acid), **3:67–69,** *68;* **7:**188
  Human Genome Project and, **4:191–192**
  recombinant, **3:**529
  sequencing of, **5:**437
  structure of, **3:**529, 533
  studies on, **3:**533
Doane, Thomas, **8:**240
Doar, John, **2:**195
DOB. *See* Daughters of Bilitis
Dobrynin, Anatoly, **2:**471, 475
Doby, Larry, **1:**421
Dobzhansky, Theodosius, **3:**269
Doctorow, E. L., **5:**121
Documentaries, **8:**73
Documents, government, **4:24–25**
DOD. *See* Defense, Department of
Dodd, Samuel, **8:**233
Dodds, Harold, **6:**465
Dodge, D. L., **6:**267
Dodge, Grenville, **8:**181, 564
Dodge City (Kansas), **2:**158; **3:69**
  "Peace Commission of," **3:***70*
  railroads and development of, **7:**34
Dodge City Trail, **3:69**
DOE. *See* Education, Department of; Energy, Department of
Doenitz, Karl, **8:**556

Dogs, diseases in, **8:**319
Doheny, Edward L., **8:**63
DOI. *See* Interior, Department of
Doisy, Edward A., **1:**461
DOJ. *See* Justice, Department of
Dole, Elizabeth H., **5:**12
Dole, Robert (Bob)
  on Persian Gulf War, **6:**293
  in presidential campaign of 1976, **3:**167
  in presidential campaign of 1988, **3:**168
  in presidential campaign of 1996, **3:**169; **7:**114
  on Proposition 209, **6:**510
  on school vouchers, **3:**138
  as Viagra spokesman, **8:**322
Dollar
  devaluation of, **3:**21–22
  origins of term, **2:**481
Dollar diplomacy, **3:70–71**
  vs. Alliance for Progress, **1:**128
Dollar sign, **3:71–72**
Dollar-a-year man, **3:**72
Domestic Policy Council (DPC), **3:**330
Domestic trade. *See* Trade, domestic
Domestic violence, **3:72–75**
  in 19th century, **3:**312–313
  activism targeting, Coalition of Labor Union Women and, **2:**256
  child abuse, **2:136–138**
  legal remedies for, **3:**74
  prevalence of, **8:**339
  Violence Against Women Act and, **8:339–340**
Domestic workers, health hazards for, **5:**299
Dominican Republic, **3:75–77**
  U.S. occupation of, **2:**54
  U.S. relations with, **5:**47, 49
    Good Neighbor Policy and, **4:**22
    gunboat diplomacy and, **4:**76
Dominicans (Order of Preachers), **3:**77
Dominion Marine Association, **4:**54
Dominion of New England, **2:**110, 280; **3:77–78; 6:**363, 379
  Massachusetts Bay Colony and, **5:**271
  New York in, **6:**83–84
  Rhode Island in, **7:**151
Domino theory, **2:**151; **3:**78

Donaghy, Don, **1:**301
Donahue, Tom, **1:**153
Donald Duk (Chin), **5:**123
Donaldson, Thomas, **6:**531
Donelson, Fort
  siege of, **2:**212
  unconditional surrender of, **3:**79; **8:**249
Donelson, John, **2:**479
Dongan, Thomas, **2:**109, 280; **3:**79
Dongan charters, **3:**79
Donnelly, Ignatius, **1:**204
Donnelly, Lynch v., **2:**166, 170
Donner party, **3:79–80**
Donovan, Raymond, **5:**12
Donovan, William D. (Wild Bill), **6:**503
Donovan, William J., **1:**162–163; **6:**167
"Don't ask, don't tell" policy, **3:**56, 78; **5:**385
"Don't fire till you see the white of their eyes," **3:**78
"Don't give up the ship," **3:78–79**
Doolittle, James (Jimmy), **1:**86, 90; **8:**554
Doorman, Karel W. F. M., **4:**466
Dorantes, Andrés, **2:**360
Dorantes, Esteban de, **1:**47
Dorchester Company, **3:**80; **8:**174
Dorr, Thomas Wilson, **3:**82; **7:**152; **8:**194
Dorr's Rebellion, **3:80–82; 5:**175; **7:**152
  aftermath of, **3:***81*
Dorrance, John, **2:**36
Dorrance, Vanhorne's Lessee v., **8:**308
Dorsey, Thomas, **5:**497
Dos Passos, John, **5:**157; **6:**12
  The 42nd Parallel, **5:**121
  1919, **5:**121
  Big Money, **5:**121
  Manhattan Transfer, **5:**120
Dostoyevsky, Fyodor, **3:**279
DOT. *See* Transportation, Department of
Dot-coms, **2:**337; **3:**183–184
  See also Electronic commerce
DOTS. *See* Directly Observed Treatment Short Course
Doty, James, **3:**448; **8:**490
Double Indemnity (Cain), **5:**121
Doubleday, **6:**538
Doubleday, Abner, **1:**419

Double-glazing glass, **4**:4

Doubloon, **3**:82

Dougall, Sugarman v., **1**:126

Doughboy, **3**:82

Doughfaces, **3**:82

Douglas (manufacturing company), **1**:83, 84

Douglas, Aaron, **4**:96

Douglas, Ann, **4**:469

Douglas, James (Buster), **6**:485

Douglas, Stephen A.

  and Compromise of 1850, **2**:331

  debates with Abraham Lincoln (*See* Lincoln-Douglas debates)

  and Democratic Party, **2**:551

  and Freeport doctrine, **3**:467

  and Kansas-Nebraska Act, **4**:512–513

  opposition to Lecompton Constitution, **5**:73

  and popular sovereignty, **6**:415

  in presidential campaign of 1852, **3**:154

  in presidential campaign of 1860, **2**:400; **3**:154, 155

Douglas, Thomas, **6**:135

Douglas, William O., **8**:484

  on right to privacy for birth control, **4**:67; **6**:479

Douglas fir, **3**:437, *437*

Douglass, Andrew E., **1**:240

Douglass, David, **8**:113

Douglass, Frederick, **1**:477; **5**:91, 119, 199; **6**:97

  on African colonization, **1**:148

  in African Methodist Episcopal Zion Church, **1**:44, 53

  on Canaan, **1**:46

  and Colored National Labor Union, **2**:302

  on Lincoln's second inaugural address, **5**:112

  Narrative of the Life of Frederick Douglass, an American Slave, **5**:124

  newspaper of, **6**:88

  and runaway slaves, assistance to, **8**:250

  and World's Columbian Exposition, **8**:558

Douhet, Giulio, **1**:76, 495

Dove, Arthur, **1**:297

Dove (ship), **2**:290

Doves and hawks, **3**:82–83

Dow, Charles Henry, **3**:83; **8**:366–367, *367*

Dow, Neal, **1**:117; **6**:502

Dow Jones, **3**:83, 106; **7**:549

Dowell, Board of Education of Oklahoma City v., **1**:590

Dowie, John Alexander, **8**:302

Downing, Andrew Jackson, **1**:250; **3**:510

  A Treatise on the Theory and Practice of Landscape Gardening, Adapted to North America, **5**:38

Downsizing, **3**:83

Downton, R. L., **3**:390

Dozier, Edward, **1**:340

DPC. *See* Domestic Policy Council

Dr. Pepper, **2**:388

Draft. *See* Conscription and recruitment

Draft dodgers

  amnesty for, **1**:177

    Carter's proclamation on, **9**:479–480

  vs. conscientious objectors, **2**:361

  immigration to Canada, **3**:197

Draft riots, in Civil War, **2**:211; **3**:84; **7**:164, 166; **8**:338

Drago Doctrine, **4**:82

Dragoons, **2**:77

Drake, Edwin L., **6**:298, 302, 305

Drake, Sir Francis, **3**:288; **6**:382; **8**:453

  visit to Roanoke colony, **7**:47

Drama. *See* Theater

Drama, television, **8**:72

Draper, Henry, **6**:155–156

Draper, John (Blacksburg founder), **3**:84

Draper, John W. (chemist), **2**:122

Draper's Meadows, **3**:84

Drawbaugh, Daniel, **8**:70

Dreadnought, **3**:84–85

Dreadnought (British warship), **1**:266; **3**:84, *84*; **8**:406, 407

Dream Dance Drum, **6**:7

Dred Scott case, **2**:180, 193; **3**:85–86; **5**:110

  on African Americans as citizens, **4**:74

  divided opinion on, **5**:420

  due process of law argument in, **3**:90

  effects of, **4**:495

  inconsistency between popular sovereignty and, **3**:467

  judicial review in, **4**:492

  on property rights of slaveholders, **6**:10

Dred Scott v. Sandford. See Dred Scott case

Dreier, Mary, **8**:522

Dreiser, Theodore

  An American Tragedy, **5**:120; **6**:12

  The Financier, **6**:12

  Sister Carrie, **5**:119; **6**:11, 12

  The Titan, **6**:12

  "True Art Speaks Plainly," **6**:12

Dresden (Germany), destruction during World War II, **8**:553

Dress. *See* Clothing

Drew, Timothy, **1**:45

Drexel Furniture Company, Bailey v., **2**:140, **142**

Dreyfus, Henry, **8**:559

Driggs, Frederick E., and land speculation, **5**:36

Drinker, Philip, **1**:285, 303, 463

Drinking age, national, **3**:336

Drive-in restaurants, **3**:397–398

Drivers, slave, **6**:221–222

Drogher trade, **3**:86

Drougal, Christopher, **4**:422

Drought, **8**:423

  See also Dust Bowl

Drug addiction. *See* Substance abuse

Drug Enforcement Administration (DEA), **5**:511, 512, 513

Drug Enforcement Agency (DEA), **3**:86

Drug Importation Act (1848), **6**:553

Drug trafficking, **3**:86–87

  in Baltimore, **1**:393

  Customs Service's responsibility to interdict, **2**:485

  and foreign policy, **5**:511, 512–513

  Justice Department and, **4**:503–504

  major trafficking routes, **5**:*512*

  marijuana, **5**:239–240

  and organized crime, **2**:463

  See also Narcotics trade and legislation

Drugs and drug use

  and counterculture, **2**:433

  criminalization of, **2**:462

  Pure Food and Drug Movement and, **6**:553–555

recreational, **7:**66
Drugstore, **6:**308–309
Drummond, William, **1:**114
Drunk driving, **3:**336
Drury, Newton B., **5:**552
Dry docks, **3:**87
Dry farming, **3:**87–88
Dryfoos, Orvil E., **6:**89
Drying food, **3:**406–407
DSCS. *See* Defense Satellite Communications System
DSM-III. *See Diagnostic and Statistical Manual of Mental Disorders*
D'Souza, Dinesh, **6:**395
Du Bois, W. E. B., **3:**117; **5:**91, 119, 125; **6:***235*
   African American newspapers and, **5:**199–200
   in American Association for the Advancement of Science, **1:**141
   education of, **3:**126
   and NAACP, **2:**201
   Niagara movement organized by, **6:**103–104
   and Pan-Africanism, **6:**235–236
   and pluralism, **6:**375
   social survey by, **6:**533
   The Souls of Black Folk, **3:**556; **5:**124; **6:**375; **7:**451
   at Wilberforce University, **3:**125
Du Bridge, Lee, **7:**14
Du Ponceau, Peter S., **1:**166
Du Pont Company, **2:**541–542; **3:**302; **8:**110
   chemical research at, **2:**123
   commercialization of nylon by, **2:**121
Du Pont, Henry Francis, **2:**272
   home of, **8:**489
Du Pont, Lammot, **3:**301–302
Du Pont, Pierre, **1:**517
Du Pont de Nemours, Éleuthère Irénée, **3:**301
Du Simitière, Pierre Eugène, **3:**99; **5:**485
Duane, William, **1:**360–361; **2:**393; **3:**151
   as secretary of Treasury, **7:**103
Duarte, José Napoléon, **3:**143, 144
Dubček, Alexander, **2:**90
Dube, John, **7:**451–452
Dubinsky, David, **1:**152; **4:**392
Dubois, Mary Ann Delafield, **1:**308

DuBridge, Lee A., **2:**15
Dubs, Adolph, **1:**37
Dubuffet, Jean, **1:**311
Dubuque, Gelpcké v., **3:514–515**
Dubuque, Julien, **3:**503; **5:**61
Duchamp, Marcel, **5:**120; **6:**414
   in Armory Show, **1:***268*, 269
Duché, André, **1:**304; **6:**418
Ducking stool, **3:**88
Dudley, William, **8:**400
Due process of law, **3:**88–92
   for aliens, **1:**125
   Barron v. Baltimore and, **1:**419
   for children, **4:**250
   Fourteenth Amendment on, **2:**397; **3:**90
   and freedom of press, **6:**27
   procedural, **3:**90–91
   and right to counsel, **3:**575–576
   Supreme Court on, **4:**198
Dueling, **3:**92–93
   Burr-Hamilton duel, **1:577–578; 3:***92
Duer, William, and land speculation, **5:**36
Duesenberry, James, **3:**110
Duffy, Edmund, **6:**395
Duffy, John, **3:**238
Dugan, Eva, **1:**258
Dugout, **3:**93
Dukakis, Michael, in presidential campaign of 1988, **3:**168
Duke, Buck, **1:**172
Duke, David, **4:**553; **5:**161
Duke, James B., **1:**580; **2:**108; **8:**135
Duke of York's Laws, **3:**93
Duke of York's proprietary, **3:**93–94
Duke Power Company, Griggs v., **1:**36; **2:**197; **4:66; 8:**389, 390
Dulany, Daniel, **5:**167; **7:**135, 136
Dulhut, Greysolon, **3:**291–292
Dull Knife Campaign, **3:**94; **8:**404
Dulles, Allen W., **8:**394
   resignation of, **1:**431
Dulles, Avery, **4:**475
Dulles, John Foster, **3:**142; **5:**48
   at Bermuda Conference, **1:**445
   European integration and, **3:**260
   and Geneva Accords, **3:**534
   and "massive retaliation" strategy, **2:**532
   on United Fruit Company, **3:**479
   and Versailles Treaty, **8:**316
Dulles International Airport, **1:**98

Dumbarton Oaks Conference, **3:94–95; 8:**268, 272
"Dumbbell" tenement, **6:**80; **8:**82
Dummer, Fort, **8:**311
DuMont, Allen B., **8:**77
Dunant, Jean Henri, **3:**535
Dunbar, Charles, **3:**108
Dunbar, Paul Laurence, **3:**395; **5:**124
Dunbar, William, **1:**530
Duncan, David Douglas, **1:**301
Duncan, Isadora, **2:**497–498
Duncan, Thomas, **6:**500
Dunglison, Robert, **6:**348
Dunham, Katherine, **1:**131
Duniway, Abigail Scott, **6:***206*
   Path Breaking, excerpt from, **9:**334–337
   and women's suffrage, **6:**206
Dunkards, exemption from military service, **2:**361
Dunkers. *See* Brethren
Dunlap, John, **2:**522
Dunlop, John, **1:**153
Dunmore, John Murray, Lord, **1:**48; **3:**95
   Connolly's Plot and, **2:**360
Dunmore's Proclamation, **7:**8
Dunmore's War, **3:**95
Dunn, Anderson v., **2:**393
Dunn, Winfield, **8:**86
Dunn v. Blumstein, **8:**355
Duong Van Minh, **8:**334
Duplex Printing Press Co. v. Deering, **2:**229; **6:**121
"Duplex" telegraphy, **8:**69
Dupuy de Lôme, Enrique, **2:**470
Duquesne, Fort, **3:**95, 469, 470; **6:**361
   Braddock's expedition to capture, **1:530**
   building of, American colonial efforts to stop, **8:**460
Duquesne de Menneville, Marquis, **3:**95
Durand, Asher Brown, **4:**189, *189*
Durand, Elias, **6:**309
Durand, Peter, **3:**406
Durand-Ruel, Paul, **2:**272
Durang, Christopher, **8:**115
Durang, John, **2:**497
Durant, William Crapo, **3:**526
Duren v. Missouri, **8:**60
Durham, William H., **6:**287

Duryea, Charles E., **1:**366; **8:**189
Duryea, J. Frank, **1:**366; **8:**189
Duryea Motor Wagon Company, **8:**189
Dust Bowl, **2:**371; **3:**43, **95–96**, *96*; **8:**423
  causes of, **1:**65
  firsthand account of, **9:**384–385
  in Kansas, **4:**510
Dutch
  civil law of, **2:**291
  and colonial trade, **2:**282
  exploration of America by, **2:**39; **3:**286, **289–290**, *290*
  and Long Island, **5:**149
  settlement in Brooklyn, **1:**546
  settlement in Delaware, **2:**541
Dutch Anabaptists, **1:**411
Dutch bankers' loans, **3:**96
Dutch East India Company, **3:**275, 289
  and colonial settlements, **2:**289
Dutch Reformed churches, **7:**76, 89
Dutch West India Company, **3:96–97**, 289–290
  and colonial settlements, **2:**289
  land grants by, **6:**259
  New Amsterdam founded by, **6:**40, 79
  New Castle operating under, **6:**41
  New Netherland founded by, **6:**71, 79, 82
Dutchman (Baraka), **5:**126; **8:**115
Duties, ad valorem and specific, **3:**97; **8:**50
Dutton, Clarence E., **3:**552
Duvalier, François (Papa Doc), **4:**85; **8:**446
Duvalier, Jean-Claude (Baby Doc), **4:**85; **8:**446
Duveen, Sir Joseph, **2:**272
Duyckinck, Evert, **1:**294
Duyckinck, Gerrit, **1:**294
DVDs (digital versatile discs), **2:**329, 392; **3:97–98**; **8:**77
Dwight, James, **8:**89
Dwight, Jeremiah, and land speculation, **5:**36
Dwight, Theodore, **8:**145
Dwight, Timothy, **1:**377, *378*, 379
  on Bible and science, **7:**270
  The Conquest of Canaan, **5:**118
  and Hartford Wits, **4:**101
Dworkin, Andrea, **6:**419

Dyer, Mary, **8:**494, 501
Dyer Act (1919), **2:**459
Dyer Anti-Lynching Bill, **5:**180
Dyess Colony, **8:**303
Dylan, Bob, **1:**389, 441; **7:**185
"Dynamical" geology, **3:**552
Dynamite, **3:**301, 302
Dynamo, **3:**173
Dynasty (TV show), **7:***409*

E

E. C. Knight Company, United States v., **1:**20; **2:**310, 311, 418; **4:**26; **7:**343, 344; **8:**234, **274**
E. T.: The Extra-Terrestrial (film), **1:**34
"E Pluribus Unum," **3:**99
Eads, James B., **1:**538, 564; **3:**99
Eads Bridge, **1:**538, 564; **3:**99, *99*
Eagan, Eddie, **6:**192
Eagle
  American, **3:99–100**, *100*
  bald, near extinction of, **3:**232, 233
Eagleson, Alan, **4:**145
Eagleton, Thomas, **3:**100, 166
Eagleton Affair, **3:100**
Eakins, Thomas, **1:**296–297; **3:**537
Eames, Charles, **1:**293; **3:**499
Eames, Ray, **1:**293; **3:**499
Earle, Alice Morse, **2:**271
Earle, Bank of Augusta v., **1:**395
Earle, Sir Walter, **3:**80
Early, Jubal A.
  at Battle of Chancellorsville, **2:**104
  in Shenandoah Campaign, **7:**341, 342
  threat to Washington, **2:**218
Earned Income Tax Credit (EITC), **6:**438–439
Earp, Wyatt, **3:***70*
Earp brothers, **8:**141
Earth Day, **3:100**
  Bush (George H.) on, **3:**229
  first, **3:**227–228
Earth First!, **3:**229, *229*
Earth in the Balance (Gore), **4:**8
Earth Summit, **2:**238
Earth Technology Resource Satellite (ETRS), **3:**553
Earthlodges, **1:**254
Earthquakes, **3:**36–37, **100–103**
  in California, **5:**153–154

  San Francisco, **7:240**, *240*
Easley, Ralph M., **5:**530
Easley v. Cromartie, **3:**62
East Asia, dollar diplomacy in, **3:**71
East Coast Homophile Organizations (ECHO), **3:**514
East Germany, **3:**562–563; **8:**552
  CIA operations in, **2:**92
East India Company
  Dutch, **3:**275, 289
  English/British, **1:**514; **3:**103, 275
  monopoly on tea, **2:**286; **8:**60, 61
East Indies trade, **3:**103
East Jersey, **2:**289; **3:103–104**
East Tennessee, **8:**83
Eastchurch, Thomas, **2:**476
Easter Offensive, **8:**334, 335
Eastern Airlines, **1:**83
Eastern Europe
  in Cold War, Iron Curtain of, **4:429–430**
  EU expansion into, **3:**261
  immigration from, **2:**89; **4:**224–225
    to Cleveland, **2:**233
    to Iowa, **4:**415
  Orthodox churches in, **6:**216–217
  revolutions of 1989 in, **2:**270
  Soviet control over, **2:**89–90, 268, 269; **8:**574
  See also Central Europe
Eastern Railroad Conference v. Noerr Motor Freight, **6:**297
Eastern Woodlands
  Native American social life in, **4:**304
  prehistoric, **1:**246–247
    Hopewell in, **4:**163
Eastlake, Charles Lock, **3:**497
Eastman, Charles, **3:**474–475
Eastman, Crystal, **8:**499
Eastman, George, **6:**329, 366
Eastman Kodak, **6:**329–330
Eastman Kodak Research Laboratory, **6:**329
Easton, David, **6:**401, 403, 407
Easton, Edward, **1:**358
Easy chairs, **3:**495
Eating disorders, **3:104**
Eating habits
  American, **2:**98
  See also Diets
Eaton, Amos, **1:**519
Eaton, Charles, **8:**272
Eaton, Cyrus S., **6:**548

Eaton, Dorman B., **6**:275

Eaton, Hubert, **2**:81

Eaton, John, **2**:396; **3**:104–105;
    5:424

Eaton, Theophilus, **2**:289; **6**:59

Eaton affair, **3:104–105**

eBay, **3**:183

Ebbinghaus, Hermann, **6**:523

Eberly, David, on Persian Gulf War,
    9:518–520

E-book technology, **6**:539

EBWR. *See* Experimental boiling
    water reactor

Eccles, Marriner, **3**:345

ECHO. *See* East Coast Homophile
    Organizations

Eckert, J. Presper, **2**:334

Eckholm, H. Conrad, **1**:433

Eckley, Francis, **1**:514

Eclectic Reader (McGuffey), **8**:106

Eclecticism, in architecture,
    1:249–250, 253

Eclipse, solar, of 1831, **9**:45, *47*

ECOA. *See* Equal Credit Opportu-
    nity Act

Ecodevelopment, **3**:226

Ecological forestry, **3**:437–438

Ecology, **2**:370; **3**:551
    deep, **8**:479
    professionalization of, **8**:481
    See also Conservation; Environ-
        mental movement

E-commerce. *See* Electronic com-
    merce

Economic censorship, **2**:84, 85

Economic indicators, **3:105–107**
    business forecasting, **1**:586–588
    cost of living, **2**:422–424

Economic nationalism, **1**:171

Economic Opportunity, Office of,
    credit unions subsidized by,
    2:454

Economic Opportunity Act (EOA)
    (1964), **2**:328; **8**:385, 386

Economic Royalists, **3:107**

Economic sectionalism, **7**:298

Economic Stabilization Agency
    (ESA), **6**:166

Economics, **3:107–111**
    American System of, **1:171**
    business cycles, **1:582–586**, *583*
    under Hamilton, **4**:87–91
        Bank of United States in, **4**:89–90
        domestic debts in, **4**:87–88

foreign debts in, **4**:87
    vs. Jeffersonian Republicans,
        4:471
    manufacturing in, **4**:90; **5**:227
    mint in, **4**:90
    nationalism in, **1**:171; **4**:87
    state debt in, **4**:88–89
    taxation in, **4**:89
    Keynesian, **4:523**; **5**:441–442
    Nobel Prizes in, **6**:487
    politicization of, **2**:432
    statistics in, **7**:538–539
    supply-side, **5**:441; **8:21–22**, 29

Economies of scale, **3**:577

Economy
    of Confederate States of America,
        2:216–217, 342–343
    inflation in, **4:350–353**
    of Native Americans, **4**:267–269
    stagflation in, **7:516–517**

ECSC. *See* European Coal and Steel
    Community

ECT. *See* Electroconvulsive shock
    therapy

Ecuador
    commerce with, **5**:44–45
    U.S. relations with, Galápagos
        Islands and, **3**:503

Ecumenical movement, Disciples of
    Christ on, **3**:45

Eddis, William, on indentured ser-
    vants, **9**:114–116

Eddy, Arthur Jerome, **1**:316

Eddy, Mary Baker, **2**:170–171, *171*;
    8:501
    See also Church of Christ, Scientist

Edell, David J., **1**:463

Edelman, Bernard, *Dear America:
    Letters Home from Vietnam*,
    excerpt from, **9**:473–474

Eden, Anthony, at summit confer-
    ences, **8**:15

Eden Theological Seminary, **8**:264

Ederle, Gertrude, **8**:37

Edes, Benjamin, **1**:129

Edge, Walter, Port Authority of
    New York and New Jersey cre-
    ated by, **6**:421

Edger, Henry, **6**:424

Edison, Thomas Alva, **3**:173, 177,
    178, 210, 211; **5**:108; **6**:366
    carbon lamp by, **5**:24
    discovery of electricity as energy
        source by, **3**:577

in Henry Ford Museum and
    Greenfield Village, **4**:127, *127*
    and industrial development, **2**:388
    kinetoscopic records by, **3**:361
    Mimeograph by, **6**:168–169
    phonograph by, **1**:189, 357–358;
        5:502
    "quadruplex" telegraphy by, **8**:69
    stock ticker developed by, **8**:456

Edison Corporation, **3**:361

Edison Lamp Factory fire (1914),
    5:14

Editorial cartoons, **6**:395

Edmondson, William, **1**:310

Edmunds Act (1882), **5**:54; **8**:297

Edmunds-Tucker Act (1887), **5**:54;
    8:297

Education, **3:111–120**
    in 19th century, **3**:113–116
    in 20th century
        early, **3**:116–117
        later, **3**:117–119
    adult, **3**:115
        Chautauqua movement and,
            2:113
    for African Americans, **1**:482;
        3:115, 117, 118, **120–121**
    for aliens, **1**:126
    after American Revolution,
        3:112–113
    bilingual, **3:121–122**, 136
    Catholic, **4**:474–475
    Christian history in, **7**:299
    Civilian Conservation Corps and,
        2:220
    coeducation, **2:263–264**
    in colonial era, **2**:263, 291;
        3:111–112
    and college athletics, **2**:276
    district schools in, **7**:264
    hornbook in, **4**:*166*, **166–167**
    Massachusetts school law on,
        9:92–93
    cooperative, **3:122–123**
    4-H Clubs, **3:445–446**
    for deaf students, **7**:355–357
    for disabled students, **3:33–35**
        federal government and, **3**:123
    engineering, **3**:116–217
    exchange programs, Fulbright
        grants and, **3**:482–483
    experimental, **3:124–125**
    for farmers, **3**:325
    Farmers' Alliance on, **6**:416

Education, (*continued*)
  federal aid to, **2:**482; **5:**29
  federal government's role in, **3:**123
  funding for, philanthropy and, **2:**56
  higher, **3:125–133** (*See also* College[s]; Universities)
    academic freedom in, **1:10–11,** 142–143
    admissions policies in, **1:**386
    admissions testing in, **3:**139–140
      SAT in, **7:252**
    affirmative action in, **1:**37
    African American Studies in, **1:46–47; 3:**119
    agricultural and mechanical, **5:**460
    American Studies in, **1:168–171**
    associations in, **1:**142–143
    Congregationalism and, **8:**263
    for deaf students, **3:**504
    denominational colleges, **2:**70; **3:129–131**
    economics in, **3:**108
    exchange students in, **3:**274
    free, **3:461–462**
    German Reformed church and, **8:**264
    graduate schools, racial segregation in, **5:**526
    growth of, **3:**117
    military training in, **7:**119–120
    music in, **5:**492
    in Ohio, **6:**174
    religion in, **7:**98
    Rhodes scholarships, **3:**274; **7:154**
    in science, **7:271–273,** 340
    in social work, **7:**423
    in sociology, **7:**433–434, 436
    state universities, **8:279–280**
    teacher training in, **8:**62
    in Virginia, **8:**345–346
  with home schooling, **4:153–154**
  homework in, **4:158–159**
  in Kentucky, **4:**520
  in Latin schools, **5:52**
  legal (*See* Law schools)
  lifelong, **5:**365
  little red schoolhouse in, **5:133–134**
  lyceum movement and, **5:**178
  magnet schools, **5:201–202**
  McGuffey's Readers, **5:185**
  Mechanics' Institutes, **5:280**
  middlebrow culture and, **5:**365–366
  in Missouri, **5:**422
  multiculturalism in, **5:473–474**
  music, in singing schools, **7:**366
  National Education Association and, **5:**534–535
  national goals in, **3:**123–124
  for Native Americans, **3:**112, 115, 129, **133–134**
    in 19th century, **8:**226
    at boarding schools, **2:**55, 145; **3:**135–136; **4:262–263,** 286
    National Indian Youth Council and, **5:**532, **543–544**
    at tribal colleges, **8:**210–211
  in New England colonies, **6:**49–50
  parental choice in, **3:137–138; 7:**268
    busing and, **1:**589, 590
    charter schools and, **2:**110
    magnet schools and, **5:201–202**
    school vouchers and, **7:266**
    Supreme Court on, **6:**352–353
  Peabody Fund and, **6:**262
  by Peace Corps volunteers, **6:**266
  pharmaceutical, **6:**309–310
  philanthropy and, **6:**317
  preschool, Head Start program, **4:112–113**
  psychology and, **6:**524
  public (*See also* Public schools)
    in 19th century, **3:**114
    in 20th century, **3:**117
    Jefferson (Thomas) and, **3:**112–113; **8:**279
  in rural communities, **7:**208, 209
  secondary (*See* High schools)
  sex, **7:321–322**
  sexual harassment in, **7:**322–324
  special, **3:**34 (*See also* Disabled persons, education for)
  spelling bees in, **7:501**
  Teacher Corps and, **8:**61–62
  textbooks and, **8:**105–107
  transcendentalism on, **8:**180
  vocational, legislation on, **7:**401–402
  in Wisconsin, **8:**492
Education, Department of, **3:123–124,** 332
  and curriculum, **2:**482
  establishment of, **4:**114
  head of, **2:**2
  Reagan's attempt to remove, **3:**119
Education, United States Office of, **3:138–139**
Education (Mill), **6:**424
Education Alliance, **5:**166
Education for All Handicapped Children Act (1975), **3:**33, 118
  court cases leading to, **3:**34
Educational and intelligence testing. *See* Intelligence, testing of
Educational Orders Act (1938), **6:**202
Educational technology, **3:139**
Educational Testing Service (ETS), **2:**56; **3:139–140**
Edward (British sloop), **5:**87
Edward III (king of England), on treason, **8:**193
Edward VI (king of England), **3:**287
Edwards, Edwin W., **5:**161
Edwards, Jonathan, **2:**162; **3:**140, 264; **4:**38; **5:**118, 506; **6:**65, *65,* 324–325; **7:**96
  A Faithful Narrative of the Surprising Work of God, **5:**118
  mysticism of, **5:**506
Edwards, Jonathan, Jr., **7:**96
Edwards, Ninian, **4:**214–215
Edwardsean theology, **3:140**
EEC. *See* European Economic Community
EEOC. *See* Equal Employment Opportunity Commission
EFTA. *See* European Free Trade Association
Egan, Michael, **3:**453
Egleston, Nathaniel, **3:**430
Egner, Hans, **1:**13
Egypt
  foreign aid to, **3:**418
  Israel and, **3:**141; **8:**270
    Camp David Peace Accords, **2:**20; **3:**141
    conflict between, **4:**441
    peace settlement for, **1:**233; **4:**441
    in Suez Crisis, **8:**2–3
  U.S. relations with, **1:**40, 233, 234, 445; **3:140–142**
  right of extraterritoriality, **3:**304
EgyptAir Flight 990, **3:**36
Egyptian Americans, **1:**231
Ehrlich, Paul
  and chemotherapy, **2:**124
  The Population Bomb, **3:**228

Eielsen, Elling, **6:**137

Eielsen Synod, **6:**137

Eight, The. *See* Ashcan School

Eight Bells (Homer), **3:**537

Eight Men (Wright), **5:**125

Eighteenth Amendment, **1:**503–504; **6:**501

  effects of, **1:**117

  in electoral politics, **3:**162

  enforcement of, Volstead Act for, **6:**501; **8:**352

  repeal of, **1:**117

Eighth Amendment, **1:**457; **6:**552

  excessive bail prohibited by, **1:**385

Eigo, James, **1:**16

Eijkman, Christiaan, **6:**148

Einhorn, David, **4:**489–490

Einstein, Albert

  at Princeton University, **6:**465

  and Pugwash Conferences, **6:**547

  and quantum theory, **6:**345

  visits to California Institute of Technology, **2:**14

EIS. *See* Environmental Impact Statement

Eisaku, Sato, **4:**459

Eisenhower, Dwight D., **8:***503*

  on air defense, **1:**76

  and Air Force, **1:**77, 78

  anticonservation policies of, **2:**372

  antidiscrimination policies of, **3:**49

  and appearance of flag, **3:**378

  arms race under, **1:**271

  Atoms for Peace program of, **3:**208; **6:**140

  at Bermuda Conference, **1:**445

  and Camp David, **2:**20, *20*

  and Canada, relations with, **2:**27

  and civil rights, **2:**194, 202

  Council of Economic Advisors and, **2:**431

  Cuba policy of, **2:**470

  defense policy of, **2:**528

  domestic policy of, **7:**113

  and domino theory, **3:**78

  Eisenhower Doctrine of, **1:**233, 445; **3:**142

  farewell address by, text of, **9:**434–435

  and Federal Mediation and Conciliation Service, **3:**343

  and foreign aid to South Vietnam, **3:**417

  foreign policy of, **3:**426–427; **7:**113

  and Foreign Service, **3:**28

  and Geneva Accords, **3:**534

  at Geneva Conference (1954), **3:**534–535

  Health, Education, and Welfare Department under, **4:**113

  Information Agency created by, **6:**504

  Internet and, **4:**398

  interstate highway system under, **4:**403

  Israel and, **4:**440–441

  John Birch Society on, **1:**198; **4:**481

  in Korean War, **4:**549

  labor policies of, **3:**244

  Latin American policies of, **5:**48

  and Lebanon, U.S. landing in, **5:**72

  on military-industrial complex, **5:**376

  on munitions industry, **5:**482

  and NASA, **5:**523

  and National Security Council, **3:**330

  New Look policy of, **2:**528

  New York Times on, **6:**90

  in Normandy Invasion, **6:**118

  and Paris Conference (1960), **6:**247

  and Pledge of Allegiance, **6:**370

  in presidential campaign of 1952, **3:**164

  in presidential campaign of 1956, **3:**164

  presidential library of, **5:**100

  and President's Foreign Intelligence Advisory Board, **3:**330

  and prisoners of war, **6:**472

  and psychological warfare, **6:**523

  and Republican Party, **7:**113

  and road construction, **7:**178

  and school desegregation, in Arkansas, **1:**263

  space program under, **7:**479–480

  in Suez Crisis, **8:**3

  at summit conferences, **8:**15

  on tidelands, **8:**125

  and Tomb of the Unknown Soldier, **8:**285

  and Transportation, Department of, **8:**185

  U-2 incident and, **8:**247

  and Vietnam War, **8:**330

  in World War II, **1:**426, 565; **8:**549

    and American occupation of Germany, **3:**561

    Market Garden, **1:**1

    North African Campaigns, **1:**233; **6:**123

    Sicilian Campaign, **7:**353

Eisenhower, Milton S., **8:**340

Eisenhower Doctrine, **1:**233, 445; **3:142**

Eisenman, Peter, **1:**253

Eisenstadt, Alfred, **1:**300

Eisenstadt v. Baird, **5:**251

EITC. *See* Earned Income Tax Credit

EKG (electrocardiograph), **2:**53

El Caney, Battle of, **7:***241*, 241–242, *242*

El Paso (Texas), **3:142**

El Salvador

  Bryan-Chamorro Treaty and, **1:**550

  civil war in, **8:**271

  foreign aid to, **3:**418

  U.S. relations with, **3:142–144**; **5:**49

El Turco, **2:**416–417

Elbe River, **3:144**

ELCA. *See* Evangelical Lutheran Church in America

Elderly. *See* Old age

Elders, Jocelyn, **5:**511

Election(s), **3:145–148**

  canvassing prior to, **2:**38

  congressional, federal supervision of, proposal for, **2:**332

  contested, **3:**148, 152, 156–157, 169–170, 171

    Bush v. Gore, **1:**578–579; **3:**170, 171, 246

  corruption in, bosses/bossism and, **1:507–508**

  direct primary, **6:463**

  gubernatorial, voter participation in, **8:***8*

  interest groups and, **4:**381

  political action committees and, **6:**393

  and political patronage, **6:**258

  preferential voting and, **6:448–449**

  presidential, **3:148–170**

    of 1789, **3:**150, 171

    of 1792, **3:**150

    of 1796, **3:**150, 171; **8:**322

    of 1800, **3:**145, 148, **150**, 171, 351–352; **4:**471; **8:**322

Election(s), (continued)
  of 1804, **3:**150–151
  of 1808, **3:**151
  of 1812, **3:**151
  of 1816, **3:**151
  of 1820, **3:**151
  of 1824, **3:**152, 171; **5:**555;
      8:322–323
    corrupt bargain in, **2:**420
  of 1828, **3:**152; **8:**323
  of 1832, **3:**152
  of 1836, **3:**152–153
  of 1840, **2:**550; **3:**146, **153**; **8:**131
  of 1848, **3:**154
  of 1852, **3:**154
  of 1856, **1:**166; **3:**154
  of 1860, **2:**383, 400; **3:**154–155;
      5:420–421
  of 1864, **2:**218; **3:**155
  of 1868, **3:**155
  of 1872, **1:**488; **3:**155–156
  of 1876, **1:**488; **3:**148, **156–157**,
      171; **8:**560
    compromise settlement of,
        2:551
    political corruption in,
        2:420–421, 467
  of 1880, **2:**400, 467; **3:**157
  of 1884, **1:**196; **2:**453; **3:**157
  of 1888, **3:**157–158, 171; **8:**233
  of 1892, **3:**158; **6:**158
  of 1896, **2:**46, 465; **3:**158–159;
      6:398, 418; **8:**234
    populism and, **5:**366
  of 1900, **3:**159, 483; **6:**320
  of 1904, **3:**159–160; **8:**323
  of 1908, **3:**160
  of 1912, **1:**566; **3:**160–161; **6:**54,
      70, 496; **8:**43, 119
  of 1916, **3:**161
  of 1920, **3:**161; **6:**118
  of 1924, **3:**161–162; **6:**498; **8:**323
  of 1928, **2:**136; **3:**162; **6:**5
    Catholic candidate in, **2:**164,
        552
  of 1932, **1:**498; **3:**162
    Communist candidate in, **2:**326
  of 1936, **3:**162–163; **6:**409, 500,
      533, 534
  of 1940, **3:**163
  of 1944, **3:**163
  of 1948, **1:**197; **3:**163–164;
      6:409, 499, 534; **8:**323
  of 1952, **2:**553; **3:**164

  of 1956, **3:**164
  of 1960, **3:**164–165; **6:**55, 463
  of 1964, **2:**374; **3:**165
  of 1968, **1:**159; **2:**204;
      3:165–166; **8:**333
  of 1972, **3:**100, **166**; **6:**227
  of 1976, **3:**166–167; **6:**517–518
  of 1980, **3:**167, 267; **6:**534
    Moral Majority and, **2:**165
  of 1984, **1:**52; **3:**167–168
  of 1988, **3:**168
  of 1992, **2:**239, 376; **3:**168–169;
      8:118
  of 1996, **3:**169; **8:**120
  of 2000, **3:**144, 147, 148, 149,
      169–170
    ballot irregularities in, **1:**392
    candidates' responses to out-
        come, **9:**523–526
    Clinton scandals and, **2:**240
    complexity of problems with,
        8:357
    education policy issue in, **3:**119
    Florida in, **3:**388
    language issue in, **3:**221
    Nader as third-party candidate
        in, **8:**120
    National Rifle Association and,
        5:557
    political corruption in, **2:**421
    Supreme Court on, **1:**578–579;
        3:170, 171, 246; **4:**494;
        7:527; **9:**523–526
    voter registration in, **8:**354
  AFL-CIO and, **1:**151, 152, 153
  congressional caucus and, **2:**76
  Constitutional Convention on,
      2:380
  and party platforms, **6:**368–369,
      399
  and polling, **6:**409, 533–534
  primary, **3:**148
    increasing importance of, **3:**147
  public financing for, **2:**23
  sectionalism in, **7:**298
  Twelfth Amendment and, **3:**171
  proportional representation and,
      6:508
  research on, **3:**147
  soft money in, **7:**439
  state
    in Massachusetts, **5:**268
    poll taxes in, **8:**9, 344
    white primaries in, **6:**463

Election laws, **3:**144–145, 148
  gerrymandering and, **3:**564
  majority rule, **5:**211–213
Elective Governor Act (1968), **8:**341
Electoral College, **2:**350; **3:**170–172
  in 1796 election, **8:**322
  members of, state legislature selec-
      tion of, **8:**355–356
  proposal for, **2:**380
  vice president elected by, **8:**322
Electric power and light industry,
    3:172–176, 177–178
  automation in, **1:**365
  deregulation of, **3:**175–176
  and manufacturing, **5:**4
  monopolies in, **6:**535
  at Niagara Falls, **6:**103
  in North Carolina, **6:**130
  nuclear power used in, **6:**138–140
  price controls and, **6:**460
  Tennessee River and, **8:**87, 88
  See also Hydroelectric power
Electric street railways, **7:**43–44
Electric typewriters, **8:**245
Electric vehicles, **3:**480
Electrical workers, **3:**176–177
Electricity, **3:**177–178
  consumption of, **3:**180
  and demand for copper, **2:**410
  domestic uses of, **3:**175, **179–183**,
      182
  fossil fuels and, **3:**210
  in rural areas, **7:**209
  sources of, **3:**212, 213
Electrification, household,
    3:179–183, 182; **4:**535, 536
  in New Deal, **1:**67
  in Power (play), **9:**388–390
  in rural areas, **3:**180
Electrocardiograph (EKG), **2:**53
Electroconvulsive shock therapy
    (ECT), **6:**522
Electron, **6:**339, 340
Electronic cameras, **6:**330
Electronic commerce (e-commerce),
    3:183–184; **5:**206; **7:**126
  digital money in, **5:**442
  interstate barriers to, **4:**406
  public-key cryptography and,
      2:468
Electronic intelligence (ELINT),
    5:558
Electronic mail. See E-mail

Electronic Numerical Integrator and Calculator (ENIAC), **2:**334–335; **3:**25
Electronic publishing, **2:**323; **6:**539
of dictionaries, **3:**23
Electronic scanning systems, **8:**77
Electronic surveillance, **3:185–186,** 338–339
Electronics, **3:178–179**
and finance, **1:**399
research in, **1:**440
Electronics industry
automation in, **1:**365–366
foreign competition in, **7:**360–361
foreign trade and, **8:**167, 169
job mobility in, **7:**360
research and development in, **4:**339
semiconductors in, **7:306–307,** 360
in Silicon Valley, **7:**306, **360–361**
Electrotype, **6:**469
Elementary and Secondary Education Act (ESEA) (1965), **2:**196, 200; **3:**118
legislation re-authorizing, **3:**119, 124
Title VII of, **3:**122
Title IX of, **3:**118
Elementary Spelling Book (Webster), **8:434**
Elementary Treatise on Mineralogy and Geology (Cleaveland), **5:**390
Elements of Popular Theology (Schmucker), **5:**176
Elements of Style (Strunk and White), **3:**222
Elevators, **3:***186,* **186–187**
in department stores, **7:**125
grain, **3:187–188**
Eleventh Amendment, **2:**158; **7:**119
on suits against states, **1:**120; **3:**342
Elgin, Lord, **2:**28
Eli Lilly and Company, **3:**531
ELINT. *See* Electronic intelligence
Eliot, Charles W., **3:**115, 116, 274; **4:**102; **5:**56, 59
Eliot, John, **1:**431, 447; **6:**448, 536
Dialogues of, **9:**99–100
Indian Bible by, **4:262**
on influenza, **4:**353
Eliot, T. S., **3:**197; **5:**157
The Waste Land, **5:**120
"Elixir sulfanilamide," **3:**404; **6:**555

Elizabeth I (queen of England), **3:**285, 287, 288
and Raleigh, **7:**46
Elizabethan poor law, **8:**439
Elizabethtown Associates, **3:188**
Elkins, Stanley M., **4:**140
Elkins Act (1903), **3:188;** **7:**26, 27; **8:**234
Ellet, Charles, **1:**539
Ellicott, Andrew, **1:**130
Ellington, Duke, **4:***467,* 468; **8:**410
Elliot, Joel, **6:**263
Elliott, Jesse D., **4:**53
in Great Lakes Naval Campaigns of 1812, **4:**53
in Perry-Elliott Controversy, **6:290–291**
Elliott, William Yandell, **6:**403
Ellis, A. Carswell, **3:**354
Ellis, Edward S., **5:**129
Ellis Island, **3:188–189,** *189;* **4:***224;* **6:**88
examination at, **3:***258*
Ellison, Ralph, **3:**280; **8:**241
Invisible Man, **4:413–414;** **5:**121, 125
Ellsberg, Daniel, **6:**286, 287; **8:**425
Ellsworth, Henry L., **1:**71
Ellsworth, Lincoln, **6:**384
Ellsworth, Oliver, at Constitutional Convention, **2:**379
Ellwood, Isaac, **1:**416
Elmhurst College, **8:**264
Elmira College, **3:**131
Elmira Prison, **3:189–190;** **7:**75
Elssler, Fanny, **1:**389
Elton, Robert, **1:**129
Elway, John, **5:**72
Ely, Eugene B., **1:**89
Ely, Richard E., **1:**159; **7:**413
Ely, Richard T., **3:**107, 109; **8:**284
E-mail (electronic mail), **2:**337; **3:184–185;** **8:**66, 67
privacy concerns about, **6:**480
Emancipation
compensated, **2:**542; **3:190**
gradual, **1:**208
illusion of freedom after, **1:**49–51
manumission, **5:230–231**
Emancipation Proclamation, **2:**212, 217; **3:190–192,** *191;* **6:**491
Battle of Antietam and, **1:**200
experiment preceding, **2:**542
initial backlash against, **2:**218, 411

text of, **9:**300–301
Embalmed beef, **3:192**
Embargo Act (1807), **3:192–193**
and Alexandria tobacco trade, **1:**122
Chesapeake-Leopard incident and, **2:**130
effects of, **8:**164, 381
factory production and, **5:**227–228
Nonintercourse Act (1809) replacing, **6:**117
and War of 1812, **8:**381
Embassies, **3:**28, **193–194**
bombing of, **3:194**
in Africa, **6:**109
staff of, **1:**133–134
ambassadors, **1:**133
Emblem of the United States, **3:99–100**
Emergency Banking Act (1933), **6:43**
Emergency Fleet Corporation, **3:194–195;** **8:**536
Emergency Price Control Act (EPCA) (1942), **6:**165
Emergency Relief Appropriation Act (1938), **6:**44
Emergency Tariff (1921), **8:**51
Emergency Tax Relief Act (1981), **8:**59
Emerson, Irene, **3:**85
Emerson, John, **3:**85
Emerson, Ralph Waldo, **1:**509; **5:**119, 506; **6:**324
"The American Scholar," **5:**119
at Brook Farm, **1:**545; **8:**301
on cities, **8:**292
Essays, **3:195**
on individualism, **4:**332
on law, **2:**317
mysticism of, **5:**506
Nature, **5:**119; **7:**194
and pluralism, **6:**373
on property, **6:**504
"Representative Men," **5:**119
and transcendentalism, **3:**195; **7:**194; **8:**179, 180, *180,* 300, 301
as Unitarian pastor, **7:**97
on weeds, **8:**436
on Whitman's *Leaves of Grass,* **5:**71
on Young Americanism, **8:**583
Emerson, Thomas, **2:**6
Emery, Lin, **1:**309

Emigrant Aid Company, **5**:59
Emigrant Aid Movement,
    3:195–196
Emigrant-cars, **5**:*372*
Emigration, **3:196–198**
  of African Americans, **1**:147–148,
    208–209, 477; **2**:296–297;
    3:197
    to Liberia, **1**:148
  Confederate, after Civil War, **2**:340
  of Jewish Americans, **3**:197; **8**:592,
    593
  of Loyalists
    to British West Indies, **8**:446
    to Canada, **7**:137; **8**:266
Emily's List, **3:198**
Eminent domain, **3:198–199**; **6**:505
  and capitalist development, **2**:43
  United States v. Lee and, **8**:274
  and urban redevelopment, **8**:285
Emissions trading, **1**:80
Emmanuel I (king of Portugal), **3**:283
Emmett, Daniel Decatur, **3**:66
Emmons, Nathaniel, **7**:96
Emmons, Samuel F., **3**:552
Emoticon, **8**:67
Empire State Building, **3**:199, *199*;
  6:80
  airplane crash into, **3**:35
Empire style furniture, **3**:496
Employers
  blacklisting by, **1**:483
  dues checkoff and, **2**:115
  welfare capitalists, **8:437–438**
  and workers' compensation,
    3:199–200; **8:529–530**
Employers' defenses, **5**:13
Employers' liability laws,
    3:199–200; **5**:14
Employment
  affirmative action in, **1**:35–37;
    4:66; **7**:315–316
    Proposition 209 and, **6**:509–510
  business cycles and, **1**:582
  discrimination in (*See* Discrimina-
    tion, employment)
  equal opportunity, **3:243–245**
  NAFTA and, **6**:124
  seniority rights in, **7:311–312**
  sexual harassment in, **7**:322–323
Employment Act (1946), **3:200**;
  8:254
  and Council of Economic Advisors,
    2:430; **3**:307, 330

Employment Anti-Discrimination
  Act (ENDA) (1994), **3**:56
Employment Division v. Smith, **1**:162,
  494; **2**:170; **3**:374; **6**:1
Employment Retirement Income
  Security Act (ERISA) (1974),
  3:200–201; **6**:284, 493; **7**:130,
  131
Employment Service, U.S.,
  3:201–202
Empowerment Zone program,
  8:287
Empresario system, **3:202**
  in Texas, **8**:99, 101
Empress of China (U.S. ship), **2**:153
Emspak, Julius, **3**:176
ENA. *See* Experimental Negotiating
  Agreement
Enabling Acts, **3:202**
Encarta, **3**:205
Encomienda system, **3:202–203**
Encounter groups, **3:203**
Encyclopaedia Britannica, **3**:204
  online, **3**:205
Encyclopedias, **3:203–205**
Encyclopédie (Diderot and d'Alem-
  bert), **3**:204
End of Nature, The (McKibben), **4**:8
ENDA. *See* Employment Anti-Dis-
  crimination Act
Endangered species, **2**:373;
  3:205–207, *206*
  wolf as, **8**:496
Endangered Species Act (ESA) (1973),
  3:100, 205, 228; **8**:424, 482
Endangered Species Preservation
  Act (1966), **3**:432
Endara, Guillermo, **6**:241, 242
Enders, John F., **6**:388
Endicott, John, **3**:80
Endowed foundations, **3:443–445**
Enemy aliens, in world wars,
  3:207–208
  World War I, **8**:538
Energy
  consumption of, **3**:180, 211–212
    projections for, **3**:213
  policies on (*See under specific admin-
    istrations*)
  renewable, **3**:209, 212–213, *213*,
    214–215
  future of, **3**:213
Energy, Department of (DOE),
  3:208–210, 215, 332

  accelerator construction by, **6**:339
  on hydroelectric power, **4**:202
  and naval oil reserves, **6**:20
  research budget of, **5**:19
Energy crisis of 1970s
  and automobile industry, **1**:370
  Carter's address on, text of,
    9:492–494
  See also Oil crises
Energy industry, **3:210–214**
  genetic engineering and, **3**:531
  See also Petroleum industry
Energy Information Administration,
  6:140
Energy Policy Act (1992), **6**:373
Energy Policy and Conservation Act
  (1975), **8**:190
Energy Reorganization Act (1974),
  6:141
Energy Research and Development
  Administration (ERDA), **3**:209,
  215–216
Energy Star program, **3**:233
Enforcement Acts (1870), **8**:273, 275
  See also Force Acts
Enforcement Bureau of Federal
  Communications Commission,
  3:340
Engelbart, Doug, **7**:280
Engerman, Stanley, **3**:107
Engineering education, **3:216–217**;
  7:272
  at Franklin Institute, **3**:455
  at MIT, **5:272–273**
  at Naval Academy, **6**:19
  Progressive Era and, **3**:251
  at West Point, **5**:374
Engineering societies, **3:217–218**
  National Academy of Engineering,
    5:522, 523
Engineers, U.S. Army Corps of,
    3:218–220
  mapping and surveying by, **2**:62
  Missouri River dams by, **5**:220
  road-building by, **7**:181
  waterway projects of, **7**:169–170;
    8:430
  West Point and, **7**:168
England. *See* Great Britain
Engle v. Vitale, **3**:374
Engler, John, **5**:356–357
English language, **3:220–222**
  American form of, development of,
    8:434

American Sign Language and,
7:356
among Native Americans, 1:482
slang in, 7:377–378
slaves' use of, 7:395, 396
English system of measures, 5:529
Engraving
wax (cerography), 5:233
wood, 8:522–523
Engstead, John, 1:300
ENIAC (Electronic Numerical Integrator and Calculator),
2:334–335; 3:25
Enlightenment
anthropology and ethnology in,
1:191
Constitution as document of, 2:382
Monticello and, 5:452
and pluralism, 6:374
Enlistment, 3:222–223
in American Revolution, 7:140
bounties and, 1:524
in Civil War, 2:210
volunteer, 8:352
Enoch Pratt Free Library (Baltimore), 5:98
Enos, Roger, 1:281
Enron Corporation, 2:419
scandal associated with, 3:176,
223; 4:27
Ensign, 3:223
Entail of estate, 3:223–224
primogeniture, 6:463–464
Entangling alliances, 3:224
Enterprise for the Americas Initia-
tive, 6:124
Enterprise resource planning (ERP),
7:442
Enterprise software, 7:441–442
Enterprise zones, 3:224
Entertainment
as consumer good, 2:390
film industry and, 2:323
television and, 2:391
zoological parks and, 8:594–595
Entrepreneurial ethic, 8:528–529
Enumerated commodities,
3:224–225
Enumerated powers, 3:225
Environmental accidents, 3:228
Exxon Valdez oil spill, 3:39, 233,
305, 305–306
Environmental business, 3:225–226

Environmental crisis, in 1950s,
2:371–372
Environmental furniture, 3:499
Environmental Impact Statement
(EIS), 3:228
Environmental movement, 2:372;
3:226–231
and climate change, interest in,
2:237
and Earth Day celebration, 3:100,
227–228
founding texts of, 2:370
in Maine, 5:210
marine sanctuaries, 5:244
and national park system,
5:552–553
on nuclear power, 6:139, 141
origins of, 3:232
and public interest law, 6:530
and recycling, 7:67
Silent Spring in, 7:359; 8:423
in Wyoming, 8:565
See also Conservation
Environmental problems, 3:225
and climate change, 2:237–238
coal mining and, 2:253
from dam construction, 4:201–202,
436
energy consumption and, 3:213, 214
global nature of, 3:230
from hazardous waste, 4:111–112
health hazards, 5:298
Industrial Revolution and, 8:422
from introduced species,
7:499–500
from irrigation, 4:436
and Native Americans, 8:571
nitrates, 6:110
ozone depletion, 1:80; 6:*223*,
223–224; 7:246
paper industry, 6:246
See also Air pollution; Water pollution
Environmental protection, 3:226
Environmental Protection Agency
(EPA), 3:231–233, 332
and air pollution, 1:79, 362
and auto emissions, 1:362
and biological pesticides, regulation of, 1:463
and Clean Air Act enforcement,
2:230
and Clean Water Act enforcement,
2:231

establishment of, 1:362; 3:100,
228; 7:246; 8:423
and Freon, 7:246
functions of, 7:246
and hazardous waste, 4:111–112
and lead, 7:246
and noise pollution, 6:112
and pesticides, 6:210
Reagan administration and, 3:229
and Superfund, 5:164
and Times Beach, 8:127
Toxic Substance Control Act and,
8:151
Environmental Quality Act (1969),
3:432
Environmental regulations
and infrastructure, 4:356, 358
in Oregon, 6:207
See also specific laws
Environmental sanitation,
7:244–246
Envoys, diplomatic, 1:134
EOA. *See* Economic Opportunity
Act
EOP. *See* Executive Office of the
President
EPA. *See* Environmental Protection
Agency
Epaulettes, 8:256
EPC. *See* Evangelical Presbyterian
Church
EPCA. *See* Emergency Price Control Act
Ephrata Cloister, 1:534
EPIC (End Poverty in California),
3:233–234
Epidemics and public health, 3:37,
234–242
in 20th century, 5:105
AMA on, 1:165
bacteriology, 5:358
birth defects, 5:236
child mortality, 5:273–274
cholera, 2:159–160, *160*;
3:236–237; 8:576
in colonial era, 2:510; 5:104
diphtheria, 5:104
environmental health hazards,
5:298
governmental inspection and,
4:363
influenza, 3:37, *237*, 241;
4:353–354, *354*
during World War I, 8:538–539

Epidemics and public health, (*continued*)
and life expectancy, **5:**104, 105
malaria, **5:213–215,** *214*
and Native Americans, decimation of, **8:**488
polio, **5:**236; **6:388–389**
smallpox, **5:**104
social change and, **5:**305
tenements and, **8:**81–82
tuberculosis, **8:235–238,** *237*
yellow fever, **3:**37, 235–236; **8:576–577**
See also Disease(s)
Episcopalianism, **3:242–243**
African Americans in, **3:**243
membership in, **7:***87, 90, 91*
Oxford Movement in, **6:**222
upstart sects and threat to, 7:86
Epperson v. Arkansas, **1:**500
Equal Credit Opportunity Act (ECOA) (1974), **2:**452; **5:**252
Equal Employment Opportunity Act (1972), **1:**36
Equal Employment Opportunity Commission (EEOC), **3:243–245; 5:**15
establishment of, **1:**36; **2:**200; **3:**49, 52; **5:**527
functions of, **1:**36
and legal challenges to age discrimination, **3:**47
and National Organization for Women, **5:**548
statistics compiled by, **3:**52–53
Equal Pay Act (1963), **2:**330; **3:**54, **245,** 308; **5:**15; **8:**517
Equal protection of the law, **3:245–247**
Barron v. Baltimore and, **1:**419
Equal rights, and liberalism, **5:**92
Equal Rights Amendment (ERA), **3:247–248,** 249; **5:**65–66; **8:**516
in electoral politics, **3:**167
Frontiero v. Richardson and, **3:**478
General Federation of Women's Clubs and, **3:**526
Moral Majority and, **5:**456
rally for, **8:***517*
ratification by states, **8:**517
Equal Rights Party, **3:**248
Equality
concept of, **3:248–251**
and liberty, balance of, **5:**92

of women, original documents on, **9:**325–337
Equiano, Olaudah, **5:**119, 364; **6:**234; **7:**388
Equine influenza, **8:**319
Equitable Building, **6:**80
Equity Colony, **8:**303
Equity funds, **4:**413
Equity in Education Land Grant Status Act (1994), **8:**211
ERA. *See* Equal Rights Amendment
Era of Good Feeling, **2:**550; **3:**151, **251**
ERDA. *See* Energy Research and Development Administration
Erdman Act (1898), **7:**24, 25, 38
Erdrich, Louise, *Love Medicine,* **5:**129, **164–165**
Erector sets, **3:**251; **8:**153
Ergonomic workplace standards, **5:**12
Ericsson, John, **4:**54
Erie, Lake, pollution of, **8:**422
Erie Canal, **2:***31,* 31–32; **3:***251,* **251–253,** *252, 253;* **6:**87
Champlain-Hudson cutoff to, **8:**312–313
and domestic trade, **8:**160
and market shipping, **2:**387
masonry on, **2:**79
and New York City, **6:**79, 88; **8:**160
and price of flour, **3:**398
railroads and, **7:**27
and westward migration, **8:**461
Erie Railroad Company v. Tompkins, **3:253–254**
Erikson, Erik, **4:**139–140
Eriksson, Leif, **6:**122; **8:**337
ERISA. *See* Employment Retirement Income Security Act
Erlanger, Joseph, **6:**349
ERP. *See* Enterprise resource planning
Erskine, John, **4:**40
Erskine, Robert, **2:**62
Ervien v. United States, **3:**202
Ervin, Sam, **4:**231
Erwitt, Elliott, **6:**330
ESA. *See* Economic Stabilization Agency; Endangered Species Act
Escalante, Silvestre Vélez de, **2:**301
Escalator clauses, **2:**423
Esch, John Jacob, **8:**185

Esch Industrial Hygiene and Occupational Disease Act (1912), **5:**14
Esch-Cummins Act. *See* Transportation Act
Esche, Otto, **2:**19
Escort services, **6:**514
ESEA. *See* Elementary and Secondary Education Act
Eskimo. *See* Inuit
Esparza, Enrique, on Alamo Siege, **9:**212–214
Espionage
Amerasia case, **1:**134
Ames case, **1:173–174**
communist subversion and, **8:**1–2
by communists, **1:**198
domestic, Nixon administration and, **8:**425–426
Hanssen case, **4:92**
Hiss case, **4:136–137**
industrial, **3:254–255**
Rosenberg case, **7:197–198**
in World War I, **8:**537
See also Spies
Espionage Act (1917), **3:**207, **254**
and censorship, **2:**83, 84
Supreme Court on, **7:**264; **8:**195
enemy aliens and, **8:**537
Espy, James Pollard, **5:**331
Esquire (magazine), **5:**196
Essay Concerning Human Understanding, An (Locke), **5:**140
Essays (Emerson), **3:**195
Essence (magazine), **5:**198
Essential Schools, **3:**124
Essex (warship), **3:256**
Essex Junto, **3:255–256**
Estaing, Comte d', **7:**144
Estate tax laws, **4:**359
See also Inheritance tax laws
Esteban (Moorish slave), **1:**256; **6:**65–66
Estebanico, **2:**1, 173; **3:**296
Estrada, Joseph, **6:**323
Ethan Frome (Wharton), **5:**119
Ethical Culture, Society for, **1:**55; **3:256–257**
Ethics
Moral Majority and, **5:**455–456
moral societies, **5:**456
Ethiopia, invasion of, by Italy, **5:**65
Ethiopia Unbound (Casely Hayford), **6:**236

Ethnic cleansing, **3:**536
Ethnicity
  Beyond the Melting Pot on, **1:**446
  meaning of, **1:**338
  melting pot, **5:**306
  multiculturalism, **5:**473–474
  political machines and, **5:**186–187
  shares of population by, **2:***555,
    555–556, 557*
Ethnohistory, **3:**257
  of gypsies, **4:**78–79
Ethnology, **1:**191–195
Ethnology, Bureau of American,
    1:192; **3:**257–258
  on Native American languages,
    4:274
Etiquette. *See* Manners and etiquette
E*TRADE, **3:**183
ETRS. *See* Earth Technology
    Resource Satellite
ETS. *See* Educational Testing Ser-
    vice
Ettor, Joseph, **5:**59–60
EU. *See* European Union
Euclid v. Ambler Realty Company,
    6:505; **8:**593
Eugenics, **3:**258
  racial science and, **7:**13
  and wildlife management,
    2:370–371
Eugénie (empress of France), **2:**245
Eulau, Heinz, **6:**403
EURATOM. *See* European Atomic
    Energy Community
Euro, **1:**394; **3:**261
Europe
  American émigrés in, **3:**197
  foreign aid to, **3:**415, 426
  immigrants from, **7:**10, 91
  slavery in, **7:**389
  U.S. relief in, after World War I,
    8:541–542
  welfare state in, **8:**438
  World War I debts to U.S.,
    8:542–543
  See also Eastern Europe; *specific
    countries*
European Atomic Energy Commu-
    nity (EURATOM), **3:**258, 260
European Coal and Steel Communi-
    ty (ECSC), **3:**258, 260
European Common Market, **7:**54;
    8:157–158
European Community, **8:**166

European Economic Community
    (EEC), **3:**258, 260
European Free Trade Association
    (EFTA), **8:**166
European Organization for Nuclear
    Research (CERN), **6:**339
European Recovery Act (1948),
    8:166
European Recovery Plan, **3:**415
European Recovery Program (ERP).
    See Marshall Plan
European Union (EU), **3:**258–261;
    8:158
Eustis, Henry L., **5:**59
Eutaw Springs, Battle of, **3:**261
Euthanasia, **3:**261–263
  definition of, **1:**339
  "right to die" cases, **3:**262;
    7:160–161
Evacuation Day, **5:**568
Evangelical Alliance, **3:**263; **5:**532
Evangelical Lutheran Church in
    America (ELCA), **5:**177;
    6:137–138
Evangelical Presbyterian Church
    (EPC), **6:**451
Evangelical Synod of North Ameri-
    ca, **8:**264
Evangelical United Brethren, Unit-
    ed Methodist Church and,
    5:334
Evangelical United Front, **3:**264,
    265
Evangelicalism, **3:**266–267
  among African Americans, **1:**42;
    6:517
  camp meetings, **2:21–22**
  and denominational colleges,
    3:130–131
  fundamentalism and, **3:**484–485;
    6:516
  Graham and, **6:**516–517
  Great Awakening and, **4:**38–39;
    6:515–516
  growth of, **2:**165
  home missionary societies, **5:**409
  Moral Majority, **5:455–456**
  New Lights, **6:**65
  and politics, **2:**165
  resurgence of, **6:**517–518
  and televangelism, **6:**517–518;
    8:71–72
  See also Mission(s)
Evangelism, **3:**263

Evans, Alice C., **5:**358
Evans, Edgar, **6:**383–384
Evans, Frederick, **7:**334
Evans, John, **1:**440; **7:**243
Evans, Luther, **5:**101
Evans, Oliver, **1:**335, 371; **3:**187,
    389; **6:**255; **7:**77, 542, 543
Evans, Robley D., **1:**428
Evans, Romer v., **3:**56, 247;
    7:195–196
Evans, Walker, **1:**301, *302*
  *Let Us Now Praise Famous Men:
    Three Tenant Families* (with
    James Agee), **5:**83–84
Evarts, William, **1:**144
Eveleth, Jonathan G., **6:**302
Evening Transcript (newspaper), **6:**96
Evening Wind (Hopper), **6:**471
Everest, Mount, mountain climbing
    on, **5:**466
Everest, Wesley, **8:**414
Everett, Edward, **2:**383; **3:**154,
    570–571; **5:**59, 98
  and land speculation, **5:**36
Everglades National Park, **3:**268,
    268; **5:**552
  Seminole in, **3:**268; **7:**9
Evers, Medgar, **1:**332; **5:**527
  assassination of, **2:**203
Everson v. Board of Education, **2:**168
Evertsen, Cornelius, Jr., **6:**82
Evertz, Scott, **1:**18
Evolution of Civilization, The (Blash-
    field), **5:***101*
Evolution of the Igneous Rocks, The
    (Bowen), **6:**301
Evolutionism, **1:**520; **3:**268–270
  and anthropology/ethnology, **1:**192
  vs. Christianity, **2:**164
  and geography, **3:**541–G501:43
  impact on historians, **4:**138
  radio broadcasting and, **7:**274
  and religion, **7:**270
  responses to, **2:**446
  in school curriculum
    North Carolina banning, **6:**130
    Scopes trial on, **1:**146;
      7:283–284; 8:86
  social, **1:**192–193; **7:411–412**
Ewell, Richard S., **1:**567; **3:**567
  in Battle of Spotsylvania Court-
    house, **7:**512
  in Battles of the Wilderness, **8:**477

Ex Parte Bollman and Swartwout,
   3:270–271; **8:**193–194
Ex Parte Crow Dog, **3:**271
Ex Parte Endo, **4:**461, 464
Ex Parte Garland, **3:**271; **8:**96
Ex Parte McCardle, **3:**271–272; **8:**97
Ex Parte Merryman, **3:**272; **8:**374
Ex Parte Milligan, **3:**272–273; **5:**317;
   8:374
Examiner (newspaper), **6:**98
Exceptionalism, American, **1:**135,
   170
Excess profits tax, **3:**273; **8:**57
Exchange(s), **3:**274–277
  bills of, **3:**273–274
  centralization of, **2:**447
  Commodities Exchange Act and,
    2:315–316
  commodity, **2:**316
  regulation of, **4:**30
Exchange rates, International Mone-
   tary Fund in, **4:**396
Exchange students, **3:**274
  Fulbright grants and, **3:**482–483
Excise taxes, **7:**230; **8:**56
Exclusionary clubs, **2:**251
Exclusionary rule, **7:**290
Executive agent, **3:**277
Executive agreements, **3:**277–278;
   8:203–204
Executive branch, **3:**341
  legislative oversight of, **5:**77–78
  organization of, Hoover Commis-
    sions on, **4:**161
  representation in, **7:**108
  See also Cabinet; President(s)
Executive Office of the President
   (EOP), **3:**330; **6:**455
Executive Order(s), **3:**278
  No. 8802, **1:**35, 547; **2:**201; **3:**49;
    6:314
  No. 9017, **5:**564
  No. 9066, **3:**208; **4:**460, 462, 463;
    7:99
  No. 9102, **4:**460
  No. 9250, **5:**564
  No. 9312, **6:**523
  No. 9980, **2:**201; **3:**49
  No. 9981, **1:**548; **2:**201; **3:**49
  No. 10631, **6:**472
  No. 10925, **1:**36; **6:**314
  No. 10988, **1:**154, 156
  No. 11130, **8:**394
  No. 11246, **1:**36; **6:**314

No. 11967, **9:**480
No. 13007, **1:**162
No. 13083, **3:**278
Executive privilege, **3:**278–279
  HUAC on, **4:**178
  investigating committees and,
    4:411
  Lincoln and, **2:**210; **3:**272
  Supreme Court on, **4:**497
Existentialism, **3:**279–281
Exit polls, **6:**534
Exorcist, The (Blatty), **5:**130
Expansionism
  Democratic Party and, **2:**550–551
  manifest destiny, **5:**222–225, *224*
  in maps, archival, **9:**45–64
  in Open Door policy, **6:**196–197
  original documents from era of,
    9:187–265
  and slavery issue, **8:**485–486
  western, **8:**444
  See also Westward migration
Expatriation, **3:**281
Expatriation Act (1907), **6:**14
*Expedition to the Valley of the Great
   Salt Lake of Utah, An* (Stans-
   bury), excerpt from, **9:**233–237
Expenditures, federal, **3:**281–282,
   282
*Experience; Or, How to Give a North-
   ern Man Backbone* (Brown),
   5:124
Experimental boiling water reactor
   (EBWR), **6:**139
Experimental Negotiating Agree-
   ment (ENA) (1973), **7:**546;
   8:277
"Experimental Novel, The" (Zola),
   6:11
Expert systems, **1:**318
Exploration(s), **3:**283–301, *284*
  and botanical studies, **1:**518
  British, **3:**285, **287–289**, *288*
    by Cabot, **2:**4–5, *5*; **3:**285, 287
    by Cook, **2:**403–404
    by Gilbert, **3:**576
    Golden Hind, **4:**18–19
    Hakluyt's *Voyages* on, **4:**86
    in New Hampshire, **6:**56–57
    in North Pole, **6:**382
    in Oregon, **6:**204
    in Pacific Northwest, **8:**452–453
    Potomac River, **6:**433
    in South Pole, **6:**382–383

    by Vancouver, **8:306–307**
    in Washington, **8:**412
  Canadian, by Ogden, **6:**37
  Dutch, **2:**39; **3:**286, **289–290**, *290;*
    4:281
    in New Netherland, **6:**71
  French, **3:**285–286, **290–293**, *292;*
    6:51
    by Champlain, **2:103–104**, *104*
    on Great Plains, **8:**451–452
    Hennepin on, **4:**126
    by Jolliet and Marquette, **4:**214,
     486–487; **5:**416, *416*
    in Kansas, **4:**508
    by La Salle, **5:1–3**, 416
     Griffon and, **4:**66
     Mississippi River, **6:**29; **8:**99
    Lake Michigan, **4:**50–51
    Lake Ontario and Huron, **4:**50
    maps of, archival, **9:***19*, 19–22
    in Michigan, **5:**353–354
    Missouri River, **5:**425–426
    by Nicolet, **6:106**
    in North Dakota, **6:**131
    on Northwest Coast, **8:**453
    Platte River, **6:**29
    Saint Lawrence River, **3:**488; **4:**50
  geophysical, **3:**551–553
  Italian, by Verrazano, **1:**11; **2:**38;
    3:285, 291; **8:**315
    Narrows, **5:**515
    New France, **6:**51
    New York, **6:**87
  by Long (Stephen), **5:150–151**
  maps of, archival, **9:**19–24
  by Marcy, **5:238**
  by Norsemen, **6:**122–123
  portages and water routes and,
    6:422
  Portuguese, **3:**283
  river pathways to, **7:**173–174
  Russian, **1:**108, 120–121; **3:**286,
    293, **293–294**; **7:**215
    in Alaska, **1:**108, 120–121; **4:**409
    on Northwest Coast, **8:**453
  Spanish, **3:**283–285, **294–296**,
    295; **7:**206
    by Cabeza de Vaca, **2:**1–2, *2;*
     3:284, 295
    New Mexico, **6:**65
    Texas, **8:**99
    Colorado River, **2:301**
    by Columbus, **7:**249
    conquistadores in, **2:360**

by Coronado, **1**:*256*; **2**:*416,
416–417*; **4**:508
Great Plains, **4**:56
in New Mexico, **6**:66
in Texas, **8**:99
in Florida, **3**:385; **5**:308–309;
8:47
in Grand Canyon, **4**:33
in Great Plains, **4**:56
Gulf Stream, **4**:73
and Hispanic Americans, **4**:134
in Kansas, **4**:508
in New Mexico, **6**:65–66
on Northwest Coast, **8**:453
by Oñate, **6**:**194**
in New Mexico, **6**:66
in Oregon, **6**:204
Potomac River, **6**:433
by Soto, **1**:102, 264; **7**:**450–451**
in Florida, **3**:385; **8**:47
in Tennessee, **8**:84
in Southwest, **8**:451
in Texas, **8**:98–99
in Washington, **8**:412
U.S., **3**:**296–301**, *298*; **8**:453–454
Colorado River, **2**:301
by Fisk, **3**:377
by Freeman, **3**:465
by Frémont, **3**:**467–468**
Great Basin, **3**:468; **4**:39
Great Salt Lake, **3**:468; **4**:57
mountain passes, **6**:254
Nevada, **3**:468; **6**:37
Platte River, **3**:467; **6**:30
geological surveys and,
3:544–545
Great Salt Lake, **4**:57
by Greely, **4**:**59–60**
by Lewis and Clark (*See* Lewis
and Clark expedition)
by Long, in Nebraska, **6**:29
in North Pole, **6**:382
by Pike, **6**:**354–355**
in Rocky Mountains, **7**:190
in South Pole, **6**:383
by Wilkes, **8**:482
Yellowstone River, **3**:318; **8**:580
Western, **8**:**451–454**, *452*
Explosives, **3**:**301–302**
Export debenture plan, **3**:302
Export taxes, **3**:**302–303**
Export-import banks, **1**:**402–404**
Expositions. *See specific expositions*
Expunging resolution, **3**:303

Extension services, **1**:71
Extinction, species, **2**:373
Extra sessions, **3**:**303**
Extracurricular activities, **2**:276
Extradition, **3**:**303–304**
political offense exception to,
3:304
Extra-Sensory Perception (Rhine),
6:246
Extraterritoriality, right of,
3:**304–305**
Extrusion molding, **6**:366
Exxon Corporation, **1**:111
credit card offered by, **3**:368
Exxon Valdez oil spill, **1**:13, 111, 113;
3:39, 233, *305*, **305–306**; **6**:304
Ezell, Harold, **6**:509

F

F-117 Nighthawk stealth fighter,
1:496
FAA. *See* Federal Aviation Administration
Fabréga, Gilberto Guardia, **6**:241,
242
Facsimile machine. *See* Fax machine
Factories
19th-century, **2**:42
and city planning, **2**:185
industrial management in,
4:**334–335**
for leather products, **5**:68–69
and recreation, changes in, **7**:64
women in, **2**:223; **8**:505
Factors (commission merchants),
2:**312–313**
Factory farms, hogs in, **4**:146
Factory Investigating Commission,
8:209
Faduma, Orishatukeh, **6**:236
Fail-Safe (Burdick, Wheeler), **5**:121
Faint the Trumpet Sounds (Walton),
5:132
Fair(s)
county and state, **2**:436, *437*
world (*See* World's fairs)
Fair, James G., **1**:497
Fair comment, **5**:90
Fair Deal, **1**:533; **2**:274; **3**:307, *307*
Fair Employment Practices Com-
mittee (FEPC), **3**:49, 244; **6**:314
Fair Housing Act (1968), **6**:506

Fair Labor Standards Act (FLSA)
(1938), **3**:**307–309**; **5**:11, 15,
135
child labor regulated by, **2**:140,
149; **4**:27; **8**:111
and Equal Pay Act, **3**:245
and minimum wage, **3**:54; **5**:395;
8:252
National Consumers' League and,
2:392
on piecework, **6**:352
textile workers' strike and, **8**:278
on wages and hours, **8**:360
Fair Oaks, Battle of, **6**:275
Fairbanks, Charles W., **3**:159
Fairbanks, Douglas, Sr., **3**:362
Fairchild Semiconductor, **7**:360
Fairness doctrine, **3**:341
Fair-trade laws, **3**:**309–310**
domestic, **3**:309
global, **3**:309–310
*Faithful Narrative of the Surprising
Work of God, A* (Edwards), **5**:118
Fajans, Kasimir, **6**:341
Falkenstein, Claire, **1**:309
Fall, Albert, in Teapot Dome Scan-
dal, **6**:19–20; **8**:63
Fall line, **3**:**310**, *310*
Fallam, Robert, **8**:447
Fallen Angels (Myers), **5**:126
Fallen Timbers, Battle of,
3:**310–311**; **4**:63; **8**:399
Greenville Treaty after, **4**:271;
6:172
*Falvo v. Owasso Independent School
District No. I-001*, **3**:316
Falwell, Jerry, **1**:449; **2**:165, 376;
3:484, 485; **5**:455–456; **6**:518
Family(ies), **3**:**311–315**
in 20th century, **3**:313–315
abuse within (*See* Domestic violence)
church and, **8**:500–501
colonial, **3**:311–312
farm, **2**:44; **7**:207
generational conflict in, **3**:528–529
in kinship patterns, **4**:531–532
Republican, **3**:312–313
slave, **3**:313; **7**:394, 465
working-class and immigrant,
3:313
World War II's effect on,
9:403–404
See also Marriage

Family and Medical Leave Act (FMLA) (1993), **3:**55, **315**, 317, 525; **5:**15

Family Education Rights and Privacy Act (1974), **3:315–316**

Family Farm Preservation Act (1982), **6:**31

Family of Love (Children of God), **2:**477

Family of Man Exhibition, **3:316**, *316*

Family planning
  Republican vs. Democratic position on, **7:**216
  See also Birth control

Family Support Act (1988), **2:**139; **6:**438

Family values, **3:316–318**

Faneuil, Peter, **3:**318

Faneuil Hall, **1:**509; **3:**318, *318*

Fannie Mae. *See* Savings and loan associations

Fanning, Tolbert, **3:**44

Fanny (Jong), **5:**122

Far right, origins of, **2:**375

Far West, prehistoric, **1:**242

Far West (boat), **3:**318

Farabundo Martí National Liberation Front (FMLN), **3:**143

Faraday, Michael, **3:**173, 177, 211

Fard, Wallace D., **4:**437; **5:**519

Farewell to Arms, A (Hemingway), **5:**120

Fargo, William G., **8:**443

Farley, James A., **1:**97; **6:427–428**

Farm Aid concerts, **1:**441, *441*

Farm Credit Administration (FCA), **1:**60

Farm debt, mortgage relief legislation, **5:**461

Farm Eco-Village, The , **8:**303

Farm families, **2:**44

Farm Journal, **6:**409

Farm Security Act (1937), **3:**319

Farm Security Administration (FSA), **3:318–320**
  photography of, **1:**301; **3:***319*, 320
  Resettlement Administration transformed into, **6:**44

Farm subsidies. *See* Agriculture, price supports in

Farman, Joseph, **6:**384

Farmer, Fanny, **3:**400

Farmer, James, **2:**201, 355

Farmer Labor Political Federation (FLPF), **6:**500

Farmer-Labor Party of 1920, **3:**161, **320–321; 5:**16

Farmer-Labor Party of Minnesota, **3:321–323; 5:**400

Farmers
  Agricultural Adjustment Administration and, **3:**318–319
  in antimonopoly parties, **1:**204–205
  buying land, **6:**527, 528
  education of, **3:**325
  Farm Security Administration and, **3:**319–320
  Jefferson (Thomas) on, **8:**527
  number of, in 20th century, **1:***66*
  Ocala Platform of, **6:**157–158
  in Progressive movement, **6:**494, 495
  Resettlement Administration and, **3:**319
  resistance to capitalism, **2:**45–46
  Shays's Rebellion by, **7:338; 9:**154–155
  violence by, **8:**338
  See also Agriculture; Rural life

Farmers' Alliance, **1:**63; **2:**179, 227; **3:**187, **323–324; 6:**416–417
  created by African Americans, **3:**323; **6:**417
  on education, **6:**416
  in Georgia, **3:**556
  in Illinois, **3:**323
  in Indiana, **3:**323
  in Iowa, **3:**323
  in Kansas, **3:**324
  in Louisiana, **3:**323
  in New Mexico, **3:**323
  in Texas, **3:**323, 324; **6:**416; **8:**102
  on textbooks, **8:**106
  women in, **3:**323–324; **6:**416
    original document on, **9:**260–261

Farmers' cooperatives, **2:406–408**

Farmer's Educational and Cooperative Union. *See* National Farmers' Union

Farmer's frontier, **8:**463

Farmers Institutes, **3:**325
  Granger movement, **4:**36–37

Farmer's Letters, **3:**320

Farmers' Loan and Trust Company, Pollock v., **6:409–410; 8:**57

Farmers' Mutual Benefit Association, **3:**323

Farmers' Nonpartisan League. *See* Nonpartisan League, National

Farmhand, **3:325–327**, *326*

Farms and farming. *See* Agriculture

Farnsworth, Philo T., **8:**77

Farragut, David, **2:**496
  New Orleans occupied by, **6:**25, 73, 75
  in Vicksburg, **8:**324

Farrakhan, Louis, **1:**207; **4:**437; **5:***520*, 521

Farrell, James T., **5:**121

Fascism, American, **3:327–328**
  See also Nazis, American

Fashion. *See* Clothing and fashion

Fast Days, **3:328–329**

Fast food. *See* Food and cuisines, fast

"Fast track," **3:**310

FAT. *See* Frente Auténtico del Trabajo

Fate of the Earth (Schell), **5:**120

Father
  in 20th century family, **3:**314
  in colonial family, **3:**311
  in Republican family, **3:**312–313

Father Divine's Peace Mission Movement, **2:**477

Father's Day, **5:463**

Faubus, Orval, **1:**262, 263; **2:**202; **4:**29

Fauci, Anthony, **1:**16

Faulk, Andrew, **7:**459

Faulkner, William, **5:**120, 157
  As I Lay Dying, **5:**121
  Light in August, **5:**121
  Sanctuary, **5:**121

Fauna of the National Parks, The (Wright, Thompson and Dixon), **5:**552

Faunce, Thomas, **6:**379

Faunce, William Herbert Perry, **1:**548

Faure, Edgar, at summit conferences, **8:**15

Faurer, Louis, **1:**301

Fauset, Jessie Redmon, **4:**96; **5:**125

Faust, Bernard, **4:**204–205

Favored union clause, **2:**243

Fawcett, H. W., **5:**361

Fax (facsimile) machine, **3:329; 6:**169; **8:**66

Fay, Michael, **1:**173

Fayol, Henri, **7:**281
FBI. *See* Federal Bureau of Investigation
FBN. *See* Federal Bureau of Narcotics
FCA. *See* Farm Credit Administration
FCC. *See* Federal Communications Commission
FCC, Red Lion Broadcasting Co. v., **3:**341
FCCC. *See* Framework Convention on Climate Change
FDA. *See* Food and Drug Administration
FDI. *See* Foreign direct investment
FDIC. *See* Federal Deposit Insurance Corporation
FDR. *See* Roosevelt, Franklin Delano
FEA. *See* Federal Energy Administration
Feather, Norman, **6:**341
Feather River, **9:**57
FEC. *See* Federal Election Commission
FECA. *See* Federal Election Campaign Act
Fechner, Robert, **2:**220
Federal Administrative Procedure Act (1946), **3:**329, 333
Federal agencies, **3:329–333**
  accountability of, **3:**333
  adjudication by, **1:22–23**
  Clinton and, **3:**332–333
  created under New Deal, **6:**43–45
  executive power of removal in, **4:**194–195
  military intelligence in, **4:**376
  number of people employed by, **3:**330
  policy making by, **1:21–22**
  scientific research by, Allison Commission on, **1:**128
  understanding, **3:**332
  See also specific agencies
Federal Agricultural Improvement and Reform Act (1996), **6:**133
Federal aid, **3:333–335**
  dependence on, **3:**334
  estimated amount of, **3:**334
  forms of, **3:**334
  after Great Depression, **3:**334
  before Great Depression, **3:**334

vs. subsidies, **3:**333–334
Federal Aid Road Act (1916), **3:**335; **8:**190
Federal Anti-Tampering Act (1983), **6:**491
Federal Arbitration Act (1925), **1:**237
Federal Art Project, **6:**471
Federal Aviation Act (1958), **3:**336
Federal Aviation Administration (FAA), **3:336–337; 8:**191
  aid to airports by, **1:**98
  establishment of, **3:**35, 336
  functions of, **1:**98–99; **3:**336–337
  standards for airports by, **1:**98
Federal Bureau of Investigation (FBI), **3:337–339**
  in 1920s, **3:**337
  in 1930s, **3:**337–338
  in 1960s, **3:**338
  in 1970s, **3:**338
  in 1980s, **3:**338–339
  in 1990s, **3:**339
  and Abscam scandal, **1:**8; **3:**338
  and African American press, **6:**99
  in *Amerasia* case, **1:**134
  American Indian Movement and, **1:**161
  anticommunism, **5:**182, 183
  in Atlanta Olympic bombing case, **3:**339
  and Castro, arrest and interrogation of, **2:**470
  and civil rights, **3:**338
  COINTELPRO, **2:265–266; 3:**338
  during Cold War, **3:**338
  and communists in film industry, **4:**178
  criticism of, **3:**338–339
  drug enforcement by, **5:**512
  establishment of, **3:**337; **4:**503
  Hanssen espionage case in, **4:92**
  and Internet spy technologies, **3:**186
  in King's assassination, **4:**530
  after 9/11 attack, **3:**339
  in Oklahoma City bombing case, **3:**339; **6:**187–188
  against organized crime, **3:**338
  and Palmer Raids, **3:**337; **6:**232
  surveillance abuse by, **3:**338–339
  during World War I, **3:**337
  during World War II, **3:**338

Federal Bureau of Narcotics (FBN), **5:**511
Federal Bureau of Prisons, **6:**477
Federal Children's Bureau, **5:**274
Federal Coal Mine Health and Safety Act (1969), **5:**391
Federal Communications Commission (FCC), **3:339–341**
  and AT&T, **1:**346–347
  censorship by, **2:**84
  on digital television, **8:**77
  and early broadcasting, **8:**77
  establishment of, **3:**339; **7:**19
  and public interest programming, **8:**73
  regulation by, **3:**340–341
  structure of, **3:**339–340
  Telecommunications Act and, **8:**75
  and televangelism, **8:**71
Federal Council of Churches, **5:**532; **6:**451
Federal courts
  establishment of, **4:**498–499
  expansion of jurisdiction of, **4:**499–500
Federal Deposit Insurance Corporation (FDIC), **1:**398, 400–401, 402, 407, 563; **3:**345; **6:**43
Federal Election Campaign Act (FECA) (1971), **3:**144; **6:**393
Federal Election Campaign Act (FECA) (1974), **3:**144
Federal Election Commission (FEC), **3:**332
Federal Elections Bill (1890), **2:**332
Federal Emergency Management Agency (FEMA), **2:**191
Federal Emergency Relief Administration (FERA), **6:**43; **8:**440, 530
Federal employees
  gay and lesbian, **7:**327
  political activities by, regulation of, **4:**103–104
  sexual harassment of, **7:**323
  trade unions for, **7:**558–559
    collective bargaining by, **1:**154, 156
Federal Energy Administration (FEA), **3:**208–209
Federal Energy Regulatory Commission (FERC), **3:**209
Federal estate tax, **8:**57
Federal Express, **1:**97; **2:**439

Federal Farm Loan Act (1916), **1:**71; **6:**54
Federal Flood Control Act (1928), **3:**384
Federal Flood Control Act (1936), **3:**384
Federal Food, Drug, and Cosmetic Act (1938), Delaney Amendment to, **2:540**
Federal funds rate, **5:**440–441
Federal government, **3:341–343**
  and big business, regulation of, **1:**580
  branches of, **3:**341
    interpreting Constitution, **3:**342
  budget of (*See* Budget, federal)
  and business regulation (*See* Government regulation of business)
  and capitalist development, **2:**43
  changes in scope of, **3:**342–343
  and city planning, **2:**187–188
  eminent domain of, **3:**198; **6:**505
  enumerated powers of, **3:**225
  evolution of, **3:**341–342
  expenditures of, **3:**281–282, *282*
  funding by, anti-discrimination legislation associated with, **2:**196
  intervention in labor disputes by, **1:**190; **7:**557
  mapping program of, **2:**62
  ownership of (*See* Government ownership)
  powers of, Executive Order 13083 and, **3:**278
  privatization by, **6:481**
  proclamations by, **6:490–491**
  propaganda by, **6:502–504**
  and public health, **3:**239
  publications of, **3:**344; **4:**24–25
    by Office of Federal Register, **5:**525
  and railroads, **7:**35
  and retirement, **7:**129
  revenue of, **1:**558, *559;* **7:**132, 133
  role in education, **3:**123
  shutdown of (1995), **1:**229
  sovereignty of, **7:**477, 534
  spending by
    during Great Depression, **4:**47–48 (*See also* New Deal)
    Keynes on, **4:**46
    pump-priming, **6:551**

  supremacy of, **5:**184
  and trade unions, **2:**43, 274
  and westward migration, **8:**444
  women in, **8:**507
Federal Highway Act (1921), **3:**335; **8:**190
Federal Highway Administration, **3:**335
Federal Housing Administration (FHA), **2:**187
  establishment of, **7:**256
  functions of, **7:**256
Federal Insecticide, Fungicide, and Rodenticide Act (1972) (FIFRA), **1:**463; **3:**232; **8:**424
Federal Intermediate Credit Banks (FICBs), **4:**384–385
Federal Labor Relations Authority (FLRA), **7:**559
Federal Land Policy and Management Act (FLPMA), **6:**529
Federal Meat Inspection Act (FMIA) (1907), **5:**277–278
Federal Mediation and Conciliation Service (FMCS), **3:343–344**
Federal National Mortgage Administration (FNMA), **7:**256
Federal Oil Pollution Act (1990), **3:**305
Federal Open Market Committee (FOMC), **5:**440–441; **6:**198
Federal Power Act (FPA) (1935), **4:**201
Federal Power Commission (FPC), **4:**201
  and natural gas industry, **6:**9
Federal Radio Commission (FRC), **3:**339
Federal Register (newspaper), **3:344;** **5:**525
Federal Reserve Act (1913), **6:**497; **8:**196
Federal Reserve Bulletin, **3:**106
Federal Reserve System, **3:**332, **344–347**
  in 1950s, **3:**346
  in 1960s, **3:**346
  in 1970s, **3:**346–347
  in 1980s, **3:**347
  in 1990s, **3:**347
  banks and, **1:**397, 398
  chairman of, **3:**110
  and check clearing, **2:**232

  creation of, National Monetary Commission and, **1:**120; **3:**344
  Glass-Steagall Act and, **1:**400
  and Great Depression, **3:**345; **4:**4–5, 12, 46
  and inflation, **4:**351–352; **7:**516–517
  McFadden Banking Act (1927), **5:185**
  in monetary system, **5:**440–441
  and money supply, **4:**351–352
  open-market operations in, **6:**198
  and panic of 1929, **3:**367
  principal goal of, **8:**254
  during World War I, **3:**344–345
  during World War II, **3:**345–346
Federal Savings and Loan Insurance Corporation (FSLIC), **1:**398, 563
Federal Security Agency (FSA), **4:**113
Federal Trade Commission (FTC), **3:347–349**
  creation of, **3:**348; **4:**27; **8:**235
  functions of, **1:**34, 214; **8:**160
  during Great Depression, **3:**348
  Nader on, **3:**349; **5:**509
  reforms of, **3:**349
  during World War II, **3:**348
Federal Trade Commission Act (1914), **1:**34, 214–215; **3:**348; **6:**497
  Wheeler-Lea Amendments to (1938), **1:**214–215
Federal-Aid Highway Act
  of 1944, **4:**403
  of 1956, **4:**403–404
Federal-Aid Highway Program, **3:335–336; 7:**178; **8:**140
Federalism
  and economics, **3:**107
  and electoral college system, **3:**172
  fiscal, **1:**560
  marital law and, **5:**249–250
  midnight judges and, **5:367**
  militias and, **5:**386
  new, **1:**454
  transition to democracy from, **3:**152
Federalist Gazette of the United States (newspaper), **6:**96
Federalist Papers, **2:**382; **3:349–350**
  American System in, **1:**171
  on Congressional appropriations, **1:**229

on interest groups, **4**:380, 382
No. 84, text of, **9**:164–167
on religious toleration, **6**:374
on representative democracy,
    2:546–547
and republic, concept of, **7**:110
Federalist Party, **3**:350–352; **8**:243
    Alien and Sedition Acts and,
        1:123–124; **3**:351; **6**:396
    collapse of, **7**:118
    and conservatism, **2**:374
    decline of, **3**:352
    Embargo Act (1807) and, **3**:193
    emergence of, **3**:350–351
    and Essex Junto, **3**:255–256
    Hartford Convention and, **4**:101
    Jefferson on, **5**:277
    vs. Jeffersonian Republicans,
        3:351–352
    against Louisiana Purchase, **3**:352
    Maryland planters and, **5**:256–257
    moral societies and, **5**:456
    nominations by, **6**:113
    on secession, **7**:293
    Virginia dynasty and, **8**:348
Federalists, **2**:381; **3**:350
    on Bill of Rights, **1**:201
    on implied powers, **4**:247
    and Judiciary Act of 1801, **4**:499
    newspaper of, **6**:96
    in North Carolina, **6**:128
    and postal service, **6**:426
    strategy of, **1**:201
    success of, **1**:201
    See also Antifederalists
Federated Department Stores,
    Macy's, **5**:190
Federated Farmer-Labor Party,
    3:321
    See also Farmer-Labor Party
Federation of American Scientists,
    6:337
Federation of Organized Trades and
    Labor Unions (FOTLU), **4**:540
Fee Patenting, **3**:352
Feeney, Helen B., **6**:295
*Feeney, Personnel Administrator of
    Massachusetts v.*, **6**:295
Feininger, Andreas, **1**:*94*
Feinstein, Dianne, **7**:53
*Feist Publications, Inc. v. Rural Tele-
    phone Service Company*, **2**:412
Feke, Robert, **1**:294
Feld, Eliot, **1**:390

Feld, Irvin, **2**:177
Feldman, Sandra, **1**:155
Feldstein, Martin, **2**:431; **7**:421–422
Felsch, Oscar (Happy), **1**:480
FEMA. *See* Federal Emergency
    Management Agency
Feminine Mystique, The (Friedan),
    2:391; **3**:281, **353**; **4**:1; **7**:18;
    8:511, 516
Feminism
    backlash against, **8**:516–517
    and concept of gender, **3**:515–518
    definition of, **8**:515
    "difference" vs. "equality,"
        8:518–519
    on domestic violence, **3**:74
    on electrical appliances, **3**:181
    Equal Rights Amendment and,
        3:248
    individualism in, **4**:332–333
    National Organization for Women
        and, **5**:548–549
    on pornography, **6**:419; **8**:517–518
    on Promise Keepers, **6**:518
    on prostitution, **6**:514
    Quakerism and, **7**:3
    radical, **7**:18
    on rape, **7**:50
    socialist, and abortion, **1**:5
    See also Women's rights movement
Fencing and fencing laws, **3**:**353**
    of public lands, **6**:532
Fenellosa, Ernest, **2**:272
Fenian movement, **2**:26; **3**:353–354
Fenno, Veazie Bank v., **8**:**310**
Fenton, Beatrice, **1**:308
Fenton, Roger, **6**:331
Fenwick, Edward Dominic, **3**:77
Fenwick, John, **6**:60, 511
FEPC. *See* Fair Employment Prac-
    tices Committee
FERA. *See* Federal Emergency
    Relief Administration
Ferber, Edna, **1**:123
Ferber, Herbert, **1**:306
FERC. *See* Federal Energy Regula-
    tory Commission
Ferdinand (king of Spain), **3**:283,
    294
Ferguson, Adam, **7**:431
Ferguson, Homer, **1**:537
Ferguson, James, **1**:194; **3**:354;
    8:103
Ferguson, John H., **6**:370

Ferguson, Miriam, **3**:354; **8**:103, 104
Ferguson, Patrick, **1**:382
Ferguson, Plessy v., **1**:443, 549; **2**:199;
    3:121, 342; **5**:406; **6**:**370–371**
Ferguson Impeachment, **3**:354;
    8:103
Ferkauf, Eugene, **7**:126
Ferlinghetti, Lawrence, **1**:433;
    5:121–122
Fermentation, **3**:405
Fermi, Enrico, **6**:138, 341, 344, 345
Fermi National Accelerator Labora-
    tory, **6**:339
Fernandez, Simon, **7**:47
Fernow, Bernhard E., **3**:430
Ferrar, John, **8**:347
Ferrar, Nicholas, **8**:347
Ferraro, Geraldine, **5**:566
    in presidential campaign of 1984,
        3:168, 198
Ferrelo, Bartolomé, **3**:285, 296
Ferries, **3**:*354*, **354–355**
Ferris, William H., **6**:236
Ferris wheel, **3**:355; **8**:*407*, 558
    world's first, **2**:132
Fertility, **2**:557–560, *558*
    See also Childbirth; Demography
        and demographic trends;
        Reproduction
Fertilizers, **3**:355–356; **7**:444–445
    chemical, **3**:355–356
    guano, **4**:69
    Native American use of, **1**:69
    natural, **3**:355, 356
    nitrates in, **6**:110
    potash in, **6**:431
    Tennessee Valley Authority pro-
        ducing, **8**:88
Fessenden, William Pitt, **4**:485;
    5:210
Festivals. *See* Holidays and festivals
Fetter, Frank, **3**:109
Fetterman Fight, **5**:40
Fetterman Massacre, **1**:453
Feudalism, **3**:**356**
    primogeniture in, **6**:464
Feuds, Appalachian Mountain,
    3:356–357
Feulner, Edwin, **8**:118
FHA. *See* Federal Housing Adminis-
    tration
Fhimah, Lamen Khalifa, **6**:233
Fiallo v. Bell, **1**:125
Fiber attenuation, **3**:357

Fiber optics, **3:357–358**
Fiber production, **8:**107–108
FICBs. *See* Federal Intermediate
    Credit Banks
FIDER. *See* Foundation for Interior
    Design Education and Research
Field, Cyrus, **2:**3, *4*
Field, James G., **3:**158
Field, Marshall, **3:**7–8
Field, Stephen J.
    attempted assassination of, **4:**250
    legal training of, **5:**56
Field v. Clark, **3:**358
Fielding, Lewis, **8:**425
Fields, W. C., **8:**309
Fiero, C. E., **6:**182
FIFRA. *See* Federal Insecticide,
    Fungicide, and Rodenticide Act
Fifteenth Amendment, **1:***542*; **3:**250,
    342
    circumvention of, **2:**219
    and civil rights, **2:**198
    and election policies, **3:**171
    and grandfather clauses, **4:**35
    provisions of, **8:**356
    Radical Republicans and, **7:**15, 112
    and state sovereignty, **7:**534
    and voting rights, **7:**106
Fifth Amendment, **1:**457
    due-process limits of, **3:**91
    Frontiero v. Richardson and, **3:**478
    Miranda v. Arizona, **5:404–405**
"Fifty-Four Forty or Fight," **1:**188;
    2:550; **3:**358
Fighters. *See* Aircraft, fighters
Figure skating, **4:**209, 210
Filer Commission on Private Philan-
    thropy and Public Needs, **3:**444
Filibustering, **3:359–360; 5:**46
    Congressional, **2:**351; **3:358–359**
    procedure to end, **2:**250
Filipino Americans, **3:360–361**
    as farmhands, **3:***326*
    immigration patterns of, **1:**324
    nativist laws and, **6:**5
    in trade unions, **8:**172
Fillmore, Millard
    anti-Masons and, **1:**203
    and Compromise of 1850, **2:**331
    as log cabin president, **5:**145
    presidency of, **8:**322
    in presidential campaign of 1848,
    3:154

in presidential campaign of 1856,
    1:166; **3:**154, 171
Film(s), **3:361–365**
    animated, **2:***64*, 64–65
    in California, **2:**10
    Canadian complaints about, **2:**27
    censorship of, **2:**85; **6:**419
    color, **3:**362, 363
    computer graphics in, **3:**365
    cowboy, **2:**444
    foreign, **3:**365
    during Great Depression, **2:**390
    and imperialism, **4:**244
    independent, **3:**364–365
    about Indiana, **4:**320
    and interior decoration, **1:**292
    music for, **5:500–501**
    musicals, **5:**500
    as recreation, **7:**65
    sexual content in, **3:**362, 363
    silent, **3:**362
    special effects in, **3:**364
    talking, **3:**362–363
    three dimension (3-D), **3:**364
    and toys, **8:**153
    Westerns, **8:***457*, **457–459**, *458*
    See also specific films
Film industry
    Academy Awards in, **6:485–486**
    and audio technology industry,
        1:358; **3:**362–363; **4:**470
    blacklists in, **4:**178; **5:**183
    communism in
        Disney's testimony on, **9:**413–417
        HUAC on, **4:**178, 411
    development of, **3:**362
    developments in, **2:**323
    during Great Depression, **3:**363;
        8:162
    in Hollywood, **4:**150
    mass media, emergence as, **5:**261
    photographic industry and, **6:**330
    pictorial photography in, **1:**300
    technical innovations in, **3:**364
    television and, **3:**364; **8:**75
    VCRs and, **8:**328
    World War I and, **3:**362
    World War II and, **3:**363
Film noir, **3:**363
Filson, John, **9:**104–107
Finance Committee, Senate, **2:**352
Financial Institutions Reform,
    Recovery, and Enforcement Act
    (FIRREA), **1:**563

Financial markets, exchanges,
    3:274–277
Financial Modernization Act. *See*
    Gramm-Leach-Bliley Act
Financial panics, **3:365–367**
    of 1785, **3:**365
    of 1792, **3:**365
    of 1819, **1:**397, 407, 408; **3:**365
    of 1837, **1:**397, 407, 408; **3:**365
        currency shortage and, **2:**481
        political effects of, **2:**550
        and prices, **6:**461
    of 1857, **3:**366
        and prices, **6:**461
    of 1873, **1:**407; **3:**366
        depression following, **1:**484; **2:**9
    of 1893, **1:**407; **3:**366
        and consumerism, **7:**128
        and Kelly's Industrial Army,
            4:516
        and Morgan (J. P.), **6:**493
    of 1907, **1:**397, 407; **3:**366
        Aldrich-Vreeland Act for, **1:**120;
            3:344, 366
        and Morgan (J. P.), **3:**344, 366
    of 1929, **1:**398; **3:**367
        and gold standard, **4:**15
    decrease in incidence of, **1:**585
    and industrialization, **2:**388
    profiteering and, **6:**493
    savings banks during, **1:**407
Financial services industry,
    3:367–370
    convergence of companies in,
        3:368
    crises in, **3:**369
    diversification of, **3:**368
    future of, **3:**369–370
    legislation of, **3:**369
    See also Bank(s)
Financier, The (Dreiser), **6:**12
Fink, Mike, **8:**45
Finkbine, Sherri, **1:**6; **7:**192
Finland, immigration from, **2:**327;
    7:262
Finlay, Carlos J., **8:**576
Finley, John Huston, **2:**189
Finley, Karen, **8:**115
Finley, Robert, **1:**147; **3:**197
Finnegan, Joseph, **3:**343
Finney, Charles Grandison, **1:**203,
    378; **2:**163; **3:**130, 264, 370;
    7:195
    and Grahamites, **3:**24

at Oberlin College, **7**:97
and religious liberty, **7**:93
Finney revivals, **3**:370–371
Finnish Americans, **7**:262
Finnish immigrants
  in Communist Party, **2**:327
  in New Sweden, **6**:77–78
Fire(s), **3**:37–38
  in agricultural practices, **1**:69
  Chicago fire (1871), **1**:12; **2**:132, **133–134**; **3**:37
  at Edison Lamp Factory (1914), **5**:14
  forest, **8**:478
  insurance, **4**:369
  Native American use of, **4**:306–307
  at Triangle Shirtwaist Factory (1911), **1**:12; **2**:247, 249; **3**:38; **5**:14; **8**:208–209, *209*
  See also Disasters; Wildfires
Fire engines, **3**:*372*, 372–373
Fire extinguishers, **3**:373
Fire fighting, **3**:371–373, *373*
  development of, **8**:292
Fire Island, **5**:150
Fire Next Time, The (Baldwin), **5**:126
Firearms. *See* Gun(s)
Firearms Owners' Protection Act (1986), **4**:76; **5**:557
Fire-Eaters, **3**:371
Firestone, Shulamith, **7**:18
FIRREA. *See* Financial Institutions Reform, Recovery, and Enforcement Act
First Amendment, **1**:457; **2**:84, 162; **3**:373–375; **6**:96
  ACLU defense of, **1**:146
  alien rights under, **1**:125
  and American Indian sacred sites on public lands, **5**:180
  and church and state, separation of, **2**:167
  Employment Division v. Smith, **3**:374; **6**:1
  Espionage Act and, Supreme Court on, **7**:264
  Grosjean v. American Press Company and, **4**:67
  group libel laws and, **4**:67
  hate crime legislation and, **4**:104–105
  and Internet, **8**:68
  and libel, **5**:90

and limits on Congressional power, **2**:350
and minority rule on falsehoods, **5**:90
and pornography, **6**:419
and religious liberty, **2**:167; **7**:85, 93
and school prayer, **7**:265
and television programs, **8**:68
First Boston Corporation, **1**:405
First Ladies, **3**:375–376
Fischer, Bobby, **2**:130
Fischer, Michael, **1**:194
Fish, Hamilton
  on *Alabama* claims, **1**:106; **8**:416
  on communism, **1**:198
Fish, Stanley, **5**:122
Fish and fisheries
  in Alaska, **1**:109–110; **7**:231
  in Canada, **6**:53
  cod, **2**:261–262
    fishing bounties and, **3**:376–377
    on Grand Banks, **4**:32
  in colonial era, **4**:349
  in Great Lakes basin, **4**:52
  industrialization of, **5**:209
  mackerel, **5**:187–188
  in Maine, **5**:209
  in North Sea, **6**:161
  oceanographic surveys of, **6**:160
  salmon, **7**:231
    dams and, **4**:202
  U.S.-Canadian disputes over, **2**:27, 28
  See also Marine biology
Fish and Game Commission, Takahashi v., **1**:125–126
Fish and Wildlife Service (FWS), **4**:383, 384
Fisher, Carl G., **5**:109; **7**:178
Fisher, Carrie, **7**:524, *524*
Fisher, Donald, **7**:126
Fisher, Doris, **7**:126
Fisher, Florence, **1**:29
Fisher, Irving, **1**:544; **3**:108–109
Fisher, Miles Mark, **6**:236
Fisher, Osmond, **3**:552
Fisher, Sir R. A., **7**:538, 539
Fisher, Rudolph, **5**:125
Fisher, Warren, Jr., **5**:473
Fisher, Yamataya v., **1**:125
Fishing bounties, **3**:376–377
Fisk, Clinton B., **3**:158
Fisk, James, Jr., **1**:472, 473

Fisk, James Liberty, expeditions of, **3**:377
Fisk Jubilee Singers, **3**:395
Fisk University, **8**:263
Fiske, John, **4**:138
Fiske, Robert, **4**:238; **7**:496
Fitch, James, **3**:63
Fitzgerald, F. Scott, **3**:197, 280; **5**:157
  The Great Gatsby, **1**:504; **4**:49–50; **5**:120, 150
  on Jazz Age, **4**:469–470
Fitzgerald, John F., **1**:510
Fitzhugh, George, **2**:374
  Sociology for the South, **7**:431–432
    excerpt from, **9**:276–280
Fitzmaurice, William Petty, **6**:490
Fitzpatrick, John, **3**:320, 321
Fitzpatrick, Thomas, **5**:40; **9**:227
Fitzpatrick v. Bitzer, **1**:120
Five Civilized Tribes. *See* Civilized Tribes, Five
Five Nations. *See* Iroquois League
Five-and-dime stores, **2**:100, *101*; **3**:9–10, *10*, **26–27**
Five-Power Naval Treaty, **3**:377
Flag(s), **3**:379–381
  Bear, **1**:433
  Creole, **2**:457
  pine tree, **6**:357
  U.S., **3**:378–379
    burning of, **2**:85; **3**:379, 380–381
    during Civil War, **3**:380
    development of design of, **3**:378, 379
    mandatory daily salute to, **3**:380
      Jehovah's Witnesses objected to, **3**:380
    after 9/11 attack, **3**:381
    Pledge of Allegiance to, **6**:370
    protection of, **3**:380
    protest and, **3**:380–381
Flag Act (1777), **3**:378
Flag Act (1794), **3**:378, 379
Flag Act (1818), **3**:378
Flag Day, **3**:377–378; **6**:370
Flag Desecration Act (1968), **3**:380–381
"Flag of the Union, The" (Morris), **8**:279
Flag Protection Act (1989), **3**:381
Flag Protection Movement (FPM), **3**:380
Flagg, James Montgomery, **1**:277

Flagler, Henry, **3:**386–387; **5:**351

Flake, Floyd, **1:**54

Flamingo resort, Las Vegas, **5:**42

Flanagan, Hallie, **8:**531

Flannagan, John B., **1:**306

Flapper, **2:**247; **3:**381, *382*, 401

Flash floods, **3:**383

Flat glass, **4:**3

Flatboat(s), **7:**171–172

Flatboatmen, **3:**381–382

Flathead, **8:**221, 222

Flathead Indian Reservation, **5:**449

Flatiron Building, **6:**80

Flavin, Dan, **1:**307

"Flavr-Savr" tomato, **3:**531

Fleischmann, Martin, **2:**266

Fleming, Alexander, **2:**124

Fleming, Arthur, **2:**14

Fleming, Williamina P., **6:**155–156

Fletcher, Frank J., **2:**412; **4:**68

Fletcher, Horace, **3:**24

Fletcher, Joseph, **1:**462

Fletcher, Robert, **3:**382

Fletcher v. Peck, **2:**397; **3:**382–383; **5:**36; **8:**576

Fletcher v. Rhode Island, **5:**103

Flexner, Abraham, **2:**56; **6:**317

  at Institute for Advanced Study, **4:**366

Flexner, Simon, **6:**388

Flexner Report, **1:**164; **5:**282, 303; **6:**317

Flexographic printing, **6:**470

Flick, Lawrence, **8:**236

Flint, Charles L., **2:**489

Flint, Timothy, **2:**74

Flogging, **3:**383; **6:**551

Flood, Curt, **1:**422, 423

Flood, James C., **1:**497

Floods and flood control, **3:**36, 42, 43, 383–384, *384*

  in Arkansas, **1:**262

  in California, **3:***42*

    Sacramento, **7:**220–221

  human losses from, **3:**384

  Johnstown flood (1889), **3:**383; **4:***483*, 483–484

  on Mississippi River, **3:**383, 384; **5:**417

  on Missouri River, **3:**383; **5:**426

  property damage from, **3:**383–384

  types of, **3:**383

Floor leader, **3:**384–385

Flores, Boerne v., **1:**494; **2:**318

Florida, **3:**385–388

  African Americans in, **3:**386, 388

  in American Revolution, **3:**385

  annexation of, **1:**188; **3:**386–387

  Apalachee Massacre in (1704), **1:221–222**

  Bowles's filibustering expeditions in, **1:525**

  citrus industry in, **2:**181–182

  in Civil War, **3:**386

  in colonial era, **3:**385–386; **5:**308–309

  constitution of, **7:**527

  Cuban Americans in, **2:**473, 474

  de Soto in, **7:**450

  emblems, nicknames, mottos, and songs of, **7:***532*

  English acquisition of, **2:**290

  Everglades National Park, **3:268**, *268*

  exploration of, **3:**385; **8:**47

  French exploration of, **3:**285

  fruit growing in, **3:**478, 479

  Great Depression in, **3:**387

  gun control in, **4:**76

  hurricanes in, **4:**198

  immigration to, **3:**388; **5:**351

  Jackson's campaign in, **7:**10

  Jim Crow laws in, **3:**387–388

  Ku Klux Klan in, **3:**386

  Lake Okeechobee, **5:**22

  maps of, **3:***386*

    archival, **9:***12*, 12–13

  Mariel boatlift (Cuban immigrants), **5:**239

  Mayan refugees in, **9:**509–515

  Native Americans in, **8:**225

    Seminole, **7:**307–308, 309–310, 484; **8:**401–402

  New Smyrna Colony in, **6:**77

  Panama Canal and, **3:**387

  Paris, Treaty of (1763) and, **6:**248

  Pinckney's Treaty (1795) and, **6:**356; **8:**204

  in presidential election of 2000, **3:**388; **7:**527; **8:**354

  Progressive movement in, **3:**387

  Prohibition in, **3:**387

  purchase of, **1:**490

    and land claims, **5:**26

  railroads in, **3:**386–387

  Reconstruction in, **3:**386

  settlement in, **3:**385

  slavery in, **3:**385

Spanish cession of, **7:**9

Spanish conquest and colonization of, **5:**308–309

Spanish exploration of, **2:**1; **3:**294, 295–296

tidelands in, ownership of, **8:**125

tourism in, **3:**386–387, 388; **8:**145–146

as winter resort, **7:**122

in World War I, **3:**387

in World War II, **3:**387

yellow fever in, **3:**387

Florida, Gulf of, **3:**388

Florida, Hoyt v., **8:**60

Florida, McLaughlin v., **5:**165

Florida, Seminole Tribe v., **1:**120; **7:309**

Florida, Straits of, **3:388**, *389*

Florida Current, **4:**73

Florida Farmers Alliance, **3:**387

Flour milling, **3:388–392**

  in colonial era, **3:**388–389

  quality-control procedures and, **3:**391

  technology of, **3:**388–391

Flour trust, **3:**390

Flower, J. R., **1:**334

Flower Gap, **6:**254

Floyd, Carlisle, **6:**199

Floyd, John, **2:**456

FLPF. *See* Farmer Labor Political Federation

FLPMA. *See* Federal Land Policy and Management Act

FLRA. *See* Federal Labor Relations Authority

FLSA. *See* Fair Labor Standards Act

Flu. *See* Influenza

Fluorescent lamps, **3:**179

Fluoride, **3:**4

Fluoxetine. *See* Prozac

Flute, Jerry, **1:**340

Flutie, Doug, **1:**232

Flying boats, **1:**83–84

Flying the Hump, **3:**392

Flying Tigers, **3:***392*, **392–393**

Flynn, Elizabeth Gurley, **1:**147; **5:**60

Flynn, Raymond L., **1:**510

FMCS. *See* Federal Mediation and Conciliation Service

FMIA. *See* Federal Meat Inspection Act

FMLA. *See* Family and Medical Leave Act

FMLN. *See* Farabundo Martí National Liberation Front

FNMA. *See* Federal National Mortgage Administration

FNS. *See* Food and Nutrition Service

Foch, Ferdinand, **2:**112; **3:**451

Fogel, Robert, **3:**107

FOIA. *See* Freedom of Information Act

Fokine, Mikhail, **1:**389–390

Foley, Margaret, **1:**308

Foley v. Connelie, **1:**126

Folger, Emily Jordan, **3:**393

Folger, Henry Clay, **3:**393

Folger Shakespeare Library, **3:393**

Folin, Otto, **1:**460

Folk, Joseph W., **5:**421

Folk art, **1:309–313**

Folk music, **3:**395–396
  ballads, **1:388–389**
  revival, **5:**496–497

Folklore, **3:393–397**
  in 19th century, **3:**394
  African American, **3:**394–395
  and mass culture, **3:**394, 395–397
  origin of term, **3:**394
  tall stories, **8:45**

Folsom, Frances, **3:**375

FOMC. *See* Federal Open Market Committee

Fong Yue Ting v. United States, **1:**125; **3:**11

Fontaine, Pierre-François-Léonard, **3:**497

Fontainebleau, Treaty of (1762), **6:**248

Food, Drug, and Cosmetic Act (1938), **3:**404; **6:**555

Food Additives Amendment (1958), **3:**404

Food and cuisines, **3:398–403**
  anxiety about, **3:**402–403
  Arab, **1:**231
  breakfast cereals, **2:98–99**
  chemicals and, **3:**402
  class distinctions and, **3:**399, 402
  cleanliness and, **3:**400
  colonial, **3:**398
  dieting, **3:**401
  fast, **3:***397*, 397–398, 402
    McDonald's, **5:184–185**
  fish, **5:**187
  French, **3:**399

genetically engineered, **3:**531
  during Great Depression, **3:**401
  health food, **4:118–119**
  immigrants and, **3:**399–400, 401, 402
  of Italian Americans, **3:**401
  mass production and, **3:**400
  meatpacking, **5:278–280**
  mechanization of housework and, **3:**400–401
  and nutrition, **6:**148–150
  organic, **4:**118; **6:210**
  Prohibition and, **3:**401
  Pure Food and Drug Movement and, **6:**553–555
  railroads and, **3:**400
  vegetarianism, **8:310**
  war rationing, **3:**401–402

Food and Drug Act (1906), **5:**510

Food and Drug Administration (FDA), **3:403–405**
  on Alzheimer's disease treatments, **1:**132
  on azidothymidine (AZT), **1:**16
  budget for, **3:**405
  creation of, **6:**554
  on "elixir sulfanilamide," **3:**404; **6:**555
  food pyramid of, **2:**97
  jurisdiction of, **6:**555
  Nader's Raiders and, **5:**509
  on thalidomide, **3:**405
  on Viagra, **8:**322

Food and Nutrition Service (FNS), **6:**150

Food Employees v. Logan Valley Plaza, **6:**350

Food preservation, **2:**35–37; **3:405–408**
  canning and, **3:**405–406
  drying and, **3:**406–407
  health effects of, **6:**554
  irradiation and, **3:**407–408
  natural processes of, **3:**405
  and packaging, **6:**229
  refrigeration and freezing and, **3:**407

Food safety
  development of, **3:**400
  governmental inspection for, **4:**364
  legislation on, **3:**403–405; **5:**277–278
  USDA role in, **1:**71

Food Safety and Inspection Service (FSIS), **5:**278

Food Security Act (1985), **1:**72

Food Stamp Act (1977), **3:**409

Food stamp program, **3:408–409; 6:**150, 438

Food Stamp Reform Bill (1970), **3:**408–409

Food supplements, **3:**401; **4:**118

Foot-and-mouth disease, **2:**73; **8:**320

Football, **3:409–413**, *411*
  college, **2:**276; **3:**409–410, 412–413; **5:**530–531
    Ivy League, **4:**449
  development of, **3:**409–410
  high school, **3:**410
  professional, **3:**410, 411
  and social stratification, **7:**65
  on television, **3:**411; **8:**74
  after World War I, **3:**410–411
  after World War II, **3:**411–412

Foote, Andrew H., in Island Number Ten operations, **4:**438

Foote, Edward Bliss, **1:**467

Foote, Henry S., and Compromise of 1850, **2:**331

Foote, Julia A. J., **1:**44

Foote, Samuel A., **8:**434

Foraker, Joseph B., **1:**550

Foraker Act (1900), **3:**413; **6:**544

Foran Act (1885), **2:**397, 398

Forbes, Hugh, **4:**99

Forbes, John, **1:**127; **6:**277
  expedition of, **1:**530; **3:**95

Forbes Road, **8:**461

Force, Juliana, **1:**310

Force Acts, **3:413–414; 6:**145–146

Ford, Betty, **3:**376; **8:***517*

Ford, Edsel, **3:**414

Ford, Gerald R.
  and Air Force Academy, **1:**78
  amnesty granted by, **1:**177
  attempted assassination of, **1:**330–331
  on bicentennial of Declaration of Independence, **1:**450
  defense policy of, **2:**529
  education policies of, **3:**118
  energy policies of, **3:**209, 215; **6:**304
  and Federal Mediation and Conciliation Service, **3:**343
  as first unelected president, **3:**171–172

Ford, Gerald R., (*continued*)
  HUD under, **4:**183
  inaugural statement of, **6:**111
  and Japanese American incarcera-
    tion, **4:**462
  Latin American policies of, **5:**49
  Mayaguez incident and, **5:**275
  Nixon pardoned by, **8:**323, 427
    text of, **9:**491–492
  Office of Economic Opportunity
    under, **6:**164
  and Panama Canal, **6:**240, 242
  presidency of, **8:**323
  in presidential campaign of 1976,
    3:167
  presidential library of, **5:**100
  and Republican Party, **2:**376
  at summit conferences, **8:**16
  and Toxic Substance Control Act,
    8:151
  and Transportation, Department
    of, **8:**185
  vetoes cast by, **8:**321
  vice presidency of, **8:**323
  in Warren Commission, **8:**394
  in World War II, **8:**557
Ford, Harold, **8:**86
Ford, Harrison, **7:**524, *524*
Ford, Henry
  advice to unemployed by,
    9:375–376
  and America First Committee,
    1:139
  anti-Semitism of, **1:**207
  and assembly-line process, **2:**389
  automobiles of, **1:**335, 367, 368,
    371–373
  bombers of, **1:**335–336
  conditions for employment by,
    8:438
  employees of, **1:**335, 372–373
  Ford Motor Company founded by,
    3:414; **8:**189
  history museum of, **4:**127, *127*;
    5:488
  and leisure time, increase in, **7:**65
  manufacturing process of,
    1:371–373
    assembly lines in, **1:**335–336, 372;
      4:334; **8:**189
    mass production, **5:**262–263
  mass marketing, **5:**246
  tractors of, **1:**59, 65
Ford, Henry, II, **1:**373; **3:**414, 415

Ford, James A., **1:**240
Ford, John (director), **8:**458
Ford, John S. (Rip) (Texas Ranger),
    8:104
Ford, Leland, **4:**463
Ford, Mary B. Black, *Notes Illustra-
    tive of the Wrong of Slavery*,
    excerpt from, **9:**269–271
Ford, Richard, **5:**123
Ford Foundation, **3:**444; **6:**318;
    8:117
Ford Motor Company, **3:***414*,
    414–415; 8:189
  in Detroit, **3:**20
  Highland Park factory, **5:**263, *263*
  manufacturing process at,
    1:371–373
    assembly line in, **8:**189
  Model T by, **5:**262–263
  and United Automobile Workers,
    8:261, 262
    clash between, newspaper
      account of, **9:**385–387
  and University of Michigan, **8:**282
Fordney Emergency Tariff Bill. *See*
    Emergency Tariff
Forecasting, business, **1:586–588**
Foreclosure. *See* Debt(s)
Foreign aid, **3:415–419**, *416*
  to Africa, **1:**40–41; **3:**416, 418
  after Cold War, **3:**418
  during Cold War, **3:**416–418
  to Eastern Europe, **3:**418
  to Egypt, **3:**418
  to El Salvador, **3:**418
  to France, **3:**452
  to Germany, **3:**562
  to Great Britain, **4:**43
  to Greece, **3:**415, 426; **4:**59;
    8:231–232
  to Guatemala, **4:**70
  to Israel, **3:**418; **4:**440–441
  to Latin America, **1:**128; **3:**416;
    5:44
  in Lend-Lease, **5:**81–82
  Point Four, **3:**415–416; **6:381**
  to Russia, **3:**418
  to South Korea, **3:**416
  to South Vietnam, **3:**417
  to Southeast Asia, **3:**416
  to Taiwan, **3:**416
  to Turkey, **3:**415, 426; **8:**231–232
  to Ukraine, **3:**418
  to Western Europe, **3:**415, 426

  after World War II, **3:**415–416,
    426
  during World War II, **6:**36
  See also Agency for International
    Development; Marshall Plan
Foreign Assistance Act (1961), **3:**418
Foreign commentaries, on America,
    1:135–139, 148–149
Foreign direct investment (FDI),
    3:420, 423
Foreign Exchange Control Law
    (1980), **3:**422
Foreign investment in United States,
    2:516–518; 3:419–424
  in 1960s, **3:**422
  in 1970s, **3:**422
  in 1980s, **3:**422
  in 1990s, **3:**422–423
  alien landholding, **1:**124
  American Revolution and, **3:**419
  from Arab countries, **3:**422
  California Gold Rush and, **3:**420
  from Canada, **3:**421–422
  Civil War and, **3:**420–421
  in colonial era, **3:**419
  in computer industry, **3:**423
  from France, **3:**419
  from Germany, **3:**421
  from Great Britain, **3:**419, 420,
    421, 422
  Great Depression and, **3:**421
  from Holland, **3:**419, 420, 422
  from Japan, **3:**422
  in railroads, **3:**420
  from Spain, **3:**419
  from Switzerland, **3:**422
  in telecommunications industry,
    3:423
  in U.S. Steel, **3:**420
  World War I and, **3:**421
  World War II and, **3:**422
Foreign Operations Administration,
    6:381
Foreign policy, **3:424–428**
  in 1920s, **3:**426
  in 1990s, **3:**427–428
  American Revolution and, **3:**425
    Plan of 1776, **6:361**
  antiwar movements on, **1:**215
  cabinet members and, **2:**2–3
  Civil War and, **3:**425
  during Cold War, **3:**426–427
  in colonial era, **3:**425

of Confederate States of America, **2**:342

Continental Congress and, **2**:394–395

critique of, **3**:424

definition of, **3**:424

dollar diplomacy, **3:70–71**

drug trafficking and, **5**:511, 512–513

establishment of, **3**:425

foreign observers on, **1**:138

Great Depression and, **3**:426

industrialization and, **3**:425

jingoism in, **4:480**

Kennan (George F.) and, **8**:569

Monroe Doctrine, **5:446–447**

most-favored-nation principle, **5:462**

munitions, export restrictions on, **5**:479

nonintervention policy, **6:117**

Open Door, **6:196–198**

recognition in, **7:56–57**

Republican Party and, **7**:112

and secret diplomacy, **3**:27

State Department in, **7**:527–531

Vietnam syndrome and, **8**:328

during World War I, **3**:426

during World War II, **3**:426

See also under specific administrations

Foreign Service, **3**:193–194, **428–430**

in 1990s, **3**:429–430

ambassadors in, **1**:133; **7**:528

American Revolution and, **3**:428

Civil War and, **3**:428

Cold War and, **3**:429

origins of, **3**:28

professionalization of, **7**:529

World War I and, **3**:428

World War II and, **3**:429

Foreign Service Act (1924), **3**:428

Foreign Service Act (1946), **3**:429

Foreign Service Act (1980), **3**:429

Foreign trade. *See* Trade, foreign

Foreman, George, **6**:484–485

Forensic science, **6**:385

Forest(s), conservation of, **2**:367–368

Forest and Rangeland Renewable Resources Planning Act (1974), **3**:431

Forest fires, **3**:38

and early forestry, **3**:436

fighting, **3**:373

and Forest Service, **3**:431–432

Forest industries, in colonial era, **4**:350

Forest Management Act (1897), **3**:431, 433, 546; **5**:35; **6**:531

Forest Reserve Act (1891), **3**:431, 433; **5**:31

Forest Service, **3:430–433**

challenges of, **3**:431–433

fire management by, **8**:478

forest service lands of, **3**:431

headquarters of, **3**:433

history of, **3**:430–431

motto of, **3**:431

National Forest System managed by, **3**:431

under Pinchot, **2**:367

as research agency, **3**:432

utilitarian policies of, **2**:369

Forestry, **3:433–438**, *434, 435*

in 1980s, **3**:437

in 1990s, **3**:437–438

definition of, **3**:433

ecological, **3**:437–438

during Great Depression, **3**:436

Marsh (George Perkins) and, **3**:434–435

Pinchot (Gifford) and, **3**:433

in postwar era, **3**:437

in Progressive Era, **3**:435–436

Timber Culture Act (1873) and, **8**:126

during World War II, **3**:436

See also Lumber industry

Forever (Blume), **1**:500

"Forgotten Man" (Sumner), **3:438**

Formaldehyde, **6**:366

Forrest, Edwin, **1**:341; **8**:113

Forrest, Nathan Bedford, **8**:85, 473

in Fort Pillow Massacre, **6**:356

Forrestal, James V., **2**:528; **5**:560; **8**:256

Forry, Samuel, **2**:235

Forsberg, Randall, **6**:268

Forssmann, Werner, **2**:53

Forsyth, George A., **8**:562

Forsyth, John, **1**:176

Fort Berthold Indian Reservation, **5**:219, 220

Fort Mohave Reservation, **5**:434–435

Fort Worth (Texas), **3:438**; **8**:103

Forten, James, **6**:234

Fortifications, **3:438–439**, *439*

Fortress Monroe, **5:445–446**

French, **3**:469, *472*

See also Army posts; *specific forts*

Fortune (magazine), **8**:127

Fortune (ship), **5**:317

"Forty Acres and a Mule," **3:440**

Forty Years in Phrenology (Sizer), **6**:334

Forty-Eighters, **3**:320–321, **440–441**

Forty-Mile Desert, **3:441**

Forty-Niners, **3:441–442**, *442*; **4**:13

42nd Parallel, The (Dos Passos), **5**:121

Forum Journal, **5**:550

Forum News (newsletter), **5**:550

Fosdick, Harry Emerson, **5**:432

Fossett, Steve, **1**:392

Fossil fuels, **3**:214; **4**:5–6, 7

alternatives to, **3**:212–213, *213*

history in U.S., **3**:210–211

Fossils, mammalian, **5**:218

Foster, Andrew (Rube), **1**:421

Foster, George, **8**:291

Foster, Jodie, **1**:331; **2**:79

Foster, John, **1**:294; **8**:522

Foster, Stephen, **3**:395; **5**:496

Foster, William Z., **2**:326, 327; **8**:170

Foster care, **3:442–443**

African Americans in, **1**:29

FOTLU. *See* Federation of Organized Trades and Labor Unions

Foucault, Michel, **3**:516; **6**:429; **7**:332

Fouilhoux, André, **1**:252; **7**:376

Foundation for Interior Design Education and Research (FIDER), **1**:294

Foundations, endowed, **3:443–445**; **6**:317–319

medical research and, **5**:287

Four Bears (Mató-Tópe), **8**:*393*

Four freedoms, **3:445**

See also specific freedoms

Four Hundred, **3:445**

Four Minute Men program, **8**:535

401(k) Plans, **6**:493

See also Retirement Plans

4-H Clubs, **3:445–446**

Fourier, Charles, **1**:545; **3**:446; **7**:194; **8**:181, 301

Fourier, Jean-Baptiste, **4**:6

Fourierism, **3:446–447; 8:**301

Four-Power Treaty, **3:446**

Fourteen Points, **2:**552; **3:**426, **447; 5:**63; **8:**315
  and Armistice of November 1918, **1:**265
  Great Britain rejecting, **4:**42
  text of, **9:**368–370

14 Points for Management (Deming), text of, **9:**499–500

Fourteenth Amendment, **2:**180–181, 193, 523; **3:**341–342
  and apportionment, **1:**227
  and civil rights, **2:**198
  civil rights under, **7:**525–526
  congressional debate over, excerpts from, **9:**310–317
  due process clause in, **2:**397; **3:**90
  equal protection clause of, **3:**249
  Force Bill (1871) strengthening, **3:**414
  gun control laws violating, **4:**74
  and interracial marriage, **5:**165
  Joint Committee on Reconstruction proposal for, **4:**485
  and judicial review, **4:**492
  marriage and, **5:**250, 251
  and privileges and immunities of citizens, **6:**482
  racial segregation in public schools violating, **3:**341
  Radical Republicans and, **7:**112
  ratification of, **3:**86
  Reconstruction and, **7:**59
  and state sovereignty, **7:**534
  and suits against states, **1:**120
  Supreme Court on, **5:**401–402, 482–483; **7:**378
    under Warren, **4:**496
  and voting rights, **7:**105–106

Fourth Amendment, **1:**457; **3:**185
  and arrest, **1:**283
  equality principle in, **3:**245
  Supreme Court on, **1:**283; **7:**289–290

Fourth of July. *See* Independence Day

Fowle, Daniel, **1:**129

Fowler, Henry Watson, **3:**222

Fowler, John, **1:**292

Fox. *See* Mesquakie

Fox, George, **7:**1

Fox, Gilbert, **2:**302

Fox, Gustavus V., **6:**23

Fox, Kate, **7:**505

Fox, Luke, **3:**286

Fox, Margaret, **7:**505

Fox, Vicente, **5:**349

Fox Indians, in Black Hawk War, **1:**473

Fox television network, **8:**75

Fox War, **3:447–448**

Fox-Wisconsin waterway, **3:**448

Foxwoods Casino, **3:**509

FPA. *See* Federal Power Act

FPC. *See* Federal Power Commission

FPM. *See* Flag Protection Movement

Fractions of crude oil, **6:**301

Fraina, Louis, **2:**325

Framework Convention on Climate Change (FCCC), **2:**238

France
  Abenaki alliance with, **1:**1; **8:**311
  and American Revolution, **3:**449–450, **472–473; 6:**94; **9:**30
    assistance in, **2:**394; **7:**137, 144; **8:**581
    material, **7:**147
    naval, **7:**145
  anti-Americanism in, **3:**452
  birth control in, **1:**467
  Caribbean territories of, **8:445–447**, *446*
  and Chickasaws, **8:**85
  CIA operations in, **2:**92
  Code Napoléon in, **2:262**
  colonial settlements of, **3:**449, 468; **4:**282 (*See also* New France)
    in Acadia, **1:**11
    in Canada, **6:**51–53
    in Florida, **3:**385
    in Illinois, **4:**214; **6:**53–54
    in Indiana, **4:**317
    in Kansas, **4:**508
    in Louisiana, **5:**414; **6:**53, 73
    on Mackinac Island and Straits, **5:**188
    in Maine, **5:**207–208
    in Michigan, **5:**188, 353–354
    in Minnesota, **5:**398
    in Mississippi, **5:**411
    in Missouri, **5:**419
    in North Dakota, **6:**131, 132
    in Ohio, **6:**171
    in Vermont, **8:**311
  in colonial wars, **2:**293–296
    archival maps of, **9:25–28**
  and Confederate States of America, **2:**342
  cuisine of, popularity of, **3:**399
  customary law in, **2:**440
  Declaration of Rights of Woman and Citizen, **2:**524
  dentistry in, **3:**3
  in European Common Market, **8:**157
  explorations of, **3:**285–286, **290–293**, *292*; **6:**51
    by Champlain, **2:**103–104, *104*
    on Great Plains, **8:**451–452
    Hennepin on, **4:**126
    by Jolliet-Marquette, **4:**486–487; **5:**416, *416*
    by La Salle
      Griffon and, **4:**66
      Mississippi River, **6:**29; **8:**99
    Lake Michigan, **4:**50–51
    Lake Ontario and Huron, **4:**50
    maps of, archival, **9:***19*, 19–22
    by Nicolet, **6:106**
    in North Dakota, **6:**131
    on Northwest Coast, **8:**453
    Platte River, **6:**29
    Saint Lawrence River, **3:**488; **4:**50
  feudalism in, **3:**356
  foreign aid to, **3:**452
  foreign investment from, **3:**419
  foreign service to, **3:**429
  in Fox War, **3:**447–448
  fur trade of, **3:**486–487, 488
  German relations with, Morocco and, **1:**123
  and Great Britain, **3:**449, 450
    colonial wars of, **2:**293–296
    in French and Indian War (*See* French and Indian War)
    French decrees, **3:471–472**
    and neutrality of U.S., **6:**33, 34
  Huguenots from, **4:190–191**
  individualism in, **4:**331
  in Indochina War, **3:**417; **8:**329
    and Geneva Accords, **3:**534
  Jacobin clubs in, **4:**456
  in Kellogg-Briand Pact, **4:**515
  Kickapoo relations with, **4:**524
  in King George's War, **4:526**
  in King William's War, **4:527–528**
  and League of Nations, **8:**315–316

and Louisiana Purchase, **3:**425, 450; **8:**200, 204
in Mexico, **5:**446
  invasion of, **5:**345
Mississippi River and, **5:**416
Morocco and, trade between, **1:**123
in Napoleonic wars, **1:**487; **3:**192
and Natchez, **5:**517–518
Native Americans and
  Iroquois, **4:**432
  on Mackinac Island (Michigan), **5:**188
  Mesquakie, **5:**326
  Miami, **5:**352–353
  missions for, **4:**276
  policies on, **4:**282
  Shawnee, **7:**336–337
  trade between, **6:**51
  treaties between, **4:**312, 313
and NATO, **3:**452; **6:**125–126
nuclear power plants in, **6:**139
and Nuclear Test Ban Treaty, refusal to sign, **6:**143
at Paris conferences, **6:**247
Quasi-War with, **3:**425, **449**, 450
  Navy in, **6:**24–25
revolutionary, U.S. relations with, **7:**56–57
in Siberian Expedition, **7:**353
Statue of Liberty from, **3:**451; **7:**540
in Suez Crisis, **8:**2–3
trade with, **8:**198
trading posts of, **8:**175
Treaty of Alliance with, **8:**199–200
and Treaty of Paris (1783), **6:**248, 250
Tripartite Agreement with, **8:**230
U.S. relations with, **3:449–452**
  during Civil War, **3:**425, 450
  cod fishing and, **2:**261
  in colonial era, **3:**425
  Convention of 1800 and, **2:**398
  Five-Power Naval Treaty and, **3:**377
  Four-Power Treaty and, **3:**446
  isolationism in, **4:**439
  Quasi-War and, **2:**258, 398, 530
  shipping restrictions, **5:**189
  during World War I, **3:**426, 451
  during World War II, **3:**426
  XYZ affair, **2:**398; **3:**425, 450; **8:570**

in War of 1812 (*See* War of 1812)
in World War I, **3:**426, 451
  Aisne-Marne Operation, **1:**99
  American Expeditionary Forces in, **1:**149; **8:**535
  American troops in, **8:**538, 540
  Armistice of November 1918, **1:**265
  Saint-Mihiel Campaigns, **7:227–228**
  Somme Offensive, **7:447–448**
  Versailles Treaty after, **3:**451; **8:**315–316
in World War II, **3:**451–452
  liberation of, **8:**549–550, *550*
  Saint-Lô, **7:**227
Franchise. *See* Suffrage
Franchising, McDonalds, **5:184–185**
Francis, Clarence (Bevo), **1:**424
Francis, David R., **5:**163
Francis, Donald, **1:**15
Francis, Thomas, Jr., **6:**389; **8:**282
Francis, William, **8:**244
Franciscans, **3:**453
  in New Mexico, **6:**67
  in Southwest, **8:**227
  and Timucuans, **8:**129
Francisqui, Jean-Baptiste, **1:**389
Francke, August Hermann, **6:**353
Franco, Francisco, **7:**485
Frank, Jerome, **2:**317
Frank, Leo, lynching of, **3:453**
Frank, Robert, **1:**301
Frank Leslie's Illustrated (magazine), **6:**553
Frankensteen, Richard, **8:**261
Frankenthaler, Helen, **1:**298
Frankfort (Kentucky), **2:**47
Frankfurt School, **3:454**
Frankfurter, Felix, **2:**189
  ACLU and, **1:**146
  on admiralty law, **1:**23
  on congressional districts, **7:**108
  on powers of Federal Communications Commission, **3:**341
Frankland, Edward, **6:**148
Franklin (state), **1:**382; **3:454–455**
Franklin, Benjamin
  Albany Plan of, **1:**114; **6:**363
  almanacs of, **1:**129
  in American Academy of Arts and Sciences, **1:**139
  on American climate, **2:**234

  in American Philosophical Society, **1:**166; **5:**66
  apprenticeship of, **1:**228
  and Articles of Confederation, **1:**317
  Autobiography of Benjamin Franklin, **1:363**; **5:**118
  and Canada, relations with, **2:**25
  charitable trust established by, **3:**443
  on chess, **2:**130
  on colonies, relations among, **7:**139
  at Constitutional Convention, **2:**379
  and Declaration of Independence, **2:**521–522
  deism and, **2:**539
  as deputy postmaster, **6:**425
  diplomacy of, **2:**394; **3:**27; **7:**146, 147
  and electric power, development of, **3:**172, 177
  exploratory efforts of, **3:**286
  fire-fighting company formed by, **3:**371
  in France, **3:**449, *451*, 472
  as freemason, **3:**466
  General Magazine and Historical Chronicle, **5:**118
  and higher education, **8:**282
  on immigrants, **4:**221
  and land companies, **5:**35
  lightning experiments, **5:**330–331
  and mutual insurance, **2:**406
  as national hero, **5:**567
  and *New England Courant,* **6:**95
  "Observations Concerning the Increase in Mankind" by, **3:**468
  Pennsylvania Gazette and, **1:**31
  and *Die Philadelphische Zeitung,* **6:**95
  on philanthropy, **6:**316
  and Plan of 1776, **6:**361
  political cartoons by, **6:**394
  and political economics, **3:**108
  Poor Richard's Almanac, **5:**118; **6:413**, 536; **8:**528
    excerpt from, **9:**113–114
  and postal service, **6:**426
  as publisher, **6:**536
  Red Line Map of, **8:**434
  and Seal of the United States, **3:**99

Franklin, Benjamin, (*continued*)
  stove invented by, **3:456; 4:**122
  and Treaty of Paris (1783), **1:**541;
    6:248, 250
  and Vandalia Colony, **8:**308
  on virtues, **8:**528
  and work ethic, **7:**63
Franklin, James, **1:**129
  New England Courant published by,
    6:95
Franklin, Jerry F., **3:**437
Franklin, Rosalind, **3:**67, 68
Franklin, William, **5:**167; **6:**62, 520;
    7:216
  in Battle of Antietam, **1:**200
Franklin and Marshall College, **8:**264
Franklin Institute, **3:**216, **455–456**
Franklin Journal and American
    Mechanics' Magazine, **3:**455
Franklin stove, **3:456; 4:**122
Franks, Bobby, **5:**82
Franks, Frederick M., Jr., in Persian
    Gulf War, **1:**268
Franz, Frederick, **4:**472
Fraser, Douglas, **8:**262
Fraser, Laura Gardin, **1:**308
Fraternal and service organizations,
    3:456
Fraternities and sororities, **3:**456
Fraunces Tavern, **3:456–457**, *457*
  bombing of, **8:**96
Frazier, Joe, **6:**484–485
Frazier, Lynn, **3:**457; **6:**118, 132
Frazier, Thelma, **1:**304
Frazier-Lemke Farm Bankruptcy
    Act (1934), **3:457**
FRC. *See* Federal Radio Commis-
    sion
Freddie Mac. *See* Savings and loan
    associations
Frederick Douglass' Weekly (newspa-
    per), **6:**97
Frederick William III (king of Prus-
    sia), **8:**264
Fredericksburg, Battle of, **2:**213;
    3:457–458
Fredericksz, Crijn, **6:**71
Fredonia Gaslight and Waterworks
    Company, **6:**8
Free banking system, **3:458**
Free Black Militia, **5:***381*
Free School Society, **8:**62
Free silver, **2:**482; **3:458–459; 4:**10
  Crime of 1873 and, **2:464**

Democratic division over, **2:**400
  arguments for, *Coin's Financial*
    School and, **2:265**
Free Society of Traders, **3:459**
Free Soil Party, **1:**417; **3:**154,
    459–460; 5:33, 97; **7:**111; **8:**119
  antislavery in, **1:**211
  and black laws, repeal of, **1:**475
  Conscience Whigs and, **2:**361
  in homestead movement, **4:**156
  platform of, **6:**368
  in Vermont, **8:**313
Free Speech (newspaper), **5:**199
Free trade, **3:**309–310, **460–461**
  barriers to, **3:**460 (*See also* Tariff[s])
  Treasury and, **8:**197–198
  United States-Canada, **8:**276–277
  See also North American Free
    Trade Agreement
Free universities, **3:461–462**
Freeboldsen, Freebold, **8:**45
Freedman's Savings Bank, **3:462**
Freedmen
  in Arkansas, **1:**261
  in Louisiana, police regulations on,
    9:323
  in Mississippi, **5:**412–413
Freedmen's Bureau, **3:462–463;**
    6:317; **7:**59
  colleges supported by, **3:**120, 125
  creation of, **2:**218
  in Georgia, **3:**555
Freedom of Information Act (FOIA)
    (1966), **2:**85; **3:**338, **463**
Freedom of Information Reform Act
    (1986), **3:**463
Freedom of press
  Alien and Sedition Acts on,
    1:123–124; **3:**374
  Amerasia case and, **1:**134
  in colonial era, **6:**95
  Grosjean v. American Press Company
    and, **4:**67
  Near v. Minnesota and, **6:**27
  New York Times Co. v. United States
    and, **6:**287
  New York Times v. Sullivan, **6:**91
  postal service and, **6:**426–427
  See also First Amendment
Freedom of religion, **7:**85, **93–95**
  for atheism, **1:**347
  First Amendment and, **2:**167; **7:**85,
    93
  as human right, **4:**193

in Maryland, **1:**196; **9:**89–91
  for Native Americans, **3:**374; **6:**1
  legislation on, **1:**161–162
  Pinckney Plan and, **6:**356
  Quakers and, **7:**1, 2
  in Rhode Island, **7:**151
  Supreme Court on, **2:**167–168;
    7:150
  Toleration Acts and, **8:**139
  Vatican II on, **8:**308
Freedom of speech
  Alien and Sedition Acts on,
    1:123–124; **3:**374
  Espionage Act and, **7:**264
  for high school students, **1:**26
  on Internet, **8:**68
  Supreme Court on, **1:**26; **3:**374;
    7:264
Freedom of the seas, **3:463–464**
  Plan of 1776 and, **6:**361
Freedom of the Will (Edwards), **6:**325
Freedom Riders, **1:**466; **2:**202;
    3:464, *465*
  Congress of Racial Equality and,
    2:354; **3:**15
  violence against, **2:**203
Freedom Support Act (FSA), **3:**418
Freedom's Journal (newspaper),
    5:199; **6:**96
Freeh, Louis J., **8:**95
Freeholders, **3:464–465; 8:**6
  Dorr's Rebellion and, **3:**82
Freeman, Derek, **1:**194
Freeman, Edward A., **6:**402
Freeman, Orville L., **1:**72
Freeman, Thomas, **3:**297, 298, 465;
    8:453
Freeman's expedition, **3:465**
Freemasons, **3:465–467**
  rise of, **1:**203
  rituals of, **1:**203
  See also Anti-Masonic movements
Freeport Doctrine, **3:467; 5:**111
Freer, Charles Lang, **2:**272
Freeze drying, **3:**407
Freezing food, **3:**407
Frelinghuysen, Theodore, **3:**153;
    4:38
Frémont, John C., **3:***467; 5:*41
  on agriculture in West, **1:**64
  in Army of Virginia, **1:**279
  and Bear Flag revolt, **1:**433
  emancipation order of, **3:**190
  explorations of, **3:467–468**

American West, **3**:299
California, **2**:8
Great Basin, **3**:468; **4**:39
Great Salt Lake, **3**:468; **4**:57
mountain passes, **6**:254
Nevada, **3**:468; **6**:37
Platte River, **3**:467; **6**:30
in presidential campaign of 1856,
  3:154; **7**:111
in presidential campaign of 1864,
  2:218
reports of, **8**:454
slaves in Missouri, manumission
  order for, **5**:230, 231
French, Daniel Chester, **1**:306
French and Indian War (Seven
  Years' War), **1**:457, 542;
  2:285–286, 294–295;
  3:468–471, *470*; **5**:21, 162;
  7:151
  Battle at Great Meadows in, **4**:55
  Battle of the Monongahela in,
    5:443–444
  Braddock's expedition in, **1**:530
  causes of, **8**:460
  Cherokee in, **2**:128
  Fort Duquesne in, **1**:530; **3**:95
  and fur trade, **3**:490
  King William's War, **4**:527–528
  and Maine, **5**:208
  maps of, archival, **9**:26–28, *28*
  Montreal in, capture of, **5**:454
  privateering in, **6**:480
  Quebec in, capture of, **7**:4
  Rogers' Rangers in, **7**:193; **8**:257
  role of rivers in, **7**:174–175
  Treaty of Paris (1763) ending,
    6:248
  and Vermont, **8**:311
  Winnebago in, **8**:488
French Canadians
  immigration to New England,
    4:224
  in Rhode Island, **7**:153
  in Vermont, **8**:313
"French Connection," breakup of,
  3:87
French decrees, **3**:471–472
French frontier forts, **3**:469, **472**
  Fort Crèvecoeur, **5**:2
  Fort Frontenac, **5**:1–2
  Fort Miami, **5**:2–3
  Fort Saint Louis, **5**:3
French Quarter, **8**:336

French Revolution
  English phase of, **7**:56
  National Assembly during, **7**:16
Freneau, Philip, **5**:118; **7**:117
Frente Auténtico del Trabajo (FAT),
  3:177
Freon, **3**:182; **7**:78, 246
Freud, Sigmund, **6**:521, 524
  on adolescence, **1**:24
  on homosexuality, **7**:325
  on post-traumatic stress disorder,
    6:431
  psychoanalysis, **5**:314
Freytag-Loringhoven, Elsa von,
  1:309
Fri, Robert W., **3**:215
Frick, Henry Clay, **1**:181; **2**:224;
  3:*473*
  in Homestead strike, **4**:157; **7**:556
Frick Art Reference Library, **3**:473
Frick Collection, **3**:473–474
Frictional unemployment, **8**:252
Friday, Ben, Sr., **1**:*235*
Friday Harbor Laboratories, **5**:240,
  241
Friedan, Betty, **8**:*517*
  The Feminine Mystique, **2**:391;
    3:281, **353**; **4**:1; **7**:18; **8**:511,
    516
  and National Organization for
    Women, **5**:548; **8**:507
  on President's Commission on the
    Status of Women, **8**:498–499
Friedlander, Lee, **1**:301
Friedman, Bernard, **1**:386
Friedman, Milton, **1**:544; **3**:107, 346
  and conservative movement, **2**:375
  on depression, **4**:46
  monetarism of, **3**:110
  "negative income tax" coined by,
    6:31
  and school choice movement,
    3:137
Friedman, Rose, **3**:110
Friedman, William, **2**:467
Friends, Society of. *See* Quakers
Friends of Domestic Industry, **3**:474
Friends of the Earth, **3**:230
Fries, John, **3**:474
  in Chase impeachment trial, **4**:241
Fries' Rebellion, **2**:227; **3**:474, *474*
  liberty poles in, **5**:97
Frigates, **8**:405, 408
Frigidaire, **3**:182

Frisch, Otto R., **6**:342
Frishmuth, Harriet Whitney, **1**:308
Frizzell, Lodisa, **9**:229–233
Frobisher, Sir Martin, **3**:285, 289;
  8:589
Froebel, Frederick, **3**:116
Froehlke, Robert F., **1**:550
Frogmen, **8**:251
Frohnmayer, John, **5**:535
From Here to Eternity (Jones), **5**:121
From the Deep Woods to Civilization
  (Eastman), **3**:474–475
Fromme, Lynette, **1**:330
Frontenac, Fort, **5**:1–2
Frontenac, Louis de Buade, comte
  de, **2**:293; **4**:527
Frontenac (ship), **4**:53–54
Frontier, **3**:475–477
  agriculture on, **1**:62
  cattle, **8**:463
  circuit riding in, **2**:175
  closing of, **2**:366
  farmer's, **8**:463
  French and Indian War and, **8**:460
  as geographical region, **3**:476
  Johnny Appleseed and, **4**:481–482
  jumping-off places to, **4**:500
  life on
    firsthand accounts of, **9**:229–233,
      244–248
    Grund's observations on,
      9:215–218
  mining, **8**:463
  pioneers in, **6**:*358*, **358–359**
  as process, **3**:475–476, 477
  rural life on, **7**:208
  social mobility in, **2**:226
  symbolic closing of, **8**:463
  Turner's thesis on, **3**:475–476, **477**;
    4:139; **8**:463
    criticism of, **3**:476
  U.S. Army on, **1**:279–280
    firsthand account of, **9**:244–248
  violence on, **8**:338
  vs. West, **8**:443
  westward migration and, **8**:459
Frontier defense, **3**:477
  Battle of Fallen Timbers and,
    3:310–311
  fortifications in, **3**:439
  and plans of union, **6**:362
Frontier economics, **3**:226
Frontiero v. Richardson, **3**:246, **478**
Frost, Robert, **3**:195; **5**:120

Frost, Yvonne, **8**:*494*

Frosted glass, **4**:4

Fruit growing, **3**:**478–480**
 on frontier, **4**:481

Fruitlands community, **8**:179, 301

Fry, D. W., **6**:343

Fry, Joshua, **4**:55

Fry, William Henry, **5**:492; **6**:199

FSA. *See* Farm Security Administration; Federal Security Agency; Freedom Support Act

FSIS. *See* Food Safety and Inspection Service

FSLIC. *See* Federal Savings and Loan Insurance Corporation

FSLN. *See* National Sandinista Liberation Front

FTA. *See* United States-Canada Free Trade Agreement

FTC. *See* Federal Trade Commission

FTC Improvement Act (1980), **3**:349

FTC Reorganization Act (1950), **3**:349

FTC v. Gratz 253, **3**:348

FTC v. Keppel & Brothers, Inc., **3**:348

FTC v. Raladam, **3**:348

Fuchida, Mitsuo, **6**:272

Fuchs, Klaus, **7**:197

Fuel Administration, **3**:**480**

Fuels, alternative, **3**:**480–481**

Fuerst, Edwin W., **1**:290

Fugitive, The (magazine), **3**:481

Fugitive Slave Act(s), **3**:**481–482**
 of 1787, **7**:380–381
 of 1793, **3**:481–482
  Supreme Court on, **4**:487; **6**:462
 of 1850, **2**:331; **3**:482; **7**:381; **8**:490
  nullification of, **6**:146
  in Oberlin-Wellington rescue case, **6**:153
  and slaves as contraband of war, **2**:395
  Supreme Court on, **1**:2–3
  and personal liberty laws, **3**:482; **6**:294
  resistance to, **8**:248, 250

Fugitive-agrarians, **3**:**481**

Fulbright, William, **3**:482; **8**:142

Fulbright Act (1946), **3**:482

Fulbright Act and Grants, **3**:274, **482–483**

Fulbright-Hays Act (1961), **3**:482

Fuld, Caroline Bamberger, **4**:366

Fulks, Joe, **1**:424

"Full Dinner Pail," **3**:159, **483**

Full Employment Act (1946), and Federal Reserve System, **3**:346

Full Employment and Balanced Growth Act (Humphrey-Hawkins Act) (1978), **3**:347; **8**:254

Fuller, John Frederick Charles, **1**:266–267

Fuller, Margaret, **1**:509; **7**:194; **8**:179, 181
 at Brook Farm, **8**:301

Fuller, Melville W.
 on commerce clause, **2**:310
 on Sherman Antitrust Act, **7**:343–344

Fuller, Meta Vaux Warrick, **1**:308

Fuller, R. Buckminster, **3**:*539*, 539–540

Fuller, Sue, **1**:309

Fullilove v. Klutznick, **1**:36

Fulton, Robert, **3**:483; **6**:14; **7**:172; **8**:187, 405

Fulton's Folly *(Clermont)* (steamboat), **3**:**483–484**; **7**:*171*, 172; **8**:187

Fund for UFO Research, **8**:255

Fundamental Orders, **2**:357

Fundamentalism, **3**:**484–485**; **6**:516
 and creationism, **2**:446
 and denominational colleges, **3**:130–131
 and liberation theology, **5**:93
 Moral Majority, **5**:**455–456**
 Protestant modernism vs., **5**:432

Fundamentals, The (pamphlet), **6**:516

"Fundamentals of Genealogy, The: A Neglected but Fertile New Field for Professional Historians?" (Anglin), **3**:522

Fundraising, direct mail and, **3**:29

Funerary traditions, **2**:510, 511–512; **3**:486; **6**:457–458

Funk, Casimir, **3**:24; **6**:148, 149

Funston, Fredrick S., **6**:320

Fur companies, **3**:**486–488**, *487*
 American Fur Company, **1**:**157–158**; **3**:487, 494; **8**:175
 Illinois Fur Brigade of, **4**:219
 Hudson's Bay Company (*See* Hudson's Bay Company)

North West Company (*See* North West Company)

Pacific Fur Company, **3**:491–492; **6**:225

Rocky Mountain Fur Company, **1**:158; **3**:494; **8**:176

Russian-American Company, **3**:487, 491

Southwest Fur Company, **1**:158

Fur trade and trapping, **3**:**488–495**, *489*, *492*, *494*
 in Alaska, **1**:108, 121
 Albatross and, **1**:114
 beaver pelts and, **1**:434–435
 China and, **2**:153
 in Colorado, **2**:298, 301
 on Columbia River, **2**:303
 Crees and, **2**:454
 Dutch explorers and, **3**:289–290
 Fort Union and, **8**:259
 France in, **3**:486–487, 488; **4**:282; **5**:1–2
 Great Britain in, **3**:487
 in Great Lakes basin, **4**:51
 in Great Valley, **4**:58
 Hawaii in, **4**:105
 hide and tallow trade in, **4**:130
 Lewis and Clark Expedition and, **8**:307
 Mangeurs de Lard (new recruits), **5**:220
 on Missouri River, **5**:427–428
 monopolies in, **1**:158
 in Montana, **5**:448
 mountain men in, **5**:**468**
 Native Americans in, **8**:222
  economics of, **4**:268
  factory system (trading houses) and, **1**:158
 Netherlands in, **4**:281
 in New Mexico, **6**:68
 in New York Colony, **6**:83
 in Oregon, **1**:114, 157, 342; **6**:204; **8**:307
 in Pacific Northwest, **8**:453
 role in colonial era, **4**:349–350
 Russia in, **3**:487
 Russian explorers and, **3**:293
 sea otters in, **7**:287–288
 seals in, **1**:121, 122; **7**:288–289
 Spain in, **3**:486
 summer rendezvous, **5**:468
 and trading posts, **8**:174–176
 U.S. explorers and, **3**:297, 298–299

voyageurs in, **8**:358
and westward exploration, 8:453–454
in Wisconsin, **8**:489, 490
in Wyoming, **8**:563
Furman v. Georgia, **2**:40
Furness, Frank, **1**:249
Furniture, **3:495–499**
in 19th century, **3**:496–497
in 20th century, **3**:497–499
Arts and Crafts, **1**:320; **3**:498
baroque, **3**:496
Chippendale (rococo), **3**:496
collecting, **2**:271
colonial, **3**:495–496
Craftsman (Mission) style, **3**:497
Empire style, **3**:496
environmental, **3**:499
Gothic Revival style, **3**:497
in interior design, **1**:293
mail-order, **3**:498
neoclassical, **3**:496–497
plastic, **3**:499
Shaker, **1**:286, *287*; **3**:497
after World War II, **3**:498–499
Furuseth, Andrew, **2**:11
Furuseth Act. See Seamen's Act
Fussell, Solomon, **1**:286
Future in America, The (Wells), **1**:138
Future of Africa, The (Crummell), **6**:235
Future Shock (Toffler), **6**:429
Futures contracts, **2**:315
Fuzzy systems, **1**:318
FWS. *See* Fish and Wildlife Service

G

Gabriel's Insurrection, **3:501**; **7**:8, 156
Gaddis, Vincent, **1**:446
Gaddis, William, *The Recognitions*, **5**:122
Gadhafi, Mu'ammar al-, **1**:40
Gadsden, James, **1**:188; **3**:502
Gadsden Purchase (1854), **3**:425, **501–502**, *502*; **8**:204
Gag rule, antislavery, **3:502**
Gagarin, Yuri, **7**:480
Gage, Thomas, **2**:360; **6**:520; **7**:4
in American Revolution, **7**:136, 139
Battle of Bunker Hill, **7**:142
as governor of Massachusetts, **7**:134

Gaia Hypothesis, **3**:551
Gaines, Edmund, **8**:401
Gaines, Ernest J., **5**:123
The Autobiography of Miss Jane Pittman, **5**:126
Gairy, Sir Eric, **4**:65
GALAHAD (Merrill's Marauders), **5:324**
Galápagos Islands, **3:503**
Galbraith, John Kenneth, **6**:165, 436, 438
Gale, Leonard, **8**:68
Gale, Samuel, **3**:108
Galena-Dubuque mining district, **3:503**
Galey, John, **6**:302
Gall, Franz Josef, **6**:332
Gallatin, Albert, **1**:192; **3**:503; **4**:486; **5**:22, *23*
and Democratic Party, **2**:549
on nationalism, **5**:568
Report on Manufactures, **1**:485; **3:503**
Report on Roads, Canals, Harbors, and Rivers, **3:503–504**
as secretary of treasury, **8**:195
on sinking fund, **7**:366
and water routes, plan for, **7**:168
Gallaudet, Edward Miner, **2**:509; **3**:504
Gallaudet, Thomas Hopkins, **2**:508; **3**:34, 504; **7**:355
Gallaudet University, **2**:509; **3:504**
"Deaf President Now" campaign at, **3**:33
Department of Education and, **3**:123
Galley boats, **3:504**
Gallo, E., **8**:487
Gallo, J., **8**:487
Gallo, Robert, **1**:15
Galloway, Joseph, **3**:504–505; **6**:387
plan of union by, **3:504–505**
and Valley Forge, **8**:306
Gallup, George, **6**:99, 409, *533*, 533–534
Galphin, George, **1**:43
Galton, Sir Francis, **3**:258; **4**:378
Galvanized Yankees, **3:505**
Galveston (Texas), **3**:*505*, **505–506**
hurricane of 1900 in, **3**:42, *505*, 506; **4**:198; **8**:102
municipal reform in, **5**:478
Galveston Island flood, **3**:384

Gálvez, Bernardo de, **1**:257; **5**:159
New Orleans used as base by, **6**:73
Gama, Vasco da, **3**:283
Gamble, James, **6**:491
Gambling, **3:506–509**
in Atlantic City (New Jersey), **1**:353
in baseball, **1**:479–480
on horse racing, **4**:170–171
lotteries, **3**:508
in Nevada, **6**:38–39
and organized crime, **2**:463
recreational, **7**:66
on steamboats, **3**:507, *508*
tribal, **8**:489
in California, **8**:215
classes of, **3**:509
early games and, **3**:506–507
by Florida Seminoles, **7**:309
by Ojibwe, **6**:181
regulation of, **1**:160; **3**:509
Supreme Court on, **3**:509; **8**:223
and violence, **3**:508
women and, **3**:507
Game theory, **3**:110
Games. *See* Toys and games
Gamma radiation, **6**:341
Gamow, George, **1**:344; **6**:342, 344
Ganciclovir, **1**:16
Gandhi, Indira, **4**:260
Gandhi, Mohandas (Mahatma), **2**:165, 202
Gandhi, Virchand, **1**:327
Gandil, Arnold (Chick), **1**:480
Gandy, Kim, **5**:549
Gangs, Chicago, **2**:133
Gann, Paul, **6**:508–509
Gannett Corporation, **6**:99
Gans, David, **6**:341, 343
Gans, Herbert, **1**:338
Gantt, Henry L., **7**:281
GAO. *See* General Accounting Office
Gaols, **6**:476
Gap, Inc., **7**:126
GAR. *See* Grand Army of the Republic
Garcés, Francisco, **8**:451
Garden State Preservation Trust, **6**:64
Gardening, **3:509–511**
botanical gardens, **1:515–518**
hydroponic, **4:204**

Gardner, Alexander, **1:**_199_, 200, 299, 531, _531_
Gardner, Erle Stanley, **5:**129
Gardner, Howard, **3:**124
Gardner, Isabella Stewart, **2:**272
Gardner, John W., **2:**56; **6:**318
Gardner, Rulon, **6:**193
Gardoqui, Diego de, in Jay-Gardoqui negotiations, **4:**466
Garey, A. E., **1:**154
Garfield, James A.
on assassination, **1:**327
assassination of, **1:**328, _572_; **2:**23; **8:**339
Crédit Mobilier of America and, **2:**453
as log cabin president, **5:**145
in presidential campaign of 1880, **2:**400, 467; **3:**157
Garies and Their Friends (Webb), **5:**124
Garland, Augustus Hill, **1:**261; **3:**271
Garland, Benjamin S., **1:**2
Garland, Hamlin, **6:**12
Garment industry. _See_ Clothing industry
Garner, Howard, **4:**380
Garner, John Nance, **3:**162, 163
Garnet, Henry Highland, **1:**211; **6:**235
Garn-St. Germain Act (1980), **1:**563
Garrett, H. Lawrence, **8:**44
Garrett, Mary Elizabeth, **4:**482
Garrett, Stephen, **3:**565
Garrett, Wilbur E., **5:**542
Garrick, David, **4:**39
Garrison, Homer, Jr., **8:**105
Garrison, William Lloyd, **1:**510; **2:**163; **5:**96
in colonization movement, **1:**209
immediatism of, **4:**219
and Mathew (Theobald), **8:**79
New England Antislavery Society founded by, **6:**47
and peace movements, **6:**267
Garrison Dam, Fort Berthold Indian Reservation and, **5:**220
Garrison v. Louisiana, **5:**90
Garroway, Dave, **8:**44
Garvey, Marcus Moziah, **1:**477, _477_, 478; **5:**124; **6:**98, 236
and back-to-Africa movement, **2:**297; **3:**197

Gary, Elbert H., **8:**295
Gas explosions, **3:**38–39
Gas warfare, **2:**_117_, 117–118
Gas-cooled nuclear reactors, **6:**139
Gaslight, **5:**_107_, 107–108
Gasoline, **6:**301
lead in, **1:**362; **7:**246
during oil crises, **6:**178
taxes on, **3:511–512**
Gaspée (British customs vessel), burning of, **2:**286; **3:**512; **7:**152
Gass, Octavius, **5:**41
Gasser, Herbert, **6:**349
Gastonia strike (1929), **3:**512
Gates, Daryl, **5:**155
Gates, Frederick T., **8:**280
Gates, Henry Louis, Jr., **1:**47
Gates, Horatio, **1:**574; **3:**261; **6:**94
in Battle of Camden, **2:**19
in Board of War and Ordnance, **8:**373
and Conway Cabal, **2:**403
in Saratoga Campaign, **7:**251; **9:**35
Gates, Sir Thomas, **1:**445, 490; **8:**347
Gates, Thomas S., **2:**528
Gates, William H. (Bill), III, **1:**580; **2:**336; **5:**359–360
Gateway Arch, **3:**_512_, **512–513**
Gateway City (ship), **5:**320
Gatling, Richard J., **5:**185
GATT. _See_ General Agreement on Tariffs and Trade
Gauge theory, **6:**339
Gaulle, Charles de
armored warfare and, **1:**267
at Casablanca Conference, **2:**65
foreign policies of, **3:**260
government formed by, **3:**452
on NATO, **6:**125–126
presidency of, **3:**452
Gault, Gerald, **2:**149; **4:**250
Gay Academic Union, **3:**514
Gay Activists Alliance, **3:**514
Gay and Lesbian Alliance Against Defamation (GLAAD), **3:**514
Gay and lesbian movement, **3:513–514**, 520; **4:**65
AIDS and, **7:**327
neoconservatives on, **6:**32
origins of, **7:**326
protests by, **7:**165
Gay and lesbian studies, **8:**521
Gay Head Indians, **8:**368–369

Gay Liberation Front (GLF), **3:**514
Gaye, Marvin, **3:**227
Gays and lesbians
in 19th century, **7:**324–325
adoption by, **1:**29
AIDS among, **1:**15–16; **3:**514
battles over rights of, Bible in, **1:**449
Daughters of Bilitis, **2:503–504**
discrimination against, **7:**325–326
in Episcopal Church, **3:**243
on feminism, **3:**520
hate crimes against, **7:**327
homophile organizations for, **7:**326
immigration restrictions on, **7:**325
magazines for, **5:**197, 198
marriage among, same-sex, **2:532–533**, _533_; **8:**314
in military, **3:**78; **5:384–385**; **7:**326, 331
political activism among, **7:**326, 327
political divisions among, **7:**326
subculture of, **7:**324, 326
violence against, **3:**514
GCA. _See_ Gun Control Act
GDP. _See_ Gross domestic product
Geary, John W., **1:**506
Gebbie, Kristine, **1:**18
Geddes, Henry, **3:**449
Geddes, James, **2:**32
Geddes, Norman Bel, **8:**559
Geduldig v. Aiello, **3:**525
Gee, E. Gordon, **1:**548
Geertz, Clifford, **1:**194
Gehrig, Lou, alma mater of, **2:**304
Gehry, Frank, **1:**253; **7:**376–377
furniture designed by, **3:**499
Geiger, Hans, **6:**340
Geiger-Jones Co., Hall v., **1:**491
Geiogamah, Hanay, **2:**501
Gelb, Leslie H., **6:**286
Geldof, Bob, **1:**441
Gell-Mann, Murray, **6:**338
Gelpcké v. Dubuque, **3:514–515**
Gelsinger, Jesse, **3:**531
Gemini program, **7:**480
Gender: An Ethnomethodological Approach (Kessler and McKenna), **3:**516
Gender and Culture in America (Stone and McKee), **3:**518
Gender and gender roles, **3:515–521**
and abortion, **1:**4

Adams's letters on, **9:**144–145
in colonial era, **3:**518
as feminist concept, **3:**515–518
history of, **3:**518–521
as medical concept, **3:**515
in mining towns, **4:**13–14
in nursing, **6:**146, 147
segregation by, **7:**303
sexuality and, **7:**330
in Victorian era, **3:**518–519; **8:**326
Gender and Power (Connell), **3:**516
Gender and the Politics of History
    (Scott), **3:**516
Gender discrimination. *See* Discrim-
    ination, sex
"'Gender' for a Marxist Dictionary:
    The Sexual Politics of a Word"
    (Haraway), **3:**517
Gender history, **4:**141
Gender theory, **3:**517
*Gender Trouble: Feminism and the
    Subversion of Identity* (Butler),
    3:516–517
Gene therapy, **3:**531
Genealogical Proof Standard (GPS),
    3:522
Genealogy, **3:**521–523
General Accounting Office (GAO),
    3:523
  establishment of, **1:**559
  head of, **2:332–333**
General Agreement on Tariffs and
    Trade (GATT), **3:**309, 461,
    523–525; 7:54–55
  and domestic trade, **8:**163
  establishment of, **3:**523–524;
    6:124; **8:**157, 166, 198–199
  Geneva Conference (1947) and,
    3:534
  and liberalization of trade, **3:**97
  "most favored nation" clause of,
    8:52
  and NAFTA, **3:**524; **6:**124
  principles of, **3:**524; **8:**52
  rounds of, **3:**524; **8:**52
General Allotment Act. *See* Dawes
    General Allotment Act
General court, colonial, **3:525**
  Massachusetts Bay Colony, **5:**270,
    271–272
  Mayflower Compact, **5:276**
  See also Colonial assemblies
General Education Board, **6:**317

General Electric Company, **3:**172,
    173, 174, 179; **5:**108
  appliance development by, **3:**181
  chemical research at, **2:**123
  Gem lamp of, **5:**24
  J. P. Morgan and, **1:**405
  research laboratory of, **5:**18, 108
  strikes against, **3:**176
General Electric Company v. Gilbert,
    3:525–526; **6:**449
General Exchange Act (1922), **3:**432
General Federation of Women's
    Clubs (GFWC), **3:**456, **526**
General Foods, **6:**229
General Forfeiture Act (1890), **5:**30
*General History of Virginia, New Eng-
    land, and the Summer Isles, The*
    (Smith), **5:**117
General Land Office, **6:**529, 530–531
General Mining Law (1872), **5:**25
General Motors (GM), **3:**526–527
  automobiles of, **1:**368, 373;
    8:189–190
  credit card offered by, **3:**368
  mass marketing by, **5:**246
  mass production in, **5:**263
  moving jobs abroad, **8:**169
  strikes against, **8:**261, *261, 262*
    sit-down, **7:**372
  tanks of, **1:**336
General Order No. 38, **3:527**
General Revision Act (1891), **6:**528
General Sherman (ship), **4:**541, 542
General Slocum (steamship), **7:***544*
  sinking of, **3:**40, *40*
General Social Survey, **6:**534
General stores, **7:**552, *552*
General Textile Strike, **8:**111
*General Theory of Employment, Inter-
    est and Money* (Keynes), **4:**16;
    6:44
General Welfare clause, **3:**527–528
"Generation of 1776," **3:**528
"Generation touched with fire,"
    3:528
Generational conflict, **3:**528–529
Generative grammar, **5:**115
Genetic engineering, **3:**529–532
  contemporary applications of,
    3:530–532
  history of, **3:**529–530
  regulation of, **1:**462–463
  study of DNA and, **3:**67
  Supreme Court on, **3:**530

Genetic fingerprinting, **3:**67, 69
Genetics, **3:**532–533
  of Alzheimer's disease, **1:**131–132
  applied, **3:**533
  classical, **3:**532
  evolutionary theory and, **3:**269
  Human Genome Project and,
    4:191–192
  of intelligence, **4:**378, 379
  molecular, **3:**532–533
  molecular biology and, **5:**437
  of obesity, **6:**153
Geneva Accords of 1954, **3:534**
  division of Vietnam by, **3:**534;
    8:329
  Vietnamese resistance to, **8:**330
Geneva Conference(s), **3:**534–535
  of 1927, **3:**534
  of 1932, **3:**534; **6:**35
  of 1947, **3:**534
  of 1954, **3:**534–535
  of 1961, **3:**535
  of 1973, **3:**535
Geneva Convention(s), **3:**535–536
  of 1864, **3:**535
  of 1906, **3:**535
  of 1929, **3:**535
  of 1949, **2:**396; **3:**535
  on prisoners of war, **3:**535; **6:**472
Geneva Protocol (1925), **2:**117, 118
"Genius" Awards, **6:**486–487
Genocide, **3:**536–537
  definition of, **3:**536
  history of, **3:**536
Genocide Convention (1951), **3:**536
Genovese, Eugene, **4:**140
Genre painting, **3:***537*, **537–538**
Gensler, Art, **1:**293
*Gentleman and Cabinet-Maker's
    Director* (Chippendale), **3:**496
Gentleman's Agreement (film), **1:**207
Gentlemen's Agreement (1907),
    3:277; **4:**457, 463
  text of, **9:**264–265
Gentrification, **3:**538–539
  definition of, **3:**538
  disadvantages of, **3:**539
  factors encouraging, **3:**539
  process of, **3:**538–539
Genzyme Transgenics, **3:**531
Geochemistry, **5:**391
Geodesic dome, **1:**565; **3:***539*,
    539–540
Geodesy, **3:**551

Geographer's Line, **3:**540, *540*
Geographia Politica (Scherer), **9:***9*
Geographic Information Systems (GIS), **5:**234
"Geographic Pivot of History" (Mackinder), **3:**542
Geography, **3:540–544**
  advent of human, **3:**541–542
  and American expansionism, **3:**542
  institutional and intellectual origins of, **3:**540–541
  Morse (Jedidiah) and, **5:**460
  postmodern (radical), **3:**543–544
  and quantitative analyses, **3:**543
  World War I and, **3:**543
Geological Society of America (GSA), **3:**550–551
Geological Survey, U.S. (USGS), **2:**62; **3:**300, **544–547**
  as agent of national policy, **3:**546–547
  directors of, **3:**545–546
  establishment of, **8:**454
  functions of, **4:**384
  in Interior Department, **4:**383
  mapping, **5:**233
  mineralogy, **5:**391
  origins of, **3:**544–545
  and petrography, **6:**300
  Powell (John Wesley) and, **2:**301
  surveying technology of, **8:**32–33
Geological surveys, state, **3:547–549,** 550
Geology, **3:549–551**
  before Civil War, **3:**549–550
  after Civil War, **3:**550–551
  crystallography, **5:**391
  mineral springs, **5:389**
  mineralogy, **5:390–391**
  petrography in, **6:300–301**
  and petroleum industry, **6:**305–306
  U.S. Bureau of Mines, **5:391–393**
Geomorphology, **3:**541, *552*
Geophysical explorations, **3:551–553**
Geophysical Year, International, **4:388–389**
Geopolitics, **3:**542
George II (king of Great Britain)
  and fairs, **2:**436
  and King's College, **2:**304
George III (king of Great Britain), **1:**515; **7:**141
  Continental Congress's petition to, **2:**393, 520
  Jefferson's accusation of, **2:**521
  Olive Branch Petition to, **6:**190
George, Henry, **3:**107; **5:**16; **6:**493; **7:**366; **8:**303
  Progress and Poverty, **2:**10
  proposed single tax on land, **5:**37–38
George, Milton, **3:**323; **6:**416
George, Phyllis, **1:***434*
George, Walter, **1:**537
George Island, **6:**382
George Loomis (oil tanker), **6:**303
George Washington Bridge, **1:**539; **3:553,** *553*
Georgetown University, establishment of, **3:**129; **4:**474
Georgia, **3:553–558**
  African Americans in, **3:**555–558
  agriculture in, **3:**555, 556
  civil rights movement in, **3:**557–558
  in Civil War, **3:**555
    Andersonville Prison in, **1:184**
      firsthand account of, **9:**304–307
  claims to western lands, **8:**455
  Cold War and, **3:**557
  in colonial era, **3:**554
  Democratic Party in, **3:**555–556
  emblems, nicknames, mottos, and songs of, **7:***532*
  Farmers' Alliance in, **3:**556
  Federalist Party in, **3:**351
  gold in, **2:**163; **4:**10
  Great Depression in, **3:**557
  gun control in, **4:**74
  immigrants in, **3:**558
  Jim Crow laws in, **3:**556
  Ku Klux Klan in, **3:**555–556
  land grants in, annulment of, **3:**382
  map of, **3:***554*
  Native Americans in, **3:**554
    removal of, **4:**295
  Populist Party in, **3:**556
  racial segregation in, **3:**556
  Reconstruction in, **3:**555
  Republican Party in, **3:**555–556
  rice plantations in, **6:**364
  settlement of, **2:**289
  sharecroppers in, **3:**556
  slavery in, **3:**554–555
  state university of, **8:**279
  taxation abandoned in, **8:**56
  temperance movement in, **8:**79
  Union sentiment in, **8:**260
  in War of Jenkins' Ear, **2:**294
  in World War II, **3:**557
  Yazoo fraud in, **1:**489; **3:**554; **8:575–576**
Georgia, Cherokee Nation v., **2:**127–128
Georgia, Chisholm v., **1:**120; **2:158**
Georgia, Furman v., **2:**40
Georgia, Stanley v., **6:**479
Georgia, Worcester v., **2:**128
Georgia Platform, **3:558–559**
Georgia v. Stanton, **3:559**
Georgia Warm Springs Foundation, **6:**388
Georgiana, **3:559**
Geotextiles, **8:**107
Geothermal energy, **3:**212–213, 214
Gerard, Thomas, **7:**52
Germ scalpers, **3:**390
Germ theory of disease, **3:**239–240
  and bioterrorism, **1:**465
Germain, George, Lord, **7:**142, 143
German Americans, **3:559–560**
  brewing traditions of, **1:**536
  in Chicago, **2:**132
  in Cleveland, **2:**233
  forced to kiss flag, **3:**380
  Forty-Eighters, **3:440–441**
  immigration patterns of, **4:**221, 223
  in Iowa, **4:**415
  newspapers of, **6:**97, 98
  in symphony orchestras, **8:**38, 39
  World War I and, **3:**208, 559, 562; **6:**5; **8:**538
  World War II and, **3:**560
German Evangelical Synod of North America, **8:**264
German mercenaries, **3:560**
  during American Revolution, **1:**442, 532; **7:**141
German Missouri Synod, **6:**137
German Reformed church, **7:**76; **8:**263, 264
German-American Bund, **3:**328, **560**
German-American Debt Agreement (1930), **3:560**
Germantown (Pennsylvania), **3:560–561**
  during American Revolution, **7:**144
Germany
  American émigrés in, **3:**197

American occupation of, **3:561**
  Army of Occupation in, **1:278**
in American Samoa, **7:**235
anti-Semitism in, **1:**207; **3:**562
division of, **1:**444; **2:**269;
    3:562–563; **8:**552
foreign aid to, **3:**562
foreign investment from, **3:**421
foreign observers from, **1:**137
Fourteen Points and, **3:**447; **8:**315
French relations with, Morocco
    and, **1:**123
gold standard in, **4:**15
Great Depression and, **4:**48–49
immigration from, **4:**221, 223, 226
internment of aliens from,
    4:399–400
and London Naval Treaties, **5:**147
and *Lusitania*, sinking of,
    5:174–175, *175*
and NATO, **3:**562–563
Nazi
  on homosexuality, **7:**326
  refugees from, **4:**226–227
  Soviet pact with, **2:**327
Siegfried Line in, **7:**354
space program of, **7:**479
submarines of, **7:**562–563
unification of, **3:**563
U.S. policy toward, after World
    War I, **8:**316
U.S. relations with, **3:561–564**
  Berlin Treaty (1921) and, **1:443**
  Bitburg Controversy and, **1:**471
  during Cold War, **3:**562–563
  imperialism in, **4:**245
  during Weimar Republic, **3:**562
  World War I and, **3:**561–562
  World War II and, **3:**562
  Zimmermann telegram and,
    8:590–591
and Virgin Islands, **8:**341
in World War I, **3:**561–562
  Aisne-Marne Operation, **1:99**
  Armistice of November 1918,
    1:265
  Brest-Litovsk Treaty, **1:**247
  and France, **3:**451
  reparations for, **7:**104–105; **8:**316
    Dawes Plan and, **2:507**
    Young Plan and, **8:585**
  submarines used by, **7:**563; **8:**33
  Versailles Treaty after, **3:**562;
    8:315–316

and war debts, **3:**560, 562
after World War I, **8:**543
  U.S. relief in, **8:**542
in World War II, **2:**89; **3:**562;
    8:249
  air war, **8:**545–546, *552,*
    552–553, *553*
    gliders in, **4:**5
    Ploesti oil fields, air raids on,
    6:371
  Allied invasion of, **8:**550–551
  Anzio Campaign, **1:**217
  Battle of Atlantic, **1:**352
  and France, **3:**451–452
  Gothic Line, **4:**23
  Gustav Line, **4:**78
  Normandy Invasion and,
    6:119–120
  Paris Conference (1949), **6:**247
  Potsdam Conference (1945) and,
    3:426; **6:434–435,** *435*
  and prisoners of war, **6:**474
  strategic air power against, **1:**81
  submarine warfare, **8:**556
  surrender of, **8:**551
  war crimes by, **8:**378
Germ-line engineering, **3:**530
Gernsback, Hugo, **5:**130
Geronimo (Apache leader)
  campaign against, **1:**472
  capture of, **8:**404
  in Oklahoma, **6:**184
  in Roosevelt (Theodore) inaugural
    parade, **5:**164
Gerow, Frank, **1:**533
Gerry, Elbridge, **3:**151, 564
  antifederalism of, **1:**202
  at Constitutional Convention,
    2:379, 380
  and districting map, **7:**107
  and XYZ affair, **8:**570
Gerrymandering, **3:**564, *564;* **6:**394
  origins of term, **7:**107
  racial, **3:**62
  Supreme Court's prohibition of,
    5:79
Gershman, Carl, **6:**32
Gershwin, George, **3:**395, 396;
    6:199
Gestalt therapy, **3:**203
Gesture painters, **1:**9
Getty, Jean Paul, **3:**564–565
Getty Education Institute, **3:**566
Getty Museum, **3:564–566**

Getty Research Institute (GRI),
    3:566
Gettysburg, Battle of, **2:**214;
    3:566–569, *568–570;* **6:**278
  New Yorkers in, **6:**88
  Pickett's charge in, **6:351,** *351*
Gettysburg, National Cemetery at,
    2:82
Gettysburg Address, **2:**180;
    3:569–571; **6:**10
  text of, **9:**302
Geysers, in Yellowstone National
    Park, **8:**580
GFWC. *See* General Federation of
    Women's Clubs
Ghana, Peace Corps volunteers in,
    6:266
Ghent, Treaty of (1815), **3:571–573,**
    572; **4:**41; **6:**263; **8:**200
  and fishing privileges, **2:**261
Ghettos, **6:**440
Ghirardelli, Domenico, **4:**444
Ghost Dance, **3:**573; **4:**294; **5:**507;
    6:7, 231; **8:**562
  Wovoka's letter on, **9:**259–260
Ghost towns, **3:***573,* **573–574**
G.I. Joe, **3:574–575;** **8:**153
GI, origin of term, **3:**82
GI Bill of Rights (1944), **1:**499;
    3:118, 127, **574;** **6:**285
  administration of, **8:**317
  impact on women's education,
    3:132
  medical profession and, **5:**304
  provisions of, **8:**317
"GI generation," **3:**528
Giacconi, Riccardo, **1:**345
Giannini, A. P., **1:**394
Gibbon, John, **6:**102
Gibbons, James, **2:**69, *69*
Gibbons, Thomas, **3:**575
Gibbons v. Ogden, **1:**549; **2:**310, 405;
    3:308, 483, **575;** **4:**26; **7:**169
Gibbs, James, **5:**453
Gibbs, Josiah Willard, **2:**122; **3:**109;
    6:335
Gibbs, Lois, **3:**230
Gibraltar, **6:**248, 250
Gibran, Kahlil, **1:***231;* **5:**72
Gibson, Ernest, **8:**314
Gibson, Fort, **8:**176
Gibson, William, **8:**350
Gibson Girl, **3:**381

Giddings, Joshua, as Radical Republican, **7:**15
Gideon, Clarence Earl, **3:**575
Gideon Bibles, **3:575**
Gideon v. Wainwright, **3:575–576**
Gift of God (ship), **6:**380
Gift taxes, **4:**359
Gila River, **1:**100
Gilbert, Alfred C., **3:**251
Gilbert, Bartholomew, **7:**47
Gilbert, Cass, **2:**102
Gilbert, General Electric Company v., **3:525–526; 6:**449
Gilbert, Grove Karl, **3:**552
Gilbert, Sir Humphrey, **2:**285; **3:**285, 288, 576; **7:**46
 ship of, **2:**290
Gilbert Islands, **3:**576; **6:**26; **8:**49
Gilbert's Patent, **3:**576
Gilbreth, Frank, **4:**334; **7:**281
Gilbreth, Lillian, **4:**334
Gilded Age, **3:576–578; 6:**88
 agrarianism in, **1:**57
 literature of, **5:**124
 theater of, **8:**113–114
 Victorian culture in, **8:**325
Gildersleeve, Virginia, **8:**272
Gill, Irving, **1:**252
Gill, John, **1:**129
Gillespie, Dizzy, **4:**469, *469*
Gillespie, Marcia Ann, **5:**470
Gilman, Daniel Coit, **3:**274; **4:**482; **5:**18
Gilman, George, **7:**125
Gilman, Nicholas, **6:**58
Gilmer, Thomas W., **6:**465
Gilmer v. Interstate/Johnson Lane Corporation, **1:**237
Gilpin, Thomas, **6:**245
Gimbel, Adam, **3:**7
Gingrich, Newt, **2:**376
 backlash against, **3:**169
 and Contract with America, **2:**398; **7:**114
 and Republican majority, **7:**114
 resignation of, **4:**240
 on welfare state, **8:**442
Ginsberg, Allen, **1:**433; **2:**433; **4:**65; **5:**121, *239*
Ginsburg, Ruth Bader, **8:**276, 507
 alma mater of, **2:**304
 on presidential election of 2000, **1:**579
 on sex discrimination, **7:**73

Ginseng, American, **2:**153; **3:**578
Giovanni, Nikki, **5:**124, 126
Giovannitti, Arturo, **5:**59–60
Girard, Stephen, **1:**404
Giraud, Henri, **2:**65
Girl Guides, **4:**1
Girl Scouts of the United States of America, **1:**527; **4:**1; **7:**65
Girty, Simon, **6:**178
GIS. *See* Geographic Information Systems
Gist, Christopher, **1:**127; **6:**175
Gitlow, Benjamin, **2:**325, 326
Gitlow v. New York, **1:**453; **2:**84; **3:**373–374
Giuliani, Rudolph, **6:**108
"Give Me Liberty or Give Me Death!" (Henry), **4:**2
Given names, **5:**509
Gjoa (ship), **6:**136
GLAAD. *See* Gay and Lesbian Alliance Against Defamation
Glacier National Park, wolves in, **8:**496
Glackens, William, **1:**268, 297, 321
Gladden, Washington, **2:**164, 349; **6:**174; **7:**413; **8:**263
Glaize, the, **4:**2
Glashow, Sheldon Lee, **6:**338
Glaspie, April, **6:**292
Glass art, **1:288–290; 4:**4
 stained glass windows, **1:313–314,** *320*
Glass brick, **4:**4
Glass ceiling, **4:2–3**
Glass fiber, **4:**4
Glass wool, **4:**4
Glasser, Ira, **1:**147
Glassford, Pelham, **1:**498
Glassmaking, **4:***3,* **3–4**
Glass-Steagall Act (1932), **4:4–5**
Glass-Steagall Act (Banking Act) (1933), **1:**400, 401–402; **3:**275, 345; **4:**5
 banks exploiting loopholes in, **3:**368
 and commercial and investment banks, separation of, **1:**405
Glazer, Nathan, **1:**338; **5:**148; **6:**32
 Beyond the Melting Pot, **1:446–447**
GLBA. *See* Gramm-Leach-Bliley Act
Gleaves, Albert, **8:**540
Glebes, **4:**5
Glendale (California), Forest Lawn Cemetery in, **2:**81

Glenn, John, **5:**523
GLF. *See* Gay Liberation Front
Glidden, Joseph, **1:**416; **2:**73
Gliddon, George R., **1:**192; **7:**13
Gliders, **4:**5
Glimpse of New Mexico (Barreiro), excerpt from, **9:**201–203
Global Climate Coalition, **4:**8
Global Energy Futures and the Carbon Dioxide Problem (report), **4:**6–8
Global warming, **2:**238; **4:5–9,** 7
 Bush (George W.) administration on, **8:**424
 coal mining and, **2:**253
 developing scientific consensus on, **4:**6
 early scientific work on, **4:**6
 gasoline taxes and, **3:**511
 growing signs of, **4:**8
 and politics, **4:**6–8
Globalization, deindustrialization, U.S., **5:**229
Glorieta Pass, Battle of, **2:**298
Gloss, Molly, **6:**207
Gloucester (Massachusetts), mackerel fisheries in, **5:**187
Glovemaking, **5:**69
Glover, Joshua, **1:**2; **8:**490
Glucksberg, Washington v., **3:**263; **7:**160; **8:418**
GM. *See* General Motors
GMAT (Graduate Management Admissions Test), **3:**139
Go Tell It on the Mountain (Baldwin), **5:**121, 125
"Go West, Young Man, Go West," **4:**9
Gobitis, Minersville School District v., **3:**380
God Sends Sunday (Bontemps), **5:**125
Godcharles v. Wigeman, **5:**13
Goddard, Luther, **2:**242
Goddard, Robert H., **2:**319; **7:***188,* 189, 479
Goddard, Sarah, **1:**129
Godey, Louis, **2:**245; **4:**9
Godey's Lady's Book (magazine), **4:9;** **5:**191–192, 198
Godie, Lee, **1:**311
Godkin, Edwin L., **1:**55; **7:**181
 The Nation founded by, **5:**521
Goethals, George W., **3:**219; **6:**238; **8:**379
Goetz, Bernard, **8:**336
Goizueta, Roberto, **2:**261

Gola, Tom, **1:**424

Gold, Henry, **7:**197

Gold, in Fort Knox, **4:**541

Gold Act (1864), **4:**9

"Gold Bug, The" (Poe), **2:**467

Gold bugs, **2:**551; **4:**9–10

Gold bullion standard, **4:**15

Gold clause cases, **4:**10; **7:**118

Gold coin standard, **4:**15

Gold Democrats, **4:**10; **7:**362

Gold exchange, **4:**10

    Morgan-Belmont Agreement and, **5:**457–458

Gold Exchange Bank, **4:**10

Gold mines and mining, **4:**10–12, *11, 12*

    in Alaska, **1:**109–110

    in Colorado, **4:**314

    Comstock Lode and, **2:**338

    Cripple Creek mining boom, **2:464**

    and ghost towns, **3:**574

    in Idaho, **4:**211

    in Montana, **5:**448

        Helena mining camp, **4:123**

        women and, **9:**240–242

    and Native Americans, **4:**314–315

    prospectors and, **6:**512

    and silver, discovery of, **7:**364

    smelters in, **7:**400

Gold Purchase Plan, **4:**12, 16

Gold Reserve Act (1934), **1:**459; **4:12,** 16

Gold rush(es)

    in Alaska, Klondike, **2:**26; **4:**538–539; **8:**589, *589*

    in Black Hills, **1:**474; **2:**493

    and boomtowns, **1:**501

    in California, **1:**501; **2:**8–9; **4:**10–11, **12–14**

        archival maps of, **9:***57, 58–64, 60, 61*

    and foreign investment in U.S., **3:**420

    and Forty-Niners, **3:**441–442, *442;* **4:**13

    and geological surveys, **3:**544

    and Native Americans, **4:**14; **8:**214

    in Colorado, **2:**298

        Pikes Peak, **6:355**

    in Georgia, **2:**163

    and mining towns, **5:**396

    and Native Americans, **8:**571

    and westward migration, **8:**463

Gold standard, **4:**14–18

    in 19th century, **4:**14–15

    in 1960s, **4:**17

    in 1970s, **4:**17

    abandonment of, **1:**544; **4:**17, 93; **7:**118

    adoption of, **4:**93

    banking crisis of 1933 and, **4:**15–16

    Cross of Gold speech and, **2:**465

    debate over, **1:**459 (*See also* Bimetallism)

    Democrats on, **2:**551

    in electoral politics, **3:**158

    gold bugs supporting, **4:**9–10

    and inflation, **4:**15, 16, 17, 351

    suspension of, and Tripartite Agreement, **8:**230

    World War I and, **4:**15

    World War II and, **4:**16

Gold Standard Act (1900), **4:**15

Goldberg, Rostker v., **2:**365

Goldberg, Rube, **2:**309

Goldberger, Joseph, **6:**148

Golden Cage, The (Bruch), **3:**104

Golden Gate Bridge, **1:**539; **2:**11; **4:**18, *18*

Golden Hind (ship), **4:**18–19

Goldin, Nan, **1:**301

Golding, Edmund, **7:**361

Goldman, Emma, **1:**181, *181;* **6:**232

    and birth control movement, **1:**467

    and peace movement, **8:**499

Goldman, Ron, **7:**365

Goldman, Sylvan, **7:**125

Goldman Sachs, **1:**404, 405

Goldman Sachs Trading Corporation (GST), **4:**412

Goldmark, Peter, **8:**77

Goldsborough, T. Allan, **2:**254

Goldstein, Israel, **1:**445

Goldwater, Barry M., **1:**259

    National Review supporting, **5:**556

    in presidential campaign of 1964, **2:**374; **3:**165

    and Republican Party, **7:**113

Golf, **4:***19,* 19–20

Golle, John, **7:**267

Gollub, Leon, **1:**311

Gomes, Esteban, **2:**38; **6:**87

Gómez, Máximo, **2:**469; **5:**47

Gompers, Samuel, **1:***150;* **5:**7, 16; **8:**262, 522

    American Federation of Labor and, **8:**171

    American Federation of Teachers and, **1:**155

    American Railway Union and, **1:**168

    anticommunism of, **1:**197

    on Clayton Act, **2:**228

    ideology of, **1:**150

    National Civic Federation and, **5:**530

    pure and simple unionism coined by, **6:**552

Gone with the Wind (film), **3:**363; **4:**20, *20, 21*

Gone with the Wind (Mitchell), **1:**348; **4:**20–21; **5:**130

Gonorrhea, **6:**513; **7:**332, 333

Gonzáles, Rodolfo (Corky), "Chicano Nationalism: The Key to Unity for La Raza," excerpt from, **9:**484–486

González, Elián, case, **2:**472; **4:21–22**

González, Julio, **1:**306

Good, Sarah, **7:**229

Good Morning America (TV show), **8:**73, 138

Good Neighbor policy, **1:**560; **2:**54; **3:**426; **4:22–23,** 77; **5:**47

Goodbye, Columbus (Roth), **5:**121

Goode, W. Wilson, **6:**279, 313

Goodell, William, and Liberty Party, **5:**96

Goodhue, Benjamin, **3:**255

Goodman, Andrew, **1:**332; **2:**203

Goodnight, Charles, **7:**339–340

Goodnight Moon (Brown), **5:**128

Goodrich, Samuel, *Parley's Magazine,* **5:**127

Goodspeed, Thomas W., **8:**280

Goodwin, W. A. R., **6:**452; **8:**484

Goodyear, Charles, **1:**371

Goodyear, Charles, Jr., **1:**503

Goodyear, Nelson, **3:**3

Gorbachev, Mikhail, **2:**93, 266, 270

    arms race and disarmament under, **1:**272; **3:**427

    and invasion of Afghanistan, **1:**37

    and nuclear arms control, **7:**149–150

    at summit conferences, **8:**16

    U.S. Communist Party's response to, **2:**328

Gordon, Anna, **8**:497

Gordon, E. F., **1**:445

Gordon, George A., **8**:263

Gordon, John B., **3**:555–556; **8**:264

Gordon, Kermit, **8**:117

Gordon, Milton M., **1**:336, 337

Gordon, Thomas, **7**:148

Gordy, Berry, Jr., **3**:20

Gore, Albert (Al), Jr.
  Earth in the Balance by, **4**:8
  and image of Tennessee, **8**:86
  in presidential campaign of 1992,
    3:169
  in presidential campaign of 2000,
    1:578; **3**:119, 144, 148, 149,
    169–170, 171
    concession speech by, **9**:523–525
  "Staffing Reinvention Program"
    of, **3**:122

Gore, Bush v., **1:578–579**; **3**:170,
    171, 246
  Bush's response to, **9**:525–526
  Florida constitution in, **7**:527
  Gore's response to, **9**:523–525
  judicial review in, **4**:494

Gorgas, Josiah, **2**:342

Gorgas, William Crawford, **5**:294;
    6:238

Gorges, Sir Ferdinando, **2**:289, 430;
    6:56, 380, 511

Gorham, Nathaniel, and land specu-
    lation, **5**:36

Göring, Hermann, **8**:378

Gorman, Francis, **8**:278

Gorman, William, **2**:450, 451

Gorrie, John, **7**:77

Gorsuch, Anne M., **2**:392

Gorton, Samuel, **7**:151

Gosnold, Bartholomew, **2**:38, 261;
    5:510

Gospel music, **4**:206–207;
    5:497–498

Goss, A. H., **3**:182

Gothic Line, **4:23**

Gothic Revival style furniture, **3**:497

Gottlieb, Michael, **1**:15

Gottlieb, Robert, **6**:92

Gough, John B., **8**:79

Goulburn, Henry, **4**:486

Gould, Charles, **6**:305

Gould, James, **5**:116

Gould, Jay, **1**:472, 473; **8**:233
  labor policies of, **7**:29

Gould, Samuel B., **7**:535

Gould, Stephen Jay, **7**:13; **8**:597–598

Gould Amendment (1913), **6**:554

Gove, Philip, **3**:23

Gover, Kevin, **1**:572

Government
  after American Revolution,
    7:137–138
  balanced, checks and balances and,
    2:116–117
  in colonies, **2**:291; **7**:200
  Constitution on, **2**:382
  county, **2:436–439**
  delegation of powers within, **2:545**
  federal (*See* Federal government)
  metropolitan (*See* Metropolitan
    government)
  municipal (*See* Municipal govern-
    ment)
  representative, **7:109–110**
  revenue sharing by, **7:133**

Government corporations, **3**:332

Government employment
  of aliens, **1**:125, 126
  of communists, **1**:198
  and loyalty oath, **8**:96
  number of people in, **3**:330, 342
  trade unions for, **1**:154
  in Virginia, **8**:346
  See also Civil service; Federal
    employees

Government ownership, **4:23–24**
  conservation and, **6**:528
  of railroads, proposal for, **6**:371
  United States v. Lee and, **8:274**
  See also Eminent domain

Government Printing Office (GPO),
    4:24–25

Government publications, **3**:344;
    4:24–25
  by Office of Federal Register,
    5:525
  Statutes at Large, **7:540–541**

Government regulation of business,
    3:13; **4:25–28**
  in 19th century, **4**:26
  in 20th century, **4**:27–28
  during American Revolution,
    4:25–26
  codes of fair competition and,
    2:263
  in colonial era, **4**:25
  oil industry, **6**:303–304
  under OSHA, **6**:158–159
  Supreme Court on, **5**:482–483

telecommunications industry,
    1:381
  See also Antitrust legislation

Governors, **4:28–30**
  American Revolution and, **4**:28–29
  in colonial era, **4**:28
    instructions to, **4:366–367**
  elections for, voter participation in,
    8:8
  Great Depression and, **4**:29
  in Jacksonian era, **4**:29
  modern, **4**:29–30
  as presidential candidates, **3**:148,
    149
  in Progressive Era, **4**:29
  term limits for, **5**:80

GPO. *See* Government Printing
    Office

GPS. *See* Genealogical Proof Stan-
    dard

Grace, Daddy, **2**:477

Grace, Robert, **3**:456

Grace, W. R., **5**:46

Graduate Management Admissions
    Test (GMAT), **3**:139

Graduate Record Exam (GRE),
    3:139, 140

Graduation Act (1854), **5**:37; **6**:527

Grady, Henry W., **1**:348; **7:467–468**

Grady, James, **5**:130

Graffiti, **4:30**
  "Kilroy Was Here," **4:526**

Grafting. *See* Transplants and organ
    donation

Graham, Bill, **1**:441

Graham, Billy, **2**:165; **3**:267;
    6:516–517; **8**:71

Graham, Katharine, **8**:506

Graham, Martha, **2**:498, 499;
    5:252–253

Graham, Sylvester, **3**:24; **5**:291

Graham v. Richardson, **1**:126

Grain elevators, **3:187–188**

Grain Futures Act (1922), **4:30**

*Grammatical Institute of the English
    Language, A* (Webster), **8**:106

Gramme, Zénobe T., **3**:173

Gramm-Leach-Bliley Act (GLBA)
    (Banking Modernization Bill)
    (1999), **1**:402; **3**:369; **4**:5

Gramm-Rudman-Hollings Act
    (1985), **1**:560; **2**:515; **4:31**

Gramophone, **1**:357

Granada, encomienda system in, **3**:202–203

Grand Army of the Republic (GAR), **4**:31–32; **8**:265, 318
  and Flag Protection Movement, **3**:380

Grand Banks, **4**:32

Grand Canyon, **4**:32–33, *33*
  exploration of, **3**:296, 300
  as monument, under Antiquities Act, **1**:205–206
  National Game Preserve in, **2**:370

Grand Canyon National Park, **4**:33; **5**:553

Grand Central Terminal, **4**:33–34, *34*; **6**:453

Grand Coulee Dam, **4**:200–201; **8**:414

Grand Forks Herald (newspaper), **6**:132

Grand National Lottery, **5**:156

Grand Ohio Company, **8**:307–308

Grand Old Party, **7**:112
  See also Republican Party

Grand Ole Opry (radio program), **4**:34–35; **5**:515, *515*

Grand Portage, **4**:35

Grand Prairie, **4**:35

Grand Prix, **1**:376

Grand Slam, **8**:90, *90*

Grand Staircase–Escalante National Monument, **8**:298

Grand Teton National Park, **8**:565

Grand unified theories (GUTs), **6**:339

Grandfather clause, **4**:35, 73; **5**:526

Grange, Harold (Red), **3**:410

Grange, the, **2**:227, 407

Granger, Francis, **3**:153

Granger, Gideon, **6**:426

Granger, Gordon, **8**:101

Granger cases, **4**:35–36

Granger laws, **7**:26

Granger movement, **2**:389; **3**:187; **4**:36–37; **6**:259
  antimonopoly parties and, **1**:204
  mail order business and, **3**:9; **5**:206
  and tobacco cooperatives, **2**:408

Grant(s)
  by National Endowment for the Arts, **5**:535
  by National Endowment for the Humanities, **5**:537
  by philanthropic foundations, **3**:444

Grant, Cary, **8**:309
  LSD use by, **5**:169

Grant, John D., **3**:212

Grant, Julia, **3**:376

Grant, Madison, **2**:366, 371

Grant, Susan-Mary, **5**:568

Grant, Ulysses S., **2**:212
  attempted assassination of, **1**:328
  Black Friday and, **1**:472, 473
  on bonus payments to veterans, **1**:499
  in Civil War, **2**:212–213
    Battle of Cold Harbor, **2**:266
    Battle of Shiloh, **7**:346
    Battle of Spotsylvania Courthouse, **7**:512
    Battles of the Wilderness, **8**:477
    Chattanooga campaign, **2**:113
    and prisoners of war, **6**:472
    raiding strategy of, **2**:217–218
    Shenandoah Campaign, **7**:341
    Siege of Petersburg, **6**:295–296
    and unconditional surrender, **8**:249
    Vicksburg, **6**:25; **8**:324
  and contrabands of war, **2**:395–396
  Court packing by, **5**:76
  and Dominican Republic, annexation of, **3**:75
  Indian policies of, **1**:492, 571; **4**:262, 276
  internment of, **6**:458
  Liberal Republican Party and, **5**:90
  memoirs of, **5**:390
  and national park system, **8**:579
  and Philadelphia fair, **8**:558
  photo of, **5**:390
  political scandals and, **1**:440
  in presidential campaign of 1864, **3**:155
  in presidential campaign of 1868, **3**:155
  in presidential campaign of 1872, **3**:156
  in presidential campaign of 1880, **3**:157
  riots and, **8**:325
  as secretary of war, Johnson's appointment of, **4**:236
  special prosecutors under, **7**:495

Grants-in-aid, **4**:37
  for agricultural education, **7**:401–402
  for vocational education, **7**:401–402

Grapes of Wrath, The (Steinbeck), **2**:10–11; **5**:120

Grasse, Comte de, **3**:473; **7**:145

Grasshoppers, **4**:37

Gratz 253, FTC v., **3**:348

Graves, James R., **1**:412

Graves, Michael, **1**:253

Graves, Nancy, **1**:307

Graves, Thomas, **8**:581

Graves, William S., **7**:353

Graves v. New York, **2**:276

Gravity's Rainbow (Pynchon), **5**:122

Gravure, **6**:470

Gray, Anna, **3**:323

Gray, Asa, **1**:140, 141, 519, 520; **2**:446; **3**:269; **7**:270

Gray, Elisha, **1**:440; **8**:456

Gray, Hanna H., **8**:281

Gray, Robert, **2**:153, 303
  explorations by
    in Aleutian Islands, **1**:121
    in Oregon, **6**:204

Gray, William, **8**:412

Gray Panthers, **4**:37–38

Gray propaganda, **6**:503

Gray v. Sanders, **3**:556

Grayson, William, and land speculation, **5**:36

Grazing lands, **6**:529, 532

GRE (Graduate Record Exam), **3**:139, 140

Great American Desert, **5**:150; **8**:462, 486

Great Awakening, **2**:162, 292; **4**:38–39; **5**:118
  Arminianism and, **1**:265
  and Congregationalism, **2**:349
  Edwardsean theology and, **3**:140
  First, **3**:264
  mysticism and, **5**:506
  and philanthropy, **6**:316
  and Princeton University, **6**:465
  and Protestantism, **6**:515–516
  Second, **1**:377–379; **2**:163; **3**:264, 265; **6**:516; **7**:84, 93
  and Republican Party, **7**:111
  and Yale University, **8**:572–573

Great Basin, **3**:468; **4**:39–40
  prehistoric, **1**:242

Great Books programs, **4**:40; **8**:281

Great Britain
  Alabama claims against, **1**:106

Great Britain, (*continued*)
    Treaty of Washington on, **1**:106;
      8:416
    during American Revolution (*See
      also specific battles and
      campaigns*)
    advantages over colonies,
      7:141–142
    in Maine, **5**:208
    in American Samoa, **7**:235
    anti-Catholicism in, **1**:196
    Aroostook War with, **1:282–283**
    Balfour Declaration by, **8**:592
    boycotts against, **1**:528
    Caribbean territories of,
      8:445–447
    in cattle industry, **4**:157
    in Civil War, **1**:105, 106
    classes in, **2**:222, 223
    Clayton-Bulwer Treaty (1850)
      with, **6**:237
    and colonial commerce, **2**:282
    colonial offices of, **1**:493
    colonial policies of, **1**:542–543;
      2:285–287; **7**:134–135
      Coercive Acts, **1**:509, 515, 542;
        2:264
        Massachusetts Government Act
          (1767), **5:272**
      colonial agents and, **2**:279–280
      colonial charters and, **2**:281–282
      Commander in Chief of British
        Forces, **2:309**
      committees of correspondence
        and resistance to, **2**:314
      Declaratory Act, **2**:286, **525**
      direct royal power, **3**:77
      Duke of York's proprietary,
        3:93–94
      Hutchinson letters and, **4:199**
      manufacturing, American, **5**:227
      mercantilism, **5**:271, **315–316**
      Mutiny Act (1765), **5:505**
      resistance to, **7**:135
      royal disallowance, **7:201**
      rum trade and, **7**:204
      and smuggling, **7**:405–406
      taxation, **2**:286; **5**:272; **7**:134
        protests against, **1**:514–515
    colonial settlements of, **2**:*61*;
      3:468; **4**:40
    cuisine in, **3**:398
    in Florida, **3**:385–386
    in Maryland, **5**:255–256

    in Massachusetts, **5**:265, 269–272
    in Michigan, **5**:354
    in North Dakota, **6**:131
    in Ohio, **6**:171
    in Oregon
      joint occupation of, **4**:41, **486**;
        6:205
      Oregon Treaty and, **6**:205,
        209–210
      Sagadahoc Colony, **7:223**
    in South Carolina, **7**:453–454
    in Vermont, **8**:311
    in colonial wars, archival maps of,
      9:25–28
    and Confederate States of America,
      2:342
    and convict transportation,
      2:401–402
    debts to, **1:540–541**
    at Dumbarton Oaks Conference,
      3:94
    Empire of, concept of, **1:541–543**
    and European Union, **3**:259–260
    explorations of, **3**:285, **287–289**,
      288
      Cabot voyages, **2**:4–5, *5*; **3**:285,
        287
      Cook voyages, **2:403–404**
      by Gilbert, **3**:576
      Golden Hind, **4**:18–19
      Hakluyt's *Voyages* on, **4:86**
      New Hampshire, **6**:56–57
      North Pole, **6**:382
      in Oregon, **6**:204
      in Pacific Northwest, **8**:452–453
      Potomac River, **6**:433
      South Pole, **6**:382–383
      by Vancouver, **8:306–307**
      in Washington, **8**:412
    feudalism in, **3**:356
    foreign aid to, **4**:43
    foreign investment from, **3**:419,
      420, 421, 422
    foreign observers from, **1**:136–137,
      138
    foreign service to, **3**:429
    and France, **3**:449, 450
      colonial wars of, **2**:293–296
      French and Indian War (*See
        French and Indian War*)
      French decrees, **3:471–472**
      and neutrality of U.S., **6**:33, 34
    fur trade of, **3**:487
    gold standard in, **4**:15

    gun control in, **4**:74
    Hay-Pauncefote Treaties with,
      4:110
    Iceland occupied by, **4**:211
    immigrants from, **4**:220–221
    and India, **4**:258
      political subordination of, **2**:45
    Irish relations with, **4**:423, 426
    Jay's Treaty with, **1**:124; **3**:450;
      4:41, **466–467**; **6**:263; **8**:200,
      204
    judiciary in, **4**:494
    in King George's War, **4:526**
    in King William's War, **4:527–528**
    in Latin America, **5**:46, 52
    and League of Nations, **8**:315–316
    Lend-Lease aid to, **5**:81–82
    London Crystal Palace Exhibition
      in, **8**:558
    and London Naval Treaties, **5**:147
    Magna Carta, **5:201**
    in Napoleonic wars, **1**:487; **3**:192
    Native Americans and
      Iroquois, **4**:283, 432
      policies on, **4**:283
      Shawnee, **7**:336–337
      treaties between, **4**:312–313
    Navy of, American Revolution and,
      5:208
    Nuclear Non-Proliferation Treaty
      with, **6**:138
    nuclear power plants in, **6**:139
    Nuclear Test Ban Treaty with,
      6:143
    overseas expansion of, **2**:402–403
    at Paris conferences, **6**:247
    Parliament of, **6:251–252**
    radar system of, **7**:14
    in SEATO, **7**:470
    in Siberian Expedition, **7**:353
    in slave trade, **5**:363, 364; **7**:384,
      386, 387
    submarines of, **7**:562–563
    in Suez Crisis, **8**:2–3
    swimming in, **8**:36
    trade with
      in 19th century, **8**:164
      after American Revolution,
        4:40–41; **8**:164
      in colonial era, **8**:163–164
        balance of, **1**:386–387
        naval stores, **6**:20
        Navigation Acts and, **4**:25;
          6:21–22

tea, **8:**60, 61, 150

textiles, **8:**108

tobacco, **8:**134

Townshend Acts and (*See* Townshend Acts)

Trade with Enemy Acts and, **8:**173

potash, **6:**431

trading posts of, **8:**175

Treaty of Ghent with, **3:571–573,** *572;* **4:**41; **6:**263; **8:**200

Treaty of Paris (1763) and, **6:**248

Treaty of Paris (1783) with, **6:**248–250; **8:**200

Treaty of Washington (1871) with, **6:**263

Tripartite Agreement with, **8:**230

U.S. relations with, **4:40–44**

after American Revolution, **3:**425; **4:**40–41

during American Revolution, **4:**40

Bermuda Conferences, **1:444–445**

Blount conspiracy, **1:489–490**

during Civil War, **3:**425; **4:**41–42

Clayton-Bulwer Treaty, **1:**439; **2:229–230**

cod fishing and, **2:**261

during Cold War, **4:**43–44

Convention of 1818 and, **2:**261, **398**

Fenian movement and, **3:**354

Five-Power Naval Treaty and, **3:**377

Four-Power Treaty and, **3:**446

during Great Depression, **4:**42

during Gulf War, **4:**44

House-Grey Memorandum and, **4:179**

impressment of seamen and, **4:248–249**

Olney-Pauncefote Treaty and, **6:191**

Oregon Territory and, **3:**358

shipping restrictions, **5:**189

Suez Crisis and, **4:**43

Trent affair and, **8:**207–208

Venezuela crisis and, **4:**42

Webster-Ashburton Treaty, **2:**26; **8:434**

during World War I, **3:**426; **4:**42

during World War II, **3:**426; **4:**43

Venezuela and, **4:**42

Olney Corollary on, **6:**191

Victorian era in, **8:**325

in War of 1812 (*See* War of 1812)

in War of Jenkins' Ear, **4:**473

warships of, **8:***406*

in World War I

aircraft carriers in, **1:**89

Armistice of November 1918, **1:**265

and Fourteen Points, **4:**42

Versailles Treaty after, **8:**315–316

in World War II

naval warfare, **8:**556

Normandy Invasion, **6:**119–120

Great Compromise. *See* Connecticut Compromise

"Great Corporation," **6:**58

Great Depression, **4:44–49,** *45, 47, 48*

abortion during, **1:**5

adolescence in, **1:**25

African Americans in, **1:**51; **5:**563

and agriculture, **8:**162

aircraft industry in, **1:**93

in Alabama, **1:**104

and antitrust legislation, **8:**235

bank failures during, **4:**45

and big business, **1:**580

birth control during, **1:**5

Bonus Army in, **1:498,** 499

and business cycles, debate on, **1:**584

causes of, **4:**45–46

and class structure, **2:**224, 227

Communist Party on, **2:**326

conservationism during, **2:**371

conservatism in response to, **2:**375

and consumerism, **2:**390

Coxey's Army during, **2:444–445**

diet during, **3:**401; **6:**150

documentary photography in, **1:**301, *302*

and domestic trade, **8:**159, 161–162

and economic indicators, importance of, **3:**105

effects of, **4:**46–49

cultural, **4:**47

by gender and race, **4:**47

on individuals, **4:**47

international, **4:**48–49

emigration during, **3:**197

and Employment Act (1946), **3:200; 8:**254

and Fair Labor Standards Act, **3:**307–308

and family life, **3:**314

and fascist movement, **3:**327–328

federal aid before and after, **3:**334

Federal Reserve System during, **3:**345; **4:**4–5, 12

Federal Trade Commission during, **3:**348

film industry during, **3:**363

in Florida, **3:**387

and foreign investment in U.S., **3:**421

and foreign policy, **3:**426

and foreign trade, **8:**165–166

forestry during, **3:**436

in Georgia, **3:**557

and "GI generation," **3:**528

Girl Scouts volunteering during, **4:**1

government communities during, **8:**303

and governors, **4:**29

and Great Britain, U.S. relations with, **4:**42

Hoover Moratorium (1931), **5:456**

in Idaho, **4:**213

infrastructure in, **4:**355

international response to, World Economic Conference, **8:532**

and liberalism, **5:**92

literature in, **5:**120

livestock industry in, **5:**135–136

in Maryland, **5:**258

merchant marine during, **5:**319–320

Mexican American community and, **5:**344

in Minnesota, **5:**400

minorities during, **3:**50

in Mississippi, **5:**413

in Montana, **5:**450

Mormon church in, **5:**54

mortgage relief legislation, **5:**462

National Youth Administration during, **8:**586

in Nebraska, **6:**30

in Nevada, **6:**38

in New York (state), **6:**88

and newspapers, **6:**99

in North Carolina, **6:**130

in North Dakota, **6:**132, 133

original documents from, **9:**375–392

Great Depression, (*continued*)
  and paper industry, **6:**245
  and prices, **6:**461
  and prisoner population, **6:**477
  public works projects of, **3:**211
  and publishing industry, **6:**538
  riots during, **7:**166
  socialism in, **7:**427
  and tariffs, **8:**52
  and taxation, **8:**58
  and theater, **8:**115
  and toys, **8:**153–154
  unemployment during, **4:**44, 45, 47
    among African Americans, **4:**47;
      5:563
    Ford (Henry) on, **9:**375–376
    rate of, **8:**251, 440
    among women, **4:**47
  Utah during, **8:**297–298
  in Vermont, **8:**314
  in Washington (state), **8:**414
  and wheat production, **3:**391
  and world's fair, **8:***559*, 559–560
  See also New Deal
Great Embargo of 1808, **7:**118
Great Gatsby, The (Fitzgerald), **1:**504;
  4:49–50; **5:**120, 150
Great Lakes, **4:50–53**
  and agriculture, **4:**51–52
  development of, **4:**50
  exploration of, **3:**291–292;
    4:50–51; **6:**106, 422
  ferries crossing, **3:**355
  and fishing, **4:**52
  and fur trade, **4:**51
  Lakes-to-Gulf Deep Waterway
    and, **5:**22–23
  Mackinac Island and Straits,
    5:188–189
  Native Americans living by, **4:**50
  physical features and population of,
    4:*51*
  Saint Lawrence Seaway to, **7:**225
  survey of, **7:**169
  U.S.-Canadian border on, **2:**26
  and U.S.-Canadian relations, **2:**29
Great Lakes Naval Campaigns of
    1812, **4:**53; **8:**432
  Battle of Lake Erie, **4:**51, 53; **6:**290
  Battle of the Thames, **8:**64,
    111–112
Great Lakes steamships, **4:53–55**
Great Law of Pennsylvania, **4:**55;
  6:276

Great Meadows (Pennsylvania), **4:**55
Great Migration, **4:55–56**
  and urbanization, **8:**290–291
Great Northern Railroad, surveys
    preceding, **3:**299
Great Plains, **4:***56*, **56–57**
  agriculture in, **4:**57
    cereal grains, **2:**97
    dry farming, **3:**88
    rise of, **1:**64
  boundaries of, **1:**244
  buffalo on, **1:**561–562
  exploration of, **4:**56; **8:**451–452
  Long's explorations of, **5:**150
  midcontinent oil region,
    5:361–362
  mortgage relief legislation, **5:**462
  mule skinners, **5:**472
  Native Americans in
    missions for, **4:**277
    sign language of, **7:357–358**
    social life of, **4:**304–305
    sun dances of, **8:**18–19
  prehistoric, **1:**244–246; **4:**56
  scouting in, **7:286–287**
  settlement of, **4:**56–57; **8:**462–463
  tornadoes in, **8:**143
  See also Dust Bowl
Great Powers, principle of concerted
    action of, **8:**269
Great Republic (steamboat), **3:**507
Great Salt Lake, **3:**468; **4:**57, *57*
  Stansbury's expedition to, excerpt
    from account of, **9:**233–237
Great Serpent Mound, **1:***246*
Great Sioux Reservation, **1:**474;
  8:275
Great Smoky Mountains, **4:**57
Great Smoky Mountains National
    Park, **5:**553
Great Society, **2:**228; **4:57–58**, *58*;
  6:55, 438; **8:**323
  goals of, **2:**228
  Highway Beautification Act in,
    4:132
  idea for, **8:**282
  Kennedy's New Frontier and, **6:**55
  legislation of, **7:**416
  neoconservatives on, **6:**32
  Office of Economic Opportunity
    in, **6:**163
  in presidential campaign of 1964,
    3:165
  War on Poverty in, **7:**416

Great Train Robbery, The (film), **4:**58,
  58; **6:**105; **8:**457
Great Union Flag, **3:**379
Great Valley, **4:59–60**
Great War for Empire. *See* French
    and Indian War
Greathead, James H., **8:**240
Greece
  Civil War in (1946-1949), **4:**59
  foreign aid to, **3:**415, 426; **4:**59;
    8:231–232
  immigrants from, **4:**59
  U.S. relations with, **4:**59
  War of Independence in (1821-
    1832), **4:**59
Greek Orthodox Church, member-
    ship in, **7:***91*
Greeley, Horace, **1:**129; **5:**90; **8:**259
  campaign for land grants for edu-
    cation, **5:**29
  and Crystal Palace Exhibition,
    2:468; **8:**558
  and Davis (Jefferson), bond for,
    2:505
  on divorce law, **3:**64
  "Go West, Young Man, Go West"
    phrase used by, **4:**9
  and *New York Log Cabin* (newspa-
    per), **3:**146
  and Peace Movement of 1864,
    6:266
  and phrenology, **6:**333
  "Prayer of Twenty Millions," **3:**191
  in presidential campaign of 1872,
    3:156
  on public lands, **4:**156
  and Yosemite National Park, **8:**581
Greely, Adolphus W., arctic expedi-
    tion by, **4:59–60**
Green, Andrew Haswell, **6:**80
Green, Charles Sumner, **3:**497
Green, Colegrove v., **1:**385
Green, Donald P., **6:**405
Green, Duff, **3:**146
Green, Edith, **8:**386
Green, Henry Mather, **3:**497
Green, Samuel, **6:**468
Green, Theodore Francis, **7:**153
Green, Timothy, **1:**129
Green, Tom, **5:**55; **6:**410
Green, William, **2:**227
Green Bay (Wisconsin), **4:**52, 60, *60*
  La Salle's trading post at, **5:**2
Green Berets, **7:**494

Green card, **4:60–61**
Green Mountain Boys, **4:61–62;**
8:311
Green Mountain Rangers, **8:**312
Green Party, **3:**230
Green Revolution, **7:**187
"Green Tree Flag," **3:**378
*Green v. School Board of New Kent
County,* **3:**16
Greenback Labor Party, **5:**16; **7:**124;
8:259
Greenback movement, **4:**62
Greenback Party, **4:**62; **8:**119
Greenbacks, **4:**9, 62; **5:**75–76;
7:118, 124
gold exchange for, **4:**10, 14
as monetary standard, **4:**14
Greenbelt (Maryland), **4:**63
Greenbelt communities, **4:**63, *63;*
5:39
Greenberg, Clement, **1:**10
Greenberg, Hank, **1:**421
Greenblatt, Richard, **2:**130
Greendale (Wisconsin), **4:**63
Greene, Francis V., **7:**181
Greene, Harold H., **1:**347
Greene, Maurice, **6:**192
Greene, Nathanael, **2:**19; **3:**261; **8:**581
and Articles of Confederation,
7:152
in Battle of Cowpens, **2:**444
in Battle of Guilford Courthouse,
4:72; **6:**128
after loss of New York City, **7:**141
in southern campaigns, **7:**145, 472
Washington's trust in, **7:**142
Greenfield Village, **4:**127, *127*
Greenglass, David, **7:**197
Greenhills (Ohio), **4:**63
Greenhouse gases emission, **1:**80;
3:511; **4:**5–6, 7, 8
Greenland
Inuit in, **4:**408–409, 410
Viking settlement in, **3:**283
Greenman, Juilliard v., **4:**500; **5:**76
Greenough, Horatio, **1:**305
Greenpeace, **3:**230; **8:**304
Greenspan, Alan, **1:**544
as chairman of Council of Eco-
nomic Advisors, **2:**432
on social security, **7:**421
Greenville Treaty (1795), **2:**509;
4:63–64, *64*
land cessions in, **4:**271; **6:**172

Greenway, Isabella Selmes, **1:**259
Greenwich Village, **4:**64–65, *65;*
8:115
Gregg, Josiah, **7:**248
Gregorian, Vartan, **1:**548
Gregory, John H., **6:**355
Grenada, invasion of, **2:**55, 270;
4:65–66; **5:**49; **8:**447
Cuban resistance to, **2:**472
press blackout during, **2:**83
Grenville, George, **2:**286; **7:**517,
518; **8:**12
Grenville, Lord, **4:**467
Grenville, Richard, **3:**288; **7:**47
Gresham, Isaac Newton, **1:**63–64
Gresham, Walter Q., **3:**157
Grey, Sir Edward, and House-Grey
Memorandum, **4:**179
Grey, Zane, *Riders of the Purple Sage,*
5:129
GRI. *See* Getty Research Institute
Gridiron, **3:**409
Grier, Robert C., **5:**76
Grievance arbitration, **1:**237
*Griever: An American Monkey King in
China* (Vizenor), **5:**129
Griffith, David Wark, **3:**362; **4:**552;
5:569
The Birth of a Nation, **1:**469,
469–470
and Western genre, **8:**457
Griffiths, Clyde, **6:**12
Griffiths, Fred, **3:**67
Griffiths, John, **5:**495
Griffon (sailing vessel), **4:**66; **5:**2
Griggs v. Duke Power Company, **1:**36;
2:197; **4:**66; **8:**389, 390
Grimes, Frances, **1:**308
Grimké, Angelina, **1:***209;* **7:**2, 3; **8:**506
on human rights, **9:**327–329
Grimké, Sarah M., **5:**91; **6:**333; **7:**2,
3, *3;* **8:**506
and abolitionism, **8:**512
Grinnell, George Bird, **1:**359; **2:**366
Griscom, John, **3:**238
Grissom, Gus, **7:**480
Griswold, Fort, **2:**357
Griswold, Frank, **3:**243
Griswold, Hepburn v., **5:**76
Griswold v. Connecticut, **1:**6, 466, 468;
4:66–67; **6:**479; **7:**192
Grocery Manufacturers of America,
3:531

Gropius, Walter, **1:**293
Gros Ventre Indians, Fort Laramie
Treaty with, text of, **9:**227–229
Groseilliers, Médard Chouart des,
3:291, 489
Grosjean v. American Press Company,
4:67
Gross, Robert, **2:**53
Gross domestic product (GDP),
real, **1:**582
Grossman, Sid, **1:**301
Grosvenor, Gilbert Hovey, **5:**541,
542
Grosvenor, Gilbert Melville, **5:**542
Grosvenor, Melville Bell, **5:**542
Grotell, Maija, **1:**304
Grotius, Hugo, **6:**33, 34; **8:**370
Ground Zero, **8:**533
Group insurance, **4:**371
Group libel laws, **4:**67
Grove City College v. Bell, **2:**206
Grove Press v. Christenberry, **1:**500
Groves, Leslie R., **5:**221–222
Groves v. Slaughter, **3:**90
Grueby, William Henry, **1:**287, 304
Gruelle, Johnny, **8:**153
Gruen, Victor, **5:**216
Grund, Francis J., *Americans in Their
Moral, Social and Political Rela-
tions,* excerpt from, **9:**215–218
Grutter v. Bollinger, **1:**386
GSA. *See* Geological Society of
America
GST. *See* Goldman Sachs Trading
Corporation
Guadalcanal Campaign, **4:**68; **6:**26;
8:556
Guadalupe Hidalgo, Treaty of
(1848), **2:**8; **3:**501; **4:**68; **5:**46,
342; **6:**68; **8:**200, 204
and Colorado, **2:**298
and Rio Grande, **7:**163
Guale, **8:**225
Guam, **4:**68–69; **8:**232
annexation of, **1:**189; **2:**470; **8:**92,
94, 109
Marine Corps on, **5:***243*
Treaty of Paris (1898) and, **6:**250
Guano, **4:**69
Guantánamo Bay, **4:**69
Guardian spirit complex, **6:**6
Guatemala
CIA operations in, **2:**92
foreign aid to, **4:**70

Guatemala, (*continued*)
  Mayan immigration from, **9**:509–515
  U.S. relations with, **2**:54; **4**:69–70;
    5:48
    Good Neighbor policy and, **4**:22
Guderian, Heinz, **1**:267
*Guerra, California Federal Savings
    and Loan Association v.*, **6**:449
Guerrilla Girls, The, **5**:337
Guerrilla warfare, **4**:70–71
  in American Revolution, **2**:19, 444
  booby traps used in, **1**:500
  in Civil War, **2**:217
  in Vietnam War, **8**:330
Guffey, Joseph, **4**:71
Guffey Coal Act (1935), **4**:71
Guffey Coal Act (1937), **4**:71
Guffy, James, **6**:302
Guggenheim, Peggy, **1**:10
Guggenheim, Simon, **6**:486
Guggenheim, Solomon R., **4**:71
Guggenheim Awards, **6**:486
Guggenheim Museum, **4**:71–72, *72*
Guide to Confident Living (Peale),
    6:442
Guideposts (magazine), **6**:442
Guiding Light, The (soap opera),
    7:408
Guilford Courthouse, Battle of,
    4:72–73; **6**:128; **7**:145
Guinn and Beal v. United States, **4**:35,
    73; **5**:526
Guiteau, Charles, **1**:328
Gulf + Western, **6**:538
Gulf Coastal Plain, **8**:83
Gulf Intracoastal waterway, **8**:430
Gulf of Sidra shootdown, **4**:73
Gulf of Tonkin Resolution. *See*
    Tonkin Gulf Resolution
Gulf Stream, **4**:73–74
Gulf Stream, The (Homer), **4**:73
Gulf War of 1991. *See* Persian Gulf
    War
Gulick, Charlotte, **2**:21
Gulick, Luther, **2**:21
Gullah culture, **7**:155
Gumbel, Bryant, **8**:*138*
Gun(s)
  Colt six-shooter, **2:302**
  rifle, **7**:*159*, **159–160**
  and violent crime, **2**:460
  See also Weapons
Gun control, **4**:74–76
  in 19th century, **4**:74

  in 20th century, **4**:74–76; **5**:557
  assassinations and, **4**:75; **5**:557
  Brady bill and, **1:530**; **6**:213
  in colonial era, **4**:74
  Columbine school massacre and,
    2:305
  legislation expanding, **6**:212–213
Gun Control Act (GCA) (1968),
    4:76; **5**:557; **6**:212
Gunboat diplomacy, **4**:76–77
Gunboats, **4:77–78**
  Princeton, **6**:464–465
Gunnison, John W., **7**:30
Gunpowder
  manufacturing of, **2**:542; **3**:301
  potash in, **6**:431
  saltpeter (potassium nitrate) in,
    6:110; **8**:243
  sodium nitrate in, **8**:243
Gupta, Akhil, **1**:194
Gurney, Joseph John, **7**:2
Gurney, R. W., **6**:342
Gurteen, Stephen Humphreys,
    2:106
Gustav Line, **4:78**
Gutenberg, Johannes, **6**:467–468
Guthrie, Woody, **1**:441; **3**:396;
    8:414
Gutiérrez, Gustavo, *A Theology of
    Liberation: History, Politics, and
    Salvation*, **5**:93
GUTs. *See* Grand unified theories
Guttmann, Allen, **1**:169
Guy, William L., **6**:132
Guyana
  People's Temple in, **2**:478; **7**:94
  See also Jonestown Massacre
Guyot, Arnold, **3**:541
Guzmán, Jacobo Arbenz, **2**:92; **4**:70
Guzzoni, Alfredo, in Sicilian Cam-
    paign, **7**:353–354
Gypsies, **4:78–79**

H

H. D. (Hilda Doolittle), **5**:120
Haacke, Hans, **1**:307
Habeas corpus, writ of, **3**:271–272;
    4:81–82
  history of use of, **4**:81
  Lincoln's suspension of, **1**:284,
    393; **4**:81; **6**:482
  Supreme Court on, **1**:284; **4**:81–82

Haber, Al, **7**:561
Habermas, Jürgen, **3**:454
Habitat Conservation Plan (HCP),
    3:206
Hackers, computer, **7**:219
Hackett, A. J., **1**:569
Hadacheck v. Sebastian, **6**:505
Hadden, Briton, **8**:127
Hadfield, George, **2**:49
Hadley, Arthur, **3**:108
Haftand, Thomas, **2**:242
Hagen, Walter, **4**:19, *19*
Hagenbeck, Carl, **8**:594
Haggenmacher, Carl, **3**:390
Haggin, James B., **1**:180
Hague, Frank, **4**:82–83; **6**:63
Hague Peace Conferences, **4:82**
  of 1899, **4**:82
  of 1907, **4**:82
  and gas warfare, attempt to ban,
    2:117
  Geneva Conventions adopted by,
    3:535
  on neutrality, **6**:34
*Hague v. Committee on Industrial
    Organization*, **4:82–83**; **5**:546
Hahn, Nancy Coonsman, **1**:308
Hahn, Otto, **6**:342
Haida, **8**:211, 213
"Hail, Columbia," **2**:302
Hair (musical), **8**:115
Hairstyles, **4**:*83*, **83–84**
  in mid-19th century, **2**:245, 246
Haiti
  dollar diplomacy in, **3**:71
  and Dominican Republic, **3**:75
  human rights in, **4**:85
  independence of, **8**:446
  refugees from, **4**:85, *85*
    U.S. policies regarding, **7**:81
  slave insurrections in, **5**:50, 163;
    7:379
  trade with, **4**:84
  UN forces in, **4**:85–86
  U.S. occupation of, **2**:54, 55; **4**:85
  U.S. relations with, **4:84–86**;
    5:46–47, 49; **8**:446–447
  gunboat diplomacy and, **4**:77
Hakluyt, Richard, **3**:287
  Voyages, **4**:86, *86*
Haldeman, H. R., **6**:111; **8**:425
Haldimand Negotiations (1781),
    8:312

Hale, Creighton J., **5**:133

Hale, David, **6**:458

Hale, George Ellery, **1**:344; **2**:14

Hale, John Parker
  and Democratic Party, **6**:58
  and Free Soil Party, **3**:154, 459
  and Republican Party, **6**:58

Hale, Matthew, **2**:316

Hale, Nathan, **7**:502

Hale, Sarah Josepha, **4**:9; **5**:198;
  8:112

Hale, William Harlan, **8**:350–351

Hale Observatories, **6**:156

Haley, Alex, **1**:363; **3**:523
  Roots, **7**:*197*

Half a Century (Swisshelm), excerpt
  from, **9**:255–257

Half Moon (ship), **4**:86–87, 187

Half-breeds. *See* Native American(s),
  intermarriage by

Halfway Covenant, **2**:349; **4**:87

Hall, A. Oakey (O.K.), **7**:162

Hall, Charles Francis, **6**:382

Hall, Charles Martin, **1**:130; **5**:330

Hall, Felix, **1**:442

Hall, Granville Stanley, **1**:24; **2**:137,
  144; **3**:73, 274

Hall, Gus, **2**:328

Hall, Prince, **3**:466

Hall, Radclyffe, **7**:325

Hall v. Geiger-Jones Co., **1**:491

Hallalhotsoot (Nez Perce leader),
  6:100, 102

Hallam, Lewis, **8**:113

Hallam, Lewis, the Younger, **8**:113

Halleck, Henry W., **2**:213;
  8:370–371
  in Peninsular Campaign, **6**:275
  and Red River Campaign, **7**:71

Hallet, Stephen, **2**:49

Hallidie, Andrew S., **4**:11; **7**:43

Hallucinogens, **7**:569

Halogen lamps, **3**:179

Halsey, William F., **5**:89; **6**:523;
  8:547, 557

Hamada, Shoji, **1**:305

Hamburg Riot (1876), **4**:87

Hamer, Fannie Lou, transcript of
  interview with, **9**:447–452

Hamill, Curt, **6**:303

Hamill, Mark, **7**:524, *524*

Hamilton, Alexander, **4**:*88*
  affair of, **6**:400
  agrarianism and, **1**:56

alma mater of, **2**:304

in American Revolution, **8**:581

on American System, **1**:171

at Annapolis Convention, **1**:187

arms policy, **5**:481

caucus supporting, **6**:113

and Coast Guard, establishment of,
  2:258

and coinage system, **2**:481

and Compromise of 1790, **2**:*330*

at Constitutional Convention,
  2:378, 379

customs officers appointed by,
  2:485

debt policies of, **2**:515, 518

duel with Burr, **1**:577–578; **3**:*92*

economic policies of, **2**:374, 386;
  3:108; **4**:87–91
  Bank of United States in, **4**:89–90
  domestic debts in, **4**:87–88
  and emergence of Federalist
    Party, **3**:350–351
  foreign debts in, **4**:87
  vs. Jeffersonian Republicans,
    3:351; **4**:471
  manufacturing in, **4**:90; **5**:227
  mint in, **4**:90
  nationalism in, **1**:171; **4**:87
  state debt in, **4**:88–89
  taxation in, **4**:89

on enumerated powers, **3**:225

Essex Junto and, **3**:256

Federalist Papers by, **2**:382;
  3:349–350
  No. 84, text of, **9**:164–167

fiscal policies of, **1**:395, 396, 458

and Great Britain, U.S. relations
  with, **4**:466, 467

on implied powers, **4**:247

on judicial review, **4**:492

and land companies, **5**:26

legal training of, **5**:56, 73

opposition to, **7**:117
  Democratic Party and, **2**:549

on police power, **6**:387

on presidency, **6**:454

in presidential campaign of 1792,
  3:150

on public lands, disposal of, **6**:527

Report on Manufactures by, **3**:527

and republic, concept of, **7**:110

and Society for the Establishment
  of Useful Manufactures, **6**:62

on subsidies, **7**:564

and tariffs, **8**:50

and taxation, **8**:56

as treasury secretary, **8**:195

on treaties with France, **7**:56–57

and Whiskey Rebellion, **8**:469

at Zenger trial, **5**:90; **8**:590

Hamilton, Alice, **5**:297

Hamilton, C. H., **3**:181

Hamilton, Henry, **2**:222

Hamilton, Richard, **6**:414

Hamilton, Thomas, on Nat Turner's
  Rebellion, **9**:287–288

Hamilton, Virginia, *M. C. Higgins
  the Great*, **5**:126

Hamilton v. Kentucky Distillers, **8**:374

Hamlin, Hannibal, **5**:210
  in presidential campaign of 1860,
    3:155

Hamm, Mia, **7**:*410*

Hammarskjöld, Dag, **8**:271

Hammer v. Dagenhart, **2**:140, 142,
  149, 311; **3**:308

Hammerstein, Oscar, **8**:115

Hammett, Dashiell, **5**:120
  Red Harvest, **5**:129

Hammon, Jupiter, **5**:124

Hammond, Georgia, **5**:135

Hammond, James, antislavery movement and, **1**:210

Hammond, William, **3**:238

Hampton, Fred, murder of, **2**:266

Hampton, James, **1**:312

Hampton, Wade, **2**:302
  supporters of, **7**:72

Hampton Normal and Agricultural
  Institute, **3**:126

Hampton Roads, Battle of, **6**:25

Hampton Roads Conference (1865),
  4:91

Hampton v. Mow Sun Wong, **1**:126

Hanaman, Franz, **5**:24

Hancock, John, **1**:512; **2**:522; **3**:256;
  6:520
  British attempt to arrest, **2**:287
  commercial motivation of, **2**:286
  and Federalists, **2**:381
  revolutionary committees and,
    7:149

Hancock, Thomas, **7**:202

Hancock, Walter, **1**:371

Hancock, Winfield Scott
  in Battle of Gettysburg, **3**:569
  in Battle of Spotsylvania Court-
    house, **7**:512

Hancock, Winfield Scott, (*continued*)
  in presidential campaign of 1876,
    3:156
  in presidential campaign of 1880,
    3:157
Handcarts, Mormon migration and,
  5:458
Handgun Violence Prevention Act.
  See Brady Bill (1993)
Handicapped. *See* Disabled
Handler, Elliot, **1:**417
Handler, Ruth, **1:**417
Handley, John J., **6:**500
Handsome Lake (Seneca leader),
  1:116; **6:**6, 7
Handy, W.C., **5:**308, *308*
Hanford Nuclear Facility,
  8:414–416
Hanging, **4:91–92**
  execution by, **2:**40
Hankey, Maurice, **1:**266
Hanks, John, **7:**23
Hanna, Bill, **2:**64
Hanna, Marcus A., **2:**23; **3:**158, 159;
  5:530
Hanna, Richard T., **4:**543
Hanoi (North Vietnam), Christmas
  bombing of, Kissinger on,
  9:475–477
Hansberry, Lorraine, *A Raisin in the
  Sun*, **5:**126
Hansell, Clarence W., **3:**357
Hansell, Haywood S., **8:**554
Hansen, Alvin, **3:**110
Hansen, Gerhard Armauer, **5:**83
Hansen, James, **2:**238; **4:**8
Hansen, Olof, **2:**509
Hansen, W. W., **6:**343
Hansen's disease. *See* Leprosy
Hanson, Duane, **1:**307
Hanson, J.C.M., **5:**101
Hanson, Phil, **1:**311
Hanssen, Robert, espionage by,
  3:339; **4:**92; **7:**503
Hantavirus, **4:92–93**
Happersett, Minor v., **5:401–402;**
  8:11
Haraway, Donna, **3:**517
Harbord, James, **1:**441
Harbors
  improvements of, **7:168–171;**
    8:430
  See also Port(s)
Hard money, **2:**550; **4:**93; **7:**439

Hardee, William J., **8:**87
Harder, Dale S., **1:**364
Hardin, Leisy v., **6:**213
Harding, Florence, **3:**376
Harding, Warren G.
  and Berlin Treaty (1921), **1:**443
  corruption in administration of,
    1:504; **2:**421
  death of, **3:**161
  and FBI, **3:**337
  illegitimate children of, **6:**400
  and naval oil reserves, **6:**19
  in presidential campaign of 1920,
    3:161; **6:**118
  Railway Shopmen's strike and, **7:**40
  and Republican Party, **7:**113
  and Tomb of the Unknown Sol-
    dier, **8:**284
Hardware trade, **4:93–94**
Hardwick, Bowers v., **6:**480
Hardy, Harriet, **5:**297
Hardy, Holden v., **1:**21; **3:**308; **5:**14
Hardy, James, **4:**121
Hare, Nathan, **1:**46
Hare, Robert, **5:**331
Hare Krishnas, **1:**326; **2:**477; **4:**133
Hare quota, **6:**508
Hargous, P. A., **3:**501–502
Hargreaves, James, **2:**424
Harisiades v. Shaughnessy, **1:**125
Harkavy, Minna, **1:**308
Harkins, William D., **6:**340, 341, 343
Harlan, John Marshall, on Sherman
  Antitrust Act, **7:**343–344
Harlan County (Kentucky), La Fol-
  lette Civil Liberties Committee
  investigation in, **5:**1
Harlem (New York), **4:**94
  Metropolitan Museum of Art exhi-
    bition on, **5:**337
Harlem, Battle of, **4:94–95**
Harlem Renaissance, **4:**94, **95–97**
  African American folklore and,
    3:395
  literature of, **4:**95–96
  members of, **4:**94, 95
  music of, **4:**96
  and nightclubs, **6:**107
  origins of, **4:**95
  visual art of, **4:**96–97
Harmar, Josiah, **6:**178; **8:**399
Harmonialism, **7:**505
Harnett, William M., **1:**295
Harper, Frances Ellen Watkins, **5:**124

Harper, Robert Goodloe, **3:**351
Harper, William Rainey, **8:**280
Harper Bros., **6:**536–537
Harper v. Virginia Board of Elections,
  5:415; **6:**508
Harpers Ferry (West Virginia)
  Brown's raid at, **1:**332; **2:**192;
    4:97–100; 8:448
  in Civil War, capture of, **4:**97
Harper's Weekly (magazine)
  on Tammany Hall, **8:**46
  on World's Columbian Exposition,
    2:271
Harriman, Edward H., **6:**135
Harriman, Mary, **3:**258
Harriman, W. Averell
  ambassadorship of, **1:**134
  as commerce secretary, **2:**310
  and Nuclear Test Ban Treaty, **6:**143
Harrington, Henry B.
  *Battles of the American Revolution,
    1775–1781*, **5:**145
  on logistics, **5:**145
Harrington, Mark, **1:**16
Harrington, Michael, **6:**31, 436–437,
  438; **7:**428
  The New American Poverty, excerpt
    from, **9:**500–504
  The Other America, **2:**228
Harrington, Oliver W., **6:**395
Harriot, Thomas, **2:**233; **9:**8–10
Harris, Barbara, **8:***500*
Harris, Benjamin, **6:**94–95
Harris, Benjamin G., **2:**411
Harris, E. Lynn, **5:**123
Harris, Eric, **2:**305
Harris, Isham G., **8:**85
Harris, Joel Chandler, **3:**395; **5:**119
  Uncle Remus, **5:**119
Harris, John, **3:**204; **6:**105
Harris, Kevin, **7:**203
Harris, Marvin, **1:**193–194
Harris, Patricia Roberts, **4:**114
Harris, Townsend, **2:**189; **4:**457
Harris, United States v., **8:**274
Harris, William Torrey, **3:**116
Harris v. McRae, **4:100**
Harrisburg Convention (1827),
  4:100
Harrisburg Pennsylvanian (newspa-
  per), **6:**533
Harrison, Benjamin
  anti-imperialism of, **1:**202

conservation policies of, **2**:367; **8**:480

and forest conservation, **3**:431, 433

Latin American policies of, **5**:46

and Louisiana lottery, **5**:156

in presidential campaign of 1888, **3**:157–158, 171; **8**:233

in presidential campaign of 1892, **3**:158

and tariffs, **8**:51

Harrison, Carter H., **4**:109

Harrison, Elizabeth, **8**:295

Harrison, Francis Burton, **6**:322

Harrison, Frederic, **6**:423

Harrison, George, **1**:441

Harrison, H., **1**:358

Harrison, Katherine, **8**:494

Harrison, Peter, **1**:249

Harrison, William Henry (Old Tippecanoe), **2**:534

in Battle of the Thames, **8**:111

in Battle of Tippecanoe, **8**:131

death of, **8**:322

as log cabin candidate, **5**:145

Native Americans and

in Battle of Tippecanoe, **8**:399

land cessions by, **4**:271–272, 314, 317

Perry's message to, **8**:432

in presidential campaign of 1836, **3**:153

in presidential campaign of 1840, **2**:550; **3**:146, 153; **8**:131

Virginia dynasty and, **8**:348

in War of 1812, **5**:21

Whig Party and, **8**:467

Harrison Narcotics Act (1914), **5**:510–511

Harrod, James, **4**:518

Harsanyi, John, **3**:109

Hart, Frederick, **1**:307; **8**:*335*

Hart, Gary, **3**:168

and charter schools, **2**:110

Hart, Oliver, **1**:412

Hart, Thomas, **1**:158

Hart, William A., **6**:8

Hart, William S., **8**:457

Hart-Celler Act. *See* Immigration Act (1965)

Harte, Bret, **5**:119

Hartford, George Huntington, **7**:125

Hartford Convention (1814–1815), **3**:151, 256; **4:101**

Hartford Wits, **4:101–102**

Hartley, Marsden, **1**:297

Hartley, Robert M., **2**:489

Hartman, Geoffrey, **6**:429

Hart-Scott-Rodino Antitrust Improvement Act (1976), **3**:349

Hartsfield, William B., **3**:557

Hartshorne, Richard, **3**:543

Hartz, Louis, **4**:139; **7**:428

The Liberal Tradition in America, **5**:140

Hartzog, George B., **5**:552

Harvard, John, **6**:316

Harvard Divinity School, **7**:96, 97

Harvard University, **4:102–103**

African American Studies at, **1**:47

and Arnold Arboretum, **1**:517

athletic program at, **2**:276

engineering program at, **3**:216, 217

establishment of, **1**:509; **2**:18, *18*; **3**:111, 127, 129; **4**:102; **8**:263

law school of, **5**:56–58

Lawrence Scientific School, **5**:59

lottery use by, **5**:156

pragmatism at, **6**:444, 445

Radio Research Laboratory at, **7**:14

sociology at, **7**:433–434

Harvey, John, **2**:280

Harvey, W. H. (Coin), *Coin's Financial School*, **2:265**

Harvey, William (colonel), **3**:268

Hasbro, **8**:153

G.I. Joe developed by, **3**:574–575

Hascall, John, **1**:59

Haskin, De Witt C., **8**:240

Haslam, John, **8**:319

Hassam, Childe, **1**:296; **3**:537

Hassler, Ferdinand Rudolph, **2**:257; **6**:155

Hat(s)

beaver, **1**:434, **435**

manufacture of, colonial restrictions on, **4**:103; **6**:22

Hatch, Carl, **4**:103–104

Hatch, Orin, and Civil Rights Act of 1991, **2**:197

Hatch Act (1939), **4:103–104**

Hatch Experiment Station Act (1887), **1**:63, 71; **8**:279

Hatcher, Richard, **1**:52

Hate crimes, **4:104–105**; **7**:12

against Asian Americans, **1**:323–324

definition of, **4**:104

against gays and lesbians, **7**:327

and group libel laws, **4**:67

incidence of, **4**:104

legislation on, **4**:104–105

Supreme Court on, **4**:104, 105

against women, **4**:104

Hate that Hate Produced, The (documentary), **5**:520

Hatfield, Mark O., **1**:388; **6**:207

Hatland, Thomas, **2**:241

Hauge, Frank, **1**:507

Hauge, Hans Nielsen, **6**:137

Hauge's Synod, **6**:137

Haupt v. United States, **8**:194

Hauptmann, Bruno, **5**:113

Hauteval, Lucien, **8**:570

Havasupais, **8**:228

Havemeyer, Mrs. Henry O., **2**:272

Haven, Samuel F., **2**:271

Havens, Richie, **1**:546

Havlicek, John, **1**:424

Hawaii, **4:105–108**, *106*

annexation of, **1**:189; **4**:107; **6**:225; **8**:94

astronomical observatories in, **6**:157

Chinese immigrants in, **2**:154

emblems, nicknames, mottos, and songs of, **7**:*532*

governors of, **4**:108

gun control in, **4**:75

introduced species in, **7**:500

Japanese Americans in, **4**:462–463, 464

Korean Americans in, **4**:543

land law in, **4**:106

merchant trade in, **4**:105–106

native Hawaiians in, **4**:105–107, 108

reciprocal trade agreement with, **8**:156

statehood for, **4**:108

sugar industry in, **4**:106–107, 108

surfing in, **8**:27–28

tourism in, **4**:108

volcanoes in, **8**:*351*, 351–352

Westernization of, **4**:106

whaling in, **4**:106

in World War II, **4**:107

Hawes-Cutting Act (1933), **8**:244

Hawkers. *See* Peddlers

Hawkins, Augustus F., **1**:550

Hawkins, Benjamin, **2**:456

Hawkins, Jane, **8**:494
Hawkins, John, **3**:288
Hawkins, Sir John, **5**:363
Hawkins, John H. W., **8**:79
Hawks. *See* Doves and hawks; War hawks
Hawley-Smoot Tariff Act (1930). *See* Smoot-Hawley Tariff Act (1930)
Haworth, James M., **7**:72
Hawthorne, Charles, **1**:320
Hawthorne, Nathaniel, **1**:509; **2**:375; **3**:195, 197
   The Blithedale Romance, **7**:194; **8**:292
   at Brook Farm, **1**:545; **8**:301
   as customs officer, **2**:485
   The Scarlet Letter, **5**:119; **7**:263
   "Young Goodman Brown," **5**:119
Haxel, O., **6**:344
Hay, George Dewey, **4**:34
Hay, John M., **2**:470
   and foreign policy, **3**:425; **4**:42
   and Hay-Bunau-Varilla Treaty, **4**:108
   and Hay-Herrán Treaty, **4**:109
   and Hay-Pauncefote Treaties, **4**:110
   Open Door policy of, **6**:196–197
   and Panama Canal, **6**:237
   on Spanish-American War, **1**:189
   and Virgin Islands, **8**:340–341
Hay-Bunau-Varilla Treaty (1903), **4**:108–109; **6**:238; **8**:201, 205
Hayburn's case, **4**:109
Haycox, Ernest, **5**:130
Hayden, Carl, **1**:259
Hayden, Ferdinand V., **1**:167; **3**:300, 544; **8**:454, 579
Hayden, Michael V., **3**:186
Hayden, Tom, **7**:561
Hayden's Case, **7**:312
Hayek, Friedrich, **3**:109
Hayes, Elvin, **1**:425
Hayes, Ira, **6**:247
Hayes, Lucy Webb, **3**:375
Hayes, Max S., **3**:321
Hayes, Rutherford B., **8**:560
   fiscal policies of, **1**:484
   immigration restriction under, **4**:232
   in presidential campaign of 1876, **2**:420, 467; **3**:148, 156, 171
   presidential library of, **5**:99
   on silver coinage, **3**:458

Hay-Herrán Treaty (1903), **4**:109; **6**:237
Haymarket riot (1886), **1**:181; **2**:132, 227; **4**:109, *110;* **8**:95, 259
Hayne, Robert Y., **6**:220; **8**:434–435
Haynes, George Edmund, **5**:563
Hay-Pauncefote Treaties (1900–1901), **2**:229; **4**:110; **6**:237; **8**:140, 205
Hays, Fort, **4**:110–111
Hays, Isaac, **1**:164
Hays, John Coffee, **8**:104
Hayter, William Stanley, **6**:471
Hayward, Richard, **1**:305
Haywood, William D. (Big Bill), **4**:111, *346;* **5**:60
   in Industrial Workers of the World, **4**:346; **7**:426
   in Russia, **4**:349
Haywood-Moyer-Pettibone case, **4**:111
Hazard, Paul H., **1**:389
Hazardous waste, **4**:111–112; **6**:139
   cleanup of, **8**:21
   in Love Canal, **5**:164
   regulation of, **4**:111–112
   in Times Beach, **8**:127
Hazelwood, Joseph, **3**:305
Hazlitt, Henry, **5**:556
HBC. *See* Hudson's Bay Company
HBO (Home Box Office), **2**:322
HCP. *See* Habitat Conservation Plan
Head Start, **3**:118; **4**:112–113; **8**:293, 386, 441
   as child care, **2**:139
Head taxes. *See* Poll taxes
Heald, Nathan, **2**:509
Health. *See* Epidemics and public health; Women's health
Health, Education, and Welfare, Department of (HEW), **4**:113–114
   Medicare and Medicaid, **5**:289–290
Health and Human Services, Department of (HHS), **3**:332; **4**:113–115
   Administration for Children and Families, **2**:147
   establishment of, **4**:113, 114
   functions of, **4**:113, 114–115
   head of, **2**:2
   organization of, **4**:114
   origins of, **4**:113–114

   See also National Institutes of Health
Health care, **4**:115–118
   access to, lack of, **4**:116
   alternative medicine, **5**:290–292
   AMA on, **1**:164–165
   Clinton plan for, **1**:153; **4**:114, 120, 372
   costs of, **4**:116–118, *117,* 119–120, 121, 173–174; **5**:304–305
      fee-for-service model and, **5**:285
   delivery of, **4**:115
   economics of, **4**:120–121
   financing of, **4**:115
   future of, **4**:117–118
   general practice in, **4**:115
   hospital system, expansion of, **5**:302
   hygiene in, **4**:204–205
   Indian medicine, **5**:292–293
   infrastructure of, **4**:356
   managed, **4**:117, 121, 173–174
      cost controls, **5**:285
   March of Dimes, **5**:236
   Maternal and child, **5**:273–275
   mental illness, **5**:312–315
   nursing and, **6**:146–148
   occupational medicine, **5**:296–299
   organization of, **4**:115
   patients' rights, **6**:257–258
   in South Dakota, **7**:461
   specialty medicine in, **4**:115–116, *116*
   for union members, AFL-CIO on, **1**:151–152, 153
   for veterans, **8**:317
   after World War II, **4**:116–117
Health food industry, **4**:118–119
   origins of, **3**:24
   vegetarianism and, **8**:310
   vitamins, **6**:149
Health food movement, and breakfast cereal, **2**:98, 99
Health insurance, **4**:119–120, 371–372
   AMA on, **4**:119
   collective bargaining and, **2**:274
   company-sponsored, **5**:297
   history of, **5**:303
   by HMOs, **4**:120–121; **5**:305
   and hospitals, **4**:173–174
   managed care, **4**:117, 121, 173–174
      medical education and, **5**:284
   origins of, **4**:116, 371

people without, **4:**116, 119, 120
rise of, **4:**371–372
Health maintenance organizations
(HMOs), **2:**406; **4:120–121**
history of, **5:**305
Healy, Bernadine, **3:**531; **8:**511
Hearne, Eddie, **1:**375
Hearnes, Warren, **5:**422
Hearst, George, **1:**180
Hearst, Patricia, **4:**525; **8:**38, *38*
Hearst, William Randolph, **8:**577,
577
estate of, **7:243,** *243*
film depicting, **2:**178–179
and Graham (Billy), **6:**516–517
International News Service found-
ed by, **6:**458
and Pulitzer (Joseph), **6:**97–98
and "Ripley's Believe It or Not"
column, **7:**168
women's magazines by, **1:**32
Heart disease, **2:52–54**
Heart implants, **4:121–122**
Heart transplantation, **8:**183
Heath, Perry S., **7:**205
Heating, **4:***122,* **122–123**
Heaven's Gate cult, **2:**478
Hebern, Edward H., **2:**468
Hecker, Frank, **3:**20
Hecker, Isaac, **2:**69
Heckler, Margaret, **1:**15; **4:**114
Hedges, Cornelius, **8:**579
Heemskerck, Jacob van, **6:**382
Heffner, Ray L., **1:**548
Heidegger, Martin, **3:**279
Heidelberg College, **8:**264
Heim v. McCall, **1:**125
Heinlein, Robert, **5:**130
Heinous.com, **8:**304
Heinz, Henry, **2:**36
Heinz Company, **3:**400; **6:**279
Heisenberg, Werner, **6:**345
Heiser, Victor, **5:**83
Helena (Montana), **1:**501
Helena mining camp, **4:123**
Helicopters, **4:123–124**
on aircraft carriers, **1:**91
development of, **1:**94; **4:**123
in Korean War, **4:**123
in Vietnam War, **1:**73; **4:**124, *124*
"Hell on Wheels," **4:124–125**
Hellegers, Andre, **1:**461
Heller, Joseph, *Catch-22,* **2:66–67;**
5:121

Heller, Walter, **2:**431
Hellman, Lillian, **5:**121
Hellman, Martin, **2:**468
Hell's Angels, **4:125**
Helms, Jesse
and Cuba relations, **2:**472
and National Endowment for the
Arts, **5:**535
opposition to Convention on the
Elimination of All Forms of
Discrimination Against
Women, **2:**399
and tobacco industry, **8:**137
Helms-Burton Act (1996), **2:**472;
5:50
Helper, Hinton Rowan, *Impending
Crisis of the South,* **4:242**
excerpt from, **9:**280–284
Helperites. *See Impending Crisis of the
South*
Helsinki Accords (1975), **3:**427; **4:125**
Helvering v. Davis, **3:**528
Helwys, Thomas, **1:**411
Hemingway, Ernest, **3:**197, 280;
5:157
A Farewell to Arms, **5:**120
The Sun Also Rises, **5:**120
Hemlock Society, **3:**261, 262
Hemp, **4:125–126**
Hemphill, Herbert Waide, Jr., **1:**310
Henday, Anthony, **3:**490
Henderson, Alexander, at Alexandria
Conference, **1:**122
Henderson, Fletcher, **4:**468, *468*
Henderson, Leon, **6:**165
Henderson, Loy, ambassadorship of,
1:134
Henderson, Richard, **2:**480
and land companies, **5:**36
Hendricks, Thomas A., **3:**156, 157
Hendrix, Jimi, **8:**524
Hennepin, Louis
disappearance of, **4:**66
narratives of, **4:126**
Hennessey, David C, **5:**191
Hennig, Willi, **8:**596
Henri, Robert, **1:**297, 310, 320, 321,
322
Henry IV (king of England), **2:**136
Henry VII (king of England), **3:**285,
287
and shipbuilding, **3:**87
Henry VIII (king of England), **3:**287
and shipbuilding, **3:**87

Henry, Andrew, **3:**487, 493
Henry, Fort, **2:**212; **4:126–127**
capture of, **3:**79
Henry, Joseph, **1:**141, 167; **2:**235;
3:172; **5:**331; **6:**335; **8:**68
Henry, O., **5:**119
Henry, Patrick, **2:**381
and American Revolution, beginning of, **8:**483
antifederalism of, **1:**201
at First Continental Congress,
2:393
on Galloway's plan of union, **3:**505
"Give Me Liberty or Give Me
Death" speech by, **4:**2
and Madison, debate between,
2:381
Virginia Resolves by, **8:**349
text of, **9:**120
Henry Ford Museum and Green-
field Village, **4:127,** *127*
Henry Frank (towboat), **8:**147
Henry Street Settlement, **5:**166;
8:114
Henry the Navigator (prince of Por-
tugal), **3:**283
Henschel, Milton, **4:**472
Hensley, Willie, **1:**112
Hepburn Act (1906), **4:127–128,**
401; **6:**494–495; **7:**26, 27
Hepburn v. Griswold, **5:**76
Hepplewhite, George, **1:**291; **3:**496
Heraldic star, **3:**378
Herberg, Will, **1:**337; **5:**556
Herbert, Hilary A., **1:**128
Herbicides. *See* Insecticides and her-
bicides
Herder, J. G., **6:**374
Heredity
molecular basis of, **3:**67
See also Genetics
Heritage Foundation (HF), **1:**545;
8:118
Herjulfsson, Bjarni, **8:**337
Herkimer, Nicholas, **1:**574; **6:**213
Hermaphroditism, **3:**515
Hermitage (Tennessee), **4:128,** *128*
Heroin, **5:**512; **7:**569
Herold, David, **1:**328
Héroult, Paul, **1:**130
Herpetology, **4:128–130; 8:**596
Herrán, Tomás, **4:**109; **6:**237
Herrera, Joe, **1:**315
Herrick, James, **2:**53

Herrnstein, Richard J., **1:**194
The Bell Curve, **7:**13
Herron, George, **2:**164
Hersey, John, **6:**92
Hershberger, W. D., **7:**14
Hershey, Alfred D., **3:**533
Hershey, Milton S., **6:**279
Hershey Chocolate Company, **6:**279
Herskovits, Melville J., **1:**193; **2:**457
Herter Brothers, **3:**497
Hertz, Heinrich, **7:**19
Herzl, Theodore, **8:**591
Hesse, Eva, **1:**307, 309
Hesselius, Gustavus, **1:**294
Hesselius, John, **1:**294
Hessians. *See* German mercenaries
Hetch Hetchy Valley dam,
 2:368–369
HEW. *See* Health, Education, and
 Welfare, Department of
Hewitt, Don, **8:**73
Heye, George Gustav, **5:**547
Hezbollah, hostages taken by, **4:**174
Hezeta, Bruno, **2:**303
HF. *See* Heritage Foundation
HGP. *See* Human Genome Project
H-Hour, **2:**507
HHS. *See* Health and Human Ser-
 vices, Department of
*Hialeah, Church of the Lukumi Babalu
 Aye, Inc. v.*, **3:**374
Hibbens, Ann, **8:**494
Hickok, James Butler (Wild Bill),
 3:508; **4:**110–111
Hicks, Edward, **1:**295
Hicks, Elias, **7:**2
Hicks, Karen, **2:***493*
Hidalgo y Costilla, Miguel, **5:**50
Hidatsa Indians, **5:**219–220, *220*;
 8:218
 Fort Laramie Treaty with, text of,
 9:227–229
 Lewis and Clark expedition and,
 5:219
Hidden Persuaders, The (Packard),
 4:130
Hide and tallow trade, **4:130**
Hiezer, Michael, **1:**307
Higginbotham, A. Leon, **8:**340
Higgins, Andrew Jackson, **5:**161
Higgins, Mary, **1:***6*
Higgins, Patillo, **6:**302, 305
Higginson, Henry L., **8:**38
Higgison, Stephen, **3:**255

"High" milling, **3:**390
High Plains, **6:**28
High schools
 in 19th century, **3:**114
 in 20th century, **1:**25
 football played at, **3:**410
 freedom of speech, Supreme Court
 on, **1:**26
 intelligence testing in, **4:**379
 introduction of, **2:**144
 peer culture in, **1:**25
 sex education in, **7:321–322**
High-energy physics, **6:338–339**
Higher criticism, **4:130–131**
Higher Education Act (1965), **8:**61
Higher-law doctrine, **4:131–132**
Highland Games, **8:**154, 155
Highland Rim, **8:**83
"Highlanders," **8:**83
Highway(s)
 cross-continent, **7:***179*
 and trucking industry, **7:**178–179
 See also Interstate highway system;
 Roads; Transportation
Highway Act (1956), **8:**286
Highway Act (1962), **3:**335
Highway Beautification Act (1965),
 1:34; **4:132**
Highway Trust Fund, **3:**511
Hijacking
 of *Achille Lauro*, **1:**13
 of airplanes, **4:132–133**
Hilgard, Ernest R., **6:**525
Hilgemeier, Edward, **7:**6
Hill, Ambrose P.
 in Battle of Antietam, **1:**200
 in Battle of Gettysburg, **3:**566–567
 in Battle of Spotsylvania Court-
 house, **7:**512
 in Battles of the Wilderness, **8:**477
Hill, Anita, **3:**198, 221; **5:**549; **7:**323;
 8:121, *121*
Hill, Carla, **8:**507
Hill, David B., **3:**158
Hill, Isaac, **3:**146
Hill, James J., **1:**168; **6:**135
Hill, Joe, **4:**348, *348*
Hill, TVA v., **3:**206
Hillard, Henry W., **1:**102
Hill-Burton Act (1947), **5:**304
Hillerman, Tony, **5:**130
Hillman, Sidney, **1:**132, 151; **3:**163;
 5:17
Hillquit, Morris, **7:**426

Hillsborough Convention (1788),
 6:128
Himes, Chester, **5:**122
 If He Hollers Let Him Go, **5:**125
Himes, Joshua V., **1:**30
Himmelfarb, Gertrude, **8:**326
Hinckley, Gordon B., **5:**55
Hinckley, John, Jr., **1:**331; **2:**79
Hinduism, **4:***133*, 133–134; **7:**91, 94
 forms of, **1:**326; **4:**133
Hine, Lewis, **1:**300
Hines, John, **3:**243
Hinmahtooyahlatkekht (Nez Perce
 leader), **6:**101, 102
Hinneys, **5:**472
*Hints on Household Taste in Furniture,
 Upholstery and Other Details*
 (Eastlake), **3:**497
Hipert, Johann Gottfried, **8:**153
Hippies, **2:***433*; **4:134**, *134*
 and cults, **2:**477
 and recycling, **7:**66
 and Utopian communities, **8:**303
 and Woodstock, **8:**524
Hippocratic Oath, **1:**461
Hirabayashi v. United States, **3:**272;
 4:461
Hiroshima (Japan), atomic bombing
 of, **1:**494; **3:**302; **5:**222; **6:**143;
 8:551, 555
Hirsch, E. D., Jr., **2:**478, 483
Hirsch, Joseph, **1:**298
Hirschfeld, Magnus, **7:**326
Hirschman, Albert O., **3:**110
Hispanic Americans, **4:134–136**
 in baseball, **1:**422
 in California
 Los Angeles riots of 1992, **7:**165
 Proposition 187 and, **4:**229;
 6:509
 Chicano movement among,
 9:484–486
 as farmhands, **3:**327, *327*
 gender roles of, **3:**520
 in Illinois, Chicago, **2:**133
 immigration patterns of, **4:**135
 in Iowa, **4:**417
 as law students, **5:**58
 military service of, **5:383–384**
 nativist movements against, **6:**5
 in New Jersey, **6:**63–64
 in New Mexico, **6:**68, 69
 number of, **4:**134
 in old age, **6:**189

in Oregon, **6**:207
poverty rate of, **6**:437
steelworkers, compensation of, **8**:278
in Texas, **8**:103
in trade unions, **8**:172
in Virginia, **8**:346
women, **3**:520; **5**:531
Hispaniola, Napoleon's ambitions for, **5**:163
Hiss, Alger, **4**:*136*
espionage case against, **4:136–137**, 178; **5**:182; **7**:113
Historic preservation, **6**:452–453
Antiquities Act on, **1**:205–206
of archives, **1**:255–256
National Trust for Historic Preservation and, **5:562**
of Native American heritage, **1**:240
national park system and, **5**:550
and tourism, **8**:146
Historic Sites Act (1935), **5**:551; **6**:452
Historical and Statistical information Respecting the History, Condition, and Prospects of the Indian Tribes of the United States (Schoolcraft), **5**:128
Historiography, American, **3**:257; **4:137–143**
History (academic discipline)
American Historical Association and, **1:158–159**
consensus, **4**:139
history of field, **4:137–143**
postmodern, **4**:141–142
Progressive, **4**:138–139
radical, **4**:140
as science, **4**:138
of slavery, **4**:140
social sciences and, **4**:139–140
statistics in, **7**:539
women's and gender, **4**:141
History and Present State of Virginia, The (Beverly), **1**:191; **9**:109–111
History of England from the Accession of James II (Macaulay), **6**:537
History of Experimental Psychology, A (Boring), **6**:526
History of New England, The (Winthrop), **8**:576
History of New York, A (Irving), **5**:118
History of Psychology, A (Brett), **6**:525
History of Science (journal), **6**:526

History of the Navy of the United States of America (Cooper), **6**:290
Hitchcock, Edward, **3**:548, 549
Hitchcock, Ethan Allen, **7**:55
Hitchcock, Henry-Russell, **1**:249, 251; **8**:326
Hitchcock, Lambert, **3**:496
Hitchcock, Lone Wolf v., **5:147–148**
Hitchhiker's Guide to the Galaxy, The (Adams), **2**:338
Hitchman Coal and Coke Company v. Mitchell, **8**:579
Hitler, Adolf
and Battle of the Bulge, **1**:565–566
Ford (Henry) and, **1**:207
National Socialist German Workers' Party of, **3**:562
rise to power of, **8**:543
after Versailles settlement, **8**:249
HIV. *See* Acquired Immune Deficiency Syndrome; Human immunodeficiency virus
Hmong Americans, **7**:471
HMOs. *See* Health maintenance organizations
Ho Chi Minh, **3**:534; **8**:330
Ho Chi Minh Trail, **8**:*329*, 330, 332, 333
Hoard, William D., **2**:490; **8**:491
Hoare-Laval Pact, **5**:65
Hoban, James, **2**:49; **8**:470
Hobart, Garret A., **3**:158
Hobart, John H., **6**:222
Hobbes, Thomas, **3**:248; **5**:92; **7**:431
on leisure, **8**:526
Hobby, Oveta Culp, **4**:113; **8**:*503*, 507; **9**:398–401
Hobby, William P., **3**:354
Hoboken (New Jersey), **6**:62
Hobson, James, **8**:240
Hobson, Richmond Pearson, **5**:325
Hochschild, Arlie, **3**:519
Ho-Chunk. *See* Winnebago/Ho-Chunk
Hockey, **4**:*143*, **143–145**
development of, **4**:143, 209–210
professional leagues for, **4**:143–145
Hodge, Archibald Alexander, **1**:449
Hodge, Charles, **7**:97
Hodges, Courtney, **1**:1
Hodur, Francis, **6**:391
Hoe rotary press, **6**:*468*, 469
Hoen, August, **2**:61
Hoff, Philip, **8**:314

Hoffa, James P. (Jimmy), **4**:386, *387*; **5**:183; **8**:172
Hoffer, Eric, **8**:340
Hoffman, Julius J., **2**:135
Hoffman, Malvina, **1**:308
Hoffman, Paul G., **8**:166
Hoffman, William, **6**:474
Hoffmann, Heinrich, **1**:313
Hofmann, Hans, **1**:298
Hofstadter, Richard, **4**:139
on third parties, **8**:118
Hog(s), **4:145–146**
commercial production of, **4**:145–146
disease in, **8**:320
as introduced species, **4**:145
in Iowa, **4**:415
Hog cholera, **8**:320
Hogarth, William, **2**:308; **6**:393
Hogg, Ima, **2**:272
Hohokam, **1**:244; **4**:146
O'odham and, **1**:100
Holand, Hjalmar Rued, **4**:516–517
Holbrook, John Edwards, **4**:129
Holbrook, Josiah, **5**:178
HOLC. *See* Home Owners' Loan Corporation
Holcombe, James P., **6**:266
Holden, William W., **6**:129
Holden v. Hardy, **1**:21; **3**:308; **5**:14, 139
Holding companies, **4:146–148**; **6**:535
advantages of, **4**:147
in aircraft industry, **1**:93
definition of, **4**:146–147
public utility, investment companies and, **4**:411–412
regulation of, **4**:147
rise of, **4**:147
Holiday Inns, **7**:53
Holidays and festivals, **4:148–149**
Christmas, **2**:166
in colonial era, **4**:148–149
controversy over, **4**:148
family, **7**:64
and fast days, **3**:328–329
Father's Day, **5**:463
Independence Day, **4**:149, *256*, **256–257**
Kwanzaa, **4**:148, **553**
Mardi Gras, **5**:238
May Day, **5**:275
Memorial Day, **5:306–307**, *307*

Holidays and festivals, (*continued*)
  Mother's Day, **5:**463
  music festivals, **5:**501–502
  and nationalism, **5:**568
  origins of, **4:**148
  Thanksgiving Day, **3:**328–329;
    8:112
Holiness movement, **3:**265; **8:**302
Holistic healing, **6:**462–463
Holladay, Ben, **5:**204; **6:**220–221;
  7:515
Holland. *See* Dutch; Netherlands
Holland (ship), **6:**25
Holland, John P., **7:**562, *563*
Holland Tunnel, **8:**240
Hollerith, Herman, **6:**169
Holley, Alexander, **4:**427
Holley, Myron, **1:**211
Holliday, Doc, **8:**141
Hollinger, David, **1:**338
Hollywood, **4:**149–150
  Academy Awards and, **6:**485–486
  and fashion, **2:**247
  Golden Age of, **2:**390
  television industry in, **4:**209
  See also Film industry
Hollywood Ten, **1:**483
  blacklisting of, **5:**183
Holm, Jean, **8:**504
Holm, Thomas Campanius, **2:**234
Holman, Frank E., **1:**537
Holme, Thomas, city plan for
  Philadelphia, **2:**184
Holmes, Arthur, **6:**344
Holmes, John Haynes, **1:**146
Holmes, Joseph A., **5:**391
Holmes, Larry, **6:**485
Holmes, Oliver Wendell, Jr.
  agnosticism of, **1:**55
  on antitrust legislation, **1:**214
  on censorship, **2:**84
  "clear and present danger test"
    established by, **3:**374; **7:**264
  on commerce clause, **2:**311
  The Common Law, **2:**317
  on due process of law, **3:**90
  on eminent domain, **3:**198
  on Espionage and Sedition Acts,
    3:254
  on eugenics, **3:**258
  existential perspective of, **3:**280
  on judicial review, **4:**492
  on Migration Bird Treaty Act, **8:**481
  on minimum-wage legislation, **1:**21

on police power, **6:**387
on regulatory takings, **6:**505
Holmes, Oliver Wendell, "Old Iron-
  sides," **2:**378
*Holmes County Board of Education,
  Alexander v.*, **1:**122
Holmes v. Walton, **4:**150
Holocaust
  anti-Semitism and, **1:**207
  refugees from, **4:**226–227
Holocaust Museum, **4:***150*, **150–151**
Holt, Henry, **1:**389; **2:**497
Holt, John (home schooling advo-
  cate), **4:**153
Holt, John C. (combine inventor),
  1:59
Holt, Nancy, **1:**307
Holton, A. Linwood, **8:**344
Holy Cross, Priests of, **4:**151
Holy Experiment, **4:**151
Holyfield, Evander, **6:**485
*Holyfield, Mississippi Band of Choctaw
  Indians v.*, **4:**263
Holzer, Jenny, **1:**299, 307
Home: Social Essays (Baraka), **5:**126
Home Box Office (HBO), **2:**322
*Home Building and Loan Association v.
  Blaisdell et al.* (Minnesota mora-
  torium case), **5:**401
Home Depot, **7:**126
Home economics, **3:**117
Home mortgage loans, **2:**450
Home Owners' Loan Corporation
  (HOLC), **4:151–152**
Home rule, **2:**112, 438–439;
  4:152–153
  in Washington (D.C.), **4:**153;
    8:411–412
Home schooling, **4:153–154**
Home shopping networks, **4:**154
Home Start, **4:**113
Homeland Security, Office of, **2:**191
Homelessness, **6:**437
Homeopathy, **4:154–155**; **5:**291, 301
Homer, **1:**575
Homer, Winslow, **1:**296, 322
  Eight Bells by, **3:**537
  The Gulf Stream by, **4:**73
  printmaking by, **6:**470
  Snap the Whip by, **3:***537*
Homestead Act (1862), **5:**25, 29, 31,
  33–34, 37; **6:**507, 527–528;
  7:33; **8:**463
  agrarianism and, **1:**57

and agricultural development,
  1:64; **5:**29
and land speculation, **5:**36
provisions of, **4:**156
Homestead Act (1872), **5:**35
Homestead Act, Enlarged (1909),
  1:65
Homestead Act, Stock Raising
  (1916), **1:**65
Homestead movement, **1:**64;
  4:155–157
  "Go West, Young Man, Go West"
    and, **4:**9
  in Montana, **5:**450
Homestead strike (1892), **2:**224;
  4:157; **5:**141; **7:**38, 545; **8:**277
  and presidential election of 1892,
    3:158
  violence in, **4:**157; **5:**141; **7:**545,
    556; **8:**339
Homesteaders
  and cattle industry, **4:157–158**
  subsistence, **7:566–567**
Homesteading, urban, **8:**287
Homework, **4:158–159**
Homma, Masaharu, **1:**427; **5:**115
Homologous transplantation, **8:**182
Homosexuality
  anticommunists on, **3:**513
  Boy Scout position on, **1:**527
  communism and, **7:**326
  Kinsey Report on, **4:**531;
    7:326–327
  legislation on, **7:**326, 327
  and male prostitution, **6:**514
  military on, **3:**513
  plays dealing with, **8:**115
  Salvation Army on, **7:**234
  Uniform Code of Military Justice
    on, **8:**256
  See also Gay and lesbian movement;
    Gays and lesbians; Sexual ori-
    entation
Honduras
  dollar diplomacy in, **3:**71
  Nicaraguan contras in, **2:**395
Hong Kong, immigration from,
  2:155–156
Honky-tonk girls, **4:**159
Honolulu (Hawaii), **4:159–160**
  diversity in, **4:**160
  population density in, **4:**159–160
Hood, John B., **2:**214, 506
  and Army of Tennessee, **8:**87

in Atlanta Campaign, **1:**351
in Battle of Nashville, **5:**516
in Tennessee Campaign, **4:160**
Hood, Raymond, **1:**252; **7:**376
Hook, Sidney, **6:**445
Hooker, Evelyn, **7:**327
Hooker, Joseph
  in Battle of Antietam, **1:**200
  at Battle of Chancellorsville, **2:**104
  at Battle of Fredericksburg, **2:**213
  and Battle on Lookout Mountain,
    5:151
  in Chattanooga campaign, **2:**113
  and invasion of Pennsylvania,
    6:280
  replaced by Meade, **3:**566
Hooker, Thomas, **2:**289, 357;
    7:95–96; **8:**459
Hooker Chemical Company, and
    Love Canal, **5:**164
Hooker Jim, **5:**433
Hooker Telescope, **6:***156*
Hoosac Tunnel, **4:**161, *161*; **8:**240
Hoosiers, **4:**318–319
Hoover, Edgar J., on Castro, **2:**470
Hoover, Herbert
  and American Relief Administra-
    tion, **8:**541
  banking reform under, **7:**256
  and Belgian Relief, **1:**439
  Bonus Army and, **1:**498, 499
  and "Chicken in Every Pot" slo-
    gan, **2:**136
  and China, relations with, **2:**151
  as commerce secretary, **2:**310
  economic policies of, **5:**55
  and employment service, **3:**201
  and engineering societies, **3:**218
  Great Depression policies of, **8:**440
  in Hoover Commissions, **4:**161
  and Hoover Dam, **4:**161–162
  Indian policies of, **1:**571
  Latin American policies of, **5:**47
  on military pensions, **6:**285
  moratorium on debt (1931), **5:456**
  on philanthropy, **6:**318
  in presidential campaign of 1928,
    3:162
  in presidential campaign of 1932,
    3:162
  presidential library of, **5:**100
  public land commission appointed
    by, **6:**531
  pump-priming by, **6:**551

and Reconstruction Finance Cor-
    poration, **7:**62
  and Republican Party, **7:**113
  at Stanford University, **7:**523
  and tariffs, **8:**52
  and taxation, **8:**58
  and White House visits, **8:**471
  and Wickersham Commission,
    8:475
Hoover, J. Edgar
  anarchism and, **1:**181
  and COINTELPRO, **2:**266
  as director of FBI, **3:**337–338
  and Palmer Raids, **3:**337; **6:**232
  on wartime internment, **4:**400
Hoover, Lou Henry, **3:**376
Hoover, W. H., **3:**182
Hoover Commissions, **4:161**
Hoover Dam, **2:**10; **3:**211;
    4:161–162, *162, 200*; **7:**56
  and economy of Nevada, **6:**38
Hoover Moratorium, **8:**543
Hope of Liberty, The (Horton), **5:**124
Hopewell (Virginia), **1:**502
Hopewell culture, **1:**247; **4:162–164**
Hopi, **4:164–166**
  agriculture among, **4:**165
  clans of, **4:**164
  education among, **4:**165
  emergence story of, **4:**164
  gambling by, **3:**507
  language of, **4:**165–166
  marriage among, **4:**164, *165*
  population of, **4:**165
  on reservation, **8:**228
  villages of, **4:***164*, 164–165
Hopkins, Harry L., **2:**138; **5:**82;
    8:197, 530, 531
  as commerce secretary, **2:**310
  and Federal Emergency Relief
    Administration, **8:**440
  and Works Progress Administra-
    tion, **2:**371; **8:**441
Hopkins, John P., **6:**549
Hopkins, Johns, **4:**482
Hopkins, Pauline, **5:**124
Hopkins, Samuel, **3:**140; **7:**96
Hopkins, Sarah Winnemucca, **6:**231;
    8:217
Hopkins, Yick Wo v., **1:**125, 324;
    2:155
Hopkins Marine Station, **5:**240, 241
Hopkinson, Joseph, **2:**302

Hopper, Edward, **1:**297; **6:**471;
    8:474, 475
Hopperdozer, **4:**37
Hopwood v. State of Texas, **1:**386
Hopwood v. Texas, **1:**37
Horiuchi, Lon, **7:**203
Horizontal Tariff Bill (1872), **4:166**
Horkheimer, Max, **3:**454
Hornaday, William Temple, **8:**594
Hornbook, **4:***166*, **166–167**; **8:**106
Horner, Charles, **1:**77
Hornet (aircraft carrier), **1:***90*
Hornig, Donald F., **1:**548
Horowitz, Daniel, **3:**353
Horr, Alexander, **8:**303
Horse(s), **4:167–169**
  American breeds of, **4:**167–168,
    168
  disease in, **8:**319
  economics of industry, **4:**169
  gypsies trading, **4:**78
  introduction of, **4:**167, 324
  legal protection of, **4:**168–169
  mustangs, **5:**504
  of Native Americans, **4:**167,
    324–325; **8:**222, 224
    and Blackfeet culture, **1:**481
    and culture, **1:**562; **2:**297
    and social life, **4:**304, 305
    and Ute culture, **8:**299
    and Yakama culture, **8:**571
  racing, **4:**168, **169–171**; **7:**510
    gambling on, **4:**170–171
  saddles for, **7:221–222**
  showing, **4:**169–171
  stealing, **4:171–172**
  transportation by, **4:**167
  uses for, **4:**167, 168
Horse catarrh, **8:**319
Horse cavalry, **2:77–78**
Horse Marines, **4:**169
Horse Protection Act (HPA) (1970),
    4:168
Horse-drawn vehicles, **2:**59–60
Horsford, Eben N., **5:**59
Horsmanden, Daniel, **6:**85
Horst, Louis, **2:**498
Horstmann, Dorothy, **6:**388
Horti, Paul, **3:**498
Horton, George Moses, *The Hope of
    Liberty*, **5:**124
Horton, James Edwin, **7:**286
Horton, Lester, **1:**131
Horvitz, Wayne, **3:**343

Horwitz, Morton, **2:**43
Hosack, David, **1:**516
Hosmer, Harriet, **1:**308
Hospitals, **4:172–174**
  Civil War, **2:**216
  costs in, **4:**173–174
  insurance and, **4:**173–174
  Johns Hopkins, **4:**482
  nurses in, **6:**147
  and patients' rights, **6:**257
  physician assistants in, **6:**334
  rise of, **4:**115, 172
  specialization in, **4:**172–173
  surgery in, **4:**173
Hostage crises, **4:174**
  on *Achille Lauro*, **1:13**
  Iran hostage crisis, **4:**174, 252, 418, **420–421**
    firsthand account of, **9:**494–495
Hostile takeovers, **5:**322, 323
"Hot Oil" case. *See Panama Refining Company v. Ryan*
Hot springs
  in Utah, **8:**295
  in Yellowstone National Park, **8:**580
"Hot type," **6:**469
Hot Wheels, **8:**153
Hotchkiss, Hazel, **8:**90
Hotel Del Coronado, **8:**305
Hotel Del Monte, **8:**305
Hotel Dieu Convent, **5:**238
Hotelling, Harold, **3:**110
Hotels and hotel industry, **4:174–177**
  in 19th century, **4:**175–176
  in 20th century, **4:**176–177
  in colonial era, **4:**175
  origins of, **7:**52–53
  resort, **7:***121*, 122
  types of, **4:**175–176
  in Virginia, **8:**346
  in West, **8:**305
Hottinguer, Jean, **8:**570
Hotze, Henry, **2:**342
Houdon, Jean-Antoine, **1:**305
Hough, Franklin B., **3:**430
Houghton, Walter, **8:**326
Houma, **4:177**
Hour of Power, The (TV show), **8:**71
Hours. *See* Wages and hours of labor
House, Edward M., **3:**277
  and Armistice of November 1918, **1:**265
  and House-Grey Memorandum, **4:**179

House Committee on Un-American Activities (HUAC), **1:**198; **4:178; 6:5; 7:17**
  ACLU investigated by, **1:**147
  on communist infiltration, **4:**411; **8:**1–2
  of film industry, **4:**178; **5:**183
  Disney's testimony before, text of, **9:**413–417
  on executive privilege, **4:**178
  Hiss case in, **4:**136, 178
  investigation process, **5:**182–183
  loyalty hearings in, **4:**178
  and National Lawyers Guild, **5:**546–547
  Nixon in, **1:**197; **4:**178
House Divided speech, Lincoln's, **4:178–179**
  text of, **9:**284–286
House Made of Dawn (Momaday), **4:179; 5:**129
House of Burgesses, **1:**333; **2:**280, 314; **4:179; 8:**342, 348, 349
House of Commons, **6:**251–252
House of Industry, **2:**138
House of Lords, **6:**251
House of Representatives, U.S., **2:**350–351; **3:**341
  apportionment in, **1:**227
  appropriations by, **1:**229
  caucuses in, **2:**77
    Black Caucus in, **1:**471
  Committee on Ways and Means, **2:**352; **8:432**
  congressional districts represented by, **3:62**
  in impeachment, **4:**234
    of Chase, **4:**241
    of Clinton, **2:**240; **4:**235, 240
    of Johnson, **4:**236–237
  intelligence oversight by, **4:**377
  membership denied by, **6:**441
  presidential elections decided by, **3:**152, 171
  Reed Rules adopted by, **7:73**
  rules of, **7:203–204**
  Speaker of, **2:**351, 352; **7:493**
  system of representation in, **3:**170; **7:**106–108
House of Wax (film), **3:**364
House Un-American Activities Committee. *See* House Committee on Un-American Activities

House-Grey Memorandum (1916), **4:179**
Household manufacturing, **5:229–230**
Household production, **2:**44, 45
Houser, Allan, **1:**315
Housing, **4:179–183**
  air conditioning in, **1:**74
  apartments, **1:222–224; 4:**182
  building materials, **1:563–565**
  in colonial era, **4:**179–180
  cost of, **4:**182
  discrimination in, prohibition of, **2:**200
  dugout, **3:**93
  federal government and, **2:**187–188
  Federal Housing Administration and, **7:**256
  heating for, **4:122–123**
  Home Owners' Loan Corporation and, **4:**151–152
  home ownership rates for, **4:**152, 182–183
  kitchens in, **4:534–536**
  in Levittown, **5:***85*, 85–86
  low-income, **6:**438
  mass production of, **7:**574
  Native American, **4:**179; **8:**475
    Inuit, **4:***408*
    Iroquois, **4:**431
  in New York City, **6:**80; **8:**81–82
  plumbing, **6:371–373**, *372*
  public, **8:**293
    debacle of 1950s, **8:**286–287
  segregation in, **4:**182; **7:**302
  suburban, **4:**181, 182; **7:**574
  tenements, **8:81–83**, *82*
  trailer parks, **8:178**
  urban redevelopment and, **2:**188; **8:285–288**
  after World War II, **4:**181–182
  between world wars, **4:**181
  See also Architecture
Housing Act (1949), Title I of, **8:**285
Housing Act (1954), **4:**355
  Title III of, **8:**285
Housing and Community Development Act (1974), **8:**287
Housing and Urban Development, Department of (HUD), **2:**188; **3:**331; **4:183; 6:**438
  establishment of, **4:**183
  functions of, **4:**183

head of, **2**:2
municipal government, housing projects and, **5**:475
Housing Choice Voucher Program, **6**:438
Housing cooperatives, **2**:406
Houston (Texas), **4**:*184*, **184–186**, *185*; **8**:103
Houston, Charles Hamilton, **5**:526
and *Brown* case, **1**:549
Houston, E. J., **3**:173
Houston, Sam, **1**:106, 107; **4**:185; **7**:99
in Battle of San Jacinto, **7**:240–241
as president of Republic of Texas, **8**:100
and secession by Texas, **8**:101
and Texas Rangers, **8**:104
Hoving, Thomas, **5**:337
How the Other Half Lives (Riis), **1**:299–300; **5**:166; **6**:80; **8**:82
"How to Make Our Ideas Clear" (Peirce), **6**:445
How to Win Friends and Influence People (Carnegie), **4**:186
Howard, A. W., **3**:391
Howard, Sir Albert, **6**:210
Howard, Ebenezer, **2**:186
Howard, Edward, **2**:242
Howard, Fort, **4**:186
Howard, Jesse, **1**:312
Howard, Oliver O., **3**:125
at Battle of Chancellorsville, **2**:104
in Battle of Gettysburg, **3**:567
as commissioner of Freedmen's Bureau, **3**:462
and Nez Perces, **6**:102
Howard Stern Show (radio program), **8**:45
Howard University, **1**:50; **8**:263
Department of Education and, **3**:123
establishment of, **3**:125
Howe, Elias, Jr., **2**:246; **7**:320
Howe, George, **1**:252
Howe, Irving, **2**:189; **5**:121
Howe, Julia Ward, **1**:429; **4**:100
Howe, Oscar, **1**:315
Howe, Richard, **7**:143; **9**:33
Howe, Samuel Gridley, **1**:429, 509; **2**:508; **3**:34; **6**:333
Howe, Sir William, **1**:569, 574; **7**:142, 143–144
in Battle of Long Island, **5**:150

in Battle of Oriskany, **6**:213
in Battle of Trenton, **8**:208
in Battle of White Plains, **8**:473
Howell, David, **8**:208
Howell, Mary, **8**:511
Howell, William, **6**:349
Howells, William Dean, **1**:351; **8**:292
Rise of Silas Lapham, **6**:12
Howlin' Wolf, **7**:185
Hoyt, Jesse, **2**:485
Hoyt v. Florida, **8**:60
HPA. *See* Horse Protection Act
Hsu, Francis L. K., **1**:138
Hsuan-hua, **1**:326
Hu Yaobang, **8**:123
HUAC. *See* House Committee on Un-American Activities
Hualapais, **8**:228
Hubbard, Gardiner Greene, **5**:541
Hubbard, L. Ron, **7**:283
Hubbard, William, **9**:14
Hubbell, Webster, and exclusionary clubs, **2**:251
Hubble, Edwin, **1**:344
Hubble Space Telescope, **1**:345; **4**:186–187, *187*; **6**:157
virtual reality and, **8**:350
Hubert, Philip G., **1**:223
Huckabee, Mike, **1**:263
Huckleberry Finn (Twain), **4**:187; **5**:119, 120, 127; **8**:325
HUD. *See* Housing and Urban Development, Department of
Hudson, Henry, **3**:286, 289; **6**:71, 87
colonial settlements following, **2**:289
discovery of Delaware River by, **2**:540
on Hudson River, **4**:187
river exploration by, **7**:173
ship used by, **4**:86–87
Hudson, Rock, **1**:17
Hudson River, **3**:286, 289; **4**:187–188, *188*; **6**:86; **7**:173
exploration of, **6**:71, 87
steamboat traffic on, **3**:483
tunnels under, **8**:240
Hudson River School, **4**:188–190
Hudson's Bay Company (HBC), **1**:434–435; **3**:289, 489–490; **4**:190
and Columbia River, overexploitation of, **2**:303
and exploration of Pacific Northwest, **8**:453

North West Company and, **3**:487; **6**:134–135
as royal monopoly, **3**:487
trading posts established by, **7**:124; **8**:175–176
Huerta, Dolores, **5**:*3*; **8**:266
Huerta, Victoriano, **7**:57
and Veracruz incident, **1**:1; **8**:311
Hughes, Charles Evans
in American Bar Association, **1**:145
on commerce clause, **2**:311
and Four-Power Treaty, **3**:446
on labor relations, **8**:445
on National Industrial Recovery Act, **7**:264
in presidential campaign of 1916, **3**:161
at Washington Naval Conference, **8**:418
Hughes, George, **3**:181
Hughes, Henry, **7**:431–432
Hughes, Howard, **1**:83
Hughes, John, **2**:68, 69; **3**:114
on religion in public schools, **2**:167
and religious learning, **7**:97
Hughes, Langston, **2**:205; **4**:96; **5**:121, 125, *125*
Hughson, John, **6**:85
Huguenots, **4**:190–191
Huizar, Pedro, **1**:249
Hulbert, William, **1**:419
Hull, Cordell, **1**:560; **4**:458; **5**:47, 482; **8**:86
on *Panay* incident, **6**:244
and reciprocal trade agreements, **7**:54
and tariffs, **3**:460–461; **8**:156
Hull, Jane, **1**:259
Hull, William, **3**:21; **8**:383
Hull-House, **2**:132; **6**:317, 440; **7**:317–318, *318*, 414; **8**:114
Hull-House Maps and Papers (survey), **6**:533
Human Experimentation. *See* Clinical Research
Human Gene Therapy Subcommittee, **3**:531
Human Genome Project (HGP), **3**:533; **4**:191–192
Human immunodeficiency virus (HIV), **1**:15; **3**:241
prostitution and, **6**:514
See also Acquired immune deficiency syndrome

Human Physiology (Dunglison), **6:**348
Human resources management,
    4:337–338
  See also Industrial relations
Human rights, **4:192–194**
  evolution of concept, **4:**192–194
  in Haiti, **4:**85
  international institutions for,
    4:193–194
  religious freedom as, **4:**193
  State Department reports on,
    4:192–193
  torture and, **4:**194
  for women, **4:**193
    original documents on,
      9:327–329
  for workers, **4:**194
Humane Slaughter Act (1958), **1:**185
Humanistic psychology, **6:**525
Humanities councils, **5:**537
Humboldt, Alexander von, **3:**541,
    551
Humboldt River, **6:**37
Hume, David, **3:**108, 262
  on divorce, **3:**65
Humiliation days, **3:**328–329
Hummert, Anne, **7:**409
Hummert, Frank, **7:**409
Humphrey, Hubert H., **5:**400
  in presidential campaign of 1964,
    3:165
  in presidential campaign of 1968,
    2:204; **3:**165, 166
  in presidential campaign of 1972,
    3:166; **8:**425
Humphrey, William E., **4:**194–195
  firing of, **7:**101
Humphrey-Hawkins Act. *See* Full
    Employment and Balanced
    Growth Act (1978)
Humphrey's Executor v. United States,
    4:194–195; **3:**348; **7:**101
Humphry, John, **6:**518
Huncke, Herbert, **1:**433
Hundred, **4:195**
Hungarian Reformed church, **7:**76
Hungary
  1956 revolt in, **6:**504
  after Cold War, **2:**90–91
  independence after World War I,
    2:89
  liberation movement in, **2:**88–89
  "most favored nation" status to,
    8:198

refugees from, **2:***90*
Hunger, **6:**437
Hunkers, **2:**400; **4:195**
Hunt, Commonwealth v., **2:319**
Hunt, E. Howard, Jr., **8:**425, 426,
  427
Hunt, Freeman, **2:**514
Hunt, J. B., **1:**263
Hunt, Lamar, **3:**411
Hunt, Richard Morris, **1:**222, 249
Hunt, William Morris, **1:**297, 319
Hunt, Wilson Price, **1:**342, 452
Hunter, David, **3:**190; **5:**230–231
  in Shenandoah Campaign, **7:**341
Hunter, Robert, **6:**436, 440
Hunter, Robert M. T., **2:**341
Hunter's Lessee, Martin v., **2:**381;
  5:255
Hunting
  Native American
    prehistoric, **1:**242, 244–245
    technology in, **4:**307
  recreational, **7:**64
Huntington, Anna Hyatt, **1:**308, *309*
Huntington, Collis, **8:**181
Huntington, Ellsworth, **2:**371; **3:**543
Huntington, Henry Edwards, **1:**517;
  4:195–196; **7:**42
Huntington, Samuel P., **6:**405
Huntington Botanical Gardens,
  1:517
Huntington Library and Museum,
  4:195–196
Huntington's disease, genetics of,
  4:191
Huntsville (Alabama), **1:**105
Hupa, **8:**221
Hurd, Clement, **5:**128
Hurok, Sol, **1:**390
Huron/Wyandot, **4:***196*, **196–197**
  and Champlain explorations, **2:**103
  and fur trade, **3:**488–489
Hurrell, George, **1:**300
Hurricanes, **3:**42, 43; **4:197–198**
  and floods, **3:**383
  in Galveston, **3:***505*, 506; **8:**102
  and insurance industry, **4:**372
  in Rhode Island, **7:**153
Hurston, Zora Neale, **2:**205; **3:**396;
  4:95, *95*; **5:**121, 124, 125
  Jonah's Gourd Vine, **5:**125
  Mules and Men, **5:**125
  Their Eyes Were Watching God,
    5:125

Hurtado v. California, **4:198**
Hus, Jan, **6:**515
Huss, Magnus, **1:**118
Hussein, Saddam
  Iraq-gate and, **4:**421–422
  in Persian Gulf War, **1:**77;
    6:292–293
Husserl, Emund, **3:**279
Hussey, Obed, **1:**58; **5:**183
Hutcheson, Joseph, **2:**317
Hutcheson, William L., **8:**263
Hutchins, Robert M., **4:**40; **8:**281
  and *Encyclopaedia Britannica*, **3:**204
Hutchins, Thomas, **2:**62; **3:**540
Hutchinson, Anne, **1:**508; **5:**271,
  506; **8:**494, 501
  in Antinomian controversy, **1:**205;
    5:271
  mysticism of, **5:**506
  trial of, **1:**205
    transcript of, **9:**87–89
Hutchinson, Charles L., **1:**316
Hutchinson, Francis, **6:**83
Hutchinson, Thomas, **1:**513, 515;
  5:167
  impact on struggle for indepen-
    dence, **4:**254
  letters of, **4:199**
Hutchison, Kay Bailey, **6:**292
Hutter, Jakob, **8:**301
Hutterites, **8:**301–302, 304
Huxley, Aldous, *Brave New World*,
  8:599
Huxley, Thomas H., **1:**55; **6:**423
Hyatt, John Wesley, **6:**366
Hybrid cars, **1:**79
Hyde, Henry, **4:**100
Hyde Amendment, **4:**100
Hydroelectric power, **3:**214;
  4:199–203, *203*; **8:**428
  economics of, **4:**202
  future of, **4:**202–203
  geographic distribution of, **4:**202
  growth of, **3:**175
  and Johnstown flood, **4:**483–484
  Niagara Falls and, **6:**103
  in North Carolina, **6:**130
  vs. nuclear power, **6:**139
  origins of, **4:**199–200
  regulation of, **4:**201–202
  Tennessee River and, **8:**87, 88
  types of installations, **4:**199
  in Wyoming, **8:**565
Hydrogen atom, **6:**341

Hydrogen bomb, **4:**203–204; **6:**144, 342
  in arms race, **1:**271
Hydroponics, **4:**204
Hygiene, **4:**204–206
  bathtubs and bathing, **1:**427–428
Hygienic Laboratory, **5:**544
Hylton, Ware v., **8:**390
Hylton v. United States, **4:**206, 251
Hymns and hymnody, **4:**206–207
  America the Beautiful, **1:**139
  in eighteenth century, **5:**494
  "My Country, Tis of Thee," **5:**505
  psalm singing, **5:**491

I

I, the Jury (Spillane), **5:**130
I AM, **2:**477
I Know Why the Caged Bird Sings (Angelou), **1:**500; **5:**126
I Love Lucy (TV show), **4:**209, *209;* **8:**72
i2 Technologies, **3:**184
IACC. *See* International America's Cup Class
Iacocca, Lee, **1:**374
IAEA. *See* International Atomic Energy Agency
Iberville, Pierre Le Moyne d', **3:**291; **5:**158
IBEW. *See* International Brotherhood of Electrical Workers
IBM (International Business Machines) Corporation, **1:**580; **2:**335
  antitrust suit against, **8:**235
  computers developed by, **2:***334,* 336; **6:**170; **7:**442; **8:**245
  electric typewriter by, **8:**245
  Microsoft and, **5:**360
  office equipment by, **6:**169
  in Vermont, **8:**314
IBT. *See* International Brotherhood of Teamsters
ICAA. *See* Intercollegiate Athletic Association of the United States
ICBMs. *See* Intercontinental ballistic missiles
ICC. *See* Indian Claims Commission; Interstate Commerce Commission

ICCPR. *See* International Covenant on Civil and Political Rights
Ice skating, **4:**209–211, *210*
Icebreakers, **6:**382
Ice-jam floods, **3:**383
Iceland, U.S. forces in, **2:**531; **4:**211
ICFTU. *See* International Confederation of Free Trade Unions
ICJ. *See* International Court of Justice
Ickes, Harold, **2:**371; **5:**31
ICPSR. *See* Inter-University Consortium for Political and Social Research
ICRA. *See* Indian Civil Rights Act
ICRC. *See* International Red Cross Commission
Idaho, **4:**211–214, *212*
  agriculture in, irrigation for, **4:**212, 213
  Coeur d'Alene riots, **2:**264
  Democratic Party in, **4:**213–214
  emblems, nicknames, mottos, and songs of, **7:***532*
  gold mining in, **4:**11, 211
  Great Depression in, **4:**213
  industry in, **4:**212, 213
  lumber production in, **4:**212
  Mormons in, **4:**211, 212
  Native Americans in, **4:**211
  politics in, **4:**213–214
  population of, **4:**211
  railroads in, **4:**212
  Republican Party in, **4:**213–214
  silver mining in, **4:**212, 213; **7:**364
  statehood for, **4:**211–212
  in World War I, **4:**213
  in World War II, **4:**213
IDEA. *See* Individuals with Disabilities Education Act
Identity Christians, **8:**303
Identity theft, **6:**480
Ideographs, **6:**466
IEP. *See* Individualized educational program
If He Hollers Let Him Go (Himes), **5:**125
Igloos, **1:**254
IGRA. *See* Indian Gambling Regulatory Act
IGY. *See* International Geophysical Year
ILA. *See* Institute for Legislative Action

ILD. *See* International Labor Defense
ILGWU. *See* International Ladies Garment Workers Union
I'll Take My Stand: The South and the Agrarian Tradition (article), **3:**481
Illiberal Education (D'Souza), **6:**395
Illinois, **4:**214–218, *215*
  African Americans in, **4:**217
  agriculture in, **4:**216, 217
  alien landholding in, **1:**124
  Cahokia Mounds in, **2:**6, *6–7*
  canals in, **4:**219
  Democratic Party in, **4:**216
  earthquakes in, **3:**101
  emblems, nicknames, mottos, and songs of, **7:***532*
  Farmers' Alliance in, **3:**323
  French colonial settlements in, **6:**53
  gun control in, **4:**74, 75
  industry in, **4:**216, 217
  juvenile courts in, **4:**504–505
  maps of, **4:***215*
    archival, **9:**49, *49*
  in Midwest, **5:**368–369
  Mormons in, **4:**215; **5:**459–460
  Native Americans in, **4:**214–215
  Polish Americans in, **6:**391, 392
  politics in, **4:**215, 216
  population of, **4:**215, 217
  railroads in, **4:**215–216
    regulation of, **4:**35, 36
  Republican Party in, **4:**216
  settlement patterns in, **4:**215
  slavery in, **4:**215, 216
  statehood for, **4:**215
  women in, **4:**217
Illinois, Beauharnais v., **4:**67; **6:**91
Illinois, Munn v., **2:**134; **3:**187; **4:**35, 36; **7:**26
Illinois, Pope v., **6:**419
Illinois, Presser v., **4:**74
Illinois, Wabash, St. Louis, and Pacific Railway Company v., **2:**310; **7:**26, 37
Illinois and Michigan Canal, **2:**132; **4:**219
Illinois Central Railway, **5:**30
Illinois Fur Brigade, **4:**219
Illinois Indians, **4:**218–219, *219;* **8:**224

Illinois State Federation of Labor, **3:**320

Illustrations of Masonry (Morgan), **3:**466

ILO. *See* International Labor Organization

ILWU. *See* International Longshoremen's and Warehousemen's Union

Imanishi-Kari, Thereza, **7:**279

IMF. *See* International Monetary Fund

Immediatism, **1:**209–210; **4:219**

Immigrants
  American Republican Party on, **1:**168
  and American society, **2:**290
  bossism and, **2:**388
  in Boston, **1:**510
  children of, **2:**145
  cholera among, **3:**236–237
  in cities, **5:**4, 165–166
  and class system, **2:**224
  in Cleveland, **2:**233
  in Communist Party, **2:**325, 327
  and cuisine, **3:**399–400, 401, 402
  Democratic Party and, **5:**187
  in Detroit, **3:**20
  employment of, **5:**4–5
  and Erie Canal, building of, **3:**252
  family life of, **3:**313
  as farmhands, **3:***326,* 326–327, *327*
  Federalist Party and, **6:**396
  hostility towards (*See* Nativism)
  illegal
    reducing public services for, **6:**509
    in "sweat shops," **6:**289
  Know-Nothing Party on, **1:**166; **4:**540
  music and, **5:**495
  in New Orleans, **6:**73, 74
  in New York City, **6:**79, 80, 81, 88
  non-Protestant, **6:**516
  objections to (*See* Anti-immigrant sentiment)
  origins of, **5:**4
  political exiles, **6:396–397**
  Progressives and, **6:**496
  and racial conflict, **5:**4–5
  repatriation of, **3:**196
  in settlement houses, **7:**317
  and tenements, **8:**81
  in trade unions
    in American Federation of Labor, **1:**150
    in clothing industry, **1:**132
    in United Automobile Workers union, **8:**261
  YMCA and, **8:**584
  See also Alien(s)

Immigration, **4:219–230**
  in 17th century, **4:**220–222
  in 18th century, **4:**220–222
  in 19th century, **4:***221, 222,* 222–225, *225*
  in 20th century, **4:**220, 224–229, *225, 227, 228;* **5:**5
  in 21st century, **4:**220
  from Africa, **4:**221
  African American, **5:**369 (*See also* Slave trade)
  to American West, **8:**445
  from Arab nations, **1:**230–231
  from Asia, **1:**322, 324; **5:**5
    Southeast, **7:**470–471
  birds of passage and, **1:465**
  and bossism, **1:**507
  of Brethren, **1:**534
  to California, **2:**10
  from Canada, **2:**27
  and Catholicism, **2:**71
  of Catholics, **1:**196; **2:**68
  from China, **2:**150–151, 154–156
  contract labor system and, **2:**397
  of convicts, **2:**401
  from Cuba, **2:**472, 473
    to Florida, **5:**351
    Mariel boatlift, **5:238–239**
  and demographic trends, **2:**556–557
  and deportation, **3:11–12**
  from Eastern Europe, **2:**89; **4:**224–225, 415; **5:**4
    and Lower East Side, **5:**166
  Ellis Island and, **3:188–189,** *189*
  exclusion policies, **3:**207
  from Finland, **7:**262
  to Florida, **3:**388; **5:**351–352
    by Mayan refugees, **9:**509–515
  and foreign-language newspapers, **6:**95, 97
  of French Canadians, **4:**224
  to Georgia, **3:**558
  from Germany, **3:**559–560, 561; **4:**221, 223, 226
    Civil War and, **5:**421
    and Lower East Side, **5:**166
  in Gilded Age, **3:**577
  from Great Britain, **4:**220–221
  from Greece, **4:**59
  and green card, **4:**60–61
  from Guatemala, **9:**509–515
  of gypsies, **4:**78–79
  of Hispanic Americans, **4:**135
  illegal, **4:**228–229
  from India, **1:**324, 325
  industrialization and, **4:**223–226; **5:**4–5
  to Iowa, **4:**415
  from Iran, **4:**421
  from Iraq, **4:**422
  from Ireland, **2:**163; **4:**221, 222–223, 423–425
    and Lower East Side, **5:**166
  from Italy, **4:**225, 444–445, 448
  of Jews, **1:**206–207; **4:**225, 226–227, 476–477, 488–489
    from Iraq, **4:**422
    and Lower East Side, **5:**165–166
  from Korea, **4:**542, 543–544
  and labor, **5:**4–5
  and labor force, **2:**42
  from Lebanon, **5:**71–72
  legislation on, **4:**228–229, 230–231, 232–233
  marriage and, **5:**250
  to Maryland, **4:**220
  to Massachusetts, **4:**220; **5:**266–267
  "melting pot," **5:306**
  of Mennonites, **5:**309–310
  merchant marine and, **5:**318
  from Mexico, **3:**142; **4:**227; **5:**343–345, **343–345**
  to Milwaukee, **5:**388
  to Minnesota, **5:**397, 398, 399
  municipal government and, **5:**475
  of Muslims, **4:**436
  from Netherlands, **4:**221–222; **7:**262
  to New England, **4:**220–221
  to New Jersey, **6:**60, 62–64
  from Norway, **7:**262
  to Oregon, **6:**206, 207
  to Pennsylvania, **4:**221
  from Philippines, **3:**360–361
  from Poland, **4:**225; **6:**389–392
  political machines and, **5:**186, 187
  and racial discrimination, **3:**48
  rates of, **4:**220, 222, *222*

and religious affiliation, shifts in, 7:88–89, 91
restrictions on, **4:232–234**
　for China, **1:**324; **4:**224, 227, 232; **6:**5, 14, 396 (*See also* Chinese Exclusion Act)
　for gays and lesbians, **7:**325
　general, **4:**232–233
　intelligence-based, **4:**379
　for Iran, **4:**421
　for Iraq, **4:**422
　for Japan, **4:**457, 463; **6:**5; **9:**264–265
　McCarran-Walter Act (1952), **5:181**
　repeal of, **4:**227, 228, 233
　Roosevelt's (Franklin Delano) proclamation on, **9:**390–392
　after World War I, **4:**226
　during World War II, **4:**226–227
to Rhode Island, **7:**152, 153
from Russia/Soviet Union, **7:213–214**
from Scandinavia, **4:**223; **5:**4; **7:**262
of Scotch-Irish, **7:**284–285
to South, **4:**220; **7:**464
to South Carolina, **4:**220; **7:**453–454
to South Dakota, **7:**458
of Spanish speakers, **7:**492
and suburbanization, **7:**573
from Sweden, **7:**262
and tuberculosis, **8:**237
and urbanization, **8:**291
to Utah, **8:**297
to Virginia, **4:**220
of Walloons, **8:**368
to Washington (state), **8:**413
to Wisconsin, **8:**490–491
during World War I, **4:**226
during World War II, **4:**226–227
after World War II, **4:**228–229; **5:**5
See also Emigration
Immigration Act (1903), **6:**396
Immigration Act (1917), **4:**232
Immigration Act (1924), **4:**233
Immigration Act (1990), on naturalization, **6:**14
Immigration Act (Hart-Cellar Act) (1965), **4:230–232; 6:**81
　impact of, **4:**231
　provisions of, **4:***230*, 230–231, 233

Immigration and Nationality Act (INA) (1952). *See* McCarran-Walter Act (1952)
Immigration and Naturalization Service (INS)
　drug enforcement by, **5:**512
　wartime internment by, **4:**400
Immigration Reform and Control Act (IRCA) (1986), **4:**228–229
Immunity
　of citizens, **6:481–482**
　diplomatic, **1:**134
　sovereign, **7:**477, 534–535
Immunization. *See* Vaccination
Impeachment, **4:234–236**
　Constitution on, **4:**234
　of Ferguson (James), **3:**354; **8:**103
　hearings, on Nixon, **4:**235
　of Pickering (John), **4:**234
　trials, **2:**352–353
　　of Chase (Samuel), **4:**234, **241**
　　of Clinton, **2:**240, 353; **3:**169; **4:**235–236, **238–241; 7:**114
　　of Johnson (Andrew), **2:**353, 505; **4:**234–235, **236–238; 7:**60, 100
　separation of powers in, **7:**312
Impending Crisis of the South (Helper), **4:242**
　excerpt from, **9:**280–284
Imperial Tobacco, **8:**135
Imperialism, **4:242–246**
　and arms race, **1:**270
　in Asia, **4:**242–243
　British, **1:**541–543
　cultural, **5:**261
　definition of, **4:**242
　in electoral politics, **3:**159
　foreign resistance to, **4:**245, 246
　formal, **4:**242
　informal, **4:**242, 244–246
　liberal, **4:**244–245
　manifest destiny, **5:222–225,** *224*
　mapmaking and, **5:**232
　maps of, archival, **9:**2
　"new," **1:**189
　and terrorism, **4:**246
　in World War II, **4:**244–245
See also Anti-imperialism
Implied powers, **4:246–248**
　McCulloch v. Maryland, **5:184**
Import Administration, **3:**309
Impressment
　Confederate, **4:**248

of seamen, **4:248–249**
　and Chesapeake-Leopard incident, **2:129–130**
　press gangs and, **6:**459
In Cold Blood (Capote), **5:**122
"In God We Trust," **4:249**
In Re Debs, **2:**228; **4:249–250**
In Re Gault, **2:**149; **4:250,** 505
In Re Neagle, **4:250**
In the Luxembourg Gardens (Sargent), **3:**537
INA (Immigration and Nationality Act). *See* McCarran-Walter Act
Inauguration, presidential, **4:250–251**
Incandescent lighting, **3:**173, 177, 179
Ince, Thomas, **8:**457
Incidents in the Life of a Slave Girl (Jacobs), **3:**518–519
Income
　gap in American society, **2:**226
　per capita, in standard of living, **7:**521–522
Income tax
　Laffer curve theory and, **5:**20
　negative, **6:**31
　progressive, **8:**55, 196
　　during Civil War, **8:**56
　　federal, **8:**57–58
　　during World War II, **8:**58
　Supreme Court on, **4:251–252; 6:**409–410; **7:**512–513
Incorporated territories of the United States, **8:**92, 94
Inde. *See* Apache
Indemnities, **4:252**
Indentured servants, **2:**223, 226, 290; **4:252–254,** *253*
　as agricultural workers, **3:**325
　classes of, **4:**253
　convicts compared with, **2:**401
　decline of, and slavery, **1:**47–48
　distribution of, **4:**253
　Eddis (William) on, **9:**114–116
　first Africans as, **7:**7
　in New Smyrna Colony, **6:**77
　on plantations, **6:**364
　vs. slavery, Beverly (Robert) on, **1:**191; **9:**109–111
　treatment of, **4:**253
　in Virginia, **8:**342–343
Independence, **4:254–255**
　debate over, **7:**136–137

Independence, (*continued*)
Declaration of (*See* Declaration of Independence)
development of, **2:**520–521
support for, **2:**522
Independence (Missouri), **4:255–256**
Independence Day, **4:**149, *256*, **256–257; 5:**568
Independence Hall, **4:***257*, **257–258**
Independence National Historical Park, **4:**257–258
Independence Rock, **4:258**
Independent counsel. *See* Special prosecutors
Independent Counsel Act (1978), **7:**313, 496
Independent films, **3:**364–365
Independent Fundamental Churches of America, **3:**484
Independent Living Movement, **6:**389
Independent treasury system, **3:**344; **4:258**
Index, economic indicator, **3:**105–107
India
capitalist development in, **2:**44
under Great Britain, **4:**258
political subordination of, **2:**45
immigration from, **1:**324, 325
and religious affiliation, **7:**91
independence for, **4:**258–259
nuclear weapons of, **4:**261; **6:**138
Pakistani relations with, **4:**259–260
religions of, **1:**326; **4:**133
Soviet relations with, **4:**259, 260
U.S. relations with, **4:258–261**
Indian agents, **4:261–262**
Indian Americans. *See* Native American(s)
Indian Americans, Asian, **1:**325
in California, **1:**324, 325
number of, **1:**325
religious practices of, **4:**133
Indian Bible, Eliot's, **4:262; 6:**536
Indian Brigade, **4:263**
Indian Child Welfare Act (1978), **4:263–264**
Indian Civil Rights Act (ICRA) (1968), **2:**200; **4:264–265**
provisions of, **4:**264–265
Supreme Court on, **4:**264, 265
Indian Civilization Fund Act (1819), **3:**134

Indian Claims Commission (ICC), **4:***265*, **265–266**, 273–274; **5:**532; **8:**275
Indian Claims Commission Act (1946), **5:**25; **8:**215
Indian Country, **4:266–267**
Indian Education Act (1972), **3:**136
Indian Gambling Regulatory Act (IGRA), **3:**509
Indian Indenture Law (1850), **8:**214
Indian Intercourse Act (1834), **6:**29
Indian Peace Commission, **4:**272
Indian Removal Act (1830), **3:**554; **4:**295–296; **8:**206, 224
Indian Reorganization Act (IRA) (1934), **1:**482, 492; **2:**506; **4:297; 8:**206
and Alaska, **1:**110
and Northwestern Indians, **8:**223
opposition to, **4:**297
provisions of, **4:**288, 297
and Southeastern Indians, **8:**226
Indian Reorganization Act (IRA) (1948), Nez Perce rejection of, **6:**101
Indian Rights Association (IRA), **4:302–303**
Indian Scout uniform, **8:**257
Indian Self-Determination and Education Assistance Act (1975), **3:**136; **4:303; 5:**25
Indian Shaker religion, **4:**293; **6:**7
Indian Territory, **4:309; 6:**183–185
opening to colonization, **1:**501, 502
schools in, **3:**135
settlers in, **6:**185
sooners in, **7:**450
Indian Trade and Intercourse Act (1790–1847), **4:309**
Indiana, **4:317–320**
admission to Union, **1:**522
African Americans in, **4:**317, 319
agriculture in, **4:**318, 320
capital of, **2:**47
in Civil War, **4:**318
in colonial era, **4:**317
Democratic Party in, **4:**320
education in, **4:**319
emblems, nicknames, mottos, and songs of, **7:***532*
Farmers' Alliance in, **3:**323
films about, **4:**320
industry in, **4:**318–320

maps of, archival, **9:**49, *49*
in Midwest, **5:**368–369
Native Americans in, **4:**317
New Harmony Community in, **3:**107, 113; **8:**300
politics in, **4:**320
population of, **4:**317, 320
Republican Party in, **4:**320
rural areas of, **4:**318–319
sports in, **4:**320
State Bank of, **1:**408
state university of, **8:**279
statehood for, **4:**317
Indiana Company, **1:**432; **4:320**
and Vandalia Colony, **8:**308
Indianapolis (Indiana), **2:**47; **4:320–321**, *321*
industry in, **4:**318, 320–321
Indianapolis 500, **1:**375
Indians of All Tribes, **7:**70
Indigo cultivation, **4:330; 8:**164
Individual retirement account (IRA), **4:330; 6:**282; **7:**132
Individualism, **4:330–334**
in Christianity, **1:**196; **4:**331, 332
definitions of, **4:**330–331
development of, **4:**332–334
in transcendentalism, **8:**179, 300
Individualized educational program (IEP), **3:**34–35
Individuals with Disabilities Education Act (IDEA), **3:**34
Indochina, U.S. imperialism in, **4:**245
Indochina War, **8:**329
foreign aid in, **3:**416–417
Geneva Accords and, **3:**534; **8:**329
Industrial accidents
and labor legislation, **5:**14
Safety First Movement and, **7:**222
Industrial decline, in Rust Belt, **1:**561; **7:215–216**
Industrial democracy, **2:**273
Industrial disasters, **3:**38–39
Industrial ethic, **8:**529
Industrial hygiene, in lead industry, **5:**62
Industrial management, **4:334–335**
mass production, **5:261–264**
quality circles and, **7:**3–4
scientific, **7:280–283**
Industrial relations, **4:335–338**
Industrial research, **4:338–342**
definition of, **4:**338

distributed approach to, **4**:340–341
funding for, **4**:339, *341*, 342
  venture capital in, **4**:*340*, 341–342
growth of, **4**:339
roots of, **4**:338–339
Industrial revolution, **4:342–345**
cotton in, **4**:343–344, 345
definition of, **4**:342
as economic and social revolution,
    4:342–343
and environmental damage, **8**:422
industrial management in,
    4:334–335
and Native American economy,
    4:268–269
and printing industry, **6**:469
railroads in, **4**:344, 345
and suburbanization, **7**:573
and textile industry, **8**:108–109
Industrial Workers of the World
    (Wobblies) (IWW), **4:345–349;
    5**:7, *8;* **6**:257; **8**:263
in California, **2**:10
capitalism targeted by, **2**:45
and Communist Party, **2**:326
formation of, **2**:227
goals of, **4**:346, 347
and Lawrence (Massachusetts)
    strike, **5**:59
membership in, **4**:347, 348
origins of, **4**:345–346
sabotage by, **7**:219
socialism in, **4**:346–347; **7**:424, 426
strikes by, **4**:347
suppression of, **3**:207
syndicalism of, **8**:39–40
violent repression of, **4**:348; **8**:414
in Washington (state), **8**:414
Industrialization
and advertising, **1**:32
and apprenticeship, **1**:228
and Christianity, **2**:164
and class relations, **2**:223, 227
and consumerism, **2**:387
and decorative arts, **1**:287
deindustrialization, **5**:229
and department stores, **3**:6–7
and education, **3**:113
and environmental devastation,
    2:366
and foreign policy, **3**:425
in Gilded Age, **3**:577
and household manufacturing,
    5:229–230

and housing, **4**:180–181
and immigration, **4**:223–226
and individualism, **4**:333
and industrial relations, **4**:335
judiciary's role in, **5**:13
of Latin America, **5**:44, 45
lumber industry and, **5**:172
manufacturing, **5:227–229**
in Missouri, **5**:421
in New Jersey, **6**:62–63
in New York (state), **6**:88
in Pennsylvania, **6**:278–279
and recreation, changes in, **7**:64
steel, **5**:228
technological developments and,
    2:388
and tobacco industry, **8**:134–135
See also Mass production; Rust Belt
Industries
colonial, **4**:*349,* **349–350**
See also specific types
INF (Intermediate-Range Nuclear
    Forces) Treaty, **7**:150
Infant and toddler mortality
maternal and child health care,
    5:273–274
rates of, **5**:105
Infanticide, **3**:261
in colonial era, **1**:3
Infantile paralysis. *See* Poliomyelitis
Infectious disease, control of, **5**:105
Inflation, **4:350–353**
in 1970s, **3**:367; **4**:17
in 1980s, **3**:367
American Revolution and, **6**:461
causes of, **4**:351–352
in Confederacy, **2**:216, 343; **4**:353
and consumer purchasing power,
    2:385
Fed regulation and, **3**:346;
    4:351–352; **7**:516–517
gold standard and, **4**:15, 16, 17
history of, **4**:352–353
measurement of, **2**:424; **4**:350–351
and price and wage controls, **6**:460
in stagflation, **7**:516
and unemployment, relationship
    between, **8**:254
*Influence of Sea Power upon History,
    The* (Mahan), **3**:577
Influenza, **4:353–354**, *354*
pandemic of 1918-1919, **3**:37, *237,*
    241
during World War I, **8**:538–539

Infomercials, **4:354–355**
Information Age, **2**:333
Information Security (INFOSEC),
    5:559
Information Security Oversight
    Office, **5**:525
Information Service, U.S. (USIS),
    6:503
Information technology, future
    directions for, **5**:19
INFOSEC. *See* Information Securi-
    ty
Infrastructure, **4:355–358**
  port authorities and, **6**:420–421
Ingalls, John J., **3**:324
Ingles, Thomas, **3**:84
Ingles, Mrs. William, **3**:84
Ingresoll, Jared, **3**:151
Ingresoll, Robert G., **3**:156
Ingstad, Helge, **8**:337
Inhalants, **7**:569
Inherent powers, **4:358**
Inheritance laws
on alien landholding, **1**:124, 126
primogeniture, **6:463–464**
Inheritance tax, **8**:57
Inheritance tax laws, **4**:359
Initiatives, **4:359–360**
in Oregon System, **6**:208
See also Proposition
Injection molding, **6**:366
Injunctions, labor, **4:360–361**
Norris-LaGuardia Act and, **6**:121
Inkpaduta (Dakota leader), **7**:503
Inland lock navigation, **4:361**
Inland waterways. *See* Waterways,
    inland
Inland Waterways Commission,
    4:361; 5:565; **8**:147, 429
In-line skating. *See* Rollerblading
Inner cities, **7**:576
urban redevelopment and,
    8:285–286
Inness, George, **6**:507
Innis, Roy, **2**:355
Inoculation, **3**:235
See also Vaccines
Inönü, Ismet, **2**:7
Inoue, T., **6**:344
*Inquiry into the Effects of Spirituous
    Liquors on the Human Mind and
    Body* (Rush), **8**:78

INS. *See* Immigration and Naturalization Service; International
News Service
Insanity. *See* Mental illness
Insect(s)
boll weevil, **1:**495
in Black Belt, **1:**471
European corn borer, **2:**415
introduced species of, **7:**500
Insecticides and herbicides,
4:361–362
Agent Orange, **1:54–55**
in agriculture, **1:**67; **4:**361–362
biological, regulation of, **1:**463
dangers of, **1:**67; **4:**362; **7:**359
and foods, **3:**402
against grasshoppers, **4:**37
vs. organic farming, **6:**210
Silent Spring on, **7:**359
use in Vietnam War, **2:**537–538
Insider trading, **4:362–363**
Inspection, governmental,
4:363–364
Inspirationists, **1:**133
Installment buying, selling, and
financing, **4:364–366**
Installment credit, **2:**449–450
Institute for Advanced Study, **4:**366
Institute for Colored Youth, **3:**125
Institute for Legislative Action
(ILA), **5:**557
Institute for Policy Research (IPR),
1:545
Institute for Social Research. *See*
Frankfurt School
Institutional Revolutionary Party
(PRI), **5:**349
Institutionalism, **3:**109
Instructions, **4:366–367**
Instrumentalism, **6:**326, 445
Insular cases, **3:**413; **4:**367; **8:**92, 94
De Lima v. Bidwell, **2:545**
Insulin, transgenic, **3:**531
Insull, Samuel, **3:**175; **6:**535
Insurance, **4:367–372**
automobile, **4:**370
aviation, **4:**368–369
cooperative, **2:**406
fire, **4:**369
group, **4:**371
health (*See* Health insurance)
life, **4:**370–371
marine, **4:**367–368
inland, **4:**368

old-age (*See* Social security)
unemployment, **8:**253–254
workers' compensation, **4:**369–370
Insurrections
domestic, **4:372–373**
Bacon's Rebellion, **1:382–383**
Nat Turner's Rebellion,
5:516–517, *517*
Shays's Rebellion, **7:338;**
9:154–155
slave (*See* Slave insurrections)
See also Riots
Integrated pest management (IPM),
4:362
Integration, **4:373–375**
in Bermuda, **1:**445
in Dallas (Texas), **2:**495
definition of, **3:**15
See also Desegregation
Intel Corporation, **2:**336
Intellectual property, **4:375–376**
GATT and, **3:**524
Intellectuals, Jesuit, **4:**475
Intelligence
artificial, **1:318**
military and strategic, **4:376–377**
assuring integrity of, **5:**559
communications, **5:**558
electronic, **5:**558
National Security Agency,
5:558–559
photography in, **6:**331–332
signals, **5:**558–559
robots used in, **7:**184
testing of, **4:378–380; 6:**524
Intelligence organizations
Office of Strategic Services,
6:167–168; 7:502
spies in, **7:**502–503
See also Central Intelligence
Agency
Intelligence quotient (IQ), **4:**378,
380; **6:**524
Interchangeable parts
invention of, **1:**335, 371
in textile industry, **2:**387
in watch manufacture, **2:**242
Interchurch Center, **6:**516
Intercollegiate Association of Amateur Athletics, **8:**154
Intercollegiate Athletic Association
of the United States (ICAA),
3:410; **5:**530

Intercollegiate Football Association,
3:409
Intercolonial Congress, **6:**362
Intercontinental ballistic missiles
(ICBMs), **1:**75; **2:**528, 532;
5:407; **6:**144
Interest arbitration, **1:**236–237
Interest groups, **4:380–382**
definition of, **4:**380
effects of, **4:**381–382
membership in, **4:**380
representation by, **7:**108
role in politics, **4:**380–382
tactics of, **4:**381
See also Lobbies and lobbying
Interest laws, **4:382–383**
Interest rates
business cycles and, **1:**582
in monetary system, **5:**440–441
Interesting Narrative (Equiano),
6:234
Interests, vested, **4:383**
Intergovernmental Panel on Climate
Change (IPCC), **4:**8
Interior, Department of (DOI),
3:331; **4:383–384**
bureaus of, **4:**383–384
establishment of, **4:**383
functions of, **4:**383–384
and geological surveys, **3:**544, 546
head of, **2:**2
and Indian affairs, **1:**570
organization of, **4:**383
and public lands management, **5:**31
and U.S. territories, **8:**93
Interior decoration, **1:**290–292
Interior design, **1:**292–294
Intermediate credit banks,
4:384–385
Intermediate-Range Nuclear Forces
(INF) Treaty (1987), **7:**150;
8:203, 206
Intermittent fever, **5:**300
Intermodal Surface Transportation
Efficiency Act (ISTEA) (1991),
3:336; **4:**404; **8:**191, 231
Intermodal trucking, **8:**231
Internal combustion engine, patent
on, **7:304**
Internal Revenue Service (IRS)
narcotics division of, **5:**510–511
Whiskey Ring and, **8:**470
Internal Security Act (1950), **1:**197

Internal Security Act (McCarran Act) (1950), **2:**85
and passports, **6:**255
International agreements. *See* Treaties, with foreign nations
International America's Cup Class (IACC), **7:**223–224
International arbitration
development of, **4:**394
international law in, **4:**394
by joint commissions, **4:**484–485
International Atomic Energy Agency (IAEA), **6:**138–139
International Bank for Reconstruction and Development. *See* World Bank
International Banking Act (1978), **3:**347
International Bible Society, **3:**575
International Boot and Shoe Workers Union, **1:**503
International Brotherhood of Electrical Workers (IBEW), **3:**176
International Brotherhood of Teamsters (IBT), **4:**385–387; **5:**8, 17
in AFL-CIO, **1:**151; **4:**386
corruption of, **8:**172
decline of, **4:**386–387
discrimination in, **4:**387
establishment of, **4:**385
growth of, **4:**385–386
McClellan Committee Hearings, **5:**183
strikes by, **4:**386, *386*
UPS strike (1997), **2:**226
International Brotherhood of Teamsters v. United States, **4:**387
International Bureau of Federal Communications Commission, **3:**340
International Business Machines. *See* IBM
International Confederation of Free Trade Unions (ICFTU), **1:**151, 152
International Convention on the Prevention and Punishment of the Crime of Genocide, **3:**536
International Copyright Act (1891), **6:**537
International Court of Justice (ICJ), **4:**387–388
establishment of, **4:**394; **8:**272
functions of, **4:**387–388

jurisdiction of, **4:**387–388
U.S. in, **4:**388, 394
International Covenant on Civil and Political Rights (ICCPR), **4:**193
International Criminal Court, **1:**354; **4:**194; **8:**372
International Federation of Business and Professional Women, **5:**538
International Federation of Red Cross and Red Crescent Societies, **7:**70
fundamental principles of, **7:***70*
International Geophysical Year (IGY), **3:**552; **4:**388–389; **5:**523
International Harvester Company, **4:**389
International Labor Defense (ILD), **4:**389
in Scottsboro case, **4:**389; **7:**286
International Labor Organization (ILO), **4:**389–390; **5:**64; **8:**269
International Ladies Garment Workers Union (ILGWU), **2:**246, 249; **4:**390–393, *391,* 478
and Amalgamated Clothing Workers of America, merger with, **2:**250
plays produced by, **8:**115
International law, **4:**393–395
copyright, **6:**537
Declaration of London and, **5:**146
laws of war and, **8:**370–372
mixed commissions, **5:**428
on neutrality, **6:**33–37
retaliation in, **7:**126–127
on seizure of ships, **6:**483
and state boundary disputes, **1:**522–523
on territorial sea, **8:**93
on tidelands, **8:**124–125
International Lawn Tennis Federation, **8:**90
International Longshoremen's and Warehousemen's Union (ILWU), **2:**11; **4:**395–396
International Monetary Fund (IMF), **1:**536; **4:**396–397; **8:**166, 198, 269
establishment of, **3:**110; **4:**396; **8:**531
floating exchange rates established by, **4:**17
and foreign aid, **3:**415

functions of, **2:**517; **4:**16, 396
and Third World, **8:**271
International News Service (INS), **6:**458
International Olympic Committee (IOC), **6:**191
International Paper Company, **6:**245
International Polar Year (IPY), **4:**59
International Printing Pressmen's and Assistant's Union, **5:**17
International Red Cross Commission (ICRC), **6:**472
International Refugee Organization, **7:**80
International Society for Krishna Consciousness (ISKCON), **2:**477
International Space Station (ISS), **5:**524; **7:**184, 481
International Telephone and Telegraph Corporation (ITT), **4:**449
International Trade Organization (ITO), **3:**524
International Union of American States, **6:**236
International Union of Electrical, Radio, and Machine Workers (IUE), **3:**176
International Union of Mine, Mill, and Smelter Workers (IUMM-SW), **4:**397; **8:**454
Internationalism, rise of, **4:**440
Internet, **2:**337; **4:**397–399
access to, **8:**67
advertising on, **1:**34
and communications industry, **2:**321
and computer viruses/worms, **2:**338
and cults, **2:**478
culture and, **5:**366
development of, **3:**185; **4:**397–399; **8:**66, 70
e-commerce, **3:**183–184; **5:**206
in education, **3:**139
encyclopedias on, **3:**205
and English language, **3:**222
fiber optics technology and, **3:**357–358
growth of, **4:**399
households with access to, **2:**323
libraries and, **5:**99
Library of Congress and, **5:**102
magazines, **5:**195

Internet, (*continued*)
  maps on, **5:**234
  marketing research and, **5:**248
  privacy on, **6:**480
    FBI and, **3:**339
  and publishing industry, **6:**470, 539
  regulation of, **8:**68
  scientific information retrieval on,
    7:279–280
  self-help groups on, **7:**305
  and software industry, **7:**443
  spy technologies on, **3:**186
  as telecommunications tool, **8:**65,
    66
  and Utopian communities, **8:**304
  and video game industry, **8:**327
  and virtual reality systems, **8:**350
Internet Protocol (IP), **8:**66
Internment, wartime, **4:399–400**
  in World War I, **4:**399
  in World War II, **4:**399–400
    of Japanese Americans,
      4:459–462, *463–464;* **5:**168
      firsthand account of, **9:**405–406
      reparations for, **4:**461–462,
        464–465; **8:**415
    in Washington (state), **8:**415
Internships, medical, **5:**282
Interpreter of Maladies (Lahiri), **5:**123
Interpretive dance, **2:**497–498
Interstate commerce
  barriers to, **4:405–406**
  laws on, **2:**310; **4:401–402; 7:**26,
    514
    Populists and, **2:**389
    Supreme Court on, **3:**575; **4:**26;
      7:352, 514
  original package doctrine on,
    6:213
Interstate Commerce Commission
  (ICC), **3:**188; **4:400–401; 7:**26
  authority of, Motor Carrier Act
    (1980), **5:463**
  closure of, **4:**400–401
  functions of, **4:**128, 401
  Hepburn Act on, **4:**128, 401
  Nader's Raiders and, **5:**509
  powers of, expansion of, **2:**383
  Supreme Court on, **7:**352; **8:**234
Interstate compacts, **4:403**
  Bank of Augusta v. Earle and, **1:**395
Interstate Highway Act (1956),
  8:190

Interstate highway system,
  4:403–405, *404, 405;* **8:**190
  beautification of, **1:**34; **4:**132
  creation of, **4:**355–356
  Federal-Aid Highway Program
    and, **3:**335–336; **8:**140
  gasoline taxes and, **3:**511
  and trucking industry, **8:**231
  and vacation activities, **8:**305
  in Vermont, **8:**314
Interstate Oil Compact (1935),
  6:303
Interstate trade barriers, **4:405–406**
*Interstate/Johnson Lane Corporation,
  Gilmer v.,* **1:**237
Inter-University Consortium for
  Political and Social Research
  (ICPSR), **6:**403
Interurban electric railways. *See*
  Railways, interurban
Intervention, U.S., **4:406–408**, *407*
  in 19th century, **4:**406
  in 20th century, **4:**244, 406–407
  definition of, **4:**406
  imperialism and, **4:**244
  purposes of, **4:**406
  See also specific countries
Intolerable Acts (1774), **4:408**
  See also Coercive Acts
Intracoastal Waterway, **7:**169
Intrauterine device (IUD), **1:**469
  Dalkon Shield, **1:**469; **2:**493–494
Intrepid (ship), **1:**415; **4:**408
Introduced species, *7:499,* **499–500**
Introduction to Psychology (Hilgard),
  6:525
Intuitionism, **8:**180
Inuit (Eskimo), **4:408–410; 6:**381;
  8:211
  education for, **4:***409*
  European colonization and,
    4:409–410
  European exploration and,
    4:408–409
  housing of, **4:***408*
  social organization of, **4:**409
Inupiaq (language), **8:**211
Inupiat, **8:**212
Invasive species, **8:**437
*Invention of Women, The: Making
  African Sense of Western Gender
  Discourses* (Oyewùmí), **3:**517
Investigating committees,
  4:410–411

Investment
  business cycles and, **1:**582
  direct vs. portfolio, **3:**419
  foreign (*See* Foreign investment in
    United States)
Investment bank(s), **1:404–406**
  Jay Cooke and Company,
    2:404–405
  regulation of, **1:**405–406
Investment companies, **4:411–413**
Invisible Man (Ellison), **4:413–414;
  5:**121, 125
IOC. *See* International Olympic
  Committee
Iowa, **4:414–417**
  African Americans in, **4:**417
  agriculture in, **4:**414–417
  Amana Community in, **1:**133
  antimonopoly parties in, **1:**204
  in Civil War, **4:**415
  in colonial era, **4:**414
  Democratic Party in, **4:**416
  emblems, nicknames, mottos, and
    songs of, **7:***532*
  Farmers' Alliance in, **3:**323
  4-H Clubs in, **3:**445
  Hispanic Americans in, **4:**417
  immigrants in, **4:**415
  industry in, **4:**415
  in Midwest, **5:**368–369
  missionaries in, **4:**417
  Native Americans in, **4:**414
    Mesquakie, **5:**326–327
  political issues in, **4:**416
  population of, **4:**416–417
  railroads in, **4:**414–415
  Republican Party in, **4:**416
  Spirit Lake Massacre in,
    7:503–504
  state university of, **2:**263; **8:**279
  statehood for, **4:**414
  urbanization in, **4:**416
  women in, **4:**415
Iowa Band, **4:417**
Iowa Injunction and Abatement Law
  (1909), **6:**513
Iowa State University, **8:**319
Ioway, **8:**223
IP. *See* Internet Protocol
IPCC. *See* Intergovernmental Panel
  on Climate Change
IPM. *See* Integrated pest manage-
  ment

IPR. *See* Institute for Policy Research
Ipswich Protest (1687), **4:**417
IQ. *See* Intelligence quotient
IRA. *See* Indian Reorganization Act; Indian Rights Association; Individual retirement account
Iran
  CIA operations in, **2:**92
  hostage crisis in, **3:**194; **4:420–421**; **8:**96
    Carter's role in, **4:**174, 418, 420–421
    and electoral politics, **3:**167
    firsthand account of, **9:**494–495
    indemnities in, **4:**252
    mixed commission and, **5:**428
    motivations for, **4:**174, 418
  immigration from, **4:**421
    restrictions on, **4:**421
  oil in, **6:**298
  Soviet occupation of, **4:**418
  U.S. intervention in, **4:**418
  U.S. relations with, **4:418–419**
Iran-Contra Affair, **2:**395; **3:**278; **4:419–420**; **5:**49; **6:**401
  and congressional oversight of intelligence, **4:**377
  and electoral politics, **3:**168
  Report on the Iran-Contra Affair, text of, **9:**504–509
  special prosecutors in, **7:**496
  and Tower Commission, **8:**148
Iranian Americans, **4:**421
  geographic distribution of, **4:**421
  number of, **4:**421
Iran-Iraq war, chemical weapons used in, **2:**119
Iraq
  immigration from, **4:**422
    restrictions on, **4:**422
  International Atomic Energy Agency inspections in, **6:**140
  nuclear weapons capacity of, **6:**138, 293
  oil in, **6:**298
  in Persian Gulf War, **1:**77, 465, 496; **6:**292–293
Iraq-gate, **4:421–422**
Iraqi Americans, **4:**422
  geographic distribution of, **4:**422
  number of, **4:**422
IRCA. *See* Immigration Reform and Control Act

Iredell, James, on judicial review, **2:**7
Ireland
  British relations with, **4:**423, 426
  immigration from, **2:**163; **4:**221, 222–223, 423–425
  nationalism in, **4:**423
  population of, **4:**222
  potato famine in, **4:**222–223, 424; **6:**432
  U.S. relations with, **4:423**
Ireland, John, **2:**69
Irish, Edward (Ned), **1:**423, 424
Irish Americans, **4:423–426**
  Catholic, **4:**223, 423, 424–425
  in Chicago, **2:**132
  in Civil War, **4:**424
  in Connecticut, **2:**358
  culture of, **4:**425–426
  in Fenian movement, **3:**353–354
  geographic distribution of, **4:**223, 423, 424
  impact of, **4:**221
  in Iowa, **4:**415
  in New York City riot of 1871, **7:**164
  number of, **4:**222, 423, 424
  in Pennsylvania, **6:**278
  in policy and bookmaking syndicates, **2:**463
  political machines and, **5:**186, 187
  in politics, **4:**425
  professional activities of, **4:**424–425, *425*
  Protestant, **4:**221, 223, 423
  Scotch-Irish, **7:**284–286
  in Vermont, **8:**313
  and whiskey making, **8:**468
  women, **4:**223, 425
Iron
  as building material, **1:**564
  from Latin America, **5:**45
Iron Act (1750), **4:**426
Iron and steel industry, **4:426–429**, *427*
  in 19th century, **4:**426–427
  in Birmingham, **1:**466
  blast furnaces in, **1:485**
  in colonial era, **4:**350, 426
  companies in, **8:**295
  decline of, **4:**429; **7:**546
  expansion of, **4:**426–427, *427*
  foreign competition in, **4:**429
  growth of, **5:**228
  ironworks, **5:**329–330

Memorial Day Massacre (1937), **5:307**
Menominee Iron Range, **5:311–312**
  mergers in, **4:**428
Mesabi Iron Range, **5:326**
  in Michigan, **5:**355
  mini-mills in, **4:**429
  in Pittsburgh, **6:**360–361
  puddling in, **4:**426–427
  in Rust Belt, **7:**215
  shipbuilding and, **5:**319
  trade unions in, **4:**427–429; **7:**545–546; **8:277–278**
  in World War II, **4:**428–429
Iron Curtain, **3:**426; **4:429–430**
  Churchill on, **8:**574
Iron lung, **6:**388
Iron Mountains. *See* Great Smoky Mountains
Iron stoves, **3:**398, 399
Ironclad Oath, **3:**271; **4:430**; **8:**96
Ironclad warships, **4:430–431**
  Battle of the *Monitor* and the *Merrimack*, **5:442–443**
  of Confederate Navy, **6:**23, 25
  of Union Navy, **6:**25
Ironwork, **5:***329*, 329–330
Iroquois, **4:431–433**, *432*
  Abenaki and, **5:**21; **8:**311
  Albany Plan and, **1:**113–114
  architecture of, **1:***238*
  art of, **4:***431*
  British relations with, **4:**283, 432
  in colonial wars, **2:**293
  Dutch relations with, **4:**281, 432
  Erie Canal and displacement of, **3:**251
  in French and Indian War, **3:**469, 471
  French relations with, **4:**432
  and fur trade, **3:**488–489
  housing of, **4:**431
  in maps, archival, **9:**17
  nation members of, **4:**431
  in Onondaga, **6:**195–196
  on reservations, **4:**432–433
  resistance to white migration, **8:**459
  social life of, **4:**304, 431
  teachers among, **3:**133
  in Tennessee, **8:**84
  treaties with, **4:**316
  and Underground Railroad, **8:**249

Iroquois League (Five Nations),
6:86–87
in Civil War, 6:184
and New York Colony, 6:83
origins of, 9:81–82
treaty with (1784), text of,
9:153–154
warfare and, 4:431–432
Irradiation of food, 3:407–408
"Irrepressible conflict," 4:433
Irrigation, 3:18, 19; 4:433–436
dependence on, 4:434
environmental problems with,
4:436
federal role in, 4:435
in Idaho, 4:212, 213
in Kansas, 4:509, 510
legislation on, 1:65; 4:435
Native American use of,
4:307–308, 433–434
in Nebraska, 6:30
and reclamation of arid lands,
7:55–56
Rio Grande and, 7:163
social problems with, 4:435–436
in Spanish colonial settlements,
7:207
in West, 1:65; 4:434–436
windmills and, 8:486
Irrigation survey, 3:545
IRS. See Internal Revenue Service
Irvine (California), 2:188
Irving, Washington, 3:197; 5:118;
7:397
exploration of American West and,
3:299
A History of New York, 5:118
"The Legend of Sleepy Hollow,"
5:118
"Rip Van Winkle," 5:118
The Sketchbook of Geoffrey Crayon,
Gentleman, 5:118
Irwin, Robert, 1:307
Isabel (queen of Spain), 3:283
ISKCON. See International Society
for Krishna Consciousness
Islam, 4:436–438; 7:91, 94
among African Americans, 1:45,
45; 4:436–437, 438
in Arab nations, 1:234; 4:436
Bahá'í, 1:384
and black nationalism, 1:478
early American, 4:436
forms of, 4:437–438

fundamentalist, 1:234
See also Nation of Islam
Island Number Ten, operations at,
4:438
Isobe, Hosen, 1:325
Isolationism, 4:438–440
in 19th century, 4:438
in 20th century, 4:439–440
of America First Committee,
1:139; 4:440
Bricker Amendment and, 1:537
in colonial era, 4:438
foreign observers on, 1:138
Ludlow resolution and, 5:170
origins of, 4:438–439
terminology of, 3:224
after World War I, 8:543
in World War I, 4:439
in World War II, 4:440
Isostasy, 3:552
Israel
American émigrés in, 3:197; 8:592,
593
in Arab-Israeli wars, 1:233, 234;
4:440–441
arms sold to, 4:441
in Cold War, 4:440
creation of, 1:207
Egypt and, 3:141; 8:270
Camp David Peace Accords,
2:20; 3:141
conflict between, 4:441
peace settlement for, 1:233; 4:441
in Suez Crisis, 8:2–3
foreign aid to, 3:418
at Geneva Conference (1973),
3:535
neoconservatives and, 6:31–33
nuclear weapons of, 6:138
Palestinian negotiations with,
4:442–444
United Nations and, 8:270
U.S. aid to, 4:440–441
U.S. recognition of, 1:207; 4:440
U.S. relations with, 4:440–443;
8:592–593
and Liberty incident, 5:95–96
moral commitment in, 4:440
and U.S.-Arab relations, 1:233
Israeli-Palestinian Peace Accord
(1993), 4:443–444
ISS. See International Space Station
ISTEA. See Intermodal Surface
Transportation Efficiency Act

Isthmian Canal Commission, 6:105
ITA. See Teachers Insurance Annuity
Association
Italian Americans, 4:444–448
in 19th century, 4:444
in 20th century, 4:447
Catholicism of, 4:445
in colonial era, 4:444
in Connecticut, 2:358
cuisine of, 3:401
culture of, 4:445
geographic distribution of, 4:225,
444, 447
in New Jersey, 6:63
number of, 4:225, 445, 447
and organized crime, 2:463
in politics, 4:447
professional activities of, 4:225,
446
public image of, 4:447
relocation of, 7:99
social mobility of, 4:447
in World War II, 4:445
Italy
in European Common Market,
8:157
explorations of, by Verrazano,
1:11; 2:38; 3:285, 291; 8:315
Narrows, 5:515
New France, 6:51
New York, 6:87
immigration from, 4:225, 444–445,
448
internment of aliens from,
4:399–400
Monte Cassino, 5:451–452
under Mussolini, 4:448
in slave trade, 7:386
Stazione Zoologica (Naples), 5:240
U.S. relations with, 4:448–449
Five-Power Naval Treaty and,
3:377
Mafia incident and, 5:191
after World War I, 2:89
in World War I, American Expeditionary Forces in, 1:149
in World War II, 4:448; 8:549, 549
Anzio Campaign, 1:217–218
Gothic Line, 4:23
Gustav Line, 4:78
Salerno, 7:230
Sicilian Campaign, 7:353–354
ITO. See International Trade Organization

Itoyatin, **6**:442
ITT. *See* International Telephone and Telegraph Corporation
ITT Affair, **4**:449
IUD. *See* Intrauterine device
IUE. *See* International Union of Electrical, Radio, and Machine Workers
IUMMSW. *See* International Union of Mine, Mill, and Smelter Workers
Ives, Charles, **5**:492
Ives, James M., **2**:484; **6**:470
  See also Currier and Ives
Ives, Joseph, **2**:242
Ives, Joseph C., **4**:33
Ivy League, **4**:449–450
Iwo Jima, **4**:*450*, 450–451
  assaults on, **8**:556
  landing on, **8**:547
IWW. *See* Industrial Workers of the World
Izaak Walton League, **2**:367

J

J. A. Croson Company, Richmond v., **1**:581; **7**:157
J. Allen Hynek Center for UFO Studies, **8**:255
J. C. Penney, **7**:125
  origins of, **3**:*8*, 9
J. P. Morgan Company, **1**:405
Jack Paar Show, The (TV show), **8**:142
Jackling, D. C., **6**:115
Jackson, Alan, **1**:388
Jackson, Andrew, **2**:534
  Albany Regency and, **1**:114
  on appointments, **1**:225
  attempted assassination of, **1**:327–328
  backwoodsmen under, **1**:382
  vs. Bank of the United States, **1**:395, 397; **3**:152; **7**:103
    and antibank movement, **1**:195; **3**:365
    and pet banks, **6**:295
  banks under, **4**:258
  in Battle of New Orleans, **6**:73, 75
  censure of, **3**:303
  in Creek War, **1**:102; **2**:456
  and Democratic Party, **2**:550
  and Democratic-Republican Party, **5**:555
  duel with Dickinson, **3**:93
  Eaton affair and, **3**:105
  economic policies of, **4**:453
  on enumerated powers, **3**:225
  Florida campaign of, **7**:10
  and Force Act (1833), **3**:413–414; **6**:145–146
  and government jobs, **1**:572
  Hermitage of, **4**:128, *128*
  Indian policies of, **2**:128, 158; **3**:278; **4**:285, 295, 298; **7**:102; **8**:401
  and Indian Removal Act (1830), **8**:226
  invading Florida, **3**:385
  Jacksonian Democracy and, **4**:453–455; **5**:159–160
  "Kitchen Cabinet" of, **3**:146; **4**:534
  marriage of, **6**:400
  Maysville Veto, **5**:277
  as national hero, **5**:567
  and nationalism, **8**:435
  as Old Hickory, **6**:190
  opposition to, Whig Party and, **8**:467
  "Our Federal Union! It Must Be Preserved!", **6**:220
  and Panama Canal plans, **6**:237
  party nomination of, **2**:399
  and political patronage, **2**:22
  in presidential campaign of 1824, **3**:152, 171; **5**:555; **8**:322–323
  in presidential campaign of 1828, **3**:152; **8**:323
  in presidential campaign of 1832, **3**:152
  and Radical Republicans, **5**:550
  in Seminole Wars, **7**:9, 309–310, 484
  and spoils system, **7**:198–199
  spoils system under, **4**:453; **6**:426; **7**:507
  and tariffs, **8**:50
  and Treasury, **8**:196
  tribal land annexation under, **1**:188
  in War of 1812, **5**:159; **9**:42
Jackson, Charles, **1**:184, 185
Jackson, David, **3**:493
Jackson, Helen Hunt, *A Century of Dishonor*, **2**:95
  excerpt from, **9**:257–259
Jackson, Henry, **6**:32
Jackson, Howell E., **6**:410
Jackson, Jesse, **2**:*205*; **7**:46
  in presidential campaign of 1984, **1**:52; **3**:168
  in presidential campaign of 1988, **3**:168
  and Rainbow Coalition, **7**:46
Jackson, John G., **8**:448
Jackson, Jonathan, **3**:255
Jackson, Kenneth T., **7**:572, 573
Jackson, Mahalia, **5**:497
Jackson, Maynard, **1**:349; **3**:558
Jackson, Michael, **5**:490
Jackson, Phil, **1**:426
Jackson, Shoeless Joe, **1**:421, 480, *481*
Jackson, Thomas J. (Stonewall)
  in Battle of Antietam, **1**:199–200
  at Battle of Chancellorsville, **2**:104, 213
  in Capture of Harpers Ferry, **4**:97
  in First Battle of Bull Run, **1**:567; **2**:211
  in Peninsular Campaign, **6**:275
  in Second Battle of Bull Run, **1**:568
  in Seven Days' Battles, **7**:319
Jackson, Thomas Penfield, **5**:360
Jackson, William H., **1**:299
Jacksonian Democracy, **4**:453–455; **5**:159–160
  agrarianism and, **1**:56–57
  alternative medicine and, **5**:291
  Benton and, **5**:420
  definition of, **4**:453
  governors in, **4**:29
  and postal service, **6**:426
  and state geological surveys, **3**:548
Jacksonville (Florida), **4**:455–456
JACL. *See* Japanese American Citizens League
Jacobin clubs, **4**:456
Jacobs, Harriet, **1**:49; **2**:18; **3**:518–519; **8**:512
Jacobson, Matthew Frye, **1**:338
Jacobson v. Massachusetts, **3**:239
Jacobus, Donald Lines, **3**:522
Jacquet-Droz, Pierre, **8**:244
Jaffe, Philip, **1**:134
Jails. *See* Prison(s)
Jainism, **1**:327
JAMA. See Journal of the American Medical Association
Jamaica, buccaneers in, **1**:550
James I (king of England), **2**:110
  charters issued by, **2**:287

James I (king of England), (*continued*)
  and Virginia, **8:**341
James II (king of England), **2:**280;
  3:77, 94
  and Dominion of New England,
    6:379
  New York land grant to, **6:**82, 87;
    8:311
  representative legislature to New
    York guaranteed by, **6:**83
James, Daniel (Chappie), **8:**241
James, Edwin, **5:**150
James, Henry, **3:**197; **5:**119
  The Turn of the Screw, **5:**119
James, Jerry, **7:***18*
James, Jesse, **8:***178*, 179
James, Thomas, **3:**286
James, William, **3:**116, 195, 280;
  6:*325*, *445*
  and parapsychology, **6:**246
  and pluralism, **6:**374–375
  and positivism, **6:**424
  and pragmatism, **6:**445
  and psychology, **6:**523
  Varieties of Religious Experience,
    5:118
James River and Kanawha Company,
  4:456–457
Jameson, Fredric, **6:**430
Jameson, John Franklin, **1:**159
Jamestown (Virginia), **2:**290
  burning of, **1:**383
  establishment of, **2:**287
  vs. Plymouth Colony, **8:**528
  Powhatans and, **4:**283
  problems in, **4:**283; **8:**341
  Starving Time at, **7:525; 9:**84–86
Jamison, Judith, **1:**131
Janet, Pierre, **6:**431
Janiger, Oscar, **5:**169
Janov, Arthur, **6:**462
Jansky, Karl, **1:**344
Japan
  Allied occupation of, **4:**458
  automobile industry of, **1:**336,
    373–374; **3:**422
  biological warfare against China,
    2:118
  bioterrorism in, **1:**465
  capitalist development in, **2:**44
  cherry trees given by, **4:**465
  China invaded by, **4:**457–458
  commercial treaty with, **8:**198
  economic power of, **4:**458–459

electronics industry in, **7:**360–361;
  8:167, 169
foreign investment from, **3:**422
Kanagawa Treaty with, **4:**457
Korea and, **4:**457, 541–542, 545
and London Naval Treaties, **5:**147
Lytton Commission and, **5:**428
Manchuria and, **5:**218–219
Perry's expedition to, **4:**457; **6:291;**
  8:198
religions of, **1:**325–326, 327
robotics in, **1:**365
and Russia, war with, **7:**210–211
in Russo-Japanese War, **4:**457
  Portsmouth, Treaty of (1905)
    ending, **6:**423
semiconductor industry in, **7:**307,
  361
in Sino-Japanese War, **7:367**
soybeans in, **7:**478
trade with, **4:**458–459
  in electronics industry, **7:**360–361
U.S. relations with, **4:457–459**
  Five-Power Naval Treaty and,
    3:377
  Four-Power Treaty and, **3:**446
  imperialism in, **4:**242, 245
  Open Door policy and, **4:**457;
    6:197
  Panay incident and, **6:243–244**
  right of extraterritoriality in,
    3:304
  Root-Takahira Agreement, **7:197**
  Sino-Japanese war and, **5:**219
  Taft-Katsura Memorandum and,
    8:43
  trade deficit with, **2:**517
  U.S. shipping in, **5:**320
in World War I, **4:**457
in World War II, **1:**470; **4:**458;
  8:249
  aerial bombing of, **1:**495
  air war, **8:***554*, 554–555, *555*
    atomic bombings, **6:**143; **8:**551,
      555
    Battle of the Philippine Sea,
      6:320–321; 8:557
    Flying the Hump and, **3:**392
    Flying Tigers in, **3:**392–393
    Peleliu, **6:**274
    Tarawa, **8:**49
    Tinian, **8:**130
  aircraft carriers of, **1:**90–91

atomic bombing of, **1:**494, 495;
  3:302; **5:**222; **6:**143; **8:**551,
  555
Battle of Coral Sea, **2:412–413**
Battle of Java Sea, **4:**465–466
Battle of Leyte Gulf, **6:**26; **8:**557
Battle of Midway, **5:367–368**
Gilbert Islands, **3:**576; **6:**26; **8:**49
Guadalcanal Campaign, **4:**68;
  6:26; **8:**556
invasion of Philippines, **6:**322;
  8:546, *547*
Iwo Jima, **4:**450
Marshall Islands, **3:**576; **6:**26
Pearl Harbor attack, **6:***272,*
  272–273; **8:**543–545,
  555–556
Potsdam Conference and,
  6:434–435
and prisoners of war, **6:**472, 474
Rabaul Campaign, **7:**6–7
Saipan, **7:228**
strategic air power against, **1:**81
surrender of, **8:**551–552
U.S. counteroffensive, **8:**547–548
U.S. submarine warfare and,
  8:556–557
Yap Mandate and, **8:**575
Japanese American Citizens League
  (JACL), **4:**464
Japanese Americans, **1:***322*; **4:***462,*
  462–465
  discrimination against, **4:**463
  educational trends among, **4:**464
  gender roles of, **3:**520
  immigration patterns of,
    4:462–463, 464
  immigration restrictions on, **4:**463;
    6:5
  in California, **4:**457
  Gentlemen's Agreement on,
    4:457, 463
    text of, **9:**264–265
  internment of, **2:**11; **3:**208, 278;
    4:*400,* **459–462,** *460, 461,*
    463, 463–464; **5:**168; **8:**578
  Colorado and, **2:**300
  court cases involving, **3:**91
  firsthand account of, **9:**405–406
  reparations for, **4:**461–462,
    464–465; **8:**415
  Supreme Court on, **3:**272
  in Washington (state), **8:**415
  in Los Angeles, **5:**153

loyalty questionnaires administered to, **5:**168
as "model minority," **4:**464, 465
nativist laws and, **6:**5
in New Jersey, **6:**63
number of, **4:**462
postwar acculturation of, **4:**464
racism against, **2:**11, 13; **7:**11
in Washington (state), **8:**415
Japanese Buddhism, **1:**552
Japanese cherry trees, **4:**465, *465*
Jarves, J. J., **2:**272
Jarvik, Robert, **1:**463; **2:**53
Jarvis, Gregory B., **2:**102
Jarvis, Howard, **6:**508–509
Jaspers, Karl, **3:**279
Java (programming language), **2:**337
Java Sea, Battle of, **4:**465–466
Jaworski, Leon, **1:**145; **7:**495; **8:**427
Jay, John, **3:**225; **8:**200
  alma mater of, **2:**304
  diplomacy of, **2:**394; **3:**28; **7:**146, 147
  Federalist Papers by, **2:**382; **3:**349–350; **6:**374
  in Jay-Gardoqui negotiations, **4:**466
  and Jay's Treaty, **4:**41, 467; **8:**200, 204
  legal training of, **5:**56
  Metropolitan Museum of Art, proposal for, **5:**335
  and Olive Branch Petition, **6:**190
  and republic, concept of, **7:**110
  and Treaty of Paris (1783), **1:**541; **6:**248, 250
Jay Cooke and Company, **2:**404–405
Jaycees, **7:**183
Jay-Gardoqui negotiations (1785), **4:**466
Jayhawkers, **4:**466
Jayne, William, **7:**459
Jay's Treaty (1794), **1:**124, 541; **4:**41, **466–467**; **5:**26; **8:**200, 204
  as arbitration agreement, **6:**263
  and emergence of Federalist Party, **3:**350
  France and, **2:**398; **3:**450
  and Greenville Treaty, **4:**63
  mixed commissions and, **5:**428
  Monroe-Pinkney Treaty and, **5:**447
  and XYZ affair, **8:**570
Jazz, **1:**491; **4:**467–469
  African American folklore and, **3:**395

and audio technology industry, **1:**358
  big-band swing and, **4:**468–469
  free, **4:**469
  in Harlem Renaissance, **4:**96
  origins of, **4:**467–468
  ragtime and, **4:**468
Jazz Age, **4:**469–470
  literature in, **5:**120
  modernity and, **4:**468
Jazz Singer, The (film), **4:**470, *470*
JCS. *See* Joint Chiefs of Staff
JDL. *See* Jewish Defense League
Jefferson, Blind Lemon, **1:**492
Jefferson, Thomas, **4:***471*
  and African American relocation, idea for, **2:**296
  agrarianism of, **1:**55, 56–57, 62
  on Alien and Sedition Acts, **6:**145
  on American climate, **2:**234
  in American Philosophical Society, **1:**166; **5:**66
  anarchism and, **1:**180
  anthropological studies of, **1:**191
  antiurbanism of, **8:**291
  archaeological studies of, **1:**239
  architecture of, **1:**249
  and Army Corps of Engineers, **3:**219
  Aurora and, **1:**360
  and Bank of the United States, opposition to, **1:**395
  Banneker (Benjamin) and, **1:**48
  on bill of rights, **1:**455
  on capital punishment, **2:**40
  caucus supporting, **6:**113
  on Charlotte Town Resolves, **2:**109
  on citizenship, **2:**179, 180
  and coinage system, **2:**481
  collecting by, **2:**272
  and Compromise of 1790, **2:330**
  cypher system invented by, **2:**468
  and Declaration of Independence, **2:**287, 394, 521–522; **3:**89; **7:**136
  defense policy of, **2:**530
  deism and, **2:**539
  and Democratic Party, **2:**549–550
  on disposal of public lands, **6:**527
  economic policies of, **1:**458; **2:**386; **3:**108; **4:**89
  and Embargo Act (1807), **2:**130; **3:**192, 193; **8:**164
  on entangling alliances, **3:**224

on enumerated powers, **3:**225
  vs. Essex Junto, **3:**256
  exploration in age of, **3:**297–298
  factory system of, **1:**281
  on farmers, **8:**527
  foreign policy of, **7:**126
  fur trade and, **1:**157
  and Gabriel's Insurrection, **3:**501
  garden of, **3:**510
  and Great Britain, relations with, **4:**466
  on implied powers, **4:**247
  and Indian emigration, **7:**102
  Italian influence on, **4:**444
  Jeffersonian democracy and, **4:**471–472
  Kentucky Resolutions by, **1:**124; **8:**349
  land policy of, **6:**201
  and landscape design, **5:**38
  legal training of, **5:**56, 73
  Lewis and Clark expedition under, **5:**87–88; **8:**307
    message on, **9:**187–191
  Locke's political philosophy and, **5:**141
  on Louisiana, **3:**18
  Louisiana Purchase by, **1:**187; **2:**550; **3:**450; **5:**159, 162–163; **8:**200, 204
  mammalogy, fostering of, **5:**217
  Mazzei letter, **5:**277
  on mercantilism, **5:**316
  and meteorological research, **2:**235
  meteorology and, **5:**331
  Monroe-Pinkney Treaty, **5:**447
  Monticello, **5:**452–453, *453*
  as national hero, **5:**567
  Native Americans and, **8:**64
    land cessions by, **4:**271, 313–314
    languages of, **4:**274
    policies on, **4:**284, 295, 313–314
  Navy under, **1:**269
  and neutral rights of U.S., **6:**34
  Notes on the State of Virginia, **5:**118; **6:**374, 396
  on patents, **6:**255
  personal librtary of, **5:**100
  on philanthropy, **6:**316
  on political exiles, **6:**396
  and political offense exception to extradition, **3:**304
  and political patronage, **2:**22
  on potatoes, **6:**432

Jefferson, Thomas, (*continued*)
  as president, **2:**549–550
  in presidential campaign of 1796,
    3:150, 171; **8:**322
  in presidential campaign of 1800,
    3:148, 150, 351–352; **4:**471;
    8:322
  in presidential campaign of 1804,
    3:151
  on property, **6:**507
  and public education, **3:**112–113;
    8:279
  and racial science, **7:**12
  and religious liberty, **2:**167; **7:**93
  on representative government,
    7:109
  on right of revolution, **7:**148, 149
  and Seal of the United States, **3:**99
  Spanish Conspiracy and, **3:**270
  subpoena to, **6:**457
  on subsidies, **7:**564
  A Summary View of the Rights of
    British America, **7:**136
  and surveying activities, **2:**256
  and taxation, **8:**56
  on treaties with foreign nations,
    7:57
  and tribute to pirate-states, **8:**229
  on uniform system of measures,
    5:528–529
  and University of Virginia, **8:**279,
    283
  Vancouver explorations and,
    8:306–307
  in Virginia dynasty, **8:**343, 348
  Virginia Resolves and, **8:**349–350
  Virginia State Capitol designed by,
    2:*47*; **7:**146
  on war hawks, **3:**82
  and War of 1812, **8:**381
  and Washington (D.C.), choice as
    capital, **2:**519
  and westward exploration,
    8:453–454, 461
Jefferson Davis, United States v.,
  8:194
Jefferson Territory, **4:470–471**
Jeffersonian democracy, **2:**549–550;
  4:471–472
  Adams judicial appointments and,
    5:367
Jeffersonian National Gazette (newspaper), **6:**96

Jeffersonian Republicans, **2:**549;
  7:117–118
  and classical republicanism, **7:**116
  vs. Federalist Party, **3:**351–352
  Hartford Convention and, **4:**101
  Jeffersonian democracy of,
    4:471–472
  newspaper of, **6:**96
  in North Carolina, **6:**128
  and postal service, **6:**426
  Quids as, **7:**5
Jefferson-Jenkins, Carolyn, **5:**66
Jeffords, James M., **2:**197; **8:**314
  defection of, **7:**114
Jeffreys, Herbert, **1:**383
Jeffries, G., **8:**319
Jeffries, Jim, **6:**484
Jehovah's Witnesses, **4:472–473**
  growth of, **7:**90
  membership in, **7:***91*
  objected to mandatory recitation of
    Pledge of Allegiance, **3:**380;
    6:370
Jellinek, E. M., **1:**119
Jemison, Mary, **2:**51–52
Jencks, Christopher, **3:**137
Jenkins, Charles F., **8:**76
Jenkins, Charles J., **3:**558
Jenkins, Frederick, **6:**47
Jenkins, John, **2:**476
Jenkins, Robert, **4:**473
Jenkins' Ear, War of, **4:**473
Jenner, Edward, **3:**235; **7:**399
Jennewein, Paul, **1:**306
Jenney, William Le Baron, **2:**132
Jennings, May Mann, **3:**387
Jennings, Robert, **8:**319
Jennison, Charles R., **4:**466
Jensen, Arthur, **7:**13
Jensen, J. H. D., **6:**344
Jerome, Chauncey, **2:**241–242
Jerry Springer Show (TV show), **8:**44
Jersey City (New Jersey), **6:**62, 63
Jersey Prison Ship, **4:**473; **6:**475
Jesuits, **4:***473,* **474–475**
  explorations of, **3:**291; **4:**50–51
  O'odham and, **1:**100
  Relations reports by, **4:**473–474
  schools founded by, **4:**474–475
Jesup, Thomas Sidney, **8:**402
Jesus Freaks, **8:**303
Jesus People Movement, **2:**477;
  8:303
Jet fuel, **6:**301

Jeter, Mildred, **5:**165
Jew(s), **4:476–479**
  Chanukah, **2:104–105**
  at City University of New York,
    2:189
  in Communist Party, **2:**327
  culture of, **4:**478
  in Florida, **5:**351
  German-made products boycotted
    by, **1:**529
  Holocaust Museum and,
    4:150–151
  immigration patterns of,
    1:206–207; **4:**225, 226–227,
    476–477, 488–489
    from Germany, **3:**559
    from Iraq, **4:**422
  immigration to Israel, **3:**197
  neighborhoods of, **4:**477, 478
    in Lower East Side, **5:**165–166
  as neoconservatives, **6:**31–33
  as New York intellectuals, **6:**84–85
  number of, **4:**477
  professional activities of, **4:**476,
    477–478
  refugees during World War II,
    4:226–227
    U.S. response to, **1:**444–445
  religious affiliation of, diversity of,
    7:89
  in Rhode Island, **7:**151
  and slavery, **4:**476
  Soviet, emigration of, **7:**213, 214
  in trade unions, **5:**166
    International Ladies Garment
      Workers Union, **4:**390–392,
      478
  women, **5:**534
  Young Men's and Young Women's
    Hebrew Association,
    8:583–584
  Zionism, **8:591–593**
  See also Anti-Semitism; Judaism
Jewell, Richard, **3:**339
Jewell Ridge Coal Corporation v. Local
  Number 6167, United Mine
  Workers of America, **3:**308
Jewelry, Art Deco, **1:**288
Jewish defense groups, **1:**206–207
Jewish Defense League (JDL),
  4:475–476
Jewtraw, Charles, **6:**192
Jiang Jieshr (Jie-shi), **2:**151, 152
Jicarilla Apaches, **1:**218–219, 221

Jig, **2**:497

Jim Crow laws, **1**:472; **2**:201;
   4:479–480
   Buchanan v. Warley and, **5**:526
   in Florida, **3**:387–388
   in Georgia, **3**:556
   See also Segregation

Jingoism, **4:480**

JNH. See Journal of Negro History

Job Corps, **4:480–481**; **5**:11; **8**:386,
   441

Job training, federal, **2**:330

Job Training Partnership Act (1982),
   5:12

Jobs, Steven P., **2**:336, *337*

Jodo Shinshu (Pure Land), **1**:326

Joel, Billy, **1**:389

Joffrey Ballet, **1**:390

Jogging, **7**:*204*, 205

Jogues, Isaac, **4**:51

John (king of England), **5**:201

John II (king of Portugal), **3**:283

John XXIII, Pope, **2**:70; **8**:308

John, Elton, **1**:388

John Birch Society, **1**:198; **4:481**
   excerpt from manifesto of,
      9:429–433
   protests against water fluoridation,
      3:4

John D. and Catherine T.
   MacArthur Foundation, **5**:181

John Paul II, Pope, **6**:392

Johnny Appleseed, **4:481–482**

*Johns Hopkins Studies in Historical and
   Political Science*, **6**:402

Johns Hopkins University,
   4:482–483; **8**:280
   educational model used by,
      5:17–18
   establishment of, **3**:115, 127
   and learned societies, **5**:67
   Medical School, **5**:281–282

Johnsen, Heather Lynn, **8**:*284*

Johnson, Sir John, **5**:167

Johnson, Sir William, **5**:167

Johnson, Adelaide, **1**:308

Johnson, Alvin, **3**:204; **6**:445

Johnson, Andrew
   Alabama claims and, **1**:106
   amnesty granted by, **1**:177
   attempted assassination of, **1**:328
   Civil Rights Act vetoed by, text of,
      9:317–318

and civil rights legislation, **2**:193;
   3:49

in Committee on the Conduct of
   the War, **2**:313

and Fourteenth Amendment,
   opposition to, **7**:59

and Freedmen's Bureau, **3**:462

impeachment trial of, **2**:353, 505;
   4:234–235, **236–238**, *237*;
   7:60, 100

   separation of powers in, **7**:312

as log cabin president, **5**:145

and loyalty oaths, **8**:96

presidency of, **8**:322

in presidential campaign of 1864,
   3:155

Proclamation of Amnesty by, **6**:491

Radical Republicans and, **7**:15, 16

Reconstruction under, **4**:236–237;
   7:15, 58, 59–60

   in North Carolina, **6**:129

Tenure of Office Act and, **8**:91

Johnson, Ban, **1**:420

Johnson, Charles S., **5**:123, 125

Johnson, Charlotte, **1**:417

Johnson, E. R., **1**:167

Johnson, Earvin (Magic), **1**:17, 425

Johnson, Eastman, **5**:510

Johnson, Elridge, **1**:358

Johnson, F. Ross, **5**:85

Johnson, Frank M., **6**:477

Johnson, Henry, **5**:87

Johnson, Herschel V., **3**:154

Johnson, Hiram, **2**:10; **3**:161; **4**:29
   and proposition, **2**:12

Johnson, Hugh S., **1**:490; **5**:555

Johnson, J. B., **3**:94

Johnson, Jack, **6**:484

Johnson, James Weldon, **4**:96;
   5:125, 526
   *Autobiography of an Ex-Colored
      Man*, **5**:124

Johnson, Jim, **1**:263

Johnson, Joe, **8**:87

Johnson, John, **1**:299

Johnson, Sir John, **2**:314; **6**:213

Johnson, Joseph, **8**:448

Johnson, Joseph E., **1**:567

Johnson, Lady Bird, **3**:376; **4**:*58*

Johnson, Louis A., **2**:528; **5**:558

Johnson, Lyndon B., **4**:*58*
   Alliance for Progress under, **1**:128
   Baker Case and, **1**:385

and civil rights, **2**:194, 195, 199,
   203, 553

Community Action Program
   under, **8**:386

and consumer protection, **2**:384

contracting guidelines of (Executive Order 11246), **1**:36

Council of Economic Advisors and,
   2:431

and credibility gap, **2**:447

Cuba policy of, **2**:471

and Dominican Republic, occupation of, **3**:76

education policies of, **3**:118

environmental policies of, **3**:227

fiscal policies of, **2**:431

on food stamp program, **3**:408

foreign policy of, **3**:427

Great Society of (*See* Great Society)

Highway Beautification Act under,
   4:132

HUD under, **4**:183

immigration reform under, **4**:231

Indian policies of, **4**:289

Israel and, **4**:441

Job Corps under, **4**:480

Kerner Commission under, **4**:522

Latin American policies of, **5**:49

and *Liberty* incident, **5**:96

manipulating public opinion, **6**:534

National Review and, **5**:556

and National Traffic and Motor
   Vehicle Safety Act (1966),
   5:561

The New Republic on, **6**:77

and nondiscriminatory employment, **6**:314

and Nuclear Non-Proliferation
   Treaty, **6**:138

Office of Economic Opportunity
   under, **6**:163

and Panama Canal, **6**:239, 242

presidency of, **8**:323

in presidential campaign of 1960,
   3:164

in presidential campaign of 1964,
   2:24; **3**:165

presidential library of, **5**:100

SALT under, **7**:552–553

speech at University of Michigan,
   8:282

speech declining to seek re-elec-
   tion, **9**:462–463

Johnson, Lyndon B., (*continued*)
  at summit conferences, **8**:15–16
  and tariffs, **8**:52, 158
  and Teachers Corps, **8**:61
  and termination policy, **8**:91
  and Tonkin Gulf Resolution, **8:142–143**
  and trade unions, **8**:262, 263
  and Transportation, Department of, **8**:185
  and Treasury, **8**:197
  and Vietnam War, **1**:77; **3**:427; **8**:331–333, *332*
    policies of, **2**:151, 365, 528, 532; **7**:212
  and Violence Commission, **8**:340
  and Voting Rights Act, **3**:144; **8**:357
  War on Poverty, **1**:571–572; **2**:328; **6**:438, 551; **8**:293, 385, 441
  war powers under, **8**:388
  Warren Commission and, **8**:394
  and Washington (D.C.) home rule, **8**:411
  and Wise Men, **8**:493
  workplace safety under, **6**:158
  in World War II, **8**:557
Johnson, Marietta, **3**:116
Johnson, Michael, **6**:192; **7**:205
Johnson, Mississippi v., **3**:559; **5**:418; **8**:97
Johnson, Oliver, **6**:47
Johnson, Opha Mae, **5**:243
Johnson, Philip, **1**:251, 253, 494; **6**:430
Johnson, Richard, **1**:191
Johnson, Richard M., **3**:153, 171
Johnson, Robert, **1**:492
Johnson, Robert Underwood, **2**:369
Johnson, Samuel, **3**:220; **6**:387; **7**:137
Johnson, Samuel, Jr., **3**:22
Johnson, Samuel William, **3**:325
Johnson, Tom, **2**:233; **5**:477; **6**:174
Johnson, United States v., **6**:554
Johnson, Sir William, **1**:432; **6**:490
Johnson, William, on due process of law, **3**:89
Johnson, William D., **1**:65
  and land speculation, **5**:36
Johnson Controls, Inc., Automobile Workers v., **1**:377
Johnson County War (1892), **8**:565

Johnson Debt-Default Act (1934), **5**:81
Johnson v. McIntosh, **6**:506
Johnson v. Transportation Agency of Santa Clara County, **1**:36–37
Johnson-Clarendon Convention (1868), **1**:106
Johnson-Reed Act (1924), **4**:59
Johnston, Albert Sidney, **2**:212–213
  in Battle of Shiloh, **7**:346
Johnston, Henrietta, **1**:294
Johnston, Henry, **6**:186
Johnston, Joseph E., **2**:212, 214, 215
  in Atlanta Campaign, **1**:350–351
  capitulation of, **2**:343
  and Davis (Jefferson), controversy between, **1**:567; **2:505–506**
  in First Battle of Bull Run, **1**:567; **2**:211
  in Peninsular Campaign, **6**:275
Johnston, Kathryn, **5**:133
Johnston, Mary, **5**:129
Johnston, Philip, **6**:17
Johnston Atoll, **1**:189
Johnstown flood, **3**:383; **4**:*483*, **483–484**
JOIDES. *See* Joint Oceanographic Institute's Deep Earth Sampling Program
Joint Chiefs of Staff (JCS), **4:484**
Joint commissions, **4:484–485**
Joint Committee on Reconstruction, **4:485–486**
Joint occupation, of Oregon territory, **4**:41, **486**; **6**:205
Joint Oceanographic Institute's Deep Earth Sampling Program (JOIDES), **3**:552
Joint-stock companies, **2**:111; **8**:174
Joint-stock land banks, **4:486**
Joliot, Frédéric, **6**:340, 341
Jolliet, Louis, **2**:131; **3**:285, 291; **5**:22
  explorations with Marquette, **4:486–487**, *487*
  on Arkansas River, **1**:264
  in Illinois, **4**:214
  on Mississippi River, **3**:472; **4**:51; **5**:416
  and Wisconsin River, discovery of, **8**:489
Jolly Flatboatmen (Bingham), **3**:537
Jolson, Al, **4**:470, *470*
Jomini, Henri, **5**:145

Jon, Gee, **2**:40
Jonah's Gourd Vine (Hurston), **5**:125
Joncaire, Daniel de, **6**:102
Joncaire, Louis Thomas de, **6**:102
Jones, Abner, **8**:263
Jones, Alex S., **6**:90
Jones, Bobby, **4**:19, *19*
Jones, Catesby, **5**:442
Jones, Charles Colcock, **1**:42
Jones, Charles O., **6**:453
Jones, Charles Price, **1**:45; **2**:172
Jones, Chuck, **2**:64
Jones, Cleve, **1**:72
Jones, Clinton v., **2:240–241**
Jones, Edward Davis, **3**:83; **8**:366–367
Jones, Evan, **2**:163
Jones, Gayl, *Corregidora*, **5**:126
Jones, George, **6**:89
Jones, James, *From Here to Eternity*, **5**:121
Jones, Jesse, **7**:63
Jones, Jim, **4**:488; **7**:94; **8**:339
Jones, John Paul, **1**:497, *497*; **6**:24, 57
Jones, LeRoi. *See* Baraka, Imamu Amiri
Jones, Margaret, **8**:494
Jones, Marion, **6**:192; **7**:205
Jones, (Mother) Mary, in Industrial Workers of the World, **4**:346
Jones, Paula Corbin, **2**:239; **4**:239, 240; **7**:496
  legal suit against Clinton, **2:240–241**
Jones, Rufus M., **7**:2
Jones, S. J., **5**:59
Jones, Samuel M. (Golden Rule), **6**:174
Jones, Thomas Hudson, **8**:285
Jones, William, **3**:300
Jones Act (1916), **4:487**
  and Philippines, **6**:322
Jones Act (1917), and Puerto Rico, **6**:542, 544–545
Jones and Laughlin Steel Corporation, National Labor Relations Board v., **2**:311; **3**:90; **8**:274
  effects of, **4**:493
Jones v. Van Zandt, **3**:482; **4:487**
Jonestown Massacre, **4**:488, *488*; **8**:339
Jones-White Act (1928), **3**:195
Jong, Erica, *Fanny*, **5**:122

Joplin, Scott, **7**:22
Jordan, Barbara, "Constitutional Faith" speech by, text of, **9**:489–491
Jordan, David Starr
anti-imperialism of, **1**:202
at Stanford University, **7**:523
Jordan, I. King, **3**:504
Jordan, June, **5**:126
Jordan, Michael, **1**:52, 426; **2**:79
Jordan, W. K., **3**:133
Joseph, Ruth, **5**:72
Joseph (Nez Perce chief), **6**:101, *101*, 102; **8**:404
Josephson, Brian D., **6**:347
Josephson, Matthew, **7**:181
Josephson effect, **6**:347
Journal(s), scholarly, African American, **5**:200
Journal of Congress, **4**:488
Journal of Negro Education, **5**:200
Journal of Negro History (JNH), **5**:200
Journal of Parapsychology, **6**:246
Journal of the American Medical Association (JAMA), **1**:164
Journal of the American Veterinary Medical Association, **8**:319
Journal of the Franklin Institute, **3**:455
Journal of the History of the Behavioral Science, **6**:526
Journalism
broadcast, **7**:20
Cold War and, **6**:99
muckrakers, **5**:470–471
photojournalism, **1**:301
Pulitzer Prizes for, **6**:488–489
science, **7**:273–277
women in, **8**:506
yellow, **8**:577
Journey of Reconciliation, **2**:354
Journeymen, **2**:223
Journeymen Barbers, Messner v., **6**:350
Jowers, Lloyd, **4**:530
Joy, Henry B., **3**:20
Joy Luck Club, The (Tan), **5**:123
Joyce, James, **5**:157, 194; **6**:419, 427
Ulysses, obscenity suit against, **2**:84
Joyner, Florence Griffith, **7**:205
JR, Parham v., **2**:149
Juáres, Juan, **3**:453
Juárez, Benito, **5**:46, 345
Judaism, **4**:488–491
in colonial era, **4**:476

Conservative, **4**:490, 491
early American, **4**:477
membership in, **7**:*91*
Orthodox, **4**:489, 490–491
Reconstructionist, **4**:490
Reform, **4**:489–490, 491
and religious learning, **7**:97
women's role in, **8**:500
after World War II, **4**:478–479
See also Anti-Semitism; Jew(s)
Judd, Donald, **1**:307
Judges
impeachment of, **4**:234, 241
midnight, **4**:499; **5**:367
nomination of, judicial ideology and, **7**:313
Judicial activism, and Supreme Court nominations, **4**:497
Judicial branch of federal government, **3**:341
See also Supreme Court, U.S.
Judicial circuits, **2**:175–176
Judicial review, **4**:491–494, 495; **8**:208
Calder v. Bull and, **2**:7
in Hayburn's case, **4**:109
in *Marbury v. Madison*, **4**:491–492; **5**:235–236; **8**:23
of taxation legislation, **4**:206
Judiciary, **4**:494–498
administrative adjudication and, **1**:22
Burger Court and, **4**:497
Constitutional Convention on, **2**:380–381
laissez-faire conservatism and power of, **2**:375
representation in, **7**:108
tribal, **4**:265, **316–317**
Warren Court and, **4**:496–497
Judiciary Act (1789), **2**:381; **3**:253–254; **4**:498–499
on admiralty law, **1**:23
provisions of, **4**:499
review of state court decisions, **5**:255
Supreme Court on, **8**:36
on writs of mandamus, **5**:235
Judiciary Act (1801), **4**:499–500
goal of, **8**:26
provisions of, **4**:499–500
Judiciary Act (1802), **4**:500; **8**:26
Judson, E. Z. C., **5**:129
Judson, Harry Pratt, **8**:281

Juglar, Clément, **1**:582
Juice industry, **2**:182
Juilliard v. Greenman, **4**:500
Juin, Alphonse, **4**:78
Julian, George W., **2**:313
as Radical Republican, **7**:15
Julian, Percy L., **1**:*50*
Julius Rosenwald Fund, **6**:317
Julliard v. Greenman, **5**:76
Jumping-off places, **4**:500
Jung, Carl G., psychoanalysis, **5**:314
Junge, Ember Reichgott, **2**:110
Jungle, The (Sinclair), **2**:37, 227, 389; **4**:27, **500–501**; **5**:120, 135, 277, 280; **6**:11, 12, 352, 554; **8**:285
excerpt from, **9**:360
Junior Chamber of Commerce (Jaycees), **7**:183
Junior colleges, **3**:117, 127
Junior Leagues International, Association of, **4**:501
Junk bonds, **1**:563; **4**:501–502; **5**:84
Juntas, in Latin America, **5**:50–51
Jurisdictional Act (1928), **8**:215
Jury trial, **4**:502–503
African Americans as jurors, **4**:503; **7**:555
plea bargain and, **6**:369
women as jurors, **8**:60
Jussieu, Antoine Laurent de, **1**:519
Just, Alexander, **5**:24
Just What Is It That Makes Today's Homes So Different, So Appealing? (Hamilton), **6**:414
Justice, Department of (DOJ), **3**:331; **4**:503–504
corporations investigated by, **2**:419
establishment of, **4**:503
functions of, **4**:503–504
head of, **2**:2
in ITT Affair, **4**:449
organization of, **4**:503
specialized police agencies of, **6**:385
Strike Force Against Organized Crime, **2**:377
Justice of the peace, **4**:504
Jutland, Battle of, **1**:266
Juvenile courts, **2**:137, 146, 149, 461; **4**:250, **504–506**
Juvenile Delinquency and Youth Offenses Control Act (1961), **6**:212

Juvenile Justice and Delinquency
    Prevention Act (1974), **4**:505
Juvenile Miscellany, **5**:127
Juveniles
    detention facilities for, **7**:74–75
    prosecution as adults, **2**:461

K

Kabila, Joseph, **1**:39
Kabila, Laurent-Désiré, **1**:39
Kaczynski, David, **8**:247
Kaczynski, Theodore John (Ted),
    8:*247*, **247–248**
    anarchism and, **1**:182
Kaempffert, Waldemar, **7**:274
Kagahi, Soryu, **1**:325
Kahanamoku, Duke, **8**:37
Kahane, Meir, **4**:475
Kahn, Louis, **1**:253
Kainai (Blood) Indians, **1**:481
Kaiser, Henry, **1**:373; **4**:120; **8**:414
Kaiser Aluminum and Chemical
    Company, **6**:116
Kaiser Permanente, **4**:117
Kajioka, Sadamichi, **8**:365
Kalakaua (king of Hawaii), **4**:107
Kallen, Horace, **1**:337, 338; **6**:375
Kalm, Pehr, **1**:519
Kalm, Peter, **6**:432
Kamehameha, **4**:105–106
Kan, Gene, **4**:*398*
Kanagawa, Treaty of (1854), **4**:457
Kandinsky, Wassily, **1**:297
    in Armory Show, **1**:268
Kane, Elisha Kent, **6**:382
Kansa Indians, **8**:223
Kansas, **4:507–511**
    agriculture in, **4**:508, 509, 510
    alien landholding in, **1**:124
    antislavery settlers in, **3**:195–196
    in Border War, **1:506**; **7**:4
    boundary disputes in, **4**:466
    in Civil War, **4**:509
    in colonial era, **4**:508
    constitution of, **4**:510; **8**:563
    Dust Bowl in, **4**:510
    emblems, nicknames, mottos, and
        songs of, **7**:*532*
    Farmers' Alliance in, **3**:324
    Free-State Party in, **4:512**
    geography of, **4**:507
    governors of, **4**:510

Kansas-Nebraska Act and,
    4:508–509, 512–513
    legislature of, **4**:509, 510
    Native Americans in, **4**:507–508,
        509
    New England Emigrant Aid Com-
        pany and, **6**:49
    population of, **4**:510
    Pottawatomie Massacre in, **4**:98,
        509
    prehistoric, **4**:507–508
    segregation in, **4**:510
    slavery in, **4**:508–509, 512–513;
        5:110–111
        conflicts over, **1**:505, 506
        and Lecompton Constitution,
            5:73
    Sons of the South in, **7**:449–450
    statehood for, **4**:509; **8**:143
    tornadoes in, **8**:143
    wheat production in, **3**:390
    women's suffrage in, **4**:509–510
    in World War II, **4**:510
    Wyandotte Constitution and,
        8:563
Kansas, Coppage v., **2**:408; **8**:578
Kansas City (Missouri), **4**:511, *511*
    Pendergast machine in, **6:274–275**
Kansas Committee, National,
    4:511–512
Kansas Free-State Party, **4:512**
Kansas People's Party, **3**:324
Kansas-Nebraska Act (1854), **1**:505,
    506; **3**:195; **4:512–513**;
    5:58–59, 73, 110
    debate over passage of, **4**:512–513
    and Kansas, **4**:508–509
    and Missouri, **5**:420
    and Nebraska, **6**:30
    provisions of, **4**:512
    Sumner's "Crime Against Kansas"
        speech on, excerpt from,
        9:288–292
    and Vermont, **8**:313
Kant, Immanuel, **3**:262; **6**:324;
    8:180
Kao, Charles K., **3**:357
Kapany, Narinder, **3**:357
Kaplan, Mordecai M., **4**:490
Kapleau, Philip, **1**:552
Kaposi's sarcoma (KS), **1**:15
Karbowiak, Antoni E., **3**:357
Karcher, Alan, **6**:62
Kardiner, Abram, **6**:431

Kareline, Alexandre, **6**:193
Karenga, Maulana, **4**:553
Karenga, Ron, **1**:46, 47
Karlsefni, Thorfinn, **8**:337
Karmal, Babrak, **1**:37
Kármán, Theodore von, **3**:217
Kashevarov, Aleksandr, **3**:294
Kashim, **8**:212
Kashmir, struggle over, **4**:259–260
Kasparov, Gary, **2**:130, 338
Kasserine Pass, Battle of,
    4:513–514; **6**:124
Katz v. United States, **6**:479
Katzenbach, South Carolina v., **8**:357
Kaufman, George S., **1**:123
Kaufmann, Craig, **1**:299
Kaufmann, Walter, **3**:280
Kawaida, **1**:46
Kawakita v. United States, **8**:194–195
Kaweah Co-Operative Common-
    wealth, **8**:303
Kay, John, **2**:424
Kayak, **2**:37
Kazanjian, Varaztad, **2**:422
Kazin, Alfred, **2**:189; **5**:121
KCA Indians. *See* Kiowa,
    Comanche, and Plains Apache
    coalition
Kearney, Denis, **2**:10; **4**:514
    and anti-Chinese movement, **2**:154
Kearneyites, **4**:514
Kearny, Lawrence, mission to China
    by, **2**:153; **4**:515
Kearny, Stephen Watts, **6**:68
    in Arizona, **1**:257
    march to California by, **4:514–515**
    Stockton and, **4**:515; **7**:551
Kearsarge (ship), **1**:105
Keating, William H., **3**:455
Keayne, Robert, **7**:478
Keck, Fred, **3**:498
Keck, George, **3**:498
Keck Observatory, **6**:157
Keefe, Dan, **4**:395
Keelboat, **4**:515; **7**:22, 171
Keeley, Leslie, **1**:119
Keeling, Charles David, **2**:237; **4**:6
Keeling curve, **2**:237, *237*
Keeney, Barnaby, **5**:537
Kefauver, Estes
    and investigation of organized
        crime, **2**:463
    in presidential campaign of 1956,
        3:164

Kefauver Committee, **2:**463

Kehler, Randy, **6:**268

Keith, Benjamin Franklin, **8:**309

Keith, George, **7:**2

Keith, Minor, **5:**46

Keller, Louis, **7:**417

Kelley, Abby, **7:**3

Kelley, Alfred, **2:**32

Kelley, David, **6:**154

Kelley, Florence, **2:**147
   and National Consumers' League, **2:**392

Kelley, Oliver Hudson, **4:**36

Kellogg, Frank B., **7:**196
   in American Bar Association, **1:**145
   and Farmer-Labor party of Minnesota, **3:**322
   and Kellogg-Briand Pact, **4:**515

Kellogg, John H., **1:**31; **2:**98; **3:**24

Kellogg, W. P., **6:**76

Kellogg, William K., **2:**98

Kellogg-Briand Pact (1928), **3:**426; **4:515; 6:**35, 36, 197, 264; **8:**205, 371

Kelly, Charles T., **4:**516

Kelly, Ellsworth, **1:**298

Kelly, Joan, **8:**520

Kelly, John (Honest), **3:**157; **8:**46

Kelly, King, **1:**420

Kelly, Oliver Hudson, **2:**407

Kelly Act. *See* Airmail Act

Kelly's Industrial Army, **4:516**

Kelso, Frank B., **8:**44

Kelvin, William Thomson, Lord, **6:**160

Kelvinator, **3:**182

Kemble, Frances, **1:**136–137

Kemp, Jack, **3:**169; **4:**184; **5:**20

Kendall, Amos, **3:**504; **6:**426

Kendall, George, **2:**40

Kendrick, John, **2:**153
   explorations by, in Aleutian Islands, **1:**121

Kenesaw Mountain, Battle of, **4:516**

Kennan, George F.
   ambassadorship of, **1:**134
   "American Diplomacy," excerpt from, **9:**411–413
   and containment strategy, **2:**268; **7:**212
   "X" article, **8:569**

Kennebec River settlements, **4:516**

Kennedy, Anthony M.
   on line-item vetoes, **8:**321
   on presidential election of 2000, **1:**579
   on Religious Freedom Restoration Act, **1:**394
   on sexual orientation, discrimination based on, **7:**196
   on state sovereignty, **1:**120

Kennedy, Edward M.
   and bioethics, **1:**462
   and Chappaquiddick incident, **2:105**
   in presidential campaign of 1980, **3:**167
   and Teachers Corps, **8:**61

Kennedy, Jacqueline (Jackie), **3:**375, 376
   and White House furnishings, **8:**471

Kennedy, John F., **5:***533*
   and Alliance for Progress, **1:**127–128; **3:**143, 417–418
   anti-Catholicism and, **1:**196
   in Arlington National Cemetery, **1:**264
   assassination of, **1:**330; **2:**495; **8:**339
      conspiracy theories on, **1:**330; **2:**378
      and gun control, **4:**75
      Malcolm X on, **5:**520
      media coverage of, **8:**339
      and Vietnam War, **8:**331
      Warren Commission on, **8:394–395**
   birthplace of, **1:**508
   at Camp David, **2:***20*
   campaign song for, **2:**24
   and church-state separation, **2:**169
   and civil rights, **2:**195, 199; **3:**49
   Cold War policies of, **1:**444
   and collective bargaining, by federal employees, **1:**154, 156; **7:**558
   and communication satellites, **2:**319
   and consumer protection, **2:**384, 391
   on consumer rights, **6:**555
   Council of Economic Advisors and, **2:**431, 432
   Cuba policy of, **2:**470–471
      Bay of Pigs invasion and, **1:**430–431; **2:**470–471
   Cuban missile crisis and, **2:**471, 474, 475
   defense policy of, **2:**528
   and Democratic Party, **2:**553
   and employment discrimination, **6:**314
   on employment discrimination, **1:**36
   environmental policies of, **3:**227
   fiscal policies of, **2:**431
   and food stamp program, **3:**408; **6:**438
   foreign policy of, **3:**427
   and GATT, **3:**524
   and gold reserves, **4:**17
   inauguration of, **4:***251*
   Indian policies of, **4:**289
      termination in, **8:**91
   internment of, **6:**458
   Israel and, **4:**441
   and Khrushchev, **7:**212, *212*
   labor policies of, **3:**244
   Latin American policies of, **5:**48–49
   on moon landing, **5:**523
   and National Endowment for the Arts, **5:**535
   and National Endowment for the Humanities, **5:**536
   and National Security Council, **5:**560
   Navy and Marine Corps Medal for, **2:**527
   and New Frontier, **6:**55
   The New Republic on, **6:**77
   and *New York Times*, **6:**90
   and Peace Corps, **6:**265–266
   in presidential campaign of 1960, **1:**507; **3:**164–165; **6:**55, 463
   presidential library of, **5:***99*, 100
   and President's Commission on the Status of Women, **8:**498, 516
   religious affiliation of, **2:**164
   and South Vietnam, foreign aid to, **3:**417
   space program under, **7:**480
   speech at University of Michigan, **8:**282
   at summit conferences, **8:**15
   on supersonic transport, **8:**21
   and tariffs, **8:**52, 157, 166
   and Trade Expansion Act, **7:**54
   and trade unions, **8:**172
   Vietnam War policies of, **2:**151; **7:**212; **8:**330–331

Kennedy, John F., (*continued*)
 Voter Education Project of, **2**:354
 and Washington (D.C.) home rule,
  8:411
 and Women's Bureau, **8**:508
 in World War II, **8**:557
Kennedy, Robert F., **3**:165
 assassination of
  and gun control, **4**:75
  and Violence Commission, **8**:340
 civil rights movement and, **2**:202
 Cuban missile crisis and, **2**:471,
  475
 and FBI, **3**:338
 influence of, **2**:2
 outlawing segregation on trains
  and buses, **3**:464
 in presidential campaign of 1968,
  3:165
Kennedy, Ruby Jo Reeves, **1**:337
Kennedy Round, **3**:524; **8**:52, 158,
 166
Kenner, Duncan F., **2**:342
Kenney, David D., **3**:182
Kenny, Elizabeth, **6**:388
Kensington Stone, **4**:516–517
Kent, Jacob F., **7**:486
Kent State University, protest at,
 2:16; **3**:119; **4**:517–518
Kentucky, **4**:518–521, *520*
 African Americans in, **4**:521
 agriculture in, **4**:519
  hemp, **4**:126
 art and literature in, **4**:520–521
 Bluegrass country in, **1**:491, *491*
 capital of, **2**:47
 in Civil War, **4**:519
  Bragg's Campaign in, **7**:35, 157
  Richmond Campaigns in,
   7:156–157
  Union sentiment in, **8**:260
 in colonial era, **4**:518
 constitution of, **4**:519
 as "Dark and Bloody Ground,"
  2:501–502
 earthquakes in, **3**:101
 education in, **4**:520
 emblems, nicknames, mottos, and
  songs of, **7**:*532*
 gun control in, **4**:74
 horses in, **4**:168
 and Missouri, boundary dispute
  between, **1**:522
 Morgan's raids into, **5**:458

 motto of, **8**:279
 mountain feuds in, **3**:356–357
 Native Americans in, **4**:518
 politics in, **4**:519, 521
 population of, **4**:521
 prehistoric, **4**:518
 slavery in, **4**:519–520
 statehood for, **4**:518
 violence in, **4**:520
 voice voting in, **3**:146
 whiskey industry in, **7**:504; **8**:78,
  468
 women in, **4**:521
Kentucky boats. *See* Flatboat(s)
Kentucky Conventions (1780s),
 4:522
Kentucky County, **1**:382
Kentucky Distillers, Hamilton v., **8**:374
Kentucky Resolutions (1798), **1**:124;
 8:349
 in southern rights movement, **7**:473
Keogh plans. *See* Retirement plans
Keokuk (Sauk chief), **1**:473
Keppel, Frederick P., **2**:56
Keppel & Brothers, Inc., FTC v., **3**:348
Kerbschnitt, **3**:495
Kerenga, Maulana, **4**:148, 553
Kerenski, Aleksandr F., **7**:211
Kerkorian, Kirk, **5**:42
Kern, Edward, **4**:39
Kern, Stephen, **3**:542
Kernell, Samuel, **6**:454
Kerner, Otto, **4**:522
Kerner Commission, **4**:522; **6**:438
Kerosine oil, **4**:522–523; **6**:298, 301
Kerouac, Jack, **1**:433; **2**:433; **4**:65
 alma mater of, **2**:304
 On the Road, **5**:122
Kerr, Robert S., **1**:385
Kerrey, Bob, **1**:354
Kerry, John, **6**:241
Kerry, Peggy, **6**:85
Kerst, Donald W., **6**:343
Kertwig, Oskar, **2**:142
Kesey, Ken, **6**:207
 One Flew Over the Cuckoo's Nest, **5**:122
Kesselring, Albert, **1**:217
 and Gustav Line, **4**:78
Kessler, David, **1**:16
Kessler, Suzanne, **3**:516, 517
Ketchum, William C., Jr., **1**:303
Kettering, Charles F., **6**:174
Kevorkian, Jack, **1**:339; **3**:262;
 7:160–161

Key, Francis Scott, **1**:328; **3**:378,
 379; **5**:185; **7**:524
 "Star-Spangled Banner"
  inspiration for, **7**:188
  Ripley (Robert LeRoy) on, **7**:168
Key, V. O., **3**:147; **6**:398, 403
Keynes, John Maynard, **3**:109, 345;
 4:523; **5**:441–442; **8**:254
 on business cycles, **1**:584
 *General Theory of Employment,
  Interest and Money*, **4**:16; **6**:44
 on gold standard, **4**:15
 on government spending, **4**:46
 on interest rates, **3**:345
 and International Monetary Fund,
  3:110
 on investment, **4**:45
 and New Deal, **6**:44
Keynesianism, **3**:110; **4**:523;
 5:441–442
 at Brookings Institution, **8**:117
 Council of Economic Advisors and,
  2:431
 and Employment Act (1946), **3**:200
 and Federal Reserve System,
  3:345–346
 and government spending, **4**:46
Keyserling, Mary Dublin, **2**:392
KGC. *See* Knights of the Golden
 Circle
Khalid Shaikh Mohammed, **3**:41
Khe Sanh, siege at, **1**:77
Khmer Rouge, **2**:16
 Mayaguez incident, **5**:275
Khoury, Callie, **5**:72
Khrushchev, Nikita, **2**:269; **3**:427
 Bay of Pigs invasion and, **1**:430
 and Berlin Wall, **1**:444
 at Camp David, **2**:20
 Cuban missile crisis and, **2**:471,
  474, 475
 and de-Stalinization, **2**:327
 and Kennedy, **7**:212, *212*
 and Paris Conference (1960), **6**:247
 at summit conferences, **8**:15
 U-2 incident and, **8**:247
 visit to U.S., **2**:20; **7**:212
Khyatt, Robert, **3**:381
Kickapoo, **4**:524, *524*; **8**:224
 and Greenville Treaty, **4**:64
Kidder, Alfred V., **1**:240
Kidnapping, **4**:524–526
 in colonial era, **4**:525
 firsthand account of, **9**:101–103

of free African Americans, **6**:294, 462

Lindbergh, **4**:525; **5**:113

by UFOs, **8**:255

Kidney transplantation, **8**:183

Kieft, Willem, **4**:282; **6**:71–72

Kieft's War, **6**:72

Kier, Samuel M., **4**:522, 523; **6**:302

Kierkegaard, Søren, **3**:279, 280

Kilauea (volcano), **8**:351, *351*, 352

Kilborne, Fred L., **8**:320

Kilgore, Bernard, **8**:367

Kilgore, Harley, **5**:557

Kilocalories, **6**:148

Kilroy, James J., **4**:526

"Kilroy Was Here" graffiti, **4**:526

Kilson, Martin, **1**:46

Kim, Elaine H., "War Story," **9**:419–424

Kim Il Sung, Soviet Union and, **4**:546

Kimball, Kate F., **2**:113

Kimball, Spencer, **5**:55; **8**:298

Kimmel, Husband E., **6**:272, 273

Kimpton, Lawrence, **8**:281

Kincaid, Jamaica, **5**:123

Kind, Phyllis, **1**:311

King, B. B., **1**:492; **7**:185

King, Billie Jean, **7**:511, *511*; **8**:90

King, Clarence, **3**:300, 544, 545, *545*, 552; **6**:300; **8**:454

King, Coretta, **2**:*203*

King, Ernest J., **8**:546, 557

as chief of naval operations, **6**:20

King, Martin Luther, Jr., **1**:*52*; **2**:*203*; **4**:*529*; **5**:*533*

in Alabama, **1**:104

assassination of, **2**:204; **4**:528–530; **8**:339

conspiracy theories on, **4**:530

FBI and, **3**:338

and gun control, **4**:75

prosecution of Ray after, **4**:529–530

riots after, **4**:528; **7**:*164*; **8**:338

trade union support and, **1**:154

and Violence Commission, **8**:340

Bible's influence on, **1**:449

Christian teachings of, **2**:164–165

and civil rights movement, **2**:199

education of, **3**:126

as FBI target, **2**:266

"I Have a Dream" speech, **5**:237

Montgomery bus boycott and, **1**:529; **2**:202; **3**:557

National Baptist Convention and opposition to, **1**:413

and Nobel Peace Prize, **3**:557

nonviolent strategies of, **2**:192

"Poor Peoples' Campaign" of, **3**:50

in Progressive National Baptist Convention, **1**:45

and radicalism, **7**:17–18

resistance to draft, **2**:364–365

in Saint Augustine, **3**:388

in Southern Christian Leadership Conference, **3**:557; **7**:472–473

teachings of, **6**:517

in Tennessee, **8**:86

on Vietnam War, **1**:216; **2**:204

King, Rodney, **5**:155, *155*; **6**:385, *386*; **7**:12; **8**:339

See also Los Angeles, riots in

King, Rufus, **5**:424

at Constitutional Convention, **2**:379

in presidential campaign of 1804, **3**:151

in presidential campaign of 1808, **3**:151

in presidential campaign of 1816, **3**:151

in Second Battle of Bull Run, **1**:568

King, Stephen, **5**:122, 130

King, William Lyon Mackenzie, **2**:27

King, William R., **3**:154

King and I, The (film), **8**:248

"King Cotton," **4**:526

King Cotton diplomacy, **2**:342, 344

King Features, **6**:458

King George's War, **2**:294; **3**:469; **4**:526

Aix-la-Chapelle Treaty and, **1**:99–100; **4**:313

feud over conduct of, **6**:83

privateering in, **6**:480

King Philip's War, **4**:313, **526–527**; **6**:379, 448; **7**:151; **8**:459

fast followed by, **3**:329

Mount Hope, **5**:464

and Narragansetts, **5**:513

New England Confederation in, **6**:49

King William's War, **2**:293; **4**:527–528

end of, **7**:217

Kingdom and the Power, The (Talese), **6**:90

King's College, **2**:304

See also Columbia University

King's Highway, **7**:176

King's Mountain, Battle of, **1**:382; **7**:145

King's Province, **4**:528

Kingsbury, Nathan, **8**:65

Kingsley, Clarence, **3**:117

Kingsley, Sidney, **5**:121

Kinkaid, Thomas C., **5**:89

Kinkaid Act (1904), **1**:65

Kino, Eusebio, **1**:256; **4**:474; **8**:227, 238

Kinsey, Alfred, **4**:530–531; **7**:326

Kinsey Report, **4**:530–531

on homosexuality, **4**:531; **7**:326–327

Kinship, **4**:531–532

Kinsman, Delos O., **8**:493

Kintpuash (Modoc leader), **5**:433; **8**:404

Kiowa, **4**:532–534, *533*; **8**:218

alliances of, **4**:532

belief systems of, **4**:533

kinship system of, **4**:532–533

migrations by, **4**:532

on reservations, **6**:263

treaty with, Congressional violation of, **5**:147–148

Kiowa, Comanche, and Plains Apache coalition (KCA Indians), **4**:532

Kiowa Apaches, **1**:218, 219

Kirby, James B., **3**:182

Kirby, Rollin, **6**:395

Kirby-Smith, Edmund

in Battle of Perryville, **6**:291

in Red River Campaign, **7**:71

in Richmond Campaigns, **7**:156–157

Kirchwey, Freda, **5**:522

Kirk, Claude, **3**:388

Kirk, Russell, **5**:556

Kirkland, Lane, **1**:152, 153

Kirkpatrick, Jeane, **5**:49; **6**:32

Kirstein, Lincoln, **1**:390; **2**:498; **6**:81

Kissinger, Henry A.

and African policies, **1**:38

on Christmas bombing of Hanoi, **9**:475–477

and Cuba policy, **2**:471

and European relations, **3**:260

Kissinger, Henry A., (*continued*)
  as executive agent, **3:**277
  and Latin America, **5:**49
  and Panama Canal, **6:**240, 242
  and prisoners of war in Vietnam, **6:**475
  in SALT, **7:**553
  at summit conferences, **8:**16
  in Vietnam War peace negotiations, **8:**334
"Kitchen Cabinet," **3:**146; **4:**534
Kitchens, **4:534–536**
Kitchin, Joseph, **1:**582
Kitchin, Thomas, **9:**23, *23*
Kitson, Theo Alice Ruggles, **1:**308
Kitt Peak National Observatory, **6:**156
Kittinger, Joe, **1:**392
KKK. *See* Ku Klux Klan
Klamath-Modoc, **4:536–538**
  termination policy and, **8:**91
Klebold, Dylan, **2:**305
Kleburg, Robert, **5:**135
Klein, Lawrence R., **1:**587; **3:**110
Klein, William, **1:**301
Kleindienst v. Mandel, **1:**125
Kleinrock, Leonard, **4:**398
Kline, Franz, **1:**298
Klinkhammer, Stephen, on fall of Saigon, **9:**477–479
Klondike gold rush, **2:**26; **4:538–539,** *539;* **8:**589, *589*
Kluckhohn, Clyde, **1:**193
Klutznick, Fullilove v., **1:**36
K-Mart, **3:**10, 26; **7:**126
Knapp, Isaac, **6:**47
Knauss, Friedrich von, **8:**244
Knickerbocker Club, **2:**251
Knickerbocker Theater (Washington, D.C.), collapse of, **3:**36
Knight, Bobby, **1:**425
Knight, Etheridge, **5:**126
Knight, Frank, **3:**109
Knight v. Board of Regents of University of State of New York, **8:**62
Knights of Labor (KOL), **2:**254; **3:**466; **4:539–540; 5:**7, 10, 16; **8:**171
  and boycotting, **1:**528
  Burlington strike and, **1:**576
  campaign for child labor legislation, **2:**140
  inclusiveness of, **2:**224
  and Labor Day, **5:**12

and railroad strike of 1886, **7:**29
Knights of Mary Phagan, **3:**453
Knights of Reliance, **3:**323
Knights of the Golden Circle (KGC), **2:**411; **4:540**
Knoedler, Michael, **2:**272
Knoll, Florence, **1:**293
Knorr, Nathan Homer, **4:**472
Knowland, William F., **1:**537
Knowlton, Charles, **1:**467
Knowlton v. Moore, **8:**57
Know-Nothing Party, **1:**165–166; **4:540–541,** *541;* **8:**260
  anti-Catholicism of, **2:**69, 163; **6:**4
  ideology of, **1:**166; **4:**540
  organizations in, **1:**165–166
  platform of (1856), **9:**242–243
  in presidential campaign of 1856, **3:**154
  Tammany Hall and, **8:**46
Knox, Fort, **4:541**
Knox, Frank, **8:**543
  in presidential campaign of 1936, **3:**162
Knox, Henry, **7:**142; **8:**124, 318
  Indian policies of, **4:**284; **6:**178
  Indian agents in, **4:**261
Knox, John, on right of revolution, **7:**148
Knox, John Jay, **1:**400
Knox, Philander, and dollar diplomacy, **3:**70, 71
Knox v. Lee, **5:**76
Knutson-Vandenberg Act (1930), **3:**432
Koch, Bill, **1:**173
Koch, Edward, **2:**189
Koch, Robert, **1:**465; **3:**239; **8:**236
Kodak camera, **6:**329
Koh Tang (island), **5:**275
Kohl, Helmut, **1:**471
Kohlberg Kravis Roberts & Company, in RJR Nabisco takeover battle (1988), **5:**85
Kohler, Kaufman, **4:**490
Kohut, Alexander, **4:**490
KOL. *See* Knights of Labor
Kolchak, Aleksandr V., **7:**353
Kolmer, John A., **6:**388
Kondratiev, Nikolai, **1:**582
König, Friedrich, **6:**469
Konko Kyo, **1:**327
Koons, Jeff, **1:**307
Koop, C. Everett, **1:**17

Koopmans, Tjalling, **3:**109, 110
Kopechne, Mary Jo, **2:**105
Korea
  capitalist development in, **2:**44
  division of, **4:**545; **8:**120
  immigrants from, and Christian churches, **7:**91
  Japanese power in, **4:**457, 541–542, 545
  trade with, **4:**541, 542
  U.S. relations with, **4:541–542**
  Pueblo incident and, **6:541**
  See also North Korea; South Korea
Korea War of 1871, **4:542**
Korea-gate, **4:542–543**
Korean Airlines flight 007, **4:543**
Korean Americans, **4:543–544**
  immigration patterns of, **4:**542, 543–544
  during Korean War, firsthand account of, **9:**419–424
  professional activities of, **4:**543, 544
Korean War, **2:**531; **4:544–550,** *545, 546, 548*
  African Americans in, **5:**382
  air combat in, **1:**76–77; **4:550–551**
  aircraft carriers in, **1:**91–92
  anticommunism during, **2:**327
  armored warfare in, **1:**267; **4:***546*
  beginning of, **2:**269
  biological weapons experimentation in, **2:**118
  China in, **2:**151
  and Chinese Americans, **2:**155
  Chosin Reservoir Campaign in, **2:160–161,** *161*
  cost of, **8:**377
  course of, **4:**546–548
  defoliation used in, **2:**537
  desertion in, **3:**17
  excess profits tax in, **3:273**
  firsthand accounts of, **9:**417–424
  guerrilla warfare in, **4:**70
  helicopters in, **4:**123
  Hispanic Americans in, **5:**384
  impact of, **4:**549
  logistics in, **5:**146
  MacArthur's speech to Congress on, text of, **9:**427–428
  medical research, army, **5:**295
  munitions in, **5:**479, 480
  Native Americans in, **4:**329
  origins of, **4:**545–546
  paratroops in, **6:**247

peace negotiations in, **4:**548–549, *549*

price controls in, **6:**166

prisoners of war in, **4:***548,* 548–549; **6:**472, 473

thirty-eight parallel and, **8:**120

underwater demolition teams in, **8:**251

United Nations and, **8:**270

U.S. Air Force in, **1:**76–77

U.S. Army in, **1:**277; **4:***547*

U.S. Marine Corps in, **5:**242

war powers in, **8:**374, 388

women in, **8:**503–504

Korematsu v. United States, **3:**272; **4:**461

Koresh, David, **2:**478; **8:**359

Koreshan Unity community, **8:**302

Kościuszko, Thaddeus, **6:**390

Kosloff, Theodore, **1:**390

Kosovo, NATO bombing campaign in (1995), **1:**496; **4:551**; **8:**588

Kosuth, Joseph, **1:**307

Kosygin, Alexei, **7:**212

at summit conferences, **8:**15–16

Kotzebue, Albert L., **3:**144

Kovacs, Ernie, **8:**142

Kowinski, William Severini, **5:**215

Kraemer, Shelley v., **6:**506

Kramer, Hilton, **6:**32

Kramer, Larry, **1:**18, *19*

Kramer, Stanley, **4:**125

Krasner, Lee, **1:**10

Krayzelburg, Lenny, **6:**192

Krentz, Jane Anne, *Sweet Starfire,* **5:**130

Kresge, Sebastian S., **3:**26; **7:**126

Kress, Samuel H., **3:**26; **5:**539

Krieger, Alex D., **1:**240

Krim, Mathilde, **1:**15

Kristol, Irving, **6:**31–33

Kroc, Ray A., **5:**184

Kroeber, Alfred, **1:**193

Kroes, Rob, **1:**138

Kroll, Leon, **1:**297

Krstic, Radisav, **1:**354–355

Kruger, Barbara, **1:**299

Kruszka, Wenceslaus, **6:**391

Krutch, Joseph Wood, **5:**120

Krzyzewski, Mike, **1:**425

KS. *See* Kaposi's sarcoma

Ku Klux Klan (KKK), **4:551–553**; **8:**473

in 20th century, **4:**552–553

in Alabama, **1:**103, 104

anti-Catholicism of, **1:**196

in *The Birth of a Nation,* **1:**470

in Colorado, **2:**299

conservatism and, **2:**375

denunciation of, Democratic Party and, **3:**162

devoted to flag, **3:**380

and disfranchisement, **3:**57

in Florida, **3:**386

in Georgia, **3:**555–556

in Indiana, **4:**319

legal cases involving, **8:**273, 274

in North Carolina, **6:**129

in Ohio, **6:**174

in Oregon, **2:**167

origins of, **4:**551

in Reconstruction, **4:**551–552

targets of, **1:**104; **4:**551, 552

in Tennessee, **8:**85

as terrorist group, **8:**95

Kubicki, Frances M., letter to Roosevelt on job discrimination, **9:**376–377

Kucinich, Dennis, **7:**53

Kuh, Katherine, **1:**316

Kuhn, Fritz, **3:**560

Kühn, Justus Engelhardt, **1:**294

Kuhn, Maggie, **4:**37–38

Kuhn, Thomas, **3:**543; **6:**327, 404, 446

Kunin, Madeleine, **8:**314

Kunstler, William M., **2:**135

Kurita, Takeo, **5:**89

Kurland, Bob, **1:**424

Kurtzman, Lemon v., **2:**169; **3:**374

Kuskov, Ivan, **3:**294

Kutenais, **8:**221

Kuwait, in Persian Gulf War, **1:**77; **6:**292–293

Kuznets, Simon, **1:**582; **3:**109, 110

Kwajalein atoll, **5:**252

Kwanzaa, **4:**148, **553**

Kyoto Protocol (1997), **2:**238; **3:**230, 231; **4:**8; **8:**424

L

La Bodega y Quadra, Juan Francisco de, **8:**453

La Condamine, Charles-Marie de, **3:**551

La Croix, Edmund, **3:**390

La Farge, John, **1:**289, 296, 313

La Farge, Oliver, **1:**159, 340

La Follette, Philip, **6:**499–500; **8:**492

La Follette, Robert M., Jr. (Young Bob), **5:1**, 77; **6:**499–500; **8:**492

presidential candidacy of, **5:**16

La Follette, Robert M., Sr. (Fighting Bob), **6:***497*

in presidential campaign of 1912, **3:**160; **6:**496

in presidential campaign of 1924, **2:**548; **3:**162; **8:**119

Progressive Party of, **6:498–499**

and progressive reform, **8:**492, 493

and University of Wisconsin, **8:**284

as Wisconsin governor, **4:**29

La Follette Civil Liberties Committee, hearings held by, **5:**1

La Follette Seamen's Act. *See* Seamen's Act

La Guardia, Fiorello H., **1:**162

and civil defense, **2:**191

and Lincoln Tunnel, **5:**110

as mayor of New York City, **6:**81

La Guardia Airport bombing, **8:**96

La Harpe, Bénard de, **3:**292

La Jolla (California), Scripps Institution of Oceanography, **5:**241

La Mama, Café, **8:**115

La Mama Experimental Theater Club, **8:**115

La Mothe Cadillac, Antoine de, **3:**19

La Pérouse, Jean-François de Galaup, comte de, **8:**453

La Salle, Robert Cavelier, Sieur de, **3:**285, 291; **5:1–3**

disappearance of, **4:**66

explorations of, **5:**1–3, 158

Griffon and, **4:**66

Hennepin on, **4:**126

Mississippi River, **5:**416; **6:**29; **8:**99

La Vérendrye, Pierre Gaultier de Varennes, **3:**292, 490; **6:**131; **8:**451–452

Labels on packaging, **6:**229

Labino, Dominick, **1:**290

Labor, **5:3–10**

vs. big business, **1:**580

capitalism and, **2:**44, 46

child, **2:140–141**, *141*, 146

Clayton Act and, **2:228–229**

and Democratic Party, **2:**23

employer initiatives and, **5:**5

Labor, (*continued*)
  foreign, **2:**397–398
  forms of, capitalist world-economy
      and, **2:**44
  in Great Depression, **5:**7
  lockouts and, **5:**141
  May Day, **5:**275
  organized, **5:**6, 17 (*See also* Trade
      union[s])
    employers' counter-measures
        against, **5:**9
    in lumber industry, **5:**174
  political activism by, **5:**7
  postwar, **5:**8–10
  Puritan work ethic and, **7:**63–64
  and railroads, **7:**37–38
  statistics on, **3:**106
  Taft-Hartley Act and, **5:**11
  unrest, **5:**6 (*See also* Strike[s])
  "yellow-dog" contract and,
      8:578–579
Labor, Department of, **3:**331;
      5:10–12
  and employment services, **3:**201–202
  head of, **2:**2
  Women's Bureau in, **8:**508
Labor conditions
  hour limitations for women,
      5:472–473
  human rights and, **4:**194
  occupational medicine, **5:**296–299
  and violence, **8:**338–339
Labor Day, **5:**12–13
  establishment of, **8:**263
Labor disputes
  arbitration of, **1:**236–237
  conciliation and mediation in,
      2:338–339
  federal intervention in, **1:**190
  Federal Mediation and Concilia-
      tion Service and, **3:**343
  Memorial Day Massacre (1937),
      5:307
  in mining towns, **5:**396–397
  Molly Maguires, **5:**438
  Mooney bombing case, **5:**455
  in Pennsylvania, **6:**278–279
  picketing, **6:**350–351; **8:**230
  See also Boycotting; Strike(s)
Labor injunctions, **4:**360–361
Labor legislation and administra-
      tion, **5:**13–16, 21
  Fair Labor Standards Act and,
      3:307–308

Family and Medical Leave Act and,
      3:315, 317, 525
  labor provisions of Clayton Act
      and, **6:**121
  National Labor Relations Act,
      5:544–546
  National War Labor Board and,
      5:564–565
  Norris-LaGuardia Act and, **6:**121
  Taft-Hartley Act (*See* Taft-Hartley
      Act)
  for women, **7:**303
Labor Management Relations Act.
      See Taft-Hartley Act
Labor parties, **5:**16
  Union Labor Party, **8:**259
Labor Party of Illinois, **3:**320
Labor spies, **3:**255
Labor standards, International
      Labor Organization on, **4:**390
Laboratories
  Bell Telephone, **1:**440–441
  industrial, **4:**339
  marine biology, **5:**240–241
  medical, animals in, **1:**185, 186
  of National Bureau of Standards,
      5:529–530
  of National Institutes of Health,
      5:544
  research, **5:**17–19
    in 19th century, **5:**17–18
    in Cold War, **5:**19
    future directions for, **5:**19
    industrial, **5:**18
    military patronage of, **5:**18
    war and, **5:**18–19
Laboratory of Hygiene, **5:**544
"Laboring Classes" (Brownson),
      8:181
Labor-management relations, in
      1930s, La Follette Civil Liber-
      ties Committee hearings on, **5:**1
Labor-Management Reporting and
      Disclosure Act. *See* Landrum-
      Griffin Act
Labor's Non-Partisan League, **5:**17
Labov, William, **5:**115
Labrador Current, **4:**73
Lacey, John F., **8:**480
Lacey Act (1900), **8:**479–480
Lackawanna Valley, The (Inness),
      6:507
Ladd, Anna Coleman Watts, **1:**308
Ladd, William, **1:**216; **6:**267

Ladies' Home Journal, **6:**554
  advertising in, **1:**32
  circulation of, **5:**198
Lady Chatterley's Lover (Lawrence),
      1:146, 500
*Lady's Magazine and Repository of
      Entertaining Knowledge,* **5:**197
Lafayette, Marquis de, **8:**306, 581
  in American Revolution,
      3:449–450, 473
  name of National Guard honoring,
      5:542
  "stars and stripes" coined by, **3:**378
  visit to America (1824-1825), **5:**20
"Lafayette, we are here," **5:**19–20
Lafayette Escadrille, **5:**20
Laffer, Arthur, **5:**20
Laffer curve theory, **5:**20
Laffite, Jean, **1:**432
Lafitte, Pierre, **6:**423
LaFollette, Robert, **3:**320, 321
LaGuardia, Fiorello, burlesque
      houses closed by, **1:**575
LaHarpe, Bernard, **5:**134
LaHaye, Tim, **3:**485
Lahiri, Jhumpa, *Interpreter of Mal-
      adies,* **5:**123
Laird, Melvin, **2:**528; **8:**335
Laissez-faire, **5:**20–21, 91
  and privatization, **6:**481
Laissez-faire conservatism, **2:**375
Lake(s), eutrophication of, **8:**422
Lake Carriers' Association, **4:**54
Lake Champlain, **5:**21
  Indian wars at, **8:**395–396, *396*
Lake Erie, **4:**50, *51*
  pollution of, **8:**422
Lake Erie, Battle of, **4:**51, 53;
      5:21–22; **6:**290; **8:**432
Lake Huron, **4:**50, *51;* **6:**106
Lake Mead, **4:**162
Lake Michigan, **4:**50–51, *51*
  Lakes-to-Gulf Deep Waterway
      and, **5:**22–23
Lake Okeechobee, **5:**22
Lake Ontario, **4:**50, *51*
Lake Pontchartrain, **5:**22
Lake Superior, **4:**50, *51*
Lakes-to-Gulf Deep Waterway,
      5:22–23
Lakota. *See* Sioux
Lakota language, **5:**23–24
Lam Son 719, **8:**335
Lamar, Joseph R., **1:**532

Lamar, Mirabeau B., **8**:100, 104
Lamarck, Jean-Baptise de, **3**:530, 542
Lamas, Carlos Saavedra, **1**:560
Lamb, Floyd, **1**:*324*
Lambert, Ward (Piggy), **1**:423
Lame Bull (Blackfeet chief), **1**:481
Lame-duck amendment, **5**:24
Lamm, Heinrich, **3**:357
Lamon, Harry V., Jr., **6**:493
L'Amour, Louis, **5**:130
Lamp(s)
  Argand, **5**:107
  carbon, **5**:24
  electric, **5**:108, *108*
  energy-efficient, **5**:108
  fluorescent, **5**:24, 108–109
  halogen, **5**:24
  incandescent, **5**:24, 107–108
  kerosine, **5**:107
  oil, **5**:107
Lampman, Robert J., **6**:437
Lancaster, Joseph, **3**:113
Lancaster (Mercerburg) Theological Seminary, **8**:264
Lancey, James de, **2**:444
Land
  public (*See* Public land)
  single tax on, **7**:366
Land, Edwin, **1**:140
Land acts, **5**:25
  of 1796, **5**:36
Land and Water Fund Conservation Act (1965), **3**:431
Land bounties, **5**:25
Land cessions. *See* Native American(s), land cessions by
Land claims, **5**:25–26
  by Alaska Natives, **1**:110, 111, 112
  in archival maps, **9**:37
  Louisiana Purchase and, **5**:26
  by Native Americans, **4**:273–274
  of thirteen colonies, after independence, **8**:454–455
  in Vermont, **8**:311
Land companies, **5**:26–27, 35–38
Land disputes. *See* Boundary disputes
Land Forfeiture Act (1890), **5**:37
Land grant(s), **3**:127; **5**:25, **27–31**
  in Alaska, **5**:30
  by Charles II, **6**:126, 276, 511, *511*, 512

by Dutch West India Company, **6**:259
  for education, **5**:28, **29–30**, 33, 34–35, 460
    and black colleges, **3**:126
    for 4-H Clubs, **3**:445
    and state universities, **8**:279
  for homesteads, **5**:28, 29
  in Kansas, and Lecompton Constitution, **5**:73
  as military bonuses, **1**:498
  as old-age pensions, **5**:28, 34
  overview, **5**:27–29
  proprietary colonies, **6**:510–512
  to railroad companies, **2**:43, 94; **5**:27, 28, **30–31**, 37, 38; **7**:32; **8**:181
    Mussel Slough incident, **5**:503–504
  recipients of, **5**:28
  to states, by Congress, **5**:28
  and westward migration, **8**:444
  See also Morrill Land Grant Act
Land of the Spotted Eagle (Standing Bear), excerpt from, **9**:379–384
Land Office, U.S. General and Bureau Plans Management, **5**:31, 33; **6**:529
  land patents granted by, **5**:32
Land Ordinance (1785), **5**:25, 29, 36
Land patents, **5**:31–32
  of Gilbert, **3**:576
Land policies, **5**:32–34
  entailing of estates, **3**:224
  under Jefferson, **6**:201
  under Monroe, **6**:201
  Ordinances of 1784, 1785, and 1787 on, **6**:200–201
  primogeniture, **6**:463–464
  public domain, **6**:527, **527–529**
  public land commissions reviewing, **6**:530–532
Land reform movement, **5**:37
Land scrip, **5**:34–35
Land speculation, **5**:35–38
  public domain, **6**:527–528
  public land commissions on, **6**:530–531
  in undeveloped lands, **5**:36–37
  in urban property, **5**:37–38
  and Vandalia Colony, **8**:308
  Yazoo fraud, **1**:489; **8**:575–576
Land tenure
  among aliens, **1**:124, 126; **4**:464

among Native Americans, **1**:69
Lander, Louisa, **1**:308
Landes, Bertha Knight, **8**:509
Landgraf v. USI Film Products, **2**:197
Land-Grant College Act. *See* Morrill Act
Landis, James M., and civil defense, **2**:191
Landis, Kenesaw Mountain, **1**:421, 479
Landmarks Preservation Commission, **6**:453
Landon, Alfred M., **6**:409
  in presidential campaign of 1936, **3**:162; **8**:298
Landon v. Plasencia, **1**:125
Landrum-Griffin Labor-Management Reporting and Disclosure Act (1959), **2**:116; **5**:11, 15; **7**:558
  McClellan Committee and, **5**:183
  and trade unions, **5**:545; **8**:172
Landscape architecture, **5**:38–39
  in cemeteries, **2**:80, 81, *81*
  modern, **5**:39
  picturesque style of, **5**:38–39
Landsteiner, Karl, **6**:388
Lane, Charles, **8**:301
Lane, Harriet, **3**:375
Lane, James H., **8**:143
Lane, Joseph, **3**:154; **6**:205
Lane, Ralph, **7**:47
Lane, William Henry, **2**:497
Lane Theological Seminary, **6**:152
Lang, Michael, **8**:524
Langdell, Christopher Columbus, **5**:56–58
Langdon, John, **3**:151; **6**:58
Langdon, William Chauncy, **2**:21
Lange, Dorothea, **1**:301; **3**:396
Lange, Oskar, **3**:109
Langer, William
  as governor of North Dakota, **6**:132
  in Nonpartisan League, **6**:118
Langford, Nathaniel, **8**:579
Langley (aircraft carrier), **1**:89
Langmuir, Irving, **2**:123; **3**:175; **5**:18, 24, 108
Langston, John Mercer, **8**:345
Langstroth, Lorenzo L., **1**:436
Language(s)
  American Sign, **7**:355–357
  English, **3**:220–222

Language(s), (*continued*)
  American Sign Language and,
    7:356
    slang in, **7:377–378**
    slaves and, **7**:395, 396
  Native American, **1**:482;
    4:274–275; **8**:571
    Cherokee, **2**:124–125, **126–127**,
      127
    classification of, **4**:274–275
    and culture, **4**:275
    decline of, **4**:275
    Hopi, **4**:165–166
    Navajo, **2**:468
    Ojibwe, **6:181–182**
    in oral literature, **4**:279–280
    in oratory, **4:281**
    sign, **7:357–358**
    written, **4**:275
  Spanish, **7:490–492**
Lanham Act (1946), **8**:174
Laniel, Joseph, **1**:445
Lannuier, Charles-Honoré, **3**:497
LANs. *See* Local area networks
Lansdale, Edward, **2**:471
Lansing, John, at Constitutional
  Convention, **2**:379
Lansing, Robert, **5**:146
  and Virgin Islands, **8**:341
Lansing-Ishii Agreement (1917),
  3:277
Lansky, Meyer, **5**:41–42
Laos
  Geneva Conference (1961) and,
    3:535
  immigration from, **7**:470–471
  independence for, **8**:329–330
  in Vietnam War, **8**:332, 334, 335
Laotian Americans, **7**:471
LaPierre, Wayne, **5**:557
Lapwai, Fort, **6**:102
Laqueur, Thomas, **3**:516
Laramie, Fort, **5:39–40**; **8**:563
Laramie, Fort, Treaty of (1851),
  1:481; **5:40**; **8**:402
  Arapaho and, **1**:235
  Mandan Hidatsa and, **5**:220
  Sioux and, **7**:370
  text of, **9**:227–229
Laramie, Fort, Treaty of (1868),
  1:474; **2**:298; **5:40–41**, 130;
  8:219, 275
  and Crow Indians, **2**:466
Larimer, William, **3**:5

Larsen, Carl, **6**:383
Larsen, Nella, **4**:*96*; **5**:125
Las Vegas (Nevada), **5:41–43**; **6**:38
  age of legitimacy for, **5**:42
  casinos in, **5**:42
  gambling in, **5**:41–42
  nightclubs in, **6**:107
  prewar and postwar boom in,
    5:41–42
  segregation in, **5**:42
Las Vegas Land and Water Company, **5**:41
Lasagna, Louis, **1**:16
Lasansky, Mauricio, **6**:471
Lasch, Christopher, **4**:334; **6**:429
Laser technology, **5**:43; **6**:337
  applications of, **5**:43
  physical principles of, **5**:43
Laslett, Peter, **5**:140
Last of the Mohicans, The (Cooper),
  5:70, 119
Lathrop, Gertrude Katherine, **1**:308
Lathrop, Julia Clifford, **2**:147
Lathrop, Mary Frances, **1**:145
Latin America
  in American Studies, **1**:170
  bananas imported from, **3**:479
  commerce with, **5:43–46**, 47
    trade agreements and, **6**:124–125
  dollar diplomacy in, **3**:71
  economic instability in, **5**:45
  filibuster armies targeting,
    3:359–360
  foreign aid to, **1**:128; **3**:416; **5**:44,
    47–49
  foreign incursions in, **5**:46
  foreign observers from, **1**:136–137
  Great Depression and, **4**:48–49
  immigration from, **4**:135; **8**:291
    (*See also* Hispanic Americans)
  and religious affiliation, **7**:91–92
  industrialization of, **5**:44, 45
  juntas in, **5**:50–51
  Monroe Doctrine and, **5:446–447**
  Olney Corollary on, **6**:191
  reciprocal trade agreements with,
    7:54
  U.S. investment in, **5**:45, 46, 47
  U.S. relations with, **5:46–50**
    Alliance for Progress and,
      1:127–128; **3**:417–418; **5**:48
    Clayton-Bulwer Treaty and,
      2:229
    drug trafficking and, **5**:512–513

  Good Neighbor policy in, **1**:560;
    3:426; **4**:22–23, 77
  Grenada invasion, **4**:65
  gunboat diplomacy and, **4**:76–77
  Pan-American Union and,
    6:236–237
  Polk Doctrine and, **6**:408
  Rio de Janeiro Conference (1947)
    and, **7:163**
  wars of independence in, **5**:46,
    50–52
  chronology of, **5**:*51*
  See also specific countries
Latin American immigrants. *See*
  Hispanic Americans
Latin schools, **5**:52
Latinismo, **6**:544
Latinos. *See* Hispanic Americans
Latitudinarians, **5**:52
Latrobe, Benjamin H., Jr., **5**:52
Latrobe, Benjamin Henry, **1**:249,
  292; **2**:49; **8**:471
Latrobe, J. H. B., **1**:148
Latrobe's folly, **5:52–53**
Latta, Alexander, **3**:372
Latter-day Saints, Church of Jesus
  Christ of, **5:53–55**; **8**:296
  in 19th century, **5**:54
  division within, **7**:103
  early years of, **5**:53
  founding of, **5**:53
  in Great Depression, **5**:54
  growth of, **7**:90
  internationalism of, **5**:54–55
  membership in, **7**:*91*
  migration to Utah
    Mormon handcart companies,
      5:458–459
    Mormon trail, **5**:459, *459*
    Mountain Meadows Massacre,
      5:467–468
  missionary work of, **5**:53, 54
  Mormon War, **5:459–460**
  in politics, **5**:55
  polygamy in, **5**:250
  in Progressive Era, **5**:54
  Relief Society of, **5**:53, 54
  Serviceman's Committee of, **5**:54
  Social Welfare Department of, **5**:54
  tenets of, **5**:53
  United Orders of, **5**:54
  Welfare Plan of, **5**:54
  in World War I, **5**:54
  See also Mormon(s)

Lau v. Nichols, **3**:122
Laud, William, **4**:55
Laudonnière, René Goulaine de, **3**:285
Laughlin, Laurence, **3**:109
Laughlin, Robert, **1**:440
Laurel, Jose, **6**:322
Laurence, William L., **6**:90
Laurens, Henry, **7**:147
  and Treaty of Paris (1783), **6**:248
Laurent, Robert, **1**:306
Lauretis, Teresa de, **3**:516
Lauritsen, Charles C., **6**:342
Lausanne Agreement, **5**:55
LAV. *See* Lymphadenopathy-associated virus
Lavoisier, Antoine-Laurent, **6**:148
Law(s)
  enforcement of (*See* Police)
  rule of reason in, **7:203**
  vocation of (*See* Legal profession)
  See also specific laws
Law, James, **8**:319
Law, John, **2**:262; **5**:158, 414
Law firms, growth of, **5**:58, 75
Law School Admissions Test (LSAT), **5**:58
Law schools, **5:55–58**, 74
  accreditation of, **5**:56–57
  in colonial era, **5**:55–56, 73
  curricula of, **5**:57
  development of, **5**:56–57
  faculty of, demographics of, **5**:58
  Harvard model for, **5**:56–58
  Litchfield model for, **5**:56
Law student(s)
  demographics of, **5**:58
  first female, **5**:75
Lawlor, Loewe v. See Danbury Hatters' Case
Lawrence (Kansas)
  Quantrill's Raid on, **7:4**
  sack of, **1**:506; **3**:196; **5:58–59**
Lawrence, Abbott, **5**:59; **6**:317
Lawrence, Amos, and land speculation, **5**:36
Lawrence, Amos Adams, **5**:266; **6**:49
Lawrence, Charles, **1**:11
Lawrence, D. H., **1**:146
  Lady Chatterley's Lover, **1**:500
Lawrence, Ernest O., **2**:487, *487*; **6**:336, 342
Lawrence, Jacob, **1**:298; **5**:*370*
Lawrence, James, **3**:78–79

Lawrence, Mary, **1**:308
Lawrence, Matilda, **5**:96
Lawrence, Richard, **1**:327–328
Lawrence, Sir Thomas, **1**:295
Lawrence (ship), **5**:21; **6**:290
Lawrence (Massachusetts) strike, **5:59–61**, *60*, *61*
Lawrence Scientific School, **5**:59
Lawson, Ernest, **1**:268, 297, 321
Lawsuits
  consumer safety, **2**:384
  See also specific cases
Lawton, Henry W., **7**:486
Lawyer(s)
  apprenticeship of, **5**:55–56
  colonial, training of, **5**:55–56
  education of, **5**:55–58 (*See also* Law schools)
  See also Legal profession
"Lawyer" (Nez Perce leader), **6**:100, 102
Lay, Kenneth, **3**:223
LCD. *See* Liquid crystal display
LDS. *See* Latter-day Saints, Church of Jesus Christ of
Le Duc Tho, **8**:334
Le Guin, Ursula, **6**:207
Le Maire, Jakob, **2**:39
Le Moyne, Jacques, **9**:13
Le Moyne, Jean Baptiste, **6**:213
Le Witt, Sol, **1**:298
Lea, Isaac, **1**:167
Leach, Bernard, **1**:305
Lead and lead industry, **5:61–63**; **6**:114–115
  blast furnace for, **5**:62
  consumer use of, **5**:63
  EPA regulation of, **7**:246
  in Galena-Dubuque mining district, **3**:503
  in gasoline, **1**:362; **7**:246
  prospecting and mining, **5:61–63**
  secondary recovery of, **5**:62–63
  toxicity of, **6**:115
  in Wisconsin, **8**:490
Lead colic, **5**:62
Lead glass, **4**:3
Lead (tin) soldiers, **8**:153
Leadbelly (Ledbetter), Huddie, **1**:389, 441
Leaded gasoline, **1**:362; **7**:246
Leadville (Colorado), **1**:502, *502*; **5**:62
  strike at, **8**:454

Leadville Mining District, **5**:63
Leaf, June, **1**:311
League of Nations, **5:63–65**; **8**:315–316
  Covenant of, **8**:268
  debate on, and U.S. electoral politics, **3**:161, 162
  end of, **5**:65
  establishment of, **5**:64
  Geneva Conference (1932) called by, **3**:534
  operations and activities of, **5**:64–65
  organization of, **5**:64
  origins of, **5**:64
  United Nations as improvement on, **8**:269
  U.S. Senate's rejection of, **8**:316, 543
  Wilson's compromises to achieve, **2**:151
  Wilson's proposal for, **3**:426; **5**:63; **6**:264; **8**:201, 205, 315–316, 539
League of United Latin American Citizens (LULAC), **5**:344
League of Women Voters, **5:65–66**
League to Enforce Peace, **6**:449
Lear, Norman, **1**:126
Learned societies, **5:66–68**
  American Academy of Arts and Sciences, **1:139–140**
  American Association for the Advancement of Science, **1:140–142**
  American Historical Association, **1:158–159**
  American Philosophical Society, **1:166–167**
  National Academy of Sciences, **5:522–523**
Learning from Las Vegas (Venturi), **6**:430
Leary, Timothy, **5**:169, *169*
Lease, Mary E., on women in Farmers' Alliance, **9**:260–261
Leather and leather products industry, **5:68–70**
  decline of, **5**:69–70
  employment in, **5**:69
  factory system and, **5**:68–69
  mechanization and, **5**:68–69
Leatherstocking Tales (Cooper), **5:70**, 119; **8**:457, 479

"Leave No Child Behind Act" (2001), **3:**119, 124
Leavenworth, Fort, **4:**508
Leavenworth, Henry, **5:**70
Leavenworth expedition, **5:70**
Leaves of Grass (Whitman), **5:71**, 119; **6:**537
Lebanese Americans, **5:71–72**
  culture of, **5:**72
  immigration of, **5:**71
  in politics, **5:**72
  prominent individuals of, **5:**72
Lebanon
  Beirut bombing in, **1:438–439**
  U.S. landing in, **3:**142; **5:**72
    Marine Corps in, **5:**242–243
  U.S. relations with, **5:**71
Lebergott, Stanley, **8:**251, 252
Leche, Richard, **5:**161
Lechmere, Winthrop v., **1:**225
LeClerc, Charles, **5:**163
LeCocq, Louis, **1:**375
Lecompton Constitution, **5:72–73**, 110
LeConte, Joseph, **7:**270
Lederberg, Joshua, **3:**529
Ledo Road, **1:**576–577; **7:**180, *181*
Ledyard, John, **3:**140–141; **4:**105
Lee, Ann, **7:**333; **8:**501
Lee, Arthur, **6:**190
  diplomacy of, **3:**27; **7:**147
Lee, Don L., **5:**126
Lee, Edward M., **8:**564
Lee, George, **1:**332
Lee, George Washington Custis, **8:**274
Lee, Gypsy Rose, **1:**575, *575*
Lee, Harold B., **5:**54
Lee, Jarena, **8:**501
Lee, Jason, **6:**205
Lee, John D., **5:**467–468
Lee, Knox v., **5:**76
Lee, Mary Ann, **1:**389; **2:**497
Lee, Richard Henry, **1:**512; **2:**381
  antifederalism of, **1:**201, 202
  at First Continental Congress, **2:**393
  on Galloway's plan of union, **3:**505
  and independence, goal of, **2:**520
  and land companies, **5:**35
Lee, Robert E., **2:**212; **3:**567; **8:**344
  Arlington House estate of, **2:**82; **8:**274

Arlington National Cemetery and, **1:**264
Army of Northern Virginia under, **1:**278
  vs. Army of the Potomac, **1:**279
  in Battle of Antietam, **1:**199–200
  in Battle of Bull Run, Second, **1:**568
  in Battle of Chancellorsville, **2:**104, 213
  in Battle of Fredericksburg, **3:**457
  in Battle of Gettysburg, **3:**566–569; **6:**351
  in Battles of the Wilderness, **8:**477
  as engineer commander, **3:**219
  extra power to, granting of, **2:**341
  farewell speech by, **9:**308
  at Harpers Ferry raid, **4:**97, 99
  in Maryland, invasion of, **5:**259
  in Peninsular Campaign, **6:**275
  in Pennsylvania invasion, **6:**280
  Pennsylvania raid of, **2:**213–214
  in Seven Days' Battles, **7:**319; **9:**67
  in Shenandoah Campaign, **7:**341
  in Siege of Petersburg, **6:**295
  surrender of, **1:***226,* **226–227**; **2:**215, 343; **8:**344
Lee, Russell, **1:**301
Lee, Spike, **3:**364
Lee, United States v., **8:274**
Lee, Wen Ho, **3:**210
Lee Optical, Williamson v., **3:**247; **8:484–485**
Leedskalnin, Edward, **1:**312
Legal and Educational Defense Fund of National Organization for Women, **5:**549
Legal education. *See* Law schools
Legal profession(s), **5:73–75**
  American Bar Association for, **1:144–145; 5:**74
  in colonial era, **5:**73–74
  National Lawyers Guild for, **5:546–547**
  professional standards for, enhancement of, **5:**74–75
Legal Realists, **5:**57
Legal system, on domestic violence, **2:**136
Legal tender, **5:75–76**
  cases, **5:**76–77; **7:**118
    Supreme Court on, **4:**500; **5:**76
Legal Tender Act (1862), **5:76**, 76

"Legend of Sleepy Hollow, The" (Irving), **5:**118
Leger, Fernand, **1:**310
Leggett, William, **5:**142
Legion of Merit, **2:**526–527
Legionnaires' disease, **2:**88; **5:**77
Legislation
  rule of reason in, **7:203**
  See also specific laws
Legislative branch of federal government, **3:**341
  See also Congress; House of Representatives; Senate
Legislative Reorganization Act (1946), **5:77–78**
  Title III, **5:**137
Legislature(s)
  bicameral, **5:**78
  Charter of Privileges and, **2:**110
  Constitutional Convention on, **2:**379–380; **3:**170
  Madison (James) on, **1:**456; **7:**107
  state, **5:78–81** (*See also under specific states*)
    of first states, **5:**79
    party control of, **5:**80
    professionalization of, **5:**79–80
    regional differences among, **5:**79
    representation in, **5:**79
    term limits in, **5:**80
  unicameral, **5:**78
  See also Congress
Leglen, Suzanne, **8:**90
Lehman, Herbert H., **1:**162; **8:**46
Lehman, John, **6:**24
Leibniz, Gottfried Wilhelm, **3:**24
Leidy, Joseph, **1:**167
Leighton, William, **1:**289
Leisler, Jacob, **5:***81;* **6:**83
Leisler Rebellion, **5:81,** *81;* **6:**83–84
Leisure. *See* Recreation; Vacation and leisure
Leisure class, Veblen's theory of, excerpt from, **9:**347–351
Leisy v. Hardin, **6:**213
Leiter, Saul, **1:**301
Leland, John, **1:**412
Leland, Waldo G., **1:**255
Lelyveld, Arthur J., **8:***592*
LeMay, Curtis E., **3:**165; **8:**554
  in presidential election of 1968, **1:**159
  and Strategic Air Command, **1:**81–82

Lemke, William, **3**:327, 457
  in Nonpartisan League, **6**:118
Lemlich, Clara, **3**:53
Lemon v. Kurtzman, **2**:169; **3**:374
LeMond, Greg, **1**:452
Lenape, **6**:79; **8**:459
  See also Delaware Indians
Lend-Lease Act (1941), **5**:82; **6**:36
  League of Women Voters support
    for, **5**:66
Lend-Lease program, **2**:531;
  5:81–82
L'Enfant, Pierre-Charles
  city plan for Washington (D.C.),
    2:49, 185, 187; **8**:409, 417
  and White House, site for, **8**:470
Lenin, Vladimir, **2**:267; **7**:57
  and anticommunism, **1**:198
Lennon, John, **2**:79
Leno, Jay, **8**:142
Lenoir, Étienne, **1**:371
Lenski, Gerhard, **1**:337
Lentricchia, Frank, **6**:429
Leo XIII, Pope, **2**:69
León, Alonso de, **8**:99
Leonard, Elmore, **5**:130
Leontief, Wassily, **3**:109, 110
Leopard (British ship), **2**:129
Leopold, A. Starker, **5**:552
Leopold, Aldo, **2**:370, 372, 373;
  3:227, 432; **8**:481
Leopold, Nathan, **4**:525; **5**:82–83,
  83
Leopold-Loeb case, **4**:525; **5**:82–83
Leprosy, **5**:83
Lepton, **6**:339
Lermond, Wallace, **8**:303
Lescaze, William, **1**:252; **7**:376
Lescoulie, Jack, **8**:142
Lesley, Craig, **6**:207
Leslie, Sir John, **7**:77
Lesquereux, Leo, **1**:167
Lesseps, Ferdinand de, **6**:237
Lessons from the Intersexed (Kessler),
  3:517
Lester, Charles Edwards, **1**:299
*Let Us Now Praise Famous Men: Three
  Tenant Families* (Agee and
  Evans), **5**:83–84
Letter bombs, Unabomber and,
  8:247, *247–248*
Letter Concerning Toleration, A
  (Locke), **5**:140

"Letter from the Birmingham Jail"
  (King), **1**:104; **6**:517
Letterman, David, **8**:142
Letterman, Jonathan, **8**:375
Letterpress printing, **6**:469
Letters from an American Farmer
  (Crèvecoeur), **1**:136; **6**:373
Leukemia, childhood, **2**:35
Leupp, Francis E., **1**:571
Leutze, Emanuel, *Washington Cross-
  ing the Delaware*, **2**:543–544,
  544
Levassor, Emile Constant, **1**:366
Levees, **3**:384
Levene, Phoebus Aaron, **3**:67
Lever Act (1917), **5**:84
  and Fuel Administration, **3**:480
Lever Brothers, **7**:408
Lever Food and Fuel Control Act.
  See Lever Act
Leveraged buyouts, **5**:84–85
Levi, Edward, **3**:338; **8**:281
Levin, Ira, *Boys from Brazil*, **5**:122
Levine, Charles, **1**:83
Levine, Lawrence, **4**:470
Levinstein, Leon, **1**:301
Levitt, Alfred, **7**:574
Levitt, Helen, **1**:301
Levitt, William, **5**:149; **7**:53, 574,
  575
Levittown, **5**:*85*, 85–86, 149; **7**:*53*,
  572, 574, *575*
Levy, **5**:86
Levy, Asser, **4**:476
Levy, David, **6**:424
Lewelling, Lorenzo D., **6**:417
Lewes, G. H., **6**:423
Lewin, Arthur, **1**:47
Lewin, John, **6**:510
Lewin, Kurt, **3**:203
Lewinsky, Monica, scandal involv-
  ing, **2**:79, 240; **3**:169; **4**:238,
  239–240; **7**:496
Lewis, Andrew, **3**:95
Lewis, Carl, **7**:205
Lewis, Clarence Irving, **6**:*326*, 327,
  445–446
Lewis, Edmonia, **1**:308
Lewis, F. John, **2**:53
Lewis, Gilbert N., **2**:122; **6**:336
Lewis, John L., **1**:151; **2**:254; **3**:*255*;
  5:8, 17; **8**:171, 268, 277
  Centralia Mine disaster and, **2**:95

  and Congress of Industrial Organi-
    zations, **2**:227
  steel workers and, **7**:545
Lewis, Lennox, **6**:485
Lewis, Meriwether, **3**:297; **5**:86–87
  on Columbia River, **2**:303
Lewis, Morris, **1**:298
Lewis, Samuel, **9**:*31*
Lewis, Sinclair, **5**:120
  Arrowsmith, **5**:18
  Babbitt, **5**:120; **8**:290, 292
  on Chautauqua movement, **2**:114
  Main Street, **5**:120
Lewis, W. Arthur, **3**:110
Lewis, William H., **3**:94
Lewis and Clark expedition, **3**:297;
  8:453
  American Philosophical Society
    and, **1**:166
  Fort Mandan, **5**:219
  and fur trade, **3**:491
  Jefferson's message on, **9**:187–191
  journals of, **5**:87–88
    excerpts from, **9**:191–198
  map of, **5**:*88*
  in Montana, **5**:448
  and mountain passes, **6**:254
  Native Americans and, relations
    with, **4**:314
  in Nebraska, **6**:29
  in Oregon, **6**:204
  in Pacific Northwest, **6**:226
  river exploration by, **7**:173
  in Rocky Mountains, **7**:190
  specimens collected by, **8**:597
  Vancouver explorations and, **8**:307
LeWitt, Sol, **1**:307
Lexington (aircraft carrier), **1**:89;
  5:87
Lexington (Continental brig), **5**:87
Lexington (store ship), **5**:87
Lexington (Union sidewheeler), **5**:87
Lexington and Concord, Battles of,
  5:88, 88–89; **7**:*140*
  American and British accounts of,
    9:143–144
  maps of, **5**:*88*
    archival, **9**:30, *30*
  minutemen in, **5**:404
Leyte Gulf, Battle of, **5**:89; **6**:26;
  8:557
Liability
  of railroad company, **6**:232
  and workers' compensation, **4**:369

Liautard, Alexandre, **8**:319
Libbey, Laura Jean, **5**:129
Libby, Willard F., **1**:240; **6**:344; **7**:*21*
Libel, **5**:90
  laws on, **8**:590
  Supreme Court on, **3**:374; **4**:67
Liberal arts colleges, **8**:279
Liberal Christianity, Protestant
    modernism and, **5**:431–432
Liberal Republican Party,
    3:155–156; **5**:90
Liberal Tradition in America, The
    (Hartz), **5**:140
Liberalism
  anticommunism in, **1**:197
  Brookings Institution and, **8**:117
  and Chautauqua movement, **2**:113
  vs. conservatism, **2**:374, 375
  and consumer protection, **2**:388
  contemporary critics of, **5**:90–93,
    91
    Locke's political philosophy and,
      5:91, 140–141
  in economic theory, **3**:107
  journalistic outlets for, **6**:76, 92
  and Protestantism, **6**:516, 518
  varieties of, **5**:91–92
Liberation (magazine), **6**:269
Liberation theology, **5**:93
Liberator (newspaper), **1**:210, *210*;
    6:47
Liberia
  black migration to, **1**:148
  establishment of, **1**:148; **2**:297
  Pan-Africanism and, **6**:235
  U.S. immigrants in, **1**:477; **2**:297;
    3:197
  U.S. relations with, **5**:93–94
Libertarian Party, **8**:120
Libertarians, and freedom of speech,
    2:83
Liberty
  concept of, **5**:*94*, 94–95
  due process for protection of, **3**:91
  and equality, **3**:249
    balance of, **5**:92
  negative, **5**:94
  positive, **5**:95
  See also Freedom
Liberty (ship), Israeli attack on,
    5:95–96
Liberty Bell, **5**:95, *95*
Liberty bonds, **5**:*94*, 96; **8**:123, 542
Liberty engine, **5**:481–482

Liberty flag, **3**:378
Liberty League, **5**:97
Liberty loans, **5**:96
  role of, **7**:258
  Victory Loan of 1919, **8**:326–327
Liberty of contract, **3**:308;
    5:394–395, 472–473
Liberty Party, **5**:96–97; **8**:119
  establishment of, **1**:211; **5**:96
  goals of, **1**:211; **5**:96
  in presidential campaign of 1840,
    3:153
  in Vermont, **8**:313
Liberty Place, Battle of, **6**:74
Liberty poles, **5**:97
"Liberty" ships, **7**:347, *347*
"Liberty Song" (Dickinson), **8**:278
Liberty-cap cent, **5**:97
Libraries, **5**:97–99
  academic, **5**:97
  corporate, **5**:97
  Folger Shakespeare Library, **3**:393
  Frick Art Reference Library, **3**:473
  government publications at, **4**:24
  Huntington Library and Museum,
    4:195–196
  Internet and, **5**:99
  Newberry Library, **6**:93–94
  Presidential, **5**:99–100
  public systems, **4**:356; **5**:97–98
    Carnegie (Andrew) and, **2**:56;
      7:65
  special, **5**:97
  university, **5**:98
Library Awareness Program,
    3:338–339
Library of Congress, **5**:100–103,
    101
  collections of, **5**:101, 102
  evolution of, **5**:100–102
  foreign acquisitions by, **5**:101
  funding of, **5**:101, 102
  history of, **5**:100–102
  and Internet, **5**:102
  place in national culture and edu-
    cation, **5**:102
  poet laureate appointed by, **6**:381
Libya
  aerial bombing of, **1**:496
  U.S. relations with, **1**:40
    Gulf of Sidra shootdown and,
      4:73
    Pan Am Flight 103 and,
      6:233–234

License cases, **5**:103
Licenses to trade, **5**:103
Lichtenstein, Roy, **6**:414
Lick, James, **1**:344
Licklider, J. C. R., **4**:398
Liddell Hart, Basil H., **1**:267
Liddy, G. Gordon, **8**:425, 426
Lie, Trygve, **8**:270
Lieber, Francis, **1**:137; **3**:204; **6**:401,
    402; **8**:371
  and Civil War General Order No.
    100, **2**:220
  on neutrality, **6**:34
Lieberman, Joseph, in presidential
    campaign of 2000, **3**:170
Lieberman, Nancy, **1**:425
Life (magazine), **8**:127
*Life, History, and Travels of Kah-ge-
    ga-gah-bowh, The* (Copway),
    5:128
Life Among the Piutes (Hopkins),
    6:231; **8**:217
*Life and Adventures of Joaquin Muri-
    eta, The* (Ridge), **5**:128
Life and Labour of the People in London
    (Booth), **6**:533
Life expectancy, **2**:510; **5**:103–106;
    6:188
  in 19th century, **5**:104–105
  in 20th century, **5**:105–106
  active, **5**:106
  in colonial era, **2**:291; **5**:104
  race and, **5**:105–106
  sex and, **5**:105
  social class and, **5**:105–106
Life insurance, **4**:370–371
Life insurance companies, credit
    provided by, **2**:447
Life stages. *See* Adolescence; Child-
    hood; Old Age
Life table, **5**:103–104
Lifesaving service, **5**:106
Liggett and Myers, **8**:135
Light in August (Faulkner), **5**:121
Light industry, **3**:172–176, 179
Lighthouse Board, **5**:106–107
Lighthouse Service, **2**:258
Lighting, **5**:107–109
  fluorescent, **3**:179
  halogen, **3**:179
  incandescent, **3**:173, 177, 179
Lightner, Candy, **1**:232
Lightning, Franklin's experiments
    on, **5**:330–331

Liguest, Perre Laclede, **5**:419
Lilienthal, David, **8**:88
Liliuokalani (queen of Hawaii), **4**:107
Lillie, Gordon (Pawnee Bill), **6**:185
Lillie, May, **6**:185
Lillooet, **8**:221
Lily, The (journal), **1**:489; **6**:88, 96
Lim, Shirley, *Among the White Moon Faces*, **5**:123
Limbaugh, Rush, **7**:21; **8**:44
Limerick, Patricia Nelson, **8**:463
Limits of Growth, The , **3**:228
Lin, Maya Ying, **1**:307; **8**:335
Lincoln, Abraham
  and Agriculture, Department of, **3**:331
  American System under, **1**:171
  amnesty granted by, **1**:177
  and Arizona Territory, **1**:257
  assassination of, **1:328**; **2**:218; **8**:339
  Baltimore Riot and, **1**:393
  Battle of Antietam and, **1**:200
  and blockade of Confederate coast, **1**:487–488
  on citizenship, **2**:180
  Civil War policies of, **2**:209–210
  and colonization movement, **1**:148; **2**:297
  and Committee on the Conduct of the War, **2**:313, 314
  compared to Moses, **2**:164
  and Confiscation Acts, **2:346**
  debates with Stephen Douglas (*See* Lincoln-Douglas debates)
  on Declaration of Independence, **2**:523
  Democrats opposed to, **2**:411
  on Dred Scott decision, **3**:86
  and emancipation, **1**:49
  Emancipation Proclamation of, **2**:212, 217, 542; **3:190–192**, *191*; **6**:491
  English working-men's address to, **9**:299–300
  environmental policies of, **8**:583
  executive orders of, **3**:278
  and First Battle of Bull Run, **1**:567
  Gettysburg Address by, **2**:180; **3**:569–571; **6**:10
    text of, **9**:302
  habeas corpus suspended by, **1**:284; **4**:81; **6**:482

  at Hampton Roads Conference, **4**:91
  "House Divided" speech by, **4:178–179**; **5**:110
    text of, **9**:284–286
  land policy of, **5**:33
  as leader, **2**:219
  legal training of, **5**:56
  and liberalism, **5**:91
  as log cabin president, **5**:145
  and loyalty oaths, **8**:96
  McClellan's letter to, **9**:298–299
  and military censorship, **2**:84
  military strategy and administration of, **2**:217–218
  and national cemeteries, **2**:81–82
  as national hero, **5**:568
  nickname for, **7:23**
  opposition to, **2**:218
  and Pinkerton Agency, **6**:357
  and *Powhatan* incident, **6**:443
  in presidential campaign of 1860, **2**:23; **3**:155; **7**:111
  in presidential campaign of 1864, **2**:218; **3**:155; **7**:112
  and Radical Republicans, **2**:218; **7**:15
  and railroads, **7**:34, 40
  and Reconstruction, **7**:58
  relationship with Congress and Republican Party, **2**:218
  Republican convention of 1860 and, **2**:400
  "Right Makes Might" speech of, **2**:405
  second inaugural address by, **1**:447; **2**:192; **5:112–113**
    text of, **9**:308–309
  on Stowe (Harriet Beecher), **8**:248
  Thanksgiving Day established by, **8**:112
  and Vallandigham incident, **3**:527; **8**:306
  Wade-Davis Bill vetoed by, **8**:359
  war powers of, **8**:374
    exercise of extraordinary, **2**:210; **3**:272
  widows' letters to, **9**:303–304
  Wilmot Proviso and, **8**:486
Lincoln, Benjamin, **2**:19
Lincoln, Mary Todd, **3**:375
Lincoln County War, **6**:69
Lincoln Highway, **5**:109; **7**:178; **8**:564

Lincoln Highway Association, **5**:109
Lincoln Logs, **5:109**, 145; **8**:153
Lincoln Memorial, **8**:410
Lincoln Mills, Textile Workers v., **1**:237
Lincoln Tunnel, **5:109–110**, *110*
Lincoln University, **3**:121, 125
Lincoln-Douglas debates, **3**:467; **5:110–111**, *111*
Lind, James, **6**:148
Lindbergh, Anne Morrow, **5**:*113*
Lindbergh, Charles A., **3**:321; **5**:*114*
  in America First Committee, **1**:139
  "America First" speech by, text of, **9**:393–395
  barnstorming by, **1**:418
  trans-Atlantic flight of, **1**:82, 83, 93; **3**:31; **5:113–114**
Lindbergh, Charles A., Jr., **5**:*113*
  kidnapping of, **4**:525; **5**:113
Lindbergh Kidnapping Law (1932), **5**:113
Lindeman, Raymond, **1**:520
Lindesmith Center, **5**:513
Lindley, John, **1**:519
Lindsay, John, **4**:522
Lindsay Earls, Board of Education v., **2**:149
Linebacker I, Operation, **1**:77
Linebacker II, Operation, **1**:77
Line-item vetoes, **8:320–321**
Linen industry, **5:114**
Linenthal, Mark, **1**:375
Ling, James J., **2**:348
Lingayen Gulf, **5:114–115**
Linguistic Society of America, **5**:115
Linguistics, **5:115–116**
  descriptive (structural), **5**:115
  post-structuralism and, **6**:430
Lining, John, **2**:234
Linnaeus, Carolus (Carl), **1**:191, 516, 518–519; **8**:596
Linotype, **6**:469
Linowitz, Sol, **6**:240
Linton, Ralph, **1**:193
Linton, William J., **8**:523
Lion King, The (musical), **8**:115
Lipan Apaches, **1**:218, 219, 220–221
Lippincott, Jesse, **1**:357–358
Lippmann, Walter, **5**:120; **6**:76, 535
Lipset, Seymour, **6**:32; **7**:428
Lipton, Seymour, **1**:306
Lipton, Sir Thomas, **1**:172
Liquid crystal display (LCD), **8**:77

Liquid-drop model, **6:**343
Liquor. *See* Alcohol; Spirits industry
Liquor laws. *See* Alcohol, regulation of
Liri Valley (Italy), **5:**451–452
Lisa, Manuel, **3:**298; **6:**29
List, Friedrich, **3:**108
Lister, Joseph, **3:**239; **4:**173
Liston, Charles (Sonny), **6:**484
Liston, Robert, **1:**489
Litchfield Law School, **5:116**
Literacy
  among African Americans, **3:**120, 121
  among Cherokee, **2:**126–127
  in colonial era, **3:**112
    Puritanism and, **1:**447
  cultural, **2:478–479**
Literacy test, **5:**116, *117*
  legal challenge to, **8:**483
Literary Digest (journal), **6:**409, 533–534
Literary Guild, **6:**538
Literary Situation, The (Cowley), **5:**121
The Literary Voyager; or Muzzeniegun (magazine), **5:**192
Literature, **5:116–130**
  abolitionist, **5:**119
  African American, **2:**205; **5:**119, 121, 123, **123–126; 7:**197
    after 1960s, **5:**126
    communism and, **5:**125
    in Depression and after, **5:**125–126
    folklore, **3:**395
    in Harlem Renaissance, **4:**95–96
    from Reconstruction to World War I, **5:**124
    during slavery, **5:**124
  after American Revolution, **5:**118
  Asian American, **5:**123
  of beat generation, **1:433**
  category romance as, **5:**130
  chapbooks, **2:105**
  children's, **5:126–128**
    American, emergence of, **5:**127
    early American, **5:**127
    late 19th and early 20th century, **5:**127–128
    McGuffey's Readers, **5:185**
    Native American, **5:**127
  of Cold War, **5:**121, 130
  conservative, **2:**375
  crime novels as, **5:**122, 130
  detective fiction as, **5:**130
  dime novels, **3:25–26**
  Enlightenment and, **5:**118
  fantasy as, **5:**129–130
  frontier fiction, **8:**457
  in Great Depression, **5:**120
  of Harlem Renaissance, **5:**121, **124–125,** 124–125
  Hispanic American, **5:**123
  in Jazz Age, **5:**120
  by Kentuckians, **4:**520
  Knickerbockers and, **5:**118–119
  in magazines, **5:**191, 192–193, 194, 196
  modernists and, **5:**120–121
  Native American, **2:**484; **4:**179; **5:128–129**
    children's, **5:**127
    oral, **4:279–281**
  naturalism and, **5:**118–120; **6:11–13**
  Nobel Prizes in, **6:**487
  and nonfiction novels, **5:**122
  by Oregonians, **6:**207
  overview, **5:116–123**
  popular, **5:**122–123, 123, **129–130**
    Cooper (James Fenimore) and, **5:**70
    on Great Depression, **5:**83–84
    Lost Generation and, **5:**157
    noir, **5:**120
  postmodernist, **6:**429
  pulps as, **5:**129
  religious, **7:95–98**
  Romanticism in, **7:**194–195
  science fiction as, **5:**122, 130
  Spanish language and, **7:**492
  Transcendentalism and, **5:**119
  westerns as, **5:**129, 130
  See also specific titles
Lithography, **6:**469–470, 470–471
  of Currier and Ives, **2:***483,* **483–484**
  mapmaking and, **5:**233
Litigation
  consumer safety, **2:**384
  See also specific cases
Little, Malcolm. *See* Malcolm X
Little, Royal, **2:**348
Little Bighorn, Battle of, **1:**354, 453, 475; **3:**318; **5:130–132; 8:**275, 404
  Custer in, **1:**354; **5:**131–132; **7:**370–371
  eyewitness account of, **9:**253–255
  Sioux in, **5:**130–132; **7:**370–371
Little Bighorn National Monument, **5:132**
Little Crow (Sioux leader)
  in Sioux Wars, **7:**369, 370; **8:**403
  speech by, **9:**243–244
Little James (ship), **5:**317
Little League, **5:132–133**
Little Niagara, Fort, **6:**102
Little Raven (Arapaho chief), **2:**298
Little red schoolhouse, **5:***133,* **133–134**
Little Review, **5:**194
Little Richard, **7:**185
Little Rock (Arkansas), **2:**202; **5:134**
  establishment of, **1:**260
  school desegregation in, **1:**263; **5:**134, *134*
Little Steel Formula (1942), **8:**171
Little Steel Strike (1937), **8:**277
"Little Theaters," **8:**114
Little Turtle (Miami chief), **4:**64; **5:**353; **6:**178
Little Wolf (Cheyenne leader), **8:**404
Little Women (Alcott), **5:**127
Littlefield, Ephraim, **8:**435
Littlejohn, James, **6:**219
Littleton, Harvey K., **1:**290
Litvinov, Maxim, **7:**57
Liver transplantation, **8:**183
Livestock industry, **2:**73–74; **5:135–136**
  barbed wire in, **1:**416; **2:**73, 76
  disease in, **8:**319, 320
  in early America, **5:**135
  hogs in, **4:145–146**
  and meatpacking, **5:**135–136
  postwar developments in, **5:**136
  safety of, USDA role in, **1:**71
  in South Dakota, **7:**460
  stockyards in, **7:551–552**
  and vegetarianism, **8:**310
  See also Cattle; Meatpacking
Living Theater, **8:**115
Livingston, Robert R., **3:**450, 483
  alma mater of, **2:**304
  and Declaration of Independence, **2:**521
  and Louisiana Purchase, **5:**162–163
Llarneros, **1:**218

Llewellyn, Karl, **2:**317
Llewellyn Park (New Jersey), **5:**39
Lloyd, Earl, **1:**424
Lloyd, William, **3:**351
Lloyd George, David
　on Fourteen Points, **4:**42
　at Paris peace conference, **8:**315
Lo Pizzo, Anna, **5:**60
Loader, Jane, with Kevin Rafferty
　　and Pierce Rafferty, *The Atomic
　　Café,* **5:**121
Lobbies and lobbying, **1:**488;
　4:380–382; 5:136–137
　by American Medical Association,
　　1:164–165
　illicit, **5:**137
　Legislative Reorganization Act
　　and, **5:**77–78, 137
　for Native Americans
　　by American Indian Defense
　　　Association, **1:159–160**
　　by Society of American Indians,
　　　7:430–431
　number of, **5:**137
　objects of, **5:**136
　private vs. public, **5:**137
　regulation of, **5:**137
　for retired persons, by AARP, **1:142**
　in Senate confirmation hearings,
　　5:137
　by Sierra Club, **7:**355
　tactics of, **5:**136
Lobotomy, **6:**522
Local area networks (LANs), **8:**66
Local government, **5:137–139**
　after American Revolution, **5:**138
　civil service reform in, **2:**207
　colonial, **5:**137–138
　council-manager, **5:**138
　dependent on federal aid, **3:**334
　home rule by, **4:**152–153
　in interstate highway program,
　　4:404
　martial law and, **5:**254
　mayor-council, **5:**138
　merged, **5:**139
　metropolitan, **5:**139
　municipal, **5:**138–139
　in New England, **5:**137–139
　political subdivisions, **6:406**
　social legislation by, **7:**415
　special districts for, **5:**139
　town government, **8:148–149**
　See also Municipal government

*Local Number 6167, United Mine
　Workers of America, Jewell Ridge
　Coal Corporation v.,* **3:**308
Lochner v. New York, **1:**21, 580; **3:**90,
　308; **5:**14, **139–140**
　judicial review in, **4:**492
　liberty of contract in, **5:**394, 395,
　　473
Locke, Alain, **6:**375
　The New Negro: An Interpretation,
　　5:125
Locke, Gary, **1:**324
Locke, John, **3:**108, 248; **6:**10; **8:**179
　and checks and balances, **2:**116
　on due process of law, **3:**89
　*An Essay Concerning Human Under-
　　standing,* **5:**140
　ideas of, and Declaration of Inde-
　　pendence, **2:**287
　A Letter Concerning Toleration,
　　5:140
　political philosophy of, **5:**91,
　　140–141
　on "pursuit of happiness," **2:**284
　The Reasonableness of Christianity,
　　5:140
　on representative government, **7:**109
　on right of revolution, **7:**148
　*Some Thoughts Concerning Educa-
　　tion,* **5:**140
　Two Treatises of Government, **5:**140,
　　140; **7:**161
Lockhart Commission, **6:**420
Lockheed, **1:**83, 84
　P-80 (F-80) of, **1:***95*
Lockout, **5:**11, **141–142**
Lockwood, Belva, **3:**248; **5:**74; **8:**506
Lockwood, Charles A., **8:**557
Lockwood, Mary, **2:**504
Locofoco Party, **5:142**
Locomotives, **5:142–144,** *143*
　builders of, **5:**142–143
　development of, **7:**30
　diesel-electric, **5:**144
　electric, **5:**144
　steam, **5:**142–144
　types of, **5:**142–143
Locusts, **4:**37
Lode mining, **4:**11
Lodge, Edward, **7:**203
Lodge, Henry Cabot, **8:**316
　ambassadorship of, **1:**134
　expansionism of, and arms race,
　　1:270

and Federal Elections Bill (1890),
　2:332
in presidential campaign of 1960,
　3:164
rejecting Versailles Treaty, **8:**201
at Washington Naval Conference,
　8:418
Loeb, Kuhn, **1:**404
Loeb, Richard, **4:**525; **5:**82, *83*
Loess Hills, **6:**28
Loewe, Dietrich, **2:**496
Loewe v. Lawlor. See Danbury Hat-
　ters' Case
Log cabin, **5:145**
Log Cabin Republicans, **5:**145
Logan, Benjamin, **6:**177
Logan (Mingo chief), speech by,
　9:103–104
Logan Valley Plaza, Food Employees v.,
　6:350
Logging industry. *See* Lumber
　industry
Logistics, **5:145–146**
　grand, **5:**146
　primary and secondary, **5:**146
　strategic, **5:**146
　tactical, **5:**146
Logocentric thinking, **6:**431
Logrolling, **5:146**
Logstown, Treaty of (1748), **4:**313
Logue, Edward J., **1:**510
Lohr, Lenox, **5:**484
Loma Prieta earthquake (1989),
　3:37, 102
Lomax, Alan, **1:**169, 388; **3:**396
Lomax, John A., **1:**388, 389; **2:**442;
　3:396
Lomax, Louis, **5:**520
Lôme, Enrique Dupuy de, **5:**47
Lon Nol, **2:**16–17
London, Declaration of, **5:146–147**
London, Jack, **6:**12
　The Call of the Wild, **5:**119
　The People of the Abyss, **5:**119
　and temperance movement, **3:**60
London, Treaty of, **5:147**
London Company, **8:**174
　in Virginia, **8:**341, 342
London Conference, **6:**235
London Crystal Palace Exhibition
　(1851), **8:**558
London Magazine, maps in, **9:**23, *23*
London Merchant Adventurers,
　5:317

London Naval Treaties, **5:**147

Lone Ranger and Tonto Fistfight in Heaven, The (Alexie), **5:**129

Lone Wolf v. Hitchcock, **5:**147–148

Lonely Crowd, The (Riesman), **5:**121, **148**

Long, Alexander, **2:**411

Long, Breckenridge, **1:**207

Long, Crawford, **1:**184, 185

Long, Earl K., **5:**161; **6:**74

Long, Huey, **2:**375; **5:**160–161
  as fascist Senator, **3:**327
  and freedom of press, **4:**67
  and New Orleans, **6:**74

Long, Iris, **1:**16

Long, John, **7:**278

Long, Stephen H.
  on agriculture in West, **1:**64
  explorations of, **2:**301; **3:**299; **5:150–151**
    in Nebraska, **6:**29
    on Oklahoma, **6:**183

Long Beach (California), **5:148–149**

Long Drive, **5:**149

Long Island (New York), **5:149–150**

Long Island, Battle of, **5:**149, **150**; **7:**137

Long Island Railroad Company, Palsgraf v., **6:232**

"Long Line of Vendidas, A" (Moraga), **3:**520

"Long telegram," **8:**569

Longfellow, Henry Wadsworth, **3:***58*
  "The Slave in the Dismal Swamp," **3:**57–58

Longhouses, **1:**255; **6:**276

Longman, Evelyn Beatrice, **1:**308

Longman-Pearson, **6:**538

Long-playing (LP) record, **5:**503

Longshoremen, trade unions for, **4:**395–396

Longstreet, James
  in Battle of Antietam, **1:**199–200
  in Battle of Gettysburg, **3:**567–568
  in Battle on Lookout Mountain, **5:**151
  in Battles of the Wilderness, **8:**477
  in Chattanooga campaign, **2:**113
  in First Battle of Bull Run, **1:**567
  in Second Battle of Bull Run, **1:**568

Longwood Gardens, **1:**517

Longworth, Nicholas, **8:**486

Look Homeward, Angel (Wolfe), **5:**120

Looking Backward (Bellamy), **6:**417; **7:**424; **8:**303

Looking Glass (Nez Perce chief), **4:***325*

Lookout Mountain, Battle on, **2:**113; **5:**151

Loomis, Elias, **1:**343; **2:**235

Loomis, Orland S., **6:**500

Looney Tunes, **2:**63

Loos, Adolf, **1:**252

Lopez, Aaron, **8:**210

López, Narciso, **2:**469; **3:**359; **5:**46

Lopez, United States v., **2:**311–312; **8:274–275**
  judicial review in, **4:**493

Lorain, John, **2:**413

Lord, Nathan, **2:**502

Lord, Walter, **8:**132

Lorde, Audre, **8:**511

Lords of Trade and Plantation, **1:**493; **5:**151
  Massachusetts Bay Colony and, **5:**271

Lorimer, George Horace, **7:**252–253

Lorimier, Peter, **5:**62

Loring, Edward G., **1:**577

Los Angeles (California), **5:151–155**
  in 20th century, **5:**152–153
  air pollution in, **5:**154
  development of, **2:**10; **8:**445
  early history of, **5:**151–152, *152*
  earthquakes and, **3:**37, 102; **5:**153–154
  economy of, **5:**152–154
  Empowerment Zone program, **8:**287
  entertainment industry in, **5:***153*
  ethnic composition of, **8:**291
  founding of, **2:**8
  future of, **5:**154
  Getty Museum in, **3:564–566**
  growth of, railroads and, **5:**152
  Hollywood (*See* Hollywood)
  interurban trains in, **7:**42
  map of, **5:***153*
  McNamara bombing case, **5:**189
  Mexican Americans in, discrimination against, **9:**407–409
  racial diversity of, **5:**153
  riots in
    in 1965 (Watts), **2:**12; **8:430–431,** *431*

  in 1992 (Rodney King), **5:**155, *155*; **6:**385, *386*; **7:**12, 165; **8:**338, 339
  media coverage of, **8:**339
  segregation in, **5:**153
  social structure of, **5:**153–154

Los Angeles Times Building, bombing of, **2:**10

Losing Ground: American Social Policy (Murray), **6:**440

Lost Battalion, **5:**155

"Lost Cause," **4:**20–21; **5:155–156**

Lost Cause, The (Pollard), **5:**155

Lost Colony, **3:**288

Lost Generation, **3:**280; **5:**156

Lost in the Funhouse (Barth), **5:**122

Lotteries, **3:**508; **5:156–157**
  national (1860s–1890s), **5:**156–157
  public funds raised through, **2:**518
  as revenue source, **5:**157
  state-operated (1964–), **5:**157
  state-sanctioned (1607–1840s), **5:**156, 160

Loudon, John Campbell, Earl of, **2:**295

Louima, Abner, **6:**385

Louis, Joe, **6:**484

Louis XIV (king of France), **3:**286

Louis XVI (king of France), **7:**146, 147

Louisburg expedition, **5:**157
  archival maps of, **9:***25,* 26

Louisiana, **5:158–162**
  in 19th century, **5:**159–160
  in 20th century, **5:**160–161
  bayous in, **1:**432
  Bourbon period of, **5:**160
  Code Napoléon in, **2:**262
  Code Noir in, **2:**262–263
  in colonial era, **5:**158–159
  constitution of, **5:**160; **7:**527
  cotton plantations in, **6:**364
  Creole flag of, **2:**457
  economy of, **5:**160–161
  emblems, nicknames, mottos, and songs of, **7:***532*
  Farmers' Alliance in, **3:**323
  free blacks in, **5:**160
  French claims to, **8:**452
  French colonial settlements in, **6:**53, 73
  French legal system in, **2:**440
  Jefferson on, **3:**18
  maps of, **5:***158*

archival, **9:**20, 20–23, 21, 23, 45, 46

"Mississippi bubble" (1917), **5:414**

Natchitoches, **5:**158

Native American mounds in, **4:**278; **5:**158

police regulations in, **9:**323

Reconstruction and, **5:**160

secession of, **5:**160

Serpent lottery in, **5:**156–157, 160

slavery in, **5:**160

Spanish, **5:**158, 159

Spanish colonial settlements in, **6:**73

Spanish language in, **7:**491

statehood for, **5:**159

sugar plantations in, **6:**364

tax system of, **5:**161

Territory of Orleans in, **6:213**

tidelands in, ownership of, **8:**125

voter registration in, **8:**354

White Caps in, **8:**470

White League in, **8:472–473**

Louisiana, Allgeyer v., **1:**21

Louisiana, Garrison v., **5:**90

Louisiana, Taylor v., **8:60**

Louisiana Maneuvers, **5:**161

Louisiana Purchase, **1:**187; **3:**425, 450; **5:**159; **8:**204

boundaries of, **9:**45, 46

consequences of, **5:**163

Federalist Party against, **3:**352

Jefferson and, **2:**550

and land claims, **5:**26

map of, **5:**162

and Native Americans, **8:**217, 224

negotiation of, **5:**162–163

and New Orleans, **6:**73

and North Dakota, **6:**132

price of, **5:**162

Spain and, **7:**484

survey and exploration after, **3:**297; **8:**461

by Lewis and Clark, **5:**86–87

Louisiana Purchase Exposition (1904), **5:**163, **163–164**

furniture at, **3:**498

Louisiana Territory

French claim to, **5:**162–163

naming of, **5:**3

natural history of, **5:**162

political history of, **5:**162

Spanish claim to, **5:**162–163

See also Louisiana Purchase

Louisville (Kentucky), Southern Exposition in, **8:**558

Louverture, Toussaint, **3:**501

Love, Alfred, **1:**216; **6:**267

Love, William, **5:**164

Love Canal (New York), **3:**39, 230, 232; **5:164,** 164

Love in the Ruins (Percy), **5:**123

Love Medicine (Erdrich), **5:**129, **164–165**

Lovejoy, Arthur O., **1:**143; **7:**193

Lovejoy, Elijah, **2:**84; **5:**165; **6:**97

Lovejoy riots, **5:165**

Lovell, James, **2:**467

Lovell, Joseph, **5:**286

Lovell, Philip, **1:**252

Lovell, Solomon, **6:**281, 282

Lovelock, James, **3:**551

Lovestone, Jay, **1:**152; **2:**326; **4:**391

Lovett, Robert A., **2:**528

Loving, Richard, **5:**165

Loving v. Virginia, **5:**165, 251, 406

Low, Anne Marie, on Dust Bowl, **9:**384–385

Low, Isaac, **5:**167

Low, Juliette Gordon, **4:**1

"Low" milling, **3:**390

Lowcountry, **7:**154–155

Lowden, Frank O., **3:**161

Lowe, Stanley, **1:**446

Lowe, Thaddeus, **1:**391

Lowell (Massachusetts), **2:**185; **7:**64

Lowell, A. Lawrence, **4:**102–103

Lowell, Elizabeth, *Tell Me No Lies,* **5:**130

Lowell, Francis Cabot, **2:**245, 387; **8:**108, 109

Lowell, John, **3:**256

Lowell, John, Jr., **3:**256

Lowell, Josephine Shaw, **2:**106, 392

Lowell, Percival, **1:**344; **6:**156

Lowell, Robert, **5:**122

Lowell Mills (Massachusetts), **2:**223

Lower East Side, **5:165–167**

Orchard Street, **5:**166

Lower South, **5:167**

Lowi, Theodore J., **3:**332

Lowie, Robert, **1:**193

Lowrie, Walter, **3:**280

Lowry, Henry Berry, **5:**170

Lowry War, **5:**170

Loyalists, **5:167–168**

in American Revolution, **7:**139, 141

arguments of, **2:**284

in Canada, **2:**26

confiscated property of, **1:**541; **2:**346–347

and conservatism, **2:**374

emigration of, **3:**197

Loyalty oaths, **5:168**

for Confederate soldiers, **3:**505

for federal employees, **8:**96

Ironclad Oath, **4:430; 8:**96

Pledge of Allegiance, **6:**370

Supreme Court on, **2:**480; **8:**62, 96–97

for teachers, **8:62–63**

LPs. *See* Long-playing (LP) record

LSAT. *See* Law School Admissions Test

LSD (lysergic acid diethylamide), **5:169; 7:**569

Lubbock, John, **1:**192

Lucas, Eliza, **4:**330

Lucas, George, **3:**364; **7:**524

Lucas, Jerry, **1:**424

Lucas, John, in Anzio Campaign, **1:**217

Lucas, Robert, **3:**110

Lucas v. South Carolina Coastal Council, **2:**318; **3:**198

Luce, Henry, **8:**127

Lucent Technologies, **1:**440

Lucky Strike (cigarettes), **8:**135

Lucumi, **7:**249–250

Ludars, **4:**79

Ludlow, Louis, **5:**170

Ludlow, Roger, **5:**170

Ludlow Massacre, **2:**254, 299, 300; **5:169–170; 8:**339

Ludlow resolution, **5:170**

Ludlow's Code, **5:170**

Ludlum, Robert, **5:**130

Ludwig, Carl, **6:**349

Lugar, Richard, **4:**320

Luisetti, Hank, **1:**424

Lukban, Vicente, **6:**320

Luks, George, **1:**268, 297, 321

LULAC. *See* League of United Latin American Citizens

Lumbee, **5:170–171,** 171; **7:**47; **8:**226

Lumber industry, **5:171–174**

in Arkansas, **1:**261–262

clear-cutting by, **5:**173

Forest Service and, **3:**431

growth of, **5:**173–174

Lumber industry, (continued)
  in Idaho, **4:**212
  labor in, **5:**173
  land scrip and, **5:**35
  logging by, saws for, **5:**173
  in Maine, **5:**209
  map of, **5:***172*
  in Michigan, **5:**354
  in Minnesota, **5:**399
  in Montana, **5:**450
  in Progressive Era, **3:**435–436
  sawmills in, **7:259**
  size of, **5:**173–174
  in Wisconsin, **8:**491
Lumpkin, Joseph Henry, **8:**79
Lumumba, Patrice, **8:**271
Luna Park, **1:**179
Luna y Arellano, Tristán, **1:**102; **3:**295–296
Lundeen, Ernest, **3:**322
Lundeen Bill, **7:**129
Lundestad, Geir, **3:**259
Lundy, Benjamin, **1:**209; **6:**47
Lung cancer, **2:**34; **8:**135
Lungren, Dan, **6:**510
Lupton, Frances, **1:**308
Lusitania, sinking of, **3:**464; **5:174–175**, *175*; **8:**534
Luther, Martin, **6:**515
  Vatican II on, **8:**309
  and work ethic, **8:**526
Luther v. Borden, **5:175**
Lutheran Free Church, **6:**137
Lutheranism, **5:175–177**
  Akron Rule (1872) and, **5:**176
  and *Book of Concord*, **5:**176
  confessionalism and, **5:**176
  current status of, **5:**177
  General Synod of, **5:**175–177
  in Great Depression, **5:**177
  in late19th century, **5:**176
  membership in, **5:**177; **7:***91*
  Missouri Synod of, **5:**176–177
  Norwegian churches and, **6:**137–138
  Pietism and, **6:353–354**
  in postwar world, **5:**177
  theological disputes among, **5:**176–177
  unity in, **5:**177
Luxembourg, in European Common Market, **8:**157
Lyceum movement, **3:**115; **5:178**; **7:**64–65
Lyceum Theater School, **8:**114

Lyme disease, **5:178–179**
Lymphadenopathy-associated virus (LAV), **1:**15
Lynch, Charles, **5:**179
Lynch law, **5:**179
Lynch v. Donnelly, **2:**166, 170
Lynching, **5:179–180**; **8:**337
  capital punishment by, **2:**40
  at Fort Benning, **1:**442
  of Frank (Leo), **3:453**
  geographic distribution of, **1:**332; **5:**179
  in Georgia, **3:**556
  and NAACP, **5:**526
  as political violence, **1:**332; **5:**179
  prevention of, women in, **1:**339–340; **5:**180
  rate of, **8:**337
  statistics for, **5:**179
  targets of, **5:**179, *179*
  Till (Emmett), **8:126**
  and Tulsa race riot, **8:**239
  during World War I, **8:**537
Lynd, Helen Merrell, **4:**318–319; **7:**433
Lynd, Robert S., **4:**318–319; **7:**433
Lynds, Elam, **6:**476
Lynes, Russell, **5:**366
Lyng v. Northwest Indian Cemetery Association, **1:**161–162; **5:180**
Lyon, Irving, **2:**271
Lyon, Mary, **3:**114; **5:**464
Lyon, Matthew, **1:**124
Lyon, Phyllis, **2:**503
Lyons v. Oklahoma, **5:**526
Lyotard, Jean-François, **6:**429
Lysergic acid diethylamide. *See* LSD
Lytton Commission, **5:**65, 428

M

M. C. Higgins the Great (Hamilton), **5:**126
MAAG. *See* Military Assistance Advisory Group
McAdoo, William Gibbs, **3:**161, 162; **4:**31; **8:**196
McAllister, Ward, **3:**445
MacArthur, Arthur, **6:**320
MacArthur, Catherine T., **5:**181
MacArthur, Douglas
  Bataan-Corregidor Campaign and, **1:**427

  Bismarck Archipelago Campaign and, **1:**470
  Bonus Army and, **1:**498
  dismissal of, **2:**528
  as engineer commander, **3:**219
  in Korean War, **4:**545, 546–548
  speech to Congress on, text of, **9:**427–428
  at Lingayen Gulf, **5:**115
  occupation of Japan under, **4:**458
  and Philippines, **6:**322; **8:**547
  strategies in World War II, **8:**547, 548
MacArthur, John D., **5:**181; **6:**486
MacArthur Foundation, **5:181**
  "Genius" Awards, **6:486–487**
Macaulay, Thomas Babington, **6:**537
McAuliffe, Anthony C., **1:**426
McAuliffe, Sharon Christa, **1:**232; **2:**101; **7:**481
McBain, Ed, **5:**122
McCabe, Charles Cardwell, **1:**429
McCabe, Thomas, **3:**346
McCaffrey, Barry, **5:**511
McCain, John, in presidential campaign of 2000, **3:**170
McCain-Feingold Act (2002), **3:**144
McCall, Heim v., **1:**125
McCandless, Bruce, II, **7:**483
McCardell, Claire, **2:**247
McCardle, William, **3:**271
McCarran, Pat, anticommunism of, **1:**197
McCarran Act (Internal Security Act) (1950), **2:**85
McCarran-Walter Act (1952), **3:**12, 197; **4:**228; **5:181**
  on naturalization, **6:**14
  problems with, **4:**230, 231
  provisions of, **4:***230*
McCarthy, Eugene
  and censorship, **2:**85
  in presidential campaign of 1968, **3:**165; **8:**333
  in presidential campaign of 1976, **3:**167
McCarthy, Joseph, **5:**181, *182*
  anticommunism of, **1:**197
  and China, relations with, **2:**151
  Congressional censure of, text of, **9:**428–429
  and conservative movement, **2:**375
  and conspiracy theories, **2:**378

Democrats' inability to oppose,
2:553
hearings of, 4:411; 8:1–2
"The History of George Catlett
Marshall," 9:424–426
National Review defending, 5:556
McCarthyism, **5:181–183**
and book banning, 1:500
and economic analysis, 3:110
and FBI activities, 3:338
and National Lawyers Guild,
5:546–547
New Republic on, 6:77
New Yorker on, 6:92
and newspapers, 6:99
and trade unions, attacks on, 3:176
Yalta Conference and, 8:574
See also Anticommunism; Blacklisting; House Committee on
Un-American Activities
McCartney, Bill, 6:518
McCarty, Maclyn, 3:533
McCauley, Mary (Molly Pitcher),
8:505
McCay, Winsor, 2:63
McClellan, Brinton, in Battle of
Antietam, 1:199–200
McClellan, George B.
Army of the Potomac under, 1:279;
9:67
in capture of Harpers Ferry, 4:97
criticism of, 2:211, 212, 314
letter to Lincoln from, 9:298–299
Maryland invasion, defense of,
5:259
in Peninsular Campaign, 6:275
in presidential campaign of 1864,
2:218, 551; 3:155
in Seven Days' Battles, 7:319; 9:67
Stuart's Ride and, 7:560
McClellan Committee Hearings,
5:183
McClelland, Nancy, 1:292, 293
McClintock, Hamilton, 6:302
McCloy, John J., 8:394
McClure, Michael, 1:433
McClure, Robert J. Le M., 6:136
McCollum, Elmer V., 6:149
McCollum v. Board of Education,
2:168
McComb, H. S., 2:453
McConnell, John, 3:100
McCord, James W., Jr., 8:426
McCormack, Powell v. See Powell case

McCormick, Cyrus, Jr., 4:389
McCormick, Cyrus Hall, 1:58; 2:97,
132; 5:183
at London Crystal Palace Exhibi-
tion, 8:558
McCormick, Katharine Dexter,
1:468
McCormick, Stanley, 1:468
McCormick reaper, 1:58; **5:183–184**
McCorvey, Norma, 7:192
McCoy, Joseph G., 1:2; 2:73, 75
McCoy, Thomas P., 7:153
MacCracken, Henry, 3:410
McCracken, Henry M., 5:530
McCray v. United States, **5:184**
McCready, Benjamin W., 3:238;
5:297
McCrory, J. G., 3:26
McCulloch, Hugh, 2:404
McCulloch, John Ramsey, 3:108
McCulloch v. Maryland, 3:225; **5:184**
implied powers in, 4:247
McDade, Joseph, 5:77
McDaniel, Hattie, 6:*485*
Macdonald, Dwight, 5:365; 6:90
Macdonald, Sir John A., 2:26
McDonald Observatory, 6:157
McDonald v. Smith, 6:297
McDonald's, 3:398; **5:184–185**
MacDonald-Wright, Stanton, 2:476
Macdonough, Thomas, 6:25
McDougal, Duncan, 1:342
McDougal, John, 8:214
McDougall, Alexander, 2:83; 8:473
and Committee of Inspection,
2:313
McDougall, William, 1:438
MacDowell, Edward, 5:492
McDowell, Ephraim, 5:*285*
McDowell, Irvin
in Army of Virginia, 1:279
in First Battle of Bull Run, 1:567;
2:211
in Peninsular Campaign, 6:275
McDowell, Tremain, 1:169
McElroy, Neil H., 2:528
McEnery, John, 6:76
McEntee, Gerald W., 1:154
McFadden Banking Act (1927),
5:185
McFarland, Horace, 5:550
McGarvey, J. W., 3:45
McGee, W. J., 3:175
McGillivray, Alexander, 1:525; 2:135

McGlachlin, Edward F., Jr., Army of
Occupation under, 1:278
McGonagle, William L., 5:95–96
McGovern, George, 8:262
AFL-CIO and, 1:152
on amnesty, 1:177
as chairman of Select Committee
on Nutrition and Human
Needs, 3:409
in presidential campaign of 1972,
3:100, 166; 6:227; 8:425
McGrain v. Daugherty, 2:352
McGraw, John, 1:420
and land speculation, 5:36
McGraw-Hill Buildings, 7:376
McGreevey, James E., 6:64
McGrory, Mary, 8:506
McGuffey's Readers, 5:127, **185**;
8:106, *106*
McGuire, Mark, 1:422
McGuire, Peter J., 5:12; 8:262, 263
Machado, Gerardo, 2:470
Machen, August W., 7:205
McHenry, Fort, 5:**185**, *186*
Machiavelli, Niccolò, 8:370
Machine, political, **5:186–187**
corrupt
Tammany Hall, 8:46
Tweed Ring, 8:46, **242**
in Missouri, 5:421
municipal government and, 5:475,
477
municipal reform and, 5:**478**
Pendergast machine, 6:**274–275**
Tammany societies, 8:47
See also Bosses and bossism; Cor-
ruption, political
Machine guns, 5:**185–186**, 480
Machine Readable Cataloging
(MARC), 5:101
Machlup, Fritz, 3:109
McIntire, Samuel, 1:249, 305
Macintosh, Ebenezer, 7:135
McIntosh, Johnson v., 6:506
MacIntyre, Alasdair, 4:334
MacIver, Robert M., 6:375, 376
Mack, Alexander, Sr., 1:534
Mack, Connie, 1:420, 421
McKay, Claude, 4:96; 5:125
McKay, Douglas (Giveaway), 2:372
McKay, Gordon, 1:503; 5:59
invention of bottom-stitcher for
shoes, 5:69
Mackay, John W., 1:497; 2:3

Mackay-Bennett (ship), **8**:131
MacKaye, Benton, **1**:224
McKean, James, **5**:54; **8**:297
McKean, Thomas, **2**:541
McKee, Nancy, **3**:518, 519, 520
McKenna, Wendy, **3**:516
McKenny, Thomas L., **1**:570
McKenzie, Alexander, **6**:132
Mackenzie, Alexander, **3**:297
    explorations by
        in Aleutian Islands, **1**:121
        in Oregon, **6**:204
McKenzie, Donald, **8**:453
McKenzie, Kenneth, **1**:158; **8**:259
Mackenzie, Ranald S., **7**:72
Mackenzie, William Lyon, **2**:58
Mackerel fisheries, **5:187–188**
McKibben, Bill, **4**:8
McKim, Charles, **8**:410
Mackinac, Straits of, and Mackinac
    Island, **5:188–189**
Mackinac National Park, **5**:550
Mackinaw City (Michigan), **5**:188
Mackinder, Halford, **3**:542
McKinley, William
    American Protective Association
        and, **1**:167
    assassination of, **1:328–329**; **2**:84,
        227; **6**:236; **8**:339
        anarchism and, **1**:181
        Roosevelt (Theodore) after, **8**:323
    Cuban policy of, **2**:470
    and flag, **3**:380
    and forest conservation, **3**:431
    and gold standard, **1**:459
    and Hawaiian annexation, **1**:189;
        4:107
    and Nicaraguan Canal Project, **6**:105
    and Philippines, **6**:319–320, 321;
        8:201
    in presidential campaign of 1896,
        2:23, 46; **3**:158, 159; **8**:234
    in presidential campaign of 1900,
        3:159, 483; **6**:320
    protectionist policies of, **2**:551
    and Republican Party, **7**:112
    and Spanish-American War, **5**:47
    Taft Commission appointed by,
        8:41
    and tariffs, **3**:358; **8**:51, 156
    on world's fairs, **8**:559
    McKinley Tariff Act (1890), **3**:158,
        358; **8**:51, 156
        compromise regarding, **2**:332

MacKinnon, Catharine, **3**:54; **6**:419;
    7:323
McKissack, Jeff, **1**:312
McKissick, Floyd, **2**:355
McLain, William, **1**:148
McLane, John, **6**:423
McLane, Louis, **7**:103; **8**:196
McLaughlin, Ann Dore, **5**:12
McLaughlin, Mary Louise, **1**:304;
    6:418
McLaughlin v. Florida, **5**:165
MacLaury, Bruce, **8**:117
McLaury, Frank, **8**:141
McLaury, Tom, **8**:141
McLean, John, **6**:426, 462
    in presidential campaign of 1836,
        3:153
McLean, Malcolm, **5**:320
McLean, Wilmer, **1**:226
McLean Credit Union, Patterson v.,
    2:197
MacLeish, Archibald, **1**:450; **5**:101
MacLeod, Colin, **3**:533
McLoughlin, John, **8**:175
McLuhan, Marshall, **6**:470; **8**:67
McMahon, Thomas, **8**:278
McMillan, Edwin, **2**:123; **6**:338, 342,
    343
Macmillan, Harold, **1**:445
McMillan, James, **8**:410
McMillan, Terry, **5**:123
McMillen, Eleanor, **1**:292
MacMonnies, Frederick W., **1**:306
McMullin, Fred, **1**:480
McMurray, W. Grant, **7**:104
McMurtry, Larry, **5**:123, 130
McNair, Robert, **1**:392
McNair, Ronald E., **2**:102
McNamara, Frank, **2**:450, 451
McNamara, Robert S.
    on airpower in Vietnam, **1**:77
    on arms race, **1**:271
    influence of, **2**:2
    and National Guard, **5**:543
    and *Pentagon Papers*, **6**:286
    as secretary of defense, **2**:528
    and World Bank, **8**:532
McNamara bombing case, **5:189**
McNary-Haugen Bill, **3**:302; **5:189**
MacNeil, Carol Brooks, **1**:308
MacNeil, Hermon A., **1**:306
MacNeil, Robert, **3**:222
McNickle, D'arcy, **3**:136
    The Surrounded, **5**:128; **8**:30

Macon, Nathaniel, **8**:382
Macon's Bill No. 2 (1810), **5:189**;
    6:117; **8**:382
MacPhail, Larry, **1**:421
McPherson, Aimee Semple, **5**:*410*
McPherson, James Alan, **5**:123
McPhitrigde, C. A., **1**:58
McRae, Cora, **4**:100
McRae, Harris v., **4:100**
McRae, Milton A., **6**:459
Macready, William Charles, **1**:341
McReynolds, James Clark, **2**:167
    on parental choice in education,
        6:353
MacSparran, James, **2**:234
McSweeney-McNary Act (1928),
    3:432
McTeague (Norris), **5**:119–120; **6**:12
Macune, Charles, **3**:324; **6**:157, 416
MACV. *See* Military Assistance
    Command, Vietnam
McVeigh, Timothy, **6**:186, 187–188;
    8:339
    anarchism and, **1**:182
    The Turner Diaries and, **3**:328
McWilliams, Carey, **5**:522
McWilliams, United States v., **3**:328
Macy, Rowland H., **3**:7
Macy's, **5:189–190**, *190*
    origins of, **3**:7
MAD. *See* Mutual Assured Destruc-
    tion
Mad cow disease, **2**:73
Madar, Olga M., **2**:256
MADD. *See* Mothers Against Drunk
    Driving
Maddox (destroyer), **8**:142–143
Maddox, George, **6**:483
Maddox, Lester, **3**:558
Madero, Francisco I., **7**:57
Madison (Wisconsin), **2**:47
Madison, Dolley, **2**:245; **3**:375
Madison, James
    on Alien and Sedition Acts, **6**:145
    at Annapolis Convention, **1**:187
    on Bank of the United States,
        4:89–90
    on Bill of Rights, **1**:455; **3**:89
    Bonus Bill of 1816 and, **1**:498
    on checks and balances, **2**:116
    and Compromise of 1790, **2:330**
    on Congressional appropriations,
        1:229

in congressional campaign of 1788, **3**:145

on congressional districts, **7**:107

Constitutional amendments proposed by, **1**:455–456

at Constitutional Convention, **2**:378, 379

and Democratic Party, **2**:549

economic policies of, **2**:550; **4**:88, 89–90

on enumerated powers, **3**:225

Federalist Papers by, **2**:382; **3**:349–350; **6**:374

and General Welfare clause, **3**:527

on government, **5**:92, 95

and Henry (Patrick), debate between, **2**:381

on interest groups, **4**:382

Jeffersonian Republicans and, **4**:472; **7**:117

on legislature, **1**:456; **7**:107

and meteorological research, **2**:235

on philanthropy, **6**:316

pocket veto used by, **6**:380

in presidential campaign of 1808, **3**:151

in presidential campaign of 1812, **3**:151

on president's removal power, **7**:100

and religious liberty, **2**:167; **7**:93

on representative democracy, **2**:546–547; **7**:109, 110

and republic, concept of, **7**:110

on separation of powers, **7**:312

on subsidies, **7**:564

and tariffs, **8**:50, 195

and University of Virginia, **8**:283

in Virginia dynasty, **8**:343, 348

and Virginia Resolves, **1**:124; **8**:349

war message to Congress (1812), **1**:487

text of, **9**:183–185

in War of 1812, **8**:381, 382

Madison, Marbury v., **1**:494; **5**:235–236; **8**:208

judicial review in, **4**:491–492; **8**:23

midnight judges in, **5**:367

Madison Square Garden, **5**:*190*, **190–191**

Madriz, José, **3**:71

Maezumi Rōshi, Taizan, **1**:552

Mafia, **2**:463; **7**:158

See also Crime, organized

Mafia incident, **5**:191

Magazines, **5:191–196**

in 19th century, **5**:191–193

in 20th century, **5**:193–195

advertising in, **1**:32; **5**:193, 198; **7**:252

African American, **5**:193, 194, **199–200**

banned from mail, **6**:427

colonial, archival maps in, **9**:23, 25–26

on the Internet, **5**:195

mail-order, **5**:206

men's, **5:196–197**

muckraking, **5:470–471**

New York intellectuals publishing works in, **6**:85

photography in, **1**:300–301

political cartoons in, **6**:394

science, **7**:273–274

social surveys in, **6**:533

transcendentalist, **8**:179

women's, **1**:32; **4**:9; **5**:191–192, **197–199**

See also specific magazines

Magellan, Ferdinand, **6**:382

Magendie, François, **6**:148

Magic numbers of nucleons, **6**:344

Magic Theater, **8**:116

Magna Carta, **5:201**

due process of law in, **3**:88

right of petition in, **6**:297

Magnalia Christi Americana (Mather), **5**:118

Magnavox Odyssey, **8**:327

Magnet schools, **5:201–202**

vs. charter schools, **2**:111

Magnetic resonance imaging (MRI), **5:202**

Magnetogenerators, **3**:173

Magnuson-Moss Warranty/FTC Improvement Act (1975), **3**:349

Magoffin, James, **6**:68

Magruder, Jeb Stuart, **8**:425

Maguire, Thomas, **1**:389

Mahan, Alfred Thayer, **2**:530

and foreign policy, **3**:425

imperialism of, **4**:243

The Influence of Sea Power upon History, **3**:577

and naval reform, **1**:265, 270; **4**:243

Mahican Indians, **5**:202, **202–203**, *203*; **6**:276; **8**:220

in Stockbridge Indian settlement, **7:550**

Mahon, Pennsylvania Coal v., **3**:198; **6**:505

Mahone, William, **7**:52; **8**:344

Mahoney, William, **3**:321, 322

Mail

air transportation of (*See* Airmail)

antislavery campaign via, **1**:210

camels used for, **2**:19

Pony Express, **5**:204; **6:411–413**, *412, 413*, 427

rural free delivery of, **7:205–206**, 208

stagecoach transportation of, **5:203–204**; **7:514–516**

Star Route frauds and, **7:524**

See also Postal Service, U.S.

Mailer, Norman, **3**:280; **5**:122

The Naked and the Dead, **5**:121

Mail-order houses, **3**:9; **5:204–207**; **7**:125

Book-of-the-Month Club, **1:500–501**

vs. direct mail, **3**:29

rural areas and, **7**:208

Sears Roebuck Catalog, **7:290–291**

Main Street (Babbitt), **5**:120

Maine, **5:207–211**

agriculture in, **5**:208–209

alcohol regulation in, **1**:117

in American Revolution, **5**:208

boundary dispute in, Aroostook War over, **1**:282–283

in Civil War, **5**:209–210

in colonial era, **5**:207–208

economy of, **5**:208–209, 210

emblems, nicknames, mottos, and songs of, **7**:*532*

environmentalism in, **5**:210

founding of, **2**:289

Kennebec River settlements in, **4:516**

map of, **5**:*209*

Missouri Compromise and, **5:422–425**

Native Americans in, **5**:207–208

New Deal and, **5**:210

Penobscot region in, **6:281–282**

as proprietary colony, **6**:*510*, 511

Reconstruction in, **5**:209–210

Sagadahoc Colony in, **7:223**

shipbuilding in, **5**:210

statehood for, **5**:208

temperance movement in, **8**:80

tourist industry in, **5**:210

Maine, (*continued*)
  in War of 1812, **5:**208
  in World War II, **5:**210
Maine (battleship), **5:**47
  sinking of, **2:**470; **5:**211, *211;* **6:**25;
    7:484, 485; **8:**577
Maine, Alden v., **1:**120
Maistre, Joseph de, **4:**331
Maize, **2:**96
  See also Corn
Major, Clarence, **5:**123
Majority rule, **5:**211–213
  Mayflower Compact, **5:**276
Makah, **5:**213, *213;* **8:***221*
  in Ozette, **6:**222–223
  religious traditions of, **4:**294
Ma-ka-tai-me-she-kai-kiak. *See*
  Black Hawk
Makemie, Francis, **6:**450
*Making Sex: The Body and Gender
  from the Greeks to Freud* (Laque-
  ur), **3:**516
Malamud, Bernard, **1:**546; **5:**121
  God's Grace, **5:**122
Malaria, **5:**213–215, *214,* 294
Malaspina, Alejandro, **8:**453
Malbone, Edward Greene,
  5:393–394
Malcolm, Ellen, **3:**198
Malcolm X, **1:**478
  assassination of, **5:**520
  on assassination of Kennedy (John
    F.), **5:**520
  Autobiography of Malcolm X, **1:**363;
    5:126
  civil rights movement denounced
    by, **2:**204
  conversion of, **5:**520
  and Nation of Islam, **4:**437; **5:**520
  in Organization of Afro-American
    Unity, **6:**211
  self-naming by, **5:**509–510
*Maleska: The Indian Wife of the White
  Hunter* (Stephens), **6:**537
Malina, Judith, **8:**115
Maliseet, **8:**219
Mallet, Paul, **6:**29, 67; **8:**451
Mallet, Pierre, **6:**29, 67; **8:**451
Mallon, Mary, **3:**240–241
Mallory, S. R., **6:**23
Mallory Bill, **8:**50
Mallot, Byron, **1:**112
Malls, shopping, **5:**215–217; **7:**125–126
  See also Retailing industry

Malmédy Massacre, **5:**217
Malnutrition, **6:**437
Maloof Brothers, **5:**72
Malvar, Miguel, **6:**320
Mamachatpam. *See* Yakama
Mammalogy, **5:**217–218; **8:**596
Mammals of North America, The (Hall
  and Kelson), **5:**217
Man and Nature (Marsh), **3:**434, 541
Man Who Cried I Am (Williams),
  5:126
MANA. *See* Mexican American
  Women's National Association
Manabe, Syukuro, **2:**237
Management buyouts, **5:**85
Managerial capitalism, **2:**42
Managers, city, **2:**183–184
Manassas. *See* Bull Run
Manchild in the Promised Land
  (Brown), **5:**126
Manchuria and Manchukuo,
  5:218–219
  League of Nations and, **5:**65
  Open Door policy in, **6:**197
Mandan, Fort, **5:**219
Mandan Indians, **3:**297; **5:**219–220,
  220; **8:**218
  bullboats of, **1:**568–569
  Fort Laramie Treaty with, text of,
    9:227–229
  gambling by, **3:**507
  Lewis and Clark Expedition and,
    5:219
Mandel, Kleindienst v., **1:**125
Mandela, Nelson, **7:***452,* 453
Mandelbaum, Maurice, **6:**424
Mangeurs de Lard, **5:**220
Mangum, W. P., **3:**153
Manhattan, **1:**546; **5:**220–221
  archival maps of, **9:***70,* 70–77, *71,*
    75, 76
  Dutch colonial settlements in,
    3:286; **6:**71
  ferry connections with, **3:**354
  Greenwich Village in, **4:**64–65, *65*
  Times Square in, **8:**128, *128*
  Tin Pan Alley in, **8:**129, *129*
Manhattan Company, **5:**476
Manhattan Life Building, **6:**80
Manhattan Project, **2:**487; **5:**18,
  221–222, 482; **6:**69, 143, 336
  in Washington (state), **8:**414
Manhattan Transfer (Dos Passos),
  5:120

Manifest destiny, **5:222–225**
  and annexation, **1:**188
  in archival maps, **9:**55–56
  and Canadian-U.S. relations, **2:**25
  and Caribbean, relations with, **3:**75
  filibustering and, **3:**359–360
  and foreign policy, **3:**425
  and westward expansion, **2:**163
Manila Bay, Battle of, **5:**225
Manila Pact. *See* Southeast Asia
  Treaty Organization
Mankiller, Wilma, **2:**126, *126*
Mann, Horace, **2:**167, 508; **3:**114;
  5:178; **6:**333
Mann, Marty, **1:**119
Mann, Thomas, **6:**239
Mann Act (1910), **2:**459; **5:**225; **6:**513
Mann-Elkins Act (1910), **6:**496; **7:**26
Manners and etiquette, **5:**225–227
  foreign observers on, **1:**136
  and political correctness, **6:**395
Manning, James, **1:**548
Manpower Development and Train-
  ing Act (1962), **5:**11
Mansfield, Joseph, in Battle of Anti-
  etam, **1:**200
Manship, Paul, **1:**306
Manson, Charles, **1:**330; **2:***477*
Manson, Mahlon D., **7:**156
Mansour, Ned, **5:**72
Manstein, Erich von, **1:**267
Mantle, Mickey, **1:**421
Manuel I (king of Portugal), **3:**283
Manufacturing, **5:**227–229
  American system of, **5:**262
  cotton, **2:**426–427, *427*
  decline of, **8:**163
  factory, **5:**4
  foreign trade and, **8:**167
  Gallatin's report on, **3:**503
  in Gilded Age, **3:**577
  in Hamilton's economic policies,
    4:90; **5:**227
  household, **5:**229–230
  improvements in, and con-
    sumerism, **2:**386–387
  mass production, **5:261–264**
  mechanization of, **5:**4
  mercantilism and, **5:**316
  in Michigan, **5:**355–357
  of munitions, **5:**480–482
  nonfactory, **5:**4
  productivity in, **6:**492; **8:**361
  in World War II, **5:**5

Manufacturing Engineering Labora- tory, **5**:529–530

Manufacturing Extension Partner- ship, **5**:529

Manumission, **5**:230–231

See also Antislavery; Slavery

Manypenny, George, **4**:272

Manzhouguo, **5**:219

Mao Zedong, **2**:151, 152–153

Soviet Union and, **4**:545, 546

Maple Sugar, **5**:231

Mapplethorpe, Robert, **1**:301–302; **5**:535

Maps and mapmaking, **5**:231–234

archival, **9**:1–77

of American Revolution, **9**:29–36

of Civil War, **9**:65–67

colonial, **9**:2, 12–18

of colonial wars, **9**:*25*, **25–28**, *27, 28*

of early Republic, **9**:37–40, *40, 41*

of explorations, **9**:19–24

functions of, **9**:1

interpretation of, **9**:1–2

narratives in, **9**:2–4

Native Americans in, **9**:2, 4, 14–16, 47–52, *48*

of New York City, **9**:*70*, **70–77**, *71, 72, 74, 75, 76*

precolonial, **9**:*6*, **6–10**, *7, 8, 9*

prime meridian in, **9**:3, 35, 45

production of, **9**:4

scale of, **9**:4

transportation in, **9**:56–59

of War of 1812, **9**:42

of westward expansion, **9**:45–64

chorographical, **9**:37, *39*

Frémont explorations and, **3**:467–468

by Geological Survey, U.S., **3**:546

science of, **2**:60–63

Marable, Manning, **1**:47

Marathons, **5**:234–235

Maraziti, Joseph, **6**:64

Marbury v. Madison, **1**:494; **5**:235–236; **8**:208

discretionary authority in, **5**:418

judicial review in, **4**:491–492; **8**:23

midnight judges in, **5**:367

MARC. *See* Machine Readable Cata- loging

Marcel, Gabriel, **3**:279

Marcet, Jane, **3**:108

March, Peyton C., **8**:379

March for the Animals (1990), **1**:186

March of Dimes, **5**:236

fundraising for polio research by, **6**:388

March of Time (radio program), **5**:236–237

March on Washington (1963), **5**:237, *237;* **7**:*11*

AFL-CIO and, **1**:152

National Urban League and, **5**:563

Marchand, Roland, **1**:33

Marches, **6**:227

Marching bands, **5**:237–238

Marciano, Rocky, **6**:484

Marconi, Guglielmo, **7**:19; **8**:66

Marcos, Ferdinand, **6**:323

Marcus, Bernard, **7**:126

Marcus, George, **1**:194

Marcuse, Herbert, **3**:454, *454*

Marcy, Randolph B., explorations of, **5**:238; **8**:364

Marcy, William L., **2**:28

Albany Regency and, **1**:114

Ostend Manifesto and, **6**:219

on spoils system, **7**:507

Marden, Brice, **1**:298

Mardi Gras, **5**:238; **6**:73, *74*

Maria Monk controversy, **5**:238

Mariana Islands, in Trust Territory of the Pacific, **8**:95, 232–233

Mariel boatlift, **2**:55; **5**:238–239

Marietta (Ohio), **5**:239

Marijuana, **5**:*239*, 239–240; **7**:568

Marijuana Tax Act (1937), **5**:511

Marin, John, **1**:297; **2**:476; **6**:471

Marine, David, **6**:149

Marine Biological Laboratory (MBL), **5**:240

Marine biology, **5**:240–241

See also Oceanography

Marine Corps, U.S., **5**:241–244, *243*

capturing Gilbert Islands, **3**:576

establishment of, **2**:530

in Guadalcanal Campaign, **4**:68; **6**:26

Native Americans in, **4**:328

recruitment for, **2**:364

in Somalia, **1**:39–40; **7**:447

Special Forces of, **7**:495

and Tinian, **8**:129–130

in World War II, at Iwo Jima, **4**:450

Marine disasters, **3**:39–40, *40*

Marine Hospital Service, **3**:239

Marine insurance, **4**:367–368

Marine Protection, Research, and Sanctuaries Act (1972), **5**:244

Marine sanctuaries, **5**:244

Marion, Battle at, **5**:244

Marion, Francis, **4**:70; **7**:145

Maris, Roger, **1**:422

Marisol, **1**:306

Maritain, Jacques, **2**:165

Maritime Canal Company, **6**:105

Maritime Commission, Federal, **5**:244–245

See also Merchant marine

Maritime law, **1**:23–24

Maritime warfare, Declaration of London and, **5**:146

Mark IV, **7**:441

Market Garden, Operation, **1**:1

Marketing, **5**:245–247

cooperatives and, **2**:407, 408

direct mail, **3**:29–30

research, **5**:247–248

polling in, **6**:409, 533

See also Advertising; Direct mail

Markets, Public, **5**:248

Markham, J., **8**:319

Markham, William, **6**:41, 276

Marne, Battle of, trenches in, **8**:207

Marque and Reprisal, Letters of, **5**:248

Marquette, Jacques, **5**:158

explorations of, **1**:264; **3**:472; **4**:51, **486–487**, *487*

in Illinois, **4**:214

Mississippi River, **5**:416, *416*

Marquette, Père Jacques, **3**:285, 291; **8**:175

and Chicago, founding of, **2**:131

and Wisconsin River, discovery of, **8**:489

Marquis, Richard, **1**:290

Marriage, **5**:249–251

in 19th century, **3**:312–313

in 20th century, **3**:313–314

average age of, **1**:25, *26*

ceremonies, **8**:435–436

changing perceptions of, **5**:250

Christian understanding of, **3**:65

and citizenship, **6**:14

in colonial society, **2**:291; **3**:63, 311

historical trends in, **2**:560–561

interracial (miscegenation), **5**:405–406

Marriage, (continued)
among African Americans, **4:**479;
5:405–406
bans on, **5:**165
among Native Americans, **4:270;**
5:188, 468
in kinship patterns, **4:**531–532
marital law, **5:**249–250
among Native Americans
Hopi, **4:**164, *165*
intermarriage, **4:270; 5:**188, 468
as political model, **5:**249
polygamy, **6:410–411**
and property rights, **5:**251–252;
6:506
Protestant theology of, **5:**249, 250
same-sex, **2:532–533,** *533*
in Vermont, **3:**514; **8:**314
among slaves, **3:**313; **5:**250; **8:**436
taking husband's name after, **5:**509
Utopian communities and, **7:**94;
8:301
"Marriage trauma," **3:**312
Married Women's Property Act
(1922), **6:**14
Married Women's Property Act
(New York, 1848), **5:251–252**
Marrow of Tradition, The (Chesnutt),
5:124
Marschak, Jacob, **3:**109
Marsden, Ernest, **6:**340
Marsh, A. L., **3:**181
Marsh, George Perkins, **2:**366;
3:434–435, 541
Marsh, Grant, **3:**318
Marsh, O. C., **3:**269
Marshak, Robert E., **6:**344
Marshall, A. D., **8:**118
Marshall, Burke, **2:**195
Marshall, George C., **2:**528; **8:**546
in China, **2:**152
Marshall, George Catlett
McCarthy on, **9:**424–426
War Department under, **8:**379
Marshall, Humphry, **1:**519
Marshall, James Wilson, **4:**10,
12–13, 14
Marshall, John
on bills of credit, **2:**446
on civil rights, **2:**198
and colonization movement, **2:**296
on commerce clause, **1:**549; **2:**310,
405; **3:**575
on contract clause, **2:**107, 397

Court under, **8:**23
on due process of law, **3:**89
on enumerated powers, **3:**225
on habeas corpus, **4:**81
on implied powers, **4:**247
on interstate commerce, **4:**401
judicial review under, **3:**382;
4:491–492, 495; **8:**23, 208
late career of, **2:**127
legal training of, **5:**56
Marbury v. Madison, **5:**235
McCulloch v. Maryland, **5:**184
on national authority over states,
2:265
on Native Americans
Cherokee Nation case, **2:**128
claims of Plankasaw tribe, **6:**506
treaties with, **4:**314
on nonprofit organizations, **6:**316
on police power, **6:**387
on private-corporation charters,
2:503
on property rights, **1:**419
on racial segregation, **6:**370–371
on slave trade, **1:**190
on steamboat monopolies, **3:**483
on subpoenas to presidents, **3:**279;
6:456
on treason, **3:**270; **8:**193, 194
in *Ware v. Hylton,* **8:**390
and XYZ affair, **8:**570
Marshall, Paule, *Brown Girl, Brown-*
stones, **5:**126
Marshall, Ray, **3:**343; **5:**11
Marshall, Robert, **2:**372
Marshall, Thomas R., **3:**160, 161
Marshall, Thurgood
on abortion under Medicaid, **4:**100
and *Brown* case, **1:**549; **2:**202
education of, **3:**126
on equal protection analysis, **3:**246
as NAACP lawyer, **5:**526–527
on Supreme Court, **8:**121
Marshall Field and Company, **3:**8
Marshall Islands, **5:**252
nuclear weapons tests in, **8:**232
in Trust Territory of the Pacific,
8:95, 232–233
in World War II, **3:**576; **6:**26
Marshall Plan, **2:**268; **3:**259, 415,
426; **5:**252; **8:**166, 232
and France, **3:**452
and Germany, **3:**562
and Great Britain, **4:**43

vs. loans, **2:**517
U.S. imperialism in, **4:**245
Martel, Charles, **5:**101
Martelé silver, **5:**328
Martha Graham Dance Company,
5:252–253, *253*
Martha's Vineyard, **2:**38; **5:253–254**
Marti, Agustin Farabundo, **3:**143
Martí, José, **1:**137; **2:**469; **5:**47;
6:504
Martial law, **5:254–255**
Martin, Abraham, **1:**7
Martin, Agnes, **1:**298
Martin, Del, **2:**503
Martin, Don, **1:**131
Martin, Glenn, **1:**92
Martin, Henry Newell, **5:**18;
6:349
Martin, Homer, **8:**261
Martin, Luther, antifederalism of,
1:202
Martin, Lynn, **5:**12
Martin, Morgan, **3:**448
Martin, Walter, **2:**478
Martin, William McChesney, **3:**346
Martin v. Hunter's Lessee, **2:**381;
5:255
Martin v. Mott, **5:**255
Martineau, Harriet, **3:**2
Martinet, Louis A., **6:**370
Martinez, Estéban (Estevan José),
3:491; **8:**453
Martinez, Juan, **8:**453
Martinez, Julian, **1:**303
Martinez, Maria, **1:**303
Martinez, Maximiliano Hernandez,
3:143
Martinez, Mel, **4:**184
Martínez, Pedro, **4:**474
Martinez, Robert, **5:**511
Martinez, Santa Clara Pueblo v.,
4:265; **7:247**
Marty (TV show), **8:**72
Marvin, Lee, **6:**231
Marvin, Michelle Triola, **6:**231
Marx, Harpo, **1:**123
Marx, Karl
on capitalism, **7:**424
on classes, **2:**226
Marx, Leo, **1:**169
Marx Brothers, **8:**309
Marxism, and American Federation
of Labor, **1:**150

Mary II (queen of England), and
    colonial policies, **2**:280; **6**: 379
Mary and John (ship), **6**:380
Maryland, **5**:255–259
  agriculture in, **8**:134
  in Alexandria Conference, **1**:122
  antimiscegenation law in, **5**:405
  British convicts in, **2**:401
  Catholicism in, **1**:196
  civil rights movement in, **5**:258
  in Civil War, **5**:257, 259
    Union sentiment in, **8**:260
  colonial assembly of, **1**:333; **2**:280
  in colonial era, **1**:333; **2**:129, 162,
      171, 401; **5**:255–256; **8**:133,
      164
  constitution of, **7**:526, 527
  economy of, **5**:256–257
  emblems, nicknames, mottos, and
      songs of, **7**:*532*
  Federalist Party in, **3**:351
  in foreign trade, **8**:164
  founding of, **2**:67, 287
  geological survey of, **3**:548
  glassmaking in, **4**:3
  immigration to, **4**:220
  invasion of (1862), **5**:259
  maps of, **5**:*256*
    archival, **9**:*13*, 13–14, 37, *38*
  Maryland Charter (1632), **5**:260
  Mason-Dixon line, **5**:259–260
  poll taxes in, **6**:408
  Progressivism in, **5**:257–258
  as proprietary colony, **6**:*510*,
      511–512
  Protestantism in, **5**:256
  public works in, **5**:257
  Reconstruction in, **5**:257, 259
  religion in, **2**:162, 171
  religious freedom in, **1**:196
    colonial legislation on, **9**:89–91
  as royal colony, **6**:511
  settlement of, **5**:255–256
  sexual orientation in, ban on dis-
      crimination based on, **3**:56–57
  slavery in, **5**:256, 257
  suburbanization, **5**:257, 258
  tobacco in, **5**:256; **8**:133, 134
  War of 1812 in, **5**:256–257
Maryland (battleship), **6**:273
Maryland, Brown v., **1**:549; **6**:387
  original package doctrine in, **6**:213
Maryland, McCulloch v., **3**:225; **5**:184
  implied powers in, **4**:247

Maryland Almanac, **1**:130
Maryland School for the Blind,
    3:504
Masculinity studies, **3**:517
MASH. *See* Mobile Army Surgical
    Hospital
Mashantucket Pequots
  casino run by, **3**:509
  lawsuit filed by, **6**:289–290
Mashpee Wampanoag, **5**:259
Mason, C. H., **6**:287
Mason, Charles Harrison, **1**:45;
    2:172; **5**:260
Mason, George, **1**:454; **2**:381
  at Alexandria Conference, **1**:122
  antifederalism of, **1**:201
  surveying by, **9**:37
  Virginia Declaration of Rights by,
      2:521; **8**:348
  and Virginia Resolves, **8**:349
Mason, James M., **2**:342; **8**:208
Mason, John, **2**:289; **6**:56, 511, 512
  Ostend Manifesto and, **6**:219
Mason, Lucy, **2**:392
Mason, Max, **8**:281
Mason, Robert Tufton, **6**:512
Mason & Dixon (Pynchon), **5**:122
Mason-Dixon line, **1**:521;
    5:259–260, *260*; **9**:37
Masons. *See* Freemasons
"Mass defect," **6**:341
Mass media, **5**:260–261
  and libel, **6**:91
  magazines, **5**:191–196
  press associations and, **6**:458–459
  weather forecasts, **5**:332
  See also Media
Mass Media Bureau, **3**:340
Mass murder, **8**:339
Mass production, **5**:261–264
  assembly line in, **1**:334–336
  automation in, **1**:364–366
  in automobile industry, **1**:367,
      371–373; **5**:262–263, *263*
  of cigarettes, **8**:133, 135
  of food, **3**:400
  in Gilded Age, **3**:577
  of housing, **7**:574
  mass marketing and, **5**:245–246
  of toys, **8**:153
Massachusetts, **5**:264–269
  adoption in, **1**:27, 28
  alcohol regulation in, **1**:116

American Academy of Arts and
    Sciences and, **1**:139
in American Revolution, archival
    maps of, **9**:*29*, 29–33
animal protection laws in, **1**:186
arts in, **5**:266, 268
claims to western lands, **8**:455
in colonial era, **5**:265
  colony formed, **5**:271
  settlement of, **5**:265
Constitution in, ratification of,
    2:381
culture in, **5**:266, 268
economy of, **5**:266, 267
emblems, nicknames, mottos, and
    songs of, **7**:*532*
first government of, **6**:46
geological survey of, **3**:548
glassmaking in, **4**:3–4
Hoosac Tunnel in, **4**:161, *161*
immigration to, **4**:220; **5**:266–267
Ipswich Protest in, **4**:417
land and conservation in,
    5:268–269
in land disputes, **8**:311
life insurance in, **4**:370
and Louisburg expedition, **5**:157
map of, **5**:265
Marine Biological Laboratory
    (MBL), **5**:240, 241
Martha's Vineyard, **5**:253–254
minutemen, **5**:403–404
and New Hampshire, boundary
    dispute between, **1**:521–522
politics in, **5**:268
population of, **5**:264–265
provincial congresses in, **6**:520
race and ethnic relations in,
    5:266–267
and Rhode Island, boundary dis-
    pute between, **1**:521
sow case in, **7**:478
Suffolk Resolves in, **8**:3
sumptuary laws in, **8**:17
temperance movements in, **8**:78
topography of, **5**:264
town government in, **8**:148
Townshend Acts and, **8**:349
transportation in, **5**:267–268
universities in, **5**:267
Massachusetts, Jacobson v., **3**:239
Massachusetts, Thurlow v., **5**:103
Massachusetts Adoption Act (1851),
    1:27, 28

Massachusetts Ballot, **5:**269

Massachusetts Bay Colony, **1:**509; **3:**289; **5:**269–271

animal protection laws in, **1:**186

Antinomian controversy in, **1:**205

Hutchinson trial in, **9:**87–89

assistant in, **1:338–339**

British mercantilism and, **5:**271

and cod fishing, **2:**261

Coercive Acts and, **5:**272

colonial assembly in, **1:**333; **2:**280

colonial charter of, **2:**281

establishment of, **5:**265, 269–270; **6:**47

general court of, **3:**525

law and politics, **5:**270

Maine settlement, **5:**207

Massachusetts Body of Liberties (1641), **5:**271

patents granted by, **6:**255

and petitions, **6:**297

philanthropy in, **6:**316

pine tree flag of, **6:357**

pine tree shilling of, **6:357**

and Plymouth Colony, **6:**379

Praying Towns established by, **6:**448

Randolph Commission to, **7:47–48**

religion in, **2:**162

religious dissidents, **5:**270–271

religious persecution in, **6:**57

school law in, text of, **9:**92–93

tensions in, **6:**47–48

textile production in, **8:**108

theocracy in, **6:**50; **8:**116

Massachusetts Bay Company, **3:**525; **4:**56; **8:**174

and Cambridge Agreement, **2:**18

and settlement of New England, **2:**111, 288

Massachusetts Body of Liberties (1641), **5:**271

Massachusetts Circular Letter (1768), **5:272; 8:**349

text of, **9:**122–123

Massachusetts Emigrant Aid Company, **6:**49

Massachusetts Government Act (1767), **5:**272

Massachusetts Government Act (1774), **4:**408

Massachusetts Institute of Technology (MIT), **5:272–273; 6:**346; **7:**272

and e-mail, development of, **3:**184

engineering program at, **3:**216, 217

Internet development at, **4:**397

Lawrence Scientific School and, **5:**59

Radiation Laboratory at, **7:**14

Massachusetts Quarterly Review (magazine), **8:**179

Massachusetts Spy, The (weekly), **6:**426

Massage parlors, **6:**514

Massasoit, **6:**378

Massey, John E., **7:**52

MasterCard, **2:**450, 451

Masters, Edgar Lee, **5:**120

Masterson, Bat, **3:***70*

Matabuti, Haki, **5:**126

Matchbox Cars, **8:**153

Materials Science and Engineering Laboratory, **5:**530

Maternal and child health care, **5:273–275**

March of Dimes, **5:**236

maternal mortality rates, **5:**105

Maternity and Infancy Care Act (1921), **5:**274

Mathematical economics, **3:**109

Mathematical psychology, **6:**525

Mathematics, in statistics, **7:**538

Mather, Cotton, **2:**162; **3:***63*, 235; **5:**300; **6:**316; **7:**95, 96

on American climate, **2:**234

Magnalia Christi Americana, **5:**118

The Wonders of the Invisible World, **5:**118

and Yale University, **8:**572

Mather, Increase, **2:**162; **8:**78

on evidence used in Salem witch trials, **9:**93–95

Mather, Richard, **1:**431; **2:**19

Mather, Stephen, **1:**505

Mather, Stephen T., **5:**550–551

Matheson, Scott, **8:**298

Mathew, Theobald, **8:**79

Mathews, John Joseph, **5:**128

Mathews, Shailer, **5:**432

Mathews v. Diaz, **1:**126

Matinecooks, **6:**79

Matisse, Henri, exhibitions of, **1:**297

in Armory Show, **1:**268, 269, 297

Matles, James, **3:**176

Mató-Tópe (Four Bears), **8:***393*

Matsui, Connie, **4:**1

Matsuoka Rōshi, Soyu, **1:**552

Matsushita Corporation, **8:**327

Mattachine Society, **3:**513; **7:**326, 327

Mattel, **8:**153

Mattel Company, **1:**417

Matthaei, Heinrich, **3:**68

Matthaei, Johann H., **3:**533

Matthiessen, F. O., **1:**169, 170

Mattson, Harold, **1:**417

Mauborgne, Joseph O., **2:**468

Mauchly, John, **2:**334

Mauldin, Bill, **6:**99

Maumee, Lake, **1:**480

Mauna Kea Observatory, **6:**157

Mauna Loa (volcano), **8:**351

Maurer, Louis, **6:**394

Maury, Matthew Fontaine, **2:**235; **5:**331; **6:**159–160

Maw, Herbert, **8:**298

Mawhood, Charles, **6:**464

Maxfield, Joseph, **1:**358

Maxim, Hiram, **5:**185–186

Maximilian, Ferdinand, **5:**345

Maximilian (emperor of Mexico), Shelby's expedition and, **7:**341

Maxwell, George H., **7:**55

May, Henry, **1:**284

May, Jan Cornelisse, **6:**71

May, Samuel J., **6:**47

May Day, **5:**275

Maya in Exile: Guatemalans in Florida (Burns), excerpt from, **9:**509–515

Mayaguez incident, **5:**275

Maybach, William, **1:**366, 371

Maybeck, Bernard, **1:**293

Mayer, Louis B., **6:**485

Mayer, Maria Goeppert, **6:**344

Mayflower (ship), **2:**290; **5:**275; **6:**355, *355*, 378, 379

landing and settlement, **5:**265

See also Pilgrims

Mayflower Compact, **5:**276; **6:**378

text of, **9:**86

Mayhew, Jonathan, **7:**148

Mayo, Elton, **4:**334

Mayo, Henry T., **8:**311

Mayo Foundation, **5:276–277**

Mayors, and city councils, **2:**183

Mays, Willie, **1:**421

Maysville Veto, **5:**277

Maytag Company, **3:**181

Maywood, Augusta, **1:**389; **2:**497

Mazzei, Filippo, **4:**444

Mazzei letter, **5:**277

Mbeki, Thabo, **7**:453
MBL. *See* Marine Biological Laboratory
Mboya, Tom, **1**:138
M'Carty, William, **9**:221–222
Meacham, Joseph, **7**:333–334
Mead, Carver, **1**:463
Mead, Elwood, **7**:56
Mead, George Herbert, **6**:*446*
Mead, Lake, **4**:162
Mead, Margaret, **1**:141, 193, *193*
Meade, George G., **2**:214
  Army of the Potomac under, **1**:279
  in Battle of Gettysburg, **3**:566–569
  and invasion of Pennsylvania, **6**:280
Means, Gardiner, **6**:42
Means, Russell, **1**:161; **8**:561
Meanwell, Walter (Doc), **1**:423
Meany, George, **1**:151; **8**:172, 262
Mears, Helen Farnsworth, **1**:308
Measures
  English system of, **5**:529
  metric system of, **5**:529
Meat Inspection Act (1890), **1**:71; **6**:495
Meat Inspection Act (1906), **3**:404; **5**:135 ; **6**:554
Meat inspection laws, **2**:383; **5**:277–278, *278*
Meat production. *See* Livestock industry
Meatpacking industry, **5**:135–136, **278–280**, *279*
  Beef Trust cases, **1**:435–436
  in Chicago (Illinois), **2**:73, *73*, 132; **8**:463
  consumer protection movement and, **2**:389
  federal regulation of, **7**:514
  The Jungle on, **4**:27, 500–501; **5**:277, 280; **6**:11, 12, 554
    excerpt from, **9**:360
  monopoly in, **6**:229–230
  occupational health issues in, **5**:299
  Packers and Stockyards Act (1921) and, **6**:229
  stockyards in, **7**:551–552
MEC. *See* Methodist Episcopal Church
Mecham, Evan, **1**:259
Mechanical scanning systems, **8**:76–77
Mechanics' Institutes, **5**:280
  Franklin Institute, **3**:455–456

Mechanism of Mendelian Heredity, The (Morgan, Sturtevant, Bridges, and Muller), **3**:532
Mechelle Vinson, Meritor Savings Bank v., **3**:54–55; **5**:**324**; **7**:323
Mecklenburg Resolves (Mecklenburg Declaration of Independence), **2**:109
Medal of Honor, **2**:525–526
Medals, military. *See* Military decorations
Media
  and celebrity culture, **2**:78
  in electoral politics, **3**:149
  industry developments in, **2**:320–322
  and language standards, **3**:221
  military censorship and, **2**:83
  "order restoration" function of, **8**:74
  scandal coverage by, **7**:261–262
  sports coverage by, **7**:508–509
  violence portrayed in, **5**:261; **8**:339
  See also Mass media
Mediation, **6**:263
  domestic, **2**:339
  labor, **2**:338–339
  railroad, **7**:25–26
Medicaid. *See* Medicare and Medicaid
Medical education, **5**:280–284
  AMA standards for, **1**:164
  bacteriology, **5**:357–358
  at Dartmouth College, **2**:502–503
  early history, **5**:280–281, 300–301
  in Europe, **5**:300
  evolution and growth of, **5**:283–284, 302–303
  Flexner report on, **2**:56; **5**:282, 303
  homeopathy in, **4**:155
  internships and residency in, **5**:282–283
  at Johns Hopkins University, **4**:482
  managed care and, **5**:284
  Mayo Foundation, **5**:276–277
  modernization of, **5**:281–282
  for nurses, **6**:146–147
  at University of Pennsylvania, **8**:283
  women in, **4**:482
Medical Education in the United States and Canada (Flexner), **1**:164; **5**:282, 303; **6**:317
Medical insurance. *See* Health insurance

Medical meteorology, **2**:234–235
Medical profession, **5**:284–286
  GI Bill and, **5**:304
  licensing, **5**:302
  medical societies, **5**:288–289
  nursing, **5**:304; **6**:146–148
  obstetrics, **2**:142–143
  physician assistants, **6**:334–335
  specialization, **5**:303–304
  Surgeon General of the Army, **5**:286
Medical research, **5**:286–288
  on animals, **1**:185, 186; **5**:218; **6**:349
  double-blinded clinical trials, **5**:287
  ethics in, **1**:461–462
  on human subjects, **5**:287
  Mayo Foundation, **5**:276–277
  microbiology, **5**:357–359
  military, **5**:294–295, 296
  by National Institutes of Health, **5**:544
  in physiology, **6**:348–350
  polio vaccine, **5**:236
  statistics in, **7**:539
  therapeutics, **5**:287
  on women, Society for Women's Health Research and, **7**:430
Medical schools. *See* Medical education
Medical societies, **5**:288–289
  See also American Medical Association
Medicare and Medicaid, **5**:289–290; **6**:438
  abortion under, **1**:7; **4**:100
  establishment of, **8**:441
  limitations in coverage of, **6**:188
Medicine and surgery, **5**:299–305
  alternative, **5**:290–292
    chiropractic, **2**:157–158; **5**:291–292
    homeopathy, **4**:154–155; **5**:291, 301
    medicine shows, **5**:305–306, *306*
    New Age, **5**:292; **6**:39
  anesthesia in, **1**:184–185; **5**:301
  biochemistry and, **1**:460
  blood transfusion, **5**:*286*
  code of ethics in, **1**:461, 462
  in colonial era, **5**:299–300
  electronics and, **3**:179
  ethical codes for, **1**:164
  general practice in, **4**:115

Medicine and surgery, (*continued*)
  genetic engineering and, **3:**531
  hygiene in, **4:**204–205
  mental illness, **5:312–315**
  military, **5:293–296,** *295*
    in Civil War, lessons from, **5:**302
    and pharmaceutical industry,
      6:307
    and war casualties, **8:**375–376
    in World War II, impact of, **5:**304
  Native American, **5:292–293**
  neurology, **5:**313–314
  Nobel Prize in, **6:**349, 350, 388,
      487–488
  occupational, **5:296–299**
  ophthalmology, **5:**303–304
  osteopathy, **5:**291, 302
  ovarian surgery, first, **5:***285*
  physician assistants and, **6:**334
  physiology, **6:348–350**
  psychiatry, **6:521–522**
  robotics in, **7:**184
  Rockefeller Foundation and, **7:**187
  specialization in, **4:**115–116, *116*
    and hospitals, **4:**172–173
  technology, Magnetic Resonance
      Imaging (MRI), **5:202**
  transplants and organ donation,
      8:182–184
  virtual reality in, **8:**350
  women in, **8:**511
Medicine Lodge Treaty (1867),
    4:532
  Congressional violation of,
      5:147–148
Medicine shows, **5:305–306,** *306*
Medicines, patent, **2:**388
Medill, Joseph, **6:**458
Medina, Ernest, **2:**440
Medina, Harold, **1:**405
Mediterranean, slave trade in, **7:**389
Meek, Cora, **1:**311
Meeker, Nathan C., **8:**259
Mees, C. E. Kenneth, **6:**329
Meese, Edwin, **6:**420
Meese Commission, **6:**420
Meet the Press (TV show), **8:**44
Meetinghouse, **5:306**
Megan's Law (1996), **5:306**
Megrahi, Abdel Baset Ali al-,
    6:233–234
Meier, Richard, **3:**565
Meigs, Montgomery C., **3:**219
Meitner, Lise, **6:**342

Melamine, **6:**366
Méliès, Georges, **3:**361
Mellanby, Edward, **6:**148
Mellencamp, John, **1:**441
Mellette, Arthur, **7:**460
Mellon, Andrew W., **5:**538
  as secretary of treasury, **8:**197, 229
  and taxation, **8:**57–58
Mellon, Paul, **5:***539,* 539–540
Melting pot, **1:**337; **5:306**
  See also Multiculturalism
Melville, Herman, **2:**375; **6:**373;
    8:325
  as customs officer, **2:**485
  Moby-Dick, **3:**280; **5:**119, **430–431;**
      7:194
Melvin, People v., **5:**13
Memminger, Christopher G., **2:**341
Memorial Day, **5:306–307,** *307*
Memorial Day Massacre (1937),
    5:307; **8:**277
  La Follette Civil Liberties Com-
      mittee hearings on, **5:**1
*Memories of the North American Inva-
    sion* (Roa Barcena), **9:**224–227
Memphis (Tennessee), **5:307–308**
  zoological park in, **8:***594*
Men
  hairstyles of, **4:83–84**
  magazines for, **5:196–197**
Menard, Michel B., **3:**506
Mencken, H. L., **2:**375; **3:**220, 221,
    222; **5:**120; **6:**537
  on middlebrow culture, **5:**365
  on *The Nation,* **5:**522
  on slang, **7:**377
  on Victorianism, **8:**326
Mendel, Gregor, **1:**520; **3:**269, 532
Mendieta, Ana, **1:**307
Mendoza, Antonio de, **1:**256; **3:**296;
    6:65–66
Menéndez de Avilés, Pedro, **3:**385
  colonization efforts of, **5:308–309**
Menger, Karl, **3:**109
Menil, Dominique de, **2:**273
Menino, Thomas M., **1:**510
Menninger, William, **6:**522
Mennonites, **5:308–309**
  Amish and, **1:**174
  exemption from military service,
      2:361
  pacifism of, **6:**227
  slavery protested by, **9:**97–98
  and Underground Railroad, **8:**250

Menominee Indians, **5:310–311,**
    311
  termination policy and, **8:**91
Menominee Iron Range, **5:311–312**
Men's studies, **3:**517
Mental illness, **5:312–315**
  in Alzheimer's disease, **1:**131–132
  patients' rights in, **6:**257
  psychoanalysis, **5:**314
  treatment of, **6:**521, 522
  See also Psychiatry; Psychology
Menzel, Donald H., **6:**341
Mercantilism, **1:**542; **3:**287;
    5:315–316
  manufacturing, hindrances to,
      5:227
  Massachusetts Bay Colony and,
      5:271
  Navigation Acts and, **6:**21
Mercator, Gerhardus, **1:**135; **5:**232
Mercer, Henry, museum of, **5:**488
Mercer, Hugh, **6:**464
Mercereau, John, **8:**186
Mercersburg (Lancaster) Theologi-
    cal Seminary, **7:**97; **8:**264
Merchant adventurers, **5:316–317**
Merchant marine, **5:318–321**
  Shipping Board oversight of, **7:**350
  See also Shipping
Merchant Marine Act (1936), **5:**319
Merchant Marine Act o(1970), **5:**321
Merchantmen, armed, **5:321–322**
  and Murmanks, port of (Russia),
      5:483
MERCOSUR, **6:**125
Mercury, in dentistry, **3:**3–4
Mercury, Project, **7:**480
Mercury-gold amalgamation, **4:**11
Meredith, James, **2:**203–204
Mergens, Board of Education v., **2:**169
Mergenthaler, Ottmar, **6:**469
Mergers and acquisitions,
    5:322–323
  in 1990s, **1:**580
  Federal Trade Commission investi-
      gating, **3:**349
  in financial services industry, **3:**368
  in railroad industry, **7:**36, 39
  retail, **7:**126
  in steel industry, **4:**428
Meriam Report, **1:**492, 571; **2:**506;
    4:299; **5:323–324**
*Meritor Savings Bank v. Mechelle Vin-
    son,* **3:**54–55; **5:324;** **7:**323

Merk, Frederick, **1:**188

Mermaid Inn, **8:**54

Merriam, C. Hart, **5:**217

Merriam, Charles, **3:**220

Merriam, Charles E., **6:**402–403

Merriam, George, **3:**220

Merriam-Webster Company, **3:**23

Merrick, Samuel, **3:**455

Merrill, Eliza, **6:**29

Merrill, Moses, **6:**29

Merrill's Marauders, **5:**324

  See also Burma Road; Ledo Road

Merrimack (ship), **4:**430, *430;* **8:**405

  sinking of, **5:**325

Merrimack and *Monitor,* Battle of, **5:**442–443

Merrimack River, **6:**56; **7:**174

Merrimack River Valley, **6:**55

Merritt, Leonidas, **5:**326

Merritt, Wesley, **7:**486

  in Philippine Insurrection, **6:**319

Merryman, John, **3:**272

Merton, Thomas, **5:**507, *507*

Mesa, **5:**325

Mesa Verde, **2:**297

  prehistoric ruins of, **1:***239;* **5:***325,* **325–326**

Mesabi Iron Range, **5:**326

Mescaleros, **1:***218, 219,* 219–221

Meselson, Matthew Stanley, **3:**533

Mesons, **6:**338

Mesquakie Indians, **5:**326–327; **8:**224

  in Fox War, **3:**447–448

  and Galena-Dubuque mining district, **3:**503

Mesquite, **5:**327

Messenger, The (newspaper), **5:**200

Messner v. Journeymen Barbers, **6:**350

Metacom (King Philip) (Wampanoag chief), **6:**379; **7:**151

  Mount Hope headquarters of, **5:**464

Metacom's War. *See* King Philip's War

Metals

  and solid-state physics, **6:**345

  See also specific types

Metalwork, **5:327–330**

  aluminum, **5:**330

  blacksmithing, **1:**483–484, *484*

  brass, **5:**329

  copper, **5:**329

  iron, **5:***329,* 329–330

  pewter, **5:***327,* 328

  silver, **5:**327–328

Metamora; or, The Last of the Wampanoags (play), **8:**113

Meteor (ship), **4:**54

Meteorology, **5:330–332**

  ballooning used in, **1:**391

  medical, **2:**234–235

  and warnings of tornadoes, **8:**144

  weather satellites, **8:**432

Methane, **3:**481

Methanol, **3:**480

Methodism, **3:**264; **5:332–334**

  among African Americans, **1:**42, 43–44, 45, 53–54; **5:**333; **7:**87

  Arminianism and, **1:**265

  and camp meetings, **2:**22; **7:***86,* 87

  Christmas Conference on, **5:**333

  Church of the Nazarene and, **6:**27

  and circuit riders, **2:**175

  membership in, **7:***87,* 90, *90, 91*

  Second Awakening in, **1:**378

  spread of, **7:**86

  and Underground Railroad, **8:**250

  women ordained in, **1:**44, 53

Methodist Episcopal Church (MEC), African Americans in, **1:**44

Methylphenidate (Ritalin), **7:**568–569

Metric system, **5:**529

Metropolitan district, **8:**290

Metropolitan government, **5:334–335**

  See also Municipal government

Metropolitan Institute of Texas, **8:**302

Metropolitan Museum of Art (New York), **5:**335–338, *336*

Metz, Christian, **1:**133

Metz, Johann-Baptiste, **5:**93

Meuse-Argonne Offensive, **1:**149; **5:338–339; 8:**538

Mexican American Gorras Blancas, **3:**323

Mexican American Women's National Association (MANA), **5:343**

Mexican Americans, **5:343–345**

  in Colorado, **2:**298

  farm workers, **3:**326–327, *327*

  labor movements among, **2:**77; **8:**266

  in Los Angeles, discrimination against, **9:**407–409

Mexican American Women's National Association, **5:**343

  after Mexican-American War, **7:**10

  military service by, **5:***383,* **383–384**

  in New Jersey, **6:**63–64

  number of, **4:**134

Mexican Cession (1848), and land claims, **5:**26

Mexican-American War, **1:**433; **2:**534; **5:**46, **339–342**

  Alamo Siege and, **1:**106–107, 354

  atrocities in, **1:**354

  Battle of Buena Vista in, **1:**560; **5:***341*

  Battle of Chapultepec in, **2:**105

  Battle of Resaca de Palma in, **5:***340*

  Battles of Monterrey in, **5:**452

  and boundaries of Mexico, **9:**52–55

  bounties in, **1:**524

  causes of, **5:**339

  claims, **5:**343

  demobilization after, **2:**546

  desertion in, **3:**17

  diplomacy in, **5:**339–340, 341–342

  guerrilla warfare in, **4:**70

  immediate cause of, **7:**163

  Kearny's march to California in, **4:514–515; 5:**341

  manifest destiny and, **5:**223

  maps of, **5:***339, 342*

  Mexico City in, capture of, **5:**350

  Mexico's preparation for, **9:**218–219

  military forces in, **2:**530

  Mormon Battalion, **5:458**

  munitions in, **5:**479

  Native Americans after, **8:**571

  and New Mexico, **6:**68–69

  photography in, **6:**331

  Polk's speech on, **9:**219–221

  prisoners of war in, **6:**472

  results of, **5:**342

  Roa Barcena's history of, **9:**224–227

  and slavery issue, **8:**485–486

  songs, ballads, and poetry on, **9:**221–222

  Stockton-Kearny Quarrel in, **7:551**

  and Texas, **8:**204

  Texas Rangers in, **2:**363

  and trading with enemy, **8:**173

Mexican-American War, (*continued*)
  Treaty of Guadalupe Hidalgo ending, **3:**501; **4:68**; **5:**342; **6:**68; **8:**200, 204
  U.S. Marine Corps in, **5:**242
  U.S. Navy in, **6:**25
  Veracruz in, siege of, **5:**341
  veterans of
    land grants to, **1:**498
    organizations for, **8:**318
  Villa raid at Columbus and, **8:**336
Mexico
  American émigrés in, **3:**197
  boundaries of, **9:**52–55
  capitalist development in, **2:**44
  Confederate migration to, **5:**345; **7:**340–341
  conquest of, **3:**294
  election of 2000 in, **5:**349
  encomienda system in, **3:**203
  filibuster armies targeting, **3:**359
  under Fox, **5:**349–350
  French invasion of, **3:**450–451; **5:**345, 446
  Gadsden Purchase Treaty (1854) with, **8:**204
  Germany's anti-American alliance with, **3:**562
  immigration from, **3:**142; **4:**227
    labor shortages during World War I and, **2:**42
  independence from Spain, **2:**8; **7:**489–490
  Madero assassination, U.S. response to, **7:**57
  maps of, archival, **9:**52–55, *53, 54, 55*
  North American Free Trade Agreement with, **3:**309; **6:**124–125; **8:**199
  public murals in, **5:**483
  punitive expedition into, **5:**346–347; **8:**336
  Shelby's expedition into, **7:**340–341
  Slidell's mission to, **7:**397–398
  Texas annexation and, **1:**188; **8:**99–100, 104, 204
  trade unions in, **3:**177
  U.S. relations with, **5:**46–47, 49, **347–350** (*See also* Mexican-American War)
    border policy, **5:**350
    during Cold War, **5:**348–349

NAFTA era, **5:**349
  prior to World War II, **5:**347–348
  punitive expedition into Mexico, **5:**346
  Veracruz incident and, **1:**1; **8:311**
  Vicente Fox and, **5:**349–350
  Villa raid at Columbus and, **5:**346; **8:**336
  World War II alliance, **5:**348
U.S. territorial disputes with
  and Hispanic Americans, **4:**135
  Texas and manifest destiny, **5:**223
World War I and, **2:**467; **8:**534–535, 591
World War II and, **5:**348
Mexico, Gulf of, **5:**346
  oil in, **6:**179
Mexico City, capture of (1847), **5:**350
Meyer, Adolf, **5:**314; **6:**521
Meyer, Eugene, **7:**62
Meyer, George von Lengerke, **6:**23
Meyerowitz, Joel, **1:**301
Meyers, Anne, **1:**425
Meyers, Jerome, **1:**297
MFD. *See* Miners for Democracy
Mfume, Kweisi, **5:**527
Miami (Florida), **3:**387; **5:350–352**
  Cuban immigrants in, **2:**473; **8:**291
Miami, Fort, **5:**2–3
Miami Indians, **5:352–353**; **8:**224, 431
Miami Purchase, **5:**353
Miami University, **8:**279
Michaux, André, **1:**519
Michaux, François André, **1:**519
Micheaux, Oscar, **3:**362
Michelson, Albert A., **6:**335
Michigan, **5:353–357**
  admission to Union, **1:**522
  agriculture in, **5:**354
  automobile industry in, **5:**355–357
  banking crisis of 1933 in, **1:**402
  in colonial era, **5:**353–354
  copper mining in, **2:**409, *409*, 410
  emblems, nicknames, mottos, and songs of, **7:***532*
  government and strategy in, **5:**353–354
  Henry Ford Museum and Greenfield Village in, **4:127**, *127*
  Mackinac Island and Straits, **5:188–189**
  manufacturing in, **5:**355–357

maps of, **5:***354*
  archival, **9:**49, *49*
Menominee Iron Range, **5:311–312**
in Midwest, **5:**368–369
Polish Americans in, **6:**392
state university of, **8:**279, **281–282**
statehood for, **5:**354
timber and mineral extraction in, **5:**354–355
town government in, **8:**148, 149
Upper Peninsula of, **5:**357
and Wisconsin, boundary dispute between, **1:**523
Michigan (boat), **4:**54
Michtom, Morris, **8:**153
Mickey Mouse (cartoon), **2:**63, *63*
Micmac language, **8:**219
Microbiology, **5:357–359**
  bacteriology, Army research, **5:**294
Microchips, in automation, **1:**365–366
Micronesia, **8:**232–233
Microprocessor, **2:**336
Microscopical Petrography (Zirkel), **6:**300
Microsoft Corporation, **1:**580; **2:**336; **5:359–360**
  early products of, **7:**442
  Encarta, **3:**205
  investigation of, **2:**419
  as monopoly, **7:**443
  Windows operating system, **2:**337; **7:**442–443
Microsoft Network (MSN), **2:**323
Microwave technology, **5:361–362**
Midcontinent oil region, **5:361–362**
Middle classes
  bathing among, **1:**428
  and clothing and fashion, **2:**247
  and counterculture, **2:**433
  and domestic violence, **3:**73
  growth of, **2:**228
  identification with, **2:**225
  immigration to America, **2:**290
  industrialization and, **2:**224
  recreation among, **7:**64
  work ethic of, **7:**63
Middle Colonies, **2:**285; **5:**362
  in American Revolution, **7:**143–144
  in domestic trade, **8:**160
  families in, **3:**311–312
  in foreign trade, **8:**164

non-English settlers in, **6:**41
philanthropy in, **6:**316
religion in, **7:**84; **8:**139
settlement and migration patterns, **8:**459
Middle East
    hostage crises in, **4:**174
    oil in, **6:**298
        and U.S. oil crises, **6:**178–179
        and U.S. relations, **1:**233
    peace process in, Camp David Peace Accords and, **2:**20, *21;* **3:**141
    UN peacekeeping mission in, **6:**270–271
    U.S. relations with, **1:**445; **3:**141, 142
        Israel and, **1:**207
        oil and, **1:**233
    See also Arab nations; *specific countries*
Middle names, **5:**509
Middle Passage, **5:**362–365, *363, 364, 365;* **7:**388; **8:**209
Middle Tennessee, **8:**83
Middle years of political science, **6:**402–403
Middlebrow culture, **1:**500; **5:**365–366
Middle-of-the-road populists, **5:**366–367
Middleton, Arthur, **3:**99
Midgley, Thomas, Jr., **3:**182; **7:**78
Midnight judges, **4:**499; **5:**367
Midway, Battle of, **1:**90; **5:**367–368, *368*
Midway Islands, **5:**368
    annexation of, **1:**189; **3:**425
Midwest, **5:**368–369
    canals in, **8:**187
    managed expansion in, **8:**461
    maps of, archival, **9:**48–52, *49*
    Rust Belt in, **1:**561; **7:**215–216
    tornadoes in, **8:**143
Midwives, **2:**142, 143
Mies van der Rohe, Ludwig, **1:**223, 252, 293; **7:**376
Miescher, Friedrich, **3:**67
Migrant workers, La Follette Civil Liberties Committee hearings on, **5:**1
Migration
    by African Americans, **5:**369–371, *370*

in 20th century, **1:**51; **8:**537
    and city public schools, **3:**118
    from Georgia, **3:**557
    and urbanization, **8:**285
ancient routes of, **1:***245*
"chain," **3:**313
Great Migration from England, **4:**55–56
internal, **5:**371–374 (*See also* Suburbanization)
    to cities, **5:**373, 475
    country music and, **5:**493
    industrial decline and, **7:**215–216
    map of, **5:***373*
    by migrant workers, **5:**374
    to Minnesota, **5:**401
    Mormon
        Mormon handcart companies, **5:**458
        Mormon Trail, **5:**459, *459*
    suburban, **5:**373–374
    to Sun Belt, **5:**374
    by train, **5:***372*
    and urbanization, **8:**285, 290–291
    and voter residency requirements, **8:**355
    western frontier, **5:**371–372, *372*
by Pacific Islanders, **6:**225
See also Westward migration
Migration of the Negro, The (painting), **5:***370*
Mikan, George, **1:**424
Mikoyan, Anastas, **2:**470
Mikulski, Barbara, **6:**392
Milam, J. W., **8:**126
Miles, John D., **7:**72
Miles, Nelson
    in Apache Wars, **1:**221
    on Battle of Little Bighorn, **5:**132
    Personal Recollections, **5:**132
    in Spanish-American War, **7:**486
Miles, William H., **1:**44
Military
    bonuses in, **1:**498–499
    conscription for (*See* Conscription and recruitment)
    desertion from, **3:**16–17
    enlistment in, **3:**222–223
    hairstyles in, **4:**83, 84
    on homosexuality, **3:**513
    intelligence testing in, **4:**378–379
    mobilization, **5:**429–430
    nursing in, **6:**147
    science education and, **7:**272

trucks used by, **8:**231
    twenty-one gun salute in, **8:**243
    See also specific branches
Military Academy. *See* West Point
Military Assistance Advisory Group (MAAG), in Vietnam, **8:**329, 330
Military Assistance Command, Vietnam (MACV), **3:**417; **8:**330–331
Military base closings, **5:**375–376
Military decorations, **2:**525–527, *526*
    awarded to African Americans, **5:**381–382
    awarded to Hispanic Americans, **5:**383–384
Military intelligence. *See* Intelligence, military and strategic
Military law, **5:**378–380
    courts-martial under, **2:**440
    martial law, **5:**254–255
    Uniform Code of Military Justice, **8:**256
    See also Martial law
Military maps, archival, **9:**3
Military medals. *See* Military decorations
Military medicine. *See* Medicine, military
Military Order of the Loyal Legion of the U.S.A., **5:**380
Military photography. *See* Photography, military
Military policy, Vietnam syndrome and, **8:**328
Military Reconstruction Acts (1867), **3:**559
Military roads, **7:**180–181
    Burma and Ledo, **1:**576–577; **7:**180, *181*
    French and Indian War and, **8:**461
Military service
    by African Americans, **2:**201; **5:**380–382, *381, 382*
        black cavalry in the West, **1:**471–472
        black infantry in the West, **1:**475, *476*
        Brownsville affair, **1:**549–550
        in Vietnam War, **8:***333*
    by gays and lesbians, **3:**78; **5:**384–385; **7:**326, 331
    by Hispanic Americans, **5:***383,* **383–384**
    in militias, **5:**386–387, *387*

Military service, (*continued*)
   minorities in, **2:**364, 365
   by Native Americans, **4:327–329**
   violations of, amnesty for, **1:**177
   by women, **8:502–505**, *503, 504*
      uniforms for, **8:**257, 258, *502*
      in Women's Army Corps,
         9:398–401
Military spending, **1:**560; **3:**282
Military trials of civilians, Supreme
   Court on, **3:**271, 272
Military uniforms, **2:**246; **8:***256,*
   256–259, *257, 258*
Military-industrial complex (MIC),
   5:376–378
   in Eisenhower's farewell address,
      9:434–435
   Manhattan Project and, **5:**221
   origins of, **1:**269–271; **5:**377
Militia(s), **5:386–387**, *387*
   in American Revolution, **7:**139–140
   in Civil War, **2:**530
   in colonial era, **3:**222
   Constitution on, **5:**378
   minutemen, **5:403–404**
   mobilization and, **5:**429
   muster day, **5:504–505**
   president's power to call out, **5:**255
   right to bear arms and, **1:**456, 457
   state, in volunteer army, **8:**352
   See also National Guard
Militia Act (1792), **5:**542
Militia movement (20th century),
   5:385–386
   Ruby Ridge and, **7:203**
   See also Radical right
Milk
   pasteurized, **2:**490, *491*
   See also Dairy industry
Milk, Harvey, **3:**514
Milken, Michael, **4:**363, *363,* 501,
   502; **5:**42
Mill(s). *See* Flour milling; Gristmills;
   Sawmills; Textiles
Mill, Henry, **1:**588; **8:**244
Mill, John Stuart, **1:**500; **6:**423
Milledge, John, **3:**554
Millennialism, **5:388**
   social gospel and, **5:**431
Miller, Alfred Jacob, **1:**295; **3:**299
Miller, Ann, **1:**575
Miller, Arthur, **1:**546; **5:**121; **8:**115
   The Death of a Salesman,
      2:512–513

Miller, Charles C., **2:**422
Miller, Cheryl, **1:**425
Miller, E. L., **7:**30
Miller, Elizabeth Smith, **1:**488
Miller, Henry, **5:**121
Miller, Herman, **1:**293
Miller, Joyce, **2:**256
Miller, Lewis, **2:**113
Miller, Marvin, **1:**422
Miller, Perry, **3:**280
Miller, Phineas, **2:**429
Miller, Samuel F.
   on Fourteenth Amendment, **7:**378
   on power of state courts, **3:**515
Miller, Thomas, **2:**476
Miller, Walter M., Jr., *Canticle for
   Leibowitz,* **5:**121
Miller, William, **1:**30, 378, 447;
   8:313
Miller, William E., **3:**165
Miller v. Albright, **1:**125
Miller v. California, **6:**419
Millerites, **1:**30
   rise of, **1:**30
   in Vermont, **8:**313
Miller's Run Gap, **6:**254
Miller-Tydings Amendment to Sher-
   man Antitrust Act, **3:**309
Milligan, Lambden P., **3:**272
Millikan, Robert A., **2:**14, 15; **6:**336;
   7:278–279
Milliken v. Bradley, **1:**590; **2:**199;
   3:118
Milliken's Bend, Battle of, **2:**212
"Million Man March," **5:**521
Mills, Anson, **8:**258
Mills, C. Wright, *The Power Elite,*
   5:121
Mills, Clark, **1:**306
Mills, Enos A., **1:**434
Mills, Lowell, **3:**53
Mills, Robert, **8:**417, 472
Mills College, **3:**133
*Mills v. Board of Education of the Dis-
   trict of Columbia,* **3:**34
Milosevic, Slobodan, **1:**355; **8:**588
Milton, John, **3:**65
Milwaukee (Wisconsin), **5:***388,*
   388–389
   foundation of, **4:**52
   school choice experiment in,
      3:137–138
Milwaukee Leader (newspaper), **6:**98
Mimeograph, **6:**168–169

Mims, Fort, Massacre at, **2:**456;
   5:389
Mind and the World-Order (Lewis),
   6:327, 445
Mineral(s), and nutrition, **6:**149
Mineral Lands Leasing Act (1920),
   3:421
Mineral Leasing Act (1920), **6:**528
Mineral patent law, **5:389**
Mineral resources
   depletion allowances on, **3:11**
   Interior Department and,
      4:383–384
   U.S. Bureau of Mines and, **5:**392
Mineral springs, **5:389–390**, *390;*
   7:121
   in Antebellum period, **8:**305
   in colonial era, **8:**305
   Saratoga Springs, **7:**251–252
Mineralogy, **5:390–391**
   geology and, **3:**544, 546, 549–550
Minerals Management Service
   (MMS), **4:**383–384
Miners, trade unions of, **5:**6;
   8:267–268
Miners for Democracy (MFD),
   8:268
Minersville School District v. Gobitis,
   3:380
Mines, U.S. Bureau of (USBM),
   5:391–393
Mines and mining
   Coeur d'Alene riots, **2:264**
   in Colorado, **2:**299
   disasters involving, **3:**38–39
      Centralia Mine disaster, **2:**95
   explosives used in, **3:**301
   Guffey Coal Acts and, **4:**71
   public lands and, **5:**25
   in Utah, **8:**296, 297
   in West Virginia, **8:**449–450
   in Wisconsin, **8:**490
   See also specific metals
Minesweeping, **5:393**
Minh, Duong Van, **8:**334
Miniatures (art), **5:393–394**, *394*
Minimalism
   in music, **5:**492–493
   in sculpture, **1:**307
Minimum wage
   history of rise in, **8:**360–361
   legislation on, **5:394–396**
      Fair Labor Standards Act, **3:**54,
         307–308; **8:**252

Supreme Court on, **1:**21; **8:**360
for women, **8:**445
Mining Enforcement and Safety
Administration (MESA), **5:**391
Mining frontier, **8:**463
Mining Laws (1866, 1870, 1872),
5:25, 389
Mining towns, **4:**11; **5:***396*, **396–397**
Galena-Dubuque mining district,
3:503
gender roles in, **4:**13–14
as ghost towns, **3:**574
saloons in, **8:**54
violence in, **4:**13; **8:**54
Virginia City (Nevada), **1:**497;
2:338; **4:**11; **8:347**
women in, **4:**13–14
Minisink, **8:**220
Mink, Patsy, **8:**507
Minneapolis–St. Paul (Minnesota),
5:397–398
flour milling in, **3:**390, 391
Fort Snelling in, **7:**407
Minnesota, **5:398–401**
agriculture in, **5:**399
American settlement in, **5:**398–399
charter schools in, **2:**110
Children's Code of, **1:**28
in colonial era, **5:**398
emblems, nicknames, mottos, and
songs of, **7:***532*
Farmer-Labor party of, **3:**321–323
Great Depression in, **5:**400
immigration to, **5:**397, 398, 399
industrial growth in, **5:**399
Kensington Stone in, **4:516–517**
Mesabi Iron Range, **5:**326
in Midwest, **5:**368–369
Northwest Angle, **6:**135–136
politics in, **5:**400
Progressive Era in, **5:**399–400
Sioux uprising in, **7:***369*, **369–370**
Little Crow's speech before,
9:243–244
three-party system in, **8:**243
*Minnesota, Chicago, Milwaukee, and
Saint Paul Railway Company v.,*
2:134
Minnesota, Near v., **6:27**
Minnesota Mining and Manufactur-
ing Company, and bionics,
1:463
Minnesota Moratorium case, **5:**401
Minnesota Rate Cases, **2:**311

Minnesota State Federation of
Labor, **3:**321
Minnesota-Montana Road, **3:**377
Minor v. Happersett, **5:401–402; 8:**11
Minorities
in baseball, **1:**421, 422
during Great Depression, **3:**50
in higher education
for law, **5:**58
for sciences, **7:**273
women's colleges, **3:**132
in military, **2:**364, 365
poverty among, **2:**225
in trade unions, **3:**50
See also specific groups
Minority business, **1:581–582**
set-asides for, **7:**315–316, 398
Small Business Administration and,
7:398
Minsky, Hyman, **3:**110
Minstrel shows, **3:**66; **5:402,**
489–490; **8:**113
music industry and, **5:**502
songs of, **5:**496
Mint(s)
federal, **5:402–403**
Hamilton on, **4:**90
private, **5:**403
Minuit, Peter, **6:**40, 77
Minuteman ICBM, **2:**528
Minutemen, **1:**509; **5:403–404**
Mir space station, **7:**481
Mirabel, Robert, **2:**501
Miranda, Francisco de, **3:**274; **5:**86
Miranda v. Arizona, **5:404–405**
Mirrors, **4:**4
Miscegenation, **5:405–406**
among African Americans, **4:**479;
5:405–406
laws against, **5:**165, 405–406
in Maryland, **5:**405
among Native Americans, **4:270;**
5:188, 468
Supreme Court on, **5:**251, 406
Mises, Ludwig von, **3:**109
Miss America pageant, **1:**433, *434;*
5:406
Miss Lonelyhearts (West), **5:**121
Missile Defense. *See* Strategic
Defense Initiative
Missile gap (Cold War), **5:406–407**
Missiles, **5:407–408**
anti-ballistic missile systems,
6:144–145

defense against, **1:**75–76 (*See also*
Strategic Defense Initiative)
inter-continental ballistic missiles,
6:144
Missing children, **2:**147
Missing in action controversy, **6:**475
See also Prisoners of war
Mission(s)
circuit riders, **2:**175
domestic/Indian, **4:275–277**
in Arizona, **1:**256–257
in California, **2:**8, 67; **5:408–409**
architecture of, **1:**248–249
firsthand account of, **9:**107–109
Church of England, **7:**430
in Florida, **5:**309
government support of, **4:**276
home missionary societies, **5:**409
in Iowa, **4:**417
Jesuit, **4:**473–474
in Nebraska, **6:**29–30
and Nez Perces, **6:**100
in Oregon, **6:**205
regional differences in,
4:276–277
Spanish exploration and, **7:**206
in Washington, **8:**412
Dominican, **3:**77
foreign, **5:409–410**
in Arab world, **1:**232
Mennonite, **5:**310
Mount Holyoke College and,
5:464
and National Council of Churches, **5:**532–533
social gospel movement and, **5:**431
fundamental churches sending,
3:484
Mission 66, **5:**552
Mission Indians of California,
5:408–409
Mission (Craftsman) style furniture,
3:497
Missionary societies, home, **5:409**
and National Council of Churches,
5:532–533
Mississippi, **5:410–414**
African Americans in, **5:**412–413
agriculture in, **5:**413
antebellum period, **5:**411–412
Black Belt in, **1:**471
Black Code of, text of, **9:**319–322
civil rights movement in, **5:**413–414
firsthand account of, **9:**447–452

Mississippi, (*continued*)
  in Civil War, **5:**412; **8:324**, *324*
  in colonial era, **5:**411
  constitution of, **7:**527
  economic diversification, **5:**414
  emblems, nicknames, mottos, and
    songs of, **7:***532*
  expedition to, **3:**465
  Great Depression in, **5:**413
  Native Americans in, **5:**410
  Prohibition in, **1:**117
  riots in, **8:**324–325
  school desegregation in, Supreme
    Court on, **1:**122
  segregation at bus terminals in,
    3:464
  tidelands in, ownership of, **8:**125
  White Caps in, **8:**470
  white farmers in, **5:**413
Mississippi, Williams v., **8:483**
Mississippi Band of Choctaw Indians v.
  Holyfield, **4:**263
Mississippi Bubble, **5:**158, **414**
Mississippi Freedom Summer pro-
  ject, **2:**354–355; **7:**12
Mississippi in Time of Peace, The (Currier and Ives), **2:***483*
Mississippi Plan, **5:414–415**
Mississippi River, **5:415–418**
  American access to, in 19th centu-
    ry, **5:**162
  bayous on, **1:**432, *432*
  in Civil War, Island Number Ten
    operations, **4:**438
  course of, **5:**415
  discovery of, **3:**295
  Eads Bridge across, **1:**538; **3:**99, *99*
  in exploration of America,
    7:173–174
  flooding of, **3:**42, 383; **5:**417
    control measures for, **3:**384;
      7:170
  French exploration of, **5:**2–3, 158
  galley boats on, **3:**504
  La Salle's expeditions and, **5:**2–3
  Lakes-to-Gulf Deep Waterway
    and, **5:**22–23
  maps of, **5:***415*
    archival, **9:***19, 20,* 20–22, *22*
  Mississippi Valley, **5:***418*, **418–419**
  Pike expedition to, **6:**354
  Pinckney's Treaty and, **6:**356;
    8:200
  showboats on, **7:**350–351

Spanish discovery of, **5:**411
steamboats on, **3:**483
towboats on, **8:**147–148
See also Lake Pontchartrain
Mississippi River Commission,
  3:384; **5:**417
Mississippi Summer Project (1964),
  8:587
Mississippi v. Johnson, **3:**559; **5:**418;
  8:97
Mississippi Valley, **5:***418*, **418–419**
  Corn Belt in, **2:**413, **414–415**
  land speculation in, **5:**35
Mississippian societies, **1:**246
  mounds of, **1:**246; **4:**278
Missouri, **5:419–422**
  agriculture in, **5:**419
  Benton era in, **5:**420
  border ruffians in, **1:505**
  boundary disputes in, **4:**466
  in Civil War, **5:**420–421
    Union sentiment in, **8:**260
  constitution of, **5:**424
  earthquakes in, **3:**101
  education in, **5:**422
  emblems, nicknames, mottos, and
    songs of, **7:***532*
  gun control in, **4:**75
  industrialization in, **5:**421
  and Kentucky, boundary dispute
    between, **1:**522
  lead mines in, **5:**62; **6:**114
  map of, **5:***420*
  mules and, **5:**472
  New England Emigrant Aid Com-
    pany and, **6:**49
  people of, **5:**419
  politics in, **5:**420, 421, 422
  resources in, **5:**419
  Santa Fe Trail to, **7:247–249**
  segregation in, **5:**425
  slavery in, Tallmadge Amendment
    and, **8:**45
  slaves freed during Civil War,
    5:230
  State Bank of, **1:**408
  state university of, **8:**279
  territorial period in, **5:**419–420
  trade with New Mexico, **6:**68
  in World War I, **5:**421
  in World War II, **5:**421
  zinc mines in, **6:**115
Missouri, Cummings v., **2:480;** **8:**96
Missouri, Duren v., **8:**60

Missouri Botanical Garden, **1:**516
Missouri Compromise, **2:**351; **5:**420,
  422–425; 8:462
  Maine and, **5:**208
  map of, **5:***423*
  Nashville Convention and, **5:**516
  opposition to, Richmond Junto
    and, **7:**157
  repeal of, **4:**512–513
  Supreme Court on, **3:**85
Missouri ex. rel. Gaines v. Canada,
  3:14; **5:425,** 526
Missouri Fur Company, **3:**298, 487
Missouri Indians, **5:**419
Missouri River, **5:425–427,** *427*
  floods of, **3:**383
  fur trade, **5:427–428**
  Lewis and Clark expedition on,
    3:297
  Pick-Sloan Missouri Basin Project
    and, **6:**30
Missouri v. Holland, **5:428**
MIT. *See* Massachusetts Institute of
  Technology
Mitchel, Ormsby MacKnight, **1:**343
Mitchell, Arthur, **1:***52*
Mitchell, Elisha, **3:**547–548
Mitchell, George, **1:**160
  as Arab American, **1:**231
  and Clean Air Act, **2:**230
  on Persian Gulf War, **6:**292
Mitchell, Hitchman Coal and Coke
  Company v., **8:**579
Mitchell, John (participant in
  Whiskey Rebellion), convicted
  of treason, **2:**377
Mitchell, John (union organizer),
  1:190; **2:**254; **8:**267, 268
Mitchell, John N.
  influence of, **2:**2
  Watergate scandal and, **8:**425
Mitchell, Margaret, **1:**348; **4:**20–21
  Gone with the Wind, **5:**130
Mitchell, Maria, **1:**141; **6:***155*
Mitchell, Samuel, **9:***65,* 66
Mitchell, Silas Weir, **5:**314;
  6:348–349
Mitchell, Wesley C., **6:**403
Mitchell, William (Billy), **1:**76, 81,
  495, 496
  and air defense, **1:**86
  court-martial of, **2:**440
  Ostfriesland sunk by, **1:**266
Mitchell, Wisconsin v., **4:**105

Mitchell v. Trawler Racer, **1:**23
Mitterand, François, **3:**452
Mitterofer, Peter, **8:**244
Miwok Indians, **8:**582, 583
Mixed commissions, **5:428**
MMS. *See* Minerals Management Service
MNF. *See* Multinational Force
Moab (Utah), **8:**298
Mob rule, **5:**179
Mobile Army Surgical Hospital (MASH), **6:**147
Mobile Bay, Battle of, **2:**496; **5:428–429**
Mobile homes, **8:**178
Mobile phones, **8:**67
Mobilization, **5:429–430**
  for World War I, American Expeditionary Forces in, **1:**149; **8:**535
  See also Conscription and recruitment
Mobutu Sese Seko (Joseph), **1:**39; **8:**271
Moby-Dick (Melville), **3:**280; **5:**119, **430–431;** **7:**194
Moccasin Gap, **6:**254
Mochila, **6:**412
Model, Lisette, **1:**301
Model A Ford, **3:**414
Model Cities program, **8:**293
Model Penal Code (MPC), **7:**49–50
Model T Ford, **3:**414; **8:**189
Model Treaty (1776), **3:**425
Modern Corporation and Private Property, The (Commons and Van Hise), **6:**42
Modern dance, **2:**497–498, 499
Modern Language Association, **5:**67
Modern Maturity (magazine), **1:**142
Modernism, **6:**516
  in architecture, **1:**251–252, 288
  in decorative arts, **1:**288
  in interior design, **1:**293
  magazines and, role in nurturing, **5:**194
  Metropolitan Museum of Art and, **5:**336
  in painting, **1:**297
  in sculpture, **1:**307
  in theology, **3:**45
  Protestant, **5:431–433**
Modigliani, Franco, **3:**109, 110
Modoc, **4:536–538,** *537;* **8:**218

Modoc War, **5:**433; **8:**215, 404
Mody, Navroze, **1:**324
Moe, Terry, **3:**137
Moffat Tunnel, **8:**240
Moffatt, Michael, **1:**194
Moffett, William A., **8:**555
Mofford, Rose, **1:**259
Mohammed, Khalid Shaikh, **3:**41
Mohave Indians, **5:433–435,** *434*
Mohawk River, **3:**252
Mohawk Valley (New York), **5:**435
Mohawks, **6:**86
  after American Revolution, **7:**137
  attacks on other Native Americans, **2:**357
  as steelworkers, **6:**88
Mohegan, **2:**356–357
  in modern era, **2:**359
Mohegan tribe, **5:**435
Mohican. *See* Mahican
Moholy-Nagy, László, **1:**298
Mojave, **8:**228
Molasses Act (1733), **5:435–436;** **7:**204, 406; **8:**12, 173
Molasses trade, **5:436–437**
  duties on, **7:**406; **8:**12–13
  smuggling in, **7:**406
Molecular biology, **5:**359, **437–438**
  study of DNA and, **3:**67
Molecular genetics, **3:**532–533
Molet, **3:**378
Moley, Raymond, **8:**197
Molina, Mario, **6:**223
Molineaux, Tom, **6:**483
Moll, Hermann, **9:**16, *17*
Molly Maguires, **5:**438; **6:**279, 357
Moltmann, Jürgen, **5:**93
Moluntha (Shawnee chief), **6:**177
Molybdenum, prospecting and mining, **5:**63
MoMA. *See* Museum of Modern Art
Momaday, N. Scott, *House Made of Dawn,* **4:**179; **5:**129
  Pulitzer Prize for, **4:**179, 533
Monaco, Mississippi bonds held by, **7:**119
Monardes, Nicolás, **1:**518
Mondale, Walter F.
  in presidential campaign of 1976, **3:**167
  in presidential campaign of 1984, **3:**168, 198
  and Rust Belt, coining of term, **7:**215

Mondavi, Robert, **8:**487
"Monday Night Football," **3:**411
Mondo Nuovo (Porcacchi), **9:**7, 7–8
Mondrian, Piet, **1:**298, 306
Monetarism, **3:**110
  on depression, **4:**46
Monetary policy, **5:**440–441
Monetary theory, **5:**441–442
Money, **5:438–442**
  cotton, **2:**429–430
  counterfeiting of, **2:**433–434
  issuance of, **5:**75–76
  paper
    advocates for, **3:**108
    and public debt, **2:**514
    state issue of, **2:**446
  supply of, and inflation, **4:**351
  tobacco as, **8:133**
  wildcat, **8:**477
  See also Currency and coinage
Money, John, **3:**515
Money market, **4:**413; **5:**440
Monge, Gaspard, **1:**335
"Mongrel Tariff" (1883), **8:**51
Monism, **6:**374
Monitor (ship), **4:**430, *430;* **6:**25; **8:**405
Monitor and *Merrimack,* Battle of, **4:***430;* **5:442–443;** **8:**405
Monitorial schools, **3:**113
Moniz, Egas, **6:**522
Monk, Maria, **5:**238
Monmouth, Battle of, **5:**443; **7:**144
Monnet, Jean, **3:**259, 260
Monogenism, **1:**191
Monongahela, Battle of the, **5:443–444**
Monongahela River, **5:**444
Monopoly(ies), **5:444–445**
  AFL-CIO as, **1:**151
  AT&T as, **1:**346; **8:**65, 70
  attitudes toward, **1:**212
  in electric power industry, **6:**535
  in flour milling, **3:**390
  in fur trade, **1:**158
  in meatpacking, **6:**229–230
  Microsoft as, **7:**443
  in oil industry, **6:**303
  patents and, **6:**255
  in railroad industry, **7:**27, 36, 39; **8:**188–189
  Standard Oil Company as, **7:**521
  state-created, **1:**212
  in steamboat traffic, Supreme Court on, **3:**483, 575

Monopoly(ies), (*continued*)
  Theatrical Trust (Syndicate) as,
    8:114
  U.S. Steel as, **4:**428
  See also Antitrust legislation
Monopoly (game), **5:**445; **8:**152–153
Monroe, Fortress, **5:445–446**
Monroe, James
  antifederalism of, **1:**201, 202
  and colonization movement, **2:**296,
    297
  early presidency of, **3:**251
  economic policy of, **2:**550
  Gabriel's Insurrection and, **7:**8
  Indian policies of, **4:**295
  isolationism of, **4:**439
  land policy of, **6:**201
  and Louisiana Purchase, **5:**163
  as minister to France, **8:**570
  in presidential campaign of 1808,
    3:151
  in presidential campaign of 1816,
    3:151
  in presidential campaign of 1820,
    3:151
  Spanish relations under, **7:**484
  and University of Virginia, **8:**283
  in Virginia dynasty, **8:**343, 348
Monroe Doctrine, **2:**530; **3:**425;
    4:41; **5:**46, 52, **446–447**
  anticommunism and, **5:**447
  and Caribbean policies, **2:**54
  Clayton-Bulwer Treaty and, **2:**229
  factors leading to, **7:**210
  isolationism of, **4:**439
  manifest destiny and, **5:**223
  Monroe's speech on, **9:**204–206
  nonintervention policy in, **6:**117
  Olney Corollary to, **6:191**
  Polk Doctrine and, **6:**408
  Roosevelt Corollary to, **2:**54;
    3:75–76; **5:**47; **7:196**
  Roosevelt's speeches on,
    9:206–209
  and Spain, **7:**484
  Wilson's speech on, **9:**209
Monroe-Pinkney Treaty (1806),
    5:447
Monroney, A. S. "Mike," **5:**77
Monrovia (Liberia), founding of,
    2:297
Monsanto, petrochemical subsidiary
    of, **3:**211
Montagnier, Luc, **1:**15

Montagu, M. F. Ashley, **7:**13
Montague, Andrew J., **8:**344
Montaigne, Michel de, "On Canni-
    bals," **5:**116
Montana, **5:447–451**
  in 20th century, **5:**450–451
  agriculture in, **5:**450
  Cheyenne relocation to, **3:**94
  copper industry in, **1:**180;
    5:449–450; **6:**115
  earthquakes in, **3:**101
  emblems, nicknames, mottos, and
    songs of, **7:***532*
  expeditions to, **3:**377
  federal government in, **5:**451
  fur trade in, **5:**448
  gold mining in, **4:**11
    at Helena mining camp, **4:123**
    women and, **9:**240–242
  Lewis and Clark expedition in,
    5:448
  livestock industry in, **5:**449
  Native Americans in, **3:**94;
    5:448–449
  politics in, **5:**449, 451
  railroads in, **5:**448
  vigilantes in, **8:**336
Montcalm, Louis-Joseph de, **1:**7;
    2:295; **3:**471; **7:**4
Monte Cassino, **5:451–452**
Monterrey, Battles of, **5:**452
Montesquieu, Baron de, **2:**40; **7:**312
  on democracy, **7:**109
  on due process of law, **3:**89
Montgolfier brothers, **1:**391
Montgomery, Bernard L., **1:**565
  in Normandy Invasion, **6:**118
  in North African Campaign, **6:**124
  in Sicilian Campaign, **7:**353–354
Montgomery, Richard, **1:**281; **5:**21;
    7:142
Montgomery (Alabama), bus boycott
    in, **1:**104, 529, 548; **2:**202; **3:**15,
    557
Montgomery Convention (1861),
    5:452
Montgomery Ward & Co., **3:**9;
    7:125
  and Chicago, growth of, **2:**132
  furniture by, **3:**498
  mail-order, **5:**206
Monticello, **5:452–453,** *453*
  architecture of, **1:**249
  interior design of, **1:**292

landscape architecture of, **5:**38
Montreal, Capture of (1760), **5:454**
Montreal, Capture of (1775), **5:454**
Montreal, colonial settlements in,
    6:51–52
Montreal Protocol (1987), **6:**223;
    7:246
Montreal Protocol on Substances
    that Deplete the Ozone Layer
    (1978), **2:**238; **3:**230, 233
  implementation of, Clean Air Act
    and, **2:**230
Monts, Sieur de, **2:**103
Monument Valley, **3:***17*
Monuments, national, **2:**369, 371
  under Antiquities Act, **1:**205–206
Moody, Dwight L., **3:**265, 266;
    6:516
Moody, Paul, **2:**245; **8:**108, 109
Moody's, **5:**454
Moon, Sun Myung, **2:**477; **8:**303
Moon landing, **5:***454,* **454–455,**
    523–524, *524*
  transcript of, **9:**435–444
Moon rocks, **6:**301
Mooney, James, **6:**5
Mooney, Thomas J., **1:**146
  bombing case, **5:**455
Mooney, William, **8:**45
Moonshine, **5:**455
Moore, Annie, **3:**189
Moore, Arch Alfred, Jr., **8:**450
Moore, Charles, **1:**253
Moore, Clement, "A Visit from
    Saint Nicholas," **5:**127
Moore, E. M., **1:**184
Moore, Gordon, **2:**321, 338
Moore, Henry Ludwell, **3:**109
Moore, Hiram, **1:**59
Moore, James, **1:**221
Moore, John Bassett, **4:**484
Moore, Knowlton v., **8:**57
Moore, Marianne, **5:**120
Moore, Sara Jane, **1:**330–331
Moore, Thomas, **3:**407
Moore v. Dempsey, **4:**81
Moorhead, Warren K., **1:**492
Moraga, Cherríe, **3:**520
Morais, Sabato, **7:**97
Moral Majority, **2:**165; **3:**167, 267,
    485; **5:455–456;** **6:**518; **8:**71
  and church-state separation, oppo-
    sition to, **2:**169
  conservatism and, **2:**376

Moral societies, **5:**456
Moral therapy, **5:**312–313
Morality, in Victorian era, **8:**325–326
Moran, Thomas, **1:**295
Moratorium, Hoover, **5:**456
Moravian Brethren, **5:**456–457; **6:**353–354
Mordkin, Mikhail, **1:**390
More, Nicholas, **3:**459
More, Paul Elmer, **2:**375
More, Sir Thomas, *Utopia,* **5:**116–117
Morehead, Charles S., **1:**284
Morehead v. New York ex rel. Tipaldo, **5:**395
Morelos, José María, **5:**50–51
Moretum (Virgil), **3:**99
Morgan, Charles, **2:**260
Morgan, Clement, **6:**103–104
Morgan, Daniel, **1:**574; **7:**145
  in Battle of Cowpens, **2:**444
Morgan, George W., **2:**479
Morgan, Sir Henry, **1:**550
Morgan, J. P., **1:**110, 405, 580; **8:**233, 295
  in anthracite strike (1902), **1:**190
  and Edison Light Company, **3:**173
  gold drain and, **1:**459
  "Northern Pacific panic" of 1901 and, **6:**135
  Panic of 1893 and, **6:**493
  Panic of 1907 and, **1:**397; **3:**344, 366
  public perception of, **7:**181, 182
  and railroad mergers, **7:**36
  in steel industry merger movement, **4:**428
Morgan, J. P., Jr., **1:**405
Morgan, John Hunt, raids by, **5:**458
Morgan, Julia, **7:**243
Morgan, Junius, **1:**405
Morgan, Kemp, **8:**45
Morgan, Lewis Henry, **1:**192
Morgan, Margaret, **6:**462
Morgan, Morgan, **8:**448
Morgan, Robin, **5:**470
Morgan, Thomas Hunt, **3:**269, 532
Morgan, United States v., **1:**405
Morgan, William, **1:**203; **3:**466; **8:**584
Morgan Stanley, **1:**405
Morgan v. United States, **8:**101
Morgan v. Virginia, **5:**527

Morgan-Belmont Agreement, **5:**457–458
Morgenstern, Oskar, **3:**109, 110
Morgenthau, Henry, and Near East Relief, **8:**542
Morgenthau, Henry, Jr., **1:**544
  as secretary of treasury, **6:**44; **8:**197
Morial, Ernest F., **6:**74
Morison, S. E., **3:**283
Morlacchi, Giuseppina, **1:**389
Mormon(s), **2:**163; **3:**264
  African American, **8:**298
  attacks on, **7:**94
  and Deseret, **3:**16
  discrimination against, **4:**212
  freemasonry and, **3:**466
  during Great Depression, **8:**298
  in Idaho, **4:**211, 212
  in Illinois, **4:**215; **5:**53
  migration to Salt Lake Valley, **5:**53
  in Missouri, **5:**53
  and Native Americans, **2:**65; **8:**217, 228, 296, 300
  at Nauvoo, **6:**14–15
  in Ohio, **5:**53
  polygamy among, **2:**163; **5:**53, 55; **6:**15, 410; **8:**296, 297
    Supreme Court decision on, **2:**167; **7:**150
  war against, **5:**54
  in Utah, **5:**53–54; **8:**296
    Salt Lake City, **7:**233–234
  during World War I, **8:**297
  during World War II, **5:**54
  See also Latter-day Saints, Church of Jesus Christ of
Mormon Battalion, **5:**458
Mormon expedition, **5:**458
Mormon handcart companies, **5:**458–459
Mormon Tabernacle, **8:**41
Mormon Tabernacle Choir, **8:**297
Mormon Trail, **5:**459, *459;* **6:**30
Mormon War, **5:**53, 459–460
Morning Edition (radio program), **5:**554; **8:**44
Morning Show (TV show), **8:**44, 138
Morocco
  trade with, **1:**123
  U.S. relations with, **1:**232, 233
  in World War II, **1:**233
Morocco Agreement (1880), **1:**123
Morphine, Civil War veterans addicted to, **5:**510

Morphy, Paul, **2:**130
Morrill, Justin Smith, **3:**115; **5:**29; **8:**313
Morrill Act (1890), **3:**115
Morrill Anti-bigamy Act (1862), **8:**296
Morrill Land Grant Act (1862), **1:**63; **3:**115, 127; **5:**17, 28, 29, **460; 6:**410
  and agricultural colleges, **5:**29–30, 34–35; **8:**319
  and agricultural (land) economics, **3:**107
  and black colleges, **3:**126
  and Cornell University, establishment of, **2:**415
  and denominational colleges, **3:**130
  and engineering education, **3:**216
  and state universities, **8:**279
Morrill Tariff (1861), **8:**51
Morris, Charles, **3:**204
Morris, Colin, **4:**331
Morris, George Anthony, **1:**304
Morris, George Pope, "The Flag of the Union," **8:**279
Morris, Gouverneur
  alma mater of, **2:**304
  at Constitutional Convention, **2:**379
  and land speculation, **5:**36
  on revolutionary committees, **2:**314; **7:**136
Morris, Lewis, **8:**589–590
Morris, Mark, **2:**499
Morris, Nelson, **5:**135
Morris, Robert, **1:**307, 395, 396; **7:**148, 149
  and coinage system, **2:**481
  and land speculation, **5:**36
  and Plan of 1776, **6:**361
Morris, William, **1:**320
Morrison, deLesseps, **6:**74
Morrison, Toni, **2:**205; **5:**123, 124, 126
  Beloved, **5:**123, 126
Morrison, United States v., **2:**312; **3:**74; **8:**274
Morrissey, John, **2:**463
Morrow, Prince, **7:**321
Morrow, Prince A., **6:**513
Morse, Jedediah, Geographies of, **5:**460
Morse, O. M., **3:**390

Morse, Samuel F. B., **1**:299; **3**:183; **7**:94; **8**:65, 68–69, *69*

Morse, Wayne, **6**:207

Morse code, **8**:68

Mortality, **2**:557–560, *558*

Mortality experience, in American history, **5**:103–104

Mortars, Civil War naval, **5**:460

Mortgage lending, **2**:450

Mortgage relief legislation, **5**:460–462
  Frazier-Lemke Farm Bankruptcy Act, **3**:457

Mortgages
  Federal Housing Administration and, **7**:256
  Home Owners' Loan Corporation and, **4**:152

Morton, J. Sterling, **1**:238

Morton, Levi P., **3**:157

Morton, Oliver P., **3**:156

Morton, Samuel George, **1**:192; **7**:13

Morton, Thomas, **5**:117; **7**:63

Morton, William Thomas Green, **1**:184–185

Morton Downey, Jr. Show (TV show), **8**:44

Mosby's Rangers, **5**:462

Moscone, George, **3**:514

Moscoso, Mireya, **6**:241

Moscoso Alvarado, Luis de, **8**:99

Moscow Art Theater, **8**:114, 115

Moseley, Henry G. J., **6**:340

Moses, Robert, **2**:94; **3**:281; **4**:355; **6**:81; **8**:315
  and Lincoln Tunnel, **5**:110
  and New York parkways, **7**:178

Mosko, Charles, **3**:78

Mosley, Walter, **5**:123

Mosquitoes, and yellow fever, **8**:576

Moss, Frank, **8**:298

Moss, John, **2**:85

"Most favored nation" status, **5**:462; **8**:52, 157, 198
  to China, **8**:198
  to Hungary, **8**:198

Motels, **5**:462, **462–463**
  rise of, **4**:176
  and vacationing, **8**:305

Mother Earth (journal), **1**:181, 467

Motherhood, surrogate, **8**:29–30

Mothers Against Drunk Driving (MADD), **1**:118, 119; **3**:336

Mother's Day, **5**:463

Motherwell, Robert, **1**:10, 298

Motion pictures. *See* Film

Motley, Archibald J., **4**:96

Motor Carrier Act (1980), **5**:463; **8**:231

Motor courts, **2**:389

Motor hotels. *See* Motels

Motor vehicle safety, **5**:105

Motorcycles, Hell's Angels and, **4**:125

Motorized fire engine, **3**:372–373

Motown, **5**:490

Motown Records, **3**:20; **7**:185

Mott, John R., **8**:584

Mott, Lucretia, **6**:88; **7**:3, 310, 311; **8**:10
  and abolitionism, **8**:512
  Declaration of Rights and Sentiments by, **2**:524
    text of, **9**:332–334
  and Seneca Falls Convention, **8**:506, 512
  and women's suffrage, **7**:106

Mott, Martin v., **5**:255

Mott Foundation, **8**:282

Moulton, F. R., **3**:552

Moulton, Harold G., **1**:545; **8**:117

Moultrie, Fort, Battle of, **5**:463

Moultrie, William, **2**:108

Mounds, Native American, **4**:277–279**
  Adena, **1**:20
  archaeological studies of, **1**:239, 246, *247*; **4**:277–278
  at Cahokia, **4**:278; **8**:225
  Hopewell, **4**:163, *163*
  Mississippian, **1**:246; **4**:278
  Poverty Point, **6**:441

Mount, William Sidney, **3**:537

Mount Holyoke College, **3**:131; **5**:464; **7**:319–320
  minorities in, **3**:132

Mount Hope (Rhode Island), **5**:464

Mount Pinatubo, **8**:351

Mount Ranier Act (1899), **5**:35

Mount Redoubt, **8**:351

Mount Rushmore, **1**:474; **5**:464–465, *465*

Mount Spurr, **8**:351

Mount St. Helens (Washington), **5**:465, *466*
  eruption of, **3**:37; **8**:351
  and mudflow floods, **3**:383
  recovery after, **8**:351
  observatory at, **8**:352

Mount Vernon (Virginia), **5**:465–466, *467*
  distillery at, **3**:60
  kitchen of, **4**:*534*
  landscape architecture of, **5**:38

Mount Vernon Ladies Association, **5**:465–466; **8**:146

Mountain climbing, **5**:466–467

Mountain houses, **7**:122

Mountain Meadows Massacre, **5**:467–468

Mountain men, **5**:468

Mourning, **2**:511; **3**:486

Mourning Dove, **5**:128

Mourot, Michael, **1**:290

Mourt's Relation, **5**:468–469

Moussaoui, Zacarias, **6**:108

Movable type, **6**:466

Movies. *See* Film

Mow Sun Wong, Hampton v., **1**:126

Moyer, Charles H., **4**:111

Moyer v. Peabody, **3**:272

Moyne de Bienville, Jean-Baptiste le, **1**:102

Moynihan, Daniel Patrick, **1**:338, 441; **6**:440
  Beyond the Melting Pot, **1**:446–447
  as neoconservative, **6**:32, 33
  and transportation legislation, **3**:336

Mozoomdar, Protap Chunder, **1**:326

MPC. *See* Model Penal Code

Mr. Potato Head (toy), **8**:153

MRI. *See* Magnetic Resonance Imaging

Ms. magazine, **5**:198, *469*, **469–470**

MSN (Microsoft Network), **2**:323

MTV (Music Television), **5**:503

Mubarak, Hosni, **3**:141
  and *Achille Lauro* hijacking, **1**:13

Muckrakers, **2**:389; **5**:470–471; **6**:554; **8**:233
  on Robber Barons, **7**:181

Mudd, Samuel, **1**:328

Muddy Pass, **6**:254

Mueller v. Allen, **2**:169

Mugabe, Robert, **1**:39

Mugler v. Kansas, **5**:471

Mugwumps, **2**:551; **5**:471–472; **7**:112

Muhammad V (king of Morocco), **1**:233

Muhammad, Elijah, **1**:478; **4**:437; **5**:*519*
  and Fard (Wallace D.), **5**:519
  and Malcolm X, **5**:520

political passivity of, **5:**521

Muhammad, Wallace, **5:**521

Muhammad Speaks (newspaper), **5:**200, 520

Mühlenberg, Heinrich Melchior (Henry), **5:**175, *176;* **6:**353; **7:**83

Muhlenberg, William A., **3:**242, *243*

Muir, John, **2:***369;* **3:**227, 435; **7:***355*
 and aesthetic preservationism, **2:**368
 and Hetch Hetchy Valley dam, opposition to, **2:**369
 and Hoover Dam, opposition to, **2:**10
 Sierra Club of, **7:**354
 and Yosemite National Park, **8:**582, 583

Mulder, Gerrit Jan, **6:**148

Mule skinner, **5:**472

Mules, **5:**472, *472*

Mules and Men (Hurston), **5:**125

Mulhall, Lucille, **6:**185

Mulhall, Zach, **6:**185

Mulkey, Lincoln, **7:**82

Mulkey, Reitman v., **7:**82

Muller, Hermann Joseph, **3:**532

Muller, Kal, **1:**569

Muller v. Oregon, **1:**21; **3:**54, 247, 308; **5:**394, 395, **472–473**
 Brandeis Brief in, excerpt of, **9:**357–360

Mulligan, James, **5:**473

Mulligan letters, **2:**453; **5:**473

Mulliken, Samuel, **1:**59

Mulroney, Brian, **2:**28
 and United States-Canada Free Trade Agreement, **8:**276

Multiculturalism, **1:**338; **5:473–474**
 exchange students and, **3:**274
 Fulbright grants and, **3:**482–483
 and political correctness, **6:**395
 See also Melting pot

Multiethnic Placement Act (1994), **1:**29

Multinational Force (MNF), **6:**270

Multiple-Use Mining Law (1955), **3:**432

Multiple-Use Sustained-Yield Act (1960), **3:**431, 437

Mumbo Jumbo (Reed), **5:**126

Mumford, L. Quincy, **5:**101

Mummification, **3:**486

Municipal government, **5:474–476**
 city councils, **2:**182–183
 city manager plan, **2:**183–184

commission, **2:312**
 home rule by, **4:**152–153
 See also Metropolitan government; Town government

Municipal ownership, **5:476–478**

Municipal reform, **5:**478

Munitions, **5:478–482**; **6:**493
 See also Artillery; Gun(s); Nuclear weapons; Weapons

Munitz, Barry, **3:**566

Munk, Jens, **3:**286

Munn v. Illinois, **2:**134; **3:**187; **4:**35, 36; **5:482–483**; **7:**26

Muñoz Marín, Luis, **6:**546, 547

Munro, William B., **6:**402–403

Munsee, **8:**220, 567

Munsee Delaware, Mahican and, **5:**203

Munster, Sebastian, **9:***6,* 6–7

Murals, **5:483**

Murat, Achille, **3:**2

Murmansk (Russia), **5:483**

Murphy, Carl, **6:**98

Murphy, Charles Francis, **6:**79; **8:**46

Murphy, Charles M., **1:**451

Murphy, Eddie, **4:***149*

Murphy, Frank, on commerce clause, **2:**311

Murphy, George Lloyd, **6:**163

Murphy, George M., **6:**341

Murphy, Jim, **5:***372*

Murphy, Jimmy, **1:**375

Murray, Charles, **1:**194; **6:**440; **8:**387
 The Bell Curve, **7:**13

Murray, James, **3:**200

Murray, John, **2:**350

Murray, John Courtney, **2:**165; **4:**475; **8:**308

Murray, Judith Sargent, "On the Equality of the Sexes," excerpt from, **9:**325–327

Murray, Pauli, **8:**499

Murray, Philip, **1:**151, 197; **8:**277

Murray v. Curlett, **1:**347

Murrow, Edward R., **2:**78; **5:**554; **7:**20; **8:**73

Muscle Shoals speculation, **5:483–484**; **8:**87, 88

Museum(s), **5:485–489**
 American Museum of Natural History, **1:165**
 architecture of, **5:**485, 487
 Art Institute of Chicago, **1:316–317**

Barnum's American Museum, **1:418–419**

cabinets, semiprivate, **5:**485–486

The Cloisters (New York), **5:**336

collecting and, **2:**272, 273; **5:**486–487

"dime" museums, **5:**487

emergence of, **5:**485–486

Frick Collection, **3:**473–474

Getty Museum, **3:564–566**

Guggenheim Museum, **4:71–72**, 72

Henry Ford Museum, **4:127**

Holocaust Museum, **4:150–151**

Huntington Library and Museum, **4:195–196**

of industrialists, **5:**488

mammal specimens in, **5:**217

Metropolitan Museum of Art (New York), **5:**335–338, *336*

Modern Art, Museum of (MoMA) (New York), **5:484**

Monticello, **5:452–453**, *453*

Mount Vernon, **5:465–466**, *467*

National Gallery of Art, **5:538–541**

natural history, **5:**487–488

science, **7:**277

Science and Industry, Museum of (MSI) (Chicago), **5:484–485**

twentieth-century styles of, **5:**488

zoological, **8:**597

See also Historic preservation

Museum of Modern Art (MoMA), **3:**498–499; **5:484**

Museum of Science and Industry (MSI) (Chicago), **5:484–485**

Music
 African American, **5:489–490**
  blues, **1:**491–492
  ragtime, **7:**22
  white interest in, **5:**499
 audio technology industry and, **1:**358–359
 ballads, **1:**388–389
 "Battle Hymn of the Republic," **1:429**
 bluegrass, **5:490–491**, *491*
  Grand Ole Opry and, **4:**34–35
 blues, **5:**490
  in Memphis, **5:**308
 classical, **5:491–493**
  and symphony orchestras, **8:38–39**

Music, (*continued*)
  consumerism in, **2:**391
  country and western, **5:493–494**
    Grand Ole Opry and, **4:**34–35
    honky-tonk girls and, **4:**159
    in Nashville, **5:**515
  cowboy, **2:442–443**
  early American, **5:494–496**; **8:**575
  existentialism in, **3:**280
  festivals, **5:501–502**
  folk, **3:**395–396
  folk revival, **5:496–497**
  gospel, **4:**206–207; **5:497–498**
  of Harlem Renaissance, **4:**96
  hymns and hymnody, **4:206–207**
    America the Beautiful, **1:**139
    in eighteenth century, **5:**494
    "My Country, Tis of Thee," **5:**505
    psalms, **5:**491, 494
  jazz, **4:467–469**
    and audio technology industry,
      1:358
    in Harlem Renaissance, **4:**96
    in Kansas City, **5:**421
    types of, **5:**490
  marching bands, **5:237–238**
  minstrelsy, **5:**489–490, 496
  Native American, **5:498–499**
  New Age, **6:**39
  opera, **6:198–199,** *199*
  popular, **5:499–500**
    disco, **3:45–46**
    early American, **5:**495–496
    MTV, **5:**503
    Native American influences on,
      5:498
  in Puritan religious life, **1:**431
  quadrille bands, **5:**495
  ragtime, **5:**490
    and jazz, **4:**468
  rap, **5:**490
  rhythm-and-blues (R&B), **5:**490
  rock and roll, **1:**492; **5:**499–500;
    7:185–186
    audio technology industry and,
      1:359
    on MTV, **5:**503
  in singing schools, **7:366**
  soul, **5:**490
  theater and film, **5:500–501**
  videos, **5:**503
  at Woodstock, **7:**186; **8:***523,*
    523–524
  of World War I, **9:**364–365

Music industry, **2:**322; **5:502–503**
  in Detroit, **3:**20
Music Television (MTV), **5:**503
Musical activism, **1:**441
Musicals, **8:**115
Musick, Edwin C., **2:**153
Muskets, muzzle-loading, **5:**479
Muskie, Edmund S., **3:**165, 166;
    5:210; **6:**392; **8:**425
Muslims
  immigration of, **4:**436
  Lebanese American, **5:**72
  See also Islam
Mussel, Zebra, **7:**500
Mussel Slough incident, **5:503–504**
Mussolini, Benito, **4:**448
Mustang (Ford), **3:414–415**
Mustangs, **5:**504
Muste, A. J., **6:**266, 269
Muster Day, **5:504–505**
Muth, John, **3:**110
Mutiny Act (1765), **5:**505
*Mutual Assurance Society, Currie's
    Administrators v.,* **6:**10
Mutual Assured Destruction
    (MAD), **6:**144
Mutual Benefit Association, **6:**416
Mutual Defense Assistance Act
    (1949), **8:**329
Mutual funds, **3:**367; **4:**413
Mutual UFO Network, **8:**255
Muybridge, Eadweard, **1:**299; **2:**308
Muzzeniegun (magazine), **5:**192
Muzzle-loading muskets, **5:**479
My Army Life (Carrington), excerpt
    from, **9:**244–248
"My Country, Tis of Thee," **5:**505
My Fair Lady (musical), **8:**115
My Generation (magazine), **1:**142
My Lai incident, **1:**354; **2:**440;
    5:505, *506*
Mycobacterium leprae, **5:**83
Mycobacterium tuberculosis, **8:**236
Myer, Albert J., **2:**235
Myer, Dillon S., **1:**571; **4:**288, 461
Myers, Isaac, **2:**302
Myers, Mae Ethel Klinck, **1:**308, 309
Myers, Walter Dean, *Fallen Angels,*
    5:126
Myers v. United States, **5:**506;
    7:100–101
Myrdal, Gunnar, **2:**56
  An American Dilemma, **1:**138,
    148–149

Mystic Massacre, **6:**289, *290*
Mysticism, **5:506–507**
Myth(s), of wilderness, **1:**170
Mythology, national
  American Studies on, **1:**169
  See also Folklore
Myth-symbol school, of American
    Studies, **1:**169–170

N

NAACP. *See* National Association
  for the Advancement of Colored
  People
NAAQS. *See* National Ambient Air
  Quality Standards
Nabokov, Vladimir, **5:**121
NABSW. *See* National Association
  of Black Social Workers
NACA. *See* National Advisory Com-
  mittee for Aeronautics
NACHO. *See* North American Con-
  ference of Homophile Organi-
  zations
Nación, La (newspaper), **1:**137
NACSE. *See* National Association of
  Civil Service Employees
NACW. *See* National Association of
  Colored Women
Nadelman, Elie, **1:**310
Na-Dene, **8:**221
Nader, Ralph
  as Arab American, **1:**231
  and consumer movement, **2:**384;
    7:18; **8:**285
  and consumer protection, **6:**555
  on Federal Trade Commission,
    3:349; **5:**509
  and *The Nation,* **5:**522
  in presidential campaign of 1996,
    3:230
  in presidential campaign of 2000,
    3:170, 230
    censorship of, **2:**86
  as third-party candidate, **8:**120
  trade unions and, **3:**177
  Unsafe at Any Speed, **2:**384, 391;
    5:561; **8:**285
Nader's Raiders, **2:**384; **5:**509
NAFTA. *See* North American Free
  Trade Agreement

Nagasaki (Japan), atomic bombing of, **1**:494; **3**:302; **5**:222; **6**:143; **8**:551, 555

NAGCN. *See* National Association of Graduate Colored Nurses

NAGPRA. *See* Native American Graves Protection and Repatriation Act

Nagumo, Chuichi, **5**:367; **6**:272, 273

Nahat, Dennis, **1**:390

Nahum Keike
settlement of, **3**:80
See also Salem (Massachusetts)

Naismith, James, **8**:584

Najimy, Kathy, **5**:72

Naked and the Dead, The (Mailer), **5**:121

Nakoda, **5**:23

NALC. *See* Negro American Labor Council

NAM. *See* National Association of Manufacturers

Naming, **5**:509–510

Nanotechnology, future directions for, **5**:19

Nantucket, **5**:510; **8**:*146*

Napalm, **8**:*332*

Naples (Italy), Stazione Zoologica, **5**:240

Napoleon Bonaparte (emperor of France), **2**:35; **3**:192
legal code of, **2**:262
in Louisiana Purchase, **1**:187; **3**:450; **5**:163; **8**:200, 204
War of 1812 and, **8**:382, 384

Napoleon guns, **5**:479

Napoleon III (emperor of France), **1**:130

Napoleonic wars, blockades in, **1**:487

Napster, **2**:322

NARA. *See* National Archives and Records Administration

NARAL. *See* National Abortion and Reproductive Rights Action League

Narcotic Control Act (1956), **5**:511

Narcotics trade and legislation, **5**:510–513
in 19th century, **5**:510
in 1980s, **5**:511
in 1990s, **5**:511–512
Drug Enforcement Administration and, **5**:511, 512

Federal Bureau of Narcotics and, **5**:511

Internal Revenue Service and, **5**:510–511

major trafficking routes, **5**:*512*

Nixon and, **5**:511

Treasury Department and, **5**:510–511

See also Drug trafficking

Narragansett, **2**:356, 357; **5**:513–514; **8**:220
in King Philip's War, **4**:527
in Rhode Island, **7**:151

Narragansett Bay, **5**:514

Narragansett Planters, **5**:515

Narrative of the Life of Frederick Douglass, An American Slave (Douglass), **5**:124

Narrative of William Wells Brown, a Fugitive slave (Brown), **5**:124

Narrows, **5**:*514*, **515**

Narváez, Pánfilo de, **1**:102; **2**:360; **3**:295, 385; **6**:65; **8**:47, 99

NASA. *See* National Aeronautics and Space Administration

NASCAR. *See* National Association for Stock Car Auto Racing

NASD. *See* National Association of Securities Dealers

Nash, John, **3**:110

Nash, Philleo, **4**:289, 300

Nash, Thomas, **2**:241

Nashoba community, **8**:300

Nashua, **6**:56

Nashville (Tennessee), **5**:515–516
foundation of, **5**:515
New Deal and, **5**:515
population of, **5**:515

Nashville, Battle of, **2**:214; **5**:516

Nashville Agrarians, **2**:375

Nashville Basin, **8**:83

Nashville Convention, **5**:516

Nasir, Jamal 'Abd al-. *See* Nasser, Gamal Abdel

NASL. *See* North American Soccer League

NASPT. *See* National Association for the Study and Prevention of Tuberculosis

Nassau Hall, **6**:465

Nasser, Gamal Abdel, **1**:233; **3**:141, 142; **4**:43; **8**:2, 3, 270

Nasser, Jack, **5**:72

Nast, Thomas, **8**:46, 233

Nat Turner's Rebellion, **5**:516–517, *517*; **7**:10, 380; **8**:343
historical assessment of, **9**:287–288

Natchez, **5**:517–518, *518*
political life of, **4**:291

Natchez Campaign of 1813, **5**:518

Natchez Trace, **1**:562; **5**:518–519
bayous on, **1**:432

Natick, **6**:448

Nation, Carry A., **8**:54, *80*

Nation, The (journal), **5**:521–522; **6**:326, 375

Nation at Risk, A (report), **3**:123, 137; **8**:62

Nation Institute, **5**:522

Nation into State: The Shifting Symbolic Foundations of American Nationalism (Zelinsky), **5**:567

Nation of Islam (NOI), **1**:45, *45*, 478; **5**:519–521
civil rights movement denounced by, **2**:204
mainstream Islam on, **4**:437
prophets in, **4**:437
rise of, **4**:437

National Abortion and Reproductive Rights Action League (NARAL), **1**:6

National Academy of Engineering, **5**:522, 523

National Academy of Sciences, **5**:67, **522–523**

National Action Party (PAN) (Mexico), **5**:349

National Advisory Commission on Civil Disorders. *See* Kerner Commission

National Advisory Committee for Aeronautics (NACA), **1**:92

National Aeronautics and Space Act (1958), **5**:523

National Aeronautics and Space Administration (NASA), **5**:523–524
and aircraft industry, **1**:96
balloons used by, **1**:392
Cold War and, **5**:523
and communication satellites, **2**:319, 320
establishment of, **1**:345; **3**:300; **7**:480
functions of, **1**:345
Hubble Space Telescope by, **1**:345
and International Space Station, **5**:524

National Aeronautics and Space Administration (NASA), (*continued*)
Moon landing (*Apollo 11*), **5**:*454*, **454–455**
predecessor of, **8**:569
Project Apollo of, **5**:523–524, *524*
Project Gemini of, **5**:523
Project Mercury of, **5**:523
shuttle missions of, **2**:101; **5**:524
virtual reality used by, **8**:350
weather forecasts and, **8**:433
National Airport Act (1946), **1**:84
National Ambient Air Quality Standards (NAAQS), **1**:79
National American Woman Suffrage Association (NAWSA), **5**:565; **7**:106; **8**:11–12, 514
National and Community Service Trust Act (1993), **1**:173
National Anti-Vivisection Society, **1**:186
National Archives Act (1934), **5**:525
National Archives and Records Administration (NARA), **5**:524–526**
Nixon tapes made public by, **6**:112
and presidential libraries, **5**:99
National Army, in World War I, **8**:540–541
National Association for Stock Car Auto Racing (NASCAR), **1**:375–376
National Association for the Advancement of Colored People (NAACP), **2**:201; **5**:124, **526–527**
anti-lynching crusade by, **5**:*179*, 180
and *Brown* case, **1**:549
on Confederate flag, **3**:381
foundation of, **5**:526
leaders of, political violence against, **1**:332
Missouri ex rel. Gaines v. Canada, **5**:425
Niagara movement and, **5**:526; **6**:104
and prisons, **6**:477
and Proposition 14, challenge to, **7**:82
public interest law carried out by, **6**:530

vs. Universal Negro Improvement Association (UNIA), **1**:478
during World War I, **8**:537
National Association for the Study and Prevention of Tuberculosis (NASPT), **8**:236
National Association of Artists' Organizations, **5**:536
National Association of Black Social Workers (NABSW), **1**:29
National Association of Civil Service Employees (NACSE), **6**:283
National Association of Colored Women (NACW), **3**:526; **5**:527; **8**:510
formation of, **8**:514
National Association of Evangelicals, **6**:288
National Association of Graduate Colored Nurses (NAGCN), **6**:147
National Association of Manufacturers (NAM), **5**:527–528
lobbying by, investigation of, **5**:77–78, 137
National Association of Securities Dealers (NASD), **7**:549
National Association of Securities Dealers Automated Quotations (NASDAQ), **7**:549
National Atlas of the United States, The, **5**:234
National Bank Act (1863), **5**:528; **8**:196
National Bank Act (1864), **8**:196
National bank notes, **5**:528
National Banking System, **1**:397, 400; **3**:344
National banks, **2**:333
National Baptist Convention (NBC), **1**:44–45
National Baptist Convention of America (NBCA), **1**:44
National Bituminous Coal Commission, **4**:71
National Broadcasting Co. v. U.S., **3**:341
National Broadcasting Company. *See* NBC
National Bureau of Economic Research, **5**:528
economic indicators used by, **3**:105–106
establishment of, **3**:109

National Bureau of Standards, **5**:528–530; **6**:336, 341
National Cancer Institute, and AIDS, **1**:15–16
National Cathedral, **6**:458
National Cemetery System, **8**:317
National Civic Federation (NCF), **5**:530
National Collegiate Athletic Association (NCAA), **2**:276, 278; **5**:530–531**
and football, **3**:410, 411; **5**:530–531
television revenues of, **5**:531
National Committee for Mental Hygiene, **5**:314
National Committee on Excellence in Education, **8**:62
National Community Mental Health Centers Act (1963), **5**:315
National and Community Service Act (1990), **1**:19
National and Community Service Trust Act (1993), **1**:19
National Conference of Commissioners on Uniform State Laws, **7**:531–533
National Conference of Puerto Rican Women, **5**:531
National Congress of American Indians, **5**:531–532
National Consumers' League (NCL), **2**:392; **6**:554
National Council of Churches, **3**:2; **5**:532–533; **6**:516
National Council of Crime and Delinquency, **6**:552
National Council of Jewish Women (NCJW), **5**:534
National Council of La Raza (NCLR), **4**:135
National Council of Negro Women, **5**:534
National Council on Alcoholism and Drug Dependence (NCADD), **1**:119
National Council on the Arts, **5**:535
National Council on the Humanities, **5**:537
National Deaf-Mute College, **3**:504
National Defense Act (1916), **6**:450
National Defense Act (1920), **5**:542; **8**:352

National Defense Advisory Commission (NDAC), **6:**165

National Defense Education Act (1958), **3:**118, 127

National Defense Research Committee (NDRC), **6:**166–167

National domain, **6:**527, *527*

National Economic Council, **3:**330

National Economist (newspaper), **6:**97

National Education Association (NEA), **5:**534–535
American Federation of Teachers and, **1:**155, 156, 157
on homework, **4:**158
on sex education, **7:**321

National Election Studies (NES), **6:**534

National Emblem Act (1940), **3:**100

National Endowment for Democracy, **6:**32

National Endowment for the Arts (NEA), **5:**535
middlebrow culture and, **5:**366

National Endowment for the Humanities (NEH), **5:**536–538
middlebrow culture and, **5:**366

National Energy Plan (1977), **6:**304

National Environmental Policy Act (NEPA) (1969), **3:**228; **8:**423
and Council on Environmental Quality, **3:**330
on noise pollution, **6:**112–113

National Farm Workers' Organizing Committee, **3:**479

National Farmers' Union, **1:**64

National Federation of Business and Professional Women's Clubs, **5:**538

National Federation of Telephone Workers (NFTW), **2:**325

National Firearms Act (1934), **4:**75; **5:**557

National Flag Day Bill, **3:**377

National Football League (NFL), **3:**410–412; **8:**74

National Forest Management Act (1897), **3:**431, 433

National Forest Management Act (1976), **3:**431

National Forest Roadless Area Conservation Act (2002), **3:**431

National Forest System, **3:**431

National forests, land for, **5:**34

National Foundation for Infantile Paralysis. *See* March of Dimes

National Foundation for the Arts and Humanities Act (1965), **5:**536

National Front for the Liberation of South Vietnam (NLF), **3:**417; **8:**330

National Gallery of Art, **5:**538–541

National Gallery of Art Sculpture Garden, **5:**540

National Gardening Association, **3:**510

National Gay Task Force, **3:**514

National Genealogical Society (NGS), **3:**521

National Geographic Magazine, **5:**541, 541–542

National Geographic Society, **3:**540, 541, 542; **5:**541–542
on Bermuda Triangle, **1:**446

National Grange of the Patrons of Husbandry, **1:**63
on textbooks, **8:**106

National Guard, **2:**364, 365; **3:**223; **5:**542–543, *543*
Air Guard of, **5:**542
after Civil War, **2:**534
establishment of, **5:**542
at Kent State protest (1970), **4:**517
legislation on, **5:**387
martial law and, **5:**254
reorganization of, **5:**542–543
role of, **5:**387
in World War I, **8:**540–541
in World War II, **8:**545
See also Militia(s)

National Guard Act (1877), **5:**254

National heroes, **5:**567–569

National Highway Traffic Safety Administration (NHTSA), **1:**377; **3:**335

National Historic Preservation Act (1966), **6:**453

National Historical Publications and Records Commission, **5:**525

National Hockey Association (NHA), **4:**143

National Hockey League (NHL), **4:**143–145

National Hockey League Players Association (NHLPA), **4:**145

National Holiness Association, **6:**287

National Home for Disabled Volunteer Soldiers, **8:**317

National Housing Act (1937), **6:**44

National Imagery and Mapping Agency (NIMA), **2:**92

National Indian Youth Council, **5:**532, 543–544

National Industrial Recovery Act (NIRA) (1933), **5:**8, 555; **6:**43; **8:**278
minimum wage in, **5:**395
and oil shipments, **6:**243
on subsistence homesteads, **7:**566
Supreme Court on, **1:**21; **7:**263–264
and textile industry, **8:**111

National Institute for Allergy and Infectious Diseases (NIAID), **1:**16

National Institute for the Promotion of Science. *See* American Association for the Advancement of Science

National Institute of Standards and Technology (NIST), **5:**529–530

National Institute on Alcohol Abuse and Alcoholism (NIAAA), **1:**118, 119

National Institutes of Health (NIH), **5:**544
and clinical research, **2:**238, 239
establishment of, **5:**544
on genetic research, **1:**462–463
on human gene therapy, **3:**531
mission of, **5:**544
on obesity, **6:**153
research by, **5:**544; **6:**308
and women's health, **8:**511–512

National Intelligencer (newspaper), **6:**96

National Interest (magazine), **6:**32–33

National Investigations Committee on Aerial Phenomena (NICAP), **8:**255

National Labor Reform Party, **5:**546

National Labor Relations Act (NLRA) (Wagner Act) (1935), **1:**35, 483; **5:**5, 7–8, 14–15, 141, **544–546**; **6:**43; **7:**558; **8:**277
and collective bargaining, **2:**274
on picketing, **6:**350
provisions of, **2:**243
and restrictions on property rights, **6:**506

National Labor Relations Act (NLRA) (Wagner Act) (1935), (*continued*)
and right-to-work laws, **2:**275; **7:161**
and trade unions, **2:**325; **8:**171
Triangle Shirtwaist fire and, **8:**209
National Labor Relations Act (1947). *See* Taft-Hartley Act (1947)
National Labor Relations Board, American Ship Building Co. v., **5:**141
National Labor Relations Board (NLRB), **5:**11, 15
American Federation of Labor and, **1:**150–151
establishment of, **2:**274; **5:**544–545; **6:**43; **7:**558; **8:**42, 171
Taft-Hartley Act (1947) and, **8:**42–43
National Labor Relations Board v. Brown, **5:**141
National Labor Relations Board v. Jones and Laughlin Steel Corporation, **2:**311; **5:546; 8:**274
effects of, **4:**493
National Labor Relations Board v. Truck Drivers Local 449, **5:**141
National Labor Union (NLU), **5:**16, **546; 8:**171
National Lawn Tennis Association, U.S. (USNLTA), **8:**89, 90
National Lawyers Guild, **5:546–547**
National League (NL), **7:**509
National Liberation Front. *See* National Front for the Liberation of South Vietnam
National Lutheran Commission for Soldiers' and Sailors' Welfare, **5:**177
National Lutheran Council (NLC), **5:**177
National Marine Sanctuary System, **5:**244
National Monetary Commission, **5:547**
creation of, **1:**120; **3:**344
National monuments, **2:**369, 371
National Museum of the American Indian (NMAI), **5:547–548; 6:**1–2
National Museum of the American Indian (NMAI) Act (1989), **6:**1

National Narcotics Border Interdiction System, **5:**511
National Nonpartisan League. *See* Nonpartisan League, National
National Oceanic and Atmospheric Administration (NOAA)
Coast and Geodetic Survey at, **2:**257
National Marine Sanctuary System, **5:**244
National Weather Service at, **8:**432–433
National Opinion Research Center (NORC), **6:**534
National Organization for Women (NOW), **5:548–549; 8:**507, 510, 516
and abortion laws, **1:**6
establishment of, **5:**548
fundraising by, **5:**549
Legal and Educational Defense Fund of, **5:**549
membership of, **5:**549
as political action group, **5:**548–549
statement of purpose, text of, **9:**481–484
National Outdoors Association, **5:**557
National park(s)
in Alaska, **5:**552–553
land for, **5:**34
promoting, **5:**550–551
in Rocky Mountain region, **7:**191
Sierra Club and, **7:**355
vacationing in
railroads and, **8:**305
after World War II, **8:**305
National Park Service (NPS), **4:**383; **5:**549–553; **6:**452; **8:**146
establishment of, **6:**528
functions of, **4:**384
National park system, **5:549–554,** *553*
birth of, **5:**549–550
challenges of, **5:**553
consolidation of, **5:**550–551
environmental revolution and, **5:**552–553
expansion of, **5:**551–552
See also specific parks
National Parks Conservation Association, **5:**552

National Performance Review, **3:**332–333
National Pike, **7:**176–177
National Police Gazette, The, **5:**196
National Progressives of America, **6:**500
National Prohibition Act (1919), **8:**352
National Public Radio (NPR), **5:554; 7:**21; **8:**44
National Reclamation Act (1902), **6:**328
National Recovery Act (1933), **5:**362
National Recovery Administration (NRA), **1:**490; **5:554–555; 6:**43, 45; **7:**113
establishment of, **8:**162
Supreme Court on, **1:**21
National Republican Party, **5:555–556; 8:**467
National Research Council (NRC), **5:**18, 67, 522, 523
founding of, **2:**14
oceanographic research by, **6:**161
National Research Project, **6:**492
National Restaurant Association, **8:**310
National Retired Teachers Association, **1:**142
National Review (journal), **2:**375; **5:556**
on drug policy, **5:**513
National Rifle Association (NRA), **5:556–557**
Brady Bill and, **1:**530
National Road. *See* Cumberland Road
National Safety Council, **1:**12
National Sandinista Liberation Front (FSLN), **6:**105
National Science Foundation (NSF), **5:557–558**
accelerator construction by, **6:**339
and Internet, **4:**399
National Science Foundation Act (1950), **5:**557
National Security Act (1947), **1:**76
and National Security Council, **3:**330
National security adviser, **2:**3
National Security Agency (NSA), **5:558–559**
criticism of, **3:**185–186

National Security Council (NSC), **3:**27, 330; **5:559–561**
and Central Intelligence Agency, **2:**91
establishment of, **7:**530
evolution of, **5:**560–561
and foreign policy, **3:**28
functions of, **5:**560; **7:**530
members of, **7:**530
personnel of, **5:**560
propaganda by, **6:**503
Tower Commission and, **8:**148
National Security Council Intelligence Directive (NSCID), **5:**558
National Security League, **6:**449
National Severe Storms Forecast Center, **8:**144
National Silver party, **3:**158
National Socialist German Workers' Party (NSDAP), **3:**562
National Society of the Colonial Dames of America (NSCDA), **2:**285
National Synchrotron Light Source, **6:**348
National Tariff Act (1789), **8:**50
National Teacher Training Institute, **8:**62
National Teachers Association (NTA), **5:**534
National Technical Institute for the Deaf, **3:**123
National Television Systems Committee (NTSC), **8:**77
National Textile Workers Union, **3:**512
National Trades' and Workers' Association, **5:**561
National Trades' Union, **5:**561
National Trades' Union Convention, **8:**171
National Traffic and Motor Vehicle Safety Act (1966), **5:561–562; 8:**190, 285
National Transportation Safety Board (NTSB), **8:**241
National Trust for Historic Preservation, **5:562; 6:**452
on Vermont, **8:**314
National Union (Arm-in-Arm) Convention, **3:**155; **5:562–563**
National Union for Social Justice, **5:563**

National Union of Textile Workers, **8:**111
National Urban League, **5:**124, **563–564**
National Vietnam and Gulf War Veterans Coalition, **8:**318
National Voter Registration Act (NVRA) (1993), **8:**354, 357
National War Labor Board (NWLB)
World War I, **5:564; 8:**536
World War II, **5:564–565; 8:**171
National Waterways Commission, **5:565**
National Weather Service. *See* Weather Service, National
National Wildlife Federation, **3:**207
National Woman Suffrage Association (NWSA), **6:**278; **8:**11
National Woman's Party, **5:**65, **565–566; 8:**514
National Women's Political Caucus (NWPC), **5:**566
Nationalism, **5:566–569**
in 20th century, **5:**569
American Revolution and, **7:**146
in archival maps, **9:**3–4
black, **1:477–478**
of Malcolm X, **6:**211
Canadian, **2:**27
Chicano, **9:**484–486
at Constitutional Convention, **2:**379
definition of, **5:**566
holidays and, **5:**568
Irish, **4:**423
Jewish, **8:**592
militias and, **5:**386
national heroes and, **5:**567–568, 569
9/11 attack and, **5:**569; **6:**109
Pledge of Allegiance and, **6:**370
prizefighting and, **6:**483–484
roots of, **5:**566–567
"United We Stand, Divided We Fall," **8:**278–279
Nationalist Party, **6:**545, 546
Nations, Gilbert O., **1:**166
NationsBank, **3:**368
Native American(s), **6:**4
activism by
American Indian Movement, **1:**115–116, **160–161**

Indian Rights Association, **4:302–303**
Red Power, **7:70–71**
African Americans and, **4:**324; **7:**8–9; **8:**249
agriculture of, **1:**61, **68–71; 2:**96, 413
Akimel O'odham, **1:**100
economics of, **4:**267–269
fruit growing, **3:**478
gardening, **3:**509
in Great Plains, **8:**218
Hopi, **4:**165
irrigation in, **4:**307–308, 433–434
in New England, **8:**220
potatoes, **6:**432
on prairie, **8:**224
Pueblo, **6:**540; **8:**227
technology in, **4:**307–308
in Alabama, **1:**101–102
in Alaska, **1:**108, 109, 110, 111, 112; **8:211–214,** *212*
Alcatraz occupied by, **1:**115–116; **8:**215
alcohol and, **1:**116; **4:321–323**
American Indian Movement of (*See* American Indian Movement)
in American Revolution, **2:**360; **4:329–330; 7:**141–142, 146
animal totems of, **8:**496
animals owned by, **8:**318
anthropological studies of, **1:**191–192
archaeological studies of, **1:**239–240; **6:**441
architecture of, **1:254–255**
Ancestral Pueblo (Anasazi), **1:**182–183, *183*
Iroquois, **1:***238*
in Arizona, **1:**100–101, 256–257; **6:**230, 540
in Arkansas, **1:**260
art of, **1:314–316**
Iroquois, **4:***431*
Association on American Indian Affairs and, **1:340**
"Beaver Wars," **5:**207
in Buffalo Bill's Wild West Show, **8:**476
buffalo in culture of, **1:**561
in California, **2:**7, 8, 9, 10, 12; **8:***214*, 214–216
canoes used by, **2:**37
at Centennial Exhibition, **2:**87

Native American(s), (*continued*)
children
adoption of, **4:**263–264
removal of, **4:**262–264
Christianity and, **1:**447, 482; **2:**125, 163
in cities, **1:**160–161
citizenship of, **1:**574; **4:264,** 287, 299; **8:**215
civil rights of, legislation on, **4:**264–265; **7:**247
in Civil War, **1:**501; **2:**126, 158, 492–493; **4:326–327,** 328
Choctaw leader on, **9:**302–303
in Indian Brigade, **4:**263
from Indian Territory, **6:**184
and colonists, relations with, **2:**290–291; **7:**7
colonization of Americas and, **3:**285
in Colorado, **2:**297, 298–299; **4:**314–315; **8:**299, 300
Sand Creek Massacre of, **7:243–244**
in Connecticut, **2:**356–357; **5:**435
constitutional rights of, Supreme Court on, **7:247**
copper used by, **6:**115
creation tales and myths of, **2:**445; **4:**279
crude oil used by, **6:**298, 305
culture of, **3:**394
languages and, **4:**275
National Museum of the American Indian and, **5:**547–548; **6:**1–2
Native American Graves Protection and Repatriation Act (1990) and, **6:**1–3
dance, **2:**_500,_ 500–501, _501_
Ghost Dance, **4:**294; **5:**507
Wovoka's letter on, **9:**259–260
music and, **5:**498
sun dance, **4:**292–293; **8:18–19**
displacement of
from Minnesota, **5:**399
from Mississippi, **5:**412
economic life of, **4:267–269**
after European contact, **4:**267–268
Industrial Revolution and, **4:**268–269
education for, **1:**482; **3:**112, 115, 129, **133–134**

at boarding schools, **2:**55, 145; **3:**135–136; **4:262–263,** 286
encomienda system and, **3:**202, 203
environmental problems and, **8:**571
epidemics decimating, **8:**488
ethnological studies of, **3:**257
in Everglades, **3:**268
factory system (trading houses) for, **1:**158, 281; **4:311**
in Florida, **5:**309; **8:**225
food and cuisine of, **3:**398
food preservation methods of, **3:**405
French explorers and, **2:**103–104; **3:**290–291
in fur trade, **3:**488; **8:**222
factory system and, **1:**158
gambling on lands of, **3:**506–507, 509; **8:**489
in California, **8:**215
Florida Seminoles, **7:**309
Ojibwe, **6:**181
regulation of, **1:**160; **3:**509
Supreme Court on, **3:**509; **8:**223
gender roles of, **3:**519
genocide of, **3:**536
in Georgia, **3:**554
gold mining and, **4:**314–315
Gold Rush and, **4:**14; **8:**214
and gun control, **4:**74
horses of, **4:**167, **324–325;** **8:**222, 224
and social life, **4:**304, 305
uses for, **4:**325
housing of, **4:**179; **8:**475
Inuit, **4:**_408_
Iroquois, **4:**431
in Idaho, **4:**211
in Illinois, **4:**214–215
Indian agents and, **4:261–262**
Indian Claims Commission and, **4:265–266,** 273–274; **5:**532
Indian Country of, **4:266–267**
in Indian Territory, **4:309;** **6:**183–185
in Indiana, **4:**317
intermarriage among (miscegenation), **4:**270; **5:**188, 468
in Iowa, **4:**414
Jackson's *A Century of Dishonor* on, **9:**257–259
in Kansas, **4:**507–508, 509
in Kentucky, **4:**518
kidnapping by, **4:**525
firsthand account of, **9:**101–103

land allotment and, **4:**273, 286–287
land cessions by, **1:**188; **3:**297; **4:270–274,** _273_
and agriculture, **1:**69–70
through allotment, **4:**273, 286–287
compensation for, **8:**275
Congressional violation of, **5:**147–148
Dawes General Allotment Act and, **1:**574; **2:506–507**
doctrine of discovery and, **5:**32
Greenville Treaty and, **4:**64
Indian Claims Commission and, **4:**265–266
under Jackson, **1:**188
under Jefferson, **4:**271, 313–314
Mahican, **5:**203
Nez Perces, **6:**100, 102
process and policy for, **5:**33
and religious freedom, **1:**161–162
through removal, **4:**272
surplus land acts and, **5:**34
and Trail of Tears, **8:**177
treaties on, **4:**270–272; **5:**34, 147–148
land claims by, **4:**273–274
land tenure among, **1:**69
languages of, **4:274–275**
Apachean, **6:**18
classification of, **4:**274–275
and culture, **4:**275
decline of, **4:**275
Hopi, **4:**165–166
Mandan, Hidatsa, and Arikasa, **5:**219
Navajo, **6:18–19**
Ojibwe, **6:181–182**
in oral literature, **4:**279–280
in oratory, **4:281**
sign, **7:357–358**
written, **4:**275
literature of, **2:**484; **4:**179
oral, **4:279–281**
litigation by, **2:**127–128
lobbying for
by American Indian Defense Association, **1:159–160**
by Society of American Indians, **7:430–431**
Louisiana Purchase and, **8:**217, 224
at Louisiana Purchase Exposition, **5:**163, 164
as Loyalists, **5:**167–168

Mackinac Island, **5**:188, *188*
magazines, **5**:192
in maps
  colonial, **9**:14–16
  depiction of, **9**:4, 14–16
  making of, **5**:231–232; **9**:2
  westward expansion and,
    9:47–52, *48*
marriage ceremony among, **8**:435
in matrilineal societies, **4**:290–291
medicine, **5**:292–293
migration and, **5**:371
in military, **4**:327–329
  Navajo Code Talkers, **6**:16,
    17–18, *18*, 19, 69
in Minnesota, **5**:398, 399
missions to (*See* Mission[s], domes-
    tic/Indian)
in Missouri, **5**:419
in Montana, **5**:448
and Mormons, **8**:217, 228
mounds of, **4**:277–279
  Adena, **1**:20
  archaeological studies of, **1**:239,
    246, 247; **4**:277–278
  at Cahokia, **2**:*6*, 6–7; **4**:278;
    8:225
  Hopewell, **4**:163, *163*
  Mississippian, **1**:246; **4**:278
  Poverty Point, **6**:441
mountain men and, **5**:468
museums displays and, **5**:488
music of, **5**:498–499
National Congress of American
    Indians and, **5**:531–532
National Indian Youth Council
    and, **5**:532, **543–544**
in Nebraska, **6**:29–30, 261
in Nevada, **6**:230–231; **8**:216
New Deal for, **1**:571; **4**:288, 297
in New Hampshire, **6**:56, 57
in New Mexico, **6**:65, 67, 68–69,
    69, 230, 540; **8**:47–48
in New Netherland, **6**:71–72, 79
in New York (state), **6**:86–87
in New York Colony, **6**:83
in North Dakota, **6**:131, 132, 134
in Ohio, **4**:278; **6**:171–172,
    177–178
in Ohio Valley, **6**:176–177
in Oklahoma, **6**:183–185, 262, 444;
    7:308–309; **8**:239
oratory among, **4**:281

in Oregon, **6**:203–204, 205, 207,
    231
on Oregon Trail, **6**:209
in Pennsylvania, **6**:276
peyote use by, **1**:162; **3**:374;
    4:292–293; **6**:1, 8; **7**:401
and Plymouth Colony, **6**:378–379
policies on
  Board of Indian Commissioners,
    1:492
  British, **4**:283
  colonial, **4**:281–283
  Dutch, **4**:281–282
  French, **4**:282
  Meriam Report, **5**:323–324
  Modoc War (1872–1873), **5**:433
  reform of, **2**:95
  Spanish, **4**:282–283
  U.S., **4**:284–290
    1775-1830, **4**:284–285
    1830-1900, **3**:271; **4**:285–287
    1900-2000, **4**:287–290; **8**:91–92
political life of, **4**:290–292
  after European contact,
    4:291–292
  in matrilineal societies,
    4:290–291
  sachem in, **7**:220
pottery of, **1**:303
powwows, **5**:498
prehistoric, **1**:241–247
  Mesa Verde cliff dwellings, **5**:*325*,
    325–326
preservation of heritage of, **1**:240
  national park system and, **5**:550
recreation among, **7**:63
relations with, **7**:8–9
  captivity narratives, **2**:50–52, *51*,
    52; **3**:84
religious conversion of
  forced, **6**:101, 541, 542
  by Franciscans, **6**:67; **8**:129, 227
  of Nez Perce, **8**:222
  Praying Towns and, **6**:448
  by Puritans, **6**:48, 448
  in Southwest, **8**:227, 238
religious freedom for, **3**:374; **6**:1
  legislation on, **1**:161–162
religious life of, **2**:544; **4**:292–294;
    7:85
  alcohol in, **4**:322
  boarding schools and, **4**:262–263
  Eliot's *Dialogues* on, **9**:99–100
  Eliot's Indian Bible in, **4**:262

Mohave, **5**:434
  music and, **5**:498
  mysticism and, **5**:507
  Native American Church, **6**:1, 8
  new movements in, **4**:293–294
  peyote use in, **1**:162; **4**:292–293;
    7:401
  restrictions on, **4**:293; **7**:401
  revival movements and, **6**:5–8
  traditional, **4**:292–293
removal of, **2**:125; **4**:295–297, *296*;
    7:9, *102* (*See also* Trail of
    Tears)
  Army in, **1**:280
  courts supporting, **6**:506
  development of policy, **4**:295
  and economic life, **4**:268–269
  effects of, **4**:285–286
  to Indian Territory, **4**:309;
    6:183–184
  Jackson on, **4**:285, 295, 298
  land cessions through, **4**:272
  legislation on, **4**:295–296
  in maps, archival, **9**:47–52
  Natchez Campaign of 1813 and,
    5:518
  in Northwest Territory, **6**:137;
    8:222
  of Prairie Indians, **8**:224
  Removal Act of 1830 and,
    7:101–103
  resistance to, **4**:285
  in South, **8**:226
  Supreme Court on, **4**:285; **6**:183
  and Tecumseh's Crusade, **8**:64
  treaties on, **4**:296
republicanism of, **7**:116
reservations, **1**:492; **4**:297–302
  in 1900, **4**:*299*
  agriculture on, **1**:70
  Arapaho on, **1**:235
  Blackfeet on, **1**:481–482
  in California, **8**:215
  Cheyenne escape from, **3**:94
  Comanche on, **2**:308
  establishment of, **1**:570–571;
    4:298
  Flathead (Montana), **5**:449
  Fort Berthold, **5**:219, 220
  in Great Basin, **8**:217
  as Indian Country, **4**:266
  Iroquois on, **4**:432–433
  Klamath (Oregon), **5**:433
  land cessions for, **4**:272–273

Native American(s), (*continued*)
legislation on, **4:**298–299, 301
Meriam Report on conditions,
1:492; **5:323–324**
Navajo on, **6:**15, 17, *17*, 19
in North Dakota, **6:**132
in Northwest, **8:**222, 223
objectives of creating, **4:**298–299
Onondaga, **6:195–196**
Peace Commission (1867) and,
6:263
policies on, **4:**298–301
population of, **4:**301–302
Proclamation of 1763 and, **6:**490
resistance to, **4:**299
Seminole on, **7:**308, 309
Sioux on, **7:**369–370
in Southwest, **8:**228
treaties on, **4:**272–273
revival movements of, **6:5–8**
Ghost Dance, **3:**573; **6:**7; **8:**562
in Northwest, **8:**223
in Rhode Island, **7:**151
running traditions of, **8:**154
in scouting corps, **4:**328
secret societies of, **7:**295
self-determination for, **4:**289, 301,
303
Sequoyah (proposed state) for,
7:314
sexuality of, **7:**328–329
sign language of, **7:357–358**
slavery and, **4:323–324**
smallpox in, **5:**219–220; **7:**399
social life of, **4:303–306**
in South Carolina, **7:**453, 454
in South Dakota, **7:**458, 459, 461
sovereignty of, **7:**477
Spanish explorers and, **3:**296
speeches
by Little Crow, **9:**243–244
by Logan, **9:**103–104
by Powhatan, **9:**98
by Tecumseh, **9:**199–200
Spirit Lake Massacre by,
7:503–504
sports among, **7:**63, 507
state intervention in life of, **3:**271
structures built by, **1:**563
technology of, **4:306–309**
in Tennessee, **8:**83–84
termination of services to,
4:288–289; **5:**128
legislation on, **4:**300

opposition to, **1:**340; **4:**288–289
origins of, **4:**288, 300
in Texas, **8:**98, 100
and Texas Rangers, **8:**104
theater of, **8:**112
tobacco and, **4:325–326; 8:**133
tomahawks of, **8:**140–141
trade with, **4:309–311; 8:**160
alcohol in, **4:**322–323
after American Revolution,
4:310–311
Charleston (South Carolina) and,
2:108
in colonial era, **4:**267–268, 310,
322–323
economics of, **4:**267–268
in Great Basin, **8:**216
Indian agents in, **4:**261
in New France, **6:**51
in New Hampshire, **6:**57
Panton, Leslie and Company,
6:244
in trading houses (factory system), **1:**158, 281; **4:**311
and trading posts, **8:**174, 176
Virginia Indian Company and,
8:349
wampum in, **8:369–370**
trails of, **4:311–312**
treaties with, **4:312–315;**
8:206–207, 217
in 18th century, **4:**313
in 19th century, **4:**313–315
in 20th century, **4:**315
colonial, **4:**312–313, **315–316**
Congressional violation of,
5:147–148
end of, **4:**315
Fort Laramie (1851), **5:**220
Greenville Treaty, **4:63–64**, 271;
6:172
on Indian Country, **4:**266
Indian Treaty at Prairie du Chien
and, **6:447–448**
Iroquois League, **9:**153–154
on land cessions, **4:**270–273; **5:**34
in Montana, **5:**449
Neah Bay, **5:**213
Ojibwe, **6:**180–181
origins of, **4:**312–313
on removal, **4:**296
on reservations, **4:**272–273
Seminole, **7:**308
Sioux, **4:**315; **7:**368, 369, 370

by Stevens (Isaac), **7:**547–548
Supreme Court on, **4:**314, 315;
5:147–148
Treaty of Fort Laramie, **1:**235;
7:370; **8:**402; **9:**227–229
Treaty of Medicine Lodge, **5:**148
tribal courts of, **4:**265, **316–317**
tribal governments of, constitutional rights and, **4:**264–265
tribal membership for, **4:**264;
7:247
and Underground Railroad, **8:**249
in Utah, **6:**230; **8:**217, 296, 299
in Vermont, **8:**311
in Virginia, **6:**442; **8:**341, 349
in War of 1812, **4:**272; **8:**382,
399–400
warfare of, **8:390–394**
with colonists, **8:**391–393
indigenous, **8:**390–391
motivations for, **8:**390–391
weapons in, **8:**391–392
wars with, **8:395–405** (*See also*
Frontier defense)
in 16th century, **8:**395
in 17th century, **8:**395–397
in 18th century, **8:**397–399
in 19th century, **8:**399–405, *400,
403*
Apache Wars, **1:220–221**
atrocities in, **1:**353–354; **8:**337
Battle of Fallen Timbers,
3:310–311; 4:63
Battle of Little Bighorn, **1:**354;
8:404
eyewitness account of,
9:253–255
Sioux in, **7:**370–371
Battle of Tippecanoe, **8:**131
Black Hawk War, **1:473–474;**
8:300
Black Hills War, **1:**474–475
Chickasaw-Creek War,
2:135–136
in colonial era, **8:**395–399, *397*
Dull Knife Campaign, **8:**404
Dunmore's War, **3:**95
Fox War, **3:447–448**
French and Indian War (*See*
French and Indian War)
horse cavalry in, **2:**78
in Kansas, **4:**509
King Philip's War, **4:526–527**
King William's War, **4:527–528**

Logan's speech on, **9:**103–104
in Maine, **5:**207–208
Massacres in, **8:**337
Modoc War, **5:**433; **8:**404
Mountain Meadow Massacre,
   5:467–468
Natchez Campaign of 1813, **5:518**
Navajo War, **6:**16, 19; **8:**404
Ohio Wars, **6:177–178; 8:**399
Patriot War, **7:**8
Pequot War, **6:289**, 379
Pontiac's War (*See* Pontiac's War)
Pueblo Revolt, **6:**67, **542; 8:**47
Red River Indian War, **7:72**
Red River War, **8:**404
scalping in, **7:260–261**
Seminole Wars, **3:**385, 386;
   7:309–310, 484; **8:**226,
   401–402
Sioux Wars, **7:370–371; 8:**403
tactics in, **8:**390–394
Tecumseh's Crusade, **8:64**
Yakima Indian Wars, **8:**402–403,
   571–572
in Washington (state), **8:**415, 571
water supply for, **1:**100; **8:**415
whaling by, **8:**465, *465*
in Wisconsin, **8:**488, 489
women
  farming by, **1:**68–69
  in matrilineal societies,
    4:290–291
  in World War I, **4:**328
  in World War II, **4:**328–329
  in Wyoming, **8:**563, 564, 566
YMCA and, **8:**584
See also Paleoindians; Tribes; *specific*
   tribes
Native American Church, **6:1**, 8
ceremonial protocol in, **4:**292
Comanche and, **2:**308
Ghost Dance and, **5:**507
Native American Graves Protection
  and Repatriation Act (NAG-
  PRA) (1990), **6:1–3**
Native American Party, **1:**168
Native American Rights Fund, **6:3**
Native American studies, **6:3–4**
ethnohistory in, **3:257**
Native Son (Wright), **5:**121, 125; **6:**12
Nativism, **6:4–5; 7:**16
of American Republican Party, **1:**168
and immigration restriction,
   4:232–233

of Know-Nothing Party, **1:**166;
   4:540
Maria Monk controversy, **5:238**
and political violence, **1:**331–332
and Republican Party, **7:**111
Nativist movements (American Indian revival movements), **6:5–8**
Ghost Dance, **3:573; 6:**7; **8:**562
in Northwest, **8:**223
NATO. *See* North Atlantic Treaty
  Organization
Natural gas, **3:**212
as alternative fuel, **3:**480
discovery of, **6:**8
future of, **3:**213
in petrochemical industry, **6:**298
in tidelands, **8:**124
transportation of, **6:**9
Natural Gas Act (1938), **6:**9
Natural gas industry, **6:8–10**
development of, **6:**8–9
growth of, **6:**9
regulation of, **6:**9
Natural history
mammalogy, **5:217–218**
marine biology, **5:240–241**
museums of, **5:**487–488; **8:**597
Natural language processing, **1:**318
Natural rights, **6:10–11**
Paine (Thomas) on, **7:**162
Natural selection, **3:**269
Naturalism, **6:11–13**
in literature, **5:**118–120
in sculpture, **1:**306
Naturalization, **3:**281; **6:13–14**
McCarran-Walter Act (1952),
   5:181
requirements for
  in 18th century, **1:**123
  American Republican Party on,
    1:168
Naturalization Act (1790), **6:**396
Naturalization Act (1798), **1:**123
Naturalization Act (1870), **6:**14
Nature (Emerson), **5:**119; **7:**194;
   8:180
Nature Conservancy, **2:**372; **3:**206
Nature of Geography, The
  (Hartshorne), **3:**543
Nauman, Bruce, **1:**307
Nautilus (submarine), **6:**14, 382
Nauvoo, Mormons at, **5:**53; **6:14–15**
Mormon Trail, **5:**459
Mormon War, **5:**459–460

Navajo, **6:15–17**, *16;* **8:**228
in Arizona, **1:**257
art of, **1:**315, *315*
campaigns against, **2:**537
code talkers, **6:**16, **17–18**, *18*, 19, 69
Fort Defiance and, **2:**537
language of, **6:18–19**
in New Mexico, **6:**65, 69
on reservations, **8:**228
seminomadic lifestyle of, **8:**227
as slaves, **6:**15
Spain and, **6:**15
in World War II, **2:**468
Navajo Community College (Diné
  College), **8:**210
Navajo Nation, **6:**15, 17, *17*
Navajo War, **6:**16, 19, 69; **8:**404
Naval Academy, **6:**19
during Civil War, **7:**153
establishment of, **2:**530
Naval Appropriation Bill (1851),
   3:383
Naval Appropriations Act (1916),
   6:450
Naval blockades, **1:487**
Naval oil reserves, **6:19–20; 8:**63
Naval operations, chief of (CNO),
   6:20
Naval stores, **1:**523; **6:20–21**
Navasky, Victor, **5:**522
Navassa Island, **1:**189
Navigation
projects aimed at improving,
   7:168–171
See also River(s), navigation on
Navigation Act(s), **4:**25; **6:21–23**
of 1660, **6:**21
of 1817, **6:**21
and colonial commerce, **2:**282
mercantilism, **5:315–316**
and piracy, **6:**360
and smuggling, **6:**22, 360;
   7:405–406
Navy, Confederate, **6:23**, 25
Alabama in, **1:105–106**
armored ships in, **1:**265
ironclad warships in, **4:**430–431
rams used by, **7:47**
Navy, Department of, **6:23–24**
and naval oil reserves, **6:**19
Navy, Royal
impressment of seamen by,
   4:248–249
in War of 1812, **8:**384

Navy, Union, **2:**214; **6:**25
  armored ships in, **1:**265
  ironclad warships in, **4:**430–431
  naval mortars, **5:460**
  in Vicksburg, **8:**324
Navy, U.S., **6:24–27**
  aircraft carriers of, **1:89–92**
  in American Revolution, **6:**24
  armored ships of, **1:265–266**
  arms control in, **1:**269–270
  Battle Fleet Cruise Around the
      World, **1:428–429**, *429*
  Civil War and, **6:**25
  in Cold War, **6:**26–27
  dirigibles in, **3:**30
  early history of, **2:**530
  ensigns in, **3:223**
  gunboats, **4:77**
  in imperialism, **4:**243–244
  under Jefferson, **1:**269
  Liberty incident, **5:**95–96
  liquor ration for, **3:**59
  medicine in, **5:**296
  Merrimac, sinking of, **5:325**
  in Mexican-American War, **6:**25
  and national defense, **2:**531
  and Naval Academy, **6:**19
  oceanographic research by,
      6:159–161, *162*
  ordnance of, **6:**202–203, *203*
  in Persian Gulf War, **6:**27
  pilot charts, **5:**331
  Princeton, explosion on, **6:464–465**
  Pueblo incident, **6:541**
  in Quasi-War with France,
      6:24–25
  recruitment for, **2:**364
  under Roosevelt (Theodore), **1:**270
  sexual harassment in, Tailhook
      incident, **7:**323; **8:43–44**
  in Spanish-American War, **6:**23,
      25; **7:487–488**
  Special Forces of, **7:**494–495
  submarines of, **7:**562–563
  Thresher disaster in, **8:122–123**
  underwater demolition teams
      (UDTs) of, **8:251**
  uniforms in, **8:**257
  vessels, types of, **5:**480
  warships of, **8:405–409**
  in World War I, **6:**24, 25–26;
      8:540
    and North Sea mine barrage,
        6:134

  in World War II, **6:**24, 26;
      8:555–558
    Battle of Atlantic, **1:**352
    Battle of Java Sea, **4:**465–466
    Battle of Leyte Gulf, **6:**26; **8:**557
    Battle of the Philippine Sea,
        6:320–321; 8:557
    capturing Gilbert Islands, **3:**576;
        6:26
    capturing Marshall Islands,
        3:576; **6:**26
    Guadalcanal Campaign, **4:**68;
        6:26; **8:**556
    gunboats, **4:**77
    Pearl Harbor, **6:**272, 272–273;
        8:543–545, 555–556
    Task Force 58, **8:**53
Navy and Marine Corps Medal,
    2:527
Navy Cross, **2:**526
Navy Nurse Corps, **6:**147
NAWSA. *See* National American
    Woman Suffrage Association
Naylor, Gloria, *The Women of Brew-
    ster Place*, **5:**126
Nazarene, Church of the, **6:27**
Nazi Party, **8:**543
Nazis, American
  ACLU on, **1:**147
  German-American Bund and,
      3:560
  See also Fascism, American
NBC. *See* National Baptist Conven-
    tion
NBC television network, **8:**72
  cartoons on, **2:**64
  early commercial broadcasting by,
      8:77
  foundation of, **8:**66
  news programs on, **8:**73
  Today on, **8:**138
  Tonight Show on, **8:**142
  westerns on, **8:**73
NBCA. *See* National Baptist Con-
    vention of America
NCAA. *See* National Collegiate Ath-
    letic Association
NCADD. *See* National Council on
    Alcoholism and Drug Depen-
    dence
NCF. *See* National Civic Federation
NCJW. *See* National Council of
    Jewish Women

NCL. *See* National Consumers'
    League
NCLR. *See* National Council of La
    Raza
NDAC. *See* National Defense Advi-
    sory Commission
NDRC. *See* National Defense
    Research Committee
NEA. *See* National Education Asso-
    ciation; National Endowment
    for the Arts; Newspaper Enter-
    prise Association
Neagle, David, **4:**250
Neah Bay, Treaty of (1855), **5:**213
Near East Relief, **8:**542
Near v. Minnesota, **6:**27
NEAS. *See* New England Antislav-
    ery Society
Nebbia v. New York, **6:28**
Nebraska, **6:**28, *28*–31
  African Americans in, **6:**31
  agriculture in, **6:**30, 31
  in Civil War, **6:**30
  in colonial era, **6:**29
  constitution of, **6:**30
  emblems, nicknames, mottos, and
      songs of, **7:***533*
  explorations in, **6:**29
  Great Depression in, **6:**30
  irrigation in, **6:**30
  Kansas-Nebraska Act and,
      4:512–513; **6:**30
  Native Americans in, **6:**29–30, 261
  prehistoric, **6:**28–29
  slavery in, **4:**512–513
Necessary and proper clause,
    Supreme Court on, **4:**247–248
Necessity, Fort, **3:**469
Necotowance, **6:**443
Neddermeyer, Seth H., **6:**344
Needham, John, **8:**85
"Needless War" doctrine, **4:**20, 21
Neel, Alice, **1:**298
Ne'eman, Yuval, **6:**338
Negative income tax (NIT), **6:31**
Negative liberty, **5:**94
Negro American Labor Council
    (NALC), **8:**172
"Negro Family, The: The Case for
    National Action" (Moynihan),
    6:440
Negro World (newspaper), **6:**98
NEH. *See* National Endowment for
    the Humanities

Nehru, Jawaharlal, **4**:259

Neighborhood Youth Corps, **8**:293, 386

Neighborhoods, preservation of, **8**:287

Neighbors, and property law, **6**:506

Neiman-Marcus, **3**:8–9

Neisser, Ulric, **6**:525

Nelson, Gaylord A., **3**:100, 228
  hearings on pill safety, **1**:468
  and Teachers Corps, **8**:61

Nelson, George, **3**:499

Nelson, Lemrick, **2**:466

Nelson, Ted, **7**:280

Nelson, William, **7**:156

Nelson, Willie, **1**:441, *441*

Nemours, Pierre Samuel du Pont de, **3**:108

Neoclassical furniture, **3**:496–497

Neoconservatism, **6**:31–33
  National Review and, **5**:556

Neo-fascist communities, **8**:303

Neolin (prophet), **6**:7, 411

Neo-Lutherans, **5**:176

Neon, **6**:341

NEPA. *See* National Environmental Policy Act

NEPTEC. *See* Nez Perce Tribal Executive Committee

Nerve gas, **2**:118

NES. *See* National Election Studies

Nesters. *See* Homesteaders

Nestlé
  boycott of, **1**:529
  and wine industry, **8**:487

Netanyahu, Benjamin, **4**:442, 444

Netherlands
  birth control in, **1**:467
  colonial settlements of, **4**:281–282
  in European Common Market, **8**:157
  explorations of, **4**:281; **6**:71
  foreign investment from, **3**:419, 420, 422
  fur trade of, **3**:488–489
  immigration from, **4**:221–222; **7**:262
  Native Americans and
    Iroquois, **4**:281, 432
    policies on, **4**:281–282
    treaties between, **4**:312
  in slave trade, **7**:384
  trading posts of, **8**:175
  See also Dutch

Netscape Communications, **2**:337

Networks, media. *See* Radio; Television

Neuerburg, Norman, **3**:565

Neuharth, Allen, **6**:99–100

Neumann, John von, **3**:109, 110

Neurath, Otto, **3**:204

Neurology, **5**:313–314

Neustadt, Richard, **6**:453, 454

Neutra, Richard, **1**:252

Neutral rights, **6**:33–34
  Plan of 1776 and, **6**:361

Neutrality, **6**:34–37
  international law and, **4**:393–394

Neutrality Act (1935), **5**:170

Neutrality Act (1936), **5**:170

Neutrality Act (1937), **5**:170

Neutrality Proclamation, **6**:491

Neutrino, **6**:339, 341

Neutrons, **6**:338, 340–341

Nevada, **6**:37–39
  in Civil War, **6**:37–38
  Comstock Lode in, **1**:497; **2**:9, 338; **3**:300
  earthquakes in, **3**:101
  emblems, nicknames, mottos, and songs of, **7**:*533*
  explorations in, **3**:468; **6**:37
  gambling in, **6**:38–39
  gold mining in, **4**:11
  Great Depression in, **6**:38
  military bases in, **6**:39
  mining towns in, **8**:347
  Native Americans in, **6**:230–231; **8**:216
  nuclear testing in, **6**:38
  prehistoric, **6**:37
  prostitution in, **6**:513
  public domain in, **6**:529
  reclamation projects in, **7**:55
  silver industry in, **6**:37, 38
  tourism in, **6**:38
  in World War II, **6**:38
  Yucca Mountain, **3**:209

Nevada (battleship), **6**:273

Nevada, Crandall v., **6**:297

Nevada Test Site, radiation from, **3**:209; **8**:298

Nevelson, Louise, **1**:307, 309

Neville, John, **8**:469

Nevin, Blanche, **1**:308

Nevin, John W., **7**:76, 97; **8**:264

New, Wilson v., **1**:19

New Age movement, **6**:39; **8**:303
  alternative medicine, **5**:292

primal therapy, **6**:462–463

New Albion colony, **6**:39–40

New American Atlas (Tanner), **5**:233

New American Poverty, The (Harrington), excerpt from, **9**:500–504

New Amsterdam, **3**:289; **6**:40, 40–41, 79, 87
  burghers in, **1**:573
  founding of, **2**:289
  Jews in, **4**:476
  and Long Island, **5**:149
  recaptured by Dutch, **6**:82
  Stuyvesant and, **6**:40, 72

New Bahama Channel, **3**:388

New Castle, **6**:41

New Christian Right, **2**:376

New Classicism, in economics, **3**:110

New Criterion (magazine), **6**:32

New Criticism, **5**:122

New Deal, **4**:47–48; **6**:41–46
  in action, **6**:42–43
  administrative agencies created under, **1**:21; **6**:43–45 (*See also specific agencies*)
  on agriculture, **1**:66–67, 71; **7**:474
  American Federation of Labor and, **1**:150–151
  American Studies and, **1**:169
  and antitrust legislation, **8**:235
  Blue Eagle emblem in, **1**:490
  Brain Trust of, **1**:532
  Brookings Institution on, **8**:117
  and child care, **2**:138–139
  and Civilian Conservation Corps, **2**:220
  and collective bargaining, **2**:274
  and commerce clause, **2**:311
  Communist Party on, **2**:326
  conservationism during, **2**:371
  conservatism in response to, **2**:374, 375
  and domestic trade, **8**:162
  and Federal Deposit Insurance Corporation, creation of, **1**:402, 407
  final phase of, **6**:44–45
  General Accounting Office during, **3**:523
  and government jobs, **1**:572
  and government regulations, **3**:13
  and greenbelt communities, **4**:63
  Home Owners' Loan Corporation in, **4**:151–152

New Deal, (*continued*)
  Indian, **1:**571; **4:**288, 297
  industrial relations in, **4:**337
  inflation and, **4:**352
  Keynes and, **6:**44
  and labor movement, **5:**7–8
  and labor violence, **8:**339
  Labor's Non-Partisan League and, **5:**17
  and liberalism, **5:**92
  in Maine, **5:**210
  malaria aid, **5:***214*
  in Maryland, **5:**258
  in Michigan, **5:**356
  and minorities, **3:**50
  in Montana, **5:**450
  murals and, **5:**483
  and national parks, **5:**552
  National Union for Social Justice challenging, **5:**563
  The New Republic on, **6:**76
  opposition to, by American Liberty League, **1:**163–164
  origin and design of, **6:**41–42
  political cartoon on, **6:***43*
  political machines and, **5:**187
  and Postal Service, U.S., **6:**427–428
  in presidential campaigns, **3:**162, 163
  Progressive Party supporting, **6:**499
  public works programs of, **8:**441
  realignment of, **6:**43–44
  and Resettlement Administration, **7:**120
  resistance to, **6:**43
  Second, **6:**43
  social legislation in, **7:**415–416
  Supreme Court on, **8:**24
    definition of business affected with public interest, **6:**28
    Federal Trade Commission, **3:**348
    interpretive shift in, **4:**493, 496
    judicial review and, **4:**492–493
    National Industrial Recovery Act, **1:**21; **7:**263–264
    National Recovery Administration, **3:**348
  and tariffs, **8:**156
  and Tennessee Valley Authority, **8:**83, 88
  Third, **6:**45
  trade unions in, **4:**391–392
  United States v. Butler and, **8:**273
  and welfare system, **8:**440–441
  and Works Progress Administration, **6:**43; **8:530–531**
  See also specific laws
New Deal Liberty League, **2:**375
New Deal Revenue Act (1938), **6:**44
New Directions, **3:**418
New Divinity, **7:**96
New England, **6:46–47**
  American Revolution in, **7:**142
  cod fisheries in, **2:**261
  in domestic trade, **8:**160
  Dominion of, **2:**110
  earthquakes in, **3:**101
  Federalist Party in, **3:**351
  floods in, **3:**383
  Hartford Convention and, **4:**101
  immigration to, **4:**220–221
  isolation of, **6:**46
  liberal Christianity in, **5:**431
  local government in, **5:**137–139
  lumber industry in, **5:**171–172
  mackerel fisheries in, **5:**187–188
  newspapers published in, **6:**95
  prisons in, **6:**476
  schools in, **3:**111, 112
  secessionist movement in, **3:**256
  selectmen in, **7:304**
  in slave trade, **8:**209
  and tariffs, **3:**460
  textile industry in, **8:**109
  town government in, **8:**148–149
  transcendentalism in, **8:**179
  See also New England colonies; *specific states*
New England Antislavery Society (NEAS), **6:**47
New England colonies, **2:**285, 287–289; **6:47–48**, *48*
  agriculture in, **1:**62
  Aix-la-Chapelle Treaty and, **1:**99
  architecture in, **1:**248, 249
  assemblies in, **2:**280
  city planning in, **2:**184
  direct royal power in, **3:**77
  divine providences in, **3:**63
  education in, **6:**49–50
  families in, **3:**311–312
  in foreign trade, **8:**164
  Great Migration to, **4:**55–56
  Ipswich Protest in, **4:**417
  King Philip's War in, **4:526–527**
  maps of, archival, **9:***14*, 14–17, *15, 16, 17*
  marriage in, **3:**63
  philanthropy in, **6:**316
  plans of union in, **6:**362–363
  primogeniture in, **6:**464
  Puritans in, **6:**46, 47, 555, 556
  religion in, **7:**83, 84, 93
  religious liberty offered by, **8:**139
  rum trade in, **7:**204
  settlement and migration patterns, **8:**459
  slavery in, **5:**515
  sumptuary laws in, **8:**17
  theocracy in, **6:**50, 60; **8:116**
  toll bridges in, **8:**139
  witchcraft in, **7:**83; **8:**494–495
  See also specific colonies
New England Company, **3:**80; **6:**48
New England Confederation, **6:48–49**, 379
New England Courant (newspaper), **6:**95
New England Emigrant Aid Company, **6:**49
New England Glass Company, **4:**3
New England Primer (textbook), **3:**112; **5:**127; **6:49–50**, *50*; **8:**106
New England school of composers, **5:**492
New England Theology, **7:**96
New England Way, **6:50**; **8:**116
New Era, **6:50–51**
New France, **2:**329; **3:**471, 472; **5:**21; **6:51–54**, *52, 53*
  early settlement of, **6:**51
  population of, **6:**51–54
  trade in, **6:**51–53
    with Native Americans, **6:**51
    with New Mexico, **6:**67–68
New Freedom, **6:54–55**, 70, 495
New Frontier, **6:55**
New Hampshire, **6:55–59**, *56*
  African Americans in, **6:**58
  agriculture in, **6:**58–59
  in American Revolution, **6:**57–58
  child labor regulation in, **6:**58
  in Civil War, **6:**58
  in colonial era, **6:**56–57
  constitution of, **6:**58
  emblems, nicknames, mottos, and songs of, **7:***533*
  founding of, **2:**289

Green Mountain Boys in, **4**:61; **8**:311

in land disputes, **8**:311

lottery in, **5**:157

and Massachusetts, boundary dispute between, **1**:521–522

Native Americans in, **6**:56, 57

prehistoric, **6**:56

as proprietary colony, **6**:*510*, 511, 512

provincial congresses in, **6**:520

railroads in, **6**:58

ski resorts in, **7**:122

slavery in, **6**:57, 58

textile industry in, **6**:58

tourism in, **6**:59

New Hampshire, Peirce v., **5**:103

New Hampshire, Sweezy v., **1**:10, 143

New Harmony Community (Indiana), **3**:107, 113; **8**:300

New Haven (Connecticut)

city plan for, **2**:184

founding of, **2**:289

New Haven Colony, **6**:*59*, **59–60**

basis of government of, **1**:449

Blue Laws in, **1**:490

theocracy in, **6**:60; **8**:116

New International Economic Order, call for, **8**:271

New Jersey, **6**:**60–65**, *61*

in 20th century, **6**:63–64

African Americans in, **6**:63

agriculture in, **6**:61

air pollution in, **6**:64

airports in, **1**:98

in American Revolution, **6**:62

Battle of Monmouth, **5**:**443**

in colonial era, **6**:60–62

in foreign trade, **8**:164

freedom of religion in, **8**:139

constitution of, **6**:63

East Jersey incorporated in, **3**:103

emblems, nicknames, mottos, and songs of, **7**:*533*

Federalist Party in, **3**:351

first settlers in, **2**:289; **3**:188

gun control in, **4**:75

immigrants in, **6**:60, 62–64

industrialization in, **6**:62–63

in Middle Colonies, **5**:362

population density in, **6**:60

porcelain industry in, **6**:418

as proprietary colony, **6**:*510*, 511

provincial congresses in, **6**:520

redevelopment of, **6**:64

as royal colony, **6**:*510*

silk production in, **7**:361–362

suburbanization in, **6**:63

urbanization in, **6**:63

women's voting rights in, **3**:145; **7**:105

New Jersey Plan, in Constitutional Convention, **2**:380

New Jewel Movement, **4**:65

New Left, **7**:18; **8**:587

food protest by, **3**:402

See also Students for a Democratic Society

New Lights, **6**:**65**, 515

and Princeton University, **6**:465

New Mexico, **6**:**65–70**, *66*

Barreiro on, **9**:201–203

cession by Mexico of, **2**:550

in Civil War, **6**:69

Cold War and, **6**:69

in colonial era, **6**:66–67

emblems, nicknames, mottos, and songs of, **7**:*533*

encomienda system in, **3**:203

explorations of, **6**:65–66

Farmers' Alliance in, **3**:323

Hispanic Americans in, **6**:68, 69

under Mexican rule, **6**:68

Mexican-American War and, **6**:68–69

Native Americans in, **6**:65, 67, 68–69, 69, 230, 540; **8**:47–48

reconquest of, **6**:67

Spanish colonial administration in, **2**:279

Spanish explorations in, **3**:296

Spanish language in, **7**:491

statehood of, **6**:69–70

and Texas, **6**:68, 69

tourism in, **6**:69

trade of, **6**:67–68

as U.S. territory, **6**:68–69

Utopian communities in, **8**:303

White Caps in, **8**:470

in World War II, **6**:69

New Nationalism, **1**:566; **6**:54, **70–71**, 495

New Negro: An Interpretation, The (Locke), **5**:125

New Netherland, **2**:289; **6**:40, 71, **71–72**, 82, 87; **7**:200

architecture in, **1**:248

British conquest of, **3**:93

Native Americans in, **6**:71–72, 79

Nicolls' Commission and, **6**:106–107

origins of, **3**:96–97

Petition and Remonstrance of, **6**:**296–297**

slavery in, **6**:72

southern extension of, **2**:541

trade in, **6**:71, 72

New Netherland Company, **6**:71

New Orange, **6**:82

New Orleans (Louisiana), **6**:*73*, **73–75**, *74*

African Americans in, **6**:74

during American Revolution, **6**:73

architecture in, **6**:73

capture of, **6**:73, **75–76**

naval mortars and, **5**:460

cholera epidemics in, **2**:159

during Civil War, **6**:73–74, 75–76

Butler's Order No. 28, **1**:590

French colonial settlement in, **6**:53, 73

furniture manufacturing in, **3**:497

Houma and, **4**:177

immigrants in, **6**:73, 74

jazz in, **4**:467–468

and Louisiana Purchase, **5**:162

Lower Garden District in, **8**:288

Mafia incident, **5**:191

mint at, **5**:403

revolt against Spanish rule, **5**:159

riots in, **5**:160; **6**:76

slavery in, **6**:73

Spanish colonial settlement in, **6**:73

street railway service in, **7**:43

as terminal for flatboat commerce, **3**:382

tourism in, **6**:74

Vieux Carré in, **6**:73, *73*, 74; **8**:336

World's Industrial and Cotton Centennial Exposition in, **8**:558

yellow fever epidemics in, **8**:576

See also Lake Pontchartrain

New Orleans (steamboat), **3**:483; **6**:75, **7**:172

New Orleans, Battle of, **1**:382; **5**:159; **6**:25, 73, **75**, *75*

maps of, **8**:*385*

archival, **9**:42, *43*, *44*

New Panama Canal Company, **6:**237, 238

New Progressive Party (PNP), **6:**547

New Republic, The (magazine), **6:**33, **76–77,** 90, 326

New Right, The: We're Ready to Lead (Viguerie), excerpt from, **9:**495–499

New Smyrna Colony, **6:77**

New South. *See* South, New

New Sweden Colony, **2:**541; **6:77–78,** 276

New Theology, **8:**263

New York (state), **6:86–89,** *87, 88*

in 19th century, **6:**88

in 20th century, **6:**88–89

abolitionism in, **6:**88

airports in, **1:**98

Amana Community in, **1:**133

American Labor Party in, **1:**162

in American Revolution, **6:**87

animal protection laws in, **1:**186

Anti-Rent War in, **1:206**

anti-Semitism in, **1:**206

Apalachin Conference in, **1:222**

Attica State Prison in, **1:355–356**

canal system of, **2:**31–32; **3:**251–253

in Civil War, **6:**88

claims to western lands, **8:**455

climate of, **6:**86

in colonial era (*See* New Netherland; New York Colony)

and Connecticut, boundary dispute between, **1:**521; **2:**355–356

constitution of, **7:**525, 526

dairy industry in, **2:**489

Democratic Party in, Hunkers in, **4:195**

emblems, nicknames, mottos, and songs of, **7:***533*

Federalist Party in, **3:**351

geography of, **6:**86

geological survey of, **3:**548

Great Depression in, **6:**88

gun control in, **4:**75

higher education in, at State University of New York, **7:535–536**

Hudson River in, **4:**187–188

industrialization in, **6:**88

infrastructure in, **4:**355

Irish Americans in, **4:**424

in land disputes, **8:**311

life insurance in, **4:**370

location of, **6:**86

Long Island, **5:**149–150

maps of, archival, land holdings in, **9:**37, *39*

Mohawk Valley, **5:**435

Native Americans in, **6:**86–87

Oneida Colony in, **6:194–195**

Onondaga reservation in, **6:195–196**

polio epidemic in, **6:**388

Polish Americans in, **6:**392

prehistoric, **6:**86–87

prisons in, **6:**476

as proprietary colony, **6:***510*, 511, 512

provincial congresses in, **6:**520

ratification of Constitution in, **2:**382

as royal colony, **6:***510*, 512

Saratoga Springs in, **7:251–252**

Sing Sing in, **7:365–366**

Son-of-Sam Law in, **7:448–449**

strikes in, **7:**556

toll roads in, **8:**140

tourism in, **6:**89

town government in, **8:**148, 149

women's rights movement in, **6:**88

New York, Gitlow v., **1:**453; **2:**84; **3:**373–374

New York, Graves v., **2:**276

New York, Lochner v., **1:**21, 580; **3:**90, 308; **5:**14

judicial review in, **4:**492

liberty of contract in, **5:**394, 395, 473

New York, Nebbia v., **6:**28

New York and Boston Illinois Land Company, **5:**36

New York Athletic Club (NYAC), **8:**154

New York Children's Aid Society, **1:**27

New York City, **6:78–81,** *78–81*

in 19th century, **6:**79–80

in 20th century, **6:**80–81

African Americans in, **4:**94

air pollution in, **1:***79*

Algonquin Round Table in, **1:**123

American Museum (of P. T. Barnum), **5:**487

American Museum of Natural History in, **1:**165

in American Revolution, **6:**79; **7:**137, 141, 143, *143*

amusement parks in, **1:***179*

anti-Catholicism in, **1:**196

apartments in, **1:**222–223; **4:***181*

architecture of, **1:**252; **6:**80

Armory Show in (1913), **1:268–269**

Astor Place riot, **1:341–342**

blizzards in, **1:**486, *487;* **3:**42

botanical gardens in, **1:**517

Bowery in, **1:525**

bridges in, **1:**539

Broadway in, **1:***543,* 543–544; **8:**115

Brooklyn in, **1:***546,* 546–547

capture of, by Dutch, **6:**82

Central Park in, **2:***94,* 94–95; **6:**453

Menagerie in, **8:**594

cholera epidemics in, **2:**159, *160*

city plan for, **2:**185

in Civil War, **6:**80, 82, 84

plot to burn, **6:**82

colonial charter of, **2:**111

in colonial era, **8:**289

Committee of Inspection in, **2:313**

Cooper Union for the Advancement of Science And Art, **2:***405,* 405–406

crime in, **2:***459*

Crown Heights riots, **2:466–467**

Crystal Palace Exhibition in, **2:**468; **8:**558

elevator demonstration at, **3:**186

development of, **9:**70–77

Dongan charter and, **3:**79

draft riots in, **3:**84; **7:**164, 166; **8:**338

embargo on British imports in, **6:**116

Empire State Building in, **3:199,** *199*

Empowerment Zone program in, **8:**287

Erie Canal and, **6:**79, 88; **8:**160

ferry system in, **3:**354

fires in, **3:**37

Frick Collection in, **3:473–474**

furniture manufacturing in, **3:**496, 497, 498

gays and lesbians in, **7:**325, 326

Grand Central Terminal in, **4:33–34,** *34;* **6:**453

Greenwich Village in, **4:64–65**, *65;* **8:**115

Guggenheim Museum in, **4:71–72**, *72*

Harlem neighborhood, **4:94**

Harlem Renaissance in, **4:**94, **95–97**

housing in, **6:**80; **8:**81–82

immigrants in, **6:**79, 80, 81, 88

infrastructure in, **4:**355

Korean Americans in, **4:**544, *544*

land speculation in, **5:**37

Long Island and, **5:**149–150

Lower East Side of, **5:165–167**

Macy's, **5:189–190**, *190*

Madison Square Garden, **5:***190*, **190–191**

Manhattan, **5:220–221**

maps of, archival, **9:**70, **70–77**, *71, 72, 74, 75, 76*

maritime influence on, **9:**71, 73

Metropolitan Museum of Art, **5:335–338**

Modern Art, Museum of (MoMA), **5:484**

paving streets in, **6:**260

Pearl Street Station in, **3:**178

Pennsylvania Station in, **6:**452–453

police forces of, **6:**385

polio epidemic in, **6:**388

as publishing capital, **6:**536–537

Puerto Ricans in, **6:**542; **8:**291

race riot in, pre-Revolution, **7:**166

religious life in, **9:**72, 73

riot of 1871, **7:**164

sanitation in, **7:**245

skyscrapers in, **6:**80–81; **7:**376–377

  Chrysler Building, **7:***376*

slave insurrections in, **7:**379

slavery in, **6:**79, 85–86

Stamp Act Riot in, **7:519**

Statue of Liberty in, **7:540**, *540*

strikes in, **7:**559

  by teachers (1968), **4:**475

symphony orchestras in, **8:**38

Tammany Hall in, **6:**79; **8:45–47**, *46*

Tammany Society museum, **5:**486

Times Square in, **8:**128, *128*

Tin Pan Alley in, **5:**502; **8:**129, *129*

trade unions in

  for public sector employees, **1:**154

  for teachers, **1:**156–157

Triangle Shirtwaist fire in, **1:**12

tunnel system of, **8:**240

Tweed political machine, **5:**186–187

urban renewal program in, **8:**286

Verrazano-Narrows Bridge in, **1:**539; **8:315**

Wall Street Explosion in (1920), **8:366**

water system of, **8:**292

World Trade Center in, **6:**80–81, 421; **8:532–533**, *533*

  1993 bombing of, **6:**109; **8:**96, 339, 532, **533–534**

  2001 attack on, **6:**81, 89, 108, 421; **8:**339, 533; **9:**73–77, *76* (*See also* 9/11 attack)

See also New Amsterdam

New York City Ballet (NYCB), **1:**390; **2:**498; **6:81–82**, *82*

New York City Tenement House Act (1867), **8:**81

New York Clearing House (NYCH), **2:231**

New York College of Veterinary Surgeons, **8:**319

New York Colony, **6:**40, 79, **82–84**, *83, 84,* 87

  Charter of Liberties of, **2:109–110**

  in Dominion of New England, **6:**83–84

  Duke of York's Laws in, **3:93**

  ethnic and religious heterogeneity of, **6:**82

  founding of, **2:**289

  freedom of religion in, **8:**139

  in Middle Colonies, **5:362**

  Native Americans in, **6:**83

  See also New Netherland

New York Council of Revision, **2:433**

New York Evening Post, The Nation as weekly supplement of, **5:**521–522

New York ex rel. Tipaldo, Morehead v., **5:**395

New York Examiner (newspaper), **6:**96

New York Herald (newspaper), **6:**96

New York Intellectuals, **6:**31, **84–85**

New York Journal (newspaper), **6:**97–98

New York Log Cabin (newspaper), **3:**146

New York Morning Herald (newspaper), **8:**577

New York Morning Journal (newspaper), **8:**577

New York Philharmonic Society, **8:**38

New York Review of Books, **6:**85

New York Shakespeare Festival, **8:**115

New York Slave Conspiracy (1741), **6:***85,* **85–86**

New York State Tenement House Law (1901), **8:**285

New York Stock Exchange (NYSE), **2:**447; **7:**548, 549

  establishment of, **3:**275

  government regulation and, **3:**276

New York Sun (newspaper), **1:**137; **6:**96

New York Symphony, **8:**38

New York Times (newspaper), **6:89–91**, *90,* 97, 98

  architecture of headquarters, **7:**376–377

  Pentagon Papers published by, **6:**90, 286–287

  personal ads in, **6:**294

  on Tammany Hall, **8:**46

  Unabomber's manifesto in, **8:**247

New York Times Co. v. United States, **6:**287

New York Times v. Sullivan, **3:**374; **5:**90; **6:91**, 297–298

New York Tribune (newspaper), **1:**123; **3:**146

New York Trilogy (Auster), **5:**122

New York Weekly Journal (newspaper), **2:**292; **6:**83; **8:**590

New York World (newspaper), **6:**97–98

New York Yacht Club, **7:**223

New Yorker, The (magazine), **6:91–92**

New Zealand

  in ANZUS Treaty, **1:**361–362

  U.S. relations with, **1:361–362**

  in World War II, **1:**361

Newark (New Jersey), **6:**62, 63, **92–93**, *93*

  race riots in, **7:**166

Newberry, J. S., **4:**33

Newberry, Walter Loomis, **5:**37; **6:**93

Newberry Library, **6:93–94**

Newburgh addresses, **6:94**

Newcomb, Simon, **1**:343, 544; **3**:108

Newcomen steam engines, **7**:541, 542

Newell, Frederick Haynes, **3**:218; **7**:55

Newfoundland, **6**:53
  Viking settlement in, **3**:283

Newlands, Francis G., **7**:55

Newlands Act (1913), **7**:25, 38

Newlands Reclamation Act (1902), **1**:65; **4**:435; **5**:33–34; **6**:30, 528

Newman, Barnett, **1**:9; **3**:280

Newman, Pauline, **3**:53; **8**:522

Newmann, John von, **2**:335

Newport (Rhode Island)
  French Army at, **6**:94
    archival maps of, **9**:30, *31*
  Naval Academy at, **7**:153
  settlement of, **7**:151

Newport, Christopher, **2**:290

News agencies. *See* Press associations

News programming
  on radio, **5**:236–237
  on television, **8**:73–74

Newsome, A. R., **1**:255–256

Newson, Henry W., **6**:341

Newspaper(s), **6**:94–100
  advertising in, **1**:31, 32; **6**:96, 97
  African American, **5**:193, 194, **199–200**; **6**:88, 96–97, 98
  censorship of, **6**:99
  Alien and Sedition Acts (1798) and, **3**:351
  American Revolution and, **6**:95
  banned from mail, **6**:427
  Civil War and, **6**:97
  in colonial era, **2**:292; **6**:94–95
  comics in, **2**:308–309
  early influences on, **8**:577
  election, **3**:146
  first opposition, **8**:590
  foreign-language, **6**:95, 97, 98
  Great Depression and, **6**:99
  industry developments, **2**:321
  and Lovejoy riots, **5**:165
  middlebrow culture and, **5**:366
  penny press and, **6**:96
  Pentagon Papers in, **6**:90, 99, 286–287
  personal ads in, **6**:294
  political cartoons in, **6**:394–395
  polls by, **6**:409, 533–534
  postmasters and, **6**:426

press associations and, **6**:458–459
and Pulitzer Prizes, **6**:488–489
reporting and, **6**:96–98
"Ripley's Believe It or Not" column, **7**:168
science in, **7**:274
social surveys in, **6**:533
special interest, **6**:96–97
subsidies for, **7**:565
television and, **8**:75
weeklies, **5**:192
on World War I, **6**:98
on World War II, **6**:90, 99
See also Journalism; *specific newspapers*

Newspaper Enterprise Association (NEA), **6**:459

Newsweek (magazine), **8**:127
  on Clinton scandals, **4**:239

Newton, Huey P., **1**:478, 479

Newton, Isaac, **1**:63; **3**:204

Newton, John, **7**:388

Ney, Elisabet, **1**:308

Nez Perce, **6**:100–101; **8**:221
  conversion of, **8**:222
  horses of, **8**:222

Nez Perce Tribal Executive Committee (NEPTEC), **6**:101

Nez Perce War, **6**:101–102

NFTW. *See* National Federation of Telephone Workers

Ngo Dinh Diem, **3**:417; **8**:330–331
  canceling 1956 elections, **3**:534
  death of, **8**:331
  Eisenhower and, **8**:330
  U.S. aid to, **8**:330
  Viet Minh and, **8**:330

NGOs. *See* Nongovernmental organizations

NGS. *See* National Genealogical Society

Nguyen Van Thieu, **8**:333, 334
  Nixon's letter to, **9**:474–475

NHA. *See* National Hockey Association

NHL. *See* National Hockey League

NHLPA. *See* National Hockey League Players Association

NHTSA. *See* National Highway Traffic Safety Administration

NIAAA. *See* National Institute on Alcohol Abuse and Alcoholism

Niagara (ship), **5**:21; **6**:290

Niagara, Carrying Place of, **6**:102

Niagara, Fort, **6**:103

Niagara Campaigns, **6**:102–103

Niagara Falls (New York), **6**:86, **103**
  and Love Canal, **5**:164

Niagara Falls Power Company, **6**:103

Niagara Falls Power project, **3**:174, 178

Niagara movement, **6**:103–104
  and NAACP, **5**:526; **6**:104

NIAID. *See* National Institute for Allergy and Infectious Diseases

Niantic, **8**:220

Niatum, Duane, **5**:128–129

Niblo's Garden, **6**:104

NICAP. *See* National Investigations Committee on Aerial Phenomena

Nicaragua
  in Iran-Contra Affair, **4**:419–420
  Sandinista revolution in, **2**:55
  suit against U.S., in International Court of Justice, **4**:388, 394
  U.S. occupation of, **2**:54
  U.S. relations with, **5**:47, 49; **6**:104–105
    Bryan-Chamorro Treaty (1914), **1**:550–551
    Contra aid and, **2**:395
    dollar diplomacy in, **3**:71
    Good Neighbor Policy and, **4**:22
    gunboat diplomacy and, **4**:77

Nicaraguan Canal Project, **6**:105

Nicaraguan Contras, **3**:278

Nichirenshu, **1**:325–326

Nicholas I, Pope, **6**:216

Nicholas II (tsar of Russia), and Hague Peace Conference, **4**:82

Nichols, Edward L., **6**:335

Nichols, Herbert, **6**:526

Nichols, Lau v., **3**:122

Nichols, Maria, **1**:304

Nichols, Terry, **6**:186, 188

Nicholson, Francis, **2**:185; **8**:349
  and New Castle, **6**:41

Nickel industry, **6**:114

Nickelodeon, **3**:362; **6**:105–106

Nicklaus, Jack, **4**:20

Nickles, Don, **8**:468

Nicol prism, **6**:300

Nicolet, Jean, **3**:291
  explorations of, **6**:106
    Lake Michigan, **4**:50–51
    in Lake Superior basin, **8**:489

and Winnebago, **8**:488

Nicolfor, William, **6**:300

Nicollet, Joseph N., **3**:465

Nicolls, Richard, **3**:188; **6**:79, 107
  and boundary disputes, settlement
      of, **3**:94
  and Duke of York's Laws, **3**:93
  and New York City government,
      3:79

Nicolls' Commission, **6**:106–107

Niebuhr, H. Richard, **2**:165; **7**:76;
    8:264
  as public theologian, **7**:98

Niebuhr, Reinhold, **2**:165; **3**:280;
    7:76, 300, 414; **8**:264
  as public theologian, **7**:98

Nielsen ratings, **5**:246

Nietzsche, Friedrich, **3**:195, 279

Night Rider (Warren), **5**:121

Night Shadows (Hopper), **6**:471

Night to Remember, A (Lord), **8**:132

Nightclubs, **6**:107

Nightingale, Florence, **8**:258

NIH. *See* National Institutes of
    Health

Niishiwa, Jo, **3**:274

Niles, Hezekiah, **2**:514

Nilsson, Gladys, **1**:311

NIMA. *See* National Imagery and
    Mapping Agency

NIMBY organizations, **3**:230

Nimiipuu. *See* Nez Perce

Nimitz, Chester W., **3**:576; **6**:26
  Midway, Battle of, **5**:367–368

Nimmo Report, **1**:124

9/11 attack, **3**:41; **6**:108–109; **8**:339
  and air defense, **1**:76
  air travel after, **1**:86; **6**:108, 109;
      8:192
  airplanes used in, **4**:133
  and Aviation and Transportation
      Security Act (2001), **8**:185
  ballads inspired by, **1**:388
  benefit concerts after, **1**:441–442
  Bush (George W.) on, **6**:108; **8**:96
  Bush's War on Terrorism address
      after, text of, **9**:526–530
  and Christian Coalition, **3**:485
  and criticism of FBI, **3**:339
  economic indicators after,
      3:106–107
  effects of, **6**:108; **8**:96
  electronic surveillance after, **3**:186
  events of, **6**:81, 89, 108; **8**:96, 533

and financial services industry,
    3:369
  media coverage of, **6**:108; **8**:339
  military response to, **2**:532
  and nationalism, **5**:569; **6**:109
  and nativist movements against
      Arab Americans, **6**:5
  and pacifists, **6**:228
  and patriotic use of flag, **3**:381
  on Pentagon, **6**:89, 108, 286
  and Protestantism, **6**:518
  robots use in rescue efforts, **7**:184
  slogan after, **8**:279
  and tourism, **8**:146
  U.S.-Arab relations after, **1**:234
  U.S.-Canadian relations after, **2**:28
  U.S.-Egyptian relations after,
      3:141
  U.S.-India relations after, **4**:261
  U.S.-Pakistan relations after, **4**:261
  on World Trade Center, **6**:81, 89,
      108, 421; **8**:339, 533
    maps of, **9**:73–77, *76*

9 to 5, National Association of
    Working Women, **6**:109–110

Nine-Power Treaty, **3**:446; **6**:250

1919 (Dos Passos), **5**:121

Nineteenth Amendment, **2**:181;
    3:250, 342
  effects of, **8**:12
  and election policies, **3**:171
  and equality of sexes, **1**:21
  National Woman's Party and,
      5:565–566
  ratification of, **8**:12, 356
    by Alabama, **1**:103
  women's rights movement and,
      8:514

Ninigret, **5**:513

Nintendo, **8**:327

Ninth Amendment, **1**:457

Nipissings, **6**:106

Nipkow, Paul, **8**:76

Nipmuck, **8**:220

NIRA. *See* National Industrial
    Recovery Act

Nirenberg, Marshall, **3**:68, 533

Nisei. *See* Japanese Americans

Nishimura, Shoji, **5**:89

Niskanen, William, **1**:573

NIST. *See* National Institute of
    Standards and Technology

NIT. *See* Negative income tax

Nitrates, **6**:110

Nitrogen oxide emissions, and acid
    rain, **1**:13, 14

Nitroglycerin, **8**:240

Niverville, Joseph-Claude Boucher
    de, **3**:292

Nixon, E. D., **1**:548

Nixon, Richard M., **8**:*138*
  ACTION under, **1**:19
  AFL-CIO and, **1**:152
  African policies under, **1**:39
  Alaska land claims under, **1**:112
  alcohol abuse research under,
      1:119
  Alliance for Progress under, **1**:128
  Amtrak under, **1**:178
  antibusing measures proposed by,
      1:589
  anticommunism of, **1**:197
  antiwar movements and, **1**:217
  arms race under, **7**:553
  attempted assassination of, **1**:330
  Checkers speech of, **2**:115
  and chemical/biological weapons
      policy, **2**:118, 119
  child care policies of, **2**:139
  and civil rights, **2**:204–205
  Council of Economic Advisors and,
      2:431
  Cuba policy of, **2**:471
  and daylight saving time, **2**:507
  drug law enforcement under,
      4:503–504; **5**:511, 513
  and Endangered Species Act, **3**:205
  energy policy of, **3**:208–209, 215;
      6:304
  environmental policies of, **3**:100,
      205, 228, 231–232
  and Environmental Protection
      Agency, **3**:100, 231–232; **8**:423
  and European Community, policies
      toward, **3**:260
  executive agents appointed by,
      3:277
  executive orders of, **3**:278
  and family assistance, **8**:441
  on federal aid, **3**:334
  and Federal Mediation and Concil-
      iation Service, **3**:343
  and Federal Trade Commission,
      3:349
  and fiscal federalism, **1**:560
  Ford's pardon of, **8**:323
    text of, **9**:491–492
  foreign policy of, **3**:427

Nixon, Richard M., (*continued*)
  and gold standard, **4**:17
  in gubernatorial race of 1962, **2**:12
  in Hiss case, **4**:136
  in HUAC, **1**:197; **4**:178
  HUD under, **4**:183
  impeachment hearings on, **4**:235
  Indian policies of, **4**:289; **7**:71
  investigating committees on, **4**:411
  Israel and, **4**:441
  Job Corps under, **4**:480–481
  and Kent State protest, **4**:517
  Latin American policies of, **5**:48, 49
  and minority enterprises, **1**:581
  National Review and, **5**:556
  and National Science Foundation, **5**:558
  and National Security Council, **5**:561
  and nondiscriminatory employment, **6**:314
  and Nuclear Non-Proliferation Treaty, **6**:138
  Office of Economic Opportunity under, **6**:163–164
  and Office of Management and Budget, **3**:330
  and Okinawa, occupation of, **4**:459
  OSHA under, **6**:158
  and Panama Canal, **6**:240
  and Peace Corps, **6**:266
  Pentagon Papers episode and, **6**:287
  Pornography Commission appointed by, **6**:420
  in presidential campaign of 1952, **2**:115; **3**:164
  in presidential campaign of 1956, **3**:164
  in presidential campaign of 1960, **3**:164
  in presidential campaign of 1968, **2**:204; **3**:165–166
  in presidential campaign of 1972, **3**:166
  presidential library of, **5**:99
  price and wage controls by, **6**:460, 461
  and prisoners of war in Vietnam, **6**:475
  "Project Independence" of, **6**:304
  and Republican Party, **2**:376; **7**:113–114
  resignation of, **6**:110–112, *111*; **8**:427
  returning Blue Lake to Pueblos, **6**:69
  revenue-sharing plan of, **7**:133
  and SALT, **1**:*272*; **7**:552–553; **8**:206
  and scandal coverage in media, **7**:261
  on silent majority, **9**:467–473
  and social programs, **2**:328
  subpoena to, **6**:457
  at summit conferences, **8**:16
  and tariffs, **8**:158
  and termination policy, **8**:91
  trade policies of, **8**:525
  trade unions and, **7**:559
  and trade with China, **8**:173
  urban policies of, **8**:293
  vetoes cast by, **8**:321
  Vietnam War policies of, **1**:77; **2**:16, 17, 365, 528, 532; **3**:27, 427; **8**:333–334, 335
    letter to Thieu, **9**:474–475
    speech by, **9**:467–473
  on Vietnamization, **9**:467–473
  and Violence Commission, **8**:340
  visit to China, **2**:151, 269
  visit to Soviet Union, **2**:269; **7**:212
  and "war on cancer," **2**:34
  and War on Drugs, **3**:86
  and Washington (D.C.) home rule, **8**:411
  in Watergate (*See* Watergate scandal)
  Watergate investigation address by, text of, **9**:486–489
  in World War II, **8**:557
Nixon, United States v., **3**:279; **6**:457
Nixon tapes, **6**:111, *112*; **8**:427
Niza, Fray Marcos de, **1**:256; **2**:1, 173, 360, 416; **3**:296; **6**:66
NL. *See* National League
NLCA. *See* Norwegian Lutheran Church in America
NLF. *See* National Front for the Liberation of South Vietnam
NLRA. *See* National Labor Relations Act
NLRB. *See* National Labor Relations Board
NLRB vs. Jones and Laughlin, **3**:90
NLU. *See* National Labor Union
NMAI. *See* National Museum of the American Indian
No Man's Land, **2**:173

NOAA. *See* National Oceanic and Atmospheric Administration
Nobel, Alfred, **3**:301
Nobel Prize(s), **6**:487–488
  for Bell Labs researchers, **1**:440
  for biochemical research, **1**:461
  for chemistry, **2**:122, 123; **6**:487
  for economics, **1**:587; **3**:110; **6**:487
  for literature, **6**:487
  for peace, **6**:487; **8**:584
  for physics, **2**:487; **6**:335, 336, 337, 487
  for physiology/medicine, **1**:463; **3**:68; **6**:349, 350, 388, 487–488
  for Rockefeller scientists, **7**:187
Nobility, titles of, **8**:132–133
Nobosuke, Kishi, **4**:458
Noerr Motor Freight, Eastern Railroad Conference v., **6**:297
Noguchi, Isamu, **1**:307
NOI. *See* Nation of Islam
Noise pollution, **6**:112–113
Noise Pollution and Abatement Act (1970), **6**:112
Noland, Kenneth, **1**:298
Nolen, John, **5**:39
Nominating system, **6**:113–114, 399, 463
Nonferrous metals, **6**:114–116
Nongovernmental organizations (NGOs), human rights work by, **4**:192
Nonimportation agreements, **6**:116–117; **8**:150
Nonintercourse Act (1809), **3**:193, 425; **6**:117; **8**:381–382
  Macon's Bill No. 2 (1810) and, **5**:189
Nonintervention policy, **6**:117
No-No Boy (Okada), **5**:123
Nonpartisan League, National, **3**:187; **6**:118, 132
  Farmer-Labor party of Minnesota and, **3**:321–322
Nonprofit organizations, **3**:443–445; **6**:315, 316–317
  public interest law carried out by, **6**:529–530
Nonrecognition policy. *See* Recognition policy
Nontariff barriers (NTBs), GATT and, **3**:524
Nonviolent resistance
  in civil rights movement, **2**:192, 202

Congress of Racial Equality
    (CORE) and, **2:**354
critics of, **2:**204
See also Civil disobedience
Nootkan subgroup of Northwest
    Coast Native cultures, Makah
    tribe, **5:**213
NORAD. *See* North American Air
    Defense Command
NORC. *See* National Opinion
    Research Center
Nordin, D. Sven, **1:**204
Norfolk (Virginia), **8:**343
in colonial era, **8:**289
Noriega, Manuel, **2:**55; **5:**49;
    6:240–241, 242–243
Normal schools, **3:**114, 131
Normalcy, **6:**118
Norman, Marsha, **8:**115
Norman, Montagu, **3:**345
Normandy Invasion, **2:**508, *508;*
    6:*118–121, 119–121;* **8:**549, *550*
See also D Day
Norofsky, Jonathan, **1:**307
Norplant, **1:**469
Norris, Frank
    McTeague, **5:**119–120; **6:**12
    The Octopus, **2:**10; **6:**12
    The Responsibilities of the Novelist,
        6:12
Norris, George W., **5:**24, 78; **6:**30
Norris, William, **5:**142
Norris-LaGuardia Act (1932),
    2:274; **5:**14; **6:**121; **8:**579
on trade union activity, **8:**171
Norsemen (Vikings), **6:***122, 122–123*
    exploration of America by, **3:**283
    Kensington Stone and, **4:**516–517
    in Vinland, **8:**337
North, Lord, **6:**252; **7:**142
North, Oliver L., **2:**395; **4:**419, 420,
    420; **6:**105, 401
North African Campaign, **6:***123,*
    123–124
    Battle of Kasserine Pass in,
        4:513–514; **6:**124
North American Air Defense Com-
    mand (NORAD), **2:**27
North American Conference of
    Homophile Organizations
    (NACHO), **3:**514
North American Free Trade Agree-
    ment (NAFTA), **3:**461; **5:**49;
    6:124–125; **8:**158, 276

and Canada, relations with, **2:**28,
    29
and domestic trade, **8:**163
effects of, **3:**142
and employment, **6:**124
environmental agreement accom-
    panying, **3:**230
establishment of, **3:**309; **5:**349;
    6:124; **8:**199
GATT and, **3:**524; **6:**124
and labor movement, **3:**177
subsidies under, **7:**566
trade unions against, **8:**172
North American Soccer League
    (NASL), **7:**411
North Atlantic Drift, **4:**73
North Atlantic Treaty Organization
    (NATO), **6:**125–126
benefits of, **6:**125
challenges of, **6:**125–126
establishment of, **2:**268, 531;
    6:125; **8:**202, 205
France and, **3:**260, 452; **6:**125–126
Germany and, **3:**562–563
Kosovo bombing campaign by
    (1995), **4:**551
Spain in, **7:**485
North Carolina, **6:**126–131, *127*
in American Revolution, **6:**128;
    7:472
Cherokee in, **2:**126
in Civil War, **6:**129
    Union sentiment in, **8:**260
in colonial era, **6:**126–128
    Albemarle settlements of, **1:**114
    tobacco as money in, **8:**133
constitution of, **6:**128
embargo on British imports in,
    6:127
emblems, nicknames, mottos, and
    songs of, **7:***533*
explorations of, **6:**126
Federalist Party in, **3:**351; **6:**128
Fundamental Constitutions in,
    2:57
geological survey of, **3:**547–548
gold mining in, **4:**10
Great Depression in, **6:**130
gun control in, **4:**74
hurricanes in, **4:***197,* 198
hydroelectric power in, **6:**130
Jeffersonian Republicans in, **6:**128
Ku Klux Klan in, **6:**129
Lumbee in, **5:**170

mountain feuds in, **3:**356–357
New Deal programs in, **6:**130
Populist Party in, **6:**129–130
as proprietary colony, **6:***510,* 511
provincial congresses in, **6:**520
ratification of Constitution in,
    2:382
Reconstruction in, **6:**129
Regulators in, **6:**127
roads in, **6:**130
as royal colony, **6:***510,* 511
schools in, **6:**128–129
settlement of, **2:**289; **8:**459–460
and South Carolina, boundary dis-
    pute between, **1:**521
and state of Franklin, **3:**454–455
state university of, **8:**279
Whig Party in, **6:**128–129
in World War II, **6:**130
North Dakota, **2:**493; **6:***131,*
    131–134
agriculture in, **6:**133
coal mining in, **6:**133
in colonial era, **6:**131–132
Democratic Party in, **6:**132–133
emblems, nicknames, mottos, and
    songs of, **7:***533*
explorations of, **6:**131
Fort Mandan, **5:**219
Fort Union, **8:**259
Great Depression in, **6:**132, 133
Native Americans in, **6:**131, 132,
    134
Nonpartisan League organized in,
    6:118, 132
oil production in, **6:**133
population trends in, **6:**133–134
Populist Party in, **6:**132
Republican Party in, **6:**132–133
statehood of, **6:**132
three-party system in, **8:**243
tourism in, **6:**133
as U.S. territory, **6:**132
North Korea
embargo against, **8:**173
International Atomic Energy
    Agency inspections in, **6:**140
in Korean War, **4:**544–550
nuclear weapons capacity of, **6:**138
U.S. relations with, **4:**542
North Pacific Sealing Convention,
    6:459
North Polar explorations, **6:**381–382
North Pole, **3:**300

North Sea
  fisheries of, **6:**161
  oil in, **6:**179–180
North Sea mine barrage, **6:134**
North Star, The (newspaper), **5:**199;
  6:88, 97
North Vietnam
  creation of, **3:**534; **8:**329
  embargo against, **8:**173
  under Ho, **8:**330
  prisoners of war in, **6:**472, 473, 475
  in Vietnam War, **8:**329–334
  See also Vietnam
North West Company (NWC),
  1:*435;* **3:**490–491; **6:134–135**
  and exploration of Pacific North-
    west, **8:**452, 453
  and Hudson's Bay Company,
    3:487; **6:**134–135
  trading posts established by, **4:**35;
    8:175
Northeast Passage, **6:**381–382
Northeastern University, co-op program at, **3:**122
Northern Alliance (farmers'
  alliance), **3:**323
Northern Alliance (in Afghanistan),
  6:109
Northern Baptist Convention,
  1:412, 413
Northern Pacific Railroad, **1:**458;
  7:35
Northern Securities Company, **4:**26;
  6:135; **8:**234
*Northern Securities Company v. United
  States,* **6:135; 8:**234
Northern Traveller, The (Dwight),
  8:145
Northfield Bank Robbery, **6:135**
Northrop, John H., **1:**461
Northwest, Pacific. *See* Pacific
  Northwest
Northwest Airlines, **1:**83, 84
Northwest Angle, **6:135–136**
Northwest conspiracy, **6:136**
Northwest Ordinance (1787), **5:**33,
  36; **6:**137; **8:**92, 94, 279
  and freedom of religion, **8:**139
Northwest Passage, **6:**136, 381–382
  search for, **3:**297; **8:**589
    Cook and, **2:**404; **8:**453
    Coronado and, **8:**451

Northwest Territory (Old Northwest), **6:136–137,** *137;* **8:**92, 94,
  455
  during American Revolution,
    2:222
  land policy for, **5:**33
  Marietta settlement, **5:239**
  Michigan, **5:**354
  settlement of, **8:**461
Norton, Andrews, **1:**448; **7:**97
Norton, Charles Eliot, **1:**55; **2:**272
Norton, Eleanor Holmes, **3:**244
Norton, John Pitkin, **7:**340
Norumbega et Virginia (Wytfliet),
  9:*8,* 8–10
Norway
  immigration from, **7:**262
  skiing in, **7:**374
  whaling by, **8:**466
Norwegian Americans, **7:**262, *263*
Norwegian churches, **6:137–138**
Norwegian Lutheran Church in
  America (NLCA), **5:**177
Norwegian Synod, **6:**137
Norwick, Ambach v., **1:**126
Notch in the White Mountains (Cole),
  6:507
*Notes Illustrative of the Wrong of Slav-
  ery* (Ford), excerpt from,
  9:269–271
Notes on the State of Virginia (Jeffer-
  son), **5:**118; **6:**374, 396
No-till farming, **7:**445
Notre Dame, College of, **3:**132
Nott, Josiah Clark, **1:**192; **7:**13
Notti, Emil, **1:**112
Nova Scotia, **6:**52
Novak, Michael, **1:**338; **6:**32
NOW. *See* National Organization
  for Women
NOW v. Scheidler, **5:**549
Noyes, Arthur A., **2:**14, 122
Noyes, George Rapall, **1:**448
Noyes, John Humphrey, **6:***195,* 410;
  7:94; **8:**301, 304, 313
  and Guiteau, **1:**328
  in Oneida Colony, **6:**194–195
NPR. *See* National Public Radio
NPS. *See* National Park Service
NRA. *See* National Recovery
  Administration; National Rifle
  Association

NRC. *See* National Research Coun-
  cil; Nuclear Regulatory Com-
  mission
NRDC, Chevron v., **3:**333
NSA. *See* National Security Agency
NSC. *See* National Security Council
NSCDA. *See* National Society of the
  Colonial Dames of America
NSCID. *See* National Security
  Council Intelligence Directive
NSDAP. *See* National Socialist Ger-
  man Workers' Party
NSF. *See* National Science Founda-
  tion
NTA. *See* National Teachers Associ-
  ation
NTBs. *See* Nontariff barriers
NTSB. *See* National Transportation
  Safety Board
NTSC. *See* National Television Sys-
  tems Committee
Nuclear accidents
  Browns Ferry fire, **6:**141
  Three Mile Island, **1:**12–13; **6:**139,
    141–142; **8:**122
  Thresher disaster, **8:122–123**
Nuclear fission, **6:**341–342
"Nuclear Freeze" campaign, **6:**268
Nuclear fusion, **6:**342
Nuclear Non-Proliferation Treaty
  (1968), **6:**138, 139–140
  resistance to
    by India, **4:**261
    by Pakistan, **4:**261
Nuclear physics, **6:339–345**
Nuclear power, **6:138–141,** *140*
  for aircraft carriers, **1:**91
  Atomic Energy Act (1954) and,
    3:213
  Department of Energy and, **3:**208
  development of, **3:**175
  environmentalists on, **6:**139, 141
  vs. hydroelectric power, **6:**139
  Reagan administration and, **3:**209
  vs. renewable energy, **3:**214
  risks of, **7:**560
Nuclear power plant(s)
  advantages of, **6:**139
  Atomic Energy Commission
    designing, **6:**138–139
  gas-cooled, **6:**139
  mechanism of, **6:**139
  in New Hampshire, **6:**59
  safety of, **6:**141–142

in Tennessee, **8**:88
water-cooled, **6**:139
Nuclear reaction
cold nuclear fusion, **2:266**
first self-sustained, site of, **8**:281
Nuclear Regulatory Commission
(NRC), **3**:215, 332; **6**:140,
141–142
Nuclear structure, **6**:343–344
Nuclear submarines, **7**:563
manufacturing of, **2**:358
Nuclear Test Ban Treaty (1963),
3:427; **6:142–143**; **8**:206
Nuclear warships, **8**:406–407
Nuclear weapons, **6:143–145**, *144*
and Air Force, **1**:76, 77
on aircraft carriers, **1**:91
in arms race and disarmament,
1:271–272; **6**:144–145
arms treaties on, **8**:202–203, 206
after Cold War, **3**:210
Department of Energy and, **3**:208,
209
development of, **5**:480; **6**:341–342
Hiroshima and Nagasaki, **5**:222
hydrogen bomb, **4:203–204**
in arms race, **1**:271
of India, **4**:261
of Israel, **6**:138
Manhattan Project, **5:221–222**
missiles, **5**:407–408
NATO and, **6**:126
in Nevada, **8**:298
of Pakistan, **4**:260–261
peace movements and, **6**:268
proliferation, **5**:408
religious protests against, **2**:165
Reykjavik Summit and, **7:149–150**
of Soviet Union, **1**:271–272; **6**:138
strontium 90 in, **7:560**
testing, **5**:221
first, **3**:302
in Marshall Islands, **8**:232
in Nevada, **6**:38
radiation associated with, **3**:209;
8:298
underwater, **6**:*144*
in Utah, **8**:298
in World War II, **1**:494, 495;
3:302; **6**:143; **7**:211; **8**:551
See also specific weapons
Nuclear-weapon states, **6**:138
Nucleus, **6**:340, 341

Nude Descending a Staircase
(Duchamp), **1**:*268*, 269
Nuisance, doctrine of, **6**:506
Nullification, **6:145–146**
Calhoun on, **7**:293, 457
Jackson on, **6**:220
vs. secession, **7**:292–293
South Carolina using doctrine of,
3:413
Numic Indians, **8**:299
language of, **6**:230; **8**:216
in Utah, **8**:296
Nunn, Sam, **3**:78
Nunn v. State, **4**:74
Nuremberg Code, **1**:461; **2**:239
Nuremberg principle, **8**:372
Nuremberg War Crimes Tribunal,
Genocide Convention and, **3**:536
Nurseries, origins of, **2**:138
Nursing, **6:146–148**
in military, **8**:*257*, 258, 502
physician assistants and, **6**:334
Nursing homes, number of seniors
in, **6**:189
Nutrition and vitamins, **6:148–150**
awareness of, **3**:400, 401
biochemistry research and, **1**:460
FDA recommendations for, **2**:97
supplements, **3**:402
vegetarianism and, **8**:310
See also Diets
Nutritional science, **3**:24
Nutt, Jim, **1**:311
Nuttall, Thomas, **1**:519; **6**:183
Nutting, Mary Adelaide, **6**:147
NVRA. *See* National Voter Registra-
tion Act
NWC. *See* North West Company
NWLB. *See* National War Labor
Board
NWPC. *See* National Women's
Political Caucus
NWS. *See* Weather Service, Nation-
al
NWSA. *See* National Woman Suf-
frage Association
NYA. *See* Youth Administration,
National
Nya Elfsborg, Fort, **6**:77
NYAC. *See* New York Athletic Club
NYCB. *See* New York City Ballet
NYCH. *See* New York Clearing
House
Nye, Gerald, **1**:270; **4**:411

Nye, Gerald P., **5**:482
Nylon, **6**:366, 367; **8**:110
synthesis of, **2**:121, 123
*Nyquist, Committee for Public Educa-
tion v.*, **3**:138
NYSE. *See* New York Stock
Exchange

O

OAAU. *See* Organization of Afro-
American Unity
OAI. *See* Old Age Insurance
Oakes, Richard, **1**:161
Oakland (California), **6:151**
Oakley, Ann, **3**:516
Oakley, Annie, **8**:476
OAS. *See* Organization of American
States
OASDI. *See* Old Age, Survivors and
Disability Insurance
OASI. *See* Old Age and Survivors
Insurance
Oates, Titus, **6**:383
Oaths. *See* Loyalty oaths
Oats, **2**:96; **6:151–152**
in breakfast cereals, **2**:98
cultivation in Corn Belt, **2**:414
O'Bannon, Frank, **4**:320
O'Barr, Jean Fox, **8**:520
Oberlin, John Frederick, **6**:152
Oberlin College, **3**:130; **6:152**
African Americans at, **3**:125
coeducation at, **2**:263
religious studies at, **7**:97
Oberlin movement, **6:152–153**
Oberlin-Wellington rescue case,
6:152, **153**
Obesity, **6:153–154**
Objectivism, **6:154**
Obregon, Alvaro, **5**:483
O'Brien, Lawrence R., **8**:426
O'Brien, William S., **1**:497
Obscenity
censorship of, **2**:84, 85
See also Censorship, press and artis-
tic; Pornography
"Observations Concerning the
Increase in Mankind"
(Franklin), **3**:468
Observatories
astronomical, **1**:343, 344, 345;
6:154–157

Observatories, *(continued)*
early, **6:**155–156
volcanic, **8:**352
Observer (newspaper), **6:**97
Obstetrics, development of,
2:142–143
Ocala Demands, **3:**387
Ocala Platform, **3:**324; **6:157–158**
Occaneechee Indians, **1:**383
Occom, Samson, **3:**134
*Collection of Hymns and Spiritual
Songs*, **5:**128
*A Sermon Preached at Execution of
Moses Paul*, **5:**128
Occupation, joint, of Oregon terri-
tory, **4:**41, **486**; **6:**205
Occupational medicine, **5:296–299**
Occupational Safety and Health Act
(OSHA) (1970), **5:**11, 15;
6:158–159; **8:**423
development of, **6:**158–159
effects of, **6:**159
Occupational Safety and Health
Administration (OSHA), **5:**15
establishment of, **4:**364; **6:**159
functions of, **6:**159
Occupational Safety and Health
Review Commission, **6:**159
Ocean Drilling Program, **3:**552
Ocean Dumping Act (1972), **3:**228
Ocean energy, **3:**214
Oceanographic surveys, **6:159–161**
early, **6:**159–160
technological advances in,
6:160–161
Oceanography, **6:161–163**
marine biology, **5:240–241**
Ochialini, G. P. S., **6:**344
Ochs, Adolph S., **6:**89
OCIAA. *See* Office of the Coordina-
tor of Inter-American Affairs
O'Connell, Dan, **1:**113
O'Connor, Basil, **6:**388, 389
O'Connor, Carroll, **1:**126, *126*
O'Connor, Flannery, **5:**121
O'Connor, Frank, **6:**154
O'Connor, Sandra Day, **7:**198; **8:**507
on abortion, **8:**434
as Arizona native, **1:**259
on line-item vetoes, **8:**321
on presidential election of 2000,
1:579
O'Connor, T. V., **4:**395
O'Conor, Hugo, **1:**257

Octopus, The (Norris), **2:**10; **6:**12
O'Daniel, W. Lee (Pappy), **8:**103
Odell, Jack, **8:**153
Odell, Moses F., **2:**313
Odets, Clifford, **8:**115
Waiting for Lefty, **5:**121
Odum, Howard, **7:**297
OECD. *See* Organization for Eco-
nomic Cooperation and Devel-
opment
OECS. *See* Organization of Eastern
Caribbean States
OEEC. *See* Organization for Euro-
pean Economic Cooperation
OEO. *See* Office of Economic
Opportunity
Oersted, Hans Christian, **1:**130;
3:172; **8:**68
Of Plymouth Plantation (Bradford),
6:363
OFCC. *See* Office of Federal Con-
tract Compliance
Off Broadway, **8:**115–116
Office of Administration, **3:**330
Office of Construction of Weights
and Measures, **5:**529
Office of Economic Opportunity
(OEO), **6:163–164**
establishment of, **6:**163; **8:**386
functions of, **6:**163; **8:**386, 387
Office of Education, **3:138–139**
Office of Faith-Based Community
Initiatives, **3:**330
Office of Federal Contract Compli-
ance (OFCC), **1:**36
Office of Federal Register, **5:**525
Office of Homeland Security, **2:**191;
3:330; **6:**109
Office of Management and Budget
(OMB), **1:**555; **3:**330;
6:164–165
budget by, **1:**229; **6:**164
establishment of, **6:**164
and fiscal policy, **2:**431
functions of, **6:**164
Office of National AIDS Policy,
3:330
Office of National Drug Control
Policy (ONDCP), **5:**511
Office of Noise Abatement and
Control, **6:**112
Office of Price Administration
(OPA), **6:165–166**, 460

Office of Price Stabilization (OPS),
6:166
Office of Public Diplomacy for
Latin America and the
Caribbean, **6:**504
Office of Research Integrity (ORI),
7:278
Office of Road Inquiry, **1:**71; **3:**335
Office of Scientific Research And
Development (OSRD),
6:166–167
Office of Standard Weights and
Measures, **5:**529
Office of Strategic Services (OSS),
6:167–168, 503, 523; **7:**502
Office of the Coordinator of Inter-
American Affairs (OCIAA),
6:503
Office of War Information (OWI),
6:503, 523
Office technology, **6:168–170**
printers, **6:**470
typewriter, **8:***244*, **244–245**, *245*
Officers' Reserve Corps (ORC),
6:170; **7:**119
Official Bulletin (newspaper), **6:**503
Official Theatrical Guide (Cahn),
8:114
Offset lithography, **6:**469–470
Offshore oil, **6:170–171**, 303; **8:**124
in Alaska, **6:**171, 180
development of, **6:**170–171
in Gulf of Mexico, **6:**179
in North Sea, **6:**179–180
Ogallala Aquifer, **4:**56, 57; **7:**56;
8:486
Ogden, Aaron, **3:**575
Ogden, David Bayard, **6:**171
Ogden, Gibbons v., **1:**549; **2:**310, 405;
3:308, 483, **575**; **4:**26; **7:**169
Ogden, Peter Skene, **6:**37; **8:**453
Ogden, William Butler, **7:**53
Ogden v. Saunders, **6:171**
Ogdensburg Declaration, **2:**27
Oglala firefight (1975), **1:**161
Oglala Sioux. *See* Sioux
Oglesby, Richard J., **7:**23
Oglethorpe, James Edward, **2:**185;
4:473
and debtors' imprisonment, **2:**513
Savannah established by, **3:**554
and settlement of Georgia, **2:**289
in War of Jenkins' Ear, **2:**294
O'Hara, John, **5:**121

Ohio, **6:171–175,** *173*
  in 19th century, **6:**172–174
  in 20th century, **6:**174
  African Americans in, **6:**174
  in American Revolution, **6:**171
  Bank of the United States taxed by, **6:**218
  black laws in, **1:**475
  Black Swamp in, **1:480**
  canals in, **6:**172
  capital of, **2:**47, *48*
  in Civil War, **6:**173
  in colonial era, **6:**171–172
  constitution of, **6:**172, 173
  Democratic Party in, **6:**172
  economy of, **6:**172, 173, 174
  emblems, nicknames, mottos, and songs of, **7:***533*
  Federalist Party in, **3:**351
  higher education in, **6:**174
  industry in, **6:**173–174
  maps of, archival, **9:**49, *49*
  in Midwest, **5:**368–369
  migration into, **5:**371–372
  military and civilian leaders from, **6:**173
  Morgan's raids into, **5:**458
  Native Americans in, **6:**171–172
    mounds of, **4:**278, *278*
    in Ohio Wars, **6:**177–178
  New Deal in, **6:**174
  population of, **6:**173, 174
  purchase of, **4:**64
  Republican Party in, **6:**172, 173
  slavery in, **6:**172–173
  statehood for, **6:**172
  trade unions in, **6:**173–174
  Western Reserve in, **8:***455,* **455–456**
  Whig Party in, **6:**172, 173
  in World War II, **6:**174
Ohio, Army of the. *See* Cumberland, Army of the
Ohio, Brandenburg v., **3:**374
Ohio Canal, **2:**32
Ohio Company of Associates, **5:**36
Ohio Company of Virginia, **6:175**
Ohio Idea, **3:**155; **6:175**
Ohio Life Insurance Company, **3:**366
Ohio River, **6:175–176,** *176*
  connection between Virginia and, **4:**456
  galley boats on, **3:**504

Indian warfare on, **7:**175
  land north of, land speculation and, **5:**36
  Monongahela River (tributary), **5:444**
  recanalization of, **8:**430
  showboats on, **7:**350–351
  Vandalia Colony on, **8:307–308**
Ohio University, **8:**279
Ohio Valley, **6:176–177**
  French and Indian War in, **3:**468–471, 472
  Indian-white competition for, **3:**95
Ohio Wars, **6:177–178; 8:**399
Ohman, Olof, **4:**516
Ohomo dance, **6:**444
OIC. *See* Open-Market Investment Committee
Oil
  kerosine, **4:522–523**
  from Latin America, **5:**44, 49
  in Louisiana, **5:**160–161
  Mexican nationalization of foreign-owned oil, **5:**348
  in Middle East, **6:**298
    and U.S. policies, **1:**233
  in North Dakota, **6:**133
  offshore, **6:170–171,** 179
  in Oklahoma, **6:**298, 303; **8:**239
  in Pennsylvania, **6:**298, 301–302, 305, 360
  politics of, **6:**303–304
  price of, and inflation, **7:**516
  in Texas, **6:**298, 302, 303, 305; **8:**102, 103
  in tidelands, **8:**124
  transportation of, **6:**303, 359
    regulation of, **6:**243
  wildcat drilling, **8:477**
  in Wyoming, **8:**564
  See also Petrochemical industry; Petroleum
Oil companies, and credit cards, **2:**451
Oil crises, **3:**211; **6:178–179**
  and energy policies, **3:**208, 213, 215
  and speed limits, **7:**500–501
  See also Energy crisis
Oil fields, **6:179–180**
  in Alaska, **1:**111, 112, 113; **6:**171, 179, 180
  in California, **6:**179

geographic distribution of, **6:**179–180, 299–300
  midcontinent oil region, **5:361–362**
  in Pennsylvania, **6:**179
  in Texas, **4:**185; **6:**179, *179*
  See also Petroleum prospecting and technology
Oil pipelines, **6:**303
  early, **6:359**
Oil spills
  Exxon Valdez, **1:**13, 111, 113; **3:**233, *305,* **305–306; 6:**304
  genetic engineering and clean-up of, **3:**531
Oil tankers, **6:**303
Oil wells, **6:**298, 302–303, 305
Ojibway Conquest, The (Copway), **5:**128
Ojibwe, **6:***180,* **180–181,** *181*
  animal totem of, **8:**496
  language of, **6:181–182**
  in Nebraska, **6:**29
  in North Dakota, **6:**131
O.K. Corral, **8:**141, *141*
O.K., origins of term, **2:**550; **3:**146
Okada, John, *No-No Boy,* **5:**123
O'Keeffe, Georgia, **1:**297, 301; **8:**475
O'Kelly, James, **8:**263
Okinawa
  U.S. occupation of, **4:**459
  in World War II, **6:***182,* **182–183**
    assaults on, **8:**556
    invasion of, **8:**547
Oklahoma, **6:***183,* **183–186**
  African Americans in, **6:**185, 186
  Cherokee Strip in, **2:**128
  in Civil War, **6:**184–185
  constitution of, **6:**185
  creation of state of, **2:**506
  Democratic Party in, **6:**185–186
  economy of, **6:**186
  emblems, nicknames, mottos, and songs of, **7:***533*
  Indian Territory in, **4:**309
  Native Americans in, **6:**183–185, 262, 444; **8:**239
    Cherokee, **2:**126
    Miami, **5:**353
    Seminole, **7:**308–309
  oil in, **6:**298, 303; **8:**239
  population of, **6:**186
  Republican Party in, **6:**185–186

Oklahoma, (*continued*)
  Spiro in, **7:506**
  statehood for, **6:**185
  and Texas, boundary dispute
    between, **1:**523
  tornadoes in, **8:**143
  wheat production in, **3:**390
  Wild West shows in, **6:**185
Oklahoma (battleship), **6:**273
Oklahoma! (Rodgers and Hammer-
  stein), **8:**115
Oklahoma, Lyons v., **5:**526
Oklahoma City, **6:186–187**
  1995 bombing in, **3:**41, 328; **6:**186,
    187, **187–188; 8:**95, 339
    and FBI, **3:**339
    militia movement and, **5:**385
Oklahoma Welfare Act (1936), **6:**262
Okun's Law, **8:**252
Old age, **6:188–190**
  AARP and, **1:142; 6:**189
  Alzheimer's disease in, **1:131–132**
  diversity in population, **6:**189
  Gray Panthers and, **4:**37–38
  life expectancy and, **6:**188
  number of people in, **6:**188
  poverty in, **6:**189; **7:**128, 131, 418;
    8:439
  public and private assistance in,
    6:188–189; **8:**440 (*See also*
    Medicare)
  social security benefits in, **7:**416,
    417–422
  See also Retirement
Old Age, Survivors and Disability
  Insurance (OASDI), **7:**419, 421
Old Age and Survivors Insurance
  (OASI), **7:**419
Old Age Insurance (OAI), **8:**440
*Old Dearborn Distributing Company v.
  Seagram Distillers Corporation,*
  3:309
Old Farmer's Almanac, **1:**129–130
Old Glory. *See* Flag, U.S.
Old Hickory, **6:190**
Old Indian Legends (Zitkala Sa), **5:**128
"Old Ironsides." *See Constitution*
"Old Ironsides" (Holmes), **2:**378
Old North Church (Boston), **6:190,**
  190
Old Northwest. *See* Northwest Ter-
  ritory
Older Americans Act (1965), **6:**188
Olds, Ransom E., **1:**367, 371

Olin, Laurie D., **5:**540
Oliphant, Pat, **6:**395
Olitski, Jules, **1:**298
Olive Branch Petition (1775),
  6:190–191
Olives, **3:**478
Olleros, **1:**219
Olmstead v. United States, **3:**185;
  6:479
Olmsted, Frederick Law, **1:**517;
  2:94; **3:**238; **5:**38–39, 550
  city plan for Washington (D.C.),
    8:410
  design for World's Columbian
    Exposition, **2:**187
  and park planning, **2:**186
Olney, Richard, **1:**168
  Olney Corollary of, **6:**191
  and Olney-Pauncefote Treaty,
    6:191
  in Pullman strike, **4:**249
Olney Corollary, **6:191**
Olney-Pauncefote Treaty, **6:191**
Olson, Brennan, **7:**193
Olson, Floyd B., **3:**322; **5:**400
Olson, Scott, **7:**193
Olympic Games, **7:**510–511
  of 1896, **8:**154
  of 1936, **8:**155
  of 1948, **8:**155
  of 1960, **8:**155
  of 1980, boycott of, **1:**37; **2:**269;
    6:193–194
  during Cold War, **7:**512
  ice skating in, **4:**210
  marathons, **5:234–235**
  organization of, **6:**191
  origins of, **6:**191
  political and economic importance
    of, **6:**193–194
  protests against, **6:**193–194; **7:**512
  skiing in, **7:**375
  Soviet Union in, **6:**193–194
  swimming in, **8:**36–37
  U.S. participation in, **6:191–194**
  U.S. records in, **6:**191–193
  in U.S. cities, **6:**191
  yacht racing in, **7:**224
Omaha, **8:**223
O'Mahoney, John, **3:**353
Omaq-kat-tsa (Blackfeet chief),
  1:*483*
OMB. *See* Office of Management
  and Budget

Omnibus, **7:**42–43
Omnibus Bill (1850), **2:**331; **6:194**
Omnibus Budget Reconciliation Act
  (1981), **8:**286
Omnibus Budget Reconciliation Act
  (1993), **4:**31
Omnibus Crime Control Act (1970),
  6:212
Omnibus Crime Control and Safe
  Streets Act (1968), **6:**212
  Title III of, **3:**185
Omnibus lines, and suburbanization,
  7:573
Omsted, Denison, **3:**547
On Religious Freedom (Murray), **8:**308
"On the Equality of the Sexes"
  (Murray), excerpt from,
  9:325–327
On the Law of War and Peace
  (Grotius), **6:**34
On the Road (Kerouac), **5:**122
Oñate, Juan de, **2:**360; **3:**203, 296;
  8:444
  and colonial administration, **2:**278
  explorations and settlements of,
    6:66, **194; 8:**451
ONDCP. *See* Office of National
  Drug Control Policy
*One Book Entitled Ulysses, United
  States v.,* **2:**84
One Flew Over the Cuckoo's Nest
  (Kesey), **5:**122
One-Dimensional Man (Marcuse),
  3:454
Oneida Colony, **6:194–195; 8:**301
  complex marriage in, **7:**94
  polygamy in, **6:**410
Oneida Company, **6:**195
Oneida Indians, **6:**86
  land claims by, **4:**274
  Mahican and, **5:**202–203
O'Neill, Eugene, **5:**120–121; **6:**519;
  8:115
O'Neill, Kevin R., **1:**326
O'Neill, Paul, **1:**41
O'Neill, Thomas P. (Tip),
  1:510–511
Onions, **6:195**
Onizuka, Ellison S., **2:**102
Onken, Oscar, **3:**498
Online booksellers, **6:**539
Online information industry,
  2:323–324
Onoko (ship), **4:**54

Onondaga, **6**:86

Onondaga reservation, **6:195–196**

Ontography, **3**:541

O'odham. *See* Akimel O'odham; Tohono O'odham

OPA. *See* Office of Price Administration

OPC. *See* Orthodox Presbyterian Church

OPEC. *See* Organization of Petroleum Exporting Countries

Opechancanough, **6**:442–443

Open Door policy, **2**:151; **6:196–198**

in China, **4**:243, 457; **5**:462; **6**:196–197

Japanese resistance to, **4**:457; **6**:197

and Manchuria, **5**:218–219

Russian rejection of, **7**:210

Open Housing Act (1968), backlash against, **1**:382

Open primary, **6**:463

Open-Market Investment Committee (OIC), **6**:198

Open-market operations, **6:198**

Open-pit mining, in Montana, **5**:450

Opera, **6:198–199**, *199*

Operation Big Switch, **6**:473

Operation Bootstrap, **6**:546

Operation Desert Shield, **6**:292

Operation Desert Storm. *See* Persian Gulf War

Operation Dixie, **6:199**

Operation Just Cause, **6**:241, 242–243

Operation Linebacker I, **1**:77

Operation Linebacker II, **1**:77

Operation Little Switch, **6**:473

Operation Market Garden, **1**:1

Operation Mongoose, **2**:471

Operation Overlord. *See* Normandy Invasion

Operation Ranch Hand, **1**:54

Operation Rescue, **5**:549; **6:199–200**, 489

Operation Rolling Thunder, **1**:77; **8**:332–333

Operation Torch, **1**:233

Operation Urgent Fury, **4**:65

Ophthalmology, **5**:303–304

Opium, **5**:510

Opium Exclusion Act (1909), **5**:510

Opium War (1839-1842), **2**:150, 153

Oppenheimer, J. Robert, **5**:221–222, *222*; **6**:336, 342

Opportunity (newspaper), **5**:200

OPS. *See* Office of Price Stabilization

Optics Technology, **3**:357

Options exchanges, **6:200**

Oral literature, Native American, **4:279–281**

Orange, Fort, **1**:113; **2**:289; **3**:488; **6**:83

Oranges, **3**:478

in California, **2**:182

in Florida, **2**:181–182

Oratory, **6:200**

Native American, **4:281**

Orbison, Roy, **1**:388

ORC. *See* Officers' Reserve Corps

Orchard, Harry, **4**:111

Orchestras, symphony, **8:38–39**

Ord, E. O. C., **3**:271

Army of the James under, **1**:279

Order of American Knights. *See* Knights of the Golden Circle

Order of Friars Minor, **3**:453

Order of United Americans, **8:260**

Ordinances of 1784, 1785, and 1787, **6:200–201**

and Geographer's Line, **3**:540

Marietta settlement, **5**:239

Ordnance, **6:201–203**

of Army, **6**:201–202

manufacture of, **6**:201–202, *202*

of Navy, **6**:202–203, *203*

Ordway, Nehemiah, **6**:132; **7**:459

Oregon, **6:203–208**, *204*

African Americans in, **6**:206, 207

agriculture in, **6**:205–206

annexation of, **1**:188

assisted suicides in, **3**:262–263

borders of, **6**:205, 209–210

claim over, **3**:358

constitution of, **6**:205

economy of, **6**:205–206

emblems, nicknames, mottos, and songs of, **7**:*533*

environmental legislation in, **6**:207

explorations of, **6**:204

flood of 1903 in, **3**:383

fur trade in, **1**:114, 157, 342; **6**:204; **8**:307

gun control in, **4**:75

Hispanic Americans in, **6**:207

Hudson's Bay Company in, **4**:190

immigration to, **6**:206, 207

industry in, **6**:*205*, 205–206

initiatives and referenda in, **6**:208

joint occupation of, **4**:41, **486**; **6**:205

Ku Klux Klan in, **2**:167

Lewis and Clark expedition in, **6**:204

literature of, **6**:207

missionaries in, **6**:205

Modoc War, **5:433**

Native Americans in, **6**:203–204, 205, 207, 231

pioneers in, **6**:205

politics in, **6**:205, 206–207, 208

Progressive movement in, **6**:206–207

railroads in, **6**:205–206

statehood for, **6**:205

territorial disputes over, **6**:204–205

wagon trains to, **8**:363

Oregon (battleship), **8**:*407*

Oregon, Muller v., **1**:21; **3**:54, 247, 308; **5**:394, 395

Brandeis Brief in, excerpt of, **9**:357–360

Oregon and California Railroad, forfeiture of land grant by, **5**:31

Oregon Boundary Treaty (1846), **8**:200

Oregon Compulsory Education Act (1922), **6**:352

Oregon Employment, Smith v., **7:401**

Oregon Parochial School case. *See Pierce v. Society of Sisters*

Oregon System, **6:208**

Oregon Trail, **3**:299; **6**:29, **208–209**, 226

challenges of, **6**:208–209, *209*

emigration along, Treaty of Fort Laramie (1851) and, **5**:40

Independence Rock on, **4:258**

route of, **6**:208–209, *209*

South Pass on, **7:462**

Oregon Trail, The (Parkman), excerpt from, **9**:222–224

Oregon Treaty (1846), **3**:358; **4**:41; **6**:205, **209–210**

O'Reilly, Alexander, **2**:440

O'Reilly, Leonora, **2**:392; **3**:53; **8**:521

Organ transplantation, **8:182–184**

autologous, **8**:182

heart implants, **4:121–122**

homologous, **8**:182

xenotransplantation, **3**:531, 532; **8**:182

Organic Act (1863), **1**:257

Organic Act (1878), **8**:410

Organic Act (1897). *See* Forest Management Act (1897)

Organic Act (1916). *See* Jones Act

Organic Act (1936), **8**:341
Revised (1954), **8**:341

Organic farming, **6**:210
natural fertilizers in, **3**:356
rise of, **4**:118; **6**:210

Organic Foods Production Act (1990), **6**:210

Organization for Economic Cooperation and Development (OECD), **1**:403; **3**:260, 415; **6**:210–211
members of, **6**:210–211
purpose of, **6**:211

Organization for European Economic Cooperation (OEEC), **3**:259, 415; **8**:166

Organization of Afro-American Unity (OAAU), **6**:211

Organization of American States (OAS), **5**:48–49; **6**:211–212, 236–237
Charter of, **6**:211–212
functions of, **6**:211–212
members of, **6**:211

Organization of Eastern Caribbean States (OECS), **4**:65

Organization of Petroleum Exporting Countries (OPEC), **6**:304
Latin American countries in, **5**:44, 49
and oil embargo of 1973, **3**:213
and U.S. inflation, **7**:516
and U.S. oil crises, **6**:178

Organized crime, **2**:462–464
Apalachin Conference (1957), **1**:222
federal measures against, **2**:377
legislation on, **6**:212–213
Prohibition and, **3**:60

Organized Crime Control Act (1970), **6**:212–213
Title Nine of (*See* Racketeer Influenced and Corrupt Organizations Act)

ORI. *See* Office of Research Integrity

Oriental decorative arts, **1**:287

Origin of Species (Darwin), **3**:269
American Academy of Arts and Sciences on, **1**:140

and anthropology/ethnology, **1**:192

Original package doctrine, **6**:213

Oriskany, Battle of, **6**:213

Orleans, Territory of, **6**:213
Code Napoléon in, **2**:262

Ornithology, **6**:213–215; **8**:596

Orogeny, **3**:552

O'Rourke, Matthew J., **8**:242

Orphan trains, **1**:27

Orphanages, **1**:27; **2**:136, 146, 148–149

Orpheum circuit, **8**:309

Orshansky, Molly, **6**:436

Ortelius, Abraham, **5**:232

Orthodox churches, **6**:215–217
membership in, **7**:*91*
Russian, **1**:121; **6**:*216*, 216–217

Orthodox Presbyterian Church (OPC), **6**:451

Orthophoto maps, **5**:234

Ortiz, Alfonso, **1**:340

Ortiz, Simon, **5**:129

Orton, Bill, **8**:298

Osage Indian School, football team at, **3**:*134*

Osage Indians, **6**:*217*, 217–218; **8**:223
in Missouri, **5**:419

Osage orange, **6**:218

Osborn v. Bank of the United States, **6**:218–219

Osborne, Sarah, **7**:229

Oscars. *See* Academy Awards

Osceola (Seminole leader), **7**:*307*, 310; **8**:401, 402

Osgood, Samuel, **6**:426

OSHA. *See* Occupational Safety and Health Act; Occupational Safety and Health Administration

Oskison, John M., **5**:128

Oslo Accords. *See* Israeli-Palestinian Peace Accord

OSM. *See* Surface Mining Reclamation and Enforcement, Office of

OSRD. *See* Office of Scientific Research And Development

OSS. *See* Office of Strategic Services

Ossipee, **6**:56

Ostend Manifesto (1854), **1**:189; **2**:469; **6**:219

Osteopathy, **5**:291; **6**:219

Ostfriesland (ship), **1**:266

Ostwald, Wilhelm, **2**:122

O'Sullivan, John L., **2**:40; **5**:222

O'Sullivan, Mary Kenny, **8**:521

O'Sullivan, Timothy, **1**:299

Oswald, Lee Harvey
Kennedy assassinated by, **1**:330
shooting of, **1**:330
media coverage of, **8**:339
Warren Commission on, **8**:394

Oswald, Russell G., **1**:355

Oswego, Fort, **6**:83

Otermín, Antonio de, **6**:67

Other America, The (Harrington), **2**:228; **6**:436–437, 438

Otis, Elisha, **3**:186, *186*

Otis, Elwell S., in Philippine Insurrection, **6**:319–320

Otis, Harrison Gray, **1**:249; **3**:352

Otis, James, **1**:512; **7**:135; **8**:563
Rights of the British Colonies Asserted and Proved, **7**:162

Oto, in Nebraska, **6**:29

Otoe-Missouria, **8**:223

O'Toole, Margot, **7**:279

Ottawa Indians, **6**:219–220
and fur trade, **3**:488, 489

Ottawa River, **4**:50

Otto, Nikolaus, **1**:371

Ouiatenons. *See* Miami Indians

Ouimet, Francis, **4**:19

Oukrainsky, Serge, **1**:390

Ouma. *See* Houma

Our Bodies, Ourselves (health text), **2**:143; **8**:511

"Our Federal Union! It Must Be Preserved!", **6**:220

Our Nig (Wilson), **5**:124

Our Town (Wilder), **5**:121

Our Young Folks, **5**:127

Ouray Reservation, **8**:300

Outcault, Richard, **6**:98; **8**:577

Outdoor relief, **6**:436

Outer Continental Shelf Lands Act (1953), **6**:303; **8**:125

Outerbridge, A. Emilius, **8**:89

Outerbridge, Mary Ewing, **8**:89

"Over There," lyrics of, **9**:364–365

Overgrazing, **6**:529

"Overhills," **8**:83

Overland companies, **6**:220
See also Wagon trains

Overland Trail, **6**:*220*, 220–221
route of, **6**:220–221
stagecoaches on, **7**:514–515

Overman, Lee, **1**:198

Overseers and drivers, slave, **6:**221–222

Owasso Independent School District No. I-001, Falvo v., **3:**316

Owen, Robert, **3:**107, 113; **8:**300

Owen, Robert Dale, **1:**467; **8:**530

Owen-Glass Act (1913), **1:**397; **3:**344

Owens, Jesse, **6:**193; **7:**205; **8:**155, *155*

OWI. *See* Office of War Information

Oxen, **6:**222

compared to mules, **5:**472

Oxford Movement, **6:**222

Oyewùmí, Oyèrónké, **3:**517

Ozawa, Jisaburo, **5:**89

Ozette, **6:**222–223

archaeological excavations, **5:**213

Ozone depletion, **1:**80; **6:***223,* 223–224, 384

EPA on, **7:**246

Freon and, **7:**246

international protocol on, **2:**238; **3:**230, 233

P

Paar, Jack, **8:**142

Pabst Building (Milwaukee), **5:***388*

Pacemakers, **2:**53

Pacheco Pereira, Duarte, **3:**283

"Pachucos in the Making" (Sanchez), **9:**407–409

Pacific Coast Hockey Association (PCHA), **4:**143

Pacific Far East Line (PFEL), **5:**320

Pacific Fur Company, **3:**491–492; **6:**225

Pacific Islanders, **6:**225–226

Pacific Northeast Plan, **3:**207

Pacific Northwest, **6:**226

British exploration in, **8:**452–453

dry farming in, **3:**88

fur trade in, **3:**491–492

Native Americans in missions for, **4:**277

social life of, **4:**305–306

prehistoric, **1:**242

Vancouver explorations in, **8:**306–307

Pacific Ocean

cables across, **2:**3–4

exploration of, Cook (James) and, **2:**403–404

Pacific Railroad Act (1862), **8:**181

Pacific Rim, **6:**226

Pacific Yuit, **8:**211, 212–213

Pacifism, **6:**227–228

of Addams (Jane), **9:**365–367

among anarchists, **1:**181

and civil disobedience, **6:**227

of conscientious objectors, **2:**361–362; **6:**227, 269

and pamphleteering, **6:**233

and peace movement, **6:**269

and "positive testimony," **6:**227–228

Quakers and, **7:**1

and social reform, **6:**227

See also Antiwar movements

Pack animals, mules as, **5:**472, *472*

Pack trains, **6:**228–229

Packaging, **6:**229

Packard, Vance, *The Hidden Persuaders,* **4:**130

Packenham, Sir Edward, **6:**75; **9:**42

Packers' Agreement, **6:**229–230

Packers and Stockyards Act (1921), **6:**229; **7:**514

Packets, sailing, **6:**230

"Packing effect," **6:**341

"Packing fraction," **6:**341

Packwood, Bob, **6:**207

PACs. *See* Political action committees

Paddock Bill (1892), **6:**554

Padelford, Seth, **7:**153

Paderewski, Ignacy Jan, **6:**391

Page, Charles G., **3:**172

Page, R. M., **7:**14

Page, Ruth, **1:**390

Paideia program, **3:**124

Paine, Sidney B., **3:**174

Paine, Thomas, **3:**108

Age of Reason, **2:**539

The American Crisis, **5:**118

Common Sense, **1:**515; **2:**318, 520; **3:**378; **5:**118; **6:**232, 396; **7:**109, 136

excerpt from, **9:**137–138

deism and, **2:**539

on representative government, **7:**109

The Rights of Man, **7:**148–149, **162**

Paint Creek Strike (1912-1913), **8:**450

Painter, Charles, **4:**303

Painting(s), **1:**294–299

abstract expressionism, **1:**8–10, 298

Hudson River School of, **4:**188–190

miniatures, **5:**393–394, *394*

murals, **5:**483

postmodernist, **6:**430

theft of, **7:**182

Pairing, **6:**230

Pais, **8:**228

Paiute, **6:**230–231, *231*

and Ghost Dance, **3:**573; **6:**231

Northern, **6:**230–231; **8:**216

Southern, **6:**230–231; **8:**216, 228

in Utah, **8:**298

Pajeau, Charles, **8:**153

Tinkertoys invented by, **5:**109

Pakenham, Sir Edward, **8:***384*

Pakistan

creation of, **4:**259

Indian relations with, **4:**259–260

nuclear weapons of, **4:**260–261; **6:**138

in SEATO, **7:**470

U.S. relations with, **4:**258–261

Palau, **8:**232–233

Paleoindians, **1:***241,* 241–247; **8:**84

in Maine, **5:**207

Paleontology, in Badlands of South Dakota, **1:**383

Palestine

Israeli negotiations with, **4:**442–444

Jewish immigration to, **1:**207

and terrorism, **4:**443, 444

UN resolution on, **8:**270

Palestine Liberation Front (PLF), and *Achille Lauro* hijacking, **1:**13

Palestine Liberation Organization (PLO), Lebanon evacuation (1982), **5:**242–243

Palestinian Americans, **1:**231

Palimony, **6:**231, 506

Palladio, Andrea, **5:**452, 453

Palleiro, Rafael, **8:**322

Palliser, John, **9:***51,* 52

Palmer, A. Mitchell, **3:**161, 337; **6:**232, 396

and raids on alien radicals, **1:**198; **2:**325, 552; **3:**12, 337; **6:**232, 232, 396

Palmer, Alice Freeman, **8:**281

Palmer, Arnold, **4**:20

Palmer, Bartlett Joshua, **2**:157

Palmer, Bertha Honoré, **1**:316

Palmer, Daniel David, **5**:291

Palmer, Erastus Dow, **1**:306

Palmer, James, **4**:84

Palmer, John M., **3**:159; **4**:10

Palmer, Mitchell, **1**:198

Palmer, Nathaniel, **6**:383

Palmer, Phoebe, **8**:501

Palmer, Potter, **3**:8

and land speculation, **5**:37

Palmer, Mrs. Potter, **2**:272

Palmer, Robert R., estimate of number of Loyalists, **5**:167

Palmer Raids, **1**:198; **2**:325, 552; **6**:232, 396

deportations following, **3**:12

FBI and, **3**:337; **6**:232

Palms, Francis, and land speculation, **5**:36

Palsgraf v. Long Island Railroad Company, **6**:232

Pamela (Richardson), **6**:536

Pamphleteering, **6**:232–233

Coin's Financial School (Harvey), **2**:265

Pamunkey Indians, **1**:383

PAN. *See* National Action Party

Pan Am Flight 103, **6**:233–234

Pan American, **1**:84

Pan Presbyterian Alliance, **6**:451

Pan water closet, **6**:372

Pan-Africanism, **1**:478; **6**:234–236

in 20th century, **6**:235–236

origins of, **6**:234–235

Panama

diplomatic recognition of, **2**:54

revolution in, **6**:238, 243

U.S. invasion of (1989), **1**:496; **6**:241, 242–243

U.S. relations with, **5**:47, 49

Panama Canal and, **6**:238–241, 242

riots and, **6**:239, 242

Panama Canal, **5**:47; **6**:105, 237–241

and Cape Horn, decline in importance of, **2**:39

Clayton-Bulwer Treaty and, **2**:229–230; **6**:237

construction of, **2**:54

elimination of mosquitoes for, **8**:576

failure in, **6**:237, *238*

successful, **6**:238, *239*

early plans for, **6**:237–238

and Florida, **3**:387

Hay-Bunau-Varilla Treaty and, **4**:108–109; **6**:238; **8**:201, 205

Hay-Herrán Treaty and, **4**:109; **6**:237

Hay-Pauncefote Treaties and, **4**:110; **6**:237; **8**:140, 205

Panama Canal Treaty and, **5**:49; **6**:240, 242

Roosevelt and, **8**:387–388

Thompson Act and, **6**:239

Tolls Exemption Act and, **8**:140

Panama Canal Authority, **6**:241

Panama Canal Company, **6**:239

Panama Canal Treaty (1977), **5**:49; **6**:240, 242

Panama Canal Zone, **6**:239–240

Panama Defense Forces (PDF), **6**:242–243

Panama Refining Company v. Ryan, **1**:21; **6**:243

Panama-California Exposition (1915), **7**:237

Pan-American Exposition, **6**:236

Pan-American Union, **6**:236–237

Pan-Atlantic Steamship Corporation, **5**:320

Panay incident, **6**:243–244

Pandering, **6**:513

Panhandle, **6**:244

Panics. *See* Financial panics

Panton, Leslie and Company, **6**:244

Papacy, and anti-Catholicism, **1**:195–196

Papago. *See* Tohono O'odham

Papal states, diplomatic service to, **6**:244–245

Paper and pulp industry, **6**:245–246

American Revolution and, **6**:245

Civil War and, **6**:245

in colonial era, **6**:245

Great Depression and, **6**:245

World War II and, **6**:245

Paper money standard, **4**:14

Paper standard, **1**:459

Paperbacks, **6**:537, 538

Papp, Joseph, **8**:115

Papst, Walter, **3**:499

Paraguay, trade agreements with, **6**:125

Paralysis, infantile. *See* Poliomyelitis

Paramilitary groups. *See* Militia movement; Minutemen

Parapsychology, **6**:246

Parasitology, **5**:294

Paratroops, **6**:246–247

Parcel post, **5**:206

Pardon. *See* Amnesty

Parham v. JR, **2**:149

Paris, Declaration of (1856), **1**:487; **6**:34, 35

Paris, Pact of (1928). *See* Kellogg-Briand Pact (1928)

Paris, Treaty of (1763), **2**:261, 295; **3**:471; **5**:162; **6**:248

and Proclamation of 1763, **6**:490

Paris, Treaty of (1783), **1**:124, 522; **3**:296; **6**:248–250, *249*

archival map of, **9**:*35*, 36

and control of Trans-Appalachian West, **8**:179

debt issue in, **1**:540, 541

and Florida ceded by Great Britain to Spain, **3**:385

and Northwest Territory ceded by Great Britain to U.S., **6**:136

and U.S.-Canadian border, **6**:135

Paris, Treaty of (1898), **3**:360; **6**:250, 321; **8**:201

Paris, Treaty of (1954), **8**:205

Paris Conference(s), **6**:247–248

Paris Conference (1949), **6**:247

Paris Conference (1960), **6**:247

U-2 incident and, **8**:15, 247

Paris Conference (1968-1973), **6**:247–248

Paris Peace Conference (1919), **8**:201, 315–316

Soviet exclusion from, **7**:57

Paris Peace Conference (1946), **6**:247

"Parity" in naval defense, **6**:250–251

Park(s)

cemetery as, **2**:81, *81*

in city planning, **2**:186

in Colorado, **2**:299

See also specific parks; specific types

Park, Edwards Amasa, **7**:97

Park, Maud Wood, **5**:65

Park, Mungo, **5**:*394*

Park, Robert E., **1**:337; **8**:291

Park, Tongsun, **4**:542, 543

Park, William H., **5**:357–358

Parke, John G., and railroad surveys, **7**:30

Parker, Alton B., **3:**159

Parker, Berkman v., **3:**199

Parker, Cynthia Ann, **2:**50

Parker, Dorothy, **1:***123*
  in Algonquin Round Table, **1:**123

Parker, Ely Samuel, **4:***327*

Parker, Francis W., **3:**116

Parker, James, **2:**50

Parker, Peter, **2:**108

Parker, Quanah, **2:**307–308; **6:***1*, 8;
  7:72

Parker, Theodore, **8:**179, 180

Parker v. Davis, **5:**76

Parkes, Alexander, **6:**366

Parkesine, **6:**366

Parkman, Francis, **4:**137–138
  The Oregon Trail, **9:**222–224

Parkman, George, **8:**435

Parks, Gordon, **1:**301

Parks, Rosa, **1:***51*, 104, 529; **2:**202,
  202
  firsthand account by, **9:**445–446

Parley's Magazine, **5:**127

Parliament, British, **6:**251–252

Parochial schools
  Catholic, **2:**68, 69; **4:**474–475;
    7:268
  decline of, **7:**267–268
  in North Carolina, **6:**129
  vouchers for, **7:**266

Parrington, Vernon L., **1:**169; **4:**138,
  139

Parris, Betty, **7:**229

Parris, Samuel, **7:**229

Parrish, West Coast Hotel v., **3:**308;
  5:395; **8:**445

Parry, William Edward, **6:**382

Parsons, C. A., **3:**174

Parsons, Edith Barretto Stevens,
  1:308

Parsons, Lucy
  in Industrial Workers of the
    World, **4:**346
  in International Labor Defense,
    4:389

Parsons, Talcott, **1:**194; **3:**515;
  7:433–434, 435

Parsons, Theophilus, **3:**256

Parson's Cause, **6:**252; **8:**243

Particle accelerators, **6:**342–343

Particle physics. *See* High-energy
  physics

Partido Revolucionario Institucional
  (PRI), **5:**349

Partisan Review (journal), **1:**198;
  6:84–85

Party platform, **6:**368–369, 399

PAs. *See* Physician assistants

Pasadena (California), **2:**10

Pascal, Blaise, **1:**588

Paschke, Ed, **1:**298

Pascua Yaqui Indians, **8:**228–229

Passamaquoddy/Penobscot,
  6:252–253, *253*; **8:**219
  in 20th century, **1:**2

Passes, mountain, **6:**253–254

Passports, **6:**254–255

Pasteur, Louis, **3:**239, 406

Pasteurization, **3:**407–408

Patch, Alexander, **4:**68

PATCO Strike. *See* Air traffic controllers strike

Patents and U.S. Patent Office,
  4:375; **6:**255–257
  in 19th century, **6:**255–256
  in colonial era, **6:**255
  for cotton gin, **2:**428, 429
  mining, **5:389**
  new technology and, **6:**256–257
  reform of, **6:**256
  telephone cases, **8:**70
  for typewriter, **8:**244

Paterson, William, **2:**379; **5:**78;
  8:308

Paterson (New Jersey), silk production in, **7:**361–362

Paterson Silk Strike, **6:**257

Path Breaking (Duniway), excerpt
  from, **9:**334–337

Pathfinder, The (Cooper), **5:**70

Pathologies of Rational Choice Theory
  (Green and Shapiro), **6:**405

Patients' rights, **6:**257–258

Patman, Wright, **1:**544; **3:**444;
  6:318; **7:**183

Patman Veterans Bill, **1:**498

Patrick, Frank, **4:**143, 144

Patrick, Lester, **4:**143, 144

Patriot Air-Defense Missile, **1:**75–76

Patriot War, **7:**8

Patrol gunboat motor (PGM), **4:**77

Patronage, political, **2:**22–23, 207;
  6:258
  Customs as source of, **2:**485

Patrons of Husbandry, **6:**259
  mail-order houses and, **5:**206
  See also Granger movement

Patroons, **6:**259

Pattee, James Monroe, **3:**508

Patten, Gilbert, **6:**537

Patten, Simon, **6:**42

Patterns of Culture (Benedict),
  6:259–260; **8:**599

Patterson, Claire, **6:**344

Patterson, Floyd, **6:**484

Patterson, Gilbert E., **2:**173

Patterson, Malcolm R., **8:**86

Patterson, Robert, **1:**567

Patterson, William, **6:**62

Patterson v. McLean Credit Union,
  2:197

Patton, George S., **8:***550*
  armored warfare under, **1:**267
  in liberation of France, **8:**549
  in Sicilian Campaign, **7:**353–354
  on trucks, **8:**231

Paul I (tsar of Russia), **7:**214

Paul III (of Russia), **1:**108

Paul, Alice, **5:**565; **7:**3; **8:**514

Paul, John R., **6:**388

Paul, Mary, on textile mills,
  9:340–341

Paul, William, **1:**18

Paul Bunyan, **8:**45, 288

Pauli, Wolfgang, **6:**341

Pauling, Linus, **2:**122; **3:**533

Paulists, **2:**69

Pauncefote, Sir Julian, **4:**110
  and Olney-Pauncefote Treaty,
    6:191

Paving, **6:***260*, **260–261**

Pavley, Andreas, **1:**390

Pavlov, Ivan, **6:**524

Pavlova, Anna, **1:**390

Pawnbrokers, **2:**447–448

Pawnee, **6:***261*, 261–262; **8:**218
  in Nebraska, **6:**29
  remains of ancestors returned to,
    6:3

Pawnee Bill's Wild West Show,
  2:436

Paxton Boys, **6:**262

Payne, Cecilia, **1:**344

Payne, Daniel, **1:**53

Payne, David L., **1:**501

Payne, Lewis, **1:**328

Payne-Aldrich Tariff (1909), **8:**51

PBS. *See* Public Broadcasting Service

PCA. *See* Presbyterian Church in
  America

PCHA. *See* Pacific Coast Hockey Association

PCIJ (Permanent Court of International Justice). *See* International Court of Justice

PCP. *See* *Pneumocystis carinii* pneumonia

PCUSA. *See* Presbyterian Church in the United States of America

PDF. *See* Panama Defense Forces

PDPs. *See* Plasma display panels

Peabody, Elizabeth Palmer, **7:**194; **8:**180

Peabody, George Foster, **6:**262
and Yaddo colony, **8:**570

Peabody, Moyer v., **3:**272

Peabody Fund, **6:262**

Peace, Treaty of (1783). *See* Paris, Treaty of (1783)

Peace and Bread in Time of War (Addams), excerpt from, **9:**365–367

Peace Commission (1867), **6:263**

Peace conferences, **6:263–265**
See also specific conferences

Peace Corps, **6:265–266**
idea for, **8:**282
Quaker youth camps and, **7:**3

Peace Democrats (Butternuts), **2:**218, 411

Peace movement(s), **6:266–270**
of 1864, **6:266**
boundaries of, **6:**269
characteristics of, **6:**269
cyclical, **6:**267–268
early, **6:**266–267
success and failure of, **6:**269–270
women in, **6:**267; **8:499–500**
after World War II, **6:**268–269
See also Antiwar movements

Peace of Paris (1763), **5:**158

Peacekeeping missions, **6:270–271**
Canada and, **2:**27
in Cold War, **6:**270
in Lebanon, **5:**242–243
Marine Corps in, **5:**242–243
in Middle East, **6:**270–271
in Somalia, **6:**271
United Nations and, **8:**270–271

"Peacemaker" (gun), **6:**464

Peacock, David, **1:**58

Peale, Charles Willson, **1:**295; **5:**393, 485–486, *486, 486;* **6:**214; **8:**593

Peale, Norman Vincent, **6:**442, *517*

Peale, Raphaelle, **1:**295

Peale, Titian, **5:**150

Pearl, Raymond, **7:**13

Pearl Harbor, **6:271–273**
Japanese attack on, **6:**272, 272–273; **8:**543–545, 555–556
armored ships after, **1:**266
Hawaii after, **4:**107
Roosevelt's speech after, text of, **9:**396–397

Pearl Street Station (New York City), **3:**178

Pearlstein, Philip, **1:**298

Pearson, Karl, **7:**538, 539

Pearson, Lester B., **2:**27

Peary, Robert E., **3:**300; **5:**542; **6:**382

Peay, Austin, **8:**86

Peck, Fletcher v., **2:**397; **3:382–383;** **5:**36; **8:**576

Peck, Jedediah, **6:**297

Peck, John, **3:**382

Peckham, Rufus, **1:**20

Peculiar Institution, **6:273**

Peddlers, **6:273–274,** *274;* **7:**124
Lebanese Americans as, **5:**71

Pedro II (emperor of Brazil), **2:**340

Peffer, William A., **3:**324; **6:**417

PEI. *See* Private Enterprise Initiative

Pei, Ieoh Ming, **5:**540

Peikoff, Leonard, **6:**154

Peiper, Joachim, **5:**217

Peirce, Charles Sanders, **5:**122; **6:**424, *444,* 445

Peirce v. New Hampshire, **5:**103

Pelby, Rosalie French, **1:**308

Pele (soccer player), **7:**411

Peleliu Island, **2:**58; **6:274**

Pelham, Henry, **6:**470

Pelham, Peter, **6:**470

Pell, Claiborne, **5:**536

Pell, Ella Ferris, **1:**308

Pelley, William Dudley, **3:**327, 328

Pelosi, Nancy, **8:**468

Peltier, Leonard, **1:**161; **7:**71; **8:**561

Pemberton, John C., in Vicksburg, **8:**324

Pemberton, John S., **2:**260

Pembroke College, **1:**548

Pembroke State College (North Carolina), **5:**170

Pena, Adarand Constructors v., **1:**581; **7:**316

Peña y Peña, Manuel de la, **9:**218–219

Pender, William, in Battle of Gettysburg, **6:**351

Pendergast, Thomas, **1:**507; **6:**275

Pendergast machine, **5:**421; **6:274–275**

Pendleton, Charles L., **2:**272

Pendleton, George H., **3:**155; **4:**62; **6:**275

Pendleton Act (1883), **2:**206, 208, 421; **6:**275
provisions of, **1:**225–226

Penguin Books, **6:**538

Penicillin, **2:**124

Peninsular Campaign (1862), **6:275**

Penitentiary, **6:**476, 552

Penkovskiy, Oleg, **2:**92

Penn, John, and Pennsylvania assembly, **2:**281

Penn, Richard, **6:**190

Penn, Thomas, **7:**2

Penn, William, **7:***1;* **8:**289
brewing business of, **1:**536
on capital punishment, **2:**40
and Charter of Privileges, **2:110**
city plan for Philadelphia, **2:**184
Delaware holdings of, **2:**541; **3:**94
and Free Society of Traders, **3:**459
and Great Law of Pennsylvania, **4:**55; **6:**276
on Holy Experiment, **4:**151
and New Castle, **6:**41
peace plans of, **6:**266
as proprietor of Pennsylvania, **6:**276
Quaker colony in West Jersey established by, **6:**60
and religious freedom, **7:**1, 2, 93
and settlement of Pennsylvania, **2:**289

Pennacook, **6:**57
in New Hampshire, **6:**56

Penney, James Cash, **3:***8,* 9

Pennock, Moses, **1:**58

Pennock, Samuel, **1:**58

Pennsylvania, **6:275–279,** *277*
African American colleges in, **3:**125
African Americans in, **6:**278, 312
in American Revolution, **6:**277–278
Amish in, **1:**174; **6:**279, 280
anthracite strike in (1902), **1:190–191**

Battle of the Monongahela,
5:443–444
canal system of, **2:**32, 33
charter (1681), **5:**260
in Civil War, **6:**278
Lee's invasion of, **3:**566
coal mining in, **2:**251, *251*
colonial assembly of, **1:**333; **2:**281
in colonial era, **6:**276–277, 476;
7:93; **8:**139, 164
constitution of, **6:**278, 279; **7:**526;
8:308
emblems, nicknames, mottos, and
songs of, **7:***533*
Federalist Party in, **3:**351
in foreign trade, **8:**164
Free Society of Traders and, **3:**459
geography of, **6:**275
geological survey of, **3:**548
glassmaking in, **4:**3
Great Law of, **4:**55
as Holy Experiment, **4:**151
immigration to, **4:**221
industrialization in, **6:**278–279
invasion of, **6:**280
Irish Americans in, **6:**278
Johnstown flood in, **3:**383; **4:***483,*
483–484
labor disputes in, **6:**278–279
Mason-Dixon line, **5:259–260,**
260
in Middle Colonies, **5:**362
Molly Maguires, **5:**438
Native Americans in, **6:**276
oil in, **6:**179, 298, 301–302, 305,
360
oil pipelines in, **6:**359
personal liberty laws of, **6:**294
prehistoric, **6:**276
prisons in, **6:**476
as proprietary colony, **6:***510,* 511,
512
provincial congresses in, **6:**520
Quakers in, **4:**151; **6:**276–277;
7:1–2
religious liberty in, **7:**93; **8:**139
as royal colony, **6:**511
settlement of, **2:**289
shipbuilding in, **7:**347
slavery in, **6:**277
state university of, **8:282–283**
Three Mile Island nuclear accident
in, **1:**12–13
toll roads in, **8:**139

whiskey production in, **8:**78, 468
Whiskey Rebellion in, **2:**97, 377;
3:59; **8:***469,* **469–470**
World War II and, **6:**279
Wyoming Valley, settlement of,
8:567
Pennsylvania (battleship), **6:**273
Pennsylvania (cruiser), **1:**89
*Pennsylvania Association for Retarded
Children v. Commonwealth of
Pennsylvania,* **3:**34
Pennsylvania Coal v. Mahon, **3:**198;
6:505
Pennsylvania Dutch (dialect), **6:**277
"Pennsylvania Farmer's Remedy,
The" (Dickinson), **9:**127–128
Pennsylvania Gazette (newspaper), **1:**31
Pennsylvania Germans, **3:**559;
6:279–280
*Pennsylvania Packet and Daily Adver-
tiser* (newspaper), **6:**96
Pennsylvania Provincial Council,
3:459
Pennsylvania Rock Oil Company,
6:302
Pennsylvania Society for the Preven-
tion of Tuberculosis, **8:**236
Pennsylvania Station, **6:**452–453
Pennsylvania troops, mutinies of,
6:280
Pennsylvania Turnpike, **6:**279;
7:178; **8:**190
Penny press, **6:**96
Penobscot. *See*
Passamaquoddy/Penobscot
Penobscot, Fort, **6:***281*
Penobscot Expedition (1779),
6:280–281, 282
Penobscot region, **6:281–282**
Penrose, R. A. F., **1:**167
Pension Act, arrears of (1879), **6:**282
Pension plans, **6:282–284**
collective bargaining and, **2:**274
current trends in, **6:**284
early, **7:**128
federal, **6:**283–284
private, **6:**283
for railroad employees, **7:**28–29
for teachers, **2:**56
Townsend Plan, **8:149–150**
See also Retirement plans; Social
security
Pensions, military and naval,
6:282–283, **284–285;** **8:**317

vs. bonuses, **1:**498
GI Bill of Rights and, **3:**574; **6:**285
Grand Army of the Republic and,
4:31
Pension Act, arrears of (1879),
6:282
Pentacostalism, in Assemblies of
God, **1:**334
Pentagon, **6:285–286,** *286*
attack on, **6:**89, 108, 286 (*See also*
9/11 attack)
Pentagon Papers, **2:**85; **6:286–287;**
8:425
excerpt from, **9:**455–459
newspapers publishing, **6:**90, 99,
286–287
Pentecostal and Charismatic
Churches of North America,
6:288
Pentecostal churches, **3:**265;
6:287–289, *288*
African Americans in, **6:**288
Assemblies of God, **6:**288
Church of God, **6:**287, 288
Church of God in Christ,
2:172–173; **6:**287
Church of the Nazarene, **6:**27
and evangelical theology, **3:**267
McPherson, Aimee Semple, **5:***410*
membership in, **7:***91*
Pentecostal Holiness Church,
6:288
women in, **8:**501
Pentecostal Fellowship of North
America (PFNA), **6:**288
Pentecostal Holiness Church, **6:**288
Penutian language, **8:**221
Penzias, Arno, **1:**344–345, 440
Peonage, **6:**289
People for the Ethical Treatment of
Animals (PETA), **1:**186
People Left Behind, The (report),
6:437
People of the Abyss, The (London),
5:119
People's Advocate, Incorporated,
6:509
People's Party (Populist Party),
6:417; **8:**119
in Georgia, **3:**556
in North Carolina, **6:**129–130
in North Dakota, **6:**132
platform of, **6:**368, 417
in Texas, **8:**102

People's Temple, **2**:478; **7**:94; **8**:303

Pepper, Beverly, **1**:307, 309

Pepper, William F., **4**:530

Pepsi, **7**:439

Pepsi-Cola, **2**:261

Pequot War, **2**:357; **6**:289, 379; **8**:459

Narragansetts in, **5**:513

Pequot-Mohegan, **8**:220

Pequots, **2**:356–357; **6:289–290**

captives of, **2**:51

Mashantucket

casino run by, **3**:509

lawsuit filed by, **6**:289–290

in modern era, **2**:359

Mohegans and, **5**:435

Peralta, Pedro de, **6**:66–67

Percier, Charles, **3**:497

Percy, Earl, **6**:483

Percy, Sir Hugh, **5**:89

Percy, Walker, **3**:280

Love in the Ruins, **5**:123

The Thanatos Syndrome, **5**:123

Peres, Shimon, **4**:443, 444

Peretz, Martin, **6**:77

Pérez, Albino, **6**:68

Pérez Jiménez, Marcos, **5**:48

Perfectionist Society, **8**:313

Perils of Pauline (film), **3**:362

Perkins, Frances, **2**:274; **6**:158; **7**:129; **8**:197, 507

women's clubs and, **8**:509

Perkins, George W., **5**:530

Perkins, Jacob, **7**:77

Perkins, R. Marlin, **8**:595

Perky, Henry, **2**:98

Perle, Richard, **6**:32

Perls, Fritz, **3**:203

Permanent Court of International Justice (PCIJ). *See* International Court of Justice

Permanent residents, **4**:60–61

Perot, H. Ross

and GATT, **3**:524

on national debt, **2**:517

and Persian Gulf syndrome research, **6**:292

politically alienated citizens and, **2**:548

in presidential campaign of 1992, **2**:517; **3**:169, 171; **8**:118

in presidential campaign of 1996, **3**:169; **8**:120

Perrot, Nicolas, **3**:503

Perry, Matthew C., expedition to Japan, **4**:457; **6**:291; **8**:198

Perry, Oliver H., in War of 1812, **8**:383

Perry, Oliver Hazard, **3**:79

in Battle of Lake Erie, **5**:21

in Battle of the Thames, **4**:53; **8**:111

in Perry-Elliott Controversy, **6:290–291**

"We Have Met the Enemy, and They Are Ours," **8**:432

Perry, William J., **2**:529

Perry-Elliott Controversy, **6:290–291**

Perryville, Battle of, **6**:291

Pershing, John J., **5**:20; **8**:336

American Expeditionary Forces and, **1**:149

Mexico, punitive expedition into, **2**:78; **5**:346–347

in Somme Offensive, **7**:447

strategy of, **1**:149

and War Department, **8**:379

in World War I, **3**:451; **8**:538

American Expeditionary Forces and, **5**:338; **8**:535

Persian Gulf region, Carter Doctrine on, **1**:233

Persian Gulf syndrome, **6:291–292**, 293

Persian Gulf War, **6:292–294**

aerial bombing in, **1**:496

air defense in, **1**:75–76

all-volunteer force in, **2**:365

armored warfare in, **1**:268

biological warfare in, threat of, **1**:465

Bush's address on, text of, **9**:515–517

Carter Doctrine and, **2**:60

conscientious objectors during, **2**:362

cost of, **6**:293; **8**:377

Egypt's support in, **3**:141

and electoral politics, **3**:168

firsthand accounts of, **9**:518–522

and Great Britain, U.S. relations with, **4**:44

intelligence activities in, **4**:377

prisoners of war in, **6**:472

propaganda in, **6**:504

U.S. Air Force in, **1**:77; **6**:293

U.S. Army in, **1**:277

U.S. Marine Corps in, **5**:243

U.S. Navy in, **6**:27

Vietnam syndrome and, **8**:328

women in, **8**:504

Person to Person (TV show), **8**:73

Personal ads, **6:294**

Personal computers, **8**:245

Personal liberty laws, **6:294**

Fugitive Slave Acts and, **3**:482; **6**:294

Personal Responsibility and Work Opportunity Reconciliation Act (PRWORA) (1996), **2**:139; **3**:317, 485; **6**:439; **7**:222

Personnel Administrator of Massachusetts v. Feeney, **6:295**

Personnel management, **4**:336, 337

Pertain, Henri Philippe, **3**:451

Peru

commerce with, **5**:44–45

Cuban immigrant incident (1980), **5**:238

Spanish conquest of, **3**:294

U.S. relations with, drug trafficking and, **5**:512

Pesler, James, **7**:*18*

Pesos. *See* Pieces of eight

Pest Control Act (1947), **3**:432

Pestalozzi, Heinrich, **3**:116

Pesticide Control Act (1972), **3**:228

Pesticides. *See* Insecticides and herbicides

PET. *See* Polyethylene terephthalate

Pet banks, **6:295**

PETA. *See* People for the Ethical Treatment of Animals

Peter, Laurence J., **6:295**

"Peter Principle," **6:295**

Peter Principle, The: Why Things Always Go Wrong (Peter), **6**:295

Peter the Great, **1**:108

Peterdi, Gabor, **6**:471

Peters, Andrew, **1**:513

Peters' Colony Company. *See* Texan Emigration and Land Company

Petersburg, Siege of, **6:295–296**, *296*

trenches in, **8**:207, *207*

Petersen, Donald, **3**:415

Petersen, Hjalmar, **3**:322

Peterson, Esther, **3**:245; **8**:498

Peterson, Roger Tory, **6**:215

Petition, right of, **6:297–298**

Petition and Remonstrance of New Netherland, **6:296–297**

Peto, John F., **1**:295
Petrochemical industry, **6**:298–300, *299*
  decline of, **6**:299
  geography of, **6**:299–300
  plastics and, **6**:299
  products of, **6**:301
  rise of, **6**:298–299
  See also Oil
Petrography, **6**:300–301
Petroleum
  boomtowns, **1**:502
  in California, **2**:10
  future of, **3**:213
  history in U.S., **3**:210–211, *212*
  See also Oil
Petroleum industry, **3**:211;
    6:301–305
  and chemical industry, **2**:121;
    3:211
  in Dallas (Texas), **2**:494
  demand and supply and, **6**:304–305
  early, **6**:301–302
  geology and, **6**:305–306
  kerosine oil in, **4**:522–523
  in Long Beach (California),
    5:148–149
  monopoly in, **6**:303
  National Recovery Act (1933),
    5:362
  rise of, **6**:302–303
  and wildcat oil drilling, **8**:477
  See also Oil
Petroleum prospecting and technol-
    ogy, **6**:302, **305–306**, 513
  midcontinent oil region,
    5:361–362
  Spindletop oil well, **5**:361
Petry, Ann, *The Street*, **5**:125
Pettibone, George A., **4**:111
Pettigrew, J. J., in Battle of Gettys-
    burg, **6**:351
Pettit, Bob, **1**:424
Petty, Sir William, **6**:248
Pew, J. Howard, **6**:306
Pew, Joseph Newton, **6**:306
Pew Memorial Trust, **6**:306–307
Peyote, **3**:374; **6**:1, 8
  in Native American religious life,
    1:162; **4**:292–293; **7**:401
Peyote Cult, **6**:1
Peyote Way, **2**:163
Peyton Place (TV show), **7**:409
Pfaelzer, Mariana R., **6**:509

Pfaff, Judy, **1**:307
PFIAB. *See* President's Foreign
    Intelligence Advisory Board
Pfizer Inc., **8**:322
PFNA. *See* Pentecostal Fellowship
    of North America
PGA. *See* Professional Golfers Asso-
    ciation
PGM. *See* Patrol gunboat motor
Phagan, Mary, **3**:453
Pharmaceutical industry, **6**:307–308
Pharmacist(s)
  changing role of, **6**:310–311
  demographics of, **6**:311
  education for, **6**:309–310
Pharmacy, **6**:308–311
  in 19th century, **6**:308–309
  legislation on, **6**:309
  science and technology and, **6**:309
  soda fountain at, **6**:309
Phelan, James D., **2**:369
Phelps, Oliver, and land speculation,
    5:36
Phenolics, **6**:366
Phi Beta Kappa Society, **6**:311
Philadelphia (Pennsylvania),
    6:311–313, *312, 313*
  African Americans in, **6**:312
  American Philosophical Society,
    5:66
  botanical garden in, **1**:516
  Centennial Exhibition in, **2**:87–88,
    88
  city plan for, **2**:184, *185*
  in colonial era, **6**:277, 312; **8**:289
  Continental Congress in, **6**:277,
    312
  decline of, **6**:312–313
  embargo on British imports in,
    6:116
  Empowerment Zone program,
    8:287
  fair in, **8**:558
  flour milling in, **3**:389, *391*
  foundation of, **6**:276, 311–312
  furniture manufacturing in, **3**:496,
    497
  growth of, **6**:312
  Independence Hall in, **4**:*257*,
    257–258
  insurance in, **4**:367–368, *369*
  as nation's capital, **6**:277, 278, 312
  newspapers published in, **6**:95

  occupation in American Revolu-
    tion, **7**:143
  philanthropy in, **6**:316
  police forces of, **6**:385
  porcelain industry in, **6**:418
  publishing in, **6**:536
  Puerto Ricans in, **6**:543
  Quakers in, **7**:2
  riots in, **6**:315
  strikes in, **7**:556
  trade unions in, **8**:170–171
  water system of, **8**:292
  yellow fever epidemic in,
    3:235–236; **8**:291, 576
Philadelphia (ship), **1**:415
Philadelphia and Lancaster Turn-
    pike, **7**:176
Philadelphia cordwainers' case,
    6:313–314
Philadelphia Gas Ring, **7**:162
Philadelphia Plan, **6**:314–315
Philadelphische Zeitung, Die (newspa-
    per), **6**:95
Philanthropist, The (newspaper), **5**:96
Philanthropy, **6**:315–319
  American Revolution and, **6**:316
  and black colleges, **3**:126
  by Bruce (Ailsa Mellon), **5**:539–540
  by Carnegie (Andrew), **2**:55–57,
    227; **6**:317
  vs. charity, **6**:315
  Civil War and, **6**:317
  in colonial era, **6**:315–316
  by Dale (Chester), **5**:539
  by Folgers, **3**:393
  foundations and, **3**:443–445;
    6:317–319
  future of, **6**:319
  by Getty (Jean Paul), **3**:565–566
  by Mellon (Andrew W.),
    5:538–539
  by Mellon (Paul), **5**:539–540
  by Peabody (George), **6**:262
  Pew Memorial Trust, **6**:306–307
  religious, and early history of edu-
    cation, **2**:106
  by Rockefeller (John D.), **6**:317,
    318; **7**:187
  by Rockefeller (Nelson), **6**:318
  by Rosenwald (Lessing J.), **5**:539
  scientific, **6**:317
  World War II and, **6**:318
  See also specific foundations

Philip (Wampanoag chief), **4:**313, 527; **9:**15–16

Philip Morris, **8:**137

Philippine Insurrection, **3:**360; **6:319–320,** 321–322
anti-imperialists and, **6:**320, 321
opposition to, **1:**203
U.S. imperialism and, **4:**244
war casualties of, **6:**320, 321–322

Philippine Sea, Battle of the, **1:**90–91; **6:320–321; 8:**557

Philippine War. *See* Philippine Insurrection

Philippine-American War. *See* Philippine Insurrection

Philippines, **6:321–324**
Anti-Imperialist League on, **9:**263–264
Battle of Manila Bay, **5:225**
immigration from, **3:**360
independence of, **6:**320, 322–323; **8:**244
Japanese invasion of, **6:**322; **8:**546, 547
Jones Act (1916) on, **4:487; 6:**322
Lingayen Gulf, **5:**114–115
Spanish-American War and, **7:**487
Taft Commission and, **8:**41
Tydings-McDuffie Act (1934) and, **6:**322
U.S. acquisition of, **1:**189; **2:**470
U.S. atrocities in, **1:**354
U.S. control of, **3:**360; **6:**250, 319–320, 321–322; **8:**41, 92, 201
U.S. imperialism in, **4:**244
in World War II, **1:**427; **5:**89

Philips, Howard, **6:**163–164

Phillips, Bert, **8:**48

Phillips, Carl, **5:**123

Phillips, Duncan, **2:**273

Phillips, Irna, **7:**409

Phillips, Sam, **7:**185

Phillips, William, **1:**282

Phillips Curve, **8:**254

Phillips Petroleum Company v. Wisconsin, **6:**9

Philosophy, **6:324–328**
deist, **2:538–540**
positivism, **6:423–425**
postmodernism, **6:**429
post-structuralism, **6:430–431**
pragmatism, **6:**325–327, 424, **444–447**
transcendentalism, **8:179–181**

Philosophy and the Mirror of Nature (Rorty), **6:**327, 446

Phinney, Archie, **6:**101

Phoenix (Arizona), **6:328**
botanical garden in, **1:**517

Phonograph, **1:**189, 357–358; **5:**502
commercial use of, **6:**168

Photius (archbishop of Constantinople), **6:**216

Photocomposition devices, **6:**469

Photographic industry, **6:328–331**

Photography, **1:299–302; 6:**330
aerial, **5:**234
documentary, **1:**299–300, 301
Family of Man exhibition, **3:**316, *316*
military, **1:**301; **6:***331,* **331–332**
in Civil War, **1:***199,* 200, 299, *530,* 530–532; **6:**329, 331–332
in Mexican-American War, **6:**331
in Spanish-American War, **6:**332
and mourning memorials, **2:**511
pictorialism in, **1:**300–301

Phrenology, **6:***332,* **332–334,** *333*

Phthisis. *See* Tuberculosis

Phyfe, Duncan, **3:**496

Phylon (journal), **5:**200

Physical Review (journal), **6:**335, 344, 347

Physician assistants (PAs), **6:334–335**

Physician-assisted suicide, **3:**261, 262–263

Physicians, prescribing narcotics, **5:**510–511

Physics, **6:335–348**
in 19th century, **6:**335
in 20th century, **6:**335–336
Big Science, **6:**337–338
biophysics, **5:**437
at California Institute of Technology, **2:**14
and cyclotron, development of, **2:486–487,** *487*
high-energy, **6:338–339**
and military, **6:**336–337
Nobel Prizes in, **6:**335, 336, 337, 487
nuclear, **6:339–345**
cold nuclear fusion, **2:**266
solid-state, **6:345–348**
microwave technology, **5:361–362**

World War I and, **6:**336
World War II and, **6:**336–337

Physics Laboratory, **5:**530

Physiocrats, **5:**20

Physiography, **3:**541

Physiology, **6:348–350**
Nobel Prize in, **6:**349, 350, 388, 487–488

Physique magazines, **5:**197

Phytoplankton, **4:**32

Piacenza, Aldo, **1:**311

Piankashaws. *See* Miami Indians

Picasso, Pablo, **2:**475; **5:**120
exhibitions of, **1:**297
in Armory Show, **1:**268

Piccard, Auguste, **1:**391

Piccard, Don, **1:**392

Pickens, Andrew, **7:**145

Pickens, Fort, **6:**443

Pickering, Edward, **1:**344

Pickering, John, impeachment of, **4:**234

Pickering, Timothy, **1:**124; **3:**256, 351, 352; **6:**426

Picketing, **6:350–351; 8:**230

Pickett, Bill, **2:***443*

Pickett, George E.
in Battle of Gettysburg, **3:**568–569; **6:**351
charge of, **3:**569; **6:**351, *351*
in Siege of Petersburg, **6:**296

Pickford, Mary, **3:**362, 401

Pickling, **3:**405

Pick-Sloan Missouri Basin Project, **6:**30

Pieces of eight, **6:**351

Piecework, **6:351–352**
in clothing industry, **2:**248

Piedmont region, **6:352**
fall line dividing tidewater from, **3:**310
settlement of, **2:**108

Piegan Indians, **1:**481

Pierce, Franklin
and Cuba, efforts to purchase, **1:**188–189; **2:**469
as dark horse, **2:**502; **3:**154
and Gadsden Purchase, **3:**502
New England Emigrant Aid Company and, **6:**49
and transcontinental railroad, **1:**188

Pierce, John D., **3:**114; **5:**317; **8:**281

Pierce, Palmer E., **5:**530

Pierce, Samuel R., Jr., **4:**183–184

Pierce, William, **3:**328

Pierce v. Society of Sisters, **2:**164, 167; **6:**352–353

Pierpont, Francis, **8:**449

Pierpont, James, **8:**572

Pierre (South Dakota), **2:**48; **7:**459

Pierre Chouteau Jr. and Company, **3:**494

Pierson, Abraham, **2:**357; **8:**572

Pietism, **1:**533; **3:**264; **6:**353–354, 515

in Amana Community, **1:**133

Pifer, Alan, **2:**56

"Piggybacking," **8:**231

Pigot, Robert, **1:**569

Pigs. *See* Hog(s)

Pike, Albert, **3:**66

Pike, Zebulon, **3:**297, 298; **6:***354;* **8:**453

on aridity of West, **1:**64

expeditions of, **6:**354–355

Colorado, **2:**298

Rocky Mountain, **7:**190

Spanish interference with, **7:**489

Pike's Peak, **6:**354, 355

first recorded ascent of, **5:**150

Pikes Peak Gold Rush, **6:**355

Pikuni Indians, **1:**481

Pilcher, Joshua, **5:**70

Pilgrims, **6:***355,* 355–356, 377–379, 515

Mayflower, **5:**265, 275

Mayflower Compact of, **5:**276

text of, **9:**86

merchant adventurers and, **5:**317

patents, **5:**317

See also Plymouth Colony

Pilgrim's Progress (Bunyan), **5:**127

Pill, birth control, **1:**466

development of, **1:**468

Pillory, **6:**356

Pillow, Fort, Massacre at, **6:**356

Pillow, G. J., **2:**105

Pillsbury, Harry Nelson, **2:**130

Pillsbury Mills, **3:**390, 391

Piltdown man, **7:**278

Pima/Tohono O'odham. *See* Tohono O'odham

Pimping, **6:**513, 514

Pinchot, Gifford, **3:**175, 226; **5:**31; **6:**529

and Ballinger-Pinchot controversy, **1:**391

and conservationism, **2:**366, 367–368; **8:**422–423

dismissal of, **2:**369

and forestry, **3:**430, 433, 435

and Hetch Hetchy Valley dam, **2:**369

in public land commission, **6:**531

Taft firing, **8:**43

utilitarian ethic of, **8:**480

Pinckney, Charles Cotesworth, **6:**356

at Constitutional Convention, **2:**379

on enumerated powers, **3:**225

on export taxes, **3:**302

in presidential campaign of 1800, **3:**150

in presidential campaign of 1804, **3:**151

in presidential campaign of 1808, **3:**151

and XYZ affair, **8:**570

Pinckney, Eliza Lucas, on plantation life in South Carolina, **9:**111–112

Pinckney, Thomas, **8:**200

in presidential campaign of 1796, **3:**150; **8:**322

Pinckney Plan, **6:**356

Pinckney's Treaty, and Spanish-U.S. relations, **7:**484

Pinckney's Treaty (1795), **3:**425; **5:**159; **6:**356–357; **8:**200, 204

Pincus, Gregory, **1:**468

Pine Ridge Indian Reservation, **1:**383, *384*

AIM occupation of Wounded Knee on, **8:**560–561, *561*

casino run by, **3:**509

Wounded Knee Massacre on, **8:***562,* 562–563

Pine tar, **6:**20

Pine tree flag, **6:**357

Pine tree shilling, **6:**357

Pineda, Alonzo Álvarez, **1:**102; **3:**294–295

Pinegar, William, **8:**210

Pingree, Hazen M., **3:**19–20

Pinkerton, Allan, **6:**357

Pinkerton Agency, **6:**357–358; **8:**178–179

in Homestead strike, **4:**157; **7:**556

Pinkham, Lydia E., **2:**388

Pinkney, William, **5:**447

Pinochet, Augusto, **2:**150; **4:**193; **5:**49

Pinto (Ford), **3:**415

Piomingo (Chickasaw chief), **2:**135

Pioneers, **6:***358,* 358–359

in Oregon, **6:**205

women, firsthand accounts by, **9:**229–233, 238–239

Pioneers, The (Cooper), **3:**434; **5:**70, 119

PIP. *See* Pro-Independence Party

Pipe smoking, **4:**326; **8:**134

Pipelines, oil

in Alaska, **1:**111, 112, **113; 6:**180

early, **6:**359

Piper, Leonora E., **6:**246

Pipes, plumbing, **6:**372–373

Pippen, Scottie, **1:**426

Piracy, **1:**551; **6:**359–360

and Barbary wars, **1:**415

privateering and, **6:**480

in Straits of Florida, **3:**388

and tribute, **8:**229

See also Privateers and privateering

Pirogue, **2:**37

Piroplasmosis (Texas fever), **8:**319, 320

Piscataqua, **6:**56, 57

Piscataqua River, **6:**56

Piss Christ (Serrano), **5:**535

Pit, **6:**360

Pitcairn, Harold, **1:**93

Pitcairn, John, **5:**88

Pitch, **6:**20

Pitchlynn, P. P., on Choctaw in Civil War, **9:**302–303

Pithole (Pennsylvania), **6:**360

Pitkin, Henry, **2:**242

Pitkin, James, **2:**242

Pitt, Fort, **3:**95

See also Duquesne, Fort

Pitt, William, **1:**305; **3:**469–470; **9:**26

the Elder, in French and Indian War, **2:**286, 295

Pitts, Hiram A., **1:**59

Pitts, John A., **1:**59

Pittsburgh (Pennsylvania), **6:***360,* 360–361

growth of, **8:**292

Hill District in, **8:**286

railroad strike of 1877, **7:**29, *29*

and westward migration, **8:**461

Whiskey Rebellion and attack on, **8:**469

Pittsburgh Courier (newspaper), **6:**98, 99

Pittsburgh Reduction Company, **5:**330

Pius VI, Pope, **4:**474

Pius VII, Pope, **4:**474

Pius XI, Pope, **1:**5

Piven, Frances Fox, **6:**440

Pizarro, Francisco, **2:**360; **3:**294

Placide, Alexander, **1:**389

Plains Apache, in KCA Indian coalition, **4:**532

Plains Indians
 defeat of, **7:**9
 and Ute, **8:**299

"Plains Woodland" culture, **6:**29

Plan of 1776, **6:**361

Plan of a Proposed Union between Great Britain and the Colonies (Galloway), **6:**387

Plank roads, **6:**361, *362*

Planned Parenthood, **1:**466, 468
 and *Griswold v. Connecticut*, **4:**66
 women's rights movement and, **1:**6

Planned Parenthood of Southeastern Pennsylvania v. Casey, **1:**7; **4:**497–498; **6:**361–362; **8:**434

Plans of union, colonial, **6:**362–363
 Albany Plan, **1:**113–114; **6:**363
 Dominion of New England, **6:**363

Plant, Henry B., **8:**47

Plant Patent Act (1930), **6:**256

Plant Variety Protection Act (1970), **6:**256

Plantation colonies, **2:**285

Plantation system of South, **6:**363–365
 economics of, **7:**463
 management in, **7:**463
 Pinckney (Eliza Lucas) on, **9:**111–112
 slavery in, **7:**394–395, 463

Plantou, A. A., **3:**3

Plants. *See* Botany

Plasencia, Landon v., **1:**125

Plasma display panels (PDPs), **8:**77

Plass, Gilbert N., **2:**237; **4:**6

Plastic surgery. *See* Cosmetic surgery

Plastics, **6:**299, 365–368, *367*
 as building material, **1:**565
 characteristics of, **6:**366
 disadvantages of, **6:**367
 furniture from, **3:**499
 future of, **6:**367–368

genetic engineering and, **3:**531
 history of, **6:**365–366
 plumbing pipes from, **6:**373
 in toy industry, **8:**153
 types of, **6:**366
 uses of, **6:**366–367

Plate glass, **4:**4

Plate tectonics, **3:**551

Platforms, party, **6:**368–369, 399
 of American Party (1856), text of, **9:**242–243

Plath, Sylvia, **5:**122

Plato, **3:**261

Platt, Orville Hitchcock, **6:**369

Platt Amendment (1901), **2:**54, 470; **4:**69; **5:**47; **6:**369

Platte River, **3:**467; **6:**29, 30
 Long's explorations of, **5:**150

Playboy, **5:**197

Playboy Entertainment Group, United States v., **8:**68

Playground movement, **7:**65

Plea bargain, **6:**369

Pleasant, Richard, **2:**498

Pleasonton, Alfred, in Battle of Antietam, **1:**200

Pledge of Allegiance, **5:**169; **6:**370
 reference to God in, **7:**94
 World's Columbian Exposition and, **8:**558

Plessy, Homer, **6:**370

Plessy v. Ferguson, **1:**443, 549; **2:**199; **3:**14, 121, 342; **5:**160, 406; **6:**370–371

Pleuropneumonia, of cattle, **8:**320

PLF. *See* Palestine Liberation Front

PLO. *See* Palestine Liberation Organization

Plockhorst, Bernard, **1:**313

Ploesti oil fields, air raids on, **6:**371

Plott, Charles, **3:**110

Plowden, Sir Edmund, **6:**39–40

Plows, **1:**58, *60*

Plumb, Glenn E., **6:**371

Plumb Plan, **6:**371

"Plumbers Unit," **6:**287

Plumbing, **1:**428; **6:**371–373, *372*

Plummer, Henry, **8:**336

Plummer, Rachel Parker, **2:**50

Plummer, William, **3:**151

Plunkitt, George Washington, **2:**453

Plural marriages, **6:**410

Pluralism, **6:**373–377
 cultural, **1:**337, 338; **6:**375–376

early perceptions of, **6:**373–374
 in late 19th century, **6:**374–375
 political, **6:**376–377

Pluralist Democracy in the United States: Conflict and Consensus (Dahl), **6:**376

Pluralistic Universe, A (James), **6:**374

Plutonium, **6:**139

Plymouth, Virginia Company of, **6:**377, **379–380**

Plymouth Colony, **2:**288; **3:**289; **6:**377–379**
 demise of, **6:**379
 economy and society of, **6:**378
 foundation of, **6:**377–378
 government and politics of, **6:**378
 growth of, **6:**378
 vs. Jamestown, **8:**528
 landing and settlement, **5:**265, 275
 Mayflower Compact and, **5:**276
 text of, **9:**86
 Mount Hope, **5:**464
 Mourt's Relation report, **5:**468–469
 and Native Americans, **6:**378–379
 See also Pilgrims

Plymouth Company, Sagadahoc Colony of, **7:**223

Plymouth Rock, **6:**379

PM. *See* Preventive mediation

PNBC. *See* Progressive National Baptist Convention

Pneumatic drill, **8:**240

Pneumocystis carinii pneumonia (PCP), **1:**15

PNP. *See* New Progressive Party

Pocahontas, **5:**117; **6:**442, *443*

Pocket vetoes, **6:**380–381; **8:**321

Pocumtuck, **8:**220

Podhoretz, Norman, **6:**32, 33

Podoloff, Maurice, **1:**424

Poe, Edgar Allan, **5:**129; **7:**194–195
 "The Fall of the House of Usher," **5:**119
 "The Gold Bug," **2:**467
 "The Purloined Letter," **5:**119
 "The Raven," **5:**119
 and University of Virginia, **8:**283

Poet laureate, **6:**381

Poetry
 African American, **4:**96
 poet laureate and, **6:**381

Poindexter, John, **6:**401
 in Iran-Contra Affair, **4:**420

Poinsett, Joel R., **1:**166–167

index

INDEX

Point du Sable, Jean Baptiste, **2**:132
Point Four, **3**:415–416; **6**:381
Pokagon, Simon, **5**:128
Pokanoket, **8**:220
Poker Alice, **3**:507
Pol Pot, **2**:16
Poland
 conquest by Germany and Soviet Union, **2**:267
 first partition of, **7**:146
 independence after World War I, **2**:89
Polanski, Roman, **3**:364
Polar exploration, **6**:381–384, *383*
 Greely's Arctic expedition, **4:59–60**
 North Polar, **6**:381–382
 Northeast Passage, **6**:381–382
 Northwest Passage, **6**:136, 381–382
 Peary (Robert E.), **5**:542; **6**:382
 South Polar, **6**:382–384
Polaroid Corporation, **6**:330
Police, **6:384–386**
 Boston, strike of, **1:513–514**; **7**:164–165
 future of, **6**:386
 history of, **6**:385
 issues of, **6**:385–386
 organization of, **6**:384–385
 statistics of, **6**:385
 strikes by, **7**:557
 technology and, **6**:385
Police brutality, **6**:385, *386*, **386–387**
Police power, **3**:198; **6:387**
 of arrest, **1:283–284**
 Miranda v. Arizona, **5:404–405**
 prohibition and, **5**:471
 prostitution and, **5**:225
 of search and seizure, **1**:283, 284; **7:289–290**
Policy and bookmaking syndicates, **2**:463
Poliomyelitis (polio), **6:388–389**, *389*
 March of Dimes and, **5:236**
 vaccine for, **5**:236; **6**:388–389, *389*
Polish Americans, **6:389–393**, *390, 392*
 in American Revolution, **6**:390
 anticommunism among, **1**:197
 in Cleveland, **2**:233
 community building by, **6**:391

contemporary, **6**:392
immigration patterns of, **4**:225; **6**:389–390, 391–392
religious and political affairs of, **6**:391
Polish National Alliance, **6**:391
Polish Peasant in Europe and America, The (Thomas and Znaniecki), **6**:391
Political action committees (PACs), **1**:488; **2**:23–24; **6**:393
 direct mail services used by, **3**:29
Political activism, folk revival music and, **5**:496–497
Political activities
 by federal employees, regulation of, **4**:103–104
 in hotels, **4**:176
Political assessments, **2**:22–23
Political Behavior (Eulau), **6**:403
Political cartoons, **6:393–395**, *394*
Political correctness, **6:395–396**
Political economy, **3:107–111**
 Christian theocratic, **1**:449
Political exiles, to U.S., **6:396–397**
 Mayans as, **9**:509–515
Political Liberalism (Rawls), **5**:92
Political machines. *See* Machine, political
Political parties, **6:397–400**
 absence of, in Confederacy, **2**:341
 alternative, call for, **2**:547–548
 and caucuses, **2:76–77**
 characteristics of, **6**:398–399
 and democracy, **2**:547
 and government jobs, **1**:572, 573
 nominating conventions of (*See* Conventions, party nominating)
 origin and development of, **6**:398
 and party platform, **6:368–369**, 399
 and presidents, **6**:454
 third parties, **8:118–120**, 243
 two-party system, **8**:119, **243**
  nominating system of, **6**:113–114, 399
 after Watergate scandal, **2**:553
 See also Third parties; *specific parties*
Political patronage, **6:258**
Political pluralism, **6:376–377**
Political representation, **7:105–108**
Political scandals, **6:400–401**
 See also Scandals

Political science, **6:401–406**
 in 1990s, **6**:405
 area studies and, **6**:404–405
 behaviorism and, **6**:403–404
 disciplinary maturity period of, **6**:403
 emergent period of, **6**:402
 formative period of, **6**:401–402
 general, **6**:405
 middle years of, **6**:402–403
 positive political theory, **6**:403, 404
Political Science Quarterly (journal), **6**:402
Political subdivisions, **6:406**
Political System, The (Easton), **6**:403
Political theory, **6**:405, **406–408**
 on right of revolution, **7:148–149**
Politics
 Christianity and, **2**:164–165
 Civil War, **2**:218
 radicalism in, **7:16–18**
Politics (Aristotle), **6**:407
Politics (magazine), **6**:85
Polk, James K.
 banking under, **1**:195
 and Cuba, efforts to purchase, **2**:469
 as dark horse, **2**:399, 502; **3**:153
 executive agents appointed by, **3**:277
 expansionist policies of, **2**:550; **3**:299
 "Fifty-four Forty or Fight!" slogan by, **3**:358
 as log cabin president, **5**:145
 Mexican-American War and, **5**:339–341; **9**:219–221
 Mexico and, Slidell's mission to, **7**:398
 Monroe Doctrine and, **5**:446
 and Oregon Treaty, **6**:205, 210
 Polk Doctrine of, **6**:117, **408**
 in presidential campaign of 1844, **3**:153
 slavery issue and, **8**:485–486
 and tariffs, **8**:51
 Texas annexation under, **1**:188; **8**:100
 and trading with enemy, **8**:173
 and Treaty of Guadalupe Hidalgo, **4**:68; **8**:200
 war powers under, **8**:387
Polk, Leonidas, **3**:324; **6**:157
Polk, Sarah, **3**:375

323

Polk Doctrine, **6:408**
  nonintervention policy in, 6:117
Poll taxes, **6:408–409**
  elimination of, 8:9
  in Louisiana, 5:160
  in Maryland, 6:408
  in Mississippi, 5:414–415
  in Virginia, 6:408; 8:344
Pollard, Edward A., *The Lost Cause,*
  5:155
Polling, **6:409**, 532–534
Pollock, Jackson, 1:9, *9,* 10, 298;
  6:471
*Pollock v. Farmers' Loan and Trust
  Company,* **6:409–410**; 8:57
Pollution
  and Canadian-American relations,
    2:27, 29
  legislation for control of, 3:227,
    228
  progress in reducing, 3:231
  See also Air pollution; Noise pollu-
    tion; Water pollution
Pollution Prevention Act (1990),
  3:233
Polycarbonates, 6:367
Polyesters, 8:110
Polyethylene, 6:367
Polyethylene terephthalate (PET),
  6:367
Polygamy, **6:410–411**
  among Mormons, 2:163; 5:250;
    6:15, 410; 8:296, 297
    Supreme Court on, 2:167; 7:150
  in Oneida Colony, 6:410
Polygenism, 1:192
Polymers, 6:366
Polystyrene, 6:366, 367
Polyvinyl chloride, 6:373
Pomerene, Atlee, 7:62
Pomo, 2:7
Ponca Indians, 8:223, 224
  in Nebraska, 6:29
  removal of, 2:95
Ponce de León, Juan, 2:1, 360;
  3:284, 294
  explorations of
    Florida, 3:385
    Gulf Stream, 4:73
Ponce Massacre, 6:545
Pond, J. B., 5:178
Pong (video game), 8:327
Pons, B. Stanley, 2:266
Pontiac, 6:411

Pontiac fever, 5:77
Pontiac's War, 1:543; **6:411**
  and Paxton Boys, 6:262
  Proclamation of 1763 and, 6:490
  tactics of Algonquians in, 8:392
  and Vandalia Colony, 8:308
PONY, 6:514
Pony Express, **6:411–413,** *412, 413,*
  427; 8:443
  discontinued, 8:456
  Southern Overland Mail and,
    5:204
Poole, Elijah. *See* Muhammad, Elijah
Poole, Frederick C., in Archangel
  Campaign, 1:247
Pools, railroad, 6:413
Poor, Henry Varnum, 7:520
Poor Clares. *See* Franciscans
Poor Law (1601), 6:316
Poor Richard's Almanac (Franklin),
  1:129; 5:118; **6:413,** 536; 8:528
  excerpt from, 9:113–114
Poor whites, **6:414**
Poore, Ben Perley, 2:271
Poorhouses, 6:436; 8:439
  elderly in, 7:128; 8:439
Pop art, **6:414–415**
Popé (prophet), 6:7, 67, 541, 542
Pope, Albert A., 1:450
Pope, Jacob, 1:59
Pope, John, 1:501
  Army of the Potomac under, 1:279
  Army of Virginia under, 1:279
  and Dakota Expeditions, 2:492
  in Island Number Ten operations,
    4:438
  and railroad surveys, 7:30
  in Second Battle of Bull Run,
    1:568; 2:212
Pope, John Russell, National
  Gallery of Art designed by,
  5:538
Pope v. Illinois, 6:419
Popenoe, David, 3:317
Popham, Sir John, 6:380, *380;* 7:223
Popham Colony. *See* Sagadahoc
  Colony
Popish Plot (1678), 5:151
Popovic, Mikulas, 1:15
Popular culture
  ecological consciousness in, 3:227
  folklore and, 3:394, 395–397
  foreign observers on, 1:138
  Frankfurt School criticizing, 3:454

UFO phenomenon in, 8:255
See also Music
Popular Democratic Party (PPD),
  6:546
Popular health movement, 5:291
Popular sovereignty, 2:331;
  6:415–416; 8:485
  inconsistency between *Dred Scott*
    case and, 3:467
Population. *See* Demography and
  demographic trends
Population Bomb, The (Ehrlich),
  3:228
Populism, 2:227; **6:416–418**
  alternative medicine and,
    5:291–292
  and Coxey's Army, 2:445
  in Gilded Age, 3:577
  of Johnson (Lyndon), 8:323
  in Oregon System, 6:208
  and progressivism, 2:389
  and Republican Party, 7:112
  sectionalism in, 7:296–297
Populist Party, 5:16
  in Alabama, 1:103
  establishment of, 6:158
  farmers and, 2:45, 46
  Granger movement and, 2:389
  middle-of-the-road populists,
    5:366–367
  presidential candidate of, 6:158
  in presidential election of 1892,
    3:158
  in South, 7:469
  See also People's Party
Porcacchi, Tomaso, 9:7, *7*–8
Porcelain, **6:418**
Porgy and Bess (Gershwin), 3:395
Pork barrel, 5:146; **6:418;**
  7:565–566
Porkbusters Coalition, 7:566
Pornography, **6:418–420**
  feminism on, 6:419; 8:517–518
  in films, 6:419
  skin magazines, 5:197
  Supreme Court on, 6:419
  women on, 6:419
Pornography Commission, 6:420
Port(s)
  cities and, 8:289
  colonial, 2:284
  Washington (D.C.) as, 8:409–410
  See also Harbors
Port authorities, **6:420–421**

Port Authority of New York and New Jersey, **6:**421
  airports operated by, **1:**98
Port Hudson, Battle of, **2:**212
Port Hudson, in Civil War, **8:**324
Port Royal, **6:**421–422
Portage Canal Company, **3:**448
Portages and water routes, **6:**422
  Fox-Wisconsin Waterway, **3:**448
  Mackinac Island and Straits, **5:**188–189
  Niagara, Carrying Place of, **6:**102
Portal-to-Portal Act (1945), **3:**308
Portal-to-Portal Act (1947), **5:**395
Porter, David, **3:**256
Porter, David Dixon, **6:**25
Porter, Edwin S., **3:**361–362; **4:**58; **6:**105
Porter, Fairchild, **1:**298
Porter, Fitz-John, **1:**568
  in Battle of Antietam, **1:**200
Porter, Katherine Anne, **3:**197; **8:**570
Porter, Peter B., **5:**22
Porter, William, **5:**328
Porter, William Sydney, **5:**119
Portfolio investment, vs. direct investment, **3:**419
Portland (Oregon), **6:**422–423
Portland cement, **2:**79
Portnoy's Complaint (Roth), **5:**121
Portola, Gaspar de, **2:**8; **8:**451
"Portolan World Chart" (map), **5:**232
Portraits, miniatures, **5:**393–394, *394*
Portsmouth, Treaty of (1905), **6:**423
Portsmouth Colony, shipbuilding in, **6:**57, 58
Portugal
  African colonies of, **1:**38
  exploration of America by, **3:**283
Positive political theory, **6:**403, 404
Positivism, **6:**423–425
Positron, **6:**339
Posse Comitatus, **5:**385
Post, Charles William, **2:**98; **5:**561
Post, Emily, **5:**226
Post, George W., **1:**251
Post roads, **6:**425; **7:**176
Postal Act (1845), **6:**427
Postal Service, U.S., **2:**439; **6:**425–428
  airmail by, **1:**97–98; **6:**427; **8:**190

  during American Revolution, **6:**425
  automation in, **1:**365
  censorship by, **2:**84; **6:**426–427
  after Civil War, **6:**427
  establishment of, **6:**425
  Federalists and, **6:**426
  in Jacksonian Democracy, **6:**426
  Jeffersonian Republicans and, **6:**426
  mail-order and, **5:**206
  in New Deal, **6:**427–428
  overland mail and stagecoaches, **5:**203–204
  parcel post, **5:**206
  stamps, **6:**427
Postman Always Rings Twice, The (Cain), **5:**121
Postmillennialists, **5:**388, 431
Post-Modern Condition, The (Lyotard), **6:**429
Postmodernism, **6:**428–430
  in architecture, **7:**376
  and historiography, **4:**141–142
  self in, and individualism, **4:**333–334
Postmodernism: or, the Cultural Logic of Late Capitalism (Jameson), **6:**430
Post-Philosophy, **6:**429
Post-polio syndrome, **6:**389
Post-structuralism, **6:**429, **430–431**
Post-traumatic stress disorder (PTSD), **6:**431
  Vietnam syndrome as, **8:**328–329
Potash, **6:**431–432
Potassium carbonate. *See* Potash
Potassium nitrate, **6:**110; **8:**243
Potatoes, **6:**432
Potawatomi, **6:**432–433, *433*; **8:**224
Potomac River, **6:**433–434, *434*; **7:**173
Potsdam Conference (1945), **3:**426; **6:**434–435, *435*; **8:**15
Pottawatomie Massacre, **1:**505, 506; **4:**98, 509; **5:**59; **6:**435–436
Potter, David, **4:**139
Potter, Van Rensselaer, **1:**461
Pottery, **1:**303–305
  art, **1:**304–305
  Arts and Crafts, **1:**321
  colonial, **1:**285–286, 303–304
  Native American, **1:**303
Poulsen, Valdemar, **1:**189

Poultry industry, **2:**542
Pound, Ezra, **3:**197; **5:**120
Pound, Roscoe, **4:**496
Poverty, **6:**436–441
  in 19th century, **6:**436
  in 20th century, **2:**225
  changing views of, **6:**440
  children living in, **6:**437; **7:**186
  in colonial era, remedies for, **8:**439
  defining levels of, **6:**436
  in Detroit, **3:**20
  among elderly, **6:**189; **7:**128, 131, 418; **8:**439
  measures against
    Catholics and, **2:**70
    charity organization movement and, **2:**105–106
    Great Society, **2:**228
    Head Start, **4:**112–113
    Job Corps, **4:**480–481
    World Bank and, **8:**532
  misconceptions of, **6:**437
  The New American Poverty (Harrington) on, **9:**500–504
  reasons for, **6:**437–438
  rural, **6:**437
  in shanty towns, **7:335**
  statistics of, **6:**436–437
  and tenements, **8:**81–82
  urban, **6:**437, 439, 440
  See also War on Poverty; Welfare system
Poverty (Hunter), **6:**440
Poverty Point, **6:**441
Poverty Social Worker (Hunter), **6:**436
Povolny, Michael, **1:**304
Powderly, Terence, **1:**528; **4:**539, 540; **5:**16
Powell, Adam Clayton, Jr., **2:**196; **6:**441
Powell, Cecil F., **6:**344
Powell, Colin
  and AIDS, **1:**18
  alma mater of, **2:**189
  on Persian Gulf War, **6:**292, 293
Powell, John Wesley, **1:**192; **3:**257, 300
  and Colorado River exploration, **2:**301
  in Grand Canyon, **4:**33
  on irrigation, **4:**435
  on preservation of environment, **2:**366
  in public land commission, **6:**530

Powell, John Wesley, (*continued*)
   *Report on the Lands of the Arid
      Region,* **3:**18
   scientific surveys of, **8:**454
   and U.S. Geological Survey, **3:**544,
      545
Powell, Lewis, Jr.
   on affirmative action, **1:**386
   retirement of, **1:**506
   on sex discrimination, **3:**478
Powell, Ozzie, **7:***286*
Powell case, **6:441**
Powell v. Alabama, **3:**575
Powell v. McCormack. See Powell case
Power. *See* Electric power; Hydro-
   electric power
Power, Katherine Ann, **7:**182
Power (Arendt), excerpt from,
   9:388–390
Power Elite, The (Mills), **5:**121
Power of Positive Thinking, The
   (Peale), **6:442**
Power of Sympathy, The (Brown),
   5:118
Powers, Francis Gary, **8:**247
Powers, Hiram, **1:**305
Powhatan (chief)
   British relations with, **4:**312–313
   leadership of, **4:**290–291
   speech to John Smith, text of, **9:**98
Powhatan Confederacy, **6:442–443,**
   443
   British relations with, **4:**283
   in Virginia, **4:**283; **8:**341
Powhatan incident, **6:**443
Powley, State of Maryland v., **5:**13
Pownall, Thomas, **3:**108
POWs. *See* Prisoners of war
Powwow, **2:**500; **6:444**
   music of, **5:**498
PPD. *See* Popular Democratic Party
PPL Therapeutics, **3:**531
Prabhupada, **1:**326; **2:**477
Pragmatism, **3:**269; **6:**325–327, 424,
   444–447
   and liberalism, **5:**91
Pragmatism (James), **6:**445
Prairie, **6:447,** *447*
   buffalo trails in, **1:562**
Prairie, The (Cooper), **5:**70, 119
Prairie du Chien, Indian Treaty at,
   6:447–448
Prairie Island Indian Community,
   revenue from gambling, **3:**509

Prairie schooner, **2:**339, 441; **6:448,**
   448
Prairie Wind Casino, **3:**509
Pratt, Caroline, **3:**116
Pratt, Enoch, **5:**98
Pratt, James, **2:**50
Pratt, John H., **3:**552
Pratt, Julius, **1:**189
Pratt, Richard Henry, **3:**115, 135
   and education of Native Ameri-
      cans, **2:**55
Pratt Free Library (Baltimore), **5:**98
Pratt Graphic Arts Center, **6:**471
Pratte, Bernard, **1:**158
Praxis Series, **3:**139
Praying Towns, **6:**448
Preble, Edward, **1:**415; **2:**378
Precipitation. *See* Rain
Preemption Act (1841), **5:**33, 37
Preface to a Democratic Theory (Dahl),
   6:376
*Preface to a Twenty-Volume Suicide
   Note* (Baraka), **5:**126
Preferential voting, **6:448–449**
Prefrontal lobotomy, **6:**522
Pregnancy
   premarital
      abortion for, **1:**3
      in adolescence, **1:**26
      rate of, **1:**26
      quickening during, **1:**3–4
Pregnancy Discrimination Act
   (1978), **3:**525; **6:449**
Prejudice. *See* Discrimination
Premillennialists, **5:**388
Prendergast, Maurice, **1:**268, 297, 321
Preparedness, **6:449–450**
Presbyterian Church in America
   (PCA), **6:**451
Presbyterian Church in the United
   States of America (PCUSA),
   6:450
Presbyterianism, **6:450–452,** 515
   and Calvinism, **2:**15
   Cambridge Platform and, **2:19**
   and Congregationalism, **2:**349
   Covenanters and Seceders,
      6:450–451
   denominations in, **6:**451
   and education for African Ameri-
      cans, **3:**125
   in Egypt, **3:**141
   influence of, **6:**451–452
   mainstream, **6:**450

   membership in, **7:***87, 90, 91*
   Reformed Christianity and, **7:**75
   revivalism and, **3:**264
   Second Awakening in, **1:**378
   upstart sects and threat to, **7:**86
   and Westminster Confession, revi-
      sion of, **3:**1
Prescott, Samuel, **7:**133
Prescott, William, **1:**569
   "Don't fire till you see the white of
      their eyes," **3:78**
"Present State of the Study of Poli-
   tics, The" (Merriam), **6:**402
Preservation, historic. *See* Historic
   preservation
Preservation (magazine), **5:**550; **6:**452
Preservation movement, **3:**227;
   6:452–453
   vs. conservation movement, **7:**355
   Sierra Club in, **7:**355
   See also Conservation; Wildlife
      preservation
Preservationism, aesthetic, **2:**368–369
President(s), U.S., **6:453–456**
   access to, **8:**471
   ambassadors appointed by, **1:**133, 134
   amnesty granted by, **1:**177
   appointments by
      power of, **1:225–226**
      removal of, Supreme Court on,
         5:506
   assassination of, **1:**327–331; **8:**339
   cabinet of, **2:**2–3
   candidates for, **3:**148–149
   censure of, **3:**303
   as chief executive officer, **3:**341
   Constitution interpreted by, **3:**342
   Council of Economic Advisors of,
      2:430–432; 3:110
   death of, vice presidential succes-
      sion after, **8:**322, 323
   election of (*See also* Election[s],
      presidential)
      Constitutional Convention on,
         2:380
   and executive agreements,
      3:277–278
   Executive Office of, **3:**330; **6:**455
   executive privilege of, **3:**278–279
      HUAC on, **4:**178
      investigating committees and,
         4:411
      Supreme Court on, **4:**497
   and federal budget, **1:**557, 559

and global issues, **6**:455–456
impeachment trials of, **2**:352–353
inauguration of, **4:250–251**
interment of, **6:457–458**
international law and, **4**:393
militia, power to call out, **5**:255
persuading politicians, **6**:454–455
powers of, **6:453–454**
recognition power of, **7**:56
removal power of, **7**:100
residence of, **8:470–472**, *471*
Scotch-Irish, **7**:285–286
Secret Service protection for, **1**:329; **7**:294
separation of powers and, **7**:312
subpoenas to, **3**:279; **6:456–457**
in treaty negotiation and ratification, **4**:393; **8**:199, 203
two-term tradition for, **3**:151; **7**:198
veto power of, **8:321–322**
  line-item, **8:320–321**
  pocket veto, **6:380–381**
Virginia dynasty of, **8**:343, **348–349**
war powers of, **8**:373–374, 387–388
wives of, **3:375–376**
See also specific presidents
Presidential Libraries Act (1955), **5**:100
Presidential Recordings and Materials Preservation Act (1974), **5**:99
Presidential Records Act (1978), **5**:100
Presidential Succession Act (1951), **8**:323
President's Commission on the Status of Women, **8:498–499**, 516
President's Foreign Intelligence Advisory Board (PFIAB), **3**:330
Presidio, **6:458**
Presley, Elvis, **5**:308; **7**:185, *185*
Press
  censorship of, **2**:83–84
  freedom of (*See also* First Amendment)
    Alien and Sedition Acts on, **1**:123–124; **3**:374
    Amerasia case and, **1**:134
    in colonial era, **6**:95
    Grosjean v. American Press Company and, **4**:67
    Near v. Minnesota and, **6**:27

New York Times Co. v. United States and, **6**:287
New York Times v. Sullivan, **6**:91
postal service and, **6**:426–427
Press associations, **6:458–459**
Press gang, **6:459**
Presser v. Illinois, **4**:74
Pressing stamps, **6**:466
Pressure cooker, **2**:36
Pressurized water reactor (PWR), **6**:139
Preston, Thomas, **1**:512, 513
Preuss, Charles, **3**:465
Preval, René, **4**:85
Preventive mediation (PM), **3**:343
PRI. *See* Partido Revolucionario Institucional
Pribilof Islands, **6:459**
Pribylov, Gerasim, **6**:459
Price(s), **6:460–462**
  definition of, **6**:460
  setting and measuring, **6**:460
  trends in American history, **6**:461
Price, Charles, **2**:466
Price, George C., **1**:439
Price, Sol, **7**:126
Price, Sterling, **6**:68
Price and wage controls, **6**:460
  agricultural, **1**:60–61, 66
  in Korean War, **6**:166
  in World War II, **6**:165
Price Club, **7**:126
Price index, **6**:460
Price levels, in inflation, **4**:350
Priceline.com, **3**:183
Priestley, Joseph, **2**:122
  on common law, **2**:316
Prigg, Edward, **6**:462
Prigg v. Commonwealth of Pennsylvania, **3**:482; **6**:278, 294, **462**
Primal therapy, **6:462–463**
Primary, white, **6:463**
Primary elections, **3**:148
  direct, **6:463**
    closed, **6**:463
    in nominating system, **6**:113–114, 463
    open, **6**:463
  increasing importance of, **3**:147
  vs. party nominating conventions, **2**:400
Primary Geography for Children (Beecher and McGuffey), **8**:106
Prime meridian, **9**:3, 35, 45

Primer of Statistics for Political Scientists, A (Key), **6**:403
Primogeniture, **6:463–464**
Prince, Robert, **1**:516
Prince, William, **1**:516
Prince William Sound, Cook's exploration of, **2**:404
Princeton, Battle of, **2**:543; **6:464**, 465
Princeton, explosion on, **6:464–465**
  Franklin Institute investigating, **3**:455
Princeton Seminary, **7**:96, 97
Princeton University, **6:465**
  establishment of, **3**:112, 127
  Institute for Advanced Study at, **4:366**
Principles of Psychology (James), **6**:523
Principles of Scientific Management, The (Taylor), **1**:63
  excerpt from, **9**:342–347
Prindle, William, **1**:290
Pring, Martin, **6**:56
Printer's devil, **6:465–466**
Printing, woodblock (xylography), in mapmaking, **5**:232
Printing Act (1895), **4**:24
Printing and printing industry, **6:466–470**, *467, 468*
  in 19th century, **6**:469
  in 20th century, **6**:469–470
  early history of, **6**:466
  Gutenberg and, **6**:467–468
  in North America, **6**:468–469
  strikes in, **7**:556
  See also Paper and pulp industry; Publishing industry
Printing press, Cherokee, **2**:127
Printmaking, **6:470–472**
  Currier and Ives, **2**:483, **483–484**
  wood engraving and, **8:522–523**
Print-on-demand, **6**:539
Printz, Johan, **2**:541; **6**:77
Prison(s), **6:476–479**
  African Americans in, **6**:477, 478
  Alcatraz, **1:115–116**; **6**:477
  Attica, **1:355–356**; **7**:165
  in Civil War, Andersonville Prison, **1**:184
    firsthand account of, **9**:304–307
  in colonial era, **6**:476, 551–552
  crowding in, **2**:461
  debtors', **2**:513, 514
  Elmira, **3:189–190**; **7**:75

Prison(s), (*continued*)
juveniles in, **4:**505
Quakers and, **6:**476, 551–552
reform of, **6:**477–478
vs. reformatories, **6:**477; **7:**74
riots in, **7:**165
San Quentin, **7:**242–243
separate and silent systems of,
6:476–477
Sing Sing, **6:**476; **7:**365–366
supermax, **6:**478
women in, **6:**478
Prisoners of war (POWs),
6:472–476
in American Revolution, **6:**472,
473, 475
atrocities against, **1:**354
in Civil War, **2:**218; **6:**472
in Andersonville Prison, **1:**184
firsthand account by, **9:**304–307
exchange of prisoners, **6:**473
prison camps, **6:**473–474
Union, **1:***567*
exchange of, **6:**473
Geneva Conventions and, **3:**535;
6:472
in Korean War, **4:***548*, 548–549;
6:472, 473
in Mexican-American War, **6:**472,
473
in Persian Gulf War, **6:**472
firsthand account by, **9:**518–520
in prison camps
Confederate, **6:**473–474
Japanese, in World War II, **1:**427
Union, **3:**189–190; **6:**474
World War II, **6:**474–475
on prison ships, **6:**475
in American Revolution, Jersey
Prison Ship, **4:**473; **6:**475
in Spanish-American War, **6:**473
in Vietnam War, **6:**472, 473, 475
POW/MIA controversy, **6:**475
in War of 1812, **6:**473
in World War I, **6:**472, 473
in World War II, **1:**427, *427*;
6:472, 473, 474; **8:***546*
Privacy, **6:**479–480
on Internet, FBI and, **3:**339
invasion of, Aid to Dependent
Children and, **8:**440
right to, **6:**479–480; **7:**192
for abortion, **4:**497; **6:**479
for birth control, **1:**6; **4:**67; **6:**479

Private banks, **1:**406
Private Enterprise Initiative (PEI),
3:418
Private investigation company. *See*
Pinkerton Agency
Private schools, **7:**267–268
Privateers and privateering, **6:**360,
480–481
Letters of Marque and Reprisal,
5:248
merchantmen, armed, **5:**321–322
Yankee, **8:**574–575
Privatization, **6:**481
Privileges and immunities of citi-
zens, **6:**481–482
Privy Council, **6:**482
Prize Act (1941), **6:**483
Prize cases, Civil War, **2:**210;
6:482–483
Prize courts, **6:**483
Prizefighting, **6:**483–485;
7:509–510
Prizes and awards
Academy Awards, **6:**485–486
Guggenheim Awards, **6:**486
MacArthur Foundation "Genius"
Awards, **6:**486–487
Nobel Prizes (*See* Nobel Prize[s])
Pulitzer Prizes, **6:**488–489
Problem of Indian Administration, The
(Meriam Report), **5:**323–324
Procedural due process of law,
3:90–91
Process of Government (Bentley),
6:376, 402
Pro-choice movement, **6:**361–362,
489
Proclamation(s), **6:**490–491
Proclamation money, **6:**490
Proclamation of 1763, **6:**490
Proclamation of Amnesty, **6:**491
Procter, Henry A., **8:**111, 400
Procter, William, **6:**491
Procter and Gamble, **1:**428; **6:**491
in soap industry, **7:**407, 408
Producer prices, **6:**460
Product placement, **1:**34
Product tampering, **6:**491–492
Production Code, **3:**363
Productivity
concept of, **6:**492
statistics on, **3:**106
Professional Golfers Association
(PGA), **4:**19

Profit sharing, **6:**492–493
Profiteering, **6:**493
Progress and Poverty (George), **2:**10;
6:493–494
Progressive Era/movement, **2:**375;
6:494–498
in Arkansas, **1:**262
in California, **2:**10
child welfare in, **2:**137
and commerce clause, **2:**311
consumerism and, **2:**386, 388
cult of wilderness, **5:**467
and domestic trade, **8:**159,
160–161
and employer's liability laws, **3:**200
engineering education in, **3:**251
farmers institutes and, **3:**325
in Florida, **3:**387
goals of, **6:**495–496
governmental inspection in, **4:**364
and governors, **4:**29
historians in, **4:**138–139
Indian policies in, **4:**287–288
individualism in, **4:**333
labor legislation in, **5:**13, 14
legislation in, **5:**84
in Maryland, **5:**257–258
maternal and child health issues,
5:274
medical education in, Flexner
report on, **5:**282
minimum-wage legislation in,
5:394
in Minnesota, **5:**399
Mormon church in, **5:**54
municipal ownership and, **5:**477
municipal reform, **5:**478
murals and, **5:**483
in Oregon, **6:**206–207
and presidential campaign of 1912,
3:160
and prisons, **6:**476
and public health work, **3:**240
reform coalitions in, **5:**14
and Republican Party, **7:**112
social legislation in, **7:**415
state legislatures in, **5:**79
supporters of, **6:**494, 495
and Treasury, **8:**196–197
in Utah, **8:**297
welfare programs in, **8:**439
Wisconsin and, **8:**492
Progressive income tax, **8:**55, 196
during Civil War, **8:**56

federal, **8**:57–58
  during World War II, **8**:58
Progressive National Baptist Convention (PNBC), **1**:45
Progressive Party
  of 1924, **6**:498–499
  of 1948, **6**:499
    establishment of, **1**:197
  Communist Party and, **2**:327
  La Follette as candidate of, **8**:119
  nickname for, **1**:566
  platform of, **6**:368
  in presidential election of 1912,
    3:160
  in presidential election of 1916,
    3:161
  in presidential election of 1924,
    3:162
  in presidential election of 1948,
    3:163
  Roosevelt (Theodore) and, **6**:496;
    7:112; **8**:119
  of Wisconsin, **6**:499–500
  and Wisconsin Idea, **8**:493
  See also Bull Moose Party
Prohibition, **1**:504; **6**:500–502, *501*
  Anti-Saloon League for, **1**:206;
    6:501
  and brewing industry, **1**:536
  and cuisine, **3**:401
  effects of, **1**:117; **8**:161
  through Eighteenth Amendment,
    1:117; **6**:501
  in electoral politics, **3**:162
  in Florida, **3**:387
  and gun control, **4**:75
  by local governments, **1**:117
  in Maryland, **5**:258
  moonshine during, **5**:455
  Mugler v. Kansas, **5**:471
  and nightclubs, **6**:107
  and organized crime, **3**:60
  and Progressive movement, **6**:496
  repeal of, **1**:117; **6**:501
  speakeasies during, **7**:492–493
  by state governments, **1**:117;
    6:500–501; **8**:80–81
  Volstead Act and, **6**:501; **8**:352
  and wine industry, **8**:487
  Woman's Christian Temperance
    Union and, **8**:497
Prohibition Party, **3**:60; **6**:502; **8**:81
Pro-Independence Party (PIP),
  6:547

Project Apollo, **5**:523–524, *524*
Project Gemini, **5**:523
"Project Independence," **6**:304
Project Mercury, **5**:523
Projection televisions (PTVs), **8**:77
Projects, the, **8**:286–287
Pro-life movement, **1**:4, *6*; **2**:165;
  6:489, *489*
  Moral Majority in, **5**:456
  Operation Rescue in, **5**:549;
    6:199–200
  *Planned Parenthood of Southeastern
    Pennsylvania v. Casey* and,
    6:361–362
Prologue (magazine), **5**:525
Promise Keepers, **6**:518
Promise of American Life, The (Croly),
  6:70, 424
Promontory Point, **2**:94; **6**:502
Propaganda, **6**:502–504
  in American Revolution, almanacs
    as, **1**:129
  black (covert), **6**:503
  in Cold War, **6**:503–504
  controversial outcomes of, **6**:504
  gray, **6**:503
  pamphleteering and, **6**:232–233
  in Persian Gulf War, **6**:504
  psychological warfare in, **6**:503,
    522–523
  white, **6**:503
  in World War I, **6**:503, 522–523;
    8:535
  in World War II, **6**:503, 523
Propane, **3**:481; **6**:301
Property, **6**:504–508
  confiscation of, **2**:346–347
    eminent domain power and,
      3:198–199
  entail of estate, **3**:223–224
  intellectual, **4**:375–376
  mortgage relief legislation,
    5:460–462
  neighbors and, **6**:506
  protection of, **6**:506–507
    contract clause and, **2**:397
  purposes of, changing ideas about,
    6:507
  real vs. personal, **4**:375
  regulatory takings of, **6**:505–506
  rights to, **6**:504–505
    restrictions on, **6**:505, 506
    Supreme Court on, **6**:505
    of women, **3**:519

Property qualifications, **6**:508
  for suffrage, **3**:145, 250; **8**:4, 6, *355*
Property Requisition Act (1941),
  4:75
Property tax, **8**:56, 57
  Proposition 13 and, **6**:508–509
Property Tax Relief Act (1978),
  6:509
Prophet, Elizabeth Clare, **2**:478
Prophet, The (Gibran), **5**:72
Prophet (Shawnee leader), **7**:337,
  337
Prophet cults, **6**:6
Proportional representation, **6**:448,
  508
Proposition 8, **6**:509
Proposition 13, **2**:12; **6**:508–509
Proposition 14, **7**:82
Proposition 187, **4**:229; **6**:509
Proposition 209, **6**:509–510
Proposition 227, **6**:510
Proprietary agent, **6**:510
Proprietary colonies, **6**:*510*,
  510–512, *511*; **7**:201
  Duke of York's, **3**:93–94
Proprietors, **6**:510–511
Pro-Slavery Argument (Dew), text of,
  9:267–269
Prospectors, **6**:*512*, 512–513
Prosser, Gabriel, **3**:501; **7**:8, 156,
  379
Prostitutes of New York (PONY),
  6:514
Prostitution, **6**:513–514
  campaigns against, **7**:64
  child, **6**:514
  Chinese immigrants and, **2**:154;
    8:436
  female, **6**:514
  male, **6**:514
  Mann Act on, **5**:225
  in mining towns, **4**:13
Protectionism. *See* Tariff
Protest movements of 1960s, and
  Earth Day, **3**:100
Protestant Reformation, and explo-
  ration of America, **3**:283, 287
Protestant Reformation Society, **6**:4
Protestantism, **6**:515–518
  arrival of, to North America,
    6:515–516
  and Catholicism, conflict of, **1**:447
  challenges to, **6**:516–517
  Civil War and, **6**:516

Protestantism, (*continued*)
  in colonial era, **7:**95–96
  conservative, **6:**516, 518
  definition of, **6:**515
  denominational colleges, **3:**129, 130
  and denominationalism, **3:**1, 2
  and evangelicalism, **6:**517–518
  Finney (Charles G.) and, **3:**370
  fundamentalism in, **2:**164; **3:**484–485; **6:**516
  gospel music, **5:**497–498
  Great Awakening and, **6:**515–516
  growth of, **7:**90
  hegemony in religious literature, **7:**95
  hymn and Psalm singing, **5:**491, 494
  ideological division within, **1:**448
  individualism in, **4:**332
  among Irish Americans, **4:**221, 223, 423
  liberal, **6:**516, 518
    vs. fundamentalist, **2:**164
  and liberation theology, **5:**93
  marriage in, theology of, **5:**249, 250
  in Middle Colonies, **5:**362
  millennialism in, **5:**388
  modernists in, **5:**431–433
  Moral Majority, **5:**455–456
  and National Council of Churches, **5:**532–533; **6:**516
  Native American missions of, **4:**276
  9/11 attack and, **6:**518
  and revivalism, **3:**263–264
  science and, **7:**271
  social gospel movement in, **7:**412–414
  Sunday schools in, **8:**19–20
  and televangelism, **6:**517–518; **8:**71–72
  and temperance movements, **8:**78
  Vatican II on, **8:**308–309
  women's role in, **8:**500, 501
  work ethic of, **8:**526–529
  See also specific denominations
Protons, **6:**338, 340
Proudhon, Pierre-Joseph, **1:**180
Prout, William, **6:**148
Providence (Rhode Island)
  in colonial era, **8:**289
  settlement of, **7:**151

Providence Island Company, **6:518–519**
  and colonization, **2:**111
Providence Plantations, Rhode Island and, **6:519**
Provincetown (Massachusetts), **2:**38
Provincetown Players, **2:**38; **6:519**; **8:**115
Provincial Congresses, **6:519–521**
  of Massachusetts, minutemen and, **5:**403–404
Provoost, Samuel, **3:**242
Provost, Étienne, **4:**57
Prozac, **6:521**, 522
Prusiner, Stanley, **5:**359
PRWORA. *See* Personal Responsibility and Work Opportunity Reconciliation Act
Pryor, David, **1:**263
Psalm singing, **5:**491, 494
PSB. *See* Psychological Strategy Board
Psychedelic drugs, **5:**169
Psychiatry, **6:521–522**
  mental illness, **5:312–315**
  modern development of, **5:**314–315
Psychic abilities, **6:**246
Psychoanalysis, **6:**521–522, 524
Psychodynamic psychiatry, **6:**521–522
Psychological Review (journal), **6:**524
Psychological Strategy Board (PSB), **6:**503
Psychological warfare, **6:**503, **522–523**
Psychology, **6:523–526**
  academic, **6:**524, 525
  of advertising, **1:**33
  applications of, in education, **6:**524
  behaviorism and, **1:437–438**; **6:**524–525
  cognitive, **6:**525
  encounter groups, **3:203**
  humanistic, **6:**525
  mathematical, **6:**525
  phrenology and, **6:**332–334
  psychoanalysis, **5:**314
  statistics in, **7:**539
  and stock market performance, **1:**476
  See also Self-help movement
"Psychology as the Behaviorist Views It" (Watson), **6:**524

Psychosocial sex identity, **3:**515
Psywar. *See* Psychological warfare
Ptolemy, **3:**283
  Geographia, **5:**232
PTSD. *See* Post-traumatic stress disorder
PTVs. *See* Projection televisions
"Public be damned," **6:526**
Public Broadcasting Act (1967), **5:**554
Public Broadcasting Service (PBS), **8:**73
  middlebrow culture and, **5:**366
  Sesame Street on, **7:**315
Public Choice (journal), **6:**404
Public Contracts Act (1936), **5:**11
Public Credit Act (1790), **6:527**
Public debt. *See* Debt(s), public
Public domain, **2:**367; **6:**527, **527–529**
Public Domain, The (Donaldson), **6:**531
Public health. *See* Epidemics and public health
Public housing, **3:**539; **8:**82, 293
  in Chicago, **2:**133
  debacle of 1950s, **8:**286–287
Public Interest (magazine), **6:**32
Public interest law, **4:**35, 36; **6:529–530**
Public land(s)
  in 19th century, **5:**28–29
  in Alaska, **5:**30
  in colonial era, **5:**32
  federal ownership of, negative reaction in Utah, **8:**298
  fencing of, **3:**353; **6:532**
  in homestead movement, **4:**155–157
  Interior Department role in, **4:**383
  land acts and, **5:**25
  land scrip and, **5:**35
  land speculation and, **5:**35–38
  management of, **5:**31
  marine sanctuaries, **5:**244
  mineral patent law, **5:**389
  Native American sacred sites on, **5:**180
  preservation of, **5:**25
  as public trust, **5:**27
  for schools, **7:**265
  single tax on, **7:**366
Public land commissions, **5:**25; **6:530–532**

Public Land Strip, **2**:173
Public opinion, **6**:409, **532–535**
  on divorce, **3**:317
  interest groups and, **4**:381
Public ownership. *See* Government ownership
Public schools
  in 19th century, **3**:114
  in 20th century, **3**:117
  alternatives to, **2**:111
  compulsory, Supreme Court on, **6**:352–353
  curriculum in, **2:482–483**
  development of, **2**:106
  evolution taught in, North Carolina banning, **6**:130
  Jefferson (Thomas) and, **3**:112–113; **8**:279
  in North Carolina, **6**:128–129, 130
  privatization proposals for, **6**:481
  religion in, controversy over, **2**:164, 167
Public transportation, **4**:356–357
Public utilities, **6:535–536**
Public utility holding companies, **4**:411–412
Public Utility Holding Company Act (PUHCA) (1935), **3**:348; **4**:147; **6:535–536**
Public Works Administration (PWA), **2**:371; **8**:441
Public works projects, **4**:48
  in Maryland, **5**:257
  Maysville Veto (1830), **5:277**
Publications, government, **3**:344; **4:24–25**
  by Office of Federal Register, **5**:525
Publicity, as advertising, **1**:32
Publick Occurrences Both Forreign and Domestick (newspaper), **6**:94
Publishing industry, **2**:322–323; **6:536–540**
  in 1920s, **6**:537–538
  almanacs in, **1**:129–130
  book reviews, **5**:192
  in colonial era, **1**:129; **6**:536
  consolidation in, **6**:538–539
  digital printing and, **3**:25
  electronic, **2**:323; **6**:539
  gift books or annuals, **5**:192
  Great Depression and, **6**:538
  Internet and, **6**:470, 539
  magazine ownership, **5**:192

McGuffey's Readers, **5:185**
  music printing, **5**:495, 502
  in New York City, **6**:536–537
  and textbooks, **8**:105
  women in, **6**:90, 95, 97
Puddling, **4**:426–427
Pueblo, **1**:563; **6**:*540*, 540–541, *541*
  agriculture of, **6**:540; **8**:227
  Apaches and, **1**:219, 220
  Blue Lake returned to, **6**:69; **8**:48
  Christianity and, **2**:163
  Franciscans converting, **6**:67; **8**:227
  irrigation by, **4**:307
  in New Mexico, **6**:65, 69, 540; **8**:47–48
  in Santa Fe region, **7**:247
  silversmithing, **5**:328
  Spanish explorers and, **3**:296
  Spanish policies and, **4**:282–283
Pueblo incident, **6:541**
Pueblo Lands Act (1924), **6**:69
Pueblo Revolt (1680), **6**:67, **542**; **8**:47, 599
Puerto Rican Americans
  military service, **5**:383–384
  number of, **4**:134
  violence by, **4**:135
Puerto Ricans, in U.S., **6:542–543**
  in Chicago, **6**:543
  communities of, **6**:543
  in New Jersey, **6**:63
  in New York City, **6**:542; **8**:291
  in Philadelphia, **6**:543
  women, **5**:531; **6**:542, 543
Puerto Rico, **5**:47; **6:543–547**, *546*
  annexation of, **1**:189; **4**:135; **6**:544–545; **8**:92, 94
  as commonwealth, **6**:546–547
  Foraker Act and, **3**:413; **6**:544
  Jones Act and, **6**:542, 544–545
  rights of citizens of, **4**:135
  under Spanish rule, **6**:544
  Spanish-American War and, **6**:542, 544
  Supreme Court on, **4**:367
  U.S. acquisition of, **2**:470
  U.S. invasion of, **4**:135
  U.S. relations with, **2**:54
Puget Sound, **6**:547, *548*
  ferry system in, **3**:355
  San Juan Islands in, **7**:242
Pugwash Conferences, **6:547–548**

PUHCA. *See* Public Utility Holding Company Act
Pujo, Arsène, **6**:548
Pujo Committee, **1**:405; **6:548**
Pujo Money Trust (1912), **3**:344
Pulaski, Casimir, **6**:390
Pulitzer, Joseph, **6**:97–98, 488, *488*
  circulation war with Hearst, **8**:577
Pulitzer Prizes, **6:488–489**
  for cartoons, **6**:395
  for comics, **2**:309
Pullis, Commonwealth v., **5**:13
Pullman (Illinois), **2**:185; **8**:303, 438
Pullman, George M., **6**:549, 550; **8**:303, 304
  and Chicago, growth of, **2**:132
  and land speculation, **5**:37
Pullman Car Works, **6**:549
Pullman cars, **6**:*550*, 550–551; **8**:*186*, 305
Pullman strike (1894), **2**:132, 227; **6**:*549*, **549–550**; **7**:38, 556–557; **8**:303
  Cleveland's response to, **4**:249
  statements by strikers and company on, **9**:353–356
  union defeat in, **7**:24
Pulp Fiction (film), **3**:364
Pulp industry. *See* Paper and pulp industry
Pulp magazines, **5**:194, 196
Pulp novels, **2**:390
Pump-priming, **6**:551
Punishment, **6:551–552**
  in colonial era, **6**:551
    flogging, **3**:383; **6**:551
    pillory, **6**:356
    prisons, **6**:476, 551–552
    stocks, **7:551**
    tar and feathers, **8**:49, *49*
  ducking stool used for, **3**:88
  nonutilitarian objectives of, **6**:551
  for rape, **7**:49
  rehabilitation and, **6**:552
  utilitarian objectives of, **6**:551
  See also Capital punishment
Purcell, John, **2**:68
Purdy, Patrick Edward, **1**:324
Pure and simple unionism, **6:552–553**
  in American Federation of Labor, **1**:150; **6**:552

Pure Food and Drug Act (1906),
  2:238, 383; **3:**403–404; **5:**135;
  6:495, 554
  alcohol in, **1:**117
  and cleanliness, **3:**400
  consumer protection movement
    and, **2:**389
  The Jungle (Sinclair) and, **4:**27
  and role of federal government,
    3:341
Pure Food and Drug Movement,
  6:553–555
Pure Land (Jodo Shinshu), **1:**326
Puritans and Puritanism, **5:**117–118;
  6:515, **555–557**, *556*
  anti-Catholicism in, **1:**195–196
  Bay Psalm Book of, **1:**431
  Calvinism and, **6:**556
  disciplining of children by, **2:**136
  on drunkenness, **8:**78
  emphasis on Scripture, **1:**447
  and existentialism, **3:**280
  and family life, **3:**312
  and fast days, **3:**328–329
  funerary traditions of, **3:**486
  and general court, **3:**525
  and Great Migration, **4:**55–56
  hairstyles of, **4:**83
  in Hawaii, **4:**106
  heretics, **5:**270–271, 506
  hymns of, **4:**206
  immigration to New England,
    2:18–19
  Magna Carta and, **5:**201
  manifest destiny, **5:**223
  Massachusetts Bay Colony, **5:**265,
    269–271
  meetinghouses of, **5:306**
  membership in, Halfway Covenant
    on, **4:87**
  moral societies, **5:456**
  Native Americans and
    conversion of, **6:**48, 448
    in King Philip's War, **4:**313
    missions for, **4:**276–277
    in New England, **6:**46, 47, 555,
      556
  and New England Way, **6:**50
  in New Haven Colony, **6:**59–60
  and philanthropy, **6:**316
  Praying Towns established by,
    6:448
  and Quakers, relations between,
    7:1

religion in lives of, **2:**162
  and revivalism, **3:**263–264
  The Scarlet Letter on, **7:**263
  separatism in, **7:313–314**
  and settlement of New England,
    2:288
  and theater, **8:**113
  vacationing and, **8:**305
  on witchcraft, **2:**162; **8:**494
  work ethic of, **7:**63–64
*Purple and Rose: The Lange Leizen of
  the Six Marks* (Whistler), **3:**537
Purple Heart, Order of the, **2:**527
Pursh, Frederick, **1:**519
Puryear, Martin, **1:**307
Push polls, **6:**534
Putin, Vladimir, at summit confer-
  ences, **8:**16
Putnam, Brenda, **1:**309
Putnam, Frederick Ward, **1:**141
Putnam, George Palmer, **6:**536, 537
Putnam, Herbert, **5:**101
Putnam, Israel, **1:**569
  "Don't fire till you see the white of
    their eyes," **3:**78
Putnam, Robert, **1:**526
PVC, **6:**366
PWA. *See* Public Works Administra-
  tion
PWR. *See* Pressurized water reactor
Pyle, Ernie, **6:**99, 183
Pynchon, Thomas
  Gravity's Rainbow, **5:**122
  Mason & Dixon, **5:**122
Pynchon, William, **5:**135
Pyramid schemes, **6:557**
  of investment companies, **4:**412
Pyrex, **4:**4

and family life, **3:**312
  in New Jersey, **3:**103
  pacifism of, **2:**281; **6:**227
  in Pennsylvania, **2:**289; **4:**151;
    6:276–277
  and prisons, **6:**476, 551–552
  in Rhode Island, **7:**151
  in Swarthmore College, **8:**33–34
  and theater, **8:**113
  and Underground Railroad,
    8:249–250
  and war relief, **8:**542
Qualified gold-bullion standard,
  4:16
Quality circles, **7:3–4**
*Quantitative Classification of Igneous
  Rocks, The* (U.S. Geological Survey), **6:**301
Quantrill, William Clarke, **4:**509;
  7:4
Quantrill's Raid, **4:**509; **7:**4
Quantum mechanics, **6:**341
Quantum physics, **6:**338–339
Quapaw, **8:**223
Quarks, **6:**338
Quartering Acts, **8:**150
  of 1774, **4:**408; **7:**4
Quasi War, **2:**258, 530
  end of, **2:**398
Quay, Matthew S., **3:**157
Quayle, Danforth (Dan)
  in presidential campaign of 1988,
    3:168
  in presidential campaign of 1992,
    3:169
  speech on family values, **3:**317
Quebec
  Arnold's march to, **1:281–282**;
    9:*34*, 36
  British occupation of, **2:**295
  capture in French and Indian War,
    7:4
  colonial settlements in, **6:**52
  founding of, **2:**103; **3:**286, 291
  Montreal, Capture of (1760),
    5:454
  Montreal, Capture of (1775),
    5:454
  under siege (1759), **3:**470–471
Quebec Act (1774), **4:**408; **6:**490
Quechan, **8:**228
Queen Anne's War, **2:**294
  Deerfield Massacre in, **2:**527
Queen Charlotte (ship), **5:**21

Q

Qaddafi, Muammar, **1:**496
Qaeda. *See* Al Qaeda
Quadrille, **5:**495
"Quadruplex" telegraphy, **8:**69
Quaker Oats Company, **2:**98;
  6:151–152
Quakers, **6:**515; **7:1–3**
  antislavery among, **1:**208; **6:**277
  and education for African Ameri-
    cans, **3:**120, 125
  exemption from military service,
    2:361

Queensberry Rules, **6**:483
Quids, **3**:151; **7**:4–5
Quill, Mike, **1**:151
Quilting, **7**:5, 5–6
 AIDS Quilt, **1**:72–73, *73*; **7**:6
Quimby, Phineas P., **2**:170
Quinby, Moses, **1**:436
Quincy, Josiah, Jr., **1**:513
Quine, Willard, **6**:446
Quiner, Joanna, **1**:308
Quinlan, Karen Ann, **1**:462; **3**:262;
 7:160
Quinn, John, **2**:273
Quinn, Robert Emmet, **7**:153
Quinn, William, **4**:108
Quinnipiac Indians, **6**:59
Quintpartite Deed, **6**:60
Quitman, John A., **2**:105; **5**:350
Quiz show scandals, **7**:6
Quota sampling, **6**:534
Qwest, **1**:381

R

R. J. Hackett (ship), **4**:54
RA. *See* Resettlement Administration
Rabaul Campaign, **7**:6–7
Rabe, David, **8**:115
Rabi, I. I., **6**:344
Rabies, **8**:319
Rabin, Yitzhak, **4**:442, *442*, 443, 444
RAC. *See* Russian-American Company
Race
 anthropological theories of, **1**:192
 assimilation and, **1**:337–338
 equal protection cases in context of, **3**:246
 historical writings on, **4**:142
 and life expectancy, **5**:105–106
 multiculturalism and, **5**:473–474
 politics of, **5**:187
 shares of population by, **2**:*555*, 555–556, *557*
 unemployment rate by, **8**:253
 in Victorianism, **8**:325
 See also Civil rights movement
Race discrimination. *See* Discrimination, race
Race relations, **7**:7–12, *11*
 in Atlanta, **1**:348–349
 in colonial era, **7**:7–8

 foreign observers on, **1**:138, 148–149
 in Haiti, **4**:84
 immigration and, **5**:4–5
 in Louisiana, **5**:161
 in Missouri, **5**:421
 music and, **5**:499
 NAACP and, **5**:526–527
 political violence and, **1**:332–333
 suburbanization and, **5**:356
Race riots, **7**:*9*; **8**:337–338
 in 1960s, **7**:165, 166–168
 in Arkansas, **1**:262
 in Chicago, **2**:133, **134**
 in Detroit, **3**:21, *22*
 after King's assassination, **4**:528; **8**:338
 in Los Angeles, **2**:12
  in 1965 (Watts), **2**:12; **8**:430–431, *431*
  in 1992 (Rodney King), **5**:155, *155*; **6**:385, *386*; **7**:12, 165; **8**:338, 339
 in Michigan, **5**:356
 and police, **6**:385
 in Toledo, **8**:138
 in Tulsa (1921), **8**:239, *239*
 during World War I, **8**:537
Racial discrimination, **3**:48–51
 benign neglect, **1**:442
 combating, **3**:48–49
 labor and, **5**:9, *9*
 redlining, **7**:72–73
 reverse, claims regarding, **1**:386
 in voting, elimination of, **3**:144
 See also Racism
Racial gerrymandering, **3**:62, 564
Racial injustice, newspapers and, **5**:200
Racial nationalism, **1**:477–478, 479
Racial science, **3**:258; **7**:12–13
 intelligence testing in, **4**:379
Racial segregation. *See* Desegregation; Segregation
Racial stereotypes
 in *The Birth of a Nation*, **1**:469
 and Brownsville affair, **1**:549–550
Racially restrictive covenant, **6**:506
Racial-religious communities, **8**:303
Racism
 affirmative action and, **1**:35–37
 African American migration and, **5**:369–371

 anti-Catholicism compared to, **1**:195
 against Asian Americans, **2**:10, 157; **8**:577–578
 against Chinese Americans, **2**:154; **5**:250
 in colonial society, **2**:291
 constitutionalized, Dred Scott case and, **3**:85–86
 at country clubs, **4**:19–20
 in education
  American Federation of Teachers on, **1**:155
  higher, **1**:37
  in graduate schools, **5**:526
 in employment, **1**:35–37
 and picketing, **6**:350
 Supreme Court on, **4**:66
 in films, **3**:362, 363
 against Japanese Americans, **2**:11, 13; **4**:463
 militia movement and, **5**:385
 in Mississippi, **5**:412–413
 in museums, **5**:487
 National Review and, **5**:556
 persistence of, **2**:205
 police brutality and, **6**:385, 386–387
 in prizefighting, **6**:484
 by property owners, **6**:506
 scientific, **1**:192–193; **7**:12–13
 in sports
  football, **3**:412
  track and field, **8**:155
 state-mandated, Supreme Court on, **5**:165
 in war industries, Roosevelt (Franklin Delano) on, **1**:35
 in Wyoming, **8**:566
 See also Racial discrimination
Racketeer Influenced and Corrupt Organizations Act (RICO) (1970), **2**:377; **3**:338; **6**:212; **7**:157–159
Rackham, Jack, **1**:550
Radar, **7**:13–15
 in air defense, **1**:75
 and aircraft armament, **1**:88
 bomber detection by, **1**:87
 microwave technology and, **5**:361
 in oceanographic surveys, **6**:160
 and weather tracking, **8**:433
Radar room, **7**:*14*
Radburn (New Jersey), **2**:186

Radcliffe College, **3**:133; **7**:319–320
  establishment of, **3**:131
  minorities in, **3**:132
Radiation
  and cancer risks, **2**:34
  experiments, **3**:210
  nuclear weapons testing and, **3**:209; **8**:298
Radical history, **4**:140
Radical Republicans, **7**:**15**, 16, 112
  Lincoln and, **2**:218; **7**:15
  on loyalty oaths, **8**:96–97
  opposition of, **5**:563
Radical Right, **7**:**15–16**
  anarchism and, **1**:182
  militia movement, **5**:**385–386**
  Ruby Ridge, **5**:385
  Waco Siege, **5**:385
Radicals and radicalism, **7**:**16–18**
  government anticommunism and, **1**:198
  Palmer Raids and, **6**:232
Radio, **7**:**18–21**; **8**:66
  advertising on, **1**:34
    for soap, **7**:408
  All Things Considered on, **5**:554; **8**:44
  and audio technology industry, **1**:358
  citizens band (CB), **2**:179
  and consumerism, **2**:390
  early days of, **7**:19, *19*
  in electoral politics, **3**:149
  Grand Ole Opry on, **4**:**34–35**; **5**:515
  Howard Stern Show on, **8**:45
  industry developments, **2**:321–322
  invention of, **1**:440
  March of Time, **5**:**236–237**
  mass media, emergence as, **5**:261
  modern, **7**:20–21
  Morning Edition on, **5**:554; **8**:44
  music on, **5**:493, 499
  National Public Radio, **5**:**554**
  oldest operating station, **8**:492
  propaganda on, **6**:503, 504
  and recreation, **7**:66
  regulation of, **2**:84; **3**:339, 340
  in rural life, **7**:209
  science on, **7**:274–275
  short-wave, **7**:*20*
  soap operas on, **7**:408–409
  symphony orchestras on, **8**:39
  talk shows on, **8**:44–45
  television and, **8**:75

  Voice of America on, **8**:**350–351**
  Westerners for, **8**:458
Radio Act (1927), **3**:339, 340
Radio astronomy, **1**:344
Radio Corporation of America (RCA), **5**:502; **8**:65, 66
Radio Free Europe (RFE), **6**:503
Radio in the American Sector (RIAS), **6**:503
Radio Liberty (RL), **6**:503, 504
Radio Shack, **7**:126
Radioactivity, **6**:340
Radiocarbon dating, **7**:**21–22**
Radiotelegraphy, **8**:69
Radisson, Pierre, **3**:291, 489
Radurization, **3**:407–408
Rafts and rafting, **7**:22, *22*, 171
Raggedy Ann, **8**:153
Ragoné, Helena, **8**:30
Ragsdale, Lincoln, **1**:258
Ragtime, **7**:22
  as African American music, **5**:490
  and jazz, **4**:468
Rahal, Bobby, **5**:72
Rahman, Omar Abdel, **3**:41; **8**:533
Rahv, Philip, **5**:121
Raich, Truax v., **1**:125
"Rail Splitter," **7**:23
Railroad(s), **7**:**30–40**; **8**:187–189
  to 1850, **7**:*31*
  and agriculture, **8**:165
  airplanes and, **8**:191
  in Alaska, **1**:110
  Amtrak, **1**:*178*, **178–179**
  antitrust legislation and, **6**:135; **8**:275
  automobiles and, **8**:191
  building of
    Chinese coolies and, **2**:*156*; **8**:578
    investment banks and, **1**:404–405; **2**:405
  vs. canals, **2**:33; **3**:253
  and city planning, **2**:185
  during Civil War, **1**:*568*; **7**:35, *36*, **40**, *41*
  commuter lines, **5**:373–374
  competition among, **7**:27
  and consumerism, **2**:387
  deregulation of, **7**:39–40, 517
  disasters involving, **3**:41
  and domestic trade, **8**:160
  "emigrant-cars," **5**:*372*
  and farmers, enslavement of, **2**:388, 389

  federal government and, **7**:35
  first, **8**:187
  in Florida, **3**:386–387
  and food and cuisines, **3**:400
  foreign investment in, **3**:420
  and fossil fuel development, **3**:210
  freight service, **7**:39
  government ownership of, proposal for, **6**:371
  and hotel industry, **4**:175
  in Idaho, **4**:212
  in Illinois, **4**:215–216
  in industrial revolution, **4**:344, 345
  in Iowa, **4**:414–415
  labor and, **7**:37–38 (*See also* Railroad strikes)
  land grants to, **2**:43, 94
  lumber industry and, **5**:172
  in maps, archival, **9**:*56*, 56–59, *58*
  in Minnesota, **5**:399
  in Missouri, **5**:421
  monopolies, **8**:188–189
  in Montana, **5**:448
  Mussel Slough incident, **5**:**503–504**
  in New Hampshire, **6**:58
  operations of, computers and, **5**:144
  in Oregon, **6**:205–206
  passenger service, **7**:38–39
  and pension plans, **7**:128
  pools, **6**:413
  Pullman cars, **6**:*550*, **550–551**
  regulation of, **4**:26, 35, 36; **7**:36–37
  standardization of, **7**:32
  and steamboats, competition with, **7**:173
  and steamship lines, **2**:260
  stockyards and, **7**:551
  strikes against (*See* Railroad strikes)
  Supreme Court on liability of, **6**:232
  surveys preceding, **3**:299, 300; **7**:30
  technological developments and, **2**:388
  in Texas, **8**:101
  and tourism, **8**:145
  trade unions for, **5**:7
    American Railway Union, **1**:**167–168**
  Transportation Act (1920) and, **8**:185, 493
  trucking industry and, **8**:191

tunnels for, Hoosac Tunnel, **4:161**,
  161
U.S.-Mexican network, **5**:343
in Utah, Salt Lake City, **7**:233–234
and vacation trends, **8**:305
in Vermont, **8**:313, 314
in Washington (state), **8**:413
and waterway transportation, com-
  petition between, **8**:429
in World War I, **8**:536
See also Transcontinental railroad
Railroad Administration, U.S., **7:23**
Railroad brotherhoods, **7:23–25**, 38
eight-hour day for, **1**:19
Railroad Conventions, **7:25**
Railroad Labor Board, **8**:185
Railroad Mediation Acts, **7:25–26**
Railroad Rate Law, **3**:188; **7:26–27**;
  8:493
Railroad rate wars, **7:27–28**
Railroad Retirement Acts, **7:28**, 38
Railroad Retirement Board v. Alton
  Railroad Company, **7:28–29**
Railroad strikes, **2**:9, 224; **7:38**
of 1877, **7:29**, *29*, 38
of 1886, **7:29**, **29–30**
of 1948 and 1950, **7:35**
American Railway Union and,
  1:168
Pullman strike (1894), **2**:132, 227;
  7:38, 556–557; **8**:303
  Cleveland's response to, **4**:249
  union defeat in, **7**:24
Railway Shopmen's, **7:40–41**
violence in, **8**:339
Railroad towns, **7**:32, 33–34
Railway Labor Act (RLA) (1926),
  7:558
Railway Shopmen's strike, **7:40–41**
Railways
cable, **7**:43
electric, **7**:43–44
elevated, **7**:44
horse-powered, **7**:43
interurban, **7:41–42**
urban and rapid transit, **3**:173–174;
  4:356–357; **7:42–46**
Rain, acid, **1:13–14**, *14*, 80
Rainbow Coalition, **7**:46
Raines v. Byrd, **8**:320–321
Rainey, Ma, **1**:492
Raisin in the Sun, A (Hansberry),
  5:126
Raitt, Bonnie, **1**:441

Rajneeshee cult, **1**:465
Raladam, FTC v., **3**:348
Râle, Sébastian, **4**:474
Raleigh (North Carolina), **6**:130;
  7:46
Raleigh, Sir Walter, **2**:285; **3**:289,
  576; **7**:46; **8**:341
charter to, text of, **9**:82–84
and Roanoke colony, **2**:287; **3**:285,
  288
Raleigh colonies, **3**:288; **7:46–47**
Rall, Johann, **8**:208
"Rally effect," **6**:454
Ramberg, Christina, **1**:311
Ramirez, Michael, **6**:395
Ramis, Harold, **5**:72
Ramos, Fidel, **6**:323
Rampton, Calvin, **8**:298
Rams, Confederate, **7:47**
Ramsay, John, **1**:58
Ramsey, Paul, **1**:462
Ranch Hand, Operation, **1**:54
Rancherias, **8**:215
Ranching. *See* Cattle; Livestock
  industry
Rand, Ayn, **6**:154
Rand, Sally, **1**:575; **8**:559
Rand Corporation, **3**:110; **8**:117
Randall, Benjamin, **1**:412
Randall, C. H., **1**:166
Randall, Fort, **1**:475
Randolph, A. Philip, **1**:547–548;
  2:201; **5:9**; **8**:172
and March on Washington, threat
  of, **3**:49
Randolph, Edmund, **3**:225; **5**:78
at Annapolis Convention, **1**:187
at Constitutional Convention,
  2:379
Randolph, Edward, **5**:151; **7**:47
Randolph, Jennings, **7**:106
Randolph, John, **3**:151; **4**:241
and "doughfaces," coining of term,
  3:82
duel with Clay, **3**:93
on war hawks, **8**:379
Randolph, Thomas Jefferson, **8**:343
Randolph, Vance, **3**:394
Randolph Commission, **7:47–48**
Random House, **6**:537, 538
Ranger (warship), **6**:57
Rangers, **7:48**
Rogers' Rangers, **7:193**; **8**:257
Texas Rangers, **8:104–105**

Rankin, Jeanette, **8**:499
Ransdell Act (1930), **5**:544
Ransom, John, Andersonville Prison
  diary of, excerpts from,
  9:304–307
Ransom, John Crowe, **3**:481; **5**:122;
  7:297
Rap music, **5**:490; **7**:186
Rape, **7:48–51**
marriage and, **5**:249
Scottsboro case, **7**:49
Rape Crisis Centers, **7:51**
Rapid transit. *See* Railways, urban
  and rapid transit
Raskin, A. H., **1**:151
Raskob, John J., **3**:199
Rathbone, Henry R., **1**:328
Rational choice theory, **6**:404, 407
Ratner, Sarah, **1**:460
Rattlesnakes, **4**:129–130
Ratzel, Friedrich, **3**:542
Rauschenberg, Robert, **6**:414, 471
Rauschenbusch, Walter, **1**:413;
  2:164; **5**:431; **6**:495; **7**:413, *414*
R.A.V. v. City of St. Paul, **4**:67, 105
Ravazza, Giuseppe, **8**:244
Rawlinson, Sir Henry, in Somme
  Offensive, **7**:447
Rawls, John
  Political Liberalism, **5**:92
  A Theory of Justice, **5**:92
Ray, Charlotte E., **5**:75
Ray, James Earl, **4**:529–530
Ray, Man, **1**:301
Rayburn, Sam, **2**:194
Raymbault, Charles, **4**:51
Raymond, Daniel, **3**:108
Raymond, Henry J., **6**:89, 97
Raymond, Rossiter Worthington,
  3:217
Rayon, **3**:421; **8**:110
R&B. *See* Rhythm-and-blues
RCA. *See* Radio Corporation of
  America; Reformed Church of
  America
RCRA. *See* Resource Conservation
  and Recovery Act
rDNA. *See* Recombinant DNA
REA. *See* Rural Electrification
  Administration
Read, George, **2**:541
Read, George W., in Somme Offen-
  sive, **7**:447–448
Read, Mary, **1**:550

Reader's Digest (magazine), **7:51**
 advertising, lack of, **5:**194
Readjuster movement, **7:52; 8:**344
Readjustment Benefits Act (1966),
  3:574
Reagan, Nancy, **3:**376; **4:***43*
Reagan, Ronald, **4:***43;* **5:**92
 AARP and, **1:**142
 and abortion, **6:**361
 and acid rain, **1:**13
 and ACTION, **1:**19
 AFL-CIO and, **1:**152
 African policies of, **1:**39
 AIDS research under, **1:**15, 16–17
 and air traffic controllers strike,
  1:82; **8:**172
 anticommunism of, **1:**199
 antitrust legislation under, **1:**215
 arms race under, **1:**272
 assassination attempt against,
  1:*330*, 331, 530; **2:**79; **8:**339
 and AT&T divestiture, **1:**347
 Beirut bombing and, **1:438–439**
 and bureaucracy, **1:**573
 as California governor, **2:**12
 Cold War policies of, **2:**269–270;
  7:212–213
 conservatism of, **2:**376
 and Contra aid, **2:**395
 Cuba policy of, **2:**472
 defense policy of, **2:**529
 and deficit spending, **2:**515
 and draft registration, **2:**365
 drug law enforcement under,
  5:511, 513
 economic policies of, **2:**385–386,
  517; **3:**224; **5:**9, 20; **8:**21–22
  (*See also* Reaganomics)
 educational policies of, **3:**119, 137
 and Emergency Tax Relief Act
  (1981), **8:**59
 and Energy, Department of, **3:**209
 energy policy of, **6:**304
 and environmental backlash,
  3:228–229
 environmental policies of, **2:**230
 and European Community, policies
  toward, **3:**260
 and federal aid, **3:**334
 and Federal Trade Commission,
  3:349
 fiscal policies of, **1:**544; **2:**423
 and food stamp program, **3:**409;
  6:150

 and foreign aid, **3:**418
 foreign policy of, **3:**427; **7:**114
 and Freedom of Information Act,
  3:463
 and gasoline tax, **3:**511
 gays and lesbians and, **7:**331
 and Grenada invasion, **4:**65
 and Guatemala, **4:**70
 and gun control, **5:**557
 Health and Human Services
  Department under, **4:**114
 hostage crises and, **4:**174
 HUD under, **4:**183–184
 intelligence community under, **4:**377
 and Intermediate Nuclear Forces
  Treaty, **8:**206
 Iran-Contra Affair and, **3:**278;
  4:*419*, 419–420; **6:**401
 Iraq-gate and, **4:**422
 Israel and, **4:**441–442
 Japanese relations under, **4:**459
 labor policies of, **2:**275; **3:**244; **5:**11
 Latin American policies of,
  3:143–144; **5:**49
 and Libya, aerial bombing of, **1:**496
 Moral Majority and, **3:**485
 NAACP and, **5:**527
 and National Endowment for the
  Arts, **5:**537
 and National Endowment for the
  Humanities, **5:**537; **6:**33
 and national parks, **5:**553
 National Review and, **5:**556
 and National Security Council,
  3:330; **5:**561
 and neoconservatives, **6:**32
 and Nicaragua, **6:**105
 and nonprofit organizations, **6:**319
 and nuclear arms control,
  7:149–150
 Office of Economic Opportunity
  and, **6:**163, 164
 and Panama Canal, **6:**240–241, 242
 and Philippines, **6:**323
 Pornography Commission
  appointed by, **6:**420
 in presidential campaign of 1968,
  3:165
 in presidential campaign of 1976,
  3:167
 in presidential campaign of 1980,
  2:23; **3:**167
 in presidential campaign of 1984,
  3:167–168

 presidential library of, **5:**100
 on prisoners of war in Vietnam,
  6:475
 privatization by, **6:**481
 public debt under, **7:**367
 and regulatory relief, **5:**11–12
 Religious Right and, **1:**449
 and Republican Party, **7:**114
 South African policy of, **7:**452
 on Soviet Union
  "Evil Empire" speech, **1:**37, 272
  invasion of Afghanistan, **1:**37
  "Star Wars" proposal of, opposition to, **7:**18
 and states' rights to set speed limit,
  3:336
 and Strategic Arms Limitations
  Talks II, **8:**202
 Strategic Defense Initiative of,
  1:75; **6:**145; **7:554–555**
 at summit conferences, **8:**16
 Supreme Court nominations by,
  4:497
 and tariffs, **3:**461
 tax cuts under, **7:**132
 and Teacher Corps, **8:**61–62
 on territorial sea, **8:**93
 and Thatcher, **4:**44
 and Tower Commission, **8:148**
 and Treasury, **8:**197
 and United States-Canada Free
  Trade Agreement, **8:**276
 urban policies of, **8:**293–294
 and Veterans Affairs Department,
  8:317
 vetoes cast by, **8:**321
 visit to Germany, **1:**471
 and War on Poverty, **8:**387
 and welfare system, **6:**439; **8:**442
Reaganomics, **2:**517; **7:52; 8:**229
Real estate development, shopping
  malls, **5:215–217**
Real estate industry, **7:52–53**
Ream, Vinnie, **1:**308
Reapers, **1:**58
Reapportionment. *See* Apportionment
Reason, rule of, **7:203**
Reasonableness of Christianity, The
  (Locke), **5:**140
Rebay, Hilla, **4:**71
Rebellion(s)
 vs. revolution, **7:**148
 slave (*See* Slave insurrections)

Reber, Grote, **1**:344
Recall, **7:53–54**
Recent Social Trends (report), **6**:318
Recessions
  factors leading to, **1**:585–586
  See also Business cycles
Recipe books, **3**:398, 399
Reciprocal trade agreements, **7:54–55**
  with Hawaii, **8**:156
Reciprocal Trade Agreements Act (1934), **1**:386; **3**:426, 524; **8**:52, 156, 165–166
Reciprocal Trade Agreements Act (1962), **8**:157
Reciprocity treaties, U.S.-Canada, **2**:28
Reclamation
  of arid lands, **7:55–56**; **8**:565
    windmills and, **8**:486
  legislation on, **1**:65
  of wetlands, **8**:464
Reclamation, Bureau of (BOR), **1**:65; **4**:383
  dams built by, **4**:200–201, 435
  functions of, **4**:384
  and irrigation, **4**:435
Reclamation Act (1902), **1**:65; **4**:435; **5**:33–34; **6**:30, 528
Reclamation Service. *See* Reclamation, Bureau of
Recognition policy, **7:56–57**
Recognitions, The (Gaddis), **5**:122
Recollects. *See* Franciscans
Recombinant DNA (rDNA), **3**:529
Reconstruction, **3**:271; **7:57–62**, *60*
  African Americans during, **1**:49–50; **4**:374
    political participation, **7**:*61*
    voting rights, **7**:58, 59, *59*, 62
  in Alabama, **1**:103
  in Arkansas, **1**:261
  black codes during, **1**:472
  carpetbaggers during, **2**:59
  civil rights legislation during, **2**:193, 194
  Compromise of 1890, **2:332**
  Congress and, **7**:59–61
  and domestic trade, **8**:159, 160
  in election politics, **3**:155
  in Florida, **3**:386
  Freedman's Savings Bank and, **3**:462
  Freedmen's Bureau, **3**:462–463

  in Georgia, **3**:555
  integration during, **4**:374
  Ironclad Oath in, **4:430**
  under Johnson (Andrew), **4**:236–237; **7**:15, 58, 59–60
  Joint Committee on, **4:485–486**
  Ku Klux Klan during, **4**:551–552
  Lincoln (Abraham) and, **7**:58
  and Louisiana, **5**:160
  in Maine, **5**:210
  in Maryland, **5**:257
  in Mississippi, **5**:413–414
  Mississippi v. Johnson, **5:418**
  and New Orleans, **6**:74
  in North Carolina, **6**:129
  Peabody Fund and, **6**:262
  riots during, **8**:337
    in Vicksburg, **8:324–325**
  scalawags in, **7:260**
  Slaughterhouse Cases in, **7**:378
  in South Carolina, **7**:455–456
  in Texas, **8**:101
  Wade-Davis Bill on, **8**:359
  waning of, **7**:61–62
  in West Virginia, **8**:449
Reconstruction Act(s), **7**:59–60
  of 1867, **3**:555
Reconstruction Finance Corporation (RFC), **1**:402; **6**:551; **7:62–63**; **8**:440
  Gold Purchase Plan and, **4**:12
Record industry, **1**:358–359; **5:502–503**
  See also Music
Record of a School (Peabody), **8**:180
Recreation, **7:63–66**
  bowling, **1**:525–526, *526*
  home-based, **7**:64
  outdoor
    mountain climbing, **5:466–467**
    rise of, **8**:305
  See also Sports
Recreational vehicles (RVs), **8**:178
Recruitment. *See* Conscription and recruitment
Recycling, **7:66–68**, *67, 68*; **8**:420
  of aluminum, **6**:116
  of glass, **4**:4
  of lead, **5**:62–63
  of packaging, **6**:229
  of plastics, **6**:368
Red Badge of Courage, The (Crane), **5**:119

Red Cloud (Sioux chief), **7**:*367*, 370; **8**:404
Red Cloud, Mitchell, **4**:*328*
Red Cloud's War, **5**:40
Red Cross, American, **7:68–70**, *69*
  establishment of, **8**:502
  after World War I, **8**:542
  in World War II, **8**:257
Red Cross and Red Crescent, International, **7**:70
  fundamental principles of, **7**:*70*
Red Harvest (Hammett), **5**:129
Red Lion Broadcasting Co. v. FCC, **3**:341
Red Power, **7:70–71**
Red River
  Long's explorations of, **5**:150
  Marcy expedition, **5**:238
Red River Campaign, **7**:71
Red River cart traffic, **7:71–72**
Red River Indian War, **7**:72; **8**:404
Red Scare, **2**:378; **7**:17; **8**:539
Red Shirts, **7**:72
Red Stick War. *See* Creek War
Red Summer of 1919, **2**:134
Redburn (Melville), **6**:373
"Redeemers," **3**:556
Redeye, Edwin S., **6**:236
Redfield, William, **1**:141; **5**:331
Redford, Robert, **7**:6
"Red-light" districts, **6**:513
Redlining, **7:72–73**
Redpath, James, **5**:178
Redwoods, **7**:314
Reece Committee, **6**:318
Reed, Charles, **4**:34
Reed, Esther, **7**:146
Reed, Harrison, **3**:386
Reed, Ishmael, **5**:123
  Mumbo Jumbo, **5**:126
Reed, John, **2**:325
Reed, Ralph, **2**:161; **3**:485
Reed, Rebecca Theresa, **8**:295
Reed, Thomas B., **7**:73
Reed, Walter, **5**:294; **8**:576, *576*
  and University of Virginia, **8**:283
Reed, Willis, **1**:425
Reed Rules, **7**:73
Reed v. Reed, **2**:445; **3**:478; **7:73**
Reeder, A. H., **1**:505
Reel, Estelle, **8**:564
Reese, United States v., **8**:275
Reeve, Tapping, **5**:56
Reeves, Joseph M., **8**:555

Reference books, **6**:539

Referendum, **3**:144; **7:73–74**
  direct democracy and, **2**:548
  in Oregon System, **6**:208

Reflections on the Revolution in France (Burke), **7**:149, 162

Reflexology, **6**:39

Reform movements. *See* Progressive Era

Reformatories, **6**:477, 552; **7:74–75**

Reformed Church of America (RCA), **7**:76, 89

Reformed churches, **7:75–76**, 89; **8**:263, 264

Reformed Presbyterian Church of North America (RPCNA), **6**:450

Refrigeration, **3**:407, *407*, 479; **7:76–78**, 77, *78*
  development of, **3**:182
  meatpacking and, **5**:279

Refugee(s)
  after American Revolution, **7**:137
  Cuban, **2**:*471*, 472, 473
  Guatemalan, **9**:509–515
  Haitian, **4**:85, *85*
    U.S. policies regarding, **7**:81
  Hungarian, **2**:*90*
  Jewish, **4**:226–227
    during World War II, **7**:*79*, 79–80
    U.S. response to, **1**:444–445
  from Nazi Germany, **4**:226–227
  political exiles, **6:396–397**
  from Southeast Asia, **7**:470–471
  Soviet, **7**:213

Refugee Act (1980), **7:78–79**, 80–81

Refugee Convention, **6**:397

Refugee Relief Act (1953), **6**:397

Regents of the University of California, Bakke v., **1**:37, 386; **3**:119

Regional floods, **3**:383

Regionalism
  cultural, **7**:297–298
  in painting, **1**:297–298

Regulating the Poor: The Functions of Public Welfare (Piven and Cloward), **6**:440

Regulators, **7:82**
  in North Carolina, **6**:127

Regulatory takings, **6**:505–506

Rehabilitation, **6**:552

Rehabilitation Act (1973), **5**:15

Rehm, Diane, **7**:21

Rehnquist, William H., **8**:274
  on abortion, **6**:361; **8**:433
    right to privacy for, **6**:479
  as Arizona native, **1**:259
  on assisted suicide, **3**:263; **8**:418
  on commerce clause, **2**:312
  Court under, **4**:493–494; **8**:25
  on doctrine of free speech, **3**:374
  on homosexuality and Boy Scouts, **1**:527
  judicial review under, **4**:493–494
  on line-item vetoes, **8**:320, 321
  nomination of, **4**:497
  on presidential election of 2000, **1**:579
  on separation of church and state, **3**:374
  on sex discrimination, **3**:478, 525
  on sexual orientation, discrimination based on, **7**:196

Reich, Otto J., **6**:504

Reich, Richard, **5**:12

Reich, Robert, **4**:481

Reid, Bill, **3**:410

Reid, Harry, **8**:468

Reid, Margaret, **3**:110

Reid, Robert, **2**:413

Reid, Thomas, **6**:402; **8**:179

Reid v. Covert, **3**:272

Reilly, Edward J., **5**:113

Reineman, R. G., **3**:499

Reiner, Rob, **1**:*126*, 127

Reinolds v. United States, **2**:167

Reinventing Government Program. *See* National Performance Review

Reitman v. Mulkey, **7:82**

Relacion, La (Cabeza de Vaca), **2**:1, *1*

Relational database software, **7**:441–442

Relations (Jesuit reports), **4:473–474**

Relativism, cultural, **1**:192–193

Relief. *See* Welfare System

Religion, **7:82–93**
  in 2002, **7**:*85*
  African American, **1:41–46**
  Asian, **1:325–327**
  assimilation and, **1**:337
  civil, **2:192–193**
  in colonial society, **2**:291–292; **7**:83–85, *88*
  and conscientious objection, **2**:361
  deist, **2:538–540**
  discrimination based on, **3:51–53**

  diversity of (denominationalism), **3:1–3**
  ecumenicalism in, Vatican II and, **8**:308
  in electoral politics, **3**:168
  and existentialism, **3**:279–280
  and fast days, **3**:328–329
  freedom of (*See* Religious liberty/freedom)
  hymns in, **4:206–207**
  immigration and shifts in, **7**:88–89
  millennialism, **5:388**
  mysticism, **5:506–507**
  National Council of Churches and, **5**:532–533
  of Native Americans (*See under* Native American[s])
  and pacifism, **6**:227
  participation in, rise in, **7**:*83*, 299
  in schools, debate on, **2**:164, 167, 168–169
  science and, relations of, **7:269–271**
    agnosticism and, **1**:55
  vs. secularization, **7**:299–300
  suffrage based on, **1**:206; **8**:6
  sumptuary laws on, **8**:17
  Sunday schools, **4**:206; **8:19–20**
  televangelism and, **8**:71–72
  Utopian communities based on, **8**:302
  in Victorianism, **8**:325
  See also Christianity; Islam; Judaism; *specific denominations*

Religious Affections (Edwards), **6**:325

Religious Freedom Restoration Act (RFRA) (1993), **1**:494; **6**:1

Religious Freedom Restoration Act (RFRA) (1997), **1**:162

Religious liberty/freedom, **7**:85, **93–95**
  for atheism, **1**:347
  First Amendment and, **2**:167; **7**:85, 93
  as human right, **4**:193
  in Maryland, **1**:196; **9**:89–91
  for Native Americans, **3**:374; **6**:1
    legislation on, **1**:161–162
  Pinckney Plan and, **6:356**
  Quakers and, **7**:1, 2
  in Rhode Island, **7**:151
  Supreme Court on, **2**:167–168; **7**:150
  Toleration Acts and, **8**:139
  Vatican II on, **8**:308

Religious Right, **1:**449; **3:**267
Religious thought and writings, **7:95–98**
Religious tolerance, **3:**2; **7:**84
"Remember the Alamo," **7:99**
Remington, Frederic, Indian and western images of, **7:99–100,** *100*
Remington typewriters, **8:**244–245
Remnick, David, **6:**92
Removal
  of aliens (*See* Deportation)
  of deposits, **3:**303; **7:**103
  executive power of, **7:100–101**
    Johnson's use of, **4:**234–235, 236–238
    Supreme Court on, **4:**194–195; **5:**506
  of Native Americans (*See* Native American[s], removal of)
Removal Act (1830), **7:101–103**
  Indian relocation districts, **7:***102*
Remsen, Ira, **5:**18
Remus, George, **1:**504
Rendell, Edward G., **6:**313
Renfrow, William C., **6:**185
Reno (Nevada), **6:**38
Reno, ACLU v., **3:**340
Reno, Janet
  accusation of congressional contempt, **2:**393
  and Elián González case, **4:**21
  special prosecutors under, **7:**496
  in Waco Siege, **8:**359
Reno, Marcus, **3:**318; **5:**131–132
Reno, Shaw v., **3:**62; **8:**358
Reno brothers, **8:**178
Reno v. American Civil Liberties Union, **2:**85; **3:**374; **8:**68
Reno v. American-Arab Anti-Discrimination Committee, **1:**125
Rensselaer, Kiliaen van, **6:**71, 259
Rensselaer Polytechnic Institute, **3:**216
Renwick, James, **1:**250
Reorganized Church of Jesus Christ of Latter-day Saints (RLDS), **7:103–104**
  headquarters of, **7:***104*
Reparation(s)
  by Germany, for World War I, **8:**316
  vs. indemnities, **4:**252
  for Japanese American internment, **4:**461–462, 464–465; **8:**415

Reparation Commission, **7:104–105; 8:**316
Repeating rifles, **5:**479
Report on Manufactures (Hamilton), **3:**527
Reporting
  and newspapers, **6:**96–98
  See also Journalism
Representation, **7:105–108**
  Articles of Confederation and, **3:**170; **7:**109
  in House of Representatives, **3:**170; **7:**106–108
  in Senate, **3:**170; **7:**108
  taxation without, **8:**59–60
Representationalism, **6:**445
Representative democracy, **2:**546–547; **7:**109–110
  republic as, **7:**110
Representative government, **7:109–110**
"Representative Men" (Emerson), **5:**119
Reprisal, **7:**126
Reproduction, **2:142–144**
  surrogate motherhood, **8:**29–30
Reproductive Health Services, Webster v., **1:**7; **8:433–434**
Reproductive rights. *See* Birth control
Reptiles, scientific study of, **4:128–130**
Republic, **7:110–111**
Republic of West Florida, **3:**385
Republic Steel (Chicago), and Memorial Day Massacre, **5:**1
Republic Steel Company, **5:**307
Republican family, **3:**312–313
Republican Party, **7:111–114**
  and abolition of slavery, **2:**208
  African Americans in, **8:**356
  anticommunism in, **1:**197
  antislavery in, **1:**212; **5:**110
  in Arizona, **1:**259
  in Arkansas, **1:**263
  birthplace of, **8:**490
  business and, **2:**23
  in California, **2:**9, 10, 11
  and "Chicken in Every Pot" slogan, **2:**136
  Christian Coalition and, **2:**161; **3:**485
  and civil rights legislation, **2:**193, 194

  and civil service assessments, **2:**23
  in Clinton impeachment trial, **4:**240–241
  conservatism of, **2:**376
  and consumer movement, attacks on, **2:**384–385
  Contract with America, **2:**384, **398; 3:**485; **7:**114; **8:**442
  domination period for, **3:**158
  economic strategy of, **6:**494
  education policies of, **3:**119
  electoral base of, **3:**149
    19th-century, **3:**146
  and emancipation of slaves, **3:**190, 191
  on family values, **3:**317
  and federal agencies, **3:**332
  and federal aid, **3:**334
  and foreign policy, **7:**112
  founding principle of, **8:**486
  and Free Soil Party, **3:**459–460
  in Georgia, **3:**555–556
  and Grand Army of the Republic, **4:**31
  and homesteading, **5:**33
  in Idaho, **4:**213–214
  ideological roots of, **7:**111
  in Illinois, **4:**216
  in Indiana, **4:**320
  in Iowa, **4:**416
  labor policies of, **5:**12, 15
  Lincoln's relationship with, **2:**218
  in Louisiana, **5:**160, 161
  in Maine, **5:**210
  in Michigan, **5:**355, 356
  in Mississippi during Reconstruction, **5:**412
  national conventions of, **2:**399; **6:**113–114
    of 1896, **7:**365
    of 1920, **7:**404
  National Review and, **5:**556
  New Right in, Viguerie on, **9:**495–499
  New York Times and, **6:**89
  nominations by, **6:**113–114
  in North Dakota, **6:**132–133
  in Ohio, **6:**172, 173
  in Oklahoma, **6:**185–186
  platform of, **6:**368
  political action committees and, **6:**393
  post-Watergate, **2:**553
  and Prohibition, **6:**502

Republican Party, (*continued*)
  Radical faction of, **7:15**, 16, 112
    Lincoln and, **2**:218; **7**:15
  and Reconstruction, 7:59–61
  and Religious Right, 3:267
  on separation of powers, 7:313
  Silver, **7:364–365**
  and slavery, **6**:416
  in South, **2**:59
  Stalwarts in, **7:517**
  in state legislatures, **5**:80
  steering committees in, 7:546–547
  on subsidies, 7:564–565
  and tariffs, **8**:51, 57, 156
  and taxation, **8**:57, 58
  in Tennessee, **8**:86
  in Texas, **8**:101, 103
  as third party, **8**:119
  in two-party system, **6**:398; **8**:243
  and Union Party, **8:259–260**
  in Utah, **8**:297, 298
  in Vermont, **8**:313, 314
  in Virginia, **8**:344–345
  Whig Party and, **8**:468
  and women's suffrage, **8**:356
Republicanism, **7:114–117**
  Washington's transfer of power
    and, **8**:419
Republicans, Jeffersonian. *See* Jeffer-
    sonian Republicans
Repudiation
  of public debt, **7:118–119**
  of state debts, **7:119**
Resaca de la Palma, Battle of, **5**:340,
    340
Research
  federal government support for,
    5:17–18
  learned societies and, **5**:67
  by think tanks, **8:117–118**
  See also Industrial research; Labo-
    ratories; Medical research; Sci-
    entific research
Reservations. *See* Native
    American(s), reservations
Reserve Forces Act (1955), **5**:542
Reserve Officers' Training Corps
    (ROTC), **6**:170; **7:119–120**
Reservoirs, in West, 7:55–56
Resettlement Administration (RA),
    3:319; **4**:63; **6**:44; **7:120**; **8**:303
Residency training, medical,
    5:282–283
Resin, **6**:20, 365

Resnick, Judith A., **2**:102
Resolutions, Congressional,
    7:120–121
Resorts and spas, **7:121–122**
  American plan at, **8**:305
  mineral springs, **5:389**
  rise of, **8**:305
Resource Conservation and Recov-
    ery Act (RCRA) (1976), **3**:232;
    4:111
Resource management, **3**:226
Responsibilities of the Novelist, The
    (Norris), **6**:12
Reston (Virginia), **2**:188
Restraint of trade, **7:122–124**
  Sherman Antitrust Act and, **7**:203
Resumption Act (1875), **3**:156; **4**:14;
    7:124
Retailing industry, **7:124–126**
  chain stores, **2:100–101**, *101*; **3**:26;
    5:206–207; **7**:125
  country stores, **2:434–436**, *435,
    436*
  department stores, **3:6–11**;
    7:124–125
  dime stores, **2**:100, *101*; **3**:9–10,
    10, **26–27**; **7**:125
  discount stores, **7**:126
  distributors in, **3:61–62**
  e-commerce, **5**:206
  mail-order houses, **3**:9; **5:204–207**;
    7:125
    Book-of-the-Month Club,
      1:500–501
    vs. direct mail, **3**:29
  malls, **5:215–217**; **7**:125–126
  marketing, **5:245–247**
  marketing research, **5:247–248**
  self-service stores, **7**:125–126
Retaliation, in international law,
    7:126–127
Retirement, **7:127–131**
  AARP and, **1:142**
  activities after, **6**:189
  federal government and, **7**:129
  Gray Panthers and, **4**:37–38
  income during, **7**:417–418
  mandatory, **6**:189
    origins of, **7**:127–128
  rates of, **7**:417
  recreation after, **7**:66
  scientific business management
    and, **7**:128–129
  See also Old age

Retirement plans, **7:131–132**
  Employment Retirement Income
    Security Act and, **3:200–201**
  individual retirement accounts in,
    4:330
  profit sharing, **6:492–493**
  See also Pension plans
Reuters, **6**:458
Reuther, Walter, **1**:151, 197; **8**:172,
    261
Revelle, Roger, **4**:6
Revels, Hiram, **1**:50
Revenue, public, **7:132–133**
  Committee on Ways and Means
    and, **8**:432
  federal, **1**:558, *559*; **7**:132, 133
  state and local, **7**:132–133
Revenue Act (1767), **8**:60, 150
Revenue Act (1950), **3**:444
Revenue Act (1978), **6**:493
Revenue sharing, **7:133**
Revere, Paul, **1**:509; **2**:314; **6**:470;
    7:133, 136
  metalsmithing, **5**:329
  trade of, **8**:522, 528
Revere's Ride, **5**:88; **7:133–134**, *134*
  Old North Church and, **6**:190
  Revere's account of, **9**:141–142
Revival movement, Native Ameri-
    can. *See* Nativist movements
    (American Indian revival move-
    ments)
Revivalism, **3:263–266**, *265*; **7**:85;
    8:263
  among African Americans, **1**:42
  in Appalachian frontier, **3**:44
  camp meetings, **2**:21–22; **7**:*86*
  Great Awakening and, **4**:38–39
  and Quakerism, **7**:2
  and religious liberty, **7**:93–94
  of Second Awakening, **1**:377–378
  and Yale University, **8**:572–573
  See also Great Awakening
Revolution(s)
  American (*See* Revolution, Ameri-
    can)
  French (*See* French Revolution)
  right of, **7:148–149**
Revolution, American, **7:134–148**
  1775-1778, **7**:*142*
  1779-1783, **7**:*144*
  African Americans in, **1**:48; **5**:380;
    7:116, 146, 152
  aftermath of, **7**:137

agriculture during, **1**:62
and Army Corps of Engineers, **3**:219
Army in (*See* Army, Continental)
Arnold's march to Quebec, **1:281–282**
Arnold's raid in Virginia, **1**:282
associations in, **1**:340
backwoodsmen during, **1**:382
Battle of Bennington in, **1:442–443; 4**:61
Battle of Brandywine Creek in, **1**:532; **7**:143
Battle of Bunker Hill in, **1**:509, 511, **569–570,** *570;* **7**:142; **9**:*33,* 33–35
   "Don't fire till you see the white of their eyes," **3**:78
Battle of Camden in, **2**:19
Battle of Cowpens in, **2:444**
Battle of Eutaw Springs in, **3:261**
Battle of Fort Moultrie in, **5:463**
Battle of Guilford Courthouse in, **4:72–73; 6**:128; **7**:145
Battle of Harlem in, **4:94–95**
Battle of King's Mountain in, **1**:382; **7**:145
Battle of Long Island in, **5**:149, 150
Battle of Monmouth in, **5:443;** **7**:144
Battle of Oriskany in, **6:213**
Battle of Princeton in, **6:464,** 465
Battle of Trenton in, **8:208**
Battle of Valcour Island in, **4**:77
Battle of White Plains in, **8:473**
Battles of Lexington and Concord in
   American and British accounts of, **9**:143–144
   archival maps of, **9**:30, *30*
beginning of, **1**:509; **2**:287
Boston during, **1**:509, 511–512
Boston Massacre, **1**:458, 509, **512–513,** *514*
Boston Tea Party, **1**:509, **514–515,** *515;* **3**:103
Burgoyne's invasion, **1:573–574**
business regulation during, **4**:25–26
causes of, **4:254–255**
censorship during, **2**:83
Charleston Harbor defense in, **2:108**

Cherokee in, **2**:128; **6**:128; **8**:85
Clark's Northwest Campaign in, **2:222**
and clothing and fashion, **2**:244–245
confiscation of property during, **2**:346–347
Connecticut during, **2**:357
Connolly's Plot in, **2:360**
Continental Congress during, **2**:394
correspondence during
   Scammell's love letter, **9**:146–147
   by Washington, **9**:152
   by Wilkinson (Eliza), **9**:150–151
cost of, **8**:377
cryptology during, **2**:467
debts in, **2:518–519**
   Hamilton on, **4**:87–89
defense system in, **2**:534
desertion in, **3**:17
diplomatic aspects of, **7**:146–147
and domestic trade, **8**:159, 160
events leading up to, **2**:283–284
financial aspects of, **1**:395, 396, 558; **7**:147–148
   Public Credit Act, **6:527**
Florida in, **3**:385
and foreign investment in U.S., **3**:419
and foreign policy, **3**:425
and foreign service, **3**:428
and foreign trade, **8**:164
France and, **3**:449–450, **472–473;** **6**:94; **9**:30
and freedom of religion, **8**:139
and "generation of 1776," **3**:528
German mercenaries in, **1**:442, 532; **3**:560; **7**:141
"Give Me Liberty or Give Me Death" speech in, **4**:2
Green Mountain Boys in, **4**:61
guerrilla warfare in, **2**:19, 444; **4**:70
historiography of, **4**:137
independence as goal of, **4:254–255**
inflation in, **4**:352
and inheritance laws, **6**:464
internationalization of, **7**:144–145, 147
laws of war in, **8**:370
Loyalists and, **5**:167–168
Maine in, **5**:208
manufacturing and, **5**:227

maps of, archival, **9:29–36**
Marine Corps in, **5**:241
Maryland in, **5**:256
Massachusetts in, **9**:*29,* 29–33
mercantilism as cause of, **5**:316
Middle Colonies in, **7**:143–144
military history of, **7**:139–146
military uniforms in, **8**:257
militias in, **5**:386
minutemen, **5:403–404**
Montreal, capture of, **5:454**
munitions, **5**:479
and nationalism, **5**:566–567
Native American policies during, **4**:284
Native Americans in, **2**:360; **4:329–330; 7**:141–142, 146
   wars with, **8**:398
and nativism, **6**:4
Navy in, **6**:24
in New England, **7**:142
New Hampshire in, **6**:57–58
New Jersey in, **3**:104; **6**:62
New Orleans during, **6**:73
New York Campaign in, **7**:137, 141, 143, *143*
New York City in, **6**:79, 84
New York (state) in, **6**:87
Newburgh addresses in, **6**:94
newspapers and, **6**:95
North Carolina in, **6**:128
Ohio in, **6**:171
organizing prior to, **2**:314–315
original documents on, **9**:127–152
pamphleteering in, **6**:232–233
and paper and pulp industry, **6**:245
peace agreement following, **7**:147
Pennsylvania in, **6**:277–278
Pennsylvania troops, mutinies of, **6:280**
Penobscot Expedition (1779), **6:280–281**
and philanthropy, **6**:316
and pluralism, **6**:373
Polish Americans in, **6**:390
political history of, **7**:134–139
postal service during, **6**:425
preconditions for, **1**:457–458
and prices, **6**:461
prisoners of war in, **6**:472, 473
   on Jersey Prison Ship, **4:473;** **6**:475
privateering in, **6**:480
profiteering during, **6**:493; **7**:148

Revolution, American, (*continued*)
  provincial congresses in, **6:519–521**
  publishing industry in, almanacs in,
    1:129
  Rangers in, **7:48**
  vs. reconciliation, **4:**255
  recruitment for, **2:**363
  Rhode Island in, **9:**30, *31*
  role of rivers in, **7:**175
  Russia during, **7:**210
  Saratoga Campaign in, **7:**137, 143,
    250, **250–251**; **9:***34*, 35–36
  Scotch-Irish in, **7:**285
  and secession in Civil War,
    7:292–293
  sectionalism in, **7:**295
  Siege of Savannah in (1779), **7:255**
  slavery and, **7:**392
  social impact of, **7:**146
  Sons of Liberty in, **7:449**
  South Carolina in, **7:**454–455
    Wilkinson (Eliza) on, **9:**150–151
  South in, **7:**145–146
  Southern Campaigns in, **7:472**
  Spain in, **7:**483
  spies in, **7:**501–502
  stature of soldiers in, **3:**398
  surrender in, correspondence lead-
    ing to, **9:**152
  Sweden and, **6:**78
  and tariffs, **8:**50
  and taxation, **8:**55
  and theater, **8:**113
  Ticonderoga in, capture of, **8:124**
  Treaty of Paris in, **9:***35, 36*
  trenches in, **8:**207
  United Empire Loyalists during,
    8:266
  Valley Forge in, **8:**306
    firsthand account of conditions
      at, **9:**147–149
  Vermont in, **8:**311–312
  veterans' organizations for, **8:**318
  Virginia in, **8:**343
  volunteerism during, **8:**352–353
  in West, **7:***145*
  westward migration during, **8:**461
  women during, **7:**146; **8:**505
  Wyoming (Pennsylvania) Mas-
    sacre, **8:566–567**
  Yorktown Campaign, **7:**137;
    8:580–582, *581*
Revolution (newspaper), **6:**97

Revolutionary committees,
  2:314–315; **7:**149
  committees of correspondence,
    2:314–315; 7:135, 149
    Boston, **1:512**
    New York (Committee of Inspec-
      tion), **2:**313
  committees of safety, **1:**512; **2:315;**
    7:136, 149
Revolutionary Communist Party,
  3:381
Reykjavik Summit, **1:**75; **7:149–150;**
  8:16
Reynolds, George, **2:**167; **7:**150
Reynolds, John, **3:**567
Reynolds, Robert, **7:***18*
Reynolds, United States v., **3:**279
Reynolds Metals Company, **6:**116
Reynolds v. Sims, **1:**227; **3:**246; **7:**108;
  8:357
Reynolds v. United States, **1:**494; **5:**54;
  7:150
RFC. *See* Reconstruction Finance
  Corporation
RFD. *See* Rural free delivery
RFE. *See* Radio Free Europe
RFRA. *See* Religious Freedom
  Restoration Act
Rhee, Syngman, **4:**546, 549
Rhine, Joseph Banks, **6:**246
Rhoads, Everette, **4:**533
Rhode, Paul, **6:**391
Rhode Island, **7:***150*, **150–154**
  in American Revolution, **7:**152
    archival maps of, **9:**30, *31*
  boundary disputes in, over King's
    Province, **4:**528
  colonial assembly in, **1:**333; **2:**280
  colonial charter of, **2:**281
  Dorr's Rebellion in, **3:80–82**
  early settlers of, **7:**151
  economy of, **7:**152
  emblems, nicknames, mottos, and
    songs of, **7:***533*
  established as colony, **5:**271
  founding of, **2:**288
  freedom of religion in, **8:**139
  geography of, **7:**150
  and Massachusetts, boundary dis-
    pute between, **1:**521
  in modern era, **7:**153
  Narragansett Planters in, **5:**515
  Providence Plantations in, **6:**519
  Quakerism in, **7:**1

  ratification of Constitution in,
    2:382
  in slave trade, **8:**210
Rhode Island, Fletcher v., **5:**103
Rhode Island system (management
  style), **8:**110–111
Rhodes, Cecil J., **7:**154
Rhodes, James A., **6:**174
Rhodes scholarships, **3:**274; **7:154**
Rhyolite signals intelligence satel-
  lite, **2:**93
Rhythm-and-blues (R&B), **5:**490
RIAS. *See* Radio in the American
  Sector
Ribault, Jean (Jan), **3:**285, 291
Ribbentrop, Joachim von, **8:**378
Ricardo, David, **8:**169
Rice, Abraham, **4:**489
Rice, Elmer, **5:**121
Rice, Thomas D., **5:**402
Rice culture and trade, **2:**96, 97;
  7:154–155
  on plantations, **6:**364
  and slavery, **7:**391, 392
  in Southern colonies, **2:**289
Rich, Daniel Catton, **1:**316
Rich, Lorimer, **8:**285
Rich, Marc, **2:**240
Richard, Little, **7:**185
Richards, Dickinson, Jr., **2:**53
Richards, Ellen, **3:**117
Richardson, Elliot, **7:**495
  as commerce secretary, **2:**310
  as defense secretary, **2:**528
  Watergate scandal and, **8:**427
Richardson, Frontiero v., **3:**246, **478**
Richardson, Graham v., **1:**126
Richardson, Henry Hobson, **1:**252,
  510
Richardson, Samuel, **6:**536
Richie v. People, **5:**13
Richmond (Virginia), **7:155–156**
  colonial, **8:**343
  as Confederate capital, **2:**209, 340;
    7:156
  devastation in Civil War, **7:***156*
  flour milling in, **3:**391
  State Capitol in, **2:***47;* **7:**146
  White House of the Confederacy
    in, **8:472**, *472*
Richmond, Bill, **6:**483
Richmond, Mary, **2:**106
Richmond (Kentucky) Campaigns,
  7:156–157

Richmond Enquirer (newspaper), **7**:157

Richmond Junto, **7:157**

Richmond v. J. A. Croson Company, **1**:581; **7:157**

Richter, Charles, **3**:100

Richter magnitude scale, **3**:100–101

Rickard, Tex, **5**:191

Rickenbacker, Eddie, **1**:375

Ricketts, John Bill, **2**:176

Rickey, Branch, **1**:421

Rickover, H. G., **6**:139

Ricks, Willie, **1**:479

RICO. *See* Racketeer Influenced and Corrupt Organizations Act

Riddle, Toby (Winema), **5**:433

Riddleberger, H. H., **7**:52

Ride, Sally K., **7**:481, 483

Riders, legislative, **7:159**

Riders of the Purple Sage (Grey), **5**:129

Ridge, Cane, **7**:87

Ridge, John Rollin, *The Life and Adventures of Joaquin Murieta,* **5**:128

Ridge, Tom, **6**:109

Ridgway, Matthew B., in Korean War, **4**:547, 548

Riesman, David, *The Lonely Crowd,* **5**:121, **148**

Rifles, **7**:*159*, **159–160**
  recoilless, **7:160**
  repeating, **5**:479

Riggs, Bobby, **8**:90

Right to bear arms, **1**:456, 457

"Right to die" cases, **3**:262; **7:160–161**

Right to privacy. *See* Privacy, right to

Right Wing. *See* Radical Right

Rights
  of aliens, **1:125–126**
  of Englishmen, **7:161–162**
  of individuals, **4**:332
  See also Human rights; Natural rights

Rights arbitration, **1**:236, 237

Rights of Man, The (Paine), **7**:148–149, **162**

Rights of the British Colonies Asserted and Proved (Otis), **7:162**

Right-to-work laws, **2**:275; **7:161**

Riis, Jacob, **1**:299–300; **6**:80; **8**:82, 291; **9**:351–353
  How the Other Half Lives, **5**:166

Rijp, Jan Corneliszoon, **6**:382

Riker, William H., **6**:404

Riley, Joseph P., Jr., **2**:108

Rinehart, William, **1**:306

Ringling Brothers, **2**:177

Ringmann, Mathias, **1**:135

Rings, political, **7:162**
  corrupt
    Tammany Hall, **8**:46
    Tweed Ring, **1**:*508*; **7**:162; **8**:46, **242**
  Tammany societies, **8**:47

Rio de Janeiro Conference (1947), **4**:8; **7:163**

Rio Grande, **7:163**, *163*

Rio Pact (1947), **3**:464; **5**:47, 447

Riots, **7:163–165**
  anti-Catholic, Philadelphia, **6**:315
  Chicago, **2**:133, **134**
  Cincinnati, **2**:175
  Civil War, **2**:216
  Coeur d'Alene, **2**:264
  Crown Heights, **2:466–467**
  Detroit, **3:21**, *22*; **7**:166, *167*
  draft, **8**:338
  Hamburg riot (1876), **4**:87
  Haymarket riot (1886), **1**:181; **4:109**
  media coverage of, **8**:339
  in Panama, **6**:239, 242
  prison, at Attica State Prison (1971), **1**:355–356
  race (*See* Race riots)
  during Reconstruction, **8**:337
    in Vicksburg (1874), **8:324–325**
  Stonewall riot, **3**:*513*, 514, 520; **4**:65
  urban, **7:165–166**, *166*; **8**:337–338
    of 1967, **7:166–168**, *167*
      Kerner Commission on, **4**:522
      in Newark, **6**:93
    Astor Place riot (1849), **1:341–342**
    Washington (D.C.), **7**:*164*, 167–168
    Wilmington (North Carolina), **8:485**
  See also Insurrections

"Rip Van Winkle" (Irving), **5**:118

Ripken, Cal, Jr., **1**:422

Ripley, George, **3**:204; **7**:194; **8**:179, 181, 301

Ripley, Robert LeRoy, **7**:168

Ripley, Sophia Dana, **8**:179, 181

"Ripley's Believe It or Not," **7:168**

Ripper legislation, **7:168**

Risberg, Charles (Swede), **1**:480

Rise of Silas Lapham (Howells), **6**:12

Ritalin (methylphenidate), **7**:568–569

Ritchey, George Willis, **1**:344

Ritchie, Eugene Robert, **1**:300

Ritchie, Thomas, **7**:157

Rittenberg, David, **1**:460

Rittenhouse, David, **1**:342; **2**:292

Rittenhouse, William, **6**:245

Ritter, Karl, **3**:541

Ritter, William Emerson, **5**:241; **6**:161

River(s), **7:173–175**
  cities on, **8**:289
  cleanup of, **3**:231
  crossing by ferries, **3**:354–355
  in exploration of America, **7**:173–174
  Gallatin's report on, **3**:503
  hydroelectric power from, **4**:199
  improvements of, **7:168–171**; **8**:430
  interstate compacts on, **4**:403
  navigation on, **7:171–173**, *172*
    bargemen and, **1:417**
    on keelboats, **4**:515
    maps for, archival, **9**:59
    Mississippi River, **5**:416, 417
    rafts and rafting, **7:22**, *22*
    on Tennessee River, **8**:87
  role in warfare, **7**:174–175
  as transportation routes, **7**:174
  See also specific rivers

River and harbor improvements
  flood control measures in, **3**:384
  Gallatin's report on, **3**:503
  Inland Waterways Commission on, **4**:361

Rivera, Geraldo, **8**:44

Rivera, Jacob Rodriguez, **8**:210

Rivera, Rafael, **5**:41

Rivingston's New York Gazetter (newspaper), **6**:95

Rivington, James, **6**:95

Rizzo, Frank, **6**:313; **7**:53

R.J. Reynolds, **8**:135, 137

RJR Nabisco, takeover battle (1988), **5**:85

RL. *See* Radio Liberty

RLA. *See* Railway Labor Act

RLDS. *See* Reorganized Church of Jesus Christ of Latter-day Saints
RMFC. *See* Rocky Mountain Fur Company
Roa Barcena, José María, **9:**224–227
Road Construction Project, **6:***260*
Roads, **7:175–180**
  in 19th century, **7:***177*
  in Allegheny Mountains, **1:**127
  American Automobile Association and, **1:**144
  building of, chain gangs and, **2:**100
  in colonial era, **7:***175*, 175–176; **8:**186
  Cumberland Road, **2:479–480; 7:***177, 181
  development of, bicycling and, **1:**451; **7:**178
  Federal-Aid Highway Program and, **3:**335–336
  first transcontinental, **8:**564
  Gallatin's report on, **3:**503
  gasoline taxes and, **3:**511
  military, **7:180–181**
    Burma and Ledo, **1:576–577; 7:**180, *181*
    French and Indian War and, **8:**461
  in North Carolina, **6:**130
  paving, **6:***260*, **260–261**
  plank, **6:361,** *362*
  post, **7:**176
  rural, **7:**208
  speed limits on, **7:500–501**
  toll, **8:***139,* **139–140,** 186–187
  and trucking industry, **8:**231
  turnpikes, **8:**139–140, 186–187
  Wilderness, **2:**479; **8:**478
  See also Interstate highway system
Roane, Spencer, **7:**157
Roanoke (Virginia), **8:**344
Roanoke Colony, **2:**287; **3:**285, 288
  Drake's visit to, **7:**47
  settlement attempts, **7:**47
Robber Barons, **7:181–182; 8:**233
  utilities, **6:**536
Robberies, **7:182–183**
  Northfield Bank Robbery, **6:135**
  train robberies, **8:178–179**
Robbins, Frederick C., **6:**388
Robbins, Jerome, **1:**144, 390; **2:**499
Robbins v. Taxing District, **8:**192
Roberson, Lizzie, **2:**172
Robert brothers, **1:**391

Roberts, Ed, **6:**389
Roberts, John, **8:**523
Roberts, Lawrence, **4:**398
Roberts, Oral, **8:**71
Roberts, Owen Josephus, on religious freedom, **2:**167–168
Roberts et al. v. United States Jaycees, **7:183,** 198
Robertson, A. Willis, **8:**344
Robertson, James, **2:**479, 480; **5:**515
Robertson, Marion (Pat), **1:**449; **2:**376; **3:**485; **6:**288; **8:**71
  and Christian Coalition, **2:**161
  in presidential campaign of 1988, **3:**168
Robertson, Oscar, **1:**424, *425*
Robertson, William D., **3:**144
Robeson, Paul, alma mater of, **2:**304; **7:**217
Robespierre, Maximilien, **4:**456
Robineau, Adelaide Alsop, **1:**304; **6:**418
Robins, Margaret Dreier, **8:**521
Robins Corporation, **2:**493–494
Robinson, Albert, **7:**299
Robinson, Bill (Bojangles), **8:**309
Robinson, Charles, **3:**196
Robinson, Doane, **5:**464
Robinson, Dollie Lowther, **8:**498
Robinson, Edward, **1:**448
Robinson, Edward G., **2:**189
Robinson, Frank, **2:**260
Robinson, Frederick J., **4:**486
Robinson, Henry R., **4:***454*
Robinson, Jackie, **1:**421, 547
Robinson, John, **5:**317
Robinson, Joseph, **7:**183
Robinson, Marilyn, **5:**122
Robinson, Reid, **4:**397
Robinson, Samuel M., **8:**555
Robinson, Sugar Ray, **6:**484
Robinson, Theodore, **1:**296
Robinson-Patman Act (1936), **1:**215; **3:**348; **7:183; 8:**235
Robotics, **7:183–185,** *184*
  in assembly lines, **1:**336
  automation in, **1:**365
Robsjohn-Gibbings, Terence Harold, **1:**292
Rochambeau, Jean Baptiste Donatien de Vimeur, Comte de, **6:**94; **7:**145; **8:**581
Rochester (New York), **1:**501
Röck, Fritz, **3:**257

Rock, John, **1:**468
Rock and roll, **1:**492; **7:185–186**
  audio technology industry and, **1:**359
  Rock and Roll Hall of Fame and Museum, **2:***232;* **7:**186
Rock Springs Massacre (1885), **8:**566
Rockaways, **6:**79
Rockefeller, John D., **1:**580; **4:**26; **6:**298, 303; **8:**233
  and Chautauqua movement, **2:**114
  oil refining empire of, **2:**232
  philanthropy of, **6:**317, 318; **7:**187
  public perception of, **7:**181, 182
  in Standard Oil Company, **7:***520,* 521
  and University of Chicago, **8:**280, 281
  and Williamsburg, restoration of, **8:**484
Rockefeller, John D., Jr., **7:**187
  and College of William and Mary, **8:**483
  and Ludlow Massacre, **5:**169–170
  real estate transactions by, **5:**37
  and Williamsburg, **6:**452
Rockefeller, John D. (Jay), IV, **7:**186
Rockefeller, Nelson, **1:**355; **3:**167, 171
  philanthropic work of, **6:**318
  in presidential campaign of 1964, **3:**165; **7:**113
  in presidential campaign of 1968, **3:**165
  and State University of New York, **7:**535–536
Rockefeller, William, **6:**303
Rockefeller, Winthrop, in Arkansas, **1:**262, 263
Rockefeller Brothers Fund, **6:**318
Rockefeller Commission Report, **7:186**
Rockefeller Foundation, **3:**443; **6:**317, 318; **7:186–187**
  and biochemistry research, **1:**460
  and corn production, **2:**414
  molecular biology and, **5:**437
  and nuclear research, **6:**344
  oceanography centers of, **6:**162
Rockefeller Institute for Medical research, **5:**18
Rockefeller University, **7:187–188**
Rockets, **7:***188,* **188–190,** *189*
  development of, **7:**479

Rockingham, Charles, **6:**248

Rocks, description of. *See* Petrography

Rockwell, George Lincoln, **3:**328

Rocky Mountain Fur Company (RMFC), **1:**158; **3:**494; **8:**176

Rocky Mountains, **7:190–191**
  Big Horn range of, **1:***452,* **452–453**
  exploration of, **3:**299, 300; **5:**150
  mountain passes in, **6:**254
  national park in, **2:**299

Rococo furniture, **3:**496

Rodale, J. I., **6:**210

Rodeos, **2:**444; **7:***191,* **191–192**

Rodes, Bronson v., **1:545**

Rodgers, Jimmie, **3:**395

Rodgers, John, **1:**415

Rodgers, Richard, **8:**115

Rodia, Simon, **1:**312

Rodman, T. J., **1:**319

Rodney, Caesar, **2:**541

Rodriguez, Richard, **5:**123

Roe, Saenz v., **7:222**

Roe v. Wade, **1:**6–7; **7:192–193**; **8:**517
  challenge to, **8:**433–434
  decision in, **1:**6
  Griswold v. Connecticut and, **4:**67
  judicial review in, **4:**493
  Planned Parenthood of Southeastern Pennsylvania v. Casey and, **6:361–362**
  reaction to, **1:**6–7
  right to privacy in, **4:**497; **6:**479

Roebling, John A., **1:**539, 547, 564

Roebling, Washington, **1:**547

Roebuck, Alva C., **3:**9

Roebuck, John A., **2:**342

Roethke, Theodore, **5:**122

Rogers, H. G., **6:**288

Rogers, Henry Darwin, **1:**140; **3:**548

Rogers, John, **1:**306

Rogers, Moses, **7:**254

Rogers, Randolph, **1:**306

Rogers, Robert, **7:**193

Rogers, Will, **6:**185

Rogers, William Barton, **1:**140; **3:**548; **5:**272

Rogers, William P., **2:**102

Rogers Act (1924), **7:**529

Rogers Brothers Silverware Company, **8:**192

Rogers' Rangers, **7:**193; **8:**257

Rogers v. Bellei, **2:**181

Rogue River War, **8:**402–403

Rohlfs, Charles, **3:**498

Rohrabacher, Dana, and National Endowment for the Arts, **5:**535

Rolf, Ida P., **6:**39

Rolfe, John, **6:**442

Rolfing, **6:**39

Roll of Thunder, Hear My Cry (Taylor), **5:**126

Roller coasters, **1:**179

Rollerblading, **7:193,** *193*

Rolling Thunder, Operation, **1:**77; **8:**332–333

Roma, **4:**78

Roman Catholicism. *See* Catholicism

Romania
  air raids on Ploesti oil fields in, **6:371**
  during Cold War, **2:**90

Romantic fiction, pulp magazines, **5:**194

Romantic history, **4:**137–138

Romanticism, **7:193–195**
  anthropology/ethnology and, **1:**192
  and Hudson River School, **4:**189
  and transcendentalism, **8:**179–181

Romer, Christina, **8:**252

Romer v. Evans, **3:**56, 247; **7:195–196**

Romero, Oscar, **3:**143, *143*

Rommel, Erwin, **1:**267
  in Battle of Kasserine Pass, **4:**513–514
  North African campaign and, **6:**124

Romnichels, **4:**78

Rony, Hugo, **6:**153

Rood, Florence, **1:**155

Rooney, Andy, **7:***372,* 373

Rooney, J. Patrick, **3:**138

Rooney, Mickey, **1:**575

Roosevelt, Adelheid Lange, **1:**309

Roosevelt, Edith Kermit, **3:**375

Roosevelt, Eleanor, **3:**376; **6:**42; **8:***499*
  and Civilian Conservation Corps, **2:**220
  in Junior League, **4:**501
  and League of Women Voters, **5:**66
  and National Youth Administration, **8:**586
  and peace movement, **8:**499
  and President's Commission on the Status of Women, **8:**498, 516
  women's clubs and, **8:**509
  and Women's Trade Union League, **8:**522

Roosevelt, Franklin Delano
  agrarianism and, **1:**57
  agricultural reforms of, **1:**66
  alma mater of, **2:**304
  ambassadors under, **1:**134
  on American Liberty League, **1:**164
  amnesty granted by, **1:**177
  anti-Semitism and, **1:**207
  Arab nations and, **1:**233
  arms race under, **1:**270–271
  Atlantic Charter and, **1:**353
  and atomic bomb, **8:**551
  attempted assassination of, **1:**329
  Bank Holiday Proclamation by, **6:491**
  banking collapse of 1933 and, **7:**62–63
  Brain Trust of, **1:532**
  and Brownsville affair, **1:**550
  and Buenos Aires Peace Conference, **1:**560
  business regulation under, **4:**27
  at Cairo Conferences, **2:**7
  and Camp David, **2:**19
  at Casablanca Conference, **2:**65
  childhood of, **6:**42
  and China, relations with, **2:**151
  and Church of Jesus Christ of Latter-day Saints, **8:**298
  and Churchill, **8:**543
  civil rights and, **5:**237
  civil servants under, political activities by, **4:**103, 104
  and civil service, **2:**207
  and Civilian Conservation Corps, **2:**220
  and Coast Guard, establishment of, **2:**258
  and commerce clause, **2:**311
  communism and, **1:**198
  Communist Party and, **2:**326, 327
  conservation program of, **2:**371
  on corruption, **1:**475
  Cuba policy of, **2:**470
  defense policy of, **2:**531

Roosevelt, Franklin Delano, (*continued*)
and Democratic Party, **2**:552
and disability rights movement, **3**:32
economic policies of, **1**:386; **2**:385, 552
on economic royalists, **3**:107
embassies established by, **3**:193
and employment discrimination, **6**:314
energy policies of, **3**:211
Executive Office of the President created by, **3**:330
executive orders of, **1**:547; **3**:208, 278
  No. 8802, **2**:201; **3**:49
  No. 9066, **3**:208
on fascist movement, **3**:328, 562
and FBI, **3**:337–338
Federal Security Agency under, **4**:113
fireside chats of, **7**:20
  on bank crisis by, text of, **9**:377–379
fiscal policies of, **1**:400, 402, 459, 544; **4**:12, 15–16
and Flying Tigers, **3**:392
and food safety, **3**:404
foreign policy of, **1**:537; **3**:426; **4**:22; **7**:118
"forgotten man" term used by, **3**:438
funeral procession for, **3**:*486*
Georgia and, **3**:557
Good Neighbor Policy of, **1**:560; **2**:54
and Haiti, occupation of, **4**:85
Hawaii under, **4**:107
immigration under, **4**:226–227
  quotas on, proclamation on, **9**:390–392
imperialism of, **4**:244
internationalism of, **4**:440
on Japan, **4**:458
and Japanese American internment, **3**:208; **4**:460, 463
Junior League and, **4**:501
and labor movement, **5**:7
labor policies of, **2**:11, 255; **3**:244, 308; **5**:544–546; **8**:586
and Labor's Non-Partisan League, **5**:17
labor's support of, **5**:16, 17

Latin American policies of, **5**:47
Lend-Lease program, **5**:81–82
letter on job discrimination to, **9**:376–377
and liberalism, **5**:92
and Ludlow resolution, **5**:170
March of Dimes and, **5**:236
on military pensions, **6**:285
on "monopoly press," **6**:98–99
Monroe Doctrine and, **5**:447
and National Gallery of Art, **5**:538, 539
as national hero, **5**:569
and national park system, **5**:551
and National Recovery Administration, **5**:555
and National War Labor Board, **5**:564; **8**:171
and natural resource preservation, **8**:423
and naval development, **8**:555
and New Deal, **2**:390; **3**:162, 163; **6**:42–45
The New Republic on, **6**:76
nomination acceptance speech of, **2**:400
and Office of War Information, **6**:503
Ogdensburg Declaration, **2**:27
and Olson (Floyd B.), **3**:322
on *Panay* incident, **6**:244
Pearl Harbor speech by, text of, **9**:396–397
polio rehabilitation center established by, **6**:388
poliomyelitis in, **6**:388
Polish Americans and, **6**:391
in presidential campaign of 1920, **3**:161
in presidential campaign of 1932, **1**:498; **2**:24; **3**:162
in presidential campaigns of 1936, 1940, and 1944, **3**:163
presidential library of, **5**:99–100
on racism in war industries, **1**:35
and railroad retirement act, **7**:28
and Republican Party, **7**:113
and Resettlement Administration, **3**:319; **7**:120
scientific research under, **6**:166–167
Second Bill of Rights of, **5**:92

social security under, **6**:283; **7**:129, 418
socialism and, **7**:427
and Soviet Union, **7**:57, 211
Supreme Court and, **4**:492–493, 496; **5**:57
  court-packing plan for, **7**:312–313; **8**:24, **26–27**
and Tammany Hall, **8**:46
and tariffs, **3**:461; **8**:52
and taxation, **8**:58
and telecommunications industry, **7**:19
and Tennessee Valley Authority, **8**:88
and Thanksgiving Day, **8**:112
third term of, **2**:552
on thirty-hour week, **8**:120
and Treasury, **8**:197
and United Nations, **6**:264; **8**:202
  establishment of, **8**:268, 273
vetoes cast by, **8**:321
and welfare system, **8**:440
and Works Progress Administration, **8**:530
in World War II, **4**:43; **8**:249, 543, 546
  air war against Japan, **8**:554
  at Casablanca Conference, **8**:549
  internment under, **4**:399–400, 460, 463
  policies of, **2**:118; **8**:588
  strategic air power under, **1**:81
  summits with Stalin and Churchill, **8**:15
  at Teheran Conference, **8**:64
  at Yalta Conference, **8**:573, 574, *574*
See also New Deal
Roosevelt, Franklin Delano, Jr., **3**:244
Roosevelt, Nicholas J., **6**:75
Roosevelt, Quentin, diary of, excerpts from, **9**:367–368
Roosevelt, Theodore, **2**:*369*; **7**:*513*
Alaska coal lands under, **1**:110
and Algeciras Conference, **1**:123
in anthracite strike (1902), **1**:190; **6**:279; **7**:557
antitrust laws under, **4**:26–27; **8**:233, 234
assassination attempt against, **1**:329, 566

and Battle Fleet Cruise Around the
World, **1:**428
on big business, **1:**214
and Bull Moose Party, **1:**566
on Chautauqua movement, **2:**113
and conservation, **2:**366, 367, 368,
369; **3:**226, 430, 433;
6:528–529; **8:**422–423, 480
and consumer protection, **2:**389
expansionism of, and arms race,
1:270
and FBI, **3:**337
and football, **3:**410
foreign policy of, **3:**425
Gentlemen's Agreement by, **4:**457,
463
text of, **9:**264–265
Grand Canyon preservation by,
1:205–206
on Hague Peace Conference, **4:**82
and Hay-Bunau-Varilla Treaty,
6:238; **8:**201
immigration policies of, **2:**84
imperialism of, **4:**244
inland waterways under, **4:**361
and Japan, relations with, **4:**457;
7:211
Labor Day speech of, **8:**527
and labor movement, **5:**6
Latin American policies of, **5:**47
laws of war and, **8:**371
and log cabin as political icon,
5:145
at Louisiana Purchase Exposition,
5:164
and monopolies, dissolution of,
7:36
on Monroe Doctrine, Roosevelt
Corollary to, **3:**425; **5:**446;
6:117; **9:**206–209
on muckrakers, **5:**470
as national hero, **5:**569
national monuments designated by,
5:550
Navy under, **1:**270; **6:**25
New Nationalism campaign of,
6:54, 70, **70–71**
Open Door policy of, **6:**197
and Panama Canal, **2:**54; **6:**105,
237–238, 242; **8:**387–388
and Philippines, **6:**320, 321, 322
and Portsmouth, Treaty of (1905),
6:423
and preparedness, **6:**449

presidency of, **6:**494–495; **8:**323
in presidential campaign of 1900,
3:159
in presidential campaign of 1904,
2:23; **3:**159; **8:**323
in presidential campaign of 1912,
2:548; **3:**160; **6:**54, 70, 496;
8:43, 119
in presidential campaign of 1916,
3:161
public land commission appointed
by, **6:**531
at Republican convention of 1912,
2:400
and Republican Party, **7:**112
and road construction, **7:**178
Rough Riders of, **2:**364; **7:***199,* 200
in Spanish-American War, **7:**486
Square Deal of, **7:513–514**
State Department under, **7:**528
vs. Taft (William H.), **1:**391
and trade unions, **8:**268
war powers under, **8:**387–388
Wells (H. G.) and, **1:**138
and wildlife preservation, **2:**366,
367
Winning of the West, **8:**288
Roosevelt, Theodore, Jr., in American Legion, **1:**162
Roosevelt Corollary, **2:**54; **3:**75–76,
425; **6:**117; **7:196**
Roosevelt's speeches on, **9:**206–209
Root, Ed, **1:**312
Root, Elihu, **2:**530; **7:**196
agreement with Japan, **7:**197
in American Bar Association, **1:**145
in anthracite strike (1902), **1:**190
arbitration agreements negotiated
by, **6:**263
Army under, **1:**276
mission to Russia, **7:**196–197
as secretary of state, **7:**528
War Department under, **8:**378
at Washington Naval Conference,
8:418
Root Arbitration Treaties, **7:196**
Root Mission, **7:196–197**
Roots (Haley), **3:**523; **7:197**
Roots (TV program), **8:**75
Root-Takahira Agreement, **7:197**
Roper, Elmo, **6:**409, 533–534
Rorimer, James, **5:**337
Rorty, Richard, **5:**92, 122; **6:**327,
429, 446

Rose, John, **8:**416
Rosecrans, W. S., **2:**113, 135
and Army of the Cumberland,
2:479
in Battle of Chickamauga, **2:**135
Rosemeyer, Bernd, **1:**375
Rosenbaum, Yankel, **2:**466
Rosenberg, Anna, **8:**503
Rosenberg, Ethel, **7:**197–198, *198*
Rosenberg, Harold, **1:**10; **3:**280
Rosenberg, Julius, **7:**197–198, *198*
Rosenberg, United States v., **8:**195
Rosenberg case, **7:197–198**
McCarthyism and, **5:**182
Rosenman, Joel, **8:**523–524
Rosenquist, James, **6:**414
Rosenthal, Joe, **6:**99
Rosenwald, Julius, **3:**444; **7:**290–291
Rosenwald, Lessing J., **5:**539
Rosofsky, Seymour, **1:**311
Ross, Betsy, **3:**378, 379
Ross, Charley, **4:**525
Ross, Edward A., **1:**142–143; **6:**424;
7:412; **8:**284
Ross, Harold, **1:**123; **6:**91–92, *92*
Ross, James Clark, **6:**383
Ross, John, **2:**125; **6:**183
Ross, Lewis, **5:**361
Ross, Nellie Tayloe, **8:**564
Ross, Robert, **8:**417
Ross Ice Shelf, **6:**383
Rosseau, Jean-Jacques, and deism,
2:539
Rostker v. Goldberg, **2:**365
Rostow, Walt Whitman, **3:**417
Roszak, Theodore, **1:**306
*Rotary Club of Duarte, Rotary Interna-
tional v.,* **3:**456
*Rotary International v. Rotary Club of
Duarte,* **3:**456; **7:198**
Rotation in office, **7:198–199**
ROTC. *See* Reserve Officers' Train-
ing Corps
Roth, Henry, **6:**13
Roth, Philip
Goodbye Columbus, **5:**121
Portnoy's Complaint, **5:**121
Roth IRA. *See* Taxpayer Relief Act
(1997)
Roth v. United States, **2:**85
Rothko, Mark, **1:**9, 298; **3:**280
Rothstein, Arnold, **1:**480
Rothstein, Arthur, **1:**301

Rouault, Georges, in Armory Show, **1**:297

Rough Riders, **2**:364; **7**:*199*, **199–200**
  eyewitness account of, **9**:261–263

Roughing It (Twain), **4**:13; **7**:516
  excerpt from, **9**:248–252

Rountree, Martha, **8**:44

Rourke, Constance, **1**:169

Rousseau, Jean Jacques, **1**:191

Rowland, Henry A., **5**:18; **6**:335

Rowland, Sherwood, **6**:223

Rowlandson, Mary, captivity narrative of, **9**:101–103

Rowlandson, Mary White, **2**:51; **5**:117–118

Rowlandson, Thomas, **2**:308

Rowlett, Frank B., **2**:467

Rowson, Susanna Haswell, *Charlotte Temple*, **5**:118

Roxas, Manuel, **6**:322

Roy, Bob, on Korean War, **9**:417–419

Royal colonies, **2**:281; **6**:*510*; **7**:**200–201**
  New Jersey as, **2**:289

Royal disallowance, **6**:252; **7**:**201**; **8**:243

Royal George (ship), **4**:53

Royce, Josiah, **6**:445

Royer, Daniel, **8**:562

Rozelle, Pete, **3**:411

Rozier, Jean-François Pilâtre, **1**:391

RPCNA. *See* Reformed Presbyterian Church of North America

Rubber, **7**:**201–203**

Rubin, Gayle, **3**:516

Rubin, Irv, **4**:475

Rubin, Robert, **8**:197

Rubincam, Milton, **3**:521

Ruby, Jack, **1**:330; **8**:339, 394

Ruby Ridge (Idaho), **3**:339; **5**:385; **7**:**203**

Ruckelshaus, William D., **3**:232; **7**:495; **8**:423
  Watergate scandal and, **8**:427

Rudd, Mark, **1**:182

Rudolph, Paul, **1**:253

Rudolph, Wilma, **7**:205; **8**:155

Ruebiz, Faud, **5**:72

Ruether, Rosemary Radford, **5**:93

Ruffin, Frank G., **7**:52

Ruffin, Josephine St. Pierre, **3**:526; **8**:510

Rugby, **3**:409

Ruggles, John, **6**:255

Ruhlmann, Jacques-Émile, **3**:498

Rule of reason, **7**:**203**

Rule of War (1756), **8**:173

Rules of the House, **7**:**203–204**

Rum industry, **7**:504

Rum trade, **7**:**204**
  Bermuda and, **1**:446
  Molasses Act (1733), **5**:**435–436**
  molasses trade and, **5**:436–437
  and slave trade, **8**:164, 209–210

Ruml, Beardsley, **6**:44

Rumsey, James, **6**:255

Rumsey, Mary Harriman, **4**:501

Rumsfeld, Donald H., **2**:529

Running, **7**:*204*, **204–205**
  marathons, **5**:**234–235**

Running a Thousand Miles for Freedom (Craft), excerpt from, **9**:272–274

Rupertus, William H., **6**:274

Rupp, Adolph, **1**:424, 425

Rural education
  4-H Clubs, **3**:445
  free universities, **3**:461–462

Rural Electrification Administration (REA), **1**:67; **3**:175, 211; **7**:209

Rural free delivery (RFD), **6**:425, 427; **7**:**205–206**, 208

Rural life, **7**:**206–210**
  automobiles in, **1**:368
  poverty and, **6**:437

Rural Post Roads Act (1916), **6**:425

Rural Telephone Service Company, Feist Publications, Inc. v., **2**:412

Rusch, Herman, **1**:312

Rush, Benjamin, **1**:119; **3**:113; **5**:*313*; **6**:316; **8**:319
  on capital punishment, **2**:40
  and chemical science, **2**:121–122
  pamphlet on alcohol by, **8**:78

Rush, Richard, **4**:486

Rush, William, **1**:305

Rush-Bagot Agreement (1817), **2**:26, 29; **3**:277

Rush-Bagot Treaty (1817), **3**:425; **4**:41

Rusk, Dean, **6**:318

Ruskin, John, **1**:250

Russell, Bertrand, **6**:547

Russell, Bill, **1**:424

Russell, Charles Taze, **4**:472

Russell, Daniel, **4**:62

Russell, Frederick F., **5**:294

Russell, H. H., **1**:206

Russell, Lillian, **3**:401

Russell, Morgan, **2**:476

Russell, Richard B., **8**:394

Russell, Steve, **8**:327

Russell, William G., **6**:355

Russell, William H., **3**:375; **5**:204

Russell Sage Foundation, **3**:444

Russia, **7**:**210–213**
  Alaska purchased from, **8**:201, 204
  and education in U.S., **4**:158
  explorations by, **3**:286, *293*, **293–294**; **7**:215
    in Alaska, **1**:108
    impact on Aleut, **1**:120–121
    impact on Inuit, **4**:409
    on Northwest Coast, **8**:453
  foreign aid to, **3**:418
  fur trade of, **3**:487, 491
  Murmansk, port of, **5**:483
  Revolution of 1917 in, and anticommunism, **1**:197, 198
  Root Mission to, **7**:**196–197**
  in Russo-Japanese War, **4**:457
    Portsmouth, Treaty of (1905) ending, **6**:423
  space program of, **7**:481
  in summit conferences, **8**:**15–17**
  territorial claims in North America, **7**:**214–215**
  U.S. intervention in, **7**:*352*
  U.S. relations with
    Manchuria and, **5**:218
    Open Door policy and, **6**:197
  in World War I
    Archangel Campaign, **1**:247–248
    Brest-Litovsk Treaty, **1**:247; **8**:315
  See also Soviet Union

Russian and Soviet Americans, **7**:**213–214**, *214*
  in Communist Party, **2**:327

Russian ballets, **1**:389–390

Russian Orthodox Church, **6**:*216*, 216–217
  Aleut in, **1**:121

Russian Revolution (1917), and League of Nations, **5**:64

Russian-American Company (RAC), **3**:294, 487, 491

Russo, Anthony J., **6**:287

Russo-Japanese War (1904), **4**:457
  Manchuria and, **5**:218

Portsmouth, Treaty of (1905) ending, **6:**423
Russwurm, John, **5:**199; **6:**96
Rust Belt, **1:**561; **7:215–216**
  Michigan, **5:**356
Rust v. Sullivan, **6:**362; **7:216**
Rustin, Bayard, **6:**269
  on Vietnam War, **1:**216
Rutgers, Henry, **7:217**
Rutgers University, **7:216–217**
  economic indicators developed at, **3:**105
  establishment of, **3:**112, 127
Ruth, Babe, **1:**421, 480
Ruthenberg, Charles, **2:**325
Rutherford, Ernest, **2:**486; **6:**340, 342, 343
Rutherford, Griffith, **6:**128
Rutherfurd, Joseph Franklin, **4:**472
Rutherfurd, Lewis, **1:**343
Rutledge, John, **3:**99
  at Constitutional Convention, **2:**379
RVs. *See* Recreational vehicles
Rwanda
  U.S. relations with, **1:**40
  war crimes in, **1:**354
Ryan, John, **2:**70
Ryan, Joseph, **4:**395
Ryan, Leo, **2:**478; **4:**488; **7:**94
Ryan, Panama Refining Company v., **1:**21; **6:243**
Ryan, W. Carson, **3:**136
Rybczynski, Witold, **8:**287
Rycraft, John, **1:**2
Ryerson, Martin A., **1:**316; **2:**272
Ryman, Robert, **1:**298
Ryswick, Peace of, **7:217**

S

SAA. *See* Society of American Archivists
Saarinen, Eero, **1:**253; **3:**499, 513
Saarinen, Eliel, **1:**293
Sabbath (Sunday) laws, **1:**490–491
Sabin, Albert, **6:**389
Sabotage, **7:219**
SAC. *See* Strategic Air Command
Sac Indians. *See* Sauk Indians
Sacagawea, **5:**86
Sacco, Nicola. *See* Sacco-Vanzetti case

Sacco-Vanzetti case, **7:219–220**, *220*
  ACLU in, **1:**146
  anarchism in, **1:**181; **7:**220
  International Labor Defense in, **4:**389
  Vanzetti's last statement after, text of, **9:**361–362
Sachem, **7:220**
Sackville-West, Lord, **3:**158
Sacramento (California), **7:220–221**, *221*
  as capital, **2:**9
Sadat, Anwar al-, **3:**141
SADC. *See* Southern African Development Community
Saddles, **7:221–222**
Saenz v. Roe, **7:222**
Safe Drinking Water Act (SDWA) (1974), **3:**228, 232; **8:**424
Safety First Movement, **7:222**
Safety Fund System, **1:**397; **7:222**
Safety glass, **4:**4
Safford, Laurence F., **2:**467
Safire, William, **3:**222; **6:**90
Sagadahoc Colony, **7:223**
Sagamores, **8:**219
Sagas, Nordic, **8:**337
Sage, Henry W., **2:**415
  and land speculation, **5:**36
Sage, Margaret Olivia, **6:**317
SAGE air-defense system, **7:**440
Sage Foundation, **3:**444
Sagebrush Rebellion, **3:**228–229; **5:**553; **6:**38
Sahaptian languages, **8:**571
SAI. *See* Society of American Indians
Saigon (South Vietnam), fall of, firsthand account of, **9:**477–479
Sailing and yacht racing, **7:223–224**
  America's Cup, **1:***172*, **172–173**; **7:**223–224
Sailing warships, **8:**405
Sailors, Kenny, **1:**424
St. Clair, Arthur, **3:**279; **6:**172, 178; **8:**399, 456
  in Battle of Princeton, **6:**464
  and Fort Ticonderoga, **8:**124
  territorial government established by, **6:**137
St. Denis, Ruth, **2:**498
St. James, Margo, **6:**514
St. John, John P., **3:**157
St. John, Vincent, **4:**347
St. Leger, Barry, **1:**573, 574; **6:**213

St. Leger Eberle, Abastenia, **1:**308–309
St. Valentine's Day Massacre, **2:**133
Saint Albans (Canada), Civil War raid on, **7:**224; **8:**313
Saint Augustine (Florida), **2:**67; **3:**296; **7:**224
  during Civil War, **3:**386
  establishment of, **3:**385
  King (Martin Luther) visiting, **3:**388
  New Smyrna colonists in, **6:**77
  tourism in, **8:**145
  in War of Jenkins' Ear, **2:**294
Saint Clair Tunnel, **8:**240
Saint Domingue (West Indies), **8:**446, *446*
Saint Eom, **1:**312
Saint Francis River Farms, **8:**303
Saint Ignace (Michigan), **5:**188
Saint John's College, **8:**281
Saint Landry Parish (Louisiana), police regulations of, text of, **9:**323
Saint Lawrence River, **4:**50; **6:**86; **7:**174, 225, *225*
  exploration of, **3:**291, 488; **4:**50
  and U.S.-Canadian relations, **2:**29
Saint Lawrence Seaway, **2:**27, 29; **7:225–226**
  development of, **8:**430
Saint Louis (Missouri), **7:***226*, **226–227**
  in archival maps, **9:***58*, 59
  Clark's Museum, **5:**487
  in colonial era, **7:**226
  Eads Bridge at, **3:***99*, *99*
  fur trade and, **5:**427, 468
  furniture manufacturing in, **3:**498
  Gateway Arch in, **3:***512*, **512–513**
  industry in, **7:**227
  Louisiana Purchase Exposition in, **5:**163–164
  population of, **7:**226, 227, *227*
  Pruitt-Igloe project in, **8:**286
  slavery in, **7:**226–227
Saint Louis, Fort, **5:**3
Saint Petersburg (Florida), **8:**47
Saint-Denis, Louis Juchereau de, **3:**292
Sainte-Claire Deville, Henri, **1:**130
Saint-Gaudens, Annetta Johnson, **1:**308

Saint-Gaudens, Augustus, **1**:306, 308
city plan for Washington (D.C.), **8**:410
Saint-Lô (France), **7:227**
Saint-Mihiel (France), campaigns at, **7:227–228**
Saipan (Japan), **7**:228; **8**:554
invasion of Tinian and, **8**:129–130
Sakata, S., **6**:344
Saks Fifth Avenue, **3**:7
Salam, Abdus, **6**:338
Salameh, Mohammed, **8**:533
Salaries. *See* Wages and salaries
Salem (Massachusetts), **7:228–229**
settlement of, **3**:80
Salem witch trials, **5**:118; **7**:228–229, *229*, 229–230; **8**:495, 501
evidence used in, Mather on, **9**:93–95
Salerno, United States v., **1**:385
Salerno (Italy), **7:230**
Sales taxes, **7:230–231**
Salinas de Gortari, Carlos, **6**:124
Salinger, J. D., **5**:121
Salinger, Pierre, **8**:241
Salisbury, Robert Gascoyne-Cecil, Lord, **6**:191
Salish language, **8**:221
Salk, Jonas, **2**:189; **6**:389
polio vaccine, **5**:236
Salmon, Daniel E., **5**:358; **8**:319
Salmon fisheries, **7:231**
dams and, **4**:202
Saloons, **8**:54, 81
Salt, **7:232–233**
production of, **7**:232–233
uses for, **7**:233
SALT I and II. *See* Strategic Arms Limitation Talks
Salt Lake City (Utah), **7**:*233*, **233–234**
city plan for, **2**:185
Mormon Tabernacle in, **8**:41
Progressive Era in, **8**:297
world's fair in, **8**:*559*
Salton Sea, **7:234**
Saltonstall, Dudley, **6**:281, 282
Saltonstall, Gurdon, **8**:572
Saltpeter (potassium nitrate), **6**:110
Salvation Army, **7:234–235**
Salyer, J. Clark, **8**:481
Sam, Alfred C., **6**:236

Samoa, American, **6**:225; **7:235–236; 8**:95
Samplers, **7:236**
Sampson, William, on common law, **2**:317
Sampson, William T., in Spanish-American War, **7**:486, 488
Sampson-Schley controversy, **7:236**
Samuelson, Paul, **3**:107, 109–110
San Andreas fault, **7**:240
San Antonio (Texas), **7:236–237; 8**:103
San Diego (California), **7**:*237*, **237–238**
in colonial era, **7**:237
population of, **7**:237
San Diego Marine Biological Laboratory (Scripps Institution), **5**:241
San Fernando Valley, earthquake of 1971, **3**:102
San Francisco (California), **2**:9; **7**:*238*, **238–240**
boom of, **1**:501
bridges in, **1**:539
cable cars in, **7**:*239*
development of, **8**:444–445
Earth Day celebration in, **3**:100
earthquakes in, **3**:37, 101–102; **7**:240, *240*
Bank of America after, **1**:394
ferry system in, **3**:355
fire fighting in, **3**:373
furniture manufacturing in, **3**:497
gold rushes and, **4**:13, *13*; **9**:59
Golden Gate Bridge in, **4**:18, *18*
Haight-Ashbury district of, **2**:433, *433*
liberalism of, **7**:239
maps of, archival, **9**:59, 64, *65*
population of, **7**:239
streetcar network in, **7**:43
tourism in, **7**:239
vigilantes in, **8**:336, 338; **9**:239–240
San Francisco Ballet, **1**:390
San Francisco Conference (1945), **2**:467–468
San Francisco State University, **1**:46
San Francisco Vigilance Committee, **8**:336, 338
constitution of, text of, **9**:239–240
San Idefonso, Treaty of, **5**:162

San Jacinto, Battle of, **7:240–241; 8**:100
San José (California), **7:241**
founding of, **2**:8
San Juan Hill and El Caney, Battles of, **7**:*241*, **241–242**, *242*
San Juan Islands, **7:242**
San Lorenzo, Treaty of. *See* Pinckney's Treaty
San Miguel Mission, **1**:24
San Quentin State Prison, **7:242–243**
San Simeon, **7**:243, *243*
Sanatorium, for tuberculosis patients, **8**:236
Sanborn Map and Publishing Company, **5**:233
Sanchez, George I., "Pachucos in the Making," **9**:407–409
Sánchez, José, **3**:453
Sánchez, Oscar Arias, **2**:395
Sanchez, Sonia, **5**:126
Sanctuary (Faulkner), **5**:121
Sand Creek Massacre, **2**:298; **4**:326; **7:243–244**, *244*
effects of, **8**:404
Sand Hills, **6**:28
Sandblasting glass, **4**:4
Sandburg, Carl, **5**:120
Sanders, George Nicholas, on Young Americanism, **8**:583
Sanders, Gray v., **3**:556
Sanders, Wesberry v., **1**:227
Sandford, Dred Scott v. See Dred Scott case
Sandinistas, **6**:105
Sandino, Augusto, **6**:104–105
Sandler, Irving, **1**:9
Sandoval, Alexander v., **2**:196
Sandys, Sir Edwin, **8**:347–348
Sanford, John F. A., **3**:85
Sangalli, Rita, **1**:389
Sanger, Margaret, **1**:4, 5, 466, 467–468; **7**:321, 330
Sanger, W. W., **6**:513
Sanitary Commission, United States, **7:244**
Sanitation
environmental, **7:244–246**
in 19th century, **7**:245–246
in 20th century, **7**:246
in colonial era, **7**:245
development of, **7**:245–246
and public health, **3**:237–238

Sanpoil, **8:**221

Santa Anna, Antonio López de
  at Alamo, **1:**106–107; **8:**100
  in Battle of San Jacinto, **7:**240–241;
    8:100
  centralized power of, **8:**100
  and Gadsden Purchase, **3:**502
  in Mexican-American War, **1:**560
  in Mexico City, capture of, **5:350**
  restoration to power, Polk and,
    5:340–341
  Texas Navy and, **8:**104

Santa Clara Pueblo v. Martinez,
  4:265; **7:247**

Santa Cruz River, **1:**100

Santa Fe (New Mexico), **7:247**
  colonial settlements in, **2:**67; **6:**67
  founding of, **8:**444
  tourism in, **6:**69–70
  trade in, **6:**68; **7:**248

Santa Fe Trail, **2:**128; **6:**68; **7:**247,
  247–249, *248*
  and Colorado, development of,
    2:298
  and Comanches, **2:**308
  and fur trade, **3:**493

Santa Maria (ship), **7:249**

Santería, **7:**249, *249*–250

Santiago, Battle of, Sampson-Schley
  controversy in, **7:**236

Sapir, Edward, **1:**193; **5:**115

Sapiro, Aaron, **2:**408

SARA. *See* Superfund Amendments
  and Reauthorization Act

Saratoga (aircraft carrier), **1:**89

Saratoga Campaign, **7:**137, 143, *250,*
  250–251
  archival maps of, **9:***34,* 35–36

Saratoga Springs (New York),
  7:251–252

Sargent, Charles Sprague, **1:**517

Sargent, John Singer, **1:**296; **3:**537

Sargent, Thomas, **3:**110

Sargent, Winthrop, **5:**411

Sarin, **2:**118

Sarin gas attack, **1:**465

Sarnoff, David, **8:**77

Sartre, Jean-Paul, **3:**279, 280, 452

SAT, **3:**139; **7:252**
Satellite(s)
  communication, **2:**319–320, *320*
  weather, **8:432,** 433
Satellite direct broadcasting services
  (DBS), **2:**322

Satrom, Leroy, **4:**517

"Saturday Club," **8:**179

Saturday Evening Post (magazine),
  7:252, **252**–253

Saturday Night Live (SNL) (TV
  show), **7:**253, *253*

Saud, Ibn (king of Saudi Arabia), **1:**233
Saudi Arabia
  oil in, **6:**298, 300
  U.S. relations with, **1:**233
    Persian Gulf War and, **6:**292

Sauer, Carl, **3:**543

Sauer, Christopher, **3:**561

Sauk (Sac) Indians, **7:**254; **8:**223
  in Black Hawk War, **1:**473; **8:**490

Sauk Prairie, **7:**254

Saulnier, Raymond J., **2:**431

Saulsbury, William, **2:**542

Saunders, Clarence, **7:**125

Saunders, Ogden v., **6:171**

Saunders, Richard, **1:**129

Savage, L. J., **3:**110

Savannah (Georgia), **7:255**
  city plan for, **2:**185
  in colonial era, **8:**289

Savannah, Siege of (1779), **7:**255

Savannah, Siege of (1864),
  7:255–256

Savannah (ship), **7:**254–255, 543

"Save our State" initiative, **6:**509

Savery, William, **3:**496

Savimbi, Jonas, **1:**39

Saving, drop in, **2:**452

Savings and loan associations
  (S&Ls), **1:**399, 401, 407;
  7:256–258
  deregulation of, **3:**13
  failure of, **3:**369

Savings bank, **1:406**–408; **2:**447

Savings bonds, **7:**258–259
  Thrift Stamps, **8:**123

Sawmills, **7:**259

Sawyer, Philetus, **8:**491

Saxton, Joseph, **3:**173

Say, Jean-Baptiste, **3:**108

Say, Thomas, **5:**150

Saybrook Platform, **2:**19; **7:259**

Saylor, David O., **2:**79

SBA. *See* Small Business Administration

Scab, **7:**259–260

Scalawag, **3:**386; **7:260**

Scalia, Antonin
  on line-item vetoes, **8:**321

on presidential election of 2000,
  1:579
on religious practices, **1:**494
on sexual orientation, discrimination based on, **7:**196

Scalping, **7:***260,* 260–261

Scammell, Alexander, love letter by,
  9:146–147

Scandals, **7:**261–262
  Abscam, **1:**8; **3:**338
  accounting, **4:**27–28
  Baker Case, **1:385**
  baseball (Black Sox), **1:479**–480
  basketball, **1:**424
  Belknap, **1:**440
  Clinton, **2:**239–240; **6:**400, 401
    extramarital affairs, **4:**238–240;
      7:496
    media coverage of, **7:**261
    Rose Garden statement on,
      9:522–523
    Whitewater, **4:**238; **7:**496
  of corporate accounting practices,
    2:419
  Crédit Mobilier, **2:452**–453
  Enron, **3:**176, 223; **4:**27
  Iran-Contra Affair, **4:**377,
    419–420; **6:**401
    and congressional oversight,
      4:377
    Report on the Iran-Contra Affair,
      text of, **9:**504–509
    special prosecutors in, **7:**496
  Iraq-gate, **4:421**–422
  ITT Affair, **4:449**
  Korea-gate, **4:**542–543
  media coverage of, **7:**261–262
  Mulligan letters, **5:473**
  political, **6:400**–401
  quiz show, **7:**6
  Tailhook scandal, **7:**323
  Teamsters Union, **8:**172
  Teapot Dome Oil, **6:**19–20, 400;
    8:63
  special prosecutors on, **7:**495
  televangelism, **8:**72
Watergate
  investigating committees in, **4:**411
  Jordan's "Constitutional Faith"
    speech on, text of, **9:**489–491
  media coverage of, **7:**261
  newspapers on, **6:**99
  and Nixon impeachment hear-
    ings, **4:**235

Scandals, (*continued*)
   Nixon's investigation address on,
      text of, **9**:486–489
   and resignation of Nixon,
      6:110–112
   significance of, **6**:400–401
   special prosecutors in, **7**:495
   tape recordings in, **7**:495
   and Vietnam War, **8**:334
   Whitewater, **4**:238
   Starr investigation of, **7**:496
Scandinavian Americans, **7:262–263**
   in Chicago, **2**:132
   immigration patterns of, **4**:223;
      7:262
   in Iowa, **4**:415
   number of, **7**:262
Scandinavian nations
   exploration of America by, **3**:286
   See also specific countries
Scaravaglione, Concetta, **1**:308
Scarlet Letter, The (Hawthorne),
      5:119; **7:263**
Schaefer, Jack, **5**:130
Schaefer, William, **1**:393
Schaff, Philip, **7**:76, 97; **8**:264
*Schechter Poultry Corporation v. Unit-
   ed States*, **1**:21; **3**:348; **5**:395,
   555; **7:263–264**
Schecter, Arnold J., **2**:538
Scheidler, Joseph, **6**:489
Scheidler, NOW v., **5**:549
Schell, Jonathan, *Fate of the Earth*,
   5:120
Schelling, Thomas, **3**:110
Schenck, Charles, **7**:264
Schenck v. United States, **7:264**
Scherer, Heinrich, **9**:*9*
Scherer, James A. B., **2**:14
Scherman, Harry, **1**:500
Schieffelin, Ed, **8**:141
Schiffer, Michael, **1**:240
Schindler, Rudolph, **1**:252
Schizophrenia, treatment of, **6**:522
Schlesinger, Arthur M., Jr., **1**:338;
   4:139
Schlesinger, James R., **2**:528–529
Schley, Winfield Scott, in Spanish-
   American War, **7**:486, 488
   Sampson-Schley controversy of,
      7:236
Schlink, F. J., **2**:390
Schmeling, Max, **6**:484
Schmidt, Clarence, **1**:312

Schmitt, Friedrich A., **5**:177
Schmitz, John G., **1**:166; **3**:166
Schmoke, Kurt, **1**:393
Schmucker, Samuel, **5**:176
   Elements of Popular Theology, **5**:176
Schnabel, Julian, **1**:307
Schnackenberg, Henry, **1**:310
Schneider, David M., **1**:194; **5**:251
Schneiderman, Rose, **3**:53; **8**:522
Schoenheimer, Rudolf, **1**:460
Schofield, J. M., in Tennessee Cam-
   paign, **4**:160
Scholarships, Rhodes, **3**:274; **7:154**
Scholastic Aptitude Test. *See* SAT
Schönbein, Christian Friedrich,
   6:366
School(s)
   boarding, for Native Americans,
      2:55, 145; **3**:135–136
   charity, **2**:106
   charter, **2:110–111**; **3**:119
      states with, **2**:*110*
   co-ed, **3**:131
   community, **7:266–267**
   dame, **2**:138, **495–496**; **3**:112
   for deaf, **2**:509; **7**:355–357
   desegregation of (*See* Desegrega-
      tion, of schools)
   district, **7:264–265**
   for-profit, **7**:267
   land for, **7:265**
   magnet, **5:201–202**
      vs. charter schools, **2**:111
   marching bands in, **5**:238
   medical, **5**:281–284
   monitorial, **3**:113
   normal, **3**:114, 131
   parochial
      Catholic, **2**:68, 69; **4**:474–475
      decline of, **7**:267–268
      vouchers for, **7**:266
   prayer in, **7:265–266**
      Supreme Court on, **1**:347;
         7:265–266
   private, **7:267–268**
   public
      in 19th century, **3**:114
      in 20th century, **3**:117
      alternatives to, **2**:111
      compulsory, Supreme Court on,
         6:352–353
      curriculum in, **2:482–483**
      development of, **2**:106
      evolution taught in

      North Carolina banning, **6**:130
      Scopes trial and, **8**:86
   Jefferson (Thomas) and,
      3:112–113; **8**:279
   in North Carolina, **6**:128–129
   privatization proposals for, **6**:481
   reform, **7**:74–75
   religion in, debate on, **2**:164, 167,
      168–169
   secondary (*See* High schools)
   segregation in, **3**:118, 121
   for singing, **5**:494; **7:366**
   single-sex, **7:268–269**, 303
   suburban, **7**:575
   summer programs in marine biolo-
      gy, **5**:240
   Sunday, **2**:106; **8:19–20**
      Chautauqua movement and,
         2:113
   violence in
      Columbine school massacre,
         2:305
      and interstate commerce, **8**:274
   vouchers for, **3**:119, 137–138;
      7:266
School and Society (Dewey), **8**:106
*School Board of Education of Richmond
   County, Georgia, Cumming v.*,
   3:115
*School Board of New Kent County,
   Green v.*, **3**:16
School choice movement, **3**:137–138
   See also Education, parental choice
      in
School districts, **5**:138–139
School lands, **7:265**
School of the Americas, **1**:442
Schoolbooks, **8**:106
Schoolcraft, Henry Rowe, **1**:192
   *Historical and Statistical information
      Respecting the History, Condition,
      and Prospects of the Indian Tribes
      of the United States*, **5**:128
Schooner, **2**:259; **7:269**
Schott, Charles A., **2**:235
Schouten, Willem, **2**:39
Schreckengost, Viktor, **1**:304
Schrieffer, Robert, **6**:337, 346
Schrödinger, Erwin, **6**:345
Schroeder, Theodore, **2**:84
Schuller, Robert, **8**:71
Schultz, Augustus, **5**:69
Schultz, Henry, **3**:110
Schultz, Theodore J., **6**:112

Schumacher, Ferdinand, **2**:98
Schumpeter, Joseph, **3**:109; **4**:45
Schurman, Jacob Gould, **2**:415
Schurz, Carl, **3**:440–441, *441*; **5**:90;
  7:181
  anti-imperialism of, **1**:202
  and forest conservation, **3**:434
  on Grand Army of the Republic,
    4:31
Schurz, Margarethe Meyer, **3**:440
Schutz, Will, **3**:203
Schuyler, George, *Black No More*,
  5:125
Schuyler, Philip, **1**:574
Schuylkill Canal, **8**:239
Schwarschild and Sulzberger, **5**:135
Schwartz, Anna, **3**:110
  on depression, **4**:46
Schwartz, Delmore, **5**:121
Schwarz, Berthold, **3**:301
Schwarzkopf, H. Norman, in Per-
  sian Gulf War, **6**:292, 293
Schwarzmann, J. H., **2**:87
Schwei, Barbara, **2**:501
Schweiker, Richard, **4**:114
Schwerner, Michael, **1**:332; **2**:203
Science(s)
  ballooning used in, **1**:391
  in colonial era, **2**:292
  in creationism vs. evolutionism
    debate, **2**:446
  history as, **4**:138
  journalism and television on,
    7:273–277
    National Geographic Society
      and, **5**:541–542
  and religion, relations of, **7**:269–271
    agnosticism and, **1**:55
    fundamentalism vs. modernism,
      5:432
  statistics in, **7**:539
Science (journal), **1**:141
Science education, **7**:271–273
  California Institute of Technology
    (Caltech), **2**:14–15; **3**:217
  4-H Clubs and, **3**:445
  at Franklin Institute, **3**:455
  marine biology, **5**:240
  at Sheffield Scientific School, **7**:340
Science museums, **7**:277
  American Museum of Natural His-
    tory, **1**:165
  Franklin Institute, **3**:455–456
  Henry Ford Museum, **4**:127

Museum of Science and Industry
  (MSI) (Chicago), **5**:484–485
Science Service, **7**:274
Science–The Endless Frontier (Bush),
  5:19, 557
"Scientific" charity, **6**:436
Scientific fraud, **7**:277–279
Scientific information retrieval,
  7:279–280
Scientific management, **4**:334;
  7:280–283
  diffusion of, **7**:281
  in industry, **7**:281–282
  mass production and, **5**:264
  origins of, **7**:280–281
  Taylor on, **4**:334; **7**:280–282
    excerpt of, **9**:342–347
Scientific racism, **1**:192–193
Scientific research
  by federal agencies, Allison Com-
    mission on, **1**:128
  federal support for, **6**:166–167
  fraud in, **7**:277–279
  Human Genome Project,
    4:191–192
  information retrieval of,
    7:279–280
  International Geophysical Year,
    4:388–389
  oceanographic, **6**:159–162
  by universities, **7**:272
Scientific societies
  American Academy of Arts and
    Sciences, **1**:139–140
  American Association for the
    Advancement of Science,
    1:140–142
  American Philosophical Society,
    1:166–167
Scientology, **7**:283, *283*
Scioto Company, **5**:26, 36
SCLC. *See* Southern Christian
  Leadership Conference
Scobee, Francis R., **2**:102
Scofield Reference Bible, **3**:484
Scopes, John T., **2**:446
  trial of, **2**:164, 446; **3**:270, 484;
    7:283–284; **8**:86
  ACLU in, **1**:146; **7**:283–284
  radio coverage of, **7**:274
Scorsese, Martin, **3**:364
Scotch pine, **3**:*436*
Scotch-Irish, **7**:284–286
  and Presbyterianism, **6**:450–451

in South Carolina, **7**:453–454
  and whiskey making, **8**:468
Scots Highlanders, **8**:257
Scott, Dred, **3**:85, *85*
Scott, Frank J., **3**:510
Scott, Howard, **8**:63
Scott, Joan, **3**:516, 517
Scott, Robert C., **8**:345
Scott, Robert Falcon, **6**:383–384
Scott, Walter Dill, **1**:33
Scott, Winfield, **1**:*276*
  Anaconda Plan of, **2**:217
  in Aroostook War, **1**:282–283
  in Battle of Chapultepec, **2**:105
  and Cherokees, **8**:177
  on laws of war, **8**:370
  vs. McClellan, **2**:211
  in Mexican-American War, **1**:560;
    2:105; **5**:341–342
  in Niagara Campaigns, **6**:103
  in presidential campaign of 1852,
    3:154
  in Seminole Wars, **8**:401–402
  in War of 1812, **8**:384
Scottsboro case, **1**:104; **7**:49, **286**
  ACLU in, **1**:146
  International Labor Defense and,
    4:389; **7**:286
  and race relations, **1**:104
Scouting
  Boy Scouts of America, **1**:527
  Camp Fire Girls, **2**:21
  Girl Scouts of the United States of
    America, **1**:527
  in Great Plains, **7**:286–287
  by Native Americans, **4**:328
Scovill Manufacturing Company,
  6:329; **8**:192
Scrabble (board game), **7**:287
Scream therapy, **6**:462
Screen printing, **6**:470
Scribner, Charles, **6**:536
Scripps, George, **6**:459
Scripps, Robert P., **6**:459
Scripps Institution of Biological
  Research, **6**:161
Scripps Institution of Oceanography
  (SIO), **5**:241; **6**:162
SCS. *See* Soil Conservation Service
Scudder, Janet, **1**:308
Scully, William, **1**:124
Sculpture, **1**:305–309
  colonial, **1**:305
  minimalism in, **1**:307

Sculpture, (*continued*)
  modernism in, **1:**307
  naturalism in, **1:**306
  by women, **1:**307–308
Scurlock, Robert S., **1:**301
Scurvy, **7:**287
  on colonial ships, **2:**290
SDC. *See* Systems Development
  Corporation
SDI. *See* Strategic Defense Initiative
SDS. *See* Students for a Democratic
  Society
SDWA. *See* Safe Drinking Water
  Act
*Sea as a Source of the Greatness of a
  People, The* (Ratzel), **3:**542
Sea Lion Park, **1:**179
Sea otter trade, **7:**287–288
  China and, **2:**153
Seaborg, Glenn, **2:**122–123; **6:**342
Seabury, Samuel, **3:**242
*Seagram Distillers Corporation, Old
  Dearborn Distributing Company
  v.*, **3:**309
Seal(s)
  of Confederate States of America,
    7:288
  of United States, **7:288,** *288*
    American eagle on, **3:**99
    motto on, **3:99**
SEAL (Sea, Air, Land) teams,
  7:494–495
  in Vietnam War, **8:**251
Sea-Land company, **5:**320–321
Seale, Bobby, **1:**478, *479*; **2:**135
Sealing, **7:288–289**
  in Alaska, **1:**121, 122
  in Pribilof Islands, **6:**459
Sealing wax, **6:**365
Seaman, Barbara, **8:**511
Seamans, Robert C., Jr., **3:**215
Seamen's Act (1915), **7:**289
Search and seizure, unreasonable,
  7:289–290
  arrest as, **1:**283; **7:**290
  in colonial era, **8:**563
  Fourth Amendment on, **1:**283,
    284; **7:**289–290
  Supreme Court on, **1:**283, 284
Searing, Laura Redden, **2:**509
Sears, F. R., Jr., **8:**89
Sears, Isaac, and Committee of
  Inspection, **2:**313
Sears, Richard D., **8:**90

Sears, Richard W., **3:**9; **5:**206; **7:**125,
  290
Sears, Roebuck and Company, **3:**9,
  26; **7:**125
  and Chicago, growth of, **2:**132
  and *Encyclopaedia Britannica*, **3:**204
  expansion of, **1:**405
  and mail order, **1:**428
Sears Roebuck Catalog, **5:***205,* 206;
  7:290–291, *291*
  furniture in, **3:**498
Sears Tower (Chicago), **7:***291,*
  291–292
Seasonal unemployment, **8:**252
  gradual decline in, **8:**253
SEATO. *See* Southeast Asia Treaty
  Organization
Seattle (Washington), **7:**292, *292*
  Century 21 Exposition in, **8:**560
  ferry system in, **3:**355
  WTO protests in (1999), **2:**226;
    7:165
Sea-Wolf, The (London), **6:**12
Sebastian, Hadacheck v., **6:**505
Sebrell, W. Henry, **2:**97
SEC. *See* Securities and Exchange
  Commission
Seceders, **6:**450–451
Secession, **7:292–294**
  by Alabama, **1:**102
  by Arkansas, **1:**261
  definition of, **7:**292
  Fire-Eaters advocating, **3:**371
  Lower South and, **5:167**
  precedent for, **7:**292–293
  prior to Civil War, **2:**208
  by South Carolina, **7:**293–294, 455
    Declaration of Causes, **9:**292–294
  by Texas, **8:**101
  as treason, **2:**505
  United Confederate Veterans'
    defense of, **8:**265
Second Amendment, **1:**457; **4:**74
Second Great Awakening,
  1:377–379; **2:**163; **3:**264, 265;
  6:516; **7:84,** 93
  and Republican Party, **7:**111
Second New Deal, **6:**43; **8:**197
Second Sex, The (Beauvoir), **3:**281
Second Treatise on Government
  (Locke), **6:**10
Secret Service, **7:***294,* **294–295**
  establishment of, **7:**294
  functions of, **7:**294

presidential protection by, **1:**329;
  7:294
Secret societies, **7:295**
  freemasons, **3:**465–467
  Molly Maguires, **5:**438
  Phi Beta Kappa Society, **6:**311
  Sons of the South, **7:**449–450
Secretary of state, vs. national secu-
  rity adviser, **2:**3
Sectionalism, **7:295–299**
  economic, **7:**298
  Webster-Hayne debate and,
    8:434–435
Sects, **2:**476; **7:**83
  Weber on, **3:**1
  See also Cults
Secular City, The (Cox), **5:**93, 432
Secularization, **7:299–301**
Securities, regulation of, **1:**491
Securities Act (1933), **1:**405; **3:**345;
  7:548
Securities and Exchange Act (1934),
  3:345, 348; **7:**548
Securities and Exchange Commis-
  sion (SEC), **2:**419; **3:**275, 276
  establishment of, **7:**548
  functions of, **7:**548
Seddon, James A., **2:**341
Sedgwick, Ellery, **1:**351
Sedimentation, **6:**301
Sedition Act(s), **3:**254; **7:301**
  of 1798, **1:**457; **2:**377; **5:**90; **7:**301
  of 1918, **7:**301; **8:**537
  See also Alien and Sedition Acts
See It Now (TV show), **8:**73
Seeger, Pete, **1:**389; **5:***496*
Seeger, United States v., **2:**361–362
Sega, **8:**327
Segal, George, **1:**306
Segregation, **7:**301–304, **301–304**
  in Alabama, **1:**104
  de facto, **3:**16; **4:**375; **7:**301–302
  de jure, **7:**301–302
  definition of, **7:**301
  emergence of, **4:**374; **7:**302
  by gender, **7:**303
  in Georgia, **3:**556
  in graduate schools, **5:**526
  in hotels, **4:**176
  in housing, **4:**182; **7:**302
  Jim Crow laws on, **4:**374, 479–480
  in Las Vegas, **5:**42
  in Louisiana, **5:**160, 161
  in Missouri, **5:**421

private, exclusionary clubs and, 2:251
in schools, 2:144–145; 3:118, 121
Berea College v. Kentucky, 1:443
separate-but-equal doctrine and, 2:199
Supreme Court on, 3:14; 4:374; 5:425; 7:302
in Tennessee, 8:85–86
on trains and buses, 3:464
Morgan v. Virginia and, 5:527
Plessy v. Ferguson and, 6:370–371
voluntary, 7:303–304
Wilson (Woodrow) and, 2:552
See also Desegregation
Segundo, Juan Luis, 5:93
Seicho-No-Le, 1:327
Seitz, Collins J., 2:543
Seitz, Frederick, 6:345
Seitz, Peter, 1:423
SEIU. *See* Service Employees International Union
Selden, Baker v., 2:412
Selden, David, 1:157
Selden, George Baldwin, 1:367, 371; 7:304
Selden patent, 1:367, 371; 7:304
Seldon, George B., 1:552
Selective incorporation, 1:453
Selective serotonin reuptake inhibitors (SSRI), 6:521
Selective Service Act (1917), 8:352
Selective Service System, 8:352
Selectmen, 7:304
Self-determination, for Native Americans, 4:289, 301, 303
Self-help movement, 7:304–306
areas of support in, 7:305–306
How to Win Friends and Influence People (Carnegie) in, 4:186
impact of, 7:305–306
origins of, 7:304–305
phrenology and, 6:333
The Power of Positive Thinking (Peale), 6:442
Self-naming, 5:509–510
"Self-Reliance" (Emerson), 8:180
Selfridge, Thomas E., 3:35
Self-service stores, 7:125
Self-taught artists, 1:309–313
Seligman, Edwin, 3:204
Selkirk, Thomas Douglas, Lord, 4:190
Sellars, Wilfrid, 6:327

Seller, John, 9:15, *15*
Selling of Joseph, The (Sewall), 5:118
Sells, Cato, 1:571; 4:288, 299
Selma (Alabama), civil rights movement in, 1:104
Selvy, Frank, 1:424
Semiconductors, 7:306–307, 360–361
Seminaries, theological, 7:96–97
Seminole, 3:385; 7:307–309, *308*; 8:47, 225, 249
adaptation of, 8:226
in Everglades, 3:268; 7:9
in Florida, 7:307–308, 309–310, 484; 8:401–402
gambling on lands of, 7:309
in Oklahoma, 7:308–309
reservation of, 7:308, 309
treaties with, 7:308; 8:206
wars with, 7:8–9, **309–310**, 484; 8:401–402
Seminole Tribe v. Florida, 1:120; **7:309**
Seminole Wars, 3:385, 386; 5:22; **7:309–310**, 484; 8:226, 401–402
Semmes, Raphael, 1:105; 6:23
Semple, Ellen, 3:542–543
Senate, U.S., 2:350, 351; 3:341
in appointing power, 1:225
appropriations by, 1:229
and Clinton impeachment trial, 2:240
cloture procedure used by, **2:250**
confirmation hearings by (*See* Confirmation)
Constitution on, 8:243–244
extra sessions of, **3:303**
filibuster in, 3:358–359
Finance Committee, 2:352
on Gadsden Treaty, 3:502
in impeachment, 4:234
of Chase, 4:241
of Clinton, 4:235, 240–241
of Johnson, 4:237–238
intelligence oversight by, 4:377
League of Nations rejected by, 8:543
majority leader of, 2:352
McClellan Committee, 5:183
Missouri Compromise, 5:422–425
pairing in, 6:230
presidential elections decided by, 3:171

system of representation in, 3:170; 7:108
in treaty negotiation and ratification, 8:199, 203
United Nations Charter approved by, 8:202
Versailles Treaty rejected by, 3:451; 8:201–202, 205, 316
Senators, as presidential candidates, 3:149
Sendak, Maurice, *Where the Wild Things Are*, 5:128
Seneca, 6:86
in American Revolution, 8:566
Seneca Falls Convention (1848), **6:88; 7:310–311; 8:506**, 512–513
Declaration of Rights and Sentiments at, text of, 9:332–334
and women's suffrage, 8:10
Seneca Oil Company, 6:302, 305
Senefelder, Aloys, 6:469
Senex, John, 9:20, *20*, 20–21
Seniority rights, 7:311–312
Separate system of prisons, 6:476–477
Separate-but-equal doctrine, 2:199
Separation of powers, 7:312–313
Mississippi v. Johnson, 5:418
veto power and, 8:321–322
line-item, 8:321
Separatists
African American, 4:375
Puritan, 6:378, 555; 7:313–314
September 11 attacks. *See* 9/11 attack
Sequestration Act (1802), 4:5
Sequins (Quinnipiacs), 2:357
Sequoia (tree), 7:314
Sequoia National Park, 8:303
Sequoyah, proposed state of, 7:314
Sequoyah (Cherokee farmer), 2:*124*, 125, 126
Serapis (warship), 6:24
Serbia. *See* Yugoslavia
Serial killings, 7:315
Sermon Preached at Execution of Moses Paul, A (Occom), 5:128
Serpent (lottery), 5:156
Serpent Mound, 1:*246*
Serra, Junipero, 2:8, 67; 3:296; 8:451; 9:107–109
Serra, Richard, 1:307
Serrano, Andres, 5:535

Servants
  domestic, and kitchen design, **4:**535
  indentured (*See* Indentured servants)
Service Employees International
  Union (SEIU), **1:**153
Service industry, employment in,
  5:8, 9
Service organizations, **3:**456
Servicemen's Readjustment Act. *See*
  GI Bill of Rights
Sesame Street (TV show), **7:**315, *316*
Set-asides, **7:315–316**, 398
Seton, Elizabeth Ann, **2:***68*
Seton, Ernest Thompson, **1:**527;
  2:21
Settlement house movement, **2:**146;
  7:316–319
  and Lower East Side, **5:**166
Settlement patterns, townships, **5:**362
Sevareid, Eric, **7:**20
Seven Days' Battles, **2:**212; **6:**275;
  7:319
  archival map of, **9:**67, *68*
Seven Sisters Colleges, **3:**132;
  7:319–320
Seven Years' War. *See* French and
  Indian War
Seventeenth Amendment, **6:**496
Seventh Amendment, **1:**457; **2:**351;
  7:108
Seventh-day Adventist Church,
  1:30–31
  origins of, **8:**501
Severance tax, **5:**160
Sevier, Ambrose, **1:**261
Sevier, John, **3:**455; **5:**484
Sewage treatment, **4:**356; **7:**245
Sewall, Samuel, **5:**118
  The Selling of Joseph, **5:**118
Seward, William H., **3:**155, 191
  Alabama claims by, **1:**106
  and Alaska, **1:**108, 189; **8:**201, 204
  anti-Masons and, **1:**203
  and Asia policies, **4:**242–243
  on assassination, **1:**327
  attempted assassination of, **1:**328
  and foreign policy, **3:**425
  at Hampton Roads Conference, **4:**91
  imperialism of, **4:**242–243
  on "irrepressible conflict," **4:433**
  and *Powhatan* incident, **6:**443
  Republican convention of 1860
    and, **2:**400

  as secretary of state, **7:**528
  and Virgin Islands, **8:**340
Sewing
  samplers of, **7:236**
  See also Quilting
Sewing machine, **7:320–321**
  and clothing industry, **2:**248
  invention of, **2:**246
Sex
  and life expectancy, **5:**105
  shares of population by, **2:**557
Sex, Gender, and Society (Oakley),
  3:516
Sex discrimination. *See* Discrimination, sex
Sex education, **7:321–322**
  and AIDS, **1:**17, 18
Sex offenders, Megan's Law (1996),
  5:306
Sexism, civil rights movement and,
  8:515–516
Sexton, Anne, **5:**122
Sexual abuse
  Catholic Church scandal involving,
    2:71
  See also Rape
Sexual harassment, **3:**54–55;
  7:322–324; 8:517
  in education, **7:**322–324
  *Meritor Savings Bank v. Mechelle
    Vinson*, **5:**324
  and political scandals, **6:**400
  Tailhook incident, **8:**43–44
  Thomas (Clarence) hearings on,
    3:198, 221; **8:**121
  in workplace, **7:**322–323
Sexual orientation, **7:324–328**
  discrimination based on, **3:56–57;**
    7:196, 325–326
  emergence of concept, **7:**324
  in hate crime legislation, **7:**327
  and identity, **7:**324, 325
  military service and, **5:**384–385
  politics of, **7:**326–328
  psychology of, **7:**325, 327
  See also Gays and lesbians; Homosexuality
Sexual preference, **7:**324
Sexual television programming, **8:**68
Sexual violence, feminism on, **8:**517
Sexuality and sexual behavior,
  7:328–332
  in 19th century, **7:**329–330
  in 20th century, **7:**330–332

  abortion and, **1:**4–5
  academic study of, **7:**330, 331–332
  in adolescence, **1:**25, 26
  of African Americans, **7:**329
  in Catholicism, **1:**196
  in colonial era, **7:**328–329
  history of, **7:**328
  and identity, **7:**324, 325, 328–329,
    330
  Kinsey Report on, **4:530–531**
  legislation on, **7:**326, 327
  of Native Americans, **7:**328–329
  Uniform Code of Military Justice
    on, **8:**256
  Viagra and, **8:322**
Sexually transmitted diseases
  (STDs), **7:332–333**
  incidence of, **7:**332–333
  types of, **7:**332
  See also specific types
Seymour, Horatio, **3:**155
Seymour, Samuel, **3:**299; **5:**150
Seymour, William J., **2:**172; **6:**287
Seyss-Inquart, Artur von, **8:**378
Shackleton, Ernest, **6:**383
Shafter, William R., in Spanish-
  American War, **7:**486
Shaheen, Jeanne, **6:**59
Shahn, Ben, **1:**298, 301; **6:**428
Shakers, **7:333–335**, *334*; **8:**301
  chairs of, **1:**286, *287*
  establishment of, **8:**501
  furniture of, **3:**497
  and Underground Railroad, **8:**250
Shaku, Soyen, **1:**325
Shalala, Donna, **1:**231
Shaler, Nathaniel S., **3:**541; **5:**59, 240
Shamans, **8:**213
Shane (film), **8:**458, *458*
Shange, Ntozake, **5:**124
Shanker, Albert, **1:***156*, 156–157
Shannon, Charles, **1:**310
Shannon, Claude, **2:**130, 468
Shannon, Wilson, **5:**59
Shanty towns, **7:335**
Shapiro, Harold, **1:**462
Shapiro, Ian, **6:**405
Shapiro, Joel, **1:**307
Shapley, Harlow, **1:**344
Sharecroppers, **1:**63; **3:**325, 462;
  7:208, **335–336**, *336*
  and cotton plantations, **6:**365
  in Georgia, **3:**556
  New Deal and, **7:**474

and peonage, **6**:289

Share-the-wealth movements, **5**:160–161; **7**:335

Sharon, Ariel, **4**:443

Sharp, Granville, **6**:234

Sharpe, Bolling v., **3**:245

Sharpe, Cecil, **3**:394

Shasta Dam, **4**:*201*

Shattuck, Lemuel, **3**:238

Shaughnessy, Harisiades v., **1**:125

Shaw, George Bernard, **3**:220; **6**:537

Shaw, Henry, **1**:516

Shaw, Irwin, *The Young Lions*, **5**:121

Shaw, Leander, **3**:388

Shaw, Lemuel, **2**:319

on police power, **6**:387

Shaw, Louis A., **1**:463

Shaw, Robert Gould, **1**:510

statue of, **1**:512

Shaw v. Reno, **3**:62; **8**:358

Shawk, Able, **3**:372

Shawn, Edwin Meyers (Ted), **2**:498

Shawn, William, **6**:92

Shawnee, **7**:336–338

in American Revolution, **4**:329; **7**:337

in colonial era, **7**:336–337

in Dunmore's War, **3**:95

in Pennsylvania, **6**:276

relations with white settlers, **3**:84

in Tecumseh's Crusade, **8**:64

in Tennessee, **8**:85

westward migration and, **8**:459

Shays, Daniel, **2**:345; **7**:338, *338*

Shays's Rebellion, **2**:45, 227, 345; **5**:265–266; **7**:338; **9**:154–155

debt execution and, **2**:514

Sheehan, Neil, **6**:286

Sheeler, Charles, **1**:297, 301, 310; **6**:471

Sheen, Fulton J., **2**:70; **8**:71

Sheep, **7**:339

introduction of, **7**:339

merino, **7**:339; **8**:312

in Montana, **5**:449

in Vermont, **8**:312

and wool growing, **7**:339; **8**:524, *525*

Harrisburg Convention on, **4**:100

Sheep wars, **7**:339–340

Sheerer, Mary G., **1**:304

Sheet glass, **4**:4

Sheffield Scientific School, **7**:340

Shehab, Fuad, **5**:72

Shelburne, Earl of, **7**:147

Shelby, Evan, **8**:85

Shelby, Joseph O., Mexican expedition of, **7**:340–341

Sheldon, Edward, **3**:116

Shelekhov, Grigory, **1**:108

Shell, **2**:121

Shell model, **6**:344

Shell shock, **8**:539

Shellac, **6**:365–366

Shelley v. Kraemer, **6**:506

Shenandoah Campaign, **7**:341

Sheridan's Ride in, **7**:342

Shenandoah Valley (Virginia), **7**:341

Shepard, Alan, **5**:523; **7**:480

Shepard, Matthew, **5**:179; **8**:566

Shepard, Sam, **8**:115

Shepherd, (Boss) Alexander, **8**:410

Sheppard-Towner Maternity and Infancy Protection Act (1921), **5**:65–66; **7**:342, 415; **8**:297

General Federation of Women's Clubs and, **3**:526

Sheraton, Thomas, **1**:291; **3**:496

Sherbert v. Verner, **2**:169

Sheridan, Philip H., **2**:215

and Battle of Little Bighorn, **5**:131–132

at Fort Hays, **4**:110–111

in Red River Indian War, **7**:72

in Shenandoah Campaign, **7**:341, **342**

in Siege of Petersburg, **6**:296

Sheridan's Ride, **7**:342

Sherman, Cindy, **1**:301

Sherman, Goody, **7**:478

Sherman, James S., in presidential campaign of 1908, **3**:160

Sherman, John, **1**:213, 484; **3**:157; **7**:342, 343, 345; **8**:233

and Sherman Silver Act, **2**:332

Sherman, Roger, **1**:456; **2**:357–358

and Connecticut Compromise, **2**:359

at Constitutional Convention, **2**:379

and Declaration of Independence, **2**:521

Sherman, Sidney, **7**:99

Sherman, Stuart, **6**:494

Sherman, William Tecumseh, **2**:213; **7**:*346*

in Atlanta Campaign, **1**:350–351

Army of the Cumberland in, **2**:479

Battle of Kenesaw Mountain, **4**:516

railroads in, **7**:35

and burning of Columbia, **2**:302–303

"forty acres and a mule" phrase by, **3**:440

on logistics, **5**:146

March to the Sea by, **2**:214; **7**:*345*, **345–346**

and Navajos, **6**:16

raiding strategy of, **2**:214–215, 217–218

in Siege of Savannah, **7**:255

in Tennessee Campaign, **4**:160

as Union Pacific's chief engineer, **8**:181

in Vicksburg, **8**:324

Sherman Antitrust Act (1890), **2**:418; **5**:21; **7**:342–344; **8**:233–234, 274, 275

commerce clause and, **2**:310

common law in, **1**:213–214

conditions leading to, **1**:580

economists' reaction to, **3**:108

effects of, **7**:343

formative period of, **7**:123

and free trade, **3**:460

Miller-Tydings Amendment to, **3**:309

and *Northern Securities Company v. United States*, **6**:135

opposition to, **7**:343

and organized labor, **2**:496

passage of, **1**:213; **4**:26; **7**:343

provisions of, **1**:213–214; **5**:445; **7**:342

and Pullman strike, **4**:249

and railroad pools, **6**:413

and restraint of trade, **7**:122

rider exempting labor unions from, **7**:159

rule of reason in interpretation of, **7**:203

strikes outlawed by, **2**:228

support for, **7**:343

Supreme Court on, **1**:20, 172, 214; **4**:26

debate in, **7**:343–344

in International Harvester Company case, **4**:389

See also Monopoly(ies)

Sherman Silver Purchase Act (1890), **1**:459; **2**:332; **3**:158, 366, 458; **7**:344–345

Sherwood, Maude, **1**:308

Sherwood, Robert E., **1**:123; **5**:121

Shigeru, Yoshida, **4**:458

Shi'ite Islam, **1**:384

Shiloh, Battle of, **2**:213; **7:346–347**

Shiloh National Military Park, **2**:*82*

Shima, Kiyohide, **5**:89

Shinn, Everett, **1**:268, 297, 321

Shintoism, **1**:327

Ship(s)

  armored, **1:265–266**

  clipper, **2:241**

  colonial, **2:290**

  disasters involving, **3**:39–40, *40*

  insurance on, **4**:367–368

  of the line, **7:350**; **8:407**

  naval vessels, **5**:480

  research, **3**:546, *546*

Shipbuilding, **7:347–348**

  blacksmithing and, **1**:484

  in colonial era, **4**:349; **7**:347

  dry docks used in, **3**:87

  early, **7**:171

  Emergency Fleet Corporation and, **3:194–195**

  Great Lakes steamships, **4:53–55**

  in Portsmouth, **6**:57, 58

  in Rhode Island, **7**:153

  tar and, **8**:48

  Titanic, sinking of, **8:131–132**, *132*

  in World War I, **8**:536

  in World War II, **5**:210; **7**:347; **8**:557

Shipherd, John J., **6**:152

Shipp, J. F., **8**:318

Shippen, William, **2**:142

Shipping

  containerization, **5**:320

  Federal Maritime Commission, **5:244–245**

  mercantilism and, **5**:315–316

  merchant marine, **5:318–321**

  merchantmen, armed, **5:321–322**

  Monroe-Pinkney Treaty (1806), **5**:447

  ocean, **7:348–350**

  packet ships for, **6**:230

Shipping Board, U.S., **7:350**

Shipstead, Henrik, **3**:321–322

Shirley, William, **5**:157

Shockley, William, **1**:346, 440; **2**:335; **6**:337, 346; **7**:360

Shockley Semiconductor Laboratories, **7**:360

Shoemaking industry, **1:502–503**; **5:68–69**

Shoes, imports of, **5**:70

Sholes, Christopher Latham, **8**:*244*, 244–245

Shopping malls, **5:215–217**

Short, Luke, **3**:*70*

Short, Thomas, **6**:153

Short, Walter C., **6**:272, 273

Short Cuts (Altman), **5**:123

Shorter, Eli, and land speculation, **5**:36

Shortridge, Eli, **6**:132

Shoshone, **2**:307; **7**:350, *351*; **8**:216

  Arapaho and, **1**:235

  in New Mexico, **6**:65

Show, Armory, **2**:476

Showboats, **7:350–352**; **8**:112, 113

Shrank, John N., **1**:329

Shreve, Henry Miller, **7**:*171*, 172, 543

Shreveport rate case, **2**:311; **7:352**

Shriver, R. Sargent, Jr., **3**:100, 166; **6**:163, 265–266; **8**:386

Shultz, George, **3**:343

Shultz, Theodore W., **3**:110

Shute, Samuel, **6**:57

Siad Barre, Muhammad, **1**:39

Siberian Expedition (1918), **7**:*352*, **352–353**

Sibley, Charles, **6**:215

Sibley, George C., **6**:183

Sibley, Henry Hastings, **2**:492; **5**:399; **7**:369

Sibley, Henry S., **2**:298

Sibley, Hiram, **8**:456

Sicilian Campaign, **7:353–354**, *354*

Sickles, Daniel, in Battle of Gettysburg, **3**:568

Sidbury, James, **7**:8

Sidney, Algernon, **7**:109; **8**:193

Siegel, Benjamin (Bugsy), **5**:41–42; **6**:38

Siegel, Jerry, **2**:*309*

Siegfried Line, **7:354**

Siemens, Werner, **7**:43

Sienkiewicz, Henryk, **6**:391

Sierra Club, **3**:206; **7:354–355**; **8**:304

  and aesthetic preservationism, **2**:368

  membership of, growth in, **3**:227, 228, 229

  and National Park Service, **5**:552

Sierra Leone, African American emigration to, **2**:296, 297

SIGINT. *See* Signals intelligence

Sigman, Morris, **4**:391

Sign language

  American, **2**:508, 509; **3**:504; **7:355–357**

  opposition to, **3**:32

  Indian, **7**:*357*, **357–358**

Signal Corps, U.S. Army, **7:358**

Signals intelligence (SIGINT), **5**:558–559

"Significance of the Frontier in American History, The" (Turner), **3**:475–476, 477; **8**:559

Sigsbee, Charles, **6**:160

Sihanouk, Norodom, **2**:16

Sikhism, **1**:326–327

Sikorsky, Igor, **1**:94; **4**:123

Siksika Indians, **1**:481

Sildenafil citrate. *See* Viagra

Silent films, **3**:362

Silent majority, Nixon's speech on, **9**:467–473

Silent Spring (Carson), **1**:67; **3**:205, 227, 232; **4**:362; **6**:210; **7:359**; **8**:285, 423

Silent system of prisons, **6**:476–477

Silhouettes, **7:359**

Silicon, **7**:306, 307

Silicon chip, **2**:336

Silicon Valley, **2**:12; **6**:347; **7**:306, **360–361**

Silicone, **6**:366

Silicone breast implants, **1:533**

Silk culture and manufacture, **7:361–362**

  Lebanese Americans in, **5**:71

Silko, Leslie Marmon, *Ceremony*, **5**:129

Silliman, Benjamin, **1**:141, 435; **3**:549; **5**:327–328, 390–391

Silliman, Benjamin, Jr., **6**:302; **7**:340

Sills, David L., **3**:204

Silver

  coinage

    Bland-Allison Act and, **1**:484

    controversies over, **1**:458–459

    insufficient amount of, **2**:481

    legislation on, **7**:363–364

    Sherman Silver Purchase Act, **7:344–345**

  collecting, **2**:272

  in decorative arts, **1**:286–287

prospecting and mining, **5:**62, 63; **7:**364
  in Arizona, **1:**257; **8:**141
  Bonanza Kings and, **1:497**
  in Colorado, **7:**364
  Comstock Lode and, **2:338**
  in Idaho, **4:**212, 213; **7:**364
  in Montana, **5:**448
  in Nevada, **6:**37, 38
  silversmiths, **5:**327–328
Silver City (Idaho), **3:**574
Silver Democrats, **7:**344–345, **362–363**
Silver legislation, **3:**458–459
Silver Republican Party, **3:**158; **7:364–365**
Silver Star, **2:**526
Silverman, Fred, **2:**64
Silvers, Phil, **8:**309
Silviculture, **3:**433
Simcoe (ship), **4:**53
Simcoe, John, **1:**282
Simkin, William, **3:**343
Simmons, Ruth J., **1:**548
Simmons, William, **3:**556
Simmons-Harris, Zelman v., **3:**138
Simon, Herbert, **3:**110
Simon, John, **3:**222
Simon, Théodore, **3:**116
Simon and Schuster, **6:**538
Simons, Henry, **3:**109
Simons, Menno, **1:**174; **5:**309
Simpson, George, **3:**492
Simpson, James, **7:**139
Simpson, Kirke E., on Tomb of the Unknown Soldier, dedication of, **9:**370–373
Simpson, Nicole Brown, **7:**365
Simpson, O. J., murder trials of, **2:**12; **7:**365, *365*
Simpson, "Sockless Jerry," **6:**417
Sims, Edwin W., **5:**225
Sims, Reynolds v., **1:**227; **3:**246; **7:**108; **8:**357
Sims, William S., in Spanish-American War, **7:**488
Sinatra, Frank, **8:***142*
Sinclair, Harry F., **8:**63
Sinclair, Upton
  and EPIC movement, **3:**233, 234
  The Jungle, **2:**37, 227, 389; **4:**27, **500–501**; **5:**120, 135, 277, 280; **6:**11, 12, 352, 554; **8:**285
    excerpt from, **9:**360

social activism of, **2:**10, 11
Sinclair v. United States, **2:**352
Siney, John, **2:**254
Sing Sing, **6:**476; **7:365–366**
  women at, **7:**75
Singer, Isaac Bashevis, **5:**121
Singer, Isaac Merrit, **2:**246
Singer sewing machines, **7:**320, *320*, 321
Singing schools, **7:366**
Single tax, **6:**493; **7:366**
Singleton, Bayard v., **1:431**
Singleton, James Washington, **7:**366
Singleton Peace Plan, **7:**366
Sinking fund, national, **7:366–367**
Sino-Japanese War, **7:367**
  U.S.-Japan relations and, **5:**219
Sintering, **5:**62
SIO. *See* Scripps Institution of Oceanography
Sioux, **5:**23; **7:367–369**; **8:**218, 275
  at Battle of Little Bighorn, **5:**130–132
    eyewitness account of, **9:**253–255
  and Black Hills, importance of, **1:**474; **8:**275
  in Black Hills War, **1:474–475**
  Chiwere, **8:**224
  in Dakota Territory, **2:**493
  Dhegiha, **8:**223
  Fort Laramie Treaty with (1851), **5:**40
    text of, **9:**227–229
  Fort Laramie Treaty with (1868), **5:**40–41, 130
  and Ghost Dance, **3:**573
  Indian Treaty at Prairie du Chien and, **6:447–448**
  land claims by, **4:**274
  languages of, **8:**223
    Lakota, **5:23–24**
  in Nebraska, **6:**29
  in North Dakota, **6:**131, 132
  schoolchildren, **3:***135*
  Seven Councilfires of, **5:**23
  in South Dakota, **1:**383
  Spirit Lake Massacre by, **7:503–504**
  Stoney, **5:**23
  treaties with, **4:**315; **7:**368, 369, 370
  tribes of, **7:**367–368
  uprising in Minnesota, **5:**399; **7:***369*, **369–370**

Little Crow's speech before, **9:**243–244
  at Wounded Knee, **7:**368, *368;* **8:**562–563
Sioux Nation, United States v., **8:275**
Sioux Wars, **5:**41; **7:370–371**; **8:**403
Siphon toilet, **6:**372
SIR. *See* Society for Individual Rights
Sirica, John J., **6:**457; **8:**426
Sister Carrie (Dreiser), **5:**119; **6:**11, 12
Sit-down strikes, **7:***371*, **371–372**
Sit-ins, **6:**227
Sitting Bull (Sioux chief), **1:**475; **3:**573; **5:***131*
  in Battle of Little Bighorn, **8:**404
  death of, **8:**404, 562
  in Wild West Show, **8:**476
Situation comedies (sitcoms), **2:**391; **8:**72
Six Nations, and Vandalia Colony, **8:**308
Six-Day War (1967), Arab immigration after, **1:**231
Sixteenth Amendment, **3:**342; **6:**496; **8:**196
Sixteenth Street Baptist Church, bombing of, **1:**332
Sixth Amendment, **1:**457
60 Minutes (TV show), **7:372–373**; **8:**73
Sizer, Nelson, **6:**334
Sizer, Theodore, **3:**124
Skate (submarine), **6:**382
Skateboarding, **7:373**, *373*
Skating, in-line. *See* Rollerblading
Sketchbook of Geoffrey Crayon, Gentleman, The (Irving), **5:**118
Skid row, **7:***373*, **373–374**
Skiing, **7:**122, *374*, **374–375**
Skin cancers, **2:**34
Skin of Our Teeth, The (Wilder), **5:**121
Skin transplantation, **8:**183
Skinner, B. F., **1:**437–438; **6:**524–525
Skinner, Cortland, **2:**444
Skinner, John S., **4:**69
Skinners, **2:444**
Skolaskin (prophet), **6:**7
Skyllas, Drossos, **1:**311
Skyscrapers, **1:**252; **7:375–377**
  in Boston, **1:**510, *510*
  building materials for, **1:**564

Skyscrapers, *(continued)*
  in Chicago, **2:**132; **8:**290
  Chrysler Building, **7:***376*
  in New York City, **3:**199, *199;*
    6:80–81
  plumbing in, **6:**373
  Sears Tower, **7:***291*, **291–292**
SLA. *See* Symbionese Liberation
    Army
Slang, **7:377–378**
  in dictionaries, **3:**23
Slater, Don, **2:**390
Slater, Samuel, **2:**245; **7:**152
  and Amoskeag Manufacturing
    Company, **6:**58
  and Rhode Island system,
    8:110–111
  and Slater mill, **8:**108–109
Slaton, John M., **3:**453
Slaughter, Alanson, **2:**490
Slaughter, Groves v., **3:**90
Slaughterhouse 5 (Vonnegut), **5:**121
Slaughterhouse cases, **3:**90; **6:**482;
    7:62, **378**
Slave(s)
  in agriculture, **3:***325*
  American Revolution and, **7:**152,
    392
  and Christianity, **2:**163
  during Civil War, **2:**209, 343,
    395–396
  in colonial society, **2:**291
  compensation for, **3:**440
  as contraband of war, **2:395–396**
    Butler's report on, **9:**294–296
  and cotton production, **2:**425, 429
  courtship among, **8:**436
  culture of, **7:**395–396
  drivers of, **6:221–222**
  education for, **3:**120
  emancipation of, **3:**190–192
  escape by (*See also* Underground
    Railroad)
    firsthand accounts of, **9:**272–276
  family life of, **3:**313; **7:**394, 465
  freed
    discrimination of, **1:**472, 475
    emigration of, **3:**197
  fugitive (*See* Fugitive Slave Act)
  and gender roles, **3:**518–519
  and gun control, **4:**74
  vs. indentured servants, Beverly
    (Robert) on, **1:**191; **9:**109–111
  industrial work by, **7:**463–464

  languages of, **7:**395, 396
  in Louisiana, **2:**262–263
  as Loyalists, **5:**167–168
  marriage among, **5:**250; **8:**436
  Navajo as, **6:**15
  overseers of, **6:221–222**
  as property, **6:**505
  quality of life for, **7:**393–394, 464
  religious life of, **1:**41–43; **7:**396,
    465–466
  rights of, **7:**389
  smuggling of, **7:406–407**
  social life of, **7:**465
  social standing of, **7:**389
  stature of, **3:**398, 399
  women, **7:**207–208
    institutionalized rape of, **7:**49
  vs. working class, **2:**224
"Slave in the Dismal Swamp, The"
    (Longfellow), **3:**57–58
Slave insurrections, **7:**8, **378–380,**
    379, 380
  on *Amistad,* **1:176–177**
  and antislavery movement,
    7:387–388
  Brown (John) and, **4:**97–100
  Christianity among slaves and,
    1:42
  Creole, **2:457**
  Fugitive Slave Acts and, **3:**482
  Gabriel's Insurrection, **3:501; 7:**8,
    156
  Nat Turner's Rebellion,
    5:516–517, *517;* **7:**10, 380;
    8:343
    historical assessment of,
      9:287–288
  New York Slave Conspiracy
    (1741), **6:***85,* **85–86**
  number of, **7:**379
  Vesey Rebellion, **6:**235; **7:**380, 455;
    8:316–317
Slave rescue cases, **3:**482; **7:380–382**
  Oberlin-Wellington, **6:**152, **153**
  See also Underground Railroad
Slave ships, **7:382,** *382*
  Amistad, **1:176–177**
  Antelope, **1:190**
  Bance-Island, **5:***365*
  Brookes, **5:***364*
  conditions on, **5:**363–364, *364;*
    7:382, 388; **9:**95–96
  slave resistance on, **7:**388

  Voyages of the Slaver St. John excerpt
    on, **9:**95–96
Slave trade, **7:382–389,** *384, 386*
  abolition of, **7:**387
    enforcement of, **7:**406–407
  advertising flier, **5:***365*
  African tribes involved in,
    7:384–385
  Amistad case and, **1:176–177**
  Antelope case and, **1:190**
  in Caribbean, **7:**387, *387*
  character of, **7:**386–387, 388
  decline of, **7:**385–386, 388
  firsthand account of, **9:**112–113
  as forced migration, **5:**368
  illegal (after 1808), **1:**48; **7:**387
    smuggling in, **7:406–407**
  internal (domestic), **7:**387, 394
  Mediterranean, **7:**389
  Middle Passage, **5:362–365,** *363,
    364, 365*
  molasses trade and, **5:**436
  origins of, **5:**363; **7:**383–385
  size of, **1:**47; **7:**386
  Supreme Court on, **1:**190
  transatlantic, **7:***383,* 383–388,
    389–390
  triangular trade in, **8:**164, 209–210
Slavery, **7:389–397**
  in 1860, **7:***391*
  abolition of, **2:**193, 218
    after American Revolution, **7:**137
    Republican Party and, **2:**208
  within Africa, **7:**386–387, 389–390
  African American literature about,
    5:124
  agriculture and, **7:**383–384, 385
  in Alabama, **1:**102
  American Revolution and, **7:**392
  arguments in favor of, **1:**192;
    7:386, 392, 466
    in original documents,
      9:267–269, 276–280
  in Arkansas, **1:**260, 261
  in Bermuda, **1:**445
  in Brazil, **2:**340
  in California, ban on, **2:**9
  capitalist economy and, **2:**44
  and child care, **2:**138
  Christiana fugitive affair,
    2:161–162
  Christianity on, **1:**41–42
  and Civil War, **2:**208
  Clayton Compromise on, **2:229**

cotton and, **1**:48; **6**:364; **7**:393

crime and, **2**:458

debate on

    Bible's influence on, **1**:447–448

    and Compromise of 1850, **2**:331

decline of, in North, **7**:*393*

definitions of, **7**:389

dehumanization in, **7**:389

in Delaware, **2**:542

Democratic Party and, **2**:551;

    6:415–416

Douglas on, **5**:110–111

ecclesiastical opponents to, **2**:349

economy of, **7**:394–395

and electoral politics, **3**:154

extension of, Wilmot Proviso and,

    8:485–486

in Florida, **3**:385

foreign commentaries on,

    1:136–137

in Georgia, **3**:554–555

historical reenactment of, **8**:484

historical writings on, **4**:140

in Illinois, **4**:215, 216

indentured servants and, decline of,

    1:47–48

in independence debate, **7**:136–137

integration during, **4**:373–374

Jews and, **4**:476

in Kansas, **4**:508–509, 512–513

in Kentucky, **4**:519–520

Knights of the Golden Circle and,

    4:540

Lincoln on, **5**:110–111

    in his second inaugural address,

        5:112

    in "House Divided" speech,

        9:284–286

in Louisiana, **5**:159, 160

magazines and newspapers, on,

    5:192, 199

in Maryland, **5**:256, 257

Methodism and, **5**:333

in Missouri, **5**:420

    Saint Louis, **7**:226–227

    Tallmadge Amendment and, **8**:45

Missouri Compromise, **5**:422–425

Native Americans and, **4**:323–324;

    8:249

natural rights and, **6**:10

in Nebraska, **4**:512–513

in New England, **5**:515

in New Hampshire, **6**:57, 58

in New Netherland, **6**:72

in New Orleans, **6**:73

in New York City, **6**:79, 85–86

in Ohio, **6**:172–173

opposition to (*See* Antislavery)

origins of, **1**:47–48; **7**:389

as peculiar institution, **6**:273

in Pennsylvania, **6**:277

plantation system and, **6**:364

on plantations, **7**:394–395, 462

Quaker opposition to, **7**:2

religious groups' positions on,

    3:44–45

Republican Party and, **6**:416

rice culture and, **7**:155, 391, 392

scientific racism and, **1**:192

slave resistance to, **1**:48, 49; **7**:378,

    464 (*See also* Slave insurrec-

    tions)

vs. slave society, **7**:391–392

slaveholders in

    culture of, **7**:396–397

    on plantations, **7**:463

slaves' accounts of, **5**:124

in South Carolina, **7**:454

state bans on, **5**:230

sugar industry and, **7**:383–384,

    389–390, 392; **8**:13

task system of, **7**:155

in Tennessee, **8**:83, 85

in Texas, **8**:101

tobacco and, **6**:364; **7**:391, 392;

    8:134, 341

transcendentalism on, **8**:181

United Confederate Veterans'

    defense of, **8**:265

in Virginia, **8**:341, 342–343

in Washington (D.C.), **8**:410

westward expansion of, **7**:392–393;

    8:461–462

Whig Party on, **2**:361

White Slave Traffic Act (1910),

    5:225

Wilmot Proviso and, **6**:415

Slee, J. Noah, **1**:468

Sleepy Hollow (New York), **7**:397

Slichter, Sumner, **2**:273

Slick, Sam, **6**:274

Slidell, John, **2**:342; **8**:208

    and land speculation, **5**:36

    mission to Mexico by, **5**:340;

        7:397–398

Sloan, Alfred P., Jr., **1**:373; **3**:526

Sloan, John, **1**:268, 297, 321; **6**:471

Sloat, John Drake, **2**:8; **7**:551

Slocum, John, **4**:293; **6**:7, *8*

Slogans, advertising, **1**:33

Sloo, A. G., **3**:501–502

Sloss, James, **1**:103

Sloughter, Henry, **6**:84

Slovak Republic, creation of, **2**:91

Slovaks, in Cleveland, **2**:233

Slovenes, in Cleveland, **2**:233

SLP. *See* Socialist Labor Party

S&Ls. *See* Savings and loan associa-

    tions

Slums. *See* Tenements

Small, Albion, **6**:424; **7**:432

Small, Mary J., **1**:44

Small Business Administration

    (SBA), **7**:398

Small claims courts, **2**:339

Smallpox, **3**:235; **7**:398–400

    in colonial era, **5**:300

    elimination of, **2**:88

    in Native Americans, **5**:219–220;

        7:399; **8**:488

    pandemic of 1836-1837, **1**:481

    resistance to quarantining of

        patients, **3**:*235*

    vaccine for, **5**:300; **7**:*399*, 399–400

Smelser, Neil J., **7**:436

Smelters, **6**:114–115; **7**:400–401

Smet, Pierre-Jean De, **4**:474; **8**:412

Smibert, John, **3**:318

Smirnov, E. S., **8**:596

Smith, Adam, **1**:228; **3**:108; **5**:20;

    6:387, 481

    on mercantilism, **5**:316

    Wealth of Nations, **3**:107

Smith, Al, **2**:164; **7**:113

    and Democratic Party, **2**:552

Smith, Alfred, in *Smith v. Oregon*

    Employment, **7**:401

Smith, Alfred E., **1**:196; **3**:161, 162;

    8:46

    and Empire State Building, **3**:199

    Port Authority of New York and

        New Jersey created by, **6**:421

    in presidential campaign of 1928,

        6:5

Smith, Amanda Berry, **8**:501

Smith, Andrew Jackson, in Red

    River Campaign, **7**:71

Smith, Anna Deavere, **8**:115

Smith, Bessie, **1**:492

Smith, Billy, **6**:302

Smith, Charles Shaler, **1**:538

Smith, Cheryl K., **3**:262

Smith, Coyle v., **3:**202
Smith, David, **1:**306, 307
Smith, Dean, **1:**425
Smith, Edward, **6:**148
Smith, Edwin Burritt, anti-imperialism of, **1:**202
Smith, Elias, **8:**264
Smith, Employment Division v., **1:**162, 494; **2:**170; **3:**374; **6:**1
Smith, Francis (Borax), **1:**505
Smith, Fred, **1:**312
Smith, Frederick M., **7:**104
Smith, Frederick W., **2:**439
Smith, George Otis, **3:**546
Smith, George T., **3:**390
Smith, Gerald L. K., **1:**198; **3:**327, 328
Smith, Gerrit, **1:**209, 211; **3:**154; **6:**502
  and Davis (Jefferson), bond for, **2:**505
  and Liberty Party, **5:**96, 97
Smith, Harry, **3:**396
Smith, Henry Boynton, **7:**97
Smith, Henry Nash, **1:**169, 170
Smith, Howard W., **8:**344
Smith, Hulett Carlson, **8:**450
Smith, Jacob, **1:**354
Smith, James, **2:**52
Smith, Jedediah Strong, **2:**301; **3:**299; **7:**190; **8:**454
  trapping in Great Valley, **4:**58
  trapping in Rocky Mountains, **3:**493
Smith, John, **4:**137
  Cape Cod exploration by, **2:**38
  captivity narrative by, **2:**51
  fishing ventures of, **2:**261
  The General History of Virginia, New England, and the Summer Isles, **5:**117
  New Hampshire mapped by, **6:**56
  Pocahontas and, **6:**442, *443*
  Potomac River mapped by, **6:**433
  Powhatan's speech to, text of, **9:**98
  river exploration by, **7:**173
  on Starving Time, **9:**84–86
  A True Relation of Virginia, **5:**117
Smith, Joseph, **2:**163; **5:***53;* **8:**296
  The Book of Mormon and, **1:**447; **2:**163; **5:**53
  as freemason, **3:**466
  and Grahamites, **3:**24
  in Illinois, **5:**459

murder of, **7:**94
  at Nauvoo, **6:**14–15
  on polygamy, **6:**15, 410
  in Vermont, **8:**313
Smith, Joseph, Jr., **7:**103
Smith, Joseph, III, **7:**103, 104
Smith, Kirby, **2:**479
Smith, Mamie, **1:**492
Smith, Margaret Chase, **8:**507
Smith, Marvin, **1:**301
Smith, McDonald v., **6:**297
Smith, Melancton, antifederalism of, **1:**201; **9:**160–164
Smith, Michael J., **2:**102
Smith, Morgan, **1:**301
Smith, Neil, **3:**543
Smith, O. P., **2:**160
Smith, Peter, and land speculation, **5:**36
Smith, Robert Angus, **1:**13
Smith, Robert H., **1:**118, 119
Smith, Samuel Francis, **5:**505
Smith, Samuel Stanhope, **7:**12
Smith, Theobold, **5:**358; **8:**320
Smith, Sir Thomas, **8:**347
Smith, Tommie, **6:**193, *193*
Smith, Vernon, **3:**110
Smith, Wallace B., **7:**104
Smith, William, **6:**219, 382
Smith, William, Jr., **5:**167
Smith, William Kennedy, **7:**50
Smith, William W., **7:**104
Smith, Willoughby, **8:**76
Smith Act (1940), **3:**207, 208, 338; **6:**99; **7:**401
  convictions under, **8:**1
  as sedition act, **7:**301, 401
  Supreme Court on, **8:**1
Smith College, **3:**131; **7:**319–320
  athletic program at, **2:**277
  botanical garden at, **1:**517
Smith Paper Company, **6:**245
Smith v. Allwright, **3:**147; **5:**526; **6:**463
Smith v. Oregon Employment, **7:**401
Smith-Hughes Act (1917), **7:401–402**
Smith-Lever Act (1914), **1:**71; **3:**325, 432; **7:**402
  and 4-H Clubs, **3:**445
Smith-Mundt Act (1948), **8:**351
Smithson, James, **6:**317; **7:**402
Smithson, Robert, **1:**307

Smithsonian Institution, **3:**257; **7:402–403**; **8:**597
  collections of, **5:**487
  establishment of, **1:**192; **6:**317; **7:**402
  functions of, **7:**402–403
  mammal specimens, **5:**217
  meteorological project, **5:**331
  and meteorological research, **2:**235
  museums under, **7:**403
  National Gallery of Art, **5:538–541**
  National Museum of the American Indian, **5:547–548**; **6:**1–2
  and National Zoological Park, **8:**594
  organizational structure of, **7:**402
  publications of, **7:**403
  research centers under, **7:**403
  returning Native American remains, **6:**2
  U.S. National Museum, biology collection, **5:**217
Smog. *See* Air pollution
Smohalla (prophet), **6:**7
Smoke Signals (Alexie), **5:**129
Smoke-filled room, **7:404**
Smokey Bear, **3:**432, 436
Smoking (food preservation method), **3:**405
Smoking (tobacco), **7:404–405**
  advertising for, **1:**34; **7:**404, 405; **8:**136
  anti-tobacco campaigns and, **7:***404,* 404–405
  health hazards of, **7:**404–405; **8:**133, 135–137
  history of, **8:**134–135
  rates of, **7:**404, 405
  second-hand, **8:**136
"Smoking gun" tape, **6:**111, 112
Smoky Mountain Boys (Crazy Tennesseans), **5:***491*
Smoot, Reed, **5:**54; **8:**297
Smoot-Hawley Tariff Act (1930), **1:**386; **3:**460; **4:**49; **8:**52, 165
  duties under, **3:**97
Smuggling
  colonial, **3:**103; **7:405–406**; **8:**12
  and burning of *Gaspée,* **3:**512
  Navigation Acts and, **6:**22, 360
  tea, **8:**61
  of slaves, **7:406–407**
  See also Drug trafficking

Smuts, Jan Christian, **5**:63
Smyth, Alexander, **8**:383
Smyth, John, **1**:411
Smyth, William Henry, **8**:63
Snake(s), **4**:129–130
Snake River, **7**:407
Snap the Whip (Homer), **3**:*537*
SNCC. *See* Student Nonviolent
    Coordinating Committee
Snelling, Fort, **7**:407
SNL. *See Saturday Night Live*
Snorkel truck, **3**:373
Snow, Elisha, **8**:574
Snow, Samuel, **1**:30
Snuff, **8**:134
Snyder, Gary, **1**:433
Snyder, John W., Jr., **8**:44
Snyder, Ralph, **2**:450, 451
Soap and detergent industry,
    7:407–408
  borax in, **1**:505
  Procter and Gamble, **6**:491
Soap operas, **6**:491; **7**:408–410
Sobell, Morton, **7**:197
Sobrero, Ascanio, **3**:301
Sobrino, Jon, **5**:93
Soccer, **3**:409, 412; **7**:410–411
Social class. *See* Class(es)
Social Control (Ross), **6**:424
Social darwinism, **1**:192–193; **2**:227;
    3:269; **7**:411–412
Social Democratic Party, **7**:412
  in Socialist Party of America, **7**:429
Social deviancy, **5**:313
Social evolutionism, **1**:192–193
Social gospel, **1**:413; **3**:265;
    7:412–414; **8**:263
  and Congregationalism, **2**:349
  creation of, **2**:164
  Methodism and, **5**:333
  Protestant modernism and,
    5:431–432
Social Gospel, The, **8**:302
Social Justice (magazine), **5**:563
Social legislation, **7**:415–417
  in 19th century, **7**:415
  in New Deal, **7**:415–416
  in Progressive Era, **7**:415
  See also Welfare system
Social mobility
  frontier and, **2**:226
  upward, faith in, **2**:227
Social Register, **7**:417

Social Science Research Council,
    5:67
Social sciences
  encyclopedia of, **3**:204
  and historical writing, **4**:139–140
Social security, **7**:129–130, 131,
    417–422; **8**:440
  administration of, **4**:114; **7**:419
  for elderly, **7**:416, 417
  establishment of, **4**:48; **6**:43, 283;
    7:416, 417, 418–419; **8**:58
    finding funding needed for, **8**:197
  expansion of, **7**:*419*, 419–420, *420*
  growth of, **8**:441
  number of beneficiaries of, **7**:419,
    419
  operating procedures of,
    7:420–421
  plans predating, **2**:11
  problems with, **7**:421–422
  purposes of, **7**:417
  rates of return from, **7**:420–421,
    421
  reform of, **7**:421–422
  and sex discrimination, **3**:54
Social Security Act (1935), **6**:283;
    8:440
  Aid to Dependent Children, **2**:146
  amendment to (1939), **2**:207
  and family values, **3**:317
  League of Women Voters support
    for, **5**:66
  provisions of, **7**:416, 417
  and state employment services,
    3:201
  Supreme Court on, **7**:416, 419
  unemployment insurance under,
    8:253–254
Social settlements. *See* Settlement
    house movement
Social surveys, **6**:533
Social work, **7**:422–423
  in adoption, **1**:28–29
  predecessor of, **2**:106
Socialism, **3**:107; **7**:424–429
  adherents to, **7**:425–426
  anarchism and, **1**:180
  anticommunism in, **1**:197–198
  decline of, **7**:427–428
  definition of, **7**:424
  exclusion policy for individuals
    supporting, **3**:207
  in Great Depression, **7**:427
  ideology of, **7**:424, 426

  in Industrial Workers of the
    World, **4**:346–347; **7**:424
  internal divisions in, **7**:426–427
  legacy of, **7**:428
  May Day, **5**:275
  origins of, **7**:424
  peak of, **7**:424–426
  publications of, **7**:426
  repression of, **7**:427
  in Social Democratic Party, **7**:412
  trade unions associated with, **3**:176
  utopias of, **7**:424; **8**:303
Socialist feminism, and abortion, **1**:5
Socialist Labor Party (SLP), **5**:16;
    7:423–424
  decline of, **7**:423–424
  origins of, **7**:423
  in presidential elections, **2**:227;
    3:159, 160, 161
  in Socialist Party of America, **7**:429
  in Wisconsin, **8**:492
Socialist movement. *See* Socialism
Socialist Party of America (SP),
    1:467; **2**:325; **7**:429; **8**:119
  anticommunism of, **1**:197–198
  antiwar sentiment in, **7**:426–427
  Debs in, **7**:425
  establishment of, **7**:17, 425, 429
  internal divisions in, **7**:426–427,
    429
  and labor, **5**:16
  members of, **7**:425–426
  and peace movements, **6**:267
  political candidates from, **7**:425,
    426, 427, 429
  repression of, **7**:427
Socialist Trade and Labor Alliance
    (STLA), **4**:346
Social-reform pacifists, **6**:227
La Société des Nations (Bourgeois),
    5:63
Society for Christian Union and
    Progress, **8**:179
Society for Establishing Useful
    Manufactures, **5**:227
Society for Ethical Culture, **1**:55;
    3:256–257
Society for Individual Rights (SIR),
    3:514
Society for the Establishment of
    Useful Manufactures, **6**:62
Society for the Prevention of Cruel-
    ty to Animals (SPCA), **1**:185,
    186; **7**:429–430

Society for the Prevention of Cruelty to Children, **7:**430
Society for the Propagation of the Gospel in Foreign Parts (SPG), **3:**112; **7:**430
Society for the Propagation of the Gospel in New England. *See* New England Company
Society for Women's Health Research, **7:**430
Society of American Archivists (SAA), **1:**255–256
Society of American Indians (SAI), **7:**430–431
Society of Associated Teachers, **8:**62
Society of Friends. *See* Quakers
Society of Sisters, Pierce v., **2:**164, 167; **6:**352–353
Sociology, **7:**431–437
   The Lonely Crowd, **5:**148
   urban, **8:**291
Sociology for the South (Fitzhugh), **7:**431–432
   excerpt from, **9:**276–280
Sod house, **3:**93
Soda fountains, **6:**309; **7:**437, 438, *438*
Soddy, Frederick, **2:**486; **6:**341
Sodium carbonate, **6:**431
Sodium nitrate, **8:**243
Sodomy laws, **7:**326, 327
Sōen, Shaku, **1:**552
SOF. *See* Special Operations Forces
Soft drink industry, **2:**388; **7:**437–439
   Coca-Cola in, **2:**260–261; **7:**438–439
   soda fountains in, **7:**437, 438, *438*
Soft money, **2:**23; **3:**147; **7:**439
   policy of, **7:**439
   in political campaigns, **7:**439
Software industry, **7:**439–443
   companies in, **7:**441
   enterprise software in, **7:**441–442
   Internet and, **7:**443
   personal computers and, **7:**442–443
   programming services in, **7:***440,* 440–441
   sectors of, **7:**439–440
   shrink-wrapped software in, **7:**442–443
   video games in, **8:**327
Soil, **7:**443–445
   classification of, **7:**444

conservation of, **7:**445
erosion of, **7:**445
fertility of, **7:**444
management of, **7:**444–445
mapping of, **7:**444
Soil Conservation Service (SCS), **7:**445
Soja, Edward, **3:**543
Soka Gakkai International, **1:**326
Solar eclipse, of 1831, **9:**45, *47*
Solar power, **3:**209, 214, 216
Soldiers' and Sailors' Additional Homestead Act of 1872, **5:**35
Soldiers' homes, **7:**445–446; **8:**317
Soldier's Medal, **2:**527
Soliah, Kathleen, **8:**38
Solid South, **7:**446
Solid waste disposal, **4:**356
Solidarity Day (1981), **1:**152
Solid-state physics, **6:**345–348
Solomon, Isaac, **2:**36; **3:**406
Solow, Robert, **3:**110
Somalia, **7:***447*
   Marines killed in, **1:**39–40; **7:**447
   peacekeeping mission in, **6:**271; **8:**271
   U.S. relations with, **1:**39–40; **7:**446–447
Sombart, Werner, **3:**400
Some Thoughts Concerning Education (Locke), **5:**140
Somers, Sir George, **1:**445; **8:**347
Somervell, Brehon B., **3:**219; **6:**285
Somit, Albert, **6:**401
Somme Offensive, **7:**447–448, *448*
Sommerville, Chris, **3:**531
Somoza, Anastasio, **2:**54, 395
Somoza Debayle, Anastasio, **5:**49
Somoza García, Anastasio, **6:**104–105
Son of the Forest, A (Apess), **5:**128; **7:**448
Sonar, in oceanographic surveys, **6:**160
Song(s)
   cowboy, **2:**442–443
   in Puritan religious life, **1:**431
   See also Music; *specific songs*
Sonneborn, Harry, **5:**184
Sonnenshein, Hugo F., **8:**281
Son-of-Sam Law, **7:**448–449
Sons of Confederate Veterans, **8:**265
Sons of Liberty
   in American Revolution, **1:**514, 528; **7:**135, **449**

Boston's, **7:**149
founding of, **2:**357
in Civil War, **7:**449
   Copperhead Order of, **2:**411
   in Northwest conspiracy, **6:**136
liberty poles of, **5:**97
Sons of Temperance, **8:**79
Sons of the South, **7:**449–450
Sontag, Susan, **5:**122
Sony
   Betamax by, **8:**327
   video games by, **8:**327
Sooners, **1:**501; **7:**450
Sorby, Henry C., **6:**300
Sorghum, **7:**450
Sororities, **3:**456
Soros, George, Lindesmith Center established by, **5:**513
Sosa, Sammy, **1:**422
Soto, Gary, **5:**123
Soto, Hernando de, **2:**360; **3:**295; **5:**158
   and Choctaw Indians, **2:**158
   explorations of, **7:***450,* 450–451
      in Alabama, **1:**102
      on Arkansas River, **1:**264
      in Florida, **3:**385; **7:**450; **8:**47
      in Mississippi, **5:**411
      in Tennessee, **8:**84
Soul music, **5:**490
Soule, George, **6:**76
Soule, John Babsone Lane, **4:**9
Soule, Michael, **2:**373
Soulé, Pierre, **1:**188–189; **2:**469
   Ostend Manifesto and, **6:**219
Souls of Black Folk, The (Du Bois), **3:**556; **5:**124; **6:**375; **7:**451
Sound. *See* Audio technology industry
Sousa, John Philip, **5:**237–238
Souter, David
   on presidential election of 2000, **1:**579
   on state sovereignty, **1:**120
South, the, **7:**462–469
   African American emigration from, **5:**369–371
   agriculture in, **2:**413
      in 19th century, **1:**63
      antebellum, **7:**463–464
      in Civil War, **1:**63
      in colonial era, **1:**62
      cotton, **2:**424–426, *426,* 429; **3:**555; **7:**463

plantation system, **6:363–365**
sugar, **8**:13
during American Revolution,
  7:145–146
antebellum, **7:462–467**
  and Nat Turner's Rebellion,
    5:516–517
black codes in, **1**:472
during Civil War (*See also* Confed-
    erate States of America)
  Union sentiment in, **8:260**
after Civil War (*See* Reconstruction)
class divisions in, **7**:464
cultural regionalism in, **7**:297
Democratic Party in, **2**:551; **7**:446
disfranchisement in, **3**:57, 146, 147
in domestic trade, **8**:160
dueling in, **3**:92–93
economic development in,
  7:467–468, 473
economy of
  in antebellum South, **7**:463–464
  in New South, **7**:467–468
education in, **3**:115, 120, 121, 126
Fugitive-Agrarians on, **3**:481
geographic borders of, **7**:462–463
Gone with the Wind portraying,
  4:20–21
honor code in, **7**:464
immigration to, **4**:220; **7**:464
industry in, **7**:467, 468
intellectual life in, **7**:465–466
Lower, **5:167**
Mason-Dixon line, **5:259–260**, *260*
Middle, **5**:167
Nashville Convention and, **5**:516
Native Americans in, removal of,
  8:226
New, **1**:50; **7:467–469**
opposition of tariffs in, **3**:460;
  6:145; **8**:50
  Force Acts and, **3**:413–414;
    6:145–146
peonage in, **6**:289
plantations in, **7**:462
  slavery on, **7**:394–395, 462
politics in, **7**:465
poor whites in, **6:414**
population of, **7**:464
Populist Party in, **7**:469
prisons in, **6**:477
Progressive Party in, **6**:499
on property taxation, **8**:56
religion in, **7**:465–466

sectionalism in, **7**:296, 297, 298
social life in, **7**:464
Solid, **7:446**
southern rights movement in,
  7:473–474
sports in, **7**:507–508
state flags in, **3**:381
states' rights in, **7**:536–537
in Sun Belt, **8**:18
temperance movements in, **8**:79
textile industry in, **7**:467, 468
third parties in, **8**:119
women of, **7**:464
work ethic in, **8**:528
South Africa
  apartheid in, **1**:38, 39; **7**:452–453
    student activism against, **8**:587
  in Cold War, **7**:452
  U.S. relations with, **1**:39;
    7:451–453
South America. *See* Latin America
South Carolina, **7:453–457**, *454*
  African Americans in, **7**:456–457
  agriculture in, **7**:454
  in American Revolution,
    7:454–455, 472
    Wilkinson (Eliza) on, **9**:150–151
  Battle of Fort Moultrie, **5:463**
  Cherokee war with, **2**:128
  civil rights movement in,
    7:456–457
  in Civil War, **7**:455
  in colonial era, **7**:453–454
  Confederate flag in, **3**:381
  constitution of, **7**:527
  economy of, **7**:454, 456
  emblems, nicknames, mottos, and
    songs of, **7**:*533*
  Federalist Party in, **3**:351
  Force Act (1833) and, **3**:413
  4-H Clubs in, **3**:445
  Fundamental Constitutions in, **2**:57
  geological survey of, **3**:548
  gun control in, **4**:75
  Hamburg Riot in (1876), **4:87**
  hurricanes in, **4**:198
  immigration to, **4**:220; **7**:453–454
  industry in, **7**:456
  Native Americans in, **7**:453, 454
  and North Carolina, boundary dis-
    pute between, **1**:521
  nullification of federal tariff by,
    6:145; **8**:50
    Force Acts and, **3**:413; **6**:145–146

plantation life in, Pinckney (Eliza
    Lucas) on, **9**:111–112
politics in, **7**:454
as proprietary colony, **6**:*510*, 511
provincial congresses in, **6**:520
ratification of Constitution in,
  2:381
Reconstruction in, **7**:455–456
rice plantations in, **6**:364
as royal colony, **6**:*510*, 511
secession by, **7**:293–294, 455
  Declaration of Causes, **9**:292–294
settlement of, **2**:289
slave insurrections in, **7**:379, 380,
  455; **8:316–317**
slavery in, **7**:454
State Bank of, **1**:408
state university of, **8**:279
textile industry in, **7**:456
*South Carolina Coastal Council, Lucas
  v.*, **2**:318; **3**:198
South Carolina Exposition and Protest
  (Calhoun), **7:457**
South Carolina Gazette (newspaper),
  6:95
South Carolina v. Katzenbach, **8**:357
South Dakota, **2**:493; **7:457–462**,
  458
  agriculture in, **7**:460
  Badlands in, **1:383–384**, *384*
  banking industry in, **7**:460–461
  Black Hills in, **1:474**; **8**:275
  constitution of, **7**:525
  economy of, **7**:460–461
  education in, **7**:461
  emblems, nicknames, mottos, and
    songs of, **7**:*533*
  gold mining in, **4**:11
  health care industry in, **7**:461
  immigration to, **7**:458
  livestock industry in, **7**:460
  Mount Rushmore, **5:464–465**, *465*
  Native Americans in, **7**:458, 459,
    461
  politics in, **7**:460
  population of, **7**:458
  statehood for, **7**:459
  tourism in, **7**:460
South Florida Task Force, **5**:511
South Korea
  foreign aid to, **3**:416
  in Korean War, **4:544–550**
  U.S. relations with, **4**:542
    and Korea-gate, **4**:542–543

South Pass, **7:**462, *462*
South Polar explorations, **6:**382–384
South Vietnam
  creation of, **3:**534; **8:**329
  under Diem, **8:**330–331
  foreign aid to, **3:**417
  under Thieu, **8:**333, 334
  in Vietnam War, **8:**329–334
  See also Vietnam
Southampton, earl of, **8:**347
Southard, E. E., **6:**521
Southdale Mall (Edina, Minnesota), **5:**216
Southeast Asia
  foreign aid to, **3:**416
  immigration from, **7:**470–471
Southeast Asia Treaty Organization (SEATO), **7:**469–470; **8:**202
  establishment of, **7:**469
  internal divisions in, **7:**470
  members of, **7:**469
Southeast Asian Americans, **7:**470–472, *471*
  geographic distribution of, **7:**471
  number of, **7:**471
  professional activities of, **7:**471
Southern African Development Community (SADC), **1:**40
Southern Agrarianism, **3:**481
Southern Alliance, **3:**323; **6:**416–417
Southern Arizona Water Rights Settlement Act (1982), **1:**100
Southern Baptist Convention, **1:**412, 413; **3:**485
  boycott of Disneyland by, **1:**529
  membership in, **7:***91*
Southern Campaigns, **7:**472
Southern Christian Leadership Conference (SCLC), **3:**557; **7:**18, **472–473**
Southern Commercial Conventions, **7:**473
Southern Exposition, **8:**558
Southern Homestead Act (1866), **1:**63
Southern Overland Mail Company, **5:**204
Southern Pacific Company, Mussel Slough incident, **5:503–504**
Southern Pacific Railroad, **2:**10; **7:**35
Southern rights movement, **7:473–474**

Southern Tenant Farmers' Union (STFU), **7:474**
Southern Unionists, **7:474–475**
Southwell, Sir Robert, **5:**151
Southwest, **7:475–476**
  boundaries of, **1:**242–243; **7:**475
  Catholic presence in, **2:**67
  culture of, **7:**476
  economic history of, **7:**475–476
  Mesa, **5:**325
  Mesa Verde, prehistoric ruins of, **5:***325*, **325–326**
  Mesquite, **5:**327
  Native Americans in
    missions of, **4:**276
    social life of, **4:**305
    treaties with, **4:**314–315
  political influence of, **7:**475, 476
  prehistoric, **1:**242–243
  silversmithing, **5:**328
  in Sun Belt, **8:**18
Southwest Fur Company, **1:**158
Southwest Territory, **7:**476
Southwestern Cable Co., United States v., **3:**340
Sovereign immunity, **7:**477, 534–535
Sovereigns of Industry, **7:**476
Sovereignty
  doctrine of, **7:476–477**
  popular, **2:**331; **8:**485
  state (*See* State sovereignty)
Soviet Union
  Afghanistan invaded by, **1:37–38**, *38*
  and U.S. relations with Pakistan and India, **4:**260
  and African policies of U.S., **1:**38, 39
  Ames' espionage for, **1:173–174**
  arms race and disarmament in, **1:**271–272
    SALT and, **7:**552–554
    SDI and, **7:**554–555
  atomic bomb in, **1:**271
  and Berlin blockade, **1:**443
  CIA operations in, **2:**92, 93
  and Communist Party, U.S., **2:**326, 327–328
  and Cuba, **1:**430; **2:**470, 474
  decline of, **2:**270
  diplomatic recognition of, **7:**57, 211
  dissolution of, **2:**270

  at Dumbarton Oaks Conference, **3:**94
  and Eastern/Central Europe, control over, **2:**89–90, 268, 269; **8:**574
  imperialism of U.S. and, **4:**245
  Indian relations with, **4:**259, 260
  Iran occupied by, **4:**418
  Iron Curtain of, **4:429–430**
  and Korea, **8:**120
  in Korean Airlines flight 007 crash, **4:**543
  in Korean War, **4:**544–549
  Lend-Lease aid to, **5:**82
  and Middle Eastern policies of U.S., **1:**233
  missile development in, **5:**407
  missile gap with U.S., **5:406–407**
  and Nazi Germany, pact with, **2:**327
  Nuclear Non-Proliferation Treaty with, **6:**138
  nuclear power plants in, **6:**139
  Nuclear Test Ban Treaty with, **6:**143
  nuclear weapons of, **1:**271–272; **6:**138
  in Olympics, **6:**193–194
  origins of, **2:**267
  at Paris conferences, **6:**247
  at Reykjavik Summit, **1:**75
  satellite launched by, **2:**319
  serial killings in, **7:**315
  smallpox in, **7:**398–399, 400
  space program of, **7:**479–480
  in Suez Crisis, **8:**3
  in summit conferences, **8:15–17**
  and United Nations, **8:**270
  U.S. relations with, **7:211–213** (*See also* Cold War)
    containment policy in, Kennan on, **9:**411–413
    and Internet development, **4:**397, 398
    Nixon's visit, **2:**269; **7:**212
    telephone hotline, **2:**320, 475
    trade, **7:**211
    U-2 incident and, **8:**247
    during World War II, **2:**267; **3:**426; **7:**211
    "X" article and, **8:**569
    Yalta Conference and, **2:**267; **8:573–574**

U.S. relief in, after World War I,
  8:541–542
in World War II, **2:**89, 267; **3:**144;
  7:211
and prisoners of war, **6:**474
See also Cold War; Russia
Sow case, **7:478**
Soybeans, **2:**414; **7:478–479**
SP. *See* Socialist Party of America
S&P. *See* Standard & Poor's
Spa(s). *See* Resorts and spas
Space Needle, **8:**560
Space program, **5:**523–524;
  7:479–482
in Alabama, **1:**105
Moon landing *(Apollo 11)*, **5:***454,*
  454–455
Space shuttle(s), **5:**524; **7:**190, 481,
  482, *483*
Challenger disaster, **2:101–102,**
  102; **3:**41
Discovery, **2:**102; **3:**46
robotics in, **7:**184
Spacewar (computer game), **8:**327
Spain
Adams-Onís Treaty with, **1:**188;
  3:386, 425; **8:**204
American Revolution and, **7:**147,
  483
Catholic missions of, in California,
  9:107–109
Civil War in (1936)
  Abraham Lincoln Brigade in,
    1:7–8
  and relations with U.S., **7:**485
colonial settlements of, **7:**489–490
  administration of, **2:**278–279
  in Alabama, **1:**102
  architecture in, **1:**248–249
  in Arizona, **1:**256–257
  borderlands of, **7:488–490**
  in California, **2:**8
  and city planning, **2:**185
  and encomienda system,
    3:202–203
  in Florida, **3:**385
  independence of, **5:**50–52
  in Kansas, **4:**508
  in Louisiana, **6:**73
  in New Mexico, **6:**66–67
  in North Dakota, **6:**132
  Oñate in, **6:**194
  rural life in, **7:**206–207
  in South Carolina, **7:**453

wedding rituals in, **8:**436
convoy system used by, **2:**402
and Cuba, **2:**469–470
and Dominican Republic, **3:**75
explorations of, **3:**283–285,
  294–296, *295;* **7:**206, 488–489
  by Cabeza de Vaca, **2:1–2,** *2;*
    3:284, 295
  in New Mexico, **6:**65
  in Texas, **8:**99
  on Colorado River, **2:301**
  by Columbus, **7:**249
  conquistadores in, **2:360**
  by Coronado, **1:**256; **2:***416,*
    416–417; **4:**508
    in Great Plains, **4:**56
    in New Mexico, **6:**66
    in Texas, **8:**99
  in Florida, **3:**385; **8:**47
  in Grand Canyon, **4:**33
  in Great Plains, **4:**56
  Gulf Stream, **4:**73
  and Hispanic Americans, **4:**134
  in Kansas, **4:**508
  in New Mexico, **6:**65–66
  on Northwest Coast, **8:**453
  by Oñate, **6:194**
    in New Mexico, **6:**66
  in Oregon, **6:**204
  on Potomac River, **6:**433
  by Soto, **1:**102, 264; **7:450–451**
    in Florida, **3:**385; **8:**47
    in Tennessee, **8:**84
  in Southwest, **8:**451
  in Texas, **8:**98–99
  in Washington, **8:**412
foreign investment from, **3:**419
fur trade of, **3:**486
Jay-Gardoqui negotiations with,
  4:466
in Jenkins' Ear, War of, **4:**473
Louisiana Purchase and, **7:**484
Mississippi River and, **5:**416
Native Americans and
  Hopi, **4:**165
  missions for, **4:**276
  Navajo, **6:**15
  policies on, **4:**282–283
  relations with, **2:**135, 136
  treaties between, **4:**312
  wars between, **6:**67
    Apache Wars, **1:**220
and Paris, Treaty of (1783), **6:**248,
  250

Pinckney's Treaty with,
  6:356–357; 8:200, 204
power in North America, decrease
  in, **3:**298
in slave trade, **5:**363; **7:**383–384,
  387
Treaty of Paris (1763) with, **6:**248
Treaty of Paris (1898) with, **3:**360;
  6:250, 321; **8:**201
U.S. relations with, **7:483–485**
  Bowles's filibustering expeditions
    and, **1:**525
  Pinckney's Treaty and, **7:**484
  Spanish Conspiracy and, **7:**490
  territorial disputes in, **7:**484,
    489–490
  U.S. imperialism and, **4:**244;
    7:489–490
  war with (*See* Spanish-American
    War)
in World War II, **7:**485
Spalding, Eliza, **6:**100, 205; **8:**412
Spalding, Henry, **6:**100; **8:**412
Spander, Murray, **3:**182
Spanish Borderlands, **7:488–490,**
  491
  Franciscans in, **3:**453
Spanish Conspiracy, **3:**270; **7:490**
Spanish dollars. *See* Pieces of eight
Spanish language, **7:490–492,** *491*
Spanish Trail, **6:**254
Spanish-American War, **2:**470, 530;
  5:47; **7:485–487,** *486, 487*
  African Americans in, **5:**380–381
  Battle of Manila Bay in, **5:**225
  Battle of San Jacinto in, **7:**240–241
  Battles of San Juan Hill and El
    Caney in, **7:241–242**
  causes of, **7:**484, 485
  censorship during, **2:**83
  close of, **3:**360
  Cuba in, **6:**369; **7:**484, 485–486
  demobilization after, **2:**546
  desertion in, **3:**17
  enlistment for, **2:**364
  eyewitness account of, **9:**261–263
  and Guam, **4:**68
  Hispanic Americans in, **5:**383
  Maine, sinking of, **5:211,** *212*
  military uniforms in, **8:**258
  mobilization for, **5:**429
  munitions in, **5:**479
  new imperialism and, **1:**189
  peace treaty in, **7:**486–487

Spanish-American War, (*continued*)
  and Philippines, **3:**360; **6:**319–320,
    321–322; **8:**41
  photography in, **6:**332
  prisoners of war in, **6:**473
  and Puerto Rico, **6:**542, 544
  Rough Riders in, **2:**364; **7:***199*,
    199–200
  Sampson-Schley controversy in,
    7:236
  State Department in, **7:**528
  Teller Amendment and, **8:**78
  Treaty of Paris (1898) ending,
    6:250
  U.S. Army in, **1:**276; **7:**486
  U.S. Navy in, **6:**23, 25; **7:487–488**
  warships in, **8:**406, *407*
  women in, **8:**502
  yellow journalism and, **8:**577
Sparks, William A. J., **5:**31
SPCA. *See* Society for the Preven-
    tion of Cruelty to Animals
Speakeasy, **1:**504; **7:492–493**, *493*
Speaker of the House of Representa-
    tives, **2:**351, 352; **7:493**
  Mulligan letters scandal, **5:473**
Special districts, **6:**406
Special education, **3:**34
Special effects in films, **3:**364
Special interest groups. *See* Interest
    groups
Special Operations Forces (SOF),
    7:494–495
Special prosecutors, **7:495–497**
  and Tower Commission, **8:**148
Special Weapons and Tactics
    (SWAT), **3:**338
Specie circular, **7:497**
Specie payments, **1:**396, 458, 484
  suspension and resumption of,
    7:124, 497–499
  See also Currency and coinage
Species
  endangered, **2:**373; **3:205–207**,
    206
    wolf as, **8:**496
  introduced, **7:***499*, **499–500**
  invasive, **8:**437
Specific duties, vs. ad valorem duties,
    8:50
Speck, Frank, **6:**443
Specter, Arlen, **2:**197
Speech, freedom of

Alien and Sedition Acts on,
    1:123–124; **3:**374
  Espionage Act and, **7:**264
  for high school students, **1:**26
  on Internet, **8:**68
  Supreme Court on, **1:**26; **3:**374;
    7:264
Speech codes. *See* Group libel laws
Speeches. *See* Oratory
Speed, John, **9:**13, *13*
Speed limits, **7:***500*, **500–501**
  national, **3:**335–336
Speed skating, **4:**209, 210
Speedwell (ship), **5:**275; **6:**378
Speer, Robert, **3:**5–6
Spelling bee, **7:501**
Spencer, Herbert, **2:**227; **3:**269;
    6:424
Spender, John Alfred, **1:**138
Spener, Philipp Jakob, **6:**353, *353*
Sperry, Charles S., **1:**428
Sperry, Elmer A., **3:**173
SPG. *See* Society for the Propaga-
    tion of the Gospel in Foreign
    Parts
Spiegler, Caesar, **3:**30
Spielberg, Steven, **3:**364
  Close Encounters of the Third Kind,
    1:446
Spies, **7:501–503**
  in American Revolution,
    7:501–502
  in Civil War, **7:**502
  in Cold War, **2:**92; **7:**503
  in intelligence organizations,
    7:502–503
  motivations of, **7:**503
  in World War I, **7:**502; **8:**538
  in World War II, **3:**338; **7:**502
  See also Espionage; *specific people*
Spies, August, and Haymarket riot,
    4:109
Spillane, Mickey, *I, the Jury*, **5:**130
Spilsbury, John, **1:**411
Spindletop, **6:**302–303, 305
Spindletop oil well (Beaumont,
    Texas), **5:**361
Spinelli, Altiero, **3:**259
Spingarn, Arthur B., **5:**526
Spinks, Leon, **6:**485
Spinning Jenny, **8:***109*
Spira, Henry, **1:**186
Spirit Lake Massacre (1857),
    7:503–504

Spirit of St. Louis, **5:**113–114, *114*
Spirits industry, **7:504–505**
Spiritual Milk for Boston Babes (Cot-
    ton), **5:**127
Spiritualism, **7:505–506**
  African American folklore and,
    3:395
  New Age movement, **6:**39
  parapsychology, **6:**246
  women's rights advocates and,
    8:513
Spiro, **7:506**
*Splicing Life: The Social and Ethical
    Issues of Genetic Engineering with
    Human Beings* (report), **3:**530
Spock, Benjamin, **2:**144; **6:**268, *268*
  alma mater of, **2:**304
  *Common Sense Book of Baby and
    Child Care*, **2:**318–319
Spock, Jane Cheney, *Common Sense
    Book of Baby and Child Care*,
    2:318–319
Spofford, Ainsworth Rand, **5:**100
Spoils system, **2:**22, 206; **7:506–507**
  in Democratic Party, **4:**453
  under Jackson, **4:**453; **6:**426;
    7:198–199, 507
  Pendleton Act (1883) and, **6:**275
Spokane (ship), **4:**54
Spooner, Lysander, **5:**96
Spooner Act (1902), **6:**237
Sports, **7:507–512**
  in 19th century, **7:**508–509
  African Americans in, **7:**510, 511
    football, **3:**412
    prizefighting, **6:**483, 484, 485
    track and field, **8:**154–156
  arenas, Madison Square Garden,
    5:*190*, **190–191**
  baseball, **1:419–422**
    in 19th century, **7:**508
    in 20th century, **7:**509
    salaries in, **8:**361
  basketball, **1:423–426**
  bicycle racing, **1:**451, *451*
  bowling, **7:***508*
  college, **2:**276–278; **7:**511
    football, Ivy League, **4:**449
  in colonial era, **7:**507–508
  football, **3:409–413**, *411*
    at college, **3:**409–410, 412–413;
      5:530–531
    development of, **3:**409–410
    at high schools, **3:**410

Ivy League, **4**:449
professional, **3**:410, 411
after World War I, **3**:410–411
after World War II, **3**:411–412
golf, **4**:*19*, **19–20**
hockey, **4**:*143*, **143–145**, 209–210
horseracing, **4**:168, **169–171**; **7**:510
ice skating, **4**:**209–211**
in Indiana, **4**:320
magazines, **5**:196
marathons, **5**:**234–235**
media coverage of, **7**:508–509
mountain climbing, **5**:**466–467**
Native American, **7**:63, 507
prizefighting, **6**:**483–485**; **7**:509–510
professional, rise of, **7**:509–510
as recreation, **7**:65
"Ripley's Believe It or Not" column, **7**:**168**
rollerblading, **7**:*193*, *193*
rugby, **3**:409
running, **7**:*204*, **204–205**
sailing and yacht racing, **7**:**223–224**
America's Cup, **1**:**172–173**; **7**:223–224
skateboarding, **7**:*373*, *373*
skiing, **7**:*374*, **374–375**
soccer, **3**:409, 412; **7**:**410–411**
surfing, **8**:**27–28**
swimming, **8**:**36–37**
on television, **8**:74
tennis, **8**:**89–91**, *90*
track and field, **8**:**154–156**, *155*
trade unions in, **7**:511
baseball, **1**:**422–423**
strikes by, **7**:559
women in, **7**:509, *510*, 511–512
golf, **4**:19
swimming, **8**:37
tennis, **8**:90
track and field, **8**:155
See also Olympic Games
Spotsylvania Courthouse, Battle of, **2**:214; **7**:**512**
Sprague, Frank J., **3**:173–174; **7**:41
Sprague, William, **7**:153
Spray drying, **3**:407
Springer v. United States, **4**:251; **7**:**512–513**
Springs. *See* Mineral springs
Spruance, Raymond A., **5**:367; **8**:557
in Battle of the Philippine Sea, **6**:320

and capture of Gilbert Islands, **3**:576
Spurzheim, Johann Christoph, **6**:332
Sputnik, **7**:479; **8**:560
impact on astronomy, **1**:345
impact on education, **4**:158
impact on space program, **7**:479
Squanto, **1**:69
Mayflower Pilgrims and, **5**:265
Square Deal, **7**:**513–514**
Squash, Indian cultivation of, **1**:68
Squatters, **6**:527
land policy and, **5**:33
SQUID. *See* Superconducting Quantum Interference Device
SRC. *See* Survey Research Center
SSC. *See* Superconducting Super Collider
SSI. *See* Supplemental Security Income
SSRI. *See* Selective serotonin reuptake inhibitors
SST. *See* Supersonic transport
St. *See* Saint
Stack v. Boyle, **1**:385
Stafford v. Wallace, **7**:**514**
Stag at Sharkey's (Bellows), **3**:538
Stagecoach travel, **7**:177, **514–516**, *515*; **8**:186
and mail delivery, **6**:425
overland mail, **5**:**203–204**
and taverns, **6**:425; **8**:53–54
Stagflation, **3**:13; **7**:**516–517**
Staggers Rail Act (1980), **7**:39, 517; **8**:231
Stahl, Franklin William, **3**:533
Stained glass windows, **1**:**313–314**, *320*
Stalin, Joseph, **2**:267
arms race and, **1**:271
discrediting of, **2**:327
in Korean War, **4**:545, 546
at Potsdam Conference, **6**:434
at summit conferences, **8**:15
at Teheran Conference, **8**:64
and Tito, **8**:588
United Nations and, **8**:272
and U.S. Communist Party, **2**:326
World War II and, **7**:211; **8**:249
at Yalta Conference, **8**:573, 574, *574*
Stalwarts, **7**:**517**
Stamp Act (1765), **2**:286; **4**:25; **5**:97; **7**:134, *517*, **517–518**; **8**:55
denunciation of, **8**:483
Muntiny Act (1765) and, **5**:505

newspapers on, **6**:95
and nonimportation agreements, **6**:116
North Carolina protesting, **6**:127
opposition to, **4**:254; **7**:518
by Stamp Act Congress, **7**:**518–519**
Stamp Act Riot in, **7**:519
Virginia Resolves on, **8**:349
provisions of, **8**:349
purposes of, **7**:517–518
text of, **9**:117–119
Stamp Act Congress, **2**:286; **7**:**518–519**
Stamp Act Riot, **7**:**519**, *519*
Stampedes, **7**:**519–520**
Stampp, Kenneth M., **4**:140
Stamps, **6**:427
Standard & Poor's (S&P), **3**:106; **7**:**520**
Standard Oil Co. v. United States, **6**:303; **8**:235
Standard Oil Company, **3**:366; **4**:26; **6**:298, 303; **7**:**520–521**; **8**:233
antitrust litigation against, **2**:418; **7**:521
breakup of, **7**:521
establishment of, **7**:520
growth of, **7**:520–521
muckraking and, **5**:471
stock held by, **7**:520–521
Standard Oil Company of New Jersey v. United States, **7**:203, **521**
Standards of living, **2**:385, 422; **7**:**521–522**
definition of, **7**:521
measurement of, **7**:521–522
productivity and, **6**:492
Standing Bear, Luther, *Land of the Spotted Eagle*, excerpt from, **9**:379–384
Standing Bear (chief), **8**:224
Stanford, Jane, **1**:143; **7**:523
Stanford, Leland, **2**:9; **6**:502; **7**:*37*, 522, 523; **8**:181, 188
Stanford Linear Accelerator, **6**:339
Stanford University, **7**:**522–523**; **8**:280
academic freedom at, **1**:142–143
establishment of, **7**:522–523
founder of, **7**:*37*
research at, **7**:523
science education at, **7**:272
Silicon Valley and, **7**:360

Stankiewicz, Richard, **1**:307
Stanley, Ann Lee, **8**:301
Stanley, Wendell M., **1**:461
Stanley Steamer (automobile), **3**:480
Stanley v. Georgia, **6**:479
Stansbury, Howard, **3**:299; **4**:57;
    9:233–237
Stanton, Charles E., **5**:20
Stanton, Edwin M., **2**:220, 420;
    3:559
  Johnson's removal of, **4**:234–235,
    236–238
  suspension of, **7**:60, 100
Stanton, Elizabeth Cady, **3**:248;
    6:88, 97; **7**:310, 311, *311*; **8**:10,
    11
  and bloomers, **1**:488–489
  critique of churches, **8**:501
  Declaration of Rights and Senti-
    ments by, **2**:524
  text of, **9**:332–334
  on divorce, **3**:65, 66
  on Scriptures, **1**:449
  and Seneca Falls Convention,
    8:506, 512
  and voluntary motherhood, **1**:467
  and women's suffrage, **7**:106; **8**:513
Stanton, Georgia v., **3**:559
Stapleton, Jean, **1**:*126*, 126–127
Star of the West (ship), **7**:523
Star Route frauds, **7**:524
"The Star Spangled Banner," **5**:185
Star Wars. *See* Strategic Defense Ini-
    tiative
Star Wars (film), **7**:524, *524*
  and toys, **8**:153
Stare decisis, **7**:525
Stark, John, **1**:442, 569, 574;
    6:57–58; **8**:312
Starr, C., **1**:*6*
Starr, Ellen Gates, **8**:114
Starr, Kenneth W., **2**:240; **7**:*496*
  Clinton investigation by, **4**:235,
    238, 239, 240
  Starr Report on, **4**:240; **7**:496
Stars and Stripes. *See* Flag, U.S.
Stars and Stripes (newspaper), **6**:91
"Star-Spangled Banner," **3**:378, 379;
    7:524
  Hendrix (Jimi) rendition of, **8**:524
  inspiration for, **7**:188
  Ripley (Robert LeRoy) on, **7**:168
START. *See* Strategic Arms Reduc-
    tion Talks

Starving Time, **7**:525
  Smith on, **9**:84–86
Stassen, Harold E., **3**:322; **8**:272
State(s)
  boundary disputes between,
    1:521–523, *522*; **2**:355–356
  and business regulation, **4**:26
  capitals of, **2**:47–48
  and church, separation of,
    2:167–170, *168*; **7**:82, 93
  civil service reform in, **2**:207
  debt of, **2**:519–520
    under Hamilton, **4**:88–89
  dependent on federal aid, **3**:334
  emblems, nicknames, mottos, and
    songs of, **7**:531, *532–533*
  flags of, **3**:381
  governors of, **4**:28–30
  grants-in-aid for, **4**:37
  in interstate compacts, **4**:403
  litigation against, Supreme Court
    on, **3**:342–343
  maps of, archival, **9**:3, 37, 40
  and ownership of tidelands,
    8:124–125
  power of, vs. federal power,
    Supreme Court on, **7**:378;
    8:23
  production by, **2**:44, 45
  prohibition by, **6**:500–501; **8**:80–81
  recall of officials in, **7**:53–54
  regulating private industries, **4**:35,
    36
  revenue of, **7**:132–133
  speed limits set by, **7**:501
  suffrage determined by, **8**:4, 6–7, 9
  taxation by
    of Bank of the United States,
      4:247; **6**:218
    capitation, **2**:48
    sales, **7**:230–231
    trade among (*See* Interstate com-
      merce)
State, Department of, **7**:527–531
  African Americans in, **7**:530
  Amerasia Case and, **1**:134
  in Cold War, **7**:529–530
  communists in, **4**:136; **7**:530
  establishment of, **7**:527
  expansion of, **7**:528, 529
  and foreign policy, **3**:28
  functions of, **7**:527
  head of, **2**:2

  human rights reports by,
    4:192–193
  organizational structure of, **7**:528,
    529, 530
  secretaries of, **7**:527–528
  in Spanish-American War, **7**:528
  women in, **7**:530–531
  in World War I, **7**:528–529
State, Nunn v., **4**:74
State banks, **1**:406, **408–409**
  and check currency, **2**:114
State constitutions, **7**:525–527
  after American Revolution, **7**:138
  bills of rights in, **1**:453–454; **7**:525
  civil rights under, **7**:525–526
  after Civil War, **7**:527
  line-item veto in, **8**:320
  in Revolutionary era, **7**:526
  specificity of provisions of, **7**:525
  vs. state laws, litigation on, **8**:308
  See also under specific states
State fairs. *See* County and state fairs
State judiciary
  on civil justice reform, **4**:498
  vs. U.S. Supreme Court
    Ableman v. Booth on, **1**:2
    Gelpcké v. Dubuque on, **3**:514–515
State laws
  antitrust, **1**:213; **7**:343
  vs. federal law, Supreme Court on,
    4:250; **8**:390
  judicial review of, **4**:250, 492, 495
  vs. state constitutions, litigation on,
    8:308
  uniform, **7**:531–534
*State of Maryland v. Baltimore and
  Ohio Railroad*, **2**:438
State of Maryland v. Powley, **5**:13
State of Missouri, Craig v., **1**:540;
    2:446
State parks, vacationing in, after
    World War II, **8**:305
State sovereignty, **7**:477, **534–535**
  vs. federal sovereignty, **7**:477, 534
  and state immunity, **1**:120
  Supreme Court on, **1**:120; **7**:534
State universities, **3**:127; **8**:279–280
State University of New York
    (SUNY), **7**:535–536
States' rights, **7**:536–537
  and Civil War, **2**:208
  commerce clause and, **2**:310–312
  in Confederacy, **7**:537

at Constitutional Convention, **2**:379

implied powers of Congress and, **4**:247

Jackson on, **6**:220

and state sovereignty, **7**:534

Webster-Hayne debate and, **8**:435

States' Rights Democratic Party, **3**:164; **8**:119

State-War-Navy Coordinating Committee (SWNCC), **5**:560

Statistics, **7**:**537–540**

Census Bureau and, **2**:87

early use of, **7**:537–538

in political science, **6**:403

in polling, **6**:409, 533

professionalization of, **7**:538

in psychology, **6**:525

tools and strategies of, **7**:538–539

Statler, E. M., **4**:176

Statue of Liberty, **3**:188, 451; **7**:**540**, *540*

Status of Forces Agreements (SOFA), **5**:379

Statutes at Large, United States, **7**:**540–541**

Statutes of limitations, **7**:541

Statutory law, **7**:541

Staudinger, Hermann, **6**:366

Staunton, Howard, **2**:130

Staupers, Mabel Keaton, **6**:147

Stazione Zoologica (Naples), **5**:240

STDs. *See* Sexually transmitted diseases

Stead, Eugene A., **6**:334

Stead, W. T., **8**:291

Steam power and engines, **7**:**541–543**

in agriculture, **1**:59

vs. electric power, **3**:172, 174–175

elevators powered by, **3**:186

and manufacturing, **5**:4

in suburbanization, **7**:573

Steam warships, **8**:405–406

Steamboats and steamships, **2**:258, 259; **7**:**543–544**; **8**:187, 429

coastwise voyages of, **2**:260

development of, **7**:541–542, 543

disasters involving, **3**:39–40

and domestic trade, **8**:160

explosion on, **7**:172–173

first, **7**:*171*, 172

gambling on, **3**:507, *508*

and market shipping, **2**:387

merchant marine and, **5**:318–319

on Mississippi River, **5**:416

on Missouri River, **5**:426

monopolies in, Supreme Court on, **3**:483, 575

New Orleans, **5**:416

and packet ships, **6**:230

railroad competition and, **7**:173

and river transportation, **7**:174

routes of, archival maps of, **9**:*58*, 59

Savannah, **7**:**254–255**, 543

and tourism, **8**:145

Steam-pump fire engine, **3**:372

Stearns, J. B., **8**:69

Stearns, Shubael, **1**:412

Stebbins, Emma, **1**:308

Steel, as building material, **1**:564; **2**:388

Steel industry. *See* Iron and steel industry

Steel strikes, **7**:**544–546**; **8**:277

Homestead strike (1892), **4**:**157**; **7**:545, 556; **8**:339

Little Steel strike (1937), **7**:*545*, 545–546

in Pennsylvania, **6**:279

Steelworkers Organizing Committee (SWOC), **4**:428; **7**:545–546; **8**:277

Memorial Day Massacre (1937), **5**:**307**

Steeplechase Park, **1**:179

Steering committees, **7**:**546–547**

Steffens, Joseph Lincoln, **5**:470, *470*; **6**:360

Stegner, Wallace, **5**:549

Steichen, Edward, **1**:300; **3**:316, *316*

Steiger, William, **6**:158

Stein, Clarence, **2**:186

Stein, Gertrude, **3**:197; **5**:157

Tender Buttons, **5**:120

Stein, Herbert, **2**:431

Steinbeck, John, *The Grapes of Wrath*, **2**:10–11; **5**:120

Steinberger, Albert, **7**:235

Steinem, Gloria, **5**:*469*, 469–470

Steinman, David B., **3**:218

Steinmetz, Charles P., **3**:174, 211

Stella, Frank, **1**:298

Stella, Joseph, **1**:297, 298; **2**:476

Stem, Alan, **4**:34

Stem cell transplantation, **8**:183

Stempel, Herb, **7**:6

Stengrum, Henry, **3**:182

Stephens, Alexander H.

in Confederacy, **2**:208, 340, 341

election to U.S. Congress, **7**:58–59

at Hampton Roads Conference, **4**:91

Stephens, Anne S. W., **6**:537

Stephens, Uriah, **4**:539

Stephenson, Benjamin F., **8**:318

Stephenson, Jean, **3**:521, 522

Sterilization laws, **1**:469; **3**:32; **8**:511

Sterling, George, **1**:320

Sterling, Lindsey Morris, **1**:308

Stern, David, **1**:425

Stern, Howard, **7**:21

Stern, Robert A. M., **1**:253

Stern, Wilhelm, **4**:378

Sternberg, George M., **5**:294

Sternberg, Robert, **4**:379–380

Stethoscope, invention of, **2**:53

Stettinius, Edward R., **5**:82

Steuben, Friedrich Wilhelm von, **2**:174, 403; **7**:141, 144; **8**:306, 447

Steuben Glass, **4**:4

Steunenberg, Frank, **2**:264

Stevens, Ernest L., **1**:572

Stevens, Isaac, **8**:571

mission by, **7**:547–548

as Washington governor, **8**:413, 415

Stevens, J. P., mills of, **8**:278

Stevens, John (railroad magnate), **4**:344; **5**:142

Stevens, John C., **7**:508

Stevens, John F., **6**:238

Stevens, John Paul

on Civil Rights Act of 1991, **2**:197

on line-item vetoes, **8**:320, 321

on presidential election of 2000, **1**:579

on welfare system, residency requirements in, **7**:222

Stevens, Lillian M., **8**:497

Stevens, Nettie, **3**:532

Stevens, Thaddeus, **1**:57

in Joint Committee on Reconstruction, **4**:485

as Radical Republican, **7**:15, 112

Stevens, Thomas, **1**:451

Stevens, Wallace, **5**:120

Stevenson, Adlai E.

Cuban missile crisis and, **2**:475

in presidential campaign of 1892, **3**:158

Stevenson, Adlai E., (*continued*)
  in presidential campaign of 1952, **3**:164
  in presidential campaign of 1956, **3**:164
Stevenson, Noel, **3**:521
Stevenson, Robert Louis, *Treasure Island*, **1**:550
Stevenson, William E., **8**:449
Stewart, Alexander, **3**:261
Stewart, Alexander Turney, **3**:7
Stewart, Alvan, **1**:211; **5**:96
Stewart, Archibald, **5**:41
Stewart, Dugald, **8**:179
Stewart, Ellen, **8**:115–116
Stewart, George E., in Archangel Campaign, **1**:247
Stewart, Helen, **5**:41
Stewart, Maria W., **8**:506
  on women's rights, **9**:331–332
Stewart, Philo P., **6**:152
Stewart, Potter
  on abortion under Medicaid, **4**:100
  on right to privacy for birth control, **4**:67
  on sex discrimination, **3**:478, 525
Stewart, Robert, **7**:483
Stewart J. Cort (ship), **4**:55
STFU. *See* Southern Tenant Farmers' Union
Stickley, Gustav, **1**:287, 293, 320; **3**:497–498
Stickley, John George, **3**:497
Stickley, Leopold, **3**:497
Stickney, Josiah H., **8**:319
Sticks and Bones (Rabe), **8**:115
Stiegel, Henry William, **4**:3
Stieglitz, Alfred, **1**:297, 300, *300*, 301; **5**:336
Stigler, George, **3**:109
Still, Andrew Taylor, **5**:291, 302
Still, William Grant, **4**:96
Stillman, Charles, **1**:155
Stillman's Run, Battle of, **8**:401
Stilwell, Joseph, **5**:324
  in China-Burma-India Theater, **1**:576; **2**:152
Stimson, Henry L., **2**:151, 467; **5**:482
  and Japanese American incarceration, **4**:460
  and U.S.–Japanese relations, **4**:457–458; **6**:197

  and U.S.–Nicaraguan relations, **4**:22; **6**:104
  War Department under, **8**:378, 379, 543
Stimson Doctrine, **3**:426
Stine, Anne, **8**:337
Stites, Benjamin, **5**:353
STLA. *See* Socialist Trade and Labor Alliance
Stock car racing, **1**:375–376
Stock market, **7:548–550**
  AMEX in, **7**:548–549
  blue sky laws and, **1:491**
  contractionary impact of crashes in, **1**:585
  crash of 1929 in, **7**:548
    government regulation following, **3**:275
    and Great Depression, **1**:585
    and Reconstruction Finance Corporation, **7**:62
  crash of 1987 in (Black Monday), **1:476–477**, 563, 585
  economic indicators and behavior of, **3**:106
  growth of, **7**:549–550
  insider trading in, **4:362–363**
  investment companies in, **4**:411–413
  junk bonds in, **4:501–502**
  Moody's ratings, **5:454**
  NASDAQ in, **7**:549
  after 9/11 attack, closed, **6**:108
  NYSE in, **7**:548, 549
  origins of, **7**:548
  Standard & Poor's and, **7:520**
  Wall Street Journal on, **8**:366–367
Stock Raising Homestead Act (1916), **1**:65
Stockbridge Indian settlement, **7:550**
Stockbridge-Munsee. *See* Mahican Indians
Stocking, George W., Jr., **1**:194
Stocks, **6**:356; **7:551**
Stockton, Robert F., **2**:297; **4**:515; **7**:551
  on flogging, **3**:383
  "Peacemaker" (gun) devised by, **6**:464
Stockton-Kearny Quarrel, **7:551**
Stockyards, **7:551–552**
Stoddard, Solomon, **4**:38
Stoddert, Benjamin, **6**:23

Stoekl, Eduard von, **7**:210
Stoessel, Walter, ambassadorship of, **1**:134
Stokes, Carl, **1**:52
Stokoe, William C., **7**:356
Stoller, Robert, **3**:515
Störner, Horst, **1**:440
Stone, Barton W., **3**:44; **7**:87; **8**:263
Stone, Edward Durell, **1**:253
Stone, Harlan Fiske, **3**:337
  on freedom of contract, **5**:395
Stone, Linda, **3**:518, 519, 520
Stone, Lucy, **6**:97; **8**:506
Stone, Ralph, **4**:*478*
Stone, Thomas, at Alexandria Conference, **1**:122
Stoneman, George, **5**:244
Stonewall riot, **3**:*513*, 514, 520; **4**:65; **7**:165
Stoney Creek, Battle of, **7:552**
Stoney Sioux, **5**:23
Stono Rebellion, **7**:379
Storm warning system, **2**:235
Storms
  meteorology, **5:330–332**
  See also Blizzards; Hurricanes
Storm-surge floods, **3**:383
Story, Joseph, **2**:316; **3**:89
  on fugitive slaves, **3**:482; **6**:294, 462
  judicial review by, **4**:495
Story, William Wetmore, **1**:306
Stotz, Carl, **5**:132
Stout, Rex, **5**:130
Stowe, Calvin, **3**:114
Stowe, Harriet Beecher, **3**:180; **8**:106, 113, 506
  Congregationalism and, **2**:349
  Uncle Tom's Cabin, **2**:163; **5**:119; **7**:195, 381; **8:248–249**
Strachey, William, **1**:445
Straight, Dorothy, **6**:76
Straight, Willard, **3**:71; **6**:76
Strand, Paul, **1**:300
Strassmann, Fritz, **6**:342
Strategic Air Command (SAC), **1**:77, 81–82
Strategic Arms Limitation Talks (SALT), **7:552–554**
  SALT I, **1**:272, *272*; **7**:553; **8**:202, 206
    ABM Treaty in, **1**:75; **7**:553
    Interim Agreement in, **7**:553
    shortcomings of, **7**:553
  SALT II, **1**:272; **7**:553; **8**:202, 206

Strategic Arms Limitation Treaty, **2:**269

Strategic Arms Reduction Talks (START), **1:**272; **7:**553–554; **8:**203

Strategic Defense Initiative (SDI), **1:**75; **5:**43; **6:**145, 337; **7:**149, **554–555**
  opposition to, **7:**18

Strategic Hamlet Program, **3:**417

Strategy, in warfare, **5:**145–146

Stratton, Mary Perry, **1:**304

Stratton, W. S., **2:**464

Strauch, Adolph, **2:**81

Strauder v. West Virginia, **4:**503; **7:555**

Straus, Lazarus, **5:**190

Strauss, Levi, **2:**245; **4:**14

Strauss, Nathan, **2:**490

Straw poll, **6:**533

Strawbridge, Robert, **2:**175

Street, Sidney, **3:**380–381

Street, The (Petry), **5:**125

Street railways. *See* Railways, urban and rapid transit

Streetcar Named Desire, A (Williams), **8:**115

Streetcars
  electric, **8:**188
  horse-drawn, **8:**188

Streeter, Alson J., **3:**158; **8:**259

Streetwalkers, **6:**514

Streisand, Barbra, **1:**546

Streptomycin, **8:**237

Stresemann, Gustav, **3:**562

Strickland, William, **1:**250; **2:**32

Strike(s), **7:555–560**
  by air traffic controllers, **1:**82; **2:**275; **5:**11; **7:**559; **8:**172
  and antistrike decrees, **6:**121
  by athletes, **7:**559
  by automobile workers, **7:**372; **8:**261, *261,* 262
    newspaper account of, **9:**385–387
  by baseball players, **1:**422
  by Boston police, **1:**513–514
  Burlington, **1:**576, *576*
  child participation in, **2:**140
  by coal miners, anthracite strike (1902), **1:**190–191; **5:**6; **6:**279; **7:**557
  collective bargaining and, **2:**274
  by communication and media workers, **2:**324, 325

economic, **7:**555
  by electrical workers, **3:**176
  by farm workers, **8:**266, *267*
  by garment workers, **1:**132; **2:**247; **3:**512; **4:**390, 391; **8:**111, 521–522
  in Gilded Age, **3:**577
  goals of, **7:**555
  government neutrality in, **7:**557
  in Great Depression, **5:**17
  grievance, **7:**555
    arbitration for, **1:**237
  Homestead strike (1892), **4:157;** **8:**339
  industrial employment and, **5:**6
  by Industrial Workers of the World, **4:**347
  injunctions against, **4:**360–361
  interest arbitration for, **1:**236
  by Knights of Labor, **4:**540; **5:**7
  La Follette Civil Liberties Committee hearings on, **5:**1
  in Lawrence (Massachusetts), **5:**59–61, *60, 61*
  legislation on, **7:**557–558
  lockouts and, **5:**141
  by longshoremen, **4:**395, 396
  and Ludlow Massacre, **5:**169–170
  by meatpacking workers, **5:**280
  Memorial Day Massacre (1937), **5:307**
  by mine workers, **2:***255,* 264, 299; **4:**397; **8:**268
    Coeur d'Alene, **2:264;** **8:**454
    Colorado coal, **2:300–301**
    Cripple Creek, **2:464–465;** **8:**454
    Leadville (Colorado), **8:**454
  national, **1:**181; **4:109**
  number of, **7:***556*
  organizing, **7:**555–556
  outlawed, **2:**228
  Paterson Silk Strike, **6:**257
  Philadelphia cordwainers' case, **6:313–314**
  Pinkerton Agency and, **6:**357
  by police, **7:**557
  by public sector employees, **7:**558–559
  Pullman, **6:***549,* **549–550; 8:**303
  by railroad workers, **2:**9, 224
  scabs and, **7:**259–260
  sit-down, **7:***371,* **371–372**
  by steelworkers, **4:**429; **8:**277
  Taft-Hartley Act on, **8:**171

  by teachers, **1:**156–157
    in New York City (1968), **4:**475
  by teamsters, **4:**386, *386*
  by textile workers, **4:**347; **8:**278
  Truax v. Corrigan and, **8:**230
  violence in, **7:**556; **8:**339
  whipsaw, **5:**141
  after World War I, **8:**536
  after World War II, **7:**558
  See also Labor disputes; Railroad strikes; Steel strikes

Strikebreakers, African Americans as, **3:**49

Stringfellow, B. F., **1:**505

Strip joints, **6:**514

Strip mining, **2:***251, 252*

Striptease artists, **1:**575

Stroke, **5:**105

Strong, Benjamin, **3:**345

Strong, Caleb, and War of 1812, **4:**101

Strong, George Templeton, **5:**568

Strong, Josiah, **2:**349; **8:**263

Strong, William, **1:***146*

Strontium 90, **7:**560

Structural integration, **6:**39

Structural unemployment, **8:**252

Structuralism, **6:**430

Structure of Scientific Revolutions (Kuhn), **3:**543; **6:**327, 404, 446

Strunk, William, **3:**222

Struthers, Sally, **1:***126,* 127

Strutt, Jedediah, **8:**108

Stryker, Roy Emerson, **1:**301; **3:**320

Stuart, Gilbert, **1:**295

Stuart, J. E. B., **4:**99; **5:**462; **7:**560
  and invasion of Pennsylvania, **6:**280
  in Peninsular Campaign, **6:**275

Stuart, Moses, **1:**448

Stuart, Robert, **1:**342; **3:**492; **6:**29

Stuart's Ride, **4:**99; **7:**560

Student activism, **8:**586–587

Student Education Employment Program, **3:**122

Student Nonviolent Coordinating Committee (SNCC), **2:**202; **3:**557; **7:561;** **8:**587
  and Black Panthers, **1:**478
  and Black Power, **1:**479
  dissolution of, **2:**204
  establishment of, **7:**18, 561
  founding statement of, text of, **9:**446

Student Nonviolent Coordinating
    Committee (SNCC), (*continued*)
  Freedom Summer drive of, **2:**203
  resistance to draft, **2:**364–365
  separatism of, **4:**375
  women in, **8:**516
Students for a Democratic Society
    (SDS), **7:**18, **561–562**; **8:**587
  in civil rights movement,
    7:561–562
  establishment of, **7:**561
  Vietnam War opposition by,
    7:561–562
  and Weathermen, **1:**182
Stumpf, William, **3:**499
Sturgeon, William, **3:**180
Sturges v. Crowninshield, **7:**562
Sturtevant, Alfred Henry, **3:**532
Stuyvesant, Peter, **1:**206; **4:**476
  New Amsterdam government led
    by, **6:**40, 296
  New Castle captured by, **6:**41
  New Netherland led by, **6:**72, 87
  New Sweden captured by, **6:**276
  portrait of, **1:**294; **6:**72
Styrofoam, **6:**367
Styron, William, **5:**122
Sublette, William L., **3:**493; **8:**176,
    363
Submarines, **7:562–564**
  aircraft carriers and, **1:**91
  in Civil War, **7:**562
  in Cold War, **7:**563
  vs. convoy systems, **2:**403, *403*
  destroyed by North Sea mine bar-
    rage, **6:**134
  development of, **5:**480
  Nautilus, **6:**14
  and naval blockades, **1:**487
  in North Polar exploration, **6:**382
  nuclear, **7:**563
    manufacturing of, **2:**358
  Thresher disaster, **8:122–123**
  in torpedo warfare, **8:**144
  in World War I, **2:**3; **7:**562–563;
    8:33, 540, 590
  in World War II, **7:**563; **8:**556–557
Submerged Lands Act (1953), **6:**303;
    8:125
Subpoenas, to presidents, **3:**279;
    6:456–457
Subsidies, **3:**309–310; **7:564–566**
  vs. federal aid, **3:**333–334
  shipping, **5:**319–320, 321

Subsistence homesteads, **7:566–567**
Substance abuse, **7:567–571**
  during Civil War, **5:**510
  forms of, **7:**568–569
  prevention of, **7:**570–571
  treatments for, **7:**569–570
  See also Alcoholism
Substitutes, Civil War, **7:571**
Subtreasuries, **7:571**
Suburbanization, **7:571–576**
  automobiles in, **7:**573–574
  and city planning, **2:**185–187
  commuter railroads, **5:**373–374
  highways and, **7:**179
  and housing, **4:**181, 182; **7:**574
  Levittown as example of, **5:**85–86
  in Maryland, **5:**257, 258
  and metropolitan districts, **8:**290
  metropolitan government,
    5:334–335
  in Michigan, **5:**356
  as migration, **5:**373–374
  municipal government and,
    5:475–476
  in New Jersey, **6:**63
  problems with, **7:**574–576
  real estate industry and, **7:**53
  shopping malls and, **5:**215, 216;
    7:125
  transportation advances in,
    7:572–574
  urban redevelopment and, **8:**286
Subversion, Communist, **8:1–2**
Subways, **7:**44, *44*
  tunnels for, **8:**240
Sudden Infant Death Syndrome
    (SIDS), **8:2**
Suess, Hans E., **4:**6; **6:**344
Suez Crisis, **3:**141; **4:**43; **8:2–3**, 270
  U.S. response to, **1:**445
  and U.S. electoral politics, **3:**164
Suffixes, **5:**509
Suffolk Banking System, **1:**397; **8:3**
Suffolk Resolves, **8:3–4**
Suffrage, **8:4–12**
  for African Americans, **1:***542*;
    3:145; **7:**106; **8:6–9**, 355, 356
  in 20th century, **8:**9
  after Civil War, **7:**58, 59, *59*
  Federal Elections Bill (1890) and,
    2:332
  Mississippi Plan and, **5:414–415**
  in Reconstruction, **8:**7–9

  resistance to, **3:**146, 147; **7:**58;
    8:8–9, 273, 275
  almost universal, **3:**250
  in colonial era, **3:**145; **8:**4, **6**, 355
  definition of, **8:**4
  democracy and, **2:**547
  exclusion from, **8:4–6**
  property requirements for, **6:508;**
    8:4, 6, 355
  religious requirements for, **1:**206;
    8:6
  and representation, **7:**105–106
  residency requirements for, **8:**355
  as test of political equality, **3:**250
  white primaries and, **6:**463
  for women, **3:**145, 147, 519; **7:**106;
    8:9–12, *10*, 356
    Equal Rights Party and, **3:**248
    freedom of contract and,
      5:394–395
    in Kansas, **4:**509–510
    magazine publications, **5:**192
    Minor v. Happerset, **5:401–402**
    National Woman's Party and,
      5:565–566
    in New Jersey, **3:**145; **7:**105
    newspapers and, **6:**97
    Nineteenth Amendment on,
      2:181
    organizations on, **8:**11–12
    original documents on,
      9:332–337
    Supreme Court on, **8:**11
    Woman's Christian Temperance
      Union and, **8:**497
    women activists and, **7:**106;
      8:513–514
    in Wyoming, **8:**564
  See also League of Women Voters
Sugar Acts, **2:**283, 286; **7:**134;
    8:12–13
  and cod fishing trade, **2:**261
  and Rhode Island economy, **7:**152
Sugar industry, **8:13–15**
  in colonial era, **8:**12–13
  in Hawaii, **4:**106–107, 108
  importation from Latin America,
    5:45
  maple sugar, **5:**231
  Molasses Act (1733), **5:435–436**
  and slavery, **7:**383–384, 389–390,
    392; **8:**13
  sorghum in, **7:**450
Sugar plantations, **6:**364–365

"Sugar Trust Case, The," **4**:26

Sugarman v. Dougall, **1**:126

Suicide

assisted (*See* Assisted suicide)

laws on, **1**:339

mass, People's Temple and, **2**:478; **7**:94; **8**:303

Sulfur dioxide emissions, and acid rain, **1**:13, 14

Sullivan, Ed, **8**:72

Sullivan, John, **1**:532; **8**:208; **9**:30

Sullivan, John L., **6**:484, *484*

Sullivan, L. B., **6**:91

Sullivan, Louis, **1**:293; **7**:375

Sullivan, New York Times v., **3**:374; **5**:90; **6**:91, 297–298

Sullivan, Rust v., **6**:362; **7:216**

Sullivan, Timothy, **4**:75

Sullivan Law (1911), **4**:75

Sully, Alfred, **2**:492–493; **3**:377

Sully, Thomas, **1**:295

Sulzberger, Arthur Hays, **6**:89

Sulzberger, Arthur Ochs, Jr., **6**:89

Sulzberger, Arthur Ochs (Punch), **6**:89

Sulzberger, Iphigene, **6**:90

Summary View of the Rights of British America, A (Jefferson), **7**:136

Summerlin, William A., **7**:278

Summit conferences, U.S. and Russian, **8:15–17**

Sumner, Charles, **2**:194; **5**:90

on *Alabama* claims, **1**:106

Brooks' caning of, **1**:332

"Crime Against Kansas" speech by, excerpt from, **9**:288–292

and Democratic Party, **2**:551

in Free Soil Party, **2**:361; **3**:459

as Radical Republican, **7**:15, 112

Sumner, Edwin, in Battle of Antietam, **1**:200

Sumner, Fort, **6**:16, 19

Sumner, James B., **1**:461

Sumner, William Graham, **2**:227; **3**:109, 438; **6**:424; **7**:412, 432

and laissez-faire conservatism, **2**:375

Sumptuary laws and taxes, colonial, **8:17**

Sumter, Fort, **2**:209; **6**:443, 482; **8:17–18**

Sumter, Thomas, **7**:145

Sun Also Rises, The (Hemingway), **5**:120

Sun Belt, **8:18**, 291

migration to, **5**:374

Sun dance, **4**:292–293; **8:18–19**, *19*, 223

Sun Microsystems, **2**:337

Sunday, Billy, **3**:265–266

Sunday laws, **1**:490–491

Sunday schools, **2**:106; **8:19–20**

Chautauqua movement and, **2**:113

hymns in, **4**:206

Sunrise Community, **8**:303

Sununu, John, **1**:231

SUNY. *See* State University of New York

Super Bowl, **3**:411

"Super Tuesday," **6**:114

Superconducting Quantum Interference Device (SQUID), **6**:347

Superconducting Super Collider (SSC), **6**:339; **8:20**

Superconductivity, **6**:337, 347

Superfund, **3**:39, 231; **8:20–21**, 424

functions of, **8**:21

funding for, **4**:112

legislation authorizing, **4**:111–112; **8**:20–21

limitations of, **4**:112; **8**:21

and Times Beach, **8**:127

Superfund Act (1980), **3**:228, 232

Superfund Amendments and Reauthorization Act (SARA) (1986), **4**:111–112; **8**:21

Supermarkets, **2**:100; **7**:125

Supermax prisons, **6**:478

Supersonic transport (SST), **8:21**

Superstore book retailing, **6**:538–539

Supplemental Security Income (SSI), **6**:438; **8**:441

Supply-side economics, **2**:517; **8:21–22**, 29, 229

in monetary theory, **5**:441

"Supra-Constitutional principles," **6**:10

Supremacy clause, in Constitution, **2**:380

Supreme Court, U.S., **3**:341; **8:22–26**

on abortion

discussion of, **7**:216

legalization of, **1**:6–7; **7:192–193**; **8**:517

as litmus test for Court nominees, **1**:7

under Medicaid, **4**:100

reactions to, **1**:6–7

restricted access to, **1**:7, 45–46; **6**:361–362; **8**:433–434

right to privacy and, **4**:497

on academic freedom, **1**:10, 143

on administrative adjudication, **1**:22

on admiralty law, **1**:23

on affirmative action, **1**:36–37, 386; **4**:66; **7**:157

on African Americans

on juries, **7**:555

during Reconstruction, **8**:23

on alien landholding, **1**:124; **4**:464

on alien rights, **1**:125–126

on *Amistad* case, **1**:176

on antimiscegenation laws, **5**:165

on antitrust legislation, **1**:436; **2**:418–419; **8**:274

and International Harvester Company, **4**:389

and interstate commerce, **4**:26; **6**:135; **8**:234

Sherman Antitrust Act, **1**:20, 172, 214; **4**:26

debate over, **7**:343–344

and Standard Oil Company, **6**:303; **7**:521; **8**:235

on appointments, presidential, **5**:506

on apportionment, **1**:227; **8**:357

on arrest, **1**:283, 284; **7**:290

on Asian Americans, discrimination against, **1**:324

on assisted suicide, **3**:263; **8**:418

on bail, **1**:385

on Bank of the United States, state taxation of, **4**:247; **5**:184; **6**:218

on Bible reading, **1**:449

on bigamy, **5**:54

on Bill of Rights, **1**:453, 457; **2**:198

on bills of credit, **2**:446

on birth control, **1**:6; **4**:66–67; **6**:479

on book banning, **1**:500

on boundary disputes, **1**:521, 522–523

on Buckley Amendment, **3**:316

under Burger, **4**:497; **8**:25

on doctrine of free speech, **3**:374

on business regulation, **5**:482–483

on capital punishment, **2**:40–41; **6**:552

Supreme Court, U.S., (*continued*)
on censorship, **2**:84, 85; **3**:374;
    6:419
on Cherokee Nation cases,
    2:127–128
on child abuse, **2**:137
on child labor, **2**:140, 142, 149
on children's rights, **2**:149; **4**:250
on Chinese Exclusion Act, **8**:276
on Christian symbols, public dis-
    play of, **2**:166, 170
on church-state separation,
    2:168–170
on civil rights, **2**:194, 195, 197,
    198, 199; **7**:62; **8**:24–25, 273,
    274
on civil servants, political activities
    of, **4**:104
on Clayton Act, **6**:121
on clear and present danger, **7**:264
on commerce clause, **2:310–312,**
    405; **3**:575; **4**:26; **8**:274–275
on common law, **2**:317, 318
Congress and, relationship
    between, **8**:22
on congressional administrative
    discretion, **1**:21
on congressional authority over
    monetary policy, **4**:10
on congressional contempt, **2**:393
on congressional districts, **7**:108
on congressional violation of Indi-
    an treaties, **5**:147–148
on conspiracy, **2**:377
Constitution interpreted by, **3**:342
on constitutional facts, **5**:473
on contract clause, **2**:107, 397
on contracts, **3**:382
    liberty of, **3**:308; **5**:394, **472–473**
on copyright, **2**:412
on county government, **2**:438
on county-unit system in Georgia,
    3:556
on Debs (Eugene V.), **4**:249
on deportation, **3**:11
on desegregation, **3**:14–15
on disabilities, **1**:172
distinction between attorneys and
    counselors at law, **5**:73
on diversity-of-citizenship cases,
    3:254
on domestic violence, **3**:74
on due process of law, **2**:134;
    3:89–91; **4**:198

on economic regulations,
    8:484–485
on education
    parental choice in, **6**:352–353
    policies, **3**:115, 118, 119, 121,
        122, 138
on electronic surveillance, **3**:185
on eminent domain, **3**:198; **8**:274
on employment discrimination,
    2:196
    gender-based, **1**:377
    pregnancy and, **3**:525; **6**:449
    standards for evaluating,
        8:389–390
on enumerated powers, **3**:225
on environmental policies, **3**:206
on equal family benefits for women
    and men, **3**:478
on equal protection, **3**:245–247
on Espionage and Sedition Acts,
    3:254
establishment of, **2**:380, 381
on executive privilege, **3**:279; **4**:497
on fairness doctrine, **3**:341
on fair-trade laws, **3**:309
on Federal Communications Com-
    mission, **3**:340, 341
on federal estate tax, **8**:57
on Federal Power Commission, **6**:9
on Federal Trade Commission,
    3:348
on Fifth Amendment, **5:404–405**
on First Amendment, **3**:373–374;
    6:1, 91; **8**:68
on flag
    burning of, **3**:381
    mandatory daily salute to, **3**:380
on food labels, **6**:554
on Fourteenth Amendment, **7**:62,
    378
    Loving v. Virginia, **5**:251
    Minor v. Happerset, **5:401–402**
    Munn v. Illinois, **5:482–483**
    under Warren, **4**:496
on Fourth Amendment, **1**:283;
    7:289–290
on freedom of press
    *Grosjean v. American Press Compa-
    ny* and, **4**:67
    Near v. Minnesota and, **6**:27
    *New York Times Co. v. United
    States* and, **6**:287
    New York Times v. Sullivan, **6**:91,
        297–298

on freedom of speech, **3**:374
    Espionage Act and, **7**:264
    in high schools, **1**:26
    on Internet, **8**:68
on fugitive slaves, **1**:2–3; **3**:482;
    4:487; **6**:278, 294, 462
on General Welfare clause,
    3:527–528
on genetic engineering, **3**:530;
    6:256
on gerrymandering, **3**:62; **5**:79
on Gold Clause cases, **7**:118
on grandfather clauses, **4**:35, 73;
    5:526
on grievance arbitration, **1**:237
on Guffey Coal Acts, **4**:71
on gun control, **4**:74
on habeas corpus, **1**:284; **3**:270,
    271, 272; **4**:81–82
on hate crimes, **4**:105
    against women, **4**:104
on hours of labor, **5**:14, 139–140
on implied powers, **4**:247–248
on income tax, **4:251–252;**
    6:409–410; **7**:512–513; **8**:57
on inherent powers, **4:358**
on Insular cases, **4**:367
on interstate comity, **1**:395
on interstate commerce, **2**:60;
    4:401, 402
    barriers to, **4**:406
    federal control over, **7**:352, 514
    original package doctrine of,
        6:213
on Interstate Commerce Commis-
    sion, **4**:401
on investigating committees, **4**:411
on investigative powers of Con-
    gress, **2**:352
on Japanese American internment,
    3:272; **4**:461, 464
on judicial review, **2**:7
judicial review by, **4:491–494**, 495;
    6:10
on jurors, **4**:503; **7**:555
    women as, **8**:60
on juvenile justice, **4**:505
on labor issues, **1**:580; **2**:228, 229,
    275, 408, 496; **8**:578–579
    industrial court, **8**:495
on legal-tender, **4**:500; **5**:76
on libel, **3**:374; **4**:67; **5**:90; **6**:91
on license cases, **5**:103
on line-item veto, **8**:320–321

on literacy tests, **5:**116
on lockouts, **5:**141
on loyalty oaths, **2:**480; **8:**62, 96–97
on marriage, interracial (miscegenation), **5:**251, 406
under Marshall, **8:**23
on martial law, **5:**254
on military law jurisdiction, **5:**379
on Military Reconstruction Acts (1867), **3:**559
on military trials of civilians, **3:**271, 272
on minimum wage, **1:**21; **8:**360, 445
on Minnesota moratorium case, **5:401**
on miscegenation, **5:**251, 406
and Mormons, **5:**54
on national authority over states, **2:**265
on Native Americans, **1:**474; **3:**271
  children, **4:**263
  constitutional rights of, **4:**264, 265; **7:247**
  gambling on lands of, **3:**509; **7:**309; **8:**223
  lands of, compensation for, **8:**275
  peyote use by, **1:**162; **7:**401
  religious freedom for, **1:**161–162; **5:**180; **7:**401
  removal of, **4:**285; **6:**183; **8:**224
  and sacred sites on public lands, **5:**180
  treaties with, **4:**314
on necessary and proper clause, **4:**247–248
on New Deal, **8:**24
  agricultural, **8:**273
  definition of business affected with public interest, **6:**28
  Federal Trade Commission, **3:**348
  interpretive shift in, **4:**493, 496
  judicial review and, **4:**492–493
  National Industrial Recovery Act, **1:**21; **7:**263–264
  National Recovery Administration, **3:**348
nominations to
  abortion issue and, **1:**7
  judicial activism and, **4:**497
  Senate confirmation of, **2:**353
on nonprofit organizations, **6:**316

nullifying treaties, **8:**199
number of justices in, **8:**26–27
on oil shipments, **6:**243
on one-person-one-vote, **5:**79
original package doctrine of, **6:213**
packing bills, **8:**24, **26–27**
  separation of powers in, **7:**312–313
on patents, **6:**256
on picketing, **6:**350; **8:**230
on Pledge of Allegiance, **6:**370
on police power, **6:**387
on poll taxes, **2:**48; **5:**415
on popular sovereignty, **3:**82
on pornography, **6:**419
on pregnant women, benefits to, **3:**525; **6:**449
on presidential election of 2000, **4:**494; **7:**527
  candidates' responses to, **9:**523–526
presidential elections decided by, **1:**578–579; **3:**148, 170, 171
on president's power to call out militia, **5:**255
on president's removal power, **7:**100–101
on private-corporation charters, **2:**503
on privileges and immunities of citizens, **6:**482
Prize Cases of, **2:**210
on prohibition, **5:**471
on property rights, **6:**505
on public health, **3:**239
on Public Interest Doctrine, **4:**35, 36
on racial discrimination
  in employment, **4:**66
  in Jim Crow laws, **4:**479–480
on racial segregation, **1:**443, 549; **2:**199; **3:**341; **4:**374; **5:**406, 425; **6:**370–371; **7:**302
on racially restrictive covenant, **6:**506
on Racketeer Influenced and Corrupt Organization Act (RICO), **7:**158
on railroad liability, **6:**232
on railroad rates, **7:**26; **8:**493
on Reconstruction, **5:**418; **7:**61–62
on regulatory takings, **6:**505–506
on rehabilitation, **6:**552
under Rehnquist, **4:**493–494; **8:**25

on doctrine of free speech, **3:**374
  on separation of church and state, **3:**374
on religion in schools, **2:**164
on religious freedom, **2:**167–168; **7:**150
  for Native Americans, **1:**161–162; **5:**180; **7:**401
on religious practices, **1:**494
on restraint of trade, **7:**123
reversing previous rulings, **3:**342
on right to counsel, **3:**575–576
and "right to die" cases, **3:**262; **7:160–161**
on right to petition, **6:**297–298
on right to privacy, **6:**479–480
role of, **8:**22
  evolution of, **4:**495–498
  Roosevelt (Franklin Delano) and, **4:**492–493, 496; **5:**57
  court-packing plan for, **7:**312–313; **8:**24, **26–27**
on school desegregation, **1:**589–590; **2:**108–109, 202; **3:**16, 341; **4:**374; **5:**526, 527
  in public schools, **5:**425
  speed of, **1:**122
  and state sovereignty, **7:**534
on school prayer, **1:**347; **7:**265–266
on school vouchers, **7:**266
on Scottsboro case, **7:**286
on search and seizure, **1:**283, 284
on sedition acts, **7:**301, 401; **8:**1
on seniority rights, **7:**311–312
on separation of church and state, **3:**374
separation of powers and, **7:**312–313
on set-asides, **7:**316, 398
on sex discrimination, **2:**206, 445–446; **3:**478, 525; **6:**295; **7:**73, 183; **8:**275–276
on sexual harassment, **3:**54–55; **5:**324; **7:**323–324
on sexual orientation, discrimination based on, **3:**56; **7:**196
on sexual television programming, **8:**68
on sit-down strikes, **7:**372
on Slaughterhouse cases, **3:**90; **7:**62
on slave trade, **1:**190
on slavery, **3:**85–86
on social security program, **7:**416, 419

Supreme Court, U.S., (*continued*)
on special prosecutors, **7**:313, 496
on state admittance procedures,
  3:202
on states
  bankruptcy laws of, **6**:171; **7**:562
  constitutions of, **7**:527
  vs. federal law, **4**:250; **8**:390
  vs. federal power, **7**:378; **8**:23
  power of courts of, **1**:2–3;
    3:514–515; **5**:255
  regulation of private industry,
    4:35, 36
  sovereignty of, **1**:120; **2**:158;
    7:534–535
  suits against, **3**:342–343
on steamboat monopolies, **3**:483,
  575
on steel industry, **7**:546
on subpoenas to presidents,
  6:456–457
under Taney, **8**:23
on tariffs, **3**:358
on taxation, by Congress, **5:184**
on Tenth Amendment, and treaty-
  making power, **5**:428
on territories of U.S., **3**:413; **8**:92,
  94
on tidelands, **8**:124–125
on tort case, **6**:232
on trade unions, **4**:82–83; **5**:546
  seniority systems of, **4**:387
  strikes by, **7**:559
on trademark, **8**:173
on treason, **3**:270; **8**:194
on Vallandigham incident, **8**:306
on voting practices and rights,
  1:385; **3**:144, 147; **8**:273, 275
  discrimination in, **8**:9
  election districts in, **8**:357
  poll taxes in, **8**:9, 344
  property requirements for, **6**:508
  residency requirements in, **8**:355
  Voting Rights Act, **8**:9, 357
on wages and hours, regulation of,
  1:19, 21; **3**:308; **5**:394–395;
  7:303; **8**:360
on war powers, **8**:373–374, 388
under Warren, **4**:493, 496–497;
  8:24–25
  on separation of church and state,
    3:374
on welfare system, residency
  requirements in, **7**:222

on West Virginia's debt, **8**:350
on white primaries, **6**:463
on wildlife
  preservation of, federal authority
    in, **8**:481
  state ownership of, **8**:479
on women
  labor laws for, **5**:394, 472–473
    minimum wage and, **5**:394–395
  protective legislation for, **3**:247
  segregation of, **7**:303
  suffrage for, **8**:11
  women justices in, **5**:566; **8**:507
on workers' right to demonstrate,
  5:546
on Yazoo fraud, **5**:36; **8**:576
on zoning ordinances, **8**:593
Surface Mining Reclamation and
  Enforcement, Office of (OSM),
  4:383, 384
Surfing, **8**:27, *27*–28
Surnames, **5**:509
Surplus, federal, **8:28–29**
  and Deposit Act of 1836, **3**:12
Surplus Property Act (1944), **3**:483
Surratt, Mary, **1**:328
Surrogate motherhood, **8:29–30**
Surrounded, The (McNickle), **5**:128;
  8:30
Surveillance, by FBI, **3**:337, 338–339
Survey Act (1824), **8:30–31**
Survey Research Center (SRC),
  6:534
Surveying, **8**:*31*, **31–33**, *32*
  and cartography, **2**:62
  Coast and Geodetic Survey and,
    2:256–257
  in exploration of American West,
    3:297, 299, 300
  under Jefferson, **6**:201
  legislation on, **8**:30
  Mason-Dixon line, **5:259–260**
  oceanographic, **6:159–161**
  railroad, **7:30**
  state geological, **3:547–549**, 550
  tools for, **8**:31–33
  See also Polling
Suspending Act, **8**:150
Susquehannock, **6**:276
Sussex case, **8**:33
Sustainable development, goal of,
  3:231
Sutherland, George, **2**:60
  on minimum-wage legislation, **1**:21

on zoning, **6**:505
Sutter, Johann, **2**:8, 9
Sutter, John, **4**:12–13, 14; **8**:33
Sutter's Fort, **8:33**, *33*
Suttle, Charles F., **1**:577
Sutton, May, **8**:90
Sutton, Walter S., **3**:532
Suzuki Rōshi, Shunryu, **1**:552
Swaine, Charles, **3**:286
Swamp, Dismal, **3:57–58**
*Swan v. Charlotte-Mecklenburg Board
  of Education*, **1**:589; **2**:108–109,
  199; **3**:118
Swanson, Claude A., **8**:344
Swanton, John, **4**:177
Swanwick, Helena, "The War in Its
  Effect Upon Women," excerpt
  from, **9**:363–364
Swarthmore College, **8:33–34**
Swartout, Samuel, **2**:485
Swartwout, Samuel, **3**:270
SWAT. *See* Special Weapons and
  Tactics
Swayne, Noah H., on power of state
  courts, **3**:515
Swearer, Howard R., **1**:548
Sweatshops, **6**:289; **8:34–35**, *35*
  bowling alleys as, **1**:526
  child labor in, **2**:140
  clothing industry and, **2**:247,
    248–249
  shoemaking industry and, **1**:503
  student protests against, **8**:587
Sweden
  and American Revolution, **6**:78
  colonial settlements of, **6**:77–78
  in Delaware, **2**:541
  foreign observers from, **1**:138,
    148–149
  immigration from, **7**:262
Swedenborg, Emanuel, **8:35–36**
Swedenborgian Churches, **8:35–36**
Swedish Americans, **7**:*262*
Swedish West India Company, **3**:286
Sweeney, John, **1**:153
Sweeney, Peter B. (Brains), **7**:162
Sweet, Ossian, **4**:75
Sweet potatoes, **6**:432
Sweezy v. New Hampshire, **1**:10, 143
Swidler, Ann, **1**:338
Swift, Gustavus, **5**:135
Swift, Louis, **1**:258
Swift and Company v. United States,
  1:436; **2**:311

Swift v. Tyson, **3:**254; **8:36**
Swilling, Jack, **1:**256
Swimming, **8:36–37**, *37*
Swing music, big-band, **4:**468–469
Swink, George Washington, **1:**64
Swinnerton, James Guilford, **2:**309
Swinton, Ernest D., **1:**266
Swisshelm, Jane, *Half a Century*, excerpt from, **9:**255–257
Switzerland, foreign investment from, **3:**422
SWNCC. *See* State-War-Navy Coordinating Committee
SWOC. *See* Steelworkers Organizing Committee
Swope, Gerard, **5:**555
Sylvester, J. J., **5:**18
Sylvis, William, **5:**546
Symbionese Liberation Army (SLA), **8:38**, 95
Symington, Fife, **1:**259
Symmes, John Cleves, **5:**36, 353
Symphony orchestras, **8:38–39**
Synchrotron, **6:**338
Syndicalism, **8:39–40**
Syntroleum, **3:**480
Syphilis, **6:**513; **7:**332, 333, *333*
Syrian Americans, **1:***230*, 230–231
System of Mineralogy (Dana), **5:**390
Systems Development Corporation (SDC), **7:**440

T

Taber, John, **6:**44
Tabernacle, Mormon, **8:41**
Tactics, in warfare, **5:**145–146
Taft, Lorado, **1:**316
Taft, William Howard, **5:**63
  in American Bar Association, **1:**145
  antitrust legislation under, **8:**234
  and appearance of flag, **3:**378
  and Arizona statehood, **1:**258
  and baseball tradition, **1:**420
  on child labor tax, **2:**142
  and Children's Bureau, **2:**147
  on Clayton Act, **2:**228, 229
  and conservation legislation, **8:**437, 480
  and dollar diplomacy, **3:**70, 71
  and FBI, **3:**337
  and government pensions, **6:**283

  and Labor Department, **3:**331; **5:**10
  Latin American policies of, **5:**47
  on minimum-wage legislation, **1:**21
  and naval oil reserves, **6:**19
  and Philippines, **6:**320, 322
  in presidential campaign of 1908, **3:**160
  in presidential campaign of 1912, **3:**160; **6:**70, 496; **8:**43, 119
  and Progressives, **6:**496
  at Republican convention of 1912, **2:**400
  vs. Roosevelt (Theodore), **1:**391
  State Department under, **7:**528
  War Department under, **8:**378
Taft Commission, **8:41**
Taft-Hartley Act (1947), **2:**43, 275; **3:**176; **5:**11, 15; **7:**558; **8:41–43**
  on checkoff, **2:**116
  closed shop banned by, **2:**243; **7:**161
  and Federal Mediation and Conciliation Service, **3:**343
  National Association of Manufacturers and, **5:**528
  and National Labor Relations Board, **8:**42–43
  provisions of, **5:**141; **7:**558
  on trade union activity, **8:**42–43, 171–172
  Truman's veto of, **8:**321, 322
  and workers' rights, **5:**545
Taft-Katsura Memorandum (1905), **8:43**
Taft-Roosevelt Split, **6:**70, 496; **8:43**, 119
TAG. *See American Genealogist, The*
Tagliacozzi, Gasparo, **2:**422
Tailhook incident, **7:**323; **8:43–44**
Tainter, Charles, **1:**357
Taiwan
  capitalist development in, **2:**44
  foreign aid to, **3:**416
  immigration from, **2:**155
  U.S. relations with, **2:**152
Takagi, T., **4:**466
Takahashi v. Fish and Game Commission, **1:**125–126
Talbot, Marion, **8:**281
Talbot, Silas, **2:**378
Talese, Gay, **5:**122; **6:**90
Taliban, **6:**109

Talk shows, **2:**78, *78*; **8:44–45**
  vs. soap operas, **7:**409
Talking films, **3:**362–363
Tall stories, **8:45**
Tallchief, Maria, **2:**501
Tallchief, Marjorie, **2:**501
Talleyrand-Périgord, Charles Maurice de, **2:**398
Tallmadge, James, **3:**82; **8:45**
Tallmadge Amendment (1819), **5:**423, 424; **8:45**
Talmadge, Eugene, **3:**556
Talon, Jean, **6:**51
Tamarind Workshop, **6:**471
Tammany Hall, **1:**507; **6:**79; **8:45–47**, *46*
  draft held by, **3:**84
  political machine predating, **3:**150
  in presidential campaign of 1884, **3:**157
Tammany societies, **8:47**
  museum of (New York), **5:**486
Tampa-St. Petersburg (Florida), **8:47**
Tampons, and toxic shock syndrome, **8:**150–151
TAN. *See* Temporary Assistance for Needy Families
Tan, Amy
  The Bonesetter's Daughter, **5:**123
  The Joy Luck Club, **5:**123
Tanainas, **8:**213
Tandy, Charles, **7:**126
Tanenhaus, Joseph, **6:**401
Taney, Roger B., **3:**272; **8:**196
  and Bank of the United States, campaign against, **7:**103
  on commerce clause, **2:**310
  on contract clause, **2:**107
  Court under, **8:**23
  on *Dred Scott* case, **4:**74, 492, 495; **6:**10
  on Fugitive Slave Acts, **1:**2; **6:**462
  on habeas corpus, suspension of, **1:**284
  on judicial review, **4:**492, 495
  and *Luther v. Borden*, **5:**175
  on Missouri Compromise, **5:**425
  on popular sovereignty, **3:**82
  on slavery, **3:**85–86
  on wildlife, state ownership of, **8:**479
TANF. *See* Temporary Assistance for Needy Families

Tanguy, Yves, **1:**298
Tanks. *See* Armored vehicles
Tanner, Henry Schenk, **5:**233
Tanner, John, **2:**51
Tanning and tanneries, for leather products, **5:**68–69
Taoism, **1:**327
Taos (New Mexico), **6:**68, 69; **8:47–48,** *48*
Taos Fair, **8:**47
Taos Society of Artists, **6:**69; **8:**48
Tap dance, **2:**497
Tappan, Henry Philip, **3:**274; **8:**282
Tappan, Lewis, **1:**210
  and Navajos, **6:**16
Tar, **6:**20; **8:48–49**
Tar and feathers, **8:**49, *49*
Taraki, Noor Mohammed, **1:**37
Tarantino, Quentin, **3:**364
Tarawa, **3:**576; **8:49**
Tarbell, Edmund Charles, **1:**297
Tarbell, Ida, **5:***471;* **7:**521
Target (discount store), **7:**126
Tariff(s), **5:**21; **8:49–52**
  ad valorem duties, **8:**50
  American Revolution and, **8:**50
  in American System, **1:**171
  Calhoun (John C.) and, **3:**460; **6:**145
  Civil War and, **8:**51, 156
  Clay (Henry) and, **7:**111
  during Cold War, **3:**461
  in colonial era, **8:**49–50
  Compromise Tariff (1833), **8:**50–51
  Democratic Party and, **8:**51, 57, 156
  Dingley Act (1897) and, **8:**51
  in electoral politics, **3:**157, 158, 162
  Emergency Tariff (1921), **8:**51
  fair-trade laws and, **3:**309–310
  Friends of Domestic Industry and, **3:**474
  GATT and, **3:**524; **8:**52, 157, 198–199
  Great Depression and, **8:**52
  Horizontal Tariff Bill (1872) and, **4:166**
  McKinley Tariff Act (1890) and, **3:**358; **8:**51, 156
  Molasses Act (1733), **5:435–436**
  "Mongrel Tariff" (1883), **8:**51
  Morrill Tariff (1861), **8:**51

National Association of Manufacturers and, **5:**528
National Tariff Act (1789) and, **8:**50
New Deal and, **8:**156
North American Free Trade Agreement and, **3:**309; **6:**124
Payne-Aldrich Tariff (1909), **8:**51
Republican Party and, **8:**51, 57, 156
Smoot-Hawley Tariff Act (1930) and, **1:**386; **4:**49; **8:**52, 165
South opposing, **3:**460; **6:**145; **8:**50
  Force Acts and, **3:**413; **6:**145–146
specific duties, **8:**50
as subsidies, **7:**565
Tariff Act (1816), **8:**50
Tariff Act (1824), **8:**50
  Harrisburg Convention on, **4:**100
Tariff Act (1828), **8:**50
Tariff Act (1832), **8:**50
Tariff Act (1842), **6:**419; **8:**51
Tariff Act (1909), **3:**460
Tariff Act (1930), **8:**156
Tariff of Abominations (1828), **5:**228
trade agreements and, **8:**156–158
Underwood-Simmons Act (1913) and, **6:**497; **8:**51, 57, 156
Walker Tariff (1846), **8:**51
Wilson-Gorman Tariff Act (1894) and, **8:**51, 156
World War II and, **8:**157
Tarleton, Banastre, in Battle of Cowpens, **2:**444
Task Force 58, **8:53**
Task plantation system, **6:**363, 364
Tate, Allen, **3:**481
Tatum, Edward Lawrie, **3:**533
Taub, Edward, **1:**186
Taussig, Frank, **3:**109
Taverns and saloons, **6:**425; **8:***53,* **53–54**
  Fraunces Tavern, **3:456–457,** *457*
Tawney, Lenore, **1:**309
Tax in Kind, Confederate. *See* Tithes, Southern Agricultural
Tax Reform Act (1969), **3:**444
Tax Reform Act (1986), **8:**59
Taxation, **8:54–59**
  American Revolution and, **8:**55
  of Bank of the United States, by states, **4:**247; **6:**218
  of banks, Supreme Court on, **5:**184

British colonial, **2:**286; **7:**134
  protests against, **1:**514–515
and budget surplus, **8:**28–29
Bush (George, H. W.) and, **8:**59
Bush (George, W.) and, **8:**59
capitation, **2:**48
child labor, **2:142**
during Civil War, **2:**215, 216; **7:**132; **8:**56–57
  Confederacy and, **2:**342–343
Clinton and, **8:**59
colonial, **8:**55
  Ipswich Protest against, **4:417**
  Massachusetts Circular Letter on, **5:272; 8:**349
    text of, **9:**122–123
  Mutiny Act as, **5:**505
  under Stamp Act, **7:517–518; 8:**55, 349
  under Townshend Acts, **8:**49–50, 55, 150, 349
  Virginia Resolves on, **8:**349
by Congress, Supreme Court on, **5:184**
Constitution on, **8:**55
definition of, **8:**54
as economic regulation, **5:**184
as election issue, **3:**168
excess profits, **3:**273; **8:**57
excise, **8:**56
export taxes, **3:302–303**
gasoline, **3:511–512**
Great Depression and, **8:**58
in Hamilton's economic policies, **4:89**
of inheritance, **4:**359; **8:**57
intergovernmental exemption from, **2:**275–276
as interstate trade barrier, **4:**405–406
legislation on, judicial review of, **4:**206
Proposition 13 and, **6:**508–509
Reagan and, **8:**59
sales, **7:230–231**
single tax, **7:**366
in social security program, **7:**420
of spirits, **7:**504, 505
of state bank notes, **8:**310
vs. state investment, **1:**408
in supply-side economics, **8:**21–22
tobacco, **8:**136
undistributed profits, **8:**58
on whiskey, **6:**278

World War I and, **8:**57

World War II and, **8:**58

See also Income tax; Poll taxes

"Taxation without representation," **7:**135; **8:59–60**

and independence, struggle for, **4:**254

Virginia Resolves on, **8:**349

Tax-exempt status of endowed foundations, **3:**444

Taxing District, Robbins v., **8:**192

Taxonomy, mammals, **5:**217–218

Taxpayer Relief Act (1997), **4:**330

Taylor, Andrew, **6:**219

Taylor, Edward, **5:**118

Taylor, Elizabeth, **1:**17

Taylor, Frederick W., **4:**334; **5:**264; **7:**280–282; **8:**529

The Principles of Scientific Management, **1:**63

excerpt from, **9:**342–347

Taylor, Glen, **3:**163; **6:**499

Taylor, Graham, **7:**317

Taylor, John

and Arkansas, **1:**260

and Virginia Resolves, **8:**349

Taylor, John W., **5:**423–424

Taylor, Major, **1:**451

Taylor, Mildred, *Roll of Thunder, Hear My Cry,* **5:**126

Taylor, Myron, **8:**277

Taylor, Nathaniel William, **1:**377, 378; **7:**97

Taylor, Richard, **8:**87

in Red River Campaign, **7:**71

Taylor, Roger E., **1:**240

Taylor, Sidney, **5:**324

Taylor, Zachary

and Compromise of 1850, **2:**331

on Madison (Dolley), **3:**375

in Mexican-American War, **1:**560; **5:**339, 340, 341

and Omnibus Bill, **6:**194

in presidential campaign of 1848, **3:**154

in Seminole Indian Wars, **5:**22

in Texas, **1:**188

Whig Party and, **8:**467

Taylor Grazing Act (1934), **2:**371; **5:**31, 34

Taylor v. Louisiana, **8:**60

TCP. *See* Transmission Control Protocol

TCU. *See* Tribal College and University

TDIU. *See* Team Drivers International Union

Tea

duty on, **3:**103; **8:**60

prerevolutionary trade, **8:**61

Tea Act (1773), **8:**61, 150

TEA-21. *See* Transportation Equity Act for the 21st Century

Teach, Edward (Blackbeard), **1:**550, *550*

Teach for America, **8:**62

Teacher Corps, **8:61–62**

Teachers

academic freedom for, **1:10–11,** 142–143

loyalty oath for, **8:62–63**

Native American, **3:**133

pension plans for, **2:**56

strikes by, **1:**156–157

in New York City (1968), **4:**475

trade unions for, **1:**154–157

training for, **8:**62

women as, **3:**112, 114, 131

Teachers Insurance and Annuity Association College Retirement Equities Fund (TIAA-CREF), **6:**282

Teachers Insurance Annuity Association (TIAA), **2:**56

Team Drivers International Union (TDIU), **4:**385

Teamsters. *See* International Brotherhood of Teamsters

Teamsters v. Vogt, **6:**350

Teapot Dome oil scandal, **6:**19–20, 400; **7:**113; **8:**63

special prosecutors on, **7:**495

Technical Cooperation Administration, **6:**381

Technocracy Movement, **8:**63

Technologies of Gender (Lauretis), **3:**516

Technology

advances in, and structural unemployment, **8:**252

business machines, **1:**588–589

and changing character of work, **5:**4

communication satellites, **2:319–320,** *320*

and consumerism, **2:**388, 392

digital, **3:**24–25

compact discs (CDs), **2:328–329**

educational, **3:**139

electrical appliances, **3:179–183,** *182*

electronics, **3:178–179**

law enforcement, **3:185–186**

in lead industry, **5:**62

and lumber industry, **5:**174

in military intelligence, **4:**376

Native American, **4:306–309**

Tecumseh (Shawnee chief), **2:**456; **4:**284; **6:**7; **7:**337

in Battle of Tippecanoe, **8:**131, 382, 392, 399

death of, **8:**392, 400

speech by, text of, **9:**199–200

on Treaty of Fort Wayne, **4:**314

in War of 1812, **8:**131, 382, 399, 400

Tecumseh's Crusade, **8:64**

Teddy bear (toy), **8:**153

Teed, Cyrus, **8:**302

Teenagers. *See* Adolescence

Teepee. *See* Tipi

Teeth. *See* Dentistry

Teflon, **6:**366

Tehachapi Pass, **6:**254

Teheran Conference (1943), **7:**211; **8:64–65**

Tekumtha. *See* Tecumseh

Telecommunications, **8:65–67**

access to, **8:**67

Baby Bells, **1:381**

digital technology and, **3:**24–25

fiber optics and, **3:**357–358

foreign investment in, **3:**423

government regulation of, **1:**381; **7:**19

microwave technology, **5:**361

Telecommunications Act (1996), **1:**381; **3:**339, 340; **7:**21; **8:67–68,** 75

Telegraph, **8:**65, **68–69,** *69*

commercial use of, **6:**169

and electronic commerce, **3:**183

transoceanic cables and, **2:**3–4

See also Western Union Telegraph Company

Telegraphone, **1:**189

Telemaque. *See* Vesey, Denmark

Telephone(s), **8:**65–66, **69–70,** *70*

answering machines for, **1:189–190**

AT&T and, **1:**346; **8:**65

Telephone(s), (*continued*)
  cellular, **6:**169
  at Centennial Exhibition, **2:**87
  commercial use of, **6:**169
  and electronic commerce, **3:**183
  growth of industry, **8:**456
Telephone cases, **8:70–71**
Telephone company cooperatives,
    2:406
Telephone sex, **6:**514
Telepresence systems, **8:**350
Telescopes
  Hooker Telescope, **6:***156*
  Hubble Space Telescope, **1:**345;
    4:186–187, *187;* **6:**157; **8:**350
  in observatories, **6:**156–157
  production of, **1:**343–344, 345
  technological improvements in,
    6:156
Televangelism, **6:**517–518; **8:71–72**
Television, **8:**66, **72–78**
  advertising on, **1:**34; **8:**72, 73,
    75–76
    infomercials, **4:354–355**
  cable, **1:**381; **2:**322; **8:**74
    advertising on, **8:**76
    MTV, **5:**503
  and cartoons, **2:**64
  and celebrity culture, **2:**78
  censorship of, **2:**85
  children's, marketing and, **5:**246
  and civil rights movement, **2:**201
  color, **8:**77
  consumerism in, **2:**391
  documentaries on, **8:**73
  dramas on, **8:**72
  in electoral politics, **3:**147, 149
  and film industry, **3:**364; **8:**75
  Hollywood in industry, **4:**209
  home shopping networks on, **4:**154
  impacts of, **8:**75–76
  industry developments, **2:**321–322
  invention of, **1:**440
  and language standards, **3:**221
  music on, **5:**493
  news on, **8:**73–74
  and newspapers, **8:**75
  Nielsen ratings, **5:**246
  propaganda on, **6:**504
  and quiz show scandals, **7:**6
  rating system for, **8:**68
  reality shows, **5:**503
  and recreation, **7:**66
  regulation of, **8:**68

science on, **7:**275–276
situation comedies on, **8:**72
soap operas on, **7:408–410**
sports on, **1:**421; **7:**511; **8:**74
  football, **3:**411; **8:**74
symphony orchestras on, **8:**39
talk shows on, **8:**44
technology of, **8:**76–78
televangelism on, **6:**517–518;
    8:71–72
and toys, **8:**153
variety shows on, **8:**72
VCRs and, **8:**327–328
violence on, **3:**340; **8:**339
Westerners for, **8:**458
westerns on, **8:**73
See also Media
Television programs, **8:**72–76
  All in the Family, **1:126–127**
  Good Morning America, **8:**73, 138
  The Hour of Power, **8:**71
  I Love Lucy, **4:209**; **8:**72
  The Jack Paar Show, **8:**142
  Jerry Springer Show, **8:**44
  Marty, **8:**72
  Meet the Press, **8:**44
  Morning Show, **8:**44, 138
  Morton Downey, Jr. Show, **8:**44
  Person to Person, **8:**73
  Roots, **8:**75
  Saturday Night Live, **7:**253, *253*
  See It Now, **8:**73
  Sesame Street, **7:**315, *316*
  60 Minutes, **7:372–373**; **8:**73–74
  Today, **8:**44, 73, **138,** *138*
  Tonight Show, **8:**44, **142,** *142*
  *Tell Me How Long the Train's Been
    Gone* (Baldwin), **5:**126
Teller, Edward, **6:**342, 344
Teller, Henry M., **8:**78
Teller Amendment (1898), **8:78**
Temperance movements, **3:**60; **7:**64;
    8:78–81, *79*
  early, **1:**116; **8:**78
  growth of, **8:**78–80
  moral persuasion vs. coercion in,
    1:116–117
  Native Americans in, **4:**323
  and saloons, **8:**54, 81
  Union Colony, **8:259**
  in Vermont, **8:**313
  women in, **1:**117; **8:**80, 81, 512
  See also Prohibition
Temple University, **1:**47

Temporary Assistance for Needy
    Families (TANF), **6:**439; **7:**222;
    8:442
Temporary National Economic
    Committee (TNEC), **6:**44
Ten Bears, Yamparika, **2:**307
*Ten Nights in a Bar-Room, and What I
    Saw There* (Arthur), **8:**80
Tender Buttons (Stein), **5:**120
Tender offers, **5:**322
Tenement Act (1901), **8:**82
Tenement House Law (1867), **8:**82
Tenements, **8:81–83,** *82,* 285
  demolition of, **8:**285
  firsthand account of, **9:**351–353
  in New York City, **6:**80; **8:**81–82
  reputation of, **1:**222, *222*
Ten-forties, **8:81**
Tennent, Gilbert, **4:**38; **6:**65
Tennent, William, **4:**38
Tennessee, **8:83–87,** *84*
  African Americans in, **8:**85–86
  civil rights movement in, **8:**86
  in Civil War, **8:**85
    Hood's Campaign in, **4:**160
    Union sentiment in, **8:**260
  constitution of, **7:**527
  Democratic Party in, **8:**86
  emblems, nicknames, mottos, and
    songs of, **7:***533*
  geography of, **8:**83
  geological survey of, **3:**548
  Ku Klux Klan in, **8:**85
  mountain feuds in, **3:**356–357
  Native Americans in, **8:**83–84
    mounds of, **4:**278
  New Deal and, **6:**43
  power production in, **8:**87, 88
  prehistoric, **8:**83–85
  reapportionment in, **1:**385
  Republican Party in, **8:**86
  school desegregation in, **8:**86
  Scopes trial in, **8:**86
  sections of, **8:**83
  slavery in, **8:**83, 85
  in Southwest Territory, **7:**476
  state university of, **8:**279
  Utopian communities in, **8:**303
  whiskey production in, **8:**78
  in World War I, **8:**86
Tennessee (battleship), **6:**273
Tennessee, Army of, **8:87**
Tennessee River, **8:**83, **87**
  dam on, **4:**200

Muscle Shoals speculation, **5:483–484**
Tennessee Valley Authority (TVA), **3**:175, 211; **8**:83, *88*, **88–89**, *89*
establishment of, **2**:371; **4**:200
functions of, **4**:200
League of Women Voters support for, **5**:66
and Nashville, **5**:515
and natural resources, **8**:423
Power (play) on, **9**:388–390
and rural electrification, **1**:67
Tellico Dam project of, **3**:206
Tennessee Valley Authority Act (1933), **6**:43
Tennis, **8:89–91**, *90*
Tennis Educational Association, **8**:90
Tennis rackets, **8**:91
Tenrikyo, **1**:327
Tenskatawa (Shawnee leader), **1**:116; **6**:7; **8**:64, 382
Tenth Amendment, **1**:457
and limits on Congressional power, **2**:350
sovereignty in, **7**:477
states' rights in, **7**:536
treaty-making power in, **5**:428
Tenure of Office Act (1867), **7**:100; **8:91**
and impeachment trial of Johnson, **4**:234–235, 236–238
Terman, F. E., **7**:14
Terman, Lewis, **3**:116; **4**:378; **6**:524
Termination policy, **4**:288–289; **8:91–92**
legislation on, **4**:300
opposition to, **4**:288–289
by Association on American Indian Affairs, **1**:340
origins of, **4**:288, 300
Termination Resolution (1953), **5**:128
Terminus (Georgia), **7**:32
Terrell, Mary Church, **2**:138; **3**:125; **8**:510
Terrestrial magnetism, **3**:551
Territorial expansion. *See* Expansionism; Westward migration
Territorial governments, **8:92–93**
Territorial sea, **8:93**
tidelands, **8:124–125**
Territories, U.S., **8**:*94*, **94–95**
Alaska as, **8**:94
American Samoa, **8**:95

Florida as, **3**:386–387
Guam, **4**:68–69; **8**:92, 94, 232
Hawaii as, **8**:94
incorporated, **8**:92, 94
New Mexico as, **6**:68–69
North Dakota as, **6**:132
Northwest Ordinance and, **6**:137; **8**:92, 94
Philippines, **8**:92
Puerto Rico, **8**:92, 94
Supreme Court on, in insular cases, **4**:367
unincorporated, **8**:92, 94
Virgin Islands, **8**:94
Territory of Orleans, **5**:159
Terrorism, **3**:41; **8**:*95*, **95–96**, 339
Achille Lauro hijacking, **1:13**
airplane hijacking, **4:132–133**
bioterrorism, **1:464–465**
CDC activities aimed to prevent, **2**:88
and conservation of resources, **8**:424
history of, **8**:95
imperialism of U.S. and, **4**:246
Iran hostage crisis, **3**:194; **4:420–421**; **8**:96
Justice Department and, **4**:504
labor unrest
Molly Maguires, **5:438**
Mooney case, **5:455**
in Libya, **1**:40
and Gulf of Sidra shootdown, **4**:73
as organized crime, **2**:463
by Palestinians, **4**:443, 444
Pan Am Flight 103, **6:233–234**
by Symbionese Liberation Army, **8:38**
TWA Flight 800, **8**:*241*, **241–242**
war on (*See* War on Terrorism)
See also Bombing(s); 9/11 attack
Terry, Alfred H., **3**:318
and Battle of Little Bighorn, **5**:131
Terry, David S., **4**:250
Terry, Eli, **2**:241; **6**:274
Terry, Mary Sue, **8**:345
Terry, Peggy, on working women in World War II, **9:397–398**
Terry, Randall, **6**:199, 489
Tesla, Nikola, **3**:174, 178, 181, 211
Test laws, **8:96–97**
Test of English as a Foreign Language (TOEFL), **3**:139, 140

Testing, standardized
development of, **3**:116
Educational Testing Service (ETS) and, **3**:139–140
Tet Offensive, **1**:77; **2**:447, 532; **3**:427; **8**:*97*, **97–98**, *98*, 333
Tetzel, Johannes, **6**:515
Tevis, Lloyd, **1**:180
Texan Emigration and Land Company, **8**:98
Texas, **8:98–103**, *102*
African Americans in, **8**:101
agriculture in, **8**:101–102
annexation of, **1**:188; **2**:550; **8**:98, 100–101, 104, 204
and land claims, **5**:26
astronomical observatories in, **6**:157
cattle drives in, **2**:74, 75
cattle in, **1**:64; **8**:101
in Civil War, **8**:101
Democratic Party in, **8**:101, 102, 103
emblems, nicknames, mottos, and songs of, **7**:*533*
expeditions of, **8**:98–99
Farmers' Alliance in, **3**:323, 324; **6**:416; **8**:102
Ferguson removed from governorship of, **3**:354
flood of 1900 in, **3**:384
geography of, **8**:98
Grand Prairie in, **4**:35
Hispanic Americans in, **8**:103
honky-tonk girls in, **4**:159
independence from Mexico for, **1**:106; **8**:99–100, 104, 204
manifest destiny and, **5**:223
maps of, **8**:*102*
archival, **9**:52–56, *53*
under Mexican rule, **8**:99
Mexican-American War and, **5**:339, 340
Native Americans in, **8**:98, 100
and Texas Rangers, **8**:104
and New Mexico, **6**:68, 69
oil in, **4**:185; **6**:179, *179*, 298, 302, 303, 305; **8**:102, 103
Spindletop gusher, **5**:361
and Oklahoma, boundary dispute between, **1**:523
Polish Americans in, **6**:391
Populist Party in, **8**:102
railroads in, **8**:101

Texas, (*continued*)
 Reconstruction in, **8**:101
 Red River land dispute, **5**:238
 Republic of, **8**:*100*, 100–101
 Republican Party in, **8**:101, 103
 settlement of, **3**:202
 slavery in, **8**:101
 Spanish explorations in, **3**:296
 under Spanish rule, **8**:99
 statehood of, **8**:101
 tidelands in, ownership of, **8**:125
 tornadoes in, **8**:143
 U.S. settlements in, **1**:188
 wheat production in, **3**:390
 white primaries in, **6**:463
 in World War II, **8**:103
Texas, Hopwood v., **1**:37
Texas Centennial Exposition,
 2:494–495
Texas Exchange, **3**:324
Texas fever. *See* Piroplasmosis
Texas Navy, **8**:104
Texas public lands, **8**:104
Texas Rangers, **2**:363; **8**:104–105
Texas Revolution, **8**:99–100, 104
Texas v. White, **8**:97, **105**
Textbooks, **8**:105–106
 vs. CD-ROMs, **3**:139
 early, **8**:*106*, **106–107**
 McGuffey's Readers, **8**:106, *106*
 New England Primer, **6**:49–50, *50*;
  8:106
Textile Workers v. Lincoln Mills, **1**:237
Textiles and textile industry, **4**:*343*;
 8:*107*, **107–111**
 in 19th century, **2**:42
  conditions in, firsthand account
   of, **9**:340–341
 in 20th century, **2**:45
 British, Civil War and, **2**:342
 in Charlotte (North Carolina),
  2:108
 in colonial era, **4**:350; **8**:108
 cotton in, **2**:427–428
 development of, **8**:108–110
 fiber production in, **8**:107–108
 foreign trade and, **8**:167
 growth of, **5**:227–228
 interchangeable parts in, **2**:387
 labor practices in, **8**:110–111
 Lebanese Americans in, **5**:71
 linen production in, **5**:114
 in Massachusetts, **5**:266
 in New Hampshire, **6**:58

 piecework in, **6**:352
 products and services of, **8**:107
 silk in, **7**:361–362
 in South, **7**:467, 468
 in South Carolina, **7**:456
 statistics of, **8**:110
 strikes by, **4**:347
 trade unions in, **8**:278
 in Vermont, **8**:312
 See also Clothing industry
Textron Incorporated, **2**:347–348
Thalidomide, **1**:6; **3**:405
Thames, Battle of the, **8**:64,
 111–112
Thanatos Syndrome, The (Percy),
 5:123
Thanksgiving Day, **3**:328–329;
 4:148; **8**:112
 Delaware Indians and, **2**:544
Thanksgiving Day Proclamation,
 6:490
Tharp, Twyla, **1**:144; **2**:499
Thatcher, Harvey D., **2**:490
Thatcher, Margaret, **4**:*43*, 44
Thayer, Eli, **3**:195–196, *196*; **6**:49
Thayer, Sylvanus, **3**:216; **5**:374
Theater, **8**:112–116
 African Americans in, **8**:113
 American Revolution and, **8**:113
 Broadway, **1**:*543*, 544; **8**:115, 128,
  129
 burlesque, **1**:575
 in colonial era, **8**:112–113
 Death of a Salesman, The (Miller),
  2:512–513
 of Gilded Age, **8**:113–114
 Great Depression and, **8**:115
 "high," **8**:112
 "Little Theaters," **8**:114
 "low," **8**:112
 minstrel shows, **5**:402, 489–490,
  496; **8**:113
 music for, **5**:499, **500–501**
 musical, **5**:499, 500
 Native American, **8**:112
 Off Broadway, **8**:115–116
 political, **8**:115
 Provincetown Players, **6**:519;
  8:115
 on showboats, **7**:350–352
 "Tom Shows," **8**:113
 vaudeville, **8**:113
 Wild West shows, **8**:113

Theatre Owners Booking Associa-
 tion (TOBA), **8**:309
Theatrical Trust (Syndicate), **8**:114
theglobe.com, **3**:184
Their Eyes Were Watching God
 (Hurston), **5**:125
Theme parks, **1**:179–180
Theocracy
 in New England, **6**:50, 60; **8**:116
 in Utah, **8**:295
Theology, **6**:324–325; **7**:95–98
 See also Religion
*Theology of Liberation: History, Politics,
 and Salvation, A* (Gutiérrez),
 5:93
Theory of Justice, A (Rawls), **5**:92
Theory of the Leisure Class, The
 (Veblen), excerpt from,
 9:347–351
Theosophy, **8**:116–117
 as mysticism, **5**:506–507
Theravada Buddhism, **1**:326, 553
Thérèse Raquin (Zola), **6**:11
Thermoplastics, **6**:365, 366–367
Thermoset plastics, **6**:365, 366–367
TheStreet.com, **3**:183
Thieu, Nguyen Van, **8**:333, 334
 Nixon's letter to, **9**:474–475
Think tanks, **8**:117–118
 Brookings Institution, **1**:545–546
 Carnegie Institution of Washing-
  ton, **2**:57
Third Amendment, **1**:457, 458
Third New Deal, **6**:45
Third parties, **8**:118–120, 243
 in 20th century, **8**:119–120
 after Civil War, **8**:119
 See also specific parties
Thirteenth Amendment, **2**:193, 523;
 3:341; **6**:10
 and civil rights, **2**:198
 Lincoln and, **2**:218; **3**:192
 and Underground Railroad, dis-
  banding of, **8**:250
Thirty-eighth parallel, **8**:120
Thirty-hour week, **8**:120–121
Thomas, Adele, **1**:*6*
Thomas, Benjamin, **2**:260
Thomas, Clarence, **8**:274
 confirmation hearings for,
  8:121–122
 CORE support for, **2**:355
 Equal Employment Opportunity
  Commission under, **3**:244

hearings on sexual harassment, **3**:198, 221

on line-item vetoes, **8**:321

nomination of, **7**:323; **8**:121

on presidential election of 2000, **1**:579

on sexual orientation, discrimination based on, **7**:196

Thomas, Cyrus, **1**:239

Thomas, Elbert D., **5**:1

Thomas, George H.

and Army of the Cumberland, **2**:479

in Battle of Chickamauga, **2**:135

in Battle of Nashville, **2**:214; **5**:516

in Chattanooga Campaign, **2**:113

in Tennessee Campaign, **4**:160

Thomas, Helen, **1**:231

Thomas, Isaiah, **1**:129; **6**:426

Thomas, Jesse B., **5**:424, 425

Thomas, Marlo, **5**:72

Thomas, Norman

and ACLU, **1**:146

anticommunism of, **1**:197–198

socialism of, **7**:427

Thomas, R. J., **8**:261

Thomas, Robert Bailey, **1**:130

Thomas, Ross, **5**:130

Thomas, Seth, **2**:241

Thomas, William I., **6**:391

Thomas Amendment to Agricultural Adjustment Act (1933), **4**:15

Thomas Aquinas, Saint, **3**:261

Thomas v. Collins, **6**:297

Thomas Viaduct, **5**:52–53

Thompson, Ben, **5**:552

Thompson, Benjamin (Count Rumford), **1**:140

Thompson, David, **1**:481; **8**:452–453

and Columbia River exploration, **2**:303

Thompson, Dorothy, **8**:506

Thompson, Hunter S., **4**:125; **5**:122

Thompson, Jacob, **6**:266

Thompson, John (Snowshoe), **1**:58; **7**:374

Thompson, Lydia, **1**:575

Thompson Act (1950), **6**:239

Thomson, Charles, **3**:99; **4**:488; **7**:288, *288*

Thomson, David, **6**:56–57

Thomson, Elihu, **3**:173

Thomson, J. J., **6**:340, 341

Thomson, Samuel, **5**:291, 301

Thomson, Virgil, **6**:199

Thomson, William, **3**:552

Thong Popham. *See* Tohono O'odham

Thoreau, Henry David, **1**:509; **7**:194; **8**:180

on American Philosophical Society, **1**:167

on birds, **6**:215

at Brook Farm, **8**:301

cabin at Walden Pond, **7**:66

Cape Cod, **2**:38

"Civil Disobedience," **5**:119; **7**:194; **9**:339–340

civil disobedience by, **2**:191–192

and deep ecology, **8**:479

and Grahamites, **3**:24

and Hudson River School, **4**:189

and peace movements, **6**:267

on preservation of environment, **2**:366

Walden, **5**:119; **8**:366

Thorn, Jonathan, **1**:342

Thornburgh, Richard L., **8**:122

Thorndike, Edward, **3**:116

Thorndike, Israel, **3**:256

Thornhill v. Alabama, **6**:350

Thornton, Charles (Tex), **2**:348

Thornton, Sir Edward, **8**:416

Thornton, William, **2**:49

Thornwell, James, **2**:374

Thoroughgood, Adam, **1**:248

Thorpe, Jack, **2**:442

Thorpe, Jim, **2**:55; **8**:154

Thoughts on African Colonization (Garrison), **6**:47

Thoughts on Government (Adams), **7**:136

Three Affiliated Tribes of Fort Berthold Indian Reservation, **5**:219–220

Three dimension (3-D) films, **3**:364

Three Mile Island nuclear accident, **1**:12–13; **3**:175, 233; **6**:139, *139*, 141–142; **8**:122, *122*, *122*

Three Years in Europe; Or, Places I Have Seen and People I Have Met (Brown), **5**:124

Thresher disaster, **3**:40; **8**:122–123

Threshing machines, **1**:59

Thrift Stamps, **8**:123

Throckmorton, James, **8**:101

Throop, Amos Gager, **2**:14

Through English Eyes (Spender), **1**:138

Thurlow v. Massachusetts, **5**:103

Thurman, Allen G., **3**:156, 158

Thurman, Arthur, **1**:375

Thurman, Wallace, **5**:125

Thurmond, J. Strom, **3**:358

and flag protection, **3**:381

in presidential campaign of 1948, **3**:164, 171

as States' Rights Democratic Party candidate, **8**:119

Thurston, Robert, **3**:217

Thwaites, Reuben G., **4**:474

TIAA-CREF. *See* Teachers Insurance and Annuity Association College Retirement Equities Fund

Tiananmen Square protest, **8**:*123*, **123–124**

Tibetan Buddhism, **1**:326, 553

Ticknor, George, **5**:98

Ticonderoga, Fort, **5**:21; **8**:*124*

in American Revolution, **8**:311–312

capture of, **8**:124

Tidal energy, **3**:214

Tidal wave, **3**:102

Tidelands, **8**:124–125

Tidewater, **8**:125–126

fall line dividing Piedmont from, **3**:310

wheat growing in, **8**:466

Tiegan, Henry, **3**:322

Tiffany, Louis Comfort, **1**:288, 289, 313; **4**:4

Tiffany glass, **1**:288, *289*, 289–290, 313

Tiffin, Edward, **6**:172

Tifft, Susan E., **6**:90

Tijerina, Reies Lopes, **6**:69

Tilden, Bill, **8**:90

Tilden, Samuel J., **8**:*242*

in presidential campaign of 1876, **2**:420, 467, 551; **3**:148, 156, 171

Till, Emmett, lynching of, **8**:**126**, *126*

Tillamook, **8**:221

Tillich, Paul, **2**:165; **5**:121

Tillman, Benjamin R. (Pitchfork), **7**:456; **8**:126

Tillman Act (1907), **2**:421; **3**:144

Tillmanism, **8**:126

Tilsdale, Elkanah, **6**:394

Tilton, James, **2**:235

Timber and Stone Act (1878), **5**:37; **6**:528, 531

Timber Culture Act (1873), **1**:65; **5**:25, 37; **6**:528; **8**:126

Timberlake, John B., **3**:104

Timberlake, Margaret, **3**:104

Time, Inc., **8**:127

Time (magazine), **8**:126–127

March of Time (radio program), **5**:236–237

Time Warner, **8**:127

Time zones, **2**:507

Times Beach (Missouri), **3**:233; **8**:127–128

Times Square, **8**:128, *128*

Timmons, Bill, **6**:111

Timoshenko, Stephon, **3**:217

Timothy, Elizabeth, **6**:95

Timucua, **8**:128–129, *225*

Tin industry, **6**:114

Tin Pan Alley, **5**:502; **8**:129, *129*

Tin soldiers, **8**:153

Tindal, Matthew, **2**:539

Ting, Samuel C. C., **6**:338

Tinian, **8**:129–130

Tinker v. Des Moines Independent Community School District, **1**:26; **2**:149; **3**:119

Tinkertoys, **5**:109; **8**:153

Tintype, **6**:329

Tipi, **1**:254; **8**:*130*, 130–131

Tippecanoe, Battle of, **8**:131, 382, 392, 399

"Tippecanoe and Tyler Too!", **2**:24; **3**:153; **8**:131

Tipton, John, **3**:455

Titan, The (Dreiser), **6**:12

Titanic, sinking of, **8**:131–132, *132*

Titanic (film), **8**:132

Titanium, **6**:114

Tithes, Southern agricultural, **8**:132

Title IX of Education Amendments, **2**:277

Titles of nobility, **8**:132–133

Tito, Josip Broz, **8**:588

Tituba (slave), **7**:229

Tlingit, **8**:211, 213, 221

TNEC. *See* Temporary National Economic Committee

TNT (trinitrotoluene), **3**:302

TOBA. *See* Theatre Owners Booking Association

Tobacco cooperatives, **2**:408

Tobacco industry and use, **8**:133–137, *134, 136*

in 20th century, **8**:133, 135–137

antitrust litigation against, **1**:172; **8**:135

and cancer risks, **2**:34, 35

in Chesapeake colonies, **2**:129, 287

chewing, **8**:134, 135

in colonial era, **1**:62; **7**:404; **8**:133

early production and consumption of, **8**:133–134

geographic distribution of, **4**:325

health risks of, **5**:105; **7**:567, 568; **8**:133, 135–137

industrialization and, **8**:134–135

limits on production of, **1**:396

in Maryland, **5**:256

as money, **8**:133

Native Americans and, **4**:325–326; **8**:133

origins of, **4**:325–326

on plantations, **6**:363–364

salaries of clergy fixed in terms of, **6**:252; **8**:243

and slavery, **6**:364; **7**:391, 392; **8**:134, 341

as substance abuse, **7**:567, 568

types of tobacco, **4**:325

in Virginia, **1**:62, 122; **8**:134, 341, 342

See also Smoking

Tobacco Institute, **8**:136

Tobey, Mark, **1**:298

Tobin, Daniel J., **4**:385; **5**:17

Tobin, J. Austin, **6**:421

Tobin, James, **3**:109; **5**:441

Tocqueville, Alexis de

on American uniqueness, **1**:169

Democracy in America, **1**:137; **2**:548–549; **3**:249, 450; **4**:331; **7**:82

on democracy's reign, **4**:454–455

on "democratic" corruption, **2**:420

on gambling spirit, **8**:529

on generations, **3**:528

on individualism, **4**:331

and Jacksonian Democracy, **4**:453

on judiciary, **4**:494

on philanthropy, **6**:316

on representative government, **7**:110

on social sciences, **6**:407

on U.S. Congress, **2**:351

Today (TV show), **8**:44, 73, **138**, *138*

Todd, John B. S., **7**:459

Todd, T. Wingate, **7**:13

TOEFL (Test of English as a Foreign Language), **3**:139, 140

Toffler, Alvin, **6**:429

Tohono O'odham, **1**:**100–101**, *101*; **8**:227, 238

gambling by, **3**:507

language of, **1**:100

water rights for, **1**:100–101

Toilets, **6**:372, 373

Tojo, Hideki, **8**:378

Tokamak, **6**:337

Tokyo Round, **3**:524; **8**:52

Toledo (Ohio), **8**:138–139

founding of, **4**:52

Toleration Acts, **8**:139

Toll bridges and roads, **7**:180; **8**:*139*, **139–140**, 186–187

Toll canals, **8**:140

Tolliver, Mose, **1**:311

Tolls Exemption Act (1912), **8**:140

Tolman, Richard, **6**:336

Tom Sawyer (Twain), **5**:127; **8**:325

"Tom Shows," **8**:113

Tom Thumb locomotive, **7**:30

Tomahawk, **8**:140–141

Tombstone (Arizona), **1**:502; **8**:141, *141*

Tomlinson, Ray, **3**:184, 185

Tomomi, Iwakura, **4**:457

Tompkins, D. A., **2**:108

Tompkins, Daniel D., **3**:151

Tompkins, Erie Railroad Company v., **3**:253–254

Tompkins, Jane, **8**:248

Tonight! America After Dark (TV show), **8**:142

Tonight Show (TV show), **8**:44, **142**, 142, *142*

Tonka trucks, **8**:153

Tonkin Gulf Resolution, **3**:165; **8**:142–143, 332

Tonti, Henri de, **1**:260, 264

Toombs, Robert, **2**:341

Toomer, Jean, **8**:410

Cane, **5**:125

Topeka Constitution, **8**:143

Topographical Engineers, Corps of, **3**:544

Torch, Operation, **1**:233

Tordesillas, Treaty of (1494), **3**:284

Tories. *See* Loyalists

Tornadoes, 3:41–42, 43; **8:143–144,** *144*
  and trailer parks, **8:**178
Torpedo warfare, **8:144–145**
  in Battle of Mobile Bay, **5:**428–429
  destroyers in, **8:**408
  Nautilus, **6:**14
Torresola, Griselio, **1:**329
Torrey, John, **1:**516, 519
Torrijos, Omar, **6:**240, 242
Tort cases, **6:**232
Torture, **4:**194
  in prison, **6:**477
"Total Victory" speech, Truman's, text of, **9:**401–402
"Totally administered society," **3:**454
Tour de France, **1:**452
Tourgee, Albion W., **6:**370
Tourism, **8:***145,* 145–147, *146*
  in 19th century, **8:**145–146
  in 20th century, **8:**146
  automobile and, **8:**146
  in Bermuda, **1:**446
  in Colorado, **2:**300
  and excursion ferries, **3:**355
  in Florida, **3:**386–387, 388; **8:**145–146
    Miami, **5:**351
  in Hawaii, **4:**108
  historic preservation and, **8:**146
  in Louisiana, New Orleans, **6:**74
  in Maine, **5:**210
  in Massachusetts, Nantucket, **5:**510
  in Montana, **5:**450
  in national parks, **5:**551, 552
  in Nevada, **6:**38
  in New Hampshire, **6:**59
  in New Jersey, Atlantic City, **1:**353
  in New Mexico, **6:**69
  in New York (state), **6:**89
  Niagara Falls and, **6:**103
  9/11 attack and, **8:**146
  in North Dakota, **6:**133
  and powwows, **6:**444
  in South Dakota, **7:**460
  in Vermont, **8:**314
  in Virginia, **8:**346
  in West, **8:**146
  in Wyoming, **8:**565
  See also Vacation and Leisure
Toussaint L'Ouverture, François Dominique, **5:**163
Tovar, Pedro de, **2:**416; **3:**296
Towboats and barges, **8:***147,* **147–148**

Tower, John, **8:**148
Tower Commission, **8:148**
Town(s)
  colonial, **1:**507
  company, **2:**387; **8:**437–438
  cow, **2:442**
  railroad, **7:**32, 33–34
  See also Cities
Town government, **8:148–149**
  See also Metropolitan government; Municipal government
Town meetings, in New England, **5:**137–139
Townes, Charles H., **6:**337
Townley, Arthur C., **6:**132
  and Nonpartisan League, **6:**118
Townsend, Francis E., **2:**11; **8:**149, *149*
Townsend Plan (1934), **7:**129; **8:149–150**
  National Union for Social Justice supporting, **5:**563
Townshend, Charles, **2:**286
Townshend Acts (1767), **2:**286; **4:**25; **7:**134; **8:**49, 55, **150**
  Massachusetts Circular Letter on, **5:272; 8:**349
    text of, **9:**122–123
  and nonimportation agreements, **6:**116; **8:**150
  North Carolina protesting, **6:**127
  opposition to, **4:**254
    Virginia Resolves on, **8:**349
  provisions of, **8:**349
  repeal of, **4:**254
  resistance to, **3:**320; **8:**49–50
  and tea trade, **8:**61, 150
  and writs of assistance, **8:**563
Townshend Revenue Act (1767), text of, **9:**121–122
Township settlement type, in Middle Colonies, **5:**362
Townsley, James, **6:**435
Toxic shock syndrome (TSS), **2:**88, 384; **8:150–151**
Toxic Substance Control Act (TSCA) (1976), **1:**463; **3:**232; **8:151,** 424
Toy Story (film), **8:**153
Toynbee Hall, **7:**317
Toyota, assembly lines at, **1:**336
Toys and games, **8:151–154**
  in 20th century, **8:**152–153
  Barbie doll, **1:417; 8:**153

  chess, **2:***130,* **130–131**
  erector sets, **3:251; 8:**153
  G.I. Joe, **3:574–575; 8:**153
  history of, **8:**151–152
  mass production of, **8:**153
  Monopoly, **5:445; 8:**152–153
  proliferation of, **2:**145
  Scrabble, **7:**287
  video games, **8:**153, **327**
Trace elements, **6:**149
Trachtenberg, Allen, **1:**169
Track and field, **7:**204–205; **8:154–156,** *155*
  in college athletics, **2:**276
Tractors, **1:**59, 65
Tracy, Destutt de, **3:**108
Tracy, Nathaniel, **3:**256
Trade
  balance of, **1:**386–387; **2:**517
    with Japan, **4:**459
  chambers of commerce and, **2:102–103**
  and colonization, **2:**111
  domestic, **8:159–163,** *161, 162*
    (*See also* Interstate commerce)
    American Revolution and, **8:**159, 160
    Civil War and, **8:**159, 160
    in colonial era, **8:**159–160
      Alexandria Conference on, **1:122**
    fair-trade laws and, **3:**309
    GATT and, **8:**163
    Great Depression and, **8:**159, 161–162
    NAFTA and, **8:**163
    with Native Americans, **8:**160
      in Great Basin, **8:**216
      in New France, **6:**51
      in New Hampshire, **6:**57
      Panton, Leslie and Company, **6:**244
      and trading posts, **8:**174, 176
    present, **8:**159, 163
    in Progressive Era, **8:**159, 160–161
    Reconstruction and, **8:**159, 160
    regulation of, **8:**160
    Santa Fe Trail in, **7:247–249**
    World War I and, **8:**159, 161
    World War II and, **8:**159, 162–163
  drogher, **3:86**
  electronic, **3:183–184**

Trade, (*continued*)
  Embargo Act (1807), **3:192–193**
  enumerated commodities in,
    3:224–225
  export-import banks and,
    1:402–404
  foreign, **8:163–170**, *165* (*See also*
      Slave trade; Tariff[s]; Treaties,
      commercial)
    American Revolution and, **8**:164
    with Canada, **2**:27–28; **6**:124
    with Caribbean territories, **2**:54
    with China, **2**:150, **153**; **6**:226
      Cushing's Treaty on, **4**:515
      Hawaii in, **4**:105–106
      Wangxia Treaty (1844), **5:462**
    Civil War and, **8**:165
    during Cold War, **8**:166–168
    in colonial era, **4**:25; **6**:20, 21–22;
        8:163–164 (*See also* Colonial
        commerce)
      Trade with Enemy Acts and,
        8:173
    and domestic industries, **8**:167, 168
    with European Union, **3**:259
    fair-trade laws and, **3**:309–310
    with France, **8**:198
    GATT and, **3**:524; **8**:169
    with Great Britain
      in 19th century, **8**:164
      after American Revolution,
        4:40–41
      in colonial era, **8**:163–164
        naval stores, **6**:20
        Navigation Acts and, **4**:25;
          6:21–22
        tea, **8**:60, 61, 150
        textiles, **8**:108
        tobacco, **8**:134
        Townshend Acts and (*See*
          Townshend Acts)
        Trade with Enemy Acts and,
          8:173
        potash, **6**:431
    Great Depression and, **8**:165–166
    with Haiti, **4**:84
    with Japan, **4**:458–459
      electronics industry in,
        7:360–361
    with Korea, **4**:541, 542
    Macon's Bill No. 2 (1810), **5:189**
    with Mexico, **6**:124
    with Morocco, Algeciras Confer-
      ence on, **1:123**
    NAFTA and, **5**:349; **8**:169

    National Association of Manufac-
      turers and, **5**:528
    and public debt, **8**:168
    with Soviet Union, **7**:211
    transpacific, **6**:226
    U.S. interventions for, **4**:406
    with Vietnam, **8**:328
    World War I and, **8**:165
    World War II and, **8**:166
    WTO and, **8**:169
  free, **3**:309–310, **460–461**
    barriers to, **3**:460 (*See also*
      Tariff[s])
    Treasury and, **8**:197–198
  licensing of, **5**:103
  merchant marine, **5**:318–321
  with Native Americans, **4**:309–311
    alcohol in, **4**:322–323
    Charleston (South Carolina) and,
      2:108
    in colonial era, **4**:267–268, 310,
      322–323
    economics of, **4**:267–268
    Indian agents in, **4**:261
    after Revolution, **4**:310–311
    in trading houses (factory sys-
      tem), **1**:158, 281; **4:311**
    Virginia Indian Company and,
      8:349
    wampum in, **8:369–370**
  reciprocal agreements, **7:54–55**
  restraint of, **7:122–124**
  triangular, **2**:282; **7**:204
  See also Colonial commerce
Trade Acts, **6**:22
Trade agreements, **8:156–158**
  reciprocal, **7:54–55**
  with Hawaii, **8**:156
  See also General Agreement on
    Tariffs and Trade
Trade Agreements Act (1934), **3**:461;
  8:156
Trade Agreements Extension Act
  (1945), **8**:157
Trade dollar, **8:158**
Trade Expansion Act (1962), **3**:461;
  7:54; **8**:52, 156, 157, 166
Trade secrets, **4**:376
Trade union(s), **8:170–172**
  in 18th century, **5**:13
  in 19th century, **5:6–7**, 13
  in 20th century, **5:7–8**
  African Americans in, **2**:301–302;
    3:49–50; **8**:172, 263

    for agricultural workers, **3**:326
    in arbitration, **1**:236–237
    for athletes, **7**:511, 559
    automation and, **1**:364
    for automobile workers, **1**:373;
      5:356; **8**:172, **260–262**
      sit-down strikes by, **7**:372
    blacklisting as weapon against,
      1:483
    boycotts used by, **1**:528–529
    and business unionism, **1**:589
    "buy American" phrase by, **8**:169
    in California, **2**:10, 11
    for carpenters and joiners,
      8:262–263
    checkoff provisions and,
      2:115–116
    for child workers, **2**:140
    and closed shop arrangement,
      2:242–244
    for clothing workers, **1:132–133**
    for coal miners, **2:253–256**
      establishment of, **1**:190
    Cold War and, **5**:545
    and collective bargaining,
      2:273–275
    communications and media,
      2:324–325
    company, **8**:277
    corruption of, **8**:172
    and cost-of-living adjustment
      clauses, **2**:424
    Danbury Hatters' case and, **2**:228,
      496
    decline of, **2**:275
    definition of, **8**:170
    Democratic Party and, **8**:172
    for electrical, radio, and machine
      workers, **3:176–177**
    espionage against, **3**:255
    exclusionary policies of, **2**:243
    for farm workers, **2**:77; **3**:326;
      8:172, **266–267**
    federal government and, **2**:43, 274
    Filipino Americans in, **8**:172
    for garment workers, **1**:132; **2**:247,
      249–250; **4:390–393**, 478
    globalization and, **2**:226
    for government employees, **1**:154,
      154, 156; **7**:558–559
    growth of, **2**:224–225
    in Haywood-Moyer-Pettibone
      case, **4**:111
    Hispanic Americans in, **8**:172

immigrants in
in American Federation of Labor, **1:**150
in clothing industry, **1:**132
industrial big business and, **5:**228
industrial relations and, **4:**335–338
for industrial workers, **4:345–349;**
7:424, 426; **8:**414
as interest groups, **4:**380–381
Jews in, **4:**390–392, 478
La Follette Civil Liberties Committee hearings on, **5:1**
Landrum-Griffin Act (1959) and, **5:**545; **8:**172
in leather industry, **5:**69
legislation on, **5:**14–15; **8:**171
lockouts and, **5:**141
for longshoremen, **4:395–396**
Ludlow Massacre and, **5:**169–170
McClellan Committee hearings, **5:183**
McNamara bombing case, **5:189**
for meatpackers, **5:**135
membership in, decline in 1990s, **1:**580
for mine workers, **1:**190;
4:346–347, **397; 5:**6; **7:**557;
8:171, **267–268,** 454
and Guffey Coal Acts, **4:**71
in Minnesota, **5:**399–400
against NAFTA, **8:**172
National Civic Federation and, **5:**530
National Labor Relations Act and, **5:**544–545; **8:**42
National Labor Union (NLU), **5:546; 8:**171
National Trades' and Workers' Association against, **5:**561
National Trades' Union, **5:561**
Negro American Labor Council, **8:**172
in Ohio, **6:**173–174
origins of, **8:**170–171
for packinghouse workers, **5:**280
political action committees formed by, **2:**24; **6:**393
and pure and simple unionism, **6:552–553**
and racial discrimination, **3:**49
for railroad workers, **1:167–168,**
547, **547–548; 7:23–25,** 38;
8:172
recognition of, **7:**555–556

right-to-work laws and, **7:**161
sabotage by, **7:219**
seniority systems of, discrimination in, **4:**387
for shoe workers, **1:**503; **5:**69
Social Democratic Party and, **7:**412
Socialist Labor Party and, **7:**423–424
for steel workers, **4:**427–429;
7:545–546; **8:277–278**
Supreme Court on, **4:**82–83, 387;
5:546
tactics used against, "yellow-dog" contract, **8:578–579**
Taft-Hartley Act and, **5:**11;
8:42–43, 171–172
for teachers, **1:154–157**
for teamsters, **1:**151; **4:385–387**
for textile workers, **6:**58; **8:**111, 278
and violence, **8:**339
walking delegates in, **8:**366
in Washington (state), **8:**414
women in, **2:**256; **8:521–522**
in World War I, **1:**155; **8:**536
in World War II, **1:**237; **7:**558;
8:171
See also American Federation of Labor–Congress of Industrial Organizations; Collective bargaining
Trade Union Educational League (TUEL), **8:**170
Trade Union Unity League (TUUL), **8:**170
Trade with the Enemy Acts, **8:**173
Trademarks, **1:**33; **6:**256; **8:173–174**
functions of, **4:**376
Trading companies, **8:**174
Baynton, Wharton, and Morgan, **1:431–432**
See also specific companies
Trading houses, Native American, **4:311**
Trading posts, frontier, **1:**537; **7:**124;
8:174–175, *175*
Trading stamps. *See* Thrift stamps
Trading with the Enemy Act (1917), **8:**173
Trading with the Enemy Act (1950), **8:**173
Traffic congestion, **7:**180

"Traffic in Women, The: Notes on the Political Economy of Sex" (Rubin), **3:**516
Traffic jams, **6:***81*
Trafficking, human, **4:**193
Trail(s), Native American, **4:311–312**
Trail drivers, **8:**176
"Trail of Broken Treaties," **8:177**
Trail of Tears, **2:**125, 127, 128;
6:183; **8:**177
Trailer parks, **8:**178, *178*
Train robberies, **8:178–179**
Trainbands, **5:***81*
Trans World Airlines. *See* TWA
Trans-Appalachian West, **8:**179
"Transcendental Club," **8:**179
Transcendentalism, **7:**194;
8:179–181
Emerson and, **3:**195; **8:**300, 301
and literature, **5:**119
and Utopian movements, **8:**300–301
Transcontinental and Western Air. *See* TWA
Transcontinental railroad, **2:**9; **7:***33,*
34–35
building of, **5:**30, 33; **6:**502;
8:181–182, *182,* 187–188
Chinese coolies and, **2:***156*
and cattle drives, **5:**149
choice of route for, **7:**30
and consumerism, **2:**387
Golden Spike Ceremony, **7:***34*
"Hell on Wheels" and, **4:124–125**
Kansas-Nebraska Act and, **4:**512
land for, **1:**188; **4:**512; **5:**28, 33
in maps, archival, **9:***56,* 56–58
and tourism, **8:**305
Transgenic foods, **3:**531
Transistor, **6:**337, 346
invention of, **2:**335–336
Transmission Control Protocol (TCP), **8:**66
Trans-Missouri Freight Association,
United States v., **8:**275
Transplants and organ donation, **8:182–184**
autologous, **8:**182
heart implants, **4:121–122**
homologous, **8:**182
xenotransplantation, **3:**531, 532;
8:182

Transportation, Department of (DOT), **3**:331; **8:184–185**
  establishment of, **8**:185, 190
  Federal Highway Administration in, **3**:335
  head of, **2**:2
  mission of, **8**:184
  structure of, **8**:184
Transportation Act (1920), **7**:26, 37; **8:185**, 493
  and Inland Waterways Commission, **8**:147
  and Railroad Labor Board, **7**:38
  and railroad pools, **6**:413
Transportation Act (1958), **7**:45
Transportation Agency of Santa Clara County, Johnson v., **1**:36–37
Transportation and travel, **8:185–192**, *186–191*
  in 19th century, **8**:186–189
  in 20th century, **8**:189–192
  of agricultural products, **1**:63; **3**:390
  in colonial era, **8**:186
  Congress regulating, **4**:26
  and consumerism, **2**:387
  desegregation of, Montgomery bus boycott and, **1**:529, 548; **2**:202; **3**:15
  and domestic trade, **8**:160
  by ferries, **3**:354–355
  Great Lakes steamships, **4:53–55**
  by horse, **4**:167
  and hotel industry, **4**:175–176
  in industrial revolution, **4**:344, 345
  interstate
    ICC in, **4**:400–401
    laws on, **4**:401–402
  land-grant support of, **5**:28
  maps and mapmaking, **5:231–234**
    archival, **9**:56–59
  in Massachusetts, **5**:267–268
  meatpacking industry and, **5**:279
  merchant marine, **5:318–321**
  Mississippi River, **5**:416, 417
  Missouri River, **5**:426
  motels, **5**:*462*, **462–463**
  in New Jersey, **6**:62
  of oil, **6**:303, 359
  overland mail and stagecoaches, **5:203–204**
  port authorities and, **6**:420–421
  prairie schooner, **6:448**, *448*
  public, **4**:356–357

Pullman cars, **6**:*550*, **550–551**
recreational vehicles, **8**:178
Red River cart traffic, **7:71–72**
regional transit, **5**:477
speed of, **8**:*187*, *188*
by stagecoach, **7:514–516**
subsidies for, **7**:564
suburbanization and, **5**:373–374; **7**:572–573
technological advances in, and westward migration, **8**:461
toll bridges and roads, **8**:*139*, **139–140**
urban streetcar lines, **5**:476–477
in Vermont, **8**:313, 314
water, **8**:429–430
  canals and, **2**:29
  rivers and, **7**:174
in Wyoming, **8**:564
See also Migration; Railroad(s)
Transportation Equity Act for the 21st Century (TEA-21), **3**:336; **8**:191
Transportation Security Administration (TSA), **8**:185
Transylvania Company, **2**:480
Trappers, **3**:488–495
"Trash TV," **8**:44
Trask, James D., **6**:388
Trask, Katrina (Kate) Nichols, **8**:570
Trask, Spencer, **8**:570
Trask, Thomas, **1**:334
Traumatic Neuroses of War, The (Kardiner), **6**:431
Trautmann, Thomas, **1**:194
Travel Industry Association of America, **8**:145
Traveling salesmen, **8:192–193**
  See also Peddlers
Travis, Maurice, **4**:397
Travis, William Barret, **1**:106–107
Trawler Racer, Mitchell v., **1**:23
Traylor, Bill, **1**:310
Treason, **8:193–195**
  by Arnold (Benedict), **1:282**
  capital punishment for, **2**:40
  conspiracy to commit, **2**:377
  secession as, question of, **2**:505
  Supreme Court on, **3**:270
Treasure Houses of Britain, The: 500 Years of Patronage and Collecting (exhibition), **5**:540
Treasure Island (Stevenson), **1**:550

Treasures of Tutankhamun (exhibition), **5**:540
Treasury, Department of, **3**:331; **8:195–198**
  Assay Offices of, **1**:333
  Civil War and, **8**:196
  and fiscal policy, **2**:431
  on foreign investment, **3**:422
  and gold standard, **4**:16, 17
  head of, **2**:2
  implementing Harrison Narcotics Act (1914), **5**:510–511
  Morgan-Belmont Agreement (1895), **5:457–458**
  in Progressive Era, **8**:196–197
  and public lands management, **5**:31
  responsibilities of, **8**:195
  specialized police agencies of, **6**:384–385
  T-bills, **5**:440
  Thrift Stamps of, **8**:123
  and uniform weights and measures, **5**:529
Treasury system, independent, **4:258**
Treaties
  commercial, **8:198–199**
  vs. executive agreements, **3**:277
  with foreign nations, **8:199–203**
    (*See also* Foreign policy)
    early Republic and, **7**:56–57
    international law in, **4**:393
    mixed commissions and, **5**:428
    negotiation and ratification of, **8**:199, **203–206**
  with Native Americans (*See* Native American[s], treaties with)
  negotiation and ratification of, Supreme Court on, **5**:428
  See also specific treaties
Treatise on the Theory and Practice of Landscape Gardening, A (Downing), **3**:510; **5**:38
Treatment Action Group, **1**:16
Treatment and Data Subcommittee, **1**:16
Treaty councils (Indian treatymaking), **8:206–207**, 217
Treaty War (1855), **8**:571
Tree(s)
  Osage orange, **6**:218
  sequoias, **7**:314
Trench method of tunneling, **8**:240
Trenchard, Sir Hugh, **1**:76, 81, 495

Trenchard, John, **7:**148

Trenches, in American warfare, **8:**207 **8:***167, 538*

Trent, William, **8:**308

Trent Affair, **3:**464; **8:207–208**

Trenton, Battle of, **8:208**
  and Battle of Princeton, **6:**464

Tresaguet, Pierre-Marie, **8:**140

Trescott, William, **2:**374

Trevett v. Weeden, **8:208**

Triangle Shirtwaist fire (1911), **1:**12; **2:**247, 249; **3:**38; **5:**14; **8:208–209,** *209*
  investigating committee for, **8:**522

Triangular trade, **2:**282; **7:**204; **8:209–210,** *210*
  Middle Passage, **5:362–365,** *363, 364, 365*
  molasses trade, **5:436–437**
  Spanish official's account of, **9:**112–113
  sugar in, **8:**13
  See also Molasses trade; Rum trade; Slave trade

Tribal College and University (TCU), **8:**210

Tribal colleges, **8:210–211**

Tribally Controlled Community College Assistance Act (1978), **3:**136; **8:**211

Tribes
  Alaskan, **8:211–214,** *212*
  California, **8:***214,* **214–216**
  Great Basin, **8:***216,* **216–218**
  Great Plains, **2:**131; **8:***218,* **218–219**
    resistance to white settlement, **8:**462–463
    Treaty of Fort Laramie (1851) and, **5:**40
  Northeastern, **8:219–221,** *220*
  Northwestern, **8:221–223,** *222*
  Prairie, **8:223–225,** *224*
  Southeastern, **8:***225,* **225–227**
  Southwestern, **8:***227,* **227–229**
  See also specific tribes

Trickle-down economics, **6:**551; **8:**197, **229**

Tri-County Pact (1935), **6:**30

Trilling, Diana, **5:**121

Trilling, Lionel, **5:**121
  alma mater of, **2:**304

Trinitrotoluene (TNT), **3:**302

Trinity, Fort, **6:**41

Trinity College, **3:**132

Tripartite Agreement (1936), **8:230**

Tripoli, **8:**229
  in Barbary Wars, **4:**408
  war with, **1:**415; **2:**378

Tripp, Linda, **4:**239

Trippe, Juan, **1:**83

Trist, Nicholas P., **3:**277; **4:**68; **5:**341–342

Troeltsch, Ernst, **3:**1

Trolleys, **7:**43
  trackless, **7:**44

Trollope, Frances, **1:**136; **3:**2

Troops of Teachers program, **8:**62

Tropical cyclones, **4:**197

Trotsky, Leon, **2:**326; **7:**57

Trotter, William Monroe, **6:**103–104

Truax, Robert, **7:**189

Truax v. Corrigan, **8:230**

Truax v. Raich, **1:**125

Truck Drivers Local 449, NLRB v., **5:**141

Trucking industry, **8:230–231**
  CB radio use in, **2:**179
  deregulation of, **5:**463
  interstate highways and, **7:**178–179
  and railroads, **8:**191

Trudeau, Edward Livingston, **8:**236

Trudeau, Garry, **2:**309; **6:**395

Trudeau, Pierre, **2:**27

Trudell, John, **1:**161

Trudgen, J. Arthur, **8:**36

True: The Man's Magazine, **5:**196

"True Art Speaks Plainly" (Dreiser), **6:**12

True Relation of Virginia, A (Smith), **5:**117

Trugpa, Rinpoche Chogyam, **1:**326

Truitte, James, **1:**131

Trujillo Molina, Rafael Leónidas, **2:**54; **3:**76, *76;* **5:**47

Truman, Harry S., **1:***448;* **5:**82
  amnesty granted by, **1:**177
  anticommunism and, **1:**197, 198; **2:**327; **7:**17
  arms race under, **1:**271
  and atomic bomb, **7:**211; **8:**551
  attempted assassination of, **1:**329; **4:**135
  and Berlin Airlift, **1:**443
  Council of Economic Advisors and, **2:**431
  and Democratic Party, **2:**552

  and domino theory, **3:**78
  and Employment Act (1946), **3:**200
  and European integration, **3:**259, 260
  and European Recovery Act (1948), **8:**166
  Executive order No. 9980, **2:**201; **3:**49
  Executive order No. 9981, **1:**548; **2:**201; **3:**49
  extra sessions convened by, **3:**303
  Fair Deal of, **1:**533; **2:**274; **3:**307
  and Federal Mediation and Conciliation Service, **3:**343
  Federal Security Agency under, **4:**113
  foreign policy of, **2:**553
  and Genocide Convention, **3:**536
  health insurance under, **4:**119
  and hydrogen bomb, **6:**144
  in Independence (Missouri), **4:***255, 256*
  and Indochina War, **8:**329
  and intelligence services, **2:**91
  Iranian relations under, **4:**418
  and Israel, relations with, **8:**592
  Israel recognized by, **1:**207; **4:**440
  and Japanese Americans, **4:**461–462
  in Korean War, **4:**545, 547–548
    price controls during, **6:**166
  labor policies of, **2:**95; **3:**244
  Latin American policies of, **5:**47–48
  loyalty security program of (Executive Order 9835), **5:**168
  Manual for Courts-Martial, **8:**256
  Marshall Plan of, **3:**259
  and National Security Agency, **5:**558
  and National Security Council, **3:**330; **5:**560
  and national security system, **2:**528
  The New Republic on, **6:**77
  Office of War Information eliminated by, **6:**503
  and Pendergast machine, **6:**274
  Point Four program of, **3:**415–416; **6:**381
  at Potsdam Conference, **6:**434; **8:**15
  presidency of, **8:**323
  in presidential campaign of 1944, **1:**507; **3:**163

Truman, Harry S., (*continued*)
  in presidential campaign of 1948,
    3:163, 164; **6**:409, 499; **8**:323
  presidential library of, **5**:100
  on racism in war industries, **1**:35
  and reciprocal trade agreements,
    7:54
  and Republican Party, **7**:113
  at Rio de Janeiro Conference,
    7:163
  segregation under, **4**:374
  on territorial sea, **8**:93
  "Total Victory" speech by, text of,
    9:401–402
  and trade union relations, **8**:262
  and Transportation, Department
    of, **8**:184
  vetoes cast by, **8**:321, 322
  war powers and, **8**:374, 388
Truman Doctrine, **3**:415, 426; **4**:59;
    8:231–232
  and Cold War, **2**:268
Trumbull, John, **1**:295; **2**:272; **5**:393
Trumbull, Lyman, **2**:346; **7**:59
Trumka, Richard L., **5**:12
Truong, Hung, **1**:324
Truscott, Lucian, Jr., in Anzio cam-
    paign, **1**:218
Trust(s), **8**:233–235
  Married Women's Property Act,
    New York State, **5**:251–252
  problems with, **7**:342–343
  Pujo Committee on, **6**:548
  railroad, **7**:36
  regulation of, **8**:160, 233–235
  rise of, **1**:213; **4**:26; **7**:342; **8**:233
  See also Antitrust legislation;
    Monopoly(ies)
Trust, The (Jones and Tifft), **6**:90
Trust Territory of the Pacific, **6**:225;
    8:95, 232–233
  Marshall Islands, **5**:252
"Trust-busting," **4**:26; **8**:233,
    234–235
*Trustees of Dartmouth College v.
    William H. Woodward. See* Dart-
    mouth College Case
Truteau, Jean Baptiste, **2**:493
Truth, Sojourner, **8**:506, 512
  on women's rights, **9**:329–330
Truxtun, Thomas, **8**:405
Tryon, William, **6**:127
TSA. *See* Transportation Security
    Administration

TSCA. *See* Toxic Substance Control
    Act
Tshombe, Moise, **8**:271
Tsiolkowsky, Konstantin, **7**:479
TSS. *See* Toxic shock syndrome
Tsui, Daniel, **1**:440
Tsunami, **3**:102
Tubbs, Alice, **3**:507
Tuberculin skin test, **8**:237
Tuberculosis, **8**:235–238, *237*
  in 19th century, **8**:236
  cause of, **8**:236
  diagnosis of, **8**:236, 237
  disease control efforts against,
    3:239
  treatment of, **8**:236–237
  after World War II, **8**:237
Tubman, Harriet, **8**:250, 506
  in African Methodist Episcopal
    Zion Church, **1**:44, 53
Tubman, William V. S., **5**:94
Tucker, Benjamin R., **1**:181
Tucker, George, **8**:292
Tucker, Henry St. George, **8**:283
Tucker, Jim Guy, **1**:263
Tucker, Nathan Beverly, **6**:507
Tucson (Arizona), **8**:*238*, 238–239
Tudor, William, **5**:379
Tuekakas (Nez Perce leader), **6**:101,
    101, 102
TUEL. *See* Trade Union Education-
    al League
Tugwell, Rexford, **6**:555; **7**:120
  in Brain Trust, **6**:42
  and Farm Security Administration,
    3:320
  and National Recovery Adminis-
    tration, **5**:555
  and Resettlement Administration,
    3:319
Tulsa (Oklahoma), **8**:239
Tulsa Race Riot (1921), **8**:239, *239*
Tungsten, **3**:179
Tungsten filament, ductile, **5**:18, 24,
    108
Tunica, **5**:*518*
Tunisia, in World War II, **1**:233
  Battle of Kasserine Pass,
    4:513–514; **6**:124
Tunnel-driving shield, **8**:240
Tunnels, **8**:239–241
  Hoosac Tunnel, **4**:161, *161*; **8**:240
  methods of building, **8**:240
Tupac Amaru Rebellion, **5**:50

Turbogenerators, **3**:174
Turé, Kwame. *See* Carmichael,
    Stokely
Turing, Alan, **1**:318; **2**:334
Turk (slave), **6**:66
Turkey
  capitalist development in, **2**:44
  foreign aid to, **3**:415, 426;
    8:231–232
  Nixon pressuring to destroy poppy
    crops, **5**:511, 512
  U.S. relations with, Cairo Confer-
    ence and, **2**:7
  U.S. right of extraterritoriality in,
    3:304
Turn of the Screw, The (James), **5**:119
Turnbull, Andrew, **6**:77
Turner, Frederick Jackson, **1**:169;
    4:138–139; **8**:284
  and Kennedy's New Frontier, **6**:55
  on sectionalism, **7**:297
  "The Significance of the Frontier
    in American History,"
    3:475–476; **8**:288, 463, 559
Turner, James, **8**:522
Turner, James E., **1**:46
Turner, Jonathan Baldwin, campaign
    for land grants for education,
    5:29
Turner, Nat, **3**:120; **7**:10
  insurrection led by, **5**:516–517;
    7:380; **8**:343
Turner, Richmond K., **4**:68
Turner, Ted, Cartoon Network of,
    2:65
Turner Diaries, The (Pierce), **3**:328
Turner Thesis, **8**:463
Turners, **3**:440
Turnpikes, **7**:176, 177; **8**:139–140,
    186–187
Turpentine, **6**:20
Tuscaroras, and Underground Rail-
    road, **8**:249
Tuskegee Airmen, **5**:382, *382*
Tuskegee syphilis study, **1**:462; **2**:88
Tuskegee University (Institute),
    3:126; **8**:241
  establishment of, **1**:50
  veterinary medicine at, **8**:319
Tustenugge, Halleck, **8**:402
Tuttle, Julia, **3**:387
Tutwiler, Julia S., **1**:104
TUUL. *See* Trade Union Unity
    League

Tuve, Merle A., **6**:342
TVA. *See* Tennessee Valley Authority
TVA v. Hill, **3**:206
TWA, **1**:83
TWA Flight 800, **3**:36; **8**:*241*, **241–242**
Twain, Mark, **3**:220
  in anti-imperialist movement, **6**:320, 321
  Huckleberry Finn, **4**:**187**; **5**:119, 120, 127; **8**:325
  popularity of, **8**:325
  Roughing It, **4**:13; **7**:516
    excerpt from, **9**:248–252
  Tom Sawyer, **5**:127
Tweed, William Marcy (Boss), **1**:507; **5**:186–187; **6**:79, 89; **7**:162; **8**:*242*
  draft held by, **3**:84
"Tweed Days in St. Louis" (Steffens), **5**:470
Tweed Ring, **1**:*508*; **5**:186–187; **7**:162; **8**:46, **242**
Twelfth Amendment, **3**:171
  presidential campaign of 1800 and, **3**:150
Twentieth Amendment, **3**:303
  as lame-duck amendment, **5**:24
Twenty-Eight Hour Law (1873), **1**:185
Twenty-Eighth Congregational Society, **8**:179
Twenty-fifth Amendment, **3**:342
  and election policies, **3**:171
  on extra sessions, **3**:303
Twenty-first Amendment, **6**:501
Twenty-fourth Amendment, **6**:508
Twenty-one gun salute, **8**:**243**
Twenty-second Amendment, **3**:342
Twenty-seventh Amendment, **1**:457
Twenty-sixth Amendment, **3**:342
  and election policies, **3**:171
Twenty-third Amendment, and election policies, **3**:171
Twining, Alexander C., **7**:77
Twining, Nathan F., **6**:371
"Two Dogmas of Empiricism" (Quine), **6**:446
Two Moon (Cheyenne chief), on Battle of Little Bighorn, **9**:253–255
Two Penny Act (1755), **8**:**243**
Two Treatises of Government (Locke), **5**:140, *140*; **7**:161

Two Years Before the Mast (Dana), **3**:86, 383
Two-party system, **8**:119, **243**
  challenges to, **3**:149
  nominating system of, **6**:113–114, 399
Two-thirds rule, **8**:**243–244**
Tydings-McDuffie Act (1934), **6**:322; **8**:**244**
Tylenol incident, **6**:491
Tyler, John
  and Border Slave State Convention, **1**:505
  Dorr's Rebellion and, **3**:82; **5**:175
  presidency of, **8**:322
  in presidential campaign of 1840, **8**:131
  and tariffs, **8**:51
  Texas annexation and, **1**:188; **8**:100, 204
  and Whig Party, **8**:467
Tyler, Julia, **3**:375
Tyler, Royall, **8**:113
Tyler, Scott, **5**:535
Tylor, Edward Burnett, **1**:192
Tyndall, John, **3**:239
Typesetting, **6**:469
Typewriter, **6**:168; **8**:*244*, **244–245**, *245*
  invention of, **1**:588
Tyson, Don, **1**:263
Tyson, John, **1**:263
Tyson, Mike, **6**:485; **7**:50
Tyson, Swift v., **8**:36

U

U-2 incident, **7**:212; **8**:15, **247**
UAW. *See* United Automobile Workers of America
U-boats
  in Battle of Atlantic, **1**:352
  vs. convoy systems, **2**:403, *403*
UCC. *See* Uniform Commercial Code; United Church of Christ
UCMJ. *See* Uniform Code of Military Justice
UCV. *See* United Confederate Veterans
Udall, Steward, and Alaska Native land claims, **1**:111, 112
Udin, Sala, **8**:286

UDTs. *See* Underwater Demolition Teams
UE. *See* United Electrical, Radio, and Machine Workers of America
Uemura, Naomi, **6**:382
UFCO. *See* United Fruit Company
UFOs. *See* Unidentified Flying Objects
UFW. *See* United Farm Workers of America
UGW. *See* United Garment Workers
Uintah Valley Reservation, **8**:300
Ukraine, foreign aid to, **3**:418
Ulbricht, Walter, **1**:444
Uloa, Francisco de, **2**:301
Ulysses (Joyce), **6**:419, 427
  obscenity suit against, **2**:84
  serialized in *Little Review*, **5**:194
Umialik, **8**:212
UMWA. *See* United Mine Workers of America
UN. *See* United Nations
Unbending Gender (Williams), **3**:517–518
Uncas (Mohegan leader), **5**:435
Uncle Remus (Harris), **3**:395; **5**:119
Uncle Sam, **1**:277; **5**:567; **8**:248, *248*
Uncle Tom's Cabin (Stowe), **2**:163; **5**:119; **7**:195, 381; **8**:113, **248–249**
Uncle Tom's Children (Wright), **5**:125
Unconditional surrender, **2**:65; **8**:249
Underground Railroad, **8**:**249–251**, *250*
  firsthand account of, **9**:274–276
  in Wisconsin, **8**:490
Underwater Demolition Teams (UDTs), **7**:494; **8**:251
Underwood, John C., **2**:505
Underwood, Oscar W., at Washington Naval Conference, **8**:418
Underwood Constitution, of Virginia, **8**:344
Underwood Tariff, **3**:161
Underwood-Simmons Act (1913), **6**:497; **8**:51, 57, 156
Underworld (DeLillo), **5**:122
Undistributed profits tax, **8**:58
UNEF. *See* United Nations Emergency Force
Unemployment, **8**:**251–254**
  decadal estimates of, **8**:*251*
  in Great Depression, **4**:44, 45, 47; **8**:251, 440

Unemployment, (*continued*)
 among African Americans, **4:**47;
  5:563
 Ford (Henry) on, **9:**375–376
 among women, **4:**47
 inflation and, **4:**351–352
 after 9/11 Attack, **3:**106–107
 and psychological problems, **4:**47
 reduction in, mandatory retirement and, **7:**128
 in stagflation, **7:**516
Unemployment insurance,
 8:253–254
 American Federation of Labor on,
  2:227
 Social Security Act and, **8:**440
UNHCR. *See* United Nations High
 Commissioner for Refugees
UNIA. *See* Universal Negro
 Improvement Association
Unicameralism, **5:**78
Unidentified flying objects (UFOs),
 8:*255,* **255–256**
 Bermuda Triangle and, **1:**445, **446**
 in Nevada, **6:**39
Unification Church, **2:**477; **8:**303
Uniform Anatomical Gift Act
 (1968), **8:**183
Uniform Code of Military Justice
 (UCMJ), **2:**440; **8:**256
Uniform Commercial Code (UCC),
 7:531
Uniform Determination of Death
 Act (1981), **1:**339
Uniform state laws, **7:531–534**
Uniforms, military, **2:**246; **8:***256,*
 256–259, *258*
 for women, **8:***257, 258, 502*
Unincorporated territories, U.S.,
 8:92, 94
Union, Fort, **2:**493; **8:**259
Union (Civil War)
 comparative advantages of, **2:**209
 conscription by, **2:**211
 foreign policy of, **3:**425
 military strategy and administration of, **2:**217–218
 politics in, **2:**218
 prison camps of, **3:**189–190; **6:**474
 sentiment, in South, **7:474–475**
 support for
  in border states, **8:**260
  in North, **8:**313
  in South, **8:**260

and taxation, **8:**56
veterans' organizations, **8:**265
See also Army, Union; Navy, Union
Union Canal, **8:**239
Union Carbide, **2:**121
Union Colony, **8:**259
Union Labor Party, **5:**16; **8:**259
Union League, Metropolitan Museum of Art, proposal for, **5:**335
Union League Club, **2:**251
Union of American Republics,
 6:236–237
Union of Needletrades, Industrial
 and Textile Employees, **2:**250
Union Pacific Railroad, **2:**9; **8:**181,
 188
 exploration along, **3:**300
 financing of, and political corrup-
  tion, **2:**452–453
 route to southern California, **7:**35
 and transcontinental roadway, **7:**34
  Golden Spike Ceremony, **7:***34*
  race with Central Pacific Rail-
   road, **2:**94
 in Wyoming, **8:**564
Union Party, **8:259–260**
Union Seminary, **7:**97
Union sentiment, in South,
 7:474–475
Unions. *See* Labor; Trade union(s)
Union-shop agreement, **2:**243
Unit rule, **6:**113; **8:**260
Unitarianism, **5:**431
 split with Congregationalism,
  2:349, 350
 and transcendentalism, **7:**194–195;
  8:179–180
Unitas Fratum. *See* Moravian
 Brethren
United Airlines, **1:**83
United Americans, Order of, **8:**260
United Artists, **3:**362
United Automobile Workers of
 America (UAW), **5:**8, 356;
 8:172, **260–262**
 Ford Motor Company and, clash
  between, newspaper account
  of, **9:**385–387
 Polish Americans in, **6:**391
 relations with other unions, **3:**176;
  8:266
 sit-down strikes by, **7:**372
 strike against General Motors,
  7:166; **8:**261, *261*

United Brotherhood of Carpenters
 and Joiners, **8:262–263**
United Church of Christ (UCC),
 2:349; **8:263–264**
 membership in, **7:***91*
United Colonies of New England.
 See New England Confedera-
 tion
United Confederate Veterans
 (UCV), **8:264–265,** 318
United Copper Company, **3:**366
United Daughters of the Confedera-
 cy (UDC), **8:265–266**
United Electrical, Radio, and
 Machine Workers of America
 (UE), **3:176–177**
United Empire Loyalists, **8:**266
United Farm Workers of America
 (UFW), **2:**77; **3:**326, 479; **8:**172,
 266–267
 boycotts by, **1:**529; **5:***3*
 and grape strike, **5:***3;* **8:***267*
 minorities in, **3:**50
United Fruit Company (UFCO),
 2:54; **3:**479; **4:**69–70; **5:**46, 48
United Garment Workers (UGW),
 1:132
United House of Prayer for All Peo-
 ple, **2:**477
*United Jewish Organization of
 Williamsburg, Inc. v. Hugh L.
 Carey,* **5:**79
United Kingdom. *See* Great Britain
United Lutheran Church in America
 (ULCA), **5:**177
United Mine Workers of America
 (UMWA), **1:**190; **2:**254–255;
 5:6, 17; **8:**171, **267–268**
 Centralia Mine disaster and, **2:**95
 and dues checkoff, **2:**115
 and Guffey Coal Acts, **4:**71
 and Ludlow Massacre, **5:**169–170
 strike by, **7:**557
 and United Steelworkers of America, **8:**277
 in Utah, **8:**297
 in West Virginia, **8:**450
United Nations (UN), **8:268–272**
 Charter of, **8:**268, 272
 on children's rights, **2:**149–150
 during Cold War, **8:**269–270
 after Cold War, **8:**271–272

Convention on the Elimination of All Forms of Discrimination Against Women, **2:**398–399
creation of, **1:**271; **2:**11, 467–468; **3:**94; **6:**264; **7:**212; **8:**202, 268–269
decolonization and, **8:**270–271
General Assembly of, **5:**64; **8:**269, 272
on genocide, **3:**536
in Haiti, **4:**85–86
and human rights, **4:**192, 193
International Court of Justice in, **4:**387–388, 394
International Labor Organization in, **4:**390
and Korean War, **4:**545–549, 546
and laws of war, **8:**372
League of Nations and, **5:**64, 65
limitations of, **1:**271
membership in, **8:**268
on neutrality, **6:**34, 36
and nonintervention policy, **6:**117
and Nuclear Non-Proliferation Treaty (1968), **6:**138
origins of, **8:**268–269
peacekeeping missions of, **6:**270–271
and Refugee Convention, **7:**80
in Rwanda, **1:**40
Security Council of, **8:**269, *269*, 272
  international criminal tribunals under, **8:**372
in Somalia, **1:**39
on territorial sea, **8:**93
and Third World, **8:**271
and Trust Territory of the Pacific, **8:**95, 232
war crimes trials by, **8:**378
United Nations Charter, **6:**264; **8:**202, 205
United Nations Conference (1945), **8:**272
United Nations Conference on Environment and Development (Earth Summit) (1992), **2:**238
United Nations Declaration, **8:**273
United Nations Emergency Force (UNEF), **8:**270
United Nations High Commissioner for Refugees (UNHCR), **7:**80
United Network for Organ Sharing (UNOS), **8:**183

United Organization of Taxpayers, **6:**508
United Packinghouse Workers of America, **5:**280
United Parcel Service (UPS), **1:**97; **2:**439
  strike at (1997), **2:**226
United Presbyterian Church of North America (UPCNA), **6:**451
United Press Association (UP), **6:**459
United Press International (UPI), **6:**458, 459
United Spanish War Veterans (USWV), **8:**318
United States and Foreign Securities Company (US&FS), **4:**412
United States Civil Service Retirement Association (USCSRA), **6:**283
United States ex rel. Standing Bear v. Crook, **8:**224
United States Exploring Expedition (1840), **6:**383
United States Flour Milling Company, **3:**390
United States Geological Survey (USGS). *See* Geological Survey, U.S.
United States Golf Association (USGA), **4:**19
United States Government Manual, **3:**329, 332
United States Information Agency (USIA), **6:**504
  abstract expressionism exhibited by, **1:**10
  Voice of America under, **8:**350, 351
United States Jaycees, Roberts et al. v., **7:**183, 198
United States Statutes at Large, **7:**540–541
United States Steel Corporation, **8:**277
United States v. American Tobacco Company, **1:**172
United States v. AT&T, **1:**347
United States v. Burr, **3:**279; **6:**456; **8:**194
United States v. Butler, **1:**396; **3:**527; **8:**273
United States v. California, **8:**124

United States v. Carolene Products Co., **3:**246
United States v. Cooper, **6:**456
United States v. Cruikshank, **6:**297; **8:**273
United States v. Curtiss-Wright Export Corporation, **8:**198, 388
United States v. Darby Lumber Company, **3:**308
United States v. Dennis, **2:**377
United States v. E. C. Knight Company, **1:**20; **2:**310, 311, 418; **4:**26; **7:**343, 344; **8:**234, **274**
United States v. Harris, **8:**274
United States v. Jefferson Davis, **8:**194
United States v. Johnson, **6:**554
United States v. Lee, **8:**274
United States v. Lopez, **2:**311–312; **8:**274–275
  judicial review in, **4:**493
United States v. McWilliams, **3:**328
United States v. Morgan, **1:**405
United States v. Morrison, **2:**312; **3:**74; **8:**274
United States v. Nixon, **3:**279; **6:**457
United States v. One Book Entitled Ulysses, **2:**84
United States v. Playboy Entertainment Group, **8:**68
United States v. Reese, **8:**275
United States v. Reynolds, **3:**279
United States v. Rosenberg, **8:**195
United States v. Salerno, **1:**385
United States v. Seeger, **2:**361–362
United States v. Sioux Nation, **8:**275
United States v. Southwestern Cable Co., **3:**340
United States v. Trans-Missouri Freight Association, **8:**275
United States v. Virginia, **8:**275–276
United States v. Washington, **8:**415
United States v. Wong Kim Ark, **2:**155; **8:**276
United States v. Zenith Radio Corp. et. al., **3:**340
United States-Canada Free Trade Agreement, **2:**28; **8:**276–277
United Steelworkers of America (USWA), **5:**8; **8:**277–278
  relations with other unions, **3:**176
  strikes by, **4:**429; **7:**546
  in World War II, **4:**428
United Steelworkers of America v. Weber, **1:**36

United Textile Workers (UTW), **6:**58; **8:**111, **278**

"United We Stand, Divided We Fall," **8:278–279**

Unity of Brethren. *See* Moravian Brethren

Universal Automatic Computer (UNIVAC), **2:**335

Universal Declaration of Human Rights, **4:**192

Universal Limited Art Editions, **6:**471

Universal Military Training and Service Act (1951), **5:**430

Universal Negro Improvement, **6:**236

Universal Negro Improvement Association (UNIA), **1:**477, 478

Universal Peace Movement, **6:**267

Universal Peace Union (UPU), **1:**216

"Universalis Cosmographic" (map), **5:**232

Universalist church, **2:**350

Universities, **3:127–129**
 economics at, **3:**108
 exchange students in, **3:**274
 industrial research at, **4:**340
 Ivy League, **4:449–450**
 in Massachusetts, **5:**267
 Morrill Act (1862) and, **5:460**
 religious learning in, **7:**98
 scientific research at, **7:**272
 segregation in, **5:**425
 state, **3:**127; **8:279–280**
 See also Education, higher; *specific universities*

University of Alabama, **1:**104

University of California, **2:13–14**; **3:**127
 affirmative action in, court case addressing, **1:**386
 botanical garden of, **1:**517
 free university movement at, **3:**462

University of Chicago, **8:280–281**
 athletic program at, **2:**277
 economics department of, **3:**109
 and *Encyclopaedia Britannica*, **3:**204
 financial support for, **7:**187
 Laboratory School at, **3:**116
 pragmatism at, **6:**444, 445

University of Delaware
 desegregation of, **2:**543
 and Winterthur Museum, **8:489**

University of Florida, **3:**387, 388

University of Michigan, **8:**279, **281–282**

University of Minnesota, American Studies at, **1:**169

University of North Carolina, **6:**130

University of Pennsylvania
 establishment of, **3:**112, 127
 museum of, **5:**486
 veterinary medicine at, **8:**319

University of Virginia, **8:283**
 Jefferson (Thomas) and, **8:**279, 283

University of Wisconsin, **8:**279, **284**, 492
 and Wisconsin Idea, **8:**493

University of Wyoming, **8:**565
 Black 14 incident at, **8:**566

Unknown Soldier, Tomb of the, **8:***284*, 284–285
 dedication of, firsthand account of, **9:**370–373

UNOS. *See* United Network for Organ Sharing

Unsafe at Any Speed (Nader), **2:**384, 391; **5:**561; **8:**285

Untouchables, The (film), **1:**504

UP. *See* United Press Association

Up From Slavery: An Autobiography (Washington), **5:**124

UPCNA. *See* United Presbyterian Church of North America

Updike, John, **5:**121

Upham, James P., **6:**370

UPI. *See* United Press International

Upjohn, Richard, **1:**250

UPS. *See* United Parcel Service

Upshur, Abel P., **6:**465

UPU. *See* Universal Peace Union

Upward Bound program, **8:**293, 441

Uranium, **6:**138–139, 341–342
 Manhattan Project and, **5:**221
 See also Nuclear weapons

Urban areas. *See* Cities

Urban homesteading, **8:**287

Urban League. *See* National Urban League

Urban mass transit, **3:**173–174; **7:42–46**
 decline of, **7:**44–45
 patronage of, **7:***45*

Urban planning. *See* City planning

Urban redevelopment, **2:**188; **3:**538–539; **6:**438; **8:285–288**, 293
 eminent domain for, **6:**505
 and historic preservation, **6:**453

Urbanization, **2:**388; **8:288–294**
 19th-century, **8:***290*

20th-century, **8:***293*
 and American society, **8:**294
 in Confederate States of America, **2:**343
 critics of, **8:**291–292
 in Gilded Age, **3:**577
 government policies and, **8:**292–294
 and housing, **4:**180–181
 migration and, **8:**285, 290–291
 in New Jersey, **6:**63
 and newspapers, **6:**97
 shopping malls and, **5:**215
 stages of, **8:**289–291
 supporters of, **8:**292
 of Virginia, **8:**346
 and waste disposal, **8:**419

U'Ren, William S., **6:**206, 208

Urey, Harold C., **6:**341

Ursuline Convent, burning of, **1:**196; **8:**295

Uruguay
 commerce with, **5:**44
 trade agreements with, **6:**125

Uruguay Round, **3:**524; **8:**52

Ury, John, **6:**85

U.S. Special Forces (USSF), **7:**494

U.S. Steel, **8:**295
 creation of, **4:**428
 decline of, **4:**429
 foreign investment in, **3:**420
 as monopoly, **4:**428
 trade unions and, **7:**545

U.S. Veterinary Medical Association (USVMA), **8:**319

U.S.A. (Dos Passos), **6:**12

USA Patriot Act (2001), **3:**369; **6:**109

USA Today (newspaper), **6:**99–100

USAF. *See* Air Force, U.S.

USAID. *See* Agency for International Development

USAirways, **2:**109

USCSRA. *See* United States Civil Service Retirement Association

USDA. *See* Agriculture, Department of

Use tax, **7:**230

Usery, W. J., **3:**343

USES. *See* Employment Service, U.S.

US&FS. *See* United States and Foreign Securities Company

USGA. *See* United States Golf Association

USGS. *See* Geological Survey, U.S.
Ushijima, Mitsuru, **6:**182–183
USI Film Products, Landgraf v., **2:**197
USIA. *See* United States Information Agency
USIS. *See* Information Service, U.S.
USNLTA. *See* National Lawn Tennis Association, U.S.
Usselinx, William, **6:**77
USSF. *See* U.S. Special Forces
Ussher, James, **1:**30
Usury. *See* Interest Laws
USVMA. *See* U.S. Veterinary Medical Association
USWA. *See* United Steelworkers of America
USWV. *See* United Spanish War Veterans
USX Corporation, **8:**295
Utah, **8:**295–299
 Ballet West of, **1:**390
 capital punishment in, **2:**40
 constitution of, **8:**297
 copper mining in, **6:**115
 culture of, **8:**297, 299
 earthquakes in, **3:**101
 economy of, **8:**296–297, 298
 emblems, nicknames, mottos, and songs of, **7:***533*
 during Great Depression, **8:**297–298
 minorities in, **8:**298
 modern, **8:**298–299
 Mormon migration to
  Mormon handcart companies, **5:**458–459
  Mormon trail, **5:**459, *459*
  Mountain Meadows Massacre, **5:**467–468
 Mormons in, **5:**53–54; **8:**296
 Native Americans in, **6:**230; **8:**217, 296, 299, 300
 Progressive Era in, **8:**297
 Stansbury's expedition to, excerpt from account of, **9:**233–237
 during World War I, **8:**297
 during World War II, **8:**298
Utah (battleship), **6:**273
Ute, **8:**216, *299*, **299–300**
 in Colorado, **2:**299
 Mormons and, **8:**296
Utility companies, municipal ownership and, **5:**476
Utopia (More), **5:**116–117

Utopian communities, **2:**476; **8:300–304**
 Amana Community, **1:133**
 antebellum, **8:***302*
 Brook Farm, **1:545; 8:**301
 city planning for, **2:**185
 pacifism and, **6:**228
 religious, **8:**302
 secular, **8:**302–303
 socialist, **7:**424
 technology-based, **8:**304
 transcendentalism and, **8:**179, 181
 Union Colony, **8:259**
UTW. *See* United Textile Workers

V

VA. *See* Veterans Administration; Veterans Affairs, Department of
Vacation and leisure, **8:305**
 in antebellum period, **8:**305
 in colonial era, **2:**292; **8:**305
 commercialization of, **7:**65
 Hobbes (Thomas) on, **8:**526
 motels in, **5:***462*, **462–463**
 privatization of, **7:**66
 See also Tourism
Vaccination, **3:**235, 239, 241; **5:**105
 Centers for Disease Control and, **2:**88
 development of, **2:**144
Vaccines
 attenuated, **6:**389
 Bacillus-Calmette-Guérin (BCG), **8:**237
 polio, **5:**236; **6:**388–389, *389*
 smallpox, **5:**300; **7:***399*, 399–400
 yellow fever, **8:**576
Vacuum cleaners, development of, **3:**182–183
Vail, Alfred, **8:**68
Vail, Theodore, **1:**346; **8:**67
Valcour Island, Battle of, **4:**77
Valentine, Allan, **6:**166
Valentine, Robert G., **1:**571
Valentino, Rudolph, **3:**401
Vallandigham, Clement L., **2:**218, 411; **8:**305–306
 banishment of, **3:**527
 as Sons of Liberty leader, **6:**136
Vallandigham incident, **3:**527; **8:305–306**

Vallejo, Mariano Guadalupe, **1:**433; **2:**9; **9:**62
Valley Forge, **7:**144; **8:306**
 conditions at, firsthand account of, **9:**147–149
Value America, **3:**184
Values, Native American, **1:**482
Van Buren, Martin
 in Albany Regency, **1:**114
 banking under, **1:**195
 Caroline affair and, **2:**58
 on congressional elections of 1838, **2:**23
 and Democratic Party, **2:**551
 Eaton affair and, **3:**105
 Free Soil Party and, **7:**111; **8:**119
 on hours of labor, **8:**360
 on Maysville veto, **5:**277
 nickname of, **2:**550; **3:**146
 party nomination of, **2:**399
 and presidential campaign of 1812, **3:**151
 in presidential campaign of 1832, **3:**152
 in presidential campaign of 1836, **3:**153
 in presidential campaign of 1840, **3:**146, 153
 in presidential campaign of 1848, **1:**417; **3:**154
 and slavery, **5:**97
Van Dam, Rip, **8:**589–590
Van de Graaff, Robert J., **6:**342
Van Der Zee, James, **1:**301
Van Doren, Charles, **7:**6, *6*
Van Hise, Charles R., **6:**42
 and University of Wisconsin, **8:**284
Van Leewenhoek, Anton, **1:**3
Van Rensselaer, Stephen, **8:**383
Van Schaick, William, **3:**40
Van Slyke, D., **1:**460
Van Syckle, Samuel, **6:**359
Van Tyne, Claude H., **1:***255*
Van Vechten, Carl, **1:**300
Van Voorhis, Westbrook, **5:**236
Van Wyck, Robert A., **8:**46
Van Zandt, Jones v., **3:**482; **4:487**
Vance, Cyrus, **6:**239–240
 and Cuba policy, **2:**471
Vance, Zebulon B., **6:**129
Vancouver, Fort, **8:**176
Vancouver, George, **3:**297; **8:**453
 explorations by, **8:306–307**, *307*
 in Aleutian Islands, **1:**121

Vancouver, George, (*continued*)
  of Columbia River, **2:**303
  in Oregon, **6:**204
Vandalia Colony, **8:307–308**
Vandegrift, Alexander A., **1:**520;
  4:68
Vanden Heuvel, Katrina, **5:**522
Vandenberg, Arthur, **7:**106; **8:**272
  and Republican Party, **7:**113
Vanderbilt, Cornelius, **1:**580; **3:**360
  and Davis (Jefferson), bond for,
    2:505
Vanderbilt, Cornelius, Jr., **1:**258
Vanderbilt, W. H., **6:**526
Vanderbilt, William K., **1:**375
Vanderhorst, Richard H., **1:**44
Vanderlyn, John, **1:**295
Vane, Henry, **1:**205
Vanhorne's Lessee v. Dorrance, **8:308**
Vann, Robert L., **6:**98
Vanuxem, Lardner, **3:**548
Vanzetti, Bartolomeo
  last statement by, text of,
    9:361–362
  See also Sacco-Vanzetti case
Vardaman, James K., **5:**413
Vargas, don Diego de, **6:**67
Varick, James, **1:**44, 53
Varieties of Religious Experience
  (James), **5:**118
Variety programs, **8:**72
Variety stores. *See* Dime stores
Varner, Robert, **6:**477
Vasquez, Louis, **1:**537
Vassar College, **3:**131, 132, 133;
  7:319–320
Vatican II, **2:**70; **3:**267; **8:308–309**
  goals of, **8:**308
  impact of, **8:**308–309
  on religious freedom, **4:**475; **8:**308
Vaudeville, **1:**575; **8:**113, **309–310**
  African Americans in, **8:**309
  decline of, **8:**309
Vaughan, Thomas Wayland, **6:**162
Vaughn, George, **6:**57
Vaugondy, Didier Robert de, **9:***11, 24*
Vaux, Calvert, **1:**250; **2:**94; **5:**38–39
Vauxcelles, Louis, **2:**475
VAWA. *See* Violence Against
  Women Act
VC. *See* Viet Cong
V-chip technology, **3:**340
VCR. *See* Videocassette recorder
Veatch, John A., **1:**504–505

Veazie Bank v. Fenno, **8:310**
Veblen, **3:**109
Veblen, Thorstein, *The Theory of the
  Leisure Class*, excerpt from,
    9:347–351
Vegetarian Resource Group, **8:**310
Vegetarianism, **8:310**
  in Seventh-day Adventist Church,
    1:31
Veksler, Vladimir I., **6:**338, 343
Velocity of money, **5:**440
Venable, James, **1:**184
Venerable Society. *See* Society for
  the Propagation of the Gospel
  in Foreign Parts
Venereal disease
  prostitution and, **6:**513, 514
  See also Sexually transmitted dis-
    eases
Venezuela
  commerce with, **5:**44–45
  Great Britain and, **4:**42
    Olney Corollary on, **6:**191
  independence of, **5:**50
  U.S. relations with, **5:**47, 48, 49
    Monroe Doctrine and, **5:**446
Venture capital, in industrial
  research, **4:***340*, 341–342
Venturi, Robert, **1:**253; **6:**430
Veracruz incident, **1:**1; **8:311**
Vergennes, Charles Gravier, comte
  de, **3:**472, 473; **6:**250;
  7:146–147, 210
Verhulst, Willem, **6:**71
Verizon, **1:**381
Vermont, **8:311–315,** *312*
  in 19th century, **8:**312–314
  in 20th century, **8:**314
  agriculture in, **8:**313, 314
  in American Revolution, **1:**442;
    8:311–312
    committee of safety in, **7:**149
  in Civil War, **8:**313
    Saint Albans Raid, **7:**224; **8:**313
  in colonial era, **8:**311
  Democratic Party in, **8:**314
  economy of, **8:**312–313
  emblems, nicknames, mottos, and
    songs of, **7:***533*
  governors of, **8:**312, 314
  Great Depression in, **8:**314
  in Haldimand Negotiations, **8:**312
  independence of, Green Mountain
    Boys and, **4:**61–62

  industry in, **8:**313, 314
  in land disputes, **8:**311
  legislature of, **8:**313, 314
  maple sugar in, **5:**231
  Native Americans in, **1:**2; **8:**311
  personal liberty laws of, **6:**294
  polio epidemic in, **6:**388
  population of, **8:**312, 314
  Republican Party in, **8:**313, 314
  same-sex unions in, **3:**514
  ski resorts in, **7:**122
  state university of, **8:**279
  statehood for, **8:**312
  tourism in, **8:**314
  town government in, **8:**148
  transportation in, **8:**313, 314
  Utopian communities in, **8:**303
  World War II and, **8:**314
Vernam, Gilbert S., **2:**468
Verner, Sherbert v., **2:**169
Vernon, Edward, **4:**473
Vernon, Lillian, **3:***29*
Verrazano, Giovanni da, **1:**11; **2:**38;
  3:285, 291; **8:**315
  explorations of
    Narrows, **5:**515
    New France, **6:**51
    New York, **6:**87
Verrazano-Narrows Bridge, **1:**539;
  8:315
Versailles, Treaty of (1919), **1:**394;
  8:315–316
  financial provisions of, **8:**316
  Hitler's claim regarding, **8:**249
  International Labor Organization
    in, **4:**390
  League of Nations in, **8:**315–316
  and Poland, **6:**391
  territorial provisions of, **8:**316
  U.S. rejection of, **3:**451;
    8:201–202, 205, 316
  war guilt clause of, **3:**562
  and Yap Mandate, **8:**575
VerticalNet, **3:**184
Vesey, Denmark, **2:**107; **6:**235;
  7:380; **8:**317
Vesey, Joseph, **8:**317
Vesey Rebellion, **6:**235; **7:**380, 455;
  8:316–317
Vespucci, Amerigo, **1:**135; **3:**284
Vestal, David, **1:**301
Veterans
  bonuses for, **1:498–499**
  in civil service, **6:**295

Civil War
 bonuses for, **1:**499
 organizations for, **8:**264–265
 pensions for, **7:**127
 GI Bill for, **3:574; 6:**285; **8:**317
 health care for, **8:**317
 homes for, **8:**317
 Mexican-American War, land
  grants to, **1:**498
 organizations for, **8:**318
  American Legion, **1:162–163**
  Grand Army of the Republic,
   4:31–32
  Society of Cincinnati, **2:**173, **174**
  United Confederate Veterans,
   8:264–265
 pension plans for, **4:**109;
  6:282–283, **284–285; 8:**317
 Persian Gulf syndrome in,
  6:291–292, 293
 post-traumatic stress disorder in,
  6:431
 soldiers' homes for, **7:445–446;**
  8:317
 substance abuse in, **5:**510
 Vietnam War
  benefits to, **1:**499
  health problems of, **2:**538
  Vietnam syndrome in, **8:328–329**
 War of 1812, land grants to, **1:**498
 World War I, Bonus Army of,
  1:498, 499
 World War II, compensation for,
  1:499
Veterans Administration (VA),
 6:285; **8:**317
Veterans Affairs, Department of
 (VA), **3:**332; **8:317–318**
 establishment of, **8:**317
 head of, **2:**2
Veterans Benefits Administration,
 8:317
Veterans of Foreign Wars of the
 United States, **8:**318
Veterans Health Services and
 Research Administration, **8:**317
Veterans of Vietnam War (organiza-
 tion), **8:**318
Veterinary College of London, **8:**319
Veterinary medicine, **8:318–320**
 disease treatment in, **8:**318–320
 educational system for, **8:**318–319
 microbiology in, **5:**358
Veto(es), **8:321–322**

by Bush (George H. W.), **8:**321
by Carter, **8:**321
by Clinton, **1:**7, 229; **8:**321
Congressional overriding of, **8:**321
Constitution on, **8:**321
in divided government, **8:**321
by Ford, **8:**321
by Johnson (Andrew), **9:**317–318
line-item, **8:320–321**
Maysville, **5:277**
by Nixon, **8:**321
pocket, **6:380–381; 8:**321
presidential defense of, **8:**322
by Reagan, **8:**321
by Roosevelt (Franklin Delano),
 8:321
by Truman, **8:**321, 322
by Wilson, **8:**352
Viacom, Inc., **6:**538
Viagra, **8:322**
Viburnum Trend, **5:**62
Vice president, U.S., **8:322–324**
 in 18th century, **8:**322
 in 19th century, **8:**322–323
 in 20th century, **8:**323
 functions of, **8:**322
 presidency after serving as
  through death of president,
   8:322, 323
  through election, **8:**322
 resignation of, **8:**323
Vickery, William, **3:**110
Vicksburg (Mississippi)
 in Civil War, **2:**213; **5:**412, 460;
  6:25; **8:**324, *324*
 riots in (1874), **8:324–325**
Victor Emmanuel III (king of Italy),
 1:329
Victor Talking Machine Company,
 5:502
Victoria (queen of Great Britain),
 8:325
 on Civil War, **1:**106
Victorianism, **8:325–326**
 20th-century interpretations of,
  8:326
 characteristics of, **8:**325–326
 and gardening, **3:**510
 and gender roles, **3:**518–519
Victorio (Apache leader), **1:**472, 475;
 8:404
"Victory garden" campaigns, **3:**510
Victory Loan of 1919, **8:326–327**
Video cameras, **6:**331

Video games, **8:**153, **327**, *327*
Videocassette recorder (VCR),
 2:392; **8:**77, **327–328**
 and advertising, **1:**34
Viet Cong (VC), **8:330–334**
 and Tet Offensive, **8:**97–98
Viet Minh, **3:**534; **8:**329, 330
Vietnam
 division of, by Geneva Accords,
  3:534; **8:**329
 immigration from, **7:**470–471
 in Indochina War, **3:**416–417;
  8:329
 road-building in, **7:**181
 in SEATO, **7:**469–470
 U.S. relations with, after Vietnam
  War, **8:**328
 U.S. shipping in, **5:**320
 U.S. trade with, **8:**328
Vietnam syndrome, **8:328–329**
Vietnam Veterans of America, **6:**475;
 8:318
Vietnam War, **8:329–335,** *330*
 adolescents and, **1:**26
 aerial bombing in, **1:**496, *496*
 African Americans in, **5:**382; **8:***333*
 Agent Orange in, **1:54–55**
 air war in, **8:***331*
 aircraft carriers in, **1:**91–92
 aircraft industry in, **1:**96
 anarchism in, **1:**182
 antiwar movement in, **1:**216–217,
  217; **6:**268
 atrocities by U.S. troops in, **1:**354;
  8:*333*
 ballads inspired by, **1:**388
 biological warfare in, **2:**119
 booby traps used in, **1:**500
 Cambodia operations in, **2:**16–17
 campus protests during, **8:**587
 casualties in, **2:**537; **8:**329, 332,
  333, 334, *376*
 Christmas bombing of Hanoi in,
  Kissinger on, **9:**475–477
 Cold War and, **2:**269
 conscientious objectors during,
  2:362
 costs of, **8:**334
 and counterculture, **2:**433
 and defense policy, **2:**536
 defoliation used in, **2:**537–538
 desertion in, **3:**17
 draft during, **2:**364–365; **5:**430;
  8:352

Vietnam War, (*continued*)
  amnesty for evasion of, **1:**177
    Carter's proclamation on,
      9:479–480
    resistance to, **1:***278*
  Easter Offensive in, **8:**334, 335
  Eisenhower and, **8:**330
  emigration during, **3:**197
  escalation of, **8:**332–333
  fall of Saigon in, firsthand account
    of, **9:**477–479
  federal expenditures during, **3:**282
  guerrilla warfare in, **4:**70
  gunboats in, **4:**77
  helicopters in, **1:**73; **4:**124, *124*
  Ho Chi Minh Trail in, **8:***329*, 330,
    332, 333
  and immigration to U.S., **7:**470
  imperialism in, **4:**245
  Indochina War and, **8:**329
  Johnson and, **1:**77; **3:**427;
    8:331–333
  Kennedy and, **8:**330–331
  laws of war in, **8:**372
  letters from soldiers in, **9:**473–474
  munitions in, **5:**479, 480
  My Lai incident in, **1:**354; **2:**440;
    5:505, *506*
  Native Americans in, **4:**329
  Nixon and, **1:**77; **3:**427;
    8:333–334, 335
    letter to Thieu by, **9:**474–475
    speech by, **9:**467–473
  Operation Linebacker I in, **1:**77
  Operation Linebacker II in, **1:**77
  Operation Ranch Hand in, **1:**54
  Operation Rolling Thunder in,
    1:77; **8:**332–333
  opposition to, **8:**333
    Kent State protest, **4:517–518**
    by Students for a Democratic
      Society, **7:**561–562
  original documents from,
    9:455–480
  paratroops in, **6:**247
  peace negotiations in, **8:**333, 334
    at Paris Conference, **6:**247–248
  Pentagon Papers on, **6:286–287**
    excerpt from, **9:**455–459
  press releases during, **2:**83
  prisoners of war in, **6:**472, 473, 475
    population of, **6:**477
  SEALs in, **8:**251
  support for, public, **9:**459–462

Tet Offensive in, **1:**77; **2:**447, 532;
  3:427; **8:**97, **97–98**, *98*, 333
and theater, **8:**115
Time on, **8:**127
Tonkin Gulf incident and,
  8:142–143, 332
troop withdrawal from, **8:**333–334
U.S. Air Cavalry in, **1:**73
U.S. Air Force in, **1:**77
U.S. Army in, **1:**277
U.S. Coast Guard in, **2:**259
U.S. Marine Corps in, **5:**242
U.S.-Vietnam relations after, **8:**328
and U.S. electoral politics, **3:**165,
  166
veterans of
  benefits to, **1:**499
  health problems of, **2:**538
  memorial to, **8:335**, *335*
  organizations for, **8:**318
  post-traumatic stress disorder in,
    6:431
  Vietnam syndrome in, **8:328–329**
Vietnamization in, **8:**333, **335–336**
  Nixon's speech on, **9:**467–473
war powers in, **8:**374, 388, 389
women in, **8:**504
Vietnam War Memorial, **8:335**, *335*
Vietnamese Americans, **7:**471
Vietnamization, **3:**427; **8:**333,
  335–336
  Nixon's speech on, **9:**467–473
Vieux Carré, **6:**73, *73*, 74; **8:**336
Vigilantes, **8:336**, 338
  and bank robbers, **8:**179
  Regulators, **7:82**
  in San Francisco, **8:**336, 338;
    9:239–240
  White Caps, **8:**470
Vigils, **6:**227
Vignali, Carlos, **2:**240
Viguerie, Richard A., **3:**29
  The New Right: We're Ready to Lead,
    excerpt from, **9:**495–499
Vikings, **6:**381
  exploration of America by, **3:**283
Vilaboa, Napoleón, **5:**239
Villa, Francisco (Pancho), raid on
  Columbus by, **5:**346; **8:336–337**
Village Voice (newspaper), personal
  ads in, **6:**294
Villard, Oswald Garrison, **5:**521–522
Villasur, Pedro de, **6:**29
Villegas, Daniel Cosío, **1:**137–138

Vincent, John, **7:**552
Vincent, John Heyl, **2:**113
Vinegar, **3:**405
Viner, Jacob, **3:**109
Vinland, **6:**122–123; **8:**337
Vinson, Carl, **8:**555
Vinson, Mechelle, **3:**54–55; **5:**324
Vinyl, **6:**366
Violence, **8:337–339**, *338*
  against African Americans,
    1:332–333; **8:**337–338
  lynching of Till (Emmett), **8:**126
  NAACP and, **5:**526
  in antislavery movement, **1:**211
  against Asian immigrants, **2:**154;
    8:578
  in Chicago, **2:**133
  against Chinese Americans, **2:**154
  against civil rights activists,
    2:203–204
  domestic, **3:72–75**
    activism targeting, Coalition of
      Labor Union Women and,
      2:256
  child abuse, **2:136–138**
  farmer/frontier, **8:**338
  gambling and, **3:**508
  against gays and lesbians, **3:**514
  in Kansas Territory, **1:**505, 506;
    3:196
  in Kentucky, **4:**520
  labor, **8:**338–339
  mass, **8:**339
  media portrayal of, **5:**261; **8:**339
  in mining towns, **4:**13; **8:**54
  against Native Americans, **8:**337
  objection to, **6:**227
  political, **1:331–333**; **8:**339
  rise in 20th century, **2:**459–460
  school, Columbine school mas-
    sacre, **2:**305
  serial killings, **7:315**
  sexual, feminism on, **8:**517
  in strikes, **7:**556; **8:**339
  on television, **8:**339
    public outcry against, **2:**64
  urban, **8:**337–338
  in video games, **8:**327
  See also Assassination(s); Domestic
    violence; Hate crimes; Riots;
    Terrorism
Violence Against Women Act
  (VAWA) (1994), **3:**74, 317;
  5:548; **8:**274, **339–340**

commerce clause and, **2**:312
Violence Commission, **8:340**
Violent Crime Control and Law
  Enforcement Act (1994), **8**:339
Violet-le-Duc, Eugène-Emmanuel,
  1:250
Virgil, *Moretum*, **3**:99
Virgin Islands, **8:340–341**
  annexation of, **1**:189; **8**:94,
    340–341
  economy of, **8**:341
Virgin Land (Smith), **1**:170
Virginia, **8:341–346**
  in 19th century, **8**:343–344
  in 20th century, **8**:344–346
  African Americans in
    education for, **8**:344, 346
    number of, **8**:346
    in politics, **8**:345
    white flight from, **8**:347
  agriculture in, **8**:341–342, 343, 346
    tobacco, **1**:62, 122; **8**:133, 134,
      341, 342
  in Alexandria Conference, **1**:122
  in American Revolution, **8**:343
    Arnold's raid in, **1**:282
  antimiscegenation laws of, **5**:165
  Bacon's Rebellion in, **1:382–383**
  Blue Laws in, **1**:490
  British convicts in, **2**:401
  in Civil War, **8**:344
    Battle at Marion, **5:244**
    Capture of Harpers Ferry, **4:97**
    Union sentiment in, **8**:260
  claims to western lands, **8**:454–455
  in colonial era, **2**:129; **8**:341–343
    Beverly (Robert) on, **1**:191;
      9:109–111
    charter of, **2**:281
    House of Burgesses in, **2**:280, 314
    slaves in, **7**:8
  constitution of, **8**:343, 344, 348
  Declaration of Rights by, **8:348**
    text of, **9**:135–136
  Democratic Party in, **8**:344–345
  economy of, **8**:346
  education in, higher, **8**:345–346
  emblems, nicknames, mottos, and
    songs of, **7**:*533*
  Federalist Party in, **3**:351
  in foreign trade, **8**:164
  founding of, **3**:289
  geological survey of, **3**:548

"Give Me Liberty or Give Me
  Death" speech and, **4**:2
government employment in, **8**:346
governors of, **8**:344, 345
Hampton Roads Conference in,
  4:91
immigration to, **4**:220
Indiana Company in, **4**:320
Kentucky Conventions and, **4**:522
legislature of, **8**:343, 344–345
  General Assembly, **8**:342, 343
  House of Burgesses, **1**:333;
    4:179; **8**:342, 348, 349
  reapportionment in, **8**:344
maps of, **8**:*342, 345*
  archival, **9**:*12*, 12–14, *13*
Mason-Dixon line in, **5**:260
Monticello in, **5:452–453**
Mount Vernon in, **5:465–466**, *467*
mountain feuds in, **3**:356–357
Native Americans in, **6**:442; **8**:341,
  349
Ohio River and, connection
  between, **4**:456
origins of, **7**:46
poll taxes in, **6**:408
population of, **8**:343, 346
presidential dynasty of, **8**:343,
  348–349
provincial congresses in, **6**:520
ratification of Constitution in,
  2:381
readjuster movement in, **7:52**;
  8:344
Republican Party in, **8**:344–345
school desegregation in, **8**:344
Shenandoah Valley in, **7:341**
slave insurrections in, **7**:379, 380;
  8:343
slavery in, **8**:341, 342–343
theater in, **8**:113
toll roads in, **8**:139
tourism in, **8**:346
urbanization of, **8**:346
Virginia Company of London in,
  8:347–348
Virginia Indian Company in, **8:349**
Virginia Resolves and, **1**:124;
  8:349–350
women in
  education for, **8**:346
  in political office, **8**:345
Virginia (warship), **6**:25
Virginia, Cohens v., **2:265**, 381

Virginia, Loving v., **5:165**, 251, 406
Virginia, Morgan v., **5**:527
Virginia, United States v., **8:275–276**
Virginia Association, **1**:340
Virginia Beach (Virginia),
  8:346–347
Virginia Board of Elections, Harper v.,
  5:415; **6**:508
Virginia City (Nevada), **1**:497;
  2:338; **4**:11; **6**:37; **8**:347
Virginia Company of London,
  2:111; **3**:289; **8:347–348**
  charter issued to, **2**:285
  and colonial settlements, **2**:287
  dissolution of, **8**:348
  establishment of, **8**:347
  as foreign investment, **3**:419
  management of, **8**:347
  Pilgrims and, **5**:317
  Plymouth branch of, **2**:430
Virginia Company of Plymouth,
  6:377, **379–380**; **8**:347
Virginia Declaration of Rights,
  1:454; **2**:521; **8:348**
  text of, **9**:135–136
Virginia dynasty, **3**:151; **8**:343,
  348–349
  Democratic party during, **2**:549
Virginia Indian Company, **8:349**
Virginia Military Institute, **8**:276
Virginia Plan, in Constitutional
  Convention, **2**:379
Virginia Resolves, **8:349–350**
  on Alien and Sedition Acts, **1**:124;
    8:349
  passage of, **8**:349
  in southern rights movement,
    7:473
  on Stamp Act, **8**:349
  text of, **9**:120
  on Townshend Acts, **8**:349
Virginia v. West Virginia, **8:350**
Virginian, The (Wister), **5**:129
Virology. *See* Microbiology
Virtual reality, **8:350**
  applications for, **8**:350
  critics of, **8**:350
Virtues, Franklin's (Benjamin) list of,
  8:528
Viruses, hantavirus, **4:92–93**
Visa (credit card), **2**:450, 451
VisiCalc, **7**:442
VISTA. *See* Volunteers in Service to
  America

Vitale, Engle v., **3**:374

Vitamines, The (Funk), **6**:148

Vitamins, **6**:148–150
    biochemistry research and, **1**:460
    and nutritional science, **3**:24
    vitamin C deficiency, **7**:287

Vivekananda, **1**:326; **4**:133

Vivisection. *See* Medical research, on
    animals

Vizcaíno, Sebastián, **8**:451

Vizenor, Gerald
    Darkness in Saint Louis BearHeart,
        5:129
    *Griever: An American Monkey King
        in China*, **5**:129
    Winter in the Blood, **5**:129

Vlaminck, Maurice de, in Armory
    Show, **1**:297

VOA. *See* Voice of America

Vocational education, legislation on,
    7:401–402

Voelter, Heinrich, **6**:245

Vogt, Teamsters v., **6**:350

Voice of America (VOA), **6**:503–504;
    8:350–351

Volcanoes, **8**:351–352
    disasters involving, **3**:37
    Mount St. Helens (Washington
        state), **5**:465, *466*

Volk, Leonard W., **1**:316

Vollard, Ambroise, **2**:272

Volleyball, invention of, **8**:584

Volstead, Andrew J., **8**:352

Volstead Act (1919), **2**:458; **6**:501;
    8:352

Volta, Alessandro, **3**:172, 177; **8**:68

Voltaire, and deism, **2**:539

Voluntarism. *See* Pure and simple
    unionism

Volunteer Army, **8**:352
    See also Conscription and recruit-
        ment; Enlistment

Volunteer firefighters, **3**:371

Volunteer Hospital Corps, **6**:147

Volunteerism, **8**:352–353
    in ACTION, **1**:19
    in AmeriCorps, **1**:173
    Big Brother movement, **1**:452
    Big Sisters, **1**:453
    March of Dimes, **5**:236
    nursing, **6**:147
    Peace Corps, **6**:265–266
    during World War I, **3**:72

Volunteers. *See* Conscription and
    recruitment; Enlistment

Volunteers in Service to America
    (VISTA), **1**:19, 173; **8**:386

Von Braun, Wernher, **7**:189

Von Karman, Theodore, **7**:189

Von Pufendorf, Samuel, **5**:91

Von Raasloff, General, **8**:340

Vonnegut, Kurt, **1**:364
    Cat's Cradle, **5**:121
    Slaughterhouse 5, **5**:121

Vonnoh, Bessie Potter, **1**:308

Voter Education Project, **2**:354

Voter registration, **8**:353–355
    in 19th century, **8**:354
    by African Americans, **8**:*354*, 357
        Student Nonviolent Coordinat-
            ing Committee in, **7**:561
    laws on, disfranchisement through,
        8:354

Voting, **8**:355–357
    by African Americans
        constraints on, **8**:356
        in Georgia, **3**:555–556, 557–558
        grandfather clause used to pre-
            vent, **4**:35, 73; **5**:526
        NAACP and, **5**:526–527
    in Alabama, **1**:103
    by ballot (*See* Ballot)
    in colonial era, **8**:355
    and democracy, **2**:547–548
    poll tax as prerequisite for, **2**:48;
        6:408; **8**:9
        Supreme Court on, **8**:9, 344
        in Virginia, **8**:344
    preferential, **6**:448–449
    property qualifications for, **3**:145,
        250
    rates of participation in,
        2:547–548; **8**:4, 5, 353, 355
    regulation of, **3**:144–145; **8**:356
    religious requirements for, **1**:206;
        8:6
    residency requirements for, **8**:355
    right to (*See* Suffrage)
    by women, **8**:356–357
    See also Disfranchisement; Suffrage

Voting Rights Act (VRA) (1965),
    1:385; **2**:200; **3**:57, 144; **5**:116;
    8:357–358
    1970 amendment to, **8**:9, 354, 355
    1975 amendment to, **8**:9
    1982 amendment to, **8**:9, 357–358
    backlash against, **1**:382

civil rights movement and, **2**:204
    effects of, **7**:106; **8**:9
    and Georgia politics, **3**:557–558
    provisions of, **8**:9, 357
    purpose of, **8**:357
    resistance to, **8**:357
    and role of federal government,
        3:341
    Supreme Court on, **8**:9, 357

Voting Rights Act (1970), **2**:200

Vouchers, school, **3**:119, 137–138;
    7:266

Voulkos, Peter, **1**:305

Voyage of Discovery (Vancouver),
    8:306–307

Voyages (Hakluyt), **4**:86, *86*

Voyages of the Slaver St. John
    (O'Callaghan), **9**:95–96

Voyageurs, **3**:490, 491; **4**:35; **8**:358

VRA. *See* Voting Rights Act

Vubu, Kasa, **8**:271

Vulcanite, invention of, **3**:3

Vulcanization, discovery of, **7**:202

W

Wabanakis, in Maine, **5**:207–208

*Wabash, St. Louis, and Pacific Railway
    Company v. Illinois*, **2**:310; **7**:26,
    37

WAC. *See* Women's Army Corps

Waco Siege, **3**:339; **5**:385; **8**:359,
    359
    and Oklahoma City bombing,
        6:187

Wadd, William, **6**:153

Wade, Benjamin F., **2**:313; **8**:359

Wade, Roe v. See Roe v. Wade

Wade-Davis Bill (1864), **7**:58; **8**:359

Wadsworth, James S., and land spec-
    ulation, **5**:36

Wadsworth, Joseph, **2**:281

Wage Stabilization Board (WSB),
    6:166

Wages
    collective bargaining and, **2**:274
    comparable worth principles and,
        2:329–330
    Equal Pay Act (1963) and, **2**:330;
        3:54, 245
    stagnation of, in 1990s, **1**:580;
        2:225

"stickiness" of, and unemployment, **8:**252
trade unions and, **2:**325; **3:**176; **8:**261, 268
See also Minimum wage
Wages and Hours Act. *See* Fair Labor Standards Act
Wages and hours of labor
in industrial revolution, **4:**343
piecework and, **6:351–352**
regulation of, **5:**11, 13, 14–15; **8:359–361**
under Adamson Act, **1:**19; **8:**360
under Fair Labor Standards Act, **3:**307–308; **8:**360
Lochner v. New York and, **5:**139–140
under National War Labor Board, **5:**564–565
Supreme Court on, **1:**19, 21; **5:**14; **8:**360
for women, **1:**21; **5:**5; **7:**303; **8:**360
Brandeis Brief on, **9:**357–360
Wages and salaries, **8:361–362**
control of, **6:**460
productivity and, **6:**492
in standard of living, **7:**521–522
Wagner, Fort, Battle of, **2:**212
Wagner, Honus, **1:**420
Wagner, Richard, **6:**198
Wagner, Robert, **1:**154; **2:**274; **6:**43; **8:**46
on Factory Investigating Commission, **8:**209
Wagner Act (1935)
and AFL growth, **1:**151
See also National Labor Relations Act
Wagner-Peyser Act (1933), **3:**201; **5:**11
Wagon(s), **8:**186
Conestoga, **2:**339, 441; **7:**177; **8:***462*
covered, **2:**441, *441;* **8:***463*
Dearborn, **2:510**
Wagon manufacture, **8:**362
Wagon trains, **2:**441; **8:363–365,** *364*
decline of, **8:**365
firsthand account of, **9:**229–233
number of, **8:**364
on Oregon Trail, **6:**209
organization of, **8:**364

of overland companies, **6:220**
oxen in, **6:**222
prairie schooner, **6:448,** *448*
routes of, **8:***363,* 363–364
Wagoners of the Alleghenies, **8:**365
Wainwright, Gideon v., **3:575–576**
Wainwright, Jonathan M., **1:**427
Waite, Davis, **6:**417
Waite, Morrison, **7:**150; **8:**275
Waiting for Lefty (Odets), **5:**121; **8:**115
Wakarusa War, **1:**506
Wakashan, **8:**221
Wake, Defense of, **8:365–366**
Wakefield, Sarah F., **2:**51
Waksman, Selman, **7:**217; **8:**237
Walcott, Charles D., **3:**545–546
Wald, Abraham, **3:**109, 110
Wald, Lillian D., **2:**147; **8:**521
Walden (Thoreau), **5:**119; **8:**180, **366**
Waldenbooks, **6:**538
Waldo, Albigence, on life at Valley Forge, **9:**147–149
Waldseemüller, Martin, **1:**135; **3:**284; **5:**232
Walker, Alice, **2:**205; **5:**123, 124, 126
Walker, Amasa, **3:**108
Walker, David, **6:**235
Walker, Edwin A., **1:**330
Walker, Francis A., **3:**108
Walker, Frank, **3:**208
Walker, James Dent, **3:**522
Walker, James J., **8:**46
Walker, John H., **3:**320
Walker, Joseph, **3:**299; **8:**582
Walker, Leroy P., **2:**341
Walker, Mort, **2:**308
Walker, Nellie Verne, **1:**308
Walker, Quok, **1:**48
Walker, Robert J., **8:**51
Walker, Thomas, **2:**479
Walker, William (filibuster), **3:**359–360; **5:**46; **6:**104
Walker, William H. (camera maker), **6:**329
Walker Tariff (1846), **8:**51
Walker War (1853-1854), **8:**296, 300
Walking delegate, **8:**366
Walk-in-the-Water (ship), **4:**53–54
Wall Street. *See* Stock market
Wall Street explosion (1920), **8:**366
Wall Street Journal (newspaper), **8:366–367**
Walla Walla settlements, **8:367–368**

Wallace, Dewitt, **7:**51, *51*
Wallace, George C., **8:***119*
American Independent Party of, **8:**119
assassination attempt against, **3:**166
career of, **1:**104
and conservative movement, **2:**376
fundraising for, **3:**29
presidential candidacy of, **1:**382; **2:**204; **3:**165, 166, 171
in presidential election of 1968, **1:**159
right-wing forces and, **7:**16
on school desegregation, **1:**104; **4:**29
Wallace, Henry A.
as agriculture secretary, **1:**71
as commerce secretary, **2:**310
Communist Party and, **2:**327
as editor of *The New Republic,* **6:**77
in presidential campaign of 1940, **3:**163
in presidential campaign of 1948, **3:**163, 164; **6:**499
in presidential election of 1948, **1:**197
Wallace, Irving, **6:**539
Wallace, Lew, **7:**157
in Battle of Shiloh, **7:**346
in Shenandoah Campaign, **7:**341
Wallace, Mike, **5:**520
Wallace, Neil, **3:**110
Wallace, Stafford v., **7:514**
Wallerstein, Immanuel, **2:**44
Walloons, **8:368**
Wal-Mart, **3:**10; **7:**126; **8:368**
and Arkansas economy, **1:**263
Walpole, Sir Robert, **6:**252
Walpole Company. *See* Grand Ohio Company
Walsh, John, **3:**565
Walsh, Lawrence, **6:**401; **7:**496
Walsh, Thomas J., **8:**63
Walsh-Healey Act (1936), **3:**308; **8:368**
Walter, Thomas U., **2:**49
Walters, Alexander, **6:**235
Walters, Barbara, **2:**78
Waltham (Massachusetts), **2:**387
Waltham Mills, **5:**4
Walther, C. F. W., **5:**177
Walton, Bill, **1:**425
Walton, E. T. S., **6:**342–343

Walton, G., *Faint the Trumpet Sounds*, **5**:132
Walton, Holmes v., **4:150**
Walton, John, **6**:186
Walton, Sam, **1**:263; **3**:10, 26; **7**:126; **8**:368
Walworth, Ellen Hardin, **2**:504
Walzer, Michael, **5**:92
Wambaugh, Joseph, **5**:122
Wampanoag Indians, **6**:378; **8:368–369**, *369*
  Mount Hope, **5:464**
  Puritan settlements and, **2**:288
  in Rhode Island, **7**:151
  treaties with, **4**:313
Wampum, **6**:86; **8:369–370**
Wanamaker, John, **3**:7; **5**:206; **7**:205
Wanghia, Treaty of. *See* Cushing's Treaty
War
  archival maps of, **9**:3
  atrocities in (*See* Atrocities in war)
  casualties of (*See* War casualties)
  civil liberties during, **8**:374–375
  conscientious objection to, **2:361–362**
  Constitution on, **8:373–375**
  costs of, **3**:282; **8:376–377**, *377*
    Civil War, **2**:219
    in Vietnam War, **8**:334
    debts, in World War I, **8:542–543**
    and Dawes Plan, **3**:562
    and German-American Debt Agreement, **3**:560, 562
    and Young Plan, **3**:562
  declarations of, **5**:378; **8**:373
  defoliation used in, **2:537–538**
  laws of, **8:370–373**
  mobilization for, **5:429–430**
  and post-traumatic stress disorder, **6**:431
  role of rivers in, **7**:174–175
War and Ordnance, Board of, **8**:373
War bonds, **1**:397–398
  See also Savings bonds
War Brides Act (1945), **2**:155
War casualties, **8:375–376**
  in Civil War
    at Battle of Antietam, **1**:199, *199*, 200
    at Battle of Fredericksburg, **3**:457
    at Battle of Gettysburg, **3**:569–570
  definition of, **8**:375

number of, by conflict, **8**:*375*
  of Philippine Insurrection, **6**:320, 321–322
  in Vietnam War, **8**:329, 332, 333, 334, *376*
  in World War II, **8**:*551*
  on D Day, **6**:120
War crimes trials, **1**:354; **8:378**
  in Civil War, **1**:184
  for ethnic cleansing in Yugoslavia, **1**:354–355
  Genocide Convention and, **3**:536
  My Lai incident (Vietnam), **5**:505
  after World War II, **8**:378
  See also Atrocities in war; International Criminal Court
War dance, **6**:444
War Democrats, **2**:551; **8:378**
  and Union Party, **8**:259
War Department, **8:378–379**
  air defense systems by, **1**:75
War Finance Corporation, **8:379**
War guilt clause of Versailles Treaty, **3**:562
War hawks, **3**:82; **8:379–380**
  and presidential campaign of 1812, **3**:151
  and Uncle Sam nickname, **8**:248
  in War of 1812, **8**:379, 382–383
"War in Its Effect Upon Women, The" (Swanwick), excerpt from, **9**:363–364
War industries, racism in, **1**:35
War Industries Board (WIB), **2**:552; **5**:377; **8:380**, 536, 539
  and appliance industry, **3**:181
  and National Recovery Board, **5**:554
War Labor Board. *See* National War Labor Board
War Labor Disputes Act (1943), **5**:564
War memorials, **8**:*380*, 380–381
  Vietnam War Memorial, **8:335**, *335*
War of 1812, **2**:530; **4**:41; **8:381–385**
  and antiwar movements, **1**:216
  and ban on trading with enemy, **8**:173
  Battle of Lake Erie in, **4**:51; **5**:21
  Battle of New Orleans in, **5**:159; **6**:73, **75**, *75*
  maps of, **8**:*385*
  archival, **9**:42, *43, 44*

Battle of Stoney Creek in, **7:552**
Battle of the Thames in, **8**:64, **111–112**
Battle of Tippecanoe in, **8**:399
bounties in, **1**:524
British blockade in, **8**:384
Canadian invasion in, **8**:383–384
Capitol damage in, **2**:48, 49
causes of, **8**:381–383
declaration of war in, **8**:383
desertion in, **3**:17
Detroit surrender in, **3:21**
disease in, **2**:235
Essex during, **3**:256
events leading to, **2**:129
Fort McHenry, **5**:185
Great Lakes Naval Campaigns of 1812, **4:53**
guerrilla warfare in, **4**:70
gunboats in, **4**:77
Madison's speech on, **9**:183–185
Maine in, **5**:208
maps of
  archival, **9:42**, *43, 44*
  battles from 1812-1813, **8**:*381*
  battles from 1814-1815, **8**:*382*
  Niagara Frontier, **8**:*382*
Marine Corps in, **5**:241
in Maryland, **5**:256–257
Monroe-Pinkney Treaty and, **5:447**
munitions manufacture and, **5**:481
and nationalism, **5**:568
Native Americans in, **4**:272; **8**:382, 399–400
New England opposition to, **4**:101
Niagara Campaigns, **6:102–103**
peace negotiations in, **8**:384–385
Perry-Elliott Controversy, **6:290–291**
piracy in, **6**:359
press gangs and, **6**:459
prisoners of war in, **6**:473
privateering in, **5**:248; **6**:480
rockets used in, **7**:188
and tariffs, **8**:50
Tecumseh in, **8**:131
Treaty of Ghent ending, **3**:571–573; **4**:41; **6**:263; **8**:200
and Uncle Sam nickname, **8**:248
U.S. Army in, **1**:275–276
and Vermont, **8**:312
veterans of, land grants to, **1**:498; **5**:28–29

war hawks in, **8:**379, 382–383

warships in, **8:**405

Washington burning in, **8:417**

women in, **8:***383*

Yankee (privateer brig) in, **8:**574

War of Austrian Succession. *See* King George's War

War of Jenkins' Ear, **2:**294

War of Spanish Succession. *See* Queen Anne's War

War of the League of Augsburg. *See* King William's War

War on Drugs, **3:**86

War on Poverty, **1:**571–572; **6:**438, 551; **8:**293, **385–387**, 441

Community Action Program in, **2:328**

Head Start in, **4:**112–113; **8:**386

Job Corps in, **4:**480; **8:**386

Office of Economic Opportunity in, **6:**163; **8:**386

programs in, **7:**416; **8:**386–387

War on Terrorism, **8:**96

Bush's address on, text of, **9:**526–530

Egypt's support in, **3:**141

and Labor Department, **5:**12

War powers, **8:387–388**

Constitution on, **8:373–375**, 387

War Powers Act (1973), **5:**378; **8:388–389**

loopholes in, **8:**388

presidential resistance to, **8:**321, 374, 388, 389

provisions of, **8:**373–374, 389

War Relocation Authority (WRA), **4:**460–461, 463

War Savings Stamps, **8:**123

War Settlements Act (1928), **3:**560

"War Story" (Kim), **9:**419–424

War Trade Board, **8:389**

Ward, Aaron Montgomery, **3:**9; **7:**125

Ward, Clara, **1:**441

Ward, Elsie, **1:**308

Ward, John Quincy Adams, **1:**306

Ward, John William, **1:**169

Ward, Lester Frank, **6:**424; **7:**412, 432

Ward, S. A., **1:**139

Ward's Cove Packing Co., Inc., v. Atonio, **2:**196, 197; **8:389–390**

Ware, Caroline, **8:**498

Ware v. Hylton, **8:390**

Warfield, Benjamin Breckinridge, **1:**449

Warfield, Edward, **1:**550

Warhol, Andy, **1:**301; **6:**330, 414, 415, *415*

Warley, Buchanan v., **5:**526

Warm Springs Reservation, **8:**223

Warner, Elizabeth Stewart, letters of, **9:**238–239

Warner, Glenn Scobie (Pop), **3:**410

Warner, Mark R., **8:**344

Warner, Olin L., **1:**306

Warner, Sam Bass, Jr., **8:**294

Warner, Seth, **1:**442, 574; **4:**61; **8:**312

Warner Brothers, cartoons of, **2:**63, 64

Warnerke, Leon, **6:**329

Warr, Lord de la, **2:**540

Warren, Earl, **1:**457; **3:**164

as California governor, **2:**11

on censorship, **2:**85

on citizenship, **2:**198

Court under, **4:**493, 496–497; **8:**24–25

on natural rights, **6:**10

on separation of church and state, **3:**374

crafting doctrine of speech, **3:**374

critics of, **2:**169

judicial review under, **4:**493

in *Loving v. Virginia,* **5:**165

on segregation, **1:**549

in Warren Commission, **8:**394

Warren, Edward, **1:**391

Warren, Fiske, **8:**303, 304

Warren, George F., **1:**544

Warren, Gouverneur K., in Battle of Gettysburg, **3:**568

Warren, John Collins, **1:**184–185

Warren, Joseph, **8:**3

Warren, Josiah, **8:**303

Warren, Mercy Otis, **4:**137; **8:**505

Warren, Robert Penn, **3:**481; **4:**520; **5:**102, 122

All the King's Men, **5:**121

Night Rider, **5:**121

Warren, Samuel D., on right to privacy, **6:**479

Warren, Whitney, **4:**34

Warren Bridge, **2:**107

Warren Commission, **8:394–395**

Warren Plan. *See* Gold Purchase Plan

Warsaw Pact, **2:**89, 268; **6:**125

disintegration of, **2:**90

Warships, **8:405–409**

armored, **1:265–266**

battleships, **8:**407

British, **8:***406*

cruisers, **8:**407–408

destroyers, **8:**408

Dreadnought, **3:84–85**

frigates, **8:**405, 408

ironclad, **4:430–431**

nuclear, **8:**406–407

radar on, **7:**14

rams, **7:47**

sailing, **8:**405

steam, **8:**405–406

in torpedo warfare, **8:**144

types of, **5:**480

"White Squadron," **8:473**

See also specific ships

Wasatch Mountains, **8:**295

Wascoe, **8:**221

Washburn, Cadwallader, **8:**491

Washing machines, development of, **3:**181–182

Washington (D.C.), **8:***409,* **409–412**

African Americans in, **8:**410

Bonus Army in, **1:498,** 499; **7:**166

botanical garden in, **1:**516

burning of, in War of 1812, **8:417**

capitol at, **2:48–50,** *49*

choice as capital, **2:**519

city plan for, **2:**49, 185, 187; **7:**52; **8:**409, 410

in Civil War, **8:**410

Compromise of 1790 and, **2:330**

demonstrations in, **8:***411*

early history of, **8:**409–410

in electoral college, **3:**171

Folger Shakespeare Library in, **3:393**

founding of, **8:**409

home rule in, **4:**153; **8:**411–412

Knickerbocker storm (1922) in, **1:**486

Lincoln Memorial in, **8:**410

local government of, **8:**410, 411–412

March for the Animals in (1990), **1:**186

March on Washington (1963), **1:**152; **5:237,** *237,* 563

National Gallery of Art in, **5:538–541**

National Museum of the American Indian in, **5:547–548**

Washington (D.C.), (*continued*)
population of, **8:**410, 411–412
as port city, **8:**409–410
riots in, **7:***164,* 167–168
slavery in, **8:**410
Vietnam War Memorial in, **8:335,** *335*
in War of 1812, burning of, **8:417**
White House in, **8:**470–472, *471*
Washington (state), **8:**412–416, *413*
agriculture in, **8:**413
in colonial era, **8:**412
economy of, **8:**414
emblems, nicknames, mottoes, and songs of, **7:***533*
environmental issues in, **8:**415
Friday Harbor Laboratories, **5:**240, 241
Great Depression in, **8:**414
health care in, **8:**415
immigration to, **8:**413
industry in, **8:**414–416
Japanese Americans in, **8:**415
missionaries in, **8:**412
Mount St. Helens in, **5:**465, *466*
Native Americans in, **8:**415, 571
population of, **8:**416
railroads in, **8:**413
San Juan Islands in, **7:**242
statehood for, **8:**413
trade unions in, **8:**414
water resources in, **8:**415
in World War I, **8:**414
in World War II, **8:**414–415
Washington, Booker T., **3:**117, 126; **5:**119
"Atlanta Compromise" speech by, **3:**556
and Du Bois, **6:**103
and newspapers, African American, **5:**199–200
as principal of Tuskegee University, **8:**241
Up From Slavery: An Autobiography, **5:**124
Washington, Bushrod, **2:**297
and African colonization, **1:**148
on privileges and immunities of citizens, **6:**482
Washington, Eugenia, **2:**504
Washington, Fort, **7:**143
Washington, George
and Agriculture Department, **1:**71
at Alexandria Conference, **1:**122

in Allegheny Mountains, **1:**127
in American Academy of Arts and Sciences, **1:**139
in American Revolution, **1:**509, 511, 532; **7:**136, 137, 140–141, 142–146; **8:**581
amnesty granted by, **1:**177
appointments by, **1:**225
and Arnold's march to Quebec, **1:**281
Aurora on, **1:**360
and Bank of the United States, **1:**395
in Battle of Bunker Hill, **8:**207
in Battle of Harlem, **4:**94–95
in Battle of Long Island, **5:**150
in Battle of Princeton, **6:**464
in Battle of Trenton, **8:**208
in Battle of White Plains, **8:**473
cabinet of, **2:**2
and Capitol building, **2:**48
and civil service, **2:**206
as commander in chief, appointment of, **2:**394; **7:**139
Connolly's Plot and, **2:360**
at Constitutional Convention, **2:**379
and Continental Congress, **7:**140
Conway Cabal and, **2:403**
correspondence with Cornwallis, **9:**152
Delaware River crossing, **2:543–544,** *544;* **8:**208
distillery opened by, **3:**60
on enumerated powers, **3:**225
executive agents appointed by, **3:**277
on executive privilege, **3:**279
farewell address of, **8:418–419**
on foreign policy, **3:**425
text of, **9:**179–183
and Federalist cause, **2:**381
and France, **3:**472–473
in French and Indian War, **3:**469; **4:**55
and gardening, **1:**516; **3:**509–510
Great Union Flag by, **3:**379
inauguration of, **4:**250–251
Indian policies of, **4:**313; **6:**177–178
internment of, **6:**457
on isolationism, **4:**439
in James River Company, **4:**456

and Jay's Treaty, **4:**41, 467; **8:**200, 204
and land companies, **5:**26, 35, 36
and liquor ration for Army, **3:**59
on militias, **5:**386
Mount Vernon, **5:465–466,** *467*
mules and, **5:**472
and national census, **2:**86
as national hero, **5:**567
and national identity, **7:**141
and neutral rights of U.S., **6:**33, 34
neutrality order of, **3:**278
Neutrality Proclamation by, **6:**491
in New York City, **1:**544
and Newburgh addresses, **6:**94
and Order of the Purple Heart, **2:**527
and pine tree flag, **6:**357
and political patronage, **2:**22
presidency of, **7:**138
in presidential campaign of 1789, **3:**150, 171
in presidential campaign of 1792, **3:**150
and presidential open house, **8:**471
against prison ships, **6:**473
in Quasi-War, **3:**449
spies used by, **7:**501–502
teeth of, **3:**3
in treaty negotiation and ratification, **8:**199
trip to Barbados, **1:**414
and two-term tradition for presidency, **7:**198
on uniform system of measures, **5:**528–529
at Valley Forge, **8:**306
in Virginia dynasty, **8:**343, 348
and Virginia Resolves, **8:**349
and Washington (D.C.) founding, **8:**409
on waterways, **7:**168
and West Point, **8:**447
Whiskey Rebellion and, **2:**97; **8:**469
martial law in, **5:**254
and White House, site for, **8:**470
Washington, Harold, **2:**133
Washington, Henry S., **6:**300–301
Washington, Madison, **2:**457
Washington, Martha, **3:**375
Washington, Treaty of (1871), **1:**106; **2:**26; **6:**263; **8:416–417**
Washington, United States v., **8:**415

Washington Conference (1922), **3**:304
and China policy, **2**:151
and national defense, **2**:531
Washington Crossing the Delaware (Leutze), **2**:543–544, *544*
Washington Monument, **8**:417, *417*
Washington Naval Conference, **8:417–418**, 575
arms control at, **1**:270; **6**:264; **8**:555
and Five-Power Naval Treaty, **3**:377
and Four-Power Treaty, **3**:446
"parity" in naval defense and, **6**:250
Washington Post (newspaper)
publishing *Pentagon Papers*, **6**:99, 287
Unabomber's manifesto in, **8**:247
Washington v. Davis, **3**:247
Washington v. Glucksberg, **3**:263; **7**:160; **8:418**
Washingtonian movement, **8**:79
Washoe, **8**:216
Waste disposal, **8:419–420**
genetic engineering and, **3**:531
hazardous, **4**:111–112; **8**:21
plastics and, **6**:367–368
recycling, **7:66–68**, *67, 68*; **8**:420
sanitation systems for, **7**:245–246
sewage, **4**:356; **7**:245
solid, **4**:356
Waste Land, The (Eliot), **5**:120
Wataugans, **3**:454–455
Watchmaking, **2:241–242**
Water, sanitation systems for, **7**:245–246
Water closet, **6**:372
Water law, **8:420–421**
Water outlets, cities on, **8**:289
Water pollution, **8:421–422**
Exxon Valdez oil spill and, **3**:233, *305*, **305–306**
in Hudson River, **4**:188
legislation for control of (*See* Clean Water Act)
Manhattan Company and, **5**:476
in Mississippi River, **5**:417
non-point sources of, **3**:233
sewage disposal and, **4**:356
Water rights
arguments over, in Colorado, **2**:299

for Native Americans, **1**:100–101; **8**:415
Water supply and conservation, **2**:368; **8:422–425**
urbanization and, **8**:292
in Washington (state), **8**:415
See also Irrigation
Water-cooled nuclear reactors, **6**:139
Watergate scandal, **2**:23, 421; **3**:279; **8**:*425*, **425–428**
campaign finance reform attempts after, **3**:147
investigating committees in, **4**:411; **8**:*426*
Jordan's "Constitutional Faith" speech on, text of, **9**:489–491
media coverage of, **7**:261
newspapers on, **6**:99
and Nixon impeachment hearings, **4**:235
Nixon's investigation address on, text of, **9**:486–489
and presidential campaign of 1972, **3**:166
and president's removal power, **7**:101
and resignation of Nixon, **6:110–112**
significance of, **6**:400–401
special prosecutors in, **7**:495
and subpoena to Nixon, **6**:457
tape recordings in, **7**:495
and Vietnam War, **8**:334
Waterhouse, Benjamin, **5**:390
Waterpower, **8:428–429**
Ballinger-Pinchot controversy on, **1:391**
and manufacturing, **5**:4
windmills and, **8**:486
Waters, Ethel, **8**:309
Waters, Muddy, **1**:492
Waterways
Canadian-American, **2**:29
improvements of, **7:168–171**
inland, **8**:187, 192, **429–430** (*See also* Canal[s]; River[s])
and domestic trade, **8**:160
Fox-Wisconsin Waterway, **3:448**
Inland Waterways Commission on, **4:361**
insurance for, **4**:368
Muscle Shoals region (Alabama), **5**:483–484

towboats and, **8**:147–148
See also River(s)
Watie, Stand, **6**:184
Watkins, Arthur V., **1**:537; **4**:288; **8**:298
Watkins, Carleton, **1**:299; **8**:583
Watkins v. United States, **2**:352
Watson, Ella (Cattle Kate), **2**:*75*
Watson, James, **3**:67–68, *68*, 529, 533
Watson, John, **5**:393
Watson, John B., **1**:437, *437*, 438; **6**:524
Watson, Lloyd R., **1**:436
Watson, Philip, **6**:509
Watson, Thomas Augustus, **8**:69
Watson, Thomas E., **3**:556; **5**:366; **6**:417; **7**:205
Watson, Thomas J., Jr., **2**:335
Watson, Thomas J., Sr., **2**:335
Watson-Watt, Robert, **7**:14
Watt, James, **3**:229; **7**:541, 542, 543
Watts riots (1965), **2**:12; **5**:153; **8:430–431**, *431*
Wax engraving (cerography), **5**:233
Wax portraits, **8:431**
Waxman, Harry, **2**:230
Waxman, Henry A., **1**:15
Wayland, Francis, **1**:548; **3**:108, 115
Wayland, Julius A., **8**:303
Wayne, (Mad) Anthony
in Battle of Fallen Timbers, **3**:310–311
and Fort Defiance, **2**:537
and Fort Wayne, **8**:431
and Greenville Treaty, **2**:509; **4**:63–64, 271; **6**:172
in Ohio, **2**:537; **6**:172, 178; **8**:399
Wayne, Fort, **8:431–432**
Wayne, Fort, Treaty of (1809), **4**:314
Wayne, John, **3**:363; **8**:288, 458
Ways and Means, Committee on, **2**:352; **8**:432
WCAR. *See* Women's Central Association for Relief
WCIW. *See* World Community of Islam in the West
WCTU. *See* Woman's Christian Temperance Union
"We have met the enemy, and they are ours," **5**:21; **8**:432
WEAL. *See* Women's Equity Action League
"Wealth" (Carnegie), **6**:317

Wealth of Nations (Smith), **1:**228; **3:**107; **6:**481

Weapons
  in Civil War, **5:**479
  in Indian warfare, **8:**391–392
  manufacture of, **5:**480–481
  of merchantmen, armed, **5:321–322**
  prehistoric, **1:**242, *242*
  in Revolution, **5:**479
  See also Arms race and disarmament; Artillery; Military-industrial complex; Munitions; Nuclear weapons; Ordnance; *specific types*
Weas. *See* Miami Indians
Weather Bureau, U.S., **1:**71
  history of, **5:**331–332
Weather satellites, **8:432,** 433
Weather Service, National (NWS), **8:432–433**
  Coast Guard and, **2:**259
  establishment of, **2:**235; **5:**331, 332
  See also Meteorology
Weatherford, William, **8:**400
Weathermen (anarchist group), **1:**182; **4:**65; **7:**166; **8:**95
Weather-related disasters, **3:**41–43
Weaver, Buck, **1:**480
Weaver, James B., **6:**417; **8:**119
  presidential bid of, **2:**227; **3:**158
  in presidential campaign of 1892, **6:**158
Weaver, Randy, **7:**203
Weaver, Richard, and conservative movement, **2:**375
Weaver, Sylvester, **8:**138, 142
  Today developed by, **8:**138
  Tonight Show developed by, **8:**142
Weaver, Vicky, **7:**203
Weaver, Warren, **1:**460; **5:**437; **6:**315
Weavers, the, **1:**441
Webb, Alexander, **2:**189
Webb, Beatrice, **2:**273
Webb, Electra Havemeyer, **1:**310
Webb, Frank J., *Garies and Their Friends*, **5:**124
Webb, James, **5:**523
Webb, Joseph, **8:**572
Webb, Sidney, **2:**273
Webb, Walter Prescott, **3:**475
Webb-Kenyon Act (1913), **1:**117
Weber, Max, **1:**572; **2:**41; **6:**471
  and cubism, **2:**475–476

on dichotomy between church and sect, **3:**1
Weber, United Steelworkers of America v., **1:**36
Web-fed newspaper press, **6:**469
Webster, Daniel
  and Compromise of 1850, **2:**331
  conservatism of, **2:**374
  Creole slave case and, **2:**457
  and Dartmouth College Case, **2:**503
  debate with Hayne, **8:434–435**
  on due process of law, **3:**89
  and land speculation, **5:**36
  and lyceum movement, **5:**178
Webster, John White, **8:**435
Webster, Noah, **3:**22–23, 113, 204, 220; **8:**106
  on Bill of Rights, **9:**167–169
  Elementary Spelling Book, **8:**434
  and medical meteorology, **2:**235
  Webster's American Spelling Book, **5:**127
Webster v. Reproductive Health Services, **1:**7; **6:**361; **8:433–434**
Webster-Ashburton Treaty (1842), **2:**26; **8:**200, **434**
  Aroostook War and, **1:**283
Webster-Hayne debate, **8:434–435**
Webster-Parkman Murder Case, **8:435**
Webster's American Spelling Book, **5:**127
Webster's blue-backed speller, **8:**434
Wechsler, David, **4:**379
Wedding traditions, **8:435–436**
Weddington, Sarah, **7:**192
Wedemeyer, Albert C., in China-Burma-India Theater, **2:**152
Wedgwood pottery, **1:**286
Weed, Thurlow, **2:**23; **3:**466
Weeden, Trevett v., **8:**208
Weeds, **8:436–437**
Weegee, **1:**301
Weekend, origins of, **7:**65
Weeks, Edward A., **1:**351
Weeks, John W., **8:**437
Weeks Act (1911), **3:**432; **8:**423, **437**
Weems, Ward Lane, **1:**308
Wefald, Knud, **3:**322
Wegener, Alfred, **3:**551
Weidenbaum, Murray, **2:**431
Weigle, Luther A., **1:***448*
Weimar Republic, **3:**562

Weinberg, Steven, **6:**338
Weinberger, Caspar, **2:**529
  in Iran-Contra Affair, **4:**419, 420
  Vietnam syndrome and, **8:**328
Weinberger v. Wisenfeld, **3:**54
Weisskopf, Victor F., **6:**344
Weissman, Julia, **1:**310
Weissmuller, Johnny, **2:**98; **8:**37
Weitzel, Godfrey, **8:**472
Welch, James, **5:**129
Weld, Theodore Dwight, **1:**209; **6:**152
Weld, Thomas, **6:***153*
Welde, Thomas, **1:**431
Welfare and Pension Plans Disclosure Act (1958), **5:**11
Welfare capitalism, **2:**43; **5:**5; **8:437–438**
Welfare Reform Act (1996), **3:**409
Welfare system, **6:**438–439; **8:438–443**
  aliens in, **1:**126
  and children, **2:**137
  Clinton and, **6:**439
  conservative backlash against, **2:**228; **8:**442
  food stamp program in, **3:**408–409; **6:**150, 438
  foster care in, **3:**442–443
  legislation on, **7:**415
  privately negotiated, **2:**274
  Reagan and, **6:**439
  reform of, and child care, **2:**139
  residency requirements in, **7:**222
  See also Federal aid
Well of Loneliness, The (Hall), **7:**325
Wellek, René, **5:**122
Weller, Thomas H., **6:**388
Welles, Gideon, **3:**191; **8:**208
Welles, Orson, **3:**363
  Citizen Kane, **2:***178,* **178–179**
  radio dramatization by, **7:**19
Wellesley College, **3:**131, *132,* 133; **7:**319–320
  minorities in, **3:**132
Wells, Edward, **9:***16*
Wells, Fargo and Company, **8:443**
Wells, Henry, **8:**443
Wells, Herbert George (H. G.), **1:**138
Wells, Horace, **1:**184, 185
Wells, Ida B., **2:**201; **5:**199
  anti-lynching crusade by, **5:**180

and World's Columbian Exposition, **8:**558

Wells, Robert W., **3:**85

Welsh, Herbert, **4:**302–303

Welsh v. United States, **2:**362

Welter, Barbara, **3:**518

Wendt, Julia Bracken, **1:**308

Wentworth, Benning, **4:**61; **6:**57; **8:**311

Wentworth, John (Long John), **2:**502; **6:**57

Wentworth, John (The Elder), **6:**57

Werden, Sir John, **6:**510

Wesberry v. Sanders, **1:**227

Wesley, Charles, **3:**264

Wesley, John, **1:**43, 265; **2:**175; **3:**264; **5:**332; **6:**287; **8:**528

Wessells, Henry W., **3:**94

West, American, **8:443–445**

  agriculture in, **1:**64–65; **3:**18

    irrigation for, **4:**434–436

  alien landholding in, **1:**124

  American Revolution in, **7:***145*

  barbed wire in, **1:**416

  black regiments in, **1:**471–472

  camels in, **2:**19

  cattle ranching in, **4:**157–158

  climate in, **2:**236

  conservation in, opposition to, **2:**367

  cultural regionalism in, **7:**297–298

  development of, Bank of America and, **1:**394

  expansion into (*See* Expansionism; Westward migration)

  exploration of, **3:**297–301; **5:**150

  ghost towns in, **3:**574

  herpetology expeditions in, **4:**129

  housing in, **4:**180

  maps of, archival, **9:**24, *24*

  overland mail and stagecoaches, **5:203–204**

  pioneers in, **6:**358–359

  reclamation of arid lands in, **7:55–56**

  Remington's images of, **7:99–100,** *100*

  sectionalism in, **7:**296–298

  seismic activity in, **3:**101–102

  settlement of, **1:**501

    and environmental devastation, **2:**366

    land speculation and, **5:**36–37

    railroads and, **7:**33

sheep in, **7:**339

sheep wars in, **7:339–340**

stagecoach travel in, **7:**514–515

survey and management of, Land Office in, **5:**31

tourism in, **8:**146, 305

vigilantes in, **8:336,** 338

West, Benjamin, **1:**129; **3:**197

West, Candace, **3:**516

West, Cornel, **1:**47

West, Jerry, **1:**424, 425

West, Nathanael

  The Day of the Locust, **5:**121

  Miss Lonelyhearts, **5:**121

West Coast Hotel Company v. Parrish, **3:**308; **5:**395; **8:445**

West Germany, **3:**562–563; **8:**552

  in European Common Market, **8:**157

  in NATO, **6:**125

West India Company

  Danish, **3:**286

  Dutch, **3:96–97,** 289–290

    and colonial settlements, **2:**289

  Swedish, **3:**286

West Indies, **8:445–447,** *446*

  Barbados, **1:413–415,** *414*

  British and French

    molasses trade, **5:**436–437

    Paris, Treaty of (1763) and, **6:**248

    in slave trade, **8:**164, 209

  colonial trade with, **2:**261

West Point (Military Academy), **5:374–375; 8:447**

  Arnold (Benedict) at, **1:**282

  and corps of engineers, **7:**168

  engineering education at, **3:**216, 219

  establishment of, **2:**530

  military uniforms at, **8:**257, *257*

West Tennessee, **8:**83

West Virginia, **8:447–451**

  capital of, **8:**449

  constitution of, **8:**350

  debt assumed by, **8:**350

  emblems, nicknames, mottos, and songs of, **7:***533*

  mountain feuds in, **3:**356–357

  statehood for, **8:**344

West Virginia (battleship), **6:**273

West Virginia, Strauder v., **4:**503; **7:555**

West Virginia, Virginia v., **8:350**

West Virginia State Board of Education v. Barnette, **3:**374; **6:**370

Westergaard, Harald, **3:**217

Westermann, H. C., **1:**311

Western Apaches, **1:**219, 220

Western Associated Press, **6:**458

Western Electric, **1:**440

Western exploration, **8:451–454,** *452*

  Fisk expeditions, **3:**377

  Frémont explorations, **3:467–468**

  by Great Britain, **8:**306–307

  Pike expeditions, **6:354–355**

  Yellowstone River expeditions, **3:**318; **8:**580

  See also Exploration(s)

Western Federation of Miners (WFM), **5:**6; **8:**454

  Industrial Workers of the World and, **4:**346–347

  International Union of Mine, Mill, and Smelter Workers and, **4:**397

Western hemisphere, Monroe Doctrine on, **5:446–447**

Western historians, new, **3:**476

Western Land Company, **5:**36

Western lands, **8:454–455**

  Claim associations for, **2:**221

  mineral patent law, **5:**389

  public land commissions and, **6:**530–531

  settlement of, **5:**30–31

  See also Northwest Territory

Western Museum (Cincinnati), **5:**487

Western Reserve, **8:***455,* 455–456

Western Union Telegraph Company, **2:**439; **3:**183; **8:**69, **456–457**

  AT&T and, **8:**70

  and cable advances, **2:**3

Westerns, **8:***457,* **457–459,** *458*

  The Great Train Robbery, **4:**58, *58;* **6:**105

  on television, **8:**73

Westheimer, Irvin F., **1:**452

Westinghouse, George, **2:**388; **3:**173; **5:**108

Westinghouse Electric Company, **3:**172, 173, 174

  appliance development by, **3:**181

Westmoreland, William C., in Vietnam War, **1:**77; **8:**331, 332

Weston, Brett, **1:**301

Weston, Edward, **1:**301; **6:**330
Weston, Thomas, **5:**317; **6:**377–378
Westward migration, **1:**382;
    8:459–464, *460*
  Adams (John Quincy) and,
    1:187–188; **8:**307
  Donner party, **3:79–80**
  federal government and, **8:**444
  Forty-Mile Desert and, **3:**441
  frontier, moving, **5:**371–372
  and fur trade, **3:**490
  "Go West, Young Man, Go West"
    and, **4:**9
  Gold Rush and, **4:**13, 14
  homestead movement in,
    4:155–157
  manifest destiny, **5:222–225**
  maps of, archival, **9:**2
  Miami Purchase, **5:353**
  to Michigan, **5:**354
  to Minnesota, **5:**398
  Mormon
    handcart companies, **5:458–459**
    Mormon trail, **5:459,** *459*
    Mountain Meadows Massacre,
      5:467–468
  original documents on
    Frizzell's journal, **9:**229–233
    Grund's observations, **9:**215–218
    Warner's letters, **9:**238–239
  vehicles used in, **8:**462, *463*
  Wilderness Road and, **8:**478
  See also Oregon Trail
Wetherald, Richard T., **2:**237
Wetherford, William, **1:**102
Wetherill, Samuel, **8:**591
Wetlands, **8:***464,* 464–465
  and ague, **1:**72
  Dismal Swamp, **3:57–58**
Wetzel, Don, **1:**363
Wexler, Harry, **2:**237
Wexner, Lex, **7:**126
Weyerhauser, Frederick, **5:**173
Weyerhauser Company
  formation and growth of, **5:**173
  land acquisition by, **5:**35
Weyl, Walter, **6:**76
Weyler y Nicolau, Valeriano, **2:**470
Weyrich, Paul, **8:**118
WFM. *See* Western Federation of
  Miners
WHA. *See* World Hockey Associa-
  tion
Whaam! (Lichtenstein), **6:**414

Whaling, **8:***465,* **465–466**
  in colonial era, **4:**349
  in Hawaii, **4:**106
  in Nantucket, **5:**510
  Native American, by Makah, **5:**213
Wharton, Edith, **1:**292
  Ethan Frome, **5:**119
Wharton, Samuel, **8:**308
*What Is the Proper Way to Display a
  U.S. Flag?* (Tyler), **5:**535
Wheat, **8:466–467**
  export of, **3:**390
  growing of, **2:**96, 97
  McCormick reaper, **5:183–184**
  production of
    during Great Depression, **3:**391
    during World War I, **3:**390
  storage of, **3:**187
  winter, **3:**88
Wheatley, Phillis, **1:**48; **5:**119, 124
Wheeler, Burton, **6:**498
  in presidential campaign of 1924,
    3:162
Wheeler, George, **3:**300, 545
Wheeler, John A., **6:**343
Wheeler, Joseph, **7:**486
Wheeler, William A., **3:**156
Wheeler-Howard Act. *See* Indian
  Reorganization Act
Wheeler-Lea Act (1938), **3:**348
Wheelock, Eleazar, **2:**502; **3:**133, 134
Wheelock, John, **2:**502, 503
Wheelwright, John, **1:**205
Where the Wild Things Are (Sendak),
  5:128
Whiffen, Marcus, **1:**251
Whig Almanac, **1:**129
Whig Party, **3:**152–153, 154;
  8:467–468
  antibanking movement in, **1:**195
  antislavery in, **1:**211
  in Arkansas, **1:**260
  Conscience Whigs, **2:360–361**
  and conservatism, **2:**374
  Cotton Whigs, **2:**361
  vs. Jackson (Andrew), **7:**103
  in Louisiana, **5:**159–160
  in North Carolina, **6:**128–129
  in Ohio, **6:**172, 173
  panic of 1837 and, **2:**550
  platform of, **6:**368
  in presidential campaign of 1840,
    8:131
  and Republican Party, **7:**111

  on subsidies, **7:**564
  tariffs and, **5:**228
  in Vermont, **8:**313
Whip, party, **8:468**
Whipple, Abraham, **3:**512
Whipple, Amiel W., **7:**30
Whipple Observatory, **6:**157
Whipsaw strikes, **5:**141
Whiskey, **8:**78, **468–469**
  consumption of, **7:**504
  distilling of, **2:**97; **3:**59
  production of, **7:**504
  tax on, **7:**504
Whiskey Rebellion, **2:**97, 377; **3:**59;
  6:278; **8:**56, *469,* **469–470**
  government agents tarred and
    feathered during, **8:**49
  liberty poles in, **5:**97
  martial law and, **5:**254
Whiskey Ring, **8:470**
  special prosecutor on, **7:**495
"Whisky Trust, The," **4:**26
WHISPER, **6:**514
Whistler, James A. McNeill, **1:**296;
  3:537; **6:470–471**
White, Andrew Dickson, **2:**415;
  3:274
  as AHA president, **1:**159
  at Hague Peace Conference, **4:**82
White, Canvass, **2:**79
White, Caroline Earle, **1:**186
White, E. B., **3:**222; **6:**92
  Charlotte's Web, **5:**127
White, Edward D., **8:**275
  on antitrust legislation, **1:**214
White, Elijah, **8:**363
White, Ellen, **8:**501
White, Ellen Harmon, **1:***30,* 30–31
White, Frank, **1:**263
White, George, Jr., **5:***253*
White, George S., **1:**162
White, Henry Dexter, **8:**531
White, Hugh, **5:**413, 414
White, Hugh L., in presidential
  campaign of 1836, **3:**153
White, James, **1:**30, 31
White, John, **3:**80; **9:**8–10, 13
  as governor of Roanoke colony,
    7:47
White, Kevin H., **1:**510
White, Richard, **8:**463
White, Stanford, **2:**251
White, Texas v., **8:**97, **105**
White, William, **3:**242

White, William Alanson, **5**:314
White Bird (Nez Perce chief), **6**:101
White Caps, **8**:470
White Citizens Councils, **8**:470
White Fish River, archival maps of,
  9:*51, 52*
White flight
  in Philadelphia, **6**:313
  in Virginia, **8**:347
White House, **8**:470–472, *471*
  staff of, vs. cabinet, **2**:2–3
White House of the Confederacy,
  8:472, *472*
White League, **6**:76; **8**:472–473
White Mountains, **6**:55, 56, 59
White Plains, Battle of, **8**:473
White propaganda, **6**:503
White Slave Traffic Act (Mann Act)
  (1910), **2**:459; **5**:225; **6**:513
"White Squadron," **8**:473
White supremacy, **8**:472, **473–474**
  antimiscegenation laws and,
    5:405–406
  and lynching of Till (Emmett),
    8:126
  militia movement and, **5**:385
  Tillmanism and, **8**:126
  Vardaman, in Mississippi, **5**:413
  See also Ku Klux Klan; Racism
White-collar crime, **2**:461–462
Whitefield, George, **2**:162; **3**:264;
  4:*38,* 38–39; **6**:65, 316, 450;
  7:85; **8**:71
  and Great Awakening, **2**:292
Whitehead, Joseph, **2**:260
Whitehead, Mary Beth, **8**:29–30
Whitehead, Robert, **8**:144, 408
Whitely, William, **2**:542
Whiteness studies, **4**:142
Whitewater Canal, **8**:239
Whitewater scandal, **2**:239; **4**:238
  Starr investigation of, **7**:496
Whitman, C. O., **5**:240
Whitman, Charles Otis, **6**:349
Whitman, Christie Todd, **6**:64;
  8:424
Whitman, Marcus, **6**:205;
  8:367–368, 412
Whitman, Narcissa, **6**:205; **8**:412
Whitman, Walt, **1**:322, 546; **3**:195;
  6:537; **8**:292
  on individualism, **4**:332
  Leaves of Grass, **5**:*71,* 119
Whitman Sisters, **8**:309

Whitney, Anne, **1**:308
Whitney, David M., **3**:20
Whitney, Eli, **2**:387, 428–429; **6**:364
  inventions of
    cotton gin, **1**:63; **8**:109
    interchangeable parts, **1**:335, 371;
      5:481
Whitney, Gertrude Vanderbilt,
  1:308, 310; **8**:474, *474*
Whitney, Mount, **3**:300
Whitney, W. R., **3**:175
Whitney, William Dwight, **3**:23
Whitney, Willis R., **5**:18, 24, 108
Whitney Museum, **8**:474–475
Whittier, John Greenleaf, **7**:2
Whittle, Christopher, **7**:267
Whittlesey, Charles W., **5**:155
WHO. *See* World Health Organization
WHOI. *See* Woods Hole Oceano-
  graphic Institution
*Whole Book of Psalmes Faithfully
  Translated into English Metre,
  The* (Daye), **6**:468, 536
Whorf, Benjamin Lee, **4**:275
Who's Afraid of Virginia Woolf?
  (Albee), **5**:122
WIB. *See* War Industries Board
Wickersham, George W., **8**:475
Wickersham Commission, **8**:475
Wideman, John Edgar, **5**:123
Widnall, Sheila E., **8**:505
Wiener, Myron, **7**:101
Wiener, Norbert, **2**:486
Wiesel, Elie, **4**:150
Wieselthier, Valerie, **1**:304
Wigeman, Godcharles v., **5**:13
Wigfall, Louis, **2**:341
Wiggins, Ella May, **8**:111
Wigglesworth, Edward, **5**:104
Wigglesworth, Michael, *The Day of
  Doom,* **5**:117
Wightman Cup, **8**:90
Wigner, Eugene P., **6**:343, 345
Wigwam, **1**:254; **6**:276; **8**:475
Wilberforce University, **1**:53; **3**:125
Wilbur, James, **8**:571
Wilbur, John, **7**:2
Wilbur, Ray Lyman, **7**:523
Wilcox, Howdy, **1**:375
Wild One, The (film), **4**:125
Wild West shows, **2**:436; **7**:191;
  8:113, 457, 475, **475–477**
  in Oklahoma, **6**:185

Wildavsky, Aaron, **1**:554
Wildcat (Seminole warrior), **8**:402
Wildcat money, **8**:477
Wildcat oil drilling, **8**:477
Wildcaters, **6**:302
Wildenhain, Marguerite, **1**:304
Wilder, L. Douglas, **8**:345
Wilder, Laura Ingalls, **5**:127
Wilder, Thornton, **5**:157
  The Bridge at San Luis Rey, **5**:120
  Our Town, **5**:121
  The Skin of Our Teeth, **5**:121
Wilderness
  of Alaska, **1**:108, 109, 111
  cult of, in Progressive Era, **5**:467
  myth of, **1**:170
  preservation of, **2**:372
    national park system and,
      5:549–550
Wilderness, Battles of the, **2**:214;
  8:477–478
Wilderness Act (1964), **3**:227, 432
Wilderness Road, **2**:479; **6**:254;
  8:478
Wilderness Society, **2**:372
  membership of, growth in, **3**:227,
    229
Wildfires, **8**:478
  fighting, **3**:373
Wildlife, introduced species of,
  7:*499,* **499–500**
Wildlife management, **2**:370
  and eugenics, **2**:370–371
Wildlife preservation, **2**:366–367,
  369; **8**:479–482
  Audubon Society and, **1**:359–360
  and overpopulation problem, **2**:370
  in Yellowstone National Park,
    8:580
Wiley, Harvey W., **2**:122;
  3:403–404; **6**:553, 554
Wiley, John, **6**:536
Wiley Act. *See* Pure Food and Drug
  Act (1906)
Wilkes, Charles, **2**:303; **3**:299;
  6:383; **8**:207
  expedition of, **8**:482
Wilkes, John, **3**:378
Wilkins, Maurice, **3**:67, 68
Wilkins, Roy, **1**:332; **5**:527
Wilkinson, Eliza, letters of,
  9:150–151
Wilkinson, James, **3**:270, 359; **4**:84;
  6:183; **7**:490; **8**:383–384

Wilkinson, John, on blockade running, **9**:296–297

Wilkinson, Signe, **6**:395

Willard, Benjamin, **2**:241, 242

Willard, Emma, **3**:114, 131
  Congregationalism and, **2**:349

Willard, Frances, **8**:81, *496*, 496–497

Willard, Simon, **2**:242

Willard, Xerxes A., **2**:490

Willet, William, **1**:314

Willey, Waitman T., **8**:449

Willhoite, Michael, *Daddy's Roommate*, **1**:500

William II (emperor of Germany)
  and Algeciras Conference, **1**:123
  and Armistice of November 1918, **1**:265

William III (king of Great Britain)
  and colonial charters, **2**:281
  and colonial policy, **2**:280, 285; **3**:77
  and Plymouth colony, **6**:379
  on treason, **8**:193

William, Fort, **8**:176

William and Mary, College of, **8**:343, **482–483**, 484
  establishment of, **3**:112, 127, 129
  first professor of law at, **5**:56, 73
  Native Americans at, **3**:134

William Carter Fund, **3**:443

Williams, Abigail, **7**:229

Williams, Anna W., **5**:358

Williams, Annette (Polly), **3**:137

Williams, Claude (Lefty), **1**:480

Williams, Esther, **8**:37

Williams, Eugene, **2**:134

Williams, Eunice, **2**:51

Williams, Fannie Barrier, **3**:526

Williams, G. Mennen ("Soapy"), **5**:356

Williams, George, **8**:584

Williams, H. L., **6**:179

Williams, Harold M., **3**:565, 566

Williams, Harrison A., **1**:8; **6**:158

Williams, Henry, **8**:483

Williams, Henry Sylvester, **6**:235

Williams, Jesse, **2**:490

Williams, Joan, **3**:517–518

Williams, John A., **5**:123
  Man Who Cried I Am, **5**:126

Williams, Kenny, **1**:46

Williams, Micajah, **2**:32

Williams, Moses, **7**:*359*

Williams, Peter, **1**:53

Williams, Raymond, **2**:222; **8**:326

Williams, Robin M., **6**:375, 376

Williams, Roger, **1**:411, *411*, 412, 508; **5**:117, 270–271; **6**:47, 515, 519
  and religious liberty, **7**:93, 151
  and settlement of New England, **2**:288

Williams, Ted, **1**:421

Williams, Tennessee, **5**:122; **8**:115

Williams, Wayne B., **3**:338

Williams, William Appleman, **4**:140

Williams, William Carlos, **3**:195; **5**:120

Williams Act, **5**:323

Williams v. Mississippi, **8**:483

Williamsburg (Virginia), **6**:452
  city plan for, **2**:185
  colonial, **8**:343, **483–484**

Williamson, Charles, **5**:86

Williamson, Hugh, **6**:201
  on American climate, **2**:234

Williamson v. Lee Optical, **3**:247; **8**:484–485**

Williams-Steiger Act. *See* Occupational Safety and Health Act

Willis, Dorsie, **1**:550

Willisch, Marianne, **3**:498

Willkie, Wendell L., in presidential campaign of 1940, **3**:163; **7**:113

Wills, Helen, **8**:90

Willson, Robert, **1**:290

Willys, John, **2**:449

Wilmington (Delaware), **2**:543

Wilmington (North Carolina), riot in, **8**:485

Wilmot, David, **3**:459; **6**:278, 415; **8**:485
  and Democratic Party, **2**:551
  and Free Soil Party, **7**:111

Wilmot Proviso, **1**:417; **6**:415; **8**:485–486**
  vs. Clayton Compromise, **2**:229
  debates over, Whig Party and, **2**:361
  and Free Soil Party, **3**:459

WILPF. *See* Women's International League for Peace and Freedom

Wilson, Alexander, **6**:214

Wilson, August, **5**:123

Wilson, Caroline Davis, **1**:308

Wilson, Charles E., **2**:528

Wilson, E. D., **6**:341

Wilson, E. O., **1**:194

Wilson, Edith, **3**:376

Wilson, Edmund Beecher, **3**:532

Wilson, Edward, **6**:383

Wilson, Edward Osborne, **2**:373; **8**:598

Wilson, Edwin, **6**:383

Wilson, George, *American Class Reader*, **5**:127

Wilson, Harriet E., *Our Nig*, **5**:124

Wilson, Henry, **2**:453

Wilson, Jack. *See* Wovoka (Paiute prophet)

Wilson, James, **1**:454–455; **8**:193
  at Constitutional Convention, **2**:379, 380
  legal training of, **5**:56

Wilson, John, **5**:31

Wilson, John (Moonhead), **2**:544

Wilson, Joseph, **1**:305; **5**:31

Wilson, Kenmmons, **7**:53

Wilson, Mary Jane, **1**:161

Wilson, Pete, **2**:12
  and Proposition 187, **6**:509
  and Proposition 209, **6**:509–510

Wilson, Richard (Dick), **8**:560, 561

Wilson, Robert O., **2**:487

Wilson, Robert W., **1**:344–345, 440

Wilson, Samuel (Uncle Sam), **8**:248b

Wilson, William G., **1**:118, 119

Wilson, William Julius, **1**:47; **6**:440

Wilson, William L., **7**:205; **8**:51

Wilson, Woodrow
  American Federation of Labor and, **1**:150
  antitrust legislation under, **1**:214–215; **2**:418; **3**:348; **6**:54, 63; **7**:344; **8**:235
  and Arab world, **1**:233
  arms control under, **1**:270
  and Balfour Declaration, **8**:592
  on big business, **1**:214
  Bryce (James) and, **1**:137
  and child labor laws, **4**:27
  and Committee on Public Information, **2**:313; **6**:503
  declaration of war against Germany, **8**:591
  and Democratic Party, **2**:551–552
  and Dominican Republic, occupation of, **3**:76
  executive agents appointed by, **3**:277
  and FBI, **3**:337

and Federal Reserve Act (1913),
6:497; **8**:196
and Federal Trade Commission,
8:160
foreign policy of, **2**:552; **3**:426
Fourteen Points of, **2**:552; **3**:426,
447; **5**:63; **8**:315
  and Armistice of November 1918,
1:265
  Great Britain rejecting, **4**:42
  text of, **9**:368–370
and government pensions, **6**:283
and Haiti, occupation of, **4**:85
House-Grey Memorandum and,
4:179
imperialism of, **4**:244
internment of, **6**:458
isolationism and, **4**:439
labor policies of, **2**:228
Latin American policies of, **5**:47;
7:57
and League of Nations, **2**:151;
3:426; **5**:63–64; **6**:264; **8**:201,
205, 539
and Ludlow Massacre, **5**:169–170
and military pensions, **4**:31
on Monroe Doctrine, **9**:209
and National Park Service, **5**:550
and National Research Council,
5:522
and National War Labor Board,
5:564
New Freedom campaign of,
6:54–55, 70
as New Jersey governor, **4**:29
The New Republic on, **6**:76
and Nineteenth Amendment,
5:565–566
at Paris peace conference, **3**:426;
8:315
and Philippines, **6**:322
and preparedness, **6**:449
as president of Princeton University, **6**:465
in presidential campaign of 1912,
1:566; **3**:160; **6**:54, 70, 496;
8:43
in presidential campaign of 1916,
3:161
in presidential campaign of 1920,
6:118
and Progressives, **6**:497
and rail system, **7**:23, 24
and railway work hours, **1**:19

and Russia, mission to, **7**:196
Russian Revolution (1917) and,
1:198
segregationism of, **2**:552
and self-determination principle,
2:89
Siberian Expedition and,
7:352–353
and sinking of *Lusitania*, **5**:174
State Department under,
7:528–529
and Transportation Act (1920),
8:185
and University of Virginia, **8**:283
Veracruz incident and, **1**:1; **8**:311
vetoes by, **8**:352
Virginia dynasty and, **8**:349
on Volstead Act, **8**:352
war powers under, **8**:388
and women's suffrage, **8**:*11*
in World War I, **3**:426; **8**:534, 535,
539
  Archangel Campaign, **1**:248
  Armistice of November 1918,
1:265
  policies of, **2**:89
  Yap Mandate and, **8**:575
Wilson Act (1890), **1**:117
Wilson Dam, **8**:87, 88
Wilson v. New, **1**:19
Wilson-Gorman Tariff Act (1894),
8:51, 156
Winchester rifle, **5**:479
Wind power, **3**:*213*, 214–215
Wind River Indian Reservation,
1:235
Wind River Shoshone, **2**:307
Winder, William H., **7**:552
Windmills, **3**:388, 389; **8**:*486*, *486*
Windows on the Millennium (market
study), **5**:248
Windows operating system, **2**:337;
5:360; **7**:442–443
Windsor chair, **3**:496
Wine industry, **3**:479; **7**:567;
8:486–488
Winema (Toby Riddle), **5**:433
Winesburg, Ohio (Anderson), **5**:120;
6:13
Winfrey, Oprah, **1**:52; **2**:*78*
Wingate, George, **5**:556
Wingfield, Walter Clopton, **8**:89

*Winnebago County Department of
Social Services, DeShaney v.*,
2:137; **3**:74
Winnebago/Ho-Chunk, **8**:*488*,
488–489
  in Minnesota, removal from, **5**:399
  Nicolet visiting, **6**:106
Winner-take-all system, **3**:171
Winning of the West (Roosevelt), **8**:288
Winnipesaukee, **6**:56
Winograd, Garry, **1**:301
Winrod, Gerald B., **3**:327
Winship, George, **6**:132
Winslow, Erving, anti-imperialism
of, **1**:202
Winslow, John S., **1**:105
Winsor, Jackie, **1**:307
Winter, Edward, **1**:304
Winter in the Blood (Vizenor), **5**:129
Winter resorts, **7**:122
Winter storms, **1**:485–487, *486*, *487*
Winters, Jeannette L., **5**:243
Winterthur Museum, **8**:489
Winthrop, Fritz-John, **8**:572
Winthrop, John, **1**:508; **2**:17; **5**:91
  and Antinomian controversy, **1**:205
  astronomical observations by,
1:342
  and Cambridge Agreement, **2**:18,
19
  "city on a hill," **1**:169; **2**:184
  and colonial assembly, **2**:280
  and general court, **3**:525
  The History of New England, **8**:576
  and Hutchinson (Anne), **8**:494
  manifest destiny and, **5**:223
  Massachusetts Bay Colony founded
by, **4**:56; **6**:47
  and New Haven Colony, **6**:60
  on philanthropy, **6**:316
  and settlement of New England,
2:288
  on smallpox, **7**:399
  and theocracy, **8**:116
Winthrop v. Lechmere, **1**:225
Wire chairs, **3**:499
Wireless communications, **1**:381
Wireless technology, **8**:67
Wireless Telecommunications
Bureau, **3**:340
Wirsum, Karl, **1**:311
Wirt, William, **1**:203; **3**:116, 466
  and Cherokee Nation cases, **2**:127,
128

Wirt, William, (*continued*)
  party nomination of, **2**:399
  in presidential campaign of 1832, **3**:152
Wirth, Conrad L., **5**:552
Wirth, Louis, **8**:291–292
Wirtz, Willard, **6**:158
Wirz, Henry, **1**:184; **6**:473
Wisconsin, **8**:*489–493, 490*
  admission to Union, **1**:522
  antimonopoly parties in, **1**:204
  capital of, **2**:47
  dairy industry in, **2**:489, 490; **8**:491
  economy of, **8**:491–492
  emblems, nicknames, mottos, and songs of, **7**:*533*
  Fox-Wisconsin Waterway in, **3**:448
  ginseng production in, **3**:578
  Menominee Iron Range, **5**:311–312
  and Michigan, boundary dispute between, **1**:523
  in Midwest, **5**:368–369
  Native Americans in, **8**:488, 489
  Progressive Party of, **6**:499–500
  Sauk Prairie in, **7**:254
  school choice experiment in, **3**:137–138
  sexual orientation in, ban on discrimination based on, **3**:56
  state university of, **8**:279, **284**
  Stockbridge Indian settlement in, **7**:550
  Supreme Court of, *Ableman v. Booth* in, **1**:2
  three-party system in, **8**:243
Wisconsin, Phillips Petroleum Company v., **6**:9
Wisconsin, Yoder v., **2**:170
Wisconsin Idea, **8**:284, **493**
Wisconsin Railroad Commission v. Chicago, Burlington and Quincy Railroad, **2**:311; **8**:493
Wisconsin v. Mitchell, **4**:105
Wisdom of the Body, The (Cannon), **6**:349
Wise, Gene, **1**:170
Wise, Isaac Mayer, **4**:489, *489*, 490; **7**:97
Wise, John, **1**:392; **3**:30; **4**:417; **5**:91
Wise, Kendall D., **1**:463
Wise Men, **8**:493
Wise use movement, **7**:355; **8**:482
Wisenfeld, Weinberger v., **3**:54

Wistar, Caspar, **1**:289
Wister, Owen, *The Virginian*, **5**:129
Witchcraft, **8**:*494*, **494–495**
  in colonial era, **7**:83; **8**:494–495
  in Puritans' world, **2**:162; **8**:494
  Salem witch trials, **7**:228–229, **229–230**; **8**:495, 501
  evidence used in, Mather on, **9**:93–95
Witchita Indians, **8**:218
Witherspoon, John, **3**:220; **6**:450
  as president of Princeton University, **6**:465
Witmer, David J., **6**:286
Wittenmyer, Annie, **8**:496
Wizard of Oz, The (film), **3**:363
W.J. Barta (towboat), **8**:147
Wobblies. *See* Industrial Workers of the World
Wodziwob (prophet), **3**:573; **6**:7
Wofford, Harris, **1**:173
Wolcott, Alexander S., **1**:299
Wolcott, Marion Post, **1**:301
Wolcott, Oliver, **3**:352
Wolf, Fred D., **3**:182
Wolfe, George C., **8**:115
Wolfe, James, **1**:7; **2**:286, 295; **3**:470, 471; **9**:26, 28
  and capture of Quebec, **7**:4
Wolfe, Thomas, **5**:122, 157
  Look Homeward, Angel, **5**:120
Wolff, Alfred, **1**:74
Wolff Packing Company v. Court of Industrial Relations, **8**:495
Wolfle, Dael, **1**:141
Wolves, **8**:495–496, 565
  in Yellowstone National Park, **8**:580
Womack, Robert, **2**:464
Woman in the Nineteenth Century (Fuller), **8**:181
Woman's Bible, The, **1**:448–449
Woman's Christian Temperance Union (WCTU), **3**:73; **8**:81, **496–497**, 514
Woman's Exchange movement, **8**:497
Women
  in 19th century, **3**:312–313, 518–519
  in 20th century, **3**:314, 519–520
  in 1920s, **3**:381
  and abolitionism, **8**:505–506, 512
  as advertisers' targets, **2**:390–391
  affirmative action for, **1**:36–37

African American
  activists, **8**:510, 512
  clubs for, **8**:514
  double jeopardy for, **8**:521
  on mainstream women's right movement, **3**:519, 520
  in military, **8**:505
  National Association of Colored Women and, **5**:527
  National Council of Negro Women and, **5**:534
  as nurses, **6**:146–147
  suffrage organizations of, **8**:514
  in track and field, **8**:155
  in workforce, **8**:507
in American Bar Association, **1**:145
in American Revolution, **7**:146; **8**:505
in Arizona, **1**:258–259
Asian American, **3**:520
assembly line and, **1**:336
in astronomy, **1**:344
birth control for, **1**:466–469
in Chautauqua movement, **2**:113–114
and child care, **2**:138
in churches, **6**:518; **8**:*500*, **500–502**, *501*
  Catholic, **2**:71
  Christian Science, **2**:171
  Church of God in Christ, **2**:172
  Episcopal, **3**:243
  ordination of, in Methodism, **1**:44, 53
citizenship of, **2**:180, 181
  married, **6**:14
in Civil War, **2**:215; **8**:502, 509
in Civilian Conservation Corps, **2**:220
clothing and fashion for, **2**:245–247, *246*
  bicycling and, **1**:451
  bloomers, **1**:488–489, *489*
  hairstyles, **4**:83–84
  women's rights movement and, **8**:513
colleges for, **3**:131–133
in colonial era, **2**:291; **3**:311, 518; **7**:206
common law and, **2**:291
in Congress, **8**:507, 517
and Consumers Leagues, **2**:392
discrimination against (*See* Discrimination, sex)

displaced homemakers, **3**:59
domestic violence and, **3**:72, 73
in economics, **3**:110
education of
  in 19th century, **3**:114–115
  in 20th century, **3**:117, 119
  after American Revolution, **3**:113
  higher, **3**:132; **8**:280–281, 282
    at Air Force Academy, **1**:78
    associations for, **1**:143
    for medicine, **4**:482
    for sciences, **7**:273
in educational reform, **3**:116
in elected office, in Kansas, **4**:510
employment discrimination
    against, pregnancy and, **3**:525;
    6:449
in engineering, **3**:217
equal pay for, legislation requiring,
  3:245
equal rights for, legislation requiring, **3**:247–248
equality of, original documents on,
  9:325–337
exclusionary clubs for, **2**:251
in factories, **2**:223; **8**:505
and farmers' alliances, **3**:323–324;
  6:416
  original document on, **9**:260–261
as farmhands, **3**:326
on frontier, firsthand accounts of,
  9:244–248, 255–257
and gambling, **3**:507
glass ceiling and, **4**:2–3
in gold mining towns, **9**:240–242
during Great Depression, **4**:47
hairstyles of, **4**:83–84
hate crimes against, **4**:104
Hispanic American, **3**:520; **5**:531
human rights for, **4**:193
  original documents on,
    9:327–329
in Illinois, **4**:217
in Iowa, **4**:415
Irish American, **4**:223, 425
Jewish, **5**:534
as jurors, **8**:60
in Kansas, **4**:510
in Kentucky, **4**:521
in Korean War, **8**:503–504
labor by, liberty of contract issues,
  5:394–395, **472–473**
as law students, **5**:58
as lawyers, **5**:58

and liberated consumerism, **2**:391
and lynching prevention,
  1:339–340
magazines for, **5:197–199**
married, citizenship of, **8:497–498**
maternal and child health care,
  5:273–275
medical research on, **7**:430
in medicine, **8**:511
in military service, **8:502–505**,
  503, *504*
  Marine Corps, **5**:243
  at Naval Academy, **6**:19
  sexual harassment of, Tailhook
    incident, **8:43–44**
  uniforms for, **8**:257, 258, *502*
minimum-wage legislation for,
  8:445
in mining towns, **4**:13–14
National Women's Political Caucus and, **5**:566
Native American, **3**:519
  farming by, **1**:68–69
  in matrilineal societies,
    4:290–291
  Ute, **8**:299
9 to 5, National Association of
  Working Women for,
  6:109–110
Nobel Prize winners, **1**:461
nonworking (housewives), *The*
  Feminine Mystique on, **3**:353
as nurses, **6**:146, 147
and peace movements, **6**:267;
  8:499–500
in Persian Gulf War, **8**:504
as pharmacists, **6**:311
as pioneers, firsthand accounts by,
  9:229–233, 238–239
pirates, **1**:550
as police officers, **6**:385
in politics, **3**:198
on pornography, **6**:419
poverty among, **2**:225
at Princeton University, **6**:465
in prison, **6**:478
property rights of, **3**:519
as prophets, **6**:7
in prostitution, **6**:513–514
in publishing, **6**:90, 95, 97
Puerto Rican, **5**:531; **6**:542, 543
in Pure Food and Drug Move-
  ment, **6**:554
Quaker, **7**:3

and recreation, **7**:64
reformatories for, **7**:75
republicanism of, **7**:116
rights of, and liberalism, **5**:92
in rodeos, **7**:191
rural, **7**:206, 207, 209
in Sanitary Commission, **7:244**
sculptors, **1**:307–308
segregation of, **7**:303
in settlement house movement,
  7:318
slave, **7**:207–208
smoking, **8**:135, 136, 137
soap operas and, **7**:409
in sociology, **7**:435
of South, **7**:464
in sports, **7**:509, *510*, 511–512
  basketball, **1**:425–426
  bicycling, **1**:451, *451*
  college, **2**:276–277, *277*
  golf, **4**:19
  swimming, **8**:37
  tennis, **8**:90
  track and field, **8**:155
in State Department, **7**:530–531
suffrage for, **3**:145, 147, 519;
  7:106; **8:9–12**, *10*, 356
  in Kansas, **4**:509–510
  National Woman's Party and,
    5:565–566
  in New Jersey, **3**:145; **7**:105
  newspapers and, **6**:97
  Nineteenth Amendment on,
    2:181
  organizations on, **8**:11–12
  original documents on,
    9:332–337
  Supreme Court on, **5**:401–402;
    8:11
  Woman's Christian Temperance
    Union and, **8**:497
  women activists and, **7**:106;
    8:513–514
  in Wyoming, **8**:564
surrogate motherhood by, **8:29–30**
as teachers, **2**:495–496; **3**:112, 114,
  131
in temperance movements, **1**:117;
  8:80, 81, 512
United Daughters of the Confederacy (UDC), **8:265–266**
in Utopian communities, **8**:301
veterinarians, **8**:320
in Victorian era, **3**:518–519; **8**:326

Women, (*continued*)
  in Vietnam War, **8:**504
  violence against (*See also* Domestic violence)
    in 19th century, **3:**312–313
    pornography and, **6:**419
  in Virginia, **8:**345, 346
  volunteerism among, **8:**353
  voting by, **8:**356–357
  wages and hours of labor, regulation of, **1:**21; **5:**5; **7:**303; **8:**360
    Brandeis Brief on, **9:**357–360
  in War of 1812, **8:***383*
  in workforce, **2:**256; **3:**55, 520; **5:**9; **8:**505, **505–508,** 507
    business machines and, **1:**588
    exploitation of, **2:**223–224
    organization for, **5:**538
    during World War II, firsthand account of, **9:**397–398
  in World War I, **8:**502, 536–537
    effect of war on, **9:**363–364
  in World War II, **8:***257,* 502–503
    military service by, **9:**398–401
    in workforce, **9:**397–398
Women, President's Commission on the Status of, **8:498–499,** 516
Women Hurt in Systems of Prostitution Engaged in Revolt (WHISPER), **6:**514
Women in Industry (Brandeis), excerpt of, **9:**357–360
Women Marine Corps Reserve, **5:**243
Women of Brewster Place, The (Naylor), **5:**126
Women's Army Corps (WAC), **9:**398–401
Women's Bill of Rights (1967), **3:**118
Women's Bureau, **3:**526; **8:508**
  of Department of Labor, **5:**11
Women's Central Association for Relief (WCAR), **7:**244
Women's Christian Temperance Union, **1:**117
  and Pure Food and Drug Movement, **6:**554
Women's clubs, **3:**456, 526; **8:508–510**
  black, **8:**514
Women's Educational Equity Act (1974), **8:**510

Women's Equity Action League (WEAL), **8:510**
Women's health, **8:511–512**
  childbirth and reproduction, **2:142–144**
  clinical research on, **7:**430
  eating disorders, **3:104**
  legislation on, **7:**342
  maternal and child health care, **5:273–275**
  toxic shock syndrome, **8:**150–151
Women's health movement, **1:**468
  Dalkon Shield protests and, **2:**494
Women's history, **4:**141
Women's International League for Peace and Freedom (WILPF), **8:**499
Women's Journal (newspaper), **6:**97
Women's Organization for National Prohibition Reform, **6:**501
Women's Professional Football League (WPFL), **3:**412
Women's rights movement, **8:**507, **512–519**
  in 19th century, **3:**519; **8:512–515**
  in 20th century, **3:**519–520; **5:**548–549, 565–566; **8:***513,* **515–519**
  and abortion, **1:**6; **8:**511, *518*
  African American women on, **3:**519, 520
  and anti-abortion movement, **1:**4
  and Convention on the Elimination of All Forms of Discrimination Against Women, **2:**398–399
  and Declaration of Sentiments, **2:524–525**
  and divorce law, **3:**64
  on domestic violence, **3:**73
  Equal Credit Opportunity Act (1974), **5:**252
  Equal Rights Amendment (ERA), **5:**456
  as human rights movement, **4:**193
  Johns Hopkins University in, **4:**482
  and labor conditions, **5:**297–298
  magazines, **5:**192, 194, *469,* 469–470
  marriage and, **5:**250
  Married Women's Property Act, New York State, **5:**251–252
  Metropolitan Museum of Art and, **5:**337

Mexican American Women's National Association, **5:**343
Ms. magazine, **5:***469,* **469–470**
  National Organization for Women and, **5:**548–549
  National Woman's Party and, **5:**565–566
  National Women's Political Caucus and, **5:**566
  neoconservatives on, **6:**32
  in New York (state), **6:**88
  and newspapers, **6:**97
  original documents from, **9:**325–337
  origins of, **8:**506
  in Pennsylvania, **6:**278
  and Pregnancy Discrimination Act (1978), **3:**525; **6:449**
  pro-choice movement, **6:489**
  against prostitution, **6:**513
  reproductive rights, **5:**274
  Seneca Falls Convention in, **7:310–311;** **9:**332–334
  See also Suffrage, for women
Women's studies, **3:**119; **8:519–521**
  funding for, **2:**56
Women's Trade Union League (WTUL), **8:521–522**
Wonderful Wizard of Oz, The (Baum), **5:**127
Wonders of the Invisible World, The (Mather), **5:**118
Wong, Anna May, **3:**362, 364
Wong Kim Ark, United States v., **2:**155; **8:276**
Wong Wing v. United States, **1:**125
Wood, Abraham, **8:**85, 447
Wood, Donna, **1:**131
Wood, Eric Fisher, **1:**162
Wood, Fernando, **2:**411, 551; **6:**79; **8:**46
Wood, Grant, **1:**298; **3:**538; **6:**471; **7:**297, 298
Wood, James, **1:**316
Wood, Jethro, **1:**58
Wood, Leonard, **3:**161
Wood, Peter, **1:**392
Wood, Ruby Ross, **1:**293
Wood block printing, in mapmaking, **5:**232
Wood engraving, **8:522–523**
Wood paving, **6:**260
Wood turpentine, **6:**20
Wood v. Broom, **1:**227

Woodard, Lynette, **1**:425
Woodbury, Levi, **4**:487
Woodcock, Leonard, **8**:262
Wooden, John, **1**:425
Wooden blocks, printing of books
    from, **6**:466
Woodhull, Victoria, **8**:506
Woodruff, Ernest, **2**:260
Woodruff, Robert W., **2**:260;
    7:438–439
Woodruff, Wilford, **5**:54; **8**:297
Woods, Dave, **1**:312
Woods, Tiger, **4**:20
Woods, William B., **8**:274
Woods Hole (Massachusetts), **5**:240,
    241
Woods Hole Oceanographic Institu-
    tion (WHOI), **6**:162
Woodson, Carter G., **5**:199
Woodstock, **7**:186; **8**:*523*, **523–524**
Woodward, August, **3**:19
Woodward, Dartmouth College v. See
    Dartmouth College Case
Woodward, Robert S., **3**:552
Woodward, Samuel, **1**:119
Woodward, William H., **2**:503
    See also Dartmouth College Case
Woodworth-Etter, Mary, **8**:302
Wool growing and manufacture,
    7:339; **8**:**524–526**, *525*
    in colonial era, **8**:108
    Harrisburg Convention on, **4**:**100**
    tariffs and, **8**:50
Woollcott, Alexander, **1**:123
Woolman, John, **6**:227; **7**:2
Woolsey, John M., **6**:419
Woolsey, R. James, **1**:174
Woolsey, Theodore S., **2**:271–272
Woolworth, Frank Winfield, **2**:100;
    3:9–10, 26; **7**:125
Woolworth Building, **6**:80
Woolworth Building (Marin), **6**:471
Worcester, Joseph, **3**:23
Worcester, Samuel Austin, **2**:128;
    6:183
Worcester v. Georgia, **2**:128
Word processors, **6**:170
Worden, John, **5**:443
WordStar, **7**:442
Work, **8**:**526–529**
    alien right to, **1**:125
    changing character of, **5**:3–4
      in late 20th century, **5**:9
      technology and, **5**:4

cooperative, **1**:436–437
    through Job Corps, **4**:480–481
    motivational content of, **4**:334
    and recreation, separation of, **7**:64
Work, Hubert, **7**:*55*, 56
Work, Jim, **1**:311
Work ethic
    geographic variation in, **8**:528
    Protestant, **8**:526–529
    Puritan, **7**:63–64
Work Incentives Improvement Act
    (1999), **5**:15
Work systems, high-performance,
    4:337–338
Workday
    in early 19th century, **7**:64
    minimum hours legislation, **3**:53–54
    reduction of, **7**:65
Workers, consumerism and entrap-
    ment of, **2**:388
Workers' compensation, **3**:199–200;
    5:14; **8**:**529–530**
    insurance, **4**:369–370
    introduction of, **5**:5
Workers Party of America, **2**:326
Working class
    families, **3**:313
    identification with, **2**:225
    recreation among, **7**:64
    vs. slaves, **2**:224
Working Men's movement, **5**:142
Working People's Nonpartisan
    Political League, **3**:321
Workingmen's Benevolent Associa-
    tion, **2**:254
Workingmen's Party, **8**:**530**
    and anti-Chinese movement, **2**:154
    Kearney (Denis) and, **2**:10
Workmen's Compensation Act
    (1908), **5**:14
Works Progress Administration
    (WPA), **2**:371; **6**:43; **8**:441,
    530–531, 586
    Federal Art Project, **5**:483
    function of, **3**:396
    and gypsies, **4**:78–79
    National Research Project of,
      6:492
    and paving roads, **6**:*260*
    political activities by, **4**:103–104
    and post offices, **6**:428
    and printmaking, **6**:471
    regionalist painting and, **1**:298
    supporting artists, **5**:536

World Bank, **1**:536; **8**:166, 198, 269,
    531–532
    and foreign aid, **3**:415
    and Third World, **8**:271
World Community of Islam in the
    West (WCIW), **5**:521
World Council of Churches, **5**:532
World Court. *See* International
    Court of Justice
World Cup, **7**:410–411
World Economic Conference, **8**:**532**
World Federation of Trade Unions,
    1:151
World Health Organization (WHO)
    poliomyelitis eradication by, **6**:389
    smallpox eradication by, **7**:400
    on tuberculosis, **8**:237
World Hockey Association (WHA),
    4:144
World League of American Football,
    3:411
World Trade Center, **6**:80–81, 421;
    8:**532–533**, *533*
    1993 bombing of, **3**:41; **6**:109;
      8:96, 339, 532, **533–534**
    2001 attack on, **6**:81, 89, 108, 421;
      8:339, 533 (*See also* 9/11
      attack)
World Trade Organization (WTO),
    3:309; **7**:55; **8**:169
    creation of, **8**:52
    and liberalization of trade, **3**:97
    objectives of, **8**:52
    protests against, **2**:226; **7**:165
World War I, **8**:**534–539**
    Addams (Jane) on, **9**:365–367
    advertising during, **1**:33
    aerial bombing in, **1**:495
    African Americans during, **8**:537,
      537
      migration of, **5**:369
      military service by, **5**:381, *381*
    aircraft armament in, **1**:88
    aircraft industry in, **1**:92
    Aisne-Marne Operation in, **1**:99
    American battlefields in, **8**:*534*,
      536
    American Expeditionary Forces in,
      1:149; **8**:535
    Archangel Campaign in,
      1:247–248
    Armistice of November 1918 in,
      1:265
    armored ships in, **1**:266

World War I, (*continued*)

armored vehicles in, **1:**266–267

banking during, **1:**397–398

Battle of Belleau Wood in, **1:441**

Battle of Jutland in, **1:**266

biological weapons used in, **1:**465

blockades in, **1:**487

British blockade in, **2:**396

censorship during, **2:**83, 84

Champagne-Marne operation in, **2:103; 5:**338

Château-Thierry Bridge defense in, **1:**441; **2:112**

chemical warfare in, **2:**117, *117*

China after, **2:**151

Choctaw encoding messages during, **6:**17

code breaking in, **2:**467

commerce with Latin America during, **5:**44, 47

confiscation of property during, **2:**347

conscientious objectors during, **2:**361

convoy systems during, **2:**403

and copper industry, **2:**410

cost of, **3:**282; **8:**377

cost of living during, **2:**423

debts, **8:542–543**

and Dawes Plan, **3:**562

and German-American Debt Agreement, **3:**560, 562

and Lausanne Agreement, **5:**55

Young Plan and, **3:**562; **8:585**

demobilization after, **2:**546

desertion in, **3:**17

and domestic trade, **8:**159, 161

drafted men in, **2:**364

economic mobilization for, **3:**72, 194–195; **8:**535–536, **539–540**

and Fuel Administration, **3:**480

enemy aliens during, **3:**207–208, 254; **8:**538

espionage in, **8:**537

explosives used in, **3:**302

FBI activities during, **3:**337

Federal Reserve System during, **3:**344–345

and film industry, **3:**362

and foreign investment in U.S., **3:**421

and foreign service, **3:**428

and foreign trade, **8:**165

gas attack in, **8:***535*

and geography, **3:**543

and German Americans, **3:**559, 562; **6:**5; **8:**538

Girl Scouts volunteering during, **4:**1

and gold standard, **4:**15

Hispanic Americans in, **5:**383

immigration during, **4:**226

inflation in, **4:**352

internment in, **4:**399

isolationism in, **4:**439

Lafayette Escadrille in, **5:**20

liberty loans in, **5:**96; **7:**258

and Lost Generation, **5:**157

marine insurance in, **4:**368

merchant marine and, **5:**319

Meuse-Argonne Offensive in, **1:**149; **5:**338–339; **8:**538

and Lost Battalion, **5:**155

military uniforms in, **8:**258

military-industrial complex and, **5:**377

mobilization for, **5:**429–430

American Expeditionary Forces in, **1:**149; **8:**535

economic, **5:**84

liberty loans in, **5:**96

Victory Loan in, **8:326–327**

Mormon church in, **5:**54

multilateral treaties after, **8:**201, 205

munitions, **5:**186, 479, 480, 481–482

Murmansk, port of (Russia), **5:**483

National Army in, **8:**540–541

National Guard in, **8:**540–541

National War Labor Board in, **5:564; 8:**536

Native Americans in, **4:**328

and nativism, **6:**4–5

neutrality of U.S. in first years of, **6:**35

newspapers on, **6:**98

organized labor in, **5:**7

original documents on, **9:**363–373

"Over There" in, lyrics of, **9:**364–365

paratroops in, **6:**246

and preparedness, **6:**449–450

press associations during, **6:**459

prices during, **6:**461

prisoners of war in, **6:**472, 473

propaganda in, **6:**503, 522–523; **8:**535

public information during, **2:**313

race riots during, **8:**537

railroads in, **7:**35; **8:**536

Red Cross in, **7:**68

research laboratories in, **5:**18

road building during, **7:**180

Saint-Mihiel Campaigns in, **7:227–228**

Sedition Act in, **7:**301

sexuality in, **7:**330

shipbuilding in, **8:**536

Somme Offensive in, **7:447–448**

spies in, **7:**502; **8:**538

State Department in, **7:**528–529

strategic air power in, **1:**81

submarines in, **2:**3; **7:**562–563; **8:**33, 590

symphony orchestras in, **8:**39

and taxation, **8:**57

Thrift Stamps financing, **8:123**

torpedos used in, **8:**144

trade unions in, **1:**155; **8:**536

trading with enemy in, **8:**173

training camps, **8:**540–541

trench warfare in, **8:***538*

and trucking industry, **8:**231

U.S. entry in, **2:**89; **8:**535, 590–591

U.S. Marine Corps in, **5:**242

U.S. Navy in, **6:**24, 25–26; **8:**540

and North Sea mine barrage, **6:134**

U.S. participation in, **2:**535

U.S. relief in, **8:541–542**

Belgian, **1:**439

and U.S. military forces, expansion of, **2:**530–531

Versailles Treaty after, **3:**451, 562; **8:315–316**

veterans of, Bonus Army of, **1:498,** 499

"victory garden" campaigns during, **3:**510

War Finance Corporation in, **8:379**

War Industries Board in, **8:380**

and wheat production, **3:**390

women in, **8:**502, 536–537

effect of war on, **9:**363–364

Zimmermann telegram and, **3:**562; **8:**534–535

World War II, **8:543–552**

Aachen (Germany) in, **1:**1

adolescence during, **1:**25

in Africa, **8:**549

African Americans in, **1:**49, 51; **8:**545
  military service by, **5:**381–382, 382
and agriculture, **8:**162
air war, **1:**495
  against Germany, **8:**545–546, 552, **552–553,** 553
    gliders in, **4:**5
    Ploesti oil fields, air raids on, **6:**371
  against Japan, **1:**495; **3:**302; **8:**554, **554–555,** 555
    atomic bombings, **6:**143; **8:**551, 555
    Battle of the Philippine Sea, **6:**320–321; **8:**557
    Flying the Hump and, **3:**392
    Flying Tigers in, **3:**392–393
    Peleliu, **6:**274
    Tarawa, **8:**49
    Tinian, **8:**130
aircraft carriers in, **1:**89–91
aircraft industry in, **1:**93–94
aircraft used in, **1:**493, 494
and American occupation of Germany, **3:**561
anti-Semitism in, **1:**207
antiwar movements in, **1:**216
Anzio (Italy) in, **1:217–218**
armored vehicles in, **1:**267, 267
arms race in, **1:**270–271
assembly lines and, **1:**335–336
Atlantic Charter in, **1:353**
atomic bomb in, development of, **6:**143, 336, 342; **8:**414–415
  (See also Manhattan Project)
Australia in, **1:**361
banking during, **1:**398
Bastogne defense in, **1:**426–427
Bataan-Corregidor Campaign in, **1:**427; **8:**547
Battle of Atlantic in, **1:**352–353
Battle of Bismarck Sea in, **1:**470
Battle of Coral Sea in, **2:412–413**
Battle of Java Sea in, **4:465–466**
Battle of Kasserine Pass in, **4:513–514; 6:**124
Battle of Leyte Gulf in, **6:**26; **8:**557
Battle of Midway in, **5:**367–368, 368
Battle of the Bulge in, **1:**426, 565, **565–566; 5:**217; **8:**550–551, 551

Malmédy Massacre in, **5:217**
Bismarck Archipelago Campaign in, **1:470**
bombers in, **1:**86, 86
Bougainville landing in, **1:520–521,** 521
casualties in, **8:**551
censorship during, **2:**83, 84
Cherbourg capture in, **2:124**
China during, **2:**152
Chinese Americans in, **2:**155
code breaking in, **2:**334, 467
commerce with Latin America during, **5:**44, 47
confiscation of property during, **2:**347
conscientious objectors during, **2:**361
conscription and recruitment in, **8:**543
and consumerism, **2:**390–391
convoy systems during, **2:**403, 403
and copper industry, **2:**410
cost of, **3:**282; **8:**377
cost of living during, **2:**423
D Day, **6:**118–120, 119; **8:**549
  casualties on, **6:**120
  Navy in, **6:**26
  use of gliders on, **4:**5
defoliation used in, **2:**537
demobilization after, **2:**546
desertion in, **3:**17
dirigibles in, **3:**31
and domestic trade, **8:**159, 162–163
drafted men in, **2:**364
economic mobilization for, **8:**546
Elbe River dividing line in, **3:144**
enemy aliens during, **3:**208
engineering projects of, Burma Road and Ledo Road, **1:576–577**
European Theater, **8:**544, 549–551
Excess Profits Tax in, **3:**273
and executive agreements, **8:**203
and families, effect on, **3:**314; **9:**403–404
FBI activities during, **3:**338
Federal Reserve System during, **3:**345–346
Federal Trade Commission during, **3:**348
and film industry, **3:**363
foreign aid after, **3:**415–416

foreign aid during, **6:**36
and foreign investment in U.S., **3:**422
foreign policy during, **3:**426
and foreign service, **3:**429
and foreign trade, **8:**166
forestry during, **3:**436
fortifications during, **3:**439
gays and lesbians in, **3:**513
General Accounting Office during, **3:**523
and German Americans, **3:**560
German Enigma code in, breaking, **2:**334, 467
and "GI generation," **3:**528
Girl Scouts volunteering during, **4:**1
and gold standard, **4:**16
Gothic Line in, **4:**23
and Guam, **4:**69
guerrilla warfare in, **4:**70
Gustav Line in, **4:**78
Hispanic Americans in, **5:**383, 383–384
Iceland in, **4:**211
immigration during, **4:**226–227
imperialism in, **4:**244–245
inflation in, **4:**352
intelligence activities in, **6:**167
internment in, **4:**399–400
  of Japanese Americans, **4:459–462,** 463–465; **5:**168
    firsthand account of, **9:**405–406
    in Washington (state), **8:**415
isolationism in, **4:**440
Italian Americans in, **4:**445
  relocation of, **7:**99
Iwo Jima in, **4:450–451**
"Kilroy Was Here" graffiti in, **4:526**
laws of war in, **8:**371–372
Lend-Lease in, **5:**81–82
Malmédy Massacre in, **5:217**
Manhattan Project in, **5:221–222**
marine insurance in, **4:**368
Marshall Islands in, **5:**252
Marshall Plan, **5:**252
and medical practice, impact on, **5:**304
medical research in, army, **5:**295
merchant marine during, **5:**320
merchantmen, armed, **5:**322–323
Merrill's Marauders (GALAHAD), **5:324**

World War II, (*continued*)

meteorology, **5**:332

military production by GM during, **3**:526–527

military uniforms in, **8**:258

military-industrial complex and, **5**:377

missile development, **5**:407

mobilization for, **5**:430

Monte Cassino, **5:451–452**

Mormon church in, **5**:54

multilateral treaties after, **8**:202, 205

munitions, **5**:479, 480, 482

"Murmansk run," **5**:483

National Guard in, **8**:545

National War Labor Board in, **5:564–565**

Native Americans in, **4**:328–329

Navajo Code Talkers, **6**:16, **17–18**, *18*, 19, 69

naval aircraft in, **1**:89–90

neutrality of U.S. in first years of, **6**:36

and New Orleans, **6**:74

New York Times on, **6**:90

New Zealand in, **1**:361

newspapers on, **6**:90, 99

Normandy Invasion, **6:118–121**, *119–121*; **8**:549, *550*

North African Campaign in, **1**:233; **6**:*123*, **123–124**

nuclear weapons used in, **3**:302

occupation of Berlin in, **1**:443

oceanography in, **6**:160, 162

Okinawa in, **6:182–183**; **8**:547, 556

Operation Dixie in, **6:199**

Operation Market Garden in, **1**:1

Operation Torch in, **1**:233

organized labor in, **5**:8

original documents on, **9**:393–409

Pacific Theater in, **2**:58; **8**:546–548, *547, 548*, 556

and paper industry, **6**:245

paratroops in, **6**:246

and Paris conferences, **6**:247

Pearl Harbor attack, **6**:*272*, 272–273; **8**:543–545, 555–556

and petrochemical industry, **6**:298

and philanthropy, **6**:318

and political exiles, **6**:397

Potsdam Conference (1945) and, **3**:426; **6:434–435**, *435*

price and wage controls during, **6**:165, 460

prices during, **6**:461

and prisoner population in, **6**:477

prisoners of war in, **6**:472, 473, 474; **8**:*546*

propaganda in, **6**:503, 523

Rabaul Campaign in, **7:6–7**

radar in, **7**:14

radio reports during, **7**:20

railroads during, **7**:35

rationing in, **3**:401–402; **6**:165

Red Cross in, **7**:69

refugees, **7**:*79*, 79–80

U.S. response to, **1**:444–445

research laboratories in, **5**:18–19

road-building during, **7**:180–181

Saint-Lô in, **7:227**

Saipan in, **7:228**

Salerno in, **7:230**

savings bonds in, **7**:258, *258*

science education in, **7**:272

science journalism in, **7**:275

sexuality in, **7**:330–331

shipbuilding in, **5**:210; **7**:347; **8**:557

Sicilian Campaign in, **7:353–354**

Soviet Union in, **2**:89, 267; **3**:144; **7**:211

Spain in, **7**:485

spies in, **7**:502

steel industry in, **4**:428–429

strategic air power in, **1**:81

strategy and logistics in, **5**:145

submarines in, **7**:563; **8**:556–557

summit conferences in, **8**:15

and tariffs, **8**:157

and taxation, **8**:58

Teheran Conference and, **8**:64

torpedoes used in, **8**:145

trade unions in, **1**:237; **7**:558; **8**:171, 261, 277

trading with enemy in, **8**:173

treason trials in, **8**:194–195

and trucking industry, **8**:231

Truman's "Total Victory" speech in, text of, **9**:401–402

unconditional surrender policy in, **2**:65; **8**:249

unemployment rate during, **8**:252

U.S. Air Force in, **8**:545

U.S. Army in, **1**:277

U.S. entry into, **8**:545–546

Roosevelt's speech on, **9**:396–397

U.S. Marine Corps in, **5**:242, *243*

U.S. Navy in, **5**:146; **6**:24, 26; **8:555–558**

Battle of Leyte Gulf, **5**:89; **6**:26; **8**:557

Battle of the Philippine Sea, **6:320–321**; **8**:557

capturing Gilbert Islands, **3**:576; **6**:26

capturing Marshall Islands, **3**:576; **6**:26

Guadalcanal Campaign, **4:68**; **6**:26; **8**:556

gunboats, **4**:77

at Lingayen Gulf, **5**:114–115

Pearl Harbor, **6**:*272*, 272–273; **8**:543–545, 555–556

Task Force 58, **8**:53

U.S. participation in, **2**:531, 535

veterans of

compensation for, **1**:499

organizations for, **8**:318

"victory garden" campaigns during, **3**:510

Wake Atoll in, **8:365–366**

war crimes trials after, **8**:378

women in, **8**:*257*, 502–503

military service by, **9**:398–401

in workforce, firsthand account of, **9**:397–398

World Wide Web

development of, **7**:280

See also Internet

World Wildlife Fund, **3**:206

WorldCom, Incorporated, **2**:419

World's Columbian Exposition (1893), **1**:179, 251; **2**:178; **3**:174; **5**:39; **8**:290, 297, 558–559

buildings housing, **2**:132, 187

Ferris Wheel at, **3**:355; **8**:*407*, 558

Fine Arts Building at, **2**:272, *272*

Harper's Weekly coverage of, **2**:*271*

household appliances at, **3**:181

model day nursery at, **2**:138

protests against, **8**:558

Wild West Show at, **8**:476

World's fairs, **2**:177–178; **8:558–560**

Centennial Exhibition, **2**:87–88, *88*

Crystal Palace Exhibition, **2:468**

elevator demonstration at, **3**:186

furniture at, **3**:498

of Great Depression, **8:**559, 559–560
Louisiana Purchase Exposition, **5:**163–164
museums and, **5:**487
World's Industrial and Cotton Centennial Exposition, **8:**558
Wormley Conference, **8:560**
Worth, Charles, **2:**245
Worth, Jonathan, **6:**129
Worth, William J., **2:**105; **8:**402
Worthington, Thomas, **6:**172
Wouk, Herman, *The Caine Mutiny*, **5:**121
Wounded Knee, AIM occupation of (1973), **1:**161; **7:**70, 71, 165; **8:560–561,** 561
 Ghost Dance movement and, **5:**507
Wounded Knee Massacre (1890), **8:**562, **562–563**
 Ghost Dance and, **3:**573; **8:**562
 Sioux after, **7:**368, 368
Wovoka (Paiute prophet), **3:**573; **4:**293–294; **6:**7, 7, 231
 letter from, **9:**259–260
Wozniak, Stephen G., **2:**336
WPA. *See* Works Progress Administration
WPFL. *See* Women's Professional Football League
WRA. *See* War Relocation Authority
Wren, Christopher, **1:**251; **2:**185
 and College of William and Mary, **8:**483
Wright, Alice Morgan, **1:**309
Wright, Allen, **6:**184
Wright, Benjamin, **2:**32
Wright, Carroll D., **6:**492
Wright, Chauncey, **6:**424
Wright, Fanny, **8:**530
Wright, Fielding L., **3:**164
Wright, Frances (Fanny), **1:**136
Wright, Francis, **8:**300
Wright, Frank Lloyd, **4:**72
 architecture of, **1:**252, 320
 furniture of, **3:**498
 Guggenheim Museum designed by, **4:**71
 interior design of, **1:**293
 stained glass of, **1:**314, 320
 and suburban housing, **4:**181
Wright, Gavin, **2:**42, 43
Wright, George, **5:**552
Wright, George E., **8:**403

Wright, Hendrick B., **2:**411; **6:**553
Wright, Henry, **2:**186
Wright, John Lloyd, **8:**153
 Lincoln Logs invented by, **5:**109
Wright, Lucy, **7:**334
Wright, Orville, **1:**92; **3:**35; **6:**174
Wright, Patience, **1:**308; **8:**431
Wright, Richard, **3:**280; **6:**12
 Black Boy: A Recollection of Childhood and Youth, **5:**125
 Eight Men, **5:**125
 Native Son, **5:**121, 125
 Uncle Tom's Children, **5:**125
Wright, Russell, **1:**304
Wright, Sewall, **3:**269
Wright, Silas, **1:**114
Wright, Wilbur, **1:**92; **6:**174
Wrigley, William, Jr., **1:**258
Wriston, Henry Merritt, **1:**548
Wriston Report (1954), **3:**429
Writs of Assistance, **8:563**
 sample text of, **9:**116–117
Writs of mandamus, Judiciary Act of 1789, **5:**235
Wrought iron, **5:**329, 330
WSB. *See* Wage Stabilization Board
WTO. *See* World Trade Organization
WTUL. *See* Women's Trade Union League
Wuertzbach, Frederick, **6:**245
Wundt, Wilhelm, **6:**524
Wurf, Jerry, **1:**154
Wyandot, **4:196–197**
Wyandotte Constitution, **8:563**
Wyatt, Addie, **2:**256
Wyatt, Francis, **6:**432
Wycliffe, John, **6:**515
Wyeth, Andrew, **1:**298
Wyllis, John, **8:**399
Wyman, Grace L., **6:**331
Wyneken, Friedrich, **7:**89
Wynkoop, Edward, **7:**243
Wynn, Steve, **5:**42
Wyoming, **8:563–566**
 African Americans in, **8:**566
 agriculture in, **8:**565
 Big Horn Mountains in, **1:**452, **452–453**
 coal mining in, **8:**564, 565
 economy of, **8:**564–565
 emblems, nicknames, mottos, and songs of, **7:**533
 environmental movement in, **8:**565

 fur trade in, **8:**563
 Independence Rock in, **4:**258
 Native Americans in, **8:**563, 564, 566
 oil in, **8:**564
 South Pass in, **7:462**
 tourism in, **8:**565
 transportation in, **8:**564
 women's suffrage in, **2:**547; **3:**147; **8:**564
Wyoming (Pennsylvania) Massacre, **8:566–567**
Wyoming Valley (Pennsylvania), settlement of, **8:**567
Wytfliet, Cornelius van, **9:**8, 8–10
Wythe, George, **5:**56

X

"X" article, **8:569**
X-1 plane, **8:**569, **569–570**
Xenotransplantation, **3:**531, 532; **8:**182
Xerox Corporation
 copiers by, **1:**588; **6:**169
 and graphic user interface (GUI) concept, **2:**337
 industrial research by, **4:**340
X-ray diffraction, **3:**533
X-ray studies
 in astronomy, **1:**345
 in physics, **6:**345
 in physiology, **6:**349
X-rays, for dental use, **3:**4
Xylography (wood block printing), **6:**466
 in mapmaking, **5:**232
XYZ affair, **2:**398; **3:**425, 450; **8:570**

Y

Yablonski, Joseph, **8:**268
Yacht racing, **7:223–224**
Yaddo, **8:570–571**
Yakama, **8:571**
Yakima Indian Wars, **8:**402–403, **571–572**
Yale, Elihu, **2:**357; **8:**572
Yale Divinity School, **7:**97
Yale University, **8:572–573**
 athletic program at, **2:**276

Yale University, (*continued*)
  engineering program at, **3:**216
  establishment of, **2:**357; **3:**111, 127
  Hartford Wits at, **4:101–102**
  lottery use by, **5:**156
  Sheffield Scientific School at, **7:340**
Yalta Conference (1945), **3:**426;
      7:211; **8:**15, 272, **573–574**, *574*
  and U.S.-Soviet relations, **2:**267
Yamamoto, Isoroku, **5:**367–368;
      6:272
Yamasaki, Minuro, **1:**253
  World Trade Center designed by,
      8:532
Yamasee War (1715), **8:**225
Yamashita, Tomoyuki, **5:**115
Yamataya v. Fisher, **1:**125
Yanagi, Soetsu, **1:**305
Yancey, William L., **1:**102, 106
Yandell, Enid, **1:**308
Yankee, **6:**46; **8:**575
Yankee (privateer brig), **8:574–575**
"Yankee Doodle," **8:575**
Yap Mandate, **8:575**
Yaqui, **8:**228–229
Yard, Robert Sterling, **2:**372; **5:**550
Yardley, Herbert O., **2:**467
Yasuhiro, Nakasone, **4:**459
Yasutani Rōshi, Hakuum, **1:**552
Yates, Robert, at Constitutional
      Convention, **2:**379
Yavapais, **8:**228
Yazoo fraud, **1:**489; **3:**554; **5:**26, 36;
      8:575–576
Ybor City (Florida), **8:**47
Yeager, Chuck, **8:***569*, 569–570
Yeardley, Sir George, **1:**333; **2:**280
Yellow fever, **3:**37, 235–236;
      8:576–577
  in biological warfare, **2:**118
  in Florida, **3:**387
  research on, **5:**294
  sanitary reform and, **7:**245
Yellow journalism, **8:577**
Yellow Kid, The (comic), **2:**308; **6:**97,
      98; **8:**577
"Yellow Peril," **8:***577*, **577–578**
Yellow-dog contract, **5:**14;
      8:578–579
Yellowstone National Park, **5:**550;
      8:146, 565, *579*, **579–580**
  establishment of, **2:**366; **8:**480
  survey of, **3:**300
  as wildlife refuge, **3:**205

Yellowstone River expeditions,
      3:318; **8:**580
Yeltsin, Boris, at summit confer-
      ences, **8:**16
Yemen, *Cole* bombing in, **2:270–271**
Yerkes, Charles, **1:**344
Yes I Can (Davis), **5:**126
Yick Wo v. Hopkins, **1:**125, 324; **2:**155
Ylvisaker, Paul, **6:**318
YMCA. *See* Young Men's Christian
      Association
YMHA. *See* Young Men's Hebrew
      Association
Yoakum, Joseph E., **1:**311
Yoder v. Wisconsin, **2:**170
Yoeme. *See* Pascua Yaqui Indians
Yogananda, Paramahansa, **1:**326;
      4:133
Yokich, Steven, **8:**262
Yom Kippur War, contraband ship-
      ments during, **2:**396
York, Alvin, **8:**86
York, James Stuart, Duke of, **2:**280,
      289
  proprietary of, **3:93–94**
  See also James II
Yorktown Campaign, **3:**473; **7:**137;
      8:580–582, *581*
  French in, **6:**94
Yosemite National Park, **5:**550;
      8:*145*, **582–583**
  dam in, controversy over,
      2:368–369
Yoshida, Ray, **1:**311
Yost, Ed, **1:**392
Youk, Thomas, **3:**262
Young, Andrew, **1:**39; **2:**349; **3:**558
  on South Africa, **7:**452
Young, Bennett H., in Saint Albans
      Raid, **7:**224
Young, Brigham, **2:**163; **3:**16; **6:**410;
      8:296
  as freemason, **3:**466
  Las Vegas mission, **5:**41
  Mormon Battalion and, **5:**458
  Mormon migration, **5:**459
  at Nauvoo, **6:**15
  opposition to, **7:**103
  and settlement of Utah, **5:**53–54
  in Vermont, **8:**313
Young, Chic, **2:**308
Young, Coleman, **3:**20
Young, David, **1:**59
Young, Ella Flagg, **3:**116

Young, James, **6:**302
Young, John Russell, **5:**101
Young, John W., **7:**480, 482
Young, Milton R., **6:**132
Young, Owen, **7:**105
Young, Robert M., **6:**526
Young, Whitney M., Jr., **5:**563
Young, William J., **8:**31
"Young America," **8:583**
Young Americans for Freedom,
      2:375
"Young Goodman Brown"
      (Hawthorne), **5:**119
Young Joseph (Nez Perce leader),
      6:101, 102
Young Lions, The (Shaw), **5:**121
Young Men's Christian Association
      (YMCA), **7:**65; **8:**583, **584–585**
  and war relief, **8:**542
Young Men's Hebrew Association
      (YMHA), **8:583–584**
Young Mill-Wright and Miller's Guide
      (Evans), **3:**389
Young Plan (1929), **2:**507, 516;
      3:426, 562; **5:**55; **7:**105; **8:**585
Young Women's Christian Associa-
      tion (YWCA), **8:585–586**
  and voting rights for women, **8:**514
  and war relief, **8:**542
Young Women's Hebrew Association
      (YWHA), **8:584**
Younger, Thomas (Cole), **6:**135
Youngstown (Ohio), **7:**215
Yousef, Ramzi Ahmed, **3:**41; **8:**96,
      533–534
Youth, **2:**144
  See also Adolescence; Childhood
Youth Administration, National
      (NYA), **8:586**
Youth counter-culture, and Utopian
      communities, **8:**303
Youth movements, **8:586–588**
  4-H Clubs, **3:445–446**
  National Indian Youth Council,
      5:532, **543–544**
Youth's Companion, The (magazine),
      5:127; **6:**370
Yowaluck, Louis, **6:***8*
Yuba River, **9:**57
Yucca Mountain (Nevada), **3:**209
Yugoslavia
  ethnic cleansing in, **1:**354–355
  independence after World War I,
      2:89

NATO bombing campaign in,
   1:496; **4:**551
   maps used in, **2:**63
   U.S. relations with, **8:588–589**
Yuit, **8:**211, 212–213
Yukawa, Hideki, **6:**344
Yukon region, **8:**589, *589*
   Klondike Rush in, **4:538–539**
Yuman-speaking tribes, **5:**433–434
Yung Wing, **3:**274
YWCA. *See* Young Women's Christ-
   ian Association
YWHA. *See* Young Women's
   Hebrew Association

Z

Zadvydas v. Davis et al., **1:**125
Zaharias, Babe Didrikson, **4:**19,
   8:155
Zaidan, Mohammed Abul Abbas, **1:**13
Zaire, U.S. relations with, **1:**39
Zander, Arnold, **1:**154
Zangara, Giuseppe, **1:**329

Zangwill, Israel, **1:**337; **5:**306
Zappa, Frank, **1:**231–232
Zebra mussel, **7:**500
Zelaya, José Santos, **3:**71; **6:**104
Zelinsky, Wilbur, **5:**567
Zelman v. Simmons-Harris, **3:**138
Zen Buddhism, **1:**552
Zenger, John Peter, **2:**292; **5:**90;
   6:83, 95; **8:**590
Zenger trial, **5:**90; **8:589–590**, *590*
Zenith Electronics Corporation,
   8:169
*Zenith Radio Corp. et. al., United
   States v.*, **3:**340
Zimbabwe, U.S. relations with, **1:**39
Zimmerman, Don, **3:**516
Zimmermann telegram, **3:**562;
   8:534–535, **590–591**
Zinc industry, **5:**62; **6:**114, 115; **8:**591
Zinn, Walter H., **6:**139
Zinzendorf, Nikolaus Ludwig von,
   5:456, *457*; **6:**353
Zion City, **8:**302
Zionism, **8:591–593**
   of Jewish Defense League, **4:**475

Zirkel, Ferdinand, **6:**300
Zitkala Sa, *Old Indian Legends*, **5:**128
Znaniecki, Florian, **6:**391
Zogby, James, **5:**72
Zola, Émile, **6:**11
Zoning ordinances, **2:**187; **5:**38;
   6:505; **8:**593
Zoological parks, **8:593–596**, *594*
Zoology, **8:596–598**
   mammalogy, **5:**217–218
Zorach, William, **1:**306
Zorin, Valerian, **2:**475
Zouave uniform, **8:***256*, 257
Zubieta, Albert Alemán, **6:**241
Zuckerman, Morton, **1:**351
Zukor, Adolph, **3:**362
Zumwalt, Elmo R., Jr., **2:**537, 538
Zuni, **8:***598*, **598–599**
   gambling by, **3:**507
   in New Mexico, **6:**66
   sacred objects returned to, **6:**2–3
   Spanish explorers and, **2:**173, 416;
      3:296
Zworykin, Vladimir K., **8:**77
Zygilbojm, Szmul, **1:**445

ISBN 0-684-80532-4

90000